BENSON and HEDGES
CRICKET YEAR

FOURTEENTH EDITION
SEPTEMBER 1994 to SEPTEMBER 1995

EDITOR–DAVID LEMMON
FOREWORD BY GRAHAM GOOCH

HEADLINE

Editor's note

The aim of *Benson and Hedges Cricket Year* remains to give the cricket enthusiast an opportunity to read through the happenings in the world of cricket from each October until the following September (the end of the English season). Certain changes have been made this year in an effort to make information more accessible and to give more substance to comment and reports. Within the England section and elsewhere, there are sub-sections so that, for example, the Ashes series and the West Indies tour of England are clearly defined. First-class form charts remain, covering the Britannic Assurance County Championship and matches against touring and representative sides. (In the batting table a blank indicates that a batsman did not play in a game, a dash (–) that he did not *bat*. A dash (–) is placed in the batting averages if a player has no average, and in the bowling figures if no wicket was taken.) The structure of the book, as ever, is to present a three-dimensional look at the year – in words, pictures and statistics.

There is additional comment this year from Alan Lee of *The Times*, Derek Pringle of the *Independent on Sunday* and Frank Hayes, the former Lancashire and England batsman.

The symbol * indicates 'not out' or 'wicket-keeper' according to context.

This book would not be possible without the support of Brian Croudy whose untiring efforts and encouragement throughout the year are much appreciated. Equally, I must thank Les Hatton, the master of Sunday League statistics and information, for his help and encouragement. My continued thanks are also given to my friend Sudhir Vaidya for his meticulous work on India, to Anthony Lalley who gives so much time and energy to cricket in Australia, and to Qamar Ahmed of Pakistan, Andrew Samson of South Africa, and Ian Smith of New Zealand.

DAVID LEMMON

First published in 1995
by HEADLINE BOOK PUBLISHING

10 9 8 7 6 5 4 3 2 1

A CIP catalogue record for this book is available from the British Library

ISBN 0-7472-1471-9

Designed and produced by Book Production Consultants PLC,
25–27 High Street, Chesterton, Cambridge CB4 1ND

Printed and bound in Great Britain by
BPC Hazell Books Ltd
Member of BPC Ltd

Headline Book Publishing
A division of Hodder Headline PLC
338 Euston Road
London
NW1 3BH

Contents

Sponsor's message

Welcome to the 14th edition of the *Benson and Hedges Cricket Year*. The dust has hardly settled on one of the best English cricket seasons for many years and we already have the opportunity to relive the season, thanks to all those involved in producing this valuable book. Congratulations to editor David Lemmon, who has once again produced a complete record of first-class cricket around the world over the past 12 months. This year he has expanded the England section in order to do justice to a magnificent season and he has also commissioned several stimulating articles by well-respected cricket writers. Full marks to Ian Marshall and his team at Headline, the publishers, who have pulled out all the stops to get this book to you so soon after the end of the season.

A great deal has been happening in the world of cricket in the 12 months since we launched the 13th edition. In all, 38 Test matches and 87 limited-over internationals have been played, and reports and scorecards are included for every one. The book contains the results from all first-class matches played around the world (Sri Lanka, Pakistan, India, Zimbabwe, South Africa, New Zealand, West Indies and Sharjah), with the largest chapter in the international section of the book featuring the Australian season and England's attempt to regain the Ashes. Alan Lee explains where it went wrong in his review of the series.

Over half the book is devoted to the domestic season and each competition is now given its own section to make it much more readily accessible, as well as distinguishing the successes and failures of your favourite county in the four competitions. The Test series against the West Indies naturally receives significant coverage, and Frank Hayes' article on the relationship between Mike Atherton and Ray Illingworth makes fascinating reading. Graham Gooch's foreword stimulates the Lara versus Richards debate, and Derek Pringle writes on the current and future issues for English cricket.

I hope you enjoy this latest edition of the *Benson and Hedges Cricket Year*, and approve of the changes we've made. Work on next year's edition has already begun and, again, it will be the first cricket review of the season available when published in October 1996.

PHIL TRITTON
Marketing Manager
Benson and Hedges

Comment

A member and supporter of a county club in England must be as perplexed as a batsman facing Shane Warne. On the one hand, he is told that by allowing men like Mark Waugh, Keith Boyce, Larry Gomes, Winston Benjamin, Peter Kirsten, Kepler Wessels, Waqar Younis, Allan Donald and many others to operate within the structure of the game in England, he has been responsible for helping to turn those players into Test cricketers; on the other hand, he is told that that very same structure does not produce Test cricketers for the home country.

He is told, too, that cricketers are tired, that they are overworked, and that they play far too much cricket. 'The English game must be restructured!' is the constant cry, and then we will have a good Test team, for that is all that matters.

Statistical evidence has long since proved – and it has been accepted – that no cricketer today bowls as many overs nor plays as many innings as cricketers did 50 years ago – not even if one adds together all four of our domestic competitions. Perhaps at this point we should look at how many days a cricketer spends working during the summer.

In 1995, the English season lasted for 158 days. If a cricketer played in all 17 championship matches and all 17 of them lasted four days (highly unlikely); and if he appeared against both universities, the West Indian tourists and the Young Australians (which nobody did); and if his county reached the finals of the Benson and Hedges Cup and the NatWest Trophy *and* played the maximum number of matches in getting to Lord's (which nobody did); and if he appeared in all 17 Sunday League games and played for the TCCB XI against the Young Australians *and* made an appearance at the Scarborough or Harrogate Festivals – then he would have played 117 days' cricket. In other words, he would work a five-day week and have a week's holiday. As a truer estimate would reveal that he plays something closer to 100 days' cricket at maximum, he gets three weeks free in the summer, even allowing for travelling. Perhaps Alec Bedser is correct when he advocates that cricketers should be playing more, not less.

One of the many suggestions with regard to restructuring which has resurfaced is the establishment of regional cricket. The fact that Test trials of the past proved to be futile exercises, that selectors learnt nothing from them and that the public disregarded them has been ignored.

The motivation for all these ideas, of course, is that all must be geared to international cricket, which has now reached an indigestible level, and the television money which, at present, it engenders.

One would recommend those whose privilege it is to guide and guard the game to reread the D.H. Lawrence short story, *The Rocking Horse Winner*. You may remember that the story concerns a boy who has powers to foretell the winners of horse races. His family is comfortable, upper middle class, but in spite of all the money he brings, there is a constant cry from the house – 'There must be more money. There must be more money.'

In the end, of course, the mother becomes a millionaire, but the boy dies.

DAVID LEMMON

Who has sponsored cricket for the last 15 years?

NatWest

More than just a bank

National Westminster Bank Plc, 41 Lothbury, London, EC2P 2BP.

Foreword

by Graham Gooch, OBE

Another blazing hot summer, another West Indies visit and another batting genius blitzing England's bowlers with an unbelievable array of shots and a flurry of centuries. Impressive though he was, the 1995 Brian Lara was not as good as the Viv Richards of 1976. That does not mean that Lara is not a batsman of the very highest quality or that I would dispute he is No. 1 in the world at the moment or that he saved the West Indies from defeat in England. The tourists' batting was dependent totally on his contribution. It is a mark of the respect and esteem in which Lara is held that bowlers talk about trying to contain him, to keep him quiet and hope he might get himself out. That is a compliment to his great ability. I don't think I have ever seen a batsman pick the gaps with the precision that Lara displayed last summer.

But it is too early to call him a great, great player. His tally of 765 runs, averaging 85.00 with three centuries and three fifties is very impressive and Lara seems to have taken a special liking to England's bowlers. Lara has seven hundreds in 31 Tests; unfortunately for Mike Atherton, that includes five in 11 appearances against England. His 798 runs in the Caribbean in 1994, including that world record 375 at Antigua, coupled with the fact that Lara is still 26, means England have a problem that has not yet been solved.

However, Lara's display here this summer merely helped put the remarkable achievements of Richards' summer 19 years ago in true context. Richards was just 24 when he came to England with Clive Lloyd's side and, despite missing the Lord's Test through injury, scored 829 runs in four matches, including 291 at The Oval and 232 at Trent Bridge, at an average of 118.42. In the first eight months of 1976, Richards scored 1,710 Test runs. There is no doubt that Richards was the most destructive batsman I have ever seen; during the late seventies and early eighties, the Master Blaster from Antigua was almost impossible to bowl to. He did not choose the gaps as carefully as Lara, but his immense power more than compensated. Deliveries just outside the off-stump would disappear through mid-wicket like a bullet. There was the supreme confidence and the arrogance that declared: 'I'm the boss'.

Lara is not so obvious in his mannerisms, but that inner belief is there. Richards did have one big advantage; he did not have to carry the West Indies batting, with Gordon Greenidge, Desmond Haynes, Larry Gomes, Clive Lloyd and Alvin Kallicharran also in the line-up. This summer was conclusive proof to me that the West Indies can no longer say they are the supreme champions of Test cricket. The Aussies have definitely got one hand on that trophy with the best batting line-up around and two match-winning bowlers, Shane Warne and Craig McDermott.

England did well to recover from the Ashes debacle last winter to give the West Indies a tough series. My 20-year Test career came to a close in Australia in Perth. I have no doubt I made the right decision. This season went well for me, apart from a run-less July. On my day, I have no doubt that I can still score runs at the highest level, but the body, at 42, does not recover as quickly and easily as it used to. There is nothing like the atmosphere on the first day of a Test match, but there was no pang of regret this summer as I watched the series from the sidelines.

It was a great summer for the spectator, in person or watching on TV. Great weather seems to produce great cricket. England did well to battle back twice in the West Indies series. The star newcomer was undoubtedly Dominic Cork. He did the job that everyone was expecting Darren Gough would do. He scored runs, took wickets and made things happen. That's the toughest job in cricket – put in performances that match expectations. Gough missed the second half of the summer through injury, but he is too bubbly a character to be kept out of the limelight for long.

Two world-class performers returned for England, as everyone hoped they would. Robin Smith must have wondered whether the Young Guns had ended his career, while Jack Russell's career was on hold with Alec Stewart behind the stumps. Smith was the foundation of England's victory at Lord's and was only forced out of the series at Old Trafford with a broken cheekbone. Old Trafford was Russell's first Test for 18 months and it was the Gloucestershire skipper's undefeated 31 there that steadied nerves and took England to victory. Jack's absences have had nothing to do with his form; it was tactics. If England wanted six batsmen and five bowlers, Jack had to be fall guy. The England batting heroes this summer were the captain Mike Atherton and Graham Thorpe. Athers are providing the solid base at the top of the order that every side needs. Considering the many batting changes because of injury, England did well to post those big totals in the second half of the summer.

England's 2–2 result against the West Indies appears to have silenced all the talk of revolution that was rampant after our poor tour of Australia. However, I still believe there are too many county cricketers. We need fewer teams and fewer players. There are too many professionals who are not up to standard and would not get a game of first-class cricket in any other part of the world. The toughest thing I have found on my full-time return to the county circuit is without doubt playing a 40-over Sunday League after three days of a four-day county match.

The domestic competitions have been dominated by the counties most predicted would feature at the start of the summer. Lancashire's teamwork took the Benson and Hedges trophy, despite Aravinda de Silva's outstanding innings – one of the most brilliant ever seen in a one-day final at Lord's. But Kent did win their first trophy for 17 years when they won the AXA Equity amd Law League. Warwickshire's all-round strength edged out Northamptonshire in the NatWest final, which was carried over to Sunday for the second successive year, as the side batting second won for the tenth successive year. Warwickshire also took the Britannic Assurance County Championship for the second year running.

International rankings

As an innovation in this year's *Benson and Hedges Cricket Year*, we offer a statistical assessment of countries' achievements at international level during the period covered by this book. The method employed is simple in that it gives two points for a win and one for a draw or for an abandoned match. Points obtained are divided by points possible to arrive at a percentage.

One does not offer these as an official verdict on the year. Four of South Africa's five Tests, for example, were played against a New Zealand side very much in a state of reconstruction, while West Indies took on India, New Zealand, Australia and England in the same period. With what is probably the best Test side in their history, India played only a three-match series against West Indies and,

like Zimbabwe, did not play a Test match outside their own country. Nevertheless, the figures offer some interesting comparisons.

In contrast to 38 Test matches played in the period covered by this book, there were, during that time, 87 one-day internationals, and this figure does not include the matches played by Australia 'A' in the Benson and Hedges World Series, for these were not recognised as full internationals. As countries travelled far and wide to compete in limited-over international tournaments, the rankings in this type of cricket probably have more relevance than the Test rankings.

DAVID LEMMON

TEST RANKINGS

	P	W	L	D	Pts won	/	Pts poss	%
South Africa	5	4	1	–	8		10	80.00
Pakistan	9	5	2	2	12		18	66.66
Australia	12	5	3	4	14		24	58.33
West Indies	15	5	5	5	15		30	50.00
India	3	1	1	1	3		6	50.00
Sri Lanka	7	1	2	4	6		14	42.85
Zimbabwe	6	1	2	3	5		12	41.66
England	11	3	5	3	9		22	40.90
New Zealand	8	1	5	2	4		16	25.00

LIMITED-OVER RANKINGS

	P	W	L	D	Pts won	/	Pts poss	%
India	21	14	6	1	29		42	69.04
Pakistan	28	16	10	2	34		56	60.71
Australia	22	13	9	–	26		44	59.09
England	7	4	3	–	8		14	57.14
West Indies	21	11	9	1	23		42	54.76
Sri Lanka	25	11	13	1	23		50	46.00
South Africa	17	7	10	–	14		34	41.17
Zimbabwe	10	3	6	1	7		20	35.00
New Zealand	20	4	14	2	10		40	25.00
Bangladesh	3	–	3	–	0		6	0.00

Benson and Hedges Cricket Year World XI 1995

The World XI is chosen to reflect performances during the period covered by this book. It embraces all Test cricket from Pakistan's visit to Sri Lanka and Australia's visit to Pakistan to the series between England and West Indies. Consideration is also given to performances in one-day internationals and in domestic cricket.

Boon, Ambrose and Waqar Younis are the only members of last year's side not to retain their places. The reason for Waqar's exclusion, obviously, is due to injury.

Craig McDermott, too, comes into the same category as Waqar. He more than earned a place on his form against England, but injury marred his year and deprived him of three Test series. Allan Donald missed much international cricket and played little in South Africa before coming to England to play a vital role in Warwickshire's triumphs. Many consider him the fastest bowler in the world, and he would feature in most world elevens selected by lovers of the game, but, over the past 12 months, he did not play enough to push aside Courtney Walsh.

Azharuddin and Inzamam-ul-Haq are unlucky not to be included, particularly as Inzamam carried the Pakistan batting through a difficult period. Mark Waugh is still the most exciting batsman in the world excepting Lara, and to omit him is difficult, but he could not find consistency. He played some memorable innings, and one could dream of a partnership between him and Lara in anyone's world team.

Jimmy Adams arrived in England ranked number one

LEFT: *Michael Atherton. (Paul Sturgess/Sportsline)*

TOP: *Michael Slater. (David Munden/Sportsline)*

ABOVE: *Brian Lara. (Patrick Eagar)*

in the world, but fatigue and injury robbed him of his place. He will figure prominently in the restructuring of the West Indies side.

Graham Thorpe has shaken off the doubts one had of him as a Test player, but he cannot yet be considered world class. One would hesitate to deny Dominic Cork that title.

Michael Atherton (England) (8)

Atherton's path as captain of England has not been strewn with roses, but the man has met every adversity and criticism with great fortitude. His batting has remained as resilient as it has consistent, and, at the start of the England season, the West Indians considered that if they dismissed him, England had little else to offer.

Michael Slater (Australia) (9)

Sound in defence, belligerent in attack, Michael Slater has now established himself as the most consistent and attractive opening batsman in world cricket. He was a major reason for Australia reaching the point where they were acclaimed as world champions.

Brian Lara (West Indies) (2)

Lara had an indifferent tour of India, showed better form in New Zealand and finished top of the averages against Australia. It is a mark of the man's genius that he suffered criticism in the series against Australia, yet still came out as the leading batsman. In the last three Tests against England, he was glorious, and there is no more exciting player in world cricket. It is not that he accumulates records, but the way in which he scores his runs that invigorates.

Sachin Tendulkar (India) (6)

Tendulkar has matured into Lara's premier challenger for the title of the world's number one batsman. The amount of Test cricket that India played in 1994–5 was very limited, but Tendulkar batted brilliantly in all forms of cricket, and his rate of scoring in the Ranji Trophy and in one-day internationals was astonishing.

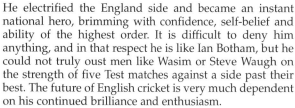

He electrified the England side and became an instant national hero, brimming with confidence, self-belief and ability of the highest order. It is difficult to deny him anything, and in that respect he is like Ian Botham, but he could not truly oust men like Wasim or Steve Waugh on the strength of five Test matches against a side past their best. The future of English cricket is very much dependent on his continued brilliance and enthusiasm.

One last omission that saddens – Aravinda de Silva. He illuminated the English summer, and one will remain ever grateful to Kent for granting us a season of his breath-taking stroke-play. If only Sri Lanka were accorded a rightful and meaningful place in the Test world, what thrills there could be. They *did* beat England last time the two nations met.

So to the chosen eleven. The Coopers and Lybrand ratings are in brackets.

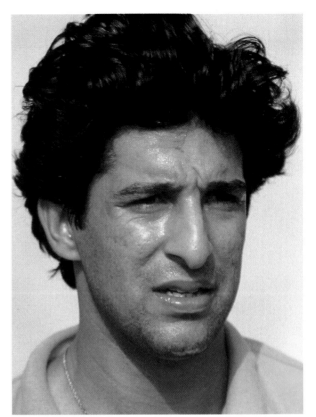

Hansie Cronje (South Africa) (11)

Not a spectacular player, but a man of great skill and the utmost determination. He is a leader by example, and his centuries brought South Africa Test victories. His total commitment to county cricket with Leicestershire was typical of the man and his passion for the game.

Steve Waugh (Australia) (1)

Steve Waugh's outstanding all-round efforts against England and West Indies lifted him to number one in world rankings as a batsman. He displayed the greatest courage in dealing with the West Indian pace bowlers and led Australia to a memorable win in the final Test. Calm, cool and consistent, he has thrived at all levels and excelled on his appearances for New South Wales.

Ian Healy (Australia)

Coopers and Lybrand give no rankings for wicket-keepers, but if they did, Ian Healy would maintain an unassailable lead. He has no peer in world cricket, with Richardson of South Africa, Mongia of India and, possibly, the up-and-coming Adam Gilchrist of Australia but distant threats to his eminence. He drives the Australian out-cricket, providing dynamism from behind the stumps. His runs in the late middle-order have been a constant source of irritation to opponents and inspiration to his side.

LEFT: *Anil Kumble. (David Munden/Sportsline)*

ABOVE: *Courtney Walsh. (Patrick Eagar)*

Wasim Akram (Pakistan) (8)

In a troubled year for Pakistan, Wasim Akram has remained a match-winner even when deprived of his new-ball partner Waqar Younis. He scores violent and vital runs, and for Lancashire he enjoyed a magnificent all-round season in all types of cricket. He played a major part in a semi-final victory in the Benson and Hedges Cup and led the side with zest and intelligence on occasions.

Shane Warne (Australia) (4)

Shane Warne continues to bemuse and bewilder all the world's leading batsmen. He is now justly recognised as not only the leading spinner of his day, but among the greatest the world has ever known.

Anil Kumble (India) (5)

Anil Kumble has been the master bowler for India in all forms of cricket, and one can only relish his contest with the England batsmen in 1996. He is hard to define, for he is a quick spin bowler of leg-breaks who does not use the leg-break very often. His season for Northamptonshire was memorable. He was the leading wicket-taker in English cricket, and he helped lift his county to great heights.

Courtney Walsh (West Indies) (9)

An inspirational captain who led by example in the earlier part of the year, Walsh produced some magnificent bowling to help defeat India and New Zealand, and he was the backbone of the attack against Australia and England. His work-load was immense, but he maintained consistency and fire when others flagged. For many years in a support role, he found himself the spearhead of the West Indian attack.

Readers may be interested to note that the Coopers and Lybrand World XI based on current ratings would differ in five places from the one above. Their rules are that the team must include the two highest-rated openers and four other top-rated middle-order batsmen, together with the top four fit bowlers. Their team is – Atherton (8) (capt), Slater (9), Lara (2), Thorpe (4), Inzamam-ul-Haq (3), Steve Waugh (1), Healy (36), Warne (4), de Villiers (3), Waqar Younis (2), Ambrose (1). Kumble or Bishop would replace an unfit Waqar. The debate continues.

DAVID LEMMON

AUSTRALIA

The end of one of the great Test careers of modern times. Graham Gooch is caught and bowled for four in the final Test at Perth. The bowler, Craig McDermott, was Man of the Series. (Patrick Eagar)

A mood of buoyancy pervaded Australian cricket at the beginning of the 1994–5 season. The national side, narrowly defeated in Pakistan, was confident of retaining the Ashes in the series against Atherton's men, and several young players had emerged as serious contenders for a place in the Test team. Two of them, Fleming and Bevan, had already proved their worth in Pakistan.

New South Wales were named as favourites to retain the Sheffield Shield, but the Blues were likely to be hard-pressed by the Queensland Bulls, who were to be assisted for one last season by Allan Border. Geoff Marsh, one of the most popular and dedicated of cricketers, had surprised many by announcing his retirement from first-class cricket. He was succeeded as captain of Western Australia by Damien Martyn, one of Australia's younger talents striving to win a regular Test place. Three of Martyn's team-mates, Zoehrer, Julian and Moody, were released from their contracts with the Australian Cricket Board, and Zoehrer lost his place in the state side to Adam Gilchrist who had moved to the Warriors from Sydney.

For the first time, some Shield games at the WACA Ground in Perth, the SCG in Sydney and the MCG in Melbourne were to be day/night affairs with coloured clothing, floodlights and white ball. Each state would play in at least one of the matches.

Peter Taylor, the former Test off-spinner, became a surprise addition to the panel of Test selectors. He replaced Bobby Simpson who felt that the dual role of selector and coach resulted in a conflict of interests.

ENGLAND TOUR OF AUSTRALIA
The Ashes Series

25 October 1994 *at Lilac Hill, Perth*

Australian Cricket Board Chairman's XI 232
 (R.T. Ponting 82, D. Gough 5 for 32)
England XI 236 for 3 (G.A. Gooch 129, G.P. Thorpe 61 not out)

England XI won by 7 wickets

27 October 1994 *at WACA Ground, Perth*

Western Australia 248 for 5 (M.P. Lavender 83,
 D.R. Martyn 51)
England XI 197

Western Australia won by 51 runs

29, 30, 31 October and 1 November 1994 *at WACA Ground, Perth*

England XI 245 (M.A. Atherton 68, B.A. Reid 4 for 71) and 393
 for 6 dec. (G.A. Hick 172, G.A. Gooch 68, J.P. Crawley 67
 not out)
Western Australia 238 (M. Goodwin 91, M.R.J. Veletta 67,
 D.E. Malcolm 6 for 70) and 272 for 5 (M. Goodwin 77,
 M.P. Lavender 51, P.A.J. DeFreitas 4 for 60)

Match drawn

England began their tour of Australia with a 50-over match against an eleven which included Greg Chappell, Geoff and Rodney Marsh, Dennis Lillee and Jeff Thomson. Gooch hit 129 off 130 balls with 19 fours and 2 sixes and added 169 in 30 overs with Thorpe.

Cricket in Australia is nothing if not inventive. The Mercantile Mutual Cup saw Victoria take the field in blue shorts, and the match between Western Australia and England was played under the experimental format of being quartered. After 25 overs, the home side were 90 for 1. England then made 83 for 4 in 25 overs before Western Australia batted for another 25 overs. England were eventually dismissed in 45.5 overs. The experiment had nothing to commend it.

England got down to proper cricket in the third match.

By mid-afternoon on the first day, they were 149 for 1, but the middle-order was destroyed by Cary and Reid, and they finished on 241 for 9. Returning after injury, Bruce Reid took four wickets, and the slim left-arm pace bowler performed well. At the age of 31, however, it seemed unlikely that he would force his way back into the Australian side. England had certainly suffered severe setbacks during the first week of the tour as Stewart had sustained a broken finger and Udal a fractured thumb. These misfortunes were forgotten on the second day when Devon Malcolm bowled with pace and aggression to put the home state to flight after Mike Veletta, Murray Goodwin and Damien Martyn had threatened to run riot, McCague being particularly severely punished. England's joy increased on the third day when Hick batted majestically to reach the 78th century of his career. Crawley, too, and Gooch gave Atherton encouragement, and Western Australia were left a day in which to score 401 to win. Although, on the last morning, DeFreitas had Hogg caught behind with the second ball of the day, the Australians had no difficulty in saving the match, and Benjamin limped off with a groin strain.

2, 3, 4 and 5 November 1994 *at Adelaide Oval*

South Australia 102 (M.J. McCague 5 for 31) and 480
 (J.D. Siddons 121, J.A. Brayshaw 101, P.C. Nobes 72,
 T.J. Nielsen 52, D. Gough 5 for 143)
England XI 323 (G.A. Hick 101, G.P. Thorpe 80, G.A. Gooch
 50, P.E. McIntyre 4 for 48, S.P. George 4 for 114) and 262
 for 6 (G.A. Gooch 101, M.W. Gatting 56)

England XI won by 4 wickets

Led by Mike Gatting, England asked South Australia to bat first in Adelaide where the weather was cold and the pitch damp. McCague, looking a different bowler from the one who had operated in Perth, made his first ball lift sharply and had Nobes caught in the gully. His third ball had Brayshaw taken at slip. Soon the state side were 21 for 6.

Skipper Siddons offered the only positive resistance before he was yorked to become McCague's fifth victim, and White polished off the tail. Crawley went cheaply, but Gooch and Hick, both in good form, hit fifties before the close, and England led by 12 runs. Hick moved to 101 off 123 balls before falling to Hickey, and, with Thorpe and Gatting going well, the tourists were 271 for 3. The introduction of leg-spinner Peter McIntyre brought disaster, and seven wickets fell for 52 runs. South Australia showed greater resolution when they batted a second time. Nobes and Faull added 126 for their second wicket, and thereafter Brayshaw and Siddons reached centuries and shared a fifth-wicket stand of 102. Gough brought the home side's second innings to a quick end on the last day, and England needed 260 to win. Crawley was out for 0 for the second time in the match, and the spinners, McIntyre and Minagall, troubled all batsmen. Gooch and Gatting righted matters, however, and the visitors registered their first significant win of the tour.

9 November 1994 *at Manuka Oval, Canberra*

England XI 143

Prime Minister's XI 144 for 8

Prime Minister's XI won by 2 wickets

12, 13, 14 and 15 November 1994 *at Newcastle Sportsground*

England XI 328 (G.A. Hick 73, J.P. Crawley 71,
G.P. Thorpe 67, B.E. McNamara 4 for 50) and 244

New South Wales 365 (M.A. Taylor 150, M.E. Waugh 80,
D.E. Malcolm 4 for 81) and 211 for 6 (M.J. Slater 94)

New South Wales won by 4 wickets

The Prime Minister's XI, led by Allan Border, bowled England out on an uncertain pitch and went on to win by two wickets with 14 balls to spare. The Australians used an all-seam attack. Darren Lehmann was top scorer in the match with 43.

After two club matches Phil Alley, the left-arm pace bowler, was deemed unfit for the remainder of the season due to a recurrent back injury, so putting a further strain on New South Wales' resources. For the match against the England tourists, however, the Blues were able to welcome back Taylor, Slater, Mark Waugh, Bevan and Robertson. Emery and Steve Waugh were still nursing injuries, but England now had a clear picture of how difficult their task in Australia would be.

The first day of the game against New South Wales gave every indication that England would cope well with the task ahead. They were not opposed by McGrath, and Rhodes, promoted to open, soon fell to Lee, but Atherton, Hick, Thorpe and Crawley all showed sound temperament and resolution, and the tourists ended the day on 318 for 9. Indeed, Crawley gave his best performance of the tour. The second day was a disaster for England. They bowled indifferently, fielded badly, and Taylor was quick to seize the initiative. He and Slater, 18, put on 54 for the first wicket, and he and Mark Waugh then added 163 in 36 overs. England wilted. Carelessly, New South Wales

allowed them back into the game, but England's second-innings batting lacked confidence and authority. Gatting, in particular, had a wretched time and was one of three to fall to the impressive left-arm spin of Anthony Kershler.

The last five England wickets fell for 44 runs, and, needing 208 to win, New South Wales, with Slater following Taylor's first-innings example, were only 50 runs short of their target at tea on the final day with eight wickets standing. Tufnell and Malcolm caused some havoc in the last session, but England's generally sub-standard performance had made defeat inevitable.

18, 19, 20 and 21 November 1994 *at Bellerive Oval, Hobart*

Australian XI 386 for 7 dec. (D.R. Martyn 103, R.T. Ponting 71,
S.G. Law 68, G.S. Blewett 53, M.N. Atkinson 51 not out)
England XI 209 (G.A. Gooch 50, S.J. Rhodes 50, M.G. Hughes
4 for 51) and 207 for 1 dec. (A.J. Stewart 101 not out)

Match drawn

On the eve of the first Test match, England had mixed feelings about their game in Hobart. Damien Martyn had impressed as Western Australia's youngest captain, and he led the Australian XI with considerable flair. He also scored a most attractive century on the opening day. Equally impressive was Ponting – surely a batsman destined for the very highest honours – and Law showed why he had been chosen as a member of the Australian squad for the one-day series. On the second day, Martyn declared at the fall of the seventh wicket, and his bowlers immediately had England in trouble. Merv Hughes, positive about his fitness and his right to face England in the Test series, soon accounted for Atherton, and the batting of the tourists was quite pathetic, lacking application and endeavour. The one consolation was that Stewart was passed fit to play and on the fourth morning when England followed on, only 21 balls having been possible on the third day, he shared an opening stand of 131 with Atherton and went on to reach a purposeful century.

 FIRST TEST MATCH
AUSTRALIA *v.* ENGLAND, at Brisbane

For England, the start of the Ashes series was a disaster. In London, the chairman of selectors lost another opportunity to keep quiet and levelled criticisms at Atherton for not informing him of all that was happening. Atherton, one felt, had enough problems to cope with without maintaining a constant communication service with a man whose job was done once the party had been selected. More significantly, England lost the services of Devon Malcolm with chicken-pox, and Martin McCague came into the side. Rather surprisingly, Gatting was preferred to Crawley whose technical imperfections gave cause for concern. Australia, less troubled than England, played McGrath rather than Fleming and included two spinners. None of the eleven who had done so well against England

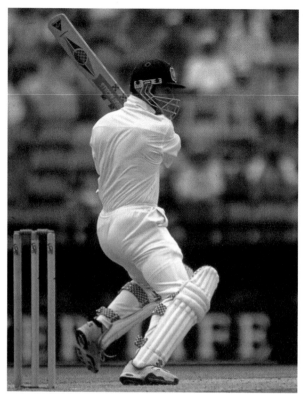

Thorpe is beaten and bowled by Shane Warne after a valiant innings of 67. (Ben Radford/Allsport)

Michael Slater hit the highest score of his Test career, 176, in the first match of the series. Here, he slashes a ball from DeFreitas to the boundary. Slater also scored centuries in the third and fifth Tests. (Stephen Laffer/Sportsline)

in Hobart was in the squad, a reminder of Australia's strength.

The final setback for England was that Taylor won the toss, and Australia batted on a pitch that was dry and true. The England new-ball attack of DeFreitas and McCague was dreadful. McCague, in particular, could find neither length nor direction, and 26 runs came from the first four overs of the day. Gough and Tufnell brought some restraint to the run-scoring, but the first wicket did not fall until after lunch. Taylor drove Tufnell hard to Gough at mid-off and set off on a silly run. Slater did not respond, and Gough's quick throw, off-balance, left Taylor stranded. It was the first success for Gough, who had become a father some hours before the start of the match, but it was not to be the last.

In four overs after lunch, DeFreitas was hit for 5 fours, and Slater knocked him out of the attack. Later DeFreitas limped off the field, and with McCague in tatters after a three-over spell which cost 29 runs, the England attack had very limited options.

Gough, brave and dependable, induced Boon to play on, but this only brought in Mark Waugh who, in partnership with Michael Slater, gave a magnificent display of varied stroke-play which realised 182 in 2½ hours. Slater reached his second century against England before tea, and in the half-hour after the break 50 runs were scored.

Another 44 came in the next half-hour. Atherton was forced to entrust the second new ball to Gough and Gooch, and, to the surprise of many, it was Gooch who dismissed Slater. The batsman drove loosely into the hands of Gatting at mid-off, but by then he had reached the highest score of his Test career and had hit 25 fours in a display of dazzling footwork and exquisite strokes.

Bevan did not last long, edging Gough's away-swinger to second slip. Waugh ended the day on 82, and Australia were a formidable 329 for 4.

Night-watchman Warne became Gough's third victim early on the second morning, but Mark Waugh had already hit McCague for three boundaries by then, and he moved to his seventh Test century, the 50th of his first-class career, with that elegant aggression which makes him one of the most attractive batsmen in world cricket. DeFreitas had recovered from whatever had afflicted him mentally and physically on the first day and accounted for both Healy and Steve Waugh, caught at slip. Mark Waugh had had a narrow escape when on 98, and he was missed by Rhodes, but by then Australia's position was an impregnable one. Eventually, Waugh was caught off a leading edge. He had hit 14 fours and a six and faced 215 deliveries. Like Slater, he had provided an innings to cherish. McCague had some late, hardly deserved consolation, and Australia were out for 426 on the second afternoon.

By the close, England were in disarray, 133 for 6, with Atherton unbeaten on 49. Stewart was caught behind by Healy, playing his first match since being injured in Pakistan, and Hick also gave the wicket-keeper a catch when he mis-hooked a bouncer. Thorpe was bemused by Warne and offered a return catch, and Gooch, having begun in blistering mood, was out to a wretched shot. Gatting was leg before to McDermott who then knocked back McCague's off stump with the last ball of what had been an awful day for England.

The position did not improve on the third morning, for McDermott and Warne took only 12.2 overs to complete the rout of England on a true pitch. Taylor did not enforce

Ian Healy catches Graeme Hick off the bowling of Shane Warne for 80. Warne took a career-best 8 for 71 in the innings, and his bowling played a major part in Australia's success in the first two Tests. He was admirably supported behind the wicket by Healy throughout the series. (Graham Chadwick/Allsport)

the follow-on, to the surprise of the majority, but he and Slater soon put England's batting performance in mocking perspective as they scored 100 inside 24 overs when Australia batted a second time.

The next 51 overs of the day brought a remarkable change as England captured seven wickets for the addition of 94 runs. Tufnell bowled admirably, allying wit to control, and, in the absence of the injured McCague, Gough and DeFreitas performed well.

Taylor declared after 55 minutes on the fourth morning, setting England 508 runs to win or, realistically, challenging them to survive more than five sessions. In the space of 15 balls either side of lunch, Shane Warne bowled Stewart with a flipper as the batsman tried to pull and trapped Atherton leg before with a ball that went straight on. Defeat, it seemed, would come in four days, but Hick and Thorpe played with the utmost resolution and good sense. McDermott was finally withdrawn from the attack, tired and wicketless, and Taylor failed to use May and Warne in tandem as much as he might have done. The end of the day came with Hick on 72,

Thorpe on 66, and England at 211 for 2. There were even whispers of an historic and impossible victory.

The whispers were soon silenced on the last morning, and the dreams faded. Only eight runs had been added when Thorpe was yorked by Warne. Hick also fell to the leg-spinner, bemused and bizarrely caught off pad, chest and bat. The two veterans, Gooch and Gatting, now stood between Australia and victory, but on the stroke of lunch, having batted for 76 minutes, Gatting was completely outwitted by McDermott and caught behind. This left Gooch and the tail, and when, in mid-afternoon, Gooch had a

FIRST TEST MATCH – AUSTRALIA v. ENGLAND
25, 26, 27, 28 and 29 November 1994 at Woolloongabba, Brisbane

AUSTRALIA

	FIRST INNINGS		SECOND INNINGS	
M.J. Slater	c Gatting, b Gooch	176	(2) lbw, b Gough	45
M.A. Taylor (capt)	run out	59	(1) c Stewart, b Tufnell	58
D.C. Boon	b Gough	3	b Tufnell	28
M.E. Waugh	c Stewart, b Gough	140	b Tufnell	15
M.G. Bevan	c Hick, b Gough	7	c Rhodes, b DeFreitas	21
S.K. Warne	c Rhodes, b Gough	2	(8) c sub (White), b DeFreitas	0
S.R. Waugh	c Hick, b DeFreitas	19	(6) c sub (White), b Tufnell	7
*I.A. Healy	c Hick, b DeFreitas	7	(7) not out	45
C.J. McDermott	c Gough, b McCague	2	c Rhodes, b Gough	6
T.B.A. May	not out	3	not out	9
G.D. McGrath	c Gough, b McCague	0		
Extras	b 5, lb 2, nb 1	8	b 2, lb 9, w 2, nb 1	14
		426	(for 8 wickets, dec.)	248

ENGLAND

	FIRST INNINGS		SECOND INNINGS	
M.A. Atherton (capt)	c Healy, b McDermott	54	lbw, b Warne	23
A.J. Stewart	c Healy, b McDermott	16	b Warne	33
G.A. Hick	c Healy, b McDermott	3	c Healy, b Warne	80
G.P. Thorpe	c and b Warne	28	b Warne	67
G.A. Gooch	c Healy, b May	20	c Healy, b Warne	56
M.W. Gatting	lbw, b McDermott	10	c Healy, b McDermott	13
M.J. McCague	b McDermott	1	(10) lbw, b Warne	0
*S.J. Rhodes	lbw, b McDermott	4	(7) c Healy, b McDermott	2
P.A.J. DeFreitas	c Healy, b Warne	7	(8) b Warne	11
D. Gough	not out	17	(9) c M.E. Waugh, b Warne	10
P.C.R. Tufnell	c Taylor, b Warne	0	not out	2
Extras	lb 1, nb 6	7	b 9, lb 5, nb 12	26
		167		323

	O	M	R	W	O	M	R	W
DeFreitas	31	8	102	2	22	1	74	2
McCague	19.2	4	96	2				
Gough	32	7	107	4	23	3	78	2
Tufnell	25	3	72	–	38	10	79	4
Hick	4	–	22	–	2	1	1	–
Gooch	9	2	20	1	3	2	5	–

	O	M	R	W	O	M	R	W
McDermott	19	3	53	6	23	4	90	2
McGrath	10	2	40	–	19	4	61	–
May	17	3	34	1	35	16	59	–
Warne	21.2	7	39	3	50.2	22	71	8
M.E. Waugh					7	1	17	–
Bevan					3	–	11	–

FALL OF WICKETS
1–99, 2–126, 3–308, 4–326, 5–352, 6–379, 7–407, 8–419, 9–425
1–109, 2–117, 3–139, 4–174, 5–183, 6–190, 7–191, 8–201

FALL OF WICKETS
1–22, 2–35, 3–82, 4–105, 5–131, 6–133, 7–140, 8–147, 9–151
1–50, 2–59, 3–219, 4–220, 5–250, 6–280, 7–309, 8–310, 9–310

Umpires: C.J. Mitchley & S.G. Randell

Australia won by 184 runs

rush of blood and was splendidly caught by Healy there was no more hope for England.

Shane Warne, a cricketer of true genius, finished with 8 for 71, his best figures in Test cricket, but the career of this marvellous bowler is still young, and who would dare to predict what wonders lie ahead...?

2 December 1994 *at Bowral*

Sir Donald Bradman's XI 205 for 4 (J.L. Arnberger 79)

England XI 208 for 6 (J.P. Crawley 91 not out)

England XI won by 4 wickets

With Crawley displaying good form, England beat a team of young cricketers led by Allan Border. Victory came with eight balls to spare.

4 December 1994 *at Manuka Oval, Canberra*

England XI 253 for 5 (M.A. Atherton 53 retired, A.J. Stewart 53, G.A. Hick 50)

Australian Capital Territory 153 (D. Gough 4 for 19)

England XI won by 100 runs

The first four England batsmen gained useful practice and Darren Gough bowled well in a game which had little significance. The former Lancashire and Worcestershire all-rounder Steve O'Shaughnessy was in the Australian side.

10 December 1994 *at North Sydney Oval*

England XI 231 for 4 (G.A. Hick 118, G.P. Thorpe 62)

Australian Cricket Academy 234 for 5 (I.J. Harvey 80, R.J. Baker 57)

Australian Cricket Academy won by 5 wickets

11 December 1994 *at North Sydney Oval*

England XI 245 for 7 (M.A. Atherton 95, M.W. Gatting 62)

Australian Cricket Academy 249 for 4 (B.J. Hodge 96 not out, R.M. Campbell 57)

Australian Cricket Academy won by 6 wickets

England were originally scheduled to play a three-day match against the Cricket Academy, but bad weather caused the abandonment of this fixture and two one-day matches were arranged in compensation. England suffered great humiliation as the young Australians won both matches. They were better in all departments and won the second match with 41 balls to spare.

17, 18, 19 and 20 December 1994 *at Heritage Oval, Toowoomba*

England XI 507 for 6 dec. (M.W. Gatting 203 not out, J.P. Crawley 91, A.J. Stewart 53 not out, G.A. Gooch 50) and 236 for 8 dec. (J.P. Crawley 63, D. Tazelaar 4 for 56)

Queensland 392 for 4 dec. (A. Symonds 108 not out, J.P. Maher 100 not out, S.G. Law 91) and 314 (M.L. Hayden 119, T.J. Barsby 101, P.C.R. Tufnell 5 for 71)

England XI won by 37 runs

In their final match before the second Test, England gained a remarkable and welcome victory. With Crawley and Gatting adding 202 off 50 overs for the fourth wicket, England reached 355 for 5 on the first day against Queensland. Crawley's innings was flawed, but Gatting's was more confident and purposeful, and he reached 203 with 30 fours on the second day. The same afternoon, Law hit 91 in a session, and Gatting was hit in the mouth while fielding. Batsmen continued to enjoy the true pitch and the fast outfield, and Symonds and Maher put on 205 joyful runs. They were undefeated, although Maher was badly missed by Rhodes who should have stumped him off Tufnell when on 29. The left-handed Maher had a Shield century to his credit, but Symonds' previous highest score in first-class cricket was 26. England's second-innings batting was not distinguished, and Atherton left the state side a daunting target of 352 in 70 overs. Barsby and Hayden showed Queensland's positive approach to the task by scoring 231 for the first wicket, but once they were separated the innings fell apart. Healy, at number three, called Barsby for a run and saw the opener run out by Fraser's direct hit on the stumps. Tufnell then displayed his talent to bemuse, and the last eight wickets fell in under an hour and a half.

Mark Ilott joined the England party as stand-by because White and Benjamin were both doubtful as to fitness, while Merv Hughes became unavailable for selection for the Australian Test side because of a muscle strain.

 SECOND TEST MATCH
AUSTRALIA *v.* ENGLAND, at Melbourne

Fleming for McGrath was the one change that Australia made to the side that won the first Test, while Malcolm replaced McCague in the England side. White was unfit, and Gatting, by virtue of his double century against Queensland, continued to keep out Crawley. Atherton won the toss and took the bold step of asking Australia to bat first on a pitch that showed signs of dampness. His gamble was well repaid, for the first day belonged to England, morally if not totally.

Slater gifted his wicket to England when he hit to DeFreitas at cover and set off on a suicidal run. Boon played in a positive manner, but Taylor had been in for 73 minutes when he fell leg before to DeFreitas for nine. Mark Waugh was missed by Gooch at third-man, and, momentarily, it looked as if he and Boon would build a big total. Tufnell's clever flight accounted for Boon, however. The batsman was lured down the pitch, and Tufnell turned the ball sufficiently to find the edge of the bat for Hick to take a good catch at slip. Bevan, ill at ease with himself, was taken in the gully off the admirable Gough's lifter, and Australia were 100 for 4.

Much depended on the Waugh twins, and for a time they suggested that they would take control. They added 71, and their separation came through temperament rather than through the skill of the bowlers. Mark Waugh, frustrated by the shackling to which his eager stroke-play had been subjected, slashed a wide long-hop into the hands of point. The batsman left the field in a mood of obvious self-disgust. He can be the most exciting batsman in the world, and the most profligate.

Healy stayed for an hour before being caught off his glove by Rhodes who had earlier missed a hard chance Healy had given off Malcolm. Warne fell to what was the last ball of the day. He was splendidly caught at slip off Gough, the best bowler in the England side, and Australia were 220 for 7.

Steve Waugh, unbeaten on 61 overnight, saw May and McDermott fall in the same Gough over on the second morning, but Fleming, in his second Test match, gave Waugh mature support in a last-wicket stand of 37. Fleming could not stay quite long enough to help Waugh to his century, but he did a very good job. Steve Waugh remained undefeated on 94 which had come from 191 balls and occupied 266 minutes. Australia would have been in a sorry state without him.

England *were* in a sorry state immediately after lunch when, with 10 on the board, Stewart was struck on the same right index-finger that had been fractured in practice earlier in the tour and again suffered a breakage. Hick was assertive until he was adjudged caught behind off McDermott by umpire Randell, a decision which did not please the England camp. Neither did Bucknor's decision

against Atherton although there seemed less cause for complaint here. Atherton played forward to a leg-break which straightened and kept low.

This was the first of three Warne wickets on the second day. The three wickets came in 40 balls at a personal cost of eight runs. Thorpe pushed forward and was caught at silly-point off bat and pad. Gatting swept and skied to Steve Waugh at short fine-leg. England closed on 148 for 4 with hopes resting on Gooch.

Those hopes evaporated with the first ball of the third day, a gentle loosener from McDermott, a full toss which Gooch drove politely back to the bowler. Within four overs Rhodes, too, was gone, and the injured Stewart returned to a hero's welcome. He drove Warne back over his head, increased his score by 15 and added 34 with Gough, a cricketer of great determination. They were dismissed within four runs of each other, and England subsided. Once more, Warne, 6 for 64, had proved too good for England's batsmen, and Australia led by 67 runs, a disappointing and demoralising state of affairs for England.

Australia now set about consolidating their advantage. Gough, a man of constant endeavour with fire in his belly, had Taylor leg before, and Tufnell, in an impressive but mainly defensive spell, had Slater stumped. Gough, who should have been given the new ball, accounted for the

SECOND TEST MATCH – AUSTRALIA v. ENGLAND
24, 26, 27, 28 and 29 December 1994 at MCG, Melbourne

AUSTRALIA

	FIRST INNINGS		SECOND INNINGS	
M.J. Slater	run out	3	(2) st Rhodes, b Tufnell	44
M.A. Taylor (capt)	lbw, b DeFreitas	9	(1) lbw, b Gough	19
D.C. Boon	c Hick, b Tufnell	41	lbw, b DeFreitas	131
M.E. Waugh	c Thorpe, b DeFreitas	71	c and b Gough	29
M.G. Bevan	c Atherton, b Gough	3	c sub (Crawley), b Tufnell	35
S.R. Waugh	not out	94	not out	26
*I.A. Healy	c Rhodes, b Tufnell	17	c Thorpe, b Tufnell	17
S.K. Warne	c Hick, b Gough	6	c DeFreitas, b Gough	0
T.B.A. May	lbw, b Gough	9		
C.J. McDermott	b Gough	0	(9) not out	2
D.W. Fleming	c Hick, b Malcolm	16		
Extras	lb 7, nb 3	10	b 1, lb 9, w 1, nb 6	17
		279	(for 7 wickets, dec.)	320

ENGLAND

	FIRST INNINGS		SECOND INNINGS	
M.A. Atherton (capt)	lbw, b Warne	44	(2) c Healy, b McDermott	25
A.J. Stewart	c and b Warne	16	(7) not out	8
G.A. Hick	c Healy, b McDermott	23	b Fleming	2
G.P. Thorpe	c M.E. Waugh, b Warne	51	c Healy, b McDermott	9
G.A. Gooch	c and b McDermott	15	(1) c Healy, b Fleming	2
M.W. Gatting	c S.R. Waugh, b Warne	9	(5) c Taylor, b McDermott	25
D. Gough	c Healy, b McDermott	20	(9) c Healy, b Warne	0
*S.J. Rhodes	c M.E. Waugh, b Warne	0	(6) c M.E. Waugh, b McDermott	16
P.A.J. DeFreitas	st Healy, b Warne	14	(8) lbw, b Warne	0
D.E. Malcolm	not out	11	c Boon, b Warne	0
P.C.R. Tufnell	run out	0	c Healy, b McDermott	0
Extras	lb 7, nb 2	9	lb 2, nb 3	5
		212		92

	O	M	R	W	O	M	R	W
Malcolm	28.3	4	78	1	22	3	86	–
DeFreitas	23	4	66	2	26	2	70	1
Gough	26	9	60	4	25	6	59	3
Tufnell	28	7	59	2	48	8	90	3
Hick	2	–	9	–	3	2	5	–

	O	M	R	W	O	M	R	W
McDermott	24	6	72	3	16.5	5	42	5
Fleming	11	5	30	–	9	1	24	2
M.E. Waugh	3	1	11	–				
Warne	27.4	8	64	6	13	6	16	3
May	18	5	28	–	4	1	8	–

FALL OF WICKETS
1–10, 2–39, 3–91, 4–100, 5–171, 6–208, 7–220, 8–242, 9–242
1–61, 2–81, 3–157, 4–269, 5–272, 6–316, 7–317

FALL OF WICKETS
1–40, 2–119, 3–124, 4–140, 5–148, 6–151, 7–185, 8–189, 9–207
1–3, 2–10, 3–23, 4–43, 5–81, 6–88, 7–91, 8–91, 9–91

Umpires: S.U. Bucknor & S.G. Randell

Australia won by 295 runs

ABOVE: *Solid as a rock, David Boon reached his 20th Test century and put Australia in an impregnable position in the second Test. Boon lost form in the last three encounters. (Stuart Milligan/Sportsline)*

The Warne hat-trick – Shane Warne finished the second Test match in spectacular style, dismissing DeFreitas, Gough and Malcolm with successive deliveries to perform the second hat-trick for Australia in a Test match within the space of three months.

TOP LEFT: *DeFreitas is leg before. (Patrick Eagar)*

LEFT: *Gough is caught behind by Healy. (Patrick Eagar)*

BELOW LEFT: *Devon Malcolm is caught at short-leg by David Boon. (Patrick Eagar)*

dangerous Mark Waugh, but Australia closed on 170 for 3. Ominously, Boon was on 64.

The inevitable Boon century arrived on the fourth morning. He and Bevan, who struggled for form, added 112 before Bevan drove Tufnell to mid-off six overs after lunch. Bevan should have been caught by Rhodes earlier in the day, but the wicket-keeper, like others in the England side, was having a poor tour. Boon was out soon after Bevan. His 131 came off 277 balls and included 14 fours. It was his 20th Test century, his first at Melbourne, and was another model of technical competence and admirable application. England could only look on in envy. What they did most of the time was to slow the game to a snail's pace and be thankful for the crumbs that came their way such as the fast leg-break from Gough which accounted for Warne. Taylor declared at tea, and England needed 388 to win in four sessions.

In the first nine overs of their innings, England lost three wickets. Gooch aimed lavishly at Fleming's third delivery and was splendidly caught in front of first slip by

Healy. In his next over, Fleming turned Hick square and scattered his stumps. Thorpe batted in a frenzy, confusing positivity with neurosis, and he might have been out two or three times before driving firm-footed at McDermott and presenting the pace bowler with his 250th Test wicket.

Atherton and Gatting, through effort and example, stood head and shoulders above the rest of the England side, and as wickets were wasted at the other end, Atherton offered stern resistance. His innings came to an end in a sad and controversial manner, adjudged caught behind by umpire Bucknor off a ball that went down the leg-side and, in the opinion of the England camp, touched the batsman's pad, not his bat or glove. Unfortunately, poor and losing sides always blame umpiring decisions for their plight. Gatting and Rhodes survived the last 15 overs of the day, and England closed on 79 for 4.

The match was over inside an hour on the last day. In 12.5 overs, England's last six wickets fell for the addition of 13 paltry runs. Gatting was caught at slip off the second ball of the day. Stewart entered and survived bravely in obvious pain. Rhodes was taken at second slip to give McDermott a well-deserved fourth wicket, for the Queensland pace bowler had performed outstandingly, but, as yet, nothing had fallen to the demon Warne. The leg-spinner was to change that state of affairs in dramatic fashion.

He trapped DeFreitas on the back foot with a ball that kept low and hurried through. The next ball was a highly flighted leg-break which found the edge of Gough's bat and had him caught behind. Malcolm trudged in, pushed tentatively forward and nudged the ball low to the right of short-leg where Boon dived to hold a fine catch. An Australian bowler had performed the hat-trick in a Test match for the second time in three months. Warne had accomplished the feat in an Ashes series for the first time in 90 years. For Australia, the Test ended with a bang; for England, it was whimper all the way.

THIRD TEST MATCH
AUSTRALIA *v.* ENGLAND, at Sydney

England's troubles mounted. White was now out of the tour, and Russell had joined the party as wicket-keeping cover in view of Stewart's broken finger. Crawley came in for Stewart for the third Test, but it is likely that he would have played in any case in place of Gatting. DeFreitas reported a strain, and Fraser was brought in. Australia were unchanged.

Nothing in the first hour of the match suggested that England's troubles were at an end. Atherton won the toss and, rightly, chose to bat first on a good pitch. In the

ABOVE RIGHT: *Mike Atherton batted with determination and skill throughout the series. His second innings of 67 comes to an end when he is caught at slip by Taylor off Fleming. (David Munden/Sportsline)*

RIGHT: *Graeme Hick hits out at Craig McDermott. Hick was left unbeaten on 98 when Atherton declared. (David Munden/Sportsline)*

ABOVE: *Angus Fraser, who came into the England party as replacement for the injured McCague, traps Mark Waugh leg before for 25 and gives England a brief scent of victory. (Patrick Eagar)*

ABOVE RIGHT: *Darren Gough was the England hero of the third Test. He hit a ferocious 51 and then took six wickets. Here, he has Healy caught at slip by Hick. (Graham Chadwick/Allsport)*

second over of the morning, Fleming bowled an out-swinger which mesmerised Gooch, and Healy took the catch. Five overs later, McDermott ripped through Hick's defence with an in-swinger and wrecked his stumps. Six overs more and an in-swinging yorker accounted for Thorpe. England were 20 for 3 from 13 overs.

Atherton had watched the carnage and had scored seven. He was now joined by Crawley, and the England batting showed a refreshing determination. McDermott's admirable opening spell had come to an end – 2 for 14 in nine overs – but Warne and May posed problems which were countered with patience. McDermott was forced to leave the field in the afternoon because of a stomach upset, but this should not detract from the quality and deter-mination of the batting of Atherton and Crawley. They added 174, and both looked set for centuries, but the return of McDermott with the second new ball altered the complexion of the game.

In the first over of what was, in effect, his third spell, McDermott took the wickets of both Atherton and Gatting. Having been at the crease for 331 minutes, faced 267 balls and hit 8 fours, Atherton had his off stump knocked back by a late in-swinger. Four balls later, a fast out-swinger took the edge of Gatting's bat and was caught by Healy, whose wicket-keeping was a constant inspiration to Australia in the field.

Crawley had not added to his score when Fleming turned him square, found the edge, and Mark Waugh took a good catch at second slip. Crawley had batted for 291

minutes, faced 226 balls and hit 6 fours. There was still a technical worry in his tendency to try to play so much to leg, but in character and temperament he had proved him-self a Test cricketer. Sadly, his departure did not end England's troubles. A bizarre mix-up left Rhodes stranded and run out. England closed on a dismal 198 for 7. Four wickets had fallen in the last half-hour of the day for just three runs.

If McDermott had been the outstanding player of the opening day, the second day, which was brought to an end by rain shortly after lunch, belonged to Darren Gough and England. Contrary to expectation, Fraser and Gough did not capitulate on the Monday morning. Fraser stood res-olute; Gough thrashed all about him. The Yorkshireman hit a six and 4 fours in his 51 off 56 balls. He and Fraser added 58 in 72 minutes. Fraser scored only seven, but his stay was invaluable. Gough treated McDermott as none had dared treat him before, and 26 runs came from the pace man's first three-over spell. McDermott finally got his reward when Fleming took a good catch at long-leg to account for Gough, but by then England's spirits had been lifted.

Nor were they to diminish. Malcolm hit his highest score in Test cricket, 29 in 23 minutes with 2 sixes and 3 fours; and the admirable Fraser cajoled 14 for the last wicket with Tufnell. Fraser batted for 141 minutes, and England reached 309, undreamed-of heights at the end of the first day. Australia faced 21 balls, scored four, and then came the rain.

Gough had been a hero on the second day, and by the end of the third he was, wrongly, being compared to Botham. It was Malcolm, however, who started the Australian decline when he persuaded Slater to drag the ball into his stumps. Gough's first strike came when Boon offered no shot to a ball that came back at him. Mark Waugh went fourth ball to a good delivery from Malcolm which went low to the wicket-keeper off the face of the bat. Bevan batted for nearly an hour before square-cutting Fraser for four. Next ball he was caught at slip. Like Boon, Steve Waugh offered no shot to a ball from Gough which clipped his off stump. Healy hinted at recovery before driving loosely at Gough in the last over of the morning, and Australia were 57 for 6, with Taylor surveying the wreckage on 19.

Warne and May quickly departed, and the follow-on seemed certain. McDermott countered with the positive approach – 21 off 30 balls – but Malcolm failed to move for a catch at mid-on and then dropped Taylor's caught-and-bowled offering. The Derbyshire pace bowler, a Jekyll and Hyde cricketer, completed his trio of gifts by bowling a bouncer which went over the heads of both Taylor and Rhodes for four byes and saved the follow-on. Gough ended Taylor's 209-minute innings with a fine caught-and-bowled and then yorked Fleming first ball. He had taken a Test-best 6 for 49, and England led by 193. This was extended by another 90 runs for the loss of Gooch before rain returned to bring a premature close.

England built solidly on their lead on the fourth day when Australia's time-wasting tactics were similar to those England had adopted at Melbourne. Having played

another fine, unselfish innings and added 104 with Hick, Atherton steered Fleming to first slip. Hick had an astonishing escape when he played on to May without dislodging a bail, and his innings was far from flawless. Nevertheless, it came as something of a surprise and cause for comment when Atherton declared with Hick only two short of his century. Hick had become static in the nineties and Thorpe was monopolising the strike, but, most importantly, Atherton wanted his bowlers to have a few overs at Australia before the tea interval, and to delay the declaration much longer would not have allowed for that. Hick left the field with bowed head amid general sympathy.

Atherton gained no reward for his declaration. The quicker bowlers tended to bowl short while Slater produced some glorious shots against the spinners. Needing 449 to win, Australia scored 139 in 38 overs before the close, and even the impossible looked probable.

Taylor and Slater led their side in pursuit of a world record, and they added 67 in the morning session. Rain fell during and after lunch, and this meant that play would be extended for an hour. Almost immediately on the resumption, Slater, who had faced 237 balls and hit 10 fours, hooked Fraser towards square-leg where Tufnell ran some 15 yards and took a very good catch. Slater had batted with much charm, but he had been dropped by Crawley off Tufnell when on 72.

THIRD TEST MATCH – AUSTRALIA v. ENGLAND
1, 2, 3, 4 and 5 January 1995 at SCG, Sydney

ENGLAND

		FIRST INNINGS		SECOND INNINGS	
G.A. Gooch	c Healy, b Fleming	1	lbw, b Fleming	29
M.A. Atherton (capt)	b McDermott	88	c Taylor, b Fleming	67
G.A. Hick	b McDermott	2	not out	98
G.P. Thorpe	lbw, b McDermott	10	not out	47
J.P. Crawley	c M.E. Waugh,			
	b Fleming	72		
M.W. Gatting	c Healy, b McDermott	0		
A.R.C. Fraser	c Healy, b Fleming	27		
*S.J. Rhodes	run out	1		
D. Gough	c Fleming,			
	b McDermott	51		
D.E. Malcolm	b Warne	29		
P.C.R. Tufnell	not out	4		
Extras	b 8, lb 7, nb 9	24	lb 6, w 1, nb 7	14
		309	(for 2 wickets, dec.)	**255**

AUSTRALIA

		FIRST INNINGS		SECOND INNINGS	
M.J. Slater	b Malcolm	11	(2) c Tufnell, b Fraser	103
M.A. Taylor (capt)	c and b Gough	49	(1) b Malcolm	113
D.C. Boon	b Gough	3	c Hick, b Gough	17
M.E. Waugh	c Rhodes, b Malcolm	3	lbw, b Fraser	25
M.G. Bevan	c Thorpe, b Fraser	8	c Rhodes, b Fraser	7
S.R. Waugh	b Gough	1	c Rhodes, b Fraser	0
*I.A. Healy	c Hick, b Gough	10	c Rhodes, b Fraser	5
S.K. Warne	c Gatting, b Fraser	0	not out	36
T.B.A. May	c Hick, b Gough	0	not out	10
C.J. McDermott	not out	21		
D.W. Fleming	b Gough	0		
Extras	b 6, lb 1, nb 3	10	b 12, lb 3, w 1, nb 12	28
		116	(for 7 wickets)	**344**

	O	M	R	W	O	M	R	W
McDermott	30	7	101	5	24	2	76	–
Fleming	26.2	12	52	3	20	3	66	2
Warne	36	10	88	1	16	2	48	–
May	17	4	35	–	10	1	55	–
M.E. Waugh	6	1	10	–	2	1	4	–
Bevan	4	1	8	–				

	O	M	R	W	O	M	R	W
Malcolm	13	4	34	2	21	4	75	1
Gough	18.5	4	49	6	28	4	72	1
Fraser	11	1	26	2	25	3	73	5
Tufnell					35.4	9	61	–
Hick					5	–	21	–
Gooch					7	1	27	–

FALL OF WICKETS
1–1, 2–10, 3–20, 4–194, 5–194, 6–196, 7–197, 8–255, 9–295
1–54, 2–158

FALL OF WICKETS
1–12, 2–15, 3–18, 4–38, 5–39, 6–57, 7–62, 8–65, 9–116
1–208, 2–239, 3–265, 4–282, 5–286, 6–289, 7–292

Umpires: S.U. Bucknor & D.B. Hair   *Match drawn*

Taylor duly reached his century and looked ready to carry on the fight, but the new ball was taken with the score on 234 for 1, and suddenly there was a dramatic change of events. Taylor and Slater had made the bowling look easy to deal with, but Malcolm's persistent hostility was rewarded when Taylor shouldered arms to a fast in-swinger and was bowled. Taylor, 248 balls and 9 fours, had been somewhat fortunate earlier in the day when umpire Hair had declined to call upon the third umpire's television evidence to answer a very close run-out appeal.

Mark Waugh and Boon gave no hint of troubles to come before Gough, who had not found his first-innings control, made a ball swing late and had Boon caught at second slip. Fraser now extracted life from the pitch, and he had both Bevan and Steve Waugh caught behind by Rhodes, who enjoyed a better match behind the stumps than in the first two Tests. Mark Waugh had appeared to be in prime form, but he moved across his stumps to a ball from Fraser and was palpably leg before. Healy drove and edged, and, in little over an hour, Australia had slipped from 234 for 1 to 292 for 7. The decline had been engineered mainly by Angus Fraser who exploited the juice in the pitch and gave England a chance of victory.

It was not to be. Warne and May held out for 77 minutes. Malcolm dropped a catch off what many – including umpires and groundsman – thought was the last ball of the match until Atherton pointed out that time for one more over remained. However, the match was drawn, and Australia retained the Ashes. But England had regained some pride and deserved a halt to much of the hostile and vindictive criticism that had been levelled at them. Gough was named Man of the Match, but the determination and example of the England skipper warranted recognition.

Atherton was still, perhaps, burdened by the presence of Illingworth. It was learned that Neil Fairbrother was to replace Craig White, but who had made the decision and offered the invitation to Fairbrother remained less clear. Ilott was to join the 'A' side in India after his period on stand-by in Australia.

21, 22, 23 and 24 January 1995 *at Queen Elizabeth Oval, Bendigo*

Victoria 246 and 334 for 8 dec. (B.J. Hodge 104, M.T.G. Elliott 73)

England XI 329 (G.A. Hick 143, P.R. Reiffel 4 for 63) and 139 for 1 (M.A. Atherton 59 not out)

Match drawn

England took the field for the final match before the last two Tests without Udal, who had followed the path back to England to recover from injury. Like Benjamin, who appeared in the game against Victoria, he had been but a shadowy figure on the tour. At Bendigo, England began well enough, reducing Victoria to 106 for 6 and dismissing them on the second morning after they had effected something of a recovery. Victoria's batting was rather laborious but, in contrast, England batted with some dash, passing the state's total with only five wickets down, in spite of losing Atherton for 0. The England success was mainly due to Hick who hit 17 fours and 3 sixes in his 177-ball innings. Sadly, this was to be Hick's last contribution to the tour. He joined the injured list and returned to England with a back problem. If this was sad for England, there was more cruelty to come. Stewart was struck on the twice-broken finger, and his tour, too, was at an end. The two batsmen who headed the first-class averages for the tour were unavailable for the last two Tests. At one time, England fielded three substitutes in Victoria's second innings, and the state side batted briskly with Hodge in fine form. To Dean Jones' disgust, England declined the offer of scoring 252 to win and settled for practice.

FOURTH TEST MATCH
AUSTRALIA *v.* ENGLAND, at Adelaide

The England XI virtually chose itself: it was the eleven who were still standing. Australia elected to bring in Blewett – who had excelled in the one-day games – for Bevan, and to play a second leg-spinner, McIntyre. Atherton won the toss, and England batted.

England had shown failings and weaknesses in abundance on the tour, but the strength, courage, determination and ability of the captain had never slackened, and at Adelaide he once more led from the front. An opening

Debutant Greg Blewett reached a magnificent century on his home ground, Adelaide. (Ben Radford/Allsport)

DeFreitas hits McDermott for six in his whirlwind 88 which made England's victory possible. (David Munden/Sportsline)

Australia played two leg-spinners in the Adelaide Test. Peter McIntyre of South Australia won his first Test cap. (Patrick Eagar)

stand of 93 was ended when Gooch was adjudged caught at slip, although some believed he had not touched the ball with bat or glove. Atherton batted on phlegmatically, and he looked set for a well-deserved century when he fell to a sucker punch. Fleming had moved Boon back to the square-leg boundary. He then dropped a ball short, and Atherton obligingly hooked as requested. It was a moment of aberration, and a disappointing end to a very fine innings which had spanned 273 minutes. A storm spectacularly halted play, but on the resumption Gatting reached his fifty, Thorpe hit 3 fours and England reached 196 for 2.

The second day was a disappointment for England. Thorpe edged Warne to slip in the third over, but Gatting and Crawley added 68 before lunch. In the afternoon session, four wickets went down as 67 runs were scored. McDermott looked particularly hostile during this period and had Rhodes taken at slip and Lewis caught off an all-too-characteristically reckless pull. Lewis' dismissal left England on 307 for 6, and Gatting on 99. He had moved snail-like through the nineties and had spent 35 minutes on 95, but the century came when he jabbed McDermott to Steve Waugh at gully and went for a quick single. DeFreitas just made his ground as Waugh's throw missed the stumps. Gatting had reached his first Test century for eight years.

The last three wickets fell at 353, with Gatting the last man out. He had batted for 410 minutes, faced 286 balls and hit 14 fours. Had Hick been fit, it is certain that Gatting would not have played, and certainly he was to play no more Tests after this tour, but he showed those qualities which have been his strength in a rugged, distinguished career. He is a man of resolve and determination, a great fighter, brave in battle. He had served England well. Slater and Taylor altered the perspective of the match before the close with 81 from 22 overs.

They did not quite recapture their initial flamboyance on the third morning and, 15 overs into the day, Slater edged

an out-swinger to slip. Boon lasted only five balls before he, too, fell to a DeFreitas out-swinger. The afternoon session belonged to England. The four quicker bowlers rotated in turn, and Lewis accounted for Taylor who had been at the crease for 267 minutes and faced 200 balls after a period of slow scoring and a slow over rate. Mark Waugh was beaten by Fraser's bouncer in the very next over, and when Steve Waugh was taken well at slip Australia were 232 for 5. Blewett and Healy scratched three more runs before tea so that Australia entered the final session 118 runs adrift with no recognised batsman to come.

In that last session, from 36 overs, Blewett and Healy cracked 159 runs. The England attack was routed. Healy ended the day on 71, and the debutant Blewett finished just nine short of his century.

Malcolm, who had erred badly when England bowled tardily on the Saturday, had Healy caught down the leg side in his first over on the Sunday. Shane Warne flailed wildly at Fraser and was taken at slip, and Fleming fell to another leg-side catch off Malcolm. The Australian innings was crumbling, and Blewett was still six short of his century, but McIntyre did remain long enough for the local hero to reach the three figures he so much deserved. He ended the innings unbeaten on 102, which included 12 fours and came from 180 balls. His outstanding innings had been full of lavish strokes and had confirmed the strength in depth that Australia possessed in batting. Bevan and Langer fretted in the wings, and Ponting, arguably the most promising of them all, still yearned for Test baptism.

For England, there was some consolation after the ragged performance in the field and the dreadfully slow over rate of Saturday: they captured the last five Australian wickets for 23 runs.

Immediately after lunch, Taylor brought on Mark Waugh. This was a surprise to all, not least to the batsmen, for, in his first over, he trapped Atherton leg before and, in his second, he bowled Gatting for 0. Gooch and Thorpe cleared the arrears before Gooch was caught behind for the fifth time in the series.

Thorpe batted impressively. His 83 was rich in punishing shots and occupied only 140 minutes, but once again he perished to a rash shot. Rhodes and Lewis quickly followed so that three wickets had fallen in 40 minutes before Crawley and DeFreitas batted steadily to the close with England 220 for 6.

The final day began with, seemingly, only two results likely: a draw or a win for Australia. That an England victory soon became a third possibility was due primarily to DeFreitas. Resuming with his score on 20, he hit another 68 off 57 balls. He destroyed McDermott, who was far from fit, by hitting 22 off one over of the second new ball. Crawley gave sensible and authoritative support until he fell to an unwise pull, and Malcolm hit Warne out of the ground so that he, DeFreitas and England went into the final phase of the match in good heart.

Australia lunched at 16 for 0, but Malcolm, having changed ends, gave them an uncomfortable start to the afternoon. He disturbed Taylor with a bouncer and then had him caught at slip chasing a wide delivery. Boon lasted five balls before being taken down the leg side off Fraser. Slater perished when he hooked Malcolm and Tufnell took a splendid running catch at fine leg. Malcolm followed this by bowling Steve Waugh first ball with a delivery of full length. It was his third wicket in 12 balls, and the cost to the bowler was four runs.

Mark Waugh looked in good form, but Tufnell joined the attack, and Waugh turned his first ball to leg. It hit Gatting on the boot and jumped up into his hands. This was a sure sign that the day did not belong to Australia. Lewis was

FOURTH TEST MATCH – AUSTRALIA v. ENGLAND
26, 27, 28, 29 and 30 January 1995 at Adelaide Oval

ENGLAND

	FIRST INNINGS		SECOND INNINGS	
G.A. Gooch	c M.E. Waugh, b Fleming	47	c Healy, b McDermott	34
M.A. Atherton (capt)	c Boon, b Fleming	80	lbw, b M.E. Waugh	14
M.W. Gatting	c S.R. Waugh, b McIntyre	117	b M.E. Waugh	0
G.P. Thorpe	c Taylor, b Warne	26	c Warne, b McDermott	83
J.P. Crawley	b Warne	28	c and b M.E. Waugh	71
*S.J. Rhodes	c Taylor, b McDermott	6	c Fleming, b Warne	2
C.C. Lewis	c Blewett, b McDermott	10	b Fleming	7
P.A.J. DeFreitas	c Blewett, b McIntyre	21	c Healy, b M.E. Waugh	88
A.R.C. Fraser	run out	7	c McDermott, b M.E. Waugh	5
D.E. Malcolm	b McDermott	0	not out	10
P.C.R. Tufnell	not out	0	lbw, b Warne	0
Extras	b 2, lb 5, w 2, nb 2	11	b 6, lb 8	14
		353		**328**

AUSTRALIA

	FIRST INNINGS		SECOND INNINGS	
M.J. Slater	c Atherton, b DeFreitas	67	(2) c Tufnell, b Malcolm	5
M.A. Taylor (capt)	lbw, b Lewis	90	(1) c Thorpe, b Malcolm	13
D.C. Boon	c Rhodes, b DeFreitas	0	c Rhodes, b Fraser	4
M.E. Waugh	c Rhodes, b Fraser	39	c Gatting, b Tufnell	24
S.R. Waugh	c Atherton, b Lewis	19	b Malcolm	0
G.S. Blewett	not out	102	c Rhodes, b Lewis	12
*I.A. Healy	c Rhodes, b Malcolm	74	not out	51
S.K. Warne	c Thorpe, b Fraser	7	lbw, b Lewis	2
D.W. Fleming	c Rhodes, b Malcolm	0	(10) lbw, b Lewis	24
P.E. McIntyre	b Malcolm	0	(11) lbw, b Malcolm	0
C.J. McDermott	c Crawley, b Fraser	5	(9) c Rhodes, b Lewis	0
Extras	b 2, lb 7, nb 7	16	b 3, lb 5, nb 13	21
		419		**156**

	O	M	R	W	O	M	R	W
McDermott	41	15	66	3	27	5	96	2
Fleming	25	6	65	2	11	3	37	1
Blewett	16	4	59	–	4	–	23	–
Warne	31	9	72	2	30.5	9	82	2
McIntyre	19.3	3	51	2	8	–	36	–
M.E. Waugh	9	1	33	–	14	4	40	5

	O	M	R	W	O	M	R	W
Malcolm	26	5	78	3	16.1	3	39	4
Fraser	28.5	6	95	3	12	1	37	1
Tufnell	24	5	64	–	9	3	17	1
DeFreitas	20	3	70	2	11	3	31	–
Lewis	18	1	81	2	13	4	24	4
Gooch	5	–	22	–				

FALL OF WICKETS
1–93, 2–175, 3–211, 4–286, 5–293, 6–307, 7–334, 8–353, 9–353
1–26, 2–30, 3–83, 4–154, 5–169, 6–181, 7–270, 8–317, 9–317

FALL OF WICKETS
1–128, 2–130, 3–202, 4–207, 5–232, 6–396, 7–405, 8–406, 9–414
1–17, 2–22, 3–22, 4–23, 5–64, 6–75, 7–83, 8–83, 9–152

Umpires: P.D. Parker & S. Venkataraghavan

England won by 106 runs

introduced and puffed away Blewett, Warne and McDermott either side of tea. Healy, a wonderful fighter, and Fleming halted the England charge. They were together for 112 minutes, and when Fleming fell to Lewis only eight overs remained. Healy completed his fifty, but the recall of Malcolm brought the end of McIntyre and the match.

DeFreitas was named Man of the Match. Lewis was fined for gesturing at McDermott, and Atherton was reprimanded for the way in which he had conducted the game. England were lucky to be fined for a mere three-over shortfall in their rate on the Saturday. They deserved to be more harshly treated for such shabby cricket. But they had won, and that brought a breath of life to the game as a whole.

FIFTH TEST MATCH
AUSTRALIA v. ENGLAND, at Perth

An early success for England as Lewis – another not chosen in the original party – has Taylor caught behind. (David Munden/Sportsline)

Fleming was unfit for the Australian side and was replaced by Angel while pace man McGrath took over from spinner McIntyre. England included an extra batsman, Ramprakash, at the expense of Tufnell. As ever at Perth, pace was to be the dominant factor. Gooch and Gatting had both announced that this was to be their last Test match, and Gooch was the first to come under the spotlight.

Taylor had won the toss, and Australia batted. The fourth ball of the match saw Slater edge Malcolm to third slip where Gooch got both hands to the ball but spilled the catch. Slater, twice dropped later by Malcolm himself – one a simple chance of caught-and-bowled – went on to make 124. It was a pugnacious innings, and he was on 33 when Taylor was caught behind off Lewis for nine. Boon was out 10 minutes later, and Australia were 55 for 2. England had every chance to grab the initiative, but they could not grab the catches. The third-wicket stand was worth only 25 when Mark Waugh cut Lewis straight to Crawley in the gully. Again the catch was spilled, and Slater and Mark Waugh were not separated until they had added another 158. They were out in quick succession, but Slater had hit 13 fours in his third hundred of the series, and Mark Waugh had revealed more of that masterly power of his with 10 fours in his 177-ball innings. Steve Waugh and Blewett took Australia to a contented close, 283 for 4.

Blewett was adjudged caught behind early on the second day – a harsh decision – and England, again resorting to a wretchedly slow over rate, began to gnaw away at the Australian tail. In spite of some ineffective swats at Malcolm, Steve Waugh hustled towards his century, but he was to be denied at the last. McDermott, suffering from a variety of ailments, was forced to call on Mark Waugh as runner. On 99, Steve Waugh seemed pinned down. When he turned Lewis to leg, brother Mark essayed a run. Steve sent him back, but Mark, slithering and diving, failed to make his ground.

McDermott did not take the field when England batted. He was not missed, for McGrath's third ball brushed

Atherton's glove and was taken down the leg side by Healy, and the fourth was edged into his stumps by Gatting. When Mark Waugh joined the attack he was hit for 11 in his first over, but the first ball of his second over trapped Gooch leg before. Three balls later, Crawley prodded hesitantly to slip where Warne took a splendid catch. In the last 43 minutes of the day, Thorpe and Ramprakash took the score to 110 in a refreshingly positive manner.

On the third day, Thorpe and Ramprakash gave more credibility to Atherton's assertion that England would have been better served by a policy of youth. For more than three hours, the two young batsmen not only held Australia at bay but were quick to punish the bowling at every opportunity. Thorpe drove and pulled fiercely, and his excellent 123 included 19 fours. Ramprakash hit 11 fours in his four-hour innings, and the pair added 158. Sadly, the dismissal of Thorpe heralded a collapse, four wickets going down for 12 runs. Lewis clouted 40 in an hour, enjoying considerable fortune, but England ended 107 adrift of Australia.

Slater began Australia's second innings with his usual aggression, but he fell to Fraser, and night-watchman Angel was run out by Gooch to leave the home side 87 for 2 at stumps.

In a tour noted for England low spots, the fourth day of the final Test saw the tourists descend to a depth that, even by their standards, was unexpected. Catches were spilled in abundance, yet five Australian wickets went down for 123 runs. DeFreitas was economical, Fraser naggingly accurate and Malcolm was hostile, but the list of fielding aberrations grew by the over. England's fielding had become a music-hall joke on the tour, and the top-of-the-bill performance came 10 minutes after lunch. Steve Waugh edged Malcolm to slip where Thorpe dropped the catch. It was not the first he had missed, and he petulantly kicked the ball away. His football was better than his

The twins' tragedy. Runner Mark Waugh is run out to leave brother Steve 99 not out at the end of the Australian first innings. (David Munden/Sportsline)

fielding, and he drove his shot wide of cover so that the batsmen were able to take two runs. Atherton sank to his knees with his head in his hands; Malcolm ranted angrily and justifiably in mid-pitch. It was a scene that symbolised England's tour.

Blewett reached his second century in Test cricket in his second Test. It was a blazing, mature affair – 19 fours, 157 balls – as he and Steve Waugh added a ruthless and highly entertaining 203. This was vintage stuff, however bedraggled the opposition. Healy batted with a runner, and why Warne batted at all none could understand. Taylor delayed his declaration until England had only the last 65 minutes of the day to bat.

In those 65 minutes, 14 overs, the England batting disintegrated much as the fielding had done. Gooch, in his last Test innings, was roundly cheered. The innings lasted 12 balls, and he was woefully dropped by the floundering Angel at mid-on before Boon missed a more difficult

FIFTH TEST MATCH – AUSTRALIA v. ENGLAND
3, 4, 5, 6 and 7 February 1995 at WACA Ground, Perth

AUSTRALIA

	FIRST INNINGS		SECOND INNINGS	
M.J. Slater	c Lewis, b DeFreitas	124	(2) c Atherton, b Fraser	45
M.A. Taylor (capt)	c Rhodes, b Lewis	9	(1) b Fraser	52
D.C. Boon	c Ramprakash, b Lewis	1	(4) c Rhodes, b Malcolm	18
M.E. Waugh	c DeFreitas, b Lewis	88	(5) c Rhodes, b DeFreitas	1
S.R. Waugh	not out	99	(6) c Ramprakash,	
			b Lewis	80
G.S. Blewett	c Rhodes, b Fraser	20	(7) c Malcolm, b Lewis	115
*I.A. Healy	c Lewis, b DeFreitas	12	(8) not out	11
S.K. Warne	c Rhodes, b DeFreitas	1	(9) c Lewis, b Malcolm	6
J. Angel	run out	11	(3) run out	0
G.D. McGrath	run out	0		
C.J. McDermott	run out	6		
Extras	b 14, lb 4, w 4, nb 9	31	b 1, lb 9, nb 7	17
		—		—
		402	(for 8 wickets, dec.)	345

ENGLAND

	FIRST INNINGS		SECOND INNINGS	
G.A. Gooch	lbw, b M.E. Waugh	37	c and b McDermott	4
M.A. Atherton (capt)	c Healy, b McGrath	4	c Healy, b McGrath	8
M.W. Gatting	b McGrath	0	b McDermott	8
G.P. Thorpe	st Healy, b Warne	123	(5) c Taylor,	
			b McGrath	0
J.P. Crawley	c Warne, b M.E. Waugh	0	(6) c M.E. Waugh,	
			b McDermott	0
M.R. Ramprakash	b Warne	72	(7) c S.R. Waugh,	
			b M.E. Waugh	42
*S.J. Rhodes	b Angel	2	(8) not out	39
C.C. Lewis	c Blewett, b McGrath	40	(9) lbw, b McDermott	11
P.A.J. DeFreitas	b Angel	0	(10) c Taylor,	
			b McDermott	0
A.R.C. Fraser	c Warne, b Angel	9	(4) lbw, b McGrath	5
D.E. Malcolm	not out	0	b McDermott	0
Extras	b 4, lb 1, nb 3	8	lb 1, w 1, nb 4	6
		—		—
		295		123

	O	M	R	W	O	M	R	W
Malcolm	31	6	93	–	23.3	3	105	2
DeFreitas	29	8	91	3	22	10	54	1
Fraser	32	11	84	1	21	3	74	2
Lewis	31.5	8	73	3	16	–	71	2
Gooch	1	1	0	–				
Ramprakash	11	–	43	–	8	1	31	–

	O	M	R	W	O	M	R	W
Angel	22.3	7	65	3	3	–	20	–
McGrath	25	6	88	3	13	4	40	3
Blewett	4	1	9	–				
M.E. Waugh	9	2	29	2	3	–	13	1
Warne	23	8	58	2	7	3	11	–
McDermott	13	5	41	–	15	4	38	6

FALL OF WICKETS
1–47, 2–55, 3–238, 4–247, 5–287, 6–320, 7–328, 8–386, 9–388
1–75, 2–79, 3–102, 4–115, 5–123, 6–326, 7–333, 8–345

FALL OF WICKETS
1–5, 2–5, 3–77, 4–77, 5–235, 6–246, 7–246, 8–247, 9–293
1–4, 2–17, 3–26, 4–26, 5–27, 6–27, 7–95, 8–121, 9–123

Umpires: K.E. Liebenberg & S.G. Randell

Australia won by 329 runs

chance at short-leg. Finally, Gooch swatted the magnificent McDermott straight, and the bowler took the catch. A great Test career was at an end. Gatting had been off the field throughout the Australian innings, but he came in at number three and was bowled off his pads as he played across the line. Half an hour still remained, but Fraser appeared as night-watchman and was quickly despatched by McGrath. Thorpe completed a dreadful day when he edged to slip first ball, and Crawley, who had had an awful match, was out for a 'pair' when he, too, edged to slip. England ended the day on 27 for 5.

Any hopes that were nurtured of the captain playing a saving innings were dashed when he was caught down the leg side off the 12th ball of the final day. Rhodes belatedly made a contribution to the series, and Ramprakash gave further indication of what youth might have achieved, but Man of the Series McDermott quickly brought an end to the match to leave Australia worthy victors by 3–1.

Gooch and Gatting departed from Test cricket, but the question as to why *both* veterans were selected for the tour was not answered by the chairman of selectors. England had been dreadfully unlucky with injuries, particularly those which had deprived them of Stewart, Gough and Hick, but what a difference Hussain and Ramprakash would have made in the field where the veterans laboured and England became figures of fun.

Like Gooch, Gatting had a generally sad tour and announced his retirement from Test cricket. McGrath bowls him for 0 in the first innings of the final Test. (David Munden/Sportsline)

TEST MATCH AVERAGES – AUSTRALIA v. ENGLAND

AUSTRALIA BATTING

	M	Inns	NO	Runs	HS	Av	100s	50s
G.S. Blewett	2	4	1	249	115	83.00	2	–
M.J. Slater	5	10	–	623	176	62.30	3	1
S.R. Waugh	5	10	3	345	99*	49.28	–	3
M.A. Taylor	5	10	–	471	113	47.10	1	4
M.E. Waugh	5	10	–	435	140	43.50	1	2
I.A. Healy	5	10	3	249	74	35.57	–	2
D.C. Boon	5	10	–	246	131	24.60	1	–
T.B.A. May	3	5	3	31	10*	15.50	–	–
M.G. Bevan	3	6	–	81	35	13.50	–	–
D.W. Fleming	3	4	–	40	24	10.00	–	–
C.J. McDermott	5	8	2	42	21*	7.00	–	–
S.K. Warne	5	10	1	60	36*	6.66	–	–
G.D. McGrath	2	2	–	0	0	0.00	–	–

Played in one Test: J. Angel 11 & 0; P.E. McIntyre 0 & 0

ENGLAND BATTING

	M	Inns	NO	Runs	HS	Av	100s	50s
G.P. Thorpe	5	10	1	444	123	49.33	1	3
G.A. Hick	3	6	1	208	98*	41.60	–	2
M.A. Atherton	5	10	–	407	88	40.70	–	4
J.P. Crawley	3	5	–	171	72	34.20	–	2
G.A. Gooch	5	10	–	245	56	24.50	–	1
D. Gough	3	5	1	98	51	24.50	–	1
A.J. Stewart	2	4	1	73	33	24.33	–	–
M.W. Gatting	5	9	–	182	117	20.22	1	–
P.A.J. DeFreitas	4	8	–	141	88	17.62	–	1
C.C. Lewis	2	4	–	68	40	17.00	–	–
D.E. Malcolm	4	7	3	50	29	12.50	–	–
A.R.C. Fraser	3	5	–	53	27	10.60	–	–
S.J. Rhodes	5	9	1	72	39*	9.00	–	–
P.C.R. Tufnell	4	7	3	6	4*	1.50	–	–

Played in one Test: M.R. Ramprakash 72 & 42; M.J. McCague 1 & 0

AUSTRALIA BOWLING

	Overs	Mds	Runs	Wkts	Av	Best	10/m	5/inn
M.E. Waugh	53	11	157	8	19.62	5-40	–	1
S.K. Warne	256.1	84	549	27	20.33	8-71	1	2
C.J. McDermott	232.5	56	675	32	21.09	6-38	–	4
D.W. Fleming	102.2	30	274	10	27.40	3-52	–	–
J. Angel	25.3	7	85	3	28.33	3-65	–	–
G.D. McGrath	67	16	229	6	38.16	3-40	–	–
P.E. McIntyre	27.3	3	87	2	43.50	2-51	–	–
T.B.A. May	101	30	219	1	219.00	1-34	–	–
M.G. Bevan	7	1	19	–	–	–	–	–
G.S. Blewett	24	5	91	–	–	–	–	–

ENGLAND BOWLING

	Overs	Mds	Runs	Wkts	Av	Best	10/m	5/inn
D. Gough	125.5	33	425	20	21.25	6-49	–	1
C.C. Lewis	78.5	13	249	11	22.63	4-24	–	–
A.R.C. Fraser	129.5	25	389	14	27.78	5-73	–	1
P.A.J. DeFreitas	184	39	558	13	42.92	3-91	–	–
P.C.R. Tufnell	207.4	45	442	10	44.20	4-79	–	–
D.E. Malcolm	181.1	32	588	13	45.23	4-39	–	–
G.A. Gooch	25	6	74	1	74.00	1-20	–	–
G.A. Hick	16	3	58	–	–	–	–	–
M.R. Ramprakash	19	1	74	–	–	–	–	–

Bowled in one innings: M.J. McCague 19.2–4–96–2

AUSTRALIA FIELDING FIGURES

25 – I.A. Healy (ct 23/st 2); 8 – M.E. Waugh; 7 – M.A. Taylor; 5 – S.K. Warne; 3 – S.R. Waugh, G.S. Blewett and C.J. McDermott; 2 – D.W. Fleming and D.C. Boon

ENGLAND FIELDING FIGURES

21 – S.J. Rhodes (ct 20/st 1); 9 – G.A. Hick; 5 – G.P. Thorpe; 4 – M.A. Atherton and D. Gough; 3 – M.W. Gatting, C.C. Lewis and subs (J.P. Crawley and C. White 2); 2 – M.R. Ramprakash, A.J. Stewart, P.A.J. DeFreitas and P.C.R. Tufnell; 1 – J.P. Crawley and D.E. Malcolm

FIELDING FIGURES

46 – S.J. Rhodes (ct 40/st 6)
16 – G.A. Hick
9 – G.P. Thorpe
8 – M.A. Atherton
7 – Subs
5 – P.C.R. Tufnell, D. Gough and M.W. Gatting
3 – J.P. Crawley, M.J. McCague, A.J. Stewart and C.C. Lewis
2 – C. White, P.A.J. DeFreitas and M.R. Ramprakash
1 – S.D. Udal, A.R.C. Fraser, J.E. Benjamin and D.E. Malcolm

†A.J. Stewart retired hurt

ENGLAND IN AUSTRALIA, 1994-95 — BATTING

Summary

Batsman	M	Inns	NO	Runs	HS	Av
G.A. Gooch	10	19	1	685	101	36.05
M.A. Atherton	10	20	1	755	88	39.73
G.A. Hick	8	15	1	877	172	62.64
G.P. Thorpe	8	20	3	756	123	44.47
M.W. Gatting	9	16	1	532	203*	35.46
J.P. Crawley	9	15	2	563	91	43.30
S.J. Rhodes	9	13	4	240	50	14.11
P.A.J. DeFreitas	7	11	1	190	88	15.83
M.J. McCague	4	5	1	29	16	7.25
J.E. Benjamin	4	5	1	11	7	2.75
D.E. Malcolm	8	12	4	91	29	11.37
C. White	3	5	1	125	51	25.00
D. Gough	5	8	2	114	46	19.00
P.C.R. Tufnell	5	13	7	30	16	7.50
S.D. Udal	2	4	1	291	101*	58.20
A.J. Stewart	5	9	1	60	27	12.00
A.R.C. Fraser	2	6	4	68	40	17.00
C.C. Lewis	2	4	–	114	72	57.00
M.R. Ramprakash	1	2	–			

BOWLING — Bowler's average

Bowler	O–M–R–W	Average
P.A.J. DeFreitas	299.1–67–852–24	35.50
D.E. Malcolm	340.3–55–1133–34	33.32
M.J. McCague	125.2–21–487–14	34.78
J.E. Benjamin	105.5–23–341–6	56.83
G.A. Hick	61–8–224–2	112.00
C.C. Lewis	78.5–14–249–11	22.63
D. Gough	222.5–44–688–26	26.46
C. White	60.5–10–195–7	27.85
P.C.R. Tufnell	384.2–70–1018–27	37.70
S.D. Udal	81.5–4–345–5	69.00
G.A. Gooch	27–7–79–2	39.50
A.R.C. Fraser	157.5–30–504–14	36.00

A M.A. Atherton 2–0–6–0
B G.P. Thorpe 2–1–6–0
C M.R. Ramprakash 11–0–43–0; 8–1–31–0

REVIEW OF THE ASHES SERIES
Alan Lee, Cricket Correspondent of *The Times*

Before the Ashes series of 1994–5 had reached its midway point, influential voices were raised in anguished warning. Much more of this, they cried, and nothing could protect the sanctity of cricket's greatest and most glorious institution. In other words, could it be justified that England and Australia must meet every two years, claiming the highest profile available to the sport, if the cricket was no longer competitive?

So it had come to this. As England groped their way towards their fourth consecutive Ashes series loss of emphatic – not to say embarrassing – proportions, the status of the event, bedrock of international cricket, was being questioned. It was unthinkable and yet, given the evidence, almost forgivable.

The fact that the series did not proceed to script, that England won one Test match and might quite conceivably have won two and entered the final match at 2–2, quietened the heretics but did not entirely negate their point. Australia took the rubber 3–1 and were not flattered one bit by the margin; now, since 1989, they have won 14 and lost only two of the 22 Tests played between the founder members of the international circuit. If that is not one-sided, I do not know what is.

For an Englishman, the worst of it is that it comes as a nasty surprise every time. As each Ashes series approaches, it is possible, from the shires and cities of the old country, to identify any number of sound reasons why things will now be different, why the latest English personnel will be a marked improvement on the previous rabble and why Australia will be short of runs/wickets/spirit or whatever else has fuelled their remarkable – and now unprecedented – run of tyranny over England. There was plenty of such big talk in the autumn of 1994, provoked by the breathtaking win over South Africa and by the silver tongue of Raymond Illingworth, who has never made any secret of his ability to walk on water and who had a captive audience of tame and agog reporters for his every remark as chairman of selectors. This time, the propaganda plainly stated, the Australians would have their comeuppance. One of the theories most frequently cited was that the retirement of Allan Border, England's regular nemesis, must have left them a rudderless ship. This, as it transpired, was a slanderous under-assessment of the leadership ability of the new captain, Mark Taylor, and of the durable coach, Bob Simpson. For them, it was business as usual and, while Border spent his winter being paraded and fêted around each of the Test grounds in turn, the Australian dressing-room paid him the ultimate tribute by replicating the discipline, commitment and ruthlessness that he had so successfully preached against England in three preceding series.

Taylor's part in the victory cannot be overstated. His Test captaincy had begun in the most chastening way imaginable when, in Karachi in October, he not only made a 'pair' but presided over a one-wicket defeat in a match in which Australia led at every step but at the finishing tape. He is a tough character, though, and one who did not have to strive to earn the respect of his players.

Under Taylor, Australia constantly looked the more focused team. Only a fool would suggest that defeat did not matter to the England players but there were times – as there have been many in recent years – when it seemed not to matter enough, when the 'mental fibre' of which Graham Gooch spoke so eloquently during his time as captain, was conspicuously absent again.

It is simplistic to blame Mike Atherton for this, to decry his powers of motivation, the poor example of his own body language and the occasions when, by his own subsequent confession, he was tactically so cautious that windows of opportunity were missed. There is validity in all such criticisms, for Atherton in Australia was young, at 26, still inexperienced as a captain and, most importantly, lacking the background of success which, as Taylor would confirm, lends so much to the self-confidence. But he could also claim, quite reasonably, that it is difficult to be positive, aggressive and at all times bright and bountiful when the team at your disposal is inured to defeat and decimated by sickness and injury.

This last point was England's prime mitigation, and a pretty compelling one, too. From the moment that Devon Malcolm – widely, if optimistically, described as the man who would shake and shock the Australians – fell ill with chicken-pox on the eve of the first Test in Brisbane, England were scarcely ever able to put out their first-choice side. Alec Stewart, Darren Gough and Graeme Hick, key components by any estimation, all sustained injuries which discounted them from two or more Tests, and the disorientation of having to summon no fewer than five replacement players was incalculable. Even the most senior of touring observers could remember nothing like it.

How much difference this made cannot be gauged but Atherton, certainly, refused to shelter behind the excuse. In this, he was wise and correct, for the superiority of Australia was self-evident in so many areas. By common consent, they possessed easily the two best bowlers on either side in Shane Warne and Craig McDermott, and the relative paucity of the support bowling was rendered inconsequential, such was the success that this pair enjoyed. Warne was captivatingly brilliant in Brisbane and just when he seemed sure to be upstaged by McDermott in Melbourne, he finished the game with a hat-trick. When his star waned slightly in the New Year, amid fears for his shoulder and his long-term stamina, McDermott marched on, finishing up with 6 for 38 in the second innings of an overwhelming Australian win in Perth.

By then, England had shot their bolt. From the humiliation of Melbourne they had heroically regrouped to come close to victory in Sydney – even reducing Australia's first innings to 65 for 8 – and then, with the kind of irresistible cricket that had flattened South Africa five months earlier, they had won a famous victory before a series of bulging full houses in Adelaide. Perth was a match too many and there were those in the team – the captain included – who were physically and mentally incapable of doing more than go through the motions. The result was inevitable, the reasons profound and worrying.

The most fundamental difference between the two teams in this series was no single player but the systems under which they play. The England side had played plenty of international cricket over the preceding year – arguably too much. So too had the Australians. But whereas the likes of Warne and McDermott, Michael Slater and the newest tyro, Greg Blewett, were allowed to channel their energies almost exclusively into the interests of the national team, Atherton and his players were expected to fulfil absurdly arduous commitments to county clubs

whose priorities – time and decisions have shown – have never included the health of the England side. Before the final Test, there was a round of Sheffield Shield games but those Australians in need of a rest simply took one. At an equivalent stage in England, players would be expected to race off up the motorway to a spurious knock-out match, slot in a four-day championship game and a knockabout Sunday League match, before drawing breath from their Test exertions.

Until this situation changes we can expect far more English subservience in Ashes cricket, because the game and its profile have moved on and the English system has not moved with them. This, above much intriguing cricket, was the overriding message of the latest Australian win.

BENSON AND HEDGES WORLD SERIES
Phase One – Matches One to Eight

One despairs at the actions and decisions of those entrusted with the administration of cricket today, although criticism is both unwelcome and dangerous. For the 1994–5 Benson and Hedges World Series, the Australian Board took the ridiculous step of adding an Australian 'A' side to the three original competing nations of Australia, England and Zimbabwe. The decision deprived states of more of their leading players and, as the matches in which the 'A' side participated were not to be recognised as *official* one-day internationals, the credibility of the tournament suffered grievously.

The initial 'A' team squad was selected as follows – D.R. Martyn (captain), P.A. Emery, M.L. Hayden, D.S. Lehmann, J.L. Langer, R.T. Ponting, T.M. Moody, G.R. Robertson, J. Angel, M.G. Hughes, P.R. Reiffel and G.J. Rowell – but when it was later learned that there was to be an interchange of players between the 'A' side and the national team there was general disbelief, and the competition lost further credibility.

The first match of the series saw Stuart Law make his international debut and share in Australia's victory with some tidy bowling and the running out of David Houghton. Zimbabwe began well enough as the Flower brothers ran well and scored 49 for the first wicket at nearly five an over. Thereafter, promise was not fulfilled as wickets fell at regular intervals just as it seemed batsmen were getting set. Facing a moderate target, Australia were given a rollicking start by skipper Mark Taylor who hit 45 off as many deliveries. Taylor and Slater were caught in successive overs, however, and with Boon out of touch and the Zimbabwe fielding dynamic, the complexion of the game changed. Healy and Bevan restored some order with a stand of 60 before the slow left-arm bowling of Grant Flower caused more embarrassment. Mark Waugh had been forced down the order by a strained groin muscle, and, batting with a runner, he saw Australia to victory by an uncomfortably narrow margin.

The Australian 'A' side entered the fray with a win that was more convincing than that of the senior side. Again Zimbabwe flattered to deceive. The Flower brothers hit 59 off the first 10 overs, but in the next 20 overs, only 36 runs

Consistently on the fringe of the Test side, Justin Langer hit 241 not out for Western Australia against New South Wales in Perth, played for Australia 'A' in the World Series and won a place in the side to go to the West Indies. (Ben Radford/Allsport)

were scored as two wickets fell. Moody, who had 3 for 16 in his 10 overs, and Hughes, 2 for 21 in his 10, paralysed the middle-order with their accuracy, and three batsmen were run out by Matthew Hayden as they strove to break free of their shackles. When Houghton was run out in the 33rd over with the score on 101, the chances of a big Zimbabwe total disappeared. Darren Lehmann, enjoying his opening position, hit 85 off 87 balls to set up the home side's win.

England's first appearance in the tournament coincided with the news that they had lost the services of Martin McCague who was returning to England with a stress fracture of the right shin. More bad news followed as England were soundly beaten by Australia in spite of suggesting for a time that they would gain some revenge for their first

Test defeat. Taylor and Slater gave the home side their customary good start with 96 off 24 overs. Slater might have been run out had England's throwing matched that of the Australians, but at no time during the tour was the England fielding ever to approach the Australians' in quality and vitality. Mark Waugh went cheaply, but Boon had returned to the pugnacious reliability of old, and he and Bevan added 92. Nevertheless, a target of 225 did not look beyond England's capabilities, and when Atherton and Stewart launched the innings with 100 in 25 overs it seemed easily within reach. Then Stewart cut a wide ball from May into the hands of backward point, Hick went cheaply, and Atherton became static as he sought to avert collapse. Neither Gooch nor Thorpe could force the pace, and both were caught in the deep when they attempted to. Disintegration followed, and Australia won with ease without exerting themselves.

Australia emphasised their dominance of the competition with their third win in as many matches when they crushed Zimbabwe. Promoted to open, Stuart Law hit 6 fours and a six – the stroke which brought up his century – in his 110. He and Boon added 159 off 196 balls for the third wicket. Law followed his fine innings with 10 economic overs as Australia strolled to victory.

Australia 'A' completed their second win over Zimbabwe, and the result made it very difficult for Zimbabwe to reach the final, for it was their fourth defeat in succession. Zimbabwe lost four wickets for 71 runs

Rising star. South Australia's pace bowler Shane George. (Patrick Eagar)

before Houghton and Whittall added 81, the first half-century stand of the series for Zimbabwe. Chasing 202 to win, Australia 'A' lost Lehmann at 2, but Martyn hit 70 off 89 balls, and he and Hayden added 155 for the

---

BENSON AND HEDGES WORLD SERIES – MATCH ONE – AUSTRALIA v. ZIMBABWE
2 December 1994 at WACA Ground, Perth

ZIMBABWE

A. Flower (capt)	c Warne, b Fleming	29
G.W. Flower	b McGrath	20
A.D.R. Campbell	hit wkt, b Warne	22
D.L. Houghton	run out	13
M.H. Dekker	lbw, b McGrath	16
*W.R. James	run out	8
G.C. Martin	b Law	16
P.A. Strang	not out	17
E.A. Brandes	c Healy, b McDermott	5
H.H. Streak	c Fleming, b Warne	7
D.H. Brain	not out	1
Extras	lb 9, w 3	12
		—
(50 overs)	(for 9 wickets)	166

AUSTRALIA

M.J. Slater	c A. Flower, b Streak	18
M.A. Taylor (capt)	c G.W. Flower, b Brandes	45
D.C. Boon	c Houghton, b Strang	8
M.G. Bevan	c James, b Streak	30
S.G. Law	c Houghton, b Martin	7
*I.A. Healy	c Campbell, b G.W. Flower	40
S.K. Warne	c and b G.W. Flower	5
C.J. McDermott	c Dekker, b G.W. Flower	0
M.E. Waugh	not out	6
D.W. Fleming	not out	0
G.D. McGrath		
Extras	lb 6, w 1, nb 1	8
		—
(47.2 overs)	(for 8 wickets)	167

	O	M	R	W
McDermott	10	–	32	1
Fleming	10	–	45	1
McGrath	10	1	23	2
M.E. Waugh	1	–	3	–
Law	9	–	27	1
Warne	10	1	27	2

	O	M	R	W
Brain	8.2	2	39	–
Streak	10	1	31	2
Brandes	10	1	29	1
Strang	10	1	30	1
Martin	5	–	17	1
G.W. Flower	4	–	15	3

FALL OF WICKETS
1–49, 2–56, 3–83, 4–88, 5–109, 6–117, 7–144, 8–151, 9–164

FALL OF WICKETS
1–69, 2–69, 3–87, 4–96, 5–156, 6–161, 7–161, 8–164

Umpires: T.A. Prue & W.P. Sheahan   *Man of the Match: S.K. Warne*   *Australia won by 2 wickets*

BENSON AND HEDGES WORLD SERIES – MATCH THREE – AUSTRALIA v. ENGLAND
6 December 1994 at SCG, Sydney

AUSTRALIA

M.A. Taylor (capt)	c and b Hick	57
M.J. Slater	c Hick, b Udal	50
M.E. Waugh	b Udal	4
D.C. Boon	not out	64
M.G. Bevan	c Gooch, b Gough	46
S.G. Law	not out	0
*I.A. Healy		
S.K. Warne		
C.J. McDermott		
T.B.A. May		
G.D. McGrath		
Extras	lb 2, w 1	3
(50 overs)	(for 4 wickets)	224

ENGLAND

M.A. Atherton (capt)	lbw, b Law	60
A.J. Stewart	c Law, b May	48
G.A. Hick	c Boon, b May	6
G.P. Thorpe	c Bevan, b McDermott	21
G.A. Gooch	c McDermott, b Warne	21
C. White	b McDermott	0
*S.J. Rhodes	c Warne, b Law	8
P.A.J. DeFreitas	run out	6
D. Gough	not out	8
S.D. Udal	b McGrath	4
J.E. Benjamin	b McDermott	0
Extras	lb 7, w 6, nb 1	14
(48.3 overs)		196

	O	M	R	W
Benjamin	6	–	25	–
DeFreitas	9	1	43	–
Gough	10	–	51	1
White	5	–	22	–
Udal	10	1	37	2
Hick	10	–	44	1

	O	M	R	W
McDermott	9.3	–	34	3
McGrath	9	4	22	1
Warne	10	–	46	1
Law	10	–	52	2
May	10	1	35	2

FALL OF WICKETS
1–96, 2–106, 3–126, 4–218

FALL OF WICKETS
1–100, 2–112, 3–133, 4–147, 5–149, 6–164, 7–180, 8–187, 9–195

Umpires: D.B. Hair & P.D. Parker   *Man of the Match:* D.C. Boon   *Australia won by 28 runs*

BENSON AND HEDGES WORLD SERIES – MATCH FOUR – AUSTRALIA v. ZIMBABWE
8 December 1994 at Bellerive Oval, Hobart

AUSTRALIA

M.J. Slater	c Whittall, b Brain	10
S.G. Law	c G.W. Flower, b Dekker	110
M.E. Waugh	b A. Flower, b Whittall	12
D.C. Boon	not out	98
M.G. Bevan	not out	11
M.A. Taylor (capt)		
*I.A. Healy		
S.K. Warne		
D.W. Fleming		
T.B.A. May		
G.D. McGrath		
Extras	b 5, lb 2, w 5, nb 1	13
(50 overs)	(for 3 wickets)	254

ZIMBABWE

A. Flower (capt)	c Healy, b May	39
G.W. Flower	c Healy, b McGrath	8
A.D.R. Campbell	b McGrath	1
D.L. Houghton	b May	4
M.H. Dekker	run out	11
G.J. Whittall	c Healy, b Fleming	35
*W.R. James	c Healy, b Warne	15
I.P. Butchart	b Fleming	10
P.A. Strang	not out	21
H.H. Streak	not out	12
D.H. Brain		
Extras	lb 6, w 7, nb 1	14
(50 overs)	(for 8 wickets)	170

	O	M	R	W
Brain	10	1	51	1
Streak	9	–	55	–
Whittall	7	1	22	1
Dekker	10	–	42	1
Strang	9	–	51	–
G.W. Flower	5	–	26	–

	O	M	R	W
McGrath	8	2	18	2
Fleming	10	–	42	2
May	10	1	34	2
Law	10	1	25	–
Warne	9	–	23	1
Boon	2	–	11	–
Slater	1	–	11	–

FALL OF WICKETS
1–12, 2–55, 3–214

FALL OF WICKETS
1–15, 2–24, 3–47, 4–64, 5–73, 6–117, 7–129, 8–136

Umpires: A.J. McQuillan & S.G. Randell   *Man of the Match:* S.G. Law   *Australia won by 84 runs*

BENSON AND HEDGES WORLD SERIES – MATCH EIGHT – ENGLAND v. ZIMBABWE
15 December 1994 at SCG, Sydney

ZIMBABWE

*A. Flower (capt)	c Stewart, b Fraser	12
G.W. Flower	not out	84
A.D.R. Campbell	b Gough	23
G.J. Whittall	c Stewart, b Gough	0
D.L. Houghton	c Stewart, b Gough	57
M.H. Dekker	c DeFreitas, b Fraser	5
G.C. Martin	b DeFreitas	7
P.A. Strang	run out	0
H.H. Streak	run out	1
S.G. Peall	c Stewart, b Gough	0
D.H. Brain	b Gough	7
Extras	lb 7, w 1, nb 1	9
(49.3 overs)		205

ENGLAND

G.A. Gooch	c and b Strang	38
M.A. Atherton (capt)	c A. Flower, b Whittall	14
G.A. Hick	run out	64
G.P. Thorpe	lbw, b Strang	0
J.P. Crawley	lbw, b Dekker	18
*A.J. Stewart	b Streak	29
P.A.J. DeFreitas	run out	5
D. Gough	b Streak	2
S.D. Udal	run out	10
A.R.C. Fraser	b Dekker	2
P.C.R. Tufnell	not out	0
Extras	lb 5, w 5	10
(49.1 overs)		192

	O	M	R	W
DeFreitas	10	2	27	1
Fraser	10	–	45	2
Gough	9.3	–	44	5
Tufnell	10	–	43	–
Udal	8	–	31	–
Hick	2	–	8	–

	O	M	R	W
Brain	8	1	27	–
Streak	8.1	1	36	2
Whittall	4	1	21	1
Strang	10	2	30	2
Peall	10	2	29	–
Dekker	9	–	44	2

FALL OF WICKETS
1–24, 2–61, 3–61, 4–171, 5–179, 6–192, 7–192, 8–197, 9–198

FALL OF WICKETS
1–49, 2–60, 3–60, 4–105, 5–169, 6–178, 7–179, 8–181, 9–192

Umpires: D.B. Hair & C.D. Timmins   *Man of the Match:* G.W. Flower   *Zimbabwe won by 13 runs*

second wicket. Hayden went on to reach an impressive century as Australia 'A' won with seven balls to spare.

The first meeting of the two Australian sides ended with the senior side winning by six runs when Glenn McGrath took three wickets in five balls. Hughes lofted the fourth ball of the 48th over to mid-wicket and the match was over. Taylor and Slater had begun the game with a partnership of 93, but the rest of the senior side's batting faltered. Hayden and Martyn provided substance for the 'A' side with a second-wicket stand of 61, and Ponting and Emery kept hopes alive before McGrath's final burst.

The seventh game in the series saw England end their run of defeats. Atherton was unable to play because of a back injury, and neither Gooch nor Stewart lasted long. Hick, Thorpe and Gatting offered some comfort on a pitch that was never easy, but when Gatting was stumped off a walking defensive shot England were 97 for 5. White played the most purposeful cricket of the innings, hitting 43 off 63 balls before being run out off the last ball of the innings. Fraser, who had been brought into the party as a replacement for McCague, showed a welcome resolve and control. He had both Lehmann and Hayden caught behind, but Martyn and Langer added 59. Martyn made 40 off 54 balls before falling to Tufnell, who bowled splendidly but once more tarnished his image. He brushed with the umpire and was fined a third of his match fee by referee John Reid. Langer and Ponting took the score to 138, at which point White bowled the aggressive and impressive Ponting. This heralded a total collapse, seven wickets

falling for 19 runs. White accounted for Moody and Hughes, but it was Fraser's running out of Langer, a decision which needed the help of the third umpire, which really decided the match. England had come back from the dead.

Unfortunately, England's span of life lasted barely 48 hours. Moving on to Sydney, they encountered Zimbabwe who had lost all four of their previous World Series matches but who had beaten England when the two sides met in the World Cup. There were extenuating circumstances for England who had lost Joey Benjamin with chicken-pox, suspected of developing into shingles, and White with a side strain which threatened to end his tour. Stewart had to drop down the order because of back spasms, and there was the general uncertainty as to form. Zimbabwe scored 60 from their first 15 overs, but then lost two quick wickets. Grant Flower, who hit 6 fours, faced 143 deliveries and carried his bat, and Dave Houghton batted admirably in a stand of 110 in 24 overs, but the last seven wickets went down for 34 runs inside 10 overs. England faced a moderate target of 206, and Gooch began with such flourish that it seemed the game would soon be over. Atherton was out to a poor shot, but Gooch continued purposefully until, in the 17th over, leg-spinner Strang joined the attack. His first ball was a long-hop which Gooch, in two minds, flapped back to him. Thorpe misread three deliveries and was out to the fourth. Hick and Crawley added 45 in 16 overs before Crawley missed a straight ball. Stewart gave a hint of heroism, but when he lashed grotesquely at Streak it began a collapse which witnessed six wickets falling for 23 runs in five overs. Three of the wickets were run outs, a reflection of the parlous state into which England had descended.

The matches in which Australia 'A' were involved were not recognised as *official* one-day internationals although the points won and lost in these games were, of course, relevant to the competition as a whole. The results in the first phase of matches were as follows.

MATCH TWO

4 December 1994 *at WACA Ground, Perth*

Zimbabwe 166 for 9

Australia 'A' 167 for 5 (D.S. Lehmann 85)

Australia 'A' won by 5 wickets

(Man of the Match – T.M. Moody)

MATCH FIVE

10 December 1994 *at Adelaide Oval*

Zimbabwe 201 for 8 (G.J. Whittall 59 not out,
   A.D.R. Campbell 54)

Australia 'A' 202 for 3 (M.L. Hayden 101 not out,
   D.R. Martyn 89)

Australia 'A' won by 7 wickets

(Man of the Match – M.L. Hayden)

MATCH SIX

11 December 1994 *at Adelaide Oval*

Australia 202 (M.J. Slater 64)

Australia 'A' 196 (G.D. McGrath 4 for 43)

Australia won by 6 runs

(Man of the Match – G.D. McGrath)

MATCH SEVEN

13 December 1994 *at MCG, Melbourne*

England 188 for 9

Australia 'A' 157 (J.L. Langer 55)

England won by 31 runs

(Man of the Match – C. White)

BENSON AND HEDGES WORLD SERIES
Phase Two – Matches Nine to Twelve, Finals

The second phase of the World Series began with England beating Zimbabwe for the first time. Neil Fairbrother, hot from South Africa, came into the England side in place of Gatting, and Joey Benjamin, the forgotten man of the tour, was given a game in place of Fraser. Zimbabwe lacked Brandes, their main strike bowler, who had returned home injured, and Houghton, their best batsman, who had gone home for Christmas.

In sweltering heat, England began badly, losing Gooch and Hick for 20 runs in the first eight overs. Atherton and

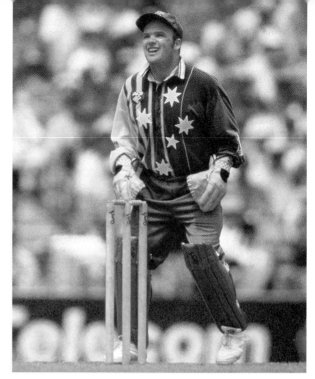

Tasmania's wicket-keeper Mark Atkinson was chosen for the Australian XI which played the England tourists and appeared in the World Series for Australia 'A'. (David Munden/Sportsline)

Thorpe restored some order, and Thorpe's 89 off 121 balls won him the individual award. It also cost him much. The heat took its toll, and he was taken to hospital with dehydration. Zimbabwe bowled tidily and fielded brilliantly.

England fielded better than they had done for most of the tour, with Fairbrother, who had dawdled in mid-pitch to run himself out, running out Butchart in exciting fashion. Andy Flower and Whittall gave the Zimbabwe mid-innings some substance, but, as a whole, the side batted very poorly and left Australia with a very disappointing record.

Mark Taylor, the Australian captain, added his voice to the general condemnation of the farce of including Australia 'A' in the World Series. The first team beat the reserves with comparative ease in their second meeting in the competition. With Healy injured, Emery was transferred to the principal side and Atkinson, the very promising Tasmanian keeper, came in to the 'A' side. Greg Blewett was also added to the 'A' side, as was Shane George. Blewett had early success when he had Taylor caught, but Mark Waugh hit 93 off 102 balls and dominated a third-wicket stand of 98 with David Boon. Hayden and Blewett began the 'A' side's reply with a partnership of 104, and Ponting batted with style and zest. Ponting and Bevan were both run out, victims of fine fielding, and the senior side's attack – even without Warne who was rested – was too much for the remainder of the batting. Law dismissed both Hayden and Blewett and finished with three wickets for 46 runs.

When England beat Australia in the penultimate match in the qualifying series, it seemed that they had won a place in the final, a supposition that was to be proved wrong two days later. Robertson, formerly of the 'A' side, was now in the senior side for Australia in place of the injured May, and McDermott was rested. Benjamin had had his outing for England and now gave way to Fraser. Gooch again went early, caught at slip, and when Mark Waugh took two wickets in nine balls England were 44 for 3 in the 14th over.

Hick and Fairbrother added 89 off 103 balls before the Lancastrian was caught behind cutting at Warne. Crawley and Rhodes departed in the final rush, but Darren Gough hit 45 off 49 balls, and when Hick was caught at long-off with nine balls of the innings remaining, he had hit 91 off 120 balls. The quality of Hick's knock can be measured from the fact that he hit Robertson's first delivery for six but only 2 fours besides. Batting was not easy, and Australia's target of 226 was formidable enough.

In fact, only four boundaries were hit in the Australian innings, three by Mark Waugh and one by Healy who scampered and scurried 63 balls for his runs in his effort to keep his side's hopes alive. Australia never really recovered from the depths of 19 for 3 in spite of Mark Waugh's 66-ball innings.

England's victory was all the more praiseworthy in that Darren Gough had run in to bowl the first ball of the innings and collapsed in pain before he could deliver the ball. He was carried from the field and a stress fracture of the foot

was diagnosed. Soon he was on his way back to England and a deserved hero's welcome at Headingley. Fairbrother's brief tour also came to an end when he injured his right shoulder as he dived to make a stop in the field. One could not say that England had enjoyed a *lucky* tour.

Whatever luck remained deserted England in the last match of the series at the SCG. Gatting returned for the injured Fairbrother, and Chris Lewis, enjoying a working holiday in Australia, was called in for Darren Gough. Lewis took the wickets of Martyn and Blewett, but he conceded 48 runs from six overs. Kept in check by Fraser and DeFreitas in the early stages, Australia 'A' ran riot in a spectacular third-wicket stand of 161 between Blewett and Bevan. Blewett batted himself into the Test side with his 113 off 133 balls, while Bevan – 105 off 102 balls – played with equal brilliance but too late to compensate for his poor showing in the first three Test matches. Blewett and Bevan hit 14 fours and a five between them, but they also ran a succession of eager, sparkling singles against a fielding side which wilted through age and bombardment. The last 15 overs of the Australian innings produced 105 runs, 81 of them coming in the last 10 overs.

There was no way that England were likely to match the highest score of the series, but they focused their attention on the 237 runs that they needed to take them into the final on run rate. England certainly started well enough, with 40 in seven overs, but both openers fell and, by 14 overs,

BENSON AND HEDGES WORLD SERIES – MATCH NINE – ENGLAND v. ZIMBABWE
7 January 1995 at Woolloongabba, Brisbane

ENGLAND			ZIMBABWE		
G.A. Gooch	b Brain	0	G.W. Flower	c Rhodes, b Udal	19
M.A. Atherton (capt)	lbw, b Martin	26	A.D.R. Campbell	c Fairbrother, b DeFreitas	3
G.A. Hick	c A. Flower, b Streak	8	M.H. Dekker	b Benjamin	5
G.P. Thorpe	c Brain, b Strang	89	*A. Flower (capt)	c Rhodes, b Gough	52
N.H. Fairbrother	run out	7	G.J. Whittall	c Rhodes, b DeFreitas	53
J.P. Crawley	lbw, b G.W. Flower	14	I.P. Butchart	run out	2
*S.J. Rhodes	st A. Flower, b Dekker	20	G.C. Martin	st Rhodes, b Hick	1
D. Gough	c Campbell, b Dekker	4	P.A. Strang	b Gough	16
P.A.J. DeFreitas	not out	12	D.H. Brain	c Hick, b Udal	2
S.D. Udal	not out	11	H.H. Streak	not out	9
J.E. Benjamin			S.G. Peall	run out	3
Extras	b 4, lb 2, w 3	9	Extras	lb 7, w 2	9
(50 overs)	(for 8 wickets)	200	(48.1 overs)		174

	O	M	R	W		O	M	R	W
Brain	8	–	27	1	Gough	9.1	3	17	2
Streak	7	1	26	1	DeFreitas	10	–	28	2
Whittall	5	–	19	–	Benjamin	6	–	22	1
Martin	5	1	15	1	Udal	8	–	41	2
Peall	5	–	19	–	Hick	7	1	29	1
Strang	10	–	42	1	Gooch	8	–	30	–
G.W. Flower	3	–	16	1					
Dekker	7	–	30	2					

FALL OF WICKETS
1–0, **2**–20, **3**–72, **4**–82, **5**–107, **6**–164, **7**–170, **8**–182

FALL OF WICKETS
1–8, **2**–16, **3**–56, **4**–103, **5**–123, **6**–124, **7**–149, **8**–156, **9**–169

Umpires: C.D. Timmins & A.J. McQuillan — *Man of the Match:* G.P. Thorpe — *England won by 26 runs*

the score was 55 for 2. Thereafter, the innings was a stop–start affair with nobody maintaining the necessary aggression. Crawley, Gatting, Lewis, DeFreitas and Rhodes all spluttered, but eventually Reiffel, in particular, had a choking effect and England ended two runs short. Australia would meet Australia 'A' in the final. The farce was complete.

BENSON AND HEDGES WORLD SERIES QUALIFYING TABLE

	P	W	L	Pts	Net R/R
Australia	6	5	1	10	0.43
Australia 'A'	6	3	3	6	0.09
England	6	3	3	6	0.08
Zimbabwe	6	1	5	2	–0.59

We had believed that the farce was complete in that the World Series Finals would be unofficial internationals, but we were wrong. There was even greater farce to come. Paul Reiffel, the medium-pacer whose efforts had thwarted England in their attempt to reach the final, was promoted from the Australian 'A' side to the senior side for the finals. Having been promoted, however, he was not picked for either of the matches.

The first game, in Sydney, was marked by some high-quality cricket, particularly in the fielding department. Bevan hit 73 off 86 balls. McDermott took four good wickets, and Warne bowled economically. Slater hit 92 off 146 balls and batted splendidly, but Australia needed 22 from the last four overs. Steve Waugh cut and pulled consecutive fours off Peter McIntyre, and three were needed from Rowell's last over. The game went to the last ball which Ian Healy sliced away for the winning run.

A second-wicket stand of 99 between Blewett and Martyn was the feature of the second game, in Melbourne, which failed to produce the excitement of the first. Taylor and Slater responded with 107 in 25 overs, after which three wickets fell for nine runs. Steve Waugh then took control, adding 56 with Boon. He took his side to victory with an over to spare.

One can only pray that the 'A' side experiment is one that is never repeated.

MATCH TEN

8 January 1995 *at Woolloongabba, Brisbane*

Australia 252 for 5 (M.E. Waugh 93, D.C. Boon 86 not out)
Australia 'A' 218 (G.S. Blewett 63, M.L. Hayden 51)

Australia won by 34 runs

(Man of the Match – M.E. Waugh)

BENSON AND HEDGES WORLD SERIES – MATCH ELEVEN – AUSTRALIA v. ENGLAND
10 January 1995 at MCG, Melbourne

ENGLAND

G.A. Gooch	c Taylor, b McGrath	2
M.A. Atherton (capt)	c S.R. Waugh, b M.E. Waugh	14
G.A. Hick	c Fleming, b Warne	91
G.P. Thorpe	c Healy, b M.E. Waugh	8
N.H. Fairbrother	c Healy, b Warne	35
J.P. Crawley	c Healy, b McGrath	2
*S.J. Rhodes	lbw, b McGrath	2
D. Gough	b McGrath	45
P.A.J. DeFreitas	not out	2
S.D. Udal	not out	2
A.R.C. Fraser		
Extras	b 4, lb 10, w 6, nb 2	22
(50 overs)	(for 8 wickets)	225

AUSTRALIA

M.A. Taylor (capt)	c Rhodes, b Fraser	6
M.J. Slater	b Fraser	2
M.E. Waugh	b Hick	41
S.R. Waugh	c Rhodes, b Fraser	0
S.G. Law	c and b Udal	17
D.C. Boon	b Hick	26
*I.A. Healy	c Atherton, b Hick	56
G.R. Robertson	run out	1
S.K. Warne	b Fraser	21
D.W. Fleming	not out	5
G.D. McGrath	b DeFreitas	10
Extras	w 3	3
(48 overs)		188

	O	M	R	W
Fleming	10	1	36	–
McGrath	10	1	25	4
M.E. Waugh	10	1	43	2
Warne	10	–	37	2
Robertson	5	–	38	–
Law	5	–	32	–

	O	M	R	W
Fraser	10	2	22	4
DeFreitas	9	–	32	1
Gooch	10	–	50	–
Udal	9	1	43	1
Hick	10	1	41	3

FALL OF WICKETS
1–11, 2–31, 3–44, 4–133, 5–136, 6–142, 7–216, 8–223

FALL OF WICKETS
1–3, 2–16, 3–19, 4–62, 5–76, 6–125, 7–131, 8–173, 9–173

Umpires: P.D. Parker & S.G. Randell — *Man of the Match: G.A. Hick* — *England won by 37 runs*

MATCH TWELVE

12 January 1995 *at SCG, Sydney*

Australia 'A' 264 for 5 (G.S. Blewett 113, M.G. Bevan 105)
England 235 for 9

Australia 'A' won by 29 runs

(Man of the Match – G.S. Blewett)

FINALS

15 January 1995 *at SCG, Sydney*

Australia 'A' 209 for 8 (M.G. Bevan 73, M.L. Hayden 50,
C.J. McDermott 4 for 25)

Australia 213 for 5 (M.J. Slater 92)

Australia won by 5 wickets

17 January 1995 *at MCG, Melbourne*

Australia 'A' 226 (G.S. Blewett 64, D.R. Martyn 58,
D.W. Fleming 4 for 28)
Australia 229 for 4 (S.R. Waugh 56 not out, M.J. Slater 56,
M.A. Taylor 50)

Australia won by 6 wickets

(Man of the Finals – S.R. Waugh)

SHEFFIELD SHIELD

13, 14, 15 and 16 October 1994 *at Woolloongabba, Brisbane*

Queensland 483 for 8 dec. (M.L. Love 187, S.G. Law 145,
C.D. Matthews 4 for 108) and 237 for 6 dec. (M.L. Love 116)
Tasmania 397 (R.T. Ponting 119, S. Young 95, J. Cox 79,
M.J. DiVenuto 52, G.J. Rowell 4 for 83) and 162 for 7
(M.J. DiVenuto 51)

Match drawn

Queensland 2 pts, Tasmania 0 pts

The opening day of the Sheffield Shield season saw
Queensland score 417 for 4 in 100 overs. This massive total
was reached mainly due to a record third-wicket stand of
326 between Martin Love and Stuart Law. Love was to hit
a century in each innings for the first time, but there was a
fine response from Tasmania. Facing a total of 483, they
reached 377 for 3 and looked likely to take first-innings
points, but they collapsed against Rackemann and
Tazelaar, seven wickets falling for 20 runs. Ponting, still
short of his 20th birthday and beginning his third season
in first-class cricket, hit the seventh century of his career.
Eventually, the match was drawn but, on the last day, Carl
Rackemann brought his total of Shield wickets for
Queensland to 332, a record.

19, 20, 21 and 22 October 1994 *at Adelaide Oval*

Tasmania 389 (M.J. DiVenuto 82, M.N. Atkinson 76 not out,
J. Cox 59, M.J. Minagall 7 for 152) and 262 (D.F. Hills 73,
S. Young 71, P.E. McIntyre 4 for 62, M.J. Minagall 4 for 111)
South Australia 390 for 9 dec. (T.J. Nielsen 74 not out,
D.S. Lehmann 70) and 148 for 3 (P.C. Nobes 63)

Match drawn

South Australia 2 pts, Tasmania 0 pts

Tasmania again finished pointless in spite of the fact that
wicket-keeper Atkinson hit the highest score of his career.
South Australia's keeper Tim Nielsen also served his side

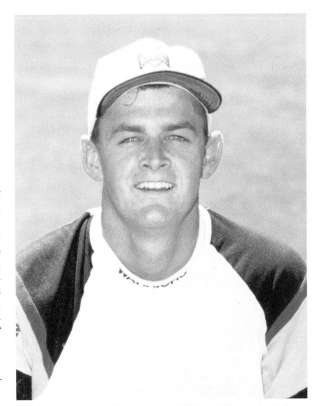

*Adam Gilchrist moved from New South Wales to Western Australia
where he became first-choice wicket-keeper. He finished the season with
55 catches and hit a maiden first-class century. (Stephen Laffer/
Sportsline)*

well, steering them to first-innings points, but the real hero
of the match was Matthew Minagall. The slow left-arm
bowler took five wickets in an innings and 10 in a match
for the first time. Needing 262 in 42 overs to win, the home
side sent Lehmann in first, but his early dismissal meant
that they settled for a draw.

26, 27, 28 and 29 October 1994 *at Woolloongabba, Brisbane*

South Australia 139 (C.G. Rackemann 7 for 43) and 147
(G.J. Rowell 4 for 42)

Queensland 488 for 6 dec. (A.R. Border 151 not out,
M.L. Love 87, M.L. Hayden 80, T.J. Barsby 76)

Queensland won by an innings and 202 runs

Queensland 6 pts, South Australia 0 pts

Queensland routed South Australia inside 2½ days. They
again owed much to their seam attack, with Rackemann
returning the best figures of his career for Queensland.
Barsby and Hayden began Queensland's innings with a
stand of 123, and Love was again in fine form. The most
impressive contribution came from Allan Border, and
there was immediate speculation that he would crown a
marvellous career by helping Queensland to win the
Sheffield Shield for the first time in his final season.

2, 3, 4 and 5 November 1994 *at MCG, Melbourne*

New South Wales 256 (S. Lee 86, P.R. Reiffel 5 for 56) and 277
(K. Roberts 51)

Victoria 255 (D.M. Jones 94, W.J. Holdsworth 5 for 70) and
281 for 2 (D.M. Jones 103 not out)

Victoria won by 8 wickets

Victoria 6 pts, New South Wales 2 pts

4, 5, 6 and 7 November 1994 *at Bellerive Oval, Hobart*

Tasmania 457 for 5 dec. (R.T. Ponting 211, R.J. Tucker
140 not out)

Western Australia 502 for 6 (T.M. Moody 272,
D.R. Martyn 113, G.B. Hogg 59 not out)

Match drawn

Western Australia 2 pts, Tasmania 0 pts

While their leading players were engaged in a tense Test
match in Lahore, New South Wales opened their Sheffield
Shield programme with a visit to the MCG. All-rounder
Shane Lee lifted the Blues from the depths of 74 for 5 with
an innings of 86. He and Maxwell added 126 for the sixth
wicket. Lee then played a major part in New South Wales
taking first-innings points. Dean Jones led Victoria to 205
for 3, but the last seven wickets went down for 50 runs.
When the eighth wicket fell Victoria needed only two runs
for the lead, but Lee dismissed Doyle and Corbett without
addition to the score. The reigning champions then succumbed to Hughes, Reiffel and Corbett. Only debutant
Kevin Roberts, a record-breaker in the Sydney grade competition the previous season, offered serious resistance.
Dean Jones was in magnificent form once more and, with
Hodge, hit off the winning runs.

The exciting Ricky Ponting hit the first double century
of his career as Tasmania reached 457 against Western
Australia. Ponting's 211 was the highest score made by a
Taswegian batsman against the Warriors, and he and Rod
Tucker added a record 319 for the fifth wicket. Tucker's

*Ricky Ponting hit the first double century of his career, for Tasmania
against Western Australia, and won a place in the Australia 'A' side
for the Benson and Hedges World Series. One of Australia's most
exciting prospects, Ponting was chosen for Australia's tour of the
Caribbean. (Laurence Griffiths/Empics)*

captaincy had been criticised for its lack of enterprise, but
he seemed to have redeemed himself when Western
Australia were reduced to 52 for 3. Martyn and Moody
then added a record 279. Tom Moody hit the highest score
of his career, a chanceless 272, but rain prevented play on
the last day.

11, 12, 13 and 14 November 1994 *at Woolloongabba, Brisbane*

Victoria 224 (C.G. Rackemann 4 for 31) and 349 for 7 dec.
(B.J. Hodge 116, M.T.G. Elliott 76, I.J. Harvey 62)

Queensland 230 for 9 dec. (S.G. Law 102, P.R. Reiffel 5 for 65)
and 344 for 5 (M.L. Hayden 201 not out, J.P. Maher 61)

Queensland won by 5 wickets

Queensland 6 pts, Victoria 0 pts

12, 13, 14 and 15 November 1994 *at WACA Ground, Perth*

Western Australia 254 (M.P. Lavender 152, T.B.A. May
4 for 77) and 266 (M.R.J. Veletta 66, B.P. Julian 51,
T.B.A. May 6 for 80)

South Australia 272 (G.S. Blewett 152, B.A. Reid 4 for 60) and
250 for 4 (G.S. Blewett 71, J.A. Brayshaw 57 not out)

South Australia won by 6 wickets

South Australia 6 pts, Western Australia 0 pts

The Australian Test team had now returned from Pakistan,
and they immediately made their presence felt, though
none was on duty at the Woolloongabba where
Queensland achieved a fine victory over Victoria to move
six points clear at the top of the Shield table. Rackemann,

Kasprowicz and Rowell contained Victoria admirably in the first innings, and skipper Law steered his side to a first-innings lead after they had lost their first three wickets for 35 runs. When Victoria batted again they lost Clarke and Jones with only five scored, but Hodge and Elliott added 169 and, with Harvey showing flourish towards the end, Jones was able to declare and leave Queensland the last day in which to score 344 to win. At 118 for 4, they seemed to have little chance, but Hayden played a devastating innings. He hit five boundaries in one over from medium-pacer Simon Cook and reached the first double century of his career to take his side to victory.

Tim May announced his return with 10 for 157 as South Australia beat Western Australia in Perth with more than three hours to spare. Mark Lavender held the Warriors' first innings together with his fifth first-class century, but Greg Blewett more than matched him and the visitors led by 18 on the first innings. The home side could never escape the stranglehold imposed upon them by May and Brad Wigney, and South Australia romped to victory. Siddons hit 4 fours and a six in his 23 off 24 balls which brought the match to its early close.

17, 18, 19 and 20 November 1994 *at MCG, Melbourne*

Victoria 293 (D.M. Jones 126, G.B. Gardiner 64, S. Young 5 for 68) and 283 (D.M. Jones 76, M.T.G. Elliott 58, I.A. Wrigglesworth 58, S. Young 5 for 56)

Tasmania 302 for 7 dec. (D.C. Boon 71, S.K. Warne 5 for 104) and 112 (T.F. Corbett 6 for 42)

Victoria won by 162 runs

Victoria 6 pts, Tasmania 2 pts

18, 19, 20 and 21 November 1994 *at SCG, Sydney*

Queensland 203 (A.J. Kershler 5 for 42) and 267 (C.J. McDermott 52)

New South Wales 469 (M.E. Waugh 113, M.G. Bevan 103, S.R. Waugh 64) and 2 for 0

New South Wales won by 10 wickets

New South Wales 6 pts, Queensland 0 pts

Tasmania fielded three first-class debutants in their side against Victoria: wicket-keeper Tod Pinnington came in for Mark Atkinson who was playing for the Australian XI at Hobart, leg-spinner Richard Allenby and left-arm spinner Mark Hatton. Allenby and Hatton were included as off-spinners Robinson (injured) and Farrell (pressure of work) were unavailable. David Boon made a welcome rare appearance, as did Shane Warne for Victoria.

Tasmania had an early strike through Leicestershire's David Millns, but the real hero of the Tasmanian attack was the medium-pacer Shaun Young who took 10 wickets in a match for the first time. Victoria recovered from 38 for 3 thanks to the efforts of Dean Jones and Gardiner who registered a maiden first-class fifty. David Boon, with solid support throughout the order, took Tasmania to first-innings points, and Victoria gave another uneven display when they batted for a second time. Elliott

and Jones, continuing in wonderful form, hit 138 for the second wicket, but three wickets then fell for 17 runs. Left-hander Ian Wrigglesworth brought some stability, but Tasmania were left to make 275 to win. They never looked like nearing their target as their batting was ripped apart by new left-arm swing bowler Troy Corbett, whose 6 for 42 came from 19 overs. Only Young, 45, offered resistance.

Leaders Queensland found the full might of New South Wales too much for them at the SCG. The Blues not only welcomed back seven men who had been in Pakistan with the national side but also found a place for Greg Matthews who had not appeared for the state since his fracas in Perth a year earlier. The Bulls batted dreadfully on the opening day against a varied attack. The honours went to left-arm spinner Kershler who took five wickets in what was only his second Shield match. Steve Waugh, unable to bowl because of his shoulder injury, began the onslaught on the Queensland bowling, and Mark Waugh and Bevan added 145 for the fourth wicket, with both batsmen reaching centuries. Greg Matthews took three wickets in Queensland's second innings, and only a belligerent fifty from McDermott saved the visitors from an innings defeat.

24, 25, 26 and 27 November 1994 *at WACA Ground, Perth*

Western Australia 284 (M.R.J. Veletta 95, A.C. Gilchrist 56, D. Tazelaar 6 for 89) and 146 (G.J. Rowell 4 for 17)

Queensland 239 (A.R. Border 73, J. Angel 4 for 53) and 192 for 3 (S.G. Law 62 not out, A.R. Border 54 not out)

Queensland won by 7 wickets

Queensland 6 pts, Western Australia 2 pts

The first ever Sheffield Shield day/night game produced an outright win for Queensland which saw them move further ahead at the top of the table. In spite of the fact that Western Australia, relying heavily on youth, led on the first innings, Queensland's victory came with more than a session to spare on the last day. The Bulls' pace trio – Rowell, Rackemann and Tazelaar – dominated, and the crucial part of the game came at the end of the second day when Western Australia had to bat the last 17 overs under lights. Rackemann and Tazelaar captured three wickets in the space of 10 balls, and the home state slipped to 31 for 4 and never really recovered.

10, 11, 12 and 13 December 1994 *at SCG, Sydney*

Tasmania 350 for 3 dec. (J. Cox 122, M.J. DiVenuto 89) and 238 for 5 dec. (D.F. Hills 53)

New South Wales 268 for 5 dec. (S. Lee 100 not out) and 269 (S.R. Waugh 52, S. Lee 52, C.D. Matthews 4 for 65)

Tasmania won by 51 runs

Tasmania 6 pts, New South Wales 0 pts

Tasmania gained an unexpected but thoroughly deserved victory over New South Wales in a rain-affected day/night match in Sydney. A second-wicket stand of 173 between

Stuart Law played superb all-round cricket in the one-day series, led Queensland to triumph in the Sheffield Shield and was chosen to captain Australia 'A' on the tour of England. (Ben Radford/Allsport)

Cox and DiVenuto gave substance to Tasmania's first innings and enabled Tucker to declare. Shane Lee hit a fierce century for the home state, and Steve Waugh conceded first-innings points in an attempt to obtain an outright result. Tucker's declaration left New South Wales a target of 321 in 68 overs. At tea, the reigning champions were 101 for 1, but the asking rate had risen appreciably. Shane Lee reached 50 off 34 balls, but he was run out. At 261 for 6, New South Wales maintained their challenge in spite of the fact that McNamara was nursing a leg injury and had to bat at number eleven with a runner. McNamara hit a four, but Matthews had Kershler caught behind with 4.4 overs remaining to give Tasmania victory. Matthews himself passed Eddie Windsor's record to become the leading first-class wicket-taker in Tasmanian history.

16, 17, 18 and 19 December 1994 *at WACA Ground, Perth*

Victoria 342 (M.T.G. Elliott 171, J. Angel 5 for 87) and 161 (J. Angel 4 for 54)

Western Australia 234 (T.M. Moody 55, D.W. Fleming 4 for 39) and 241 (T.M. Moody 81, S.K. Warne 4 for 64)

Victoria won by 28 runs

Victoria 6 pts, Western Australia 0 pts

at Adelaide Oval

South Australia 428 (D.S. Lehmann 109, P.C. Nobes 97, B.A. Johnson 56, G.S. Blewett 50, G.R. Robertson 5 for 115, G.D. McGrath 4 for 90) and 203 for 4 dec. (J.A. Brayshaw 73 not out, J.D. Siddons 60 not out)

New South Wales 245 (M.J. Slater 51, M.E. Waugh 51, G.R. Blewett 4 for 39) and 129 (S.P. George 4 for 41)

South Australia won by 257 runs

South Australia 6 pts, New South Wales 0 pts

New South Wales omitted fast bowler Wayne Holdsworth for lack of form and welcomed the return of their Test stars, but they still suffered their second successive defeat. A third-wicket stand of 175 between the increasingly impressive Lehmann and the consistent Nobes gave South Australia a substantial total which New South Wales failed to match. The top-order promised more than they achieved, and leg-spinner McIntyre and medium-pacer Greg Blewett took wickets at regular intervals. Blewett was rapidly establishing himself as an all-rounder of quality, and he finished with his best figures in first-class cricket. Siddons and Brayshaw shared an unbroken fifth-wicket partnership of 135 when South Australia batted again, and Siddons' declaration left New South Wales searching for 387 to win. They entered the last day on 20 for 3 after Shane George had dismissed Taylor, Slater and Kershler as three runs were scored. On the last morning George quickly accounted for Mark Waugh, and South Australia swept to their second win of the season.

Victoria maintained the pressure on Queensland by narrowly beating Western Australia in Perth. It was the third successive defeat for the Warriors. Victoria were put in a strong position on the opening day by Matthew Elliott's magnificent 171. Angel and Julian had reduced Victoria to 39 for 3, but Elliott found useful partners in Gardiner and Wrigglesworth, and there were 42 runs for the last wicket with Fleming. The Warriors conceded a first-innings advantage of 108, but Angel and Julian bowled them back into contention. Unfortunately, the batsmen proved vulnerable against Warne, Reiffel and Fleming. Stewart and Cary battled bravely in a last-wicket stand of 41 before Fleming had Cary caught behind.

30, 31 December 1994, 1 and 2 January 1995 *at WACA Ground, Perth*

New South Wales 205 (N.D. Maxwell 52, B.E. McNamara 50, J. Angel 5 for 62) and 360 (P.A. Emery 92, N.D. Maxwell 91, B.P. Julian 5 for 58)

Western Australia 542 for 4 dec. (J.L. Langer 241 not out, T.M. Moody 77, D.R. Martyn 62, M.P. Lavender 60) and 26 for 0

Western Australia won by 10 wickets

Western Australia 6 pts, New South Wales 0 pts

31 December 1994, **1, 2** and **3** January 1995 *at Adelaide Oval*

South Australia 524 for 8 dec. (J.A. Brayshaw 134 not out,
G.S. Blewett 112, P.C. Nobes 110, D.S. Lehmann 100,
T.F. Corbett 5 for 108)

Victoria 315 (M.T.G. Elliott 66, P.E. McIntyre 5 for 85) and 167
(W.G. Ayres 67, S.P. George 4 for 31, P.E. McIntyre
4 for 60)

South Australia won by an innings and 42 runs

South Australia 6 pts, Victoria 0 pts

A miserable first-innings batting performance by New
South Wales condemned them to their third defeat in succession. Western Australia took a complete grip on the
game through Justin Langer's second and higher double
century in first-class cricket. He shared in four century
partnerships, the last an unbroken 160 with Goodwin for
the fifth wicket. New South Wales faced humiliation when
they reached 82 for 5 in their second innings and had
McNamara retired hurt with a calf injury. Maxwell and
Emery restored some pride when they both made their
highest scores in first-class cricket, and the sixth wicket
did not fall until the total had reached 274. McNamara
returned, and Scott Thompson and Neil Jones adopted a
vigorous approach, but Western Australia were not to be
denied and were able to quieten critics with victory after
three successive defeats in a month.

South Australia drew level with Queensland at the top
of the Sheffield Shield table when they trounced Victoria
by an innings. Johnson fell at 10, but the next four batsmen
all made centuries, with Blewett and Nobes adding 207 for
the second wicket. Victoria batted consistently. Only
Hodge and last man Corbett, who had bowled well, failed
to score, but although many batsmen began promisingly,
none played the necessary big innings. Forced to follow
on, they suggested recovery when Jones and Ayres were
together, but the leg-spin of McIntyre accounted for them
both and the last eight wickets fell for 52 runs. McIntyre
had match figures of 9 for 145, and Shane George's pace,
accuracy and aggression earned him 7 for 109 and praise
from every quarter.

14, 15, 16 and **17** January 1995 *at WACA Ground, Perth*

Tasmania 236 (B.P. Julian 5 for 63) and 236 (S. Young 51,
B.P. Julian 5 for 59)

Western Australia 298 (M.R.J. Veletta 71, M.W. Goodwin 63,
S. Young 4 for 71, D.J. Millns 4 for 81) and 175 for 2
(M.P. Lavender 89)

Western Australia won by 8 wickets

Western Australia 6 pts, Tasmania 0 pts

Western Australia's second victory in succession was
brought about by Brendon Julian taking 10 wickets in
a match for the first time. Tasmania fought hard, and
wicket-keeper Mark Atkinson took seven catches in the
match, six in Western Australia's first innings.

20, 21, 22 and **23** January 1995 *at Woolloongabba, Brisbane*

Western Australia 214 (G.J. Rowell 4 for 61) and 232
(D. Tazelaar 4 for 71)

Queensland 204 (B.P. Julian 4 for 51, J. Angel 4 for 70)
and 122

Western Australia won by 120 runs

Western Australia 6 pts, Queensland 0 pts

at Bellerive Oval, Hobart

New South Wales 487 for 8 dec. (S.R. Waugh 206,
M.G. Bevan 70, S. Lee 51, P.A. Emery 50 not out) and 298
for 2 dec. (M.E. Waugh 132, M.J. Slater 70, S.R. Waugh 68
not out)

Tasmania 446 for 6 dec. (M.J. DiVenuto 119, S. Young 111 not
out, R.J. Tucker 75, R.T. Ponting 58) and 242
(R.T. Ponting 134, G.D. McGrath 5 for 50)

New South Wales won by 97 runs

New South Wales 6 pts, Tasmania 0 pts

In a match in which Hayden's first-innings 47 was the
highest score, Western Australia, put in to bat, won by a
considerable margin. It was their third win in succession
and moved them to the top of the Shield table.

Able to call upon their international players – with the
exception of Taylor – New South Wales recorded their
second win of the season. Steve Waugh hit 23 fours and a
six in making 206 off 257 balls. He and Bevan shared a
third-wicket stand of 167. Tasmania responded in positive
fashion after losing two wickets for 39 runs, and Tucker's
declaration on the third day kept the game alive. Slater
and Mark Waugh began New South Wales' second innings
with 156 in 103 minutes. Tasmania went in search of 340
for victory, but they lost four wickets for 47 runs. A brilliant 134 off 146 balls from Ponting could not save them,
but they died bravely.

27, 28, 29 and **30** January 1995 *at SCG, Sydney*

Victoria 355 (M.T.G. Elliott 99, P.R. Reiffel 55, D.S. Berry 55,
B.E. McNamara 5 for 72) and 299 for 2 dec. (D.M. Jones
154 not out, B.J. Hodge 87 not out)

New South Wales 250 (G.R.J. Matthews 59 retired hurt) and
150 (N.D. Maxwell 67)

Victoria won by 254 runs

Victoria 6 pts, New South Wales 0 pts

at Bellerive Oval, Hobart

South Australia 352 (J.D. Siddons 105, T.J. Nielsen 71,
J.A. Brayshaw 58, M.W. Ridgway 6 for 79) and 284 for 5 dec.
(J.A. Brayshaw 100 not out, T.J. Nielsen 51 not out)

Tasmania 354 for 5 dec. (J. Cox 165, R.T. Ponting 62)
and 137 for 4 (M.N. Atkinson 59 not out)

Match drawn

Tasmania 2 pts, South Australia 0 pts

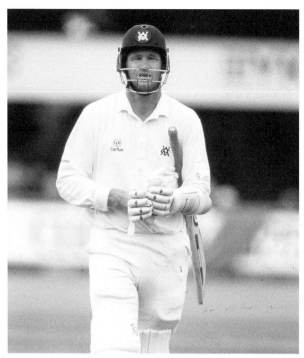

Dean Jones, captain of Victoria, hit 324 not out against South Australia in Melbourne and was voted Sheffield Shield Player of the Year. (David Munden/Sportsline)

Jamie Siddons led South Australia to the Sheffield Shield final and set a captain's example with the bat and in the field. (Stephen Laffer/ Sportsline)

Victoria went to the top of the Sheffield Shield with a resounding victory over New South Wales who were handicapped through the loss of Greg Matthews with injury. It was Victoria's first win at the SCG for 21 years, and it owed much to a third-wicket stand of 213 in 195 minutes between Dean Jones and Brad Hodge in the second innings.

South Australia failed to move ahead of Western Australia into second place when they proved unable to take a point in Hobart. Medium-pacer Mark Ridgway returned his best bowling figures for Tasmania, but his side were in danger on the last day when rain disrupted the match. Tim May ended his wicketless drought with two victims in Tasmania's second innings.

3, 4, 5 and 6 February 1995 *at MCG, Melbourne*

Victoria 572 for 4 dec. (D.M. Jones 324 not out, M.T.G. Elliott 77, R.P. Larkin 69, G.B. Gardiner 50)

South Australia 363 (J.A. Brayshaw 76, P.C. Nobes 72, P.R. Reiffel 4 for 61) and 390 for 6 (D.S. Lehmann 202 not out, J.A. Brayshaw 104)

Match drawn

Victoria 2 pts, South Australia 0 pts

Dean Jones hit 2 sixes and 28 fours in an astonishing 324 not out which came off 448 balls in 523 minutes. Jones had

enjoyed a magnificent season and had stated his willingness to return to Test cricket, but the selectors had opted for younger batsmen. South Australia batted with determination but were forced to follow on. At 65 for 4, they faced defeat, but Darren Lehmann and James Brayshaw added 270 in 191 minutes. Lehmann exposed the weakness of the Victoria attack with 202 off 208 balls, an innings which included 31 fours and a six.

8, 9, 10 and 11 February 1995 *at Woolloongabba, Brisbane*

Queensland 400 for 8 dec. (M.L. Love 98, A.R. Border 94, M.L. Hayden 52) and 34 for 0

New South Wales 196 and 237 (R.J. Davison 58, C.G. Rackemann 4 for 60)

Queensland won by 10 wickets

Queensland 6 pts, New South Wales 0 pts

Queensland moved fractionally ahead of Victoria at the top of the Sheffield Shield table when they outplayed New South Wales. The weakened New South Wales lost any hope of retaining the Shield after suffering defeat in this match. Border and Love added 141 for Queensland's fourth wicket, but the batting was consistent and the pace bowling devastating.

15, 16, 17 and 18 February 1995 *at Adelaide Oval*

South Australia 397 (P.C. Nobes 101, D.S. Lehmann 91,
B.A. Johnson 81, T.M. Moody 4 for 51) and 342 for 6 dec.
(B.A. Johnson 168, D.S. Lehmann 78)

Western Australia 333 (A.C. Gilchrist 126, T.M. Moody 75,
M.A. Harrity 5 for 92) and 398 (M.P. Lavender 90,
D.R. Martyn 89, T.M. Moody 79, S.P. George 4 for 96)

South Australia won by 8 runs

South Australia 6 pts, Western Australia 0 pts

at MCG, Melbourne

Victoria 293 (M.T.G. Elliott 111) and 201 (D.M. Jones 76,
M.S. Kasprowicz 6 for 47)

Queensland 294 for 9 dec. (M.L. Hayden 89, B. Williams 5 for
88) and 202 for 4 (M.L. Love 63, T.J. Barsby 51)

Queensland won by 6 wickets

Queensland 6 pts, Victoria 0 pts

A maiden first-class century from Johnson did much to set
up South Australia's thrilling victory over Western
Australia. There was also a maiden century from Adam
Gilchrist and a career-best bowling performance by Mark
Harrity. Western Australia were 37 runs short of victory
when their ninth wicket fell, but Coulson and Cary added
28 before Cary was leg before to Harrity.

Queensland moved clear at the top of the table with a
fine win over Victoria. Border and Rackemann nudged
Queensland to first-innings points after Elliott's second
century of the season, and Kasprowicz then produced his
best bowling performance of the season. Barsby and Love
shared a stand of 112 to set Queensland on the path to victory. With the Shield now paused for a month to accom-
modate the final stages of the Mercantile Mutual Cup,
Queensland and South Australia looked to be in strong
positions.

9, 10, 11 and 12 March 1995 *at Adelaide Oval*

South Australia 543 (J.D. Siddons 170, P.C. Nobes 70, S.P.
George 62, D.S. Lehmann 60, M.S. Kasprowicz 5 for 155)

Queensland 174 (S.G. Law 81, M.A. Harrity 4 for 39) and 281
(G.A.J. Fitness 71, S.P. George 4 for 66)

South Australia won by an innings and 88 runs

South Australia 6 pts, Queensland 0 pts

at Bellerive Oval, Hobart

Tasmania 273 (R.J. Tucker 93, M.W. Ridgway 70, J.P. Bakker 4
for 40) and 413 for 4 dec. (S. Young 152 not out, J. Cox 86,
R.J. Tucker 83 not out)

Victoria 325 (M.T.G. Elliott 140, M.W. Ridgway 6 for 29) and
304 (M.T.G. Elliott 116)

Tasmania won by 57 runs

Tasmania 6 pts, Victoria 2 pts

at SCG, Sydney

New South Wales 201 for 5 (G.R.J. Matthews 58 not out,
R.J. Davison 56) and 152 (T.M. Moody 4 for 42)

Western Australia 150 for 3 dec. (T.M. Moody 71 not out,
M.P. Lavender 66 not out) and 204 for 6 (B.J. Hogg
50 not out)

Western Australia won by 4 wickets

Western Australia 6 pts, New South Wales 2 pts

South Australia beat Queensland inside three days to draw
level with the Bulls at the top of the Sheffield Shield table.
Victoria suffered a surprise defeat in Hobart which, as it
transpired, was to cost them a place in the final. Matthew
Elliott hit a century in each innings, the first time he had
accomplished such a feat, but he was overshadowed by
Mark Ridgway's astonishing career-best performances
with both bat and ball. The left-handed Shaun Young also
capped a fine season by scoring a career-best 152.

In Sydney, another defeat for New South Wales meant
that the reigning champions were now level with
Tasmania at the bottom of the table.

16, 17, 18 and 19 March 1995 *at Bellerive Oval, Hobart*

Queensland 234 (S.G. Law 102) and 397 for 4 dec.
(S.G. Law 138, A.R. Border 124 not out, T.J. Barsby 56)

Tasmania 155 and 255 (D.F. Hills 111, A.J. Bichel 6 for 79)

Queensland won by 221 runs

Queensland 6 pts, Tasmania 0 pts

at SCG, Sydney

South Australia 301 (J.A. Brayshaw 53) and 349 for 4 dec.
(J.D. Siddons 149 not out, D.S. Webber 78 not out,
D.S. Lehmann 61)

New South Wales 305 for 9 dec. (G.R.J. Matthews 80,
M.G. Bevan 77) and 223 (J.L. Arnberger 63)

South Australia won by 122 runs

South Australia 6 pts, New South Wales 2 pts

at MCG, Melbourne

Victoria 280 (J.P. Bakker 75, R.P. Larkin 60) and 229

Western Australia 221 (G.B. Hogg 71, D.J. Saker 4 for 39) and
185 (M.P. Lavender 82, A.I.C. Dodemaide 5 for 42)

Victoria won by 103 runs

Victoria 6 pts, Western Australia 0 pts

Queensland duly claimed their place in the Sheffield
Shield final with a comfortable victory over Tasmania.
They owed much to Stuart Law who hit a century in each
innings and shared a fourth-wicket partnership of 174
with Allan Border at a crucial stage. Andy Bichel, in his
first game of the season, returned the best bowling figures
of his career.

South Australia joined Queensland in the final after

conceding first-innings points to New South Wales. Again they owed much to skipper Siddons. Victoria refound form too late, but had the consolation of skipper Dean Jones being named as Benson and Hedges Sheffield Shield Cricketer of the Year. Tony Dodemaide made his only appearance of the season and took five wickets in Western Australia's second innings.

SHEFFIELD SHIELD FINAL TABLE

	P	W	L	D	Pts
Queensland	10	6	3	1	38
South Australia	10	6	1	3	38
Victoria	10	5	4	1	33.1
Western Australia	10	4	5	1	27.7
New South Wales	10	2	8	–	18
Tasmania	10	2	4	4	16

Victoria were fined 0.9 pts, and Western Australia 0.3 pts for slow over rate

SHEFFIELD SHIELD FINAL
QUEENSLAND *v.* SOUTH AUSTRALIA, at Brisbane

History was made in Brisbane in March 1995, when Queensland won the Sheffield Shield for the first time in their 69-year history. Having finished second on 14 occasions and having failed to win any of the six finals in which they have appeared since the play-off concept was introduced in 1982, Queensland dominated the match against South Australia who failed to take advantage of a perfect pitch on the opening day. Queensland's response was for Barsby to play the innings of a lifetime and share stands of 144 with Hayden and 192 with Love.

In spite of rain on the second and third days, and in spite of the fact that stands were being demolished prior to an ambitious building programme, record crowds for a Shield final attended the match. Allan Border, who indicated that this could be his farewell to first-class cricket, played a delightful innings before dragging a wide ball into his stumps, but nothing could dampen his joy, nor that of his colleagues, in this historic victory.

SHEFFIELD SHIELD FINAL – QUEENSLAND *v.* SOUTH AUSTRALIA
24, 25, 26, 27 and 28 March 1995 at Woolloongabba, Brisbane

SOUTH AUSTRALIA

Batsman	FIRST INNINGS		SECOND INNINGS	
B.A. Johnson	c Hayden, b Bichel	4	c Hayden, b Jackson	10
P.C. Nobes	c Law, b Tazelaar	0	b Tazelaar	100
J.D. Siddons (capt)	c Border, b Rackemann	8	c Seccombe, b Rackemann	3
D.S. Lehmann	c Seccombe, b Tazelaar	12	c Tazelaar, b Bichel	62
J.A. Brayshaw	run out	53	c Seccombe, b Rackemann	16
D.S. Webber	c Seccombe, b Bichel	33	c and b Law	91
*T.J. Nielsen	b Jackson	53	lbw, b Tazelaar	0
J.N. Gillespie	c Seccombe, b Rackemann	18	c Rackemann, b Jackson	39
P.E. McIntyre	c Rackemann, b Jackson	9	c Law, b Bichel	2
S.P. George	b Rackemann	15	c Bichel, b Jackson	4
M.A. Harrity	not out	0	not out	0
Extras	b 1, nb 8	9	b 4, lb 8, nb 10	22
		214		349

QUEENSLAND

Batsman	FIRST INNINGS	
T.J. Barsby	c Gillespie, b Johnson	151
M.L. Hayden	c Nielsen, b Harrity	74
M.L. Love	c Nielsen, b Brayshaw	146
S.G. Law (capt)	c Webber, b George	11
A.R. Border	b Johnson	98
J.P. Maher	c Nielsen, b Gillespie	36
*W.A. Seccombe	c Harrity, b Gillespie	18
A.J. Bichel	c Nielsen, b Gillespie	38
P.W. Jackson	not out	11
D. Tazelaar	b McIntyre	22
C.G. Rackemann	lbw, b McIntyre	7
Extras	b 1, lb 14, w 3, nb 34	52
		664

Bowler	O	M	R	W	O	M	R	W
Bichel	19	4	54	2	29	6	90	2
Tazelaar	20	3	45	2	21	6	65	2
Rackemann	18	6	54	3	20	10	86	2
Law	10	3	26	–	3	1	14	1
Jackson	14.4	5	34	2	37.2	9	81	3
Border					1	–	1	–

Bowler	O	M	R	W
Harrity	46	12	129	1
George	33	8	102	1
Gillespie	35	10	112	3
McIntyre	49.5	10	176	2
Johnson	22	1	96	2
Brayshaw	14	5	34	1

FALL OF WICKETS
1–4, 2–6, 3–26, 4–30, 5–93, 6–128, 7–179, 8–189, 9–210
1–31, 2–34, 3–142, 4–194, 5–252, 6–253, 7–314, 8–335, 9–347

FALL OF WICKETS
1–144, 2–336, 3–376, 4–479, 5–553, 6–565, 7–618, 8–618, 9–652

Umpires: D.B. Hair & P.D. Parker

Queensland won by an innings and 101 runs

Carl Rackemann and Allan Border are clapped onto the field by their team-mates at the start of the Sheffield Shield final. Rackemann took 52 wickets in the season and became the leading wicket-taker in Queensland's history. For Border, Queensland's winning of the Sheffield Shield for the first time was a triumphant finale to a glorious career. (Allsport)

ZIMBABWE TOUR

20 **November 1994** *at Sir Richard Moore Oval, Kalgoorlie*

Western Australian XI 266 for 5 (M.P. Lavender 74,
    M. Goodwin 52)
Zimbabwe XI 236

Western Australian XI won by 30 runs

23, 24 and **25 November 1994** *at Adelaide Oval*

AIS Cricket Academy 271 for 7 dec. (D. Marsh 100 not out,
    C. Richards 60) and 189 (E.A. Brandes 4 for 49)
Zimbabwe XI 245 for 9 dec. (A. Flower 70, W.R. James 59)
    and 220 for 7 (A. Flower 78 not out)

Zimbabwe XI won by 3 wickets

27 November 1994 *at Adelaide Oval*

Zimbabwe XI 186 (A.D.R. Campbell 66, J. Gillespie 4 for 30)
South Australia 187 for 3 (D.S. Lehmann 59, G.S. Blewett 56
    not out)

South Australia won by 7 wickets

29 November 1994 *at Busselton, Western Australia*

Zimbabwe XI 269 for 7 (A. Flower 88, A.D.R. Campbell 65)
Western Australian Country XI 117

Zimbabwe XI won by 152 runs

30 November 1994 *at WACA Ground, Perth*

Zimbabwe XI 207 for 9 (D.L. Houghton 78)
Western Australia 202 for 7 (M.P. Lavender 58)

Zimbabwe XI won by 5 runs

Zimbabwe arrived in Australia to participate in the Benson and Hedges World Series. They played five warm-up matches, none of which had first-class status. They fared reasonably well in these games but were plagued by injury.

17 December 1994 *at NTCA Ground, Launceston*

Zimbabwe XI 159 (G.J. Whittall 62)
Tasmania 160 for 3 (J. Cox 57)

Tasmania won by 7 wickets

18, 19 and **20** December 1994 *at Devonport Oval*

Tasmania 257 for 5 dec. (R.J. Tucker 78 not out, D.F. Hills 50) and 136 for 3 dec. (J. Cox 63 not out)
Zimbabwe XI 141 for 3 dec. (G.W. Flower 59) and 156 for 5 (G.W. Flower 63, A. Flower 53 not out, C.R. Miller 4 for 35)

Match drawn

22 December 1994 *at Yea*

Zimbabwe XI 228 for 5 (G.W. Flower 83)
Victorian Country XI 167 for 5

Zimbabwe XI won by 61 runs

26 December 1994 *at No. 1 Oval, Dubbo*

Zimbabwe XI 277 for 5 (A. Flower 114, G.W. Flower 91)
New South Wales Country XI 195 for 9

Zimbabwe XI won by 82 runs

In the day/night match at Dubbo, the Flower brothers added 192 for the third wicket.

28, 29 and **30** December 1994 *at Newtown Oval, Maryborough*

Zimbabwe XI 294 for 6 dec. (A. Flower 139 not out, M.H. Dekker 52) and 129 (M.S. Kasprowicz 4 for 27)
Queensland 223 for 5 dec. (M.L. Hayden 64, M.P. Mott 55) and 201 for 6 (M.L. Hayden 90 not out, M.L. Love 55, S.G. Peall 4 for 52)

Queensland won by 4 wickets

1 January 1995 *at Salter Oval, Bundaberg*

Queensland 245 for 7 (M.L. Love 79, M.L. Hayden 52)
Zimbabwe XI 246 for 9 (A.D.R. Campbell 129 not out, I.P. Butchart 87)

Zimbabwe XI won by 1 wicket

4 January 1995 *at Dauth Park, Beenleigh*

Zimbabwe XI 165 (M.S. Kasprowicz 4 for 34)
Queensland 166 for 6 (M.L. Hayden 51)

Queensland won by 4 wickets

Zimbabwe's final three games of their tour outside the World Series were played in Queensland and included the second of their first-class matches. Dekker and Grant Flower put on 82 for the first wicket, and Andy Flower, at number five, played a remarkable innings, sharing an unbroken stand of 150 for the seventh wicket with Strang, who scored 37. Unfortunately, Zimbabwe collapsed against the Queensland pace attack when they batted again, and Queensland won with ease.

The first one-day game provided a sensational stand of 176 between Campbell and Butchart after five wickets had fallen for 33. The ninth wicket went down with 16 needed for victory and only the inexperienced Rowett to partner Campbell. Rowett did not score, but Campbell made the required runs and carried his bat after 49.2 overs.

MERCANTILE MUTUAL CUP

9 October 1994 *at Woolloongabba, Brisbane*

Tasmania 218 for 6 (J. Cox 75, R.T. Ponting 59)
Queensland 219 for 6 (T.J. Barsby 101)

Queensland (2 pts) won by 4 wickets

14 October 1994 *at WACA Ground, Perth*

Western Australia 177
Victoria 178 for 4

Victoria (2 pts) won by 6 wickets

16 October 1994 *at North Sydney Oval*

New South Wales 272 for 8 (M.T. Haywood 87, S.P. George 4 for 58)
South Australia 275 for 5 (D.S. Lehmann 106, J.D. Siddons 77)

South Australia (2 pts) won by 5 wickets

23 October 1994 *at Adelaide Oval*

Tasmania 215 (M.J. DiVenuto 76, S.P. George 4 for 33)
South Australia 217 for 0 (D.S. Lehmann 142 not out, P.C. Nobes 64 not out)

South Australia (2 pts) won by 10 wickets

29 October 1994 *at Bellerive Oval, Hobart*

Victoria 234 for 6 (D.M. Jones 113)
Tasmania 156 for 9 (B.A. Robinson 69 not out, P.R. Reiffel 4 for 14)

Victoria (2 pts) won by 78 runs

30 October 1994 *at Woolloongabba, Brisbane*

Queensland 245 (T.J. Barsby 84, J.P. Maher 58)
South Australia 242 for 8 (T.J. Nielsen 57, S.G. Law 4 for 47)

Queensland (2 pts) won by 3 runs

As has become customary, the Australian season opened with a batch of one-day matches for the Mercantile Mutual Cup which still seems to have an uneasy place in the cricket calendar. Trevor Barsby, having relinquished his business employment to concentrate solely on cricket, was rewarded with the individual award in the first match, in which he hit a maiden century in one-day cricket.

Like Queensland and South Australia, Victoria registered two victories. Dean Jones hit his second century in one-day domestic cricket and announced that he would again make himself available for selection for the national side.

6 November 1994 at MCG, Melbourne

Victoria 181 for 8 (D.M. Jones 76)
New South Wales 121

Victoria (2 pts) won by 60 runs

9 December 1994 at WACA Ground, Perth

Western Australia 242 for 9 (A.C. Gilchrist 60)
Queensland 241 for 9 (W.A. Seccombe 64 not out,
    T.J. Barsby 62)

Western Australia (2 pts) won by 1 run

Victoria virtually booked a place in the final with their third win in as many matches as the first phase of the domestic limited-over tournament drew to its close.

3 February 1995 at SCG, Sydney

New South Wales 116
Western Australia 117 for 4

Western Australia (2 pts) won by 6 wickets

11 February 1995 at Adelaide Oval

Victoria 236 for 7
South Australia 157 (J.C. Scuderi 51)

Victoria (2 pts) won by 79 runs

12 February 1995 at Woolloongabba, Brisbane

Queensland v. New South Wales

Match abandoned

Queensland 1 pt, New South Wales 1 pt

at Bellerive Oval, Hobart

Western Australia 240 for 9 (D.R. Martyn 57,
    C.R. Miller 4 for 48)
Tasmania 209 for 6 (J. Cox 68, S. Young 56)

Western Australia (2 pts) won by 31 runs

18 February 1995 at Bellerive Oval, Hobart

New South Wales 255 for 7 (J.L. Arnberger 73,
    M.W. Patterson 62)
Tasmania 256 for 5 (S. Young 96)

Tasmania (2 pts) won by 5 wickets

19 February 1995 at Adelaide Oval

Western Australia 213 (M.P. Lavender 100)
South Australia 214 for 6 (D.S. Lehmann 102)

South Australia (2 pts) won by 4 wickets

at MCG, Melbourne

Queensland 149 (D.J. Saker 4 for 35)
Victoria 151 for 2 (B.J. Hodge 78 not out)

Victoria (2 pts) won by 8 wickets

SEMI-FINAL
25 February 1995 at WACA Ground, Perth

Western Australia 280 for 4 (D.R. Martyn 114 not out,
    M.P. Lavender 80)
South Australia 281 for 6 (P.C. Nobes 140 not out, D.J. Marsh
    55 not out)

South Australia won by 4 wickets

FINAL
5 March 1995 at MCG, Melbourne

South Australia 169 (J.P. Bakker 4 for 15, T.F. Corbett 4 for 30)
Victoria 170 for 6

Victoria won by 4 wickets

With newcomer Jason Bakker taking four of the last five wickets, Victoria took the Cup, having won every one of their six matches.

MERCANTILE MUTUAL CUP FINAL TABLE

	P	W	L	Ab	Pts
Victoria	5	5	–	–	10
Western Australia	5	3	2	–	6
South Australia	5	3	2	–	6
Queensland	5	2	2	1	5
Tasmania	5	1	4	–	2
New South Wales	5	–	4	1	1

FIRST-CLASS AVERAGES

BATTING

	M	Inns	NO	Runs	HS	Av	100s	50s
D.M. Jones	11	21	3	1251	324*	69.50	4	3
A.R. Border	11	19	5	911	151*	65.07	2	4
S.R. Waugh	9	17	4	849	206	65.30	1	6
R.T. Ponting	7	12	–	772	211	64.33	3	3
J.A. Brayshaw	12	22	6	1012	134*	63.25	4	6
D.S. Lehmann	11	20	1	1104	202*	58.10	3	6
G.S. Blewett	9	16	2	795	152	56.78	4	3
R.J. Tucker	11	19	7	673	140*	56.08	1	4
M.J. Slater	9	17	–	896	176	52.70	3	4
S. Young	11	20	4	830	152*	51.87	2	3
G.R.J. Matthews	5	8	2	311	80	51.83	–	3
T.M. Moody	11	20	2	919	272	51.05	1	6
M.A. Taylor	8	15	–	751	150	50.06	2	2
M.T.G. Elliott	11	21	–	1029	171	49.00	3	6
M.E. Waugh	9	17	–	827	140	48.64	3	4
J.D. Siddons	12	22	3	910	170	47.89	4	1
M.L. Hayden	13	23	3	954	201*	47.70	2	6
S.G. Law	12	20	1	894	145	47.05	4	4
M.P. Lavender	11	21	2	872	152	45.89	1	6
J.L. Langer	7	12	1	485	241*	44.09	1	–
J. Cox	11	21	1	828	165	41.40	2	4
J.P. Maher	13	22	5	700	100*	41.17	1	1
P.C. Nobes	12	22	–	896	110	40.72	3	5
M.N. Atkinson	11	17	10	284	76*	40.57	–	3
P.R. Reiffel	8	10	4	242	55	40.33	–	1
B.A. Johnson	8	14	–	552	168	39.42	1	2
M.L. Love	13	23	–	1097	187	39.38	3	4
T.J. Barsby	12	22	1	827	151	39.38	2	3
R.P. Larkin	6	11	–	416	116	37.81	1	2
M.W. Goodwin	9	16	2	498	91	35.57	–	3
D.S. Webber	9	16	2	493	91	35.21	–	2
A. Symonds	4	7	1	209	108*	34.83	1	–
T.J. Nielsen	12	18	3	521	74*	34.73	–	5
N.D. Maxwell	9	17	2	498	91	33.20	–	3
M.J. DiVenuto	11	20	–	656	119	32.80	1	4
J.P. Bakker	2	4	–	127	75	31.75	–	1
G.B. Gardiner	11	19	–	596	64	31.36	–	2
A.J. Daly	5	10	1	281	48	31.22	–	–
P.A. Emery	8	14	5	274	92	30.44	–	2
D.R. Martyn	11	19	–	554	113	29.15	2	2
S. Lee	10	19	2	488	100*	28.70	1	3
M.G. Bevan	10	19	1	504	103	28.00	1	2
M.R.J. Veletta	10	19	1	493	91	27.38	–	4
B.J. Hodge	10	19	2	457	116	26.88	2	1
A.C. Gilchrist	11	17	2	398	126	26.53	1	1
D.F. Hills	11	21	–	554	111	26.38	1	3
I.A. Healy	7	13	3	260	74	26.00	–	2
D.C. Boon	7	13	–	334	131	25.69	1	1
I.A. Wrigglesworth	3	6	–	154	58	25.66	–	1
W.G. Ayres	2	4	–	100	67	25.00	–	1
G.A.J. Fitness	3	4	–	100	71	25.00	–	1
G.B. Hogg	8	13	2	265	71	24.09	–	3
R.J. Davison	7	14	–	334	58	23.85	–	2
D.S. Berry	11	18	1	399	55	23.47	–	1
C.E. Coulson	7	11	5	137	32*	22.83	–	–
I.J. Harvey	6	9	1	175	62	21.87	–	1
J.L. Arnberger	4	8	–	174	63	21.75	–	1
B.P. Julian	8	11	2	186	51	20.66	–	1
M.P. Mott	3	6	–	123	55	20.50	–	1
S.M. Thompson	6	10	2	158	29*	19.75	–	–
K.J. Roberts	5	10	–	191	51	19.10	–	1
C.R. Miller	6	8	–	146	47	18.25	–	–
W.A. Seccombe	8	11	2	164	38	18.22	–	–
D.W. Fleming	5	8	2	104	28*	17.33	–	–

	M	Inns	NO	Runs	HS	Av	100s	50s
B.E. McNamara	7	13	2	175	50	15.90	–	1
G.R. Robertson	7	11	2	120	43	13.33	–	–
C.J. McDermott	7	11	2	118	52	13.11	–	1
P.E. McIntyre	10	14	1	146	32	11.23	–	–
J. Angel	8	12	–	130	41	10.83	–	–

(Qualification – 100 runs, average 10.00)

BOWLING

	Overs	Mds	Runs	Wkts	Av	Best	10/m	5/inn
S.K. Warne	373.2	123	814	40	20.35	8-71	1	3
J. Angel	338.4	90	996	48	20.75	5-62	–	2
B.A. Johnson	88	19	282	13	21.69	3-16	–	–
M.W. Ridgway	121.1	25	402	18	22.33	6-29	–	2
P.R. Reiffel	332.4	106	806	36	23.38	5-56	–	2
C.G. Rackemann	438.1	110	1227	52	23.59	7-43	–	1
A.J. Bichel	88.5	18	285	12	23.75	6-79	–	1
C.J. McDermott	303.3	76	902	37	24.37	6-38	–	4
D. Tazelaar	398.5	106	1146	47	24.38	6-89	–	1
G.S. Blewett	136	33	399	16	24.93	4-39	–	–
M.S. Kasprowicz	195.2	56	640	25	25.60	6-47	–	2
B.A. Reid	211.3	66	515	20	25.75	4-60	–	–
G.D. McGrath	218	68	613	23	26.65	5-50	–	1
D.W. Fleming	194.3	64	457	17	26.88	4-39	–	–
T.M. Moody	319.1	93	766	28	27.35	4-42	–	–
B.P. Julian	279	68	897	32	28.03	5-58	1	3
W.J. Holdsworth	113.3	25	343	12	28.58	5-70	–	1
G.J. Rowell	355.2	104	952	33	28.84	4-17	–	–
D.J. Saker	137	39	352	12	29.33	4-39	–	–
M.E. Waugh	103	22	308	10	30.80	5-40	–	1
P.W. Jackson	374.4	115	905	28	32.32	3-54	–	–
B.A. Williams	133.5	33	362	11	32.90	5-88	–	1
S.P. George	428.5	90	1443	43	33.55	4-31	–	–
G.R.J. Matthews	208	51	608	18	33.77	3-35	–	–
A.J. Kershler	223	53	618	18	34.33	5-42	–	1
M.A. Harrity	238.1	54	767	22	34.86	5-92	–	1
P.E. McIntyre	470.1	95	1398	40	34.95	5-85	–	1
S. Young	381.3	97	1128	32	35.25	5-56	1	2
S.G. Law	128	36	353	10	35.30	2-16	–	–
M.G. Hughes	153.1	32	473	13	36.38	4-51	–	–
T.F. Corbett	261.5	56	842	23	36.60	6-42	–	2
B.E. McNamara	188	50	560	15	37.33	5-72	–	1
B.B.J. Doyle	151.2	31	492	13	37.84	3-44	–	–
C.E. Coulson	269	71	762	20	38.10	2-27	–	–
S.H. Cook	125	27	421	11	38.27	3-41	–	–
S.R. Cary	233.3	51	774	18	43.00	3-55	–	–
S.M. Thompson	153	31	611	14	43.64	3-67	–	–
D.J. Millns	205	26	805	18	44.72	4-81	–	–
M.J.P. Minagall	201.5	42	733	16	45.81	7-152	1	1
C.R. Miller	170	31	581	12	48.41	4-35	–	–
T.B.A. May	286.4	70	693	14	49.50	6-80	1	1
C.D. Matthews	199.4	39	763	13	58.69	4-65	–	–
G.R. Robertson	295.4	70	776	12	64.66	5-115	–	1
S. Lee	191	38	658	10	65.80	3-53	–	–

(Qualification – 10 wickets)

LEADING FIELDERS

55 – A.C. Gilchrist; 48 – D.S. Berry (ct 45/st 3); 44 – T.J. Nielsen (ct 39/st 5); 41 – M.N. Atkinson (ct 37/st 4); 40 – W.A. Seccombe (ct 38/st 2); 30 – I.A. Healy (ct 28/st 2); 22 – A.R. Border; 20 – J.D. Siddons; 19 – P.A. Emery (ct 14/st 5); 15 – S.G. Law and T.M. Moody; 14 – M.R.J. Veletta; 13 – M.E. Waugh; 12 – M.P. Lavender, D.R. Martyn, M.A. Taylor, J.A. Brayshaw and M.L. Hayden; 11 – M.T.G. Elliott, M.L. Love and G.A.J. Fitness (ct 10/st 1); 10 – S. Lee, G.S. Blewett and T.J. Barsby

SRI LANKA

Pakistan tour, Test and one-day international series
Singer World Series

Prolific scorer in the Test matches, Pakistan's Saeed Anwar ducks under a bouncer from Wickremasinghe. Dassanayake, who performed impressively, is the wicket-keeper. (Paul Sturgess/Sportsline)

While Pakistan's tour of Sri Lanka may have upset some in England – particularly those at Lancashire, where the absence of Wasim Akram caused them to question the advisability of overseas cricketers in the county championship – it was very necessary from the point of view of the participating countries. Sri Lanka, disgracefully neglected by the authorities in England and Australia, need all the international cricket they can get if they are to realise their undoubted potential, and Pakistan had need to re-establish good relations in Sri Lanka.

In an acerbic article in *The Cricketer Pakistan*, Anisuddin Khan compared the 'contemptuous manner in which Englishmen treat Pakistani cricket' to the way in which Pakistanis look upon Sri Lankan cricket. He cited the past behaviour of Sarfraz Nawaz while visiting the island and, in particular, the behaviour of Javed Miandad and the caustic words of Imran Khan on the 1986 tour. Happily, Salim Malik's team in 1994 was to do much to heal old wounds. Salim's party included Mohammad Kabir Khan, a left-arm fast–medium-pace bowler who had no experience at international level, and Ashfaq Ahmed, the fast–medium-pacer who had appeared in one Test match. Javed Miandad did not make himself available for selection because of a knee injury.

23, 24 and 25 July 1994 *at Matara*

Pakistanis 250 for 6 dec. (Saeed Anwar 95, Salim Malik 77 not out)

Sri Lankan Board President's XI 46 for 3

Match drawn

No play was possible on the first day, and only limited play was possible on the second when Saeed Anwar and Aamir Sohail scored 111 for the tourists' first wicket.

28, 29 and 30 July 1994 *at Welagedara Stadium, Kurunegala*

Sri Lankan Board President's XI 326 (S. Ranatunga 97, A.H. Wickramaratne 69, Wasim Akram 5 for 76, Ashfaq Ahmed 4 for 47) and 64 for 2

Pakistanis 492 (Aamir Sohail 146, Saeed Anwar 66, Salim Malik 62, H.D.P.K. Dharmasena 7 for 117)

Match drawn

The President's XI consisted of completely different players from those who had appeared in the first match. Aamir Sohail hit 2 sixes and 23 fours, and added 111 in 89 minutes with Inzamam-ul-Haq. The most impressive performer, however, was the off-break bowler Dharmasena who took seven wickets and pressed for a place in the national side.

1 August 1994 *at P. Saravanamuttu Stadium, Colombo*

Pakistanis 195 for 8 (Salim Malik 62)

Sri Lankan Board President's XI 198 for 8

Sri Lankan Board President's XI won by 2 wickets

The tourists suffered an unexpected defeat in a 47-over match. Pushpakumara, a medium-pace right-arm bowler, took 3 for 26 in his 10 overs, and the Pakistanis were restricted to 195. The President's XI were 175 for 8 in reply and, with two overs remaining, they needed 16 to win. Upashantha took 11 off Aamir Sohail, and seven came from the first three balls of the last over, bowled by Waqar Younis.

 ONE-DAY INTERNATIONAL SERIES
SRI LANKA *v.* PAKISTAN

It was originally intended that there should be three one-day internationals and three Test matches between the two countries, but the cancellation of the second Test led to the limited-over series being increased to five matches.

The first game saw two players make their debuts in one-day international cricket, Sanjeeva Ranatunga of Sri Lanka, and Ashfaq Ahmed of Pakistan. Ranatunga began impressively, sharing an opening stand of 86 with Sanath Jayasuriya when Sri Lanka decided to bat first. Jayasuriya made his highest score in one-day international cricket. His 77 came off 106 balls, and his innings included a six and 4 fours. Like fast food, one-day cricket has an instant attraction for the general public, and a near-capacity crowd of 40,000 watched the match. There was a brief stoppage for rain which reduced Pakistan's target from 201 in 50 overs to 169 in 42, but they blasted their way to victory with 11.4 overs to spare. Saeed Anwar hit 70 off 83 balls, and Inzamam-ul-Haq's 53 came off 53 deliveries. They shared an unbroken partnership of 98.

Sri Lanka levelled the series three days later. Arjuna Ranatunga again won the toss, but this time he asked Pakistan to bat first. He had immediate reward when Saeed Anwar fell to the second ball of the match. The only substance to the Pakistan innings came from a fourth-wicket stand of 74 between Basit Ali, who hit 40 off 69 balls, and Salim Malik. Salim, in splendid form on the tour, hit 3 fours and played well on a sluggish pitch to score 61 off 111 balls. Kalpage, the off-spinner, dismissed Rashid Latif and Waqar Younis with the last two deliveries of his 10-over quota to finish with 4 for 36, his best figures in a one-day international. In 27.2 overs at the start of Sri Lanka's innings, Sanath Jayasuriya and Sanjeeva Ranatunga scored 104, the first time Sri Lanka had achieved a century opening partnership against Pakistan in a one-day international. Ranatunga, with 4 fours, made 70 off 116 balls and was mainly responsible for his side's victory. He took the individual award on what was only his second appearance in international cricket.

The third match followed hot upon the second, and once again Pakistan were asked to bat first. They were in some trouble at 58 for 3 before Salim Malik and Basit Ali added 96. Salim was magnificent. His elevation to the captaincy has revitalised his batting. His unbeaten 93 came off 94 balls, and the last five overs of the innings produced 71 runs. One over by the off-spinner Muralitharan realised 27 runs. Mujtaba took five from the first two deliveries, and Salim then hit 3 sixes and a four. In all, he hit 6 fours and

FIRST ONE-DAY INTERNATIONAL – SRI LANKA v. PAKISTAN
3 August 1994 at R. Premadasa (Khetterama) Stadium, Colombo

SRI LANKA				PAKISTAN		
S.T. Jayasuriya	c Akram Raza, b Salim Malik	77		Saeed Anwar	not out	70
S. Ranatunga	st Rashid Latif, b Salim Malik	31		Aamir Sohail	c Tillekeratne, b Muralitharan	38
A.P. Gurusinha	b Akram Raza	5		Inzamam-ul-Haq	not out	53
P.A. de Silva	run out	15		Salim Malik (capt)		
A. Ranatunga (capt)	run out	33		Asif Mujtaba		
H.P. Tillekeratne	run out	13		Zahid Fazal		
R.S. Kalpage	not out	7		*Rashid Latif		
*P.B. Dassanayake	not out	5		Wasim Akram		
C.P.H. Ramanayake				Akram Raza		
G.P. Wickremasinghe				Waqar Younis		
M. Muralitharan				Ashfaq Ahmed		
Extras	lb 4, w 6, nb 4	14		Extras	b 3, lb 5	8
(50 overs)	(for 6 wickets)	200		(30.2 overs)	(for 1 wicket)	169

	O	M	R	W		O	M	R	W
Wasim Akram	10	–	38	–	Wickremasinghe	7	–	43	–
Waqar Younis	8	2	38	–	Ramanayake	7.2	–	38	–
Ashfaq Ahmed	8	1	33	–	Kalpage	9	1	34	–
Akram Raza	10	1	27	1	Gurusinha	1	–	10	–
Salim Malik	10	–	44	2	Muralitharan	4	1	21	1
Aamir Sohail	4	–	16	–	Jayasuriya	2	–	15	–

FALL OF WICKETS
1–86, 2–97, 3–133, 4–143, 5–186, 6–194

FALL OF WICKET
1–71

Umpires: K.T. Francis & W.A.U. Wickremasinghe   Man of the Match: Saeed Anwar   *Pakistan won on faster scoring rate*

SECOND ONE-DAY INTERNATIONAL – SRI LANKA v. PAKISTAN
6 August 1994 at R. Premadasa (Khetterama) Stadium, Colombo

PAKISTAN				SRI LANKA		
Saeed Anwar	c and b Wickremasinghe	0		S.T. Jayasuriya	st Rashid Latif, b Akram Raza	54
Aamir Sohail	b Vaas	11		S. Ranatunga	lbw, b Aamir Sohail	70
Inzamam-ul-Haq	c de Silva, b A. Ranatunga	14		P.A. de Silva	c Rashid Latif, b Waqar Younis	22
Salim Malik (capt)	c Wickremasinghe, b Kalpage	61		A. Ranatunga (capt)	not out	15
Basit Ali	b Kalpage	40		A.P. Gurusinha	not out	10
*Rashid Latif	c Jayasuriya, b Kalpage	27		H.P. Tillekeratne		
Wasim Akram	c Dassanayake, b Muralitharan	0		R.S. Kalpage		
Asif Mujtaba	not out	12		*P.B. Dassanayake		
Waqar Younis	c and b Kalpage	0		G.P. Wickremasinghe		
Akram Raza	not out	9		M. Muralitharan		
Ashfaq Ahmed				W.P.U.C.J. Vaas		
Extras	lb 2, w 3, nb 1	6		Extras	lb 5, w 3, nb 2	10
(50 overs)	(for 8 wickets)	180		(47.2 overs)	(for 3 wickets)	181

	O	M	R	W		O	M	R	W
Wickremasinghe	7	1	25	1	Wasim Akram	10	2	34	–
Vaas	7	–	20	1	Waqar Younis	9	–	43	1
A. Ranatunga	10	–	35	1	Ashfaq Ahmed	5	1	20	–
Muralitharan	10	1	36	1	Akram Raza	10	–	27	1
Kalpage	10	1	36	4	Salim Malik	6	–	26	–
Jayasuriya	6	–	26	–	Aamir Sohail	7.2	–	26	1

FALL OF WICKETS
1–0, 2–21, 3–39, 4–113, 5–142, 6–145, 7–163, 8–163

FALL OF WICKETS
1–104, 2–153, 3–153

Umpires: T.M. Samarasinghe & I. Anandappa   Man of the Match: S. Ranatunga   *Sri Lanka won by 7 wickets*

THIRD ONE-DAY INTERNATIONAL – SRI LANKA v. PAKISTAN
7 August 1994 at Sinhalese Sports Club, Colombo

PAKISTAN				SRI LANKA		
Saeed Anwar	c Dassanayake, b A. Ranatunga		33	S.T. Jayasuriya	c Inzamam-ul-Haq, b Akram Raza	50
Aamir Sohail	c Jayasuriya, b Wickremasinghe		4	S. Ranatunga	c Rashid Latif, b Wasim Akram	2
Inzamam-ul-Haq	c Mahanama, b Kalpage		10	A.P. Gurusinha	lbw, b Wasim Akram	0
Salim Malik (capt)	not out		93	P.A. de Silva	c Salim Malik, b Waqar Younis	21
Basit Ali	c Gurusinha, b Jayasuriya		50	R.S. Mahanama	lbw, b Salim Malik	32
*Rashid Latif	c Gurusinha, b Jayasuriya		2	A. Ranatunga (capt)	b Aamir Sohail	19
Wasim Akram	st Dassanayake, b Kalpage		23	*P.B. Dassanayake	st Rashid Latif, b Aamir Sohail	1
Asif Mujtaba	c Mahanama, b Wickremasinghe		6	R.S. Kalpage	not out	44
Waqar Younis	not out		4	G.P. Wickremasinghe	c Saeed Anwar, b Salim Malik	0
Akram Raza				W.P.U.C.J. Vaas	b Wasim Akram	33
Ashfaq Ahmed				M. Muralitharan	b Waqar Younis	1
Extras	lb 6, w 5, nb 1		12	Extras	lb 6, w 7, nb 2	15
(50 overs)	(for 7 wickets)		237	(49 overs)		218

	O	M	R	W		O	M	R	W
Wickremasinghe	8	1	26	2	Wasim Akram	9	–	24	3
Vaas	7	1	22	–	Waqar Younis	10	1	57	2
A. Ranatunga	10	–	44	1	Ashfaq Ahmed	4	1	31	–
Kalpage	10	–	48	2	Akram Raza	10	2	31	1
Muralitharan	8	1	53	–	Salim Malik	10	1	45	2
Jayasuriya	7	–	38	2	Aamir Sohail	6	–	24	2

FALL OF WICKETS
1–7, 2–50, 3–58, 4–154, 5–161, 6–193, 7–222

FALL OF WICKETS
1–13, 2–13, 3–51, 4–97, 5–118, 6–121, 7–132, 8–133, 9–209

Umpires: B.C. Cooray & P. Manuel   *Man of the Match:* Salim Malik   *Pakistan won by 19 runs*

FOURTH ONE-DAY INTERNATIONAL – SRI LANKA v. PAKISTAN
22 August 1994 at Sinhalese Sports Club, Colombo

SRI LANKA				PAKISTAN		
R.S. Mahanama	c Akram Raza, b Waqar Younis		11	Saeed Anwar	c Dassanayake, b Pushpakumara	9
S.T. Jayasuriya	lbw, b Wasim Akram		2	Aamir Sohail	c S. Ranatunga, b Kalpage	35
S. Ranatunga	c and b Akram Raza		14	Inzamam-ul-Haq	c and b Jayasuriya	33
P.A. de Silva	c Aamir Sohail, b Akram Raza		5	Salim Malik (capt)	not out	50
A. Ranatunga (capt)	run out		74	Basit Ali	st Dassanayake, b Jayasuriya	26
H.P. Tillekeratne	run out		0	Asif Mujtaba	b de Silva	3
R.S. Kalpage	c Salim Malik, b Aamir Sohail		24	Akram Raza	not out	8
*P.B. Dassanayake	b Wasim Akram		13	*Rashid Latif		
W.P.U.C.J. Vaas	not out		7	Wasim Akram		
G.P. Wickremasinghe	b Waqar Younis		11	Mushtaq Ahmed		
K.R. Pushpakumara				Waqar Younis		
Extras	lb 5, w 6, nb 2		13	Extras	lb 2, w 3, nb 6	11
(50 overs)	(for 9 wickets)		174	(41.4 overs)	(for 5 wickets)	175

	O	M	R	W		O	M	R	W
Wasim Akram	10	1	35	2	Vaas	6	1	23	–
Waqar Younis	10	1	35	2	Pushpakumara	7	–	50	1
Akram Raza	10	1	26	2	Wickremasinghe	5.4	1	26	–
Mushtaq Ahmed	10	1	28	–	Kalpage	10	–	39	1
Aamir Sohail	5	–	17	1	Jayasuriya	10	–	28	2
Salim Malik	5	–	28	–	de Silva	3	–	7	1

FALL OF WICKETS
1–5, 2–23, 3–29, 4–55, 5–55, 6–102, 7–155, 8–157, 9–174

FALL OF WICKETS
1–20, 2–61, 3–114, 4–160, 5–165

Umpires: T.M. Samarasinghe & I. Anandappa   *Man of the Match:* Akram Raza   *Pakistan won by 5 wickets*

PAKISTAN

Batsman	Dismissal	Runs
Saeed Anwar	c and b Wickremasinghe	0
Aamir Sohail	run out	25
Inzamam-ul-Haq	lbw, b A. Ranatunga	25
Salim Malik (capt)	run out	19
Basit Ali	c Vaas, b Dharmasena	31
Asif Mujtaba	c Mahanama, b Dharmasena	28
Wasim Akram	run out	0
Akram Raza	not out	33
*Rashid Latif	b Kalpage	0
Waqar Younis	b Kalpage	13
Mushtaq Ahmed	b Vaas	1
Extras	lb 5, w 3, nb 4	12
(49.5 overs)		187

SRI LANKA

Batsman	Dismissal	Runs
R.S. Mahanama	c Asif Mujtaba, b Waqar Younis	52
S.T. Jayasuriya	lbw, b Wasim Akram	0
S. Ranatunga	run out	23
P.A. de Silva	c Rashid Latif, b Aamir Sohail	6
A. Ranatunga (capt)	b Waqar Younis	32
*R.S. Kaluwitharana	lbw, b Akram Raza	4
H.P. Tillekeratne	b Waqar Younis	15
R.S. Kalpage	c Salim Malik, b Wasim Akram	4
H.D.P.K. Dharmasena	not out	3
W.P.U.C.J. Vaas	run out	1
G.P. Wickremasinghe	c Rashid Latif, b Wasim Akram	1
Extras	b 2, lb 6, w 10, nb 1	19
(48.1 overs)		160

	O	M	R	W
Wickremasinghe	3	–	9	1
Vaas	7.5	1	39	1
A. Ranatunga	10	–	23	1
Kalpage	10	1	38	2
Jayasuriya	10	–	39	–
Dharmasena	9	–	34	2

	O	M	R	W
Wasim Akram	9.1	2	20	3
Waqar Younis	8	–	33	3
Akram Raza	10	–	25	1
Mushtaq Ahmed	10	–	27	–
Aamir Sohail	10	–	41	1
Salim Malik	1	–	6	–

FALL OF WICKETS
1–1, 2–54, 3–59, 4–92, 5–130, 6–130, 7–160, 8–162, 9–184

FALL OF WICKETS
1–4, 2–58, 3–73, 4–102, 5–139, 6–140, 7–151, 8–151, 9–157

Umpires: W.A.U. Wickremasinghe & P. Manuel   *Man of the Match:* Waqar Younis   *Pakistan won by 27 runs*

these 3 sixes. Sri Lanka quickly subsided to 133 for 8 and looked well beaten, but Kalpage and Vaas shared a record stand of 76 off 100 balls to bring new hope. Wasim returned to bowl Vaas, and Waqar Younis ended an absorbing match when he bowled Muralitharan.

The final two matches in the series saw Wasim Akram first draw level with, and then beat, Kapil Dev's record of 251 wickets in one-day international cricket. His two wickets in the fourth match brought him level with Kapil Dev, and he claimed the record when he accounted for Jayasuriya in his first over in the fifth match. Pakistan won the fourth encounter with ease. Only skipper Arjuna Ranatunga offered fighting resistance to a tidy spell by Akram Raza and to the pace of Wasim. Needing 175 to win, Pakistan had reached 61 for 2 in the 15th over when Salim Malik came to the crease. He hit 4 fours, reached 50 off 75 balls and stayed until the end, the 42nd over, when Pakistan won by five wickets. Salim's 50 was his seventh half-century in eight innings.

Having dismissed Pakistan for a moderate 187 in the fifth match, Sri Lanka advanced to 122 for 4 at the end of the 40th over and looked in sight of victory. Once more, however, they were denied as their last six wickets went down for 21 runs. Wasim Akram and Waqar Younis, bowling better than he had done at any time on the tour up to this point, took the last five wickets in 39 balls. Waqar began the collapse when he bowled both Arjuna Ranatunga and Hashan Tillekeratne in the 44th over.

TEST SERIES
SRI LANKA v. PAKISTAN

Not surprisingly, the pitch for the first Test at the P. Saravanamuttu Stadium was more suitable for spin than for pace, and Sri Lanka fielded only one fast–medium bowler, Wickremasinghe. Pakistan included two front-line spinners, Akram Raza and Mushtaq Ahmed.

Salim Malik won the toss, and Pakistan batted. The lack of a pair of new-ball bowlers of quality told against Sri Lanka as Saeed Anwar and Aamir Sohail gave Pakistan a rousing start. Make-shift opening bowler Gurusinha was hit for 24 in four overs, all of the runs he conceded coming in boundaries. Aamir Sohail hit 8 fours and had scored 41 off 50 balls when he was bowled as he tried to cut a ball from Kumara Dharmasena. The opening stand had realised 65 brisk runs, and Saeed Anwar and Asif Mujtaba now set about consolidating the innings. They added 115, but Sri Lanka brought themselves back into the game when they captured five wickets for 80 runs. Saeed Anwar batted faultlessly until he was well caught in the gully six short of his century, and Salim Malik was out seven balls later. He was caught at short-leg when the ball lodged under Tillekeratne's right armpit.

Three wickets fell in the final session, but Inzamam-ul-Haq and Wasim Akram batted with sense and authority, and Pakistan closed on 297 for 6, a highly satisfactory score on a pitch which was already encouraging the spinners.

Gurusinha is caught behind off Mushtaq as Sri Lanka lose early wickets in the first Test match. (Paul Sturgess/Sportsline)

The seventh-wicket partnership became worth 85 on the second morning before Wasim was caught at long-off. Inzamam was smartly taken at short-leg, but Akram Raza played some belligerent shots, and Pakistan were all out for a commendable 390. The bowling honours went to the 23-year-old Kumara Dharmasena who bowled his off-cutters quite briskly to capture 6 for 99, his best return in his brief Test career.

Jayasuriya was taken at slip off Wasim, but it was the advent of Mushtaq Ahmed which caused Sri Lanka great problems. In eight overs he took 3 for 20, and Sri Lanka tumbled to 60 for 4. Mahanama, who was returning after a knee operation, was bowled round his legs as he tried to sweep, and Gurusinha, never comfortable against any of the bowlers, was caught behind. These wickets fell in consecutive overs from Mushtaq just before tea, and Ranatunga was caught and bowled after the break. Dehydration and cramp forced Mushtaq to leave the field after bowling eight overs, and de Silva and Tillekeratne prospered in his absence. Aravinda de Silva hit 12 fours and reached 74 by the close, when Sri Lanka were 152 for 4.

There is no more glorious sight in world cricket than de Silva in full flow, and the game has been richer for his coming. He began the third morning with 2 fours off Waqar Younis, and he reached his seventh Test century by hitting Mushtaq Ahmed over long-off for six. This gave him a world record, for it was the third occasion on which he had reached a Test century with a six. He and Tillekeratne added a record 119, and then – alas, as so often before – Sri Lanka fell apart. Their last five wickets went down for 11 runs in 29 balls. Akram Raza took three wickets in five balls, and Pakistan led by a daunting 164 runs.

They were not likely to surrender such an advantage, and Saeed Anwar and Aamir Sohail punished Sri Lanka with an opening stand of 128 in 138 minutes. If Saeed could not match de Silva in style and aggression, he still

One of the world's most exciting batsmen, Aravinda de Silva acknowledges the applause of the crowd. (Paul Sturgess/Sportsline)

played an innings of great value and deservedly took the individual award. He was studious in approach, hitting only 6 fours and remaining on 99 for 11 deliveries before flicking a single to leg. Pakistan closed on 238 for 2, in total command.

Salim Malik declared at lunch on the fourth day by which time he himself had become only the fourth Pakistani batsman to score 4,000 runs in Test cricket.

Needing 483 to win in five sessions, Sri Lanka failed to last two sessions, and the game was over with 45 minutes of the fourth day remaining. Surrounded by close catchers, the Sri Lankan batsmen surrendered in 47 overs. Wasim and Waqar quickly removed the top order, and Akram Raza thwarted middle-order resistance on a pitch which was increasingly slower and lower in bounce. Not for the first time, Sri Lanka had fought hard for two days, only to subside in the later stages of the match. They desperately need to wed a corporate professional determination to their undoubted individual brilliance.

The second Test match had been scheduled for Colombo between 18 and 23 August, but civil unrest followed the general election in Sri Lanka, and a curfew was imposed as a precautionary measure. Accordingly, the second Test match was cancelled, and the fourth and fifth

FIRST TEST MATCH – SRI LANKA v. PAKISTAN
9, 10, 11 and 13 August 1994 at P. Saravanamuttu Stadium, Colombo

PAKISTAN

	FIRST INNINGS			SECOND INNINGS	
Saeed Anwar	c Jayasuriya, b Warnaweera	94		c Dassanayake, b Warnaweera	136
Aamir Sohail	b Dharmasena	41		c Jayasuriya, b Dharmasena	65
Asif Mujtaba	c Dassanayake, b Dharmasena	44		c Dassanayake, b Warnaweera	31
Salim Malik (capt)	c Tillekeratne, b Dharmasena	1		not out	50
Basit Ali	lbw, b Warnaweera	27		b Dharmasena	11
Inzamam-ul-Haq	c Tillekeratne, b Dharmasena	81		not out	7
*Rashid Latif	c Dassanayake, b Muralitharan	0			
Wasim Akram	c Jayasuriya, b Dharmasena	37			
Akram Raza	c Tillekeratne, b Warnaweera	25			
Mushtaq Ahmed	not out	5			
Waqar Younis	c Gurusinha, b Dharmasena	2			
Extras	b 11, lb 6, nb 16	33		lb 6, nb 12	18
		390		(for 4 wickets, dec.)	318

SRI LANKA

	FIRST INNINGS			SECOND INNINGS	
R.S. Mahanama	b Mushtaq	21		c sub (Zahid), b Akram	37
S.T. Jayasuriya	c Aamir, b Wasim	9		c Rashid, b Wasim	1
A.P. Gurusinha	c Rashid, b Mushtaq	11		c Asif, b Waqar	8
P.A. de Silva	c Aamir, b Akram	127		c and b Waqar	5
A. Ranatunga (capt)	c and b Mushtaq	9	(6)	st Rashid, b Akram	41
H.P. Tillekeratne	lbw, b Waqar	34	(5)	c and b Akram	8
*P.B. Dassanayake	c Rashid, b Wasim	3		b Wasim	24
H.D.P.K. Dharmasena	c Aamir, b Wasim	1		lbw, b Wasim	30
G.P. Wickremasinghe	not out	0		b Wasim	4
M. Muralitharan	c Asif, b Akram	0		not out	20
K.P.J. Warnaweera	c and b Akram	4		b Wasim	0
Extras	b 1, lb 5, nb 1	7		lb 2, nb 1	3
		226			181

	O	M	R	W	O	M	R	W
Wickremasinghe	12	–	59	–	5	–	25	–
Gurusinha	4	1	24	–				
Dharmasena	45.3	13	99	6	31	2	84	2
Muralitharan	36	6	123	1	11	1	42	–
Warnaweera	28	5	63	3	31	1	108	2
de Silva	1	–	5	–				
Jayasuriya					13	–	53	–

	O	M	R	W	O	M	R	W
Wasim Akram	17	4	30	3	18	4	43	5
Waqar Younis	16	1	84	1	7	–	28	2
Mushtaq Ahmed	14	2	57	3	6	1	25	–
Akram Raza	19	7	46	3	16	3	83	3
Aamir Sohail	2	–	3	–				

FALL OF WICKETS

1–65, 2–180, 3–181, 4–221, 5–247, 6–260, 7–345, 8–354, 9–387
1–128, 2–202, 3–273, 4–298

FALL OF WICKETS

1–13, 2–41, 3–42, 4–60, 5–179, 6–215, 7–218, 8–222, 9–222
1–1, 2–30, 3–38, 4–52, 5–59, 6–118, 7–135, 8–160, 9–181

Umpires: K.T. Francis & I.D. Robinson

Pakistan won by 301 runs

one-day internationals were played in its stead.

For the third Test match, Sri Lanka brought in a new pair of opening bowlers, Pushpakumara and Vaas, and included another debutant in Sanjeeva Ranatunga, the younger brother of the captain. Sanjeeva's performances against the tourists had earned him his first Test cap. Pakistan replaced Akram Raza with the 19-year-old left-arm pace bowler Kabir Khan, the fourth Test debutant in the match.

One and a half hours were lost to bad weather on the opening day, but there was enough time for Pakistan to take a giant step towards winning the match. Salim won the toss and asked Sri Lanka to bat first on a green pitch in overcast conditions. In 28.2 overs, they were bowled out by Wasim Akram and Waqar Younis for 71, their lowest score in Test cricket. Waqar bowled at a ferocious pace, and the Sri Lankan batsmen found both the pace men unplayable. Ironically, the only resistance of substance came from the last-wicket pair, Dassanayake and Pushpakumara, who added 25. Dassanayake, a most promising wicket-keeper, hit 3 fours in one over from Waqar.

Saeed Anwar and Aamir Sohail soon surpassed the Sri Lankan total in a first-wicket stand of 94, and although Saeed and Mushtaq, the night-watchman, were out before the close, Pakistan ended the day 38 runs ahead with eight wickets in hand.

On the second day, Pakistan batted with good sense and sound technique. Dharmasena was again most impressive, but Basit Ali hit an elegant fifty, and Inzamam-ul-Haq played splendidly for his 100 not out off 126 balls in 194 minutes. He hit 13 boundaries, and he and Waqar added 60 for the ninth wicket.

Sri Lanka had 18 overs to face before the end of the day, and they were left in shreds. Wasim Akram bowled five maiden overs, and Waqar, bowling at great pace, removed Mahanama, Dassanayake and Sanjeeva Ranatunga before the umpires halted play – probably out of mercy – with Sri Lanka 17 for 3.

There was no respite on the third morning as Sri Lanka slumped to 78 for 6. At last, there was defiance as the left-handers Tillekeratne and Kalpage batted in an exciting manner to add 131. Kalpage hit 2 sixes and 9 fours, taking

THIRD TEST MATCH – SRI LANKA v. PAKISTAN
26, 27 and 28 August 1994 at Asgiriya Stadium, Kandy

SRI LANKA

	FIRST INNINGS			SECOND INNINGS	
R.S. Mahanama	c Rashid, b Waqar	2	c Inzamam, b Waqar	10
D.P. Samaraweera	c Rashid, b Wasim	6	lbw, b Waqar	13
S. Ranatunga	c Rashid, b Waqar	5	(4) c Wasim, b Waqar	4
P.A. de Silva	lbw, b Wasim	7	(5) c Rashid, b Wasim	5
A. Ranatunga (capt)	c Saeed, b Waqar	0	(6) c Rashid, b Waqar	34
H.P. Tillekeratne	b Waqar	9	(7) not out	83
R.S. Kalpage	c Aamir, b Wasim	6	(8) c sub (Ramiz), b Kabir	62
*P.B. Dassanayake	not out	19	(3) lbw, b Waqar	1
H.D.P.K. Dharmasena	lbw, b Waqar	0	c sub (Zahid), b Mushtaq	3
W.P.U.C.J. Vaas	c Wasim, b Waqar	0	lbw, b Mushtaq	4
K.R. Pushpakumara	c Aamir, b Wasim	6	lbw, b Mushtaq	0
Extras	b 1, lb 4, w 5, nb 1	11	lb 6, nb 9	15
		—		—
		71		234

PAKISTAN

	FIRST INNINGS	
Saeed Anwar	lbw, b Pushpakumara	31
Aamir Sohail	c Tillekeratne, b Pushpakumara	74
Mushtaq Ahmed	run out	0
Asif Mujtaba	c Dassanayake, b Pushpakumara	17
Salim Malik (capt)	c Dassanayake, b Dharmasena	22
Basit Ali	c and b Dharmasena	53
Inzamam-ul-Haq	not out	100
*Rashid Latif	c Samaraweera, b Dharmasena	7
Wasim Akram	c de Silva, b Pushpakumara	12
Waqar Younis	c Kalpage, b Dharmasena	20
Kabir Khan		
Extras	b 4, lb 3, w 1, nb 13	21
		—
	(for 9 wickets, dec.)	357

	O	M	R	W	O	M	R	W
Wasim Akram	14.2	4	32	4	26	12	70	1
Waqar Younis	14	4	34	6	18	–	85	5
Kabir Khan					10	1	39	1
Mushtaq Ahmed					7.3	1	34	3

	O	M	R	W
Vaas	22	2	80	–
Pushpakumara	26	3	145	4
Dharmasena	28.5	7	75	4
Kalpage	11	–	50	–

FALL OF WICKETS
1–12, 2–20, 3–22, 4–28, 5–28, 6–43, 7–45, 8–46, 9–46
1–11, 2–13, 3–17, 4–22, 5–42, 6–78, 7–209, 8–221, 9–234

FALL OF WICKETS
1–94, 2–94, 3–117, 4–158, 5–158, 6–256, 7–264, 8–297, 9–357

Umpires: B.C. Cooray & I.D. Robinson

Pakistan won by an innings and 52 runs

19 runs in one over by Waqar, and the stand lasted just 74 balls. It was broken when Kalpage miscued a hook to give Kabir his first Test wicket. The match was over before tea, and Waqar finished with 11 for 119.

The gap between the two sides was vast: seasoned, knowledgeable professionals against a side with an attitude that was amateur.

SINGER WORLD SERIES

The opening match of the four-nation tournament, between India and Sri Lanka, was abandoned after four overs, but the match was replayed the following day as a 25-over contest. Kambli hit 30 off 38 balls, and Bedade made 21 off 35 balls, but their efforts proved in vain. Mahanama hit a sparkling 50, and he and Arjuna Ranatunga added 88 in 17 overs for the third wicket to take Sri Lanka to the brink of victory, and the home side won with four balls to spare.

Shane Warne had a fine all-round match as Australia caused a surprise by beating the favourites, Pakistan. Put in to bat, Australia laboured somewhat until the arrival of

Bevan, but it was a 46-run stand between Warne and Healy which proved decisive. Warne's 30 came off 40 balls. Pakistan soon lost Aamir Sohail, but Saeed Anwar and Inzamam-ul-Haq added 75, and victory for Pakistan seemed assured. They were checked by the medium pace of Steve Waugh who ended their hopes when he dismissed Saeed Anwar and Salim Malik with successive deliveries. Earlier Warne had begun the collapse when he had Inzamam stumped and caught and bowled Basit Ali. Pakistan lost six wickets for 52 runs, and when Waqar was brilliantly caught at long-on by Slater there was no hope of recovery.

Australia were less successful two days later when Sachin Tendulkar hit his first century in one-day international cricket. There were 2 sixes and 8 fours in his 130-ball innings. Chasing a target of 247, Australia were well served by Mark Waugh and David Boon. They added 67, with Waugh hitting 61 off 80 balls, but both fell to Chauhan, and India won with ease.

Sri Lanka assured themselves of a place in the final when they beat Pakistan by seven wickets with 16 balls to spare. Salim Malik made 53 off 86 balls, and there was good support from Aamir Sohail, 32 off 54 balls, and Basit Ali, 39 off 63 balls, but the Pakistan innings never really came to life. When Sri Lanka slipped to 65 for 3, however, it seemed that

SINGER WORLD SERIES – MATCH ONE – SRI LANKA v. INDIA
5 September 1994 at R. Premadasa (Khetterama) Stadium, Colombo

INDIA

M. Prabhakar	c Jayasuriya, b Wickremasinghe	14
S.R. Tendulkar	c Dharmasena, b Wickremasinghe	6
N.S. Sidhu	c Mahanama, b Jayasuriya	17
M. Azharuddin (capt)	c Chandana, b Dharmasena	25
V.G. Kambli	not out	30
A.C. Bedade	b Wickremasinghe	21
Kapil Dev	not out	1
*N.R. Mongia		
A.R. Kumble		
R.K. Chauhan		
J. Srinath		
Extras	b 3, lb 7, w1	11
(25 overs)	(for 5 wickets)	125

SRI LANKA

R.S. Mahanama	not out	50
S.T. Jayasuriya	run out	3
P.A. de Silva	c Mongia, b Kumble	14
A. Ranatunga (capt)	run out	41
R.S. Kalpage	not out	3
H.P. Tillekeratne		
U.D.U. Chandana		
*P.B. Dassanayake		
H.D.P.K. Dharmasena		
W.P.U.C.J. Vaas		
G.P. Wickremasinghe		
Extras	lb 12, w 2, nb 1	15
(24.2 overs)	(for 3 wickets)	126

	O	M	R	W
Wickremasinghe	5	–	28	3
Vaas	4	–	20	–
Dharmasena	5	–	22	1
Ranatunga	2	–	11	–
Jayasuriya	5	–	17	1
Kalpage	4	–	17	–

	O	M	R	W
Prabhakar	4.2	–	17	–
Srinath	5	–	21	–
Kumble	5	–	17	1
Tendulkar	4	–	21	–
Kapil Dev	2	–	15	–
Chauhan	4	–	23	–

FALL OF WICKETS
1–20, **2**–23, **3**–55, **4**–87, **5**–122

FALL OF WICKETS
1–7, **2**–31, **3**–119

Umpires: K.T. Francis & B.L. Aldridge | *Man of the Match:* G.P. Wickremasinghe | *Sri Lanka won by 7 wickets*

SINGER WORLD SERIES – MATCH TWO – AUSTRALIA v. PAKISTAN
7 September 1994 at Sinhalese Sports Club, Colombo

AUSTRALIA

M.A. Taylor (capt)	lbw, b Wasim Akram	8
M.J. Slater	c Asif Mujtaba, b Wasim Akram	4
D.C. Boon	b Akram Raza	19
M.E. Waugh	st Rashid Latif, b Mushtaq Ahmed	23
S.R. Waugh	c Rashid Latif, b Mushtaq Ahmed	1
M.G. Bevan	c Mushtaq Ahmed, b Salim Malik	37
*I.A. Healy	not out	30
S.K. Warne	b Wasim Akram	30
C.J. McDermott	not out	2
T.B.A. May		
G.D. McGrath		
Extras	b 7, lb 9, w 9	25
(50 overs)	(for 7 wickets)	179

PAKISTAN

Saeed Anwar	c McGrath, b S.R. Waugh	46
Aamir Sohail	b McGrath	0
Inzamam-ul-Haq	st Healy, b Warne	29
Basit Ali	c and b Warne	0
Salim Malik (capt)	c Taylor, b S.R. Waugh	22
*Rashid Latif	c Taylor, b S.R. Waugh	7
Wasim Akram	b McGrath	16
Akram Raza	c Healy, b McDermott	10
Waqar Younis	c Slater, b Warne	2
Mushtaq Ahmed	not out	2
Asif Mujtaba	not out	1
Extras	b 2, lb 5, w 6, nb 3	16
(50 overs)	(for 9 wickets)	151

	O	M	R	W
Wasim Akram	10	2	24	3
Waqar Younis	8	2	43	–
Mushtaq Ahmed	10	1	34	2
Akram Raza	10	1	26	1
Aamir Sohail	7	–	17	–
Salim Malik	5	–	19	1

	O	M	R	W
McDermott	10	2	21	1
McGrath	10	3	25	2
May	10	–	53	–
Warne	10	1	29	3
S.R. Waugh	10	1	16	3

FALL OF WICKETS
1–11, **2**–34, **3**–48, **4**–49, **5**–85, **6**–128, **7**–174

FALL OF WICKETS
1–2, **2**–77, **3**–83, **4**–94, **5**–124, **6**–129, **7**–129, **8**–147, **9**–150

Umpires: W.A.U. Wickremasinghe & B.C. Cooray | *Man of the Match:* S.K. Warne | *Australia won by 28 runs*

SINGER WORLD SERIES – MATCH THREE – INDIA V. AUSTRALIA
9 September 1994 at R. Premadasa (Khetterama) Stadium, Colombo

INDIA

M. Prabhakar	c Slater, b Warne	20
S.R. Tendulkar	b McDermott	110
N.S. Sidhu	c Boon, b May	24
M. Azharuddin (capt)	c Healy, b McDermott	31
V.G. Kambli	not out	43
Kapil Dev	run out	4
A.C. Bedade	run out	1
*N.R. Mongia	c Healy, b Warne	3
A.R. Kumble	b S.R. Waugh	1
R.K. Chauhan	not out	2
Venkatapathy Raju		
Extras	lb 2, w 5	7
(50 overs)	(for 8 wickets)	246

AUSTRALIA

M.J. Slater	c Prabhakar, b Kapil Dev	26
M.A. Taylor (capt)	c and b Prabhakar	4
M.E. Waugh	b Chauhan	61
D.C. Boon	b Chauhan	40
S.R. Waugh	b Prabhakar	22
M.G. Bevan	c Sidhu, b Kumble	26
C.J. McDermott	c Kumble, b Prabhakar	2
*I.A. Healy	run out	15
S.K. Warne	b Venkatapathy Raju	1
T.B.A. May	not out	1
G.D. McGrath	run out	1
Extras	b 2, lb 10, w 2, nb 2	16
(47.4 overs)		215

	O	M	R	W
McDermott	10	1	46	2
McGrath	6	–	41	–
Warne	10	–	53	2
May	10	–	35	1
S.R. Waugh	8	–	33	1
Bevan	2	–	17	–
M.E. Waugh	4	–	19	–

	O	M	R	W
Prabhakar	8	–	34	3
Kapil Dev	8	1	44	1
Venkatapathy Raju	9.4	–	38	1
Kumble	9	–	31	1
Chauhan	10	–	41	2
Tendulkar	3	–	15	–

FALL OF WICKETS
1–87, 2–189, 3–173, 4–211, 5–216, 6–217, 7–226, 8–237

FALL OF WICKETS
1–22, 2–56, 3–123, 4–143, 5–181, 6–183, 7–209, 8–212, 9–213

Umpires: B.L. Aldridge & B.C. Cooray — *Man of the Match:* S.R. Tendulkar — *India won by 31 runs*

SINGER WORLD SERIES – MATCH FOUR – SRI LANKA v. PAKISTAN
11 September 1994 at Sinhalese Sports Club, Colombo

PAKISTAN

Saeed Anwar	c Jayasuriya, b Vaas	24
Aamir Sohail	run out	32
Inzamam-ul-Haq	run out	2
Salim Malik (capt)	c Tillekeratne, b Kalpage	53
Basit Ali	c Mahanama, b Jayasuriya	39
Zahid Fazal	run out	15
*Rashid Latif	not out	28
Akram Raza	not out	9
Waqar Younis		
Mushtaq Ahmed		
Kabir Khan		
Extras	lb 2, w 4, nb 2	8
(50 overs)	(for 6 wickets)	210

SRI LANKA

R.S. Mahanama	retired hurt	39
S.T. Jayasuriya	c Salim Malik, b Kabir Khan	4
S. Ranatunga	c Inzamam-ul-Haq, b Akram Raza	16
P.A. de Silva	c and b Mushtaq Ahmed	11
A. Ranatunga (capt)	not out	82
H.P. Tillekeratne	not out	39
R.S. Kalpage		
*P.B. Dassanayake		
H.D.P.K. Dharmasena		
W.P.U.C.J. Vaas		
G.P. Wickremasinghe		
Extras	b 5, lb 10, w 6, nb 1	22
(47.2 overs)	(for 3 wickets)	213

	O	M	R	W
Wickremasinghe	8	–	37	–
Vaas	8	–	38	1
A. Ranatunga	8	–	29	–
Dharmasena	8	–	39	–
Jayasuriya	10	–	33	1
Kalpage	8	–	32	1

	O	M	R	W
Waqar Younis	9	1	42	–
Kabir Khan	9.2	1	34	1
Akram Raza	10	–	49	1
Aamir Sohail	8	–	28	–
Mushtaq Ahmed	8	–	31	1
Salim Malik	3	–	14	–

FALL OF WICKETS
1–28, 2–31, 3–82, 4–136, 5–169, 6–171

FALL OF WICKETS
1–9, 2–44, 3–65

Umpires: B.L. Aldridge & P. Manuel — *Man of the Match:* A. Ranatunga — *Sri Lanka won by 7 wickets*

SINGER WORLD SERIES – MATCH FIVE – SRI LANKA v. AUSTRALIA
13 September 1994 at P. Saravanamuttu Stadium, Colombo

AUSTRALIA

M.A. Taylor (capt)	c de Silva, b Kalpage	41
M.J. Slater	run out	24
M.E. Waugh	st Dassanayake, b Jayasuriya	24
J.L. Langer	c Wickremasinghe, b Kalpage	9
S.R. Waugh	c Dassanayake, b Jayasuriya	30
M.G. Bevan	not out	47
*I.A. Healy	run out	28
G.R. Robertson	not out	5
S.K. Warne		
J. Angel		
D.W. Fleming		
Extras	lb 11, w 5, nb 1	17
(50 overs)	(for 6 wickets)	225

SRI LANKA

R.S. Mahanama	b Warne	20
S.T. Jayasuriya	c Taylor, b Angel	0
P.A. de Silva	st Healy, b Warne	33
A. Ranatunga (capt)	lbw, b S.R. Waugh	59
H.P. Tillekeratne	not out	29
R.S. Kalpage	not out	9
U.D.U. Chandana		
H.D.P.K. Dharmasena		
*P.B. Dassanayake		
W.P.U.C.J. Vaas		
G.P. Wickremasinghe		
Extras	lb 10, w 3, nb 1	14
(34.4 overs)	(for 4 wickets)	164

	O	M	R	W
Wickremasinghe	7	–	29	–
Vaas	9	2	26	–
A. Ranatunga	2	–	14	–
Kalpage	9	–	42	2
Dharmasena	10	1	45	–
Jayasuriya	10	–	42	2
de Silva	3	–	16	–

	O	M	R	W
Angel	7	1	29	1
Fleming	6.4	–	42	–
Warne	8	–	27	2
S.R. Waugh	6	–	32	1
Robertson	7	–	24	–

FALL OF WICKETS
1–61, 2–90, 3–100, 4–116, 5–144, 6–204

FALL OF WICKETS
1–4, 2–48, 3–102, 4–141

Umpires: B.L. Aldridge & T.M. Samarasinghe *Man of the Match:* A. Ranatunga *Sri Lanka won on faster scoring rate*

SINGER WORLD SERIES FINAL – SRI LANKA v. INDIA
17 September 1994 at Sinhalese Sports Club, Colombo

SRI LANKA

R.S. Mahanama	run out	2
S.T. Jayasuriya	c Bedade, b Prabhakar	1
P.A. de Silva	c Venkatesh Prasad, b Chauhan	10
H.P. Tillekeratne	c Kambli, b Kapil Dev	7
A. Ranatunga (capt)	c Chauhan, b Kumble	13
R.S. Kalpage	c Mongia, b Venkatesh Prasad	39
U.D.U. Chandana	run out	2
*P.B. Dassanayake	run out	1
H.D.P.K. Dharmasena	b Prabhakar	8
W.P.U.C.J. Vaas	not out	2
G.P. Wickremasinghe	not out	3
Extras	lb 2, w 5, nb 3	10
(25 overs)	(for 9 wickets)	98

INDIA

M. Prabhakar	c Jayasuriya, b Wickremasinghe	10
S.R. Tendulkar	c de Silva, b Vaas	0
N.S. Sidhu	lbw, b Wickremasinghe	24
M. Azharuddin (capt)	c Mahanama, b Vaas	45
V.G. Kambli	not out	8
A.C. Bedade	not out	4
Kapil Dev		
A.R. Kumble		
R.K. Chauhan		
*N.R. Mongia		
Venkatesh Prasad		
Extras	b 4, lb 1, w 3	8
(23.4 overs)	(for 4 wickets)	99

	O	M	R	W
Prabhakar	5	–	19	2
Venkatesh Prasad	5	–	17	1
Kumble	5	–	22	1
Chauhan	5	–	21	1
Kapil Dev	5	–	17	1

	O	M	R	W
Wickremasinghe	5	–	13	2
Vaas	5	–	16	2
Dharmasena	5	–	22	–
Jayasuriya	3	–	15	–
Kalpage	5	1	23	–
de Silva	0.4	–	5	–

FALL OF WICKETS
1–5, 2–5, 3–24, 4–28, 5–64, 6–74, 7–76, 8–91, 9–95

FALL OF WICKETS
1–6, 2–15, 3–86, 4–88

Umpires: K.T. Francis & B.L. Aldridge *Man of the Match:* M. Azharuddin *India won by 6 wickets*

A bowler of quality and success at the highest level – Dharmasena.
(Paul Sturgess/Sportsline)

Pakistan's 210 would be a winning score, for 21 overs had already elapsed. Mahanama gave Arjuna Ranatunga good support, but he was forced to retire with cramp when the score was 97. Tillekeratne replaced him, and he and Ranatunga shared an unbroken stand of 116. Arjuna Ranatunga hit 7 fours, and his 82 came from only 78 balls.

Victory over Australia in a match curtailed by rain gave Sri Lanka a 100% record in the tournament. Australia, who gave limited-over international debuts to Angel and Robertson, made 225 in 50 overs, but Sri Lanka's target was reduced to 163 in 36 overs. They won with eight balls to spare. Skipper Ranatunga was again the hero. Jayasuriya was out for 0, but Mahanama and de Silva put on 44 off as many deliveries. Ranatunga followed with 59 off 75 balls, and Tillekeratne kept his head to steer Sri Lanka to their target.

The rain continued to mar the competition, and no play was possible on 15 or 16 September in the game between Pakistan and India.

SINGER WORLD SERIES FINAL TABLE

	P	W	L	Ab	Pts	R/R
Sri Lanka	3	3	–	–	6	4.8
India	3	1	1	1	3	4.9
Australia	3	1	2	–	2	4.1
Pakistan	3	–	2	1	1	3.6

The rain persisted, and the final was reduced to 25 overs a side on a pitch that was damp, with an outfield that was soaking. Had the ground not been packed to capacity, it is unlikely that the match would have been played. Azharuddin won the toss and, not surprisingly, asked Sri Lanka to bat. The ball turned sharply from the start, and Sri Lanka lost both openers in the third over. By the ninth over, they were 28 for 4. In the next nine overs, Ranatunga and Kalpage added 36. Kalpage hit 39 off 56 balls, but Sri Lanka's total never looked as if it would be enough to win the match.

India did not begin well, losing Tendulkar in Vaas' first over, but Azharuddin scored 45 off 51 balls and added 71 with Sidhu for the third wicket. Kambli and Bedade had ample time in which to complete the victory in fading light.

Arjuna Ranatunga was named Man of the Series while the batting prize went to Tendulkar, the only centurion, and the bowling prize to Steve Waugh.

PAKISTAN

Australia tour
Triangular one-day international series
Patron's Trophy
Quaid-e-Azam Trophy
Pentagular Trophy
First-class averages

Salim Malik in action against Australia. He enjoyed a magnificent series, led his side to victory and was a national hero, but his season ended amid allegations of bribery, and he was suspended while the matter was investigated. Phil Emery, making his Test debut, is the wicket-keeper pictured. (David Munden/Sportsline)

AUSTRALIA TOUR

The Pakistan national side returned from their tour of Sri Lanka as the Australians arrived for a three-match Test series and participation in the triangular one-day tournament. At the end of the series against Australia, the Pakistan side would again set out on their travels, competing in the Mandela Trophy limited-over tournament in South Africa.

23, 24 and 25 September 1994 *at Pindi Cricket Stadium, Rawalpindi*

Australians 338 (D.C. Boon 101, M.E. Waugh 57, S.R. Waugh 53 not out, Mohsin Kamal 4 for 74) and 134 for 2 dec. (M.G. Bevan 62 not out)

BCCP President's XI 145 (G.D. McGrath 4 for 32) and 270 for 9 (Zahid Fazal 91, Shoaib Mohammad 55, G.D. McGrath 6 for 49)

Match drawn

The Australians' warm-up match before the international series was against a strong President's XI led by Rameez Raja. David Boon hit 18 fours in a century which came off 122 balls and shared a run-a-minute stand of 104 for the third wicket with Mark Waugh. The President's XI were bowled out in two sessions by McDermott, McGrath and Warne, but Taylor did not enforce the follow-on. Bevan batted excitingly, and the home side were left the last day in which to score 328 to win. McGrath claimed 10 wickets in a match for the first time, but Zahid's aggression led a recovery. He hit May, Warne and Bevan for sixes, and then hit McGrath for six only to be yorked next ball. Moin Khan and Ashfaq Ahmed held out to save the home side from defeat.

TEST SERIES
PAKISTAN v. AUSTRALIA

At Karachi, Australia introduced Michael Bevan to Test cricket and took the field without Allan Border for the first time after 153 successive Test matches. His successor as captain, Mark Taylor, won the toss, and Australia batted. Taylor did not have the services of Craig McDermott who withdrew from the side with an infected toenail and was replaced by Joe Angel.

Taylor himself suffered the worst of indignities in his first Test as Australia's captain. He played too early at the fourth ball he received and gave Wasim Akram a simple return catch. Boon soon followed, chopping the ball into his own stumps, and Slater and Mark Waugh were also out before lunch.

FIRST TEST MATCH – PAKISTAN v. AUSTRALIA
28, 29, 30 September, 1 and 2 October 1994 at National Stadium, Karachi

AUSTRALIA

	FIRST INNINGS		SECOND INNINGS	
M.J. Slater	lbw, b Wasim	36	(2) lbw, b Mushtaq	23
M.A. Taylor (capt)	c and b Wasim	0	(1) c Rashid, b Waqar	0
D.C. Boon	b Mushtaq	19	not out	114
M.E. Waugh	c Zahid, b Mushtaq	20	b Waqar	61
M.G. Bevan	c Aamir, b Mushtaq	82	b Wasim	0
S.R. Waugh	b Waqar	73	lbw, b Wasim	0
*I.A. Healy	c Rashid, b Waqar	57	c Rashid, b Wasim	8
S.K. Warne	c Rashid, b Aamir	22	lbw, b Wasim	0
J. Angel	b Wasim	5	c Rashid, b Wasim	8
T.B.A. May	not out	1	b Wasim	1
G.D. McGrath	b Waqar	0	b Waqar	1
Extras	b 2, lb 12, nb 8	22	b 7, lb 4, nb 5	16
		—		—
		337		232

PAKISTAN

	FIRST INNINGS		SECOND INNINGS	
Saeed Anwar	c M.E. Waugh, b May	85	c and b Angel	77
Aamir Sohail	c Bevan, b Warne	36	run out	34
Zahid Fazal	c Boon, b May	27	c Boon, b Warne	3
Salim Malik (capt)	lbw, b Angel	26	c Taylor, b Angel	43
Basit Ali	c Bevan, b McGrath	0	(6) lbw, b Warne	12
Inzamam-ul-Haq	c Taylor, b Warne	9	(8) not out	58
*Rashid Latif	c Taylor, b Warne	2	(9) lbw, b S.R. Waugh	35
Wasim Akram	c Healy, b Angel	39	c and b Warne	4
Akram Raza	b McGrath	13	(5) lbw, b Warne	2
Waqar Younis	c Healy, b Angel	6	c Healy, b Warne	7
Mushtaq Ahmed	not out	2	not out	20
Extras	lb 7, nb 4	11	b 4, lb 13, nb 3	20
		—		—
		256	(for 9 wickets)	315

	O	M	R	W	O	M	R	W
Wasim Akram	25	4	75	3	22	3	63	5
Waqar Younis	19.2	2	75	3	18	2	69	4
Mushtaq Ahmed	24	2	97	3	21	3	51	1
Akram Raza	14	1	50	–	10	1	19	–
Aamir Sohail	5	–	19	1	7	–	19	–
Salim Malik	1	–	7	–				

	O	M	R	W	O	M	R	W
McGrath	25	6	70	2	6	2	18	–
Angel	13.1	–	54	3	28	9	92	2
May	20	5	55	2	18	4	67	–
Warne	27	10	61	3	36.1	12	89	5
S.R. Waugh	2	–	9	–	15	3	28	1
M.E. Waugh					3	1	4	–

FALL OF WICKETS
1–12, 2–41, 3–75, 4–95, 5–216, 6–281, 7–325, 8–335, 9–335
1–1, 2–49, 3–171, 4–174, 5–174, 6–213, 7–218, 8–227, 9–229

FALL OF WICKETS
1–90, 2–153, 3–154, 4–157, 5–175, 6–181, 7–200, 8–234, 9–253
1–45, 2–64, 3–148, 4–157, 5–174, 6–179, 7–184, 8–236, 9–258

Umpires: H.D. Bird & Khizar Hayat

Pakistan won by 1 wicket

Recovery came in the form of debutant Bevan and Steve Waugh. As the fast bowlers tired, these two seized the initiative and added 121 in two hours before Waugh was deceived by Waqar's swinging yorker. Healy continued the assault with Bevan, who looked sure to reach a century so impressive and powerful was his leg-side play in particular. The pair added 65 and were in total control when Aamir Sohail plucked Bevan's fierce drive out of the air. Warne fell in the last over of the day, and Australia closed on a respectable 325 for 7.

Waqar and Wasim quickly ended the innings the next morning, and Pakistan seemingly took a grip on the game when, having lost Aamir Sohail at 90, they viewed tea just one over away with 153 on the board. At that point, three wickets fell in 25 deliveries for four runs. Saeed Anwar, having batted with zest and confidence, slashed May to short extra-cover, Zahid Fazal was taken acrobatically at short-leg to give May a second wicket, and Basit Ali drove loosely to point.

McGrath was replaced by Warne who had Inzamam and Rashid both taken at slip in an eight-over spell which cost only five runs. Salim was leg before to Angel, and Pakistan ended the day on a precarious 209 for 7. Six wickets had fallen in 90 minutes for the addition of 47 runs.

Wasim played some lusty blows before the Pakistan innings ended, and, in the second over of Australia's second innings, Taylor was caught behind to become the first man to collect a 'pair' in his first Test as captain. Slater left at 49, but Boon and Mark Waugh batted with admirable restraint and intelligence to add 122. Mark Waugh curbed his natural aggression, swatting just one six over midwicket off Mushtaq and restricting himself to 3 fours, before, on 61, leaving a gap between bat and pad which Waqar Younis pierced. In the next over, Wasim bowled Bevan first ball with a yorker and had Steve Waugh leg before with his next delivery. Australia ended on 181 for 5, Boon unbeaten on 85.

Wasim and Waqar brought the innings to a close half an hour before lunch on the fourth day. David boon was left undefeated for 114 which occupied just over five hours. It was his first century against Pakistan and a mighty effort.

Pakistan have never lost a Test in Karachi, but now they faced an immense task, a target of 314 which they had never before achieved in a fourth innings. Aamir was needlessly run out, and Shane Warne showed that he would be the Australians' main weapon when he totally deceived Zahid and had him caught at short-leg. Shortly before the close, Salim steered an Angel bouncer to slip, and Pakistan ended the day on 155 for 3, the game tantalisingly poised.

Australia were handicapped on the final day. McGrath was out of the attack with a pulled hamstring, and May had a neck injury which lessened his effectiveness. Nevertheless, the visitors soon took control. Warne immediately accounted for night-watchman Akram Raza, Saeed added 10 to his overnight score before giving Angel a return catch, and Wasim charged wildly at Warne and was also caught and bowled. When Basit Ali was leg before to a straight ball Pakistan were 184 for 7, and Australia were in sight of victory.

Shane Warne traps Akram Raza leg before for 2, and Australia seem certain of victory in the first Test, but they were to be thwarted by Inzamam-ul-Haq and Mushtaq Ahmed. (Shaun Botterill/Allsport)

Taylor decided to take the new ball and to rest Warne, and although Steve Waugh vindicated his captain by dismissing Rashid, it was not before the wicket-keeper had hit Angel for four boundaries and helped Inzamam to add 52. Angel was driven to despair when appeals for leg before and caught behind against Inzamam were rejected, but the return of Warne saw Waqar heave and sky the ball. When Mushtaq joined Inzamam Pakistan needed 56 to win. Surprisingly, Man-of-the-Match Warne now seemed less potent, and the Pakistan batting was remarkably assured. In 49 balls, the last pair won the match. Devastatingly for Australia, the end came when Warne turned a ball sharply from outside leg stump, and it evaded Healy to scuttle to the boundary with Inzamam out of his ground. So, one of the great matches in Test history was concluded. It was the seventh occasion on which a Test has been decided by one wicket, but never before had the last pair had to score more than 50 to accomplish the task.

McGrath was unfit for the second Test and was replaced by Damien Fleming, making his Test debut, while McDermott returned in place of May. In the Pakistan side, Aamir Malik reappeared after a four-year absence and took the place of Basit Ali, and pace bowler Mohsin Kamal was preferred to spinner Akram Raza. Salim Malik won the toss and asked Australia to bat first.

Salim had been deceived by the wicket, for it was fast and true, and Australia reached 305 for 3 on the opening day. Slater survived a chance to Mohsin at point off Waqar, but thereafter the opening partnership prospered. Slater reached a serene hundred off 132 balls, and his footwork was exemplary. Taylor was adjudged leg before at 176, and Boon was out second ball. Slater's innings of charm ended when he steered Mohsin to slip, but Mark Waugh and Bevan eclipsed any thought of collapse and batted soundly against some shoddy fielding and lack-lustre bowling.

Mark Waugh added nine and Michael Bevan 18 to their overnight scores, and their departures allowed Pakistan to scramble back into the game. Their tedious over rate on the first day did not merit such a reprieve, but it turned out to be short-lived. The Pakistan attack was handicapped by the absence for some time of both Wasim

Akram and Waqar Younis, but this should not detract from the achievements of Steve Waugh and Ian Healy who added 109 splendid runs.

Waugh withstood a barrage of short-pitched deliveries which went unpunished by umpire Liebenberg, and he was also the recipient of some verbal abuse. He deserved a century after his four hours at the crease but, on 98, he was turned square by a fearsome delivery from Waqar, and the ball rolled down his back, hit his heel and dislodged a bail. Taylor was able to declare on 521 for 9, and McDermott had Saeed Anwar caught in the gully before the close, which came with Pakistan 48 for 1.

By the end of the third day, Pakistan were 28 for 0 in their second innings, having been asked to follow on 261 runs in arrears. There was no indication of such a disaster early in the day when, with Aamir Sohail piercing the close field with regular fluency, Pakistan reached 119 for 2. Aamir had hit 13 fours and a six before he was bowled by a very fine delivery from Fleming, and this heralded a decline. Salim edged McDermott on to his leg stump, Inzamam swung wildly, Aamir Malik was adjudged leg before, Rashid was taken at cover, and Mushtaq limply held out his bat. Five wickets had gone down for 37 runs,

and although Wasim Akram attempted to rally the tail, McDermott and Fleming, both of whom had performed heroically, were not to be denied.

Aamir Sohail was forced to retire hurt on the fourth morning when he was hit in the face by a ball from Mark Waugh and received a cut which needed four stitches. Zahid Fazal was caught behind almost immediately, but Salim Malik then joined Saeed Anwar in a stand which realised 148 in 2¾ hours. Saeed was out when he chased a wide-ish out-swinger from Mark Waugh, but the crucial delivery of the day had come from Joe Angel who drew Salim into the drive and found the edge of the bat. The ball flew to Taylor at slip who got both hands to the ball but dropped the catch. Salim was on 20 at the time. By the end of the day, he had scored 155, Aamir Sohail was on 72, and Pakistan was 324 for 2.

The early dismissal of Aamir Sohail on the last morning briefly raised Australian hopes, but Salim and Aamir Malik added 133, and by early afternoon Pakistan were 469 for 3 and the match was meandering to a draw. Fleming had begun his fourth spell and, on the fifth ball of the over, Aamir Malik clipped the ball lazily into the hands of mid-wicket. Inzamam was palpably lbw next ball, and

SECOND TEST MATCH – PAKISTAN v. AUSTRALIA
5, 6, 7, 8 and 9 October 1994 at Pindi Cricket Stadium, Rawalpindi

AUSTRALIA

	FIRST INNINGS		SECOND INNINGS	
M.A. Taylor (capt)	lbw, b Mohsin	69	(2) not out	5
M.J. Slater	c Inzamam, b Mohsin	110	(1) b Waqar	1
D.C. Boon	b Mushtaq	4	not out	7
M.E. Waugh	c Aamir, b Mohsin	68		
M.G. Bevan	lbw, b Waqar	70		
S.R. Waugh	b Waqar	98		
*I.A. Healy	c Mohsin, b Aamir	58		
S.K. Warne	c and b Aamir	14		
J. Angel	b Wasim	7		
C.J. McDermott	not out	9		
D.W. Fleming				
Extras	b 3, lb 3, w 3, nb 5	14		1
	(for 9 wickets, dec.)	521	(for 1 wicket)	14

PAKISTAN

	FIRST INNINGS		SECOND INNINGS	
Saeed Anwar	c S.R. Waugh, b McDermott	15	c Healy, b M.E. Waugh	75
Aamir Sohail	b Fleming	80	c Healy, b McDermott	72
Zahid Fazal	b Fleming	10	c Healy, b M.E. Waugh	1
Salim Malik (capt)	b McDermott	33	c Healy, b Fleming	237
Aamir Malik	lbw, b McDermott	11	c Bevan, b Fleming	65
Inzamam-ul-Haq	lbw, b Warne	14	lbw, b Fleming	0
*Rashid Latif	c Slater, b Fleming	18	c Bevan, b Taylor	38
Wasim Akram	not out	45	c Healy, b Angel	5
Mushtaq Ahmed	c Warne, b McDermott	0	c S.R. Waugh, b McDermott	0
Waqar Younis	lbw, b Fleming	13	lbw, b Slater	10
Mohsin Kamal	run out	2	not out	0
Extras	b 10, lb 7, nb 2	19	b 17, lb 13, w 1, nb 3	34
		260		537

	O	M	R	W	O	M	R	W
Wasim Akram	23.5	2	62	1				
Waqar Younis	32	5	112	2	5	3	2	1
Mohsin Kamal	26	3	109	3				
Mushtaq Ahmed	36	2	145	1	1	–	1	–
Aamir Sohail	21	3	67	2				
Aamir Malik	5	2	16	–				
Salim Malik	1	–	4	–				
Rashid Latif					2	–	10	–
Saeed Anwar					2	2	0	–

	O	M	R	W	O	M	R	W
McDermott	22	8	74	4	33	3	86	2
Fleming	22	3	75	4	26	2	86	3
Warne	21.4	8	58	1	25	6	56	–
Angel	11	2	36	–	28	1	124	1
M.E. Waugh					16	1	63	2
Bevan					4	–	27	–
S.R. Waugh					13	2	41	–
Slater					1.1	–	4	1
Boon					3	1	9	–
Taylor					3	1	11	1

FALL OF WICKETS
1–176, 2–181, 3–198, 4–323, 5–347, 6–456, 7–501, 8–511, 9–521
1–2

FALL OF WICKETS
1–28, 2–90, 3–119, 4–152, 5–155, 6–189, 7–189, 8–189, 9–253
1–79, 2–227, 3–336, 4–469, 5–469, 6–478, 7–495, 8–496, 9–537

Umpires: K.E. Liebenberg & Mahboob Shah

Match drawn

a drinks interval followed. With the first ball of his next over, Fleming had Salim Malik caught behind to complete a hat-trick on the occasion of his Test debut. He finished the match with seven wickets, an astounding achievement on a benign pitch.

As the game died, Slater and Taylor took their first wickets in Test cricket, and all save Healy bowled. Healy had to be content with his five catches.

Salim Malik had saved his side with his remarkable 237 in seven hours 40 minutes. He hit 37 fours and was celebrated as a hero. He deserved the accolade, but his innings only served to emphasise how dreadfully his side had batted in their first innings on a pitch which held no demons whatsoever.

The third Test was separated from the second by the best part of a month during which the triangular one-day tournament was played. Victory in the competition cost Australia dear, for they lost Healy with a broken thumb and Steve Waugh with an injured shoulder. Both returned to Australia. New South Wales' captain Phil Emery won his first Test cap as replacement for Healy, while Langer took over from Steve Waugh. May and McGrath replaced Fleming and Angel in attack.

Pakistan also had acute problems. Basit Ali came back in place of Aamir Malik, and, following his success in the triangular tournament, Ijaz Ahmed was recalled in place of Zahid Fazal. An injury to Rashid Latif meant that Moin Khan returned to the side after an absence of two years. To

A hat trick on the occasion of his Test debut for Damien Fleming. (David Munden/Sportsline)

THIRD TEST MATCH – PAKISTAN v. AUSTRALIA
1, 2, 3, 4 and 5 November 1994 at Qaddafi Stadium, Lahore

PAKISTAN

	FIRST INNINGS			SECOND INNINGS	
Saeed Anwar	b Warne	30	(2) c Emery, b McGrath	32
Aamir Sohail	c Emery, b McGrath	1	(7) st Emery, b Warne	105
Inzamam-ul-Haq	lbw, b May	66	c Emery, b McDermott	3
Salim Malik (capt)	c Bevan, b May	75	b Bevan	143
Ijaz Ahmed	c Boon, b Warne	48	lbw, b McGrath	6
Basit Ali	c Waugh, b Warne	0	(1) c Emery, b McGrath	2
*Moin Khan	not out	115	(6) c McDermott, b May	16
Akram Raza	b Warne	0	lbw, b Warne	32
Mushtaq Ahmed	b May	14	c Emery, b McGrath	27
Aqib Javed	c Waugh, b Warne	2	lbw, b Warne	2
Mohsin Kamal	lbw, b Warne	4	not out	0
Extras	b 5, lb 7, nb 6	18	b 8, lb 16, w 4, nb 8	36
		373		404

AUSTRALIA

	FIRST INNINGS	
M.J. Slater	c Moin Khan, b Mohsin Kamal	74
M.A. Taylor (capt)	c Saeed Anwar, b Mushtaq Ahmed	32
D.C. Boon	c Moin Khan, b Akram Raza	5
*P.A. Emery	not out	8
M.E. Waugh	c Moin Khan, b Mohsin Kamal	71
M.G. Bevan	c sub (Nadeem Khan), b Mushtaq Ahmed	91
J.L. Langer	c Ijaz Ahmed, b Mohsin Kamal	69
S.K. Warne	c and b Mohsin Kamal	33
C.J. McDermott	c and b Mushtaq Ahmed	29
T.B.A. May	c Moin Khan, b Akram Raza	10
G.D. McGrath	b Mushtaq Ahmed	3
Extras	b 3, lb 17, w 2, nb 8	30
		455

	O	M	R	W	O	M	R	W
McDermott	24	4	87	–	19	2	81	1
McGrath	24	6	65	1	25.1	1	92	4
Warne	41.5	12	136	6	30	2	104	3
May	29	7	69	3	25	4	60	1
Waugh	2	–	4	–	6	–	22	–
Bevan					4	–	21	1

	O	M	R	W
Aqib Javed	31	9	75	–
Mohsin Kamal	28	2	116	4
Mushtaq Ahmed	45.1	6	121	4
Akram Raza	45	9	123	2

FALL OF WICKETS
1–8, 2–34, 3–157, 4–204, 5–209, 6–294, 7–294, 8–346, 9–355
1–20, 2–28, 3–60, 4–74, 5–107, 6–303, 7–363, 8–384, 9–394

FALL OF WICKETS
1–97, 2–106, 3–126, 4–248, 5–318, 6–402, 7–406, 8–443, 9–450

Umpires: C.J. Mitchley & Riaz-ud-Din

Match drawn

Saeed Anwar is bowled round his legs by Shane Warne in the third Test. Debutant Phil Emery is the wicket-keeper. (David Munden/Sportsline)

bowled with commendable persistence and accuracy, accounted for Saeed Anwar at 34. Once more Salim Malik was called upon to repair the innings, and he found a useful partner in Inzamam who was dropped at slip by Slater when he had only a single to his credit. Ijaz Ahmed was also reprieved by May at long-leg before he scored, and it was missed catches that told against Australia throughout the series.

May dismissed both Salim Malik and Inzamam, and with Basit Ali again failing, Pakistan closed on an uneasy 255 for 5.

The plague of missed chances continued on the second day. Moin was dropped by Emery off McDermott when 51, and by Bevan at deep point on 70. The Pakistan wicket-keeper went on to make 115 not out. He reached his century in 210 minutes and hit 3 sixes (all off Warne) and 13 fours. Moin's previous Test highest score was 32.

Taylor and Slater gave Australia a good start, but Boon fell just before the close, and the visitors ended the day on 107 for 2.

Struck on the thumb, Emery was forced to retire hurt, and Slater added only 14 to his overnight score. Mark Waugh and Michael Bevan, who enjoyed a most impressive first series, were in excellent form, but no batsman played the innings of real substance which could have taken Australia to a commanding lead. At 344 for 5 at the

the astonishment and chagrin of Pakistan supporters, both Wasim Akram and Waqar Younis declared themselves unfit to play shortly before the start of the match. Salim Malik won the toss, and Pakistan batted.

Emery soon claimed his first Test victim when he caught Aamir Sohail off McGrath, and Warne, who

TEST MATCH AVERAGES – PAKISTAN v. AUSTRALIA

PAKISTAN BATTING

	M	Inns	NO	Runs	HS	Av	100s	50s
Salim Malik	3	6	–	557	237	92.83	2	1
Aamir Sohail	3	6	–	328	105	54.66	1	2
Saeed Anwar	3	6	–	314	85	52.33	–	3
Wasim Akram	2	4	1	93	45*	31.00	–	–
Inzamam-ul-Haq	3	6	1	150	66	30.00	–	2
Rashid Latif	2	4	–	93	38	23.25	–	–
Mushtaq Ahmed	3	6	2	63	27	15.75	–	–
Akram Raza	2	4	–	47	32	11.75	–	–
Zahid Fazal	2	4	–	41	27	10.25	–	–
Waqar Younis	2	4	–	36	13	9.00	–	–
Basit Ali	2	4	–	14	12	3.50	–	–
Mohsin Kamal	2	4	2	6	4	3.00	–	–

Played in one Test: Aamir Malik 11 & 65; Ijaz Ahmed 48 & 6; Moin Khan 115* & 16; Aqib Javed 2 & 2

PAKISTAN BOWLING

	Overs	Mds	Runs	Wkts	Av	Best	10/m	5/inn
Wasim Akram	70.5	9	200	9	22.22	5-63	–	1
Waqar Younis	74.2	12	258	10	25.80	4-69	–	–
Mohsin Kamal	54	5	225	7	32.14	4-116	–	–
Aamir Sohail	33	3	105	3	35.00	2-67	–	–
Mushtaq Ahmed	127.1	13	415	9	46.11	4-121	–	–
Akram Raza	69	11	192	2	96.00	2-123	–	–
Salim Malik	2	–	11					

Bowled in one innings: Rashid Latif 2–0–10–0; Aamir Malik 5–2–16–0; Saeed Anwar 2–2–0–0; Aqib Javed 31–9–75–0

PAKISTAN FIELDING FIGURES

5 – Rashid Latif; 4 – Moin Khan; 3 – Aamir Sohail; 2 – Mohsin Kamal; 1 – Saeed Anwar, Inzamam-ul-Haq, Zahid Fazal, Wasim Akram, Mushtaq Ahmed, Ijaz Ahmed and sub (Nadeem Khan)

AUSTRALIA BATTING

	M	Inns	NO	Runs	HS	Av	100s	50s
M.G. Bevan	3	4	–	243	91	60.75	–	3
S.R. Waugh	2	3	–	171	98	57.00	–	2
M.E. Waugh	3	4	–	220	71	55.00	–	3
D.C. Boon	3	5	2	149	114*	49.66	1	–
M.J. Slater	3	5	–	244	110	48.80	1	1
I.A. Healy	2	3	–	123	58	41.00	–	2
C.J. McDermott	2	2	1	38	29	38.00	–	–
M.A. Taylor	3	5	1	106	69	26.50	–	1
S.K. Warne	3	4	–	69	33	17.25	–	–
J. Angel	2	3	–	20	8	6.66	–	–
T.B.A. May	2	3	1	12	10	6.00	–	–
G.D. McGrath	2	3	–	4	3	1.33	–	–

Played in one Test: J.L. Langer 69; P.A. Emery 8*; D.W. Fleming did not bat

AUSTRALIA BOWLING

	Overs	Mds	Runs	Wkts	Av	Best	10/m	5/inn
D.W. Fleming	48	5	161	7	23.00	4-75	–	–
S.K. Warne	181.4	50	504	18	28.00	6-136	–	2
G.D. McGrath	80.1	15	245	7	35.00	4-92	–	–
T.B.A. May	92	20	251	6	41.83	3-69	–	–
M.E. Waugh	27	2	93	2	46.50	2-63	–	–
C.J. McDermott	98	17	328	7	46.85	4-74	–	–
M.G. Bevan	8	–	48	1	48.00	1-21	–	–
J. Angel	80.1	12	306	6	51.00	3-54	–	–
S.R. Waugh	30	5	78	1	78.00	1-28	–	–

Bowled in one innings: M.J. Slater 1.1–0–4–1; D.C. Boon 3–1–9–0; M.A. Taylor 3–1–11–1

AUSTRALIA FIELDING FIGURES

8 – I.A. Healy; 6 – P.A. Emery (ct 5/st 1); 5 – M.G. Bevan; 3 – M.A. Taylor, M.E. Waugh and D.C. Boon; 2 – S.R. Waugh and S.K. Warne; 1 – M.J. Slater, J. Angel and C.J. McDermott

ABOVE: *Winning a place in the Australian side for the final Test, Justin Langer made an accomplished 69. (David Munden/Sportsline)*

LEFT: *The outstanding Australian batsman of the tour – Michael Bevan. (Shaun Botterill/Allsport)*

TRIANGULAR TOURNAMENT

As has now become fashionable, Pakistan chose to stage a triangular competition of limited-over cricket rather than play a straightforward series against the touring Australians, and South Africa were invited as the third nation.

It was South Africa who took on Australia in the opening match, and the Australians were given a sound start by Taylor and Slater, both of whom fell to the left-arm spin of Shaw. Boon and Mark Waugh went cheaply, but Steve Waugh revived his side with 5 fours in his 83-minute innings.

end of the third day, Australia seemed certain to be heading for a draw and defeat in the rubber.

The Australian lead was restricted to 82, and Pakistan again violated the ethic of the game with an unforgivably slow over rate. Basit Ali, who had been absent for two days with a stomach ailment, was allowed to open by referee Reid, but his miserable series was soon at an end when he was caught behind off McGrath, who took three wickets in eight overs to destroy the top order. McDermott accounted for Inzamam, and Pakistan lost four leading batsmen before clearing the first-innings arrears. Australia again had a scent of victory, and again it was Salim Malik who thwarted them. By the end of the fourth day, he had batted $2\frac{1}{2}$ hours for 59, and Pakistan were 137 for 5. Sadly, the proceedings were sullied by sledging and animosity which the umpires, who never seemed to be in agreement with each other, seemed unable or unwilling to control.

Australia were denied on the last day when Salim Malik produced his second outstanding innings of the series, batting $6\frac{1}{4}$ hours and saving his side. In spite of a stiff neck which had forced him to drop down the order, Aamir Sohail joined his captain in a record sixth-wicket stand of 196 in $3\frac{1}{2}$ hours.

So, for the third time in as many years, Australia failed to win a series which they had dominated for most of the time.

A bright moment in a bleak tournament for South Africa. Jonty Rhodes hits a boundary in his innings of 42 against Australia at Lahore, but South Africa lost by six runs. (Shaun Botterill/Allsport)

TRIANGULAR TOURNAMENT – MATCH ONE – AUSTRALIA v. SOUTH AFRICA
12 October 1994 at Qaddafi Stadium, Lahore

AUSTRALIA

M.A. Taylor (capt)	st Richardson, b Shaw	56
M.J. Slater	st Richardson, b Shaw	44
M.E. Waugh	c and b Cronje	3
D.C. Boon	run out	8
S.R. Waugh	c Kirsten, b Matthews	56
M.G. Bevan	run out	15
*I.A. Healy	not out	18
G.R. Robertson	not out	1
S.K. Warne		
D.W. Fleming		
C.J. McDermott		
Extras	b 1, nb 5	6
(50 overs)	(for 6 wickets)	207

SOUTH AFRICA

K.C. Wessels (capt)	c Healy, b Fleming	6
G. Kirsten	c Healy, b Fleming	4
W.J. Cronje	not out	98
D.J. Cullinan	c Slater, b S.R. Waugh	12
J.N. Rhodes	lbw, b S.R. Waugh	42
B.M. McMillan	b M.E. Waugh	3
E.O. Simons	b McDermott	19
*D.J. Richardson	b McDermott	4
C.R. Matthews	b McDermott	1
T.G. Shaw	not out	1
P.S. de Villiers		
Extras	b 4, lb 7	11
(50 overs)	(for 8 wickets)	201

	O	M	R	W
de Villiers	9	1	38	–
Matthews	10	1	41	1
McMillan	3	–	24	–
Simons	8	–	37	–
Shaw	10	–	34	2
Cronje	10	1	32	1

	O	M	R	W
McDermott	10	2	32	3
Fleming	10	3	29	2
S.R. Waugh	10	–	35	2
Warne	10	–	39	–
Robertson	7	–	41	–
M.E. Waugh	3	–	14	1

FALL OF WICKETS
1–98, 2–107, 3–107, 4–128, 5–160, 6–202

FALL OF WICKETS
1–8, 2–15, 3–50, 4–126, 5–143, 6–182, 7–194, 8–200

Umpires: Mian Mohammad Aslam & Athar Zaidi   *Man of the Match:* S.R. Waugh   *Australia won by 6 runs*

TRIANGULAR TOURNAMENT – MATCH TWO – PAKISTAN v. AUSTRALIA
14 October 1994 at Multan CC Stadium, Multan

PAKISTAN

Saeed Anwar	b Fleming	22
Aamir Sohail	b Fleming	5
Inzamam-ul-Haq	run out	59
Salim Malik (capt)	c Healy, b Warne	32
Ijaz Ahmed	c Healy, b McDermott	21
Aamir Malik	c Healy, b McDermott	20
Wasim Akram	b Fleming	9
*Rashid Latif	b Fleming	16
Akram Raza	not out	5
Waqar Younis	not out	0
Mushtaq Ahmed		
Extras	b 6, lb 1, w 3, nb 1	11
(50 overs)	(for 8 wickets)	200

AUSTRALIA

M.J. Slater	lbw, b Wasim Akram	0
M.A. Taylor (capt)	b Akram Raza	46
M.E. Waugh	c Rashid Latif, b Waqar Younis	0
D.C. Boon	not out	84
S.R. Waugh	not out	59
M.G. Bevan		
*I.A. Healy		
G.R. Robertson		
S.K. Warne		
C.J. McDermott		
D.W. Fleming		
Extras	b 1, lb 6, w 4, nb 1	12
(46 overs)	(for 3 wickets)	201

	O	M	R	W
McDermott	10	1	34	2
Fleming	10	–	49	4
S.R. Waugh	10	1	37	–
Warne	10	1	29	1
Robertson	5	–	24	–
M.E. Waugh	5	–	20	–

	O	M	R	W
Wasim Akram	8	3	26	1
Waqar Younis	9	–	39	1
Akram Raza	10	–	35	1
Mushtaq Ahmed	9	–	48	–
Aamir Sohail	6	–	26	–
Salim Malik	4	–	20	–

FALL OF WICKETS
1–9, 2–32, 3–113, 4–132, 5–164, 6–166, 7–184, 8–199

FALL OF WICKETS
1–10, 2–11, 3–81

Umpires: Saqib Qureshi & Riaz-ud-Din   *Man of the Match:* D.C. Boon   *Australia won by 7 wickets*

TRIANGULAR TOURNAMENT – MATCH THREE – PAKISTAN v. SOUTH AFRICA
16 October 1994 at National Stadium, Karachi

SOUTH AFRICA				PAKISTAN		
A.C. Hudson	lbw, b Akram Raza	23		Saeed Anwar	st Richardson, b Cronje	20
K.C. Wessels (capt)	c Salim Malik, b Akram Raza	33		Aamir Sohail	c and b Simons	22
W.J. Cronje	run out	21		Inzamam-ul-Haq	not out	51
D.J. Cullinan	c Ijaz Ahmed, b Aamir Sohail	10		Salim Malik (capt)	not out	62
J.N. Rhodes	c Salim Malik, b Aqib Javed	16		Asif Mujtaba		
E.O. Simons	c Salim Malik, b Wasim Akram	14		Ijaz Ahmed		
*D.J. Richardson	run out	7		*Rashid Latif		
D.N. Crookes	b Wasim Akram	10		Wasim Akram		
T.G. Shaw	run out	0		Akram Raza		
M.W. Pringle	not out	13		Waqar Younis		
P.S. de Villiers	not out	7		Aqib Javed		
Extras	lb 4, w 4, nb 1	9		Extras	lb 2, w 4, nb 5	11
(50 overs)	(for 9 wickets)	163		(44.4 overs)	(for 2 wickets)	166

	O	M	R	W			O	M	R	W
Wasim Akram	10	–	28	2		de Villiers	9.4	1	38	–
Aqib Javed	10	2	25	1		Pringle	8	–	35	–
Waqar Younis	10	2	40	–		Simons	10	2	39	1
Akram Raza	10	–	30	2		Cronje	6	1	12	1
Salim Malik	3	–	14	–		Shaw	7	1	23	–
Aamir Sohail	7	1	22	1		Crookes	4	–	17	–

FALL OF WICKETS
1–49, 2–70, 3–90, 4–90, 5–121, 6–131, 7–137, 8–137, 9–145

FALL OF WICKETS
1–41, 2–51

Umpires: Feroze Butt & Salim Badar *Man of the Match:* Salim Malik *Pakistan won by 8 wickets*

TRIANGULAR TOURNAMENT – MATCH FOUR – AUSTRALIA v. SOUTH AFRICA
18 October 1994 at Iqbal Stadium, Faisalabad

AUSTRALIA				SOUTH AFRICA		
M.A. Taylor (capt)	c Richardson, b de Villiers	4		K.C. Wessels (capt)	c Bevan, b May	30
M.J. Slater	b Eksteen	38		A.C. Hudson	run out	5
M.E. Waugh	c Richardson, b Cronje	38		W.J. Cronje	c S.R. Waugh, b McDermott	64
D.C. Boon	c Wessels, b Pringle	43		J.N. Rhodes	c Boon, b May	11
S.R. Waugh	b Simons	23		G. Kirsten	b McGrath	24
M.G. Bevan	not out	36		*D.J. Richardson	lbw, b McGrath	10
*I.A. Healy	c de Villiers, b Simons	4		E.O. Simons	st Healy, b Warne	11
S.K. Warne	not out	15		D.M. Crookes	st Healy, b Warne	20
C.J. McDermott				M.W. Pringle	lbw, b Warne	0
T.B.A. May				C.E. Eksteen	not out	0
G.D. McGrath				P.S. de Villiers	st Healy, b Warne	0
Extras	b 1, lb 2, w 3, nb 1	7		Extras	lb 7, w 3, nb 1	11
(50 overs)	(for 6 wickets)	208		(48.2 overs)		186

	O	M	R	W			O	M	R	W
de Villiers	9	2	41	1		McDermott	9	2	34	1
Pringle	9	1	49	1		McGrath	10	2	31	2
Simons	10	–	41	2		Warne	9.2	–	40	4
Cronje	10	1	31	1		May	10	–	34	2
Eksteen	8	–	26	1		S.R. Waugh	10	1	40	–
Crookes	4	–	17	–						

FALL OF WICKETS
1–6, 2–29, 3–95, 4–143, 5–160, 6–167

FALL OF WICKETS
1–7, 2–64, 3–86, 4–124, 5–138, 6–156, 7–176, 8–176, 9–185

Umpires: Khizar Hayat & Islam Khan *Man of the Match:* W.J. Cronje *Australia won by 22 runs*

TRIANGULAR TOURNAMENT – MATCH FIVE – PAKISTAN *v.* SOUTH AFRICA
20 October 1994 at Pindi Cricket Stadium, Rawalpindi

PAKISTAN

Saeed Anwar	c Cullinan, b Simons	42
Aamir Sohail	c Richardson, b Matthews	1
Inzamam-ul-Haq	run out	10
Salim Malik (capt)	c Wessels, b Eksteen	56
Ijaz Ahmed	b Matthews	110
Wasim Akram	b Matthews	12
*Rashid Latif	not out	3
Akram Raza	not out	4
Asif Mujtaba		
Waqar Younis		
Aqib Javed		
Extras	b 4, lb 4, w 1, nb 2	11
(50 overs)	(for 6 wickets)	249

SOUTH AFRICA

A.C. Hudson	c Rashid Latif, b Waqar Younis	20
K.C. Wessels (capt)	lbw, b Waqar Younis	19
W.J. Cronje	run out	53
D.J. Cullinan	run out	36
J.N. Rhodes	run out	33
G. Kirsten	not out	20
*D.J. Richardson	not out	10
E.O. Simons		
C.R. Matthews		
P.S. de Villiers		
C.E. Eksteen		
Extras	b 2, lb 12, w 3, nb 2	19
(50 overs)	(for 5 wickets)	210

	O	M	R	W
de Villiers	10	–	41	–
Matthews	10	2	50	3
Cronje	10	–	45	–
Simons	10	1	56	1
Eksteen	10	1	49	1

	O	M	R	W
Wasim Akram	10	1	40	–
Aqib Javed	10	–	36	–
Waqar Younis	10	–	35	2
Akram Raza	10	–	41	–
Salim Malik	5	–	24	–
Aamir Sohail	5	–	20	–

FALL OF WICKETS
1–2, **2**–39, **3**–61, **4**–186, **5**–232, **6**–245

FALL OF WICKETS
1–35, **2**–61, **3**–130, **4**–160, **5**–189

Umpires: Javed Akhtar & Said Ahmed Shah   *Man of the Match:* Ijaz Ahmed   *Pakistan won by 39 runs*

TRIANGULAR TOURNAMENT – MATCH SIX – PAKISTAN *v.* AUSTRALIA
22 October 1994 at Pindi Cricket Stadium, Rawalpindi

AUSTRALIA

M.J. Slater	b Aqib Javed	4
M.A. Taylor (capt)	c Akram Raza, b Aqib Javed	14
M.E. Waugh	not out	121
J.L. Langer	c Saeed Anwar, b Wasim Akram	27
S.R. Waugh	lbw, b Salim Malik	14
M.G. Bevan	b Waqar Younis	22
*I.A. Healy	run out	16
S.K. Warne	not out	11
T.B.A. May		
G.D. McGrath		
C.J. McDermott		
Extras	b 1, lb 13, w 5, nb 2	21
(50 overs)	(for 6 wickets)	250

PAKISTAN

Saeed Anwar	not out	104
Aamir Sohail	c Bevan, b May	45
Inzamam-ul-Haq	not out	91
Salim Malik (capt)		
Basit Ali		
Ijaz Ahmed		
*Rashid Latif		
Wasim Akram		
Akram Raza		
Waqar Younis		
Aqib Javed		
Extras	b 3, lb 4, w 2, nb 2	11
(39 overs)	(for 1 wicket)	251

	O	M	R	W
Wasim Akram	10	–	47	1
Aqib Javed	10	–	44	2
Waqar Younis	10	–	50	1
Aamir Sohail	5	–	25	–
Akram Raza	10	–	36	–
Salim Malik	5	–	34	1

	O	M	R	W
McDermott	8	1	54	–
McGrath	6	1	37	–
May	9	–	65	1
Warne	9	1	47	–
S.R. Waugh	5	–	26	–
M.E. Waugh	2	–	15	–

FALL OF WICKETS
1–14, **2**–50, **3**–114, **4**–140, **5**–206, **6**–234

FALL OF WICKET
1–91

Umpires: Mahboob Shah & Javed Akhtar   *Man of the Match:* Saeed Anwar   *Pakistan won by 9 wickets*

TRIANGULAR TOURNAMENT – MATCH SEVEN – AUSTRALIA v. SOUTH AFRICA
24 October 1994 at Arbab Niaz Stadium, Peshawar

SOUTH AFRICA			AUSTRALIA		
K.C. Wessels (capt)	c Bevan, b McDermott	4	M.A. Taylor (capt)	c Richardson, b de Villiers	17
G. Kirsten	b McGrath	45	M.J. Slater	run out	54
W.J. Cronje	not out	100	M.E. Waugh	c Rhodes, b Shaw	43
D.J. Cullinan	b Warne	36	D.C. Boon	run out	39
J.N. Rhodes	c Taylor, b Angel	3	M.G. Bevan	c Shaw, b de Villiers	45
*D.J. Richardson	c Slater, b Waugh	25	*J.L. Langer	not out	33
D.M. Crookes	lbw, b McGrath	0	S.K. Warne	run out	13
E.O. Simons	not out	10	J. Angel	b Matthews	0
C.R. Matthews			C.J. McDermott	not out	1
T.G. Shaw			T.B.A. May		
P.S. de Villiers			G.D. McGrath		
Extras	b 12, lb 9, w 3, nb 4	28	Extras	lb 5, w 2	7
(50 overs)	(for 6 wickets)	251	(49.4 overs)	(for 7 wickets)	252

	O	M	R	W		O	M	R	W
McDermott	9	–	48	1	de Villiers	10	2	49	2
Angel	10	1	37	1	Matthews	9.4	1	43	1
McGrath	10	2	22	2	Simons	8	–	46	–
Waugh	6	–	39	1	Cronje	10	–	46	–
May	5	–	33	–	Shaw	10	–	49	1
Warne	10	–	51	1	Crookes	2	–	14	–

FALL OF WICKETS
1–7, 2–92, 3–157, 4–167, 5–207, 6–207

FALL OF WICKETS
1–38, 2–105, 3–119, 4–186, 5–223, 6–239, 7–251

Umpires: Mohammad Nazir jr & Shakeel Khan   Man of the Match: W.J. Cronje   *Australia won by 3 wickets*

TRIANGULAR TOURNAMENT – MATCH NINE – PAKISTAN v. SOUTH AFRICA
28 October 1994 at Iqbal Stadium, Faisalabad

SOUTH AFRICA			PAKISTAN		
G. Kirsten	run out	69	Saeed Anwar	c Cullinan, b Matthews	14
K.C. Wessels (capt)	c and b Wasim Akram	51	Aamir Sohail	c Cullinan, b Simons	25
W.J. Cronje	b Salim Malik	18	Inzamam-ul-Haq	c Kirsten, b Simons	19
D.J. Cullinan	c Akram Raza, b Waqar Younis	4	Salim Malik (capt)	b Simons	7
J.N. Rhodes	not out	45	Ijaz Ahmed	not out	98
*D.J. Richardson	not out	27	Basit Ali	not out	52
C.R. Matthews			*Rashid Latif		
T.G. Shaw			Wasim Akram		
E.O. Simons			Akram Raza		
P.S. de Villiers			Waqar Younis		
C.E. Eksteen			Aqib Javed		
Extras	b 1, lb 2, w 2, nb 3	8	Extras	b 1, lb 4, w 1, nb 2	8
(50 overs)	(for 4 wickets)	222	(44.3 overs)	(for 4 wickets)	223

	O	M	R	W		O	M	R	W
Wasim Akram	10	–	36	1	de Villiers	8	–	46	–
Aqib Javed	10	–	35	–	Matthews	9	3	31	1
Waqar Younis	10	–	55	1	Cronje	2	1	10	–
Akram Raza	10	–	46	–	Simons	8.3	1	49	3
Salim Malik	8	–	37	1	Eksteen	10	1	52	–
Aamir Sohail	2	–	10	–	Shaw	7	–	30	–

FALL OF WICKETS
1–125, 2–130, 3–138, 4–166

FALL OF WICKETS
1–26, 2–47, 3–66, 4–76

Umpires: Afzaal Ahmed & Salim Badar   Man of the Match: Ijaz Ahmed   *Pakistan won by 6 wickets*

AUSTRALIA

M.A. Taylor (capt)	c and b Salim Malik	56
M.J. Slater	st Rashid Latif, b Salim Malik	66
M.E. Waugh	b Salim Malik	38
D.C. Boon	c Salim Malik, b Waqar Younis	21
S.R. Waugh	b Aamir Sohail	1
M.G. Bevan	not out	53
*P.A. Emery	not out	11
C.J. McDermott		
S.K. Warne		
D.W. Fleming		
G.D. McGrath		
Extras	b 1, lb 16, w 4, nb 2	23
(50 overs)	(for 5 wickets)	269

PAKISTAN

Saeed Anwar	c Taylor, b Fleming	0
Aamir Sohail	c S.R. Waugh, b Fleming	21
Inzamam-ul-Haq	c Emery, b McGrath	10
Salim Malik (capt)	b Fleming	35
Ijaz Ahmed	c Emery, b McGrath	4
Basit Ali	lbw, b McGrath	63
Wasim Akram	b McGrath	26
Akram Raza	c Emery, b M.E. Waugh	0
*Rashid Latif	not out	10
Waqar Younis	b McGrath	2
Aqib Javed	b M.E. Waugh	17
Extras	lb 8, w 7, nb 2	17
(46.4 overs)		205

	O	M	R	W
Wasim Akram	10	1	63	–
Aqib Javed	7	–	30	–
Waqar Younis	8	–	48	1
Akram Raza	10	–	45	–
Aamir Sohail	5	–	35	1
Salim Malik	10	–	31	3

	O	M	R	W
McDermott	9	–	32	–
Fleming	8	1	32	3
McGrath	10	–	52	5
Warne	10	2	32	–
S.R. Waugh	2	–	6	–
M.E. Waugh	7.4	–	43	2

FALL OF WICKETS
1–121, 2–146, 3–188, 4–191, 5–226

FALL OF WICKETS
1–17, 2–26, 3–43, 4–64, 5–112, 6–173, 7–174, 8–176, 9–178

Umpires: Khizar Hayat & Islam Khan *Man of the Match:* G.D. McGrath *Australia won by 64 runs*

When South Africa batted, Gary Kirsten was out in the fourth over, and Cronje batted magnificently as wickets fell regularly at the other end. Steve Waugh captured the important wicket of Cullinan, and then trapped Rhodes leg before after he and Cronje had added 76 off 94 balls. This sparked a collapse, and the last over arrived with South Africa needing 14 for victory. McDermott bowled Richardson with the first ball and Matthews with the fifth, and Australia won with more ease than a six-run margin suggests.

A keen Australian attack restricted Pakistan to 200 from 50 overs in the second match. Inzamam-ul-Haq and Salim Malik added 81 for the third wicket, but Inzamam was brilliantly run out by Mark Waugh, and Warne, far superior to Mushtaq Ahmed in the Tests and triangular series, choked the flow of runs.

Australia began badly, losing two wickets for 11 runs inside four overs, but Taylor and Boon then added 70. Boon, who faced 134 balls, and Steve Waugh took Australia to victory with an unbroken stand of 120 off 149 balls.

In the third match, South Africa gave an international debut to off-spinner Crookes, but he failed to strengthen an attack which looked very thin. South Africa's batting was equally weak and, with Salim Malik holding three fine catches close to the wicket, they were restricted to a meagre 163. Pakistan won with more than five overs to spare, Inzamam and Salim sharing an unbroken partnership of 115.

South Africa suffered their third defeat in a week when Australia trounced them in Faisalabad. The first 10 overs of the South African innings realised only 22 runs, and

Wessels' 30 occupied 70 deliveries. Cronje alone batted with purpose. Warne finished the match with four wickets in six balls, three of his victims stumped by Healy.

Recalled to the side after an absence of two years, Ijaz Ahmed hit a spectacular 110 off 111 balls with a six and 12 fours. With Salim Malik, he added 125 for the fourth wicket.

When South Africa batted, Wessels took 19 overs to realise his 19 runs, and it was left to Cronje to offer any hint of defiance. Jonty Rhodes was hurt when he ducked into a ball from Aqib Javed. It was the second time within six weeks that he had sustained injury while batting.

The sixth match was a nightmare for Australia. In spite of the fact that Mark Waugh played a glorious innings full of strokes rich in classical orthodoxy, they were beaten by nine wickets with 11 overs to spare. Waugh's 121 not out, the highest score in the tournament, came off 134 balls, but Saeed Anwar hit the first ball of the Pakistan innings for four, and the devastation continued unabated. His 104 not out came off 119 balls, while Inzamam-ul-Haq hit 3 sixes as his 91 came off just 80 deliveries. Warne was injured and, most seriously, Healy suffered a broken thumb which forced him to return to Australia.

Cronje played virtually a lone hand for South Africa throughout the series, and he was rewarded with a century in the seventh match. Wessels was out in the third over, and Cronje batted for the next 47 overs, facing 118 balls and reaching his century off the last ball of the innings. Australia batted in poor light, but they showed application and consistency. They needed 17 off two overs, but Langer took 3 fours in succession off de Villiers to relieve the pressure. One was needed from the last over, and Matthews bowled Angel with his third ball. McDermott pushed the winning single next ball.

In spite of Gary Kirsten and Kepler Wessels scoring 125 for the first wicket, South Africa plunged to their sixth defeat in as many matches. Facing a target of 223, Pakistan slumped to 76 for 4 before Ijaz Ahmed and Basit Ali put on 147 in 25 overs of spectacular batting.

This match had little meaning as Pakistan and Australia were already scheduled to meet in the final of the competition. An opening partnership of 121 in 22 overs between Taylor and Slater gave Australia the firmest of foundations, and only Steve Waugh, suffering from an injured arm, failed to prosper. Returning after injury, Fleming dismissed both Pakistan openers in his first three overs, and McGrath kept Australia in control with some hostile and accurate bowling. Basit Ali and Wasim Akram added 61 in 10 overs, but McGrath came back for his second spell and accounted for both in successive overs. When he bowled Waqar Younis, McGrath had taken three wickets in 10 balls.

The eighth match in the qualifying series was scheduled to be played between Pakistan and Australia at Gujranwala on 26 October but was abandoned without a ball being bowled.

PATRON'S TROPHY

28, 29, 30 September and 1 October 1994 *at Asghar Ali Shah Stadium, Karachi*

PNSC 190 (Zahid Ahmed 6 for 82) and 125 (Zahid Ahmed 4 for 43)
PIA 334 (Moin Khan 113, Zahid Ahmed 61, Aamir Malik 56)
PIA won by an innings and 19 runs
PIA 12 pts, PNSC 0 pts

at LCCA Ground, Lahore

Habib Bank 255 (Shahid Javed 71, Shakeel Ahmed 66, Imran Adil 5 for 72) and 307 for 7 dec. (Shahid Javed 75, Sohail Fazal 63 not out, Idrees Baig 60)
Railways 339 (Nadeem Younis 114, Majid Saeed 91, Maqsood Akbar 52, Abdul Qadir 7 for 67) and 85 for 5 (Abdul Qadir 4 for 23)
Match drawn
Railways 2 pts, Habib Bank 0 pts

at United Bank Sports Complex, Karachi

Allied Bank 143 and 264 (Rameez Raja 83, Mohammad Nawaz 68, Ijaz Ahmed jr 53, Shahid Hussain 4 for 48)
United Bank 296 (Javed Sami 102, Mansoor Akhtar 50, Aamer Nazir 6 for 58) and 112 for 4
United Bank won by 6 wickets
United Bank 12 pts, Allied Bank 0 pts

at Jinnah (Municipal) Stadium, Gujranwala

National Bank 312 (Aamer Gul 88, Saeed Azad 60, Manzoor Elahi 6 for 102) and 167 (Manzoor Elahi 4 for 52)
ADBP 283 (Atif Rauf 92, Sabih Azhar 66, Naeem Ashraf 6 for 96) and 91 (Maqsood Rana 6 for 26)
National Bank won by 105 runs
National Bank 12 pts, ADBP 0 pts

The Patron's Trophy was reduced to eight teams. HBFC, pointless in the previous season, and PACO dropped out of the competition, and Allied Bank returned. The number of points awarded for a win was increased from 10 to 12, and first-innings lead in a drawn match gained two rather than four points. The competition was again played without sides being able to call on their leading players for much of the time due to the Australian tour and the triangular one-day tournament.

The match between PNSC and PIA was played at a new first-class venue in Karachi, the Asghar Ali Shah Stadium. The match was dominated by PIA for whom slow left-arm bowler Zahid Ahmed had an outstanding game. Moin Khan, later to win a recall to the Test side, led the PIA XI and hit the third century of his career.

In Lahore, Abdul Qadir, the veteran leg-spinner, bowled magnificently, but the match between Habib Bank and Railways was drawn. United Bank revealed their strength in depth, for, having provided half the national side, they fielded a team capable of crushing Allied Bank. Javed Sami hit a maiden first-class century.

Mansoor Rana won the toss for ADBP in Gujranwala and asked National Bank to bat first. A third-wicket stand of 110 between Aamer Gul and Saeed Azad put National in a strong position. ADBP began well, but Naeem Ashraf destroyed the middle-order with his left-arm fast medium, and National took a first-innings lead. Batting last on a worn wicket, ADBP collapsed against the medium pace of Maqsood Rana and Athar Laeeq. Maqsood returned the best bowling figures of his career.

3, 4, 5 and 6 October 1994 *at United Bank Sports Complex, Karachi*

PNSC 181 (Shahid Hussain 4 for 74) and 286 (Azam Khan 121, Iqbal Imam 7 for 66)
United Bank 406 for 8 dec. (Ghulam Ali 128, Mansoor Akhtar 59, Mahmood Hamid 58) and 64 for 0
United Bank won by 10 wickets
United Bank 12 pts, PNSC 0 pts

at Jinnah Stadium, Sialkot

Railways 240 (Tariq Mahmood 64) and 157 (Raja Afaq 5 for 44)
ADBP 412 for 7 dec. (Atif Rauf 200, Mansoor Rana 57, Manzoor Elahi 57, Ghaffar Kazmi 52, Arshad Khan 5 for 138)
ADBP won by an innings and 15 runs
ADBP 12 pts, Railways 0 pts

at Jinnah (Municipal) Stadium, Gujranwala

Habib Bank 334 (Shaukat Mirza 124 not out, Asadullah Butt 51, Maqsood Rana 4 for 72) and 88 (Maqsood Rana 6 for 39, Athar Laeeq 4 for 46)

National Bank 223 (Naeem Ashraf 104, Saeed Azad 51, Asadullah Butt 4 for 62) and 201 for 6 (Saeed Azad 87, Tahir Shah 56)

National Bank won by 4 wickets

National Bank 12 pts, Habib Bank 0 pts

4, 5, 6 and 7 October 1994 *at Asghar Ali Shah Stadium, Karachi*

PIA 149 and 208 (Shoaib Mohammad 51)

Allied Bank 301 (Rameez Raja 81, Manzoor Akhtar 53, Zahid Ahmed 4 for 110) and 58 for 2

Allied Bank won by 8 wickets

Allied Bank 12 pts, PIA 0 pts

United Bank gained their second resounding win when they trounced PNSC. The ever-dependable Ghulam Ali hit the 18th century of his career and steered his side to a big first-innings lead. PNSC fought back well through Azam Khan, but the introduction of off-break bowler Iqbal Imam brought about a collapse. He returned the best figures of his career, and the last eight PNSC wickets went down for 68 runs.

Atif Rauf hit the first double century of his career as ADBP crushed Railways, and National Bank came from behind to overcome Habib Bank. Habib had recovered from 58 for 5 thanks to a magnificent 124 off 277 balls by Shaukat Mirza. National, too – 24 for 4 – had their saviour in Naeem Ashraf, but they still trailed by 111 runs on the first innings. Naeem's 104 came off only 119 balls. Batting again, Habib Bank were routed by Maqsood Rana and Athar Laeeq who bowled unchanged. Needing 200 to win, National were 42 for 4 before Saeed Azad and Tahir Shah added 137. The game was over on the third day, and National Bank had scored at four runs an over throughout the match.

In Karachi, PIA were put in to bat and succumbed to a varied attack. Allied Bank were well served by Rameez Raja and Manzoor Akhtar who added 119 for the second wicket, and they eventually won comfortably.

9, 10, 11 and 12 October 1994 *at Railway Stadium, Lahore*

National Bank 229 (Wasim Arif 65, Arshad Khan 6 for 88) and 286 for 9 dec. (Ameer Akbar 88, Wasim Arif 69 not out, Sajid Ali 51, Aamer Wasim 4 for 70)

Railways 192 (Majid Saeed 57, Nadeem Khan 5 for 65) and 128 (Hafeez-ur-Rehman 4 for 27)

National Bank won by 195 runs

National Bank 12 pts, Railways 0 pts

at United Bank Sports Complex, Karachi

United Bank 220 and 131

PIA 115 (Tauseef Ahmed 4 for 38) and 65 (Tauseef Ahmed 5 for 12, Shahid Hussain 4 for 35)

United Bank won by 171 runs

United Bank 12 pts, PIA 0 pts

at LCCA Ground, Lahore

PNSC 356 (Sohail Jaffar 96, Sajjad Akbar 81, Aamer Nazir 4 for 78) and 148 (Bilal Rana 4 for 31)

Allied Bank 280 (Ijaz Ahmed jr 130, Rafaqat Ali 55, Sajjad Ali 6 for 92) and 204 for 8 (Ijaz Ahmed jr 94 not out, Tahir Mahmood 4 for 53)

Match drawn

PNSC 2 pts, Allied Bank 0 pts

10, 11, 12 and 13 October 1994 *at Bagh-e-Jinnah Ground, Lahore*

ADBP 232 (Mansoor Rana 91, Asadullah Butt 4 for 48, Abdul Qadir 4 for 98) and 276 (Mansoor Rana 140 not out, Abdul Qadir 5 for 108)

Habib Bank 407 for 9 dec. (Tahir Rasheed 119, Idrees Baig 107, Shaukat Mirza 58, Mujahid Jamshed 53) and 102 for 1

Habib Bank won by 9 wickets

Habib Bank 12 pts, ADBP 0 pts

National Bank maintained their 100% record with an easy victory over Railways, and United Bank, too, had their third win in as many matches. Mohammad Ramzan's 38 in the second innings was the highest score of the match at the United Bank Sports Complex. Tauseef Ahmed was the Man of the Match. The veteran off-spinner took 5 for 12 in 15 overs in the second innings, and he had match figures of 9 for 50 in 48.2 overs. The match ended on the third day.

There were many more runs at the LCCA Ground where Allied Bank needed 225 in their second innings to beat PNSC. An outstanding innings of 94 off 100 balls by Ijaz Ahmed, who hit a century in the first innings, brought them close to their target, but 43 overs proved insufficient and both sides took credit from a fine match.

15, 16, 17 and 18 October 1994 *at Railway Stadium, Lahore*

PNSC 267 (Maqsood Rana 4 for 76) and 325 for 7 dec. (Sohail Jaffar 113, Azam Khan 95)

National Bank 399 (Mohammad Javed 106, Wasim Arif 90, Ameer Akbar 75, Naved Nazir 5 for 133)

Match drawn

National Bank 2 pts, PNSC 0 pts

at Multan CC Stadium, Multan

PIA 459 for 7 dec. (Rizwan-uz-Zaman 126, Shoaib Mohammad 88, Wasim Haider 70, Sagheer Abbas 68, Mohammad Asif 4 for 141) and 134 for 8 (Raja Afaq 7 for 55)

ADBP 357 (Mansoor Rana 175 not out, Manzoor Elahi 50, Zahid Ahmed 4 for 97)

Match drawn

PIA 2 pts, ADBP 0 pts

Railways 111 (Hasnain Kazim 5 for 29) and 193 (Tariq
   Mahmood 55, Hasnain Kazim 7 for 54)

United Bank 176 (Iqbal Zahoor 5 for 43) and 130 for 2

United Bank won by 8 wickets

United Bank 12 pts, Railways 0 pts

Habib Bank 139 (Aamer Nazir 5 for 67) and 242
   (Idrees Baig 58, Aamer Nazir 5 for 40)

Allied Bank 552 (Rameez Raja 300, Alay Haider 55,
   Abdul Qadir 4 for 175)

Allied Bank won by an innings and 171 runs

Allied Bank 12 pts, Habib Bank 0 pts

While National Bank were being thwarted by a second-wicket stand of 198 between Azam Khan and Sohail Jaffar, United Bank, playing their first match away from their own sports complex, were moving to a fourth resounding victory. Again they were engaged in a low-scoring match, and the honours went to their opening bowler Hasnain Kazim who had career-best performances for innings and match. He finished with 12 for 83.

Rizwan-uz-Zaman and Shoaib Mohammad, two former Test openers, began PIA's innings against ADBP with a partnership of 218. There was also some spirited middle-order batting from Sagheer Abbas and Wasim Haider who put on 124 for the sixth wicket. Once more, Mansoor Rana batted magnificently for ADBP, but the run rate throughout the match predetermined a draw.

Batting throughout the innings for 591 minutes and facing 415 balls, Allied Bank's skipper Rameez Raja hit 300 against Habib Bank and took his side to victory in three days. He completely dominated the innings in which only three other batsmen reached 30 and asserted a claim for a recall to the Test side.

21, 22, 23 and 24 October 1994 *at Multan CC Stadium, Multan*

Habib Bank 191 (Shakeel Ahmed 61, Sajjad Akbar 7 for 42)
   and 253 (Shakeel Ahmed 117, Naved Nazir 4 for 76)

PNSC 196 (Nadeem Ghauri 5 for 63, Asadullah Butt 4 for 34)
   and 208 (Sohail Jaffar 83, Nadeem Ghauri 6 for 69)

Habib Bank won by 40 runs

Habib Bank 12 pts, PNSC 0 pts

United Bank 232 (Mohammad Ramzan 81, Mahmood Hamid
   72, Raja Afaq 6 for 97) and 119 (Mohammad Asif 4 for 24,
   Javed Hayat 4 for 45)

ADBP 181 (Zahoor Elahi 86, Iqbal Imam 4 for 37, Tauseef
   Ahmed 4 for 50) and 104 (Tauseef Ahmed 6 for 28)

United Bank won by 66 runs

United Bank 12 pts, ADBP 0 pts

Railways 270 (Zahid Javed 77, Tariq Mahmood 64, Majid
   Saeed 52, Saqlain Mushtaq 7 for 66) and 231 (Shahid
   Saeed 104 not out, Saqlain Mushtaq 4 for 60)

PIA 135 (Imran Adil 6 for 44) and 274 for 9 (Zahid Ahmed 110,
   Rizwan-uz-Zaman 57)

Match drawn

Railways 2 pts, PIA 0 pts

22, 23, 24 and 25 October 1994 *at Bagh-e-Jinnah Ground, Lahore*

National Bank 224 (Ata-ur-Rehman 4 for 46, Aamer Nazir 4 for
   64) and 254 (Ameer Akbar 53, Ata-ur-Rehman 4 for 65)

Allied Bank 249 (Ijaz Ahmed jr 50) and 232 for 5
   (Ijaz Ahmed jr 62 not out, Rameez Raja 56)

Allied Bank won by 5 wickets

Allied Bank 12 pts, National Bank 0 pts

The batting of Shakeel Ahmed and the bowling of Nadeem Ghauri kept alive Habib Bank's hopes of reaching the semi-finals, but defeat virtually extinguished PNSC's chances of qualifying for the knock-out stage of the competition. More splendid bowling by Tauseef Ahmed took United Bank to their fifth victory in succession and placed them in an unassailable position at the top of the table.

National Bank meanwhile suffered their first defeat. They were put in to bat and reduced to 33 for 5 by Aamer Nazir and Ata-ur-Rehman. Mohammad Javed and Tahir Shah added 82, but a total of 224 was hard to defend. Allied Bank lost eight wickets before they claimed a first-innings lead, however, and National batted with more solidity in their second innings. An opening stand of 103 between Rameez Raja and Mohammad Nawaz gave Allied Bank the platform to press for victory, and another sparkling knock from Ijaz Ahmed jr, 62 off 89 balls, saw Allied romp home.

A second-wicket stand of 137 between Zahid Javed and Tariq Mahmood helped Railways to build a useful score against PIA who collapsed before the bowling of Imran Adil, the experienced medium-pacer. With Shahid Saeed hitting 104 not out at number seven after five wickets had fallen for 87, Railways were able to set PIA a target of 367 and leave them more than a day in which to get the runs. A 316-minute innings of 110 by Zahid Ahmed helped PIA to avoid defeat. The ninth wicket fell at 271 with eight minutes remaining, which Ayaz Jillani, 84 minutes for 36, and Shoaib Akhtar survived.

27, 28, 29 and 30 October 1994 *at National Stadium, Karachi*

United Bank 592 (Iqbal Imam 155, Ghulam Ali 120, Mahmood
   Hamid 108, Aamer Bashir 82, Mansoor Akhtar 53, Asadullah
   Butt 6 for 92) and 189 for 2 (Ghulam Ali 80, Mohammad
   Hamid 57 not out)

Habib Bank 191 (Shakeel Ahmed 59, Naved Anjum 52, Hasnain Kazim 6 for 46)

Match drawn

United Bank 2 pts, Habib Bank 0 pts

at United Bank Sports Complex, Karachi

PIA 169 (Shoaib Mohammad 52, Zafar Iqbal 5 for 32, Naeem Ashraf 5 for 53) and 293 (Zahid Fazal 65, Moin Khan 65, Naeem Ashraf 4 for 86)

National Bank 369 (Shahid Tanvir 88, Sajid Ali 79, Shahid Anwar 73) and 97 for 2

National Bank won by 8 wickets

National Bank 12 pts, PIA 0 pts

at Pindi Cricket Stadium, Rawalpindi

Allied Bank 185 (Javed Hayat 4 for 49) and 163 (Mohammad Asif 5 for 40)

ADBP 174 (Zahoor Elahi 65, Aamer Nazir 6 for 53, Mohammad Nawaz 4 for 41) and 175 for 8 (Mansoor Rana 60 not out, Sabih Azhar 59)

ADBP won by 2 wickets

ADBP 12 pts, Allied Bank 0 pts

at Arbab Niaz Stadium, Peshawar

Railways 501 for 4 dec. (Majid Saeed 163 not out, Babar Javed 101 not out, Nadeem Younis 75, Hafeez Tahir 62, Tariq Mahmood 62)

PNSC 318 for 5 (Farrukh Bari 72, Sher Ali 70, Azam Khan 60, Sohail Jaffar 53)

Match drawn

No points

United Bank hit their highest score of the season yet failed to win for the first time. Ghulam Ali and Aamer Bashir put on 162 for the second wicket, but the highlight of the innings was a fifth-wicket partnership of 179 between Mahmood Hamid and Iqbal Imam, the left-hander. Habib Bank offered little in reply against Hasnain Kazim and Mohammad Ali, but Mansoor Akhtar did not enforce the follow-on, and the match was drawn.

Put in to bat, PIA were no match for the consistency with bat and ball of National Bank; while ADBP recovered bravely to beat Allied Bank.

Meanwhile, Majid Saeed and Babar Javed shared an unbroken fifth-wicket stand of 232 for Railways. Both batsmen hit the highest scores of their careers.

1, 2, 3 and 4 November 1994 *at National Stadium, Karachi*

National Bank 365 (Sajid Ali 143, Shahid Anwar 79, Hasnain Kazim 5 for 65) and 298 for 6 (Tahir Shah 84, Mohammad Javed 70)

United Bank 386 (Umar Rasheed 91, Mahmood Hamid 59, Ghulam Ali 58, Habib Baloch 5 for 110)

Match drawn

United Bank 2 pts, National Bank 0 pts

at Arbab Niaz Stadium, Peshawar

ADBP 235 (Atif Rauf 121, Sajjad Ali 5 for 76) and 321 for 5 (Atif Rauf 100 not out, Tariq Mohammad 56, Zahoor Elahi 53)

PNSC 410 (Aamer Ishaq 106, Nasir Wasti 99, Azam Khan 59, Mohammad Asif 4 for 88)

Match drawn

PNSC 2 pts, ADBP 0 pts

at Pindi Cricket Stadium, Rawalpindi

Railways 104 (Raj Hans 5 for 31) and 201 (Aamer Nazir 6 for 52)

Allied Bank 228 (Alay Haider 65, Shahid Naqi 58, Arshad Khan 5 for 107, Iqbal Zahoor 4 for 52) and 83 for 3

Allied Bank won by 7 wickets

Allied Bank 12 pts, Railways 0 pts

at United Bank Sports Complex, Karachi

PIA 196 (Husnain Qayyum 80, Asadullah Butt 6 for 64) and 291 (Saqlain Mushtaq 50 not out, Shakeel Khan 4 for 76, Asadullah Butt 4 for 143)

Habib Bank 126 (Nadeem Afzal 6 for 63) and 259 (Mujahid Jamshed 93, Wasim Haider 5 for 74)

PIA won by 102 runs

PIA 12 pts, Habib Bank 0 pts

Railways' miserable campaign came to an end with defeat by Allied Bank, while PIA snatched the fourth semi-final spot when they crushed a weakened Habib Bank side.

PATRON'S TROPHY FINAL TABLE

	P	W	D	L	Pts
United Bank	7	5	2	–	64
National Bank	7	4	2	1	50
Allied Bank	7	4	1	2	48
PIA	7	2	2	3	26
Habib Bank	7	2	2	3	24
ADBP	7	2	2	3	24
Railways	7	–	3	4	4
PNSC	7	–	4	3	4

In the final qualifying match between Habib Bank and PIA at the United Bank Sports Complex in Karachi, Asadullah Butt, who finished with match figures of 10 for 207, was reported for ball tampering. He was warned by the umpires, but persisted even after the ball had twice been changed. The Domestic Tournament Monitoring Committee took the most severe action, suspending Asadullah for an indefinite period and fining him 5,000 rupees. The sentence was later restricted to a four-match suspension with the imposition of the fine. The judgment of Javed Zaman, chairman of the committee, was that Asadullah had violated the spirit and the laws of the game. Many felt that Asadullah was paying the price for the sins of others and that the Pakistani administration was under pressure from the ICC.

SEMI-FINALS

20, 21, 22 and 23 November 1994 *at National Stadium, Karachi*

National Bank 173 (Tahir Shah 55, Nadeem Afzal 4 for 44) and 282 (Zafar Iqbal 63 not out, Nadeem Afzal 5 for 96)

PIA 423 (Asif Mujtaba 70, Moin Khan 63, Rizwan-uz-Zaman 62, Zahid Fazal 59) and 33 for 2

PIA won by 8 wickets

at United Bank Sports Complex, Karachi

United Bank 138 (Aamer Nazir 5 for 74, Ata-ur-Rehman 4 for 41) and 441 for 4 (Mahmood Hamid 145 not out, Iqbal Imam 107 not out, Mohammad Ramzan 80, Umar Rashid 62)

Allied Bank 462 (Manzoor Akhtar 97, Raj Hans 94 not out, Mohammad Nawaz 71, Alay Haider 64, Tauseef Ahmed 4 for 124)

Match drawn

Allied Bank qualified for final on first-innings lead

Bowled out on the opening day by a varied attack spearheaded by Nadeem Afzal and Wasim Haider, National Bank never recovered. PIA batted with consistency and dominated the match.

United Bank, who had carried all before them in the qualifying rounds, also saw their hopes of reaching the final disappear on the first day. Ata-ur-Rehman and Aamer Nazir, the Allied Bank pace pair, bowled out United Bank in 39.1 overs and, by the end of the day, Allied Bank were 118 for 1. Mohammad Nawaz and Manzoor Akhtar took the score to 189, a second-wicket stand of 177, before being separated, and Raj Hans led spirited attack from the late-order. United Bank, 324 runs in arrears on the first innings, had no option but to bat out the match. Mahmood Hamid and Iqbal Imam shared an unbroken fifth-wicket stand of 210.

PATRON'S CUP TROPHY FINAL

26, 27, 28 and 29 November 1994 *at National Stadium, Karachi*

PIA 165 (Sagheer Abbas 58) and 161 (Zahid Fazal 69, Aamer Nazir 6 for 55)

Allied Bank 248 (Manzoor Akhtar 71, Saqlain Mushtaq 5 for 101) and 79 for 0

Allied Bank won by 10 wickets

Allied Bank's commitment to recruiting top players in an effort to restore their sporting division to former glories was rewarded when they took the Patron's Trophy with ease. Rameez Raja had relied on a battery of fast bowlers to take his side to the final, and although neither Aqib

Javed nor Ata-ur-Rehman was available – having left for South Africa with the national side – Aamer Nazir, who enjoyed an outstanding tournament, and Shahid Mahboob proved too much for Pakistan International Airlines. PIA threw away the final on the opening day when they were bowled out for 165 on a good pitch. Worse was to follow on the second day, when Manzoor Akhtar and Ijaz Ahmed flourished after offering simple chances which were not accepted.

Particularly disappointing for PIA was Zahid Ahmed who bowled indifferently, dropped catches and was fined by the match referee for disputing an umpire's decision.

Zahid Fazal and the patient Asif Mohammad offered a hint of recovery when PIA batted again, but Zahid and Sagheer Abbas fell in the same over bowled by part-time off-spinner Mohammad Nawaz. After this, PIA succumbed meekly.

QUAID-E-AZAM TROPHY

5, 6, 7 and 8 December 1994 *at Pindi Cricket Stadium, Rawalpindi*

Rawalpindi B 219 for 7 (Tassawar Hussain 89)

v. **Rawalpindi A**

Match abandoned

at Asghar Ali Shah Stadium, Karachi

Karachi Blues 241 (Manzoor Akhtar 113, Lal Fraz 4 for 43) and 346 for 4 (Sajid Ali 134, Shoaib Mohammad 110, Mahmood Hamid 50)

Karachi Whites 373 (Iqbal Saleem 74 not out, Kamran Hussain 58) and 108 (Haaris A. Khan 4 for 24), Nadeem Khan 4 for 25)

Karachi Blues won by 106 runs

Karachi Blues 12 pts, Karachi Whites 0 pts

at LCCA Ground, Lahore

Islamabad 69 (Naved Anjum 9 for 35) and 287 (Basit Ali 147, Abdul Qadir 5 for 86)

Lahore City 194 (Aamer Nazir 4 for 104) and 152 (Aamer Nazir 5 for 75)

Islamabad won by 10 runs

Islamabad 12 pts, Lahore City 0 pts

at Iqbal Stadium, Faisalabad

Peshawar 175 (Zafar Sarfraz 69, Nadeem Afzal 5 for 60) and 210 for 4 (Mazhar Qayyum 70, Sher Ali 65, Nadeem Afzal 4 for 49)

Faisalabad 300 for 6 (Mohammad Ramzan 126, Ijaz Ahmed jr 101 not out)

Match drawn

Faisalabad 2 pts, Peshawar 0 pts

Sargodha failed to arrive for their match in Bahawalpur. At the end of January, they also failed to arrive for their match against Rawalpindi A. As a result, they were scratched from the competition, and the points won and lost in the six matches in which they participated were deleted. They were relegated for the 1995/96 season.

11, 12, 13 and 14 December 1994 *at Bahawalpur Stadium, Bahawalpur*

Faisalabad 287 (Bilal Ahmed 52, Ijaz Mahmood 52, Imran Adil 5 for 70, Murtaza Hussain 4 for 90) and 174 (Mohammad Ramzan 83, Rehan Rafiq 4 for 28)

Bahawalpur 286 (Aamir Sohail 98, Azhar Shafiq 74, Wasim Hussain 4 for 99) and 27 for 1

Match drawn

Faisalabad 2 pts, Bahawalpur 0 pts

at Marghzar Ground, Islamabad

Islamabad 178 (Ahsan Butt 60, Shakeel Ahmed 6 for 75) and 136 for 5 (Tariq Rasheed 50 not out, Mohammad Akram 5 for 47)

Rawalpindi A 93 (Azhar Mahmood 5 for 36)

Match drawn

Islamabad 2 pts, Rawalpindi 0 pts

at LCCA Ground, Lahore

Peshawar 117 (Abdul Qadir 5 for 31) and 173 (Abdul Qadir 4 for 78)

Lahore City 124 (Tariq Mahmood 68, Arshad Khan 6 for 30) and 170 for 3 (Javed Hayat 72 not out)

Lahore City won by 7 wickets

Lahore City 12 pts, Peshawar 0 pts

at Army Cricket Ground, Rawalpindi

Rawalpindi B 183 (Aamer Bashir 51, Naeem Tayyab 6 for 56) and 262 for 9 dec. (Rana Qayyum-ul-Hasan 71, Tassawar Hussain 53, Jaffer Qureshi 4 for 56)

Karachi Whites 228 (Sohail Jaffer 77, Sabih Azhar 5 for 13) and 38 for 1

Match drawn

Karachi Whites 2 pts, Rawalpindi B 0 pts

In the match at the National Stadium, Karachi, Ghulam Ali and Shoaib Mohammad both hit centuries for Karachi Blues against Sargodha. The Blues' innings victory was later deleted from the trophy record as were all matches involving Sargodha, although the players' individual performances were retained in the averages.

17, 18, 19 and 20 December 1994 *at Bahawalpur Stadium, Bahawalpur*

Bahawalpur 127 (Tauqir Hussain 6 for 53) and 114 (Tauqir Hussain 4 for 43)

Rawalpindi B 211 (Robert Crosse 57, Tassawar Hussain 51, Murtaza Hussain 7 for 65) and 32 for 2

Rawalpindi B won by 8 wickets

Rawalpindi B 12 pts, Bahawalpur 0 pts

at Army Cricket Ground, Rawalpindi

Rawalpindi A 278 (Nadeem Abbasi 105, Raja Afaq 55, Salman Fazal 5 for 77) and 161 (Shahid Javed 88, Salman Fazal 6 for 43)

Karachi Whites 292 (Iqbal Imam 63, Iqbal Saleem 58, Raja Afaq 5 for 117) and 148 for 3 (Azam Khan 78 not out)

Karachi Whites won by 7 wickets

Karachi Whites 12 pts, Rawalpindi A 0 pts

at LCCA Ground, Lahore

Faisalabad 132 (Mohammad Hussain 4 for 35) and 272 (Ijaz Mahmood 88, Mohammad Hussain 6 for 90)

Lahore City 470 for 3 dec. (Tariq Mahmood 206 not out, Babar Zaman 101, Sohail Idrees 63)

Lahore City won by an innings and 66 runs

Lahore City 12 pts, Faisalabad 0 pts

at National Stadium, Karachi

Karachi Blues 294 (Munir-ul-Haq 62, Wasim Arif 58, Malik Rasheed 52, Arshad Khan 6 for 100) and 140 (Arshad Khan 4 for 34, Sajid Shah 4 for 45)

Peshawar 272 (Jahangir Khan 69, Hameed Gul 52) and 165 for 7 (Mazhar Qayyum 58)

Peshawar won by 3 wickets

Peshawar 12 pts, Karachi Blues 0 pts

Left-hander Tariq Mahmood hit the first double century of his career while both Mohammad Hussain and off-break bowler Tauqir Hussain took 10 wickets in a match for the first time.

23, 24, 25 and 26 December 1994 *at Arbab Niaz Stadium, Peshawar*

Bahawalpur 168 (Farrukh Zaman 7 for 63)

Peshawar 172 for 9 (Murtaza Hussain 6 for 50)

Match drawn

Peshawar 2 pts, Bahawalpur 0 pts

29, 30, 31 December 1994 and 1 January 1995 *at Arbab Niaz Stadium, Peshawar*

Peshawar 176 (Sher Ali 58, Jahangir Khan 55, Naeem Tayyab 6 for 31)

Karachi Whites 127 (Arshad Khan 5 for 58)

Match drawn

Peshawar 2 pts, Karachi Whites 0 pts

at Marghzar Ground, Islamabad

Bahawalpur 160 (Mohammad Ali 5 for 64, Azhar Mahmood 4
for 26)

Islamabad 161 for 4

Match drawn

Islamabad 2 pts, Bahawalpur 0 pts

at Pindi Cricket Stadium, Rawalpindi

Rawalpindi A 212 for 8 dec. (Shahid Naqi 52, Fazal Hussain 5
for 65)

Faisalabad 146

Match drawn

Rawalpindi A 2 pts, Faisalabad 0 pts

at National Stadium, Karachi

Rawalpindi B 242 (Pervez Iqbal 76, Tauqir Hussain 66, Athar
Laeeq 5 for 52) and 189 for 5 (Robert Crosse 73, Tassawar
Hussain 56)

Karachi Blues 324 for 8 dec. (Faisal Qureshi 80, Irfanullah 65,
Aamer Iqbal 57, Athar Laeeq 55 not out, Pervez Iqbal
5 for 59)

Match drawn

Karachi Blues 2 pts, Rawalpindi B 0 pts

Only the match in Karachi escaped the rain.

4, 5, 6 and 7 January 1995 *at Bohran Wali Ground, Faisalabad*

Karachi Whites 86 (Mohammad Wasim 6 for 50, Masood
Anwar 4 for 31) and 290 (Mohammad Javed 113 not out,
Azam Khan 77, Fazal Hussain 5 for 78)

Faisalabad 416 for 4 dec. (Mohammad Ramzan 203 not out,
Ijaz Ahmed jr 122)

Faisalabad won by an innings and 40 runs

Faisalabad 12 pts, Karachi Whites 0 pts

at LCCA Ground, Lahore

Lahore City 308 for 9 dec. (Naeem Ashraf 74 not out, Shahid
Anwar 53, Mohammad Hussain 51, Shoaib Akhtar 6 for 69)
and 64 for 0

Rawalpindi B 152 (Aamer Bashir 54, Abdul Qadir 6 for 31) and
219 (Alay Haider 87, Abdul Qadir 4 for 64)

Lahore City won by 10 wickets

Lahore City 12 pts, Rawalpindi 0 pts

at National Stadium, Karachi

Karachi Blues 492 for 7 dec. (Manzoor Akhtar 109 not out,
Ghulam Ali 108, Faisal Qureshi 107)

Islamabad 210 and 304 for 6 (Ghaffar Kazmi 110 not out,
Basit Niazi 57, Zafar Iqbal 4 for 71)

Match drawn

Karachi Blues 2 pts, Islamabad 0 pts

at Pindi Cricket Stadium, Rawalpindi

Bahawalpur 123 (Mohammad Aslam 7 for 52) and 86
(Mohammad Akram 5 for 46)

Rawalpindi A 164 (Pervez Shah 6 for 77, Azhar Shafiq 4 for 50)
and 46 for 3

Rawalpindi A won by 7 wickets

Rawalpindi A 12 pts, Bahawalpur 0 pts

Mohammad Ramzan hit the highest score of his career,
and Lahore witnessed the rebirth of the great leg-break
bowler Abdul Qadir with 10 wickets in the match. It was
the 21st occasion on which Qadir had achieved the feat.

10, 11, 12 and 13 January 1995 *at Bohran Wali Ground, Faisalabad*

Islamabad 154 (Shahid Ali Khan 4 for 32) and 198 (Masood
Anwar 8 for 72)

Faisalabad 253 (Saqlain Mushtaq 5 for 100, Mohammad Ali 4
for 48) and 101 for 7 (Saqlain Mushtaq 4 for 21)

Faisalabad won by 3 wickets

Faisalabad 12 pts, Islamabad 0 pts

at National Stadium, Karachi

Karachi Blues 258 (Irfanullah 52, Mohammad Aslam 4 for 52)
and 251 for 4 dec. (Manzoor Akhtar 88 not out, Sajid Ali 87)

Rawalpindi A 154 (Shahid Javed 52, Haaris A. Khan 4 for 44)
and 206 (Shahid Javed 73, Athar Laeeq 8 for 65)

Karachi Blues won by 149 runs

Karachi Blues 12 pts, Rawalpindi A 0 pts

at Bahawalpur Stadium, Bahawalpur

Lahore City 169 (Nadeem Mahmood 52, Faisal Elahi 5 for 46)
and 231 for 9 dec. (Shahid Anwar 110, Naeem Ashraf 53
not out)

Bahawalpur 174 (Naeem Ashraf 5 for 68) and 230 for 8 (Azhar
Shafiq 70, Rizwan Sattar 57, Javed Hayat 4 for 40)

Bahawalpur won by 2 wickets

Bahawalpur 12 pts, Lahore City 0 pts

at Arbab Niaz Stadium, Peshawar

Rawalpindi B 160 (Arshad Khan 4 for 37) and 224
(Alay Haider 72, Arshad Khan 4 for 61)

Peshawar 230 (Wajatullah 71, Mazhar Qayyum 70, Pervez
Iqbal 4 for 46) and 156 for 5 (Jahangir Khan sr 71)

Peshawar won by 5 wickets

Peshawar 12 pts, Rawalpindi B 0 pts

Bahawalpur registered their only win of the season when
they scored 230 in 53.2 overs to beat Lahore City.

16, 17, 18 and 19 January 1995 *at National Stadium, Karachi*

Lahore City 222 (Javed Hayat 102 not out, Athar Laeeq
4 for 41, Ali Gobhar 4 for 47)
Karachi Blues 331 for 9 (Aamer Iqbal 94, Mahmood Hamid 63,
Mohammad Hussain 4 for 59)

Match drawn

Karachi Blues 2 pts, Lahore City 0 pts

at Pindi Cricket Stadium, Rawalpindi

Rawalpindi A 190 (Shahid Naqi 61, Sajid Khan 6 for 64) and
168 (Sajid Shah 7 for 77)
Peshawar 162 (Mohammad Akram 4 for 40, Naeem Akhtar 4
for 61) and 121 (Mohammad Akram 5 for 40)

Rawalpindi A won by 75 runs

Rawalpindi A 12 pts, Peshawar 0 pts

at Marghzar Ground, Islamabad

Rawalpindi B 328 (Salman Shah 120, Tassawar Hussain 50,
Saqlain Mushtaq 7 for 105)
Islamabad 159 (Tauqir Shah 6 for 62) and 47 for 1

Match drawn

Rawalpindi B 2 pts, Islamabad 0 pts

at United Bank Sports Complex, Karachi

Bahawalpur 201 (Rizwan Sattar 64, Mohammad Javed
5 for 53, Mohammad Hasnain 4 for 51) and 162
(Lal Fraz 5 for 54)
Karachi Whites 298 for 7 (Mohammad Javed 61 not out,
Sohail Jaffer 55, Shaheen Malik 52) and 69 for 1

Karachi Whites won by 9 wickets

Karachi Whites 12 pts, Bahawalpur 0 pts

Rain interfered with the game at the National Stadium
where Karachi Blues took first-innings points against their
close rivals from Lahore, while Karachi Whites gained
their second win of the season to keep alive their hopes of
qualifying for the semi-finals.

21, 22, 23 and 24 January 1995 *at United Bank Sports Complex, Karachi*

Karachi Whites 146 (Sohail Jaffer 53 not out, Naeem Ashraf
7 for 53) and 208 (Naeem Ashraf 4 for 65)
Lahore City 237 (Shahid Aslam 71, Iftikhar Hussain 52,
Lal Fraz 5 for 73) and 118 for 6

Lahore City won by 4 wickets

Lahore City 12 pts, Karachi Whites 0 pts

at Bohran Wali Ground, Faisalabad

Faisalabad 479 for 8 dec. (Ijaz Ahmed jr 119, Saadat Gul 113,
Mohammad Amin 107 not out) and 47 for 0
Rawalpindi B 211

Match drawn

Faisalabad 2 pts, Rawalpindi B 0 pts

at Asghar Ali Shah Stadium, Karachi

Karachi Blues 216 (Haaris A. Khan 52, Shafiq Ahmed
8 for 111) and 288 for 7 dec. (Ghulam Ali 151 not out,
Manzoor Akhtar 51)
Bahawalpur 120 (Nadeem Khan 4 for 46) and 167
(Mohammad Khalid 61, Zafar Iqbal 7 for 60)

Karachi Blues won by 217 runs

Karachi Blues 12 pts, Bahawalpur 0 pts

at Arbab Niaz Stadium, Peshawar

Islamabad 299 (Mohammad Hassan Adnan 72, Mushtaq
Ahmed 57, Arshad Khan 8 for 115) and 81 for 4 (Sajid Shah
4 for 39)
Peshawar 140 (Azhar Mahmood 4 for 18) and 239 for 9 dec.
(Wajahatullah 103, Mazhar Qayyum 63, Mushtaq Ahmed
4 for 70)

Islamabad won by 6 wickets

Islamabad 12 pts, Peshawar 0 pts

27, 28, 29 and 30 January 1995 *at National Stadium, Karachi*

Faisalabad 460 (Ijaz Ahmed jr 194, Nadeem Afzal 100)
Karachi Blues 496 for 4 (Manzoor Akhtar 249, Munir-ul-Haq
100 not out, Ghulam Ali 72)

Match drawn

Karachi Blues 2 pts, Faisalabad 0 pts

Lahore City's victory took them to the top of the table as
Karachi Blues failed to beat Faisalabad. Manzoor Akhtar
hit the highest score of his career.

QUAID-E-AZAM TROPHY FINAL TABLE

	P	W	L	D	Ab	Pts
Lahore City	8	4	2	1	1	48
Karachi Blues	8	3	1	4	–	44
Faisalabad	8	2	1	5	–	30
Islamabad	8	2	1	4	1	28
Peshawar	8	2	3	3	–	28
Rawalpindi A	8	2	2	2	2	26
Karachi Whites	8	2	3	2	1	26
Rawalpindi B	8	1	2	4	1	14
Bahawalpur	8	1	4	3	–	12

SEMI-FINALS

7, 8, 9 and 10 March 1995 *at Pindi Cricket Stadium, Rawalpindi*

Faisalabad 461 for 8 dec. (Ijaz Ahmed jr 168, Mohammad Ramzan 114)

Lahore City 366 for 5 (Aamir Sohail 105, Shahid Anwar 92, Tahir Shah 56 not out)

Match drawn

8, 9 and 10 March 1995 *at Multan CC Ground, Multan*

Islamabad 96 (Nadeem Khan 5 for 28) and 128 (Nadeem Khan 5 for 32, Haaris A. Khan 5 for 53)

Karachi Blues 494 for 6 dec. (Asif Mujtaba 166, Munir-ul-Haq 102 not out, Sajid Ali 75, Mahmood Hamid 55)

Karachi Blues won by an innings and 270 runs

Lahore City were somewhat fortunate to qualify for the final by virtue of a faster run rate. Aamir Sohail and Shahid Anwar hit 189 for the first wicket. Karachi Blues trounced Faisalabad in three days.

QUAID-E-AZAM TROPHY FINAL

14, 15, 16, 17 and 18 March 1995 *at Arbab Niaz Stadium, Peshawar*

Karachi Blues 802 for 8 dec. (Asif Mujtaba 208, Mahmood Hamid 208, Moin Khan 107, Shoaib Mohammad 100, Munir-ul-Haq 62, Mohammad Hussain 4 for 231)

Lahore City 302 (Shahid Anwar 89, Nadeem Khan 5 for 135, Haaris A. Khan 4 for 62) and 320 (Zulqarnain 80 not out, Nadeem Khan 5 for 96)

Karachi Blues won by an innings and 180 runs

Karachi Blues dominated the final as they had dominated the semi-final, strengthened as they were by the availability of Asif Mujtaba and Moin Khan, and the Quaid-e-Azam Trophy went to Karachi for a record 14th time. Asif Mujtaba and Mahmood Hamid shared a fourth-wicket stand of 172, and Mahmood and Munir-ul-Haq then added 196. Moin Khan completed a highly successful season with a century, and his elder brother Nadeem claimed 10 wickets to add to the 10 he had taken in the semi-final.

PENTANGULAR TROPHY

20, 21, 22 and 23 March 1995 *at Pindi Cricket Stadium, Rawalpindi*

United Bank 307 (Mohammad Ramzan 91, Mansoor Akhtar 73, Naeem Ashraf 5 for 55) and 62 for 3

National Bank 208 (Umar Rasheed 6 for 64)

Match drawn

United Bank 2 pts, National Bank 0 pts

at Arbab Niaz Stadium, Peshawar

Allied Bank 345 (Rameez Raja 83, Mohammad Nawaz 62, Ijaz Ahmed jr 58, Aamir Hanif 58, Haaris A. Khan 5 for 108) and 28 for 2

Karachi Blues 298 (Sohail Jaffar 102, Munir-ul-Haq 72, Asif Mujtaba 51, Aquib Javed 6 for 77)

Match drawn

Allied Bank 2 pts, Karachi Blues 0 pts

31 March, 1, 2 and 3 April 1995 *at Pindi Cricket Stadium, Rawalpindi*

Lahore City 141 (Babar Zaman 62, Shahid Mahboob 6 for 22) and 154 (Ata-ur-Rehman 6 for 74, Shahid Mahboob 4 for 58)

Allied Bank 288 (Bilal Rana 80 not out, Mohammad Nawaz 50, Inamullah Khan 5 for 90) and 10 for 2

Allied Bank won by 8 wickets

Allied Bank 12 pts, Lahore City 0 pts

at Arbab Niaz Stadium, Peshawar

United Bank 222 (Iqbal Imam 50 not out, Tariq Hussain 8 for 97) and 122 (Ali Gohar 6 for 33)

Karachi Blues 345 (Azam Khan 144, Saad Wasim 66, Sohail Jaffar 63, Tauseef Ahmed 4 for 99)

Karachi Blues won by an innings and 1 run

Karachi Blues 12 pts, United Bank 0 pts

5, 6, 7 and 8 April 1995 *at Arbab Niaz Stadium, Peshawar*

Lahore City 139 (Tauseef Ahmed 4 for 26, Shahid Hussain 4 for 41) and 62 (Shahid Hussain 4 for 14)

United Bank 300 for 9 dec. (Iqbal Imam 68, Mansoor Akhtar 60, Saifullah 52, Mohammad Hussain 5 for 88)

United Bank won by an innings and 99 runs

United Bank 12 pts, Lahore City 0 pts

at Pindi Cricket Stadium, Rawalpindi

Karachi Blues 221 and 366 (Tahir Rasheed 99, Irfanullah 52, Sohail Jaffar 50)

National Bank 336 (Shahid Anwar 85, Tahir Shah 60, Shahid Tanvir 51, Ali Gohar 7 for 92) and 142 for 5 (Ameer Akbar 68, Shahid Anwar 56)

Match drawn

National Bank 2 pts, Karachi Blues 0 pts

10, 11, 12 and 13 April 1995 *at Arbab Niaz Stadium, Peshawar*

Lahore City 214 (Gulzar Awan 66, Hafeez-ur-Rehman 5 for 54) and 286 (Inamullah Khan 60, Tariq Humayun 60, Tahir Shah 7 for 65)

National Bank 419 (Sajid Ali 132, Saeed Azad 71, Tahir Shah 58, Shahid Anwar 57, Inamullah Khan 5 for 149) and 85 for 0 (Sajid Ali 54 not out)

National Bank won by 10 wickets

National Bank 12 pts, Lahore City 0 pts

The decision to revive the Pentagular Trophy met with little success. Three of the 10 matches scheduled were abandoned without a ball being bowled, and three sides finished level on 14 points. The trophy was awarded to National Bank for having the superior run rate, 4.63 runs per over. This was helped by scoring 85 in 9.5 overs to beat Lahore in the final match.

In the matches at Peshawar and Rawalpindi, Tauseef Ahmed and Ali Gohar both performed the hat-trick on the second day, 6 April.

FIRST-CLASS AVERAGES

BATTING

	M	Inns	NO	Runs	HS	Av	100s	50s
Asif Mujtaba	4	4	–	495	208	123.75	2	2
Salim Malik	3	6	–	557	237	92.83	2	1
Ijaz Ahmed jr	17	24	6	1573	202*	87.38	7	4
Mansoor Rana	8	14	3	685	175*	62.27	2	3
Atif Rauf	6	11	1	592	200	59.20	3	1
Munir-ul-Haq	11	12	3	508	102*	56.44	2	3
Aamir Sohail	5	9	–	506	105	56.22	2	2
Mazhar Qayyum	8	14	2	641	201*	53.41	1	4
Siddiq Javed	12	19	4	794	169	52.93	3	2
Saeed Anwar	3	6	–	314	85	52.33	–	3
Mohammad Ramzan	19	30	5	1286	203*	51.44	3	6
Mahmood Hamid	20	30	6	1183	208	49.29	3	7
Ghulam Ali	18	29	2	1222	224	45.25	5	3
Rameez Raja	11	18	1	754	300	44.35	1	4
Azam Khan	15	24	2	969	144	44.04	2	6
Mohammad Nawaz	17	30	4	1140	202*	43.84	3	5
Manzoor Akhtar	21	31	3	1220	249	43.57	3	6
Tahir Shah	12	18	3	646	84	43.06	–	6
Mohammad Javed	15	24	4	842	169	42.10	3	2
Iqbal Imam	14	20	2	751	155	41.72	2	3
Sohail Jaffer	18	29	2	1085	113	40.18	2	8
Moin Khan	11	18	2	622	115*	38.87	3	2
Shoaib Mohammad	13	23	1	816	201*	37.09	3	4
Sajid Ali	19	31	1	1110	143	37.00	3	5
Basit Niazi	5	9	–	329	147	36.55	1	2
Shahid Anwar	19	32	1	1128	110	36.38	1	9
Tariq Mahmood	15	25	1	851	206*	35.45	1	5
Sajjad Akbar	8	13	2	380	81	34.54	–	1
Majid Saeed	12	19	2	585	163*	34.41	1	3
Shaukat Mirza	7	12	1	371	124*	33.72	1	1
Alay Haider	18	27	3	806	118	33.58	1	5
Mansoor Akhtar	10	18	1	568	73	33.41	–	5
Shakeel Ahmed	9	17	1	516	117	32.25	1	3
Tassawar Hussain	9	14	2	387	89	32.25	–	5
Tahir Rasheed	9	16	–	509	119	31.81	1	1
Zahid Fazal	7	14	1	413	91	31.76	–	4
Jahangir Khan	9	15	–	474	71	31.60	–	3
Rizwan-uz-Zaman	8	15	–	473	126	31.53	1	2
Idrees Baig	10	18	3	465	107	31.00	1	2
Ameer Akbar	10	15	2	399	88	30.69	–	4
Wajahatullah	9	15	2	392	103	30.15	1	1
Saeed Azad	11	19	1	542	87	30.11	–	4
Nadeem Younis	7	13	–	369	114	28.38	1	1
Sher Ali	14	23	1	623	110	28.31	1	3
Shahid Javed	13	19	–	537	88	28.26	–	5
Haaris A. Khan	14	15	4	304	63	27.63	–	2
Ahsan Butt	7	12	1	304	60	27.63	–	1
Saifullah	11	17	2	409	52	27.26	–	1
Wasim Arif	14	20	2	478	90	26.55	–	4
Aamer Bashir	13	20	2	476	82	26.44	–	3
Babar Zaman	12	21	1	519	101	25.95	1	1
Aamir Sohail	8	14	2	308	98	25.66	–	1
Mohammad Hasnain	7	13	–	328	63	25.23	–	2
Shahid Naqi	10	16	1	361	61	24.06	–	3
Zahid Ahmed	9	16	1	351	110	23.40	1	1
Naeem Ashraf	15	21	3	400	104	22.22	1	2
Javed Hayat	15	24	4	437	102*	21.85	1	1
Sabih Azhar	9	15	–	323	66	21.53	–	2
Ghaffar Kazmi	13	21	2	401	110*	21.10	1	2
Amiruddin	10	17	1	330	42	20.62	–	–

	M	Inns	NO	Runs	HS	Av	100s	50s
Javed Sami	15	27	3	449	102	18.70	1	–
Mujahid Jamshed	12	19	2	311	93	18.29	–	2
Wasim Yousufi	16	22	1	366	51*	17.42	–	1

(Qualification – 300 runs)

BOWLING

	Overs	Mds	Runs	Wkts	Av	Best	10/m	5/inn
Hasnain Kazim	188	34	589	38	15.50	7-54	1	4
Tauseef Ahmed	389.5	130	702	45	15.60	6-28	1	2
Murtaza Hussain	191.2	59	387	24	16.12	7-65	–	2
Aamer Nazir	331	57	1163	68	17.10	6-52	1	8
Mohammad Aslam	194.2	36	535	31	17.25	7-52	1	2
Mohammad Akram	164	47	456	26	17.53	5-46	–	2
Ali Gohar	173.3	34	549	31	17.70	7-92	1	2
Saqlain Mushtaq	445	121	948	52	18.23	7-66	1	4
Maqsood Rana	151.4	29	520	28	18.57	6-26	1	2
Arshad Khan	676.5	161	1558	80	19.47	8-115	1	8
Bilal Raha	266.4	84	591	30	19.70	4-31	–	–
Azhar Mahmood	187	40	536	27	19.85	5-36	–	1
Abdul Qadir	350.3	48	1041	52	20.01	7-67	2	5
Masood Anwar	289	87	660	32	20.62	8-72	1	2
Iqbal Imam	227.3	54	533	25	21.32	7-66	–	1
Nadeem Khan	502.4	134	1196	56	21.35	5-28	2	5
Mohammad Hussain	338.1	99	857	40	21.42	6-90	1	3
Naeem Tayyab	230.1	45	579	27	21.44	6-31	–	3
Shahid Hussain	342	130	754	35	21.54	4-14	–	–
Asadullah Butt	285.4	66	907	42	21.59	6-64	1	2
Zafar Iqbal	272.5	66	906	41	22.09	7-60	–	2
Tauqir Hussain	261.1	66	606	27	22.44	6-53	1	2
Raja Afaq	387.5	66	975	41	23.78	7-55	–	4
Naeem Ashraf	421	69	1265	53	23.86	7-53	1	5
Haaris A. Khan	515.2	142	1181	49	24.10	5-53	–	2
Imran Adil	242.4	40	735	30	24.50	6-44	–	3
Mohammad Asif	665.5	168	1447	59	24.52	5-40	–	2
Javed Hayat	337	86	739	30	24.63	4-40	–	–
Sajid Shah	251.2	44	816	33	24.72	7-77	1	2
Manzoor Elahi	148	33	497	20	24.85	6-102	1	1
Mohammad Javed	210.2	34	657	26	25.26	5-53	–	1
Farrukh Zaman	337.1	71	815	32	25.46	7-63	–	1
Sajjad Ali	176.3	26	586	23	25.47	5-76	–	1
Mohammad Nawaz	214.4	45	513	20	25.65	4-41	–	–
Ata-ur-Rehman	220.4	37	783	30	26.10	6-74	–	1
Hafeez-ur-Rehman	235.2	63	575	22	26.13	5-54	–	1
Lal Faraz	211.5	46	689	26	26.50	5-54	–	2
Athar Laeeq	471	85	1617	60	26.95	8-65	1	2
Nadeem Afzal	360.3	52	1251	43	29.09	6-63	–	3
Mohammad Ali	213.3	30	802	24	33.41	5-64	–	1
Manzoor Akhtar	286.3	45	893	23	38.82	3-61	–	–
Shahid Mahmood	335	30	1224	31	39.48	4-76	–	–

(Qualification – 20 wickets)

LEADING FIELDERS

47 – Rifaqat Ali (ct 41/st 6); 39 – Moin Khan (ct 31/st 8); 38 – Wasim Arif (ct 33/st 5); 37 – Wasim Yousufi (ct 36/st 1); 30 – Saifullah (ct 26/st 4); 29 – Tahir Rasheed (ct 28/st 1); 28 – Bilal Ahmed (ct 22/st 6) and Sajid Ali; 24 – Ijaz Ahmed jr and Manzoor Akhtar; 20 – Javed Sami; 19 – Mahmood Hamid; 17 – Iqbal Saleem (ct 11/st 6) and Alay Haider; 16 – Nadeem Abbasi, Tariq Mahmood and Mohammad Ramzan

INDIA

Irani Cup

Duleep Trophy

Triangular Tournament – India, West Indies and New Zealand

West Indies tour, Test and one-day series

England 'A' tour

Ranji Trophy

First-class averages

Mohammad Azharuddin – the most successful Test captain in the history of Indian cricket.
(Adrian Murrell/Allsport)

Having returned victorious from the four-nation tournament in Sri Lanka, India faced a seemingly unending series of one-day internationals. The West Indians arrived in the country for a three-match Test series which was to be accompanied by five limited-over internationals, as well as a three-nation competition involving New Zealand. A tour by an England 'A' side was to occupy the first two months of 1995, after which India would fly to New Zealand for another four-nation one-day series. From New Zealand, they flew to Sharjah for one more limited-over competition.

The outcome of all this was that India, even with the retirement of Shastri and the fading power of Kapil Dev, able to field the strongest Test side in their history, were to play just three Tests but more than 20 one-day internationals in the space of eight months. It will therefore surprise no one to learn that the Indian season began with a one-day competition – the Wills Trophy – which was notable for the fact that both Desmond Haynes and Angus Fraser appeared in the Wills XI. Bombay won the tournament.

IRANI CUP
BOMBAY v. REST OF INDIA

12, 13, 14, 15 and 16 October 1994 *at Wankhede Stadium, Bombay*

Bombay 424 (Z. Bharucha 164 not out, S.V. Manjrekar 117, S.S. Dighe 57, Iqbal Siddiqui 4 for 106, A.R. Kapoor 4 for 121) and 151 for 4 (A.A. Muzumdar 55 not out, S.V. Manjrekar 52)

Rest of India 193 (V. Rathore 60, S.V. Bahutule 7 for 63) and 485 for 6 dec. (R.S. Dravid 132 not out, V. Rathore 115, V. Yadav 111, M.K. Obaid 69)

Match drawn

There was some anger that no selectors were present on the first day of what has always been regarded as a Test trial. They missed Manjrekar scoring 70 before lunch on a pitch on which the occasional delivery kept low. Manjrekar, dropped at slip off Obaid on 19, made 117 out of a second-wicket stand of 163 with Bharucha. Manjrekar faced 134 balls and hit a six and 21 fours before aiming to hook a ball that kept low. Muzumdar was caught behind, and Sulashan Kulkarni was caught at mid-wicket, but Dighe, out just before the close, stopped the rot. Bombay ended the day on 311 for 6.

They were all out 30 minutes after lunch on the second day when Bharucha became only the second opener to carry his bat through an innings in the Irani Cup. Gavaskar had first achieved the feat 20 years earlier. Bharucha batted for 539 minutes, faced 391 balls and hit 16 fours.

Vikram Rathore and Ajay Mehra gave the Rest a solid start with 84 in 17.4 overs, but thereafter batsmen floundered against the leg-spin of Bahutule who had been preferred to Hirwani.

Forced to follow on on the third day, which was over-

cast and on which play began late, the Rest reached 81 for 1 in their second innings. The pitch was at its best on the fourth day, and, aided by some poor fielding, Rathore and night-watchman Obaid added 116 in 31.4 overs. Rathore batted impressively, and Dravid and Yadav added a record 224 in 53 overs for the sixth wicket. Dravid hit a six and 11 fours in his 206-ball innings, but Yadav adopted a one-day approach. His swashbuckling knock occupied 164 balls and included 15 fours.

Amre's declaration left Bombay 62 overs in which to score 255 to win. The loss of two quick wickets to Prashant Vaidya put Bombay on the defensive, and although Manjrekar and Muzumdar later attempted to challenge once more, a draw was inevitable, and the match was called off after eight mandatory overs.

Bombay took the trophy on account of their first-innings lead. It was their 13th Irani Cup success since 1959–60.

DULEEP TROPHY

25, 26, 27, 28 and 29 October 1994 *at Burnpur CC Ground, Orissa*

West Zone 399 (A.A. Muzumdar 144, S.S. Dighe 102 not out, S.S. Bhave 61) and 241 for 3 (S.S. Bhave 107 not out, A.A. Muzumdar 77)

Central Zone 449 (P.K. Amre 147, R. Shamshed 127, A.R. Khurasiya 70, S.V. Bahutule 4 for 90)

Match drawn

Central Zone 2 pts, West Zone 0 pts

at Keenan Stadium, Jamshedpur

South Zone 454 (W.V. Raman 107, S. Sharath 75, R.S. Dravid 67, A. Vaidya 57, Abinash Kumar 4 for 82) and 386 for 5 dec. (R.S. Dravid 148, J. Arun Kumar 68, Robin Singh 64, S. Sharath 52 not out)

East Zone 313 (S.S. Karim 83, R. Biswal 80, Kanawaljit Singh 6 for 91)

Match drawn

South Zone 2 pts, East Zone 0 pts

Amol Muzumdar followed the 260 he scored on the occasion of his debut in the Ranji Trophy in February with an innings of 144 in his first game in the Duleep Trophy. West Zone were 8 for 2 when Muzumdar joined Surendra Bhave. The pair added 124, and Muzumdar batted into the second day. West Zone were further roused by Dighe, who was also playing in his first Duleep Trophy match. He hit 14 fours in his unbeaten 102 which came in 293 minutes. In spite of the loss of three wickets for 12 runs on the fourth day, Central took a first-innings lead, thanks to Rizwan Shamshed's responsible knock. On the last day, Surendra Bhave became the fifth centurion in a match destined to be drawn.

The loss of two wickets before lunch on the opening day

Ajay Kamar Sharma, a capable left-arm spinner and a prolific run-scorer for North Zone and Delhi. (Adrian Murrell/Allsport)

put South Zone on the defensive at Jamshedpur. They were rallied by skipper Raman and by Rahul Dravid, and consistent application saw South Zone bat into the third day. East Zone closed on a miserable 153 for 5, but a sixth-wicket stand of 164 between Karim and Biswal enabled them to avoid the follow-on on the fourth day. After this the South indulged in batting practice, with Dravid scoring the second century of the match.

3, 4, 5, 6 and 7 November 1994 *at Maligaon Railway Stadium, Guwahati*

Central Zone 205 (Abhay Sharma 73, P.K. Amre 51,
    A.R. Kapoor 5 for 86) and 311 (Abhay Sharma 85,
    R. Shamshed 70, A.R. Kapoor 5 for 121)
North Zone 600 (A.K. Sharma 202, V. Rathore 149,
    Rajesh Puri 88 not out)

North Zone won by an innings and 84 runs

North Zone 6 pts, Central Zone 0 pts

at Keenan Stadium, Jamshedpur

East Zone 306 (Snehasish Ganguly 80, Saurav Ganguly 56,
    Iqbal Siddiqui 4 for 48) and 177 (S. Banerjee 51, S.V. Jedhe
    5 for 68)
West Zone 349 (S.S. Sugwekar 84 not out, S.V. Manjrekar 73,
    U. Chatterjee 5 for 117) and 135 for 1 (S.S. Bhave 70
    not out, S.V. Manjrekar 51 not out)

West Zone won by 9 wickets

West Zone 6 pts, East Zone 0 pts

A third-wicket stand of 304 between Ajay Sharma and Vikram Rathore put North Zone in a position of total command against Central Zone. Rathore hit 3 sixes and 7 fours while Ajay Sharma, rejected by the Test selectors, hit 13 fours and 3 sixes. Off-spinner Ashish Kapoor took 10 wickets in a match for the first time to help his side to an overwhelming victory.

A ninth-wicket stand of 93 between Snehasish Ganguly and Avinash Kumar saved East Zone from complete collapse on the second day at Jamshedpur. Captain and vice-captain, Manjrekar and Sugwekar, batted with sense and flair to give West Zone first-innings points; East Zone, with Roy unable to bat, were bundled out for a paltry 177 in their second innings; and Bhave and Manjrekar scored at more than four runs an over to take the West to victory with some quarter of an hour remaining.

12, 13, 14, 15 and 16 November 1994 *at District Sports Association Ground, Silchar*

North Zone 276 (P. Dharmani 50, P. Mhambrey 5 for 68) and
    389 (Bhupinder Singh jr 91, Bhupinder Singh sr 85 not out,
    A.K. Sharma 82, S.A. Ankola 5 for 42)
West Zone 186 (S.S. Sugwekar 65, B. Vij 5 for 60) and
    318 for 5 (N.R. Odedra 90, S.S. Bhave 71, A.A. Muzumdar
    58 not out)

Match drawn

North Zone 2 pts, West Zone 0 pts

at Eden Gardens, Calcutta

Central Zone 263 (G. Khoda 73, Y. Khare 58,
    K.N.A. Padmanabhan 6 for 78) and 156 (Kanwaljit Singh
    7 for 32)
South Zone 313 (W.V. Raman 107, Robin Singh 63,
    M.S. Doshi 5 for 74, N.D. Hirwani 4 for 78) and 107 for 1
    (J. Arun Kumar 65 not out)

South Zone won by 9 wickets

South Zone 6 pts, Central Zone 0 pts

The bowling of Wassan, Bhupinder Singh senior and Vij put the North in total control, and their dominance was emphasised by a second-wicket stand of 154 between Bhupinder Singh senior and Ajay Sharma when they batted for a second time. Needing 480 to win, West Zone were given a good start by Odedra and Bhave who put on 121, but a draw became inevitable.

At Eden Gardens, a newly laid pitch gave aid to the spinners, and leg-spinner Anant Padmanabhan tore apart Central Zone's middle-order after Yadav and Khoda had put on 122 for the first wicket. A fifth-wicket stand of 95 between Raman and Robin Singh gave South Zone first-innings points. Skipper Raman hit a sparkling century, and Kanwaljit Singh returned the best bowling figures of his career with his off-breaks to set up an easy win for the South Zone.

21, 22, 23, 24 and 25 November 1994 *at Eden Gardens, Calcutta*

Central Zone 469 (S. Shukla 132, R. Shamshed 86,
    G.K. Pandey 74, A.R. Khurasiya 66) and 106 for 1
    (Abhay Sharma 53 not out)
East Zone 274 (S.S. Karim 103 retired hurt, N.D. Hirwani
    6 for 76)

Match drawn

Central Zone 2 pts, East Zone 0 pts

at Moin-ul-Haq Stadium, Patna

South Zone 315 (Robin Singh 155, M.K. Obaid 4 for 100) and
    157 (S. Sharath 54 not out, A.S. Wassan 6 for 81)
North Zone 456 (A.K. Sharma 172, A.R. Kapoor 79,
    S. Subramaniam 4 for 144) and 20 for 0

North Zone won by 10 wickets

North Zone 6 pts, South Zone 0 pts

Both East and Central Zones were out of the running for the Duleep Trophy when they met at Eden Gardens. No play was possible on the fourth day because of rain.

Coming to the wicket with the score on 23 for 3, Robin Singh played a masterly innings and shared in two century stands to take South Zone to 315. A rain-truncated third day saw North Zone take first-innings points, with Ajay Sharma, the captain, leading by example with a splendid innings of 172 which gave further embarrassment to the selectors who had omitted him from the national squad. Trailing by 141, South Zone collapsed against Wassan and Obaid, losing their first seven wickets for 74 runs, and the game was over in four days.

The win left North Zone needing just two points from their last fixture to claim the trophy.

30 November, 1, 2, 3 and 4 December 1994 *at Ispat Stadium, Rourkela*

South Zone 233 (S. Sharath 80 not out, Robin Singh 61,
    M.S. Narula 4 for 24) and 531 for 5 (W.V. Raman
    250 not out, J. Arun Kumar 117, R.S. Dravid 63)
West Zone 566 (S.S. Bhave 292)

Match drawn

West Zone 2 pts, South Zone 0 pts

at Eden Gardens, Calcutta

East Zone 250 (Saurav Ganguly 59, R.B. Biswal 58 not out,
    B. Vij 4 for 56) and 411 for 7 (Saurav Ganguly 114,
    D. Gandhi 110, C.M. Sharma 71)
North Zone 716 (Bantoo Singh 214, A.R. Kapoor 181,
    V. Rathore 75, Bhupinder Singh jr 55, U. Chatterjee 4 for 176)

Match drawn

North Zone 2 pts, East Zone 0 pts

Bowled out for a modest 233 in their first innings, South Zone were then savaged by Surendra Bhave who hit the highest score of his career and took the West Zone to their record score in the competition. Batting with more discipline at the second attempt, South Zone were indebted to Arun Kumar and Raman who added 142 for the second wicket. Both batsmen reached centuries, with skipper Raman reaching 250 on the final day.

East Zone struggled painfully against North Zone who were soon in total command. Bantoo Singh and Ashish Kapoor put on 283 for the seventh wicket. Saurav Ganguly and Devang Gandhi scored second-innings centuries to restore some pride to East Zone, who finished the competition without a point.

DULEEP TROPHY FINAL TABLE

	P	W	L	D	Pts
North Zone	4	2	–	2	16
West Zone	4	1	–	3	8
South Zone	4	1	1	2	8
Central Zone	4	–	2	2	4
East Zone	4	–	1	3	0

TRIANGULAR TOURNAMENT

The bizarre fixture schedule of the Indian season allowed the Triangular Tournament between India, West Indies and New Zealand to take place in the middle of the one-day series between India and West Indies. This meant that the opening match of the three-nation competition was actually the third one-day international to be played between India and West Indies in the space of seven days. West Indies introduced Sherwin Campbell to international cricket, but he went cheaply as he pressed for quick runs late in the innings. Put in to bat, West Indies owed much to Lara and Hooper who added 112 for the third wicket. Three wickets then fell for two runs, and the final total was disappointing. Sachin Tendulkar showed his increasing worth as a bowler in limited-over cricket. Skipper Azharuddin played by far the best innings of the day to take his side to victory with 10 balls to spare.

New Zealand felt cruelly treated in the second match of the tournament when a thunderstorm caused abandonment when they were in a winning position. Walsh had chosen to bat first when he won the toss, and West Indies seemed well placed as Williams and Lara added 67 for the second wicket. Lara was stumped off Hart, and his show of dissent cost him 50% of his match fee and a one-match suspension from referee Subba Row. Parore claimed four more victims to equal the wicket-keeping record for New Zealand in a one-day international, while Hart went on to establish a record with his 5 for 22. The New Zealand squad was weakened by the absence of both Crowe and Morrison with injuries. Larsen was unavailable for the tour.

There was more dismay for the New Zealanders at Baroda. They chose to bat first on a moist pitch, lost two wickets for 27 and were revived by Rutherford and Parore who added 180 for the third wicket. Parore, out in the last over of the innings, made his highest one-day score, and Rutherford reached his first century in one-day international cricket. His spectacular 108 came off 104 balls and included 13 fours. New Zealand were well satisfied with their 269 from 50 overs, but Tendulkar and Prabhakar began the Indian innings with a partnership of 144. Tendulkar refound the form he had discovered in Sri Lanka and hit 115 off 138 balls with 3 sixes and 9 fours. He was out when Nash diverted a fierce drive onto the stumps at the bowler's end. India won with ease, but New Zealand mused on the fact that de Groen had missed a caught-and-bowled chance offered by Tendulkar when he was on eight.

The match at Kanpur caused controversy and resulted in India being penalised two points. Simmons and Williams gave West Indies a fine start with a stand of 115, and Arthurton and Holder, playing in place of the suspended Lara, added 89 for the fourth wicket. Facing a target of 258, India appeared to be maintaining the required run rate. Tendulkar began with a flurry, and there was a positive contribution from Azharuddin. Prabhakar held the innings together, and when he was joined by Mongia 63 runs were needed from 43 balls. The pair showed no sense of urgency and were content to bat out the last seven overs for a meagre 16 runs. There was unruly crowd behaviour, and the outcome was that Prabhakar and Mongia were dropped from the rest of the competition, being replaced in the party by Dravid and Yadav, and referee Subba Row deducted two points from India as he considered their lack of effort was unfair on the other two sides engaged in the tournament.

In the next match, at Guwahati, West Indies won the toss and batted first. Nash bowled Simmons off his pads with a beautiful delivery in the opening over, but thereafter there was mayhem. Hooper reached a century of 107 balls, and he and Lara scored 111 for the third wicket in 21 overs. Arthurton also shared a century stand with Hooper, and West Indies reached a formidable 306. New Zealand were never in contention as leg-spinner Dhanraj returned the best figures of his embryo international career.

New Zealand received another mauling in the final qualifying match. Jadeja and Tendulkar began with a century stand. Jadeja was in excellent form, and the mighty Tendulkar hit 62 off 54 balls. In an unbroken fourth-wicket stand at the close of the innings, Azharuddin and Kambli

Phenomenal scoring at a rapid rate throughout the season by Sachin Tendulkar, one of the world's great batsmen. (Alan Cozzi)

scored 67 off 46 balls. When New Zealand batted, Young was out to the third ball of the innings, and only Parore and Fleming offered serious resistance in a partnership worth 79 off 88 balls. Fleming's 56 came from 48 deliveries.

TRIANGULAR TOURNAMENT QUALIFYING TABLE

	P	W	L	Ab	Pts
India	4	3	1	–	10
West Indies	4	2	1	1	10
New Zealand	4	–	3	1	2

(India deducted two points for giving up the chase against West Indies at Kanpur).

FINAL

Azharuddin won a crucial toss, and India batted. Once again, Jadeja and Tendulkar proved to be an outstanding opening pair and posted another century partnership. Tendulkar revelled in his position as opener, and he hit 66 off 68 deliveries. There was also a magical innings from Azharuddin while Kambli provided solidity in the closing

TRIANGULAR TOURNAMENT – MATCH ONE – INDIA *v.* WEST INDIES
23 October 1994 at M.A. Chidambaram Stadium, Madras

WEST INDIES		
P.V. Simmons	b Srinath	2
S.C. Williams	c Mongia, b Venkatesh Prasad	39
B.C. Lara	lbw, b Tendulkar	74
C.L. Hooper	c and b Kumble	58
*J.C. Adams	c and b Tendulkar	0
S.L. Campbell	st Mongia, b Tendulkar	3
S. Chanderpaul	b Prabhakar	19
A.C. Cummins	run out	16
K.C.G. Benjamin	b Venkatesh Prasad	2
C.A. Walsh (capt)	not out	0
B. St A. Browne	run out	0
Extras	lb 5, w 1, nb 2	8
(49.2 overs)		221

INDIA		
M. Prabhakar	lbw, b Walsh	38
N.S. Sidhu	c Lara, b Walsh	3
S.R. Tendulkar	c Hooper, b Cummins	8
M. Azharuddin (capt)	c Walsh, b Cummins	81
V.G. Kambli	c Hooper, b Benjamin	22
A.D. Jadeja	c Campbell, b Benjamin	21
*N.R. Mongia	not out	24
A.R. Kumble	not out	9
J. Srinath		
R.K. Chauhan		
Venkatesh Prasad		
Extras	lb 1, w 4, nb 14	19
(48.2 overs)	(for 6 wickets)	225

	O	M	R	W
Prabhakar	8	–	37	1
Srinath	7	–	24	1
Venkatesh Prasad	8.2	1	38	2
Chauhan	6	–	46	–
Kumble	10	–	35	1
Tendulkar	10	–	36	3

	O	M	R	W
Walsh	10	1	33	2
Benjamin	10	–	42	2
Cummins	9.2	–	50	2
Browne	8	–	38	–
Simmons	6	–	29	–
Hooper	5	–	32	–

FALL OF WICKETS
1–29, 2–64, 3–176, 4–178, 5–178, 6–202, 7–204, 8–209, 9–221

FALL OF WICKETS
1–17, 2–42, 3–80, 4–136, 5–178, 6–195

Umpires: G. Dharan & P. Saradhy   *Man of the Match:* M. Azharuddin   *India won by 4 wickets*

TRIANGULAR TOURNAMENT – MATCH TWO – NEW ZEALAND *v.* WEST INDIES
26 October 1994 at Fatorada Stadium, Goa

WEST INDIES		
S.C. Williams	run out	24
S.L. Campbell	c Parore, b Pringle	0
B.C. Lara	st Parore, b Hart	32
C.L. Hooper	b Hart	22
P.V. Simmons	c Young, b Hart	0
K.L.T. Arthurton	run out	1
*J.C. Adams	st Parore, b Hart	5
A.C. Cummins	c Parore, b Harris	11
C.A. Walsh (capt)	c Parore, b Hart	0
R. Dhanraj	b Pringle	8
C.E. Cuffy	not out	0
Extras	b 4, lb 7, w 9	20
(39.1 overs)		123

NEW ZEALAND		
B.A. Young	not out	13
B.R. Hartland	hit wkt, b Walsh	6
*A.C. Parore	not out	3
K.R. Rutherford (capt)		
S.P. Fleming		
S.A. Thomson		
C.Z. Harris		
M.N. Hart		
D.J. Nash		
C. Pringle		
R.P. de Groen		
Extras	w 2, nb 1	3
(9 overs)	(for 1 wicket)	25

	O	M	R	W
Pringle	4.1	–	19	2
Nash	8	1	25	–
De Groen	4	–	19	–
Hart	10	2	22	5
Thomson	10	5	19	–
Harris	3	–	8	1

	O	M	R	W
Walsh	5	1	17	1
Cuffy	4	1	8	–

FALL OF WICKETS
1–4, 2–71, 3–92, 4–94, 5–95, 6–97, 7–102, 8–102, 9–123

FALL OF WICKET
1–14

Umpires: K. Murali & B.A. Jamula   *Match abandoned*

TRIANGULAR TOURNAMENT – MATCH THREE – INDIA *v.* NEW ZEALAND
28 October 1994 at IPCL Ground, Baroda

NEW ZEALAND

B.A. Young	c Mongia, **b** Srinath	5
B.R. Hartland	c Kumble, **b** Prabhakar	8
*A.C. Parore	c Kumble, **b** Prabhakar	96
K.R. Rutherford (capt)	run out	108
S.P. Fleming	not out	33
S.A. Thomson	not out	0
C.Z. Harris		
D.J. Nash		
M.N. Hart		
C. Pringle		
R.P. de Groen		
Extras	b **5**, lb **7**, w **2**, nb **5**	19
(50 overs)	(for 4 wickets)	269

INDIA

M. Prabhakar	c and **b** Hart	74
S.R. Tendulkar	run out	115
N.S. Sidhu	c de Groen, **b** Hart	11
M. Azharuddin (capt)	not out	47
V.G. Kambli	not out	12
A.D. Jadeja		
*N.R. Mongia		
A.R. Kumble		
J. Srinath		
Venkatapathy Raju		
Venkatesh Prasad		
Extras	lb **3**, w **9**	12
(48.1 overs)	(for 3 wickets)	271

	O	M	R	W
Prabhakar	10	–	49	2
Srinath	10	1	41	1
Venkatesh Prasad	10	–	49	–
Venkatapathy Raju	7	–	39	–
Kumble	10	–	53	–
Tendulkar	3	–	26	–

	O	M	R	W
Pringle	9.1	–	53	–
Nash	10	–	51	–
de Groen	9	1	53	–
Hart	10	–	56	2
Harris	5	–	31	–
Thomson	5	–	24	–

FALL OF WICKETS
1–7, 2–27, 3–207, 4–268

FALL OF WICKETS
1–144, 2–162, 3–247

Umpires: S.K. Bansal & Suresh Shastri   *Man of the Match:* S.R. Tendulkar   *India won by 7 wickets*

TRIANGULAR TOURNAMENT – MATCH FOUR – INDIA *v.* WEST INDIES
30 October 1994 at Green Park, Kanpur

WEST INDIES

P.V. Simmons	c Srinath, **b** Tendulkar	65
S.C. Williams	c and **b** Tendulkar	45
C.L. Hooper	lbw, **b** Venkatapathy Raju	1
K.L.T. Arthurton	run out	72
R.I.C. Holder	**b** Srinath	32
A.C. Cummins	run out	14
K.C.G. Benjamin	not out	1
*J.C. Adams		
S. Chanderpaul		
C.A. Walsh (capt)		
C.E. Cuffy		
Extras	lb **18**, w **3**, nb **6**	27
(50 overs)	(for 6 wickets)	257

INDIA

M. Prabhakar	not out	102
S.R. Tendulkar	**b** Cummins	34
N.S. Sidhu	run out	2
M. Azharuddin (capt)	c Cummins, **b** Cuffy	26
V.G. Kambli	run out	16
A.D. Jadeja	run out	9
*N.R. Mongia	not out	4
A.R. Kumble		
J. Srinath		
Venkatapathy Raju		
Venkatesh Prasad		
Extras	lb **9**, w **5**, nb **4**	18
(50 overs)	(for 5 wickets)	211

	O	M	R	W
Prabhakar	6	–	50	–
Srinath	9	–	31	1
Venkatesh Prasad	7	–	36	–
Kumble	10	–	50	–
Venkatapathy Raju	10	1	41	1
Tendulkar	8	–	31	2

	O	M	R	W
Walsh	9	2	20	–
Cuffy	10	–	49	1
Simmons	2	–	19	–
Benjamin	10	1	39	–
Cummins	10	1	39	1
Hooper	8	–	36	–
Arthurton	1	1	–	–

FALL OF WICKETS
1–115, 2–120, 3–130, 4–219, 5–250, 6–257

FALL OF WICKETS
1–56, 2–78, 3–119, 4–169, 5–195

Umpires: Jasbir Singh & C.K. Sathe   *Man of the Match:* K.L.T. Arthurton   *West Indies won by 46 runs*

TRIANGULAR TOURNAMENT – MATCH FIVE – WEST INDIES v. NEW ZEALAND
1 November 1994 at Nehru Stadium, Guwahati

WEST INDIES				NEW ZEALAND		
P.V. Simmons	b Nash		0	B.R. Hartland	b Walsh	9
S.C. Williams	lbw, b Doull		25	B.A. Young	c Williams, b Dhanraj	33
B.C. Lara	c Hart, b Nash		69	*A.C. Parore	run out	9
C.L. Hooper	c Hartland, b Pringle		111	K.R. Rutherford (capt)	b Hooper	13
K.L.T. Arthurton	b Nash		45	S.P. Fleming	c Simmons, b Dhanraj	18
A.C. Cummins	not out		29	S.A. Thomson	st Adams, b Dhanraj	2
R.I.C. Holder	b Pringle		4	C.Z. Harris	lbw, b Arthurton	12
*J.C. Adams	not out		5	M.N. Hart	b Dhanraj	2
C.A. Walsh (capt)				D.J. Nash	not out	30
R. Dhanraj				S.P. Doull	b Arthurton	4
C.E. Cuffy				C. Pringle	not out	21
Extras	b 5, lb 6, w 7		18	Extras	b 4, lb 12, nb 4	20
(50 overs)	(for 6 wickets)		306	(50 overs)	(for 9 wickets)	173

	O	M	R	W		O	M	R	W
Nash	10	1	48	3	Walsh	6	1	18	1
Pringle	9	1	71	2	Cuffy	6	–	13	–
Doull	9	–	65	1	Simmons	7	1	14	–
Hart	5	–	34	–	Cummins	4	–	18	–
Harris	10	–	43	–	Dhanraj	10	2	26	4
Thomson	7	–	34	–	Hooper	10	1	29	1
					Arthurton	5	–	22	2
					Lara	2	–	17	–

FALL OF WICKETS
1–1, 2–45, 3–156, 4–259, 5–272, 6–281

FALL OF WICKETS
1–15, 2–33, 3–60, 4–92, 5–95, 6–95, 7–101, 8–121, 9–125

Umpires: M.R. Singh & S. Banarjee   *Man of the Match:* C.L. Hooper   *West Indies won by 133 runs*

TRIANGULAR TOURNAMENT – MATCH SIX – INDIA v. NEW ZEALAND
3 November 1994 at Ferozeshah Kotla Ground, New Delhi

INDIA				NEW ZEALAND		
A.D. Jadeja	c Hart, b Nash		90	B.A. Young	c Yadav, b Srinath	0
S.R. Tendulkar	b Hart		62	D.J. Murray	run out	3
N.S. Sidhu	c Hart, b de Groen		35	*A.C. Parore	lbw, b Venkatapathy Raju	51
M. Azharuddin (capt)	not out		58	K.R. Rutherford (capt)	c Srinath, b Venkatesh Prasad	8
V.G. Kambli	not out		36	S.P. Fleming	lbw, b Tendulkar	56
*V. Yadav				S.A. Thomson	c Venkatapathy Raju, b Tendulkar	9
C.M. Sharma				C.Z. Harris	c Srinath, b Venkatapathy Raju	16
J. Srinath				M.N. Hart	run out	16
Venkatesh Prasad				D.J. Nash	b Kumble	3
A.R. Kumble				S.B. Doull	st Yadav, b Kambli	8
Venkatapathy Raju				R.P. de Groen	not out	1
Extras	lb 3, w 4, nb 1		8	Extras	lb 3, w 5, nb 3	11
(50 overs)	(for 3 wickets)		289	(45.4 overs)		182

	O	M	R	W		O	M	R	W
Nash	10	–	50	1	Srinath	7	1	22	1
Doull	10	1	58	–	Venkatesh Prasad	7	–	27	1
de Groen	9	–	67	1	Sharma	1	–	23	–
Hart	9	–	36	1	Tendulkar	10	2	29	2
Harris	2	–	24	–	Kumble	10	1	41	1
Thomson	10	–	51	–	Venkatapathy Raju	10	–	30	2
					Kambli	0.4	–	7	1

FALL OF WICKETS
1–100, 2–175, 3–222

FALL OF WICKETS
1–0, 2–12, 3–27, 4–106, 5–132, 6–142, 7–168, 8–172, 9–173

Umpires: R.C. Sharma & P.K. Handoo   *Man of the Match:* S.R. Tendulkar   *India won by 107 runs*

TRIANGULAR TOURNAMENT FINAL – INDIA v. WEST INDIES
5 November 1994 at Eden Gardens, Calcutta

INDIA

Batsman	Dismissal	Runs
A.D. Jadeja	c Lara, b Dhanraj	58
S.R. Tendulkar	c Williams, b Cuffy	66
N.S. Sidhu	c Adams, b Cummins	28
M. Azharuddin (capt)	c Holder, b Hooper	41
V.G. Kambli	not out	58
A.C. Bedade	c Arthurton, b Dhanraj	3
*V. Yadav	lbw, b Walsh	0
A.R. Kumble	not out	1
Venkatapathy Raju		
J. Srinath		
Venkatesh Prasad		
Extras	b 10, lb 5, nb 4	19
(50 overs)	(for 6 wickets)	274

WEST INDIES

Batsman	Dismissal	Runs
P.V. Simmons	run out	21
S.C. Williams	c Azharuddin, b Srinath	29
B.C. Lara	b Venkatesh Prasad	1
C.L. Hooper	c Azharuddin, b Venkatapathy Raju	30
K.L.T. Arthurton	b Venkatapathy Raju	42
R.I.C. Holder	c Jadeja, b Tendulkar	5
*J.C. Adams	c Kumble, b Jadeja	1
A.C. Cummins	b Kumble	21
C.A. Walsh (capt)	c Tendulkar, b Venkatapathy Raju	30
R. Dhanraj	not out	0
C.E. Cuffy	c Kumble, b Venkatapathy Raju	0
Extras	b 2, lb 14, w 5, nb 1	22
(44 overs)		202

Bowler	O	M	R	W
Walsh	10	–	46	1
Cuffy	10	1	53	1
Cummins	10	–	50	1
Hooper	10	–	55	1
Dhanraj	10	–	55	2

Bowler	O	M	R	W
Srinath	7	–	25	1
Venkatesh Prasad	7	3	23	1
Kumble	7	–	27	1
Venkatapathy Raju	10	–	58	4
Tendulkar	8	2	35	1
Jadeja	5	–	18	1

FALL OF WICKETS
1–108, 2–147, 3–175, 4–237, 5–266, 6–267

FALL OF WICKETS
1–46, 2–49, 3–68, 4–101 5–116, 6–121, 7–162, 8–182, 9–202

Umpires: S. Venkataraghavan & V.K. Ramaswamy   *Man of the Match:* S.R. Tendulkar   *India won by 72 runs*

overs. West Indies batted with spirit, but the early dismissal of Lara by Venkatesh Prasad and the spin of Venkatapathy Raju were decisive factors on a pitch which now offered the bowlers some assistance.

Sachin Tendulkar was named Man of the Match and of the series. A crowd of 100,000 watched the final.

WEST INDIES TOUR

From the very beginning, this was not one of the happier tours that a side has made of India. The West Indian party was scheduled to arrive in India in early October and to play two warm-up matches before the first of *six* one-day internationals which had been arranged, as well as the triangular series. The outbreak of pneumonic plague in Surat on 20 September caused the commencement of the tour to be put back some 10 days and the one-day international at Baroda to be cancelled. The match at Jaipur was put back one month.

West Indies were without Richardson, Haynes and Ambrose, who withdrew from the party because of a shoulder injury. The side showed four newcomers in Sherwin Campbell, an opening batsman from Barbados, pace bowlers Cameron Cuffy and Barrington Browne, and leg-spinner Rajindra Dhanraj. Brian Lara, the vice-captain, and Carl Hooper were both fined for missing the team meeting in London on the eve of departure for India.

The touring party was to suffer further problems on the tour through travel arrangements, baggage transportation, theft and crowd behaviour.

14 October 1994 *at Mohali, Chandigarh*

West Indians 245 for 8 (C.L. Hooper 61, K.L.T. Arthurton 50)
Administrator's XI 246 for 5 (A.D. Jadeja 85, A.K. Sharma 65)

Administrator's XI won by 5 wickets

A strong local side led by Kapil Dev beat the tourists with five balls to spare in a 50-over warm-up match.

 ## ONE-DAY INTERNATIONAL SERIES

The first match of the series proved to be a misleading guide for things to come. It was a one-sided affair which West Indies dominated from start to finish. Simmons and Williams, after a cautious beginning which saw 23 runs come from the first 10 overs, batted well, and all the batsmen, save Lara, scored freely. The change in tempo came when Kapil Dev was introduced into the attack. Nineteen runs were hit off one of his overs. It marked the end of a great career for, a few days later, he announced his retirement from first-class cricket. Facing a total of 273, India wilted before Walsh and Cuffy. Sidhu and Bedade recovered some pride after the first four wickets had fallen for 21, but they could never hope to change the result.

At Bombay, before a crowd of 45,000, in a match played for the benefit of Dilip Vengsarkar, West Indies were put in to bat and lost Williams in the fourth over. Lara was again totally out of form, and it was left to Carl Hooper to establish a total of any worth. When India lost both openers for ducks it seemed West Indies would win, but Sidhu, Azharuddin and Kambli edged nearer the target. With rain imminent, Sidhu hit Cummins for six, and this inched India's run rate ahead of West Indies' and so gave them the match.

The third game in the series presented one of those problems that marred the tour. The start of the match was delayed for 45 minutes, and the contest was reduced to 44 overs each after it was revealed that 26 pieces of luggage belonging to the West Indian side were missing. They had inadvertently been taken to Madras and could not be returned to Vishakhapatnam until the morning of the match. Nor did West Indies' troubles end there, for they were fined one over for bowling their quota of 44 too slowly. The highlight of the Indian innings was Sidhu's 115 off 110 balls. He hit 2 sixes and 9 fours and ended his innings with a runner due to an attack of cramp. Hooper, outstanding in the series, gave West Indies hope with 74 from 47 deliveries. He hit 2 sixes and 7 fours, and the last over arrived with 13 runs needed for victory. Prabhakar bowled

Highly successful for India in the one-day triumphs – Ajay Jadeja. (Patrick Eagar)

FIRST ONE-DAY INTERNATIONAL – INDIA v. WEST INDIES
17 October 1994 at Nahar Singh Stadium, Faridabad

WEST INDIES			INDIA		
P.V. Simmons	c Mongia, b Chauhan	76	M. Prabhakar	b Walsh	3
S.C. Williams	c Kumble, b Srinath	61	S.R. Tendulkar	c Lara, b Walsh	0
B.C. Lara	c Azharuddin, b Kumble	10	N.S. Sidhu	c Cummins, b Benjamin	52
C.L. Hooper	not out	61	M. Azharuddin (capt)	c Lara, b Cuffy	1
K.L.T. Arthurton	hit wkt, b Srinath	39	V.G. Kambli	c Adams, b Cuffy	5
A.C. Cummins	c Bedade, b Srinath	0	A.C. Bedade	c Adams, b Benjamin	52
*J.C. Adams	not out	1	Kapil Dev	c Walsh, b Simmons	12
K.C.G. Benjamin			*N.R. Mongia	not out	15
C.A. Walsh (capt)			A.R. Kumble	c Simmons, b Hooper	4
C.E. Cuffy			R.K. Chauhan	c Adams, b Arthurton	20
S. Chanderpaul			J. Srinath	c Simmons, b Hooper	0
Extras	b 6, lb 12, w 5, nb 2	25	Extras	lb 2, w 2, nb 9	13
(50 overs)	(for 5 wickets)	273	(45 overs)		177

	O	M	R	W		O	M	R	W
Prabhakar	10	1	45	–	Walsh	5	–	11	2
Srinath	10	2	42	3	Cuffy	7	2	19	2
Kapil Dev	5	–	37	–	Cummins	7	–	27	–
Kumble	10	–	54	1	Benjamin	8	–	48	2
Tendulkar	5	–	32	–	Simmons	10	1	38	1
Chauhan	10	1	45	1	Hooper	6	–	23	2
					Arthurton	2	–	9	1

FALL OF WICKETS
1–132, 2–148, 3–164, 4–254, 5–254

FALL OF WICKETS
1–2, 2–5, 3–12, 4–21, 5–117, 6–129, 7–135, 8–149, 9–176

Umpires: A. Srinavasan & S.C. Sharma   *Man of the Match:* P.V. Simmons   *West Indies won by 96 runs*

SECOND ONE-DAY INTERNATIONAL – INDIA v. WEST INDIES
20 October 1994 at Wankhede Stadium, Bombay

WEST INDIES						INDIA					
P.V. Simmons	lbw, **b** Venkatesh Prasad				24	M. Prabhakar	c Lara, **b** Walsh				0
S.C. Williams	c Kambli, **b** Srinath				0	S.R. Tendulkar	c Hooper, **b** Cuffy				0
B.C. Lara	c Venkatesh Prasad, **b** Srinath				6	N.S. Sidhu	not out				65
C.L. Hooper	c Mongia, **b** Srinath				70	M. Azharuddin (capt)	c Chanderpaul, **b** Cuffy				34
K.L.T. Arthurton	c Mongia, **b** Kumble				2	V.G. Kambli	c Arthurton, **b** Cummins				17
*J.C. Adams	c Mongia, **b** Venkatesh Prasad				2	A.C. Bedade	not out				11
S. Chanderpaul	run out				22	*N.R. Mongia					
A.C. Cummins	c Tendulkar, **b** Prabhakar				34	Venkatesh Prasad					
C.A. Walsh (capt)	c Bedade, **b** Venkatesh Prasad				3	J. Srinath					
B. St A. Browne	not out				8	A.R. Kumble					
C.E. Cuffy	not out				1	R.K. Chauhan					
Extras	lb **3**, w **13**, nb **4**				20	Extras	lb **1**, w **4**, nb **3**				8
(50 overs)	(for 9 wickets)				192	(33.1 overs)	(for 4 wickets)				135

	O	M	R	W			O	M	R	W
Prabhakar	10	1	34	1		Walsh	7	1	15	1
Srinath	10	2	34	3		Cuffy	8.1	1	29	2
Venkatesh Prasad	10	1	36	3		Cummins	6	–	34	1
Kumble	10	–	42	1		Browne	7	–	27	–
Chauhan	10	1	43	–		Hooper	5	–	29	–

FALL OF WICKETS
1–3, **2**–17, **3**–33, **4**–48, **5**–51, **6**–111, **7**–154, **8**–167, **9**–182

FALL OF WICKETS
1–0, **2**–2, **3**–63, **4**–111

Umpires: R.T. Ramachandran & N. Menon   *Man of the Match:* N.S. Sidhu   *India won on faster scoring rate*

THIRD ONE-DAY INTERNATIONAL – INDIA v. WEST INDIES
7 November 1994 at SE Railway Stadium, Vishakhapatnam

INDIA						WEST INDIES					
A.D. Jadeja	c Murray, **b** Cummins				38	P.V. Simmons	**b** Tendulkar				51
S.R. Tendulkar	c Cummins, **b** Hooper				53	S.C. Williams	run out				49
N.S. Sidhu	not out				115	B.C. Lara	c Venkatapathy Raju, **b** Prabhakar				39
M. Azharuddin (capt)	c Walsh, **b** Arthurton				45	C.L. Hooper	not out				74
V.G. Kambli	c Arthurton, **b** Walsh				0	K.L.T. Arthurton	c Azharuddin, **b** Kumble				13
M. Prabhakar	not out				1	A.C. Cummins	run out				2
*N.R. Mongia						R.I.C. Holder	c Azharuddin, **b** Prabhakar				0
J. Srinath						C.A. Walsh (capt)	**b** Kumble				3
Venkatesh Prasad						*J.R. Murray	not out				3
A.R. Kumble						C.E. Cuffy					
Venkatapathy Raju						B. St A. Browne					
Extras	lb **2**, w **4**, nb **2**				8	Extras	b **2**, lb **15**, w **5**				22
(44 overs)	(for 4 wickets)				260	(43 overs)	(for 7 wickets)				256

	O	M	R	W			O	M	R	W
Browne	5	–	41	–		Prabhakar	9	1	61	2
Walsh	9	–	50	1		Srinath	8	–	31	–
Cuffy	9	–	41	–		Venkatesh Prasad	3	–	26	–
Cummins	7	–	43	1		Kumble	7	–	41	2
Simmons	5	–	23	–		Tendulkar	9	–	39	1
Hooper	7	–	46	1		Venkatapathy Raju	7	–	41	–
Arthurton	2	–	14	1						

FALL OF WICKETS
1–64, **2**–137, **3**–248, **4**–258

FALL OF WICKETS
1–87, **2**–146, **3**–179, **4**–203, **5**–216, **6**–221, **7**–231

Umpires: R.C. Sharma & H.S. Sekhan   *Man of the Match:* N.S. Sidhu   *India won by 4 runs*

FOURTH ONE-DAY INTERNATIONAL – INDIA *v.* WEST INDIES
9 November 1994 at Barbatti Stadium, Cuttack

WEST INDIES				INDIA		
P.V. Simmons	run out	32		A.D. Jadeja	c Cuffy, **b** Walsh	104
S.C. Williams	c Prabhakar, **b** Sharma	15		S.R. Tendulkar	**b** Simmons	88
B.C. Lara	st Mongia, **b** Kumble	89		V.G. Kambli	not out	40
C.L. Hooper	run out	2		M. Azharuddin (capt)	not out	17
K.L.T. Arthurton	c Mongia, **b** Venkatapathy Raju	27		A.C. Bedade		
R.I.C. Holder	not out	36		M. Prabhakar		
S. Chanderpaul	lbw, **b** Jadeja	0		*N.R. Mongia		
*J.R. Murray	c Prabhakar, **b** Jadeja	3		C.M. Sharma		
A.C. Cummins	lbw, **b** Kumble	8		J. Srinath		
C.A. Walsh (capt)	**b** Kumble	0		A.R. Kumble		
C.E. Cuffy	not out	17		Venkatapathy Raju		
Extras	lb **3**, w **10**, nb **9**	22		Extras	lb **1**, w **5**, nb **1**	7
(50 overs)	(for 9 wickets)	251		(49.2 overs)	(for 2 wickets)	256

	O	M	R	W		O	M	R	W
Prabhakar	8	–	36	–	Walsh	10	1	29	1
Srinath	7	–	32	–	Cuffy	10	1	36	–
Sharma	7	1	31	1	Cummins	9.2	–	58	–
Kumble	10	–	43	3	Hooper	4	–	34	–
Tendulkar	2	–	20	–	Arthurton	3	–	28	–
Venkatapathy Raju	6	–	33	1	Simmons	8	–	46	1
Jadeja	10	–	53	2	Chanderpaul	5	–	24	–

FALL OF WICKETS
1–47, 2–67, 3–77, 4–170, 5–191, 6–192, 7–202, 8–228, 9–228

FALL OF WICKETS
1–176, 2–222

Umpires: A.V. Jayaprakash & J. Kurushinkai   *Man of the Match:* A.D. Jadeja   *India won by 8 wickets*

FIFTH ONE-DAY INTERNATIONAL – INDIA *v.* WEST INDIES
11 November 1994 at Sawai Mansingh Stadium, Jaipur

INDIA				WEST INDIES		
A.D. Jadeja	c and **b** Hooper	31		P.V. Simmons	c Azharuddin, **b** Srinath	2
S.R. Tendulkar	**b** Browne	105		S.C. Williams	c Mongia, **b** Sharma	13
V.G. Kambli	c Lara, **b** Cummins	66		B.C. Lara (capt)	lbw, **b** Venkatapathy Raju	47
A.C. Bedade	not out	15		C.L. Hooper	lbw, **b** Venkatapathy Raju	84
M. Azharuddin (capt)	c Simmons, **b** Cummins	2		*J.C. Adams	c Kambli, **b** Kumble	51
C.M. Sharma	c Cuffy, **b** Browne	1		K.L.T. Arthurton	c Azharuddin, **b** Kumble	15
M. Prabhakar	not out	4		R.I.C. Holder	run out	9
*N.R. Mongia				S. Chanderpaul	c Bedade, **b** Prabhakar	8
A.R. Kumble				A.C. Cummins	**b** Venkatapathy Raju	1
J. Srinath				C.E. Cuffy	**b** Venkatapathy Raju	2
Venkatapathy Raju				B. St A. Browne	not out	1
Extras	b **6**, lb **11**, w **9**, nb **9**	35		Extras	b **1**, lb **12**, w **5**, nb **3**	21
(50 overs)	(for 5 wickets)	259		(49 overs)		254

	O	M	R	W		O	M	R	W
Cummins	10	–	49	2	Prabhakar	9	1	35	1
Cuffy	10	–	40	–	Srinath	7	–	42	1
Browne	10	–	50	2	Sharma	10	–	39	1
Hooper	10	1	35	1	Kumble	10	1	46	2
Simmons	5	–	25	–	Venkatapathy Raju	9	–	48	4
Chanderpaul	5	–	43	–	Tendulkar	4	–	31	–

FALL OF WICKETS
1–95, 2–212, 3–239, 4–249, 5–252

FALL OF WICKETS
1–3, 2–50, 3–90, 4–216, 5–218, 6–238, 7–247, 8–251, 9–252

Umpires: Dr S. Chowdury & S. Porel   *Man of the Match:* C.L. Hooper   *India won by 5 runs*

admirably, and only eight were scored, so giving India a narrow victory and leaving West Indies to rue their one lost over.

Brian Lara found his form at Cuttack, but India clinched an unprecedented third win in succession over West Indies. The home side owed much to a superbly controlled opening stand of 176 between Jadeja and Tendulkar who was bowled off his pads by Simmons. Walsh alone of the West Indian bowlers was able to maintain accuracy and economy, and Kenny Benjamin, out with a strained hamstring, was sorely missed. Jadeja was the Indian hero. He reached his first century in a one-day international off 112 balls. He hit 4 fours and 3 sixes, and 104 runs came off the last 21 overs of the innings. India won with four balls to spare.

In the absence of Walsh, Lara led West Indies in the final match. He lost the toss and dropped a catch in the opening over. Tendulkar was again in magnificent form, but Kambli made a vital contribution when he hit Chanderpaul for 16 in one over. Hooper and Adams brought West Indies to the brink of victory with 126 off 125 balls for the fourth wicket. The visitors needed 44 off the last seven overs in order to win the match, but left-arm spinner Venkatapathy Raju was the prime reason that the last seven wickets fell for 38 runs in six overs.

India took the series by four matches to one, and their excellent fielding played a major part in their success.

13, 14 and 15 November 1994 _at M. Chinnaswamy Stadium, Bangalore_

Board President's XI 238 (V. Rathore 64) and 234 for 7
 (P.K. Amre 90, K.C.G. Benjamin 4 for 49)
West Indians 403 (K.L.T. Arthurton 104, J.C. Adams 95,
 P.V. Simmons 91, A.R. Kapoor 6 for 102)

Match drawn

25, 26 and 27 November 1994 _at Calicut_

West Indians 176 (S. Chanderpaul 56, A. Kuruvilla 5 for 42)
Bombay 53 for 2

Match abandoned

At the conclusion of the one-day series, the tourists played a first-class fixture in Bangalore in preparation for the first Test match. Simmons, Adams, Williams and Arthurton confirmed their form while off-spinner Kapoor performed well for the Board President's XI and brought himself into contention for a place in the Indian side.

The match against the Ranji Trophy champions was played between the first and second Tests, but it was abandoned after the first day. The second day was cancelled because of political tension in Calicut, and the West Indians declined to play on the third day in spite of assurances as to their safety. Manager David Holford stated that 'events witnessed by the players standing outside the hotel have done nothing to reassure us that the situation is normal'.

TEST SERIES

In the first Test, at Bombay, West Indies gave first caps to Cameron Cuffy and Rajindra Dhanraj. The Wankhede pitch looked underprepared and was dry and crusty. Azharuddin won the toss and decided to bat, but neither captain could have relished having to make such a decision. Azharuddin must have rued his choice when Prabhakar prodded the second ball of the match, a lifting delivery from Walsh, into the hands of short-leg.

West Indies should have had more success, for Hooper dropped a simple chance at second slip offered by Sidhu off Benjamin. Kambli played a frenetic innings. When he was caught behind off Walsh he had hit 40 off 39 balls. His 7 fours had all come off Walsh in an astonishingly inappropriate innings. Tendulkar, on eight, was put down at first slip by Lara. Benjamin was again the unfortunate bowler, and Sidhu, who batted 89 minutes for his 18, and Tendulkar took India to lunch without further mishap.

The first three overs after the interval, however, appeared to turn the match completely in favour of West Indies. First, Tendulkar was leg before to Walsh. In the next over, Azharuddin was caught off Benjamin, and then Walsh trapped Sidhu leg before. At 99 for 5, with Manjrekar the only recognised batsman remaining, India were in disarray.

Manjrekar had been ignored for the one-day series and, it seemed, had been included in the Test side with some reluctance. He took 38 minutes to open his account, but he then batted with patience and good sense and played some elegant shots either side of the wicket. With Mongia, he added 136, and the wicket-keeper's 80, which included 13 fours, was his highest Test score. Manjrekar was out when he swept at Dhanraj and top-edged the ball to fine leg where Lara, running from slip, held a good catch. This was Dhanraj's first wicket in Test cricket but, like Cuffy, he had seemed overwhelmed by the occasion and had failed to make an impression during the vital stand between Mongia and Manjrekar. Benjamin and Walsh soon disposed of the tail, but India could be content with their 272 on a pitch that promised to get no easier.

Before lunch on the second day, India put down four catches. Williams was dropped twice in one over, and Lara had two escapes before reaching four. Simmons fell to Srinath, but the spinners were soon in operation, and West Indies lunched at 74 for 1. The pattern changed in the afternoon. Lara charged at Raju and was bowled. Hooper attacked, hitting 2 sixes and 3 fours in his 16-ball innings, but he was controversially adjudged caught at slip. Williams' 131-minute vigil ended when he was taken at silly point, but Arthurton and Adams – an impressive batsman on this tour – added 74. Shortly after tea, Arthurton was caught by Tendulkar off the controlled and consistent Raju, and, in spite of Murray's belligerence, the West Indies tail quickly subsided to Raju and Kumble, the last five wickets going down for 13 runs.

Leading by 29 on the first innings, India had eight overs

Inspiring leadership by example for West Indies from Courtney Walsh. (David Munden/Sportsline)

to negotiate before the close. Kenny Benjamin totally undermined India by taking three wickets in two overs, and with the home side 11 for 3, the game had swung very much in favour of West Indies.

There was more controversy at the start of the third day, which was delayed by 45 minutes because repairs to the footholes made by the bowlers had not dried sufficiently. The delay had the effect of allowing much of the moisture in the pitch to disappear before India recommenced their innings. In spite of this, West Indies remained on top. Benjamin dismissed the dogged Sidhu, and Hooper had Azharuddin caught at leg slip off an inside edge after lunch. This left India in trouble at 88 for 5, but Sachin Tendulkar seized the initiative with a masterly display of batsmanship. Using his feet to great advantage, he hit a six and 10 fours, making 85 off 139 balls before being caught as he attempted to cut a ball from Hooper some quarter of an hour before tea. It was his first error of judgement in a faultless display.

Manjrekar continued in his elegant and unhurried manner, and Kumble, having begun with nudges and deflections, hit lustily to record 42 off 68 deliveries. Both fell

FIRST TEST MATCH – INDIA v. WEST INDIES
18, 19, 20, 21 and 22 November 1994 at Wankhede Stadium, Bombay

INDIA

	FIRST INNINGS		SECOND INNINGS	
M. Prabhakar	c Adams, b Walsh	0	c Hooper, b Benjamin	7
N.S. Sidhu	lbw, b Walsh	18	lbw, b Benjamin	12
V.G. Kambli	c Murray, b Walsh	40	(4) c Hooper, b Benjamin	0
S.R. Tendulkar	lbw, b Walsh	34	(5) c Murray, b Hooper	85
M. Azharuddin (capt)	c Simmons, b Benjamin		(6) c Arthurton, b Hooper	17
S.V. Manjrekar	c Lara, b Dhanraj	51	(7) c Cuffy, b Walsh	66
*N.R. Mongia	c Murray, b Benjamin	80	(3) c Adams, b Benjamin	0
A.R. Kumble	c Hooper, b Walsh	19	c Hooper, b Cuffy	42
Venkatapathy Raju	c Hooper, b Walsh	4	(11) not out	3
R.K. Chauhan	c Williams, b Benjamin	1	c Murray, b Walsh	4
J. Srinath	not out	0	(9) st Murray, b Dhanraj	60
Extras	b 5, lb 7, nb 13	25	b 12, lb 14, nb 11	37
		272		333

WEST INDIES

	FIRST INNINGS		SECOND INNINGS	
P.V. Simmons	c Manjrekar, b Srinath	19	c Mongia, b Prabhakar	0
S.C. Williams	c Azharuddin, b Chauhan	49	lbw, b Srinath	11
B.C. Lara	b Raju	14	b Prabhakar	0
C.L. Hooper	c Tendulkar, b Raju	28	c Mongia, b Srinath	23
K.L.T. Arthurton	c Tendulkar, b Raju	42	c Azharuddin, b Raju	20
J.C. Adams	c Kambli, b Raju	39	lbw, b Srinath	81
*J.R. Murray	lbw, b Raju	23	b Chauhan	85
R. Dhanraj	c Mongia, b Kumble	1	c Tendulkar, b Raju	4
K.C.G. Benjamin	c Srinath, b Kumble	0	c Azharuddin, b Raju	2
C.A. Walsh (capt)	not out	2	c and b Srinath	11
C.E. Cuffy	c and b Kumble	0	not out	0
Extras	b 11, lb 12, nb 3	26	b 13, lb 10, nb 6	29
		243		266

	O	M	R	W	O	M	R	W
Walsh	22	4	79	6	28	6	64	2
Benjamin	21.3	8	48	3	24	3	82	4
Cuffy	18	4	63	–	12	2	46	1
Hooper	9	–	23	–	24	4	69	2
Dhanraj	15	1	47	1	10	–	46	1

	O	M	R	W	O	M	R	W
Prabhakar	4	–	18	–	3	–	17	2
Srinath	13	5	37	1	20	8	48	4
Kumble	23.5	7	48	3	12	1	39	–
Chauhan	21	7	57	1	15	3	45	1
Raju	21	7	60	5	28.4	4	85	3
Tendulkar					3	–	9	–

FALL OF WICKETS
1–0, 2–49, 3–96, 4–99, 5–99, 6–235, 7–265, 8–271, 9–272
1–8, 2–10, 3–11, 4–43, 5–88, 6–162, 7–237, 8–265, 9–309

FALL OF WICKETS
1–34, 2–82, 3–120, 4–120, 5–194, 6–230, 7–241, 8–241, 9–242
1–1, 2–2, 3–26, 4–48, 5–82, 6–244, 7–246, 8–252, 9–266

Umpires: H.D. Bird & S.K. Bansal

India won by 96 runs

An Indian hero in the Test series against West Indies, Javagal Srinath who later had considerable success for Gloucestershire. (Patrick Eagar)

before the close, Kumble at last providing Cuffy with a Test wicket, but India ended the day on 287 for 8, a mighty lead of 316.

Unbeaten on 20 at the end of the third day, Srinath launched a violent attack on the bowling on the fourth morning, and 46 runs were added at a run a minute before the innings was brought to an end. Srinath hit a six and 6 fours in his 72-ball knock, but his contribution did not end there.

The first over of West Indies' second innings was bowled by Prabhakar. The second ball of the over saw Simmons reach for an out-swinger and touch the ball to the keeper; the last was dragged into his stumps by Lara. Srinath accounted for Williams – who batted with a hair-line fracture of the thumb – and Hooper, and when Arthurton fell to Raju, West Indies were 82 for 5 three-quarters of an hour into the afternoon. Defeat seemed imminent, but the defiant Adams found a brave partner in Murray. The pair added 162 in 55 overs. Runs came at one a minute, and the bowling showed signs of fraying. Murray made his highest score in Test cricket and was out when he played back to Chauhan, to be bowled between bat and pad. Four balls later, Adams was gone too, and when Benjamin fell in the last over of the day, West Indies' hopes evaporated.

The match ended 22 minutes into the last day. Srinath was named man of an absorbing match, and India record-ed their 10th victory under Azharuddin, who thereby became the most successful captain in Indian Test history.

India were unchanged for the second Test while West Indies brought in Cummins and Chanderpaul for Cuffy and Dhanraj, neither of whom had impressed on their debuts. Azharuddin won the toss, and India batted well on a first day that was to be blighted by two interruptions due to members of the crowd throwing missiles at West Indian fielders. Almost an hour's play was lost as Walsh, rightly, led his team off the field. It was not the first time on the tour that West Indies had been subjected to such abuse.

The pitch lacked pace, and Sidhu and Prabhakar set about laying a solid foundation to the Indian innings. Prabhakar and Kambli squandered their wickets when they attempted to hit Hooper over the top of the set field and were caught. Kambli was brilliantly held by Williams at mid-off. Sidhu and Tendulkar stayed together until 10 minutes before the close when the opener was caught behind. Sidhu had hit 17 fours and faced 231 balls. He blended careful defence with his natural aggression. As an opener, he has undergone a remarkable and worthy trans-formation in the past two years.

India began the second morning on 230 for 4, having lost night-watchman Raju in the last over of the first day. Tendulkar was on 81, and he powered to his century off 184 balls early on the second day when he hooked Walsh for six. He played some imperious shots, but he was twice missed by Benjamin who failed to accept a return chance when the batsman was on 114, and failed to reach a more

difficult offering off Adams when Tendulkar was on 144. In the first session of the day, 135 runs came, and it was not until 65 minutes after lunch that West Indies had their first success.

Azharuddin had been irresistible, driving and glancing with eager majesty before being taken at backward short-leg off Hooper, but by then his magnificent batting had brought him 15 fours and his 97 runs had come from 119 balls. In 185 minutes, he and Tendulkar had added 202 runs.

The fall of Azharuddin was followed in Hooper's next over by the dismissal of Manjrekar in an identical manner; and Tendulkar was out to a spectacular catch at mid-wicket by Lara off Walsh. West Indies' troubles were far from over, however, for Mongia and Kumble now thrashed 93 in under two hours. Requiring 347 to avoid the follow-on, West Indies lost Williams, caught bat and pad, in the penultimate over of the day and closed on 15 for 1.

India's sole pre-lunch success on the third morning was night-watchman Cummins, but Simmons and Lara, who both batted with restraint and determination, were out in the afternoon. This brought together Adams and Hooper, the two batsmen who had shown consistently that they could cope with the Indian spinners. They were aided by the fact that Kumble was forced to bowl round the wicket after being warned by umpire Plews for running on the pitch, but this should not detract from the quality of their batting. In 136 minutes, they added 133 runs. Adams adopted the passive role while Hooper displayed his ele-gant belligerence with 81 off 118 balls, an innings which included 2 sixes and 10 fours. By the end of the day, West Indies were 302 for 5, and a point of safety had almost been reached.

That it was reached was due to Adams and Murray, for, on the fourth morning, with the ball turning sharply, Arthurton and Chanderpaul went quickly. Murray joined Adams to save the follow-on, and the pair added 97 in two hours. Murray bludgeoned effectively, hitting 5 fours in his second Test fifty, while Adams batted with supreme concentration and skill. He finished unbeaten on 125 which included 14 fours and came off 312 deliveries in 408 minutes.

Leading by 118 on the first innings, India ended the fourth day on 95 for 2, and there was disappointment that neither Sidhu nor Tendulkar batted with the purposeful aggression that the occasion demanded, particularly as Walsh had been forced to withdraw from the attack with a cricked neck after taking two quick wickets.

There was some urgency on the last morning, and wickets fell as India pressed for a declaration. West Indies were set the improbable task of scoring 327 in 62 overs. They negotiated three overs before lunch without difficulty, but early in the afternoon Williams was beaten in the air and bowled by Raju, Lara taken in the slips as he drove unwisely at the same bowler, and Simmons caught at mid-on when he drove across the line at Kumble. At 22 for 3, West Indies faced defeat, but Adams and Hooper again came to the rescue. They were dismissed in quick succession after adding 90 in 131 minutes, and West Indies were still in danger at 115 for 5 with 17 overs remaining. Arthurton and Chanderpaul resisted stoutly, and the match was drawn.

India should have won, but they had failed to force their advantage on the fourth afternoon, and their spinners had been below their usual standard. Hooper won the individual award.

Cuffy replaced Chanderpaul in the West Indian side for the final Test, and India made their first change in the series, Ashish Kapoor coming in for fellow off-spinner Chauhan. The new stadium at Mohali, not completely finished, became the 74th ground to stage a Test match. Walsh, who had decided to risk playing in spite of his injured neck, won the toss and chose to bat.

India had dominated the first two Tests, and there were hints that they would dominate again as the early stages of the third encounter went in their favour. Had Azharuddin persevered longer with the impressive Prabhakar, India might well have taken complete command, but the Indian skipper chose to rely mainly on Srinath for pace, and his line was wayward. Srinath, however, did make the breakthrough, having Simmons caught behind, and Williams fell to the last ball before lunch. Lara did not last long into the afternoon. Again, Hooper and Adams gave the innings substance, scoring briskly in a partnership of 92. Hooper provided Kapoor with his first Test wicket. He was beaten in the air by a beautifully flighted delivery and stumped by Manjrekar who was temporarily substituting for

SECOND TEST MATCH – INDIA *v.* WEST INDIES
1, 2, 3, 4 and 5 December 1994 at Vidarbha CA Ground, Nagpur

INDIA

	FIRST INNINGS		SECOND INNINGS	
M. Prabhakar	c Williams, b Hooper	19	c Lara, b Walsh	6
N.S. Sidhu	c Murray, b Hooper	107	c Simmons, b Hooper	76
V.G. Kambli	c Williams, b Hooper	0	b Walsh	6
S.R. Tendulkar	c Lara, b Walsh	179	c Arthurton, b Benjamin	54
Venkatapathy Raju	c Adams, b Walsh	2		
M. Azharuddin (capt)	c Simmons, b Hooper	97	(5) not out	32
S.V. Manjrekar	c Simmons, b Hooper	0	(6) c Murray, b Benjamin	5
*N.R. Mongia	c Hooper, b Cummins	44	run out	11
A.R. Kumble	not out	52	not out	3
J. Srinath	c and b Chanderpaul	6	(7) lbw, b Hooper	1
R.K. Chauhan	not out	1		
Extras	b 12, lb 9, nb 18	39	b 3, lb 5, nb 6	14
		—		—
	(for 9 wickets, dec.)	546	(for 7 wickets, dec.)	208

WEST INDIES

	FIRST INNINGS		SECOND INNINGS	
P.V. Simmons	c Manjrekar, b Kumble	50	c Sidhu, b Kumble	8
S.C. Williams	c Azharuddin, b Chauhan	12	b Raju	8
A.C. Cummins	c Manjrekar, b Raju	17		
B.C. Lara	c Mongia, b Raju	50	(3) c Tendulkar, b Raju	3
J.C. Adams	not out	125	(4) c Tendulkar, b Kumble	23
C.L. Hooper	c Prabhakar, b Srinath	81	(5) c Azharuddin, b Kumble	67
K.L.T. Arthurton	c Azharuddin, b Raju	7	(6) not out	7
S. Chanderpaul	c Azharuddin, b Raju	4	(7) not out	11
*J.R. Murray	lbw, b Raju	54		
K.C.G. Benjamin	lbw, b Kumble	0		
C.A. Walsh (capt)	b Kumble	1		
Extras	b 5, lb 14, nb 8	27	b 2, nb 3	5
		—		—
		428	(for 5 wickets)	132

	O	M	R	W	O	M	R	W
Walsh	32	7	93	2	5.5	3	2	2
Benjamin	26	4	120	2	13.4	1	69	2
Cummins	27	1	96	1	15	–	57	–
Hooper	40	8	116	5	25.1	6	62	2
Chanderpaul	20	4	63	1				
Adams	10	2	37	–	4	2	10	–

	O	M	R	W	O	M	R	W
Prabhakar	4	1	15	–				
Srinath	14	2	39	1	7	2	12	–
Chauhan	34	9	97	1	5	3	15	–
Raju	50	11	127	5	27	4	58	2
Kumble	51	15	131	3	23	7	45	3

FALL OF WICKETS
1–48, 2–49, 3–226, 4–230, 5–432, 6–434, 7–444, 8–537, 9–543
1–9, 2–24, 3–152, 4–157, 5–163, 6–174, 7–193

FALL OF WICKETS
1–15, 2–61, 3–98, 4–155, 5–288, 6–306, 7–320, 8–417, 9–422
1–18, 2–18, 3–22, 4–112, 5–115

Umpires: N.T. Plews & V.K. Ramaswamy

Match drawn

Mongia behind the stumps. Arthurton hit 2 fours and a six and perished with undue haste, while Murray continued his determined, positive and excellent work with the bat before falling to Kumble. Adams remained unbeaten on 84, and West Indies closed on 296 for 6.

Cummins stayed long enough with Adams for the seventh-wicket partnership to be worth 99, and the tail-enders offered support, if not runs, while Adams took his score to a career-best 174 not out. It was his second century in successive Tests, and it took him 452 minutes of resolution. He hit 19 fours and faced 371 balls.

Walsh achieved an instant breakthrough when he induced Sidhu to play a bouncer into his stumps, but Manjrekar was twice dropped, and India reached 95 for 1 at the end of the second day. A draw seemed to beckon.

Nothing that happened on the third day suggested a change in this view in spite of the early dismissal of Manjrekar. Tendulkar played a whirlwind innings – there were 9 fours in his 40 – but Prabhakar remained solid. He was fifth out, having hit 16 fours and faced 275 balls in 406 minutes, and although the second new ball brought five wickets, of which Prabhakar's was the second, for 61 runs, Srinath and Raju showed defiance for the last wicket which took the innings into the fourth morning and brought India to within 56 runs of West Indies' total.

With Williams unwell, Lara opened the West Indies' second innings with Simmons, and 41 runs came from the first four overs to make clear Walsh's orders and intentions. The first wicket produced 85 in as many minutes, and Lara batted better than he had done at any time on the tour, showing discipline and fluency. When he was third out, walking in response to an appeal to which the umpire could give no ready decision, West Indies were 156 for 3 from 31 overs. In the next 25 overs, Adams and Arthurton plundered 145 runs. Adams capped a marvellous series by showing that he had the very best of batting qualities, the ability to match his mood to the needs of his side.

Walsh declared 55 minutes into the final session, and India had an early mishap when Prabhakar was struck in the face by a ball from Walsh. He was taken to hospital where stitches were inserted into a wound in the nose, and he took no further part in the match. Shortly after this sad event, Sidhu was leg before to Benjamin, and India limped to the close on 37 for 1.

There seemed no reason why India should not bat out the final day and so win the series, but we had reckoned without the genius and inspiration of Walsh and the venom of Kenny Benjamin. The fast-bowling pair touched great heights of pace and hostility, and seven wickets went down in the first 10 overs of the day. India offered poor

---

THIRD TEST MATCH – INDIA v. WEST INDIES
10, 11, 12, 13 and 14 December 1994 at Punjab CA Stadium, Mohali, Chandigarh

WEST INDIES

	FIRST INNINGS		SECOND INNINGS	
P.V. Simmons	c Mongia, b Srinath	10	run out	25
S.C. Williams	lbw, b Kumble	34		
B.C. Lara	lbw, b Srinath	40	(2) c Mongia, b Raju	91
J.C. Adams	not out	174	not out	78
C.L. Hooper	st Manjrekar, b Kapoor	43	(3) lbw, b Raju	20
K.L.T. Arthurton	c Kapoor, b Raju	18	(5) not out	70
*J.R. Murray	lbw, b Kumble	31		
A.C. Cummins	lbw, b Raju	50		
C.A. Walsh (capt)	lbw, b Kumble	4		
K.C.G. Benjamin	lbw, b Kumble	0		
C.E. Cuffy	b Raju	1		
Extras	b 6, lb 13, w 5, nb 14	38	b 10, lb 4, nb 3	17
		443	(for 3 wickets, dec.)	301

INDIA

	FIRST INNINGS		SECOND INNINGS	
M. Prabhakar	c Murray, b Walsh	120	retired hurt	0
N.S. Sidhu	b Walsh	0	lbw, b Benjamin	11
S.V. Manjrekar	lbw, b Benjamin	40	c Murray, b Walsh	17
S.R. Tendulkar	c Williams, b Cuffy	40	c Arthurton, b Benjamin	10
M. Azharuddin (capt)	c Williams, b Cummins	27	c Cummins, b Benjamin	5
V.G. Kambli	c Simmons, b Benjamin	18	c sub (Campbell), b Benjamin	0
*N.R. Mongia	hit wkt, b Cummins	34	c Williams, b Walsh	14
A.R. Kapoor	c Simmons, b Cuffy	15	c Murray, b Walsh	1
A.R. Kumble	c Hooper, b Cuffy	0	b Benjamin	1
J. Srinath	not out	52	not out	17
Venkatapathy Raju	c Murray, b Benjamin	15	c Murray, b Cuffy	16
Extras	b 5, lb 3, w 1, nb 17	26	b 1, lb 13, nb 8	22
		387		114

	O	M	R	W	O	M	R	W
Prabhakar	18	3	65	–	9	1	34	–
Srinath	32	2	106	2	20	–	95	–
Raju	33.4	5	73	3	12.3	–	60	2
Kapoor	30	4	90	1	7	1	32	–
Kumble	29	3	90	4	7	–	56	–
Tendulkar					1	–	10	–

	O	M	R	W	O	M	R	W
Walsh	35	4	89	2	18	7	34	3
Benjamin	35.3	8	106	3	17	3	65	5
Cuffy	22	4	80	3	0.2	–	1	1
Cummins	16	2	45	2				
Hooper	17	1	50	–				
Adams	3	1	9	–				

FALL OF WICKETS
1–36, 2–93, 3–103, 4–195, 5–220, 6–269, 7–368, 8–406, 9–422
1–85, 2–135, 3–156

FALL OF WICKETS
1–1, 2–104, 3–168, 4–228, 5–262, 6–265, 7–305, 8–310, 9–323
1–17, 2–44, 3–46, 4–48, 5–66, 6–66, 7–68, 8–68, 9–114

Umpires: R.S. Dunne & S. Venkataraghavan

West Indies won by 243 runs

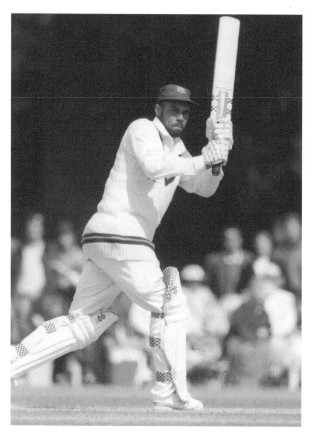

Jimmy Adams enjoyed a remarkable series with the bat for West Indies. (Empics)

resistance, but the bowling was of epic proportions. The match was over five minutes before lunch when Cuffy had Raju caught behind off a bouncer. Raju and Srinath had added 46 for the last wicket in 52 minutes to save India from total humiliation.

So West Indies drew the series to keep intact their 15-year-old unbeaten record. This was a mighty achievement at the end of an arduous and often unhappy tour. Adams was named Man of the Match and of the series, one which had seen some outstanding cricket.

ENGLAND 'A' TOUR

Tours by England 'A' sides have proliferated in recent years, but few have taken on such significance as the tour of India early in 1995. As the seniors faced a series of disasters in Australia, so the 'reserves' moved from success to success. Perhaps the most sensible choices made by the selectors were those of Phil Neale and John Barclay as managers of the party. Neale had done well enough at Northamptonshire to earn the respect of all, and he was later to be named as Woolmer's successor at Edgbaston, a coveted post. Barclay, a most likeable man, had done magnificent work since becoming director of coaching at Arundel, and both men were rich in experience of hand-

TEST MATCH AVERAGES – INDIA v. WEST INDIES

INDIA BATTING

	M	Inns	NO	Runs	HS	Av	100s	50s
S.R. Tendulkar	3	6	–	402	179	67.00	1	2
J. Srinath	3	6	3	136	60	45.33	–	2
N.S. Sidhu	3	6	–	224	107	37.33	1	1
M. Azharuddin	3	6	1	178	97	35.60	–	1
N.R. Mongia	3	6	–	183	80	30.50	–	1
M. Prabhakar	3	6	1	152	120	30.40	1	–
S.V. Manjrekar	3	6	–	179	66	29.83	–	2
A.R. Kumble	3	6	2	117	52*	29.25	–	1
V.G. Kambli	3	6	–	64	40	10.66	–	–
Venkatapathy Raju	3	5	1	40	16	10.00	–	–
R.K. Chauhan	2	3	1	6	4	3.00	–	–

Played in one Test: A.R. Kapoor 15 & 1

INDIA BOWLING

	Overs	Mds	Runs	Wkts	Av	Best	10/m	5/inn
Venkatapathy Raju	172.5	31	463	20	23.15	5-60	–	2
A.R. Kumble	145.5	33	409	13	31.46	4-90	–	–
J. Srinath	106	19	337	8	42.12	4-48	–	–
R.K. Chauhan	75	22	214	3	71.33	1-45	–	–
M. Prabhakar	38	5	149	2	74.50	2-17	–	–
A.R. Kapoor	37	5	122	1	122.00	1-90	–	–
S.R. Tendulkar	4	–	19	–	–	–	–	–

INDIA FIELDING FIGURES

7 – M. Azharuddin; 6 – N.R. Mongia; 5 – S.R. Tendulkar; 4 – S.V. Manjrekar (ct 3/st 1); 2 – J. Srinath; 1 – M. Prabhakar, N.S. Sidhu, V.G. Kambli, A.R. Kumble and A.R. Kapoor

WEST INDIES BATTING

	M	Inns	NO	Runs	HS	Av	100s	50s
J.C. Adams	3	6	3	520	174*	173.33	2	2
J.R. Murray	3	4	–	193	85	48.25	–	2
C.L. Hooper	3	6	–	262	81	43.66	–	2
K.L.T. Arthurton	3	6	2	164	70*	41.00	–	1
A.C. Cummins	2	2	–	67	50	33.50	–	1
B.C. Lara	3	6	–	198	91	33.00	–	2
S.C. Williams	3	5	–	114	49	22.80	–	–
P.V. Simmons	3	6	–	112	50	18.66	–	1
C.A. Walsh	3	4	1	18	11	6.00	–	–
K.C.G. Benjamin	3	4	–	2	2	0.50	–	–
C.E. Cuffy	2	3	1	1	1	0.50	–	–

Played in one Test: S. Chanderpaul 4 & 11*; R. Dhanraj 1 & 4

WEST INDIES BOWLING

	Overs	Mds	Runs	Wkts	Av	Best	10/m	5/inn
C.A. Walsh	140.5	31	361	17	21.23	6-79	–	1
K.C.G. Benjamin	137.4	27	490	17	28.82	5-65	–	1
C.L. Hooper	115.1	19	320	9	35.55	5-116	–	1
C.E. Cuffy	52.2	10	190	5	38.00	3-80	–	–
R. Dhanraj	25	1	93	2	46.50	1-46	–	–
A.C. Cummins	58	3	198	3	66.00	2-45	–	–
J.C. Adams	17	3	56	–	–	–	–	–

Bowled in one innings: S. Chanderpaul 20-4-63-1

WEST INDIES FIELDING FIGURES

12 – J.R. Murray (ct 11/st 1); 7 – C.L. Hooper; 6 – P.V. Simmons and S.C. Williams; 3 – B.C. Lara, K.L.T. Arthurton and J.C. Adams; 1 – C.E. Cuffy, A.C. Cummins, S. Chanderpaul and sub (S.L. Campbell)

ling promising and talented young cricketers. In this, they were superbly complemented by skipper Alan Wells who had displayed high qualities of leadership since taking over at Sussex.

Among the players closest to the senior side were Ramprakash, Salisbury, Ilott and Cork. The first three had played Test cricket, and many believed that Cork should have been in Australia ahead of Craig White. Both Ramprakash and Ilott were to spend time in Australia on stand-by and replacement in the senior squad.

2 January 1995 *at Brabourne Stadium, Bombay*

Cricket Club of India 209 for 6 (S.S. Dighe 55)

England 'A' 208 for 8 (S.V. Bahutule 5 for 41)

Cricket Club of India won by 1 run

In their opening match of the tour, the England 'A' side emulated the seniors in Australia by capitulating to leg-spin. A strong Indian side, which included the son of Sunil Gavaskar, scored 209 in their 50 overs, and, in spite of a fourth-wicket stand of 84 between Wells and Hemp, the England side fell two runs short of their target.

3, 4, 5 and 6 January 1995 *at Wankhede Stadium, Bombay*

England 'A' 283 (D.G. Cork 69, M.R. Ramprakash 59) and 204 (Balaji Rao 5 for 56)

Indian Youth XI 199 (A.A. Muzumdar 68, I.D.K. Salisbury 6 for 48) and 192 (Jitinder Singh 63, S. Sharath 59, D.G. Cork 4 for 46)

England 'A' won by 96 runs

Dominic Cork enjoyed a fine all-round match as the tourists won the first first-class match in their programme. He rescued England 'A' on the opening day when they were 125 for 5, and then took three wickets for six runs as the Youth XI lost their last seven wickets for 56 runs when in search of a target of 289. They had reached 136 for 3 and looked likely winners. England 'A' claimed a first-innings lead thanks to Ian Salisbury who took four wickets in 18 balls.

8, 9, 10 and 11 January 1995 *at M.A. Chidambaram Stadium, Madras*

Indian Board President's XI 333 for 6 dec. (R.S. Dravid 84, S. Rizwan 78, S.C. Ganguly 69, V. Rathore 59) and 204 for 4 dec. (S.C. Ganguly 65)

England 'A' 247 (J.E.R. Gallian 79, Kanwaljit Singh 4 for 56) and 168 for 9 (Kanwaljit Singh 4 for 67)

Match drawn

Having bowled a lively opening spell, Mark Ilott broke down with a side injury which, ultimately, was to force him to return to England. For much of the game, England 'A' toiled in the heat against some good batting and impressive spin bowling. Gallian batted 340 minutes and faced 280 balls to hold the 'A' side's first innings together. Needing 291 in 78 overs to win, England 'A' plunged to

138 for 8 before Johnson batted with Patel for 18 overs to add 30. Johnson scored one off 55 balls, and when he was out Patel and Ilott survived the last 22 balls to earn a draw.

14, 15, 16 and 17 January 1995 *at M. Chinnaswamy Stadium, Bangalore*

India 'A' 300 (V. Rathore 90, R.S. Dravid 60, R.D. Stemp 6 for 83) and 104 (A.A. Muzumdar 51, G. Chapple 5 for 32)

England 'A' 289 (M.R. Ramprakash 99, J.E.R. Gallian 58, N.V. Knight 50, S.V. Bahutule 4 for 96) and 117 for 6

England 'A' won by 4 wickets

England 'A' showed great character and resilience in winning the first of the three representative matches. Led by Amre, one of three Test players in the side, India 'A' were contained by the bowling of Stemp on the opening day. The home side had shown an exciting array of strokes, with Jitinder Singh and Rathore putting on 99 for the first wicket, but they were restricted to 236 for 4. Stemp had taken two wickets on the first day, but in 15.2 overs on the second, he claimed 4 for 27. England 'A' soon lost Vaughan, but Knight and Gallian added 95. Ramprakash batted into the third day and was only one short of a deserved century on a difficult pitch when he was caught behind off Chauhan. Leading by 11 runs on the first innings, India 'A' were reduced to 83 for 7 by the close as Chapple, who had batted bravely, and Cork wrecked the top-order. Chapple duly finished the innings on the fourth morning, but England 'A' faced a difficult task on a rapidly deteriorating pitch, and they needed the coolness of Ramprakash to see them through.

21, 22, 23 and 24 January 1995 *at Ferozeshah Kotla Ground, Delhi*

England 'A' 553 (M.R. Ramprakash 124, J.E.R. Gallian 100 retired hurt, P.N. Weekes 93, A.P. Wells 51) and 214 for 5 dec. (M.P. Vaughan 87, M.M. Patel 56)

Combined Universities 165 and 163 (P. Pathak 58, M.M. Patel 6 for 35)

England 'A' won by 439 runs

Joy at the England reserves' huge victory must be tempered by the fact that all 11 players in the Indian Universities' side were making their first-class debuts. Ramprakash reached the 20th first-class hundred of his career with consecutive sixes while Gallian hit 100 off 125 balls. Patel hit his first first-class fifty.

27, 28, 29, 30 and 31 January 1995 *at Eden Gardens, Calcutta*

India 'A' 216 (U. Chatterjee 72 not out) and 353 (V. Rathore 127, R.S. Dravid 52)

England 'A' 316 (A.P. Wells 93, J.E.R. Gallian 77, P.L. Mhambrey 4 for 63) and 254 for 5 (D.L. Hemp 99 not out, A.P. Wells 65)

England 'A' won by 5 wickets

With Ramprakash in Australia as reinforcement for the senior side, England 'A' brought in Glamorgan's David Hemp, and the left-hander turned out to be one of England's heroes. England took command on the first day when the Indians contributed to their own downfall against Chapple and Cork, an impressive pair, and were reduced to 95 for 7. Utpal Chatterjee hit the highest score of his career and he and Chauhan added 75 for the ninth wicket. Even so, India were out for 216 on the opening day.

England imposed a grip on the match on the second afternoon when Gallian and Wells played with refreshing positivity against the spinners to add 154 for the third wicket. Yadav twice missed stumping Wells, but the skipper batted resolutely and worked hard for his runs. Wickets tumbled after tea to the second new ball, and England closed on 275 for 6.

The tail failed to wag, and India prospered on the third day, with Vikram Rathore hitting a rasping century off 178 balls which had more than a hint of his compatriot Sidhu about it. Eventually, England needed 254 to win, and, at 82 for 4, this target looked beyond them, but Wells and Hemp added 155. On a pitch that was wearing and encouraging the spinners, Hemp batted splendidly and hit 2 sixes and 13 fours. He hit the two runs needed for victory and a winning lead in the series, but he fell one short of a deserved century.

4, 5, 6, 7 and 8 February 1995 *at Chandigarh*

India 'A' 229 (R.S. Dravid 59, G. Chapple 4 for 60) and 156
  (A.A. Muzumdar 55, G. Chapple 5 for 38)
England 'A' 209 (P.L. Mhambrey 4 for 63) and 179 for 9
  (Kanwaljit Singh 4 for 49, U. Chatterjee 4 for 71)

England 'A' won by 1 wicket

Amre, with a Test average above 40, was omitted from the Indian side, and the captaincy was handed to Rathore. The umpires chastened both sides on the opening day for their verbal intimidation. Glen Chapple had 9 for 98 in the match to give him 19 wickets in the series. On a dusty pitch, England 'A' began the last day with two wickets standing and 31 needed for victory. Johnson and Patel took the score to 168 before Patel fell to Chatterjee. Stemp, coming to the wicket with nine needed, swatted his second ball for six, took a single and drove Mhambrey through the covers for four to give England 'A' a 3–0 triumph in the series. Johnson remained bravely unbeaten on 33.

ONE-DAY SERIES

11 February 1995 *at Nehru Stadium, Indore*

India 'A' 201 for 7 (A.A. Muzumdar 79)
England 'A' 195

India 'A' won by 6 runs

14 February 1995 *at Gujarat Stadium, Motera, Ahmedabad*

India 'A' 207 for 8 (A.A. Muzumdar 69, R.S. Dravid 57)
England 'A' 208 for 7 (M.R. Ramprakash 70)

England 'A' won by 3 wickets

16 February 1995 *at Lal Bahdur, Hyderabad*

England 'A' 254 for 6 (N.V. Knight 114 not out,
  M.R. Ramprakash 57)
India 'A' 156

England 'A' won by 98 runs

England 'A' completed an outstandingly successful tour with victory in the one-day series. Ramprakash, having starred in Australia, returned to flourish in India, while Knight came out of the shadows with a century in the final match. Hemp, Ramprakash, Gallian, Cork, Nixon, Chapple and Stemp all enhanced their prospects as future Test cricketers, and the party was without its failures.

Much of the potential of the young Indians who faced the England side remained unrealised, and several of their performances were disappointing.

20 February 1995 *at Dhaka*

England 'A' 203 for 8 (J.E.R. Gallian 58)
Bangladesh 145 for 8

England 'A' won by 58 runs

22 February 1995 *at Dhaka*

England 'A' 235 for 8 (N.V. Knight 117, D.L. Hemp 52)
Bangladesh 215 (Amin-ul-Islam 52)

England 'A' won by 20 runs

24, 25 and 26 February 1995 *at Dhaka*

Bangladesh 365 for 6 dec. (Amin-ul-Islam 121, Minhazal
  Abedin 81)
England 'A' 421 for 7 (D.L. Hemp 190, N.V. Knight 150)

Match drawn

The England 'A' side played three matches in Bangladesh at the end of the tour of India.

RANJI TROPHY

CENTRAL ZONE

20, 21, 22 and 23 December 1994 *at MB College Ground, Udaipur*

Uttar Pradesh 240 (P. Agarwal 67, Mohammad Aslam 5 for 66)
  and 303 for 6 dec. (R. Sapru 106 not out, M. Mudgal 54,
  S. Yadav 52)

One of the great successes of the England 'A' tour, Glen Chapple of Lancashire. (Patrick Eagar)

Rajasthan 202 (G.K. Khoda 57, P. Krishna Kumar 53 not out, S. Kesarwani 4 for 39) and 196

Uttar Pradesh won by 145 runs

Uttar Pradesh 6 pts, Rajasthan 0 pts

at Karnail Singh Stadium, Delhi

Madhya Pradesh 479 (D.K. Nilosey 128, A.R. Khurasiya 100, M.S. Sahni 75, C.S. Pandit 66)

Railways 107 (N.D. Hirwani 4 for 44) and 302 (R. Bora 145, P. Shepherd 51, N.D. Hirwani 4 for 80)

Madhya Pradesh won by an innings and 70 runs

Madhya Pradesh 6 pts, Railways 0 pts

Pandit had joined Madhya Pradesh from Assam who had also lost Rajesh Bora to Railways for whom he hit a century on debut.

28, 29, 30 and 31 December 1994 *at BHEL Ground, Bhopal*

Madhya Pradesh 374 (K.K. Patel 93, D.K. Nilosey 92, C.S. Pandit 75, Mohammad Aslam 4 for 107) and 32 for 0

Rajasthan 168 (A. Sinha 74, N.D. Hirwani 7 for 73) and 237 (R. Kanwat 51, S.S. Lahore 5 for 92, N.D. Hirwani 5 for 95)

Madhya Pradesh won by 10 wickets

Madhya Pradesh 6 pts, Rajasthan 0 pts

at VCA Ground, Nagpur

Uttar Pradesh 366 (R. Sapru 119, S. Shukla 71 not out, S. Yadav 56, P.V. Gandhe 4 for 112) and 168 for 6 dec. (R. Shamshed 88)

Vidarbha 216 (S. Kesarwani 7 for 85) and 248 (P.K. Hedaoo 71)

Uttar Pradesh won by 70 runs

Uttar Pradesh 6 pts, Vidarbha 0 pts

Former Test leg-spinner Hirwani brought his total of wickets to 20 in two matches. He captured 10 wickets in a match for the sixth time.

5, 6, 7 and 8 January 1995 *at Indira Gandhi Stadium, Delhi*

Railways 371 (Abhay Sharma 182, Mohammad Aslam 5 for 108)

Rajasthan 392 for 5 (G.K. Khoda 187, P. Krishna Kumar 59 not out, A. Sinha 51)

Match drawn

Rajasthan 2 pts, Railways 0 pts

at Bhilai Steel Plant Ground, Bhilai

Vidarbha 132 (R.K. Chauhan 5 for 43, N.D. Hirwani 4 for 42) and 42 for 2

Madhya Pradesh 414 (K.K. Patel 168, C.S. Pandit 65, M.S. Sahni 65, P.K. Hedaoo 6 for 164)

Match drawn

Madhya Pradesh 2 pts, Vidarbha 0 pts

Abhay Sharma and Khoda both hit the highest scores of their careers in the match in Delhi.

13, 14, 15 and 16 January 1995 *at Karnail Singh Stadium, Delhi*

Railways 256 (V. Yadav 75, K. Bharathan 55, Yusuf Ali Khan 52)

Vidarbha 271 for 8 (U.S. Phate 84, P.B. Hingnikar 61, K.S.M. Iyer 57, R. Sanghvi 4 for 53, Iqbal Thakur 4 for 97)

Match drawn

Vidarbha 2 pts, Railways 0 pts

at Gandhi Bagh, Meerut

Madhya Pradesh 155 for 3 (K.K. Patel 54, A.R. Khurasiya 50 not out)

v. **Uttar Pradesh**

Twenty wickets in the first two Ranji Trophy matches for Hirwani of Madhya Pradesh. (Alan Cozzi)

CENTRAL ZONE FINAL TABLE

	P	W	L	D	Pts
Madhya Pradesh	4	2	–	2	15
Uttar Pradesh	4	2	1	1	13
Rajasthan	4	1	2	1	8
Railways	4	1	1	2	6
Vidarbha	4	–	2	2	4

EAST ZONE

11, 12, 13 and 14 December 1994 *at Keenan Stadium, Jamshedpur*

Orissa 340 (S.S. Das 132, D. Kumar 4 for 95) and 252
(M. Bhatt 62, K.V.P. Rao 6 for 81)

Bihar 217 (Abinash Kumar 68 not out, R. Seth 4 for 38)

Match drawn

Orissa 2 pts, Bihar 0 pts

at PTI Ground, Agartala

Assam 244 (Rajinder Singh 53, C. Dey 5 for 70) and 220 for
8 dec. (P. Dutta 102, D. Bora 76, C. Dey 5 for 74)

Tripura 106 (P. Dutta 4 for 30) and 124 (S.G. Chakraborty
6 for 35)

Assam won by 234 runs

Assam 6 pts, Tripura 0 pts

Assam beat Tripura by lunchtime on the third day at Agartala.

19, 20, 21 and 22 December 1994 *at Railway Stadium, Maligaon, Guwahati*

Assam 269 (S. Saikia 97) and 251 (Z. Zuffri 65, G. Dutta 55,
S. Mukherjee 5 for 70)

Bengal 503 for 6 dec. (D. Gandhi 151, C.M. Sharma
101 not out, S.J. Kalyani 73) and 21 for 1

Bengal won by 9 wickets

Bengal 6 pts, Assam 0 pts

at PTI Ground, Agartala

Orissa 379 (R. Biswal 126, S. Roul 80, A. Roy 51)

Tripura 102 (R. Biswal 5 for 33) and 189 (R. Biswal 7 for 38)

Orissa won by an innings and 88 runs

Orissa 6 pts, Tripura 0 pts

Gandhi hit 151 off 233 balls with 17 fours on the occasion of his first-class debut. The veteran Chetan Sharma hit the

---

Match drawn

Madhya Pradesh 1 pt, Uttar Pradesh 1 pt

Rain disrupted the match in Delhi and no play was possible after the first day in Meerut.

22, 23, 24 and 25 January 1995 *at Green Park, Kanpur*

Uttar Pradesh 150 (R. Shamshed 78, Iqbal Thakur 6 for 22)
and 269 (R. Shamshed 58, R. Sanghvi 4 for 52, Iqbal Thakur
4 for 99)

Railways 175 (R. Bora 54, A.W. Zaidi 4 for 44) and 248 for 6
(P.S. Shepherd 107 not out, S.S. Bangar 57 not out)

Railways won by 4 wickets

Railways 6 pts, Uttar Pradesh 0 pts

at VCA Ground, Nagpur

Vidarbha 235 (K.S.M. Iyer 88, Y.T. Ghare 65, P. Krishna Kumar
6 for 63) and 282 for 8 dec. (U.S. Phate 84, P.K. Hedaoo 69,
P. Krishna Kumar 5 for 101)

Rajasthan 189 (M.S. Doshi 4 for 53, P.V. Gandhe 4 for 70) and
330 for 9 (P. Krishna Kumar 106 not out, G.K. Khoda 66,
P.V. Gandhe 5 for 143)

Rajasthan won by 1 wicket

Rajasthan 6 pts, Vidarbha 2 pts

An unbroken last-wicket stand of 40 between Pal and Krishna Kumar gave Rajasthan victory at Nagpur and took them into the knock-out stage of the competition. Krishna Kumar, a left-hander, hit 106 off 213 balls. It was the first first-class century of his career.

second century of his career. Tripura again lost inside three days as Ranjib Biswal enjoyed a remarkable all-round match, returning his best bowling figures in the second innings.

27, 28, 29 and 30 December 1994 *at Railway Stadium, Maligaon, Guwahati*

Assam 339 (Rajinder Singh 93, N. Bordoloi 60, S. Saikia 55, S. Kumar 4 for 104, R. Biswal 4 for 125) and 242 for 7 dec. (P. Das 50 not out)
Orissa 295 (R. Biswal 66, J. Zaman 7 for 87) and 46 for 2
Match drawn
Assam 2 pts, Orissa 0 pts

29, 30, 31 December 1994 and 1 January 1995 *at Eden Gardens, Calcutta*

Bihar 79 (U. Chatterjee 4 for 13, C.M. Sharma 4 for 27) and 167 (S. Banerjee 66 not out, Sen Sharma 5 for 17)
Bengal 418 for 4 dec. (Saurav Ganguly 200 not out, S.S. Karim 67, A.O. Malhotra 63)
Bengal won by an innings and 172 runs
Bengal 6 pts, Bihar 0 pts

Javed Zaman returned the best bowling figures of his career for Assam while Saurav Ganguly equalled his highest score in first-class cricket for Bengal.

5, 6, 7 and 8 January 1995 *at Eden Gardens, Calcutta*

Bengal 250 (A. Singla 66, C.M. Sharma 50, R. Seth 4 for 84, R. Biswal 4 for 115) and 390 for 5 dec. (J. Arun Lal 113, S.J. Kalyani 85, S.S. Karim 57 not out)
Orissa 244 (R. Biswal 54) and 130 for 4
Match drawn
Bengal 2 pts, Orissa 0 pts

at Keenan Stadium, Jamshedpur

Tripura 223 (K.V.P. Rao 7 for 74) and 124 (K.V.P. Rao 6 for 50)
Bihar 309 (Satish Singh 82, Sunil Kumar 67) and 39 for 0
Bihar won by 10 wickets
Bihar 6 pts, Tripura 0 pts

Slow left-arm bowler Kashireddi Rao returned the best figures of his career for innings and match as Bihar beat Tripura at Jamshedpur.

16, 17, 18 and 19 January 1995 *at DSA Ground, Halalkandi*

Assam 201 (Rajinder Singh 75, P. Dutta 60, K.V.P. Rao 5 for 42) and 120 (G. Dutta 56, K.V.P. Rao 5 for 53, Abinash Kumar 4 for 33)

Bihar 187 (G. Dutta 5 for 46) and 135 for 7 (V. Khulkar 64)
Bihar won by 3 wickets
Bihar 6 pts, Assam 2 pts

at Eden Gardens, Calcutta

Tripura 129 (A. Sarkar 5 for 36) and 125
Bengal 276 for 9 dec. (S.J. Kalyani 78, J. Arun Lal 60, S. Mukherjee 57 not out, C. Dey 6 for 95)
Bengal won by an innings and 22 runs
Bengal 6 pts, Tripura 0 pts

By gaining first-innings points against Bihar, Assam snatched the third East Zone qualifying place ahead of Orissa. Off-break bowler Chitanjib Dey claimed his third five-wicket haul in five innings for Tripura.

EAST ZONE FINAL TABLE

	P	W	L	D	Pts
Bengal	4	3	–	1	20
Bihar	4	2	1	1	12
Assam	4	1	2	1	10
Orissa	4	1	–	3	8
Tripura	4	–	4	–	0

NORTH ZONE

10, 11, 12 and 13 December 1994 *at Indira Stadium, Una*

Himachal Pradesh 144 (R. Bittoo 63, P. Jain 5 for 35, P. Thakur 4 for 55) and 280 (R. Nayyar 120, P. Jain 5 for 67)
Haryana 434 for 6 dec. (R. Puri 134, V. Yadav 79, N. Goel 63, A. Kaypee 52)
Haryana won by an innings and 10 runs
Haryana 6 pts, Himachal Pradesh 0 pts

at Ferozeshah Kotla Ground, Delhi

Delhi 261 (A.K. Sharma 90, Bantoo Singh 62) and 260 (P. Maitreya 4 for 28)
Services 213 (R. Vinayak 90 not out, A.S. Wassan 6 for 59) and 71 (A.S. Wassan 5 for 33, F. Ghayas 4 for 30)
Delhi won by 237 runs
Delhi 6 pts, Services 0 pts

at Amritsar

Punjab v. Jammu and Kashmir
Walk-over
Punjab 6 pts, Jammu and Kashmir 0 pts

Jammu and Kashmir failed to arrive for the match at Amritsar, and the game was awarded to Punjab. In

Services' second innings against Delhi, Charles Thomson carried his bat through the 36 overs for 26 runs.

17, 18, 19 and 20 December 1994 *at Paddal, Mandi*

Himachal Pradesh 197 (Shamboo Sharma 93 not out,
    R. Bittoo 55, A.R. Kapoor 4 for 46, B. Vij 4 for 68) and 258
    (R. Nayyar 87, N. Gour 74, A.R. Kapoor 4 for 73)

Punjab 451 for 3 dec. (R. Kalsi 179, Bhupinder Singh jr 153,
    Amit Sharma 54 not out, Gursharan Singh 53 not out)
    and 6 for 0

Punjab won by 10 wickets

Punjab 6 pts, Himachal Pradesh 0 pts

at Bhiwani

Haryana v. Jammu and Kashmir

Walk-over

Haryana 6 pts, Jammu and Kashmir 0 pts

Jammu and Kashmir again failed to arrive and conceded the match against Haryana. Kalsi and Bhupinder Singh jr added 324 for Punjab's second wicket against Himachal Pradesh.

23, 24, 25 and 26 December 1994 *at Ferozeshah Kotla Ground, Delhi*

Jammu and Kashmir 210 (Kanwaljit Singh 71, K. Nath
    5 for 53) and 157 (F. Ghayas 5 for 42, A.S. Wassan 4 for 69)

Delhi 499 for 8 dec. (A. Malhotra 136, A.K. Sharma 128,
    G. Vadhera 70, Bantoo Singh 67, Arun Sharma 4 for 122)

Delhi won by an innings and 132 runs

Delhi 6 pts, Jammu and Kashmir 0 pts

at PCA Stadium, Mohali, Chandigarh

Punjab 376 (Bhupinder Singh jr 85, Amit Sharma 82)

Haryana 189 (A.R. Kapoor 5 for 43) and 266 for 7 (A.D. Jadeja
    154 not out)

Match drawn

Punjab 2 pts, Haryana 0 pts

at Air Forces Stadium, Palam Sports Complex, Delhi

Himachal Pradesh 182 (Shamboo Sharma 59, J.N. Pandey
    4 for 36) and 152 (J.N. Pandey 6 for 64)

Services 459 for 8 dec. (Suryaveer Singh 163, Chinmoy
    Sharma 115, S. Chopra 65, R. Mohsin 55 not out)

Services won by an innings and 125 runs

Services 6 pts, Himachal Pradesh 0 pts

Career-best bowling performances for match and innings by Pandey were the features of Services' victory in Delhi.

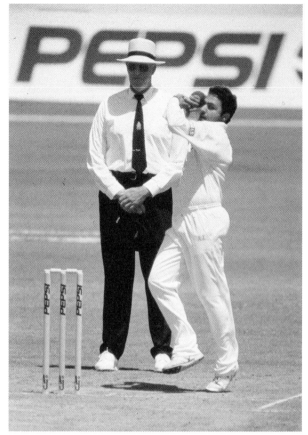

India's rising star, Ashish Kapoor of Punjab, off-break bowler and capable batsman. (Mueen-ud-din Hameed/Sportsline)

31 December 1994, 1, 2 and 3 January 1995 *at Ferozeshah Kotla Ground, Delhi*

Himachal Pradesh 205 (K. Nath 4 for 59, A.S. Wassan
    4 for 79) and 122 (F. Ghayas 4 for 39)

Delhi 637 for 3 (R. Lamba 312, R. Sehgal 216,
    Bantoo Singh 87)

Delhi won by an innings and 310 runs

Delhi 6 pts, Himachal Pradesh 0 pts

The Delhi skipper Raman Lamba and Ravi Sehgal, who had played only one match before the 1994–5 season, scored 446 in 431 minutes for their side's first wicket. Sehgal played the first three-figured innings of his career while Lamba, who missed a season through suspension, hit the second triple century of his career.

6, 7, 8 and 9 January 1995 *at Nehru Stadium, Gurgaon*

Haryana 167 (A.D. Jadeja 81, N. Chopra 7 for 66) and
    163 for 3 (A. Kaypee 62 not out)

Delhi 164 (P. Jain 5 for 46)

Match drawn

Haryana 2 pts, Delhi 0 pts

at Air Force Stadium, Palam Sports Complex, Delhi

Services 101 (A. Bedi 6 for 26) and 46 for 5

Punjab 318 (Sandeep Sharma 98, K. Mohan 84, Gursharan
Singh 73, S. Subramaniam 5 for 72)

Match drawn

Punjab 2 pts, Services 0 pts

7, 8, 9 and 10 January 1995 *at Indira Stadium, Una*

Jammu and Kashmir 579 for 5 (A. Gupta 210 not out,
V. Bhaskar 128, R. Bali 61, A. Bhatti 58)

v. **Himachal Pradesh**

Match drawn

Jammu and Kashmir 1 pt, Himachal Pradesh 1 pt

Rain affected all matches. Batting at number ten, Sandeep
Sharma hit 98 for Punjab on the occasion of his debut
while Ashwini Gupta scored the first double century
recorded for Jammu and Kashmir.

13, 14, 15 and 16 January 1995 *at Ferozeshah Kotla Ground, Delhi*

Punjab 413 (Bhupinder Singh jr 137, P. Dharmani 66,
A.S. Wassan 4 for 110)

Delhi 310 (R. Sehgal 66, A. Malhotra 62, B. Vij 4 for 86)

Match drawn

Punjab 2 pts, Delhi 0 pts

at Air Force Stadium, Palam Sports Complex, Delhi

Services 120 (S. Subramaniam 50, V. Jain 4 for 34) and 168
(Suryaveer Singh 67, P. Thakur 4 for 31, V. Jain 4 for 55)

Haryana 268 for 6 dec. (A. Kaypee 70, R. Manchanda 55) and
23 for 2

Haryana won by 8 wickets

Haryana 6 pts, Services 0 pts

22, 23, 24 and 25 January 1995 *at Air Force Stadium, Palam Sports Complex, Delhi*

Services 543 for 9 dec. (S. Chopra 152, Chinmoy Sharma 136,
R. Vinayak 75, Suryaveer Singh 63, G.S. Thapa 55)

Jammu and Kashmir 279 (A. Gupta 119 not out,
V. Bhaskat 63, J.N. Pandey 5 for 96) and 105
(S. Subramaniam 5 for 34)

Services won by an innings and 159 runs

Services 6 pts, Jammu and Kashmir 0 pts

NORTH ZONE FINAL TABLE

	P	W	L	D	Pts
Haryana	5	3	–	2	20
Delhi	5	3	–	2	18
Punjab	5	2	–	3	18
Services	5	2	2	1	12
Himachal Pradesh	5	–	4	1	1
Jammu and Kashmir	5	–	4	1	1

SOUTH ZONE

10, 11, 12 and 13 December 1994 *at Gymkhana Ground, Secunderabad*

Hyderabad 335 (M.V. Sridhar 87, V.V.S. Laxman 60,
M. Venkataramana 4 for 87) and 94 for 2

Tamil Nadu 439 (D. Vasu 132, V.B. Chandrasekhar 74,
Robin Singh 63, M. Venkataramana 60, V. Pratap 4 for 80)

Match drawn

Tamil Nadu 2 pts, Hyderabad 0 pts

at M. Chinnaswamy Stadium, Bangalore

Karnataka 545 (R.S. Dravid 191, K.A. Jeshwanth 126,
P. Prakash 4 for 147)

Andhra 187 (V.V. Kumar 53, R. Ananth 6 for 56) and 279
(B.S. Nayak 103)

Karnataka won by an innings and 79 runs

Karnataka 6 pts, Andhra 0 pts

at Regional Engineering College, Kozhikode

Kerala 346 (S. Oasis 110, S. Shankar 52, A. Shetty 4 for 80)

Goa 97 (K.N.A. Padmanabhan 6 for 26) and 201
(B. Ramprakash 5 for 48)

Kerala won by an innings and 48 runs

Kerala 6 pts, Goa 0 pts

Goa fielded three new recruits in their opening match,
V. Jaisimha from Hyderabad, and A.V. and S.V. Mudkavi
from Rajasthan.

19, 20, 21 and 22 December 1994 *at Dr Rajendra Prasad Stadium, Margao*

Karnataka 428 (S. Somsundar 112, S. Joshi 104, A. Vaidya 83,
U.S. Naik 5 for 153) and 226 for 8 dec. (K.A. Jeshwanth 50,
S.V. Mudkavi 4 for 79)

Goa 308 (S.V. Mudkavi 67, M.M. Sawkar 51) and 103
(D. Johnson 5 for 28)

Karnataka won by 243 runs

Karnataka 6 pts, Goa 0 pts

at M.A. Chidambaram Stadium, Madras

Tamil Nadu v. Andhra

Match abandoned

Tamil Nadu 2 pts, Andhra 2 pts

at Gymkhana Ground, Secunderabad

Hyderabad 227 (V.V.S. Laxman 103, R.A. Swaroop 56,
F.V. Rasheed 5 for 29) and 210 (G.A. Shetty 102)

Kerala 248 (V. Vardhan 4 for 62) and 93 for 6

Match drawn

Kerala 2 pts, Hyderabad 0 pts

Rain on all four days caused the match in Madras to be
abandoned without a ball being bowled.

28, 29, 30 and **31 December 1994** *at Indira Priyadarshini Stadium,
Vishakhapatnam*

Kerala 252 (S. Oasis 58, C. Rao 5 for 55, V. Vijaysaradhi
4 for 48) and 241 for 5 dec. (S. Oasis 81 not out)

Andhra 206 (V.V. Kumar 70, K.N.A. Padmanabhan 5 for 48)
and 206 for 9 (V.V. Kumar 61, K.N.A. Padmanabhan
4 for 70)

Match drawn

Kerala 2 pts, Andhra 0 pts

at Gymkhana Ground, Secunderabad

Goa 302 (N. Gautam 62, V. Jaisimha 58, A.V. Mudkavi 55,
N.P. Singh 4 for 71) and 157 (R. Kanwaljit 4 for 38)

Hyderabad 310 (V.V.S. Laxman 112, M.V. Sridhar 107,
N.D. Kambli 4 for 66) and 152 for 1 (M.V. Sridhar
102 not out)

Hyderabad won by 9 wickets

Hyderabad 6 pts, Goa 0 pts

at M.A. Chidambaram Stadium, Madras

Karnataka 227 (S. Somsundar 65, S. Subramaniam 7 for 68)
and 328 (K.A. Jeshwanth 154 not out, S. Joshi 53, D. Vasu
8 for 114)

Tamil Nadu 411 (S. Sharath 88, V.B. Chandrasekhar 64,
S. Ramesh 55) and 106 for 4 (Robin Singh 64 not out)

Match drawn

Tamil Nadu 2 pts, Karnataka 0 pts

Maruti Sridhar hit a century in each innings for
Hyderabad, his second century coming off 124 balls. Tamil
Nadu made a brave effort to score 145 in 11 overs to beat
Karnataka but failed.

7, 8, 9 and **10** January 1995 *at Government Victoria College Ground,
Palakkad*

Kerala 241 (M. Venkataramana 4 for 60) and 287
(P.G. Sunder 100, B. Ramprakash 56, D. Vasu 4 for 72)

Tamil Nadu 258 (W.V. Raman 93, Robin Singh 73,
M.S. Kumar 6 for 96) and 147 (M.S. Kumar 6 for 68)

Kerala won by 123 runs

Kerala 6 pts, Tamil Nadu 2 pts

at Dr Rajendra Prasad Stadium, Margao

Andhra 176 (S.V. Mudkavi 4 for 29) and 337 for 8 dec.
(V.V. Kumar 96, N.S.K. Prasad 50 not out)

Goa 137 (S. Kamat 50 not out, M. Rao 5 for 55, C.M. Raju
4 for 38)

Match drawn

Andhra 2 pts, Goa 0 pts

at Dr Ambedkar Stadium, Bijapur

Hyderabad 78 and 166 (G.A. Shetty 64, D. Johnson 5 for 48)

Karnataka 203 (A.R. Kumble 63, M. Mohi-ud-din 5 for 69) and
43 for 1

Karnataka won by 9 wickets

Karnataka 6 pts, Hyderabad 0 pts

Kerala gained a surprise victory over Tamil Nadu in spite
of more good bowling from Vasu who had had a career-
best performance against Karnataka.

15, 16, 17 and **18** January 1995 *at Municipal Stadium, Thalassery*

Karnataka 269 (J. Arun Kumar 67, A. Vaidya 57,
B. Ramprakash 6 for 101) and 233 (P.V. Shashikanth 68)

Kerala 124 (A.R. Kumble 8 for 58) and 108 (A.R. Kumble
8 for 41)

Karnataka won by 270 runs

Karnataka 6 pts, Kerala 0 pts

at Indira Gandhi Stadium, Vijayawada

Hyderabad 240 (V.V.S. Laxman 96 not out, M.V. Sridhar 54)
and 195 for 8 dec. (M. Azharuddin 74, G.V.V.G. Raju
5 for 63)

Andhra 193 (M.F. Rehman 69, Kanwaljit Singh 5 for 25) and
248 for 6 (M.F. Rehman 59, R. Sridhar 4 for 70)

Andhra won by 4 wickets

Andhra 6 pts, Hyderabad 2 pts

at Nehru Stadium, Faroda, Margao

Tamil Nadu 446 for 6 dec. (S. Sharath 121 not out,
A. Kripal Singh 101)

Goa 175 (B. Ral 4 for 39, M. Venkataramana 4 for 47) and 202
    (M. Venkataramana 6 for 86)

Tamil Nadu won by an innings and 69 runs

Tamil Nadu 6 pts, Goa 0 pts

Anil Kumble led Karnataka to the South Zone championship with the best bowling performances of his magnificent career. He took eight wickets in an innings for the first
time, and his 16 for 99 was testimony to an outstanding
achievement.

SOUTH ZONE FINAL TABLE

	P	W	L	D	Pts
Karnataka	5	4	–	1	24
Kerala	5	2	1	2	16
Tamil Nadu	5	1	1	3	14
Andhra	5	1	1	3	10
Hyderabad	5	1	2	2	8
Goa	5	–	4	1	0

WEST ZONE

23, 24, 25 and 26 December 1994 *at Indira Gandhi Stadium, Solapur*

Bombay 573 for 9 dec. (A.A. Muzumdar 220, S.S. More 166,
    M.M. Karanjkar 69, S.C. Gudge 5 for 140) and 123 for 3
    (S.K. Kulkarni 60)
Maharashtra 361 (S.S. Sugwekar 160, S.C. Gudge 55,
    P.L. Mhambrey 5 for 51)

Match drawn

Bombay 2 pts, Maharashtra 0 pts

at Sardar Patel Stadium, Motera, Ahmedabad

Gujarat 246 (P.H. Patel 66, N.S. Bakriwala 58, R. Pandit
    5 for 63, S. Pillai 4 for 59) and 358 (B. Mehta 102,
    N. Patel 55, P.H. Patel 53, D.N. Chudasama 4 for 98)
Saurashtra 350 (N.R. Odedra 142, H. Parsana 84,
    M.H. Parmar 4 for 44) and 204 for 6 (S.H. Kotak 67 not out)

Match drawn

Saurashtra 2 pts, Gujarat 0 pts

The match in Solapur caused much comment. More and
Muzumdar added 290 for Bombay's second wicket, and
Muzumdar hit his second double century in what was his
fourth Ranji Trophy match. When Maharashtra batted,
Bombay appealed for a stumping against Sugwekar when
the batsman was on 122. Umpire V.N. Kulkarni ruled not
out, but the reaction of Bombay captain Manjrekar was so
vehement and his dissent so sustained that Kulkarni had
no option but to order him from the field until the end of
the lunch session on the fourth day. It is believed that this
is the first time that an umpire has found it necessary to go
to such lengths.

31 December 1994, 1, 2 and 3 January 1995 *at Municipal Ground, Rajkot*

Maharashtra 549 (A.V. Kale 153, H.A. Kinikar 138)
Saurashtra 270 (S.S. Tanna 88) and 237 for 3
    (S. Pillai 109 not out, B. Dutta 76 not out)

Match drawn

Maharashtra 2 pts, Saurashtra 0 pts

at Shastri Ground, Vallabh Vidyanagar

Baroda 568 for 6 dec. (N.R. Mongia 152, K.S. Chavan 109,
    K.S. More 103 not out, R.B. Parikh 57, T.B. Arothe 50,
    J.J. Martin 50)
Gujarat 366 (M.H. Parmar 109, R.G.M. Patel 4 for 42, V. Buch
    4 for 105) and 289 for 9 (M.H. Parmar 155 not out)

Match drawn

Baroda 2 pts, Gujarat 0 pts

Mukund Parmar hit a century in each innings for Gujarat.
It was the second time that he had accomplished the feat
in the Ranji Trophy.

7, 8, 9 and 10 January 1995 *at University Ground, Bhavnagar*

Saurashtra 182 (S.S. Tanna 64, S.H. Kotak 51, P.L. Mhambrey
    5 for 46) and 206 (N.R. Odedra 54, S.H. Kotak 53,
    N. Kulkarni 6 for 90, S. Khartade 4 for 56)
Bombay 253 (A.A. Muzumdar 89, S.V. Manjrekar 86,
    M.M. Parsana 4 for 34) and 138 for 6

Bombay won by 4 wickets

Bombay 6 pts, Saurashtra 0 pts

at IPCL Sports Complex, Baroda

Baroda 172 (M.S. Kulkarni 6 for 67) and 256 (K.S. More 52)
Maharashtra 272 (H.H. Kanitkar 74, S.S. Sugwekar 69,
    A.V. Kale 51, Sukhbir Singh 5 for 90) and 24 for 1

Match drawn

Maharashtra 2 pts, Baroda 0 pts

15, 16, 17 and 18 January 1995 *at RCF Sports Ground, Bombay*

Baroda 301 (R. Naik 70, R.B. Parikh 67, N. Kulkarni 4 for 104)
    and 330 (N.R. Mongia 154, N. Kulkarni 6 for 119)
Bombay 348 (S.R. Tendulkar 175, V.G. Kambli 55, V. Buch
    4 for 101) and 289 for 5 (M. Joglekar 114 not out,
    S.R. Tendulkar 97)

Bombay won by 5 wickets

Bombay 6 pts, Baroda 0 pts

at Poona Club, Pune

Gujarat 199 (M.S. Kulkarni 5 for 36) and 274 (U.S. Belsare 72,
    M.H. Parmar 56, P. Kanade 4 for 65)
Maharashtra 544 for 8 dec. (A.V. Kale 141, S.C. Gudge 125,
    H.H. Kanitkar 100 not out, B. Patel 5 for 168)

Maharashtra won by an innings and 71 runs

Maharashtra 6 pts, Gujarat 0 pts

A fine century from Mongia was insufficient to halt the progress of Bombay. With Test stars available and Tendulkar captaining the side, the might of Bombay was seen most clearly. Tendulkar's 175 came off only 140 balls in 185 minutes. He hit 8 sixes and 22 fours.

21, 22, 23 and 24 January 1995 *at Wankhede Stadium, Bombay*

Gujarat 198 (N.S. Bakriwals 66, P.L. Mhambrey 4 for 60) and 161 (M.H. Parmar 56, S.A. Ankola 6 for 47)

Bombay 491 for 6 dec. (V.G. Kambli 147, S.V. Bahutule 112 not out, S.V. Manjrekar 87, M.V. Joglekar 51, H. Patel 4 for 168)

Bombay won by an innings and 132 runs

Bombay 6 pts, Gujarat 0 pts

at IPCL Sports Complex, Baroda

Saurashtra 285 (S.H. Kotak 121, N.R. Odedra 50, M.S. Narula 6 for 80) and 223 (N.R. Odedra 81, S.S. Tanna 54, V. Buch 6 for 75)

Baroda 210 (J.J. Martin 94, H. Parsana 4 for 58) and 188

Saurashtra won by 110 runs

Saurashtra 6 pts, Baroda 0 pts

Bombay beat Gujarat inside three days to take the West Zone title, which surprised no one. They scored their runs at nearly five an over, with Kambli's 147 coming off 157 balls.

WEST ZONE FINAL TABLE

	P	W	L	D	Pts
Bombay	4	3	–	1	20
Maharashtra	4	1	–	3	10
Saurashtra	4	1	1	2	8
Baroda	4	–	2	2	2
Gujarat	4	–	2	2	0

NATIONAL CHAMPIONSHIP KNOCK-OUT STAGE PRE-QUARTER-FINALS

12, 13, 14 and 15 February 1995 *at M.A. Chidambaram Stadium, Madras*

Haryana 165 (A. Kaypee 62, D. Vasu 6 for 47) and 290 (P. Thakur 60, Avtar Singh 54, D. Vasu 6 for 62)

Tamil Nadu 393 (Robin Singh 99, D. Vasu 69 not out, S. Sharath 56, V. Jain 6 for 138) and 63 for 0

Tamil Nadu won by 10 wickets

at K.D. Singh 'Bab' Stadium, Lucknow

Kerala 360 (B. Ramprakash 94, S. Oasis 52, A.W. Zaidi 5 for 89)

Uttar Pradesh 472 for 5 (S. Shukla 143 not out, J. Yadav 106, G. Pande 85)

Match drawn

Uttar Pradesh qualified for quarter-final on first-innings lead

at Municipal Ground, Rajkot

Saurashtra 321 (B. Dutta 74, P. Bhatt 65, S.S. Tanna 58, Abinash Kumar 4 for 76) and 52 (Abinash Kumar 5 for 18)

Bihar 264 (V. Khullar 104, H. Parsana 5 for 84) and 110 for 3

Bihar won by 7 wickets

at Nehru Stadium, Indore

Madhya Pradesh 291 (C.S. Pandit 122, S.V. Jedhe 4 for 58, P. Chitale 4 for 70) and 451 (M.S. Sahni 118, A.R. Khurasiya 106, H.S. Sodhi 75, M.S. Kulkarni 4 for 28)

Maharashtra 239 (H.A. Kinikar 82, A.V. Kale 82, R.K. Chauhan 6 for 97) and 216 (S.S. Bhave 72, R.K. Chauhan 6 for 88)

Madhya Pradesh won by 287 runs

at MB College Ground, Udaipur

Rajasthan 445 (A. Parmar 119, P.K. Kumar 76, V. Joshi 67, D. Kumar 60) and 389 for 5 dec. (P.K. Kumar 208 not out, R. Kanwat 66)

Assam 89 (P.K. Kumar 5 for 23, Mohammad Aslam 4 for 25) and 263 (G. Datta 73, S. Limaye 60, R. Rathore 5 for 57)

Rajasthan won by 482 runs

at PCA Stadium, Mohali, Chandigarh

Karnataka 171 (S. Joshi 72 not out, A. Bedi 4 for 31) and 85 for 2

Punjab 332 (K.K. Mohan 98, D. Johnson 5 for 93)

Match drawn

Punjab qualified for quarter-final on first-innings lead

at Ferozeshah Kotla Ground, Delhi

Delhi 464 (A.K. Sharma 170, A. Malhotra 152, C.M. Sharma 4 for 100) and 174 for 3 (V. Dahiya 76, Bantoo Singh 54)

Bengal 375 (S.S. Karim 160 not out, S. Mukerjee 65, C.M. Sharma 55, Shakti Singh 6 for 104)

Match drawn

Delhi qualified for quarter-final on first-innings lead

Divakar Vasu, Tamil Nadu's left-arm medium-pace bowler, continued with the outstanding form he had shown in South Zone matches by taking 12 for 109 in his side's victory over Haryana. Jyoti Yadav hit a century on his debut to aid Uttar Pradesh in the rain-affected match in

Lucknow, and Chandrakant Pandit scored a brisk 122 to lead his side to victory over Maharashtra.

Pudiyangam Krishna Kumar made the first double century of his career for Rajasthan, and the left-hander also had match figures of 7 for 52. Punjab had to rely on their first-innings lead in a match decimated by rain, and rain also washed out the third day's play in the game between Delhi and Bengal.

QUARTER-FINALS

26, 27, 28 February, 1 and 2 March 1995 *at Wankhede Stadium, Bombay*

Tamil Nadu 118 (P.L. Mhambrey 5 for 53) and 190
 (Robin Singh 67, N.M. Kulkarni 5 for 71)
Bombay 330 (S.R. Tendulkar 166, N.V. Joglekar 67, D. Vasu
 5 for 107)

Bombay won by an innings and 22 runs

at Keenan Stadium, Jamshedpur

Delhi 402 (R. Lamba 160, Bantoo Singh 68, Ajay Sharma 62,
 Abinash Kumar 4 for 129) and 238 (M. Prabhakar 116 not out)
Bihar 229 (Tariq-ur-Rehman 83 not out, A.K. Sharma 4 for 10)
 and 156 for 4 (Tariq-ur-Rehman 50 not out)

Match drawn

Delhi qualified for semi-final on first-innings lead

at Ordnance Equipment Factory Ground, Kanpur

Rajasthan 237 (A. Parmar 79, R.S. Rathore 54, A.W. Zaidi
 5 for 92) and 417 for 5 (G.K. Khoda 237 not out, P.K. Amre 65)
Uttar Pradesh 487 (S. Yadav 141, R. Sapru 104, S. Shukla 71,
 Mohammad Aslam 4 for 130)

Match drawn

Uttar Pradesh qualified for semi-final on first-innings lead

at PCA Stadium, Mohali, Chandigarh

Punjab 294 (P. Dharmani 114, N.S. Sidhu 71) and 353 for 5
 (K. Mohan 101 not out, A.R. Kapoor 59, P. Dharmani 55)
Madhya Pradesh 189 (K. Obaid 5 for 39)

Match drawn

Punjab qualified for semi-final on first-innings lead

Bombay, the only side to move straight into the quarter-finals, brushed aside a limp Tamil Nadu side in three days. They were helped by another spectacular century from Sachin Tendulkar, 166 off 153 balls with 27 fours and a six. Delhi were in total command against Bihar although they batted slowly in a rain-interrupted match.

There was a maiden double century for Gagan Khoda at Kanpur, but it came too late to help Rajasthan into the semi-finals. Pamkaj Dharmani reached a maiden first-class hundred for Punjab, but this was another match in which rain played a part.

SEMI-FINALS

12, 13, 14, 15 and 16 March 1995 *at Wankhede Stadium, Bombay*

Bombay 486 (S.R. Tendulkar 109, A.A. Muzumdar 69,
 V.G. Kambli 64, A.W. Zaidi 4 for 107)
Uttar Pradesh 144 (S. Shukla 72) and 109 (S. Yadav 63)

Bombay won by an innings and 233 runs

at Ferozeshah Kotla Ground, Delhi

Delhi 554 (A.K. Sharma 240, R. Lamba 165)
Punjab 780 for 8 (Bhupinder Singh jr 297, P. Dharmani 202,
 V. Rathore 74, A.R. Kapoor 52)

Match drawn

Punjab qualified for final on first-innings lead

A third century in the campaign for Tendulkar set up Bombay's crushing victory over Uttar Pradesh, but all attention was focused on Delhi. Ajay Sharma's 240 and Lamba's 165 took Delhi to a massive 554 before lunch on the third day. Sharma's runs came in four hours and included 6 sixes and 22 fours. Lamba was more circumspect, but he seemed to have taken his side to an impregnable position. First-innings lead looked certain to be Delhi's when the sixth Punjab wicket went down at 298 on the fourth day. However, this brought wicket-keeper Pamkaj Dharmani, his maiden century scored in the previous round, to join Bhupinder Singh jr. Both batsmen were to reach the first double centuries of their careers. Bhupinder Singh jr was at the crease for 785 minutes, faced 738 balls and hit 35 fours; Dharmani faced 385 balls and hit a six and 26 fours in his 580-minute stay. Together they added 460 for the seventh wicket and so beat the former world-record stand of 347 established by Depeiza and Atkinson for West Indies against Australia in May 1955.

FINAL

27, 28, 29, 30 and 31 March 1995 *at Wankhede Stadium, Bombay*

Bombay 690 for 6 dec. (S.V. Manjrekar 224,
 S.R. Tendulkar 140, S.S. Dighe 137, V.G. Kambli
 107 not out, Sandeep Sharma 4 for 155) and 513 for 6 dec.
 (S.R. Tendulkar 139, S.V. Bahutule 103 not out,
 A.A. Muzumdar 69, V.G. Kambli 64)
Punjab 371 (V. Rathore 177, N.S. Sidhu 108) and 141 for 2
 (P. Dharmani 65 not out, A. Mehra 60 not out)

Match drawn

Bombay won trophy on first-innings lead

Tendulkar won the toss and, although Joglekar was bowled by Bhupinder Singh senior at six, Bombay had one hand on the Ranji Trophy by the end of the first day, by which time Dighe was on 123, Manjrekar 110, and the score was 257 for 1. Dighe went early on the second morning, his stand with Manjrekar having realised 286, but this only brought in Tendulkar who hit 140 off 130 balls.

FIRST-CLASS AVERAGES

BATTING

	M	Inns	NO	Runs	HS	Av	100s	50s
A. Gupta	3	5	2	415	210*	138.33	2	–
S.R. Tendulkar	8	13	–	1258	179	96.76	6	3
A.K. Sharma	12	14	–	1288	240	92.00	5	3
Bhupinder Singh jr	10	12	–	952	297	79.33	3	3
S.S. Bhave	9	13	2	855	292	77.72	2	4
P. Krishna Kumar	7	12	4	607	208*	75.87	2	3
R. Lamba	8	10	–	744	312	74.40	3	–
S.S. Karim	9	12	3	641	160*	71.22	2	3
S.A. Shukla	8	11	2	608	143*	67.55	2	3
P. Dharmani	9	11	2	605	202*	67.22	2	4
K. Mohan	5	6	1	335	101*	67.00	1	2
M.H. Parmar	4	8	1	463	155*	66.14	2	2
A.V. Kale	5	7	–	458	153	65.42	2	2
C.M. Sharma	7	9	2	454	102*	64.85	2	3
A.O. Malhotra	7	9	2	443	152	63.28	2	1
K.K. Patel	6	8	1	423	168	60.42	1	2
R.S. Dravid	10	19	1	1068	191	59.33	3	6
Robin Singh	10	16	1	851	155	56.73	1	8
V. Rathore	12	21	1	1130	177	56.50	4	6
H.A. Kinikar	5	7	1	330	138	55.00	1	1
S. Sharath	11	18	4	753	121*	53.78	1	7
Abhay Sharma	7	12	1	584	182	53.09	1	3
W.V. Raman	10	15	1	738	250*	52.71	3	1
K.A. Jeshwanh	6	9	1	418	154*	52.25	2	1
Saurav Ganguly	8	14	1	677	200*	52.07	2	4
C.S. Pandit	6	7	–	364	122	52.00	1	3
S. Yadav	6	7	1	308	141	51.33	1	2
S.S. Sugwekar	10	13	2	560	160	50.90	1	3
A.A. Muzumdar	15	25	4	1068	220	50.85	2	9
R.V. Sapru	7	10	1	454	119	50.44	3	–
Rajesh Puri	7	9	1	400	134	50.00	2	–
R.B. Biswal	8	12	2	492	126	49.20	1	4
S. Joshi	6	9	1	388	104	48.50	1	2
J. Arun Kumar	8	14	2	582	117	48.50	1	3
N.R. Mongia	7	13	–	628	154	48.30	2	1
G.K. Khoda	10	18	1	815	237*	47.94	2	3
Bantoo Singh	12	16	–	765	214	47.81	1	5
J.J. Martin	5	8	1	332	94*	47.42	–	2
N.S. Sidhu	7	10	–	473	108	47.30	2	2
V.V.S. Laxman	9	17	4	607	112	46.69	2	2
A.S. Kaypee	5	8	1	316	72	45.14	–	4
S.S. Dighe	13	19	4	658	137	43.86	2	2
S. Oasis	6	10	1	394	110	43.77	1	3
Suryaveer Singh	5	8	–	350	163	43.75	1	2
V.V. Kumar	4	8	–	349	96	43.62	–	4
A.R. Khurasiya	10	14	2	518	106	43.16	2	3
R. Shamshed	11	19	1	772	127	42.88	1	6
R. Sehgal	6	8	–	342	216	42.75	1	1
N.R. Odedra	8	14	–	592	142	42.28	1	4
S.V. Manjrekar	14	24	1	961	224	41.78	2	7
A. Parmar	5	10	1	376	119	41.77	1	1
M. Prabhakar	7	11	2	371	120	41.22	2	–
V.B. Chandrasekhar	6	10	1	363	74	40.33	–	2
R. Nayyar	5	8	–	314	120	39.25	1	1
V.G. Kambli	9	15	1	545	147	38.92	2	3
M.V. Sridhar	9	17	2	573	107	38.20	2	2
A.R. Kapoor	13	16	1	561	181	37.40	1	3
S.V. Bahutule	12	16	4	441	112*	36.75	2	–
B. Ramprakash	6	10	–	365	94	36.50	–	2
Bhupinder Singh sr	11	12	3	326	85*	36.22	–	1
S.S. Tanna	5	10	–	348	88	34.80	–	4
D. Gandhi	7	11	1	348	151	34.80	2	–
S.H. Kotak	7	13	1	408	121	34.00	1	3
Rajinder Singh	5	10	–	328	93	32.80	–	3
P.K. Amre	10	17	–	526	147	30.94	1	3
S.T. Banerjee	10	14	2	314	66*	26.16	–	2
A. Vaidya	11	18	2	375	83	23.43	–	3
V.Z. Yadav	13	20	–	458	111	22.90	1	2

(Qualification – 300 runs)

BOWLING

	Overs	Mds	Runs	Wkts	Av	Best	10/m	5/inn
M. Kulkarni	108.2	14	318	22	14.45	6-67	–	2
K.V.P. Rao	273.1	88	531	36	14.75	7-74	2	5
D. Vasu	240.5	49	610	34	17.94	8-114	1	4
R. Ananth	184	48	447	24	18.52	6-56	–	2
A.R. Kumble	293.5	77	770	41	18.78	8-41	1	2
P. Jain	187	57	399	21	19.00	5-35	1	3
J.P. Pandey	134.5	14	458	21	19.08	6-64	1	2
D. Johnson	159.3	42	480	25	19.20	5-28	–	3
F. Ghayas	130	28	412	21	19.61	5-45	–	1
S.A. Ankola	196.1	51	593	30	19.76	6-47	–	2
P. Krishna Kumar	228.1	56	609	29	21.00	6-63	1	3
N.M. Kulkarni	249.5	52	694	33	21.03	6-80	1	3
C. Dey	135	15	421	20	21.05	6-95	1	3
Kanwaljit Singh	475.4	166	1002	47	21.31	7-33	–	3
H. Parsana	201.1	49	455	21	21.66	5-84	–	1
B. Ramprakash	318.3	86	658	30	21.93	6-101	1	2
A.W. Zaidi	238.2	57	627	28	22.39	5-89	–	2
A.S. Wassan	320.2	55	962	42	22.90	6-59	1	3
N.D. Hirwani	461	103	1114	48	23.20	7-83	1	3
A. Kuruvilla	200.1	35	628	27	23.25	5-42	–	1
P.L. Mhambrey	478.2	113	1264	54	23.40	5-46	–	4
Mohammad Aslam	224	40	682	29	23.51	5-66	–	2
Venkatapathy Raju	248	65	567	24	23.62	5-60	–	2
K.N.A. Padmanabhan	295	88	666	28	23.78	6-26	–	3
M. Venkataramana	250	57	631	26	24.26	6-86	1	1
R.B. Biswal	308.4	73	769	31	24.80	7-38	1	2
M. Suresh Kumar	258.4	59	637	25	25.48	6-68	1	2
S.V. Bahutule	422.4	121	1023	39	26.23	7-63	–	1
R.K. Chauhan	330.5	79	853	32	26.65	6-88	1	3
Abinash Kumar	566.1	143	1292	46	28.08	5-18	–	1
I.A. Thakur	233	42	675	24	28.12	6-22	1	1
S.V. Mudkavi	224.2	46	602	21	28.66	4-29	–	–
K. Nath	222	35	631	20	31.55	5-53	–	1
V. Chatterjee	524	125	1277	40	31.92	5-117	–	1
C.M. Sharma	240.4	42	810	25	32.40	4-27	–	–
A.R. Kapoor	569.4	112	1708	52	32.84	6-102	1	4
B. Vij	577.5	140	1545	47	32.87	5-60	–	1
Bhupinder Singh sr	291	76	771	23	33.52	3-42	–	–
S. Subramaniam	521.4	149	1174	34	34.52	7-68	–	–

(Qualification – 20 wickets)

LEADING FIELDERS

55 – S.S. Dighe (ct 47/st 8); 31 – A. Vaidya (ct 23/st 8); 30 – M.G. Chaturvedi (ct 27/st 3); 26 – V.Z. Yadav (ct 22/st 4); 22 – Abhay Sharma (ct 17/st 5); 21 – P. Dharmani (ct 17/ st 4) and S.S. Karim (ct 19/st 2); 18 – Z. Zuffri (ct 13/st 5), C.S. Pandit (ct 13/st 5) and A.A. Muzumdar; 16 – N.R. Mongia; 15 – S.V. Manjrekar (ct 14/st 1) and R. Shamshed; 14 – V. Rathore; 13 – V. Kamaruddin (ct 12/st 1), S.V. Wankhede (ct 10/st 3) and K.K. Patel (ct 12/st 1); 12 – S.S. Bhave, D.J. Jain (ct 10/st 2), S.M. Kondhalkar (ct 11/st 1), Ajay K. Sharma, P.R. Mohapatra, B.D. Moharty (ct 10/st 2) and M.M. Parmar (ct 10/st 2) and S.R. Tendulkar

It was not simply the amount of runs that Tendulkar scored in the Indian season that was impressive, but the rate at which he scored them. In his 140, he hit 5 sixes and 14 fours, and his partnership with Manjrekar was worth 221. Manjrekar batted for 548 minutes, faced 370 balls and was the backbone of Bombay's success. The massacre of the Punjabi bowling continued as Bombay were 669 for 5 at stumps on the second day, and when Tendulkar declared Kambli had hit 107 off 109 balls.

Punjab lost three wickets for 99 before Sidhu and Vikram Rathore added 218. Both reached centuries, but no one else scored 20. Tendulkar did not enforce the follow-on, and Bombay were secure. There was time for Tendulkar to hit 139 off 91 balls in just over two hours, and for Saitaj Bahutule to hit 103 off 87 balls. The rest was academic.

ZIMBABWE

South Africa 'A' tour
Sri Lanka tour, Test and one-day international series
Pakistan tour, Test and one-day international series
First-class averages

Salim Malik and Andy Flower toss up before the start of the first Test match, Zimbabwe v. Pakistan. This proved to be an historic game for Zimbabwe who gained their first Test victory. (Mueen-ud-din Hameed/Sportsline)

SOUTH AFRICA 'A' TOUR

<u>**20, 21, 22 and 23** September 1994</u> *at Old Hararians Sports Club, Harare*

Mashonaland 271 (C.B. Wishart 73, A.D.R. Campbell 53,
G.C. Martin 50, N. Boje 4 for 65) and 158 (G.W. Flower 60,
S. Elworthy 5 for 38)
South Africa 'A' 499 (J.B. Commins 164, D.J. Callaghan 104,
N. Boje 102, G.F.J. Liebenberg 84, P.A. Strang 5 for 137)
South Africa 'A' won by an innings and 70 runs

<u>**27, 28, 29 and 30** September 1994</u> *at Bulawayo Athletic Club*

Matabeleland Select XI 379 (W.R. James 107, G.J. Whittall
105, C.B. Wishart 63) and 308 (W.R. James 127)
South Africa 'A' 471 for 9 dec. (D.J. Callaghan 154, N. Boje
57, P.J.R. Steyn 51) and 219 for 4 (M.W. Rushmere 74 not
out, J.M. Arthur 53)
South Africa 'A' won by 6 wickets

<u>**4, 5 and 6** October 1994</u> *at Alexandra Club, Harare*

Zimbabwe 'A' 87 (S. Elworthy 6 for 47) and 143
South Africa 'A' 409 (G.F.J. Liebenberg 107, M.W. Rushmere
90, S.D. Jack 65 not out, B.C. Strang 5 for 95)
South Africa 'A' won by an innings and 179 runs

The fullest season of first-class cricket that Zimbabwe has experienced since attaining Test status began with a short tour by a South African 'A' side under Mark Rushmere. There were 15 players in the South African party, and they proved far too strong for the opposition that Zimbabwe provided. A Mashonaland side which included eight Test players was overwhelmed in the opening match. The home side began badly, but there was some solid middle-order batting which took them to 271 in 78 overs on the first day. The tourists, 35 for 0 overnight, lost Arthur and Rushmere early on the second morning before Liebenberg and Callaghan added 145. Leg-spinner Paul Strang destroyed the middle-order as South Africa 'A' went from 225 for 3 to 231 for 8, four wickets falling with the score on 231. By the close of play, Commins and Boje had advanced the total to 337 for 8, and they were not separated until Nick Boje, having hit the first century of his career, was caught by Grant Flower off Gary Martin for 102. The pair added 268 in 368 minutes. This was the second highest ninth-wicket partnership in the history of the game, just 15 short of the record set by Chapman and Warren of Derbyshire against Warwickshire in 1910. Mashonaland surrendered meekly in their second innings.

Matabeleland Select XI gave the tourists by far their hardest task in the second match. Guy Whittall, an all-rounder of immense promise, hit a maiden first-class hundred and shared a third-wicket stand of 166 with Wishart. Wayne James dominated a sixth-wicket stand of 102 with Ranchod, and the home side were not dismissed until early on the second morning. David Callaghan was

again in fine form and took South Africa 'A' to a first-innings lead of 92. The home side lost four wickets in clearing these arrears, but James hit his second century of the match, so becoming the first Zimbabwe batsman to score a century in each innings since independence. Needing 217 to win in 67 overs, the South Africans won with 2.4 overs to spare.

Scheduled for four days, the match with Zimbabwe 'A' was over in less than three. The home side played poor cricket on a poor pitch and were outclassed. Liebenberg and Rushmere added 167 for the tourists' second wicket, and Jack hit a fierce 65 not out at number ten.

SRI LANKA TOUR

<u>**3, 4 and 5** October 1994</u> *at Harare South Country Club*

Mashonaland Country Districts XI 177 (M. Muralitharan 6 for
55) and 125 (G.P. Wickremasinghe 4 for 20)
Sri Lankans 600 for 6 dec. (P.A. de Silva 200 retired,
S. Ranatunga 119, A.P. Gurusinha 82, S.T. Jayasuriya 58,
D.P. Samaraweera 53)
Sri Lankans won by an innings and 298 runs

<u>**7, 8 and 9** October 1994</u> *at Old Hararians Sports Club, Harare*

Sri Lankans 502 for 3 dec. (A.P. Gurusinha 141,
H.P. Tillekeratne 105 not out, R.S. Mahanama 105 retired
hurt, A. Ranatunga 100 not out)
Zimbabwe Cricket Union President's XI 96
(K.R. Pushpakumara 5 for 38, W.P.U.C.J. Vaas 5 for 41)
and 188 for 9
Match drawn

The Sri Lankans came to Zimbabwe to play three Test matches and three one-day internationals. They also had two warm-up matches of first-class status, but the opposition provided for them was woefully weak. In the first match, Stephen Peall, the off-break bowler, was the only Zimbabwe player to have bowled with any regularity in the first-class game, and he took 2 for 189 in 44 overs. Sanjeeva Ranatunga and Aravinda de Silva scored 299 – a Sri Lankan record – for the third wicket, and the Districts side sank without trace.

An opening stand of 213 in the second match was followed by a fourth-wicket stand of 160 between Tillekeratne and Arjuna Ranatunga. The Sri Lankans would have won again but for Ranchod being dropped at slip in the penultimate over of the match. He and E. Matambanadzo held out for the last 10 minutes to earn a draw.

TEST SERIES
ZIMBABWE v. SRI LANKA

A grim first Test match between the two youngest Test countries ended early when rain prevented any play on the last day. For this relief – much thanks.

Arjuna Ranatunga won the toss, and Sri Lanka batted. Mahanama was caught behind attempting a leg-glance, after which Gurusinha and Sanjeeva Ranatunga batted out the rest of the day, scoring 129 in 76 overs to end on 157 for 1. Brain retired from the Zimbabwe attack with a rib injury after bowling five overs, but Jarvis, left-arm medium pace and aggressively fit close to his 39th birthday, bowled an accurate line outside the off-stump on a flat pitch. A small crowd suffered.

They continued to suffer on the second day when Gurusinha, who hit 14 fours and a six, reached the third slowest century in Test history. In all, he batted for 607 minutes and faced 461 deliveries. Sanjeeva Ranatunga, who hit a maiden Test century in what was only his second Test, was a little quicker, facing 348 balls in 467 minutes and hitting 17 fours. Zimbabwe fielded well. Aravinda de Silva fell to a brilliant one-handed caught-and-bowled by Jarvis while Tillekeratne was splendidly caught behind down the leg side and Arjuna Ranatunga, who provided some welcome aggression, cut the ball to point. The last nine Sri Lankan wickets went down for 138 runs, and so ended the second day.

Zimbabwe were no more adventurous than Sri Lanka. Grant Flower – scoring only a single in his first 75 minutes at the crease – and Mark Dekker achieved Zimbabwe's best opening stand in their eight-Test history with 113. Flower was caught behind off a short delivery, and Dekker was out sweeping. The 19-year-old Chaminda Vaas, a left-arm seamer of genuine pace, bowled most impressively as Zimbabwe came to an early close through rain and bad light on 172 for 2 from 69 overs.

Extras totalled 65, the highest score in Zimbabwe's innings, due mainly to 18 no-balls and a wide from Wickremasinghe. In all, 44 no-balls were bowled, and batsmen scored off eight of them. Guy Whittall was fined after showing dissent at being given out caught behind, the first Zimbabwe player to be punished in this manner, and the Test died.

For the second Test, Zimbabwe replaced the injured Brain with Rennie, and Sri Lanka brought in Dharmasena for Pushpakumara. The start of the match was put back for two days because of rain. Zimbabwe won the toss and batted. They began disastrously, losing both openers for five. Campbell helped Houghton to salvage the innings with a stand of 60, but the real recovery was brought about by Houghton and Andy Flower who added 121 in 39 overs. Flower was caught off a sweep, but Zimbabwe closed on 213 for 4, with Houghton having reached his second Test century.

FIRST TEST MATCH – ZIMBABWE v. SRI LANKA
11, 12, 13, 15 and 16 October 1994 at Harare Sports Club, Harare

SRI LANKA

	FIRST INNINGS	
R.S. Mahanama	c James, b Jarvis	8
A.P. Gurusinha	c A. Flower, b Whittall	128
S. Ranatunga	c James, b Whittall	118
P.A. de Silva	c and b Jarvis	19
A. Ranatunga (capt)	c sub (Wishart), b Streak	62
H.P. Tillekeratne	c James, b Whittall	1
*P.B. Dassanayake	lbw, b Whittall	0
W.P.U.C.J. Vaas	lbw, b Streak	3
G.P. Wickremasinghe	c James, b Streak	15
M. Muralitharan	c and b Streak	0
K.R. Pushpakumara	not out	6
Extras	lb 19, w 1, nb 3	23
		383

ZIMBABWE

	FIRST INNINGS	
G.W. Flower	c Dassanayake, b Vaas	41
M.H. Dekker	c sub (Samaraweera), b Muralitharan	40
A.D.R. Campbell	c Tillekeratne, b Wickremasinghe	44
D.L. Houghton	c Dassanayake, b Vaas	58
A. Flower (capt)	c Dassanayake, b Vaas	26
G.J. Whittall	c Dassanayake, b Pushpakumara	4
*W.R. James	c Dassanayake, b Vaas	18
H.H. Streak	c Gurusinha, b Muralitharan	8
S.G. Peall	not out	9
D.H. Brain	not out	6
M.P. Jarvis		
Extras	b 10, lb 18, w 1, nb 36	65
	(for 8 wickets)	319

	O	M	R	W
Brain	5	2	9	–
Streak	42.5	14	79	4
Jarvis	41	18	76	2
Whittall	33	8	70	4
Peall	50	11	114	–
G.W. Flower	8	2	16	–

	O	M	R	W
Wickremasinghe	26	4	60	1
Vaas	37	11	74	4
Pushpakumara	20	–	68	1
de Silva	6	–	20	–
Muralitharan	32	7	60	2
A. Ranatunga	2	–	9	–

FALL OF WICKETS
1–28, 2–245, 3–281, 4–318, 5–322, 6–330, 7–361, 8–376, 9–376

FALL OF WICKETS
1–113, 2–115, 3–202, 4–259, 5–264, 6–274, 7–294, 8–307

Umpires: I.D. Robinson & L.H. Barker

Match drawn

Whittall was caught in the gully early on the second morning, but James and Houghton put on 100 in 39 overs. David Houghton was rock-like, but he was always enterprising, never dull. He was finally leg before to Vaas 20 minutes before the end of the second day, and he had led Zimbabwe from 5 for 2 to 419 for 8. He had notched up Zimbabwe's first double century in Test cricket, and he had not offered a chance against some tidy bowling until he was beyond 200. He batted for $11\frac{1}{4}$ hours and faced 541 balls. He hit 3 sixes and 35 fours in a magnificent display of concentration and quality.

Zimbabwe finished the second day on 427 for 8, and Andy Flower declared the next morning after Peall was out following some breezy hitting. The score of 462 for 9 was Zimbabwe's highest in Test cricket. By the end of the third day, with Sri Lanka reeling on 96 for 6, they seemed to be close to their first Test victory. Mahanama and de Silva were both out pulling, and James held five catches behind the stumps, four of them down the leg side, all of them good.

Zimbabwe achieved their first objective on the fourth day in forcing Sri Lanka to follow on, but it took them much longer to prise out the tail than they would have wished. They did not capture a wicket until the last ball of the morning session when Gurusinha, having offered a

dead bat for $5\frac{1}{2}$ hours, was caught at short-leg. Dharmasena continued to defend doggedly and was at the crease for five hours before being run out by Heath Streak. Sri Lanka finally followed on 244 runs in arrears, and Zimbabwe's spirits rose when Mahanama was out in the first over of the innings for the second time in the match. He was splendidly caught at slip by the diving Andy Flower, and Gurusinha perished in the last over of the day as he played a careless leg-glance.

Sri Lanka began the last day on 30 for 2, and, in the course of 100 overs, they lost only two more wickets while 163 runs were scored. Night-watchman Dharmasena batted 99 minutes for his 18, and Sanjeeva Ranatunga, having batted for 422 minutes, reached his second century in successive Tests off the last ball of the match. He had hit 15 fours, faced 352 balls and done much to ensure that Sri Lanka went into the final Test on level terms.

Dassanayake, the highly promising Sri Lankan wicketkeeper who has acquitted himself well in his brief Test career, paid the price for the inadequacies of other batsmen when he was replaced by Jayasuriya for the final Test, Tillekeratne – whose limitations as a keeper have long been well known – taking over behind the stumps. The visitors made two other changes, Pushpakumara and Kalpage replacing Muralitharan and Wickremasinghe. Brain

SECOND TEST MATCH – ZIMBABWE v. SRI LANKA
20, 21, 22, 23 and 24 October 1994 at Queen's Sports Club, Bulawayo

ZIMBABWE

FIRST INNINGS		
G.W. Flower	c Dassanayake, b Wickremasinghe	1
M.H. Dekker	c Mahanama, b Dharmasena	0
A.D.R. Campbell	st Dassanayake, b Muralitharan	18
D.L. Houghton	lbw, b Vaas	266
A. Flower (capt)	c Muralitharan, b Dharmasena	50
G.J. Whittall	c Tillekeratne, b Wickremasinghe	12
*W.R. James	c Dassanayake, b Vaas	33
H.H. Streak	c Dharmasena, b Vaas	0
J.A. Rennie	not out	19
S.G. Peall	b Vaas	30
M.P. Jarvis		
Extras	b 5, lb 11, w 2, nb 15	33
	(for 9 wickets, dec.)	462

SRI LANKA

FIRST INNINGS			SECOND INNINGS	
R.S. Mahanama	c James, b Streak	1	c A. Flower, b Streak	4
A.P. Gurusinha	c Dekker, b Peall	63	c James, b Jarvis	10
S. Ranatunga	c James, b Jarvis	4	not out	100
P.A. de Silva	c James, b Streak	0	(5) b Peall	27
A. Ranatunga (capt)	c James, b Jarvis	34		
H.P. Tillekeratne	c Dekker, b Jarvis	1	not out	15
*P.B. Dassanayake	c James, b Streak	8		
H.D.P.K. Dharmasena	run out	54	(4) c James, b Whittall	18
W.P.U.C.J. Vaas	c Dekker, b Whittall	14		
G.P. Wickremasinghe	b Whittall	7		
M. Muralitharan	not out	15		
Extras	lb 4, w 1, nb 12	17	b 5, lb 6, w 4, nb 4	19
		218	(for 4 wickets)	193

ZIMBABWE bowling

	O	M	R	W
Wickremasinghe	39	7	125	2
Vaas	44.3	14	85	4
Dharmasena	45	11	109	2
Muralitharan	55	21	108	1
de Silva	1	–	4	–
Gurusinha	4	–	15	–

SRI LANKA bowling

	O	M	R	W	O	M	R	W
Streak	28	10	68	3	14	4	28	1
Jarvis	34	22	30	3	24	14	24	1
Rennie	29	10	46	–	21	10	39	–
Peall	17	7	35	1	26	10	43	1
Whittall	17.1	6	35	2	17	7	29	1
G.W. Flower	1	1	0	–	5	2	13	–
Dekker					6	3	5	–
Campbell					2	1	1	–

FALL OF WICKETS

1–3, 2–5, 3–65, 4–186, 5–223, 6–323, 7–335, 8–419, 9–462

FALL OF WICKETS

1–4, 2–22, 3–23, 4–77, 5–79, 6–91, 7–142, 8–171, 9–193

1–4, 2–30, 3–80, 4–164

Umpires: I.D. Robinson & B.L. Aldridge

Match drawn

SRI LANKA

	FIRST INNINGS		SECOND INNINGS	
R.S. Mahanama	c Dekker, b Streak	24	(2) lbw, b Brain	0
A.P. Gurusinha	c A. Flower, b Brain	54	(1) c Whittall, b Brain	13
S. Ranatunga	c Whittall, b Strang	43	c Whittall, b Streak	8
*H.P. Tillekeratne	c Dekker, b Strang	116		
P.A. de Silva	c Dekker, b Streak	25	(4) not out	41
A. Ranatunga (capt)	c Dekker, b Streak	39	(5) not out	22
S.T. Jayasuriya	c James, b Streak	10		
R.S. Kalpage	c James, b Brain	14		
H.D.P.K. Dharmasena	c A. Flower, b Strang	21		
W.P.U.C.J. Vaas	not out	16		
K.R. Pushpakumara	c A. Flower, b Jarvis	8		
Extras	b 7, lb 11, w 4, nb 10	32	lb 2, nb 3	5
		402	(for 3 wickets)	**89**

ZIMBABWE

	FIRST INNINGS	
G.W. Flower	c Tillekeratne, b Pushpakumara	5
M.H. Dekker	lbw, b Pushpakumara	14
A.D.R. Campbell	c Tillekeratne, b Pushpakumara	99
D.L. Houghton	b Vaas	142
A. Flower (capt)	c Tillekeratne, b Vaas	10
G.J. Whittall	not out	61
*W.R. James	c Mahanama, b Pushpakumara	2
H.H. Streak	c Tillekeratne, b Pushpakumara	20
D.H. Brain	lbw, b Pushpakumara	0
P.A. Strang	b Dharmasena	6
M.P. Jarvis	b Pushpakumara	2
Extras	lb 8, nb 6	14
		375

	O	M	R	W	O	M	R	W
Brain	34	4	90	2	11	1	48	2
Streak	38	8	97	4	12	4	32	1
Jarvis	37	13	58	1	1	–	7	–
Whittall	28	5	74	–				
Strang	25	6	65	3				

	O	M	R	W
Vaas	44	12	76	2
Pushpakumara	35.4	7	116	7
Dharmasena	35	9	71	1
Gurusinha	13	3	39	–
Kalpage	12	5	31	–
Jayasuriya	2	–	12	–
A. Ranatunga	9	1	22	–

FALL OF WICKETS
1–64, 2–100, 3–149, 4–192, 5–267, 6–280, 7–329, 8–366, 9–380
1–5, 2–24, 3–36

FALL OF WICKETS
1–10, 2–25, 3–219, 4–235, 5–297, 6–305, 7–363, 8–363, 9–372

Umpires: K. Kanjee & Mahboob Shah

Match drawn

TEST MATCH AVERAGES – ZIMBABWE v. SRI LANKA

ZIMBABWE BATTING

	M	Inns	NO	Runs	HS	Av	100s	50s
D.L. Houghton	3	3	–	466	266	155.33	2	1
A.D.R. Campbell	3	3	–	161	99	53.66	–	1
S.G. Peall	2	2	1	39	30	39.00	–	–
G.J. Whittall	3	3	1	77	61*	38.50	–	1
A. Flower	3	3	–	86	50	28.66	–	1
M.H. Dekker	3	3	–	54	40	18.00	–	–
W.R. James	3	3	–	53	33	17.66	–	–
G.W. Flower	3	3	–	47	41	15.66	–	–
H.H. Streak	3	3	–	28	20	9.33	–	–
D.H. Brain	2	2	1	6	6*	6.00	–	–

Played in three Tests: M.P. Jarvis 2
Played in one Test: J.A. Rennie 19*; D.A. Strang 6

SRI LANKA BATTING

	M	Inns	NO	Runs	HS	Av	100s	50s
S. Ranatunga	3	5	1	273	118	68.25	2	–
A.P. Gurusinha	3	5	–	268	128	53.60	1	2
A. Ranatunga	3	4	1	157	62	52.33	–	1
H.P. Tillekeratne	3	4	1	133	116	44.33	1	–
H.D.P.K. Dharmasena	2	3	–	93	54	31.00	–	1
P.A. de Silva	3	5	1	112	41*	28.00	–	–
W.P.U.C.J. Vaas	3	3	1	33	16*	16.50	–	–
M. Muralitharan	2	2	1	15	15*	15.00	–	–
K.R. Pushpakumara	2	2	1	14	8	14.00	–	–
G.P. Wickremasinghe	2	2	–	22	15	11.00	–	–
R.S. Mahanama	3	5	–	37	24	7.40	–	–
P.B. Dassanayake	2	2	–	8	8	4.00	–	–

Played in one Test: S.T. Jayasuriya 10; R.S. Kalpage 14

ZIMBABWE BOWLING

	Overs	Mds	Runs	Wkts	Av	Best	10/m	5/inn
H.H. Streak	134.5	40	304	13	23.38	4-79	–	–
M.P. Jarvis	137	67	195	7	27.85	3-30	–	–
G.J. Whittall	95.1	21	208	7	29.71	4-70	–	–
D.H. Brain	50	7	147	4	36.75	2-48	–	–
S.G. Peall	93	28	192	2	96.00	1-35	–	–
G.W. Flower	14	5	29	–	–	–	–	–
J.A. Rennie	50	20	85	–	–	–	–	–

Bowled in one innings: A.D.R. Campbell 2–1–1–0; M.H. Dekker 6–3–5–0

SRI LANKA BOWLING

	Overs	Mds	Runs	Wkts	Av	Best	10/m	5/inn
K.R. Pushpakumara	55.4	7	184	8	23.00	7-116	–	1
W.P.U.C.J. Vaas	125.3	37	235	10	23.50	4-85	–	–
M. Muralitharan	87	28	168	3	56.00	2-60	–	–
H.D.P.K. Dharmasena	80	20	180	3	60.00	2-109	–	–
G.P. Wickremasinghe	65	11	185	3	61.66	2-125	–	–
P.A. de Silva	7	–	24					
A. Ranatunga	11	1	31					
A.P. Gurusinha	17	3	54					

Bowled in one innings: R.S. Kalpage 12–5–31–0; S.T. Jayasuriya 2–0–12–0

ZIMBABWE FIELDING FIGURES
13 – W.R. James; 7 – M.H. Dekker; 5 – A. Flower; 3 – G.J. Whittall; 1 – M.P. Jarvis,
H.H. Streak and sub (C.B. Wishart).

SRI LANKA FIELDING FIGURES
8 – P.B. Dassanayake (ct 7/st 1); 6 – H.P. Tillekeratne; 2 – R.S. Mahanama; 1 –
A.P. Gurusinha, M. Muralitharan, H.D.P.K. Dharmasena and sub (D.P. Samaraweera).

returned in place of Rennie and Paul Strang came in for Peall in the Zimbabwe side. Strang was making his Test debut.

Winning the toss, Sri Lanka had a solid start and, with Tillekeratne and Arjuna Ranatunga consolidating late in the day, they closed on 248 for 4. Strang had taken his first Test wicket when Sanjeeva Ranatunga hit a full toss into the hands of square-leg, and Tillekeratne suffered a similar fate on the second day. By the time he was out, however, Tillekeratne had been at the crease for 370 minutes. He reached the first Test hundred of his career, having come close on seven previous occasions, and, in all, faced 287 balls and hit 14 fours. He was the victim of a quite superb one-handed catch by Dekker, but he had led Sri Lanka to a substantial first-innings score. The strength of the Sri Lankan position was increased when Grant Flower was caught behind off Pushpakumara before the close, 10 for 1.

Dekker became Pushpakumara's second victim early on the third morning, but there followed a stand of 194 in 70 overs between Campbell and Houghton. This was the highest stand for Zimbabwe for any wicket in Test cricket. The excellent Campbell looked set for a maiden Test hundred, but he was marooned on 99 for a quarter of an hour before pushing loosely at Pushpakumara to give Tillekeratne his second catch. Andy Flower provided the wicket-keeper with his third before Whittall batted out the day with Houghton, who reached his third Test century. Zimbabwe ended the day on 276 for 4.

Houghton's second splendid innings within a week was brought to an end on the fourth morning. He faced 268 balls, hit 2 sixes and 17 fours and passed 450 runs in three innings in the series. Pushpakumara quickly disposed of the tail and finished with 7 for 116, the second-best figures for a Sri Lankan in Test cricket. Over the last two days, 104 overs were lost to rain and bad light. Only 14 overs were possible on the last morning, and the match and the series ended in a soggy draw.

If Zimbabwe could draw more comfort from the encounters than their opponents, neither side had really shown enough enterprise to deserve to win, and neither had been helped by slow, placid pitches which nullified the efforts of batsmen and bowlers.

 ## LIMITED-OVER SERIES
ZIMBABWE v. SRI LANKA

In contrast to the Test series, the one-day series offered a weekend of scintillating cricket. In the first match, Mahanama, who had struggled in the Tests, hit his highest one-day international score. His 119 came off 125 balls. He shared a stand of 119 for the second wicket with Sanjeeva Ranatunga. Facing a target of 257, Zimbabwe lost their

---

FIRST ONE-DAY INTERNATIONAL – ZIMBABWE v. SRI LANKA
3 November 1994 at Harare Sports Club, Harare

SRI LANKA

R.S. Mahanama	not out	119
A.P. Gurusinha	c Dekker, b Whittall	20
S. Ranatunga	c Houghton, b Dekker	51
A. Ranatunga (capt)	b Peall	14
P.A. de Silva	c Waller, b Whittall	35
S.T. Jayasuriya	c Waller, b Whittall	1
R.S. Kalpage	not out	0
G.P. Wickremasinghe		
*H.P. Tillekeratne		
W.P.U.C.J. Vaas		
K.R. Pushpakumara		
Extras	lb 6, w 10	16
(50 overs)	(for 5 wickets)	256

ZIMBABWE

G.W. Flower	c Tillekeratne, b Pushpakumara	0
A.C. Waller	c sub, b Wickremasinghe	40
A.D.R. Campbell	c A. Ranatunga, b Vaas	5
D.L. Houghton	c Jayasuriya, b Vaas	1
*A. Flower (capt)	b Vaas	61
G.J. Whittall	c Tillekeratne, b Wickremasinghe	0
M.H. Dekker	c Vaas, b Kalpage	20
G.C. Martin	c de Silva, b Kalpage	7
D.H. Brain	b Pushpakumara	10
H.H. Streak	not out	18
S.G. Peall	b Vaas	21
Extras	b 1, lb 8, w 7, nb 1	17
(48.1 overs)		200

	O	M	R	W
Streak	9	1	50	–
Brain	7	1	31	–
Whittall	10	1	58	3
Martin	10	1	39	–
Peall	7	–	36	1
G.W. Flower	2	–	12	–
Dekker	5	–	24	1

	O	M	R	W
Pushpakumara	10	–	51	2
Vaas	9.1	1	20	4
Wickremasinghe	8	–	42	2
A. Ranatunga	10	1	38	–
Kalpage	10	1	27	2
Jayasuriya	1	–	13	–

FALL OF WICKETS
1–40, 2–159, 3–198, 4–252, 5–255

FALL OF WICKETS
1–0, 2–12, 3–20, 4–66, 5–71, 6–129, 7–145, 8–149, 9–167

Umpires: Q. Goosen & I.D. Robinson   *Man of the Match:* R.S. Mahanama   *Sri Lanka won by 56 runs*

SECOND ONE-DAY INTERNATIONAL – ZIMBABWE v. SRI LANKA
5 November 1994 at Harare Sports Club, Harare

ZIMBABWE				SRI LANKA		
*A. Flower (capt)	b Vaas	76		R.S. Mahanama	c G.W. Flower, b Streak	108
G.W. Flower	run out	21		S.T. Jayasuriya	c Waller, b Streak	37
A.D.R. Campbell	not out	131		S. Ranatunga	run out	15
D.L. Houghton	c Kalpage, b Pushpakumara	22		P.A. de Silva	not out	97
A.C. Waller	c Tillekeratne, b Vaas	3		A. Ranatunga (capt)	c Waller, b Whittall	1
M.H. Dekker	b Vaas	9		A.P. Gurusinha	c G.W. Flower, b Streak	4
G.J. Whittall	not out	15		R.S. Kalpage	lbw, b Streak	0
G.C. Martin				*H.P. Tillekeratne	run out	7
H.H. Streak				G.P. Wickremasinghe	b Whittall	1
S.G. Peall				W.P.U.C.J. Vaas	not out	0
J.A. Rennie				K.R. Pushpakumara		
Extras	b 1, lb 8, w 3, nb 1	13		Extras	b 3, lb 3, w 10, nb 2	18
(50 overs)	(for 5 wickets)	290		(50 overs)	(for 8 wickets)	288

	O	M	R	W		O	M	R	W
Vaas	10	–	59	3	Streak	10	–	44	4
Pushpakumara	10	1	43	1	Rennie	8	–	54	–
Wickremasinghe	10	–	55	–	Whittall	8	–	57	2
A. Ranatunga	5	–	38	–	Martin	2	–	24	–
Kalpage	10	–	53	–	Peall	10	–	52	–
Gurusinha	5	–	33	–	G.W. Flower	7	–	28	–
					Dekker	5	–	23	–

FALL OF WICKETS
1–60, **2**–152, **3**–228, **4**–235, **5**–250

FALL OF WICKETS
1–66, **2**–111, **3**–233, **4**–234, **5**–245, **6**–245, **7**–276, **8**–278

Umpires: Q. Goosen & I.D. Robinson   *Man of the Match:* A.D.R. Campbell   *Zimbabwe won by 2 runs*

THIRD ONE-DAY INTERNATIONAL – ZIMBABWE v. SRI LANKA
6 November 1994 at Harare Sports Club, Harare

SRI LANKA				ZIMBABWE		
R.S. Mahanama	lbw, b Brain	40		A. Flower (capt)	c Muralitharan, b Pushpakumara	8
S.T. Jayasuriya	c A. Flower, b Brain	11		G.W. Flower	c Tillekeratne, b Vaas	0
A.P. Gurusinha	c A. Flower, b Whittall	25		A.D.R. Campbell	c Mahanama, b Vaas	2
P.A. de Silva	not out	107		D.L. Houghton	lbw, b Pushpakumara	0
A. Ranatunga (capt)	c G.W. Flower, b Brain	85		M.H. Dekker	retired hurt	23
R.S. Kalpage	not out	12		G.J. Whittall	c Gurusinha, b Pushpakumara	7
*H.P. Tillekeratne				*W.R. James	run out	29
M. Muralitharan				H.H. Streak	run out	8
G.P. Wickremasinghe				D.H. Brain	b Muralitharan	0
K.R. Pushpakumara				J.A. Rennie	not out	20
W.P.U.C.J. Vaas				S.G. Peall	b Wickremasinghe	2
Extras	lb 6, w 10	16		Extras	lb 3, w 1, nb 2	6
(50 overs)	(for 4 wickets)	296		(48.1 overs)		105

	O	M	R	W		O	M	R	W
Streak	10	1	40	–	Vaas	7	2	12	2
Brain	10	–	67	3	Pushpakumara	9	1	25	3
Rennie	7	–	60	–	Wickremasinghe	9	1	17	1
Whittall	7	–	43	1	Muralitharan	10	–	21	1
Peall	8	–	41	–	Kalpage	10	1	21	–
G.W. Flower	3	–	13	–	Jayasuriya	2	1	2	–
Campbell	3	–	14	–	Tillekeratne	1	–	1	–
Dekker	2	–	12	–	Mahanama	0.1	–	3	–

FALL OF WICKETS
1–18, **2**–76, **3**–106, **4**–249

FALL OF WICKETS
1–1, **2**–9, **3**–9, **4**–11, **5**–22, **6**–69, **7**–70, **8**–86, **9**–93

Umpires: S.N. Fleming & K. Kanjee   *Man of the Match:* P.A. de Silva   *Sri Lanka won by 191 runs*

way from the start as Grant Flower, Campbell and Houghton were all back in the pavilion with only 20 runs scored. Two of the wickets fell to Vaas who returned his best figures in a one-day international. Waller and Andy Flower halted the decline, and there was spirited batting from the tail, but Zimbabwe never looked like reaching their target. Gary Martin, a medium-pace bowler, made his international debut for Zimbabwe.

Winning the toss, Zimbabwe batted first in the second match of the series and were given a sound start by the Flower brothers. Andy Flower shared a second-wicket stand of 92 with Alistair Campbell, who played an innings of rare brilliance. He reached his first century in international cricket off 96 balls, and his 131 not out came off 115 deliveries. He hit 4 sixes and 11 fours, and it seemed that he had put victory beyond Sri Lanka's reach. Mahanama responded with his second century in succession and, with de Silva, he put on 122 for the third wicket. His dismissal by the admirable Streak signalled a collapse, and, in spite of de Silva's splendid innings, Sri Lanka finished three runs short of their target. There was some controversy, however, for the score-board was registering an incorrect score towards the end of the innings, and this may well have affected de Silva's efforts.

He made amends the following day when he made 107 not out off 100 balls, his first century in limited-over internationals. He hit 9 fours and ran brilliantly between the wickets. With Arjuna Ranatunga, he shared a fourth-wicket stand of 143. The Sri Lankan skipper hit 6 fours in his 83-ball innings. Pushpakumara and Vaas reduced the home side to 22 for 5, and there was no recovery. Zimbabwe were bowled out for their lowest score in a one-day international, and Sri Lanka won the series.

PAKISTAN TOUR

27, 28 and 29 January 1995 *at Harare South Country Club*

President's XI 301 for 4 dec. (G.W. Flower 137, G.J. Whittall 104) and 143 (M.G. Burmester 67, Akram Raza 5 for 52, Wasim Akram 4 for 26)

Pakistanis 327 for 6 dec. (Asif Mujtaba 113 not out) and 119 for 3 (Aamir Sohail 56)

Pakistanis won by 7 wickets

Pakistan arrived in Zimbabwe without the injured Waqar Younis and still smarting from their defeat in South Africa. Matters did not improve. Remarks by certain players

FIRST TEST MATCH – ZIMBABWE v. PAKISTAN
31 January, 1, 2, 3 and 4 February 1995 at Harare Sports Club, Harare

ZIMBABWE

	FIRST INNINGS	
M.H. Dekker	c Rashid, b Aqib	2
G.W. Flower	not out	201
A.D.R. Campbell	lbw, b Wasim	1
D.L. Houghton	c Sohail, b Aqib	23
*A. Flower (capt)	c Wasim, b Kabir	156
G.J. Whittall	not out	113
S. Carlisle		
P.A. Strang		
H.H. Streak		
D.H. Brain		
H. Olonga		
Extras	b 4, lb 19, w 3, nb 22	48
		—
	(for 4 wickets, dec.)	544

PAKISTAN

	FIRST INNINGS		SECOND INNINGS	
Aamir Sohail	c Houghton, b Brain	61	c Campbell, b Brain	5
Saeed Anwar	c A. Flower, b Olonga	8	lbw, b Whittall	7
Akram Raza	c Whittall, b Streak	19	(9) not out	2
Asif Mujtaba	c Carlisle, b Streak	2	(3) b Brain	4
Salim Malik (capt)	c Carlisle, b Whittall	32	(4) c A. Flower, b Brain	6
Ijaz Ahmed	c G.W. Flower, b Streak	65	(5) c Brain, b Streak	2
*Rashid Latif	c Campbell, b Whittall	6	c Houghton, b Whittall	38
Inzamam-ul-Haq	c G.W. Flower, b Streak	71	(6) c A. Flower, b Whittall	65
Wasim Akram	c Carlisle, b Streak	27	(8) c Dekker, b Strang	19
Kabir Khan	not out	2	b Streak	0
Aqib Javed	lbw, b Streak	0	b Streak	2
Extras	b 3, lb 4, w 9, nb 13	29	w 2, nb 6	8
		322		158

	O	M	R	W
Wasim Akram	39.5	12	95	1
Aqib Javed	34.1	8	73	2
Kabir Khan	35	5	142	1
Salim Malik	9	–	42	–
Akram Raza	34	6	112	–
Asif Mujtaba	7	–	30	–
Aamir Sohail	6	1	27	–

	O	M	R	W	O	M	R	W
Streak	39	11	90	6	11	4	15	3
Brain	27	4	94	1	16	4	50	3
Olonga	10	–	27	1				
Whittall	29	10	49	2	16	3	58	3
Strang	15	5	45	–	19	7	35	1
Dekker	4	1	10	–				

FALL OF WICKETS
1–4, 2–9, 3–42, 4–311

FALL OF WICKETS
1–36, 2–82, 3–88, 4–131, 5–135, 6–151, 7–271, 8–317, 9–322
1–13, 2–16, 3–26, 4–29, 5–35, 6–133, 7–142, 8–156, 9–156

Umpires: M.J. Kitchen & I.D. Robinson

Zimbabwe won by an innings and 64 runs

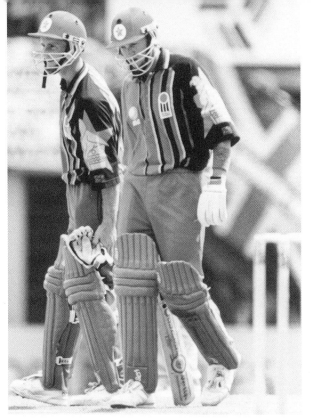

ABOVE: *Grant and Andy Flower were the backbone of the Zimbabwe side. They shared a record stand of 269 in the first Test against Pakistan. Grant Flower finished the season with 983 runs in first-class cricket, the highest number scored in a season in Zimbabwe. (Patrick Eagar)*

ABOVE RIGHT: *Henry Olonga became the first black cricketer to play for Zimbabwe, but he was no-balled for 'throwing' on the occasion of his Test debut. (Mueen-ud-din Hameed/Sportsline)*

querying why they had come to Zimbabwe did not endear them to their hosts, and, in the opening match, Henry Olonga, a black fast bowler who had been named in Zimbabwe's Test squad, was no-balled for throwing by umpire Ahmed Essat following pressure and complaints from Aamir Sohail.

In spite of this, Olonga, 18 years old, was selected for the first Test match, so becoming the first black player to represent Zimbabwe in what was the country's 11th game at the top level. There was an element of farce at the outset when the referee Hendricks missed the toss and ordered it to be retaken. Zimbabwe won the second ('real') toss, having lost the first.

The match did not begin well for the home side who lost Dekker, Campbell and Houghton for 42 before lunch, but these proved to be the sole disasters of the first day, by the end of which Grant Flower was unbeaten on 88 and skipper Andy Flower had 142. Aqib Javed had bowled a good opening spell, but he put down a simple return catch offered by Grant Flower when the opener was on 35. This was the only chance that Flower was to offer in an innings which lasted over 11 hours and contained just 10 fours.

Zimbabwe advanced from their 289 for 3 at the close of the first day to 544 for 4 – their highest ever score – before

Andy Flower declared. The captain was the only Zimbabwe batsman to lose his wicket during the day. He was out 45 minutes into the second morning when he cut a long-hop into the hands of gully, but by then his partnership with his brother was worth 269 in 83 overs. This bettered by five runs the stand by the Chappell brothers against New Zealand in 1974.

Pakistan's problems were far from over as Whittall now joined Grant Flower in an unbroken stand of 233 in 61 overs. Three catches were put down, the running between the wickets was exciting, and Pakistan disintegrated.

Olonga came on as first change and his first delivery in Test cricket went for four wides. His second was a fierce bouncer, and his third was touched to the wicket-keeper down the leg side by Saeed Anwar. Pakistan ended the day on 51 for 1.

In contrast to Pakistan, Zimbabwe were dynamic in the field and, rashly as Aamir Sohail, Salim Malik and Ijaz Ahmed batted, they were all the victims of fine catches. Pakistan moved to an uncertain close on the third day at 271 for 7, but Zimbabwe, too, had their problems. Olonga became the first bowler for 32 years to be no-balled in a Test match for throwing, and then he was forced to leave the field with a side strain. He did not appear again in the series.

Pakistan had neither the appetite nor the energy for saving the follow-on once Inzamam-ul-Haq had fallen to Heath Streak. The young pace bowler also accounted for Wasim and Aqib to give him figures of 6 for 90, the best by a Zimbabwe bowler in Test cricket. Following on, Pakistan fell apart, and they were 35 for 5 before Inzamam and Rashid gave some indication of character and determination. The match ended at 4.35 on the fourth day when Streak bowled Aqib Javed, and joyful celebrations greeted Zimbabwe's first Test victory. No side in international cricket puts more effort into a game; no side fields better.

Carlisle, debutant in the first Test, was joined by another

Heath Streak took 35 wickets in the six Test matches in which he played during the Zimbabwe season. The fast bowler later played for Hampshire. (Patrick Eagar)

newcomer in the second Test. Bryan Strang, a left-arm seamer and brother of leg-spinner Paul, came in for the injured Olonga. Andy Flower again won the toss, but Zimbabwe endured an unhappy opening day. They were bowled out for 174 as Wasim Akram found form and took his 250th wicket in Test cricket. Only Campbell, with 60 from 163 balls in 234 minutes, gave serious resistance on a green pitch, but Zimbabwe had some encouragement when Shakeel Ahmed was leg before to Streak before the close. Pakistan ended on 11 for 1, but it should have been 11 for 2 as Whittall dropped a simple catch at mid-off off the last ball of the day.

It was Aamir Sohail who escaped, but he became a Streak victim next morning, and it was Streak – more impressive with every match – who restricted Pakistan as they sought a big lead on the second day. It must be admitted that he was aided by some more irresponsible batting, and it was not until Ijaz Ahmed and Inzamam-ul-Haq came together that the batting took on an air of authority. The day ended with Pakistan claiming a first-innings lead of 86.

It proved to be sufficient for Pakistan to establish victory. On a pitch that was rapidly deteriorating, Wasim Akram bowled with controlled hostility, taking five wickets either side of lunch to wreck the Zimbabwe

SECOND TEST MATCH – ZIMBABWE v. PAKISTAN
7, 8 and 9 February 1995 at Queen's Sports Club, Bulawayo

ZIMBABWE

	FIRST INNINGS		SECOND INNINGS	
M.H. Dekker	c Shakeel, b Nazir	0	c Sohail, b Wasim	9
G.W. Flower	b Wasim	6	b Manzoor	22
A.D.R. Campbell	c Ijaz, b Manzoor	60	c Shakeel, b Wasim	0
D.L. Houghton	b Wasim	11	lbw, b Wasim	25
*A. Flower (capt)	c Ijaz, b Kabir	14	lbw, b Wasim	8
G.J. Whittall	c Sohail, b Manzoor	7	c sub (Moin Khan), b Nazir	5
S.V. Carlisle	c Kabir, b Wasim	1	not out	46
P.A. Strang	b Nazir	32	c Sohail, b Kabir	3
H.H. Streak	st Rashid, b Sohail	13	c Manzoor, b Kabir	11
D.H. Brain	c Rashid, b Sohail	5	b Kabir	0
B. Strang	not out	0	lbw, b Wasim	0
Extras	b 1, lb 9, nb 15	25	lb 6, nb 11	17
		174		146

PAKISTAN

	FIRST INNINGS		SECOND INNINGS	
Aamir Sohail	lbw, b Streak	26	c Campbell, b B. Strang	46
Shakeel Ahmed	lbw, b Streak	5	lbw, b B. Strang	7
*Rashid Latif	c A. Flower, b Streak	17	not out	1
Basit Ali	c B. Strang, b Streak	0		
Salim Malik (capt)	b Streak	44		
Ijaz Ahmed	b B. Strang	76		
Inzamam-ul-Haq	lbw, b Whittall	47		
Wasim Akram	c Dekker, b B. Strang	1		
Manzoor Elahi	c A. Flower, b B. Strang	13	(4) not out	1
Kabir Khan	not out	8		
Aamir Nazir	b Brain	7		
Extras	b 2, lb 5, w 2, nb 7	16	lb 2, w 1, nb 3	6
		260	(for 2 wickets)	61

	O	M	R	W	O	M	R	W
Wasim Akram	22	9	40	3	22.3	7	43	5
Aamir Nazir	18	4	36	2	11	1	39	1
Kabir Khan	16	2	45	1	11	3	26	3
Manzoor Elahi	21	8	38	2	14	6	32	1
Aamir Sohail	2.1	1	5	2				

	O	M	R	W	O	M	R	W
Streak	26	5	70	5	6	1	18	–
Brain	15	4	49	1	2	–	35	–
B. Strang	23	10	44	3	3.4	2	6	2
Whittall	15	3	42	1				
P.A. Strang	15	4	48	–				

FALL OF WICKETS
1–3, 2–7, 3–23, 4–56, 5–73, 6–86, 7–134, 8–167, 9–174
1–14, 2–16, 3–58, 4–73, 5–77, 6–93, 7–106, 8–145, 9–145

FALL OF WICKETS
1–9, 2–47, 3–52, 4–63, 5–133, 6–212, 7–226, 8–231, 9–246
1–56, 2–60

Umpires: B.C. Cooray & Q. Goosen

Pakistan won by 8 wickets

innings. Dekker suffered a broken finger and Houghton a broken thumb, and although Carlisle, in his second Test innings, batted with confidence and style, Zimbabwe were well beaten. Aamir Sohail launched a violent assault when Pakistan went in search of the 61 they needed for victory. Brain conceded 22 in his first over, and although both Aamir and Shakeel fell to Bryan Strang, Pakistan raced to their target in under 12 overs.

This was not a happy win for Pakistan, however, for allegations of attempted bribery and match-fixing persisted, as did rumours of division and strife within the Pakistan camp. The side was reprimanded for conduct unbecoming in the second Test, and Houghton was outspoken in his criticism of the umpires for ignoring blatant cases of sledging by the Pakistan players. Houghton was fined for his outburst, but the umpiring was severely criticised throughout the series, and the relations between the two sets of players continued to worsen. Pakistan were heavily fined for their slow over rate in the final Test.

In fact, Pakistan played their best cricket of the tour in the third encounter, in which Iain Butchart, a veteran of many a one-day international, made his Test debut. Winning the toss, Pakistan began brightly enough only for Aamir Sohail and Saeed Anwar to be out to reckless shots within the space of 12 balls. Streak was again the successful bowler, and he later captured the wickets of both Salim

Malik and Ijaz Ahmed. The only semblance of sanity in the batting came from Inzamam-ul-Haq who was last out after reaching the fourth Test century of his career. He faced 168 balls and hit 2 sixes and 12 fours.

Carlisle and Grant Flower scored four before the close, but they were soon separated on the second day. Carlisle remained, batting 172 minutes for his 31, but the Zimbabwe innings disappointed. Batsmen like Campbell and Houghton started well only to perish as patience wilted against accurate and workmanlike bowling. A first-innings lead of 12 was much smaller than Zimbabwe had anticipated and would have wished.

A wonderfully accurate spell from Bryan Strang kept Zimbabwe in contention as Pakistan threatened to build a big score. Streak was handicapped by a side injury, but some spectacular catching thwarted Pakistan when they attacked. Saeed was brilliantly taken to the right of square-leg, and Inzamam and Aamir Sohail fell to exceptional catches in the gully. Inzamam and Ijaz added 116 in 47 overs, but three wickets in the last 45 minutes of the day meant that Pakistan closed on 235 for 6.

Pakistan lost their last four wickets in nine balls for four runs on the fourth morning, and Zimbabwe needed 239 to win. Their challenge was undermined when they lost both openers to Aamir Nazir with just 12 scored. The young pace bowler also captured Campbell's wicket in his

THIRD TEST MATCH – ZIMBABWE v. PAKISTAN
15, 16, 17 and 19 February 1995 at Harare Sports Club, Harare

PAKISTAN

	FIRST INNINGS		SECOND INNINGS	
Aamir Sohail	c P.A. Strang, b Streak	21	(6) c G.W. Flower, b Whittall	19
Shakeel Ahmed	c A. Flower, b Whittall	29	c A. Flower, b B. Strang	33
Saeed Anwar	c Butchart, b Streak	4	(1) c Carlisle, b Streak	26
Salim Malik (capt)	c G.W. Flower, b Streak	20	c Carlisle, b Whittall	5
Ijaz Ahmed	lbw, b Streak	41	c Whittall, b Streak	55
Inzamam-ul-Haq	c P.A. Strang, b Brain	101	(3) c G.W. Flower, b Whittall	83
*Rashid Latif	c P.A. Strang, b B. Strang	6	c A. Flower, b Streak	6
Wasim Akram	b B. Strang	0	c Campbell, b Brain	4
Manzoor Elahi	c Streak, b B. Strang	0	c A. Flower, b Streak	0
Aqib Javed	run out	0	c A. Flower, b Brain	3
Aamir Nazir	not out	0	not out	0
Extras	lb 3, w 3, nb 3	9	lb 3, w 3, nb 10	16
		231		**250**

ZIMBABWE

	FIRST INNINGS		SECOND INNINGS	
G.W. Flower	b Nazir	6	b Nazir	2
S.V. Carlisle	c Salim, b Aqib	31	b Nazir	0
A.D.R. Campbell	c Manzoor, b Nazir	14	c Rashid, b Nazir	18
D.L. Houghton	c Rashid, b Wasim	19	(6) c Rashid, b Nazir	5
*A. Flower (capt)	c Sohail, b Manzoor	37	(4) c Nazir, b Manzoor	35
G.J. Whittall	b Aqib	34	(5) c Shakeel, b Wasim	2
I.P. Butchart	c Inzamam, b Wasim	15	c and b Nazir	8
P.A. Strang	c Sohail, b Nazir	28	c Ijaz, b Aqib	5
H.H. Streak	lbw, b Aqib	0	not out	30
D.H. Brain	not out	22	c Inzamam, b Wasim	8
B. Strang	b Aqib	6	c Shakeel, b Aqib	0
Extras	lb 4, w 1, nb 26	31	b 5, lb 5, nb 16	26
		243		**139**

	O	M	R	W	O	M	R	W
Streak	18	4	53	4	18	5	52	4
Brain	12.3	1	48	1	16.1	2	61	2
B. Strang	32	15	43	3	26	16	27	1
Whittall	18	3	73	1	22	3	66	3
Butchart	3	–	11	–				
P.A. Strang					13	3	41	–

	O	M	R	W	O	M	R	W
Wasim Akram	28	2	90	2	20	1	45	2
Aqib Javed	25	5	64	4	17.4	3	26	2
Aamir Nazir	13	3	50	3	19	3	46	5
Manzoor Elahi	10	3	28	1	3	–	12	1
Aamir Sohail	2	–	7	–				

FALL OF WICKETS
1–42, 2–46, 3–64, 4–83, 5–159, 6–180, 7–180, 8–183, 9–203
1–58, 2–72, 3–88, 4–204, 5–230, 6–233, 7–246, 8–247, 9–250

FALL OF WICKETS
1–20, 2–51, 3–79, 4–95, 5–145, 6–175, 7–193, 8–193, 9–233
1–2, 2–12, 3–37, 4–68, 5–72, 6–85, 7–95, 8–95, 9–122

Umpires: S.G. Randell & I.D. Robinson   *Pakistan won by 99 runs*

TEST MATCH AVERAGES – ZIMBABWE v. PAKISTAN

ZIMBABWE BATTING

	M	Inns	NO	Runs	HS	Av	100s	50s
G.W. Flower	3	5	1	237	201*	59.25	1	–
A. Flower	3	5	–	250	156	50.00	1	–
G.J. Whittall	3	5	1	161	113*	40.25	1	–
S.V. Carlisle	3	4	1	78	46*	26.00	–	–
A.D.R. Campbell	3	5	–	93	60	18.60	–	1
H.H. Streak	3	4	1	54	30*	18.00	–	–
P.A. Strang	3	4	–	68	32	17.00	–	–
D.L. Houghton	3	5	–	83	25	16.60	–	–
D.H. Brain	3	4	1	35	22*	11.66	–	–
M.H. Dekker	2	3	–	11	9	5.50	–	–
B. Strang	2	4	1	6	6	2.00	–	–

Played in one Test: I.P. Butchart 15 & 8; H. Olonga did not bat

PAKISTAN BATTING

	M	Inns	NO	Runs	HS	Av	100s	50s
Inzamam-ul-Haq	3	5	–	367	101	73.40	1	3
Ijaz Ahmed	3	5	–	239	76	47.80	–	3
Aamir Sohail	3	6	–	178	61	29.66	–	1
Salim Malik	3	5	–	107	44	21.40	–	–
Shakeel Ahmed	2	4	–	74	33	18.50	–	–
Rashid Latif	3	6	1	74	38	14.80	–	–
Saeed Anwar	2	4	–	45	26	11.25	–	–
Wasim Akram	3	5	–	51	27	10.20	–	–
Kabir Khan	2	3	2	10	8*	10.00	–	–
Aamir Nazir	2	3	2	7	7	7.00	–	–
Manzoor Elahi	2	4	1	14	13	4.66	–	–
Aqib Javed	2	4	–	5	3	1.25	–	–

Played in one Test: Basit Ali 0; Akram Raza 19 & 2*; Asif Mujtaba 2 & 4

ZIMBABWE BOWLING

	Overs	Mds	Runs	Wkts	Av	Best	10/m	5/inn
B. Strang	84.4	43	120	9	13.33	3-43	–	–
H.H. Streak	118	30	298	22	13.54	6-90	–	2
G.J. Whittall	100	22	288	10	28.80	3-58	–	–
D.H. Brain	88.4	15	337	8	42.12	3-50	–	–
P.A. Strang	62	19	169	1	169.00	1-35	–	–

Bowled in one innings: H. Olonga 10–0–27–1; I.P. Butchart 3–0–16–0;
M.H. Dekker 4–1–10–0

PAKISTAN BOWLING

	Overs	Mds	Runs	Wkts	Av	Best	10/m	5/inn
Aamir Nazir	61	11	171	11	15.54	5-46	–	1
Aamir Sohail	10.1	2	39	2	19.50	2-5	–	–
Aqib Javed	76.5	16	163	8	20.37	4-64	–	–
Manzoor Elahi	48	17	110	5	22.00	2-38	–	–
Wasim Akram	132.2	31	313	13	24.07	5-43	–	1
Kabir Khan	62	10	213	5	42.60	3-26	–	–

Bowled in one innings: Salim Malik 9–0–42–0; Akram Raza 34–6–112–0; Asif
Mujtaba 7–0–30–0

ZIMBABWE FIELDING FIGURES

10 – A. Flower; 5 – G.W. Flower and S.V. Carlisle; 4 – A.D.R. Campbell; 3 – P.A. Strang;
2 – D.L. Houghton, G.J. Whittall and M.H. Dekker; 1 – I.P. Butchart, H.H. Streak,
D.H. Brain and B. Strang

PAKISTAN FIELDING FIGURES

6 – Rashid Latif (ct 5/st 1) and Aamir Sohail; 4 – Shakeel Ahmed; 3 – Ijaz Ahmed;
2 – Manzoor Elahi, Inzamam-ul-Haq and Aamir Nazir; 1 – Salim Malik, Wasim
Akram, Kabir Khan and sub (Moin Khan)

---

opening spell, and he generally bowled with hostility to become the first Pakistani bowler to capture five wickets in a Test innings – Waqar and Wasim excepted – since 1989.

Andy Flower provided the only resistance as his side sank disappointingly 100 runs short of their target. Salim Malik had emulated Grace and Cronje in leading his side to victory in a three-Test series after losing the first game of the rubber, and he became the first captain to accomplish the feat away from home.

Salim's joy was short-lived. The first one-day international was tied. Seven runs were needed by Pakistan off the last over. Aamir Nazir was out to the first ball of the over, but Saeed Anwar completed a fine hundred off 131 balls after Whittall had bowled a wide. Two runs were needed off three balls, and Saeed unwisely took a leg-bye which left Wasim Akram, batting one-handed because of six stitches in his right hand, to face the bowling. He hit a full toss straight back to the bowler.

After this match, Rashid Latif and Basit Ali announced their retirements from Test cricket. Both are young, both are outstanding prospects. Rashid was Salim's vice-captain. The 'retirements' fuelled further speculation regarding rifts in the Pakistan ranks and the allegations over bribery which Salim faced. Inzamam-ul-Haq's century set up Pakistan's victory in the second match, but Zimbabwe won the third with ease to level the series.

In the third one-day international, Moin Khan held five catches to equal the world record in this form of cricket.

Pakistan's year of discontent rumbled on, but Zimbabwe could take comfort from major achievements and a significant advance after their miserable showing in the Benson and Hedges World Series in Australia.

The Logan Cup, Zimbabwe's first-class competition, failed to capture the imagination of the public or, it seems, the imagination of some of the players. A complex scoring system saw Mashonaland qualify to meet Mashonaland Under-24 in the final with the following result.

24, 25 and 26 March 1995 *at Harare Sports Club*

Mashonaland 258 (G.C. Martin 117) and 347 for 6 dec.
(A.H. Omarshah 200 not out, E.A. Essop-Adam 69)

Mashonaland Under-24 157 and 283 (G.W. Flower 145 not out, G.C. Martin 4 for 66)

Mashonaland won by 165 runs

Both Glamorgan and Northamptonshire made tours of Zimbabwe before the start of the England season, and both counties played one first-class match. In scoring 119 against Northamptonshire, Grant Flower brought his season's aggregate to 983, a record for Zimbabwe.

4, 5 and 6 April 1995 *at Harare Sports Club*

Northamptonshire 276 for 7 dec. (J.N. Snape 87, A.J. Lamb 62) and 223 (A.J. Lamb 72, B.C. Strang 4 for 83)

Mashonaland Select XI 83 (J.P. Taylor 4 for 28) and 417 for 4 (G.W. Flower 119, C.N. Evans 102, J.R. Craig 63, A. Flower 57 not out)

Mashonaland Select XI won by 6 wickets

FIRST ONE-DAY INTERNATIONAL – ZIMBABWE v. PAKISTAN
22 February 1995 at Harare Sports Club, Harare

ZIMBABWE			PAKISTAN		
A. Flower (capt)	b Aamir Nazir	25	Aamir Sohail	c and b B. Strang	7
G.W. Flower	c Rashid Latif, b Aamir Sohail	41	Saeed Anwar	not out	103
M.G. Burmester	b Aamir Sohail	25	Inzamam-ul-Haq	c Campbell, b B. Strang	0
*A.D.R. Campbell	c Ijaz Ahmed, b Aamir Sohail	21	Salim Malik (capt)	c Campbell, b Whittall	22
D.L. Houghton	c Rashid Latif, b Wasim Akram	32	Ijaz Ahmed	c B. Strang, b Peall	25
G.J. Whittall	c Inzamam-ul-Haq, b Aqib Javed	33	Shakeel Ahmed	run out	25
S.V. Carlisle	run out	0	*Rashid Latif	run out	1
P.A. Strang	c Rashid Latif, b Wasim Akram	9	Manzoor Elahi	c P.A. Strang, b B. Strang	21
S.G. Peall	b Aqib Javed	1	Aqib Javed	c A. Flower, b B. Strang	0
B. Strang	not out	4	Aamir Nazir	c Carlisle, b Whittall	3
M.P. Jarvis			Wasim Akram	c and b Whittall	0
Extras	lb 19, w 4, nb 5	28	Extras	b 4, lb 5, w 3	12
(50 overs)	(for 9 wickets)	219	(49.5 overs)		219

	O	M	R	W		O	M	R	W
Wasim Akram	8.5	–	24	2	Jarvis	7	–	30	–
Aqib Javed	10	1	43	2	B. Strang	10	1	36	4
Aamir Nazir	10	–	52	1	Whittall	9.5	–	46	3
Manzoor Elahi	8	–	36	–	Burmester	3	–	16	–
Aamir Sohail	10	–	33	3	Peall	6	–	27	1
Salim Malik	3.1	–	12	–	P.A. Strang	10	–	41	–
					A. Flower	4	–	14	–

FALL OF WICKETS
1–45, 2–105, 3–108, 4–159, 5–168, 6–170, 7–188, 8–189, 9–219

FALL OF WICKETS
1–9, 2–13, 3–68, 4–107, 5–172, 6–175, 7–209, 8–210, 9–213

Men of the Match: Saeed Anwar & B. Strang　　　　　　　　　　　　　　　　　　　　*Match tied*

SECOND ONE-DAY INTERNATIONAL – ZIMBABWE v. PAKISTAN
25 February 1995 at Harare Sports Club, Harare

ZIMBABWE			PAKISTAN		
*A. Flower (capt)	c Moin Khan, b Wasim Akram	9	Aamir Sohail	c Whittall, b Streak	7
G.W. Flower	c Moin Khan, b Manzoor Elahi	32	Saeed Anwar	c Burmester, b B. Strang	0
M.G. Burmester	c Aamir Sohail, b Manzoor Elahi	17	Inzamam-ul-Haq	not out	116
A.D.R. Campbell	c Inzamam-ul-Haq, b Salim Malik	27	Asif Mujtaba	c A. Flower, b B. Strang	0
D.L. Houghton	not out	73	Salim Malik (capt)	c A. Flower, b Streak	0
G.J. Whittall	c Ijaz Ahmed, b Wasim Akram	13	Ijaz Ahmed	b B. Strang	54
S.V. Carlisle	not out	9	*Moin Khan	c Houghton, b P.A. Strang	19
P.A. Strang			Manzoor Elahi	not out	3
H.H. Streak			Wasim Akram		
S.G. Peall			Akram Raza		
B. Strang			Aqib Javed		
Extras	lb 13, w 11, nb 5	29	Extras	lb 2, w 8, nb 1	11
(50 overs)	(for 5 wickets)	209	(48.3 overs)	(for 6 wickets)	210

	O	M	R	W		O	M	R	W
Wasim Akram	10	–	40	2	Streak	9	1	50	2
Aqib Javed	10	1	40	–	B. Strang	10	–	22	3
Manzoor Elahi	10	–	37	2	Whittall	7	–	33	–
Akram Raza	10	–	27	–	Burmester	4	–	21	–
Salim Malik	4	–	22	1	P.A. Strang	8	–	33	1
Aamir Sohail	6	–	30	–	Peall	8	–	35	–
					G.W. Flower	2	–	13	–
					Campbell	0.3	–	1	–

FALL OF WICKETS
1–26, 2–70, 3–74, 4–130, 5–185

FALL OF WICKETS
1–9, 2–17, 3–19, 4–23, 5–175, 6–206

Man of the Match: Inzamam-ul-Haq　　　　　　　　　　　　　　　　　　　　*Pakistan won by 4 wickets*

11, 12 and 13 April 1995 *at Bulawayo Athletic Club*

Matabeleland 302 for 8 dec. (H.H. Streak 98, M.D. Abrams 64) and 294 for 7 dec. (M.H. Dekker 92, M.D. Abrams 50)

Glamorgan 266 for 7 dec. (M.P. Maynard 101, R.D.B. Croft 60) and 171 (D.L. Hemp 69, G.J. Whittall 6 for 56)

Matabeleland won by 159 runs

THIRD ONE-DAY INTERNATIONAL – ZIMBABWE v. PAKISTAN
26 February 1995 at Harare Sports Club, Harare

ZIMBABWE

*A. Flower (capt)	c Moin Khan, b Manzoor Elahi	73
G.W. Flower	c Moin Khan, b Wasim Akram	6
M.G. Burmester	c Ijaz Ahmed, b Akram Raza	39
D.L. Houghton	c Aqib Javed, b Salim Malik	34
A.D.R. Campbell	c Inzamam-ul-Haq, b Aqib Javed	18
G.J. Whittall	c Moin Khan, b Manzoor Elahi	1
S.V. Carlisle	c Moin Khan, b Wasim Akram	4
P.A. Strang	c Moin Khan, b Aqib Javed	4
H.H. Streak	c Manzoor Elahi, b Aqib Javed	18
B. Strang	not out	0
M.P. Jarvis		
Extras	lb **16**, w **9**	25
(50 overs)	(for 9 wickets)	222

PAKISTAN

Shakeel Ahmed	c A. Flower, b Jarvis	36
*Moin Khan	c Whittall, b Jarvis	8
Inzamam-ul-Haq	c sub (D. Erasmus), b P.A. Strang	45
Salim Malik (capt)	c Whittall, b P.A. Strang	3
Ijaz Ahmed	c B. Strang, b P.A. Strang	12
Asif Mujtaba	run out	20
Manzoor Elahi	c Carlisle, b Whittall	10
Akram Raza	c A. Flower, b Whittall	2
Aqib Javed	not out	2
Wasim Akram	st A. Flower, b G.W. Flower	3
Aamir Sohail	absent injured	–
Extras	lb **3**, w **4**	7
(43.3 overs)	(for 9 wickets)	148

	O	M	R	W
Wasim Akram	10	1	33	2
Aqib Javed	10	1	46	3
Manzoor Elahi	10	–	41	2
Akram Raza	10	–	45	1
Aamir Sohail	6.5	–	31	–
Salim Malik	3.1	–	10	1

	O	M	R	W
Streak	6	2	7	–
B. Strang	6	1	15	–
Whittall	6	–	24	2
Jarvis	10	1	37	2
P.A. Strang	10	–	42	3
G.W. Flower	5.3	–	20	1

FALL OF WICKETS
1–15, 2–119, 3–171, 4–174, 5–175, 6–187, 7–194, 8–222, 9–222

FALL OF WICKETS
1–26, 2–73, 3–80, 4–106, 5–112, 6–138, 7–143, 8–143, 9–148

Man of the Match: A. Flower

Zimbabwe won by 74 runs

FIRST-CLASS AVERAGES

BATTING

	M	Inns	NO	Runs	HS	Av	100s	50s
A.H. Omarshah	2	3	1	215	200*	107.50	1	–
D.L. Houghton	7	10	–	627	266	62.70	2	1
A. Flower	10	15	2	768	156	59.07	3	3
G.W. Flower	12	20	3	983	201*	57.82	4	3
I.P. Butchart	3	6	1	263	117	52.60	2	–
M.G. Burmester	3	4	–	201	67	50.25	–	3
W.R. James	7	11	1	473	127	47.30	2	1
G.J. Whittall	13	22	4	762	180*	42.33	4	2
J.A. Rennie	6	10	4	224	67*	37.33	–	1
S.S. Prescott	2	4	1	103	35	34.33	–	–
G.C. Martin	5	10	1	301	117	33.44	1	1
C.N. Evans	6	11	1	305	112	30.50	2	–
G.K. Bruk-Jackson	4	8	–	239	87	29.87	–	1
A.C. Waller	2	4	–	117	53	29.25	–	1
C.B. Wishart	8	15	1	391	73	27.92	–	2
H.H. Streak	11	15	3	333	98	27.75	–	2
D.H. Brain	7	9	2	169	126	24.14	1	–
G.J. Rennie	5	9	–	215	72	23.88	–	1
P.A. Strang	9	14	2	286	97	23.83	–	2
M.P. Stannard	3	6	–	132	47	22.00	–	–
D.N. Erasmus	5	10	1	197	56*	21.88	–	1
A.D.R. Campbell	11	18	1	361	99	21.23	–	3
G.A. Briant	3	5	–	103	48	20.60	–	–
D.J.R. Campbell	5	10	1	176	60*	19.55	–	1

	M	Inns	NO	Runs	HS	Av	100s	50s
J.R. Craig	5	10	–	194	63	19.40	–	2
M.H. Dekker	11	18	–	338	92	18.77	–	1
M.D. Abrams	4	7	–	128	64	18.28	–	2

(Qualification – 100 runs, average 10.00)

BOWLING

	Overs	Mds	Runs	Wkts	Av	Best	10/m	5/inn
G.W. Flower	90.2	28	212	11	19.27	3-24	–	–
B.C. Strang	249.5	81	619	32	19.34	7-64	–	2
H.H. Streak	385.2	104	969	49	19.77	6-90	–	2
C.B. Wishart	87.5	19	281	11	25.54	5-24	–	1
M.P. Jarvis	354.3	136	726	27	26.88	7-36	1	1
G.C. Martin	120.1	36	322	11	29.27	4-66	–	–
P.A. Strang	299.3	66	934	26	35.92	7-75	–	2
D.H. Brain	193.2	34	632	17	37.17	3-50	–	–
H.R. Olonga	145	21	521	14	37.21	3-53	–	–

(Qualification – 10 wickets)

LEADING FIELDERS
27 – W.R. James (ct 26/st 1); 26 – A. Flower; 16 – G.W. Flower; 13 – D.J.R. Campbell (ct 12/st 1); 11 – M.H. Dekker

SOUTH AFRICA

A leader by example, Hansie Cronje took over the captaincy of South Africa following the retirement of Kepler Wessels and met with consistent success. (David Munden/Sportsline)

The South African season began with the departure of Mike Procter as coach of the national side and with his replacement by Bob Woolmer, whose triple success with Warwickshire had made him a man much in demand. There was a further departure in the form of Kepler Wessels who first resigned as captain of South Africa and then announced his retirement from Test cricket. Not only would the South African side miss Wessels, it would also miss Donald in the early part of the season, for the fast bowler was to undergo an operation. Wessels' successor as captain, 'Hansie' Cronje, was involved in controversy before taking up his post. He disputed an umpire's decision in the opening Castle Cup match of the season and was fined 500 rand. He later issued a statement apologising to the opposing side, Natal, and to the umpires.

With the inevitable South African emphasis on one-day cricket, the major part of the international season was the Mandela Trophy in which four nations would compete. The main tourists, New Zealand, would also play a three-Test series while Pakistan would play one Test. The other tourists, Sri Lanka, would play only in the Mandela Trophy, but they would be engaged in matches against provincial sides.

NEW ZEALAND TOUR

9 November 1994 *at Halfway House, Randjestontein*

New Zealanders 232 for 5 dec. (M.D. Crowe 61, D.J. Murray 57)
Nicky Openheimer's XI 231 for 9 (H.A. Page 59 not out)

Match drawn

11, 12 and 13 November 1994 *at Centurion Park, Verwoerdburg*

Northern Transvaal 292 (M.J.R. Rindel 91, J.J. Strydom 50, K.J. Rule 50) and 84 for 0 (C.B. Lambert 52 not out)
New Zealanders 356 for 9 dec. (S.P. Fleming 114, D.J. Murray 72, M.J. Davis 4 for 53)

Match drawn

15, 16 and 17 November 1994 *at Kimberley Country Club, Kimberley*

New Zealanders 285 for 5 dec. (C.Z. Harris 110 not out, D.J. Murray 63, K.R. Rutherford 50) and 280 for 3 dec. (D.J. Murray 109, A.C. Parore 96)
Griqualand West 218 (H.A. Page 85, R.P. de Groen 5 for 34) and 324 (V. Michau 95, H.A. Page 72, S.A. Thomson 5 for 101)

New Zealanders won by 23 runs

19, 20, 21 and 22 November 1994 *at Springbok Park, Bloemfontein*

New Zealanders 538 for 7 dec. (A.C. Parore 127 not out, B.A. Young 111, C.Z. Harris 95, M.D. Crowe 89, K.R. Rutherford 59, N.W. Pretorius 5 for 182) and 234 for 3 dec. (M.D. Crowe 124 not out, C.Z. Harris 62 not out)

Kepler Wessels retired from Test cricket, and it is believed that he will not appear in first-class cricket next season. (Alan Cozzi)

Orange Free State 392 for 5 dec. (P.J.R. Steyn 157, J.M. Arthur 83, W.J. Cronje 56, J.F. Venter 55 not out) and 383 for 8 (L.J. Wilkinson 89, J.M. Arthur 85, N. Boje 66, D.J. Nash 4 for 83)

Orange Free State won by 2 wickets

The New Zealand batsmen were in fine form in the matches that preceded the first Test. Six different players recorded centuries in the three first-class matches, a remarkable achievement. Most remarkably, Chris Harris, having hit a hundred at Kimberley, made 95 and 62 not out and performed the hat-trick in the match at Bloemfontein, yet Harris was considered a one-day cricketer and did not win a place in the eleven for the first Test. At Bloemfontein, the New Zealanders suffered their first loss in a non-Test match in South Africa. This was mainly due to Rudolf Steyn who hit the highest score made against a touring side.

FIRST TEST MATCH
SOUTH AFRICA v. NEW ZEALAND,
at Johannesburg

Playing a Test match in South Africa for the first time in 33 years, New Zealand were given a good start in that skipper Ken Rutherford won the toss and chose to bat first on a pitch which threatened to wear rapidly. The ball moved around alarmingly in the early stages, and Young was caught at slip in the fourth over. Fleming and debutant Murray lived dangerously, but they added 72 for the second wicket before falling to de Villiers, the best of the South African bowlers. Rutherford and Crowe revived New Zealand with an aggressive partnership of 126 in 42 overs. Rutherford hit 11 fours and 2 sixes, but the ball after he had hit Eksteen for his second six he skied to mid-off, so giving the left-arm spinner his first Test wicket. New Zealand closed on 242 for 4 with Crowe unbeaten on 81.

There were hopes that Crowe would become the first batsman to score a century against each of the other Test-playing nations, but these disappeared quickly on the

second morning when he suffered a harsh leg-before decision. This prompted something of a New Zealand collapse, and they slipped to 280 for 7. Nash then offered capable defence as he and Thomson added 74. Thomson's 84 came off 177 balls, and Nash resisted for 30 overs. The biggest frustration for South Africa, however, came when de Groen and Doull put on a record 57 for the last wicket. Both batsmen reached their highest Test scores.

Doull and de Groen also shone with the ball as South Africa were reduced to 73 for 4. Cullinan and Rhodes steered the score to 109 before the close, but, on the third morning, both batsmen fell to Doull in quick succession, and there seemed every possibility that South Africa would have to follow on. That they did not, they owed primarily to Richardson who, although guarding a broken thumb, batted for nearly three hours and hit 15 fours in his highest Test score of 93 off 137 balls. Crucially, he had fine support from Eksteen with whom he added 57 in 23 overs for the ninth wicket.

Trailing by 132 on the first innings, South Africa seized the initiative when de Villiers had Murray leg before with the first ball of New Zealand's second innings and then, changing ends, dismissed Young, Crowe and Rutherford –

FIRST TEST MATCH – SOUTH AFRICA v. NEW ZEALAND
25, 26, 27, 28 and 29 November 1994 at Wanderers, Johannesburg

NEW ZEALAND

	FIRST INNINGS		SECOND INNINGS	
B.A. Young	c McMillan, b Snell	7	(2) c Richardson, b de Villiers	18
D.J. Murray	c Richardson, b de Villiers	25	(1) lbw, b de Villiers	0
S.P. Fleming	b de Villiers	48	c Richardson, b Matthews	15
M.D. Crowe	lbw, b Snell	83	b de Villiers	0
K.R. Rutherford (capt)	c Cronje, b Eksteen	68	c McMillan, b de Villiers	0
S.A. Thomson	b Matthews	84	b Snell	29
*A.C. Parore	c McMillan, b Matthews	13	c Richardson, b Matthews	49
M.N. Hart	c Richardson, b Matthews	0	b Matthews	34
D.J. Nash	c Hudson, b Eksteen	18	c Richardson, b Matthews	20
S.B. Doull	not out	31	not out	14
R.P. de Groen	b Snell	26	b Matthews	0
Extras	lb 5, w 2, nb 1	8	b 9, lb 4, w 1, nb 1	15
		411		**194**

SOUTH AFRICA

	FIRST INNINGS		SECOND INNINGS	
A.C. Hudson	c Parore, b Nash	10	lbw, b Doull	2
G. Kirsten	c Crowe, b de Groen	9	lbw, b Hart	33
B.M. McMillan	c Murray, b Nash	5	lbw, b Doull	42
W.J. Cronje (capt)	lbw, b de Groen	20	c Parore, b de Groen	62
D.J. Cullinan	c Parore, b Doull	58	c Crowe, b Doull	12
J.N. Rhodes	lbw, b Doull	37	lbw, b Doull	0
*D.J. Richardson	lbw, b Nash	93	c and b Hart	6
R.P. Snell	c Crowe, b Hart	16	c Doull, b Hart	1
C.R. Matthews	c Crowe, b Hart	4	b Hart	6
C.E. Eksteen	c Fleming, b Hart	9	b Hart	0
P.S. de Villiers	not out	6	not out	1
Extras	b 6, lb 6	12	b 17, lb 6, w 1	24
		279		**189**

	O	M	R	W	O	M	R	W		O	M	R	W	O	M	R	W
de Villiers	34	8	78	2	23	9	52	4	Nash	24	6	81	3	8	2	17	–
Snell	33.5	9	112	3	16	5	54	1	Doull	21	6	70	2	15	5	33	4
Matthews	28	3	98	3	19	9	42	5	de Groen	21	2	59	2	12	3	21	1
McMillan	24	8	56	–	2	1	1	–	Hart	26	7	57	3	32.4	7	77	5
Eksteen	23	10	49	2	14	5	32	–	Thomson					11	6	18	–
Cronje	3	–	13	–	1	1	0	–									

FALL OF WICKETS

1–7, 2–79, 3–92, 4–218, 5–249, 6–280, 7–280, 8–354, 9–354
1–0, 2–32, 3–33, 4–33, 5–34, 6–103, 7–130, 8–168, 9–190

FALL OF WICKETS

1–20, 2–28, 3–38, 4–73, 5–147, 6–148, 7–173, 8–197, 9–254
1–9, 2–70, 3–130, 4–150, 5–150, 6–167, 7–175, 8–180, 9–184

Umpires: K.E. Liebenberg & I.D. Robinson

New Zealand won by 137 runs

who was out first ball – within the space of nine deliveries. Matthews had already had Fleming caught behind, and New Zealand were 34 for 5. Thomson and Parore took the total to 81 by the end of the day.

Dropped catches cost South Africa dearly on the fourth day, which saw Parore dropped off Eksteen on the second ball of the morning. Hudson, the culprit, also put down Hart off Snell. Both chances went to the slip cordon. In spite of Craig Matthews' best Test bowling performance, New Zealand's last three wickets added 64 runs, and South Africa needed 327 to win in just over 4½ sessions.

Hudson was leg before to a shooter, and Gary Kirsten was a more doubtful leg-before victim, but South Africa ended the day on 128 for 2, the game in the balance.

The pitch was difficult, but problems were exaggerated by the poor batting of the South Africans. In the third over of the final morning, McMillan was leg before to a Doull in-swinger. Cullinan cut a long-hop into the hands of Crowe at gully. It was Crowe's 67th Test catch, a New Zealand record. Rhodes was unfortunate to be adjudged leg before, but Doull's eight-over spell of 3 for 17 was to prove decisive, particularly as Nash was unfit to bowl.

Richardson played a lazy shot to give Hart a return catch, and Snell swatted horribly at the same bowler to be caught at mid-off by the ubiquitous Doull. Cronje's stubborn fighting innings came to an end when he was caught behind off a leg-glance, and Matthews and Eksteen surrendered tamely to give Hart five wickets in a Test innings for the first time. Doull was named Man of the Match, and New Zealand celebrated while South Africa lamented a poor performance.

Unfortunately, the interest and excitement generated by this Test was dissipated as the Mandela tournament took over for the month of December. New Zealand were troubled by injury and illness to Hartland, Thomson, Hart, Murray, Nash, Doull and Pringle, but Morrison, fit again, joined the tour as did left-arm spinner and capable batsman Priest.

1 December 1994 *at Soweto*

New Zealanders 252 for 6 (B.R. Hartland 81, B.A. Young 54)
Transvaal Invitation XI 243 for 8 (M.W. Rushmere 80, S.D. Jack 54)

New Zealanders won by 9 runs

3 December 1994 *at Wanderers, Johannesburg*

New Zealanders 214
Transvaal 216 for 2 (S.D. Jack 107)

Transvaal won by 8 wickets

21, 22 and 23 December 1994 *at Coetzenburg, Stellenbosch*

Boland 83 and 31 for 3
New Zealanders 86 (M. Erasmus 6 for 22)

Match abandoned

The match against the Transvaal Invitation XI marked the official opening of the Soweto Cricket Oval by the South

African Sports Minister Steve Tshwete. The New Zealanders, who lost Hart with a broken finger, were the first touring side to play at the Oval. England will play a four-day match there late in 1995.

In the match in Johannesburg, Steven Jack, promoted to open the Transvaal innings, hit 100 off 72 balls.

The match at Stellenbosch represented New Zealand's last opportunity of match practice before the second Test. Twenty-two wickets fell on the first day during which medium-pacer Marais Erasmus recorded a career-best bowling performance. In the first over of the second day, a ball from Doull reared to hit Wylie on the helmet. The batsman was caught behind next ball, and he was followed from the field by the rest of the players. Umpires Mitchley and Jerling had abandoned the match on the grounds that the pitch was too dangerous. The New Zealanders were rightly angry at being deprived of vital match practice, particularly as they were also deprived of the services of Dion Nash who was forced to return home with a persistent side strain.

SECOND TEST MATCH
SOUTH AFRICA v. NEW ZEALAND, at Durban

With Donald and Schultz injured, and Snell out of favour, South Africa gave a first Test cap to Steven Jack, the fastest bowler in the Republic. There was also a Test debut for the Boland skipper John Commins.

Rutherford won the toss, and New Zealand batted. The first day's honours went entirely to South Africa. Jack, in a lively opening spell, bowled Young through his legs, caught Fleming off de Villiers at long-leg, and had Crowe taken at long-leg off a mis-hook. Murray batted for 165 minutes for his 38, but the rest of the New Zealand batting was woeful. Rutherford hit a long-hop straight to mid-wicket, and Hart and Doull were caught playing loosely at balls outside the off stump. Thomson reached 53 off 54 balls before bad light ended play shortly before tea with New Zealand 130 for 8.

Some spirited cricket saw New Zealand claw their way back into the match on the second day. Shane Thomson and Daniel Morrison extended their ninth-wicket partnership to 66, and they were not separated until 10 minutes before lunch when Thomson, having hit 11 fours and 2 sixes and faced 135 balls, was caught off de Villiers. The pace man dismissed Pringle with the sixth ball after the interval to leave Morrison, one of Test cricket's noted 'rabbits', unbeaten for a brave and invaluable 24.

He was soon to prove his worth with the new ball, having Hudson caught at second slip in his fourth over of South Africa's innings. Kirsten, Commins and Cullinan all offered solidity, but all three fell to Doull. Commins was at the crease for 159 minutes and hit 3 fours before being caught on the long-leg boundary. Rhodes was out when he pushed forward to Hart and was caught bat-and-pad. South Africa closed on 122 for 5, and the match was finely balanced.

Three quick wickets from Morrison reduced South Africa to 182 for 9 on the third morning before Richardson, a most determined cricketer, and de Villiers added 44 for the last wicket. In the context of the match up to this point, that was a vital stand. It gave South Africa a lead of 41 and, as New Zealand slipped to 48 for 3 before bad light again brought an early end to play, it turned the game very much in favour of South Africa.

Murray was harshly adjudged leg before, and Rutherford fell to another wretched shot, pulling to mid-wicket. Crowe passed Wright's record to become New Zealand's highest run-scorer in Test cricket, but he soon fell to McMillan who also had Young dropped at slip by Hudson.

This proved to be a costly miss in terms of time, for Young's innings was to last for 333 minutes. He made just nine before lunch on the fourth day, and his 51 was the third-slowest fifty in Test cricket. Only Trevor Bailey and Chris Tavaré have occupied the crease longer in reaching fifty in a Test match. He shared a stand of 53 with Fleming, and of 63 with Thomson, but when Young finally cut McMillan into the hands of gully it heralded collapse. Six wickets fell for 48 runs, and South Africa needed 152 to win.

The out-of-form Hudson was soon out, but Kirsten and Commins took the score to 41 by the close. On the final morning, Commins was dropped at slip off Doull before a run had been added, but thereafter South Africa had no trouble and won with ease to level the series. There had been some good individual performances in the match, but much of the cricket had been mediocre.

THIRD TEST MATCH
SOUTH AFRICA v. NEW ZEALAND, at Cape Town

South Africa changed a winning side. Eksteen returned for Matthews, who was not fully fit, and Rudolf Steyn replaced Hudson whose form had deserted him totally. Steyn was winning his first Test cap. New Zealand, who were unchanged, won the toss and batted. Again they endured a miserable first day.

Morning drizzle had held up play for an hour, but a crowd of more than 17,000 had gathered to support South Africa in their effort to become the first Test side for 106 years to win a three-match series after losing the opening

---

SECOND TEST MATCH – SOUTH AFRICA v. NEW ZEALAND
26, 27, 28, 29 and 30 December 1994 at Kingsmead, Durban

NEW ZEALAND

	FIRST INNINGS		SECOND INNINGS	
B.A. Young	b Jack	2	c Cullinan, b McMillan	51
D.J. Murray	c Richardson, b de Villiers	38	lbw, b de Villiers	0
S.P. Fleming	c Jack, b de Villiers	4	(5) c Richardson, b Jack	31
M.D. Crowe	c de Villiers, b Jack	18	c Richardson, b McMillan	10
K.R. Rutherford (capt)	c Commins, b de Villiers		(3) c Commins, b McMillan	6
S.A. Thomson	c Kirsten, b de Villiers	82	b Cronje	35
*A.C. Parore	c Kirsten, b McMillan	5	run out	1
M.N. Hart	c Cronje, b McMillan	5	c Richardson, b Kirsten	6
S.B. Doull	c Richardson, b McMillan	0	c Richardson, b de Villiers	19
D.K. Morrison	not out	24	c McMillan, b de Villiers	12
C. Pringle	c Kirsten, b de Villiers	0	not out	6
Extras	lb 4, nb 3	7	lb 11, nb 4	15
		185		**192**

SOUTH AFRICA

	FIRST INNINGS		SECOND INNINGS	
A.C. Hudson	c Young, b Morrison	8	c Parore, b Doull	6
G. Kirsten	c Parore, b Doull	29	not out	66
J.B. Commins	c Hart, b Doull	30	c Young, b Hart	45
D.J. Cullinan	lbw, b Doull	34	not out	25
W.J. Cronje (capt)	c Thomson, b Morrison	19		
J.N. Rhodes	c Fleming, b Hart	1		
B.M. McMillan	b Doull	17		
*D.J. Richardson	not out	39		
C.R. Matthews	c Parore, b Morrison	7		
S.D. Jack	c Crowe, b Morrison	0		
P.S. de Villiers	c Fleming, b Doull	28		
Extras	lb 6, nb 8	14	lb 9, nb 2	11
		226	(for 2 wickets)	**153**

	O	M	R	W	O	M	R	W
Jack	16	7	32	2	15	3	45	1
de Villiers	24	7	64	5	31.2	10	56	3
Matthews	19	11	37	–	12	3	17	–
McMillan	19	8	40	3	30	8	53	3
Cronje	4	1	8	–	10	6	10	1
Kirsten					2	2	0	1

	O	M	R	W	O	M	R	W
Morrison	25	4	70	4	15	1	56	–
Doull	29.4	9	73	5	15	5	26	1
Pringle	15	5	23	–				
Hart	17	2	54	1	13.4	2	52	1
Thomson					2	1	10	–

FALL OF WICKETS
1–9, 2–19, 3–62, 4–65, 5–66, 6–102, 7–114, 8–114, 9–180
1–2, 2–11, 3–28, 4–81, 5–144, 6–144, 7–153, 8–153, 9–179

FALL OF WICKETS
1–13, 2–61, 3–110, 4–111, 5–122, 6–141, 7–168, 8–182, 9–182
1–20, 2–117

Umpires: Khizar Hayat & C.J. Mitchley

South Africa won by 8 wickets

Wicket-keeper David Richardson played a decisive part in the series victory over New Zealand. He topped the batting averages, hit a maiden Test century and held 16 catches. (David Munden/Sportsline)

New Zealand on 254 for 9, but an outrageous Test-best score of 30 by Pringle boosted New Zealand to a challenging 288.

Steyn grasped his first Test opportunity by showing confidence in an opening stand of 106 with the pragmatic Gary Kirsten. Off-spinner Thomson was belatedly introduced into the attack, and he immediately had Steyn leg before playing back. Kirsten missed a sweep, and Cullinan carelessly pulled a long-hop to mid-wicket where Young jumped high to take a good catch. Commins and Cronje suffered no more problems before the close, by which time South Africa were 136 runs behind.

During the first session of the third day, South Africa lost two wickets. Commins failed to get to the pitch of the ball and was caught at short extra-cover; and Rhodes was bowled off an inside edge by Doull. It was Doull, however, who suffered the greatest injustice of the match. Cronje attempted to pull a shorter delivery but succeeded only in looping the ball gently to mid-wicket. Even as the bowler was celebrating, Hart, the fielder, allowed the simplest of catches to slip through his hands. For New Zealand, this was a morale-sapping blow. McMillan fell to Pringle, but Cronje went on to reach his fourth Test hundred, each of which has taken South Africa to victory. His 112 came from 235 balls and included 10 fours and a straight six off Hart – who will not want to remember this match. Richardson displayed fine, positive form to reach 70 by the end of the day, by which time South Africa had a lead of 93 with three wickets standing.

They managed to add another 59 runs on the fourth morning, with Dave Richardson – who has played in all of South Africa's 20 Tests since their readmission to international cricket – reaching a maiden Test hundred. It came off 202 balls and included 6 fours. In all, he hit 53 singles, a testimony to his eager running and unflagging determination.

Trailing by 152, New Zealand lost Murray immediately after lunch. Parore batted with panache, but he was caught at fine leg off a hook shot which seemed inappropriate in the circumstances. Crowe gloved a lifting delivery to the wicket-keeper, and Rutherford offered no shot to a ball from McMillan and was adjudged leg before. Rutherford responded with a volley of abuse which cost him 75% of his match fee and a two-Test suspended sentence from referee Burge. Ending the day on 121 for 4, New Zealand faced defeat.

Twenty minutes into the final day, Bryan Young, having added nine to his overnight score, became yet another victim of the hook shot. Thomson was insanely run out by Cronje from silly point when he stood motionless after a forward defensive shot, and de Villiers deservedly mopped up the tail. Fleming showed spirit and class, but South Africa needed just 88 to win, which was never likely to trouble them.

And so Hansie Cronje equalled W.G. Grace's 106-year-old record of leading his side to victory in a three-match Test series after losing the first game of the rubber.

encounter. The match began dourly, with Murray and Young scoring 12 runs in the 15 overs possible before lunch. In the 17th over, disaster struck. Murray was taken at short-leg off McMillan and, two balls later, Parore ran himself out when turning for an ambitious third run.

Crowe fell to Jack, and Young and Thomson to the excellent McMillan to leave New Zealand on a wretched 95 for 5. Rutherford played with considerable care, and he and Fleming set about the process of resurrection. The stand ended with yet another indiscretion from Rutherford, who was out mis-hooking for the third time in successive innings. New Zealand closed on 211 for 6, which was a marked improvement on their earlier position.

Fleming added 21 to his overnight score before becoming the first of Jack's three-wicket spell in 11 balls. This left

NEW ZEALAND

	FIRST INNINGS		SECOND INNINGS	
B.A. Young	lbw, b McMillan	45	c Kirsten, b McMillan	51
D.J. Murray	c Kirsten, b McMillan	5	lbw, b de Villiers	3
*A.C. Parore	run out	2	c Eksteen, b de Villiers	34
M.D. Crowe	c Richardson, b Jack	18	c Richardson, b McMillan	5
K.R. Rutherford (capt)	c Kirsten, b McMillan	56	lbw, b McMillan	26
S.A. Thomson	b McMillan	0	run out	16
S.P. Fleming	b Jack	79	c Richardson, b de Villiers	53
M.N. Hart	c Richardson, b Jack	24	c Eksteen, b Jack	7
S.B. Doull	c Cronje, b Jack	6	c Rhodes, b de Villiers	25
D.K. Morrison	not out	0	lbw, b de Villiers	1
C. Pringle	b de Villiers	30	not out	0
Extras	lb 13, nb 10	23	b 5, lb 6, w 1, nb 6	18
		288		**239**

SOUTH AFRICA

	FIRST INNINGS		SECOND INNINGS	
G. Kirsten	b Thomson	64	lbw, b Hart	25
P.J.R. Steyn	lbw, b Thomson	38	c Doull, b Thomson	12
J.B. Commins	c Rutherford, b Hart	27	not out	10
D.J. Cullinan	c Young, b Thomson	5	hit wkt, b Hart	28
W.J. Cronje (capt)	c Pringle, b Hart	112	not out	14
J.N. Rhodes	b Doull	18		
B.M. McMillan	lbw, b Pringle	18		
*D.J. Richardson	c Crowe, b Doull	109		
C.E. Eksteen	b Hart	22		
S.D. Jack	c Murray, b Morrison	7		
P.S. de Villiers	not out	1		
Extras	b 7, lb 3, w 1, nb 8	19		0
		440	(for 3 wickets)	**89**

	O	M	R	W	O	M	R	W
de Villiers	28.5	7	90	1	28.1	9	61	5
Jack	27	7	69	4	19	7	50	1
McMillan	26	5	65	4	25	9	52	3
Cronje	5	3	8	–	7	3	15	–
Eksteen	26	10	36	–	31	16	46	–
Kirsten	2	–	7	–	1	–	4	–

	O	M	R	W	O	M	R	W
Morrison	34	7	100	1	4	1	5	–
Doull	34.2	12	55	2				
Pringle	28	5	69	1				
Hart	54	8	141	3	15.2	2	51	2
Thomson	31	7	65	3	12	3	33	1

FALL OF WICKETS

1–17, 2–19, 3–61, 4–93, 5–95, 6–179, 7–244, 8–254, 9–254

1–19, 2–63, 3–73, 4–115, 5–131, 6–154, 7–173, 8–224, 9–230

FALL OF WICKETS

1–106, 2–119, 3–125, 4–161, 5–225, 6–271, 7–325, 8–410, 9–429

1–37, 2–37, 3–69

Umpires: K.T. Francis & S.B. Lambson

South Africa won by 7 wickets

TEST MATCH AVERAGES – SOUTH AFRICA v. NEW ZEALAND

SOUTH AFRICA BATTING

	M	Inns	NO	Runs	HS	Av	100s	50s
D.J. Richardson	3	4	1	247	109	82.33	1	1
W.J. Cronje	3	5	1	227	112	56.75	1	1
G. Kirsten	3	6	1	226	66*	45.20	–	2
J.B. Commins	2	4	1	112	45	37.33	–	–
P.S. de Villiers	3	4	3	36	28	36.00	–	–
D.J. Cullinan	3	6	1	162	58	32.40	–	1
B.M. McMillan	3	4	–	82	42	20.50	–	–
J.N. Rhodes	3	4	–	56	37	14.00	–	–
C.E. Eksteen	2	3	–	31	22	10.33	–	–
A.C. Hudson	2	4	–	26	10	6.50	–	–
C.R. Matthews	2	3	–	17	7	5.66	–	–
S.D. Jack	2	2	–	7	7	3.50	–	–

Played in one Test: R.P. Snell 16 & 1; P.J.R. Steyn 38 & 12.

NEW ZEALAND BATTING

	M	Inns	NO	Runs	HS	Av	100s	50s
S.A. Thomson	3	6	–	246	84	41.00	–	2
S.P. Fleming	3	6	–	230	79	38.33	–	2
B.A. Young	3	6	–	174	51	29.00	–	2
K.R. Rutherford	3	6	–	156	68	26.00	–	2
S.B. Doull	3	6	2	95	31*	23.75	–	–
M.D. Crowe	3	6	–	134	83*	22.33	–	1
D.K. Morrison	2	4	2	37	24*	18.50	–	–
C. Pringle	2	4	2	36	30	18.00	–	–
A.C. Parore	3	6	–	104	49	17.33	–	–
M.N. Hart	3	6	–	76	34	12.66	–	–
D.J. Murray	3	6	–	71	38	11.83	–	–

Played in one Test: D.J. Nash 18 & 20; R.P. de Groen 26 & 0.

SOUTH AFRICA BOWLING

	Overs	Mds	Runs	Wkts	Av	Best	10/m	5/inn
G. Kirsten	5	2	11	1	11.00	1-0	–	–
P.S. de Villiers	169.2	50	401	20	20.05	5-61	–	2
B.M. McMillan	126	39	267	13	20.53	4-65	–	–
C.R. Matthews	78	26	194	8	24.25	5-42	–	1
S.D. Jack	77	24	196	8	24.50	4-69	–	–
R.P. Snell	49.5	14	166	4	41.50	3-112	–	–
W.J. Cronje	30	14	54	1	54.00	1-10	–	–
C.E. Eksteen	94	41	163	2	81.50	2-49	–	–

NEW ZEALAND BOWLING

	Overs	Mds	Runs	Wkts	Av	Best	10/m	5/inn
S.B. Doull	115	37	257	14	18.35	5-73	–	1
R.P. de Groen	37	5	80	3	26.66	2-59	–	–
M.N. Hart	158.4	28	432	15	28.80	5-77	–	1
S.A. Thomson	56	17	126	4	31.50	3-65	–	–
D.J. Nash	32	8	98	3	32.66	3-81	–	–
D.K. Morrison	78	13	231	5	46.20	4-70	–	–
C. Pringle	43	10	92	1	92.00	1-69	–	–

SOUTH AFRICA FIELDING FIGURES

16 – D.J. Richardson; 6 – G. Kirsten; 4 – B.M. McMillan; 3 – W.J. Cronje; 2 – C.E. Eksteen and J.B. Commins; 1 – A.C. Hudson, D.J. Cullinan, J.N. Rhodes, P.S. de Villiers and S.D. Jack

NEW ZEALAND FIELDING FIGURES

6 – M.D. Crowe and A.C. Parore; 3 – B.A. Young and S.P. Fleming; 2 – S.B. Doull, M.N. Hart and D.J. Murray; 1 – K.R. Rutherford and S.A. Thomson

SRI LANKA TOUR

30 November 1994 at Jan Smuts Ground, Pietermaritzburg

Sri Lankans 200 for 8
Natal 204 for 4

Natal won by 6 wickets

10 December 1994 at Kimberley Country Club, Kimberley

Sri Lankans 229 for 7
Griqualand West 184 for 7

Sri Lankans won by 45 runs

12 December 1994 at Harmony Ground, Virginia

Orange Free State 221
Sri Lankans 222 for 5

Sri Lankans won by 5 wickets

22 December 1994 at Zwide

Sri Lankans 202
Eastern Province Invitation XI 166

Sri Lankans won by 36 runs

26, 27, 28 and **29 December 1994** at St George's Park, Port Elizabeth

Eastern Province 198 (M. Muralitharan 6 for 42)
Sri Lankans 125 for 5

Match drawn

1, 2, 3 and **4 January 1995** at Buffalo Park, East London

Border 223 (M.P. Stonier 60, F.J.C. Cronje 51, M. Muralitharan
    7 for 57) and 225 for 3 (A.G. Lawson 77, F.J.C. Cronje 70)
Sri Lankans 454 (A.P. Gurusinha 117, A. Ranatunga 116)

Match drawn

Outside their involvement in the Mandela Trophy the Sri Lankans engaged in six matches, two of which were first-class. Unfortunately, the first of these matches, against Eastern Province, was ruined by rain. Off-spinner Muralitharan shone in both games.

MANDELA TROPHY

The month of December was given over to the Mandela Trophy in an attempt to satisfy the South African appetite for one-day cricket. The host nation took on three other Test-playing countries in what was, hopefully, the last four-team tournament outside the World Cup. Each side played the others twice, and the competition began with the two

meetings between Sri Lanka and Pakistan. Sri Lanka scored well in both of these matches but were beaten twice.

In the first game, Arjuna Ranatunga hit his first century in a one-day international – it was his 152nd match – and Salim Malik had to have six stitches in his left shin after colliding in the field with Ijaz Ahmed. This did not prevent the Pakistan captain from steering his side to victory after Aamir Sohail had hit 100 off 118 balls, his third century in this form of cricket.

In the second game, a brilliant innings by Aravinda de Silva – 95 off 105 balls – could not save Sri Lanka from a second defeat.

Under the floodlights at Newlands, South Africa ended a run of 10 consecutive defeats in one-day internationals. Cronje, leading the side for the first time in a limited-over international, hit 38 off 63 balls and set the tone for his side who applied themselves well on a difficult pitch. Mike Rindel, a left-handed all-rounder, was making his debut in international cricket and performed admirably to take the individual award. Left-arm spinner Mark Priest, a replacement for the injured Hart, appeared in the match after arriving from New Zealand earlier in the day.

The match in Bloemfontein was abandoned because of rain, and so gave New Zealand their only point of the competition. The match was notable for two events. Jayasuriya's 140 was the highest score made by a Sri Lankan batsman in a one-day international, and the game saw the debut of Lee Germon. Seen by many in his country as the best wicket-keeper and captain in New Zealand, Germon appeared in no other international match on the tour.

Outstanding fielding helped South Africa to victory over Pakistan at the Wanderers. Pakistan were 165 for 3 in the 40th over, but they lost their last seven wickets for 49 runs. Cronje completed a thousand runs in one-day internationals in 1994, but the most pleasing aspect of the game from South Africa's point of view was that Hudson ended an horrific spell by hitting 74 off 111 balls. He and Cronje put on 145 in 28 overs.

The South African high scoring continued at Verwoerdburg. Recalled to the national side and playing his first one-day international in the unaccustomed role of opener, Dave Callaghan hit the highest score made by a South African batsman in this form of cricket. He also led the side to their highest score in a one-day international. It was the second-highest team score in these matches in 1994, and the highest – 328 for 2 by Pakistan – had also been made against New Zealand. Parore also hit his first one-day international hundred before falling to Man of the Match Callaghan.

New Zealand's woes continued against Pakistan at Port Elizabeth. Crowe and Parore added 101 for the second wicket, and New Zealand reached 173 for 2, only to lose their last eight wickets for 28 runs. Pakistan won with ease, but if it was their pace men who had brought victory against New Zealand, it was Sri Lanka's spinners who strangled South Africa at Bloemfontein two days later. There were only 16 overs of pace in the South African innings. Steven Jack, in his first one-day international, dismissed both openers.

South Africa suffered another defeat at Durban, and Pakistan's victory assured them of a place in the final.

Waqar Younis and Aqib Javed reduced South Africa to 44 for 5, but Rhodes, 61 off 77 balls, and Richardson effected a recovery. Pakistan romped to their target with 15 overs to spare. Ijaz Ahmed hit 114 off 90 balls and, with his brother-in-law Salim Malik, scored 136 off 119 balls in 82 minutes. They scored the last 41 runs in three overs.

The hopes of Sri Lanka were kept alive when they beat hapless New Zealand at East London. With Rutherford and Parore sharing a third-wicket stand of 136, New Zealand reached their highest score of the tournament. In spite of this, Sri Lanka won with ease, but the match was marred by the fact that both captains were fined by referee Burge. Ranatunga lost 25% of his match fee for showing obvious dissent when adjudged caught behind. Rutherford lost half his match fee for attempting to intimidate umpire Mitchley into making a favourable decision.

New Zealand's misery continued into their final match when Waqar Younis ended their innings in the 11th game by bowling Harris, Pringle and de Groen with successive in-swinging yorkers to perform the hat-trick.

The final qualifying match was marred by two stoppages for rain. Cullinan – who retired briefly for repairs to his mouth after he had top-edged a reverse-sweep into his face – and Rhodes gave backbone to the South African innings. Dharmasena then took three wickets in an over to give Sri Lanka some joy, but the second rain stoppage left them 5.3 overs in which to score 83 runs. This was a task well beyond their capabilities.

MANDELA TROPHY QUALIFYING TABLE

	P	W	L	Ab	Pts
Pakistan	6	5	1	–	10
South Africa	6	4	2	–	8
Sri Lanka	6	2	3	1	5
New Zealand	6	–	5	1	1

Wasim Akram had recovered from illness and flew to South Africa in time for the finals. His presence made little difference. Pakistan gave two inept performances, and there were indications that off-field problems were beginning to plague the side. More happily, Donald played his first international match since injuring his foot on the tour of England. He was one of several heroes for South Africa in the second match, taking three wickets. Rindel, opening in senior cricket for the first time, shared a first-wicket stand of 190 in 38 overs with Kirsten, a South African record. Kirsten hit a six and 8 fours and made his runs off 110 balls. Richardson continued his splendid season with five catches. Pakistan were 42 for 6 and in danger of total humiliation before Asif Mujtaba and Wasim Akram added 55.

MANDELA TROPHY – MATCH ONE – PAKISTAN v. SRI LANKA
2 December 1994 at Kingsmead, Durban

SRI LANKA

R.S. Mahanama	b Waqar Younis	24
S.T. Jayasuriya	c Akram Raza, b Aqib Javed	26
A.P. Gurusinha	lbw, b Akram Raza	11
P.A. de Silva	b Aqib Javed	10
A. Ranatunga (capt)	not out	101
*H.P. Tillekeratne	retired hurt	1
R.S. Kalpage	st Rashid Latif, b Salim Malik	29
H.D.P.K. Dharmasena	not out	23
G.P. Wickremasinghe		
W.P.U.C.J. Vaas		
K.R. Pushpakumara		
Extras	b 1, lb 2, w 7, nb 3	13
(50 overs)	(for 5 wickets)	238

PAKISTAN

Aamir Sohail	c de Silva, b Kalpage	100
Saeed Anwar	b Vaas	5
Inzamam-ul-Haq	c Gurusinha, b Dharmasena	32
Salim Malik (capt)	not out	65
Ijaz Ahmed	c Mahanama, b Jayasuriya	7
Basit Ali	not out	22
*Rashid Latif		
Akram Raza		
Waqar Younis		
Ata-ur-Rehman		
Aqib Javed		
Extras	lb 5, w 3	8
(47.5 overs)	(for 4 wickets)	239

	O	M	R	W
Waqar Younis	10	–	50	1
Aqib Javed	10	–	44	2
Akram Raza	10	1	26	1
Ata-ur-Rehman	8	1	38	–
Aamir Sohail	6	–	30	–
Salim Malik	6	–	47	1

	O	M	R	W
Vaas	8	–	32	1
Pushpakumara	8	–	47	–
Wickremasinghe	6	–	28	–
Kalpage	10	–	40	1
Dharmasena	9.5	–	56	1
Jayasuriya	6	–	31	1

FALL OF WICKETS
1–44, **2**–57, **3**–68, **4**–86, **5**–172

FALL OF WICKETS
1–22, **2**–110, **3**–177, **4**–191

Umpires: K.E. Liebenberg & D.L. Orchard   *Man of the Match:* A. Ranatunga   *Pakistan won by 6 wickets*

PAKISTAN

Aamir Sohail	c and b Muralitharan	67
Saeed Anwar	c Muralitharan, b Kalpage	57
Inzamam-ul-Haq	c Dharmasena, b Vaas	62
Salim Malik (capt)	run out	20
Ijaz Ahmed	run out	1
Basit Ali	c de Silva, b Kalpage	7
*Rashid Latif	c Pushpakumara, b Vaas	7
Akram Raza	not out	8
Waqar Younis	c Mahanama, b Vaas	1
Ata-ur-Rehman	c Mahanama, b Wickremasinghe	3
Aqib Javed		
Extras	b 1, lb 7, w 3, nb 1	12
(50 overs)	(for 9 wickets)	245

SRI LANKA

R.S. Mahanama	run out	8
S.T. Jayasuriya	c Aamir Sohail, b Waqar Younis	8
A.P. Gurusinha	c and b Aamir Sohail	43
P.A. de Silva	c and b Waqar Younis	95
A. Ranatunga (capt)	b Aamir Sohail	24
R.S. Kalpage	c Rashid Latif, b Aamir Sohail	4
*H.P. Tillekeratne	run out	8
W.P.U.C.J. Vaas	run out	3
G.P. Wickremasinghe	not out	13
M. Muralitharan	c sub (Manzoor Elahi), b Aqib Javed	1
K.R. Pushpakumara	not out	14
Extras	lb 8, w 3, nb 1	12
(50 overs)	(for 9 wickets)	233

	O	M	R	W
Vaas	8	–	46	3
Pushpakumara	10	–	39	–
Wickremasinghe	10	–	39	1
Kalpage	10	–	41	2
Muralitharan	8	–	49	1
Jayasuriya	4	–	23	–

	O	M	R	W
Waqar Younis	10	–	73	2
Aqib Javed	10	2	31	1
Ata-ur-Rehman	10	–	53	–
Akram Raza	10	2	22	–
Aamir Sohail	10	–	46	3

FALL OF WICKETS
1–130, 2–130, 3–175, 4–181, 5–198, 6–229, 7–237, 8–239, 9–245

FALL OF WICKETS
1–16, 2–36, 3–95, 4–140, 5–146, 6–167, 7–179, 8–210, 9–214

Umpires: W. Diedricks & R.E. Koertzen   *Man of the Match:* Aamir Sohail   *Pakistan won by 12 runs*

SOUTH AFRICA

A.C. Hudson	lbw, b Pringle	9
G. Kirsten	lbw, b de Groen	19
W.J. Cronje (capt)	c Young, b Priest	38
D.J. Cullinan	c Young, b Doull	25
M.J.R. Rindel	run out	32
J.N. Rhodes	b Pringle	21
E.O. Simons	run out	24
*D.J. Richardson	run out	23
C.R. Matthews	not out	4
P.S. de Villiers	not out	0
C.E. Eksteen		
Extras	b 2, lb 5, w 1	8
(50 overs)	(for 8 wickets)	203

NEW ZEALAND

B.A. Young	c Rindel, b Matthews	25
S.P. Fleming	c Cronje, b de Villiers	12
M.D. Crowe	c Richardson, b Cronje	9
K.R. Rutherford (capt)	c Cronje, b de Villiers	40
*A.C. Parore	run out	13
C.Z. Harris	c Richardson, b Rindel	10
M.L. Su'a	run out	1
M.W. Priest	lbw, b Rindel	1
S.B. Doull	not out	19
C. Pringle	b Simons	1
R.P. de Groen	b Simons	0
Extras	b 3	3
(39.5 overs)		134

	O	M	R	W
Doull	7	–	35	1
de Groen	10	1	33	1
Pringle	10	3	29	2
Priest	10	–	42	1
Harris	10	–	45	–
Su'a	3	–	12	–

	O	M	R	W
de Villiers	8	2	36	2
Matthews	8	3	22	1
Cronje	5	1	10	1
Simons	8.5	1	28	2
Eksteen	5	1	20	–
Rindel	5	–	15	2

FALL OF WICKETS
1–23, 2–35, 3–83, 4–104, 5–145, 6–153, 7–199, 8–200

FALL OF WICKETS
1–39, 2–39, 3–52, 4–75, 5–101, 6–103, 7–106, 8–124, 9–134

Umpires: S.B. Lambson & C.J. Mitchley   *Man of the Match:* M.J.R. Rindel   *South Africa won by 69 runs*

MANDELA TROPHY – MATCH FOUR – SRI LANKA v. NEW ZEALAND
8 December 1994 at Springbok Park, Bloemfontein

SRI LANKA

R.S. Mahanama	c Germon, b Pringle	0
S.T. Jayasuriya	c Crowe, b Pringle	140
A.P. Gurusinha	c and b Harris	53
P.A. de Silva	c Harris, b Pringle	55
A. Ranatunga (capt)	not out	20
R.S. Kalpage	not out	4
*H.P. Tillekeratne		
H.D.P.K. Dharmasena		
G.P. Wickremasinghe		
K.R. Pushpakumara		
W.P.U.C.J. Vaas		
Extras	b 5, lb 5, w 5, nb 1	16
(50 overs)	(for 4 wickets)	288

NEW ZEALAND

B.A. Young	not out	22
S.P. Fleming	b Pushpakumara	11
A.C. Parore	not out	31
M.D. Crowe		
K.R. Rutherford (capt)		
C.Z. Harris		
*L.K. Germon		
M.W. Priest		
S.B. Doull		
C. Pringle		
R.P. de Groen		
Extras	lb 1, nb 1	2
(14.3 overs)	(for 1 wicket)	66

	O	M	R	W
Pringle	10	–	29	3
de Groen	10	–	75	–
Doull	10	1	66	–
Harris	10	–	54	1
Priest	10	–	54	–

	O	M	R	W
Pushpakumara	5	–	18	1
Vaas	7	1	33	–
Wickremasinghe	2.3	–	14	–

FALL OF WICKETS
1–1, 2–133, 3–235, 4–278

FALL OF WICKET
1–15

Umpires: W. Diedricks & R.E. Koertzen

Match abandoned

MANDELA TROPHY – MATCH FIVE – SOUTH AFRICA v. PAKISTAN
10 December 1994 at Wanderers, Johannesburg

PAKISTAN

Saeed Anwar	c Rindel, b Snell	26
Aamir Sohail	run out	23
Inzamam-ul-Haq	st Richardson, b Cronje	55
Salim Malik (capt)	c McMillan, b Snell	5
Ijaz Ahmed	c de Villiers, b Snell	73
Basit Ali	run out	2
*Rashid Latif	c Snell, b Cronje	13
Akram Raza	c Richardson, b Matthews	1
Waqar Younis	b Snell	6
Ata-ur-Rehman	run out	2
Aqib Javed	not out	1
Extras	lb 3, w 4	7
(49.1 overs)		214

SOUTH AFRICA

A.C. Hudson	lbw, b Ata-ur-Rehman	74
G. Kirsten	b Waqar Younis	9
W.J. Cronje (capt)	c Rashid Latif, b Waqar Younis	81
D.J. Cullinan	not out	18
M.J.R. Rindel	not out	13
J.N. Rhodes		
B.M. McMillan		
*D.J. Richardson		
R.P. Snell		
C.R. Matthews		
P.S. de Villiers		
Extras	lb 11, w 3, nb 6	20
(45.4 overs)	(for 3 wickets)	215

	O	M	R	W
de Villiers	10	1	25	–
Matthews	10	–	45	1
Cronje	7	–	37	2
Snell	9.1	1	37	4
McMillan	10	–	51	–
Rindel	3	–	16	–

	O	M	R	W
Waqar Younis	9.4	1	38	2
Aqib Javed	10	–	39	–
Ata-ur-Rehman	10	–	57	1
Akram Raza	10	–	40	–
Aamir Sohail	2	–	13	–
Salim Malik	4	–	17	–

FALL OF WICKETS
1–46, 2–61, 3–70, 4–165, 5–176, 6–196, 7–199, 8–205, 9–211

FALL OF WICKETS
1–18, 2–163, 3–185

Umpires: S.B. Lambson & C.J. Mitchley   *Man of the Match:* W.J. Cronje   *South Africa won by 7 wickets*

MANDELA TROPHY – MATCH SIX – SOUTH AFRICA v. NEW ZEALAND
11 December 1994 at Centurion Park, Verwoerdburg

SOUTH AFRICA

A.C. Hudson	c Priest, b Doull	3
D.J. Callaghan	not out	169
W.J. Cronje (capt)	c Young, b Thomson	68
D.J. Cullinan	c Thomson, b Su'a	38
M.J.R. Rindel	c Parore, b Su'a	1
J.N. Rhodes	c Parore, b Su'a	2
*D.J. Richardson	run out	4
E.O. Simons	c Rutherford, b Su'a	10
R.P. Snell	not out	1
C.R. Matthews		
P.S. de Villiers		
Extras	lb 14, w 1, nb 3	18
(50 overs)	(for 7 wickets)	314

NEW ZEALAND

B.A. Young	c Hudson, b Matthews	27
S.P. Fleming	c Rindel, b Matthews	0
*A.C. Parore	c Cullinan, b Callaghan	108
K.R. Rutherford (capt)	c Matthews, b Simons	14
M.D. Crowe	run out	6
S.A. Thomson	c Richardson, b Callaghan	39
C.Z. Harris	c Cronje, b Rindel	3
M.W. Priest	c and b Simons	13
M.L. Su'a	lbw, b Callaghan	1
S.B. Doull	c Richardson, b Simons	13
C. Pringle	not out	1
Extras	lb 2, w 4, nb 2	8
(40.3 overs)		233

	O	M	R	W
Pringle	10	–	40	–
Doull	9	–	70	1
Priest	5	–	35	–
Su'a	10	1	59	4
Harris	10	–	64	–
Thomson	6	–	32	1

	O	M	R	W
de Villiers	8	1	29	–
Matthews	6	1	28	2
Simons	6.3	–	46	3
Snell	4	–	32	–
Cronje	3	–	30	–
Rindel	7	–	34	1
Callaghan	6	–	32	3

FALL OF WICKETS
1–10, 2–159, 3–239, 4–261, 5–263, 6–282, 7–294

FALL OF WICKETS
1–0, 2–37, 3–60, 4–82, 5–188, 6–195, 7–215, 8–216, 9–232

Umpires: K.E. Liebenberg & D.L. Orchard   *Man of the Match:* D.J. Callaghan   *South Africa won by 81 runs*

MANDELA TROPHY – MATCH SEVEN – PAKISTAN v. NEW ZEALAND
13 December 1994 at St George's Park, Port Elizabeth

NEW ZEALAND

B.A. Young	lbw, b Aqib Javed	13
M.D. Crowe	c and b Salim Malik	83
*A.C. Parore	c Ijaz Ahmed, b Salim Malik	59
K.R. Rutherford (capt)	c Saeed Anwar, b Akram Raza	16
S.P. Fleming	lbw, b Waqar Younis	4
S.A. Thomson	b Waqar Younis	8
C.Z. Harris	c Moin Khan, b Waqar Younis	6
M.L. Su'a	b Waqar Younis	3
M.W. Priest	not out	4
C. Pringle	b Aqib Javed	0
R.P. de Groen	b Aqib Javed	0
Extras	b 1, lb 4	5
(49.4 overs)		201

PAKISTAN

Saeed Anwar	c Fleming, b de Groen	17
Aamir Sohail	b Pringle	75
Inzamam-ul-Haq	c Rutherford, b Su'a	17
Salim Malik (capt)	not out	53
Ijaz Ahmed	c Parore, b Pringle	23
Basit Ali	c Parore, b Pringle	0
Manzoor Elahi	not out	8
*Moin Khan		
Akram Raza		
Waqar Younis		
Aqib Javed		
Extras	lb 5, w 7, nb 1	13
(46.2 overs)	(for 5 wickets)	206

	O	M	R	W
Waqar Younis	10	–	32	4
Aqib Javed	9.4	1	25	3
Manzoor Elahi	10	–	40	–
Akram Raza	8	–	36	1
Aamir Sohail	4	–	30	–
Salim Malik	8	–	33	2

	O	M	R	W
Pringle	10	–	43	3
Thomson	6	–	31	–
de Groen	7.3	1	30	1
Su'a	10	2	30	1
Priest	6.3	1	26	–
Harris	6.2	–	41	–

FALL OF WICKETS
1–41, 2–142, 3–173, 4–180, 5–181, 6–194, 7–195, 8–200, 9–201

FALL OF WICKETS
1–51, 2–86, 3–142, 4–181, 5–181

Umpires: R.E. Koertzen & C.J. Mitchley   *Men of the Match:* Waqar Younis & Aqib Javed   *Pakistan won by 5 wickets*

MANDELA TROPHY – MATCH EIGHT – SOUTH AFRICA v. SRI LANKA
15 December 1994 at Springbok Park, Bloemfontein

SRI LANKA

R.S. Mahanama	c Hudson, b Jack	10
S.T. Jayasuriya	c Rhodes, b Jack	23
A.P. Gurusinha	c Rindel, b Simons	14
P.A. de Silva	c Hudson, b de Villiers	73
A. Ranatunga (capt)	run out	60
*H.P. Tillekeratne	b de Villiers	21
R.S. Kalpage	c Jack, b Simons	4
G.P. Wickremasinghe	b Simons	11
M. Muralitharan	not out	0
K.R. Pushpakumara		
W.P.U.C.J. Vaas		
Extras	lb 3, w 3, nb 4	10
(50 overs)	(for 8 wickets)	226

SOUTH AFRICA

A.C. Hudson	run out	44
D.J. Callaghan	c Ranatunga, b Vaas	9
W.J. Cronje (capt)	c Mahanama, b Muralitharan	14
D.J. Cullinan	b Kalpage	16
M.J.R. Rindel	run out	8
J.N. Rhodes	b Muralitharan	27
*D.J. Richardson	c Muralitharan, b de Silva	1
S.D. Jack	run out	1
E.O. Simons	c Ranatunga, b Kalpage	21
C.R. Matthews	not out	15
P.S. de Villiers	c Mahanama, b Jayasuriya	20
Extras	b 3, lb 12	15
(48.5 overs)		191

	O	M	R	W
de Villiers	10	1	31	2
Matthews	10	2	37	–
Cronje	3	–	23	–
Simons	10	1	51	3
Callaghan	3	–	16	–
Rindel	4	–	24	–
Jack	10	–	41	2

	O	M	R	W
Pushpakumara	3	–	20	–
Vaas	7	1	20	1
Wickremasinghe	6	–	16	–
Kalpage	10	–	42	2
Muralitharan	10	–	23	2
Jayasuriya	9.5	–	42	1
de Silva	3	–	13	1

FALL OF WICKETS
1–33, 2–44, 3–70, 4–161, 5–201, 6–214, 7–226, 8–226

FALL OF WICKETS
1–48, 2–68, 3–81, 4–96, 5–109, 6–113, 7–115, 8–152, 9–154

Umpires: S.B. Lambson & D.L. Orchard — *Man of the Match:* A. Ranatunga — *Sri Lanka won by 35 runs*

MANDELA TROPHY – MATCH NINE – SOUTH AFRICA v. PAKISTAN
17 December 1994 at Kingsmead, Durban

SOUTH AFRICA

A.C. Hudson	c Inzamam-ul-Haq, b Waqar Younis	1
D.J. Callaghan	c Inzamam-ul-Haq, b Aqib Javed	9
W.J. Cronje (capt)	c Basit Ali, b Waqar Younis	2
D.J. Cullinan	c Rashid Latif, b Aqib Javed	5
M.J.R. Rindel	run out	10
J.N. Rhodes	lbw, b Aamir Sohail	61
*D.J. Richardson	c Ijaz Ahmed, b Waqar Younis	53
E.O. Simons	b Waqar Younis	19
R.P. Snell	not out	27
C.R. Matthews	not out	3
P.S. de Villiers		
Extras	lb 4, w 8, nb 4	16
(50 overs)	(for 8 wickets)	206

PAKISTAN

Saeed Anwar	c Richardson, b de Villiers	10
Aamir Sohail	c Richardson, b Snell	44
Ijaz Ahmed	not out	114
Salim Malik (capt)	not out	36
Inzamam-ul-Haq		
Basit Ali		
Manzoor Elahi		
*Rashid Latif		
Akram Raza		
Waqar Younis		
Aqib Javed		
Extras	w 3, nb 1	4
(35 overs)	(for 2 wickets)	208

	O	M	R	W
Waqar Younis	10	–	52	4
Aqib Javed	10	3	37	2
Manzoor Elahi	10	1	27	–
Akram Raza	10	–	39	–
Aamir Sohail	7	–	34	1
Salim Malik	3	–	13	–

	O	M	R	W
de Villiers	10	–	46	1
Matthews	9	1	54	–
Snell	7	–	49	1
Simons	6	–	31	–
Callaghan	3	–	28	–

FALL OF WICKETS
1–2, 2–10, 3–20, 4–27, 5–44, 6–132, 7–174, 8–178

FALL OF WICKETS
1–13, 2–72

Umpires: W. Diedricks & K.E. Liebenberg — *Man of the Match:* Ijaz Ahmed — *Pakistan won by 8 wickets*

MANDELA TROPHY – MATCH TEN – NEW ZEALAND v. SRI LANKA
18 December 1994 at Buffalo Park, East London

NEW ZEALAND				SRI LANKA		
B.A. Young	c Tillekeratne, b Wickremasinghe		24	R.S. Mahanama	c Fleming, b Nash	1
B.R. Hartland	b Kalpage		32	S.T. Jayasuriya	c Parore, b Pringle	52
*A.C. Parore	c Tillekeratne, b Pushpakumara		67	A.P. Gurusinha	c and b Thomson	47
K.R. Rutherford (capt)	not out		102	P.A. de Silva	c Hartland, b Harris	4
S.P. Fleming	c Wickremasinghe, b Vaas		5	A. Ranatunga (capt)	c Parore, b Nash	32
S.A. Thomson	not out		11	*H.P. Tillekeratne	not out	68
C.Z. Harris				R.S. Kalpage	not out	43
M.L. Su'a				K.R. Pushpakumara		
M.W. Priest				W.P.U.C.J. Vaas		
S.B. Doull				G.P. Wickremasinghe		
C. Pringle				M. Muralitharan		
Extras	lb 11, w 3		14	Extras	b 3, lb 4, w 3	10
(50 overs)	(for 4 wickets)		255	(47.1 overs)	(for 5 wickets)	257

	O	M	R	W		O	M	R	W
Pushpakumara	10	1	50	1	Pringle	8	1	73	1
Vaas	10	1	33	1	Nash	10	–	52	2
Wickremasinghe	9	1	42	1	Su'a	3.1	–	23	–
Kalpage	7	1	42	1	Thomson	10	1	37	1
Muralitharan	9	1	50	–	Harris	10	–	40	1
Jayasuriya	5	–	27	–	Priest	6	–	25	–

FALL OF WICKETS
1–63, 2–63, 3–199, 4–220

FALL OF WICKETS
1–15, 2–102, 3–110, 4–110, 5–166

Umpires: C.J. Mitchley & D.L. Orchard   *Man of the Match:* K.R. Rutherford   *Sri Lanka won by 5 wickets*

MANDELA TROPHY – MATCH ELEVEN – PAKISTAN v. NEW ZEALAND
19 December 1994 at Buffalo Park, East London

NEW ZEALAND			PAKISTAN		
B.A. Young	c Akram Raza, b Kabir Khan	17	Saeed Anwar	c Parore, b Thomson	41
B.R. Hartland	b Akram Raza	44	Aamir Sohail	c Parore, b Harris	52
*A.C. Parore	b Aqib Javed	1	Basit Ali	c Hartland, b Priest	12
K.R. Rutherford (capt)	c Rashid Latif, b Aamir Sohail	30	Inzamam-ul-Haq	run out	15
S.P. Fleming	b Aamir Sohail	19	Salim Malik (capt)	c Su'a, b Priest	14
S.A. Thomson	c Rashid Latif, b Kabir Khan	15	Ijaz Ahmed	not out	25
C.Z. Harris	b Waqar Younis	18	*Moin Khan	not out	8
M.L. Su'a	b Waqar Younis	2	Akram Raza		
M.W. Priest	not out	17	Waqar Younis		
C. Pringle	b Waqar Younis	0	Aqib Javed		
R.P. de Groen	b Waqar Younis	0	Kabir Khan		
Extras	lb 1, w 7, nb 1	9	Extras	lb 2, w 5, nb 1	8
(47.3 overs)		172	(38.5 overs)	(for 5 wickets)	175

	O	M	R	W		O	M	R	W
Waqar Younis	8.3	1	33	4	Pringle	8	–	36	–
Aqib Javed	10	2	31	1	Su'a	6	1	26	–
Kabir Khan	10	1	32	2	de Groen	4	–	30	–
Akram Raza	7	–	25	1	Thomson	10	–	34	1
Aamir Sohail	7	–	20	2	Harris	4	–	15	1
Salim Malik	5	–	30	–	Priest	6	–	27	2
					Fleming	0.5	–	5	–

FALL OF WICKETS
1–36, 2–38, 3–82, 4–108, 5–132, 6–136, 7–145, 8–172, 9–172

FALL OF WICKETS
1–97, 2–102, 3–122, 4–126, 5–151

Umpires: W. Diedricks & S.B. Lambson   *Man of the Match:* Waqar Younis   *Pakistan won by 5 wickets*

MANDELA TROPHY – MATCH TWELVE – SOUTH AFRICA v. SRI LANKA
21 December 1994 at St George's Park, Port Elizabeth

SOUTH AFRICA

A.C. Hudson	lbw, b Wickremasinghe	27
G. Kirsten	b Dharmasena	20
D.J. Cullinan	c Gurusinha, b Dharmasena	63
W.J. Cronje (capt)	c de Silva, b Kalpage	5
J.N. Rhodes	c Mahanama, b Dharmasena	53
D.J. Callaghan	c Jayasuriya, b Dharmasena	23
*D.J. Richardson	c Ranatunga, b Vaas	7
E.O. Simons	c Kalpage, b Vaas	11
C.R. Matthews	not out	11
P.S. de Villiers	not out	7
C.E. Eksteen		
Extras	b 3, lb 7	10
(50 overs)	(for 8 wickets)	237

SRI LANKA

R.S. Mahanama	c Eksteen, b Matthews	3
S.T. Jayasuriya	c sub (Rindel), b Matthews	20
A.P. Gurusinha	lbw, b Cronje	23
P.A. de Silva	c Callaghan, b Matthews	0
A. Ranatunga (capt)	c and b Cronje	29
*H.P. Tillekeratne	not out	36
R.S. Kalpage	b Callaghan	9
H.D.P.K. Dharmasena	not out	12
W.P.U.C.J. Vaas		
G.P. Wickremasinghe		
M. Muralitharan		
Extras	b 2, lb 4, nb 1	7
(34 overs)	(for 6 wickets)	139

	O	M	R	W
Wickremasinghe	8	–	44	1
Vaas	9	–	42	2
Dharmasena	10	–	37	4
Muralitharan	10	–	32	–
Kalpage	10	1	51	1
Jayasuriya	3	–	21	–

	O	M	R	W
de Villiers	7	1	24	–
Matthews	7	–	22	3
Simons	7	–	25	–
Cronje	8	–	27	2
Callaghan	3	–	19	1
Eksteen	2	–	16	–

FALL OF WICKETS
1–30, 2–53, 3–79, 4–198, 5–200, 6–200, 7–219, 8–229

FALL OF WICKETS
1–5, 2–34, 3–34, 4–55, 5–84, 6–112

Umpires: R.E. Koertzen & K.E. Liebenberg   *Man of the Match:* C.R. Matthews   *South Africa won on faster scoring rate*

MANDELA TROPHY – FIRST FINAL – SOUTH AFRICA v. PAKISTAN
10 January 1995 at Newlands, Cape Town

SOUTH AFRICA

G. Kirsten	lbw, b Akram Raza	43
D.J. Callaghan	c Ijaz Ahmed, b Aqib Javed	4
W.J. Cronje (capt)	c Aamir Sohail, b Aqib Javed	21
D.J. Cullinan	run out	64
J.N. Rhodes	c Aamir Sohail, b Akram Raza	21
M.J.R. Rindel	run out	31
*D.J. Richardson	run out	4
E.O. Simons	c Inzamam-ul-Haq, b Waqar Younis	6
P.L. Symcox	c sub, b Waqar Younis	3
S.D. Jack	b Waqar Younis	6
P.S. de Villiers	not out	0
Extras	lb 4, w 3, nb 5	12
(49.3 overs)		215

PAKISTAN

Aamir Sohail	run out	71
Saeed Anwar	b Simons	5
Inzamam-ul-Haq	lbw, b Simons	4
Salim Malik (capt)	run out	19
Ijaz Ahmed	c Callaghan, b Jack	5
Basit Ali	c Simons, b Cronje	6
*Rashid Latif	run out	17
Wasim Akram	c Jack, b Simons	12
Akram Raza	c Jack, b Simons	12
Waqar Younis	c de Villiers, b Cronje	14
Aqib Javed	not out	6
Extras	b 5, lb 2	7
(42.5 overs)		178

	O	M	R	W
Wasim Akram	10	–	43	–
Aqib Javed	10	1	51	2
Waqar Younis	9.3	–	32	3
Akram Raza	10	–	38	2
Salim Malik	4	–	22	–
Aamir Sohail	6	–	25	–

	O	M	R	W
de Villiers	8	–	23	–
Jack	8	–	45	1
Simons	8	–	42	4
Cronje	8.5	–	31	2
Symcox	10	–	30	–

FALL OF WICKETS
1–6, 2–54, 3–89, 4–121, 5–193, 6–198, 7–200, 8–207, 9–215

FALL OF WICKETS
1–48, 2–58, 3–101, 4–105, 5–111, 6–122, 7–133, 8–149, 9–159

Umpires: C.J. Mitchley & D.L. Orchard   *Man of the Match:* E.O. Simons   *South Africa won by 37 runs*

MANDELA TROPHY – SECOND FINAL – SOUTH AFRICA *v.* PAKISTAN
12 January 1995 at Wanderers, Johannesburg

SOUTH AFRICA

G. Kirsten	st Rashid Latif, b Salim Malik	87
M.J.R. Rindel	run out	106
W.J. Cronje (capt)	c Aqib Javed, b Wasim Akram	37
D.J. Cullinan	b Waqar Younis	5
J.N. Rhodes	run out	6
D.J. Callaghan	not out	7
*D.J. Richardson	not out	1
B.M. McMillan		
E.O. Simons		
P.S. de Villiers		
A.A. Donald		
Extras	lb 9, w 6, nb 2	17
		—
(50 overs)	(for 5 wickets)	266

PAKISTAN

Aamir Sohail	lbw, b de Villiers	0
Saeed Anwar	c Richardson, b de Villiers	3
Ijaz Ahmed	c Richardson, b de Villiers	4
Inzamam-ul-Haq	c Richardson, b Donald	19
Salim Malik (capt)	c Richardson, b Donald	12
Asif Mujtaba	c Richardson, b Cronje	24
*Rashid Latif	c McMillan, b Donald	0
Wasim Akram	run out	26
Akram Raza	c McMillan, b Simons	0
Waqar Younis	c Cronje, b Simons	6
Aqib Javed	not out	4
Extras	lb 3, w 6, nb 2	11
		—
(32.2 overs)		109

	O	M	R	W
Wasim Akram	10	1	47	1
Aqib Javed	9	1	33	–
Waqar Younis	9	–	57	1
Akram Raza	8	–	44	–
Aamir Sohail	10	–	52	–
Salim Malik	4	–	24	1

	O	M	R	W
de Villiers	7	1	21	3
Donald	8	2	25	3
Simons	9.2	1	26	2
McMillan	5	–	25	–
Cronje	3	–	9	1

FALL OF WICKETS
1–190, 2–243, 3–251, 4–257, 5–260

FALL OF WICKETS
1–1, 2–7, 3–14, 4–37, 5–42, 6–42, 7–97, 8–98, 9–98

Umpires: K.E. Liebenberg & C.J. Mitchley   *Man of the Match:* M.J.R. Rindel   *South Africa won by 157 runs*

Allan Donald recovered from injury to regain his place in the South African side and help win the Mandela Trophy. (David Munden/ Sportsline)

PAKISTAN TOUR

30 **November 1994** *at Midland*

Pakistan 349 for 7 (Salim Malik 135 retired)
Nicky Openheimer's XI 168 for 5 (M.J.R. Rindel 100 not out)
Match drawn

7 **December 1994** *at Lenasia*

Pakistan 262 for 7 (Ijaz Ahmed 112, Shakeel Ahmed 58)
Transvaal Invitation XI 211 (M.W. Rushmere 55)
Pakistan won by 51 runs

20 **December 1994** *at Alice*

Pakistan 260 for 7 (Asif Mujtaba 101)
Eastern Cape Invitation XI 117 (S. Abrahams 77 not out)
Pakistan won by 143 runs

26, 27, 28 and **29** December 1994 *at Newlands, Cape Town*

Western Province 436 for 9 dec. (H.D. Ackerman 118,
    E.O. Simons 102 not out, J. Kallis 53, D.B. Rundle 50) and
    270 for 8 dec. (J. Kallis 74, A.C. Dawson 51)
Pakistan 308 (Asif Mujtaba 55, Basit Ali 53, Saeed Anwar 51)
    and 206 (Asif Mujtaba 65, Inzamam-ul-Haq 57, D.B. Rundle
    6 for 51)

Western Province won by 192 runs

4, 5, 6 and **7** January 1995 *at Kingsmead, Durban*

Natal 391 (D.N. Crookes 83, D.M. Benkenstein 76, Kabir Khan
    4 for 70) and 347 for 7 dec. (N.C. Johnson 114,
    D.N. Crookes 68, A.C. Hudson 57, Asif Mujtaba 4 for 74)
Pakistan 247 (Waqar Younis 55, L. Klusener 4 for 63) and 259
    (Inzamam-ul-Haq 77, Ijaz Ahmed 53, D.N. Crookes 4 for 40)

Natal won by 232 runs

Pakistan came to South Africa to compete in the Mandela
Trophy and to play the Inaugural Test match against South
Africa. Outside the international games they played five
matches, two of which were first-class. They lost both of
these games, and clouds began to gather over Pakistan
cricket. These clouds were on the horizon when the party
landed in South Africa. Wasim Akram had not made the
trip through illness, and Mushtaq Ahmed had been
dropped. Abdul Qadir had not made himself available for
selection, and there were persistent reports that Waqar
Younis and skipper Salim Malik were not on the best of
terms. Salim had insisted that his brother-in-law Ijaz
Ahmed should be in the side, which was regarded as
nepotism in some quarters. In the event, Ijaz justified his
selection. Rashid Latif was appointed vice-captain in an
attempt to balance the regional factions in the side, but it
was apparent by the time of the Test match that all was not
well in the Pakistan camp.

Waqar declared himself unfit because of a back strain,
and – more mysteriously – Rashid Latif also withdrew
with a back injury on the eve of the match. Most bizarre
was the decision to include medium-pace bowler Aamir
Nazir in the side at the expense of off-spinner Akram
Raza. Aamir Nazir did not arrive in Johannesburg until
the morning of the match. He had flown from Karachi 24
hours earlier and was rushed to the ground as soon as he
arrived. Play had been in progress for 36 minutes before he
was ready to take the field, and Akram Raza had been
fielding as substitute. It was no surprise that Aamir broke
down with cramp in his seventh over.

There had been early success for Pakistan after South
Africa had won the toss and batted first, but Kirsten and

ABOVE RIGHT: *Brian McMillan lost form in mid-season, but returned to
play a major part in the victory over Pakistan in the Inaugural Test. He
hit a maiden Test century and took four vital wickets. (David Munden/
Sportsline)*

RIGHT: *A tiger on the loose – Fanie de Villiers, 51 wickets in the season.
(Alan Cozzi)*

Cronje stopped the rot. The bowling was generally way-ward, and there was a liberal sprinkling of no-balls. Wasim Akram, in particular, was far from his best, and neither Aqib nor Kabir Khan had the necessary menace. The game turned completely in favour of South Africa when Rhodes and McMillan came together in a sixth-wicket stand of 157. Rhodes' position in the side had been in doubt, for he had not reached fifty in a Test match for almost a year, but he played with spirit for his 72 before being caught at slip off the returning Aamir Nazir. The young bowler also bowled Richardson first ball, but the cramp came back to haunt him.

McMillan hit strongly to reach his first Test hundred off 146 balls. South Africa ended the day on 354 for 7, and although McMillan was bowled round his legs by Wasim Akram when he was on 105, it was another of the Pakistani all-rounder's no-balls, and McMillan survived until the second morning when he was caught behind off Aqib Javed. McMillan's pugnacious approach had served his side well, and more was to come as Fanie de Villiers hit his highest Test score, 66 off 68 balls, to take the home side to an impressive 460.

Having accomplished much with the bat, de Villiers now routed Pakistan with the ball. He maintained a full length, consistently found the edge of the bat and knocked back Ijaz Ahmed's leg stump when the batsman left it exposed. The Pakistan bowlers could well have learned from watching de Villiers.

Salim Malik alone played with a sense of responsibility, and he was given some belated support by Wasim Akram so that Pakistan ended the day on 177 for 6. Salim deserved a century for his efforts but, on 99, he fell to Donald who was playing his first first-class match since the Oval Test against England in August 1994. Fanie de Villiers accounted for Wasim and Aamir Nazir to bring his total to six wickets and to give South Africa a first-innings lead of 230.

Cronje did not enforce the follow-on. He decided to go for brisk runs and a massive lead. At the beginning of the fourth day, South Africa were 161 for 3, and, thankfully, a large crowd gathered in anticipation of the last rites. Cullinan held the batting together while others plundered. Commins, batting with a runner, ran himself out in attempting a leg-bye, and Richardson, the season's hero,

---

INAUGURAL TEST MATCH – SOUTH AFRICA v. PAKISTAN
19, 20, 21, 22 and 23 January 1995 at Wanderers, Johannesburg

SOUTH AFRICA

	FIRST INNINGS		SECOND INNINGS	
G. Kirsten	c Sohail, b Kabir	62	b Wasim	42
P.J.R. Steyn	c Moin, b Wasim	1	c Moin, b Nazir	17
J.B. Commins	b Aqib	13	(6) run out	0
D.J. Cullinan	c Moin, b Aqib	0	not out	69
W.J. Cronje (capt)	c Asif, b Kabir	41	(3) c Sohail, b Aqib	48
J.N. Rhodes	c Inzamam, b Nazir	72	(5) c Moin, b Wasim	16
B.M. McMillan	c Moin, b Aqib	113	c Salim, b Kabir	33
*D.J. Richardson	b Nazir	0	lbw, b Aqib	0
C.E. Eksteen	c Moin, b Wasim	13	not out	2
P.S. de Villiers	not out	66		
A.A. Donald	c Inzamam, b Sohail	15		
Extras	b 4, lb 18, w 6, nb 36	64	b 6, lb 5, w 15, nb 6	32
		460	(for 7 wickets, dec.)	259

PAKISTAN

	FIRST INNINGS		SECOND INNINGS	
Aamir Sohail	c Richardson, b de Villiers	23	c McMillan, b de Villiers	0
Saeed Anwar	c Cullinan, b de Villiers	2	c de Villiers, b Donald	1
Asif Mujtaba	c Richardson, b de Villiers	0	c Richardson, b McMillan	26
Salim Malik (capt)	c Eksteen, b Donald	99	lbw, b de Villiers	1
Ijaz Ahmed	b de Villiers	19	(6) c Richardson, b McMillan	1
Inzamam-ul-Haq	b McMillan	19	(5) c Richardson, b de Villiers	95
*Moin Khan	c de Villiers, b McMillan	9	c Rhodes, b Eksteen	0
Wasim Akram	b de Villiers	41	c Kirsten, b Eksteen	11
Kabir Khan	c Richardson, b Donald	4	c Eksteen, b Donald	10
Aqib Javed	not out	0	c Richardson, b de Villiers	0
Aamir Nazir	b de Villiers	0	not out	1
Extras	lb 5, nb 9	14	b 8, lb 7, w 1, nb 3	19
		230		165

	O	M	R	W	O	M	R	W
Wasim Akram	36	11	113	2	23	4	53	2
Aqib Javed	29.4	6	102	3	26	2	82	2
Kabir Khan	19.1	4	60	2	18	–	58	1
Aamir Nazir	13.1	1	67	2	13	1	55	1
Aamir Sohail	14.2	2	47	1				
Salim Malik	8	–	49	–				

	O	M	R	W	O	M	R	W
Donald	17	2	63	2	15	3	53	2
de Villiers	20.5	4	81	6	19.3	11	27	4
McMillan	12	3	46	2	11	1	33	2
Eksteen	7	1	16	–	19	7	34	2
Cronje	9	5	19	–	5	2	3	–

FALL OF WICKETS
1–1, 2–55, 3–59, 4–138, 5–168, 6–325, 7–325, 8–367, 9–389
1–69, 2–96, 3–155, 4–185, 5–185, 6–251, 7–255

FALL OF WICKETS
1–20, 2–20, 3–44, 4–106, 5–134, 6–158, 7–193, 8–207, 9–230
1–3, 2–3, 3–5, 4–98, 5–100, 6–101, 7–124, 8–164, 9–164

Umpires: M.J. Kitchen & C.J. Mitchley

South Africa won by 324 runs

was out first ball for the second time in the match. Eventually, Cronje's declaration left Pakistan five sessions in which to score 490.

The attitude of the Pakistan side never suggested that they had any capacity to think of victory, and they were soon in deepest despair as de Villiers accounted for Aamir Sohail and Salim Malik with leg-cutters and caught Saeed Anwar when he mis-hooked Donald. It was nearly three hours before another wicket fell, and then Asif Mujtaba gloved McMillan to the wicket-keeper. Ijaz Ahmed went the same way, and Moin Khan fell to a spectacular catch in the covers by Rhodes. Wasim Akram was taken at short-leg, and Inzamam-ul-Haq watched all with resignation as Pakistan ended the day on 149 for 7.

South Africa duly clinched victory within half an hour on the final morning. Kabir Khan fended off a Donald lifter into the hands of short-leg, and Inzamam's tenacious effort ended when he touched a de Villiers out-swinger to Richardson. Like Salim Malik, Inzamam could claim some honour from the match. His stylish and gritty 95 had come off 179 balls. Aqib Javed became another Richardson/de Villiers victim, and so de Villiers claimed 10 wickets in a Test for the second time. He had also hit a fifty and so claimed a unique place among South African cricketers.

South African cricket was joyful. The victory by 324 runs was the highest in their history.

On and off the field, the clouds surrounding Pakistan cricket were growing darker by the hour.

CASTLE CUP

5, 6, 7 and 8 November 1994 *at Kingsmead, Durban*

Orange Free State 126 (S.M. Pollock 4 for 24, N.C. Johnson 4 for 49) and 250 (M.D. Marshall 4 for 42)
Natal 236 (F.D. Stephenson 6 for 49) and 141 for 1 (A.C. Hudson 73 not out)

Natal won by 9 wickets

Natal 16 pts, Orange Free State 5 pts

at Centurion Park, Verwoerdburg

Border 286 (P.C. Strydom 127, P.S. de Villiers 4 for 66) and 134 (P.N. Kirsten 51, R.E. Bryson 4 for 17, P.S. de Villiers 4 for 37)
Northern Transvaal 357 (M.J.R. Rindel 63, B.C. Fourie 6 for 91) and 64 for 0

Northern Transvaal won by 10 wickets

Northern Transvaal 17 pts, Border 0 pts

at Wanderers, Johannesburg

Boland 267 (J.B. Commins 77, M. Erasmus 59 not out, R.P. Snell 6 for 60, S.D. Jack 4 for 94) and 359 (J.B. Commins 93, L.D. Ferreira 71, W. Smit 52, S.D. Jack 4 for 60)

Transvaal 316 (N.H. Fairbrother 89, R.P. Snell 81, W.V. Rippon 57, H.S. Williams 4 for 59) and 154 for 4 (S.J. Cook 75 not out)

Match drawn

Transvaal 8 pts, Boland 7 pts

11, 12, 13 and 14 November 1994 *at St George's Park, Port Elizabeth*

Transvaal 396 (B.M. White 120, D.R. Laing 96, N.H. Fairbrother 66) and 224 for 9 dec. (B.M. White 68, N.H. Fairbrother 51)
Eastern Province 325 (D.J. Richardson 68, D.J. Callaghan 62, E.A.E. Baptiste 54, P.G. Amm 50, M.J. Vandrau 4 for 99) and 263 for 6 (T.G. Shaw 84 not out, D.J. Richardson 72 not out)

Match drawn

Eastern Province 5 pts, Transvaal 5 pts

at Kingsmead, Durban

Natal 179 (N.E. Wright 50, O.D. Gibson 7 for 55) and 183 (A.C. Hudson 78, O.D. Gibson 6 for 70)
Border 115 (S.M. Pollock 4 for 32, M.D. Marshall 4 for 47) and 235 (D.J. Cullinan 70, S.J. Palframan 56)

Natal won by 12 runs

Natal 15 pts, Border 5 pts

at Newlands, Cape Town

Western Province 105 (B.T. Player 4 for 34) and 386 (D.L. Haynes 96, H.D. Ackerman 58, G. Kirsten 50, F.D. Stephenson 5 for 60)
Orange Free State 215 (L.J. Wilkinson 74, C.R. Matthews 5 for 35) and 278 for 6 (W.J. Cronje 111, P.J.R. Steyn 84, G.F.J. Liebenberg 50)

Orange Free State won by 4 wickets

Orange Free State 16 pts, Western Province 5 pts

18, 19, 20 and 21 November 1994 *at Paarl CC, Paarl*

Boland 239 (J.B. Commins 86, M.W. Handman 4 for 55) and 149
Eastern Province 118 and 195 (L.J. Koen 92, C.W. Henderson 7 for 57)

Boland won by 75 runs

Boland 16 pts, Eastern Province 5 pts

at Buffalo Park, East London

Border 268 (P.C. Strydom 60) and 314 for 7 (D.J. Cullinan 150 not out, P.C. Strydom 55)
Western Province 471 (H.D. Ackerman 93, E.O. Simons 73, S.G. Koenig 64, M.W. Pringle 51 not out)

Match drawn

Western Province 6 pts, Border 4 pts

at Centurion Park, Verwoerdburg

Transvaal 360 (S.J. Cook 114, R.P. Snell 67, S.D. Jack
60 not out) and 72 for 2
Northern Transvaal 193 (R.F. Pienaar 73) and 238
(C.B. Lambert 63, M.J.R. Rindel 62, C.E. Eksteen 5 for 84)

Transvaal won by 8 wickets

Transvaal 17 pts, Northern Transvaal 4 pts

1, 2, 3 and 4 December 1994 *at Paarl CC, Paarl*

Boland 258 (K.M. Curran 104, W. Smit 54, M.J.G. Davis
4 for 60) and 100 (R.E. Bryson 5 for 25)
Northern Transvaal 213 (L.P. Vorster 64, M. Erasmus 5 for 44)
and 146 for 7 (M.J.G. Davis 68 not out)

Northern Transvaal won by 3 wickets

Northern Transvaal 16 pts, Boland 7 pts

at Springbok Park, Bloemfontein

Eastern Province 334 (K.C. Wessels 102, P.G. Amm 82, N.W.
Pretorius 5 for 96, F.D. Stephenson 4 for 83) and 126 for 3
Orange Free State 113 (T.G. Shaw 4 for 16) and 346 (G.F.J.
Liebenberg 141, P.J.R. Steyn 115, E.A.E. Baptiste 5 for 89)

Eastern Province won by 7 wickets

Eastern Province 17 pts, Orange Free State 4 pts

10, 11, 12 and 13 December 1994 *at Newlands, Cape Town*

Natal 390 (P.L. Symcox 74 not out, D.J. Watson 60,
N.C. Johnson 53, L. Klusener 50) and 246 for 5 dec.
(M.L. Bruyns 84, N.E. Wright 61)
Western Province 303 (S.G. Koenig 89, L. Klusener 4 for 62)
and 193 for 6 (S.G. Koenig 73, D.L. Haynes 70)

Match drawn

Western Province 6 pts, Natal 4 pts

15, 16, 17 and 18 December 1994 *at St George's Park, Port Elizabeth*

Eastern Province 328 (K.C. Wessels 104, P.G. Amm 65) and
268 for 5 dec. (K.C. Wessels 59 not out, P.G. Amm 58,
L.J. Koen 55)
Northern Transvaal 306 (S. Elworthy 75, E.A.E. Baptiste 5 for
62) and 196 for 7 (R.C. Ontong 75 not out)

Match drawn

Eastern Province 6 pts, Northern Transvaal 6 pts

16, 17, 18 and 19 December 1994 *at Newlands, Cape Town*

Western Province 500 for 8 dec. (B.M. McMillan 140,
H.H. Gibbs 102, M.W. Pringle 54 not out, D.L. Haynes 54)
Boland 206 (J.B. Commins 83, A.C. Dawson 4 for 51) and
271 (K.M. Curran 73, M.S. Nackerdien 54, L.D. Ferreira 52,
D.B. Rundle 5 for 76)

Western Province won by an innings and 23 runs

Western Province 17 pts, Boland 2 pts

17, 18, 19 and 20 December 1994 *at Springbok Park, Bloemfontein*

Border 380 (P.C. Strydom 100, O.D. Gibson 58) and 217 for 8
dec. (S.J. Palframan 59, N. Boje 5 for 75)
Orange Free State 294 (G.F.J. Liebenberg 126, C.F. Craven
63, O.D. Gibson 5 for 96) and 222 (L.J. Wilkinson 77,
F.D. Stephenson 52, I.L. Howell 6 for 62)

Border won by 81 runs

Border 16 pts, Orange Free State 6 pts

at Wanderers, Johannesburg

Natal 339 (M.D. Marshall 82 not out, M.L. Bruyns 71,
T.C. Webster 5 for 93) and 244
Transvaal 162 (R.E. Veenstra 4 for 36) and 177 (D.R. Laing 84
not out)

Natal won by 244 runs

Natal 18 pts, Transvaal 5 pts

6, 7, 8 and 9 January 1995 *at Centurion Park, Verwoerdburg*

Northern Transvaal 455 (C.B. Lambert 170, R.F. Pienaar 108,
J.E. Johnson 4 for 61) and 180 for 2 (C.B. Lambert 96,
R.F. Pienaar 61 not out)
Orange Free State 289 (C.F. Craven 107, S. Elworthy 5 for 55)
and 345 (G.F.J. Liebenberg 90, J.F. Venter 64,
C.F. Craven 50)

Northern Transvaal won by 8 wickets

Northern Transvaal 19 pts, Orange Free State 4 pts

13, 14, 15 and 16 January 1995 *at Buffalo Park, East London*

Transvaal 379 for 8 dec. (S.J. Cook 83, D.R. Laing 83,
M.W. Rushmere 73, C. Grainger 54)
Border 116 for 3

Match drawn

Transvaal 4 pts, Border 3 pts

at St George's Park, Port Elizabeth

Western Province 326 for 5 dec. (S.G. Koenig 149 not out,
J.H. Kallis 77) and 0 for 0 dec.
Eastern Province 0 for 0 dec. and 327 for 5 (L.J. Koen
138 not out, K.C. Wessels 107)

Eastern Province won by 5 wickets

Eastern Province 13 pts, Western Province 2 pts

at Kingsmead, Durban

Natal 450 for 8 dec. (A.C. Hudson 157, D.M. Benkenstein 71,
N.E. Wright 55) and 40 for 1 dec.
Boland 250 (K.M. Curran 85, M.S. Nackerdien 69) and 129

Natal won by 111 runs

Natal 18 pts, Boland 5 pts

26, 27, 28 and **29** January 1995 *at Kingsmead, Durban*

Northern Transvaal 270 (M.J.R. Rindel 118) and 159
  (K.J. Rule 67, M.D. Marshall 4 for 40)
Natal 208 (N.C. Johnson 71, L. Klusener 54, S. Elworthy
  7 for 65) and 223 for 5 (M.L. Bruyns 59 not out,
  J.N. Rhodes 53)

Natal won by 5 wickets

Natal 16 pts, Northern Transvaal 7 pts

27, 28, 29 and **30** January 1995 *at Paarl CC, Paarl*

Orange Free State 403 for 7 dec. (L.J. Wilkinson 101,
  W.J. Cronje 70, J.M. Arthur 61, J.F. Venter 52 not out,
  H.S. Williams 4 for 93)
Boland 227 (K.C. Jackson 52, A.A. Donald 4 for 49) and 206
  for 5 (K.M. Curran 63 not out, K.C. Jackson 58)

Match drawn

Orange Free State 7 pts, Boland 3 pts

at Buffalo Park, East London

Eastern Province 281 (D.J. Callaghan 111, D.J. Richardson
  105) and 204 for 4 dec. (K.C. Wessels 59)
Border 182 (A.G. Huckle 6 for 59) and 207 for 8
  (F.J.C. Cronje 70)

Match drawn

Eastern Province 7 pts, Border 4 pts

at Wanderers, Johannesburg

Transvaal 376 (M.W. Rushmere 134, G.A. Pollock 74,
  C. Grainger 54, A.C. Dawson 6 for 86) and 223 for 5
  (S.J. Cook 55 not out)
Western Province 442 (G. Kirsten 150, B.M. McMillan 91,
  J.H. Kallis 52, A.C. Dawson 52, C.E. Eksteen 5 for 128)

Match drawn

Western Province 5 pts, Transvaal 4 pts

3, 4, 5 and **6** February 1995 *at Paarl CC, Paarl*

Boland 228 (M.S. Nackerdien 77) and 110 (P.A.N. Emslie
  4 for 37)
Border 218 (S.J. Palframan 53, W.F. Stelling 4 for 12) and 121
  for 1 (D.J. Cullinan 78 not out)

Border won by 9 wickets

Border 15 pts, Boland 5 pts

at St George's Park, Port Elizabeth

Natal 377 (D.N. Crookes 123 not out, D.M. Benkenstein 76,
  L. Klusener 75, S. Abrahams 4 for 76) and 19 for 0
Eastern Province 218 (D.J. Richardson 51, P.L. Symcox
  4 for 47) and 175 (D.J. Richardson 54)

Natal won by 10 wickets

Natal 17 pts, Eastern Province 4 pts

at Springbok Park, Bloemfontein

Orange Free State 181 (W.J. Cronje 54 not out,
  P.J.R. Steyn 53, M.J. Vandrau 6 for 49) and 332
  (C.F. Craven 78 not out, M.J. Vandrau 5 for 79)
Transvaal 184 (N. Boje 5 for 38) and 150 (A.A. Donald 4 for 36)

Orange Free State won by 179 runs

Orange Free State 15 pts, Transvaal 5 pts

at Newlands, Cape Town

Northern Transvaal 272 (K.J. Rule 102, L.P. Vorster 56,
  D.G. Payne 4 for 50) and 216 (D.G. Payne 4 for 56,
  D.B. Rundle 4 for 91)
Western Province 286 (H.H. Gibbs 79, P.S. de Villiers 6 for 47)
  and 203 for 5 (G. Kirsten 85, H.D. Ackerman 62)

Western Province won by 5 wickets

Western Province 16 pts, Northern Transvaal 5 pts

17, 18, 19 and **20** February 1995 *at Buffalo Park, East London*

Natal 303 (M.L. Bruyns 59, B.C. Fourie 5 for 96)
Border 202 (P.N. Kirsten 60, M.P. Stonier 57)

Match drawn

Natal 8 pts, Border 6 pts

at Springbok Park, Bloemfontein

Western Province 186 (H.D. Ackerman 55, F.D. Stephenson
  5 for 61) and 287 (D. Jordaan 97, M.W. Pringle 60 not out,
  N.W. Pretorius 4 for 93)
Orange Free State 308 (G.F.J. Liebenberg 81) and 168 for 5

Orange Free State won by 5 wickets

Orange Free State 16 pts, Western Province 3 pts

at Wanderers, Johannesburg

Eastern Province 344 (E.A.E. Baptiste 75, L.J. Koen 54,
  P.G. Amm 51, R.A. Lyle 6 for 63) and 245 for 8 dec.
  (P.G. Amm 118, L.J. Koen 74, R.A. Lyle 4 for 61,
  R.P. Snell 4 for 84)
Transvaal 256 (M.J. Vandrau 59 not out, E.A.E. Baptiste
  5 for 86, M.W. Handman 4 for 95) and 289 for 9
  (A.M. Bacher 70, S.J. Cook 54, T.G. Shaw 5 for 91)

Match drawn

Eastern Province 8 pts, Transvaal 6 pts

at Centurion Park, Verwoerdburg

Boland 270 (K.C. Jackson 57, A.R. Wylie 54) and 85
  (R.E. Bryson 4 for 23)
Northern Transvaal 165 for 7 dec. (R.F. Pienaar 66) and 194
  for 9 (A.J. Seymore 84, C.W. Henderson 5 for 57)

Northern Transvaal won by 1 wicket

Northern Transvaal 14 pts, Boland 5 pts

South Africa's foremost first-class competition, the Castle Cup, has tended to become overwhelmed in the past two years by the vast amount of one-day cricket being played in the Republic. With Pakistan, Sri Lanka and New Zealand visiting the country, it was hardly likely that the domestic game would claim much interest, but it did serve to give some of the younger players the opportunity to advance their cause. Among those to win praise were pace bowler Shaun Pollock, son of Peter, Western Province's Jacques Kallis, and the young Natal wicket-keeper Mark Bruyns who took over from Errol Stewart. These young players, of course, have the chance to gain experience of international cricket at a formative age, a chance that was denied to such outstanding cricketers as Ken McEwan and Clive Rice.

While attention was focused on younger players, it was veteran West Indians who took most of the glory. Malcolm Marshall took over as captain of Natal and led them to triumph when one round of matches still to be played, while Franklyn Stephenson led Orange Free State and Desmond Haynes led Western Province for most of the season. Lambert scored heavily for Northern Transvaal, Baptiste played for Eastern Province, and Ottis Gibson had a good all-round season for Border. Gibson then returned to the Caribbean to play in the Red Stripe Cup and was chosen for the tour of England, so having the distinction of appearing regularly in three first-class cricket seasons in different continents inside a period of 12 months. And some say that cricketers play too much cricket!

The former Derbyshire player Matthew Vandrau took a career-best 11 for 128 for Transvaal against Orange Free State and still finished on the losing side. Kepler Wessels ended the season with a broken finger and is unlikely to play first-class cricket next season.

CASTLE CUP FINAL TABLE

	P	W	L	D	Pts
Natal (6)	8	6	–	2	112
Northern Transvaal (8)	8	4	3	1	88
Orange Free State (1)	8	3	4	1	73
Eastern Province (3)	8	2	2	4	65
Western Province (2)	8	2	3	3	60
Transvaal (4)	8	1	2	5	54
Border (5)	8	2	2	4	53
Boland (7)	8	1	5	2	50

(1994 positions in brackets)

FRIENDLY MATCH

1, 2 and 3 April 1995 *at Boland Bank Park, Paarl*

Warwickshire 321 for 9 dec. (D.A. Reeve 107, A.J. Moles 83, C.W. Henderson 5 for 95) and 143 for 5 dec. (T.L. Penney 77 not out)
Boland 88 and 272 (A.T. Holdstock 50, N.M.K. Smith 5 for 76)
Warwickshire won by 104 runs

UNITED CRICKET BOARD OF SOUTH AFRICA BOWL

SECTION ONE

21, 22 and 23 October 1994 *at Wanderers, Johannesburg*

Transvaal 'B' 467 for 5 dec. (C. Grainger 233, H. Engelbrecht 100, N. Pothas 76 not out) and 218 for 3 dec. (G.A. Pollock 101 not out, N.R. Rhodes 67)
Orange Free State 'B' 348 (A. Moreby 105, A. Hansen 79, M.R. Hobson 5 for 85) and 299 for 9 (C. Light 105, F. Schoeman 65, M.R. Hobson 4 for 67)
Match drawn
Transvaal 'B' 11 pts, Orange Free State 'B' 6 pts

3, 4 and 5 November 1994 *at Buffalo Park, East London*

Boland 'B' 264 (M.S. Nackerdien 62, M.S. Bredell 61, S.E. Fourie 4 for 71) and 223 for 6 dec. (M.S. Nackerdien 106)
Border 'B' 211 (S.E. Fourie 55, R.A. Smith 4 for 19) and 280 for 8 (L.M. Fuhri 84, C.F. Spilhaus 62, A.T. Holdstock 4 for 51)
Border 'B' won by 2 wickets
Border 'B' 16 pts, Boland 'B' 7 pts

4, 5 and 6 November 1994 *at Olympia Park, Springs*

Eastern Province 'B' 131 (G.K. Miller 62, S.M. Skeete 5 for 27) and 109 (L.C.R. Jordaan 5 for 40)
Eastern Transvaal 226 (S.C. Pope 5 for 30, M.W. Handman 4 for 64) and 17 for 0
Eastern Transvaal won by 10 wickets
Eastern Transvaal 16 pts, Eastern Province 'B' 5 pts

17, 18 and 19 November 1994 *at St George's Park, Port Elizabeth*

Border 'B' 254 (D.O. Nosworthy 94, G.K. Miller 4 for 57, B.S. Forbes 4 for 83) and 347 for 5 dec. (Q.R. Still 111 not out, A.G. Lawson 101)
Eastern Province 'B' 318 (G.C. Victor 139 not out, A.J. Badenhorst 4 for 67) and 63 for 2
Match drawn
Eastern Province 'B' 8 pts, Border 'B' 7 pts

30 November, 1 and 2 December 1994 *at Buffalo Park, East London*

Orange Free State 'B' 344 for 8 dec. (A. Moreby 87, C. Light 69, F. Schoeman 62) and 189 (Q.R. Still 4 for 56)
Border 'B' 300 for 3 dec. (A.G. Lawson 87, Q.R. Still 82, D.O. Nosworthy 51 not out) and 176 for 5 (Q.R. Still 55, S.E. Cronje 4 for 62)
Match drawn
Border 'B' 6 pts, Orange Free State 'B' 5 pts

1, 2 and **3** December 1994 *at Grey High School, Port Elizabeth*

Boland 'B' 302 (M.S. Bredell 99, M.S. Nackerdien 64,
B.S. Forbes 5 for 65) and 139 (J.S. Roos 74, N. Rossouw
4 for 33)

Eastern Province 'B' 252 for 6 dec. (C. Wait 97, S. Abrahams
58 not out, M.S. Bredell 5 for 57) and 193 for 4
(G.C. Victor 74, W. Terblanche 52)

Eastern Province 'B' won by 6 wickets

Eastern Province 'B' 17 pts, Boland 'B' 6 pts

2, 3 and **4** December 1994 *at PAM Brink Stadium, Springs*

Eastern Transvaal 337 (S.M. Skeete 80, B. McBride 75,
A. Norris 66)

Transvaal 'B' 171 and 346 for 8 (H.A. Manack 100,
N.R. Rhodes 77, N. Pothas 72, L.C.R. Jordaan 5 for 69)

Match drawn

Eastern Transvaal 7 pts, Transvaal 'B' 4 pts

17, 18 and **19** December 1994 *at Brackenfell Sports Field, Brackenfell*

Boland 'B' 146 (N.A. Fusedale 4 for 23) and 233
(C.S.N. Marais 107, A.V. Griffiths 5 for 78)

Transvaal 'B' 400 for 9 dec. (N.R. Rhodes 141, C. Grainger 90,
W.S. Truter 4 for 59)

Transvaal 'B' won by an innings and 21 runs

Transvaal 'B' 18 pts, Boland 'B' 2 pts

at PAM Brink Stadium, Springs

Orange Free State 'B' 111 and 282 (C. Light 121, S. Nicolson
103, L.C.R. Jordaan 6 for 93, T.A. Marsh 4 for 52)

Eastern Transvaal 240 (T.A. Marsh 65, S.A. Cilliers 4 for 88)
and 157 for 3 (C.R. Norris 51 not out)

Eastern Transvaal won by 7 wickets

Eastern Transvaal 16 pts, Orange Free State 'B' 5 pts

5, 6 and **7** January 1995 *at Springbok Park, Bloemfontein*

Orange Free State 'B' 450 for 9 dec. (A. Moreby 115,
G. van Aswegen 92, N.S. Botha 70, G.B. Shaw 4 for 103)
and 58 for 5

Eastern Province 'B' 173 (F. Botha 5 for 41) and 380
(M.G. Beamish 99, M.C. Venter 73, N. Rossouw 68 not out,
P. Wille 4 for 67, S.G. Cronje 4 for 97)

Match drawn

Orange Free State 'B' 9 pts, Eastern Province 'B' 4 pts

at Randjesfontein

Border 'B' 303 for 7 dec. (L.M. Fuhri 126, D.O. Nosworthy 89)
and 198 (G.W. Thompson 60, C.F. Spilhaus 60,
M.R. Hobson 4 for 45)

Transvaal 'B' 272 (A.M. Bacher 73, H.A. Manack 57) and
234 for 4 (A.M. Bacher 119 not out, C. Grainger 51)

Transvaal 'B' won by 6 wickets

Transvaal 'B' 16 pts, Border 'B' 7 pts

6, 7 and **8** January 1995 *at Brackenfell Sports Field, Brackenfell*

Eastern Transvaal 282 (T.A. Marsh 93) and 208 for 9 dec.
(S.M. Skeete 51, R.I. Dalrymple 5 for 48)

Boland 'B' 160 (R. Telemachus 59, L.C.R. Jordaan 6 for 59)
and 230 (C.S.N. Marais 77, L.C.R. Jordaan 6 for 88)

Eastern Transvaal won by 100 runs

Eastern Transvaal 17 pts, Boland 'B' 5 pts

26, 27 and **28** January 1995 *at St George's Park, Port Elizabeth*

Eastern Province 'B' 117 (M.R. Hobson 5 for 29,
M.J. Vandrau 5 for 46) and 336 (M.C. Venter 110,
P.I. Barclay 52, M.J. Vandrau 5 for 76)

Transvaal 'B' 249 (W.V. Rippon 115 not out, A.M. Bacher 58)
and 167 (N.D. McKenzie 53, G.B. Shaw 4 for 53)

Eastern Province 'B' won by 37 runs

Eastern Province 'B' 15 pts, Transvaal 'B' 6 pts

at Springbok Park, Bloemfontein

Boland 'B' 257 (J.S. Roos 70) and 297 for 3 dec.
(J. Henderson 122 not out, M.M. Brink 77)

Orange Free State 'B' 253 and 302 for 5 (C. Light 84,
A. Hansen 50 not out, G. van Aswegen 50)

Orange Free State 'B' won by 5 wickets

Orange Free State 'B' 17 pts, Boland 'B' 6 pts

27, 28 and **29** January 1995 *at PAM Brink Stadium, Springs*

Border 'B' 383 (M.L. Lax 90 not out, A.G. Lawson 67,
Q.R. Still 50, J.R. Meyer 4 for 51) and 269 for 6
(C. Wilson 101, A.C. Dewar 53)

Eastern Transvaal 533 (S.M. Skeete 119, C.R. Norris 107,
I.A. Hoffman 100, L.D. Botha 50)

Match drawn

Eastern Transvaal 10 pts, Border 'B' 7 pts

SECTION ONE FINAL TABLE

	P	W	L	D	Pts
Eastern Transvaal	5	3	–	2	66
Transvaal 'B'	5	2	1	2	55
Eastern Province 'B'	5	2	1	2	49
Border 'B'	5	1	1	3	43
Orange Free State 'B'	5	1	1	3	42
Boland 'B'	5	–	5	–	26

SECTION TWO

3, 4 and 5 November 1994 *at Fanie du Toit Stadium, Potchefstroom*

Northern Transvaal 'B' 271 (D.J. van Zyl 78, M.J.G. Davis 60,
A. Cilliers 4 for 54) and 145 (D.J. van Schalkwyk 4 for 34)
Western Transvaal 164 (M.J.G. Davis 8 for 37) and 137
(G.J. Smith 4 for 32, M.J.G. Davis 4 for 47)

Northern Transvaal 'B' won by 115 runs

Northern Transvaal 'B' 17 pts, Western Transvaal 5 pts

4, 5 and 6 November 1994 *at Kimberley Country Club, Kimberley*

Zimbabwe Board XI 423 for 9 dec. (E.A. Brandes 165 not out,
I.P. Butchart 99)
Griqualand West 121 (E.A. Brandes 7 for 38) and 282
(R.A. Koster 69, P.A. Strang 5 for 77)

Zimbabwe Board XI won by an innings and 20 runs

Zimbabwe Board XI 20 pts, Griqualand West 5 pts

11, 12 and 13 November 1994 *at Tigers CC, Parow*

Western Transvaal 242 (H.G. Prinsloo 82, L. Botes 64,
D. MacHelm 4 for 93) and 127
Western Province 'B' 300 for 8 dec. (B.C. Baguley
133 not out, H.H. Gibbs 60) and 70 for 1

Western Province 'B' won by 9 wickets

Western Province 'B' 16 pts, Western Transvaal 4 pts

17, 18 and 19 November 1994 *at Kingsmead, Durban*

Western Province 'B' 157 (H.H. Gibbs 59, L. Klusener
5 for 46, R.E. Veenstra 4 for 40) and 246 (B.C. Baguley 72,
R.K. McGlashan 6 for 100)
Natal 'B' 465 for 8 dec. (L. Klusener 105, R.E. Veenstra 75,
D.N. Crookes 74, D.M. Benkenstein 69)

Natal 'B' won by an innings and 62 runs

Natal 'B' 17 pts, Western Province 'B' 3 pts

1, 2 and 3 December 1994 *at Bulawayo Athletic Club, Bulawayo*

Western Transvaal 248 (L. Botes 61 not out, M.P. Jarvis 4 for
71) and 279 for 7 (H.G. Prinsloo 78, A. Cilliers 64 not out,
J.P. van der Westhuizen 51)
Zimbabwe Board XI 400 for 7 dec. (G.K. Bruk-Jackson 119
not out, S.V. Carlisle 97, K.J. Arnott 85)

Match drawn

Zimbabwe Board XI 6 pts, Western Transvaal 4 pts

2, 3 and 4 December 1994 *at Northerns-Goodwood, Cape Town*

Griqualand West 208 (H.A. Page 89, G. Bramwell 5 for 74) and
176 (R.A. Koster 64, C.V. English 4 for 30, D. MacHelm 4 for 38)
Western Province 'B' 386 (H.H. Gibbs 101, T.J. Mitchell 85)

Western Province 'B' won by an innings and 2 runs

Western Province 'B' 18 pts, Griqualand West 6 pts

9, 10 and 11 December 1994 *at Kingsmead, Durban*

Northern Transvaal 'B' 122 (W.M. Dry 51 not out) and 268
(I. Pistorius 59, A.J. Seymore 56, R.K. McGlashan 5 for 99)
Natal 'B' 362 for 9 dec. (D.M. Benkenstein 203 not out,
C. van Noordwyk 6 for 100) and 29 for 1

Natal 'B' won by 9 wickets

Natal 'B' 18 pts, Northern Transvaal 'B' 5 pts

15, 16 and 17 December 1994 *at Harare Sports Club, Harare*

Zimbabwe Board XI 317 (D.N. Erasmus 97, A.C. Waller 76,
K.G. Storey 4 for 63) and 169 (S.V. Carlisle 60, T. Bosch
4 for 44)
Natal 'B' 265 (D.N. Crookes 109, M.P. Jarvis 6 for 62) and 136
for 5

Match drawn

Zimbabwe Board XI 8 pts, Natal 'B' 7 pts

17, 18 and 19 December 1994 *at Centurion Park, Verwoerdburg*

Western Province 'B' 278 for 9 dec. (S. Conrad 61) and 181
(H.H. Donachie 66)
Northern Transvaal 'B' 241 for 7 dec. (P.H. Barnard 59) and
178 for 9

Match drawn

Western Province 'B' 6 pts, Northern Transvaal 'B' 6 pts

5, 6 and 7 January 1995 *at Harare Sports Club, Harare*

Northern Transvaal 'B' 276 for 9 dec. (I. Pistorius 84,
P.H. Barnard 78, B. Strang 4 for 59) and 227 for 7 dec.
(N. Martin 59 not out)
Zimbabwe Board XI 205 (S.V. Carlisle 74, N. Martin 4 for 67)
and 117 (C.B. Wishart 50, M.C. Krug 4 for 23)

Northern Transvaal 'B' won by 181 runs

Northern Transvaal 'B' 17 pts, Zimbabwe Board XI 4 pts

6, 7 and 8 January 1995 *at Kimberley Country Club, Kimberley*

Natal 'B' 476 for 7 dec. (E.L.R. Stewart 146, C.B. Sugden 106,
G.W. Bashford 76)
Griqualand West 453 for 7 (W.E. Schonegevel 76,
M.I. Gidley 69, F.C. Brooker 63, J. Burger 54 not out)

Match drawn

Natal 'B' 4 pts, Griqualand West 3 pts

13, 14 and 15 January 1995 *at Kimberley Country Club, Kimberley*

Western Transvaal 237 (A.J. van Deventer 57) and 143 for 3
dec. (A.J. van Deventer 68 not out)
Griqualand West 79 for 2 dec. and 159 for 6

Match drawn

Griqualand West 5 pts, Western Transvaal 2 pts

26, 27 and **28** January 1995 *at Newlands, Cape Town*

Western Province 'B' 284 for 8 dec. (C.V. English 108,
B. Strang 4 for 73) and 257 (B.C. Baguley 76, P.A. Strang
5 for 88)

Zimbabwe Board XI 260 (D.N. Erasmus 81, D. MacHelm
5 for 57) and 86 for 4

Match drawn

Western Province 'B' 7 pts, Zimbabwe Board XI 6 pts

at Fanie du Toit Stadium, Potchefstroom

Western Transvaal 184 (H.G. Prinsloo 73 not out, G.M. Gilder
4 for 42) and 208 (J.P. van der Westhuizen 105 not out)

Natal 'B' 394 for 4 dec. (E.L.R. Stewart 122 not out,
C.R.B. Armstrong 112, K.A. Forde 57)

Natal 'B' won by an innings and 2 runs

Natal 'B' 18 pts, Western Transvaal 2 pts

3, 4 and **5** February 1995 *at Centurion Park, Verwoerdburg*

Northern Transvaal 'B' 276 for 9 dec. (N. Martin 76,
I. Pistorius 54, H.A. Page 4 for 49) and 299 for 5 dec.
(P.H. Barnard 62, W.M. Dry 56 not out, A.J. Seymore 55)

Griqualand West 253 for 9 dec. (M. Michau 73, M.C. Krug
4 for 83) and 323 for 4 (M.I. Gidley 113, H.A. Page 95)

Griqualand West won by 6 wickets

Griqualand West 17 pts, Northern Transvaal 'B' 7 pts

SECTION TWO FINAL TABLE

	P	W	L	D	Pts
Natal 'B'	5	3	–	2	64
Northern Transvaal 'B'	5	2	2	1	52
Western Province 'B'	5	2	1	2	50
Zimbabwe Board XI	5	1	1	3	44
Griqualand West	5	1	2	2	36
Western Transvaal	5	–	3	2	17

Why the Bowl competition retains first-class status remains a mystery. It is, in effect, a second-eleven tournament and should be treated as such. It proved to be an interesting breeding ground for cricketers in 1994–5, however, and produced some fine performances.

Chad Grainger's maiden first-class century totalled 233 off 201 balls with 27 fours and 6 sixes. He hit 117 between lunch and tea on the first day. Even more spectacular was Eddo Brandes' maiden hundred. Batting at number eight, he hit 165 off 167 balls against Griqualand West. His innings included 15 fours and 10 sixes.

Faiek Davids did the hat-trick for Western Province 'B' against Zimbabwe Board XI when he dismissed Erasmus with the last ball of the first innings and Carlisle and Wishart with the first two balls of the second.

The Griqualand West side was captained by former Essex bowler Hugh Page and included, on occasions, Gidley – ex-Leicestershire – and van Troost of Somerset.

Skeete, the Barbadian, strengthened the Eastern Transvaal side and hit a maiden first-class hundred during the season, but was on the losing side when Natal completed the double by winning the Bowl Final.

17, 18 and **19** February 1995 *at Kingsmead, Durban*

Eastern Transvaal 212 (D.J. Pryke 4 for 50) and 81
(B.N. Benkenstein 5 for 44)

Natal 'B' 150 (K.A. Forde 59, L.C.R. Jordaan 5 for 44,
S.M. Skeete 4 for 51) and 144 for 5

Natal 'B' won by 5 wickets

The immensely popular Benson and Hedges day/night 50-over tournament which ran from October until April was won by Orange Free State who overwhelmed Eastern Province in the final, winning by 113 runs.

FIRST-CLASS AVERAGES

BATTING

	M	Inns	NO	Runs	HS	Av	100s	50s
D.J. Richardson	8	13	4	608	109	67.55	2	5
D.N. Crookes	8	10	1	600	123*	66.66	2	3
L. Klusener	8	13	5	521	105	65.12	1	3
K.C. Wessels	8	13	2	636	107	57.81	3	2
W.J. Cronje	9	16	3	726	112	55.84	2	4
M.J.R. Rindel	6	9	–	476	118	52.88	1	3
S.V. Carlisle	4	7	1	300	97	50.00	–	3
D.M. Benkenstein	10	14	2	594	203*	49.50	1	4
B.M. McMillan	8	11	–	536	140	48.72	2	1
B.C. Baguley	5	9	2	338	133*	48.28	1	2
D.J. Cullinan	9	18	4	674	150*	48.14	1	4
G. Kirsten	9	15	1	664	150	47.42	1	5
C.F. Craven	7	13	3	473	107	47.30	1	3
N. Pothas	8	14	4	472	76*	47.20	–	2
A.M. Bacher	5	10	1	423	119*	47.00	1	3
C. Light	5	10	–	468	121	46.80	2	2
S.J. Cook	7	12	2	467	114	46.70	1	4
L.J. Koen	9	16	3	604	138*	46.46	1	4
H.A. Page	6	10	–	461	95	46.10	–	4
C. Grainger	8	14	1	588	233	45.23	1	4
N.R. Rhodes	5	8	1	314	141	44.85	1	2
M.L. Bruyns	8	12	1	486	84	44.18	–	4
N.H. Fairbrother	4	8	1	308	89	44.00	–	3
A. Moreby	5	10	–	436	115	43.60	2	1
C.R. Norris	6	10	2	347	107	43.37	1	1
M. Michau	5	9	2	302	95	43.14	–	2
Q.R. Still	6	10	2	345	111*	43.12	1	3
D.L. Haynes	5	8	–	337	96	42.12	–	3
C.B. Lambert	9	18	2	674	170	42.12	1	3
E.L.R. Stewart	7	10	1	365	146	40.55	2	–
D.O. Nosworthy	6	11	1	405	94	40.50	–	3
H.D. Ackerman	9	14	–	562	118	40.14	1	4
G.C. Victor	5	9	1	321	139*	40.12	1	1
P.J.R. Steyn	9	17	–	677	157	39.82	2	2
S.M. Skeete	6	8	–	314	119	39.25	1	2
A.C. Hudson	8	15	2	496	157	38.15	1	3
P.C. Strydom	9	15	2	479	127	36.84	2	2
P.G. Amm	9	17	1	586	118	36.62	1	5
F.J.C. Cronje	8	14	1	475	70	36.53	–	3
H.H. Gibbs	10	15	–	547	102	36.46	2	3
S.G. Koenig	9	14	1	471	149*	36.23	1	3
M.S. Nackerdien	8	16	–	577	106	36.06	1	5
D.R. Laing	8	14	3	396	96	36.00	–	3
R.A. Koster	6	10	1	323	69	35.88	–	2
J.H. Kallis	9	14	1	463	77	35.61	–	4
N.C. Johnson	9	13	–	462	114	35.53	1	2
J.B. Commins	9	18	2	562	93	35.12	–	4
K.M. Curran	9	18	2	559	104	34.93	1	3
G.A. Pollock	6	11	1	345	101*	34.50	1	1
G.F.J. Liebenberg	9	17	–	585	141	34.41	2	3
M.I. Gidley	6	11	1	340	113	34.00	1	1
D.J. Callaghan	5	9	–	306	111	34.00	1	1
N.E. Wright	9	16	2	475	61	33.92	–	4
A.G. Lawson	8	15	1	471	101	33.64	1	3
R.F. Pienaar	9	16	1	472	108	31.46	1	3
G.K. Miller	7	10	–	311	62	31.10	–	1
L.J. Wilkinson	9	17	–	528	101	31.05	1	3
M.M. Brink	6	12	1	341	77	31.00	–	1
J.M. Arthur	9	17	–	523	85	30.76	–	3
M.S. Bredell	7	12	1	337	99	30.63	–	2
P.H. Barnard	6	12	–	358	78	29.83	–	3
A.J. Seymore	6	12	–	348	84	29.00	–	3
M.C. Venter	8	15	1	406	110	29.00	1	1
M.J.G. Davis	9	17	4	371	68*	28.53	–	2
S.J. Palframan	9	13	–	359	59	27.61	–	3
K.J. Rule	8	13	–	359	102	27.61	1	2
P.N. Kirsten	9	15	2	350	60	26.92	–	2
R.P. Snell	8	12	–	323	81	26.91	–	2
M.W. Rushmere	8	15	–	398	134	26.53	1	1
M. Erasmus	9	16	3	312	59*	24.00	–	1
M.P. Stonier	9	16	–	384	60	24.00	–	2

(Qualification – 300 runs)

BOWLING

	Overs	Mds	Runs	Wkts	Av	Best	10/m	5/inn
L.C.R. Jordaan	247.4	67	600	38	15.78	6-59	1	6
M.D. Marshall	263.3	98	566	35	16.17	4-40	–	–
F.D. Stephenson	214	55	492	30	16.40	6-49	–	3
M.J.G. Davis	247.5	67	585	35	16.71	8-37	1	1
S.M. Skeete	129	22	401	23	17.43	5-27	–	1
P.S. de Villiers	363.1	106	937	51	18.37	6-47	1	4
S.M. Pollock	247.5	70	591	31	19.06	4-24	–	–
N.C. Johnson	158.5	34	491	25	19.64	4-49	–	–
R.E. Veenstra	186.5	48	525	26	20.19	4-36	–	–
O.D. Gibson	166.5	35	466	23	20.26	7-55	1	3
M.J. Vandrau	225.5	42	713	34	20.97	6-49	2	4
N. Rossouw	141.5	18	483	23	21.00	4-33	–	–
D.G. Payne	222	57	623	29	21.48	4-50	–	–
M. Erasmus	220.3	56	556	25	22.24	6-22	–	2
K.G. Storey	161.1	33	450	20	22.50	4-63	–	–
M.R. Hobson	198.3	35	600	26	23.07	5-29	–	2
L. Klusener	170.1	45	502	21	23.90	5-46	–	1
D. MacHelm	231	77	552	23	24.00	5-57	–	1
R.E. Bryson	218	52	682	28	24.35	5-25	–	1
E.A.E. Baptiste	280.5	79	673	27	24.92	5-62	–	3
P.A.N. Emslie	283.5	67	707	28	25.25	4-37	–	–
B.M. McMillan	266	66	634	24	26.41	4-65	–	–
M.W. Handman	224	45	638	24	26.58	4-55	–	–
H.S. Williams	273.1	57	669	25	26.76	4-59	–	–
N.W. Pretorius	312.4	48	1079	40	26.97	5-96	–	2
J.A. Ehrke	205	54	626	23	27.21	4-85	–	–
A.C. Dawson	296.5	87	750	27	27.77	6-86	–	1
S.D. Jack	251.5	59	757	27	28.03	4-60	–	–
S. Elworthy	301	55	926	33	28.06	7-65	–	2
C.W. Henderson	370.3	91	978	34	28.76	7-57	–	–
S. Abrahams	207.3	53	579	20	28.95	4-76	–	–
B.C. Fourie	278.3	66	767	26	29.50	6-91	–	2
G.J. Smith	249.5	43	757	25	30.28	4-32	–	–
D.B. Rundle	415.3	105	1109	36	30.80	6-51	–	2
T.G. Shaw	361.1	145	658	21	31.33	5-91	–	1
C.E. Eksteen	458.2	169	891	26	34.26	5-84	–	2
R.P. Snell	288.4	69	847	23	36.82	6-60	–	1
N. Boje	357.3	100	958	25	38.32	5-38	–	2

(Qualification – 20 wickets)

LEADING FIELDERS

38 – K.J. Rule (ct 35/st 3); 34 – D.J. Richardson (ct 33/st 1); 31 – L.M. Germishuys (ct 30/st 1) and M.L. Bruyns (ct 28/st 3); 28 – R.J. Ryall (ct 26/st 2); 27 – B. McBride (ct 22/st 5); 26 – S.J. Palframan (ct 23/st 3); 25 – N. Pothas (ct 24/st 1); 20 – P.J.L. Radley (ct 18/st 2); 18 – M.M. Brink (ct 16/st 2) and S.C. Pope; 17 – C.B. Lambert and E.L.R. Stewart; 14 – C.F. Spilhaus; 13 – I.A. Hoffman; 12 – A.M. Bacher, L.J. Koen, N.C. Johnson, J.F. Venter and G.F.J. Liebenberg (ct 11/st 1)

NEW ZEALAND

West Indies tour, Tests and one-day internationals
Centenary Tournament – New Zealand, Australia, India and South Africa
Centenary Test – New Zealand *v.* South Africa
Shell Trophy
Sri Lanka tour, Tests and one-day internationals
First-class averages

A view of Lancaster Park, Christchurch, during the first Test match between New Zealand and West Indies. The ground has distinctive green sight-screens. (Philip Wilcox)

The best-laid schemes o' mice an' men
Gang aft agley,
An' lea'e us nought but grief an' pain,
For promis'd joy!

While Burns could not have been anticipating New Zealand cricket's centenary year when he wrote these lines, they are certainly appropriate for the 1995 season in the two islands. This was to have been a time of celebration and rejoicing. There were to be Test matches against three nations, one-day series against two of those nations, and a one-day international tournament involving four countries. From January to April, there would be a feast of international cricket.

There were disturbing signs from the outset when a weakened national side fared badly in a one-day tournament in India. In South Africa, there were early indications of joy, with victory in the first Test, but catastrophe followed. There was total humiliation in the four-nation Mandela Trophy and defeat in the last two Tests. Martin Crowe limped home as New Zealand's record run-scorer in Test cricket, but his great international career seemed at an end as his knee injury again reasserted itself.

Close on the failures in South Africa came the resignation of Geoff Howarth as coach to the national side, and the barring from three one-day internationals against West Indies of Fleming, Nash and Hart, arguably New Zealand's most exciting young trio of cricketers, for smoking cannabis on the South African tour.

Without the trio, New Zealand were destroyed by West Indies in the one-day series, and when they became available for selection Nash broke a finger and New Zealand suffered more defeats.

South Africa triumphed in the lone Test, and Sri Lanka won an overseas series for the first time by beating New Zealand in the first of two meetings. Coach Reid indicated that he would return to his normal business and wished to play no further part in cricketing plans, while the much-respected Graham Dowling, chief executive of New Zealand cricket, resigned his post.

This turned out to be no celebratory year. New Zealand cricket was at its lowest ebb for more than 30 years.

The first part of the season was, as usual, dominated by the Shell Cup, the 50-over competition. With the national side suffering in South Africa, the tournament took on an added significance as players strove to impress the selectors.

Andrew Jones announced that he would make himself available for international cricket, but his return – like his retirement – was to be brief. Nathan Astle produced some exciting all-round cricket for Canterbury, and Roger Twose continued for Wellington the excellent form he had shown with Warwickshire in 1994. Twose led Wellington to the final, scoring 383 runs and taking 15 wickets on the way.

There were centuries for Rod Latham of Canterbury, Graham Burnett of Northern Districts and Llorne Howell of Central Districts. Ingham, Twose, Parlane, Cooper, McMillan and McRae were worthy of note while Mark Douglas batted consistently well for Wellington. Roberts and Vaughan were among the best of the bowlers.

Perhaps the most important innings played was that by Chris Cairns for Canterbury in their semi-final win over Auckland at Lancaster Park. Cairns had been absent for six weeks with injury, and he returned against doctor's orders. The result was spectacular as he hit 143 off 105 balls. Three days later, Wellington beat Canterbury by 10 wickets to qualify to meet Northern Districts in the final. Canterbury made 202 for 7, but Wellington hit 205 without loss, Aiken scoring 101 and Douglas 93.

Northern Districts upset a few people by fielding Parore, Thomson, Simon Doull and Young in the final although none of these players had appeared in the earlier rounds, having been on tour in South Africa. None could argue with the result, for Northern Districts hit 256 for 8, Michael Parlane making 96, and bowled out Wellington for 108 to take the Cup.

WEST INDIES TOUR

15 January 1995 *at Trust Bank Park, Hamilton*

West Indians 273 for 3 (S.C. Williams 121, S.L. Campbell 108)
Sir Ron Brierley's XI 232 for 6 (N.J. Astle 59 not out)

West Indians won by 41 runs

17 January 1995 *at Eden Park, Auckland*

West Indians 206 for 9 (W.K.M. Benjamin 74)
Auckland 101 (W.K.M. Benjamin 4 for 10, K.L.T. Arthurton 4 for 26)

West Indians won by 105 runs

19 January 1995 *at Whangarei*

West Indians v. Northern Districts

Match abandoned

Under the captaincy of Courtney Walsh, West Indies welcomed the return of Curtly Ambrose from injury and Winston Benjamin from suspension, but they were to be deprived of the services of Carl Hooper through injury. In the opening match of the tour, Sherwin Campbell and Stuart Williams shared an opening stand of 237, but there was little match practice before the one-day series.

This had no effect upon the tourists who outplayed New Zealand from beginning to end. The home side brought in Astle for his international debut in the first game which also saw Jones, Vaughan, Larsen and Patel return to the New Zealand side. Unwisely, Rutherford chose to bat first when he won the toss, for, as elsewhere, television dominates international cricket in New Zealand and decrees that the match must start at 10.30 and finish no later than 5.30. When the New Zealand innings was interrupted by rain with the score on 69 for 3 from 23 overs, there was little hope that West Indies would be in search of a daunting target. So it proved, and Williams and Campbell scored 61 off 18 overs before Lara arrived to hit 55 off 32 balls, an innings which included 8 fours and a six.

FIRST ONE-DAY INTERNATIONAL – NEW ZEALAND v. WEST INDIES
22 January 1995 at Eden Park, Auckland

NEW ZEALAND				WEST INDIES		
B.A. Young	b Arthurton		42	S.C. Williams	not out	73
A.H. Jones	c Lara, b Walsh		10	S.L. Campbell	b Larsen	17
*A.C. Parore	c Adams, b Walsh		1	B.C. Lara	not out	55
K.R. Rutherford (capt)	c Adams, b Arthurton		17	K.L.T. Arthurton		
S.A. Thomson	run out		37	*J.C. Adams		
N.J. Astle	c Cummins, b Dhanraj		25	R.I.C. Holder		
J.T.C. Vaughan	not out		21	A.C. Cummins		
S.B. Doull	not out		6	C.E.L. Ambrose		
D.N. Patel				C.A. Walsh (capt)		
G.R. Larsen				K.C.G. Benjamin		
D.K. Morrison				R. Dhanraj		
Extras	lb 4, w 1, nb 3		8	Extras	lb 3, nb 1	4
(37 overs)	(for 6 wickets)		167	(27.4 overs)	(for 1 wicket)	149

	O	M	R	W		O	M	R	W
Ambrose	8	1	34	–	Morrison	5	–	19	–
Walsh	8	1	26	2	Doull	6.4	1	32	–
Cummins	7	1	25	–	Vaughan	4	–	14	–
Benjamin	6	–	32	–	Larsen	7	1	35	1
Arthurton	4	–	25	2	Patel	1	–	8	–
Dhanraj	4	–	21	1	Astle	3	–	27	–
					Thomson	1	–	11	–

FALL OF WICKETS
1–31, 2–35, 3–67, 4–80, 5–123, 6–146

FALL OF WICKET
1–61

Umpires: B.L. Aldridge & D.B. Cowie   *Man of the Match:* S.C. Williams   *West Indies won on faster scoring rate*

SECOND ONE-DAY INTERNATIONAL – NEW ZEALAND v. WEST INDIES
25 January 1995 at Basin Reserve, Wellington

WEST INDIES			NEW ZEALAND		
S.L. Campbell	b Morrison	7	B.A. Young	c Benjamin, b Cummins	39
S.C. Williams	b Doull	8	A.H. Jones	c and b Dhanraj	26
B.C. Lara	run out	72	*A.C. Parore	lbw, b Walsh	18
K.L.T. Arthurton	run out	30	K.R. Rutherford (capt)	c Adams, b Dhanraj	16
R.I.C. Holder	c Morrison, b Thomson	35	S.A. Thomson	c Adams, b Ambrose	22
W.K.M. Benjamin	b Astle	5	N.J. Astle	c Adams, b Benjamin	11
A.C. Cummins	not out	44	J.T.C. Vaughan	run out	9
*J.C. Adams	c Parore, b Morrison	8	D.N. Patel	b Walsh	25
C.E.L. Ambrose	not out	8	G.R. Larsen	c Ambrose, b Arthurton	15
C.A. Walsh (capt)			S.B. Doull	not out	9
R. Dhanraj			D.K. Morrison	st Adams, b Arthurton	2
Extras	lb 22, w 7	29	Extras	lb 3, w 5, nb 5	13
(50 overs)	(for 7 wickets)	246	(48.5 overs)		205

	O	M	R	W		O	M	R	W
Morrison	8	1	32	2	Walsh	9	1	42	2
Doull	7	–	37	1	Ambrose	8	–	29	1
Larsen	10	1	30	–	Cummins	5	–	34	1
Vaughan	6	–	30	–	Dhanraj	10	–	31	2
Patel	5	–	28	–	Benjamin	9	2	29	1
Astle	8	–	46	1	Arthurton	7.5	–	37	2
Thomson	6	–	21	1					

FALL OF WICKETS
1–15, 2–15, 3–95, 4–163, 5–173, 6–187, 7–223

FALL OF WICKETS
1–54, 2–81, 3–103, 4–109, 5–137, 6–151, 7–151, 8–193, 9–194

Umpires: R.S. Dunne & C.E. King   *Man of the Match:* B.C. Lara   *West Indies won by 41 runs*

Asked to bat in the second match, West Indies laboured somewhat. Lara hit 72 off 85 balls and Cummins hammered 44 from 38 balls, but the New Zealand fielding was sloppy and the wicket-keeping below standard. New Zealand began confidently with 54 from the first 11 overs, but leg-spinner Dhanraj began a collapse which saw three wickets fall in 10 overs for 28 runs.

The third match, in which pace bowler Roydon Hayes made his debut, saw West Indies stroll to victory, with Williams hitting 69 off 75 balls.

29, 30 and 31 January 1995 *at Carisbrook, Dunedin*

West Indians 450 for 9 dec. (J.R. Murray 141 not out,
   A.C. Cummins 107, J.C. Adams 59, S.C. Williams 54)
   and 167 for 1 (S.L. Campbell 108 not out, S.C. Chanderpaul
   50 not out)
Otago 309 (M.H. Richardson 103, K.C.G. Benjamin 5 for 97)

Match drawn

The tourists settled for batting practice in the only first-class match outside the two Tests. Sherwin Campbell's century assured him a place in the side for the first Test, where he was the only debutant.

Elation for New Zealand in the first Test against West Indies – Lara is bowled by Morrison for two. (Philip Wilcox)

THIRD ONE-DAY INTERNATIONAL – NEW ZEALAND v. WEST INDIES
28 January 1995 at Lancaster Park, Christchurch

NEW ZEALAND

B.A. Young	c Adams, **b** Arthurton	13
A.H. Jones	c Murray, **b** Arthurton	9
*A.C. Parore	c Holder, **b** Dhanraj	9
K.R. Rutherford (capt)	**b** Benjamin	30
M.W. Douglas	c Ambrose, **b** Benjamin	12
S.A. Thomson	c Murray, **b** Benjamin	3
N.J. Astle	c Holder, **b** Cummins	9
J.T.C. Vaughan	run out	9
G.R. Larsen	**b** Adams	12
D.K. Morrison	not out	14
R.L. Hayes	c Holder, **b** Arthurton	13
Extras	b **1**, lb **3**, w **6**, nb **3**	13
		——
(49 overs)		**146**

WEST INDIES

S.C. Williams	not out	69
S.L. Campbell	**b** Larsen	36
B.C. Lara (capt)	not out	34
K.L.T. Arthurton		
R.I.C. Holder		
J.C. Adams		
*J.R. Murray		
A.C. Cummins		
W.K.M. Benjamin		
C.E.L. Ambrose		
R. Dhanraj		
Extras	lb **1**, w **1**, nb **8**	10
		——
(37.4 overs)	(for 1 wicket)	**149**

	O	M	R	W
Ambrose	7	2	15	–
Benjamin	8	1	12	3
Arthurton	10	–	31	3
Cummins	8	1	23	1
Dhanraj	10	–	37	1
Adams	6	–	24	1

	O	M	R	W
Morrison	10	1	29	–
Hayes	7	–	31	–
Larsen	10	4	39	1
Vaughan	3	–	16	–
Thomson	5	1	19	–
Astle	2.4	–	14	–

FALL OF WICKETS
1–17, **2**–24, **3**–53, **4**–64, **5**–73, **6**–85, **7**–98, **8**–109, **9**–123

FALL OF WICKET
1–98

Umpires: C.E. King & D.M. Quested   *Man of the Match:* S.C. Williams   *West Indies won by 9 wickets*

TEST SERIES

Campbell duly made his debut in the first Test in which the three banished New Zealanders returned and Jones reappeared after his brief retirement from Test cricket. West Indies won the toss and asked New Zealand to bat first on a pitch full of moisture, but only 11 overs were possible on the first day, during which the home side reached 24 without loss. On the second day, they advanced to 221 for 6. Murray batted three hours for his 43, but five wickets went down for 128, and it was Fleming, a batsman of immense promise and style, and Parore who salvaged the innings with a stand of 82. Fleming surprised all by flicking lazily to slip, but Parore ended the day on 34.

There was no play on the third day, and on the fourth, New Zealand had glimpses of an unexpected victory. Parore batted boldly against the West Indian pace men, and was at the crease for five hours, facing 249 balls to reach his maiden Test century. Hart helped him to add 118 for the seventh wicket.

New Zealand fielders erupt in appeal as they claim a catch by Fleming off Hart which would have accounted for Chanderpaul, but the umpire says 'no'. (Philip Wilcox)

FIRST TEST MATCH – NEW ZEALAND *v.* WEST INDIES
3, 4, 5, 6 and 7 February 1995 at Lancaster Park, Christchurch

NEW ZEALAND

	FIRST INNINGS		SECOND INNINGS	
B.A. Young	c Murray, b Walsh	19	c Murray, b K. Benjamin	21
D.J. Murray	c Campbell, b Ambrose	43	c Murray, b Walsh	8
A.H. Jones	c Williams, b K. Benjamin	12	not out	10
K.R. Rutherford (capt)	c Murray, b Ambrose	11	not out	16
S.P. Fleming	c Lara, b Walsh	56		
S.A. Thomson	c W. Benjamin, b K. Benjamin	20		
*A.C. Parore	not out	100		
M.N. Hart	c and b W. Benjamin	45		
D.J. Nash	c Campbell, b Ambrose	3		
D.K. Morrison				
S.B. Doull				
Extras	b 12, lb 5, nb 15	32	lb 1, nb 5	6
	(for 8 wickets, dec.)	341	(for 2 wickets)	61

WEST INDIES

	FIRST INNINGS	
S.C. Williams	c Parore, b Morrison	10
S.L. Campbell	lbw, b Morrison	51
B.C. Lara	b Morrison	2
J.C. Adams	c Doull, b Morrison	13
K.L.T. Arthurton	run out	1
S. Chanderpaul	b Thomson	69
*J.R. Murray	c Murray, b Thomson	28
W.K.M. Benjamin	b Doull	85
C.E.L. Ambrose	b Morrison	33
C.A. Walsh (capt)	not out	0
K.C.G. Benjamin	c Parore, b Morrison	5
Extras	lb 11, nb 4	15
		312

	O	M	R	W	O	M	R	W
Ambrose	31.1	12	57	3	3	–	7	–
Walsh	30	5	69	2	4	1	8	1
W.K.M. Benjamin	33	4	94	1	5	1	12	–
K.C.G. Benjamin	25	7	91	2	6	–	12	1
Chanderpaul	3	1	10	–	2	2	0	–
Arthurton	2	–	3	–	5	1	9	–
Adams					3	1	4	–
Lara					4	–	8	–

	O	M	R	W
Morrison	26.2	9	69	6
Nash	5	2	11	–
Doull	22	5	85	1
Hart	25	2	75	–
Thomson	18	3	61	2

FALL OF WICKETS
1–32, 2–63, 3–92, 4–97, 5–128, 6–210, 7–328, 8–341
1–33, 2–33

FALL OF WICKETS
1–10, 2–21, 3–49, 4–54, 5–98, 6–155, 7–232, 8–299, 9–307

Umpires: B.L. Aldridge & N.T. Plews

Match drawn

Having hit 85, his highest Test score, Winston Benjamin is bowled by Simon Doull. (Philip Wilcox)

had nursed his side past the point where they would have to follow on, the game petered to the inevitable draw. The closing stages were enlivened by Winston Benjamin who hit a furious 85 off 87 balls.

Winston Benjamin was unfit for the second Test and was replaced by Dhanraj. Nash's place in the New Zealand side was taken by Su'a, but there were also fitness doubts about Rutherford, Doull and Thomson, and New Zealand paid a heavy price for fielding men who were not fully fit. The game was over in four days, and New Zealand suffered their heaviest-ever defeat in Test cricket.

Sherwin Campbell set the pattern for the West Indian innings with an aggressive 88 which included 2 sixes and 11 fours. He was hampered by a leg injury, but his runs formed the major share of a score of 134, and he was out hooking to fine leg. His dismissal brought together Lara and Adams. Brian Lara had accomplished little since his season of wonders with Warwickshire, but now he was back to his best, cutting and pulling with venom and displaying a complete range of shots. He moved faultlessly to his fourth Test century and by the time he was adjudged leg before to Morrison he had hit 24 fours and a six and had faced 181 balls. He increased the tempo of his innings as it lengthened, and nine of his boundaries came after he had reached his century. He averaged a run a ball in the later stages of his innings and added a record 221 with Adams for the third wicket. Calm and serene, Adams was unbeaten on 87 at the end of the day, and West Indies were 356 for 3.

Bowling with aggression and accuracy, Morrison captured four early wickets, and with Arthurton run out by Rutherford from mid-wicket, West Indies ended the day on 102 for 5.

New Zealand's elation was tempered by the fact that Nash broke a finger while fielding, and once Chanderpaul

---

SECOND TEST MATCH – NEW ZEALAND v. WEST INDIES
10, 11, 12 and 13 February 1995 at Basin Reserve, Wellington

WEST INDIES

	FIRST INNINGS	
S.C. Williams	c Parore, b Doull	26
S.L. Campbell	c Su'a, b Morrison	88
B.C. Lara	lbw, b Morrison	147
J.C. Adams	c Su'a, b Doull	151
K.L.T. Arthurton	run out	70
S. Chanderpaul	not out	61
*J.R. Murray	not out	101
C.E.L. Ambrose		
C.A. Walsh (capt)		
K.C.G. Benjamin		
R. Dhanraj		
Extras	lb 6, nb 10	16
	(for 5 wickets, dec.)	660

NEW ZEALAND

	FIRST INNINGS		SECOND INNINGS	
B.A. Young	lbw, b Walsh	29	b Walsh	0
D.J. Murray	lbw, b Ambrose	52	b Walsh	43
A.H. Jones	c Murray, b Walsh	0	lbw, b Benjamin	2
K.R. Rutherford (capt)	lbw, b Dhanraj	22	lbw, b Ambrose	5
S.P. Fleming	c Lara, b Walsh	47	b Walsh	30
S.A. Thomson	b Walsh	6	b Dhanraj	8
*A.C. Parore	c Adams, b Walsh	32	not out	5
M.N. Hart	c Lara, b Dhanraj	0	c Ambrose, b Dhanraj	1
M.L. Su'a	c Murray, b Walsh	6	c Adams, b Walsh	8
S.B. Doull	b Walsh	0	lbw, b Walsh	0
D.K. Morrison	not out	0	c Murray, b Walsh	14
Extras	b 1, lb 14, nb 7	22	lb 2, nb 4	6
		216		122

	O	M	R	W
Morrison	29	5	82	2
Su'a	44	4	179	–
Doull	37.2	5	162	2
Hart	46	4	181	–
Jones	13	2	50	–

	O	M	R	W	O	M	R	W
Ambrose	19	9	32	1	5	1	17	1
Walsh	20.4	7	37	7	15.2	8	18	6
Dhanraj	33	6	97	2	12	2	49	2
Benjamin	12	1	35	–	8	–	36	1

FALL OF WICKETS
1–85, 2–134, 3–355, 4–448, 5–521

FALL OF WICKETS
1–50, 2–52, 3–108, 4–135, 5–160, 6–196, 7–197, 8–207, 9–211
1–0, 2–3, 3–15, 4–70, 5–93, 6–93, 7–97, 8–106, 9–106

Umpires: R.S. Dunne & V.K. Ramaswamy

West Indies won by an innings and 322 runs

Adams, advancing in craft and confidence match after match, reached his third century in four Tests on the second morning. He was at the crease just over five hours, and his elegant 151 came off 226 balls and included 24 fours. He is a batsman of subtlety and charm. Arthurton and Chanderpaul were, perhaps, over-cautious against a weak attack which suffered from the fact that Thomson was unable to bowl or field anywhere but slip because of pre-match injury. The wisdom of selectors! Junior Murray, on the other hand, seized the opportunity to hit his first Test century, an astonishing effort which came off just 88 balls. He hit 11 fours and 2 sixes.

Walsh's declaration left New Zealand 12 overs to survive before the end of the day. Survive they did and scored 23 besides, and Young and Murray went on to make 50 for the first wicket. There was no joy thereafter for the New Zealanders as Walsh tore their innings apart with fast bowling of the very highest quality on a pitch which offered him no assistance. He captured seven wickets and then bowled Young for 0 when New Zealand were forced to follow on 444 runs in arrears. Jones and Rutherford also perished before the close which came with the home side facing a humiliating defeat, 52 for 3.

Humiliation duly arrived before lunch on the fourth day, with Walsh taking five more wickets and finishing with 6 for 18, 13 for 55 in a match in which he had passed 250 Test wickets.

New Zealand had suffered their heaviest defeat, and West Indies' 660 was the highest score made against them in a Test match. They omitted Jones and brought in Cairns and Greatbatch to the squad for the four-nation tournament. Chris Pringle, their most successful bowler in limited-over matches, was initially unavailable as he was suspended after misdemeanours in South Africa. This was a sad centenary.

CENTENARY ONE-DAY SERIES

Compounded into a fortnight, the four-nation one-day series began the day after the second Test match against West Indies was scheduled to finish. The opening match was played on the pitch that had been used for the Test. It was a dull affair which turned in Australia's favour when Warne dismissed both Cullinan and Callaghan in his first three overs at a cost of one run. Australia, without Slater who had broken a thumb in the final Test against England and without McDermott who was rested, made hard work of victory and owed much to Steve Waugh.

The second match was significant in that it brought to an end New Zealand's run of 16 limited-over matches without a victory. The return of some of New Zealand's old guard, including Martin Crowe, restored confidence. Greatbatch and Fleming were aggressive while Morrison mopped up the Indian tail as three wickets fell in five balls. Sadly, Crowe limped out of the tournament with a thigh injury.

India disappeared from the competition two days later when they lost to South Africa, but Australia virtually

assured themselves a place in the final when they beat New Zealand in a fine match at Eden Park. In spite of some controlled bowling and good fielding by the home side, Australia ran up a big score, with Taylor and Mark Waugh adding 147 for the second wicket. New Zealand responded with a third-wicket partnership of 82 off 107 balls between Greatbatch and Fleming. At 40 overs, New Zealand's run rate was ahead of Australia's, but they lost five wickets for 46 runs.

India restored some pride with victory over Australia at Dunedin. Needing 251 to win, they were given a splendid start by Tendulkar and Prabhakar who reached 50 in seven overs. The defeat did not alter the fact that Australia had qualified for the final, where they were joined by New Zealand. The match against South Africa at Christchurch was put back a day because of rain. Rutherford and Greatbatch scored 98 off 130 balls for New Zealand's second wicket, and Vaughan and Larsen bowled economically. Cairns withdrew from the attack with a side strain.

The final was a disappointment. Choosing to bat first on a lifeless wicket, New Zealand showed little enterprise against a balanced attack backed by excellent fielding. Australia raced to victory in 31.1 overs, winning ahead of the rain.

CENTENARY TOURNAMENT QUALIFYING TABLE

	P	W	L	Pts
Australia	3	2	1	4
New Zealand	3	2	1	4
India	3	1	2	2
South Africa	3	1	2	2

SOUTH AFRICA TOUR – THE CENTENARY TEST

27, 28 February and 1 March 1995 *at Trafalgar Park, Nelson*

New Zealand Academy XI 120 (A.A. Donald 4 for 39, S.D. Jack 4 for 47) and 126 (C.R. Matthews 4 for 23)

South Africans 165 (D.J. Cullinan 51, K.J. Walmsley 5 for 73) and 84 for 2

South Africans won by 8 wickets

Among the emerging players to represent the Academy against the South Africans was a six-foot five-inch fast bowler, Kerry Walmsley. Walmsley had found a place in the Auckland squad after some fine performances in club cricket, and his five-wicket haul against the South Africans was the first occasion on which he had captured five wickets in an innings in a first-class match. Indeed, he was to find a place in the New Zealand Test side against Sri Lanka after having played just three first-class matches.

Walmsley was not in the side for the Test match against South Africa. There were no debutants. New Zealand brought back Crowe, fit again, and Nash, fit again, and

CENTENARY TOURNAMENT – MATCH ONE – AUSTRALIA *v.* SOUTH AFRICA
15 February 1995 at Basin Reserve, Wellington

SOUTH AFRICA

G. Kirsten	c Healy, b Reiffel	15
M.J.R. Rindel	c Taylor, b Reiffel	14
W.J. Cronje (capt)	c Taylor, b Blewett	22
D.J. Cullinan	st Healy, b Warne	0
J.N. Rhodes	b McGrath	25
D.J. Callaghan	c S.R. Waugh, b Warne	1
*D.J. Richardson	not out	22
E.O. Simons	lbw, b McGrath	0
P.L. Symcox	c M.E. Waugh, b May	10
P.S. de Villiers	b Reiffel	8
A.A. Donald	b Reiffel	0
Extras	lb 3, nb 3	6
(46.2 overs)		123

AUSTRALIA

M.A. Taylor (capt)	c Cullinan, b de Villiers	24
G.S. Blewett	run out	14
M.E. Waugh	b Symcox	11
D.C. Boon	lbw, b de Villiers	1
S.R. Waugh	not out	44
R.T. Ponting	b Simons	1
*I.A. Healy	lbw, b Cronje	18
P.R. Reiffel	c Rhodes, b Cronje	8
S.K. Warne	not out	2
T.B.A. May		
G.D. McGrath		
Extras	b 1	1
(43.2 overs)	(for 7 wickets)	124

	O	M	R	W
McGrath	10	1	25	2
Reiffel	8.2	2	27	4
Blewett	10	–	30	1
Warne	10	3	18	2
May	8	–	20	1

	O	M	R	W
Donald	7	–	32	–
de Villiers	10	2	34	2
Simons	10	3	19	1
Symcox	10	1	23	1
Cronje	6.2	1	15	2

FALL OF WICKETS
1–20, 2–48, 3–52, 4–54, 5–55, 6–95, 7–95, 8–111, 9–121

FALL OF WICKETS
1–38, 2–39, 3–39, 4–55, 5–56, 6–103, 7–115

Umpires: B.L. Aldridge & R.S. Dunne   *Man of the Match:* S.R. Waugh   *Australia won by 3 wickets*

CENTENARY TOURNAMENT – MATCH TWO – NEW ZEALAND *v.* INDIA
16 February 1995 at McLean Park, Napier

INDIA

A.D. Jadeja	run out	7
S.R. Tendulkar	c Thomson, b Morrison	13
N.S. Sidhu	c Rutherford, b Su'a	73
M. Azharuddin (capt)	c Rutherford, b Thomson	28
V.G. Kambli	c Rutherford, b Vaughan	17
M. Prabhakar	c Rutherford, b Cairns	2
*N.R. Mongia	c Greatbatch, b Larsen	4
A.R. Kumble	not out	6
J. Srinath	run out	2
Venkatesh Prasad	lbw, b Morrison	0
Venkatapathy Raju	b Morrison	0
Extras	b 1, lb 4, w 3	8
(45.5 overs)		160

NEW ZEALAND

M.D. Crowe	c and b Srinath	7
M.J. Greatbatch	b Prabhakar	32
K.R. Rutherford (capt)	c Kambli, b Venkatapathy Raju	25
S.P. Fleming	not out	59
C.L. Cairns	c Azharuddin, b Srinath	25
S.A. Thomson	c Azharuddin, b Srinath	0
*A.C. Parore	c Mongia, b Srinath	0
J.T.C. Vaughan	not out	5
G.R. Larsen		
M.L. Su'a		
D.K. Morrison		
Extras	lb 2, w 3, nb 4	9
(32.2 overs)	(for 6 wickets)	162

	O	M	R	W
Morrison	7.5	1	22	3
Thomson	5	–	29	1
Su'a	10	1	35	1
Cairns	8	1	17	1
Larsen	10	3	28	1
Vaughan	5	–	24	1

	O	M	R	W
Prabhakar	7	1	28	1
Srinath	9.2	1	52	4
Kumble	9	–	34	–
Venkatesh Prasad	2	–	11	–
Venkatapathy Raju	5	–	35	1

FALL OF WICKETS
1–20, 2–22, 3–79, 4–104, 5–127, 6–138, 7–157, 8–160, 9–160

FALL OF WICKETS
1–42, 2–42, 3–103, 4–144, 5–144, 6–144

Umpires: D.B. Cowie & C.E. King   *Man of the Match:* S.P. Fleming   *New Zealand won by 4 wickets*

CENTENARY TOURNAMENT – MATCH THREE – SOUTH AFRICA v. INDIA
18 February 1995 at Trust Bank Park, Hamilton

SOUTH AFRICA		
A.C. Hudson	b Srinath	24
G. Kirsten	run out	80
D.J. Cullinan	c Venkatesh Prasad, b Kumble	65
W.J. Cronje (capt)	c and b Kumble	3
J.N. Rhodes	lbw, b Kumble	0
D.J. Callaghan	lbw, b Kumble	16
*D.J. Richardson	not out	11
E.O. Simons	not out	7
P.L. Symcox		
P.S. de Villiers		
A.A. Donald		
Extras	b 1, lb 7, w 4, nb 5	17
(50 overs)	(for 6 wickets)	223

INDIA		
A.D. Jadeja	c Kirsten, b Symcox	29
S.R. Tendulkar	c Symcox, b Cronje	37
N.S. Sidhu	c Callaghan, b Cronje	5
M. Azharuddin (capt)	run out	20
V.G. Kambli	c Richardson, b Donald	30
J. Srinath	c Simons, b Donald	37
M. Prabhakar	run out	6
*N.R. Mongia	run out	24
A.R. Kumble	lbw, b de Villiers	1
Venkatesh Prasad	not out	5
Venkatapathy Raju		
Extras	b 2, lb 3, w 10	15
(50 overs)	(for 9 wickets)	209

	O	M	R	W
Prabhakar	6	–	24	–
Srinath	8	–	30	1
Venkatesh Prasad	7	–	32	–
Kumble	10	–	40	4
Venkatapathy Raju	9	–	46	–
Tendulkar	10	–	43	–

	O	M	R	W
Donald	9	1	43	2
de Villiers	10	1	56	1
Simons	8	1	28	–
Cronje	10	–	34	2
Symcox	10	–	20	1
Callaghan	3	–	23	–

FALL OF WICKETS
1–47, 2–167, 3–174, 4–174, 5–201, 6–201

FALL OF WICKETS
1–61, 2–73, 3–76, 4–118, 5–148, 6–159, 7–196, 8–200, 9–209

Umpires: D.B. Cowie & E.A. Watkins   Man of the Match: G. Kirsten   South Africa won by 14 runs

CENTENARY TOURNAMENT – MATCH FOUR – NEW ZEALAND v. AUSTRALIA
19 February 1995 at Eden Park, Auckland

AUSTRALIA		
G.S. Blewett	c Fleming, b Thomson	3
M.A. Taylor (capt)	c and b Pringle	97
M.E. Waugh	c and b Vaughan	74
D.C. Boon	c Larsen, b Morrison	44
S.R. Waugh	b Pringle	13
R.T. Ponting	not out	10
*I.A. Healy	not out	4
P.R. Reiffel		
S.K. Warne		
T.B.A. May		
G.D. McGrath		
Extras	b 1, lb 5, w 2, nb 1	9
(50 overs)	(for 5 wickets)	254

NEW ZEALAND		
B.A. Young	b Reiffel	4
M.J. Greatbatch	c Healy, b Reiffel	74
K.R. Rutherford (capt)	st Healy, b Warne	7
S.P. Fleming	c Warne, b May	53
C.L. Cairns	lbw, b McGrath	22
S.A. Thomson	run out	9
*A.C. Parore	not out	27
J.T.C. Vaughan	c Healy, b Reiffel	3
G.R. Larsen	c Reiffel, b M.E. Waugh	3
C. Pringle	b McGrath	4
D.K. Morrison	not out	3
Extras	lb 12, w 4, nb 2	18
(50 overs)	(for 9 wickets)	227

	O	M	R	W
Morrison	10	1	40	1
Thomson	10	1	43	1
Pringle	10	–	54	2
Cairns	3	–	21	–
Larsen	10	–	49	–
Vaughan	7	–	41	1

	O	M	R	W
McGrath	10	–	40	2
Reiffel	10	4	35	3
Warne	10	1	40	1
May	10	–	43	1
Blewett	2	–	18	–
Boon	4	–	20	–
M.E. Waugh	4	–	19	1

FALL OF WICKETS
1–3, 2–150, 3–214, 4–238, 5–241

FALL OF WICKETS
1–19, 2–42, 3–124, 4–169, 5–181, 6–187, 7–193, 8–199, 9–217

Umpires: D.B. Cowie & D.M. Quested   Man of the Match: M.A. Taylor   Australia won by 27 runs

CENTENARY TOURNAMENT – MATCH FIVE – AUSTRALIA *v.* INDIA
22 February 1995 at Carisbrook, Dunedin

AUSTRALIA				INDIA		
D.C. Boon	c Kambli, **b** Vaidya	32		M. Prabhakar	**b** Angel	50
G.S. Blewett	c and **b** Tendulkar	46		S.R. Tendulkar	c Taylor, **b** Angel	47
R.T. Ponting	c Vaidya, **b** Prabhakar	62		N.S. Sidhu	run out	54
S.R. Waugh	c and **b** Kumble	23		M. Azharuddin (capt)	c Healy, **b** Blewett	25
M.E. Waugh	c Azharuddin, **b** Srinath	48		V.G. Kambli	not out	51
*I.A. Healy	not out	21		S.V. Manjrekar	c Healy, **b** May	14
M.A. Taylor (capt)	**b** Srinath	0		*N.R. Mongia	not out	6
S.K. Warne	not out	5		J. Srinath		
T.B.A. May				P.S. Vaidya		
G.D. McGrath				A.R. Kumble		
J. Angel				A.R. Kapoor		
Extras	b 2, lb 3, w 2, nb 6	13		Extras	lb 1, w 3, nb 1	5
(50 overs)	(for 6 wickets)	250		(47.5 overs)	(for 5 wickets)	252

	O	M	R	W		O	M	R	W
Prabhakar	10	–	61	1	McGrath	9	1	45	–
Srinath	9	–	49	2	Angel	10	1	47	2
Vaidya	7	–	36	1	Blewett	8.5	–	47	1
Kumble	7	–	28	1	Warne	10	–	61	–
Kapoor	9	–	38	–	May	10	–	51	1
Tendulkar	8	–	33	1					

FALL OF WICKETS
1–56, **2**–103, **3**–158, **4**–207, **5**–226, **6**–226

FALL OF WICKETS
1–97, **2**–100, **3**–144, **4**–213, **5**–233

Umpires: R.S. Dunne & C.E. King   *Man of the Match:* N.S. Sidhu   *India won by 5 wickets*

CENTENARY TOURNAMENT – MATCH SIX – NEW ZEALAND *v.* SOUTH AFRICA
24 February 1995 at Lancaster Park, Christchurch

NEW ZEALAND				SOUTH AFRICA		
M.J. Greatbatch	c and **b** Cronje	76		A.C. Hudson	c Douglas, **b** Morrison	10
M.W. Douglas	lbw, **b** Matthews	8		G. Kirsten	c Fleming, **b** Thomson	63
K.R. Rutherford (capt)	c Callaghan, **b** Cronje	61		D.J. Cullinan	c Vaughan, **b** Larsen	13
S.P. Fleming	c Cullinan, **b** Matthews	21		W.J. Cronje (capt)	st Parore, **b** Vaughan	34
C.L. Cairns	c Kirsten, **b** Matthews	33		J.N. Rhodes	c Greatbatch, **b** Morrison	14
S.A. Thomson	c Richardson, **b** de Villiers	6		D.J. Callaghan	lbw, **b** Larsen	23
*A.C. Parore	not out	30		*D.J. Richardson	c Thomson, **b** Vaughan	7
J.T.C. Vaughan	run out	7		E.O. Simons	c Greatbatch, **b** Vaughan	7
G.R. Larsen	not out	2		C.R. Matthews	**b** Larsen	16
C. Pringle				P.S. de Villiers	c Thomson, **b** Pringle	7
D.K. Morrison				A.A. Donald	not out	0
Extras	lb 2, w 1, nb 2	5		Extras	b 1, lb 4, w 4	9
(50 overs)	(for 7 wickets)	249		(47 overs)		203

	O	M	R	W		O	M	R	W
de Villiers	10	–	39	1	Pringle	8	–	35	1
Matthews	10	1	49	3	Morrison	8	1	30	2
Donald	10	–	50	–	Vaughan	10	–	37	3
Simons	6	–	33	–	Cairns	4	–	24	–
Callaghan	4	–	26	–	Larsen	10	–	39	3
Cronje	10	–	50	2	Thomson	7	–	33	1

FALL OF WICKETS
1–28, **2**–126, **3**–167, **4**–172, **5**–190, **6**–227, **7**–242

FALL OF WICKETS
1–28, **2**–67, **3**–117, **4**–138, **5**–143, **6**–162, **7**–173, **8**–190, **9**–197

Umpires: B.L. Aldridge & D.M. Quested   *Man of the Match:* M.J. Greatbatch   *New Zealand won by 46 runs*

NEW ZEALAND

M.J. Greatbatch	c McGrath, b Reiffel	8
M.W. Douglas	c Healy, b Reiffel	2
K.R. Rutherford (capt)	c Boon, b May	46
S.P. Fleming	c Healy, b M.E. Waugh	0
C.L. Cairns	c Taylor, b May	17
S.A. Thomson	c and b Warne	9
*A.C. Parore	c Taylor, b Warne	2
J.T.C. Vaughan	not out	20
G.R. Larsen	run out	0
C. Pringle	b May	1
D.K. Morrison	not out	4
Extras	b 1, lb 10, w 13, nb 4	28
(50 overs)	(for 9 wickets)	137

AUSTRALIA

G.S. Blewett	c and b Pringle	7
M.A. Taylor (capt)	st Parore, b Vaughan	44
M.E. Waugh	c Parore, b Morrison	46
D.C. Boon	not out	24
S.R. Waugh	c Rutherford, b Thomson	1
R.T. Ponting	not out	7
*I.A. Healy		
P.R. Reiffel		
S.K. Warne		
T.B.A. May		
G.D. McGrath		
Extras	lb 3, w 3, nb 3	9
(31.1 overs)	(for 4 wickets)	138

	O	M	R	W
McGrath	9	1	25	–
Reiffel	10	3	14	2
M.E. Waugh	10	1	38	1
Warne	10	2	21	2
May	10	2	19	3
Blewett	1	–	9	–

	O	M	R	W
Morrison	9	1	31	1
Pringle	9.1	1	52	1
Thomson	5	–	22	1
Vaughan	6	1	18	1
Larsen	2	–	12	–

FALL OF WICKETS
1–8, 2–29, 3–35, 4–81, 5–102, 6–106, 7–106, 8–106, 9–112

FALL OF WICKETS
1–15, 2–93, 3–116, 4–121

Umpires: B.L. Aldridge & R.S. Dunne   *Man of the Match:* T.B.A. May   *Australia won by 6 wickets*

Larsen and Patel. Seemingly, New Zealand were hoping that spin would play an important part in the match, but Patel, Hart and Eksteen took just four wickets between them. Thomson was declared unfit.

South Africa won the toss and batted. Larsen, a surprise choice as third seamer, bowled Kirsten with his seventh delivery, and Nash's superb out-swinger accounted for Hudson. Steyn and Cullinan added 103 before Steyn swatted unwisely at Morrison. A rain-shortened day ended with Cullinan on 82, and South Africa 153 for 3.

Cullinan batted with serene command and looked certain to reach a century of great charm when he pulled at Morrison over-ambitiously and was well caught at mid-wicket. In spite of New Zealand spilling catches in abundance, South Africa batted disappointingly, and three wickets fell on 230 when Morrison, Nash and Larsen bowled well with the second new ball.

New Zealand had 43 overs at the end of the second day and scored 94 for the loss of Murray so that they seemed well in charge. They lost their grip on the game next morning when Young, 62 not out overnight, and Crowe failed to re-establish themselves. Three wickets went down for 36 runs before Rutherford, way below his best, and Parore added 82. Parore hit a six and 12 fours before becoming one of Donald's four victims. New Zealand led by 34 runs, but the day's honours had gone to the South African attack which, on a good batting pitch, had restricted New Zealand to little more than two runs an over.

A draw seemed inevitable when South Africa ended the fourth day on 232 for 4, a lead of 198. Kirsten and Hudson

had batted fluently, and Hudson had been spectacularly caught in the covers. There had been rumours of complaints of ball-tampering against Dion Nash, but no action was taken.

Cronje led the assault on the New Zealand bowlers on the last morning. He reached his fifth Test century off 151 balls and made a declaration as bold as his batting when he left New Zealand 63 overs in which to score 275 to win.

At tea, they were 114 for 3 with 35 overs remaining, Rutherford and Fleming having added 64. Three balls after tea, Fleming drove loosely at Matthews and was caught behind. Rutherford and Parore maintained the run chase but, at 145, Rutherford spooned a catch to mid-on. His 56 had come from 60 balls, and now New Zealand faltered. Patel was brilliantly run out by Jonty Rhodes, and the rest subsided. With 43 balls remaining, Matthews trapped Nash leg before, and South Africa had won.

 SHELL TROPHY

7, 8 , 9 and 10 December 1994 *at McLean Park, Napier*

Otago 449 for 9 dec. (M.H. Richardson 122, I.S. Billcliff 121, M.G. Croy 61, A.J. Gale 60)

Central Districts 247 (W.A. Wisneski 86, S.W. Duff 62)

CENTENARY TEST MATCH – NEW ZEALAND v. SOUTH AFRICA
4, 5, 6, 7 and 8 March 1995 at Eden Park, Auckland

SOUTH AFRICA

	FIRST INNINGS		SECOND INNINGS	
G. Kirsten	b Larsen	16	c Parore, b Nash	76
P.J.R. Steyn	c Patel, b Morrison	46	c Rutherford, b Patel	13
A.C. Hudson	c Parore, b Nash	1	c Young, b Patel	64
D.J. Cullinan	c Murray, b Morrison	96	c Parore, b Hart	12
C.E. Eksteen	c Fleming, b Nash	21		
W.J. Cronje (capt)	c Crowe, b Morrison	41	(5) c Hart, b Larsen	101
J.N. Rhodes	c Parore, b Nash	0	(6) b Larsen	28
*D.J. Richardson	c Parore, b Nash	18	(7) not out	8
C.R. Matthews	c Parore, b Larsen	26	(8) not out	4
P.S. de Villiers	c Hart, b Larsen	12		
A.A. Donald	not out	4		
Extras	lb 13	13	lb 1, nb 1	2
		294	(for 6 wickets, dec.)	308

NEW ZEALAND

	FIRST INNINGS		SECOND INNINGS	
B.A. Young	c Richardson, b Donald	74	c Cullinan, b de Villiers	4
D.J. Murray	c Kirsten, b Cronje	25	c Matthews, b de Villiers	24
M.D. Crowe	c Hudson, b de Villiers	16	c Cullinan, b Matthews	14
S.P. Fleming	b Matthews	17	c Richardson, b Matthews	27
K.R. Rutherford (capt)	c Richardson, b Cronje	28	c Hudson, b de Villiers	56
*A.C. Parore	c Richardson, b Donald	89	c Cullinan, b Eksteen	24
M.N. Hart	lbw, b Matthews	28	(8) c Richardson, b de Villiers	6
G.R. Larsen	not out	26	(9) c Richardson, b Donald	1
D.N. Patel	c Richardson, b Donald	15	(7) run out	12
D.J. Nash	lbw, b de Villiers	1	lbw, b Matthews	6
D.K. Morrison	c Cullinan, b Donald	0	not out	0
Extras	lb 5, w 1, nb 3	9	b 1, lb 4, nb 2	7
		328		181

	O	M	R	W	O	M	R	W
Morrison	26	9	53	3	23	6	78	–
Nash	27	13	72	4	22	3	67	1
Larsen	24.3	7	57	3	18	6	31	2
Hart	11	3	45	–	12	3	50	1
Patel	17	2	54	–	30	6	81	2

	O	M	R	W	O	M	R	W
Donald	32.4	11	88	4	8	2	44	1
de Villiers	36	13	78	2	18	6	42	4
Matthews	32	11	66	2	12.5	3	47	3
Cronje	17	3	48	2	3	1	18	–
Eksteen	23	9	43	–	14	5	25	1

FALL OF WICKETS
1–41, 2–42, 3–145, 4–168, 5–230, 6–230, 7–230, 8–276, 9–276
1–41, 2–123, 3–135, 4–218, 5–277, 6–300

FALL OF WICKETS
1–86, 2–108, 3–137, 4–144, 5–226, 6–268, 7–303, 8–321, 9–322
1–11, 2–42, 3–50, 4–114, 5–145, 6–167, 7–174, 8–174, 9–179

Umpires: R.S. Dunne & D.B. Hair

South Africa won by 93 runs

Otago won by an innings and 12 runs

Otago 12 pts, Central Districts 0 pts

at Basin Reserve, Wellington

Northern Districts 202 (G.R. Larsen 6 for 37) and 196
(M.D. Bell 60, A.J. Bradley 57, H.T. Davis 4 for 55)

Wellington 250 (M.W. Douglas 100 not out, S. Styris 5 for 64,
C.W. Ross 4 for 94) and 149 for 3 (R.G. Twose 57,
J.M. Aiken 57)

Wellington won by 7 wickets

Wellington 12 pts, Northern Districts 0 pts

at Lancaster Park, Christchurch

Canterbury 351 (N.J. Astle 96, S.W.J. Wilson 74,
D.K. Morrison 5 for 100) and 203 (C.L. Cairns 64,
D.N. Patel 6 for 62)

Auckland 299 (A.T. Reinholds 97, J.T.C. Vaughan 60 not out,
S.J. Roberts 4 for 82)

Match drawn

Canterbury 4 pts, Auckland 0 pts

New Zealand's domestic first-class competition was overshadowed by the plethora of international cricket being played in the centenary year, but it gave great opportunity for players to improve their claims for a place in the national side. Richardson and Billcliff were early contenders with a fifth-wicket stand of 292 for Otago in their innings victory over Central Districts, as was Gavin Larsen who returned career-best figures of 6 for 37 for Wellington against Northern Districts. In this match, medium-pacer Scott Styris took 5 for 64 on the occasion of his first-class debut.

14, 15 , 16 and 17 December 1994 *at Basin Reserve, Wellington*

Otago 139 (H.T. Davis 4 for 49) and 110 (H.T. Davis 4 for 48)

Wellington 494 for 3 dec. (J.M. Aiken 138, M.H. Austen 128,
R.G. Twose 113, M.W. Douglas 52 not out)

Wellington won by an innings and 245 runs

Wellington 12 pts, Otago 0 pts

at Trust Bank Park, Hamilton

Canterbury 160 (G.R. Stead 61, S. Styris 4 for 38) and 330
  (N.J. Astle 175, D.J. Boyle 59)
Northern Districts 249 (G.P. Burnett 59, G.E. Bradburn 50)
  and 242 for 6 (M.D. Bailey 101 not out, G.P. Burnett 52)

Northern Districts won by 4 wickets

Northern Districts 12 pts, Canterbury 0 pts

at Eden Park, Auckland

Auckland 152 (W.A. Wisneski 5 for 35) and 147 (M.J. Pawson
  5 for 41)
Central Districts 166 (D.K. Morrison 4 for 67) and 137 for 9
  (J.T.C. Vaughan 7 for 34)

Central Districts won by 1 wicket

Central Districts 12 pts, Auckland 0 pts

An opening stand of 259 between Austen and Aiken, a
record for any wicket against Otago, set up Wellington's
crushing victory at Basin Reserve, while Scott Styris'
embryo career continued to flourish in Northern Districts'
win over Canterbury. This match had other heroes besides.
Nathan Astle hit a maiden first-class hundred and shared
a last-wicket stand of 101 with Michael Owens, the first
century last-wicket stand ever recorded for Canterbury.
Mark Bailey emulated Astle's performance, and his
maiden hundred took Northern to victory. Medium-
pacer Justin Vaughan, who has played for Gloucestershire,
returned the best bowling figures of his career, only to see
his side, Auckland, beaten by one wicket inside three days
by Central Districts.

22, 23, 24 and **25** January 1995 *at Trust Bank Park, Hamilton*

Northern Districts 104 (W. Watson 4 for 17) and 318
  (G.E. Bradburn 111, M.D. Bell 71, R.G. Hart 57)
Auckland 394 (C.M. Spearman 147) and 29 for 0

Auckland won by 10 wickets

Auckland 12 pts, Northern Districts 0 pts

at McLean Park, Napier

Central Districts 360 (M.J. Greatbatch 131, C.D. Ingham 76,
  G.R Jonas 5 for 60) and 45 for 1
Wellington 178 (W.A. Wisneski 5 for 21) and 226
  (R.G. Twose 79)

Central Districts won by 9 wickets

Central Districts 12 pts, Wellington 0 pts

at Centennial Park, Oamaru

Otago 172 (S.J. Roberts 4 for 69) and 177 (P.W. Dobbs 81
  not out, S.J. Roberts 5 for 56)
Canterbury 94 (R.J. Kennedy 4 for 50) and 103 (A.J. Gale 6 for 42)

Otago won by 152 runs

Otago 12 pts, Canterbury 0 pts

Skipper Grant Bradburn hit the highest score of his career
but saw his side lose to Auckland for whom Craig Spearman hit a maiden first-class century. A third centurion,
Mark Greatbatch of Central Districts, alerted the attention
of the selectors.

27, 28, 29 and **30** January 1995 *at Eden Park, Auckland*

Auckland 485 for 7 dec. (C.M. Spearman 115, A.C. Barnes 94,
  R.A. Jones 54, M.L. Su'a 52 not out) and 175 for 6 dec.
  (S.W. Brown 50 not out, G.R. Stead 4 for 58)
Canterbury 338 for 9 dec. (C.D. McMillan 110, C.L. Cairns 73,
  C.Z. Harris 60, M.W. Priest 55 not out, W. Watson 4 for 64,
  M.L. Su'a 4 for 82) and 226 for 6 (D.J. Murray 66)

Match drawn

Auckland 4 pts, Canterbury 0 pts

at Pukekura Park, New Plymouth

Central Districts 421 for 7 dec. (M.J. Greatbatch 125,
  C.D. Ingham 102, T.E. Blain 68)
Northern Districts 195 for 2 (M.E. Parlane 94, M.D. Bell 78)

Match drawn

Central Districts 2 pts, Northern Districts 2 pts

at Carisbrook, Dunedin

Otago 167 (P.W. Dobbs 65, I.S. Billcliff 60) and 229
Wellington 357 (R.G. Twose 163 not out, M.C. Goodson 61,
  E.J. Marshall 5 for 85) and 44 for 0

Wellington won by 10 wickets

Wellington 12 pts, Otago 0 pts

Inspired by skipper Roger Twose's patient innings,
Wellington gained their third victory and went clear at the
top of the table. Greatbatch and Spearman hit their second
centuries in successive matches, and there was a maiden
hundred for McMillan. Rain ruined the game in New
Plymouth.

11, 12, 13 and **14** February 1995 *at Eden Park, Auckland*

Otago 277 (M.H. Richardson 86, K.P. Walmsley 4 for 101) and
  179 (M.G. Croy 58, D.N. Patel 4 for 59)
Auckland 239 (D.N. Patel 67, A.T. Reinholds 52, E.J. Marshall
  6 for 53) and 218 for 3 (A.T. Reinholds 76, R.A. Jones 54
  not out)

Auckland won by 7 wickets

Auckland 8 pts, Otago 4 pts

at Trust Bank Park, Hamilton

Northern Districts 274 (G.P. Burnett 90, A.J. Penn 4 for 81)
  and 316 for 5 dec. (M.D. Bell 66, A.R. Tait 50 not out)
Central Districts 246 (G.R.J. Hart 55, R.P. de Groen 4 for 73,
  R.L. Hayes 4 for 76) and 274 for 7 (M.J. Greatbatch 89, L.G.
  Howell 75, W.A. Wisneski 56 not out, R.L. Hayes 4 for 70)

Match drawn

Northern Districts 4 pts, Central Districts 0 pts

at Lancaster Park, Christchurch

Canterbury 496 (N.J. Astle 191, M.W. Priest 98 not out,
R.T. Latham 59, C.L. Cairns 54) and 476 for 2 dec.
(B.R. Hartland 150, G.R. Stead 130, R.T. Latham 90 not out,
C.D. McMillan 86 not out)

Wellington 498 for 2 dec. (M.H. Austen 166, R.G. Twose 150
not out, J.M. Aiken 79, M.D. Crowe 50 not out) and 475 for
4 (M.D. Crowe 193 not out, J.M. Aiken 116, R.G. Twose 81)

Wellington won by 6 wickets

Wellington 12 pts, Canterbury 0 pts

The match at Lancaster Park produced the highest run
aggregate recorded in first-class cricket in New Zealand.
There were seven centuries in the match which equalled
the New Zealand record, while Wellington's 475 was the
best-ever chase achieved in the country. The runs came in
388 minutes, and Martin Crowe's 193 came off 179 balls.

16, 17, 18 and **19** February 1995 *at Fitzherbert Park, Hamilton North*

Central Districts 242 (A.H. Jones 78, M.W. Priest 7 for 57) and
156 (G.I. Allott 5 for 45, C.Z. Harris 4 for 74)

Canterbury 534 (D.J. Murray 130, B.R. Hartland 80,
R.T. Latham 78, L.K. Germon 60, C.D. McMillan 58,
C.Z. Harris 54, C.J.M. Furlong 4 for 204)

Canterbury won by an innings and 136 runs

Canterbury 12 pts, Central Districts 0 pts

at Queen's Park, Invercargill

Otago 183 (I.S. Billcliff 58) and 163

Northern Districts 344 (M.D. Bailey 122, P.J. Wiseman
4 for 132) and 6 for 0

Northern Districts won by 10 wickets

Northern Districts 12 pts, Otago 0 pts

at Basin Reserve, Wellington

Auckland 260 (S.W. Brown 76)

Wellington 194 for 7 (C.M. Brown 5 for 54)

Match drawn

Wellington 2 pts, Auckland 2 pts

Canterbury continued their phenomenal scoring, but this
time with resounding success. The abandoned game at
Basin Reserve made it certain that Wellington would compete in the final.

3, 4, 5 and **6** March 1995 *at Basin Reserve, Wellington*

Central Districts 225 (W.A. Wisneski 56, S.J. Hotter 4 for 54)
and 233 (S.W. Duff 59, M.A. Sigley 52, H.T. Davis 5 for 78)

Wellington 441 (S.R. Mather 126, J.D. Wells 96, R.G. Petrie 80)
and 20 for 0

Wellington won by 10 wickets

Wellington 12 pts, Central Districts 0 pts

at Lancaster Park, Christchurch

Northern Districts 254 (B.G. Cooper 72, C.W. Flanagan
4 for 37) and 178 (M.W. Priest 4 for 47)

Canterbury 256 for 8 dec. (S.W.J. Wilson 60) and 178 for 9
(R.P. de Groen 6 for 72)

Canterbury won by 1 wicket

Canterbury 12 pts, Northern Districts 0 pts

at Carisbrook, Dunedin

Auckland 299 (C.D. Lee 111 not out, J.T.C. Vaughan 59,
E.J. Marshall 4 for 76) and 99 for 2

Otago 143 and 254 (E.J. Marshall 52)

Auckland won by 8 wickets

Auckland 12 pts, Otago 0 pts

Dipak Patel was originally in the Auckland side at
Carisbrook, but he was called into the New Zealand side
against South Africa on the first morning. His place was
taken by Chris Lee who, going to the wicket with the score
on 141 for 7, hit 111, the first century of his career, off 166
balls. He then dismissed both of Otago's openers. Had
Vaughan not been dropped early in his innings, Patel
would have batted. Auckland's win took them into the
final.

SHELL TROPHY FINAL TABLE

	P	W	L	D	Pts
Wellington	7	5	1	1	62
Auckland	7	3	1	3	38
Northern Districts	7	2	3	2	30
Otago	7	2	5	–	28
Canterbury	7	2	3	2	28
Central Districts	7	2	3	2	26

National associations have a facility these days for under-
mining their domestic competitions. New Zealand is no
exception. The final of the Shell Trophy was scheduled to
coincide with the first Test match against Sri Lanka.
Auckland won the toss, and by the end of the first day,
having bowled out Wellington for 118, they had claimed a
lead of 29 for the loss of six wickets. Vaughan was out
immediately on the resumption, but Barnes and Watson,
31 off 38 balls, saw that the tail wagged effectively. Trailing
by 139 on the first innings, Wellington lost five wickets in
clearing the arrears, and they were much indebted to
Douglas and Baker. Needing 101 to win, Auckland hit off
the runs in 77 minutes.

14, 15, 16 and **17** March 1995 *at Basin Reserve, Wellington*

Wellington 118 (C. Pringle 4 for 35) and 239 (M.W. Douglas 75,
 D.N. Patel 6 for 75)
Auckland 257 and 101 for 1 (C.M. Spearman 58 not out)

Auckland won by 9 wickets

2, 3, 4 and **5** April 1995 *at Trust Bank Park, Hamilton*

New Zealand Academy 240 (C.M. Spearman 75, R. Baker
 6 for 53) and 213
Australian Academy 398 (A. Symonds 115, K. Harvey 79,
 R. Baker 56, R.L. Hayes 4 for 59) and 56 for 0

Australian Academy won by 10 wickets

The New Zealand side was composed of players who
appeared regularly in the Shell Trophy and was led by
Lee Germon. The Australian side had few with first-class
experience. Symonds, later to excel with Gloucestershire,
hit the second century of his career, 115 off 161 deliveries.

SRI LANKA TOUR

26, 27, 28 February and **1** March 1995 *at Victoria Park, Wanganui*

New Zealand Select XI 327 (D.J. Murray 182,
 L.K. Germon 64, W.P.U.C.J. Vaas 5 for 86) and
 220 for 6 dec. (A.H. Jones 66)
Sri Lankans 192 (S.T. Jayasuriya 51, H.T. Davis 5 for 46) and
 155 for 5 (H.P. Tillekeratne 68 not out)

Match drawn

4, 5, 6 and **7** March 1995 *at Fitzherbert Park, Palmerston North*

Sri Lankans 257 (M.C. Mendis 75, G.R. Jonas 4 for 67) and
 323 for 5 dec. (A. Ranatunga 107, D.P. Samaraweera 78,
 A.P. Gurusinha 63)
New Zealand Academy XI 133 (J. Silva 5 for 29,
 M. Muralitharan 4 for 45) and 205 (N.J. Astle 80,
 M. Muralitharan 5 for 56, J. Silva 5 for 77)

Sri Lankans won by 242 runs

The Sri Lankans arrived in New Zealand to play two Test
matches and three one-day internationals. They played
two first-class matches before the first Test in which there
were two debutants – Kerry Walmsley, the 21-year-old
New Zealand pace bowler, and Chamara Dunusinghe, yet
another Sri Lankan wicket-keeper.

For most of the first day all seemed to go well for New
Zealand. Rutherford won the toss and asked Sri Lanka
to bat first on a pitch that was green and hard. With his
seventh ball in Test cricket, Walmsley, six feet five inches
tall, bowled Gurusinha, and when Nash was introduced

*Chamara Dunusinghe had an outstanding Test debut for Sri Lanka
against New Zealand. (Mueen-ud-din Hameed/Sportsline)*

into the attack he dismissed Sanjeeva Ranatunga and
Aravinda de Silva in his first over. Arjuna Ranatunga
passed fifty and reached 3,000 runs in Test cricket while
the late-order batsmen scored some brisk runs, but New
Zealand could be well pleased at bowling out the visitors
for 183.

There, their pleasure ended. New Zealand had 15 overs
to negotiate at the end of the first day, and, during that
time, they lost three wickets for 33 runs. With the last ball
of the first over of the innings, Wickremasinghe had Young
caught behind off a magnificent out-swinger. He also
brought an abrupt end to Greatbatch's return to Test
cricket and, with the impressive Vaas accounting for
Murray, New Zealand had lost the advantage that was
theirs earlier in the day.

Fleming and Rutherford were soon separated on the
second morning, and thereafter there was little resistance
against the Sri Lankan pace attack. Vaas was particularly
devastating. He bowled accurately at a brisk pace, and the
left-arm bowler moved the ball late to disconcert all batsmen. It was the first time that Vaas had taken five wickets
in a Test innings.

The Sri Lankan second innings began badly and controversially. Samaraweera was given run out by umpire
Randell (with the aid of the television replay) when, having made his ground, he jumped to avoid being hit by

SRI LANKA

Batsman	FIRST INNINGS		SECOND INNINGS	
A.P. Gurusinha	b Walmsley	2	lbw, b Larsen	8
D.P. Samaraweera	c Young, b Walmsley	33	run out	6
S. Ranatunga	c Larsen, b Nash	12	lbw, b Larsen	7
P.A. de Silva	c Parore, b Nash	0	c Parore, b Morrison	62
H.P. Tillekeratne	lbw, b Morrison	9	c Young, b Nash	74
A. Ranatunga (capt)	c Young, b Walmsley	55	b Morrison	28
*C.I. Dunusinghe	c Rutherford, b Larsen	11	b Morrison	91
W.P.U.C.J. Vaas	not out	33	b Walmsley	36
G.P. Wickramasinghe	c Fleming, b Morrison	13	c sub (Hart), b Larsen	16
M. Muralitharan	c Nash, b Larsen	8	not out	10
K.R. Pushpakumara	c Larsen, b Morrison	1	c Parore, b Morrison	0
Extras	lb 6	6	b 2, lb 7, nb 5	14
		183		**352**

NEW ZEALAND

Batsman	FIRST INNINGS		SECOND INNINGS	
B.A. Young	c Dunusinghe, b Wickremasinghe	2	c Samaraweera, b Muralitharan	14
D.J. Murray	lbw, b Vaas	1	c Dunusinghe, b Vaas	36
M.J. Greatbatch	lbw, b Wickremasinghe	1	c Tillekeratne, b Muralitharan	46
S.P. Fleming	c S. Ranatunga, b Vaas	35	c Tillekeratne, b Muralitharan	0
K.R. Rutherford (capt)	c Tillekeratne, b Pushpakumara	32	c Dunusinghe, b Vaas	20
S.A. Thomson	c Muralitharan, b Vaas	8	c Gurusinha, b Muralitharan	4
*A.C. Parore	c Dunusinghe, b Wickremasinghe	7	c Tillekeratne, b Muralitharan	17
G.R. Larsen	c Dunusinghe, b Vaas	0	not out	21
D.J. Nash	lbw, b Pushpakumara	0	c Dunusinghe, b Vaas	0
D.K. Morrison	not out	7	c Gurusinha, b Vaas	0
K.P. Walmsley	b Vaas	4	c Dunusinghe, b Vaas	4
Extras	b 5, lb 1, w 1, nb 5	12	b 6, lb 11, nb 6	23
		109		**185**

Bowling	O	M	R	W	O	M	R	W
Morrison	19	5	40	3	25.3	5	61	4
Walmsley	17	3	70	3	38	7	112	1
Nash	16	4	28	2	36	12	87	1
Larsen	17	6	39	2	39	13	73	3
Thomson					6	3	10	–

Bowling	O	M	R	W	O	M	R	W
Wickremasinghe	19	7	33	3	13	2	42	–
Vaas	18.5	3	47	5	26.4	10	43	5
Pushpakumara	5	1	23	2	9	2	19	–
Muralitharan					36	15	64	5

FALL OF WICKETS
1–2, 2–40, 3–40, 4–54, 5–64, 6–88, 7–137, 8–166, 9–178
1–14, 2–21, 3–22, 4–121, 5–165, 6–205, 7–294, 8–323, 9–352

FALL OF WICKETS
1–2, 2–4, 3–6, 4–53, 5–65, 6–78, 7–79, 8–94, 9–104
1–37, 2–108, 3–108, 4–112, 5–141, 6–141, 7–166, 8–181, 9–181

Umpires: D.B. Cowie & S.G. Randell

Sri Lanka won by 241 runs

The first Sri Lankan to take 10 wickets in a Test match – left-handed pace bowler Vaas. (Mueen-ud-din Hameed/Sportsline)

Rutherford's throw. The ball hit the stumps while Samaraweera had both feet off the ground, and the batsman was given out, a decision which contravened Law 38.

Sri Lanka slipped to 22 for 3, but de Silva steered them to 92 before the close and eventually extended his partnership with Tillekeratne to 99. Sri Lanka now took total command. Dunusinghe played a determined, dogged innings to confirm an excellent Test debut, and, in spite of Morrison returning to bowl at half-pace after a back injury and taking four wickets, Sri Lanka were able to set New Zealand a target of 427.

New Zealand reached three figures for the loss of Young, and ended the fourth day on 139 for 4, but the last morning brought disaster. The left-arm seam bowling of Vaas coupled with the off-spin of Muralitharan saw the last six wickets fall for 44 runs. Vaas became the first Sri Lankan bowler to take 10 wickets in a Test match, and Sri Lanka celebrated their first Test victory on foreign soil. For skipper Arjuna Ranatunga, who, as a schoolboy, played in Sri Lanka's first Test match in 1982, it was 'the peak of my career'.

SECOND TEST MATCH – NEW ZEALAND v. SRI LANKA
18, 19, 20, 21 and 22 March 1995 at Carisbrook, Dunedin

SRI LANKA

	FIRST INNINGS			SECOND INNINGS	
A.P. Gurusinha	c Patel, b Pringle	28	b Su'a		127
D.P. Samaraweera	b Su'a	33	lbw, b Su'a		5
S. Ranatunga	c Young, b Pringle	22	c Parore, b Patel		23
P.A. de Silva	c Patel, b Walmsley	18	c Murray, b Patel		13
A. Ranatunga (capt)	c Young, b Larsen	0	(6) c Parore, b Larsen		90
H.P. Tillekeratne	c Young, b Patel	36	(5) c Murray, b Patel		108
*C.I. Dunusinghe	lbw, b Pringle	0	c Fleming, b Patel		11
W.P.U.C.J. Vaas	c Fleming, b Su'a	51	c Parore, b Walmsley		3
G.P. Wickremasinghe	c Fleming, b Patel	10	c Parore, b Walmsley		9
M. Muralitharan	c Larsen, b Patel	8	run out		7
K.R. Pushpakumara	not out	17	not out		1
Extras	lb 6, nb 4	10	b 6, lb 5, nb 3		14
		——			——
		233			411

NEW ZEALAND

	FIRST INNINGS			SECOND INNINGS	
B.A. Young	c Gurusinha, b Vaas	84	not out		0
D.J. Murray	c Dunusinghe, b Vaas	0	not out		0
M.J. Greatbatch	lbw, b Vaas	0			
S.P. Fleming	run out	66			
*A.C. Parore	c de Silva, b Vaas	19			
D.N. Patel	b Muralitharan	52			
G.R. Larsen	c Gurusinha, b Muralitharan	16			
M.L. Su'a	not out	20			
C. Pringle	c S. Ranatunga, b Vaas	4			
K.P. Walmsley	b Vaas	0			
K.R. Rutherford (capt)	absent hurt	–			
Extras	b 3, lb 28, nb 15	46			0
		——			——
		307	(for no wicket)		0

	O	M	R	W	O	M	R	W
Su'a	20.5	5	43	2	26	3	97	2
Walmsley	18	4	41	1	38	8	121	2
Pringle	15	1	51	3	22	8	55	–
Patel	21	3	62	3	57	20	96	4
Larsen	13	2	30	1	25.4	14	31	1

	O	M	R	W	O	M	R	W
Wickremasinghe	26	6	49	–				
Vaas	40	9	87	6	0.1	–	0	–
Muralitharan	50	20	77	2				
Pushpakumara	16	3	42	–				
de Silva	1	–	11	–				
Gurusinha	6	2	10	–				

FALL OF WICKETS
1–42, 2–67, 3–94, 4–97, 5–122, 6–122, 7–157, 8–178, 9–194
1–11, 2–63, 3–81, 4–273, 5–295, 6–344, 7–355, 8–377, 9–405

FALL OF WICKETS
1–26, 2–26, 3–140, 4–196, 5–197, 6–244, 7–291, 8–303, 9–307

Umpires: D.M. Quested & V.K. Ramaswamy

Match drawn

Sri Lanka's rejoicing was tempered by the New Zealand management's complaints regarding Muralitharan's action. It was not the first time that the off-spinner's action had been questioned, but he has satisfied umpires of various nationalities in different parts of the world.

Not surprisingly, Sri Lanka named an exultant unchanged side for the second Test. New Zealand made three changes. Pringle and Su'a replaced Morrison and Nash who were both injured, and Patel came in for Thomson. Rutherford again won the toss and again asked Sri Lanka to bat. There seemed little justification for his decision when the visitors were 91 for 2 at lunch, but four wickets fell in the afternoon session. Dunusinghe was out in bizarre fashion. Ducking to avoid a low, full toss from Pringle, he was hit on the ear and out leg before wicket. Sri Lanka were 138 for 6 at tea, but batted purposefully in the final session to reach 233, with Vaas hitting his first Test fifty. In truth, Sri Lanka should have been out for under 200, for New Zealand missed several chances. Rutherford split webbing on his left hand in missing one chance at mid-wicket and was unable to bat.

New Zealand closed on 7 for 0, and only 52 overs were possible on the second day. Vaas dismissed Murray and Greatbatch in the same over, and Young and Fleming advanced the score to 95 for 2 by the end of the shortened day. Already, however, it seemed that the scoring was too slow and that too much time had been lost for New Zealand to level the series.

The bowling of Vaas kept Sri Lanka in the game on the third day. He finished with a Test-best return of 6 for 87, figures which he earned fully for his continued accuracy, hostility and ability to move the ball. There was stubborn resistance from Young and Fleming, and New Zealand took a lead of 74 on the first innings, but they were never able to push the score along as quickly as they would have wished.

There were hopes for New Zealand on the fourth day when Sri Lanka were three wickets down and only seven runs ahead, but Gurusinha and Tillekeratne dug in and, by the close, the score was 210 for 3. Both batsmen reached centuries on the last day. Gurusinha batted 516 minutes for his 127, and Tillekeratne took 332 minutes over his second Test century, 108. Ranatunga hit 90, and the game passed out of New Zealand's reach. Their second innings lasted one ball before bad light ended proceedings and gave a jubilant Sri Lanka their first overseas series victory.

It was well deserved, and it added more blight to New Zealand's centenary season.

FIRST ONE-DAY INTERNATIONAL – NEW ZEALAND *v.* SRI LANKA
26 March 1995 at Lancaster Park, Christchurch

NEW ZEALAND

M.J. Greatbatch	b Pushpakumara	17
B.A. Young	run out	3
K.R. Rutherford (capt)	c Gurusinha, b Muralitharan	65
S.P. Fleming	run out	46
C.L. Cairns	c S. Ranatunga, b Pushpakumara	72
*A.C. Parore	b Vaas	31
D.N. Patel	not out	23
J.T.C. Vaughan	not out	1
G.R. Larsen		
M.L. Su'a		
C. Pringle		
Extras	b 2, lb 5, w 5, nb 1	13
(50 overs)	(for 6 wickets)	271

SRI LANKA

A.P. Gurusinha	c Greatbatch, b Vaughan	33
S.T. Jayasuriya	c Greatbatch, b Vaughan	46
S. Ranatunga	run out	11
P.A. de Silva	c and b Vaughan	54
A. Ranatunga (capt)	run out	2
*H.P. Tillekeratne	c Young, b Pringle	10
R.S. Kalpage	c Fleming, b Vaughan	35
W.P.U.C.J. Vaas	run out	27
M. Muralitharan	c Parore, b Cairns	8
K.R. Pushpakumara	c Patel, b Cairns	3
J. Silva	not out	1
Extras	lb 3, w 4, nb 1	8
(47.5 overs)		238

	O	M	R	W
Pushpakumara	10	–	53	2
Vaas	10	1	41	1
Gurusinha	4	–	19	–
Kalpage	8	–	54	–
Muralitharan	10	–	42	1
Silva	8	–	55	–

	O	M	R	W
Pringle	9	1	47	1
Su'a	3	–	35	–
Cairns	7.5	–	49	2
Vaughan	10	1	33	4
Larsen	10	1	38	–
Patel	8	–	33	–

FALL OF WICKETS
1–5, 2–28, 3–122, 4–177, 5–235, 6–265

FALL OF WICKETS
1–83, 2–96, 3–98, 4–105, 5–132, 6–193, 7–208, 8–228, 9–236

Umpires: B.L. Aldridge & D.M. Quested — Man of the Match: K.R. Rutherford — *New Zealand won by 33 runs*

SECOND ONE-DAY INTERNATIONAL – NEW ZEALAND *v.* SRI LANKA
29 March 1995 at Trust Bank Park, Hamilton

NEW ZEALAND

B.A. Young	c Tillekeratne, b Vaas	4
N.J. Astle	b Vaas	95
K.R. Rutherford (capt)	c Kalpage, b Muralitharan	34
S.P. Fleming	c Pushpakumara, b Kalpage	6
C.L. Cairns	c Gamage, b Vaas	42
*A.C. Parore	not out	61
S.A. Thomson	b Jayasuriya	1
D.N. Patel	not out	22
G.R. Larsen		
J.T.C. Vaughan		
C. Pringle		
Extras	lb 9, w 6	15
(50 overs)	(for 6 wickets)	280

SRI LANKA

A.P. Gurusinha	c Larsen, b Pringle	7
S.T. Jayasuriya	c Young, b Patel	6
S. Ranatunga	run out	15
P.A. de Silva	run out	7
A. Ranatunga (capt)	c Parore, b Larsen	27
*H.P. Tillekeratne	not out	39
R.S. Kalpage	c Patel, b Larsen	11
W.P.U.C.J. Vaas	not out	1
M. Muralitharan		
K.R. Pushpakumara		
J.C. Gamage		
Extras	b 1, lb 2, w 1	4
(31 overs)	(for 6 wickets)	117

	O	M	R	W
Pushpakumara	5	–	32	–
Vaas	10	1	36	3
Gamage	5	–	37	–
Kalpage	7	–	35	1
Muralitharan	10	1	62	1
Jayasuriya	10	–	47	1
A. Ranatunga	3	–	22	–

	O	M	R	W
Pringle	7	1	22	1
Patel	10	1	31	1
Vaughan	3	–	18	–
Larsen	6	–	20	2
Thomson	5	–	23	–

FALL OF WICKETS
1–23, 2–83, 3–94, 4–173, 5–242, 6–245

FALL OF WICKETS
1–8, 2–16, 3–30, 4–46, 5–80, 6–111

Umpires: B.F. Bowden & C.E. King — Man of the Match: N.J. Astle — *New Zealand won on faster scoring rate*

SRI LANKA

A.P. Gurusinha	b Cairns	108
S.T. Jayasuriya	c and b Patel	49
P.A. de Silva	c and b Patel	9
A. Ranatunga (capt)	b Pringle	39
R.S. Kalpage	c Rutherford, b Cairns	9
*H.P. Tillekeratne	c Fleming, b Pringle	16
M.C. Mendis	not out	3
W.P.U.C.J. Vaas	not out	1
S. Ranatunga		
M. Muralitharan		
J.C. Gamage		
Extras	b 3, lb 7, w 3, nb 3	16
(50 overs)	(for 6 wickets)	250

NEW ZEALAND

B.A. Young	b Gamage	6
M.J. Greatbatch	c de Silva, b Muralitharan	43
N.J. Astle	b Jayasuriya	35
K.R. Rutherford (capt)	c Jayasuriya, b de Silva	30
C.L. Cairns	c Gamage, b Jayasuriya	15
S.P. Fleming	b Jayasuriya	18
*A.C. Parore	c Mendis, b Kalpage	19
D.N. Patel	c Mendis, b Kalpage	11
J.T.C. Vaughan	run out	5
G.R. Larsen	not out	2
C. Pringle	lbw, b Kalpage	4
Extras	b 1, lb 5, w 4, nb 1	11
(46.3 overs)		199

	O	M	R	W
Pringle	10	–	56	2
Patel	10	1	28	2
Cairns	10	–	45	2
Vaughan	4	–	30	–
Larsen	10	–	49	–
Astle	6	1	32	–

	O	M	R	W
Vaas	8	–	34	–
Gamage	7	–	27	1
Muralitharan	10	–	32	1
Kalpage	9.3	–	47	3
Jayasuriya	10	–	35	3
de Silva	2	–	18	1

FALL OF WICKETS
1–91, **2**–106, **3**–218, **4**–224, **5**–238, **6**–246

FALL OF WICKETS
1–13, 2–80, 3–104, 4–135, 5–139, 6–173, 7–178, 8–192, 9–192

Umpires: D.B. Cowie & R.S. Dunne   *Man of the Match:* A.P. Gurusinha   *Sri Lanka won by 51 runs*

ONE-DAY INTERNATIONAL SERIES

24 **March 1995** *at Lancaster Park, Christchurch*

Canterbury 164 for 9
Sri Lankans 166 for 5 (P.A. de Silva 58 not out)

Sri Lankans won by 5 wickets

There was some consolation for Ken Rutherford and his side when they took the Bank of New Zealand Trophy by beating Sri Lanka 2–1 in the one-day series. Sent in to bat, New Zealand made their highest score in 21 one-day matches at Lancaster Park, and their highest score for 51 matches. Rutherford hit 65 off 75 balls, and Cairns scored at a run a ball after the openers had gone cheaply. Gurusinha and Jayasuriya made 83 in 10 overs, but only 25 were added in the next 10 overs as four wickets fell, a credit to accurate bowling and eager fielding. When he had Tillekeratne caught by Young, Chris Pringle became the fourth New Zealand bowler to take 100 wickets in limited-over internationals. Hadlee, Chatfield and Snedden are ahead of him.

Rain blighted the second match, but Nathan Astle gave further indication of his all-round stature.

Asanka Gurusinha dominated the final encounter in which the Sri Lankan spinners also thrived. So ended a centenary season. The fates had not been kind to New Zealand.

FIRST-CLASS AVERAGES

BATTING

	M	Inns	NO	Runs	HS	Av	100s	50s
M.D. Crowe	2	4	2	273	193*	136.50	1	–
C.D. Lee	2	2	1	120	111*	120.00	1	–
R.G. Twose	9	14	3	736	163*	66.90	3	3
M.W. Douglas	6	8	3	306	100*	61.20	1	2
C.D. McMillan	5	9	2	396	110	56.57	1	2
N.J. Astle	7	12	–	663	191	55.25	2	2
A.C. Parore	5	8	2	293	100*	48.83	1	1
M.J. Greatbatch	7	11	–	526	131	47.81	2	1
C.L. Cairns	3	5	–	227	73	45.40	–	3
J.M. Aiken	8	15	1	628	138	44.85	2	2
C.M. Spearman	10	18	2	689	147	43.06	2	2
A.R. Tait	5	6	2	170	50*	42.50	–	1
D.J. Murray	9	16	1	629	182	41.93	2	2
S.W. Brown	8	11	3	314	76	39.25	–	2
G.R. Stead	5	9	–	342	130	38.00	1	1
G.P. Burnett	7	12	1	417	90	37.90	–	3
A.T. Reinholds	8	14	1	480	97	36.92	–	3
S.P. Fleming	5	9	1	294	66	36.75	–	2
R.T. Latham	6	11	1	367	90*	36.70	–	3
M.D. Bell	6	10	–	357	78	35.70	–	4
M.H. Austen	8	14	2	423	166	35.25	2	–
R.G. Hart	7	10	3	244	57*	34.85	–	1
M.W. Priest	5	8	2	207	98*	34.50	–	2
J.T.C. Vaughan	5	8	2	202	60*	33.66	–	2
J.D. Wells	8	8	2	201	96	33.50	–	1
A.C. Barnes	6	7	1	197	94	32.83	–	1
B.R. Hartland	5	9	–	294	150	32.66	1	1
L.K. Germon	7	12	3	291	64	32.33	–	2
G.R. Larsen	6	7	3	125	33*	31.25	–	–
M.H. Richardson	9	16	–	485	122	30.31	2	1
I.S. Billcliff	8	14	–	422	121	30.14	1	3
D.J. Boyle	3	6	–	178	59	29.66	–	1
C.D. Ingham	7	13	–	374	102	28.76	1	1
P.W. Dobbs	7	12	1	313	81*	28.45	–	2
M.D. Bailey	8	13	1	333	122	27.75	2	–
M.E. Parlane	9	17	1	442	94	27.62	–	1
M.L. Su'a	5	7	2	138	52*	27.60	–	1
B.A. Young	5	10	1	247	84	27.44	–	2
R.G. Petrie	5	7	–	191	80	27.28	–	1
R.A. Jones	8	14	2	326	54*	27.16	–	2
W.A. Wisneski	8	13	1	321	86	26.75	–	3
S.R. Mather	9	14	1	347	126	26.69	1	–
K.R. Rutherford	6	8	–	210	56	26.25	–	1
A.H. Jones	7	14	1	340	78	26.15	–	2
G.E. Bradburn	7	12	1	279	111	25.36	1	1
S.W. Duff	7	12	–	304	62	25.33	–	2
C.Z. Harris	6	9	1	172	60	21.50	–	2
D.N. Patel	7	9	–	188	67	20.88	–	2
J.M. Allan	6	11	–	227	49	20.63	–	–
W. Watson	8	9	2	142	38*	20.28	–	–
A.J. Bradley	5	8	1	142	57	20.28	–	1
S.W.J. Wilson	5	10	–	190	74	19.00	–	1
G.R. Baker	8	8	–	152	47	19.00	–	–
T.E. Blain	7	12	–	220	68	18.33	–	1
L.G. Howell	8	15	1	254	75	18.14	–	1

	M	Inns	NO	Runs	HS	Av	100s	50s
A.J. Gale	7	12	1	193	60	17.54	–	1
G.R.J. Hart	5	9	1	135	55	16.87	–	1
C.J.M. Furlong	5	8	2	101	48	16.83	–	–
M.G. Croy	8	16	–	267	61	16.68	–	1
R.P. Wixon	7	13	5	128	31	16.00	–	–
M.N. Hart	6	10	–	151	45	15.10	–	–
E.J. Marshall	8	14	2	157	52	13.08	–	1
J.B. Cain	8	10	1	116	30	12.88	–	–
M.A. Sigley	7	12	–	153	52	12.75	–	1
S.J. Roberts	6	10	–	124	38	12.40	–	–
P.J. Wiseman	10	18	2	187	35	11.68	–	–

(Qualification – 100 runs, average 10.00)

BOWLING

	Overs	Mds	Runs	Wkts	Av	Best	10/m	5/inn
J.T.C. Vaughan	142.5	52	311	23	13.52	7-34	–	1
M.H. Austen	67.3	18	186	13	14.30	3-11	–	–
G.I. Allott	73.5	17	193	11	17.54	5-45	–	1
C.M. Brown	125	29	374	19	19.68	5-54	–	1
G.R. Larsen	240.1	82	495	25	19.80	6-37	–	1
R.P. de Groen	185.4	42	494	24	20.58	6-72	–	1
W. Watson	315.1	120	623	30	20.76	4-17	–	–
D.N. Patel	286.1	85	614	29	21.17	6-62	–	2
A.J. Gale	194.4	54	429	20	21.45	6-42	–	1
A.R. Tait	131	48	297	13	22.84	3-57	–	–
G.R. Jonas	258.3	69	716	31	23.09	5-60	–	1
D.K. Morrison	244.5	53	647	28	23.10	6-69	–	2
W.A. Wisneski	212	61	533	23	23.17	5-21	–	2
E.J. Marshall	220.5	35	665	28	23.75	6-53	–	2
H.T. Davis	254	58	971	40	24.27	5-46	–	2
C. Pringle	103.4	34	249	10	24.90	4-35	–	–
M.W. Priest	261.5	75	614	24	25.58	7-57	1	1
C.W. Ross	91.3	15	263	10	26.30	4-94	–	–
R.L. Hayes	179.1	35	534	20	26.70	4-59	–	–
S.J. Hotter	124.2	26	409	14	29.21	4-54	–	–
R.J. Kennedy	168.4	43	483	16	30.18	4-50	–	–
S.J. Roberts	172.3	25	680	21	32.38	5-56	–	1
K.P. Walmsley	204.3	40	701	20	35.05	5-73	–	1
A.J. Penn	130	23	398	11	36.18	4-81	–	–
C.J.M. Furlong	220.3	50	622	17	36.58	4-204	–	–
S.B. Styris	129.1	29	370	10	37.00	5-64	–	1
G.E. Bradburn	227.4	77	526	14	37.57	3-44	–	–
P.J. Wiseman	352.4	86	943	24	39.29	4-122	–	–
S.W. Duff	248.5	95	483	12	40.25	3-35	–	–
M.L. Su'a	191.5	35	613	15	40.86	4-82	–	–
M.B. Owens	146.2	35	438	10	43.80	3-45	–	–

(Qualification – 10 wickets)

LEADING FIELDERS

30 – G.R. Baker (ct 29/st 1); 29 – L.K. Germon (ct 27/st 2); 27 – R.G. Hart (ct 26/st 1); 25 – J.B. Cain (ct 23/st 2); 22 – M.G. Croy (ct 21/st 1); 18 – M.A. Sigley (ct 17/st 1); 16 – A.C. Parore; 12 – R.T. Latham; 10 – S.W. Brown.

WEST INDIES

Red Stripe Cup
Australia tour, one-day series and historic Test series
First-class averages

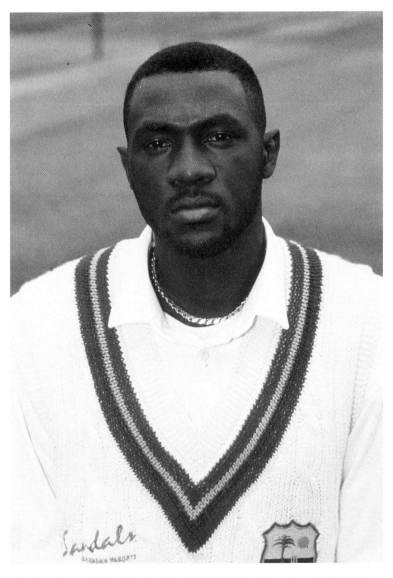

*Courtney Browne led Barbados to victory in the Red Stripe Cup and won his first Test cap
when he appeared in the final match of the series against Australia.
(Gary M. Prior/Allsport)*

The West Indian supremacy in world cricket faced a strong challenge in 1994–95. The West Indian side had fared badly in one-day cricket in India and, due almost entirely to the inspired bowling of Courtney Walsh, had managed to draw the Test series by winning the last encounter. Walsh's bowling had again been the major factor when a weak New Zealand team had been routed in both limited-over and Test cricket.

The versatile Jimmy Adams apart, the West Indian batting had been generally inconsistent, so that the return of Richie Richardson, fit again after his rest from the game through fatigue, was welcome.

Desmond Haynes had declined to make himself available for selection for the tour of India, choosing instead to play in South Africa. His contract in the Republic meant that he missed the first Red Stripe Cup match and, accordingly, the West Indian selectors refused to consider him for a place in the side to face Australia. Haynes complained bitterly at this and even threatened legal action, but the West Indies Board had made their position quite clear, and Haynes had adopted a somewhat ambivalent attitude towards international cricket, and to retirement, for some time.

None underestimated the threat that Australia posed to the crown held by West Indies, even though the Australians had not won a series in the Caribbean for 22 years.

The West Indies' one-day competition had a new format and new sponsors for 1995. The Shell/Sandals Trophy saw the six sides play in two groups with each team meeting the others twice. Carl Hooper's 97 for Guyana against Windwards was the highest score in the tournament, but it was Leeward Islands who qualified to meet Barbados in the final. Leewards won comfortably by 78 runs, with Hamesh Anthony taking 7 for 15, a record for regional limited-over cricket in the Caribbean.

Hamesh Anthony established a record for the one-day domestic competition when he took 7 for 15 for Leeward Islands in the final against Barbados. Anthony later signed to play for Glamorgan in the 1995 season in England. (David Munden/Sportsline)

RED STRIPE CUP

6, 7, 8 and 9 January 1995 *at Sabina Park, Kingston, Jamaica*

Jamaica 282 (R.C. Haynes 95, S.G.B. Ford 50,
   P.I.C. Thompson 4 for 46) and 225
Barbados 298 (F.L. Reifer 85 not out, L.K. Puckerin 55,
   P.A. Wallace 50, N.O. Perry 5 for 41) and 210 for 6
   (P.A. Wallace 71)

Barbados won by 4 wickets

Barbados 16 pts, Jamaica 0 pts

at Guaracara Park, Pointe-à-Pierre, Trinidad

Trinidad & Tobago 405 (D. Williams 112, S. Ragoonath 67) and
   226 (A. Balliram 54, J.E.S. Joseph 5 for 59)
Leeward Islands 288 (D.R.E. Joseph 131, N.B. Francis
   4 for 71) and 263 (R.B. Richardson 86, H.A.G. Anthony 66,
   I.R. Bishop 4 for 44)

Trinidad & Tobago won by 80 runs

Trinidad & Tobago 16 pts, Leeward Islands 0 pts

The most significant events in the opening matches were the return of Ian Bishop and Richie Richardson after injury and illness, a maiden first-class hundred from former Test wicket-keeper David Williams and a remarkable double-act from the Joseph brothers from Antigua, Jenson and Dave. Jenson Joseph had a five-wicket haul on his first-class debut while brother Dave hit a maiden first-class hundred.

13, 14, 15 and 16 January 1995 *at Arnos Vale, St Vincent*

Barbados 440 for 5 dec. (D.L. Haynes 201, F.L. Reifer 81,
   R.L. Hoyte 54) and 26 for 2
Windward Islands 289 (D.A. Joseph 94, W.E. Reid 6 for 73)
   and 175 (D.A. Joseph 80)

Barbados won by 8 wickets

Barbados 16 pts, Windward Islands 0 pts

at Recreation Ground, St John's, Antigua

Leeward Islands 310 (R.B. Richardson 104, D.R.E. Joseph 77,
   B.S. Browne 6 for 81)
Guyana 136 (J.E.S. Joseph 4 for 32) and 90 (L.C. Weekes
   4 for 15, J.E.S. Joseph 4 for 37)

Leewards Islands won by an innings and 84 runs

Leeward Islands 16 pts, Guyana 0 pts

at Sabina Park, Kingston, Jamaica

Jamaica 383 (W.W. Lewis 111, L.R. Williams 64) and 163 for 0
   (R.G. Samuels 77 not out, D.S. Morgan 75 not out)
Trinidad & Tobago 311 (S. Ragoonath 97, P.V. Simmons 83,
   M. Bodoe 56 not out, R.C. Haynes 4 for 95)

Match drawn

Jamaica 8 pts, Trinidad & Tobago 4 pts

The return of Desmond Haynes brought some maturity to
a young Barbados side led by Courtney Browne, the wicket-
keeper. It also brought a second victory in as many
matches and a double century for the 39-year-old opener.
The Joseph brothers again excelled for Leeward Islands
for whom Richie Richardson hit a century to confirm his
total restoration. It is worth considering that had
Leewards not had five players on tour with the Test side in
New Zealand, the Josephs would not have found a place
in the eleven.

20, 21, 22 and **23 January 1995** *at Queen's Park Oval, Port-of-Spain,*
Trinidad

Windward Islands 331 (K.K. Sylvester 73, U. Pope 67,
   R.A. Marshall 65, A.H. Gray 4 for 67) and 177 for 9 dec.
   (N.B. Francis 4 for 57)
Trinidad & Tobago 183 (K. Mason 84, C.E. Cuffy 5 for 60) and
   183 for 5 (A. Balliram 75)

Match drawn

Windward Islands 8 pts, Trinidad & Tobago 4 pts

at Kensington Oval, Bridgetown, Barbados

Guyana 160 (K.F. Semple 54, P.D. Persaud 52, V.C. Drakes
   7 for 47) and 227 (R.A. Harper 77, O.D. Gibson 4 for 52)
Barbados 230 (D.L. Haynes 74, P.A. Wallace 66, R.A. Harper 5
   for 77) and 158 for 4

Barbados won by 6 wickets

Barbados 16 pts, Guyana 0 pts

at Grove Park, Charlestown, Nevis

Leeward Islands 425 (D.R.E. Joseph 112 not out,
   H.A.G. Anthony 75, R.C. Haynes 5 for 95)
Jamaica 264 (N.O. Perry 89, R.G. Samuels 54, W.D. Phillip 8
   for 92) and 94 (W.D. Phillip 5 for 31, J.E.S. Joseph 4 for 19)

Leeward Islands won by an innings and 67 runs

Leeward Islands 16 pts, Jamaica 0 pts

Slow left-arm bowler Warrington Phillip produced not
only the best bowling performance of his career but the
best of the season in the Red Stripe Cup to keep alive
Leeward's hopes of taking the title. He became the only
bowler to take 10 wickets in a match during the season's
competition. Barbados maintained their 100% record when
Vasbert Drakes returned the best bowling performance of
his career and Guyana were beaten by six wickets.

27, 28, 29 and **30 January 1995** *at Mindoo Phillip Park, Castries, St Lucia*

Jamaica 342 (R.G. Samuels 159) and 17 for 2
Windward Islands 141 (N.O. Perry 4 for 29) and 217
   (R.C. Haynes 5 for 82)

Jamaica won by 8 wickets

Jamaica 16 pts, Windward Islands 0 pts

at Albion, Berbice, Guyana

Trinidad & Tobago 360 (P.V. Simmons 74, D. Williams 56,
   M. Bodoe 53, R.A. Harper 4 for 94) and 104 for 6
   (S. Ragoonath 55)
Guyana 171 (N.A. McKenzie 57, A.H. Gray 4 for 40) and 340
   (Sudesh Dhaniram 100, P.D. Persaud 85, I.R. Bishop
   4 for 53)

Match drawn

Trinidad & Tobago 8 pts, Guyana 4 pts

Former Test wicket-keeper David Williams hit a maiden first-class
hundred for Trinidad against Leeward Islands. (Steven Lindsell)

Outstanding all-round cricket from Vasbert Drakes earned him a place in the West Indies side in the one-day series. Drakes is to play for Sussex in 1996. (Ben Radford/Allsport)

Robert Samuels hit a career best for Jamaica, but he became a centre of controversy later when his appointment by the Jamaican selectors as captain for the one-day tournament was overturned by the Jamaica Cricket Board of Control who opted instead for Delroy Morgan. Three selectors resigned in protest.

3, 4, 5 and 6 February 1995 *at Kensington Oval, Bridgetown, Barbados*

Trinidad & Tobago 297 (S. Ragoonath 96, P.V. Simmons 63, D. Williams 61) and 289 (P.V. Simmons 92, K. Mason 64, V.C. Drakes 6 for 75)

Barbados 220 (M. Persad 5 for 63) and 237 (C.O. Browne 70 not out, P.V. Simmons 4 for 52)

Trinidad & Tobago won by 129 runs

Trinidad & Tobago 16 pts, Barbados 0 pts

at Windsor Park, Dominica

Windward Islands 263 (D.A. Joseph 64) and 151 (D. Thomas 55, J.C. Maynard 4 for 19)

Leeward Islands 457 (R.B. Richardson 122, D.R.E. Joseph 102, M.D. Liburd 77, C.E. Cuffy 7 for 80)

Leeward Islands won by an innings and 43 runs

Leeward Islands 16 pts, Windward Islands 0 pts

at Albion, Berbice, Guyana

Guyana 125 (L.R. Williams 5 for 41) and 349 (P.D. Persaud 110, K.F. Semple 57, R.A. Harper 54)

Jamaica 193 and 207 (R.G. Samuels 67, R.A. Harper 4 for 39)

Guyana won by 74 runs

Guyana 16 pts, Jamaica 0 pts

In spite of another fine bowling performance from Drakes, Barbados suffered their only defeat of the season, and, in gaining the victory, Trinidad completed the tournament unbeaten. It was Trinidad's first win at Kensington Oval since 1939. Richie Richardson and Dave Joseph equalled Ralston Otto's record of three centuries in the season for Leeward Islands. Cameron Cuffy produced the best bowling figures of his career, but he still finished on the losing side.

10, 11, 12 and 13 February 1995 *at Bourda, Georgetown, Guyana*

Windward Islands 414 (D.A. Joseph 131, U. Pope 91, R.N. Lewis 53 not out, R.A. Harper 5 for 98, M.V. Nagamootoo 4 for 130) and 10 for 0

Guyana 479 (R.A. Harper 202, Sudesh Dhaniram 79, K.F. Semple 67, R.A. Marshall 4 for 75)

Match drawn

Guyana 8 pts, Windward Islands 4 pts

at Webster Park, Anguilla

Barbados 258 (P.A. Wallace 106, H.A.G. Anthony 4 for 73) and 444 (V.C. Drakes 180 not out, C.O. Browne 74, D.L. Haynes 67, H.A.G. Anthony 4 for 112)

Leeward Islands 222 (V.C. Drakes 4 for 56) and 406 for 5 (R.B. Richardson 152, D.R.E. Joseph 85 not out, R.D. Jacobs 83)

Match drawn

Barbados 8 pts, Leeward Islands 4 pts

Barbados won the Red Stripe Cup when they took first-innings points in the drawn match with Leeward Islands. It was a remarkable match, the first first-class game to be played at Webster Park, Anguilla. Barbados lost their last six wickets for 57 runs, and Leewards their last four for 21 runs. Needing 481 to win, Leewards, inspired by Richardson, Dave Joseph and wicket-keeper Jacobs, got to within 75 of their target before time ran out. They scored at 4.3 an over. That they had been set such a task was due to an astonishing career-best innings of 180 not out by Vasbert Drakes who hit 7 sixes and 15 fours. It earned Drakes a call into the West Indies squad for the one-day internationals, but he and the Joseph brothers were the only young players to grasp the opportunities offered to them in a season when many of the leading players were absent.

In the final Red Stripe Cup match of the season, Roger Harper hit the highest score of the competition. Harper had relinquished the captaincy of Guyana in order to give opportunity to a younger man, Keith Semple.

RED STRIPE CUP FINAL TABLE

	P	W	L	D	Pts
Barbados (5)	5	3	1	1	56
Leeward Islands (1)	5	3	1	1	52
Trinidad & Tobago (2)	5	2	–	3	48
Jamaica (4)	5	1	3	1	29
Guyana (3)	5	1	2	2	28
Windward Islands (6)	5	–	3	2	12

(1994 positions in brackets)

AUSTRALIA TOUR

The Australian touring party arrived in Barbados on 1 March, played a one-day practice match four days later and then took on West Indies in a five-match one-day series.

5 March 1995 *at Kensington Oval, Bridgetown, Barbados*

Australians 330 for 7 (S.R. Waugh 117, G.S. Blewett 78, D.C. Boon 70)

Barbados 278 (A.E. Proverbs 75, T.B.A. May 4 for 50)

Australians won by 52 runs

The first match of the tour offered the Australians little other than acclimatisation to the Kensington Oval where the first one-day international and first Test were to be played. Blewett and Steve Waugh hit 175 for the Australians' second wicket, but the Barbados side was well below strength.

The first one-day international provided a sterner test and was watched by a capacity crowd. Hooper, who had excelled in India but who had missed the tour of New Zealand through malaria, returned to the West Indies side and played an exciting innings which included a six and 8 fours. Lara hit 55 off 66 balls after an uncertain start, and Australia faced a daunting target of 258. They challenged well and needed 13 from the last over, bowled by Ambrose, but they could manage only six as Boon, who had brought victory close, was left stranded at the bowler's end for much of the time in the closing stages.

Led by Healy's energetic innings, Australia took 79 runs from the last 10 overs in the second match of the series to set West Indies a target of 261. Healy's 51 came off 45 balls while, earlier, Steve Waugh had hit 58 off 59 balls. Lara and

---

FIRST ONE-DAY INTERNATIONAL – WEST INDIES v. AUSTRALIA
8 March 1995 at Kensington Oval, Bridgetown, Barbados

WEST INDIES

P.V. Simmons	c Taylor, **b** Warne	37
S.C. Williams	c Healy, **b** Reiffel	11
B.C. Lara	c Taylor, **b** Blewett	55
R.B. Richardson (capt)	run out	9
C.L. Hooper	c May, **b** McDermott	84
J.C. Adams	c M.E. Waugh, **b** McDermott	2
*J.R. Murray	c Healy, **b** M.E. Waugh	12
W.K.M. Benjamin	c May, **b** McDermott	22
V.C. Drakes	c Warne, **b** M.E. Waugh	9
C.E.L. Ambrose	c Taylor, **b** M.E.Waugh	0
C.A. Walsh	not out	6
Extras	**b** 1, **lb** 3, **w** 1, **nb** 5	10
(49.4 overs)		257

AUSTRALIA

M.A. Taylor (capt)	c Simmons, **b** Walsh	41
M.J. Slater	c Adams, **b** Benjamin	21
M.E. Waugh	c Murray, **b** Walsh	29
D.C. Boon	not out	85
S.R. Waugh	**b** Drakes	26
G.S. Blewett	c Walsh, **b** Ambrose	33
*I.A. Healy	run out	0
P.R. Reiffel	not out	10
T.B.A. May		
S.K. Warne		
C.J. McDermott		
Extras	**lb** 1, **w** 5	6
(50 overs)	(for 6 wickets)	251

	O	M	R	W
McDermott	10	–	25	3
Reiffel	10	1	50	1
M.E. Waugh	6.4	–	42	3
Warne	10	1	56	1
Blewett	8	–	44	1
May	5	–	36	–

	O	M	R	W
Ambrose	10	1	43	1
Walsh	10	1	52	2
Benjamin	6.1	–	24	1
Drakes	9.5	–	39	1
Hooper	5	–	46	–
Simmons	9	–	46	–

FALL OF WICKETS
1–26, 2–69, 3–87, 4–155, 5–158, 6–191, 7–241, 8–242, 9–246

FALL OF WICKETS
1–50, 2–94, 3–94, 4–156, 5–235, 6–236

Umpires: L.H. Barker & D. Holder   *Man of the Match:* C.L. Hooper   *West Indies won by 6 runs*

SECOND ONE-DAY INTERNATIONAL – WEST INDIES v. AUSTRALIA
11 March 1995 at Queen's Park Oval, Port-of-Spain, Trinidad

AUSTRALIA			WEST INDIES		
M.J. Slater	c and b Hooper	55	P.V. Simmons	b McGrath	34
M.A. Taylor (capt)	c Walsh, b Ambrose	16	S.C. Williams	lbw, b Reiffel	0
M.E. Waugh	b Benjamin	0	B.C. Lara	c Healy, b Blewett	62
D.C. Boon	c Benjamin, b Simmons	48	C.L. Hooper	c Blewett, b Warne	55
S.R. Waugh	b Walsh	58	J.C. Adams	run out	15
G.S. Blewett	run out	4	K.L.T. Arthurton	c Boon, b McDermott	35
*I.A. Healy	run out	51	*J.R. Murray	lbw, b Reiffel	0
P.R. Reiffel	b Benjamin	14	W.K.M. Benjamin	b Reiffel	3
S.K. Warne	not out	4	V.C. Drakes	c Reiffel, b McDermott	16
C.J. McDermott			C.E.L. Ambrose	b McDermott	1
G.D. McGrath			C.A. Walsh (capt)	not out	0
Extras	lb 3, w 6, nb 1	10	Extras	lb 8, w 4, nb 1	13
(50 overs)	(for 8 wickets)	260	(47.5 overs)		234

	O	M	R	W			O	M	R	W
Ambrose	10	–	47	1		McDermott	6.5	–	37	3
Walsh	8	–	59	1		Reiffel	10	2	32	3
Benjamin	10	–	49	2		McGrath	9	1	36	1
Drakes	10	–	47	–		Warne	10	–	63	1
Hooper	7	–	33	1		Blewett	8	–	43	1
Simmons	5	–	22	1		S.R. Waugh	4	–	15	–

FALL OF WICKETS
1–37, 2–39, 3–93, 4–153, 5–163, 6–207, 7–252, 8–260

FALL OF WICKETS
1–5, 2–79, 3–121, 4–175, 5–182, 6–185, 7–191, 8–232, 9–234

Umpires: S.U. Bucknor & C.E. Cumberbatch   Man of the Match: I.A. Healy   Australia won by 26 runs

THIRD ONE-DAY INTERNATIONAL – WEST INDIES v. AUSTRALIA
12 March 1995 at Queen's Park Oval, Port-of-Spain, Trinidad

WEST INDIES			AUSTRALIA		
P.V. Simmons	c Healy, b Fleming	6	M.A. Taylor (capt)	run out	26
S.C. Williams	run out	6	M.J. Slater	run out	1
B.C. Lara	c Reiffel, b Waugh	139	R.T. Ponting	c Drakes, b Simmons	43
C.L. Hooper	c Slater, b Reiffel	41	D.C. Boon	b Benjamin	4
J.C. Adams	not out	51	S.R. Waugh	c Hooper, b Simmons	44
K.L.T. Arthurton	c Boon, b Waugh	12	G.S. Blewett	st Murray, b Hooper	0
*J.R. Murray	not out	4	*I.A. Healy	c Williams, b Hooper	3
W.K.M. Benjamin			P.R. Reiffel	run out	1
V.C. Drakes			S.K. Warne	b Simmons	12
C.E.L. Ambrose			D.W. Fleming	not out	5
C.A. Walsh (capt)			G.D. McGrath	b Simmons	0
Extras	b 6, lb 11, w 5, nb 1	23	Extras	lb 4, w 4, nb 2	10
(50 overs)	(for 5 wickets)	282	(34.5 overs)		149

	O	M	R	W			O	M	R	W
Reiffel	10	–	36	1		Ambrose	6	1	8	–
Fleming	7.3	1	27	1		Walsh	4	1	14	–
McGrath	10	–	57	–		Benjamin	7	1	31	1
Warne	10	1	52	–		Drakes	7	–	36	–
Blewett	3	–	32	–		Hooper	6	–	38	2
Waugh	9.3	1	61	2		Simmons	4.5	–	18	4

FALL OF WICKETS
1–17, 2–26, 3–125, 4–260, 5–276

FALL OF WICKETS
1–12, 2–50, 3–59, 4–118, 5–124, 6–126, 7–127, 8–129, 9–147

Umpires: S.U. Bucknor & C.E. Cumberbatch   Man of the Match: B.C. Lara   West Indies won by 133 runs

FOURTH ONE-DAY INTERNATIONAL – WEST INDIES v. AUSTRALIA
15 March 1995 at Arnos Vale, St Vincent

AUSTRALIA

Batsman	Dismissal	Runs
M.J. Slater	b Arthurton	68
M.A. Taylor (capt)	c Simmons, b Walsh	3
M.E. Waugh	c Murray, b Benjamin	26
D.C. Boon	b Arthurton	33
S.R. Waugh	c Arthurton, b Simmons	25
G.S. Blewett	b Drakes	4
*I.A. Healy	c Simmons, b Walsh	12
P.R. Reiffel	c Murray, b Walsh	9
S.K. Warne	not out	6
C.J. McDermott	run out	11
G.D. McGrath	not out	1
Extras	lb 5, w 6, nb 1	12
(48 overs)	(for 9 wickets)	210

WEST INDIES

Batsman	Dismissal	Runs
P.V. Simmons	c Healy, b Warne	86
S.L. Campbell	st Healy, b Warne	20
J.C. Adams	b McGrath	3
C.L. Hooper	not out	60
K.L.T. Arthurton	not out	22
*J.R. Murray		
B.C. Lara		
W.K.M. Benjamin		
V.C. Drakes		
C.E.L. Ambrose		
C.A. Walsh (capt)		
Extras	b 2, lb 10, w 4, nb 1	17
(43.1 overs)	{for 3 wickets)	208

	O	M	R	W
Ambrose	8	–	22	–
Walsh	9	–	30	3
Benjamin	7	–	32	1
Drakes	7	–	36	1
Arthurton	10	–	45	2
Simmons	7	–	40	1

	O	M	R	W
McDermott	9	1	46	–
Reiffel	9	1	37	–
McGrath	10	1	40	1
Warne	9.1	3	33	2
Blewett	3	–	26	–
Boon	3	–	14	–

FALL OF WICKETS
1–6, 2–57, 3–130, 4–137, 5–152, 6–171, 7–190, 8–190, 9–209

FALL OF WICKETS
1–47, 2–56, 3–152

Umpires: L.H. Barker & G.T. Johnson   Man of the Match: P.V. Simmons   West Indies won on faster scoring rate

FIFTH ONE-DAY INTERNATIONAL – WEST INDIES v. AUSTRALIA
18 March 1995 at Bourda, Georgetown, Guyana

AUSTRALIA

Batsman	Dismissal	Runs
M.A. Taylor (capt)	c Adams, b Hooper	66
M.J. Slater	c Holder, b Drakes	41
M.E. Waugh	run out	70
S.R. Waugh	c Benjamin, b Hooper	11
R.T. Ponting	b Hooper	0
J.L. Langer	run out	6
*I.A. Healy	c Williams, b Simmons	36
P.R. Reiffel	c Campbell, b Benjamin	22
B.P. Julian	b Walsh	11
T.B.A. May	not out	3
G.D. McGrath		
Extras	b 2, lb 11, w 4, nb 3	20
(50 overs)	(for 9 wickets)	286

WEST INDIES

Batsman	Dismissal	Runs
S.C. Williams	c and b M.E. Waugh	45
S.L. Campbell	b Reiffel	9
P.V. Simmons	c Slater, b S.R. Waugh	70
C.L. Hooper	c Slater, b Reiffel	50
J.C. Adams	not out	60
K.L.T. Arthurton	c M.E. Waugh, b McGrath	0
R.I.C. Holder	not out	34
*J.R. Murray		
W.K.M. Benjamin		
V.C. Drakes		
C.A. Walsh (capt)		
Extras	lb 10, w 3, nb 6	19
(47.2 overs)	(for 5 wickets)	287

	O	M	R	W
Simmons	9	–	54	1
Walsh	8	2	38	1
Benjamin	9	–	51	1
Drakes	6	–	46	1
Arthurton	7	–	48	–
Hooper	10	–	36	3

	O	M	R	W
Reiffel	10	1	48	2
Julian	10	1	66	–
May	7	–	42	–
McGrath	8.2	–	51	1
M.E. Waugh	3	–	23	1
S.R. Waugh	9	–	47	1

FALL OF WICKETS
1–78, 2–166, 3–204, 4–204, 5–205, 6–229, 7–259, 8–276, 9–286

FALL OF WICKETS
1–17, 2–108, 3–172, 4–192, 5–193

Umpires: C. Duncan & E. Nicholls   Man of the Match: C.L. Hooper   West Indies won by 5 wickets

Brian Lara during his innings of 139 in the third one-day international. (Ben Radford/Allsport)

Hooper gave West Indies every encouragement with fluent half-centuries, but the Australian seamers maintained control and accuracy. The last seven wickets went down for 59 runs, and Australia levelled the series.

The third match, in Trinidad, belonged to Brian Lara. The left-handed maestro hit his first international century on home turf, and his 139 came off only 125 balls. He hit 3 sixes and 15 fours, displaying his full array of shots and that blend of delicate timing and sheer power which make him the great player that he is. He received splendid support from Hooper and from Adams with whom he added 135 off 115 balls. Frustrated by accurate bowling and excellent fielding, Australia lost their last seven wickets for 31 runs in the space of 41 deliveries. This was the second heaviest defeat that Australia had suffered at the hands of West Indies in a one-day international.

Australia did not simply suffer defeat at Queen's Park Oval, they also lost the services of Damien Fleming who injured his shoulder. Fleming was deemed unfit to take any further part in the tour and was sent home. Brendon Julian flew to the Caribbean as replacement.

West Indies clinched the series by taking the fourth match after Australia had chosen to bat first on a lively pitch. Rain interrupted the innings and reduced the match to a 48-over contest, and further rain reduced the West Indies' innings to 46 overs and a target of 206. At 61 for 2 after 20 overs, the home side were dithering, but the introduction of Blewett in place of Warne liberated Simmons who hit 86. He and the ever-impressively elegant Hooper added 96 off 89 balls, and Hooper remained unbeaten with 60 off 65 balls.

In Guyana, Australia made their highest-ever score against West Indies in a limited-over international and yet were beaten by five wickets with 16 balls to spare. With the series decided, both sides rested key players. Richardson, who had damaged a shoulder in the opening encounter, was still unfit and Walsh continued to lead the side. Australia began briskly, with Mark Waugh scoring 70 off 56 balls, but Carl Hooper, given a tumultuous reception on his own ground, took three middle-order wickets, and it

was left to Healy and Reiffel to rejuvenate the innings. A second-wicket stand of 91 off 13 overs between Simmons and Williams set the tone of the West Indian reply. Hooper and Adams maintained the momentum, but Simmons and Hooper were brilliantly caught by Slater, and Arthurton was out first ball. Adams and Holder sealed victory with an unbroken partnership of 94 off 17 overs. West Indies' score was the highest that they made to win a one-day international when batting second.

TEST SERIES

20, 21 and 22 March 1995 *at Bourda, Georgetown, Guyana*

Guyana 105 (G.D. McGrath 5 for 47) and 207 (K.F. Semple 67, B.P. Julian 5 for 54)

Australians 373 (G.S. Blewett 116, M.E. Waugh 75, J.L. Langer 55)

Australians won by an innings and 61 runs

26, 27 and 28 March 1995 *at Mindoo Phillip Park, Castries, St Lucia*

Australians 322 for 5 dec. (M.J. Slater 90, S.R. Waugh 73 not out, M.E. Waugh 73)

President's XI 261 for 5 (D.R.E. Joseph 83, K.L.T. Arthurton 75 not out)

Match drawn

The Australians engaged in two first-class matches in preparation for the Test series, but their joy in outplaying Guyana and in performing well in the rain-ruined match in Castries was overshadowed by the injury to Craig McDermott which was to keep him out of the series. McDermott was jogging along the sea wall in Georgetown when he tore ligaments in his left ankle. It was determined that he would not recover until the end of the tour, and it was decided that Carl Rackemann should join the party on the completion of the Sheffield Shield final. This meant that Australia entered the Test series without the services of their two main strike bowlers, McDermott and Fleming. The Australian attack would now be spearheaded by Julian, Reiffel and McGrath. As it transpired, this trio performed magnificently in the first match of the series, in Barbados.

West Indies omitted Arthurton and opted for the diminutive opening pair of Williams and Campbell. Within six overs, this pair, and Richie Richardson, were back at the pavilion, and West Indies were 6 for 3. Julian, in particular, found unexpected pace, and his accuracy and late movement accounted for Williams, taken at slip, and Richardson, cutting a wide-ish ball into the wicket-keeper's gloves.

Lara and Hooper counter-attacked majestically. They transformed the innings and, by lunch, West Indies were 116 for 3. Hooper launched a deliberately savage attack on Warne who conceded 23 runs in his first two overs, and it was apparent that the West Indian batsmen were determined to dispel the threat of Warne from the outset.

Six overs after lunch, Julian broke the stand, which had brought 124 runs at more than one a minute, when he had Hooper taken at first slip. Adams was looking fluent and positive when McGrath had him caught at third slip, and Lara was out in the next over.

Lara had passed 2,000 runs in Test cricket and had hit 8 fours when he slashed Julian to gully. Steve Waugh juggled with the ball before scooping it up in his right hand. Umpire Barker nodded that the catch had been taken, and Lara was out although television shots suggested that the ball might have touched the ground before it was caught.

Winston Benjamin hit Warne for six, but Warne claimed his revenge next ball. Murray fell to the accurate McGrath, and West Indies were bowled out in 48.1 overs for a meagre 195. This was a triumph for Australia's zest and determination in the field and for bowling that was constantly attacking, relentlessly accurate and, for the most part, totally inspired.

Australia must have been surprised to find themselves batting with 35 overs of the first day remaining. They responded positively, but Slater cut fiercely at Winston Benjamin's first ball, a long-hop, and was spectacularly caught in the gully by Stuart Williams. Boon and Taylor took the score to 72 before Boon spliced a catch to

Winston Benjamin is caught at slip by Taylor off Warne for 14. Taylor's slip-catching was a feature of the series. (Shaun Botterill/Allsport)

FIRST TEST MATCH – WEST INDIES *v.* AUSTRALIA
31 March, 1, and 2 April 1995 at Kensington Oval, Bridgetown, Barbados

WEST INDIES

	FIRST INNINGS		SECOND INNINGS	
S.C. Williams	c Taylor, b Julian	1	c Healy, b McGrath	10
S.L. Campbell	c Healy, b Reiffel	0	c S.R. Waugh, b Warne	6
B.C. Lara	c S.R. Waugh, b Julian	65	c Healy, b McGrath	9
R.B. Richardson (capt)	c Healy, b Julian	0	(5) b Reiffel	36
C.L. Hooper	c Taylor, b Julian	60	(4) c Reiffel, b Julian	16
J.C. Adams	c Warne, b McGrath	16	not out	39
*J.R. Murray	c Taylor, b McGrath	21	c S.R. Waugh, b Warne	23
W.K.M. Benjamin	c Taylor, b Warne	14	lbw, b McGrath	26
C.E.L. Ambrose	c Blewett, b McGrath	7	c Blewett, b McGrath	6
C.A. Walsh	c S.R. Waugh, b Warne	1	b McGrath	4
K.C.G. Benjamin	not out	0	b Warne	5
Extras	lb 3, w 1, nb 6	10	lb 1, nb 8	9
		195		189

AUSTRALIA

	FIRST INNINGS		SECOND INNINGS	
M.J. Slater	c Williams, b W. Benjamin	18	(2) not out	20
M.A. Taylor (capt)	c Hooper, b K. Benjamin	55	(1) not out	16
D.C. Boon	c W. Benjamin, b Walsh	20		
M.E. Waugh	c Murray, b Ambrose	40		
S.R. Waugh	c Murray, b K. Benjamin	65		
G.S. Blewett	c Murray, b Ambrose	14		
*I.A. Healy	not out	74		
B.P. Julian	c K. Benjamin, b Hooper	31		
P.R. Reiffel	b W. Benjamin	1		
S.K. Warne	c Adams, b Walsh	6		
G.D. McGrath	b W. Benjamin	4		
Extras	lb 13, nb 5	18	nb 3	3
		346	(for no wicket)	39

	O	M	R	W	O	M	R	W
Reiffel	11	2	41	1	11	6	15	1
Julian	12	–	36	4	11	2	41	1
McGrath	12.1	1	46	3	22	6	68	5
Warne	12	2	57	2	26.3	5	64	3
M.E. Waugh	1	–	12	–				

	O	M	R	W	O	M	R	W
Ambrose	20	7	41	2				
Walsh	25	5	78	2	3	–	19	–
K. Benjamin	20	1	84	2	2.5	1	14	–
W. Benjamin	23.2	6	71	3				
Hooper	12	–	59	1	1	–	6	–

FALL OF WICKETS
1–1, 2–5, 3–6, 4–130, 5–152, 6–156, 7–184, 8–193, 9–194
1–19, 2–25, 3–31, 4–57, 5–91, 6–135, 7–170, 8–176, 9–180

FALL OF WICKETS
1–27, 2–72, 3–121, 4–166, 5–194, 6–230, 7–290, 8–291, 9–331

Umpires: L.H. Barker & S. Venkataraghavan

Australia won by 10 wickets

ABOVE: *Warne bowls Kenneth Benjamin to end the West Indies' second innings, and Australia are close to victory. (Shaun Botterill/Allsport)*

RIGHT: *Man of the Match Glen McGrath. (Shaun Botterill/Allsport)*

mid-wicket, but Australia were well content to close on 91 for 2.

If the first day was much in favour of Australia, the second was conclusively theirs. A barrage of short-pitched deliveries was met by sound application. Kenny Benjamin, having dropped Mark Waugh at long-leg, had Taylor caught at second slip, and Ambrose broke a stand between the Waugh twins just as it threatened to flourish. Blewett flirted too often outside the off stump, but Steve Waugh attacked with relish. Whatever shortcomings he was once said to possess against fast bowling had disappeared. He punched 8 fours in a two-hour innings of immense character, and Australia led.

What Steve Waugh had started, Ian Healy brilliantly completed. In three hours, he drove, pulled, cajoled and ran so that 116 runs were realised for the last four wickets. He hit both Hooper and Walsh for sixes, and Australia took a commanding lead of 151 on the first innings. West Indies reduced the deficit by 13 before the end of the day.

Warne started the bowling on the third morning, and his seventh delivery, a long-hop, was hit hard by Campbell into the hands of mid-wicket. Lara survived a vociferous appeal for a bat-pad catch off Warne, but the reprieve was brief, for both he and Williams were soon gone, caught at the wicket off McGrath, destined to be Man of the Match.

Hooper drove Julian to deep mid-off and, 57 for 4, West Indies faced the humiliation of an innings defeat. Richardson and Adams briefly dismissed such thoughts until, in the last over before lunch, Richardson was bowled by Reiffel. Adams and Murray showed a resilience others had lacked and saved the ignominy of the innings defeat, but they were separated by a wonderful running, diving catch by Steve Waugh, and West Indies were doomed.

Stung by their defeat in the first Test match, West Indies dropped the inexperienced Campbell for the second encounter and recalled Arthurton. Richie Richardson himself took on the responsibility of opening the innings, and he took something of a gamble when he won the toss and asked Australia to bat. It seemed a rash decision as Taylor and Slater struck 82 in the pre-lunch session, but, on the stroke of lunch, Taylor attempted to pull Ambrose and top-edged the ball to fine-leg. In the second over after the break, Walsh had Slater taken bat and pad, and Mark Waugh caught at second slip.

Australia never totally recovered from this setback. Several batsmen promised more than they achieved, three of them were hit on the helmet, and Walsh produced another outstanding display of fast bowling to match those he had offered in India and New Zealand. The visitors were bowled out for 216, and West Indies, with Williams dropped on two by Blewett, ended the day on 14.

Although Williams soon fell to Warne on the second morning, West Indies seemed to seize the match as Lara and Richardson scored 72 in 13 overs. The dominant partner was Lara who, on the ground where he scored 375 against England a year earlier, reached 50 off 48 balls with what was his 11th four. The loss of Richardson did not hinder his flow of runs and, some three-quarters of an hour after lunch, West Indies were 168 for 2. Steve Waugh had recently joined the attack and, aided by Taylor's intelligent field-placing – soundly based on a study of his opponents – he took two vital wickets. Boon had taken up a position at short wide-ish mid-on to counter Lara's flick off his legs. When the left-hander played the shot against Steve Waugh, Boon flung himself to his left and held the catch high and wide as he tumbled backwards. In his next over, Waugh had Hooper caught by a diving Julian, and West

ABOVE: *Michael Slater in aggressive mood against Carl Hooper. (Shaun Botterill/Allsport)*

RIGHT: *David Boon has his off stump knocked out of the ground by Courtney Walsh. (Clive Mason/Allsport)*

SECOND TEST MATCH – WEST INDIES v. AUSTRALIA
8, 9, 10, 12 and 13 April 1995 at Recreation Ground, St John's, Antigua

AUSTRALIA

	FIRST INNINGS		SECOND INNINGS	
M.J. Slater	c Adams, b Walsh	41	(2) c Richardson, b Walsh	18
M.A. Taylor (capt)	c Walsh, b Ambrose	37	(1) c Murray, b Walsh	5
D.C. Boon	b Walsh	21	lbw, b W. Benjamin	67
M.E. Waugh	c Hooper, b Walsh	4	b W. Benjamin	61
S.R. Waugh	b K. Benjamin	15	not out	65
G.S. Blewett	c Murray, b W. Benjamin	11	c Williams, b Hooper	19
*I.A. Healy	c Walsh, b W. Benjamin	14	c Richardson, b Walsh	26
B.P. Julian	b Walsh	22	run out	6
P.R. Reiffel	not out	22	not out	13
S.K. Warne	c Arthurton, b Walsh	11		
G.D. McGrath	c Murray, b Walsh	0		
Extras	lb 12, nb 6	18	b 1, lb 9, nb 10	20
		216	(for 7 wickets, dec.)	**300**

WEST INDIES

	FIRST INNINGS		SECOND INNINGS	
S.C. Williams	c Boon, b Warne	16	not out	31
R.B. Richardson (capt)	c S.R. Waugh, b Julian	37	b Reiffel	2
B.C. Lara	c Boon, b S.R. Waugh	88	b Julian	43
J.C. Adams	lbw, b Warne	22	not out	3
C.L. Hooper	c Julian, b S.R. Waugh	11		
K.L.T. Arthurton	c Taylor, b Warne	26		
*J.R. Murray	lbw, b Reiffel	26		
W.K.M. Benjamin	c Taylor, b McGrath	4		
C.E.L. Ambrose	c Taylor, b Reiffel	0		
C.A. Walsh	b Reiffel	9		
K.C.G. Benjamin	not out	5		
Extras	b 6, lb 3, w 1, nb 6	16	nb 1	1
		260	(for 2 wickets)	**80**

	O	M	R	W	O	M	R	W
Ambrose	14	5	34	1	19	3	42	–
Walsh	21.3	7	54	6	36	7	92	3
K. Benjamin	16	3	58	1	15	1	51	–
W. Benjamin	15	2	40	2	24	2	72	2
Hooper	2	–	18	–	9	3	16	1
Adams					4	–	16	–
Arthurton					1	–	1	–

	O	M	R	W	O	M	R	W
Reiffel	17	3	53	3	6	2	12	1
Julian	10	5	36	1	5	2	15	1
Warne	28	9	83	3	7	–	18	–
McGrath	20.1	5	59	1	6	2	20	–
S.R. Waugh	6	1	20	2				
M.E. Waugh					6	2	15	–

FALL OF WICKETS
1–82, 2–84, 3–89, 4–126, 5–126, 6–150, 7–168, 8–188, 9–204
1–22, 2–43, 3–149, 4–162, 5–196, 6–254, 7–273

FALL OF WICKETS
1–34, 2–106, 3–168, 4–186, 5–187, 6–240, 7–240, 8–240, 9–254
1–11, 2–69

Umpires: S.U. Bucknor & D.R. Shepherd

Match drawn

Another victim for Walsh – Julian is bowled after gallant resistance.
(Shaun Botterill/Allsport)

No play was possible before lunch on the last day so that a draw became inevitable. Taylor's declaration left West Indies 36 overs in which to score 257 to win. Lara hit 5 fours in his 43 before being bowled as he drove wildly at Julian.

15, 16 and 17 April 1995 at Basseterre, St Kitts

West Indies' Board XI 262 (N.O. Perry 57, O.D. Gibson 55) and 253 for 6 (R.G. Samuels 95, S.L. Campbell 53)

Australians 317 (G.S. Blewett 93, M.A. Taylor 62, M.J. Slater 60, O.D. Gibson 4 for 45, H.A.G. Anthony 4 for 70)

Match drawn

The second and third Test matches were separated by a game between the tourists and a representative eleven in St Kitts. Ricky Ponting's hopes of winning a place in the Test side were blighted when he was taken ill on the eve of the match.

Both sides were unchanged for the third Test match which was played in Trinidad on a pitch with doubtful credentials for Test cricket. Only 40 overs were possible on the opening day, but, in that time, Australia, having been put in to bat, lost seven wickets in scoring 112 runs. Steve Waugh ended the day unbeaten after making 54 of those runs. It was another innings of tremendous courage and technical excellence.

The pitch, heavily grassed, was encouraging to the West Indian pace men from the second over of the match when Slater, caught in two minds, gave a simple catch to the keeper. In the next over, Taylor pushed the ball into the hands of short square-leg. Ambrose, it seemed, had refound the fire which he had lacked in the first two matches of the series, and his leg-cutter accounted for Mark Waugh. The field closed in, but a flurry of strokes and a stoppage for rain broke the tension.

Ambrose was seemingly incensed by the sight of Steve Waugh, but Waugh stood firm, and it was Boon, playing his 100th Test match, who was the next Ambrose victim. He was turned square and edged the ball to Richardson who took a diving catch at third slip. Blewett fell to a faint inside edge, and Healy was caught by Richardson after the ball had rebounded from Murray's gloves. Julian was taken at short square-leg, but Steve Waugh, having offered two difficult chances, remained unbeaten.

He was still unbeaten when the innings closed the following morning, Ambrose dismissing Warne and McGrath to finish with five wickets, but if West Indies believed that they had done all the hard work, they were immediately corrected. Williams and Richardson were soon gone, and Lara looked ragged before being caught at first slip off McGrath. Adams was cool and composed for $2\frac{1}{2}$ hours, displaying the class and authority which had served his side well in India and New Zealand. Hooper offered forceful support, and 30 came in three overs when Steve Waugh joined the attack, but Taylor's ploy was

Indies' dreams of a substantial lead evaporated. The last five wickets went down for 20 runs, and the lead was no more than 44. Taylor and Slater reduced this by 16 runs before the close.

Only 34 overs in four separate sessions were possible on the third day, and, although Walsh accounted for both openers, Boon and Mark Waugh batted with an authority that took the score to 134 in spite of a plethora of short-pitched deliveries to which Australian batsmen were now well accustomed.

Boon was leg before offering no stroke, and Mark Waugh was yorked when play resumed after the rest day. Both batsmen were out in the first 40 minutes, and both fell to Winston Benjamin. Steve Waugh and Blewett suffered some anxious moments, but Waugh's resolution carried him through, and Blewett fell, not to the pace bowlers, but to Hooper who, given two overs before lunch, had the South Australian caught in the second of them. It was another astonishing catch, low at slip by Williams, in a series of miraculous catches.

A fighting partnership of 58 between Steve Waugh and Ian Healy tilted the game in Australia's favour, and when rain ended play early Australia were 273 for 7, 229 runs ahead. Steve Waugh was on 52.

ABOVE: *Richie Richardson pulls Glen McGrath to the boundary during his century which was the first of the series. (Clive Mason/Allsport)*

LEFT: *Ambrose sparked West Indies to success in Trinidad with nine wickets in the match. Boon stands bewildered having been caught by Richardson. (Shaun Botterill/Allsport)*

THIRD TEST MATCH – WEST INDIES v. AUSTRALIA
21, 22 and 23 April 1995 at Queen's Park Oval, Port-of-Spain, Trinidad

AUSTRALIA

	FIRST INNINGS		SECOND INNINGS	
M.A. Taylor (capt)	c Adams, b Ambrose	2	(2) c Murray, b K. Benjamin	30
M.J. Slater	c Murray, b Walsh	0	(1) c Richardson, b Walsh	15
D.C. Boon	c Richardson, b Ambrose	18	c sub (Chanderpaul), b Walsh	9
M.E. Waugh	c Murray, b Ambrose	2	lbw, b Ambrose	7
S.R. Waugh	not out	63	c Hooper, b K. Benjamin	21
G.S. Blewett	c Murray, b W. Benjamin	17	c Murray, b K. Benjamin	2
*I.A. Healy	c Richardson, b Walsh	8	b Ambrose	0
B.P. Julian	c Adams, b K. Benjamin	0	b Ambrose	0
P.R. Reiffel	c Lara, b Walsh	11	c Hooper, b Ambrose	6
S.K. Warne	b Ambrose	0	c Hooper, b Walsh	11
G.D. McGrath	c Murray, b Ambrose	0	not out	0
Extras	lb 6, w 1	7	lb 3, nb 1	4
		128		**105**

WEST INDIES

	FIRST INNINGS		SECOND INNINGS	
S.C. Williams	c Taylor, b Reiffel	0	c Warne, b M.E. Waugh	42
R.B. Richardson (capt)	c Healy, b McGrath	2	not out	38
B.C. Lara	c Taylor, b McGrath	24	not out	14
J.C. Adams	c M.E. Waugh, b Reiffel	42		
C.L. Hooper	c Reiffel, b S.R. Waugh	21		
K.L.T. Arthurton	c M.E. Waugh, b McGrath	5		
*J.R. Murray	c Healy, b McGrath	13		
W.K.M. Benjamin	c Slater, b Warne	7		
C.E.L. Ambrose	c Slater, b McGrath	1		
C.A. Walsh	c Blewett, b McGrath	14		
K.C.G. Benjamin	not out	1		
Extras	lb 4, nb 2	6	b 4	4
		136	(for 1 wicket)	**98**

	O	M	R	W	O	M	R	W
Ambrose	16	5	45	5	10.1	1	20	4
Walsh	17	4	50	3	13	4	35	3
W. Benjamin	6	3	13	1	5	–	15	–
K. Benjamin	8	2	14	1	8	1	32	3

	O	M	R	W	O	M	R	W
McGrath	21.5	11	47	6	6	1	22	–
Reiffel	16	7	26	2	6	2	21	–
Julian	7	1	24	–	3	–	16	–
S.R. Waugh	3	1	19	1				
Warne	12	5	16	1	3.5	–	26	–
M.E. Waugh					2	–	9	1

FALL OF WICKETS
1–2, 2–2, 3–14, 4–37, 5–62, 6–95, 7–98, 8–121, 9–128
1–26, 2–52, 3–56, 4–85, 5–85, 6–85, 7–87, 8–87, 9–105

FALL OF WICKETS
1–1, 2–6, 3–42, 4–87, 5–95, 6–106, 7–113, 8–114, 9–129
1–81

Umpires: D.R. Shepherd & C.E. Cumberbatch

West Indies won by 9 wickets

rewarded as Hooper swung at a bouncer and was caught at long-leg.

The rest of the batting offered little resistance, and the tall, competitive McGrath outshone Ambrose with six wickets. West Indies led by only eight runs and, by the close, Taylor and Slater had pushed Australia 12 runs ahead.

The third day began with Australia nursing hopes of building a big score on a pitch which was easing, but this was not to be. Slater was caught off his glove off a ball which reared from a length, and Kenny Benjamin straightened a delivery to have Taylor caught behind. In the next over, Boon cut Walsh into the hands of gully. The Waugh twins responded positively, and Steve hit 21 off 19 balls, but they were out within two balls of each other, Steve steering to slip and Mark palpably leg before to the first ball of an Ambrose over. With his third ball, Ambrose wrecked Healy's stumps. Julian, too, had his stumps spreadeagled, and although Warne and Reiffel offered temporary relief, the Australian innings was over inside 37 overs in little more than two hours. The last seven wickets had fallen for a mere 20 runs.

Left 98 runs to win, West Indies began uncertainly, but the pitch had lost something of its venom. Williams gained in confidence, and Richardson, confirmed as captain for the tour of England, began to show nimble footwork. Williams was caught off his glove from a ball by Mark Waugh which lifted sharply, but this brought in Lara to complete the victory with, in view of what had gone before, remarkable ease. And so, with one match to play, the series was level.

Both sides entered the final Test with a smouldering grievance. West Indies were still upset by the catch which Steve Waugh had claimed to dismiss Lara in the first Test; Australia were less than happy about the under-prepared pitch on which they had been asked to play the third encounter. West Indies were forced to make one change on the eve of the Jamaican Test. Junior Murray was unwell, and Courtney Browne of Barbados made his Test debut. Taylor lost the toss for the fourth time in the series, and West Indies batted.

The second ball of the match saw the departure of Williams, caught at short-cover by the diving Blewett. Characteristically, Lara faced a crisis with aggression. He was soon lashing the ball to all parts of the field, but he was living dangerously, constantly encouraging the bowlers with mis-hits and edges which narrowly eluded fielders. With Richardson, who batted with restraint fitting the occasion, he added 103 at a run a minute.

The stand was broken by Warne whom West Indies had tried, unsuccessfully, to blast out of the series from the very first over he bowled in Barbados. Lara played back, got an edge onto his pads and Healy, alert as ever, nipped

---

FOURTH TEST MATCH – WEST INDIES v. AUSTRALIA
29, 30 April, 1 and 3 May 1995 at Sabina Park, Kingston, Jamaica

WEST INDIES

	FIRST INNINGS		SECOND INNINGS	
S.C. Williams	c Blewett, b Reiffel	0	b Reiffel	20
R.B. Richardson (capt)	lbw, b Reiffel	100	c and b Reiffel	14
B.C. Lara	c Healy, b Warne	65	lbw, b Reiffel	0
J.C. Adams	c Slater, b Julian	20	c S.R. Waugh, b McGrath	18
C.L. Hooper	c M.E. Waugh, b Julian	23	(6) run out	13
K.L.T. Arthurton	c Healy, b McGrath	16	(7) lbw, b Warne	14
*C.O. Browne	c Boon, b Warne	1	(8) not out	31
W.K.M. Benjamin	lbw, b S.R. Waugh	7	(5) lbw, b Reiffel	51
C.E.L. Ambrose	not out	6	st Healy, b Warne	5
C.A. Walsh	c Boon, b S.R. Waugh	2	c Blewett, b Warne	14
K.C.G. Benjamin	c Healy, b Reiffel	5	c Taylor, b Warne	6
Extras	b 1, lb 9, w 1, nb 9	20	b 13, lb 8, nb 6	27
		265		213

AUSTRALIA

	FIRST INNINGS	
M.A. Taylor (capt)	c Adams, b Walsh	8
M.J. Slater	c Lara, b Walsh	27
D.C. Boon	c Brown, b Ambrose	17
M.E. Waugh	c Adams, b Hooper	126
S.R. Waugh	c Lara, b K. Benjamin	200
G.S. Blewett	c W. Benjamin, b Arthurton	69
*I.A. Healy	c Lara, b W. Benjamin	6
B.P. Julian	c Adams, b Walsh	8
P.R. Reiffel	b K. Benjamin	23
S.K. Warne	c Lara, b K. Benjamin	0
G.D. McGrath	not out	3
Extras	b 11, lb 6, w 1, nb 26	44
		531

	O	M	R	W	O	M	R	W
Reiffel	13.4	2	48	3	18	5	47	4
Julian	12	3	31	2	10	2	37	–
McGrath	20	4	79	1	13	2	28	1
Warne	25	6	72	2	23.4	8	70	4
S.R. Waugh	11	5	14	2	4	–	9	–
M.E. Waugh	4	1	11	–	1	–	1	–

	O	M	R	W
Ambrose	21	4	76	1
Walsh	33	6	103	3
K. Benjamin	23.5	–	106	3
Hooper	43	9	94	1
Adams	11	–	38	–
Arthurton	5	1	17	1
W. Benjamin	24	3	80	1

FALL OF WICKETS
1–0, 2–103, 3–131, 4–188, 5–220, 6–243, 7–250, 8–251, 9–254
1–37, 2–37, 3–46, 4–98, 5–134, 6–140, 7–166, 8–172, 9–204

FALL OF WICKETS
1–17, 2–50, 3–73, 4–304, 5–417, 6–433, 7–449, 8–523, 9–523

Umpires: S.U. Bucknor & K.E. Liebenberg

Australia won by an innings and 53 runs

round from behind the stumps to scoop up the chance.

In contrast, Richardson had reached 68 by tea, but, in the process, he had lost Adams, who mistimed a pull, and Hooper, taken at second slip. Arthurton was taken low down by Healy, and Browne nudged Warne to short-leg. Richardson reached his patient and invaluable hundred and then, wearily, he missed a straight ball from Reiffel. The West Indian innings had fallen apart, and the Australian bowlers could be proud of a first day's work which saw their opponents out for 265 on a strip that looked full of runs.

The Australian batsmen proved that looks were not deceiving when, on the second day, they succeeded where West Indies had failed. Early signs were in favour of the home side. In the fourth over, Taylor was caught at forward short-leg off a full-blooded hit that seemed destined for the mid-wicket boundary. Adams was but three paces from the bat, yet he held on to a breathtaking catch. Boon was adjudged caught at the wicket, and Slater perished to another brilliant catch when he hooked a short ball from Walsh, and Lara sprinted in and flung himself forward. This left Australia on 73 for 3, and it brought together the Waugh twins. In 57 overs of electric stroke-play, they added 231.

Rarely can this gifted, exciting pair have batted better. They were together 3¾ hours, and they reduced the West Indian pace quartet to impotence. Mark Waugh raced to his hundred off 145 balls. Steve took 180 balls to reach three figures. This was glorious stuff, and their partnership contained a six – Steve off Hooper – 2 fives and 23 fours. The twins had tilted the match decisively and thrillingly in favour of Australia.

The Waugh twins shared a record fourth-wicket stand of 231. (Shaun Botterill/Allsport)

Mark was out before the close, having hit his eighth Test century, but Steve was unbeaten on 110, and, 321 for 4, Australia gave no hint of surrendering the initiative.

On the third morning, Blewett played just the innings that was required. He allowed Steve Waugh to adopt a more sedate, anchor role than he had done on the first day while he attacked jubilantly to make 69 out of a stand worth 113. He was out on the stroke of lunch by which time Steve Waugh had advanced to 141. By tea, Waugh was on 177.

TEST MATCH AVERAGES – WEST INDIES v. AUSTRALIA

WEST INDIES BATTING

	M	Inns	NO	Runs	HS	Av	100s	50s
B.C. Lara	4	8	1	308	88	44.00	–	3
R.B. Richardson	4	8	1	229	100	32.71	1	–
J.C. Adams	4	7	2	160	42	32.00	–	–
C.L. Hooper	4	6	–	144	60	24.00	–	1
J.R. Murray	3	4	–	83	26	20.75	–	–
W.K.M. Benjamin	4	6	–	109	51	18.16	–	1
S.C. Williams	4	8	1	120	42	17.14	–	–
K.L.T. Arthurton	3	4	–	61	26	15.25	–	–
C.A. Walsh	4	6	–	44	14	7.33	–	–
K.C.G. Benjamin	4	6	3	22	6	7.33	–	–
C.E.L. Ambrose	4	6	1	25	7	5.00	–	–

Played in one Test: S.L. Campbell 0 & 6; C.O. Browne 1 & 31*

WEST INDIES BOWLING

	Overs	Mds	Runs	Wkts	Av	Best	10/m	5/inn
K.L.T. Arthurton	6	1	18	1	18.00	1-17	–	–
C.E.L. Ambrose	100.1	25	258	13	19.84	5-45	–	1
C.A. Walsh	148.3	33	431	20	21.55	6-54	–	1
W.K.M. Benjamin	97.2	16	291	9	32.33	3-71	–	–
K.C.G. Benjamin	93.4	9	359	10	35.90	3-32	–	–
C.L. Hooper	67	12	193	3	64.33	1-16	–	–
J.C. Adams	15	–	54	–	–	–	–	–

WEST INDIES FIELDING FIGURES

12 – J.R. Murray; 7 – J.C. Adams; 5 – C.L. Hooper, B.C. Lara and R.B. Richardson; 2 – S.C. Williams, W.K.M. Benjamin and C.A. Walsh; 1 – K.L.T. Arthurton, C.O. Browne, K.C.G. Benjamin and sub (S. Chanderpaul)

AUSTRALIA BATTING

	M	Inns	NO	Runs	HS	Av	100s	50s
S.R. Waugh	4	6	2	429	200	107.25	1	3
M.E. Waugh	4	6	–	240	126	40.00	1	1
I.A. Healy	4	6	1	128	74*	25.60	–	1
M.A. Taylor	4	7	1	153	55	25.50	–	1
D.C. Boon	4	6	–	152	67	25.33	–	1
M.J. Slater	4	7	1	139	41	23.16	–	–
G.S. Blewett	4	6	–	132	69	22.00	–	1
P.R. Reiffel	4	6	2	76	23	19.00	–	–
B.P. Julian	4	6	–	67	31	11.16	–	–
S.K. Warne	4	5	–	28	11	5.60	–	–
G.D. McGrath	4	5	2	7	4	2.33	–	–

AUSTRALIA BOWLING

	Overs	Mds	Runs	Wkts	Av	Best	10/m	5/inn
S.R. Waugh	24	7	62	5	12.40	2-14	–	–
P.R. Reiffel	98.4	29	263	15	17.53	4-47	–	–
G.D. McGrath	121.1	32	369	17	21.70	6-47	–	2
B.P. Julian	70	15	236	9	26.22	4-36	–	–
S.K. Warne	138	35	406	15	27.06	4-70	–	–
M.E. Waugh	14	3	48	1	48.00	1-9	–	–

AUSTRALIA FIELDING FIGURES

10 – I.A. Healy (ct 9/st 1) and M.A. Taylor; 6 – S.R. Waugh; 5 – G.S. Blewett; 4 – D.C. Boon; 3 – M.J. Slater, M.E. Waugh and P.R. Reiffel; 2 – S.K. Warne; 1 – B.P. Julian

Healy was out soon after the break, but Julian survived 10 overs, and Reiffel stayed 26 overs while 74 runs were scored. This still left Waugh short of his double century when joined by the last man, McGrath, a noted 'rabbit', but an all-run four took him to 200. He faced 425 balls and batted for 9¼ hours. He hit a six, a five and 17 fours, and he took Australia to a massive 266-run lead. This was, indeed, a great innings.

Nor were West Indies' troubles at an end. In 14 overs before the close, they lost three wickets for 63 runs. In his fourth over, Reiffel caught and bowled Richardson; in his fifth, he skidded a ball through that trapped Lara leg before for nought; in his sixth, he persuaded Williams to chop the ball into his stumps. Australia were on the brink of an historic victory.

On the rest day, the rains came, and Australia feared that they would be thwarted by the weather, but play started on time on the Wednesday. Cracks had begun to appear, and it was apparent that survival would be no easy task as the day wore on. The Australian bowlers, unlike the West Indians, bowled a full length, but Winston

Benjamin defended well, and the only wicket to fall before lunch was that of Jimmy Adams, taken low in the gully off McGrath.

Night-watchman Winston Benjamin reached a gallant fifty soon after lunch, but he was leg before next ball. In Reiffel's next over, Hooper played the ball backward of square and went for a totally unnecessary second run. He was beaten by Julian's throw which smashed into the stumps. This was a terrible waste of a vital wicket. Arthurton hit Warne for four and six and was then leg before. Warne quickly mopped up the tail. It was inevitable he would have the last say. Kenny Benjamin was caught at slip on the stroke of tea, and West Indies were beaten in a home Test series for the first time in 22 years, and in any Test series for the first time in 15 years.

It was appropriate that Taylor should take the final catch. He had led his side with imagination, intelligence and a constant sense of purpose. But this was a memorable team effort by a party totally supportive of each other and totally committed to the ambition of beating West Indies.

FIRST-CLASS AVERAGES

BATTING

	M	Inns	NO	Runs	HS	Av	100s	50s
D.R.E. Joseph	7	10	2	606	131	75.75	3	3
D.L. Haynes	4	8	1	471	201*	67.28	1	2
S. Ragoonath	6	11	2	516	97	57.33	–	4
R.G. Samuels	7	13	2	615	159	55.90	1	4
R.B. Richardson	9	15	1	773	152	55.21	4	1
D.A. Joseph	5	10	1	443	131	49.22	1	3
F.L. Reifer	5	10	3	308	85*	44.00	–	2
B.C. Lara	4	8	1	308	88	44.00	–	3
P.V. Simmons	5	9	–	377	92	41.88	–	4
D. Williams	5	9	1	318	112	39.75	1	2
C.O. Browne	7	12	4	316	74	39.50	–	2
P.A. Wallace	6	11	–	432	106	39.27	1	3
R.A. Harper	6	11	–	396	202	36.00	1	2
D.S. Morgan	5	10	1	307	75*	34.11	–	1
K.L.T. Arthurton	4	5	1	136	75*	34.00	–	1
Sudesh Dhaniram	6	11	–	369	100	33.54	1	1
V.C. Drakes	6	9	1	268	180*	33.50	1	–
R.D. Jacobs	6	8	1	233	83	33.28	–	1
M. Bodoe	5	9	3	197	56*	32.83	–	2
J.C. Adams	4	7	2	160	42	32.00	–	–
P.D. Persaud	6	11	–	348	110	31.63	1	2
S.G.B. Ford	5	8	3	152	50	30.40	–	1
N.O. Perry	6	10	1	270	89	30.00	–	2
L.K. Puckerin	5	9	–	268	55	29.77	–	1
M.D. Liburd	5	7	–	207	77	29.57	–	1
J. Eugene	4	8	1	202	46	28.85	–	–
K.F. Semple	7	13	–	369	67	28.38	–	4
V. Pope	5	9	–	251	91	27.88	–	2
H.A.G. Anthony	6	8	1	195	75	27.85	–	2
K. Mason	5	9	–	239	84	26.55	–	2
D. Thomas	4	7	1	158	55	26.33	–	1
N.A. McKenzie	5	9	–	219	57	24.33	–	1
W.W. Lewis	5	9	–	218	111	24.22	1	–
R.C. Haynes	5	8	–	193	95	24.12	–	1
R.A. Marshall	5	9	–	217	65	24.11	–	1
C.L. Hooper	4	6	–	144	60	24.00	–	1
J.E.S. Joseph	5	7	–	151	44	21.57	–	–
A. Balliram	5	9	–	174	75	19.33	–	2
K.K. Sylvester	4	8	–	149	73	18.62	–	1
W.K.M. Benjamin	4	6	–	109	51	18.16	–	1
L.A. Harrigan	5	7	–	124	63	17.71	–	1
L.R. Williams	4	6	–	106	64	17.66	–	1
S.C. Williams	4	8	1	120	42	17.14	–	–
W.D. Phillip	5	6	–	101	39	16.83	–	–
A.H. Gray	5	8	–	131	44	16.37	–	–
F.A. Rose	5	8	1	113	26	16.14	–	–
O.D. Gibson	6	8	–	115	55	14.37	–	1

(Qualification – 100 runs, average 10.00)

BOWLING

	Overs	Mds	Runs	Wkts	Av	Best	10/m	5/inn
W.D. Phillip	167.1	48	434	28	15.50	8-92	1	2
J.E.S. Joseph	154.5	30	512	28	18.28	5-59	–	1
W.E. Reid	250.1	77	533	27	19.74	6-73	–	1
C.E.L. Ambrose	100.1	25	258	13	19.84	5-45	–	1
R.A. Harper	281.2	81	540	27	20.00	5-77	–	2
I.R. Bishop	88.3	16	345	17	20.29	4-44	–	–
C.A. Walsh	148.3	33	431	20	21.55	6-54	–	1
N.O. Perry	185.4	45	437	20	21.85	5-41	–	1
L.R. Williams	86	23	223	10	22.30	5-41	–	1
R.C. Haynes	234.4	53	550	24	22.91	5-82	–	2
V.C. Drakes	182	24	661	28	23.60	7-47	–	2
B. St A. Browne	139.3	25	455	19	23.94	6-81	–	1
I.B.A. Allen	70	5	242	10	24.20	2-11	–	–
A.H. Gray	126.2	19	447	17	26.29	4-40	–	–
M. Persad	199.1	44	500	19	26.31	5-63	–	1
O.D. Gibson	200.1	26	703	26	27.03	4-45	–	–
P.I.C. Thompson	82	10	276	10	27.60	4-46	–	–
H.A.G. Anthony	150.4	27	512	18	28.44	4-70	–	–
L.C. Weekes	116	7	470	16	29.37	4-15	–	–
C.E. Cuffy	153.1	22	513	17	30.17	7-80	–	2
P.V. Simmons	118	25	337	11	30.63	4-52	–	–
J.B. Grant	107.3	19	338	11	30.72	3-43	–	–
M.V. Nagamootoo	170.3	27	482	15	32.13	4-130	–	–
N.B. Francis	130	20	529	15	35.26	4-57	–	–
K.C.G. Benjamin	93.4	9	359	10	35.90	3-32	–	–

(Qualification – 10 wickets)

LEADING FIELDERS

24 – C.O. Browne (ct 20/st 4); 22 – D. Williams (ct 21/st 1); 19 – V. Pope (ct 18/st 1); 16 – R.D. Jacobs (ct 13/st 3); 15 – S.G.B. Ford (ct 10/st 5); 12 – J.R. Murray; 11 – D.R.E. Joseph and P.V. Simmons; 10 – R.A. Hooper

SHARJAH

The Asia Cup – India, Pakistan, Sri Lanka and Bangladesh

Sanath Jayasuriya whose brisk batting against Pakistan earned Sri Lanka a place in the final of the Asia Cup. (David Munden/Sportsline)

India won the Asia Cup for the third time in succession, but the competition tended to be overshadowed by the problems attending Pakistan. The suspension of Salim Malik while allegations of bribery were investigated – coupled with the omission of Ijaz Ahmed, the retirement of Rashid Latif and Basit Ali, and the injury to Waqar Younis – gave the side a strange appearance, with several faces new to international cricket. Moin Khan, who had lost his place to Rashid, was restored and appointed captain, but he was injured after the second match and was forced to return home. Saeed Anwar joined the long list of recent Pakistan captains, and another newcomer, Javed Qadir, arrived to keep wicket. Wasim Akram initially refused to join the side as he was in dispute with the Pakistan Board because he wanted his wife to accompany him to Sharjah and stay in the team hotel. The matter was resolved, and Wasim eventually arrived.

Meanwhile, back on the pitch, Bangladesh bowled out a Test-playing country for the first time when they dismissed Sri Lanka for 233 in the second match. Saiful Islam became the first Bangladeshi bowler to take four wickets in a one-day international.

Sri Lanka qualified for the final when they reached their target against Pakistan within 31 overs, but in the final, they were routed by the batting of Sidhu and Azharuddin.

QUALIFYING TABLE

	P	W	L	Pts	R/R
India	3	2	1	4	4.85
Sri Lanka	3	2	1	4	4.71
Pakistan	3	2	1	4	4.59
Bangladesh	3	–	3	0	2.93

ABOVE RIGHT: *Wicket-keeper Romesh Kaluwitharana was restored to the Sri Lankan side and had five catches and a stumping in the vital match against Pakistan. (David Munden/Sportsline)*

RIGHT: *Navjot Singh Sidhu – brilliant batting for India in the final. (David Munden/Sportsline)*

ASIA CUP – MATCH ONE – INDIA v. BANGLADESH
5 April 1995 at Sharjah C.A. Stadium

BANGLADESH

Athar Ali Khan	c Mongia, b Srinath	17
Mohammad Javed	run out	18
Sajjad Ahmed	c Mongia, b Prabhakar	4
Aminul Islam Bulbul	c Vaidya, b Chatterjee	30
Minhazul Abedin	run out	21
Akram Khan (capt)	c Chatterjee, b Vaidya	24
Enamul Haq	lbw, b Prabhakar	8
Mohammad Rafique	b Kumble	2
*Khalid Masud	lbw, b Kumble	4
Saiful Islam	not out	22
Anis-ur-Rehman	c Sidhu, b Vaidya	2
Extras	lb 7, w 1, nb 3	11
(44.4 overs)		163

INDIA

M. Prabhakar	not out	53
S.R. Tendulkar	b Mohammad Rafique	48
N.S. Sidhu	not out	56
M. Azharuddin (capt)		
V.G. Kambli		
S.V. Manjrekar		
*N.R. Mongia		
A.R. Kumble		
J. Srinath		
P.S. Vaidya		
U. Chatterjee		
Extras	lb 1, w 5, nb 1	7
(27.5 overs)	(for 1 wicket)	164

	O	M	R	W
Prabhakar	10	–	43	2
Srinath	8	3	21	1
Chatterjee	10	–	28	1
Vaidya	8.4	1	41	2
Kumble	8	–	23	2

	O	M	R	W
Anis-ur-Rehman	5	–	42	–
Saiful Islam	5	–	31	–
Enamul Haq	6	–	25	–
Mohammad Rafique	5	–	15	1
Athar Ali Khan	3	–	22	–
Minhazul Abedin	3	–	19	–
Aminul Islam Bulbul	0.5	–	9	–

FALL OF WICKETS
1–30, 2–40, 3–51, 4–93, 5–99, 6–114, 7–119, 8–125, 9–138

FALL OF WICKET
1–72

Umpires: N.T. Plews & I.D. Robinson   *Man of the Match:* M. Prabhakar   *India won by 9 wickets*

ASIA CUP – MATCH TWO – SRI LANKA v. BANGLADESH
6 April 1995 at Sharjah C.A. Stadium

SRI LANKA

A.P. Gurusinha	c Aminul Islam, b Saiful Islam	0
S.T. Jayasuriya	c Khalid Masud, b Saiful Islam	51
R.S. Mahanama	b Hasibul Hassan	2
P.A. de Silva	c Khalid Masud, b Minhazul Abedin	36
A. Ranatunga (capt)	b Saiful Islam	71
H.P. Tillekeratne	c Habibul Bashar, b Mohammad Rafique	37
R.S. Kalpage	run out	1
*C.I. Dunasinghe	run out	1
W.P.U.C.J. Vaas	c Mohammad Akram, b Saiful Islam	11
M. Muralitharan	c Mohammad Akram, b Mohammad Rafique	6
J.C. Gamage	not out	7
Extras	lb 5, w 5	10
(49.4 overs)		233

BANGLADESH

Athar Ali Khan (capt)	run out	2
Sajjad Ahmed	c Jayasuriya, b Muralitharan	11
Habibul Bashar	c de Silva, b Gamage	16
Aminul Islam Bulbul	lbw, b Gamage	0
Minhazul Abedin	c Dunasinghe, b Kalpage	26
Mohammad Akram	c Ranatunga, b Vaas	24
Enamul Haq	c Vaas, b Jayasuriya	1
*Khalid Masud	c and b Muralitharan	15
Mohammad Rafique	st Dunasinghe, b Muralitharan	13
Saiful Islam	c Vaas, b Muralitharan	5
Hasibul Hassan	not out	1
Extras	b 4, lb 4, w 4	12
(44.2 overs)		126

	O	M	R	W
Saiful Islam	10	2	36	4
Hasibul Hassan	6	2	29	1
Athar Ali Khan	7	–	28	–
Enamul Haq	10	–	38	–
Minhazul Abedin	6	–	30	1
Mohammad Rafique	8.4	–	50	2
Aminul Islam Bulbul	2	–	17	–

	O	M	R	W
Vaas	7	4	9	1
Gamage	7	2	17	2
Muralitharan	8.2	1	23	4
Ranatunga	5	–	24	–
Jayasuriya	7	–	19	1
Kalpage	10	1	26	1

FALL OF WICKETS
1–0, 2–8, 3–101, 4–194, 5–197, 6–198, 7–203, 8–213, 9–220

FALL OF WICKETS
1–4, 2–32, 3–32, 4–42, 5–76, 6–85, 7–100, 8–112, 9–123

Umpires: N.T. Plews & C.J. Mitchley   *Man of the Match:* A. Ranatunga   *Sri Lanka won by 107 runs*

ASIA CUP – MATCH THREE – INDIA v. PAKISTAN
7 April 1995 at Sharjah C.A. Stadium

PAKISTAN

Aamir Sohail	c Tendulkar, b Srinath	40
Saeed Anwar	c Azharuddin, b Kumble	25
Ghulam Ali	c Tendulkar, b Chatterjee	13
Inzamam-ul-Haq	b Venkatesh Prasad	88
Asif Mujtaba	run out	4
*Moin Khan (capt)	b Chatterjee	2
Wasim Akram	run out	50
Zafar Iqbal	b Kumble	18
Naeem Ashraf	not out	8
Nadeem Khan	run out	2
Aqib Javed		
Extras	lb 8, w 7, nb 1	16
(50 overs)		266

INDIA

M. Prabhakar	c Moin Khan, b Aqib Javed	0
S.R. Tendulkar	c Moin Khan, b Aqib Javed	4
N.S. Sidhu	lbw, b Zafar Iqbal	54
M. Azharuddin (capt)	c Asif Mujtaba, b Aqib Javed	11
V.G. Kambli	b Aqib Javed	0
S.V. Manjrekar	c Asif Mujtaba, b Aamir Sohail	50
*N.R. Mongia	hit wkt, b Wasim Akram	18
J. Srinath	c and b Aqib Javed	0
A.R. Kumble	run out	0
U. Chatterjee	not out	3
Venkatesh Prasad	c Moin Khan, b Aamir Sohail	3
Extras	lb 8, w 7, nb 11	26
(42.4 overs)		169

	O	M	R	W
Prabhakar	10	–	64	–
Srinath	9	–	60	1
Venkatesh Prasad	8	–	43	1
Kumble	8	–	29	2
Tendulkar	7	–	27	–
Chatterjee	8	–	35	2

	O	M	R	W
Wasim Akram	8	–	23	1
Aqib Javed	9	1	19	5
Zafar Iqbal	8	–	34	1
Naeem Ashraf	6	–	40	–
Nadeem Khan	10	–	42	–
Aamir Sohail	1.4	–	3	2

FALL OF WICKETS
1–58, 2–73, 3–104, 4–122, 5–133, 6–214, 7–255, 8–255, 9–266

FALL OF WICKETS
1–2, 2–11, 3–37, 4–37, 5–105, 6–144, 7–151, 8–151, 9–152

Umpires: I.D. Robinson & C.J. Mitchley *Man of the Match:* Inzamam-ul-Haq *Pakistan won by 97 runs*

ASIA CUP – MATCH FOUR – PAKISTAN v. BANGLADESH
8 April 1995 at Sharjah C.A. Stadium

BANGLADESH

Athar Ali Khan	c Moin Khan, b Wasim Akram	2
Javed Omar	b Aamir Nazir	9
Habibul Bashar	b Wasim Akram	0
Aminul Islam Bulbul	c and b Arshad Khan	42
Minhazul Abedin	c Moin Khan, b Aamir Nazir	0
Akram Khan (capt)	run out	44
Naimur Rehman	run out	3
*Khalid Masud	not out	27
Enamul Haq	run out	7
Saiful Islam	not out	3
Hasibul Hassan		
Extras	lb 1, w 9, nb 4	14
(50 overs)	(for 8 wickets)	151

PAKISTAN

Aamir Sohail	c Naimur Rehman, b Saiful Islam	30
Saeed Anwar	c Khalid Masud, b Hasibul Hassan	18
Ghulam Ali	c and b Naimur Rehman	38
Inzamam-ul-Haq	not out	29
Asif Mujtaba	b Athar Ali Khan	0
Wasim Akram	not out	30
*Moin Khan (capt)		
Aqib Javed		
Zafar Iqbal		
Aamir Nazir		
Arshad Khan		
Extras	lb 1, w 6	7
(29.4 overs)	(for 4 wickets)	152

	O	M	R	W
Wasim Akram	10	–	25	2
Aqib Javed	10	–	29	–
Zafar Iqbal	5	1	8	–
Aamir Nazir	7	–	23	2
Arshad Khan	10	–	29	1
Aamir Sohail	8	1	36	–

	O	M	R	W
Saiful Islam	7	–	33	1
Hasibul Hassan	8	–	43	1
Enamul Haq	4	–	20	–
Naimur Rehman	6.4	–	29	1
Athar Ali Khan	2	–	10	1
Minhazul Abedin	2	–	16	–

FALL OF WICKETS
1–12, 2–16, 3–19, 4–19, 5–91, 6–97, 7–119, 8–133

FALL OF WICKETS
1–35, 2–68, 3–106, 4–107

Umpires: I.D. Robinson & N.T. Plews *Man of the Match:* Wasim Akram *Pakistan won by 6 wickets*

ASIA CUP – MATCH FIVE – INDIA v. SRI LANKA
9 April 1995 at Sharjah C.A. Stadium

SRI LANKA

A.P. Gurusinha	c Mongia, b Srinath	15
S.T. Jayasuriya	b Kumble	31
R.S. Mahanama	c Azharuddin, b Prasad	11
P.A. de Silva	c Tendulkar, b Prasad	21
A. Ranatunga (capt)	lbw, b Srinath	5
H.P. Tillekeratne	run out	48
*R.S. Kaluwitharana	c Jadeja, b Prasad	1
H.D.P.K. Dharmasena	run out	30
W.P.U.J.C. Vaas	not out	10
C.P.H. Ramanayake	b Prabhakar	0
J.C. Gamage	not out	1
Extras	lb 12, w 12, nb 5	29
(50 overs)	(for 9 wickets)	202

INDIA

M. Prabhakar	c Tillekeratne, b Jayasuriya	60
S.R. Tendulkar	not out	112
N.S. Sidhu	c and b Jayasuriya	3
J. Srinath	not out	14
M. Azharuddin (capt)		
A.D. Jadeja		
S.V. Manjrekar		
*N.R. Mongia		
A.R. Kumble		
Venkatesh Prasad		
A.R. Kapoor		
Extras	lb 3, w 13, nb 1	17
(33.1 overs)	(for 2 wickets)	206

	O	M	R	W
Prabhakar	10	1	51	1
Srinath	10	1	35	2
Venkatesh Prasad	10	–	37	3
Kumble	10	–	37	1
Kapoor	10	–	30	–

	O	M	R	W
Vaas	9	–	67	–
Gamage	3	–	23	–
Ramanayake	4.1	–	38	–
Dharmasena	5	–	16	–
Jayasuriya	10	–	42	2
de Silva	2	–	17	–

FALL OF WICKETS
1–25, 2–60, 3–70, 4–76, 5–105, 6–113, 7–184, 8–196, 9–199

FALL OF WICKETS
1–161, 2–167

Umpires: N.T. Plews & C.J. Mitchley   *Man of the Match:* S.R. Tendulkar   *India won by 8 wickets*

ASIA CUP – MATCH SIX – PAKISTAN v. SRI LANKA
11 April 1995 at Sharjah C.A. Stadium

PAKISTAN

Aamir Sohail	c Kaluwitharana, b Vaas	0
Saeed Anwar (capt)	c Gurusinha, b Ramanayake	4
Asif Mujtaba	c Kaluwitharana, b Ramanayake	13
Inzamam-ul-Haq	c Kaluwitharana, b Vaas	73
Mahmood Hamid	run out	1
Wasim Akram	st Kaluwitharana, b Jayasuriya	6
Naeem Ashraf	c Kaluwitharana, b Muralitharan	16
Zafar Iqbal	run out	13
*Javed Qadir	c Jayasuriya, b Ramanayake	12
Arshad Khan	not out	9
Aamir Nazir	not out	9
Extras	lb 4, w 17, nb 1	22
(50 overs)	(for 9 wickets)	178

SRI LANKA

R.S. Mahanama	c Arshad Khan, b Aamir Sohail	48
S.T. Jayasuriya	c Arshad Khan, b Aamir Nazir	30
A.P. Gurusinha	run out	14
P.A. de Silva	c Javed Qadir, b Aamir Sohail	23
A. Ranatunga (capt)	not out	23
*R.S. Kaluwitharana	b Wasim Akram	17
H.P. Tillekeratne	not out	8
R.S. Kalpage		
W.P.U.C.J. Vaas		
C.P.H. Ramanayake		
M. Muralitharan		
Extras	lb 9, w 7, nb 1	17
(30.5 overs)	(for 5 wickets)	180

	O	M	R	W
Vaas	10	3	30	2
Ramanayake	10	1	25	3
Jayasuriya	10	1	31	1
Muralitharan	10	–	42	1
Kalpage	10	–	46	–

	O	M	R	W
Wasim Akram	9	–	37	1
Aamir Nazir	5	–	47	1
Zafar Iqbal	5	–	25	–
Naeem Ashraf	1	–	12	–
Arshad Khan	5.5	–	29	–
Aamir Sohail	5	–	21	2

FALL OF WICKETS
1–0, 2–19, 3–22, 4–25, 5–38, 6–74, 7–137, 8–156, 9–158

FALL OF WICKETS
1–34, 2–65, 3–118, 4–137, 5–165

Umpires: I.D. Robinson & C.J. Mitchley   *Man of the Match:* S.T. Jayasuriya   *Sri Lanka won by 5 wickets*

ASIA CUP FINAL – INDIA v. SRI LANKA
14 April 1995 at Sharjah C.A. Stadium

SRI LANKA				INDIA			
R.S. Mahanama	b Kumble	15		M. Prabhakar	c Kaluwitharana, b Vaas	9	
S.T. Jayasuriya	c Mongia, b Prasad	22		S.R. Tendulkar	c Jayasuriya, b Ramanayake	41	
A.P. Gurusinha	run out	85		N.S. Sidhu	not out	84	
P.A. de Silva	c Mongia, b Prabhakar	13		M. Azharuddin (capt)	not out	90	
A. Ranatunga (capt)	run out	3		A.D. Jadeja			
H.P. Tillekeratne	c Mongia, b Prasad	22		S.V. Manjrekar			
*R.S. Kaluwitharana	b Kumble	18		*N.R. Mongia			
R.S. Kalpage	not out	7		J. Srinath			
W.P.U.C.J. Vaas	not out	8		A.R. Kumble			
C.P.H. Ramanayake				A.R. Kapoor			
M. Muralitharan				Venkatesh Prasad			
Extras	lb 23, w 10, nb 4	37		Extras	lb 1, w 7, nb 1	9	
(50 overs)	(for 7 wickets)	230		(41.5 overs)	(for 2 wickets)	233	

	O	M	R	W		O	M	R	W
Prabhakar	10	–	45	1	Vaas	9	–	52	1
Srinath	9	2	38	–	Ramanayake	8.5	–	52	1
Venkatesh Prasad	10	1	32	2	Jayasuriya	6	–	38	–
Kumble	10	1	50	2	Muralitharan	10	–	46	–
Kapoor	10	–	32	–	Kalpage	8	–	44	–
Tendulkar	1	–	10	–					

FALL OF WICKETS
1–46, 2–46, 3–81, 4–89, 5–150, 6–192, 7–218

FALL OF WICKETS
1–48, 2–58

Umpires: N.T. Plews & C.J. Mitchley   *Man of the Match:* M. Azharuddin   *India won by 8 wickets*

Saeed Anwar, the latest captain of Pakistan. (David Munden/ Sportsline)

ENGLAND

Cricket – the world game. Northamptonshire v. Holland in the first round of the NatWest Trophy at Northampton in June.
(Ben Radford/Allsport)

INTRODUCTION TO THE SEASON
David Lemmon

English cricket took a terrible battering in the winter of 1994–5. The defeats in Australia were received with a media hostility which was severe even by English standards. Each day in the New Year brought another formula for the reconstruction of English cricket which, we were assured, would bring success. Some wanted a cricket academy, and the Australian version received plaudits and praise out of all proportion to the reality of its achievements. Some wanted the abolition of the one-day game and ignored the fact that Australian cricketers play more one-day internationals than anyone else in the world. Some wanted divisional representative matches, ignoring the fact that the Rugby Football Union, for example, were contemplating scrapping theirs because no one watched them, and they had little value in shaping an international side. The past history of Test trials should have told us that. Some wanted fewer counties although there had only recently been an increase in the number to 18. In all plans, the paying member was disregarded even though the game had been built upon his/her support and generosity.

Early in the season, there was yet another plan, this time from the counties who were privileged to have Test matches played at their headquarters. They wanted more say in affairs and a bigger slice of the cake. It seemed that they assumed their privilege as a right and that cricket essentially consisted of five days in August. They envisaged a type of premier league but forgot, perhaps, that in soccer more people value the club than the country, and that it is easier to buy a ticket for an international than it is to obtain one for Arsenal, Manchester United or Liverpool.

Once all this smoke had cleared, the counties and players could get on with playing the game, and there were many new faces to admire.

There had been some turmoil at Derbyshire which had seen Bowler leave to join Somerset, and the highly talented Chris Adams express a desire also to leave the county. He did not, and he was joined in the Derbyshire line-up by Daryll Cullinan, the South African, one of several overseas players fresh to county cricket.

Another to enjoy his first season in the county game was the Indian Manoj Prabhakar who joined Durham. Prabhakar had been set to play for Warwickshire in 1994, but he was injured and was replaced by Brian Lara who, it will be remembered, met with some success. Durham had a new captain in Mike Roseberry who had severed his connection with Middlesex to return north. Jason Boiling, too, left the London area to join the county in which he had been to university.

Most turmoil and surprise surrounded Essex. They signed Neil Williams from Middlesex, and Nicholas Derbyshire from Lancashire, but they lost three key players in Knight, Stephenson and Shahid, and they were subjected to a newspaper-article attack from the recently released Don Topley. Topley's article was rightly dismissed as nonsense, but other problems would not go away.

There had been much debate as to who should succeed

Nick Knight whose move from Essex to Warwickshire was the subject of much angry debate. (Paul Sturgess/Sportsline)

Gooch as captain, and, in the end, Paul Prichard was appointed. John Stephenson had been a main contender and, hurt at being overlooked, he left Essex to become vice-captain of Hampshire and, ultimately, to succeed Mark Nicholas as captain.

There were further complications in that young Essex batsmen asserted that they had been informed by the club that Essex intended only to register a bowler as their overseas player in the foreseeable future and that all would have an equal chance to compete for places in the side. It was then announced that Mark Waugh would rejoin Essex in 1995. This led to Nadeem Shahid asking to be released from his contract and joining Surrey. It may have also influenced Nick Knight's decision to leave Essex and join Warwickshire, although there were other more significant influences here.

It was hard to credit Knight's assertion that he felt he would have a better chance of winning an England cap at Warwickshire and that his chances had been limited at Essex. He had been promoted to open the innings, had been awarded his county cap and had won a place in the England 'A' side at the end of 1994. It transpired that

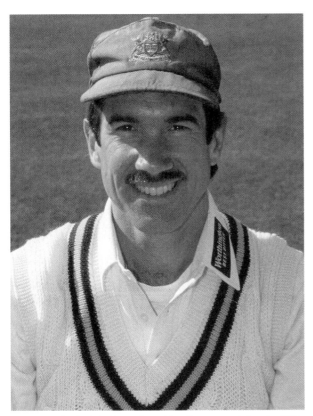

Former England wicket-keeper Bruce French announced that the 1995 season would be his last. (David Munden/Sportsline)

Knight was managed by Lara's agent and that Warwickshire were likely to offer him more money – and no one should be criticised for seeking to better his living – but there was a lack of honesty all round, and nobody came out of the affair well.

Essex's problems did not end there. Peter Edwards, a man who has done so much for the county and the game in general, underwent a series of operations and was handicapped for much of the season. There was a feeling that the Essex dressing room was not the jovial place it once had been, and none of this could have been of much help to a new captain who had been appointed amongst opposition and with two former captains, Gooch and Fletcher, very much in evidence in the club. The appointment of Nasser Hussain as vice-captain was a positive step. He has upset a few people in his career, but he has a good cricket brain and can be inspirational in the field.

Mike Garnham stood down from the side and announced that he would retire at the end of the season. Garnham had said consistently that he considered young Robert Rollins an outstanding keeper who would be pressing for an England place within two seasons – a sentiment with which the New Zealand tourists of 1994 had agreed – and Garnham stepped aside to give Rollins a chance.

Glamorgan had to rush to sign Anthony as their overseas player when Gibson was surprisingly selected for the West Indies' tour of England. Kendrick joined them from

Surrey, and there only remained the mystery as to why a side with so much talent and with such enthusiastic and warm administration do not achieve more than they do.

Gloucestershire were to be the season's great surprise, confounding all with the quality and style of much of their cricket. Russell succeeded Walsh as captain, and the Indian pace bowler Srinath joined them as overseas player. He was to be an outstanding success. His new-ball partner Mike Smith also thrived and won a place in the England 'A' side.

They signed Monte Lynch from Surrey, and the veteran brought substance and panache to the batting. Surrey could have done with him. There was also the arrival of Andrew Symonds, a graduate from the Australian Cricket Academy, who had scored a century for Queensland against the England touring side and another for a Young Australian side in New Zealand. He was able to play for Gloucestershire because he was born in Birmingham. He had a marvellous season, but his success brought conflict when he was named in the England 'A' party.

It seems that in England we are now dedicated to playing cricketers who learned the game at the expense of other countries – Hick, Caddick and White spring immediately to mind – and one hopes that this muddy problem of qualification is sorted out as soon as possible. The season was tainted by a rather unpleasant article with racial undertones which appeared in a monthly magazine. It caused a furore and clouded an issue.

A cricketer should play for the country in which he learned the game. Men like Malcolm and DeFreitas have lived and breathed the game in England; Symonds and White were tutored in Australia. One understands the lure of opting for England because here one can earn a living playing county cricket without complications, but Gallian was once captain of Australian Young Cricketers and Caddick represented New Zealand in the Youth World Cup.

Zimbabwe would certainly have been a stronger side had they been able to call on Hick, Penney and Curran. As it was, Heath Streak showed that country's rise in stock when Hampshire registered him as their overseas player. In what was destined to be Mark Nicholas' final year, John Stephenson from Essex and White from Somerset joined the side.

With Carl Hooper on duty with West Indies, Kent, like Hampshire, turned to a country which had not before provided an overseas player to English cricket and signed the Sri Lankan Test batsman Aravinda de Silva. If he was slow to start in the colder weather of early May, he warmed with the sun and his batting was the most glorious sight of the English summer.

Disappointed in the progress of left-arm spinner Alec Barnett, Lancashire acquired Gary Keedy from Yorkshire and, under coach David Lloyd, showed confidence, flair and joy in their game.

Leicestershire were strengthened by the arrival of South Africa's captain Hansie Cronje, but lost David Millns through injury early in the year and were to become a model of inconsistency.

Middlesex began the season under a cloud of uncertainty. They had lost both openers, Haynes and Roseberry, and, initially, Gatting said he would open the innings. The

Dermot Reeve – a dynamic captain who still believes that there is more room in the trophy cabinet. (Paul Sturgess/Sportsline)

New Zealand pace bowler Dion Nash was engaged as the overseas player, but, in spite of his success in 1994, he was something of an unknown quantity. Tufnell had not impressed authority in Australia, and Emburey was in his 43rd year.

The cloud soon gave way to sun. Weekes was moved up the order to open, and Jason Pooley repaid all those who had shown trust and belief in him while, whatever his failings in the England side, Ramprakash scored prolifically in the county game.

Northamptonshire gave us one of the gems of the season when they signed the Indian spinner Kumble, and, in what may be his last season, Allan Lamb led the side with intelligence and zest. The county welcomed back Neil Mallender from Somerset, and hopes were high for an exciting season.

For Nottinghamshire, Chris Cairns returned in place of Jimmy Adams, and Chris Lewis remained an enigma. His ability is unquestioned, but his appetite for the game is doubtful. There was the promise of Hindson and the reliability of Robinson – in his last year as captain – but Nottinghamshire's cricket is shrouded in uncertainty.

There was a mass exodus from Somerset at the end of the 1994 season. It began with the controversial release of wicket-keeper Neil Burns and gathered apace. Things had settled by the start of the 1995 season, by which time Bowler had arrived from Derbyshire and Batty from Yorkshire. The glories of the Botham–Richards era are now a memory, and there are none with the strength of a Roebuck or a Marks, but the county settled into a more peaceful state, with Richard Harden probably one of the most underrated batsmen in the country.

Surrey have boasted with justification of their youth policy, and the results of their under-19 sides, for example, have been good, yet there is now a frustration at the lack of success at the top level which has erupted into calls for extraordinary meetings and for the heads of the club's administrators. It was hard to see where a successful youth policy was leading when, on several occasions in early season, the new ball was being shared by three bowlers with an average age of 35, all of whom had been imported from outside the county. The non-return of Waqar Younis was a great blow, but the Surrey executive had also claimed that the county possessed the best pair of young spinners in England – Boiling and Kendrick – and both were released at the end of the 1994 season.

There was a new spinner in Richard Nowell, a good young pace bowler in Alex Tudor, and two new batsmen in Ratcliffe and Shahid, but again it was difficult to understand why these imports were to play at the expense of a popular, home-grown product like David Ward.

The 150th anniversary celebrations were to occupy much of the summer at The Oval. After that, perhaps, the county would reassess its priorities.

Alan Wells returned from his success as captain of the England 'A' side in India to a Sussex team brimming with hope. Giddins had enjoyed a fine season in 1994 and was progressing well, while Salisbury and Hemmings offered a balanced and fascinating spin attack. The season was greeted with eager anticipation.

As it was at Warwickshire who had Donald back instead of Lara and who had acquired Knight from Essex. They had three trophies in the cupboard and a dynamic captain who believed there was much room for more. Their team had few if any stars, but their spirit and self-belief were unquenchable. Every player contributed, every player worked for the other. Any side who beat them would have to play very well.

Neighbouring Worcestershire must have been less confident. They were an ageing side, and the youngsters were not quite ready, but in the one-day game, at least, they would provide stiff opposition.

Under the management of Steve Oldham, Yorkshire looked for improvement. Like Surrey, they felt starved of success, but they were producing players of quality like Gough and Vaughan, and in Michael Bevan they might at last have engaged the overseas player who could help them recapture former greatness. Only the summer would tell.

We gathered inevitably in the cold, renewed old friendships, waited for the West Indians and lived in hope.

WEST INDIES TOUR OF ENGLAND
Texaco and Test Series

Having been defeated by Australia in the Caribbean and having narrowly avoided defeat in India in a drawn series, West Indies arrived in England more vulnerable than they had been for 26 years. This vulnerability was not simply because of the disappointments in India and the Caribbean, it was also due to the failure of bowlers like Cuffy, Browne and Cummins to establish themselves. In the Red Stripe Cup, only the Joseph brothers and Vasbert Drakes could claim to have shown form enough to press for Test recognition, while men like Rose had taken a positive step in the wrong direction. There was, too, the question as to who would open the innings.

The long-running saga of Desmond Haynes seemed to be whimpering to its end rather than booming to a climax, and there was insufficient faith in Campbell and Williams. In international terms, they were inexperienced, and Richardson himself had taken over the opening role against Australia. It was unlikely that he would do this in England, and Hooper was the man most mentioned to fill the number one spot. An elegant, attacking batsman, Hooper is a joy to watch, but he is hardly blessed with strong powers of concentration and patience – qualities looked for in an opener.

In the Test arena, delightful and exciting as he is, Hooper has remained something of a nearly man. Much the same could be said about Arthurton, but Adams had enjoyed outstanding form in the months leading up to the England tour and rivalled Lara as West Indies' leading batsman. Richardson had batted splendidly in the Red Stripe Cup and had scored a century against Australia, but West Indian commentators felt that he should not have been burdened with the captaincy.

A gentle, friendly man, Richardson had been absent from the game for a long period suffering from an exhaustion that was as much mental as physical. He had made a highly successful return to first-class cricket at the beginning of the year in a tournament which was bereft of its premier players. He was then immediately returned to the firing-line to lead those players in a tense contest for what most described as 'the championship of the world'. His side had lost, and a cherished unbeaten run had been brought to an end. He was then asked – with no period of rest – to captain the side on a long and taxing tour of England, a tour which was to include *six* Tests and three one-day internationals. Most of the West Indian side had been touring the world for the past six months – India, New Zealand and the Caribbean – playing international cricket without respite. The West Indian commentators were right to think that too much was being asked of Richardson too soon.

The general feeling was that Walsh should have led the side, for he had shown admirable qualities of leadership in India and New Zealand, and in domestic competition. The problem with Walsh was that he was now the West Indies' main strike bowler and was likely to bowl more overs in the Test series than anyone else on his side. The recall of

The tour begins. Sherwin Campbell and Carl Hooper go out to open the innings against Lavinia, Duchess of Norfolk's XI at Arundel. (David Munden/Sportsline)

Ian Bishop after his lengthy back injury was correct, but Bishop's fitness for a long summer and a six-Test series was uncertain. The same could be said of Ambrose whose bowling had lost some of its spark. Most observers believed that 1995 would see the end of his Test career. Kenny Benjamin had always been in the shadows while Winston was ever a cricketer of doubtful temperament. Gibson was untried and untested at the highest level, and the spin attack was in the hands of Dhanraj and Hooper – hardly a match-winning combination.

The full West Indian party, with manager Wes Hall and coach Andy Roberts, was: R.B. Richardson (captain); C.A. Walsh (vice-captain); J.C. Adams; C.E.L. Ambrose; K.L.T. Arthurton; K.C.G. Benjamin; W.K.M. Benjamin; I.R. Bishop; C.O. Browne; S.L. Campbell; S. Chanderpaul; R. Dhanraj; O.D. Gibson; C.L. Hooper; B.C. Lara; J.R. Murray and S.C. Williams.

If West Indies were vulnerable, what about England?

They had returned from Australia beaten and bowed. Abuse came from all quarters, even from the man mainly responsible for choosing the party, Ray Illingworth, who had now achieved something akin to dictator status by having Keith Fletcher sacked.

Fletcher had been appointed to his role as 'manager', or 'coach', to the England team amid great scenes of rejoicing. A senior administrator at the TCCB had expressed how lucky they were to get him. That Fletcher had knowledge and wisdom, that he was rich in experience and could be of great assistance in advising players, was undeniable, but there were other factors that, perhaps, had not been fully considered. Fletcher was, and is, an essentially 'parochial' person. He enjoyed a highly successful career as a Test batsman, but that career had been scarred by much criticism which had been hurtful. His reign as captain of England – much acclaimed when he was first appointed – had ended abruptly and had been neither happy nor successful. He had managed an England 'A' side to Zimbabwe, and his advice to the young batsmen on the playing of spin had resulted in such tedium as to cause grave concern. His heart and soul were really in Essex and, as Trevor Bailey wryly remarked, Fletcher was all right with England as long as Gooch was captain. After that…

There was an inevitable cry for someone's head following the Australian disaster, and, as had been the case so often before in his cricketing life, Fletcher's was the head that was chosen. He returned to Essex as 'cricket consultant', although the wisdom of that appointment in a county with a coach, a new captain, and an old captain looming over all remained in question.

Illingworth also strengthened his position by tightening his grip on Atherton. There were no doubts that the Lancastrian should remain as captain of England, but the announcement that he would lead against West Indies was delayed and further delayed as if there was much to discuss, and when Atherton was finally named it was for a limited period. There were now no doubts as to who meant to be boss.

To aid Illingworth in the coaching department, Peter Lever was appointed to look after the bowlers, and John Edrich to supervise the batsmen. Boycott, it was said, had been the first choice, but had been too expensive. That was disappointing. Edrich is a good, sturdy man, but the thought of Boycott and Illingworth working together is intriguing.

All these events – and events before these, particularly the treatment of Angus Fraser – lost England a sponsor in Patrick Whittingdale. A keen cricketer and a generous man, Whittingdale had done a vast amount for the England cricket team, and he had looked for little reward. He is a serious man who does not seek self-glorification. What he provided should have been cherished by Illingworth and the rest. It was not.

So which side was the more vulnerable? The West Indies had never seemed more beatable, but a long tour lay ahead. It began with the social occasion of Arundel.

13 May at Arundel

West Indians 298 for 3 (C.L. Hooper 173 not out, R.B. Richardson 53)

Lavinia, Duchess of Norfolk's XI 196 for 8 (D.W. Randall 101)

West Indians won by 102 runs

Arundel has established itself as the welcoming ground for the season's touring side (or sides). It is a place of great beauty, and offers a delightful setting for alfresco food and drink. The cricket is of secondary importance. This is inevitable when one considers the difficulty the Duchess has in raising a good enough side to take on an eleven from abroad with the scent of battle in their nostrils. On this occasion, Paul Parker, once of Durham and Sussex, led a team which included selector David Graveney – a people's choice ahead of Illingworth's Brian Bolus – Tony Murphy, once of Surrey, Simon Hughes, earning justified fame in the press box, Norman Cowans – still on the Hampshire staff although rarely giving evidence of that fact – and Vasbert Drakes who might well have found himself playing for the opposition. Kevan James, not required by Hampshire in The Parks, took two wickets, and behind the stumps was Bobby Parks, who many felt should still be keeping for Hampshire, but the fact that Bobby was number seven in the batting order underlined the weakness of the side.

Hooper launched the festive occasion with 9 sixes and batted through the 50 overs. Randall hit 7 sixes, and a fine time was had by all.

14 May at Southampton

Hampshire 268 for 5 (G.W. White 68 not out, R.S.M. Morris 62)

West Indians 225 (O.D. Gibson 57)

Hampshire won by 43 runs

The party ended when the tourists moved along the coast to Southampton and were slain by Hampshire who, previously in the season, had been savaged by everybody that they had met. Richardson asked the county side to bat first when he won the toss. Terry and Smith went cheaply, but Morris batted through 37 of the 55 overs, and, with White, Nicholas and Udal plundering runs at the end, Hampshire made 268.

The tourists never suggested that they would approach this score. Lara was out for 14, and only Hooper batted with confidence. Gibson hit 57 off 46 balls, but by then the cause was lost, and the West Indians' innings was over in 52.1 overs.

16, 17 and 18 May at Worcester

West Indians 241 for 9 dec. (B.C. Lara 78, P.A. Thomas 5 for 70) and 0 for 0 dec.

Worcestershire 0 for 0 dec. and 86 for 5

Match drawn

The opening first-class match of the tour was ruined by rain. Only 24 overs were possible on the first day during

Paul Thomas, the Worcestershire pace bowler, took five wickets on the occasion of his first-class debut against the West Indians, 16 May. The familiar umpire is David Shepherd. (Patrick Eagar)

which the West Indians scored 114 for 2. The first wicket to fall was that of Williams who was caught in the gully off Paul Thomas, a quick bowler born in Birmingham. After a blank second day, the West Indian innings continued on the Thursday, and Thomas, making his first-class debut, finished with five wickets. It was an impressive piece of bowling, for not only was he quick, he was thoughtful.

Lara began the day with 78 joyful runs off 80 balls and he had hit 13 fours when he aimed to dab Illingworth past slip and was stumped when the ball bounced back off Rhodes' gloves and dislodged a bail. Illingworth was accurate, and Thomas was hostile, and the two captains strove to give life to the game with declarations and forfeitures.

Worcestershire went in search of 242 off 48 overs, but they were soon out of the hunt. Although he did not take a wicket, Bishop bowled tidily, and Dhanraj captured his first first-class wicket of the tour when he had Haynes stumped. Curtis was unbeaten on 37, and the match was called off after 26.3 overs.

19, 20 and **21 May** *at Taunton*

West Indians 449 for 8 dec. (C.L. Hooper 176,
S.L. Campbell 93, J.C. Adams 91) and 176 for 3 dec.
(S.L. Campbell 80, S. Chanderpaul 50 not out)

Somerset 301 for 9 dec. (P.D. Bowler 84, R.J. Harden 78,
C.A. Walsh 4 for 77) and 159 for 2 (M.N. Lathwell 76,
K.A. Parsons 52 not out)

Match drawn

The uncertainty as to a West Indian opening partnership passed away as Hooper and Campbell followed their 104 at Arundel with 242 against Somerset. The runs came in 52 overs, and the stand was dominated by Carl Hooper who played an innings of great majesty. He faced only 179 balls, and he hit 7 sixes and 24 fours. At last it seemed that Hooper's rich talent was to be revealed totally. Campbell and Adams also played some exotic strokes, but the Somerset attack was limited in the extreme. Both Caddick and van Troost were absent, and only Mushtaq Ahmed posed a major threat, well deserving his three wickets.

The first day ended with the tourists on 398 for 5 from 94 overs. Adams prospered on the second morning, but the Somerset response was positive. Lathwell and Trescothick were out for 60, and Harden and Bowler put on 150. Walsh apart, the West Indian bowling was not impressive.

Set an unrealistic target of 325 off 47 overs, Somerset were enlivened by Parsons and Lathwell after Trescothick had gone for 0. The pair added 105 in 91 minutes, and Lathwell batted with considerable zest, giving some cheer after his miserable start to the season.

TEXACO TROPHY
ENGLAND v. WEST INDIES

The selection of the England party for the Texaco Trophy was not without surprise or controversy. Peter Martin, the Lancashire pace bowler, and Alan Wells, the Sussex captain, were the two players in the thirteen who had not previously played in international cricket. Both deserved their selection.

Martin's team-mate Glen Chapple had started the season strongly favoured to win a place in the England side, but he had been troubled by injury. Martin himself had shown splendid form in a county side that was blooming in all competitions and, with Atherton and Fairbrother, he could bring the Lancashire spirit and success to the England side.

Alan Wells had done a fine job as captain of the England 'A' team in India, and many saw his selection as a form of recognition and reward for his efforts. At 34, he was rather old to be commencing an international career, but he had shown outstanding form in early-season matches.

The same could not be said of Udal who had not claimed a first-class wicket until the afternoon of his selection for the England party. His form in one-day cricket had been little better, and one remained bewildered by Illingworth's blinkered obsession regarding this off-spinner.

Udal was included in the eleven for the first match. Neither of the 'new boys' was chosen. West Indies were without Kenny Benjamin who had also not taken the field in Somerset's second innings in the match at Taunton.

Richardson won the toss, and England batted. West Indies had entered the match with little practice and indifferent form, and, with the skies looking uncertain, Richardson probably felt it better to give his bowlers a chance to settle than to expose his batsmen to the vagaries of the English weather.

Ambrose did not settle. He could not find his rhythm, and, allowed two unproductive spells, he was not given a third. Courtney Walsh was by far the best of the West Indian bowlers, and he dismissed Atherton with an excellent delivery which pitched on off stump and held its line to take the edge of the bat. Lara scooped up the catch to his right at slip.

Hick was ill at ease. He batted for 53 minutes, faced 27 balls and finally touched Winston Benjamin to the wicket-keeper. He seemed to establish a pattern of uncertainty, for Thorpe batted in that state of frenzy that sometimes consumes him, hit seven off 10 balls and committed suicide as he chased a wide delivery.

While these alarms were taking place Alec Stewart remained calm and commanding. At lunch, England were 110 for 3 from 32 overs. Stewart had hit 11 fours, and Fairbrother's arrival had, inevitably, injected a sense of urgency into the play.

Fairbrother was beginning to move up a gear when Bishop knocked back his leg stump with an in-swinger. Bishop's return to international cricket was controlled and quietly impressive, but it was Hooper who produced the most significant ball of the day. It did not seem a lethal delivery, but Stewart attempted to turn it to leg and was bowled off the back pad. He had faced 127 balls and scored 74 out of 125, and only 17 overs of the England innings remained.

Ramprakash was aware of the responsibility that was now upon him as the last recognised batsman. There were no boundaries scored in the first 11 overs after lunch, and Ramprakash's six and four were the only boundaries hit other than the 11 scored by Stewart. Ramprakash made 32 off 36 balls and added 32 with DeFreitas. Then came 29 with Cork before Ramprakash himself was bowled via his midriff by a full toss from Walsh.

Cork flailed and missed. Gough was run out, and England finished at least 30 short of hope and expectation.

There was a delay because of rain before the West Indian innings could begin. Hooper was soon in full flow; and Campbell was explosive. Cork found a scintillating leg-cutter to bowl Hooper, and West Indies were 76 for 1 from 19.5 overs when Lara accepted the offer to go off for bad light. Had West Indies stayed one ball longer, they could have claimed victory on faster run rate.

Such a ploy was unnecessary as the weather was fine on the Thursday. West Indies were in sight of victory when Lara, 70 off 95 balls, was out to a fine running catch by Atherton. Richardson had shown no sign of form in the warm-up matches on the tour, and he soon drove Gough to cover. Adams played in tired fashion at Cork, and Campbell was well run out by Udal and Stewart. It all made the score look more respectable from the England

Neil Fairbrother is bowled by Ian Bishop in the first Texaco Trophy match at Trent Bridge. (Paul Sturgess/Sportsline)

point of view, but it was really of little comfort in what had been a trouncing.

England made one change for the second match – the 1,000th limited-over international. Peter Martin made his international debut at the expense of Angus Fraser. The pitch looked superb, and it was surprising that Richardson again asked England to bat when he won the toss.

Stewart was out in the 10th over, surprised by the pace and the bounce of Bishop's second delivery. In the next 28 overs, Atherton and Hick added 144. Hick was very fortunate to be dropped by Lara when 14, and both were fortunate when Walsh was forced to withdraw from the attack with a back problem.

Hick played well, and his 66 came off 81 balls. He grew over-confident when he gambled on Hooper's throw. He was clearly out of his ground when the ball hit the stumps, but umpire Bird called for a television decision as Hick walked to the pavilion well aware of his fate.

Hick was out in the 38th over, and two overs later, Atherton's very fine innings came to an end when he was beaten by Winston Benjamin's in-swinger. He had hit 10 fours and faced 118 balls, and, with 188 runs on the board and 15 overs to come, England were in command. Those last 15 overs were to produce 118 runs.

This was due mainly to a glorious knock by Neil Fairbrother – 61 off 52 balls with a six and 5 fours – but it must be confessed that he was aided by an error of judgement on the part of umpire Bird.

When he was on 29 Fairbrother survived an appeal for run out as Ambrose kicked the ball onto the stumps in a manner once fashioned by Denis Compton. The television replay revealed that the batsman was out, but Bird had decided that he had no need to call upon the third umpire. This was a perverse decision in the extreme, for Bird had already relied on the monitor in the case of Hick whom those on the boundary or in the press box could have given out unhesitatingly. Consistency is all.

As it was, the five overs of the innings that remained after the Fairbrother incident brought England 57 runs of which the Lancastrian made 32, and England scored 306, a record total against West Indies in all limited-over internationals.

Campbell soon gave notice that the visitors were not about to surrender meekly when he hit the first ball he received, from DeFreitas, into the crowd behind square-leg for six. Hooper hit 4 fours in his 17 before impatiently lofting Gough to mid-off. Lara began sketchily, but 50 runs were posted on the board in the ninth over.

The advent of Peter Martin changed matters. His fifth ball caught Sherwin Campbell in mid-stroke, and Thorpe held the skied catch at mid-wicket. In his next over, Martin had Adams leg before, and two overs later, he hit Lara's off stump as the batsman drove loosely.

Richardson pushed the ball back into Cork's hands shortly after tea, and Arthurton became another Cork victim, only this time the batsman was run out.

Junior Murray was belligerent from the outset, and his 52-run partnership with Arthurton was followed by a stand of 47 with Winston Benjamin who swatted DeFreitas into the crowd the ball before he was out in the 44th over. Bishop helped Murray to maintain the acceleration with 18 off 16 balls in a stand which produced 48 runs and took West Indies to within 46 of their target, with five overs remaining.

Bishop stumbled as he set off for a run and was run out by Udal from mid-off. Ambrose took too much of the strike in the ninth-wicket partnership, and when Martin returned to hit his off stump all depended on Murray and Walsh.

Murray had been absolutely magnificent, and had maintained everyone's interest in the game until late in the day, but now extreme measures were needed, and he was run out by Fairbrother on the last ball of the 53rd over as he attempted to take them. He had hit 2 sixes and 4 fours and faced 77 balls for what was his first score over 50 in a one-day international.

On his first international appearance, Peter Martin rightly took the individual award.

England made two changes for the deciding match at Lord's. Wells came in for Fairbrother, who was injured, and Fraser returned at the expense of DeFreitas. Richardson again won the toss and again asked England to bat. This time there seemed justification for his action. The day had started damp, and the match began at 11.00 am with conditions in favour of the bowler.

West Indies, like England, had made two changes: Williams for Campbell, and Gibson for the injured Walsh.

ABOVE: *Phil DeFreitas is well short of the line when Junior Murray takes off the bails in the first Texaco Trophy game. (Adrian Murrell/ Allsport)*

BELOW: *Dominic Cork celebrates as he traps Jimmy Adams lbw. Cork was destined to become England's cricketer of the season. (Graham Chadwick/Allsport)*

BOTTOM: *Junior Murray pulls a ball from DeFreitas to the boundary during his gallant innings of 86 at The Oval. (Patrick Eagar)*

Mike Atherton played an outstanding innings at Lord's and was Man of the Series. He sweeps Carl Hooper, with Junior Murray closely attentive. (David Munden/Sportsline)

Gibson was making his debut in international cricket, but it was Ambrose and Bishop who caused England the early problems. They bowled quickly and extracted both bounce and movement, and the ball was swerving menacingly. All was in favour of the bowler.

Stewart hit Bishop square for four in the second over,

and two overs later, he square-cut the same bowler for four. Bishop took his revenge with the third ball of the sixth over of the match. Stewart fenced at a lifting ball and was caught at slip. The score was 12. Atherton had faced 17 deliveries and had not yet scored.

The England captain looked leg before to a no-ball and, in the seventh over, he survived a deafening appeal for a catch at the wicket. The next ball, the 27th he had faced, he turned through mid-wicket for three. It was his first scoring shot.

This was no immediate liberation for the England captain, for he went another 17 deliveries before producing his second scoring shot, but through a most difficult period, against bowling that was hostile, accurate and of high quality, he survived. This was an innings of utmost character. The man has an inner strength which few can equal, and his batting mocked those who ever doubted his fitness to lead and his aptitude for the one-day game.

In the 12th over, he square-cut Bishop gloriously to the Tavern boundary, and next over, he drove Benjamin square for four. Hick hooked and off-drove Gibson for fours in one over, and the fifty was raised off 105 balls.

In the 24th over, Hick went back, attempted to cut Hooper and was bowled. At lunch, England were 103 for 2

TEXACO TROPHY – MATCH ONE – ENGLAND v. WEST INDIES
24 and 25 May 1995 at Trent Bridge, Nottingham

ENGLAND

M.A. Atherton (capt)	c Lara, b Walsh	8
*A.J. Stewart	b Hooper	74
G.A. Hick	c Murray, b Benjamin	8
G.P. Thorpe	c Murray, b Walsh	7
N.H. Fairbrother	b Bishop	12
M.R. Ramprakash	b Walsh	32
P.A.J. DeFreitas	run out	15
D.G. Cork	b Arthurton	14
D. Gough	run out	3
S.D. Udal	not out	5
A.R.C. Fraser	not out	4
Extras	lb 11, w 5, nb 1	17
(55 overs)	(for 9 wickets)	199

WEST INDIES

C.L. Hooper	b Cork	34
S.L. Campbell	run out	80
B.C. Lara	c Atherton, b Gough	70
R.B. Richardson (capt)	c DeFreitas, b Gough	1
J.C. Adams	lbw, b Cork	2
K.L.T. Arthurton	not out	1
*J.R. Murray	not out	7
W.K.M. Benjamin		
I.R. Bishop		
C.E.L. Ambrose		
C.A. Walsh		
Extras	lb 1, w 4, nb 1	6
(52.4 overs)	(for 5 wickets)	201

	O	M	R	W
Ambrose	8	1	33	–
Walsh	10	1	28	3
Bishop	11	2	30	1
Benjamin	8	1	22	1
Hooper	10	–	45	1
Arthurton	8	–	30	1

	O	M	R	W
DeFreitas	10.4	1	44	–
Fraser	10	2	29	–
Gough	11	1	30	2
Cork	11	–	48	2
Udal	8	–	37	–
Hick	2	–	12	–

FALL OF WICKETS
1–25, 2–60, 3–85, 4–121, 5–125, 6–157, 7–186, 8–190, 9–191

FALL OF WICKETS
1–66, 2–180, 3–183, 4–191, 5–194

Umpires: N.T. Plews & D.R. Shepherd   *Man of the Match:* C.A. Walsh   *West Indies won by 5 wickets*

Angus Fraser bowls Junior Murray for 5 and puts England close to victory at Lord's. (David Munden/Sportsline)

from 30 overs, and Atherton went to his fifty immediately after the break. Thorpe helped him to add 73, but the Surrey left-hander was playing one of his frenzied, unstable innings, and it was no surprise when he skied a ball from Gibson.

Ramprakash gave his captain sensible support, and the running between the wickets was sharp and keen. The same could not be said of the West Indian fielding where the suggestion was that several players had not come to England to run about retrieving cricket balls.

Atherton's hundred came off the fourth ball of the 47th over when he took three to long-on. His century came off 144 balls and included 12 fours. He had struggled in the early part, but he had stayed. He had displayed cricketing integrity. His innings was to last 16 more balls and was to include a pulled six off Bishop and two more fours. He flicked the ball off his legs adroitly and played some magnificent cover-drives. When he was finally caught off Gibson he left the field to a standing ovation. The England supporters were well aware of his importance to English cricket whatever Illingworth's doubts may be, and if one had to be sacrificed…?

Wells had little time to acclimatise to international cricket, but he hit 15 off 10 balls before dying in the late rush for runs. The last over was typical of the end of a limited-over match. Gough hit Benjamin over cover for six, then took a single to leg. Ramprakash hit a single to long-on, and Gough swung and missed next ball. Cork was leg

TEXACO TROPHY – MATCH TWO – ENGLAND *v.* WEST INDIES
26 May 1995 at The Oval, Kennington

ENGLAND				WEST INDIES		
M.A. Atherton (capt)	b Benjamin	92		C.L. Hooper	c Atherton, b Gough	17
*A.J. Stewart	c Murray, b Bishop	16		S.L. Campbell	c Thorpe, b Martin	20
G.A. Hick	run out	66		B.C. Lara	b Martin	39
G.P. Thorpe	run out	26		J.C. Adams	lbw, b Martin	2
N.H. Fairbrother	not out	61		R.B. Richardson (capt)	c and b Cork	15
M.R. Ramprakash	c Adams, b Hooper	16		K.L.T. Arthurton	run out	39
D. Gough	not out	8		*J.R. Murray	run out	86
P.A.J. DeFreitas				W.K.M. Benjamin	c Ramprakash, b DeFreitas	17
D.G. Cork				I.R. Bishop	run out	18
P.J. Martin				C.E.L. Ambrose	b Martin	10
S.D. Udal				C.A. Walsh	not out	5
Extras	b 6, lb 5, w 6, nb 4	21		Extras	lb 6, w 7	13
(55 overs)	(for 5 wickets)	306		(53 overs)		281

	O	M	R	W			O	M	R	W
Ambrose	10	1	47	–		Gough	11	–	62	1
Walsh	5.2	–	17	–		DeFreitas	10	–	73	1
Bishop	11	–	60	1		Cork	11	–	56	1
Benjamin	10.4	–	55	1		Udal	11	–	40	–
Arthurton	8	–	48	–		Martin	10	1	44	4
Hooper	10	–	68	1						

FALL OF WICKETS
1–33, **2**–177, **3**–188, **4**–243, **5**–295

FALL OF WICKETS
1–25, **2**–69, **3**–77, **4**–88, **5**–114, **6**–166, **7**–213, **8**–261, **9**–275

Umpires: H.D. Bird & R. Palmer *Man of the Match:* P.J. Martin *England won by 25 runs*

Peter Martin, a success in both his Texaco appearances, bowls Curtly Ambrose and England win the trophy. (David Munden/ Sportsline)

before first ball, and Martin square-drove the last delivery for four. Six balls, 12 runs, two wickets.

The opening overs of the West Indian innings did not hint at the flamboyant and positive search for runs that we had seen at The Oval. Williams was out in the 10th over – Cork's first, and the Derbyshire all-rounder also accounted for Lara who slashed at a ball outside off stump and was caught off a bottom edge. Stewart took another catch, a fine one low to his left, to account for Adams. That was in the 27th over, and when, after 89 balls, Hooper finally lost patience to give the impressive Cork his third wicket, West Indies looked doomed.

Gough found the edge of Arthurton's bat, and Richardson hit Udal into the Mound Stand before missing Gough's slower ball. Fraser's accuracy presented insurmountable problems for the lower-order, and England had a joyful start to the summer by taking the Texaco Trophy.

Atherton took the individual award. His first century in a limited-over international will long remain in the memory.

30, 31 May and 1 June *at Leicester*

West Indians 468 for 7 dec. (K.L.T. Arthurton 146, S. Chanderpaul 140 not out, R.B. Richardson 60) and 143 for 4 dec. (S.C. Williams 54)

TEXACO TROPHY – MATCH THREE – ENGLAND v. WEST INDIES
28 May 1995 at Lord's

ENGLAND

M.A. Atherton (capt)	c Adams, b Gibson	127
*A.J. Stewart	c Lara, b Bishop	8
G.A. Hick	b Hooper	24
G.P. Thorpe	c Hooper, b Gibson	28
M.R. Ramprakash	not out	29
A.P. Wells	b Gibson	15
D. Gough	b Benjamin	8
D.G. Cork	lbw, b Benjamin	0
P.J. Martin	not out	4
S.D. Udal		
A.R.C. Fraser		
Extras	b 4, lb 13, w 9, nb 7	33
(55 overs)	(for 7 wickets)	276

WEST INDIES

S.C. Williams	c Atherton, b Cork	21
C.L. Hooper	c Gough, b Cork	40
B.C. Lara	c Stewart, b Cork	11
J.C. Adams	c Stewart, b Martin	29
K.L.T. Arthurton	c Stewart, b Gough	35
R.B. Richardson (capt)	lbw, b Gough	23
*J.R. Murray	b Fraser	5
O.D. Gibson	c Atherton, b Fraser	7
W.K.M. Benjamin	b Fraser	6
I.R. Bishop	not out	1
C.E.L. Ambrose	b Martin	1
Extras	lb 13, w 11	24
(48.2 overs)		203

	O	M	R	W
Ambrose	11	1	45	–
Bishop	11	2	53	1
Benjamin	10	–	61	2
Gibson	11	–	51	3
Hooper	11	–	38	1
Arthurton	1	–	11	–

	O	M	R	W
Fraser	11	3	34	3
Martin	9.2	1	36	2
Cork	9	2	27	3
Gough	10	–	31	2
Udal	8	–	52	–
Hick	1	–	10	–

FALL OF WICKETS
1–12, 2–79, 3–152, 4–244, 5–263, 6–272, 7–272

FALL OF WICKETS
1–29, 2–44, 3–94, 4–128, 5–171, 6–184, 7–190, 8–198, 9–201

Umpires: J.H. Hampshire & M.J. Kitchen   *Man of the Match:* M.A. Atherton   *England won by 73 runs*

Leicestershire 194 (J.J. Whitaker 75, R. Dhanraj 6 for 50) and
130 (K.C.G. Benjamin 4 for 50)

West Indians won by 287 runs

Whitaker was leading a Leicestershire side that included
Habib, formerly of Middlesex, and Clarke, a leg-break
bowler once of Somerset. Lara had flown home to Trinidad
for personal reasons, Cronje was absent for reasons of
honeymoon on the Continent, and the West Indians were
asked to bat first for reasons unknown. Initially, the bowling looked lively, and the tourists were 72 for 3.
Richardson brought a sense of order, but it was a stand of
223 between Arthurton and Chanderpaul in 51 overs that
revealed something of West Indian power. Arthurton hit 4
sixes and 24 fours, and Chanderpaul hit 23 fours in his
221-ball innings. His century came on the second day
when the West Indians hit another 79 runs for the loss of
two more wickets before declaring.

Leicestershire were bowled out in 47.2 overs, but it was
not the pace and fire of the fast bowlers that undermined
them, it was the leg-spin of Dhanraj who took 6 for 50 in
15 overs. There was fire from the pace men, however.
Kenny Benjamin bowled two bouncers at David Millns
and was warned. He followed by bowling two extravagant no-balls, which led to umpire Allan Jones having
words with captain Richie Richardson.

Richardson did not enforce the follow-on, and Hooper
was out as 16 runs were scored before the close. Kenny
Benjamin may have been a bad boy on the second day, but
on the third he advanced his claims for a place in the Test
side by shooting out Maddy, Smith and Habib in his first
two overs. This burst virtually settled the match.

3, 4 and 5 June *at Northampton*

Northamptonshire 281 (A.L. Penberthy 73, I.R. Bishop
4 for 64)

West Indians 286 for 5 dec. (K.L.T. Arthurton 121 not out,
J.C. Adams 93)

Match drawn

This game did not provide the practice that the West
Indians would have liked on the eve of the first Test match.
Rain prevented any play on the first day. Northamptonshire
batted with some spirit, and Penberthy hit 4 fours and 2
sixes while Mallender was unbeaten on 49.

Lara was bowled second ball for 0, but Adams and
Arthurton added 206 for the fourth wicket. Arthurton,
very much the batsman in form, hit 20 fours and 3 sixes
and batted for 260 minutes.

FIRST TEST MATCH
ENGLAND *v.* WEST INDIES, at Headingley

England made some strange decisions for the first Test
match. The first was to recall Robin Smith as an *opener*, a
position he had not filled before. The second was to name
Richard Illingworth as the spinner in the side, a bewilder-

ing choice in view of the other options available, and the
third was to omit Fraser on the morning of the match.
Martin deservedly won a first cap after his fine showing in
the Texaco Trophy, but to leave out Fraser was ludicrous,
and England paid the price accordingly. Stewart was again
pressed into service as wicket-keeper, but he dropped
down the order to number five.

West Indies chose Campbell rather than Williams as
Hooper's opening partner, and Kenny Benjamin was
preferred to his brother Winston. Ian Bishop returned to
Test cricket. Richardson won the toss – again – and
England were asked to bat.

The weather was overcast, and there were to be seven
interruptions during the day for squalls of rain, brief and
frustrating. Ambrose began with a maiden to Smith who
twice played over the ball as he attempted to cut. Atherton
opened the scoring when he turned Walsh's fourth ball
through mid-wicket for three.

The pitch looked to be without demons, but Smith was
forever hopping and fidgeting, a man not at peace with
himself. In contrast, Atherton looked unperturbed even
when Ambrose twice passed his outside edge. Walsh
retired from the attack after bowling four overs for 13
runs, and Bishop bowled his first ball in Test cricket for
two years.

Ambrose bowled with menace and economy, and his
first seven overs cost 12 runs. He should have had a
wicket in his third over when Smith was dropped by
Hooper at slip. It was a straightforward catch, shoulder
high, to which the fielder got two hands. Smith *was* caught
in the 16th over when he slashed Kenny Benjamin, who
maintained a full length, to third slip. Atherton might also
have been caught by Richardson off Benjamin in the pace
man's next over, but the ball was low to the fielder's right
and went for four.

Hick prodded and poked nervously early on, seemingly
intent on offering catching practice to the slips. He had
come through this period of uncertainty and hit 4 fours
when he played a vicious cut off Bishop. Campbell, at
backward point, flung himself to his right and held a magnificent catch. England were 91 for 2 in the 24th over.

Campbell's catch was certainly not typical of the West
Indian fielding, which was a shadow of what once it had
been. There was a general air that some of the players
would rather have been somewhere else – indifference is
too kind a word – and, for the most part, Richardson's captaincy was anonymous.

Atherton reached 53 off 82 balls in 110 minutes with 6
fours just before rain brought another interruption. Walsh
put one ball right through him, but Atherton survived the
appeal for a catch at the wicket.

Thorpe was dropped at third slip by Richardson off
Walsh. It was a low, hard chance, but it was a catch that
has to be held in Test cricket. The miss was not too costly,
for Thorpe was leg before to Bishop when the ball
straightened fractionally. Thorpe remains an enigma. He is
courageous, technically sound and has scored runs for
England (although not as many as he should have done),
but he still never suggests that he is a permanent fixture in
the England side.

Atherton's splendid innings came to an end in Bishop's

next over when a ball left him late and Murray took a good, diving catch to his right. Once again the England captain had shown constant application, the determination to get behind the ball and the equal determination to seize any scoring opportunity. He faced 145 balls, hit 8 fours and batted for 212 minutes. As he left the field, the covers came on and stayed on from 5.25 until the following morning. England were 148 for 4, Stewart not out 1, Ramprakash yet to face a ball.

If West Indies had seemed apathetic on the opening day, they sprang to life on the second – or should one say that England sank into an abyss of their own making. In Bishop's first full over of the day, Ramprakash followed the example of Smith and Hick by cutting loosely into the hands of Campbell at deepish gully. Alec Stewart then attempted to clip a straight ball through mid-wicket and was caught at slip off the edge. Gough came in to a hero's welcome and left in disbelief as he hooked his first ball to long-leg where Ambrose ran 10 yards and held the catch comfortably, two-handed in front of his face. This wicket was Bishop's fifth in 18 deliveries which had cost him five runs. As the wickets had been separated by some hours, few noticed the achievement, but it was an impressive way to return to Test cricket.

Martin heaved at Ambrose and was caught behind, and England had lost six wickets for 15 runs, four of them having fallen for nine runs since the start of play.

Illingworth and DeFreitas tried to repair some of the damage and added 42 before Kenny Benjamin, a far better bowler than he had been given credit for on this showing, claimed the last two wickets. To their delight and surprise, West Indies were beginning their innings with lunch still 35 minutes away.

They had another surprise when Malcolm's first ball of the innings pitched on off stump, climbed steeply, took the edge of Hooper's bat and was caught at first slip. England's euphoria was brief. Lara immediately carved Malcolm to third man for 2 fours, and the Derbyshire pace bowler was withdrawn from the attack after bowling two overs which had cost him 24 runs and brought the wicket of Hooper. By lunch, West Indies were an astonishing 61 for 1 at nearly seven an over.

Gough had left the field for treatment on a back problem after bowling three overs which cost 23 runs. The slaughter abated somewhat in the afternoon, but Lara reached 50 off 40 balls with his 10th four. In Illingworth's second over, however, he drove fiercely, lifted his head and Hick plucked the catch out of the air at slip.

FIRST CORNHILL TEST MATCH – ENGLAND v. WEST INDIES
8, 9, 10 and 11 June 1995 at Headingley, Leeds

ENGLAND

	FIRST INNINGS		SECOND INNINGS	
R.A. Smith	c Richardson, b Benjamin	16	c Arthurton, b Ambrose	6
M.A. Atherton (capt)	c Murray, b Bishop	81	c Murray, b Walsh	17
G.A. Hick	c Campbell, b Benjamin	18	c Walsh, b Bishop	27
G.P. Thorpe	lbw, b Bishop	20	c Campbell, b Walsh	61
*A.J. Stewart	c Hooper, b Bishop	2	c Murray, b Benjamin	4
M.R. Ramprakash	c Campbell, b Bishop	4	b Walsh	18
P.A.J. DeFreitas	c Murray, b Benjamin	23	c sub (Chanderpaul), b Walsh	1
D. Gough	c Ambrose, b Bishop	0	c sub (Williams), b Ambrose	29
P.J. Martin	c Murray, b Ambrose	2	c Lara, b Bishop	19
R.K. Illingworth	not out	17	not out	10
D.E. Malcolm	b Benjamin	0	b Ambrose	5
Extras	b 1, nb 15	16	b 1, lb 3, nb 7	11
		199		**208**

WEST INDIES

	FIRST INNINGS		SECOND INNINGS	
C.L. Hooper	c Thorpe, b Malcolm	0	not out	73
S.L. Campbell	run out	69	c Atherton, b Martin	2
B.C. Lara	c Hick, b Illingworth	53	not out	48
J.C. Adams	c Martin, b Hick	58		
K.L.T. Arthurton	c Stewart, b DeFreitas	42		
R.B. Richardson (capt)	lbw, b Martin	0		
*J.R. Murray	c Illingworth, b DeFreitas	20		
I.R. Bishop	run out	5		
C.E.L. Ambrose	c Gough, b Malcolm	15		
C.A. Walsh	c Stewart, b Gough	4		
K.C.G. Benjamin	not out	0		
Extras	b 4, lb 11, nb 1	16	b 1, lb 3, nb 2	6
		282	(for 1 wicket)	**129**

	O	M	R	W	O	M	R	W
Ambrose	17	4	56	1	20.2	6	44	3
Walsh	13	2	50	–	22	4	60	4
Bishop	16	2	32	5	19	3	81	2
Benjamin	13.5	2	60	4	6	1	19	1

	O	M	R	W	O	M	R	W
Malcolm	7.3	–	48	2	4	–	12	–
Gough	5	1	24	1				
DeFreitas	23	3	82	2	4	–	33	–
Martin	27	9	48	1	8	1	49	1
Illingworth	24	9	50	1	3	–	31	–
Hick	4	–	15	1				

FALL OF WICKETS
1–52, 2–91, 3–142, 4–148, 5–153, 6–154, 7–154, 8–157, 9–199
1–6, 2–55, 3–55, 4–82, 5–130, 6–136, 7–152, 8–193, 9–193

FALL OF WICKETS
1–0, 2–95, 3–141, 4–216, 5–219, 6–243, 7–254, 8–254, 9–275
1–11

Umpires: H.D. Bird & S. Venkataraghavan

West Indies won by 9 wickets

ABOVE: *Stewart delicately removes a bail to run Bishop out for 5. (David Munden/Sportsline)*

RIGHT: *4*
Murray leaps to catch Stewart off Kenny Benjamin, and the England innings is disintegrating. (David Munden/Sportsline)

The hundred came up in the 19th over, and Sherwin Campbell reached fifty off 71 balls. He was impressively belligerent, savaging anything short of a length, and he looked set for a century before he played a ball to the right of mid-off, only for DeFreitas to swoop on the ball one-handed and hit the stumps with his throw with Campbell just short of his ground.

Illingworth, if never looking like a wicket-taker, stemmed the constant flow of runs, but Martin was spoken to by umpire Venkataraghavan for running down the pitch. Atherton then brought on Hick who pitched a ball in the rough that Martin had created. Adams swept at the off-spinner and was caught at backward square-leg by Martin who flung himself to his right to hold the ball. It was an excellent piece of work. As if in celebration, Martin returned to have Richardson leg before playing a woeful shot. Arthurton and Murray took West Indies to the close on 236 for 5, a lead of 37, meaning that England were still in contention.

It was cold and grey on the Saturday, and England did well to capture the last five wickets for the addition of another 46 runs. Murray drove uppishly at DeFreitas, so a man was placed at extra-cover, and Murray instantly repeated the shot and was caught. Arthurton batted 196 minutes and held the innings together before he pushed forward defensively at DeFreitas and was caught behind. Bishop was run out, and Ambrose and Walsh skied the ball in frustration. Walsh was the victim of Gough who was allowed to bowl two overs at the close of the innings after his long absence.

Trailing by 83 runs, England needed a good start and a big score. They were not to get either. There was a quarter of an hour to go before lunch when they started their innings. At lunch, they were 6 for 1, Smith having cut the ball into the hands of cover.

After the interval Hick, not yet off the mark, edged Walsh high to first slip where Lara dropped a relatively simple chance. Hick responded with two thunderous pulls to the boundary, but, in the 16th over, Atherton fell to a rearing delivery from Walsh. In the next over, Hick sent a towering catch to long-leg, and England were 55 for 3.

Things could have been worse. Thorpe played on off his thigh but did not dislodge a bail, and half an hour later, he cut Bishop to Arthurton at cover point and was dropped. By this time, Stewart had already departed, edging a lifter to the keeper.

At tea, England were 90 for 4, and when the score had advanced to 109 from 34.1 overs the gloom had deepened and rain began to fall. It symbolised England's plight.

The start was delayed for an hour on the fourth day because of early-morning rain. Much depended on Thorpe and Ramprakash if England were to stay alive, but in the 10th over of the day, Walsh hit Ramprakash's off stump with an out-swinger which left the batsman groping. DeFreitas followed two overs later, spooning the ball to mid-on, and Thorpe, after much positivity and application spiced with a little fortune, was out in the third over after lunch when he played all askew at Walsh and was caught at point.

ABOVE: *An unsuccessful experiment comes to an end. Smith is caught by Richardson off Kenny Benjamin. (Patrick Eagar)*

ABOVE RIGHT: *Arthurton superbly caught by Stewart off DeFreitas for 42. Stewart's wicket-keeping was of high quality in the first two Tests. (Patrick Eagar)*

RIGHT: *A sad series for Mark Ramprakash. His off stump is knocked back by Walsh. (Graham Chadwick/Allsport)*

BELOW RIGHT: *Devon Malcolm is out! (Adrian Murrell/Allsport)*

Gough hit 3 fours and Martin a six and a four to bring light relief. It was not to be for long. Gough drove into cover's hands, Martin edged to slip, and Malcolm, after a cover-drive which had echoes of Wally Hammond, was predictably bowled.

West Indies, needing 126 to win, lost Campbell to Atherton's stunning slip catch off Martin. This had no effect on Hooper or Lara who crashed the ball in all directions. Hooper hit 18 off an over from DeFreitas, and when Illingworth came on he was hit for 2 sixes. Hooper's fifty came off 45 balls, and the hundred was up in the 16th over. Campbell had fallen to the first ball of the third over with the score at 11. The winning hit was made 16.5 overs later, 118 runs having come in that time.

Hooper hit 4 sixes and 9 fours in his 73 which came off 72 balls. Lara hit 9 fours, and his 48 came off 40 balls. Bishop was named Man of the Match, and England were massacred.

15 June *at Edinburgh*

West Indians 305 for 5 (S.C. Williams 123, J.C. Adams 57)
Scotland 258 for 5 (I.L. Philip 65, G. Salmond 61 not out,
 J.G. Williamson 57)

West Indians won by 47 runs

The 55-over match in Edinburgh provided some lively cricket. Williams hit 123 off 135 balls with a six and 22 fours while Scotland gave a most spirited reply, finding form that had eluded them in the Benson and Hedges Cup.

17, 18 and 19 June *at Chester-le-Street (Riverside)*

Durham 364 for 8 dec. (M.A. Roseberry 79, J.E. Morris 75) and
   259 (J. Boiling 69, O.D. Gibson 4 for 64)
West Indians 462 for 5 dec. (S.L. Campbell 113, C.O. Browne
   102 not out, R.B. Richardson 101 not out, B.C. Lara 91)
   and 16 for 1

Match drawn

The West Indians welcomed the opportunity of batting
practice in Durham, none more so than Brian Lara who
had not made a century on the tour. He failed again, but he
showed many of his master qualities in an innings which
occupied 90 balls. There was a maiden century for wicket-
keeper Browne, and some heroics for Durham from
Roseberry and Morris. They came together when Longley
was out in the first over and added 149. Boiling and
Killeen, making his debut, saved Durham from likely
defeat on the last day with a seventh-wicket stand of 69.
Boiling made his highest score in first-class cricket. Rain
delayed the start of the tourists' second innings.

Early success for England as Campbell is caught by Stewart off Gough.
(Patrick Eagar)

 SECOND TEST MATCH
ENGLAND *v.* WEST INDIES, at Lord's

Selectors do strange things. England chose Cork, who had
long been worthy of a place in the side, in place of
Malcolm. Rhodes – in spite of his failings in Australia, his
lack of form with the bat in the current season and the fact
that he is far from being the best wicket-keeper in the
country – was added to the party so that Alec Stewart
could open the innings without the burden of having to
keep wicket as well, and so that Robin Smith, grossly mis-
cast as an opener, could drop down the order. On the
morning of the match, the plan was changed: Rhodes was
discarded, and Stewart was asked both to open and to
keep wicket. DeFreitas was omitted from the twelve, and
Fraser returned. West Indies gave a first Test cap to Ottis
Gibson who replaced the injured Kenny Benjamin.

Atherton won the toss, and England batted on a day of
sunshine and heat. It was a good toss to win, for doubts
about the quality of the pitch, which sported a cracked
surface from the start, prevailed.

Atherton started the match by touching Ambrose's first
ball down the leg side for two. Stewart had little of the
strike and did not get off the mark until the fifth over, but
he looked sound and was severe on the bad ball, savaging
Gibson's entry into Test cricket for four to leg.

In the 13th over, Ambrose bowled Atherton with a magnificent yorker, but England were gaining momentum when,
on the stroke of lunch, Hick edged Bishop to slip. Worse was
to follow as, five balls after lunch, Stewart reached for a wide
delivery from Gibson and planted it in the hands of cover. It
was a very poor shot to a very bad delivery.

Smith entered with pressure upon him. Raymond
Illingworth had lost another opportunity to keep quiet
when, having unilaterally taken the decision to discard
Rhodes, he had publicly stated that if Smith did not score

runs, he would be out of the side, inferring that he had
been chosen on sufferance. Smith is, by nature, an uncertain starter, but he opened his score by clipping Gibson
through mid-wicket for four and then he off-drove the
same bowler for three. He also played and missed on several occasions, and he was dropped at second slip by
Richardson, but he survived, and England were 103 for 3
in 36.1 overs.

Smith had now found his touch, and he drove Ambrose
through the off side for four before hitting him through
mid-wicket for another boundary. The 150 came up in the
49th over.

It came as a surprise when Smith was bowled by
Hooper. The batsman walked into the shot with his feet
seemingly tied together. Ramprakash perished almost
immediately, driving loosely to be caught at slip.

Cork announced his arrival in Test cricket by square-
cutting Hooper for four, but he soon lost Thorpe who
sliced Ambrose's beautifully angled delivery into the
hands of slip. Gough cracked a four but was soon gone
when he fenced a short ball to gully. At 205 for 7 in the 75th
over, England were sinking fast.

It was now that Dominic Cork showed the spirit and the
tenacity for which England had been seeking.
Temperamentally he had soon proved himself well able to
cope with Test cricket, and he also revealed that he was
technically well equipped to deal with the West Indian
bowlers. Martin gave composed support, and there was a
refreshing youthfulness in their partnership of 50 in 15
overs. There seemed nothing to stop them batting into the
second day, but, with only three balls of Thursday's play
remaining, Cork was deceived by Walsh's yorker.

whose presence in the side remained a mystery, was dropped by Murray off Walsh, the ball going through the wicket-keeper's gloves for four. This was a dreadful miss, and Murray compounded his error by dropping Illingworth again, this time off the bowling of Ambrose. This was an abysmal display behind the stumps by any standards.

After 40 minutes' play, Martin was bowled by Walsh off an inside edge, and, in his next over, Walsh had Fraser leg before to close the England innings.

Campbell took a single to leg off Gough's first delivery. A single to Hooper followed, and, from the fourth ball of this opening over, Campbell hit a mighty boundary square of the wicket. He tried to repeat the shot next ball and was caught behind.

Gough was fast and aggressive. Fraser found line, length and accuracy from the start of his spell at the Nursery End. Lara drove Gough through the covers for four, but he had batted 47 minutes and faced 31 balls when he was leg before to Fraser. At lunch, West Indies trembled on 28 for 2. The morning had belonged to England.

There came another blistering day on the Friday, which England began with 255 runs on the board and with two wickets standing. West Indies were certainly leading on points, but the early events of the second day suggested that they would squander their advantage. Illingworth,

---

SECOND CORNHILL TEST MATCH – ENGLAND *v.* WEST INDIES
22, 23, 24, 25 and 26 June 1995 at Lord's

ENGLAND

	FIRST INNINGS		SECOND INNINGS	
M.A. Atherton (capt)	b Ambrose	21	c Murray, b Walsh	9
*A.J. Stewart	c Arthurton, b Gibson	34	c Murray, b Walsh	36
G.A. Hick	c Lara, b Bishop	13	b Bishop	67
G.P. Thorpe	c Lara, b Ambrose	52	c Richardson, b Ambrose	42
R.A. Smith	b Hooper	61	lbw, b Ambrose	90
M.R. Ramprakash	c Campbell, b Hooper	0	c sub (Williams), b Bishop	0
D.G. Cork	b Walsh	30	c Murray, b Bishop	23
D. Gough	c Campbell, b Gibson	11	b Ambrose	20
P.J. Martin	b Walsh	29	c Arthurton, b Ambrose	1
R.K. Illingworth	not out	16	lbw, b Walsh	4
A.R.C. Fraser	lbw, b Walsh	1	not out	2
Extras	b 1, lb 10, nb 4	15	b 6, lb 27, w 2, nb 7	42
		283		**336**

WEST INDIES

	FIRST INNINGS		SECOND INNINGS	
S.L. Campbell	c Stewart, b Gough	5	(2) c Stewart, b Cork	93
C.L. Hooper	b Martin	40	(1) c Martin, b Gough	14
B.C. Lara	lbw, b Fraser	6	c Stewart, b Gough	54
J.C. Adams	lbw, b Fraser	54	c Hick, b Cork	13
R.B. Richardson (capt)	c Stewart, b Fraser	49	lbw, b Cork	0
K.L.T. Arthurton	c Gough, b Fraser	75	c sub (Weekes), b Cork	0
*J.R. Murray	c and b Martin	16	c sub (Weekes), b Gough	9
O.D. Gibson	lbw, b Gough	29	lbw, b Cork	14
I.R. Bishop	b Cork	8	not out	10
C.E.L. Ambrose	c Ramprakash, b Fraser	12	c Illingworth, b Cork	11
C.A. Walsh	not out	11	c Stewart, b Cork	0
Extras	b 8, lb 11	19	lb 5	5
		324		**223**

	O	M	R	W	O	M	R	W
Ambrose	26	6	72	2	24	5	70	4
Walsh	22.4	6	50	3	28.1	10	91	3
Gibson	20	2	81	2	14	1	51	–
Bishop	17	4	33	1	22	5	56	3
Hooper	14	3	36	2	9	1	31	–
Adams					2	–	4	–

	O	M	R	W	O	M	R	W
Gough	27	2	84	2	20	–	79	3
Fraser	33	13	66	5	25	9	57	–
Cork	22	4	72	1	19.3	5	43	7
Martin	23	5	65	2	7	–	30	–
Illingworth	7	2	18	–	7	4	9	–

FALL OF WICKETS
1–29, 2–70, 3–74, 4–185, 5–187, 6–191, 7–205, 8–255, 9–281
1–32, 2–51, 3–150, 4–155, 5–240, 6–290, 7–320, 8–329, 9–334

FALL OF WICKETS
1–6, 2–23, 3–88, 4–166, 5–169, 6–197, 7–246, 8–272, 9–305
1–15, 2–99, 3–124, 4–130, 5–138, 6–177, 7–198, 8–201, 9–223

Umpires: D.R. Shepherd & S. Venkataraghavan

England won by 72 runs

One has complained about Stewart not being a special-ist wicket-keeper, but his work behind the stumps was infinitely better than Murray's. He was vital and kept the England fielding alert through an unusually dour period of West Indian batting. Richie Richardson grew in confid-ence and hit both Illingworth and Martin for glorious cover-drives, but Cork misjudged a chance he offered to extra-cover. Martin was the bowler to suffer, but it was he who took the only wicket of the afternoon when he bowled Hooper off an inside edge.

The doubts about the pitch were now growing, and it was apparent that West Indies would need a substantial lead if they were to win the match. Richardson and Adams batted as was most desperately required. Adams was splendid on the off side, particularly severe on Illingworth, and his fifty and the 150 were reached off suc-cessive deliveries.

England lapsed in concentration after tea, and Hick and Thorpe dropped Adams in successive Gough overs, but Fraser broke the vital stand. Richardson hooked Fraser for four, but he attempted to draw away from another short, lifting delivery only for the ball to take the shoulder of the bat and for Stewart to take the catch. It was a most intelli-gent piece of bowling. In his next over, Fraser claimed Adams leg before with a ball that held its line. West Indies were 169 for 5, and England, through Fraser, had recap-tured the initiative.

There was a vigorous appeal for leg before against Arthurton by the bowler Gough and the rest of inner field, but umpire Shepherd deemed that the batsman had got an edge on the ball. Arthurton survived until the close, but Murray did not. He gave Martin a lame return catch. West Indies were 209 for 6 at the close, and the game had swung in favour of England.

Saturday was a rogue day in every respect. The cricket was not as anticipated; and the weather was bitterly cold, a total freak in a period of sunshine and high tempera-tures. West Indies took a first-innings lead of 41. Gibson played a very useful innings of 29, hitting 6 fours and fac-ing 40 deliveries, but it was Arthurton, last out after bat-ting for 223 minutes, whom West Indies really had to thank for their advantage.

Atherton was caught behind down the leg side before the arrears were wiped off, and Stewart, after a series of sumptuous strokes, was also caught by Murray when he flicked at a ball also straying down leg side. Walsh had removed both England openers in the first 12 overs. His first ball to Thorpe temporarily removed the Surrey left-hander. Walsh lost control of what was intended to be a slow yorker. Thorpe lost sight of the ball, ducked and was hit on the helmet. Dazed, he was led away to hospital to return on the morrow.

In 26 overs, Hick and Smith restored England's fortunes with a partnership worth 99. Hick played some attacking shots which lacked conviction, but runs were valuable on a pitch roundly condemned by Andy Roberts, the West Indies coach. Hick, with a six and 10 fours to his credit, was bowled between bat and pad 10 minutes before bad light ended play early – England 155 for 3, a lead of 114.

The sun and the warmth returned on the Sunday, but the day started badly for England. In the first over,

Darren Gough is bowled by Ambrose. (Patrick Eagar)

Ramprakash played forward to Bishop and edged the ball to second slip to complete a 'pair' on his home ground.

Thorpe took his place and was assertive from the start. He pulled both Bishop and Walsh for four, and by lunch, England had advanced to 232 for 4. Hooper was unwell and off the field so that Richardson was forced to work his fast bowlers hard. The ball was lifting and moving side-ways off the seam, but Thorpe and Smith were full of determination and good sense.

They were separated shortly after lunch when Richardson took an excellent catch in the gully to dismiss Thorpe. Ambrose had maintained a full length and well deserved the wicket. Cork had batted with self-belief and self-confidence in the first innings, and he revealed those qualities again, suggesting at once that here was a young man who had a rightful place in the Test arena. In 67 minutes, he and Smith added 50, and Cork gave no in-dication that he was prepared to be a junior partner. He hit 3 fours and faced 50 balls before touching a wide-ish ball from Bishop to the keeper who took the catch in front of first slip.

The new ball was not taken until after tea, in the 94th over, and it immediately brought an end to Smith's fine innings. He was leg before to a ball of full length. He had batted for 364 minutes and hit 11 fours, and he had nursed England from a state of peril to a glimpse of fortune. He has acquired a sense of application with the years which no coach can teach, and he had resurrected his Test career when many had thought it finished.

Smith's was the first of four wickets to go down for 16

LEFT: *England level the series. Walsh, caught Stewart, bowled Cork, 0.* (Patrick Eagar)

BELOW: *Man of the Match Dominic Cork bowls Ian Bishop in West Indies' first innings. (Adrian Murrell/Allsport)*

Bowling from the Nursery End, he at once settled into a rhythm. He moved in silkily, varied pace and delivery intelligently, and proceeded to give the most sensational bowling display by an England Test debutant this century.

Adams was caught at second slip as he drove at a ball of full length, and Richardson, numbed into scorelessness by Cork's relentless probing, was leg before as he hit across the line. Shortly after lunch, Arthurton was caught bat-and-pad.

Sherwin Campbell was on 55 when Arthurton was out and was batting splendidly, meeting the wiles of Cork and the trials of the pitch with technical assurance. With the departure of Arthurton, he went onto the offensive. In the next nine overs, 39 runs were scored of which he made 30. If Murray could stay with him long enough West Indies could still win the match, but Murray was caught by Weekes – substituting for Thorpe, who was unwell – and West Indies' front-line batting, save Campbell, was at an end.

Gibson offered resolve but, with 21 added, he became another Cork victim, and in the fast bowler's next over, Campbell played across the line and gave Stewart a catch off the inside edge. It was a sad end to a very fine innings which, with more support, would have won his side the game.

Twenty minutes after tea, Cork took the last two wickets in three balls, Ambrose caught at cover and Walsh caught behind. England had beaten West Indies at Lord's for the first time since 1957. Cork's 7 for 43 was the best bowling analysis by an England player on his Test debut this century, and has only been bettered by Ferris against South Africa in 1891–2, but he had already played Test cricket for Australia. Cork was named Man of the Match, rightly so, but one must not forget Smith, Thorpe, Stewart and the leadership of Atherton. This was a team victory, a worthy one, hard earned and promising much for the future. Joy was unconfined.

This Test series was to be marked by umpiring of a poor standard, but this does not apply to the Lord's Test where the rulings of Shepherd and Venkataraghavan helped to make this a memorable match.

28, 29 and 30 June *at Oxford*

West Indians 637 for 5 dec. (C.L. Hooper 118, J.C. Adams 114 retired ill, S.C. Williams 114, K.L.T. Arthurton 102 not out, B.C. Lara 83, S. Chanderpaul 79) and 216 for 6 dec. (J.R. Murray 100, S.W.K. Ellis 5 for 59)

Combined Universities 310 (G.I. Macmillan 71, C.M. Gupte 56, R. Dhanraj 5 for 87) and 136 for 1 (I.J. Sutcliffe 63 not out)

Match drawn

The West Indians scored 493 for 4 in 105 overs in front of a large crowd in The Parks. Three batsmen hit centuries, and Arthurton became the fourth centurion when the

runs. West Indies needed 296 to win on a pitch that was worsening. It was a difficult task, and England rejoiced when Hooper, having hit 14 of the 15 runs scored, lofted Gough to mid-off. Bowler and captain had contrived this wicket intelligently. Now came Lara with 13.1 overs of the day remaining. By the close, he had hit 38 off 44 balls with 7 fours, and West Indies were 68 for 1.

Three more fours followed for Lara on the last morning. The second of them was a lavish cover-drive which took him to fifty. He repeated this beautiful shot two balls later, but Gough, the bowler, remained unbowed. He responded by giving Lara a ball which left him late off the pitch and took the outside edge. Stewart threw himself to his left and took a catch between first and second slip that was breathtaking in its brilliance. The catch was doubly important in that it disposed of the man who stood between England and any chance of victory, and by its magnificence it lifted England and their supporters to new heights. And the real hero was yet to move centre stage.

Lara was out in the seventh over of the day. Cork was not brought into the attack until play had been in progress for an hour, and he had not bowled the previous evening. In a five-over spell before lunch, he captured the wickets of Adams and Richardson at a personal cost of eight runs.

LEFT: Alec Stewart is leg before to Kenny Benjamin in what proved to be his last Test innings of the summer. (Adrian Murrell/Allsport)

Sussex ended the day on 390 for 5. They scored some brisk runs on the Sunday and then Stephenson, Jarvis and Lewry reduced the West Indians to 97 for 7. Dhanraj joined Arthurton in taking the score to 167 by the close, but Arthurton added only five to his overnight total on the Monday, and the tourists followed on.

Campbell was top scorer in their second innings with 32, eight boundaries, but the West Indians sank without trace in a gutless display. They appeared to be fatigued both mentally and physically, and, following their recent problems with Winston Benjamin, this was obviously the low point of their tour.

Sussex's win was the heaviest defeat ever inflicted on the West Indians by a county, and it was the first victory by a county side against the West Indians since 1976.

THIRD TEST MATCH
ENGLAND *v.* WEST INDIES, at Edgbaston

West Indies were supposedly in total disarray before the third Test. Winston Benjamin had been banished, and there had been an ignominious defeat at Hove. They had lost at Lord's, and they made just one change, Kenny Benjamin returning in place of Gibson.

England brought in Gallian for Ramprakash with the understanding that he could open if required. Watkinson, the Lancashire captain, had been in the original party, but he was not required on the morning of the match.

Whatever was the composition of the sides, the factor that was to dominate all else was the quality of the pitch. Raymond Illingworth had gradually come to assume dictatorial powers, a position he had demanded when he was first offered the post of England manager some years ago, and these powers extended to requesting of each of the six Test match grounds the type of pitch he would prefer. Whether there was a failure in communication or preparation, we shall never know. It was groundsman Steve Rouse, inevitably, who was to take the blame for a pitch that the West Indian pace bowlers relished.

Atherton won the toss and chose to bat. The pitch was hard. Truth was another matter. Ambrose bowled the first ball of the match. It pitched just short of a length and soared over Murray's head for four wides. The third legitimate ball of the match took the outside edge of Atherton's bat on its way to the wicket-keeper. Three overs later, Hick was caught at third slip off the shoulder of the bat. Hooper juggled the ball, and Richardson caught it.

For a time it seemed as though the Surrey pair, Stewart and Thorpe, would restore order. Each of them struck 5 fours, and Thorpe was in particularly aggressive mood, his 30 coming off 33 balls. In nine overs, they added 44 before Thorpe was out to a ball that lifted dramatically.

Stewart and Smith displayed customary grit, and they were aided by the fact that, one over after dismissing

tourists batted into the second day. Their runs came at five an over, and the students also batted enterprisingly. They were bowled out before the end of the second day, but Walsh did not enforce the follow-on. Murray, who missed out on the first innings, hit a century, and the match was drawn.

What happened in The Parks was overshadowed by what took place off field. The West Indian management announced that Winston Benjamin was being sent home for disciplinary reasons. He had refused to prove his fitness by playing against the Universities, and there was a general belief that he had been a constant irritation on the tour, responsible for factions developing within the party. Winston Benjamin, who had never fulfilled his promise at county or Test level, had been suspended some months earlier following an argument with an official in the car park at St John's, Antigua, after the Test match against England. Benjamin was replaced for the rest of the tour by Vasbert Drakes.

1, 2 and 3 July *at Hove*

Sussex 446 for 9 dec. (K. Newell 135, N.J. Lenham 128, R. Dhanraj 6 for 144)

West Indians 186 (K.L.T. Arthurton 75) and 139 (E.E. Hemmings 4 for 33, J.D. Lewry 4 for 38)

Sussex won by an innings and 121 runs

Vasbert Drakes had been scheduled to play for Sussex against the West Indians, but he now found himself a member of the touring side playing against the county for whom he has signed to play in 1996. Sussex won the toss, and Lenham and Newell made 263 for the first wicket. Newell hit the first first-class hundred of his career, and

Jason Gallian's first Test innings comes to an end – bowled Kenny Benjamin for 7. (Patrick Eagar)

Thorpe, Ambrose limped from the field with a groin strain and did not bowl again in the match. Having batted for 22 overs, Stewart mocked much of the good work he had done by playing across a ball of good length. This meant that, on his Test debut, Gallian was at the crease before lunch on the first day with the score on 84 for 4. He survived until the interval but not long after. His footwork was awry, and his mood tentative, and these combined to make him drag a ball from Benjamin into his stumps. It was later revealed that, in his 28-minute innings, he had sustained a broken finger.

The departure of Gallian virtually left Smith to fight a lone battle, which he did with considerable courage for just under 2½ hours in all. He was bruised and buffeted, but he hit 46 off 92 balls with 8 fours. It was an innings worth many a century on more friendly pitches. Its value was emphasised by the realisation that the last five batsmen scored six between them.

Smith was out in the 43rd over when he hit a long-hop to cover. The last two wickets fell in the next two overs, and England were out before tea for 147.

The England bowlers failed to present the West Indian

THIRD CORNHILL TEST MATCH – ENGLAND v. WEST INDIES
6, 7 and 8 July 1995 at Edgbaston, Birmingham

ENGLAND

	FIRST INNINGS		SECOND INNINGS	
M.A. Atherton (capt)	c Murray, b Ambrose	0	b Walsh	4
*A.J. Stewart	lbw, b Benjamin	37	absent hurt	–
G.A. Hick	c Richardson, b Walsh	3	c Hooper, b Bishop	3
G.P. Thorpe	c Campbell, b Ambrose	30	c Murray, b Bishop	0
R.A. Smith	c Arthurton, b Bishop	46	(2) b Bishop	41
J.E.R. Gallian	b Benjamin	7	(7) c Murray, b Walsh	0
D.G. Cork	lbw, b Walsh	4	(5) c sub (Williams), b Walsh	16
D. Gough	c Arthurton, b Bishop	1	c Campbell, b Walsh	12
P.J. Martin	c sub (Williams), b Walsh	1	(6) lbw, b Walsh	0
R.K. Illingworth	b Bishop	0	(9) c Hooper, b Bishop	0
A.R.C. Fraser	not out	0	(10) not out	1
Extras	lb 4, w 4, nb 10	18	nb 12	12
		147		**89**

WEST INDIES

	FIRST INNINGS	
C.L. Hooper	c Stewart, b Cork	40
S.L. Campbell	b Cork	79
B.C. Lara	lbw, b Cork	21
J.C. Adams	lbw, b Cork	10
R.B. Richardson (capt)	b Fraser	69
K.L.T. Arthurton	lbw, b Fraser	8
*J.R. Murray	c Stewart, b Martin	26
I.R. Bishop	c Martin, b Illingworth	16
K.C.G. Benjamin	run out	11
C.A. Walsh	run out	0
C.E.L. Ambrose	not out	4
Extras	b 5, lb 5, nb 6	16
		300

	O	M	R	W	O	M	R	W
Ambrose	7.5	1	26	2				
Walsh	17.1	4	54	3	15	2	45	5
Bishop	6.2	–	18	3	13	3	29	4
Benjamin	13	4	45	2	2	–	15	–

	O	M	R	W
Fraser	31	7	93	2
Gough	18	3	68	–
Cork	22	5	69	4
Martin	19	5	49	1
Illingworth	8	4	11	1

FALL OF WICKETS
1–4, 2–9, 3–53, 4–84, 5–100, 6–109, 7–124, 8–141, 9–147
1–17, 2–20, 3–26, 4–61, 5–62, 6–63, 7–88, 8–88, 9–89

FALL OF WICKETS
1–73, 2–105, 3–141, 4–156, 5–171, 6–198, 7–260, 8–292, 9–292

Umpires: M.J. Kitchen & I.D. Robinson

West Indies won by an innings and 64 runs

Saturday, 12.18 pm. Richard Illingworth, caught Hooper, bowled Bishop, and England are beaten in little over two days. (David Munden/ Sportsline)

batsmen with any great problems, whatever the state of the pitch. Gough appeared to have lost his ability to swing the ball, and Martin was wayward. In 22 overs, Hooper and Campbell scored 73. Hooper touched the first ball of the next over down the leg side where Stewart took a good catch. Lara arrived and indicated that he could not see what all the fuss had been about. In the last 12 overs of the day, he hit 4 fours and reached 21. West Indies were 104 for 1, and England already faced defeat.

Lara did not add to his overnight score, and Adams, like Lara, was leg before to Cork who gives England eternal hope in all he does. Campbell played a gem of an innings. He faced 140 balls and hit 16 fours until he was beaten by a ball which kept low. He had given the early part of the West Indian innings a bravado and, vitally, a sense of confidence. His role was now taken on by Richardson who batted as well as he has done for some years. He was dropped by Atherton at first slip when 25 and when the West Indies' lead was 76, but he played with the utmost resolution for four hours, and by the time he was last out, West Indies led by 153 runs.

Richardson hit 10 fours and faced 174 balls, and he received sound support from Murray, Bishop and Benjamin. His dismissal meant that England had 17 overs to negotiate at the end of a taxing day.

It now transpired that Stewart had aggravated the finger injury on his right hand and also had a badly bruised finger on his left hand. We did not know it at the time, but his season was over. As Gallian had a broken finger, Smith was once more forced to open. Again, he displayed the utmost courage. He lost Atherton in the seventh over to an excellent delivery which darted back at the batsman and kept low. In the next over, Hick turned away from a lifting ball from Bishop and was caught at slip off his glove. Thorpe was out to an equally wretched shot, slicing a wide ball to the wicket-keeper. Cork offered Smith some comfort, and England went to bed on 59 for 3.

The match was all over in 75 minutes, 13 overs, on the Saturday morning. Three wickets fell in Walsh's first two overs. Bishop had hit Smith painfully in the opening over of the day, and with the second ball of the second over, Walsh had Cork fend a lifter into the hands of third slip. In Walsh's next over, Martin was pinned in front of his stumps, and two balls later, Gallian edged towards first slip for Murray to take a good plunging catch.

Gough swatted a six to raise spirits. They soon subsided as Walsh, bowling round the wicket, deceived and deflated Gough with a vicious bouncer. Gough edged the next ball to gully. Smith's brave vigil came to an end after 156 minutes when he was bowled by Bishop to give the bowler his 100th Test wicket. Having been hit on the hand, Illingworth fell to a brilliant catch at second slip. The match was over.

The crowd chanted 'What a load of rubbish', and there were condemnations of the pitch and of the intimidatory nature of the West Indian bowling, especially at Smith.

Colin Croft, the former West Indian pace bowler, also made an interesting observation when he suggested that as English batsmen now play on only the most docile of wickets, they had no idea what to do when they encountered one that posed problems. Several of the shots played would support his view.

Campbell gained the individual award, but Richardson must have run him close.

10 July *at Edgbaston*

West Indians 220 for 7 (J.C. Adams 86 not out, B.C. Lara 51)
Warwickshire 198 (D.P. Ostler 63)

West Indians won by 22 runs

This match was not on the original schedule, but it was arranged when the third Test match finished so early. It was played on the Test pitch, and Warwickshire were 71 for 7 before Twose and Ostler added 71.

13 July *at Reading*

West Indians 266 for 9 (S.C. Williams 61, C.L. Hooper 54)
Minor Counties 270 for 6 (S.J. Dean 91, M.A. Fell 50)

Minor Counties won by 4 wickets

Like the game at Edgbaston, this was a 55-over contest, and Minor Counties won with 3.1 overs to spare. The West Indies conceded 78 extras which included 45 no-balls and 15 wides.

15 July *at Dublin (Castle Avenue)*

West Indians 306 for 4 dec. (S. Chanderpaul 101,
 K.L.T. Arthurton 94 not out, R.B. Richardson 57)
Ireland 187 for 3 (S.G. Smyth 98 not out, J.D.R. Benson
 74 not out)

Match drawn

Chanderpaul hit a century before lunch off 84 balls. Rain interrupted play before Ireland could begin their innings. Smyth and Benson shared an unbroken fourth-wicket stand of 161.

19, 20 and 21 July *at Canterbury*

West Indians 337 (S.C. Williams 137, J.C. Adams 77) and
92 for 4

Kent 95 (V.C. Drakes 5 for 20, O.D. Gibson 4 for 47) and 331
(P.A. de Silva 102, D.P. Fulton 89, R. Dhanraj 4 for 89)

West Indians won by 6 wickets

There was a sensational start to the game at Canterbury. In his first two overs, Dr Julian Thompson bowled Campbell off his pads and had Lara caught behind off a ball that seamed late. This left the West Indians at 0 for 2, but Williams and Adams then added 223. Williams, an exciting batsman, strong on the off side, hit 137 off 182 balls with 27 fours. He benefited from the Kent fielders who put down seven catches in the day, reprieving Williams twice. Patel and Ealham, in particular, deserved better support.

The second day began as sensationally as the first in that Kent were bowled out in 18.4 overs for 95. Their last seven wickets went down for 19 runs, and only Cowdrey and de Silva reached double figures – although 'extras' was top scorer with 24. Surprisingly, the tourists enforced the follow-on, and a two-day finish looked likely when Ward and Fleming were out for 12. Cowdrey batted stubbornly as did Fulton, who occupied the crease for 39 minutes. The sparkle, inevitably, was provided by de Silva who hit his fifth century in his last seven innings. Once again it was a thrilling affair. He hit Gibson for 14 off three balls and took 3 fours off another Gibson over. In all, he hit 2 sixes and 16 fours and reached his hundred off 98 balls. Kent ended the day with a lead of 65 and two wickets standing.

Those last two wickets fell quickly on the last morning, but the tourists then seemed too eager to get the match over and lost four wickets as they rushed to victory just before lunch. One of the wickets to fall was that of Brian Lara, leg before second ball to Thompson. This was the first time in his career that Lara had been out for a 'pair'.

22, 23 and 24 July *at Lord's*

West Indians 456 (S.L. Campbell 102, K.L.T. Arthurton 83,
S. Chanderpaul 71, B.C. Lara 62, P.C.R. Tufnell 6 for 111)
and 213 (K.L.T. Arthurton 55 not out, C.L. Hooper 53,
M.A. Feltham 6 for 41)

Middlesex 237 (J.D. Carr 115, R. Dhanraj 4 for 66) and 52 for 0

Match drawn

In their last match before the fourth Test, the West Indians settled for practice. Lara captained the side and was happy

Graham Thorpe batted with courage and skill to put England in a commanding position. He hits to leg during his innings of 94. (David Munden/Sportsline)

to reach a quick fifty on the first day. He hit 8 fours and a six, and four of his fours came in one over from Tufnell. The left-arm spinner who now, in English cricket, had become *the one we don't mention* took his revenge by bowling Lara, and he enjoyed a good match. Campbell's fine 102 included a six and 13 fours, but he did not bat in the second innings because of a swollen finger.

The tourists batted into the second day, and a draw looked certain when Middlesex closed on 215 for 7 with Carr unbeaten on 99. He reached his hundred on the Monday with his 14th four.

Lara did not enforce the follow-on, but he had little practice himself, being stumped off Weekes for 17. The greatest joy of the last day went to Mark Feltham whose 6 for 41 represented the best bowling figures of his career. Tufnell did not bowl in the second innings, and the match meandered to its slow death.

FOURTH TEST MATCH
ENGLAND *v.* WEST INDIES, at Old Trafford

England chose a strange, unbalanced party for the Old Trafford Test. Stewart was unfit – and it was later learned that his injured finger ruled him out for the rest of the season – and was replaced by Russell. The Gloucestershire captain had enjoyed a good year and had scored useful runs although it had to be admitted that his wicket-keeping was no longer of the standard it once had been. John Emburey was brought back in place of Richard Illingworth, a rather puzzling selection. Emburey was a few days short of his 43rd birthday and, presumably, this was one of those gambles which, if they come off, earn selectors the reputation of having psychic powers. As it transpired, Emburey had little influence on the outcome of the match, and one remains perplexed by Ray Illingworth's inability or unwillingness to choose the best spinners available.

On the morning of the match, Gough was omitted as there were doubts as to his fitness, and Mike Watkinson

A memorable hat trick for Dominic Cork and for England. Richie Richardson plays the ball onto his stumps. (Patrick Eagar)

TOP: *Cork flings his arms in the air as he traps Junior Murray leg before. (Adrian Murrell/Allsport)*

ABOVE: *The hat trick. Carl Hooper is palpably leg before. (Graham Chadwick/Allsport)*

was given his first Test cap. The Lancashire captain is a good, honest cricketer who bowls medium pace and off-spin and who is a very useful late middle-order batsman. Whether he is of Test quality is doubtful, particularly in the role of off-spinner.

Hick, too, was omitted on the morning of the match, a decision which brought forth some outspoken comment from the player himself, and he was replaced by Crawley who was in good form but whose appearances at the highest level had failed to convince that he was of Test class. The same could certainly be said of Craig White who took the place of the injured Peter Martin. White was not impressing with either bat or ball in the county championship, and his selection was totally incomprehensible.

As opener in place of Gallian – also injured – the selectors chose Nick Knight, the Warwickshire and former Essex batsman, who had done quite well on the England 'A' tour of India. Knight had not scored a first-class hundred in the season, but he was left-handed, and if his selection was premature – to say the least – it underlined the dearth of top-class opening batsmen in the country.

West Indies were unchanged, won the toss and batted. This should have been a good toss to win, for the pitch was fast and true and looked full of runs. Indeed, the odds were heavily in favour of West Indies winning the match when they won the toss. Hooper clipped Fraser resoundingly to the square-leg boundary, and the crowd sat back for a run feast. What they were to get was an undisciplined display of profligacy.

Campbell drove extravagantly at Fraser and edged to Russell. Hooper decided to pepper the leg-side field and mis-pulled a ball from Cork which pitched outside off stump. It was an arrogant, awful shot, and Crawley took a well-judged catch running back from square-leg.

Lara was instantly positive, and Adams bats with wisdom. Emburey bowled tidily, and the ball turned, but West Indies now seemed to be more settled. Lara restrained himself against Emburey, but was ever quick to punch the

loose ball to the boundary. He also has the ability to punch the not-so-loose ball to the ropes, and in this match he gave proof of his greatness.

Shortly before lunch, Atherton recalled Fraser who turned Adams square with a ball that left him off the pitch, found the edge and had him caught at second slip. Thirteen balls later, Fraser surprised Richardson with a little extra lift, and Thorpe held the catch at first slip. West Indies went to lunch at 94 for 4, and England could not believe their fortune.

Arthurton was missed in the gully by Cork off Fraser, and the batsman suggested that it might have been a costly miss when he hit Watkinson for six in the Lancastrian's first over in Test cricket. Cork and Watkinson soon atoned two overs later when another carelessly extravagant drive was caught low at extra-cover.

Cork covered himself in more glory when he trapped Lara leg before, the great man playing outside the ball after he had hit 16 fours off 118 deliveries.

His dismissal heralded disintegration. Murray was in a mist against spin and slogged Watkinson to mid-wicket. An early tea was taken because of sun reflecting from a nearby greenhouse, and then Cork had Bishop taken off a rebound from slip and hit the top of Benjamin's off stump. Fraser finished the job by having Walsh caught at slip. West Indies were all out 216 in 60.2 overs in $4\frac{1}{4}$ hours on a good pitch. Most of the wounds had been self-inflicted.

England had 23 overs to negotiate before the close, and both Ambrose and Walsh displayed an aggression which, in the case of Ambrose, was not always well controlled. Knight was a blend of nerves and determination, but he did have a tendency to play with the bat away from the body. Atherton might have been caught in the gully, but Richardson could not hold onto a chance when Bishop found the edge of the England captain's bat.

In the 17th over, Knight was out when he made a terrible hash of a slow full toss from Walsh. Worse followed in the last over of the day when Walsh produced a far better ball which came back off the seam and hit Crawley's off stump as he shouldered arms. England were 65 for 2, Atherton had 15.

West Indies had frittered away the advantage of winning the toss with some reckless batting on the first day; on the second morning, they surrendered any advantage they might have gained the evening before by bowling consistently short and often ill-tempered. Walsh was officially warned by umpire Bird, but it seemed to make little difference. Atherton was dropped at slip by Lara off Bishop, but he fell to Ambrose when the ball brushed his glove on the way to the keeper.

It is hard to measure Atherton's contributions in this series in terms of figures. They reveal nothing of the man's courage and determination. Once he was hit sickeningly over the heart by a ball from Walsh – the type of blow, we are told, that changed the whole course of Arthur Gilligan's career – yet next ball he was in line, on his toes, unflinching. His was the only wicket to fall in the morning session when England scored 103 runs.

Smith and Thorpe continued to defy the pace attack into the afternoon, and the bowling became as ugly as it was petulant. The batsmen met the fire and brimstone with admirable calm and courage. This was England's day. They added 104 in 31 overs before Smith was brilliantly caught at second slip by the substitute Williams. Battered and scarred, and, one felt, not relishing the fight quite as much as of yore, Smith had done a resolute job. England owed him much, and it was ironic that one ball after he was out, the players left the field because of bad light.

An early tea was taken, and four overs after the extended break Thorpe crashed four boundaries in one over from Benjamin. He seemed certain to reach his third Test century when Bishop angled the ball across him and he edged to Murray. The only blemish on his outstanding innings was that he took two paces towards the pavilion before turning back and waiting for umpire Bird's finger to be raised. The catch was so obvious that it had not been necessary.

England get the jitters on the way to their six-wicket victory. White is caught at slip by substitute Chanderpaul off the bowling of Kenny Benjamin. (David Munden/Sportsline)

One doubts if Thorpe has played better. He was at the crease for 259 minutes, faced 146 balls and hit 12 fours.

Vitally, his work was not wasted. White and Russell made useful contributions, and England closed on 347 for 7, a lead of 131. Watkinson had taken half an hour to get off the mark, and he and Cork were perhaps somewhat surprised to finish the day confronted by two part-time slow bowlers, Adams and Arthurton, in the gloom. Hooper had long been off the field with a damaged finger. The day very much belonged to England.

There was luck for England in the first over of the third day. Cork announced his intention and his exuberance with an all-run four. As he set off on his first run, he dislodged a bail with his back foot. Umpire Mitchley did not respond to Richardson's appeal. Hussain had not been so fortunate in a similar incident in the NatWest match at Chelmsford, which had also been recorded by television cameras, but Cork has the golden touch and he prospered.

The Derbyshire all-rounder was in ebullient mood. He lost Watkinson to a slip catch via Murray's gloves, and the Lancashire captain returned to his home pavilion amid a roar of approval. Non-Lancastrians reserved judgement. Emburey stayed for 12 overs while 40 were scored, and Fraser was with Cork for more than half an hour to boost the score further. There was also the great boost of 64 extras – 34 of them no-balls – and England led by 221.

Cork's first fifty in Test cricket had come off 91 balls and included 7 fours. Like Gough a few months earlier, he suffered the ludicrous comparison of being dubbed 'another

Botham'. He is not. He is Dominic Cork, very much his own man, bounding with enthusiasm, confident in his own ability, and quick to seize the chance to establish himself as a Test cricketer of outstanding ability. In this match, his best was yet to come.

In the absence of the injured Hooper, Arthurton opened with Campbell. The pair seemed unperturbed and leisurely scored 36 in 23 overs before Arthurton drove to Fraser, ran wildly, was sent back and run out by a considerable distance. After tea, 11 overs later, Campbell aimed to square-cut and was caught behind off Watkinson, and the off-break bowler claimed Adams in his next over, caught and bowled off a leading edge. Richardson played with the assurance he had shown at Edgbaston. West Indies were 159 for 3 at the close, Richardson was on 21, and Lara was on 59. He, more than anyone, stood between England and victory.

On the fourth morning, Cork opened the bowling from the Stretford End. Richardson took a single, Lara took a single. The West Indian captain lifted his bat to allow the fourth delivery of the over to pass by, and he was a little unlucky – if a little careless – when it hit the top of his pad, bounced up to hit bat and dropped down into his stumps. Murray was next in, moved across his stumps and was palpably leg before. He trudged slowly from the field. In all probability, a Test career was at an end. Hooper, nursing a chipped finger, replaced him and shuffled across his stumps in action replay. Cork had performed the third hat trick in Test cricket inside 10 months, and the first by an English Test bowler since Loader in 1957. West Indies were 161 for 6, still 60 runs adrift.

As long as Lara was at the crease, West Indies lived. His response to the critical situation was to attack with relish. He hooked and cut Cork, and he drove the ball through gaps in the field where, it had seemed, none existed. He did his best to protect his partners and added 30 in 37 minutes with Bishop who was caught off bat and pad. With Kenny Benjamin, he added 43 in 39 minutes and reached a century of the very highest quality. Records are scores of statistical interest, Lara's innings at Old Trafford was the best of batsmanship at the most crucial of times.

West Indies had now averted an innings defeat, but Benjamin was taken at slip. Ambrose whacked the ball hard, and 49 had been added in 13 overs when Lara pulled Fraser to mid-wicket where Knight ran in to take a good catch. The great man had been in for 282 minutes, faced 226 balls and hit 16 fours. With his departure, England breathed a sigh of relief, but Ambrose and Walsh were to

---

FOURTH CORNHILL TEST MATCH – ENGLAND v. WEST INDIES
27, 28, 29 and 30 July 1995 at Old Trafford, Manchester

WEST INDIES

	FIRST INNINGS		SECOND INNINGS	
C.L. Hooper	c Crawley, b Cork	16	(7) lbw, b Cork	0
S.L. Campbell	c Russell, b Fraser	10	(1) c Russell, b Watkinson	44
B.C. Lara	lbw, b Cork	87	c Knight, b Fraser	145
J.C. Adams	c Knight, b Fraser	24	c and b Watkinson	1
R.B. Richardson (capt)	c Thorpe, b Fraser	2	b Cork	22
K.L.T. Arthurton	c Cork, b Watkinson	17	(2) run out	17
*J.R. Murray	c Emburey, b Watkinson	13	(6) lbw, b Cork	0
I.R. Bishop	c Russell, b Cork	9	c Crawley, b Watkinson	9
C.E.L. Ambrose	not out	7	(10) not out	23
K.C.G. Benjamin	b Cork	14	(9) c Knight, b Fraser	15
C.A. Walsh	c Knight, b Fraser	11	b Cork	16
Extras	lb 1, nb 5	6	b 5, lb 9, nb 8	22
		216		**314**

ENGLAND

	FIRST INNINGS		SECOND INNINGS	
N.V. Knight	b Walsh	17	c sub (Chanderpaul), b Bishop	13
M.A. Atherton (capt)	c Murray, b Ambrose	47	run out	22
J.P. Crawley	b Walsh	8	not out	15
G.P. Thorpe	c Murray, b Bishop	94	c Ambrose, b Benjamin	0
R.A. Smith	c sub (Williams), b Ambrose	44	retired hurt	1
C. White	c Murray, b Benjamin	23	c sub (Chanderpaul), b Benjamin	1
*R.C. Russell	run out	35	not out	31
M. Watkinson	c sub (Williams), b Walsh	37		
D.G. Cork	not out	56		
J.E. Emburey	b Bishop	8		
A.R.C. Fraser	c Adams, b Walsh	4		
Extras	b 18, lb 11, w 1, nb 34	64	lb 2, w 1, nb 8	11
		437	(for 4 wickets)	**94**

	O	M	R	W	O	M	R	W
Fraser	16.2	5	45	4	19	5	53	2
Cork	20	1	86	4	23.5	2	111	4
White	5	–	23	–	6	–	23	–
Emburey	10	2	33	–	20	5	49	–
Watkinson	9	2	28	2	23	4	64	3

	O	M	R	W	O	M	R	W
Ambrose	24	2	91	2	5	1	16	–
Walsh	38	5	92	4	5	–	17	–
Bishop	29	3	103	2	12	6	18	1
Benjamin	28	4	83	1	9	1	29	2
Adams	8	1	21	–	2	–	7	–
Arthurton	9	2	18	–	2.5	1	5	–

FALL OF WICKETS
1–21, 2–35, 3–86, 4–94, 5–150, 6–166, 7–184, 8–185, 9–205
1–36, 2–93, 3–97, 4–161, 5–161, 6–161, 7–191, 8–234, 9–283

FALL OF WICKETS
1–45, 2–65, 3–122, 4–226, 5–264, 6–293, 7–337, 8–378, 9–418
1–39, 2–41, 3–45, 4–48

Umpires: H.D. Bird & C.J. Mitchley

England won by 6 wickets

delay them for another 24 minutes. The final victory target was 94.

Atherton and Knight gave a valuable start although tension and expectation were high. In the 13th over, Atherton glided the ball to third man and was out when he went for an unwise second run. Tea was taken shortly after, and then Knight was taken at slip. Thorpe hooked Benjamin into the hands of Ambrose, and England were 45 for 3.

Two runs later, Smith edged a lifter from Bishop into his face. He was helped from the field with a broken cheekbone. Surgery was necessary, and his season was over. A sad end for one who had shown so much courage, and

ironic that, in a match of ugly bowling, the one serious injury should come by mischance. White was caught at slip in the next over and, effectively, England were 48 for 5.

In 11 overs since tea, only 10 runs had come, but Russell met the situation with calm bordering on serenity. He pushed, dabbed, ran and hooked. Crawley took root, and England drew closer to the promised land. They reached it at ten to six, bravely, tenaciously and most deservedly.

Cork, the man with the golden arm, was once more Man of the Match, but there were many heroes at Old Trafford at the end of July 1995. The series was level.

CAPTAIN AND SELECTOR
Frank Hayes, former Lancashire and England batsman,
reflects on the relationship between captain and chief selector

---

After a truly excellent victory in the fourth Test in Manchester to level the series, Raymond Illingworth, England supremo, maintained that he was in the process of gradually weeding out players with the wrong attitude and was particularly delighted with the way in which the side had competed over the four days.

Things can change radically of course and only when the series is complete can a really true assessment be made. Cricket is notoriously fickle and England have been past masters of briefly promising much but ultimately flattering to deceive. However, at present the signs are most encouraging. Selection and management of the Test side is largely in the hands of Illingworth and the young captain Michael Atherton, and the future depends, therefore, on the capabilities of these two strong-willed Northerners. Much has already been surmised about the relationship between them. Will the partnership succeed or will it one day simply spontaneously combust? Are there in fact innate problems with such a relationship?

Although both have first-class credentials, it has already been suggested that they do not see eye to eye on many topics and that friction exists between them. Contradiction seems to reign, however, and while many suppose that only Illingworth's intervention saved Atherton's neck in the infamous 'dirt on the ball' episode, some are suggesting that Atherton now feels beholden to Illingworth and has therefore lost confidence in making his own decisions. Again, Atherton's penchant for plain speaking and his showing of dissent or disappointment – depending on one's views – have also been criticised by the England supremo.

Illingworth, himself, of course, has also been condemned, in particular by Ian Botham, for making rash critical statements in the media about Atherton and his team. Botham further maintains that Illingworth is simply too old and out of touch with the modern game to do any sort of job and also criticises him for poor selection.

All this bickering and washing of dirty linen in public is not exactly music to the ears of the cricket Establishment who are responsible for giving both Atherton and Illingworth their respective positions. This eminent group of people – once termed 'gin-slinging old dodderers' by

Botham – who many believe to be the 'old boy' network personified and Cantab based, much prefer their men to maintain a stiff upper lip, bite their tongues and fly the flag no matter what the crisis. Can, therefore, both men survive the scrutiny of the Establishment who selects them and, worse in many respects, the scrutiny and criticisms of the popular press?

Atherton is a personable young man who hails from the difficult academic background of Manchester Grammar School – to get there one must first pass the eleven-plus and then two of the hardest entrance exams in the country. Once there only the very best will do. Again, only the very best academically make it to and through Cambridge University and it is harder still for cricketers these days. He learnt his cricket via the climate of the leagues of the North and had to survive hard-bitten, 'give em nowt' adult cricketers from a young age. He is as happy in the wine bars of Bowden as he is in the taprooms of public houses in Stockport, is fiercely patriotic and has a backbone of steel. His modesty is nicely tempered by a down-to-earth honesty and he has been a great help to his county captain, Mike Watkinson. It is a quiet conviction backed up by actions, especially under stress, that give him his motivational prowess. The England captain can be trusted in the committee room to back his players to the hilt. He is learning to be consistently tactically astute and is capable of pulling the rabbit out of the hat with a change of bowling or a change in the field. On occasion, however, he can be unduly defensive and unimaginative. There is no doubting that he has a great deal of ability and will certainly recover from the recent trials and tribulations, although his voice and manner can still betray a trace of cynicism. Given the chance, he will undoubtedly become a captain of repute and one around whom a new team with refreshing belief in itself can be built.

Raymond Illingworth hails from a more modest academic background but has acquired an education from the University of Life. With Illy, what you see is what you get. He has learnt and done it all by himself. No books for him – he has been through it and worked it out for himself. 'Forget the coaching manual, lad, just listen to me.' Like

Atherton, he has the courage of his convictions and is fiercely competitive. He has the utmost confidence in his own ability and will always back his own judgement. Only on isolated occasions can he be unduly defensive. He is tactically astute and certainly one of the best captains that I had the privilege to play under. He, too, has a backbone of steel and prefers the quiet, sensible approach to motivation. As with Atherton, he backs up his statements with actions. The England supremo believes that those picked for the national side have ability and should take responsibility for their own actions. He does not mince words and what is good for the shop floor is good enough for committees also. Illingworth has a proven track record and, as a commentator and journalist, knows how to use the press and is not frightened to do so. His recent statement to the press concerning Devon Malcolm indicates the nature of the man, although showing a gathering frustration: 'The way for Devon to get in the side is to go out there and get some bloody wickets for Derbyshire. Do it out there and we pick him – that's the answer.'

These two men from the North, it seems, possess frighteningly similar attributes. However, will they, instead of recognising their common strengths and building on them, identify common weaknesses and self-destruct? Or can they knit themselves into a combination that will fortify themselves against an overcritical and sometimes diabolical press and convince, too, a cricket Establishment that can quickly make decisions when adversity and

failure strike? It is not a case of the wise old man and talented pupil but rather a case of helping each other to help oneself. One never stops learning about life or the game. Illingworth can teach Atherton much but Illingworth can also learn from Atherton. They must put their heads together and compare notes. Atherton cannot be right all of the time but neither, too, can Illingworth. If Atherton understands the wisdom of age and Illingworth the exuberance of youth, and from their own discussions they can arrive at a similar policy and speak with common tongue, then the partnership will surely thrive. If Atherton realises that it is Illingworth who carries the can for failure and Illingworth understands that only the captain and his team can get the right results on the field of play, then the partnership will blossom. The supremo and the captain must be seen to be pulling together at all times, regardless of any differences of opinion. Errors of judgement similar to that with respect to the Edgbaston pitch can only cause friction between management, captain and team, and too many errors of this nature will destroy any partnership.

In the final analysis, for the sake of English cricket, it is to be hoped that the Red Rose of Lancashire and the White Rose of Yorkshire can flower together and at least motivate a side to do as well as it can, even if the flawed structure of the English game continues to make it difficult for young talent in the country to achieve its potential. Their masters at Lord's will watch with interest.

2, 3 and 4 August *at Taunton*

West Indians 230 (S. Chanderpaul 100, J.I.D. Kerr 5 for 82)
  and 386 (S.C. Williams 119, O.D. Gibson 101 not out,
  R.B. Richardson 88, A.P. van Troost 5 for 120)
Somerset 374 (J.I.D. Kerr 80, R.J. Turner 72) and 87
  (O.D. Gibson 4 for 32)

West Indians won by 155 runs

Play started early on all three days in order to enable Somerset to travel to Holland to fulfil a fixture. The tourists were originally scheduled to play either Warwickshire or Derbyshire, but as both were engaged in the NatWest Trophy quarter-finals, Taunton became the venue. It proved to be an unlucky change for the West Indians and for Jimmy Adams in particular. Sixteen wickets fell on the first day, and, at one time, the tourists were 71 for 5. Their recovery was effected by Chanderpaul who hit 100 off 104 balls with 20 fours. Kerr returned his best bowling figures, and Somerset's much-criticised wicketkeeper Robert Turner equalled the county record with six catches. Somerset ended the day on 162 for 6, and Turner and Kerr still had honours to earn.

Jason Kerr hit the highest score of his career, and he and Turner put on 136 for the seventh wicket. Somerset took a lead of 144, thanks, in part, to 69 extras, 57 of which were no-balls.

Williams and Richardson soon wiped off the arrears in quick time, scoring 206 for the second wicket at more than

five an over. Williams hit 3 sixes and 19 fours, and his 119 came off 131 balls. Richardson was out for 88, apparently losing sight of a delivery from van Troost and offering no stroke. Jimmy Adams came in and immediately ducked into a short ball from van Troost which could have been played with a normal defensive straight bat. He was struck below the right eye and sustained a depressed fracture of the cheekbone. Surgery was necessary, and Adams' tour was over.

Gibson, batting at number eight, hit a violent century which began on the Thursday evening and outlasted the remainder of the innings. It was the first hundred of his career and came off 69 balls with 7 sixes and 8 fours. He then destroyed Somerset's upper-order, taking the first four wickets to fall. Dhanraj took the last three for two runs in three overs, and Somerset were all out in 33 overs.

5, 6 and 7 August *at Bristol*

West Indians 242 (K.P. Sheeraz 6 for 67) and 193
  (S.C. Williams 56, S. Chanderpaul 53, K.P. Sheeraz 5 for 44)
Gloucestershire 239 (A.J. Wright 73, A. Symonds 51,
  K.C.G. Benjamin 4 for 53, R. Dhanraj 4 for 110) and 122
  (K.C.G. Benjamin 5 for 52)

West Indians won by 74 runs

The West Indians were all out in 48.3 overs on the first day with 'extras', 49, being their top scorer. Kamran Sheeraz, the 21-year-old medium-pacer, was playing only his fourth first-class match, and his six wickets represented his best performance. He was also to take 10 wickets in a match for the first time.

Gloucestershire collapsed on the second day. Their last eight wickets went down for 73 runs, and Benjamin ended the innings with 4 for 0 in three overs.

The tourists batted carelessly in their second innings, and Hooper was obviously troubled by his injured finger. In spite of this, he opened the bowling when Gloucestershire batted again and took three wickets bowling medium pace. The county descended to 29 for 5 and never really recovered.

Richard Williams, the Gloucestershire wicket-keeper held seven catches in the match.

FIFTH TEST MATCH
ENGLAND v. WEST INDIES, at Trent Bridge

There were several batsmen standing by for England on the eve of the fifth Test because of injury scares, but, in the end, Hick for Smith and Illingworth for Emburey were the only changes from the side that won at Old Trafford. Alan Wells and Mark Ilott were in the original England party and were omitted on the day, while David Byas had also been called to the ground as a precaution.

West Indies made four changes. Williams replaced the injured Hooper, and neither Adams nor Ambrose was fit, and their places went to Chanderpaul and Dhanraj. As expected, Browne took over from Murray behind the stumps.

Atherton won the toss and England batted in beautiful weather on a pitch blissful for batting, but with a hint of future help for the spinners. Indeed, Dhanraj and Arthurton were in operation before lunch. Arthurton is simply a slow bowler, but Dhanraj turned the ball. Unfortunately, the leg-spinner could find no sort of length or line, and he was not encouraged by the fields his captain offered him.

Atherton and Knight began the England innings with a partnership which extended beyond tea-time, occupied 64.2 overs and realised 148 runs. It was ended when Benjamin straightened a delivery to which Knight offered no stroke. The left-hander had faced 191 balls and batted for 254 minutes for his first Test fifty, and one could not

---

FIFTH CORNHILL TEST MATCH – ENGLAND v. WEST INDIES
10, 11, 12, 13 and 14 August 1995 at Trent Bridge, Nottingham

ENGLAND

	FIRST INNINGS		SECOND INNINGS	
N.V. Knight	lbw, b Benjamin	57	(7) c Browne, b Benjamin	2
M.A. Atherton (capt)	run out	113	(1) c Browne, b Bishop	43
J.P. Crawley	c Williams, b Benjamin	14	(2) b Walsh	11
G.P. Thorpe	c Browne, b Bishop	19	c Browne, b Walsh	76
R.K. Illingworth	retired hurt	8	(11) not out	14
G.A. Hick	not out	118	(3) b Benjamin	7
C. White	c Browne, b Bishop	1	(5) c Campbell, b Bishop	1
*R.C. Russell	c Browne, b Bishop	35	(6) c Browne, b Benjamin	7
M. Watkinson	lbw, b Benjamin	24	(8) not out	82
D.G. Cork	c Browne, b Benjamin	31	(9) c Browne, b Benjamin	4
A.R.C. Fraser	b Benjamin	0	(10) c Arthurton, b Benjamin	4
Extras	b 4, lb 8, nb 8	20	lb 4, nb 14	18
		440	(for 9 wickets, dec.)	269

WEST INDIES

	FIRST INNINGS		SECOND INNINGS	
S.C. Williams	c Atherton, b Illingworth	62		
S.L. Campbell	c Crawley, b Watkinson	47	c Russell, b Cork	16
B.C. Lara	c Russell, b Cork	152	(1) c Russell, b Fraser	20
R.B. Richardson (capt)	c Hick, b Illingworth	40		
K.L.T. Arthurton	b Illingworth	13		
R. Dhanraj	c Knight, b Cork	3		
S. Chanderpaul	c Crawley, b Watkinson	18	(3) not out	5
*C.O. Browne	st Russell, b Illingworth	34	(4) not out	1
I.R. Bishop	c Hick, b Watkinson	4		
K.C.G. Benjamin	not out	14		
C.A. Walsh	b Fraser	19		
Extras	b 2, lb 7, nb 2	11		0
		417	(for 2 wickets)	42

	O	M	R	W	O	M	R	W
Walsh	39	5	93	–	30	6	70	2
Bishop	30.1	6	62	3	21	8	50	2
Benjamin	34.3	7	105	5	25	8	69	5
Dhanraj	40	7	137	–	15	1	54	–
Arthurton	9	–	31	–	13	3	22	–

	O	M	R	W	O	M	R	W
Fraser	17.3	6	77	1	6	1	17	1
Cork	36	9	110	2	5	1	25	1
Watkinson	35	12	84	3				
Illingworth	51	21	96	4				
Hick	4	1	11	–				
White	5	–	30	–				

FALL OF WICKETS
1–148, 2–179, 3–206, 4–211, 5–239, 6–323, 7–380, 8–440, 9–440
1–17, 2–36, 3–117, 4–125, 5–139, 6–148, 7–171, 8–176, 9–189

FALL OF WICKETS
1–77, 2–217, 3–273, 4–319, 5–323, 6–338, 7–366, 8–374, 9–384
1–36, 2–36

Umpires: C.J. Mitchley & N.T. Plews

Match drawn

help but admire his total dedication. He was more than fortunate that on two occasions the umpire failed to agree with bowler and fielders that Walsh's slower delivery, a yorker, would have hit the stumps but for the intervention of his pad, but this should not detract from Knight's concentration and application. Umpiring was not to be a strong point in this match.

Crawley joined Atherton and seemed untroubled until he pushed forward at Benjamin and was well caught at slip. By now, Atherton had reached an admirable century, full of character and positivity. It was easy to see why the West Indians rate him so highly and why his is their most prized wicket. It certainly did not seem that a bowler would dismiss him on this pitch and in this form. So it proved. He called for a run that was perhaps unwise, and Dhanraj fielded and hit the stumps with his throw from mid-on to catch him short of the line. It was a fine piece of fielding, and it brought an end to an innings that had lasted 247 balls and included 17 fours. Atherton had hit England's first century of the summer, and none was more worthy.

Five runs later, Thorpe prodded at Bishop and was caught behind. Four wickets had fallen in the last session, and England closed on 227 for 4, a disappointment after the excellent start given by Knight and Atherton, and disturbing in that the morrow would bring the new ball.

Richard Illingworth could not resume his innings on the second morning because it was revealed that his right index finger had been broken during his 40-minute stay at the crease the previous evening. Hick and White faced the new ball.

White, whose presence in the side was hard to justify, spent an uneasy half-hour at the crease before pushing at Bishop and giving Browne his second catch. Russell presented the West Indies with greater problems. Like Alan Knott before him, he has created his own style of batting. He crouches, nudges and pushes. He survives and accumulates. His main purpose was to support Hick and to see off the new ball. In 28 overs, he helped Hick to add 84 runs.

Certainly Hick owed Russell a debt of gratitude for the Gloucestershire wicket-keeper helped him to find composure after an uncertain start to the day which had seen him come close to playing on and equally close to being caught at short-leg. There was considerable pressure on Hick for he had openly criticised the selectors for omitting him from the previous Test. Having spoken, he was in a position where failure at Trent Bridge would have brought doom. He did not fail. Batting for 302 minutes and facing 213 balls, he hit his first century against West Indies, and his innings contained 17 fours. It must be said that eight of those fours came off Dhanraj, who looked a better bowler when Richardson was off the field and the leg-spinner was under the guidance of Walsh.

To put Hick's innings in perspective, it should be said that this was an achievement of considerable character. He confronted Raymond Illingworth and answered the manager's doubts with deeds. The pitch was easy and the opposing attack was weakened, weary and often poorly handled, but a batsman still has to score the runs – and Hick did that. He may not have convinced totally that he was sure against short-pitched fast bowling, but he nursed

Illingworth and Watkinson leave the field after their unbeaten last-wicket stand of 80 which saved England from any chance of defeat. (David Munden/Sportsline)

England through a difficult period and was there at the end when they reached a total which should, at least, have secured them from defeat.

With Watkinson, not totally convincing, he added 57, and with the ebullient Cork he put on 60. Cork was caught behind off Benjamin who bowled Fraser first ball to give him well-deserved figures of 5 for 105. A much underrated bowler, Benjamin impressed throughout the series.

West Indies scored 25 from 19 overs before the close, five of those overs being maidens bowled by Watkinson.

The opening partnership was eventually worth 77 in 45 overs, but it should never have got that far. Campbell was on 12 when he advanced down the pitch to Illingworth and was beaten by unexpected turn and bounce. Stranded, he presented Russell with the easiest of stumping chances, but the wicket-keeper failed to gather the ball. In the end, it was Williams who was the first to go. He had played some glorious shots on the off side, and his innings included 10 fours. He became over-excited and fell when he lofted Illingworth to mid-off. The rest of the day belonged to Lara.

He thrilled the Saturday crowd with a dazzling display of strokes which brought him 28 fours and 152 runs off 182

LEFT: *Nick Knight on his way to a maiden Test fifty. Knight was later injured while fielding. (David Munden/Sportsline)*

BELOW LEFT: *Mike Atherton hits England's first century of the series. (Patrick Eagar)*

Richardson joined in the fun, hitting a six and 8 fours in his 45-ball innings which ended when he surprisingly steered Illingworth to slip. Ten overs and 46 runs later, Arthurton offered no shot to a ball from Illingworth which pitched in the rough outside the left-hander's off stump and turned in to hit the wicket. It was a gross error of judgement.

Brian Lara's magnificence came to an end when he touched a leg-side long-hop to the wicket-keeper, Russell taking a good catch. Dhanraj had already come in as night-watchman, but Chanderpaul now arrived to crack two majestic boundaries, and England's hard day ended with West Indies 334 for 5.

It was difficult to understand the West Indians' batting on the early part of the Sunday morning. Dhanraj and Chanderpaul were becalmed, and the talented left-hander appeared to have no inclination to score. It took England three hours to capture the last five wickets, and the only spark of vitality was provided by Browne and the last pair.

One of this last pair, Kenny Benjamin, brought a fearful shock to England when he drove at Watkinson and hit Knight on the right side of the head. Knight was fielding as silly point and was wearing no helmet. The ball came off the meat of the bat, and that Knight did not sustain the most serious and lasting injury was a miracle. He was taken to hospital where it was discovered that there was no fracture, but it was believed that his part in the match was over.

Crawley opened with Atherton in Knight's absence, but he served only to underline his technical deficiencies. He was beaten for pace by Bishop and edged a four, and then he offered no shot at a breakback from Walsh and was bowled, an action replay of what had happened at Old Trafford. In the third over after tea, Hick played back to Benjamin and was bowled. Atherton and Thorpe now needed to play for survival, which they did, comfortably, to take England to 111 for 2 at the close.

There was less comfort the next morning. Thorpe was fortunate to survive an appeal for a catch behind off Walsh. Atherton did not have such fortune when a ball from Bishop pitched on off stump and left him late. White came and went after a painful 27 minutes, turning Bishop tamely into the hands of short-leg. How Thorpe survived only umpire Mitchley can tell us. He was beaten on the back foot by a ball from Bishop which hit his pads and seemed certain to hit middle stump. On his showing in this match, Mr Mitchley is not an umpire of Test standard.

Russell played surprisingly wildly at Benjamin and was caught behind, and the same fate befell the brave Knight who tried an injudicious cut at the same bowler. Much now depended on Benjamin, for Bishop had limped from the field with an injured ankle.

Benjamin shouldered the responsibility although it was Walsh who captured the vital wicket of Thorpe who, hav-

balls. He drove majestically through gaps on the off side which only he perceived, pulled with power and venom and late cut with a delicacy one remembered only from one's youth. With Campbell, he added 140 in 36 overs. Lara's contribution to this partnership was 104.

Sherwin Campbell was subdued and out of touch, and his innings lasted more than five hours. In the end, he was the victim more of the constant cries of 'catch it!' and of perpetual appeals than of any bowling wiles. He was adjudged caught bat-and-pad at silly point although neither bat nor glove appeared to be anywhere near the ball.

Lara peppered the boundary. Fraser was savaged out of the attack after a three-over spell. White went for 29 in four overs. Lara's hundred came off 118 balls.

Russell, caught Browne, bowled Bishop, 35. Browne took nine catches in the match and proved his worth as West Indies' keeper. (Patrick Eagar)

ing batted so well, pulled lazily at an away-swinger. Benjamin accounted for Cork and Fraser, and England were 189 for 9, with Watkinson on 20 and defeat a possibility.

That defeat came close to becoming a reality when, as soon as Illingworth arrived, Watkinson hit a simple catch to mid-wicket where Campbell misjudged the ball completely, ran in and dropped the chance. This, in effect, was the end of the match. The last pair survived for an hour and a half, and Atherton's declaration left West Indies 20 overs in which to score 293. He took the precaution of setting defensive fields when Lara opened, but the game was halted after 11 overs.

In spite of some fine individual performances by England – not the least of which was Watkinson's valiant rearguard innings, an unbeaten 82 in 165 minutes – one felt West Indies had the edge. They bowled better than England, with Man of the Match Kenny Benjamin – 10 wickets in a Test for the first time – outstanding, and they came the closer to winning.

One also felt that had either side possessed a top-class spinner, he might well have won them the match.

16, 17 and 18 August *at Southampton*

Hampshire 192 (A.C. Cummins 5 for 60) and 302 for 5
  (V.P. Terry 60)
West Indians 696 for 6 dec. (C.L. Hooper 195,
  S.L. Campbell 172, R.B. Richardson 83, C.O. Browne 74
  not out, K.L.T. Arthurton 59)

Match drawn

To relieve pressure on their walking wounded, the West Indians drafted in Phil Simmons and Anderson Cummins from league cricket. Stephenson led Hampshire for the first time, won the toss, batted and saw Terry out to the fifth ball of the match and his side reduced to 96 for 5 at lunch on an amiable pitch. Cummins took four of those wickets and added another in the afternoon when Hampshire were out for 192. The total owed a great deal to 60 extras, 40 of which were no-balls.

The tourists were 135 at the close, and the next day, in 98 overs, they scored 561 runs. Campbell and Hooper were the principal routers of the Hampshire attack. Campbell played a series of elegant strokes, and Hooper, the more belligerent, proved in exquisite fashion that he was fit for The Oval Test. He hit 20 fours and 2 sixes.

On the last day, Hampshire discovered that the pitch was friendly, and James and Aymes batted out time after five wickets had gone for 230.

19, 20 and 21 August *at Chelmsford*

West Indians 366 (P.V. Simmons 112) and 260 for 0 dec.
  (P.V. Simmons 139 not out, S. Chanderpaul 103 not out)
Essex 300 for 4 dec. (G.A. Gooch 109 retired hurt, N. Hussain
  56) and 202 for 6 (G.A. Gooch 50)

Match drawn

Large crowds flocked to see Essex play the West Indians, and the attendance brought Essex Tetley's special award, which was a bit hard on Sussex. A century in each innings by Phil Simmons – who was engaged on a two-match contract and would not appear at The Oval – and a more sedate hundred by Graham Gooch, who was also unavailable for The Oval Test, were high points of three days of entertaining batting. When the tourists batted a second time Simmons and Chanderpaul shared an unbroken first-wicket partnership of 260 at more than five runs an over. Chanderpaul was most impressive and surely he must play a major part in a restructured West Indian side.

 SIXTH TEST MATCH
ENGLAND *v.* WEST INDIES, at The Oval

Tufnell was in the England party at The Oval, but he was not in the final eleven. Knight was unfit, and Gallian was recalled. Malcolm replaced the injured Illingworth, and Wells was given his first Test cap at the expense of White. Many had pleaded Wells' cause, but one felt the selection had more of sentiment than logic about it. The claims of Hussain and Ramprakash were ignored, and Crawley retained his place.

For West Indies, Ambrose returned in place of Dhanraj, and Hooper came back to the exclusion of Arthurton.

Atherton again won the toss, and England batted on a pitch which bowlers would water with their tears. The Oval outfield gave testimony to a summer of sun and drought. Ambrose indicated that he would extract some bounce from the pitch in the opening over, and Gallian was close to being leg before to Walsh in the second. The reprieve was brief because he drove at Ambrose in the next over and edged to first slip.

Atherton and Crawley restored Lancastrian calm for the next hour and a half, and the pitch grew more docile by the minute. The two Manchester Grammar School old boys had put on 51 in 23 overs of studious batting when Atherton played at a lifting ball he might well have disregarded and was caught high at second slip.

That wicket fell shortly before lunch, and England were not to lose another until the first over after tea when Crawley drove Hooper into the hands of extra-cover. Crawley had shown sound defence and was obviously maintaining self-discipline, but steadily as Hooper bowled, he was not turning the ball to any significant degree, and Crawley was the victim of a very loose shot.

Thorpe had been both sound in defence and confident in attack. He had grown in stature through the series, and he looked set for a century before Ambrose, drawing on his inner resources, had him caught behind. Wells came next, and he turned his first ball straight into the hands of short-leg.

Hick's response was to play his natural game and attack. Russell supported him and 41 runs came in the last 50 minutes of the day to take England to 233 for 5 at the close, the innings on a knife edge.

There were definite weaknesses in West Indies' cricket throughout the series. One, it must be said, was a lack of positive leadership, for Richardson's captaincy was so often so anonymous. The other was their failure to hold vital catches. Both were in evidence on the second morning of the final Test. Hick offered two very difficult chances to short-leg, one of which hit Sherwin Campbell on the shin and should have been held. Walsh was the unlucky bowler, and it was he who saw Hick play back and lob the ball off the splice, but no fielder was able or alert enough to reach it. But it was Kenny Benjamin who had the greater cause for complaint. Russell had scored 42 when he mis-pulled a ball to square-leg where Chanderpaul – who otherwise fielded well – dropped the easiest of chances. It proved very costly.

The task confronting Hick and Russell was made easier by Richardson's bewildering captaincy. He did not call upon Benjamin until five others had been tried and Hooper had bowled seven undemanding overs. It was Benjamin who finally broke the Hick–Russell stand when he had Hick taken at second slip. The partnership was worth 144 in 41 overs and put England firmly in control.

Dropped at the wicket on 65, Hick had batted with an authority that surpassed his effort at Trent Bridge. He was confident and commanding, and one felt that at last he had begun to stand tall in Test cricket.

Watkinson was dropped three times before he reached four, and his somewhat embarrassing innings lasted an hour before, trying to withdraw his bat from a bouncer, he touched the ball to the keeper and gave Walsh his 300th Test wicket. Cork played some virile shots and, as ever, ran eagerly until he strained a groin muscle and had to employ Wells to do his running for him.

Russell's innings had lasted eight minutes under five hours when he played back to Ambrose, accurate and persevering, and lost his off stump. There is no aesthetic delight in watching Russell bat, but the man has character. He pulled and nudged as usual, and there were flicks and the occasional drive. Always he crouched, nose over the ball, the epitome of grit and determination but, like Hick, he was denied the century that his application deserved.

Ambrose bowled Cork to claim his fifth wicket in what might well be his last game against England, and Malcolm clouted 2 fours before the innings was over.

West Indies had to negotiate what one believed would be 13 difficult overs, but Stuart Williams changed that view when he smashed 5 fours through the off-side field in Devon Malcolm's first nine deliveries. Malcolm straightened his line, and the run rate slackened a little. One delivery lifted and went past Williams. Russell appealed, and Malcolm then joined the appeal. Umpire Ramaswamy raised his finger, and Williams was not the only one to look astonished. The ball certainly did not touch the bat, and the only part of the body it seemed to touch was a spot close to Williams' shoulder. The decision was particularly harsh on a young man trying to establish himself in Test cricket.

Benjamin came in as night-watchman, and West Indies had made 50 by the end of the day.

The next day was Saturday, which, of course, is Lara's day. By the close of play, West Indies were just 30 short of England's total, and their runs had come in 56 overs fewer than England had faced. Benjamin started England's problems by staying around for more than an hour in the morning, although he could have been caught at slip in the second over of the day when Thorpe and Hick left the chance to each other. He *was* caught at third slip in the 16th over of the morning, but by then he had done his job, and Lara was sufficiently prepared for his entrance.

Lara cut at Cork's first ball and missed. He padded up uncertainly to the second, but when he faced Fraser in the next over he cracked the ball to the boundary square of the wicket on the off side. In the 50 minutes before lunch, he scored 37. He might have been run out by Watkinson when 30, and he hooked over Russell's head, but such blemishes are forgotten when such a great batsman is in full flow. He was most ably supported by Campbell, one of

Graeme Hick found his best form after being dropped for the fourth Test. He played two fine innings in the sixth Test at The Oval. (David Munden/Sportsline)

West Indies' positive gains from the tour, and at lunch Campbell had 59 and West Indies were 143 for 2.

In the afternoon session, West Indies scored 116 runs for the loss of Campbell who was caught behind off an attempted pull. In the final session, from 32 overs, they made 145 and lost Lara. He had savaged each of the England bowlers. Watkinson's lack of class and experience as an off-spinner were cruelly exposed and he was rendered impotent. Gallian's figures were saved by some heroic fielding, but no dive could stop the four and six off consecutive balls. Malcolm's hostility is so often accompanied by waywardness, but Lara does not need to rely on gifts, and even the honest Fraser suffered. To his credit, Cork, injured and unwell, never lost his spirit, but how does one bowl to this left-handed genius?

The cool statistics – 179 runs, 266 minutes, 206 balls faced, 1 six and 26 fours – can convey nothing of his majesty. They cannot show the perfect timing which sends a ball racing to the boundary with fielders standing watching helpless. They cannot rekindle the gasp of pleasure the onlooker feels at the sheer beauty of the man's strokes. There is sun in his cricket, and when he was caught by Fraser as he tried to hit Malcolm over mid-off a light was extinguished.

There could have been more joy for this weary England side, but Malcolm did not accept a far from difficult return catch offered by Hooper second ball, and, at the end, Hooper was on five and Richardson had 87.

The Sunday was another hot, dry day, and England had hopes, for Lara was gone and anything was possible. When Richardson was out in the third over of the day – very well caught in the gully off a ball which he tried to cut but which came back at him – England still had their noses in front. Richardson, a gentle man who had suffered much criticism on the tour, had played splendidly and deserved a century. His support of Lara had been far from passive, and his innings included a six and 10 fours.

The dismissal of Richardson brought young Chanderpaul to the crease very early in the day, and if he or Hooper could be disposed of, England would, seemingly, have an end open. When he had made 37 Chanderpaul should have been stumped off Watkinson, whose limitations as a spinner remained apparent. As it was, Chanderpaul stayed for 46 overs with Hooper and added 196.

Chanderpaul is a calm and correct player. He is undisturbed by pace because he has so much time. He has not the flair of Lara, his bat does not yet tell fully of his

---

SIXTH CORNHILL TEST MATCH – ENGLAND v. WEST INDIES
24, 25, 26, 27 and 28 August 1995 at The Oval, Kennington

ENGLAND

	FIRST INNINGS		SECOND INNINGS	
M.A. Atherton (capt)	c Williams, b Benjamin	36	(2) c Browne, b Bishop	95
J.E.R. Gallian	c Hooper, b Ambrose	0	(1) c Williams, b Ambrose	25
J.P. Crawley	c Richardson, b Hooper	50	c Browne, b Ambrose	2
G.P. Thorpe	c Browne, b Ambrose	74	c Williams, b Walsh	38
G.A. Hick	c Williams, b Benjamin	96	not out	51
A.P. Wells	c Campbell, b Ambrose	0	not out	3
*R.C. Russell	b Ambrose	91		
M. Watkinson	c Browne, b Walsh	13		
D.G. Cork	b Ambrose	33		
A.R.C. Fraser	not out	10		
D.E. Malcolm	c Lara, b Benjamin	10		
Extras	b 15, lb 11, nb 15	41	lb 4, nb 5	9
		454	(for 4 wickets)	223

WEST INDIES

	FIRST INNINGS	
S.C. Williams	c Russell, b Malcolm	30
S.L. Campbell	c Russell, b Fraser	89
K.C.G. Benjamin	c Atherton, b Cork	20
B.C. Lara	c Fraser, b Malcolm	179
R.B. Richardson (capt)	c Hick, b Cork	93
C.L. Hooper	c Russell, b Malcolm	127
S. Chanderpaul	c Gallian, b Cork	80
*C.O. Browne	not out	27
I.R. Bishop	run out	10
C.E.L. Ambrose	not out	5
C.A. Walsh		
Extras	b 5, lb 20, w 5, nb 2	32
	(for 8 wickets, dec.)	692

	O	M	R	W	O	M	R	W
Ambrose	42	10	96	5	19	8	35	2
Walsh	32	6	84	1	28	7	80	1
Bishop	35	5	111	–	22	4	56	1
Benjamin	27	6	81	3				
Hooper	23	7	56	1	22	11	26	–
Chanderpaul					6	–	22	–
Lara					1	1	0	–

	O	M	R	W
Malcolm	39	7	160	3
Fraser	40	6	155	1
Cork	36	3	145	3
Watkinson	26	3	113	–
Gallian	12	1	56	–
Hick	10	3	38	–

FALL OF WICKETS
1–9, 2–60, 3–149, 4–192, 5–192, 6–336, 7–372, 8–419, 9–443
1–60, 2–64, 3–132, 4–212

FALL OF WICKETS
1–40, 2–92, 3–202, 4–390, 5–435, 6–631, 7–653, 8–686

Umpires: D.R. Shepherd & V.K. Ramaswamy

Match drawn

LEFT: *Brian Lara – centuries in the last three Tests, culminating in his 179 at The Oval, an innings of breathtaking brilliance. (Adrian Murrell/Allsport)*

BELOW LEFT: *John Crawley is caught behind off Curtly Ambrose who took seven wickets in the match, which was almost certainly his last Test in England. (Graham Chadwick/Allsport)*

be disdainful. The mystery regarding Hooper is why he has not scored more Test runs than he has, for he is blessed with a rare talent.

Chanderpaul was out when he drove to extra-cover, and Hooper fell to the last ball before tea, a low catch to Russell. In eight overs after tea, Browne, Bishop and Ambrose hit hard and often, and when Richardson declared West Indies had made their highest-ever total against England, led by 238 on the first innings and asked the home side to survive the last 19 overs of the day, which Atherton and Gallian did without alarm, scoring 39 on the way.

A fine spell of bowling by Ambrose in the morning accounted for Gallian, caught at slip, and Crawley, caught behind. This was a worrying period for England, and Thorpe did not ease nerves with one of his more flashy innings, but he stayed for an hour and a half before falling to Walsh.

Atherton looked set for his century, but when he was out to Bishop the game was safe. There was just time for Wells to score his first runs in Test cricket before West Indies called off the hunt. One maiden over of leg-spin from Lara hinted that his bowling could have been used to better effect.

Lara was named Man of the Match and West Indies' Man of the Series while Atherton got Wes Hall's vote as England's Man of the Series. Ambrose had walked from the field before the end of the game and had waved to the ground. It was seen as a gesture of his farewell to Test cricket, in this country at least.

West Indies have several problems, and a positive and meaningful course of action will have to be taken if they are to maintain a high place in world cricket. In four Test series, only New Zealand have bowed to them. Richardson's position is very much under threat, and well as Walsh captained in India and New Zealand, he must be close to the end of his Test career. There is a desperate need for a spinner of quality and for the utilisation of the batting talent available, which is considerable. West Indies began the tour with a feeling of vulnerability hanging over them. By the end of the tour that feeling had not disappeared, and England, having drawn the series, came out with greater hope for the future.

Dominic Cork had been an outstanding success. He is only 24 and surely the best is yet to come. Thorpe had come of age, and Atherton had survived all that had been pitched at him on and off the field and had maintained humour, dignity and top form with the bat.

From a drawn series, England could draw much comfort.

An afterthought – is the pitch that was prepared for The Oval Test really the ideal at which the TCCB aims and by which all others should be judged? Is not a true contest between bat and ball closer to the heart of the game?

personality, but he will be the despair of an army of opposing Test bowlers in the years ahead.

Carl Hooper made Malcolm and England pay dearly for dropping the catch he offered when he had scored one. From 180 balls, he hit 2 sixes and 14 fours in an innings of 127. He is a mixture of power and serenity, and one of his sixes – a straight drive off Fraser – was hit so casually as to

TEST MATCH AVERAGES – ENGLAND v. WEST INDIES

ENGLAND BATTING

	M	Inns	NO	Runs	HS	Av	100s	50s
M. Watkinson	3	4	1	156	82*	52.00	–	1
G.A. Hick	5	10	2	403	118*	50.37	1	3
R.C. Russell	3	5	1	199	91	49.75	–	1
R.A. Smith	4	8	1	305	90	43.57	–	2
G.P. Thorpe	6	12	–	506	94	42.16	–	5
M.A. Atherton	6	12	–	488	113	40.66	1	2
D.G. Cork	5	8	1	197	56*	28.14	–	1
R.K. Illingworth	4	8	5	69	17*	23.00	–	–
A.J. Stewart	3	5	–	113	37	22.60	–	–
N.V. Knight	2	4	–	89	57	22.25	–	1
J.P. Crawley	3	6	1	100	50	20.00	–	1
D. Gough	3	6	–	73	29	12.16	–	–
P.J. Martin	3	6	–	52	29	8.66	–	–
J.E.R. Gallian	2	4	–	32	25	8.00	–	–
C. White	2	4	–	26	23	6.50	–	–
A.R.C. Fraser	5	8	4	22	10*	5.50	–	–
M.R. Ramprakash	2	4	–	22	18	5.50	–	–
D.E. Malcolm	2	3	–	15	10	5.00	–	–

Played in one Test: P.A.J. DeFreitas 23 & 1; J.E. Emburey 8; A.P. Wells 0 & 3*.

ENGLAND BOWLING

	Overs	Mds	Runs	Wkts	Av	Best	10/m	5/inn
D.G. Cork	184.2	30	661	26	25.42	7-43	–	1
A.R.C. Fraser	187.5	52	563	16	35.18	5-66	–	1
R.K. Illingworth	100	40	215	6	35.83	4-96	–	–
M. Watkinson	93	21	289	8	36.12	3-64	–	–
D. Gough	70	6	255	6	42.50	3-79	–	–
D.E. Malcolm	50.3	7	220	5	44.00	3-160	–	–
P.J. Martin	84	21	241	5	48.20	2-65	–	–
P.A.J. DeFreitas	27	3	115	2	57.50	2-82	–	–
G.A. Hick	18	4	64	1	64.00	1-15	–	–
C. White	16	–	76	–	–	–	–	–
J.E. Emburey	30	7	82	–	–	–	–	–

Bowled in one innings: J.E.R. Gallian 12–1–56–0.

ENGLAND FIELDING FIGURES

10 – R.C. Russell (ct 9/st 1); 9 – A.J. Stewart; 5 – G.A. Hick and N.V. Knight; 4 – P.J. Martin and J.P. Crawley; 3 – M.A. Atherton; 2 – G.P. Thorpe, R.K. Illingworth and D. Gough; 1 – M. Watkinson, D.G. Cork, J.E. Emburey, J.E.R. Gallian, M.R. Ramprakash and A.R.C. Fraser

WEST INDIES BATTING

	M	Inns	NO	Runs	HS	Av	100s	50s
B.C. Lara	6	10	1	765	179	85.00	3	3
C.O. Browne	2	3	2	62	34	62.00	–	–
S. Chanderpaul	2	3	1	103	80	51.50	–	1
S.C. Williams	2	2	–	92	62	46.00	–	1
S.L. Campbell	6	10	–	454	93	45.40	–	4
C.L. Hooper	5	8	1	310	127	44.28	1	1
R.B. Richardson	6	8	–	275	93	34.37	–	2
J.C. Adams	4	6	–	160	58	26.66	–	2
C.E.L. Ambrose	5	7	4	77	23*	25.66	–	–
K.L.T. Arthurton	5	7	–	172	75	24.57	–	1
K.C.G. Benjamin	5	6	2	74	20	18.50	–	–
J.R. Murray	4	6	–	84	26	14.00	–	–
C.A. Walsh	6	7	1	61	19	10.16	–	–
I.R. Bishop	6	8	1	71	16	10.14	–	–

Played in one Test: O.D. Gibson 29 & 14; R. Dhanraj 3.

WEST INDIES BOWLING

	Overs	Mds	Runs	Wkts	Av	Best	10/m	5/inn
K.C.G. Benjamin	158.2	33	506	23	22.00	5-69	1	2
I.R. Bishop	242.3	49	649	27	24.03	5-32	–	1
C.E.L. Ambrose	185.1	43	506	21	24.09	5-96	–	1
C.A. Walsh	290	57	786	26	30.23	5-45	–	1
C.L. Hooper	68	22	149	3	49.66	2-36	–	–
O.D. Gibson	34	3	132	2	66.00	2-81	–	–
J.C. Adams	12	1	32	–	–	–	–	–
K.L.T. Arthurton	33.5	6	76	–	–	–	–	–
R. Dhanraj	55	8	191	–	–	–	–	–

Bowled in one innings: S. Chanderpaul 6–0–22–0; B.C. Lara 1–1–0–0.

WEST INDIES FIELDING FIGURES

14 – J.R. Murray; 13 – C.O. Browne; 9 – S.L. Campbell; 6 – K.L.T. Arthurton; 5 – S.C. Williams and subs (S.C. Williams); 4 – B.C. Lara, C.L. Hooper and R.B. Richardson; 3 – subs (S. Chanderpaul); 2 – C.E.L. Ambrose; 1 – J.C. Adams and C.A. Walsh

---

30, 31 August and 1 September *at Scarborough*

West Indians 426 (C.O. Browne 102, K.L.T. Arthurton 94, J.R. Murray 84) and 356 for 4 dec. (S. Chanderpaul 132 not out, C.L. Hooper 105)

Yorkshire 297 (M.G. Bevan 105, A.A. Metcalfe 100, R. Dhanraj 5 for 111) and 143 for 3 (M.D. Moxon 55 not out)

Match drawn

Exceptional in recent years, the West Indians' tour continued after the sixth Test, meeting Yorkshire in the Tesco Challenge at Scarborough. Darren Gough returned to first-class cricket after his long absence with a foot injury, and he dismissed both Williams and Browne on the opening day, but conceded 95 runs in 16 overs. The tourists were 25 for 3 before Murray and Arthurton added 190 in 43 overs. Browne scored his century off 72 balls and hit 3 sixes and 15 fours.

On the second day, Bevan and Metcalfe scored centuries and shared a partnership of 191 for the fifth wicket. The batting entertainment continued on the last day when Chanderpaul and Hooper put on 162 for the tourists' fourth wicket.

3 September *at Scarborough*

Yorkshire 253 for 4 (A. McGrath 106, M.G. Bevan 70 not out)

West Indians 242 (R.B. Richardson 54)

Yorkshire won by 11 runs

The West Indians' tour ended with a 40-over match for the McCain Challenge. The highlight of the game was a century from under-19 England opener Anthony McGrath who hit 3 sixes and 8 fours. The West Indians were bowled out in 39.2 overs.

A VIEW FROM THE PAVILION

Derek Pringle, former Essex and England all-rounder, now cricket correspondent of the *Independent on Sunday*, considers that the present structure of cricket in England does not help to develop players of international standard and makes his suggestions for the future

Just over a year ago, when England returned from Australia, another Ashes drubbing complete, a million microscopes suddenly seemed to turn and start scrutinising the most egregious of our national games. Within weeks, a thorough biopsy of English cricket had been carried out and a deluge of diagnostic diatribe and prognostic wherewithal followed.

Most of it was not without merit, but as in the case of most burgeoning businesses, the amount of fuss calling for change was directly proportional to the sudden availability of large amounts of cash to the game's controlling body, the TCCB. Because most of this money came from selling television rights, it was felt that if the source of such riches was to be preserved, then radical changes in the game's structure were needed in order to improve the England side's poor standing.

This argument, which has a kind of Machiavellian logic to it, preceded two important events. The first came when Australia, having just beaten England, then went on to defeat the West Indies in the Caribbean, a victory many saw as a shift in the balance of power. Then, duly shocked, and fast tiring from nearly three years on the road, the West Indians toured England, only to draw a thrilling ding-dong series at two Tests apiece. England's inconsistencies remained, but few gave them much chance of drawing the series at the outset.

What was more heartening, though, was that England showed far more resilience than of late, twice fighting back to achieve parity against a side still widely recognised as the most resilient on the planet. Indeed England's problem has never been an inability to win matches; just a tendency to lose those they should save. But now that Atherton and Illingworth had got England moving in the right direction, was there any need for the sweeping changes so many had suggested before England showed their new-found mettle?

According to most recent players the answer is still yes. As ever though, the choices seem endless, but then that has always been the first-class game's biggest problem. With 18 counties' worth of player power to choose from, the selection of a small élite, from which the national side is comprised, is a lot more difficult than people imagine.

With so many players performing to a level just below greatness, only time-wasting trial and error will eventually discover which ones cope best at Test level, unless clever judgement is brought to bear. Talent, then, is needed to spot talent, and most counties' records at producing good home-grown players, particularly in the pace and spin departments, are poor.

The real skill, however, lies in spotting those who will best cope when pressure and crisis suddenly throw invisible mountains into their path. Australia have their Cricket Academy, an establishment we in England seem much taken with, especially now that lottery money makes it a reality.

However, a word of warning – both a former pupil, Jason Gallian, and Lancashire second XI's Australian coach, Peter Sleep, think it unworkable in our sceptical isle, believing the problems of choosing fruitfully from such a large population would prove too much of a lottery, unless further millions were spent in setting up at least five academies regionally.

If anything, we English tend to put our faith in traditional systems, where sporting selection is often compromised by the self-interests of those employed to make it. Talented mavericks, particularly in team sports, are often marginalised in favour of less talented 'yes men' with more polished political skills, whose shortcomings are often cunningly obscured by endless bouts of over-keenness.

The Australians, on the other hand, seem to pre-empt this compromise by shoving people in at the deep end, ensuring those that manage to float go on to the next murky pond, where the predators are bigger and tougher, and where only the strongest survive. Instead of allowing players to proliferate as we tend to do, they prune and weed without remorse, so that when the important decisions have to be made – like who plays for New South Wales, or who gets picked for Australia – they invariably make the right ones.

For starters, what England needs is a better organised and more competitive feeder system for the county game. Too often, young players spend too long making the technical and mental adjustments necessary when they step up a level. Instead the period of acclimatisation would be drastically shortened if club cricket allowed the best teenagers and young adults to compete regularly, rather than make up the numbers. Rather too often, club cricket seems to be played for the gratification of the elders in charge and not for those coming through the ranks. The sooner this shift in emphasis is made, the better.

From then on, the path to the England team should be a meritocratic one, with if anything a faint bias towards youth. The amount of cricket must be lessened, but at the same time the intensity of competition must be increased. Good old county pros have always protested over the amount of cricket played, but their moans and groans have always been those of the dray-horse, begrudgingly compliant and always falling on deaf ears. Overseas players, however, have been flabbergasted by the workload and they complain, to a man, of mind-numbing exhaustion.

When you analyse the facts closely, there are only 18 fewer overs bowled in each four-day county match that

Derek Pringle in his England days. (Adrian Murrell/Allsport)

goes the distance (and many do) than there are during a five-day Test match. Throw in a 40-over Sunday League match in the middle of the four days, and not only are you breaking up the mental tempo of the longer game and thereby penalising the side fielding on the Monday, but the players are competing in the equivalent of a 17-Test series, with a slog in the middle, over five months – with two additional one-day knockout competitions to be fitted in as well.

It is simply too much, particularly for the Test players who rarely have enough time to recharge their batteries before they are off undertaking another punishing itinerary. In order to preserve our best players, it might be far better to institute a regional competition comprising of five sides selected from the best players (including England players) from the counties in their particular regions, and playing each other twice a season, over four days.

These players, though still belonging to their counties, would only play for them in a 50-over one-day knockout competition, or in the event of being dropped from the regional squad. For their part the counties would reduce their playing staffs, scrap the current second-team competitions, and in addition to the one-day knockout competition already mentioned, play a 17-match county championship over four consecutive days, as well as a one-day league on Sundays.

It is a system that offers minimal adjustments to both administration and infrastructure, and though it is likely to bring initial complaint from the county's membership, it is a small price to pay for the better quality of competition a regional contest would offer. It would also give the best players more time to rest and work on their game – something of a necessity if English cricket is once again to be a byword for quality.

WEST INDIANS IN ENGLAND, 1995

BATTING

Tour averages

Batsman	M	Inns	NO	Runs	HS	Av
S.C. Williams	13	20	–	770	137	38.50
S.L. Campbell	16	26	–	1225	172	47.11
B.C. Lara	13	20	1	1126	179	59.26
J.C. Adams	13	22	5	741	114*	43.58
R.B. Richardson	15	23	3	804	101*	40.20
S. Chanderpaul	15	25	8	1003	140*	59.00
J.R. Murray	12	19	3	440	100	27.50
W.K.M. Benjamin	3	3	2	11	7	5.50
O.D. Gibson	11	13	2	303	101*	27.54
I.R. Bishop	10	11	1	102	25	10.20
R. Dhanraj	10	13	3	81	22	8.10
C.L. Hooper	15	25	2	1063	195	46.21
K.L.T. Arthurton	15	23	4	1077	146	56.68
C.O. Browne	12	16	5	498	102*	45.27
C.A. Walsh	10	11	1	111	40	11.10
C.E.L. Ambrose	10	13	7	147	27*	24.50
K.C.G. Benjamin	10	12	4	154	44	19.25
V.C. Drakes	6	9	1	118	48*	14.75
P.V. Simmons	2	3	1	261	139*	130.50
A.C. Cummins	2	1	–	16	16	16.00

Match schedule (left half)

1. v. Worcestershire (Worcester) 16–18 May — D
2. v. Somerset (Taunton) 19–21 May — D
3. v. Leicestershire (Leicester) 30 May – 1 June — W
4. v. Northamptonshire (Northampton) 3–5 June — D
5. First Test Match (Leeds) 8–12 June — W
6. v. Durham (Chester-le-Street) 17–19 June — D
7. Second Test Match (Lord's) 22–6 June — L
8. v. Combined Universities (Oxford) 28–30 June — D
9. v. Sussex (Hove) 1–3 July — L
10. Third Test Match (Edgbaston) 6–11 July — W
11. v. Kent (Canterbury) 19–21 July — W
12. v. Middlesex (Lord's) 22–4 July — D
13. Fourth Test Match (Old Trafford) 27–31 July — L

Match schedule (right half)

14. v. Somerset (Taunton) 2–4 August — W
15. v. Gloucestershire (Bristol) 5–7 August — W
16. Fifth Test Match (Trent Bridge) 10–14 August — D
17. v. Hampshire (Southampton) 16–18 August — D
18. v. Essex (Chelmsford) 19–21 August — W
19. Sixth Test Match (The Oval) 24–8 August — D
20. v. Yorkshire (Scarborough) 30 August – 1 September — D

Batsman	M	Inns	NO	Runs	HS	Av
S.C. Williams	13	20	–	770	137	38.50
S.L. Campbell	16	26	–	1225	172	47.11
B.C. Lara	13	20	1	1126	179	59.26
J.C. Adams	13	22	5	741	114*	43.58
R.B. Richardson	15	23	3	804	101*	40.20
S. Chanderpaul	15	25	8	1003	140*	59.00
J.R. Murray	12	19	3	440	100	27.50
W.K.M. Benjamin	3	3	2	11	7	5.50
O.D. Gibson	11	13	2	303	101*	27.54
I.R. Bishop	10	11	1	102	25	10.20
R. Dhanraj	10	13	3	81	22	8.10
C.L. Hooper	15	25	2	1063	195	46.21
K.L.T. Arthurton	15	23	4	1077	146	56.68
C.O. Browne	12	16	5	498	102*	45.27
C.A. Walsh	10	11	1	111	40	11.10
C.E.L. Ambrose	10	13	7	147	27*	24.50
K.C.G. Benjamin	10	12	4	154	44	19.25
V.C. Drakes	6	9	1	118	48*	14.75
P.V. Simmons	2	3	1	261	139*	130.50
A.C. Cummins	2	1	–	16	16	16.00

BOWLING

Match	I.R. Bishop	O.D. Gibson	W.K.M. Benjamin	R. Dhanraj	C.E.L. Ambrose	C.A. Walsh	K.C.G. Benjamin	C.L. Hooper	K.L.T. Arthurton	S. Chanderpaul	J.C. Adams	B.C. Lara	V.C. Drakes	S.C. Williams	A.C. Cummins	P.V. Simmons	Byes	Leg-byes	Wides	No-balls	Total	Wks
v. Worcestershire (Worcester) 16–18 May	6.3-0-24-0	7-0-33-4	7-3-10-1	6-1-19-2																12		
v. Somerset (Taunton) 19–21 May				20-5-49-3	9-1-64-0 / 10-1-49-0	18-2-77-4 / 6-2-17-1	17-4-56-2	15-1-47-0 / 3-0-17-0	4-1-5-0 / 4-1-8-0								8	3		52		
v. Leicestershire (Leicester) 30 May – 1 June		12-2-55-1 / 8-1-26-3	11-3-27-0 / 1-0-1-0	12-0-32-1 / 6-1-25-0	13-6-28-0	15-4-43-2	9.2-2-58-3 / 11-3-50-4	8-1-22-3	2-0-9-0								4	4	1	8 / 38		
v. Northamptonshire (Northampton) 3–5 June	23-7-64-4			33-5-113-2			13.5-2-60-4 / 6-1-19-1			8-0-28-0	11.4-1-21-2						4	2 / 3	1	8 / 22		
First Test Match (Leeds) 8–12 June	16-2-32-5 / 19-3-81-2				17-4-56-1 / 20.2-6-44-3	13-2-50-0 / 22-4-60-4		26-3-103-3 / 23.4-3-79-3									1 / 1	3 / 13		15 / 7		
v. Durham (Chester-le-Street) 17–19 June	17-3-71-3	13.1-3-56-1	14-4-35-0	23-1-77-1				14-3-36-2	1-0-7-0 / 2-0-10-0	1-0-7-0 / 2-0-10-0							2	2		51		
Second Test Match (Lord's) 22–6 June	19-6-65-2 / 17-4-33-1	24-5-64-4 / 20-2-81-2		12-2-39-1	26-6-72-2 / 24-5-70-4	22.4-6-50-3 / 28.1-10-91-3		9-1-31-0			2-0-10-0 / 2-0-10-0						6 / 4	10 / 27	2	24 / 4		
v. Combined Universities (Oxford) 28–30 June	22-5-56-3	14-1-51-0		32.3-7-87-5 / 13-3-33-1		10-2-39-1 / 2-1-3-0		15-5-61-0 / 4-0-19-0	4-0-29-0 / 7-1-37-1		16-3-41-3 / 1-1-0-0	7-0-40-0	21-6-59-0				4 / 1			4 / 12		
v. Sussex (Hove) 1–3 July		25.3-1-110-2		36-5-144-6				13-3-58-0									3	5	1	16 / 4		
Third Test Match (Edgbaston) 6–11 July	6.2-0-18-3 / 13-3-29-4	9-1-47-4 / 13-1-75-0			7.5-1-26-2	17.1-4-54-3 / 15-2-45-5	13-4-45-2 / 2-0-15-0						4.4-0-20-5				4 / 1	4	4	10 / 12		
v. Kent (Canterbury) 19–21 July		14-5-45-3		25-8-88-4	10-6-20-1 / 4-3-1-0	5-0-20-1			9-2-18-0				17-1-78-3				1	2	2	16		
v. Middlesex (Lord's) 22–4 July				17.5-1-66-4 / 5-1-16-0	11-5-24-1	21.2-6-77-3	16-8-31-1 / 4-2-11-0	15-0-60-1	2.5-1-5-0 / 5-0-19-2		1-0-8-0 / 1-0-12-0	1-0-5-0					1			2		
Fourth Test Match (Old Trafford) 27–31 July	29-3-103-2	19-0-100-2 / 11-2-32-4		20-3-83-2 / 3-1-2-3	24-2-91-2 / 5-1-16-0	38-5-92-4 / 5-0-17-0	18-4-83-1 / 9-1-29-2	19-7-34-3			8-1-21-0 / 2-0-7-0		16.2-4-75-3 / 9-3-23-1				1 / 2	11 / 2	1 / 1	34 / 8		
v. Somerset (Taunton) 2–4 August	12-6-18-1			30-7-110-4 / 11-4-21-2				12-2-34-0					4-0-17-0				4	10	1	57		
v. Gloucestershire (Bristol) 5–7 August	10-2-24-1			40-7-137-0 / 15-1-54-0	20-5-52-2		22-8-53-4 / 16.3-4-52-5	24-3-72-0 / 5-1-15-0	5-0-19-2					1-0-2-0			4	6		22		
Fifth Test Match (Trent Bridge) 10–14 August	30.1-6-62-3 / 21-8-50-2			2.3-2-0-2		39-5-93-0 / 30-6-70-2	34.3-7-105-5 / 25-8-69-5	19-7-34-3	9-0-31-0 / 13-3-22-0						17-3-60-5	15-5-30-1	9 / 4	9 / 6	1	4 / 14		
v. Hampshire (Southampton) 16–18 August		15-6-48-2 / 9-0-43-0		28-8-68-3				12-2-34-0 / 24-3-72-0	10-6-11-1 / 7-1-13-1	4-3-3-0 / 1-0-1-0					10-0-49-1	11-0-55-0	8	12	2	40		
v. Essex (Chelmsford) 19–21 August		5-1-16-0 / 6-1-30-0		19-0-89-1 / 21-2-64-2	11-5-24-1	9-1-41-1 / 8-1-21-0		5-1-15-0					10-1-52-0 / 8-0-30-2		11-3-35-0	11-3-35-0	3 / 4	1 / 7		26 / 36		
Sixth Test Match (The Oval) 24–8 August	35-5-111-0 / 22-4-56-1			23.4-3-111-5 / 6-1-19-1	42-10-96-5 / 19-8-35-2	32-6-84-1 / 28-7-80-1	27-6-81-3	23-7-56-1 / 22-11-26-0	5-1-11-0 / 5-0-36-1	6-0-22-0 / 4-0-24-0	1-1-0-0	1-1-0-0			5-0-26-0	2-1-1-0	15 / 4	11 / 4	1	17 / 15		
v. Yorkshire (Scarborough) 30 August – 1 September		12-3-40-1 / 6-1-14-0		6-1-19-1				12-3-29-1					16-6-46-2				4	4		5 / 6		
Bowler's average	334-69-983-38 / 25.86	242.4-36-966-31 / 31.16	33-10-73-1 / 73.00	475.3-82-1596-61 / 26.16	262.1-70-744-25 / 29.76	384.2-76-1124-39 / 28.82	284.1-71-923-43 / 21.46	267.4-54-821-17 / 48.29	88.5-17-264-6 / 44.00	42-5-154-2 / 77.00	42.4-6-114-5 / 22.80	9-1-45-0 / –	106-17-400-16 / 25.00	1-0-2-0 / –	42-4-180-7 / 25.71	39-9-121-1 / 121.00						

A A.J. Stewart absent hurt
B C.O. Browne 2-0-16-0

BENSON AND HEDGES CUP

Thankfully, the Benson and Hedges Cup returned to its original format in 1995. The experiment of staging the competition on a straightforward knock-out basis had lasted just two seasons. Counties had been quick to realise that they could go several years without a home tie in either the Benson and Hedges Cup or the NatWest Trophy, and that to stage two tournaments with a similar format was not in the best interests of the game or the members whose wishes and opinions are so often disregarded.

Twenty-two teams competed for the Cup in 1995, the 18 first-class counties plus Combined Universities, Minor Counties, Scotland and Ireland who had made their debut in the tournament in 1994. The teams were divided into Northern and Southern Zones, and each zone was divided into two groups, one of six teams and one of five.

NORTHERN ZONE
Group A   Durham, Lancashire, Leicestershire, Minor Counties, Nottinghamshire and Warwickshire (the holders)
Group B   Derbyshire, Northamptonshire, Scotland, Worcestershire and Yorkshire

SOUTHERN ZONE
Group C   Combined Universities, Essex, Glamorgan, Gloucestershire, Hampshire and Middlesex
Group D   Ireland, Kent, Somerset, Surrey and Sussex

Glamorgan and Sussex have never won the trophy and, of the non-first-class counties competing, Combined Universities have the best record, for they reached the quarter-finals in 1989 when Nasser Hussain scored a century and they were narrowly beaten by Somerset. Hussain took the Gold Award in that match, but he has not won the individual honour while playing for Essex. Graham Gooch, with 21 Gold Awards, dominates the medal-winners.

23 April *at Derby*
Northamptonshire 179 (D.E. Malcolm 4 for 50)
Derbyshire 180 for 2 (C.J. Adams 94, K.J. Barnett 58 not out)
Derbyshire (2 pts) won by 8 wickets
(Gold Award – C.J. Adams)

at Stockton

Durham 165 (M. Saxelby 80 not out, D.J. Millns 4 for 26)
Leicestershire 115
Durham (2 pts) won by 50 runs
(Gold Award – M. Saxelby)

at Chelmsford

Glamorgan 277 for 7 (S.P. James 82, R.D.B. Croft 50 not out)
Essex 249 (P.J. Prichard 92)

John Stephenson took the Gold Award on the occasion of his debut for Hampshire. He scored 82 against Middlesex, and here he employs the reverse-sweep. Keith Brown is the wicket-keeper. Stephenson's fine all-round cricket was in vain as Middlesex won by six wickets. (Adrian Murrell/Allsport)

Glamorgan (2 pts) won by 28 runs
(Gold Award – S.P. James)

at Bristol

Gloucestershire 259 for 9 (A. Symonds 95)
Combined Universities 133 (J. Srinath 4 for 33)
Gloucestershire (2 pts) won by 126 runs
(Gold Award – A. Symonds)

at Lord's

Hampshire 208 for 8 (J.P. Stephenson 82)
Middlesex 212 for 4 (M.R. Ramprakash 52 not out)
Middlesex (2 pts) won by 6 wickets
(Gold Award – J.P. Stephenson)

at Leek

Minor Counties 70 (J.E.R. Gallian 5 for 15, I.D. Austin 4 for 8)
Lancashire 71 for 1
Lancashire (2 pts) won by 9 wickets
(Gold Award – I.D. Austin)

at Taunton

Somerset 241 for 7 (M.N. Lathwell 74, P.D. Bowler 52, R.J. Harden 50)
Sussex 187 (Mushtaq Ahmed 4 for 29)

Somerset (2 pts) won by 54 runs

(Gold Award – Mushtaq Ahmed)

at Trent Bridge

Nottinghamshire 230 for 6 (P. Johnson 70 not out)
Warwickshire 224 (D.P. Ostler 87, R.G. Twose 54,
   A.J. Moles 51)

Nottinghamshire (2 pts) won by 6 runs

(Gold Award – K.P. Evans)

at The Oval

Ireland 80 (S.G. Kenlock 5 for 15)
Surrey 81 for 2

Surrey (2 pts) won by 8 wickets

(Gold Award – S.G. Kenlock)

at Worcester

Scotland 118 (S.R. Lampitt 4 for 24)
Worcestershire 119 for 0 (W.P.C. Weston 54 not out,
   T.S. Curtis 54 not out)

Worcestershire (2 pts) won by 10 wickets

(Gold Award – N.V. Radford)

A sensational debut in the Benson and Hedges Cup for 'Mark' Kenlock, 5 for 15 for Surrey against Ireland and the Gold Award. (Anton Want/Allsport)

Four matches involving the two universities accorded first-class status and the game between the county champions and England 'A' were all that preceded the first round of matches in the Benson and Hedges Cup so that Sunday 23 April provided the first opportunity to assess the prospects of the counties.

Derbyshire had imposed a new code of fitness and conduct on their players after a 1994 season which skipper Kim Barnett regarded as 'a disgrace for a squad of our quality'. There was early indication that the code would pay dividends as Derbyshire beat Northamptonshire with 15.1 overs to spare. The visitors were held in check by the bowling of Devon Malcolm and Colin Wells, in particular, and although Rollins went quickly, Adams and Barnett scored 160 in 36 overs for the second wicket. Adams, an exciting batsman and fine fielder, earned his second Gold Award for his 94 off 101 balls. Having hit 14 fours, he was out when he tried to reach his century with a six, which would also have given his side victory a touch sooner.

Hansie Cronje took a wicket with the first ball he bowled for Leicestershire, but Durham won a grim struggle at Stockton. Put in to bat, the home side were reduced to 39 for 6 before Mark Saxelby stopped the rot. He added 52 with Wood, and although Boiling and Walker went for 'ducks', Brown, who scored eight, stayed 21 overs while 69 were added for the last wicket. Leicestershire reached 53 before their second wicket fell, but they subsided to 115 all out against an accurate seam attack which was well supported in the field. Saxelby tended to hit in the air, but his 80 not out deservedly won him his first Gold Award.

It is unlikely that Stephen James would have been in the Glamorgan side at Chelmsford had skipper Hugh Morris

been fit. As it transpired, his innings of 82 gave Glamorgan the substance they needed to build a good score against Essex. The home side's seam attack was not impressive, and it was left to Such and Gooch to put a break on the scoring. Even so, Croft batted most sensibly and hit the last two balls of the innings, bowled by Ilott, for six. New skipper Paul Prichard batted splendidly, but he was brilliantly caught by Maynard in the 44th over, after which, from 207 for 6, Essex slipped to 221 for 9, and, in spite of a late flurry from Ilott and Cousins, Glamorgan won a Benson and Hedges match on Essex soil for the first time.

Combined Universities had performed impressively in a warm-up match against Northamptonshire in The Parks on the Friday, but they were brushed aside by a Gloucestershire side fielding three newcomers, Lynch, Symonds and Srinath. All three acquitted themselves well. Lynch hit 28 and fielded with his customary excellence while Srinath undermined the students' innings with four wickets. The star performer, however, was Andrew Symonds who, although unable to command a regular place in the Queensland side, had hit a century against Atherton's men earlier in the year. His debut for Gloucestershire brought 95 off 70 deliveries and the Gold Award.

John Stephenson took the Gold Award on the occasion of his debut for Hampshire. He had twice won the accolade with Essex. He shared an opening stand of 94 with Terry, but he lacked support later in the order. Stephenson also dismissed Gatting and Carr in the space of four balls before Weekes and Ramprakash put Middlesex in command.

Minor Counties were bowled out in 35.5 overs for the lowest score they have ever recorded in the competition. Jason Gallian took five wickets in an innings for the first time, and Ian 'Bully' Austin, beginning his ninth season in first-class cricket, won his first Gold Award.

Darren Thomas established a Glamorgan record for the Benson and Hedges Cup when he took 6 for 20 against Combined Universities. (Allsport)

Somerset survived the early loss of Trescothick to reach a healthy 241 against Sussex. Lathwell and Bowler scored 111 for the second wicket in 28 overs. Harden maintained the momentum. Athey and Hall hit 62 in 15 overs at the start of the Sussex innings, but Mushtaq Ahmed sent back Athey and Wells, who offered no shot to a googly, in the space of three balls. He later accounted for Lenham and Remy, and his first Gold Award was some compensation for his omission from the Pakistan side.

Warwickshire's defence of the trophy began badly when, in chilly, damp conditions, they fell apart against Nottinghamshire. The home side reached 230, and they looked a beaten side when Warwickshire cruised to 172 for 2. Knight went early, but Moles and Ostler hit 113 for the second wicket in 30 overs. Twose also batted well, yet the last seven wickets went down for 26 runs, an inexplicable and inexcusable collapse.

'Mark' Kenlock, the left-arm medium-pace bowler who was playing for Spencer in the *Evening Standard* Cup final at the end of the 1994 season, made a sensational Benson and Hedges debut, taking 5 for 15 in eight overs as Ireland were bowled out for 80 before lunch at The Oval.

Scotland fared no better than Ireland as Worcestershire reached a target of 119 in 27.1 overs.

25 April *at Chelmsford*

Essex 225 for 8 (P.J. Prichard 65, N. Hussain 65)
Middlesex 228 for 3 (M.W. Gatting 93 not out, P.N. Weekes 67 not out)

Middlesex (2 pts) won by 7 wickets

(Gold Award – P.N. Weekes)

at Cardiff

Glamorgan 318 for 3 (D.L. Hemp 121, S.P. James 75)
Combined Universities 101 (S.D. Thomas 6 for 20)

Glamorgan (2 pts) won by 217 runs

(Gold Award – D.L. Hemp)

at Southampton

Hampshire 162 (A.M. Smith 6 for 39)
Gloucestershire 166 for 6 (A.J. Wright 51)

Gloucestershire (2 pts) won by 4 wickets

(Gold Award – A.M. Smith)

at Canterbury

Kent 318 for 8 (T.R. Ward 125, M.R. Benson 85)
Surrey 225 for 7 (N. Shahid 65 not out)

Kent (2 pts) won by 93 runs

(Gold Award – T.R. Ward)

at Old Trafford

Leicestershire 312 for 5 (W.J. Cronje 158, J.J. Whitaker 88)
Lancashire 318 for 5 (J.P. Crawley 89, G.D. Lloyd 81 not out, M.A. Atherton 71)

Lancashire (2 pts) won by 5 wickets

(Gold Award – W.J. Cronje)

at Leek

Minor Counties 114 (K.P. Evans 4 for 19)
Nottinghamshire 115 for 1 (R.T. Robinson 52 not out, P.R. Pollard 52)

Nottinghamshire (2 pts) won by 9 wickets

(Gold Award – K.P. Evans)

at Glasgow (Titwood)

Derbyshire 220 for 6 (D.J. Cullinan 101 not out)
Scotland 174 (D.E. Malcolm 4 for 34)

Derbyshire (2 pts) won by 46 runs

(Gold Award – D.J. Cullinan)

at Hove

Sussex 261 for 8 (J.W. Hall 59)
Ireland 198 for 9 (M.P. Rea 73)

Sussex (2 pts) won by 63 runs

(Gold Award – M.P. Rea)

at Edgbaston

Warwickshire 285 for 7 (N.V. Knight 91, R.G. Twose 90)
Durham 194 (J.E. Morris 62, D.A. Reeve 4 for 37)

Warwickshire (2 pts) won by 91 runs

(Gold Award – N.V. Knight)

Kevin Evans (Nottinghamshire) won Gold Awards in the first two rounds. (Neal Simpson/Empics)

at Leeds

Worcestershire 208 for 6 (G.A. Hick 109)
Yorkshire 212 for 4 (M.G. Bevan 83 not out)

Yorkshire (2 pts) won by 6 wickets

(Gold Award – M.G. Bevan)

Essex's chances of reaching the knock-out stage of the Benson and Hedges Cup suffered a severe setback when they were beaten at Chelmsford for the second time in three days. Gatting's decision to put the home side in when he won the toss gained rich reward when Feltham dismissed Gooch for five. Prichard again batted well, and there was an impressive innings from Hussain, but both batsmen fell to Weekes. The likeable and promising Robinson hit 21 off Fraser's last over, but Essex looked well short of a winning score. Pooley and Ramprakash did not last long, and Carr was out at 61, but thereafter Middlesex had no problems. Gatting had dropped anchor, and Weekes batted with relish. The pair added 167 to take their side to victory with 29 balls to spare.

There were records galore at Cardiff where David Hemp hit his first century in the competition, took his first Gold Award, and Glamorgan reached their highest score

in the Benson and Hedges Cup. Then Darren Thomas took 6 for 20, which established a new bowling record for Glamorgan in the Cup. Combined Universities gave a disappointing display, but the competition is played at a time when not all student cricketers can make themselves available because of examinations. Windows of Gloucestershire and Durham University was a case in point.

Gloucestershire had begun the season with few pundits – if any – giving them the slightest hope of winning one of the four trophies, but their display at Southampton caused some to rethink. Russell won the toss and asked Hampshire to bat, and Gloucestershire's confidence and eagerness in the field were soon evident. Mike Smith swung the ball appreciably with his left-arm medium pace, and he captured the first three wickets for 19 runs in seven overs. When Robin Smith was run out by Symonds' direct hit on the stumps from mid-wicket, Hampshire were 57 for 4. Russell helped Smith to a fourth wicket by catching James low to his left, but Paul Whitaker batted well for a sensible 42 before Lynch caught him low at mid-wicket. The Hampshire innings ended on the last ball of the 55th over when Lynch took another catch to dismiss Connor and so give Smith six wickets in the competition for the first time. Gloucestershire did not find the task of scoring 163 to win an easy one, particularly as Streak, strong and hostile, took a spectacular caught-and-bowled to get rid of Hancock, and then had Lynch taken at slip. At 2 for 2, the visitors had problems, but Wright and Dawson provided cement to the innings with a careful stand of 98. They fell in successive overs from Thursfield before Symonds, 33 off 25 balls, and Alleyne made possible a Gloucestershire victory with 4.5 overs to spare.

Kent opened their season with a partnership of 229 between Benson and Ward who, surprisingly for one so proficient in one-day cricket, hit his first century in the Benson and Hedges Cup. The Surrey attack relied heavily on seam, and it was not well supported in the field. Benson profited more than Ward, but Ward was well content with his 125 off 140 balls. He hit 2 sixes and 14 fours. Faced by a target of 319, Surrey lost Darren Bicknell, Thorpe and Ward with only 12 scored. There was a late flourish, but there was never a doubt about the result.

If there were records made at Cardiff, they were dwarfed by those at Old Trafford. Briers won the toss, and Leicestershire batted. Wells was out for seven in the sixth over, and Cronje replaced him. Lancashire were not to see the back of the South African until the 51st over by which time he had hit 158 off 156 balls, the highest score ever made against Lancashire in the Benson and Hedges Cup. His innings contained few blemishes, and he hit 4 sixes and 13 fours in an effortless knock on an easy-paced pitch. He and Whitaker added 175 in 22 overs, and with 104 runs coming in the last 10 overs of the Leicestershire innings, it seemed that Lancashire must be beaten. The home side, who were still without Wasim Akram – yet to arrive from Pakistan – lost Gallian at 25, but Atherton and Crawley added 124 in 21 overs to give an ideal platform for a later onslaught. Fairbrother contributed 44, but skipper Watkinson went for 0, and the last five overs arrived with

41 runs still needed for victory. Lloyd and Austin took 15 from an over bowled by Wells to make the task simpler, and Lloyd hit Parsons for six off the third ball of the final over to clinch the win and to leave him unbeaten with 81 off 73 balls. Lancashire's 318 is the highest score by a side batting second in the competition – and winning – and 630 runs for 10 wickets is a record aggregate for a Benson and Hedges Cup match.

Minor Counties were brushed aside for the second time in three days, and Kevin Evans won his second Gold Award in the same space of time for his best bowling performance in the tournament. Needing 115 to win, Nottinghamshire were given sight of victory by Pollard and Robinson who hit 92 off 33 overs. The victory came with 16.1 overs to spare. Chris Lewis took 3 for 11 in six overs before retiring with a thigh injury.

With the exception of Daryll Cullinan, the Derbyshire batsmen did not fare well against an accurate Scottish attack in Glasgow. Dropped at extra-cover off Malcolm Marshall when 13, Cullinan hit a fluent century and took his side to a reasonable total. Scotland lost four wickets for 59, and although there was some spirited batting from Marshall, Love and Stanger, they never looked likely to reach their target.

The same statement could apply to Ireland at Hove, although they had much consolation in their defeat. Rea and Warke scored 57 for Ireland's first wicket, and Rea hit a gritty 73 which brought him Ireland's first Gold Award. Earlier, Owen Butler, 19 years old and expected to join Worcestershire, bowled at a lively pace and captured three wickets – a best bowling performance for the newcomers to the competition – but Butler, like his new-ball partner Patterson, was too wayward as he strove for pace, and 26 wides were conceded.

Nick Knight hit his best score in one-day cricket at county level, and Roger Twose, another left-hander, shared a third-wicket stand of 127 in 20 overs with the new recruit to put Warwickshire on their way to their first win of the season. It seemed at one time as though the holders would pass 300, but they fell just short in spite of Reeve's typically proficient 28 off 31 balls. With Roseberry, Larkins and Prabhakar falling for 60 runs, Durham soon had problems. Morris and Longley added 71, but thereafter only Brown reached double figures, and the visitors expired with 7.3 of their quota of overs unused.

Playing his first competitive innings since returning injured from Australia, Graeme Hick hit a welcome 109 at Headingley, albeit he was twice dropped and lacked his usual command and assurance. He shared a second-wicket stand of 86 with Curtis after Weston had fallen to Robinson on two, but the rest of the Worcestershire batsmen had little to offer.

Facing a modest target, Yorkshire lost Moxon and Vaughan for 31, and Byas was run out on 66, but White joined Bevan in a stand worth 99 in 24 overs. Bevan was masterful. The left-hander took Yorkshire to victory with 20 balls to spare, and he hit 8 fours as well as the six off Illingworth with which he finished the match. In his first two matches as Yorkshire's overseas player, he had given promise of a rich return for the county's investment.

2 May *at Cambridge*

Combined Universities 209 for 7 (G.I. Macmillan 54)

Essex 213 for 2 (G.A. Gooch 115 not out, N. Hussain 81 not out)

Essex (2 pts) won by 8 wickets

(Gold Award – G.A. Gooch)

at Stockton

Durham 268 (W. Larkins 80, M. Prabhakar 69, J.E. Morris 51, C.L. Cairns 4 for 47)

Nottinghamshire 271 for 5 (R.T. Robinson 84, P. Johnson 56 not out, P.R. Pollard 56)

Nottinghamshire (2 pts) won by 5 wickets

(Gold Award – C.L. Cairns)

at Bristol

Gloucestershire 186 for 8

Middlesex 181

Gloucestershire (2 pts) won by 5 runs

(Gold Award – J. Srinath)

at Southampton

Hampshire 225 for 6 (R.A. Smith 83, J.P. Stephenson 55)

Glamorgan 227 for 3 (S.P. James 54, D.L. Hemp 52)

Glamorgan (2 pts) won by 7 wickets

(Gold Award – A. Dale)

at Canterbury

Kent 280 for 6 (T.R. Ward 113)

Somerset 161 (T.N. Wren 6 for 41)

Kent (2 pts) won by 119 runs

(Gold Award – T.N. Wren)

at Leicester

Minor Counties 224 (I. Cockbain 65 not out)

Leicestershire 198 (T.J. Boon 54, L. Potter 4 for 23, P.G. Newman 4 for 29)

Minor Counties (2 pts) won by 26 runs

(Gold Award – L. Potter)

at Northampton

Worcestershire 240 for 7 (G.A. Hick 94, K.M. Curran 4 for 38)

Northamptonshire 137 (K.M. Curran 50, R.K. Illingworth 4 for 27)

Worcestershire (2 pts) won by 103 runs

(Gold Award – G.A. Hick)

at Glasgow (Hamilton Crescent)

Scotland 129 (J.D. Love 54, P.J. Hartley 4 for 21)

LEFT: *The heroes of Minor Counties' victory over Leicestershire: skipper Ian Cockbain…*

ABOVE: *and Laurie Potter. (Both photos: Neal Simpson/Empics)*

Yorkshire 130 for 0 (M.D. Moxon 66 not out, M.P. Vaughan 50 not out)

Yorkshire (2 pts) won by 10 wickets

(Gold Award – P.J. Hartley)

at The Oval

Surrey 239 for 7 (A.D. Brown 82, D.M. Ward 60 not out)
Sussex 240 for 2 (C.W.J. Athey 97, N.J. Lenham 73 not out)

Sussex (2 pts) won by 8 wickets

(Gold Award – C.W.J. Athey)

at Edgbaston

Lancashire 305 for 2 (J.E.R. Gallian 116 not out, M.A. Atherton 114, N.H. Fairbrother 60 not out)
Warwickshire 265 (A.J. Moles 89, D.P. Ostler 73)

Lancashire (2 pts) won by 40 runs

(Gold Award – M.A. Atherton)

The Essex season had not begun well, so that victory over the Combined Universities at Fenner's was much wel-

come. Even this win, however, was not achieved with the ease that an eight-wicket margin would suggest. The students batted with confidence and ran well between the wickets. Macmillan and Sutcliffe scored 87 for the first wicket and, at lunch, the Universities were a healthy 143 for 3. Neil Williams had retired from the attack with a strained hamstring after bowling 21 innocuous deliveries for 14 runs. Peter Such later curtailed the scoring, and the students' total of 209 was disappointing. It looked more impressive when Prichard was run out for 0, and Lewis perished to a swinging ball from Renshaw. Gooch, too, was not at ease, but Hussain was in prime form and drove square of the wicket with great power and style. Gooch finally found his touch to reach his 13th hundred in the competition and to take his 22nd Gold Award. He and Hussain shared an unbroken stand of 189 to take their side to victory with 4.2 overs remaining.

Durham's hopes of qualifying for the quarter-finals took a knock when they lost to Nottinghamshire, who hit their highest score in the competition when batting second and won with seven balls to spare. Durham should certainly have set Nottinghamshire a stiffer target, for, with 13 balls of their innings to go, they were 262 for 3 with John Morris having completed fifty off 38 balls, but they proceeded to lose their last seven wickets for six runs in those 13 balls. Chris Cairns claimed four of those wickets. His contribution to the Nottinghamshire victory did not end there, for, in the 42nd over, the visitors were 169 for 3, and success looked improbable. Cairns and Johnson thought otherwise and added 81 in 10 overs before Cairns fell to Walker for 46. Evans went cheaply, but Dowman held one end as Johnson scored the runs that were needed.

The unexpected Gloucestershire resurgence continued as Middlesex were beaten to make it three wins out of the three matches played so far in the competition by the West Country side. There seemed little hope of a Gloucestershire victory when they were 106 for 5 from 38 overs at lunch, having been put in. Alleyne, Russell and, at the death, Cooper hit powerfully in the afternoon session, but 186 did not look a winning total. Srinath struck two crucial blows when, in his fourth over, he dismissed Gatting and Ramprakash with successive deliveries. Pooley and Carr added 64 before Alleyne had Pooley caught behind. Ball accounted for Carr and Weekes, and with 10 overs remaining, Middlesex needed 58 to win. This seemed to be well within their grasp until Brown was run out by Wright's direct throw and Embury fell to Srinath.

Glamorgan, another side rich in early-season promise, were still without skipper Hugh Morris, but they raced to victory over Hampshire with 8.5 overs and seven wickets to spare. Put in to bat, Hampshire could never achieve fluency against some accurate bowling and tigerish fielding. Terry went early in the innings, but Stephenson and Smith added 125 off 32 overs, never quite breaking free of the shackles imposed upon them. Both batsmen fell to Dale before lunch, and thereafter Hampshire offered little. Hemp and James began Glamorgan's innings with 116 in 23 overs. When they departed, Maynard and Cottey took over, and Dale, who earned his first Gold Award, joined Cottey for the last 39 runs.

With Trevor Ward hitting his second successive century in the competition, Kent rattled to a commanding score of 280 against Somerset at Canterbury. He dominated an opening stand of 117 with Benson in 30 overs. Ward's century came off 148 balls and, in all, he hit 15 fours and a six. Somerset were handicapped by van Troost's wayward bowling. His nine overs cost 70 runs. Walker and Fleming both hit hard and often, and Somerset became a sorry sight in the field. They were even sorrier when they batted as Tim Wren took five wickets in 17 balls to wreck their innings and decide a match which had long since been in favour of the home side. There was some recovery from the depths of 80 for 7, but all was anti-climax as Wren took his first Gold Award. Ironically, it is unlikely that he would have been in the Kent side had McCague and Igglesden been fit.

The sensation of the round came at Leicester where Minor Counties beat the home side by 26 runs. It was the sixth occasion on which Minor Counties had beaten a first-class county. Leicestershire were without skipper Nigel Briers, and his deputy, James Whitaker, used six bowlers before an opening stand of 77 between Dean and Evans could be broken. Potter and Cockbain continued the dominance of the Minor Counties over the Leicestershire attack, scoring 58 in 17 overs, but the last five wickets went down for 23 runs. A target of 225 should not have caused Leicestershire many problems, particularly as Boon and Wells scored 70 for the first wicket. Potter had Wells leg before while sweeping and, two balls later, he had Cronje,

making his home debut, taken at mid-wicket. Whitaker and Robinson quickly departed. Smith and Maddy showed positive application, but Potter caught-and-bowled Smith and later had Mullally caught to earn a famous victory. Potter took the Gold Award. It was the second time he had won the accolade. The first was in 1986 when he was playing *for* Leicestershire *against* the Minor Counties.

Northamptonshire confirmed a Jekyll-and-Hyde existence, following a wonderful championship win at Canterbury with a terrible drubbing at home to Worcestershire. It was their second defeat in the Benson and Hedges Cup and virtually put them out of the competition. Hick, batting with more freedom than he had done at Headingley a week earlier, led the Worcestershire charge after they had been put in. He and Moody scored 91 for the third wicket, but the visitors' innings never realised what it had threatened. A target of 241 looked well within Northamptonshire's reach, but Montgomerie was soon run out and Bailey caught behind off Newport, who produced a good opening spell. Indeed, Newport conceded only 13 runs from his 11 overs and claimed the wicket of Kumble as well as that of Bailey, and the match never became a true contest.

There was certainly no contest at Hamilton Crescent. Sent in on a slow wicket which offered lateral movement, Scotland stumbled to 31 for 5. Three of these wickets fell to Peter Hartley, enjoying a wonderful start to the season. Love offered resistance against his old county, but Scotland crawled to 129 in 51.1 overs. It took Moxon and Vaughan just 22.3 overs to pass this total.

Gloom descended upon The Oval. It was confirmed that Waqar Younis would not be fit for the season and that Carl Rackemann would join the side when the Australian tour of the Caribbean was completed. On the field, Surrey lost Darren Bicknell and Mark Butcher for 27 and could have lost Brown twice had Sussex held catches. As it was, Brown hit 82 off 100 balls, and Surrey lunched at 163 for 3 off 39 overs. Brown was out immediately after the interval, and only the likeable David Ward maintained the necessary acceleration, so that Surrey finished on a disappointing 239. Sussex began at four runs an over, with Athey and Hall scoring 81. Following the dismissal of Hall, Athey and Lenham added 117, and Wells joined Lenham to complete a comfortable victory with 2.5 overs remaining.

Warwickshire's chances of retaining the cup became very slim after their defeat at Edgbaston. Atherton, in fine form, and Gallian, less certain but effective, scored 210 in 43 overs for Lancashire's first wicket. Both batsmen reached centuries. It was Gallian's first in the competition. The platform that these two provided was ideal for a Red Rose plunder, and although Crawley went cheaply, Fairbrother, dropped second ball, hit 60 off 34 deliveries. For reasons which only he can tell, Reeve persisted with Welch, who had been controversially preferred to Paul Smith, and the medium-pacer was hit for 35 off his last two overs. This meant that in his full quota of 11 overs, he conceded 103 runs without taking a wicket or bowling a maiden. When one considers that Small bowled his full quota of overs for a mere 25 runs, the use of Welch seems to have been an error of great magnitude. Knight was soon out, but Moles and Ostler took Warwickshire to 178 for 1 in the 35th over. Three wickets then fell in the next three overs, and when Moles was out in the 43rd over, Warwickshire were 211 for 5, and the game swung decisively in Lancashire's favour with the rest of the visitors' batting offering little.

9 May *at Oxford*

Combined Universities 228 for 9 (G.I. Macmillan 77)
Hampshire 228 for 8 (J.P. Stephenson 98, V.P. Terry 68)

Hampshire (2 pts) won by losing fewer wickets with the scores level

(Gold Award – J.P. Stephenson)

at Chelmsford

Essex 208 for 8 (G.A. Gooch 69)
Gloucestershire 211 for 8

Gloucestershire (2 pts) won by 2 wickets

(Gold Award – R.C. Russell)

at Cardiff

Glamorgan 209 for 9 (S.P. James 90)
Middlesex 210 for 5 (M.R. Ramprakash 91 not out, P.N. Weekes 51)

Middlesex (2 pts) won by 5 wickets

(Gold Award – M.R. Ramprakash)

at Comber (North Down CC)

Ireland 146 (D.A. Lewis 67 not out)
Kent 149 for 0 (M.R. Benson 76 not out, T.R. Ward 62 not out)

Kent (2 pts) won by 10 wickets

(Gold Award – D.A. Lewis)

at Old Trafford

Lancashire 353 for 7 (J.E.R. Gallian 134, J.P. Crawley 114)
Nottinghamshire 276 for 7 (G.F. Archer 74)

Lancashire (2 pts) won by 77 runs

(Gold Award – J.E.R. Gallian)

at Leicester

Leicestershire 224 for 8 (P.E. Robinson 54, J.J. Whitaker 50)
Warwickshire 227 for 2 (A.J. Moles 78, R.G. Twose 62 not out, D.P. Ostler 52)

Warwickshire (2 pts) won by 8 wickets

(Gold Award – A.J. Moles)

at Jesmond

Durham 250 for 9 (W. Larkins 123, M. Prabhakar 58)
Minor Counties 243 for 9 (R.J. Evans 56, A. Walker 4 for 42)

Durham (2 pts) won by 7 runs

(Gold Award – W. Larkins)

at Taunton

Somerset 202 (G.D. Rose 79, J.E. Benjamin 4 for 27, S.G. Kenlock 4 for 52)
Surrey 203 for 3 (D.J. Bicknell 81 not out, A.J. Stewart 52)

Surrey (2 pts) won by 7 wickets

(Gold Award – J.E. Benjamin)

at Worcester

Worcestershire 267 for 7 (G.A. Hick 127 not out, T.M. Moody 51)
Derbyshire 135

Worcestershire (2 pts) won by 132 runs

(Gold Award – G.A. Hick)

at Leeds

Yorkshire 223 (M.G. Bevan 64)
Northamptonshire 213 (R.J. Bailey 61, K.M. Curran 53)

Yorkshire (2 pts) won by 10 runs

(Gold Award – M.G. Bevan)

Combined Universities came close to causing a surprise in The Parks where Hampshire were the visitors. The students were given a good start by Macmillan and Sutcliffe who put on 62, and all the early batsmen made useful contributions. Unfortunately, Macmillan was struck on the knee and was unable to lead his side in the field. An opening stand of 145 in 41 overs between Stephenson and Terry seemed to have assured Hampshire of victory, but Terry was leg before to Renshaw, and three more wickets fell in six overs for the addition of 19 runs. Stephenson was fifth out, in the 49th over, with the score on 184, and Udal was dropped before he had scored. He and Aymes added 33 before Udal was bowled, and the last over arrived with 10 runs needed. Killeen had Aymes caught with his first ball and bowled Maru with his fifth. Connor scrambled two runs off the last ball to level the scores and so give Hampshire victory as they had lost eight wickets to the students' nine. The win did not save Hampshire from elimination from the competition, however.

Essex, too, were eliminated when they lost at home to Gloucestershire. Prichard was leg before to Srinath at 11, but Gooch and the promising Robinson added 85. There was a typically aggressive 40 from Irani, but Essex never got on top of the Gloucestershire attack. Gooch had taken 103 balls for his 69 and was caught off Ball when he tried to reverse-sweep a delivery of very full length. Wright and Hancock scored 50 for the visitors' first wicket, but it took them 20 overs. Lynch and Dawson gave the innings impetus before Dawson and Alleyne fell at the same score. Pearson accounted for Lynch as well as Dawson, and Symonds and Srinath were out in quick succession with the result that 28 were needed from the last five overs with only three wickets standing. Ball was run out to add to the tension, but Russell remained calm and carved the last delivery of the match through the covers for four to bring victory. Russell's unbeaten 42 earned him his second Gold Award.

Glamorgan's chances of becoming quarter-finalists suffered a setback when they were beaten by Middlesex. Steve James scored his fourth successive half-century in the tournament, but some injudicious strokes from his colleagues saw Glamorgan fall well short of the total they might have expected. Their 209 seemed sufficient when Middlesex lost Pooley, Carr and Gatting for 50, but Ramprakash and Weekes added 109, and Nash blasted merrily to bring victory with nine balls to spare.

Batting first on a low, slow wicket, Ireland lost their first three wickets for 21 runs in 11 overs. Skipper Lewis remained resolute, and he and Graham added 61 for the fifth wicket, but the home side never looked likely to discomfit Kent. Ward and Benson hit off the necessary runs in 32.1 overs, and Ward may well have reached his third cen-

tury in succession had the target been more demanding. Ireland's consolation was that Lewis took their second Gold Award in three matches.

Lancashire hit their highest score in the competition, and this was also the highest score made against Nottinghamshire in the Cup. With Cairns suffering from a side strain and unable to bowl, and Lewis still absent, the Nottinghamshire attack did not look too demanding. Indeed, the new ball was taken by spinner Andy Afford but, by the time Afford bowled, Atherton was already back in the pavilion, having touched Evans' fourth delivery to wicket-keeper French. This proved to be Nottinghamshire's last piece of joy for a considerable time, for, in the next 44 overs, Gallian and Crawley added 250, a Lancashire record for any wicket in any one-day competition. Gallian beat Crawley to the three-figure mark, and it was he who took the Gold Award – his first – but both batsmen played innings of quality and demolished the Nottinghamshire bowling. Gallian's 134 came off 137 balls, and Crawley faced 120 balls for his 114. Fairbrother entered to clout, tip and run. In one over from Hindson, a great fighter, he was twice dropped on the mid-wicket boundary by Mike, off successive deliveries. The first Mike palmed for six, and 18 runs came from the over. Watkinson also scored freely, and Nottinghamshire, with Pollard having suffered a side strain and able to bat only in an emergency, could only hope to salvage some pride. This they achieved comfortably, with Archer batting well, and Evans and Hindson showing brave aggression.

Nigel Briers returned to lead Leicestershire but was out for 0. Cronje and Whitaker put on 85 for the third wicket, but thereafter only Robinson, keeping wicket as both Whitticase and Nixon were injured, showed real purpose until Parsons and Pierson hit well in the closing overs. Moles, leading Warwickshire, and Ostler made 88 for the first wicket, and Twose and Moles scored 120 for the second to enable the visitors to stroll to victory with three overs to spare. Moles claimed his second Gold Award.

Wayne Larkins kept alive Durham's hopes of a place in the last eight when he hit 15 fours and 3 sixes in his 123 against Minor Counties. His colleagues – Prabhakar, with whom he added 163 for the second wicket, apart – gave scant support, and Minor Counties had a real chance to gain their second victory in a week. Dean was out for 40 but, with Potter and Russell Evans together, they needed 118 from the last 19 overs. Potter was caught behind off Prabhakar, and Evans was bowled when he heaved unwisely at Walker, but the last five overs arrived with 31 needed and four wickets standing. Walker's accuracy and an element of panic saw three wickets fall for three runs, and Minor Counties fell eight short of their target.

With three wickets in his opening spell, Joey Benjamin undermined the Somerset innings at Taunton. Martin Bicknell and the left-arm swing bowler 'Mark' Kenlock also bowled well, and the home side were in a sorry state

Neil Killeen took two wickets in the last over for Combined Universities against Hampshire, 9 May, but just failed to bring the students victory. (Neal Simpson/Empics)

at 44 for 6. Rose and Ecclestone added 101, but a total of 202 in 54 overs presented Surrey with few problems. Somerset were without Caddick and van Troost, both injured, and Darren Bicknell and Stewart scored 98 for the first wicket. Thorpe and Brown were both out in the 42nd over, bowled by Batty, with 61 still needed, but this was the only fright that Surrey had, and victory came with 11 balls to spare. Benjamin won his first Gold Award.

Graeme Hick took his 10th award in the match at Worcester as he brought his total to 330 runs in three Benson and Hedges innings. Worcestershire lost Curtis and Weston for 25 before Hick and Moody added 89 in 19 overs. Hick dominated the rest of the innings, and his 127 came off 124 balls with 13 fours and a six. He looked completely free of the back problem that had driven him home early from Australia. Derbyshire lost their first five batsmen for 34 runs, and any recovery could not hope to alter the course of the match.

Northamptonshire's interest in the competition ended at Headingley where Bevan's batting and fielding earned him a second Gold Award. Yorkshire stumbled after lunch and lost their last eight wickets in 17 overs for 80 runs. Only Bevan kept them alive, for their innings closed with eight balls unused. Loye was soon out as Northamptonshire went in search of a moderate target, but acting-captain Bailey anchored the innings. With five wickets standing, 53 runs were needed from 50 balls, but Bailey was brilliantly run out by Bevan, and Penberthy was stumped off a wide. Snape batted encouragingly, but when he fell to Hartley it was apparent that Northamptonshire's cause was lost.

16 May *at Southampton*

Essex 211 for 4 (G.A. Gooch 117 not out)
***v.* Hampshire**

Match abandoned

Essex 1 pt, Hampshire 1 pt

at Chesterfield

Derbyshire *v.* Yorkshire

Match abandoned

Derbyshire 1 pt, Yorkshire 1 pt

at Erlington

Somerset 316 for 5 (M.E. Trescothick 122, P.D. Bowler 54)
Ireland 83 (G.D. Rose 4 for 21)

Somerset (2 pts) won by 233 runs

(Gold Award – G.D. Rose)

at Old Trafford

Durham 57 for 2
***v.* Lancashire**

Match abandoned

Durham 1 pt, Lancashire 1 pt

at Northampton

Northamptonshire 304 for 6 (A. Fordham 108, R.J. Bailey 93 not out)
Scotland 151 for 5 (G.N. Reifer 57 not out)

Northamptonshire (2 pts) won by 153 runs

(Gold Award – R.J. Bailey)

at Edgbaston

Warwickshire 100 for 1 (D.P. Ostler 54 not out)
***v.* Minor Counties**

Match abandoned

Warwickshire 1 pt, Minor Counties 1 pt

16 and 17 May *at Swansea*

Gloucestershire 176 for 8
Glamorgan 167

Gloucestershire (2 pts) won by 9 runs

(Gold Award – J. Srinath)

at Lord's

Middlesex 276 for 8 (K.R. Brown 75, D.J. Nash 54)
Combined Universities 135 for 4

Middlesex (2 pts) won on faster scoring rate

(Gold Award – K.R. Brown)

at Trent Bridge

Leicestershire 211 for 6 (J.J. Whitaker 72, D.L. Maddy 50)
***v.* Nottinghamshire**

Match abandoned

Leicestershire 1 pt, Nottinghamshire 1 pt

at Hove

Sussex 303 for 6 (C.W.J. Athey 118, J.W. Hall 67)
Kent 307 for 2 (M.R. Benson 119, T.R. Ward 76, M.J. Walker 69 not out)

Kent (2 pts) won by 8 wickets

(Gold Award – M.J. Walker)

The weather was most unkind to the last round of qualifying matches in the Benson and Hedges Cup. No play was possible at Chesterfield, and, at Southampton, Essex had scored 211 in 49 overs when rain ended the match. Gooch was unbeaten on 117, his 14th hundred in the competition. He and Hussain added 102 for the third wicket.

Only 23 overs were possible at Edgbaston, and just 18 at Old Trafford. Leicestershire had made 211 for 6 in 49.3 overs at Trent Bridge, and only the matches at Erlington and Northampton were finished on the scheduled day.

Somerset were a little fortunate. They had a resounding victory over the inexperienced Ireland side who allowed them the most runs that they had ever conceded in a one-day match. Trescothick hit a six and 15 fours in his competition-best score, 122 off 112 balls. He and Bowler shared a record second-wicket stand of 163. Rose then proceeded to return his best bowling figures in the competition, and Ireland were all out in 39.2 overs to give Somerset a massive win. This win, coupled with the defeat of Sussex at Hove, gave Somerset a surprise place in the quarter-finals.

Sussex, in contrast, could consider themselves rather unlucky. Put in to bat, they faced Igglesden, making his first appearance of the season, and McCague, the two of whom were together in the Kent side for the first time in nearly a year. Athey and Hall were undaunted by their presence and hit 145 for the first wicket. Keith Newell batted well, and Stephenson made a violent assault on McCague towards the close, enabling Sussex to reach a commendable 303. McCague's only success came when he yorked Athey in the 51st over, but by that time the Yorkshireman had reached his first century in the competition. It was also the highest score made for Sussex in the Benson and Hedges Cup. Only seven overs of the Kent innings were possible before the close but, on the second morning, Benson and Ward took their opening stand to 147 in 28 overs, their fourth century partnership in as many matches. The Ward/Benson stand was slightly below the required run rate, but Walker and de Silva soon dispelled any lingering doubts that Kent supporters may have had, and, and, incredibly, victory came with 17 balls and eight wickets to spare. Kent's 307 was their highest score when batting second in the competition.

Northamptonshire beat Scotland in a match which had no bearing on the question of who would qualify for the last eight, but the games at Swansea and Lord's were of considerable significance. At Swansea, Gloucestershire, put in to bat, scored 176 for 8 in their 55 overs on the Tuesday. The Glamorgan attack was relentlessly accurate. Watkin conceded 23 runs from his 11 overs, while Croft had 3 for 33 in his quota. Wright and Hodgson had started the Gloucestershire innings with a stand of 76, but they were out in successive overs, and the visitors were a miserable 95 for 4 in 36.5 overs when there came a stoppage. Russell helped the acceleration at the end, but 176 never seemed to be a winning score. It soon became apparent that Glamorgan would have no easy task when, on the second morning, both openers, James and Hemp, failed to score. While Maynard stayed there was hope, but he was caught by Lynch off Smith for 40, and Glamorgan were 68 for 5. Dale and Croft revived hopes with a stand of 54, but they were out in quick succession and, in spite of Metson's late flourish, Glamorgan were all out in 53.1 overs. Srinath, who took 3 for 16 in his 11 overs, took his second Gold Award of the season.

Middlesex clambered above Glamorgan by beating Combined Universities. The highlight of the Middlesex innings was a sixth-wicket stand of 119 off 97 balls between Brown and Nash. Until these two came together Middlesex were faring badly at 143 for 5, and defeat was a possibility. The students ended the day with 120 for 4 from 35.2 overs with the impressive Macmillan unbeaten on 34. Only 20 balls could be bowled on the Wednesday, and Middlesex became winners by having the faster run rate.

FINAL GROUP PLACINGS

	P	W	L	NR	Pts	Net run rate
Group A						
Lancashire	5	4	–	1	9	22.56
Nottinghamshire	5	3	1	1	7	0.70
Warwickshire	5	2	2	1	5	4.69
Durham	5	2	2	1	5	−3.18
Minor Counties	5	1	3	1	3	−11.76
Leicestershire	5	–	4	1	1	−7.58
Group B						
Yorkshire	4	3	–	1	7	17.34
Worcestershire	4	3	1	–	6	26.02
Derbyshire	4	2	1	1	5	−3.11
Northamptonshire	4	1	3	–	2	−1.49
Scotland	4	–	4	–	0	−37.35
Group C						
Gloucestershire	5	5	–	–	10	9.99
Middlesex	5	4	1	–	8	7.70
Glamorgan	5	3	2	–	6	16.45
Essex	5	1	3	1	3	−2.48
Hampshire	5	1	3	1	3	−6.10
Combined Universities	5	–	5	–	0	−28.04
Group D						
Kent	4	4	–	–	8	27.14
Somerset	4	2	2	–	4	12.17
Surrey	4	2	2	–	4	4.67
Sussex	4	2	2	–	4	0.46
Ireland	4	–	4	–	0	−46.00

QUARTER-FINALS

30 May *at Canterbury*

Kent 250 for 9 (T.R. Ward 64, M.R. Benson 56, A.R.C. Fraser 4 for 49)

Middlesex 224

Kent won by 26 runs

(Gold Award – M.A. Ealham)

at Old Trafford

Nottinghamshire 201 for 8

Lancashire 205 for 4 (G.D. Lloyd 72 not out)

Lancashire won by 6 wickets

(Gold Award – G.D. Lloyd)

at Leeds

Yorkshire 88 (S.R. Lampitt 4 for 16)
Worcestershire 89 for 2

Worcestershire won by 8 wickets

(Gold Award – S.R. Lampitt)

30 and 31 May *at Bristol*

Gloucestershire 113
Somerset 114 for 4 (M.E. Trescothick 52)

Somerset won by 6 wickets

(Gold Award – J.D. Batty)

Trevor Ward and Mark Benson shared their fifth century partnership in five Benson and Hedges Cup matches to give Kent a sound platform for victory over Middlesex at Canterbury. Road-works and poor signposting had caused traffic chaos around the St Lawrence ground before the start of the match, but Benson and Ward were untroubled by such matters as they moved to 123 in 27 overs. At this point, rain caused an interruption which lasted a quarter of an hour. Ward had by then reached 400 runs in the season's competition and so earned the bonus of £1,000 for being the first player to reach the mark. On the resumption, neither he nor Benson could quite find their touch and, at 132, Benson drove Feltham to long-on where Pooley took a good running catch. The batsmen crossed, and Ward drove the next ball to extra-cover where Nash took a low catch. Aravinda de Silva was dubiously given out caught behind, a decision balanced by the fact that umpire Bird gave Marsh dubiously *not* out

TOP: *Mark Ramprakash is bowled by Mark Ealham, and the quarter-final between Kent and Middlesex at Canterbury swings very much in favour of the home side. (Tom Morris)*

ABOVE: *Stuart Lampitt bowled splendidly for Worcestershire throughout the competition and took the Gold Award in the quarter-final. (Allsport)*

The first batsman to reach 400 runs in the Benson and Hedges Cup in 1995, Trevor Ward of Kent. (Tom Morris)

caught behind later in the innings, a decision which greatly upset Angus Fraser. Walker was legitimately caught behind, and Cowdrey also gave a catch to Brown when he attempted to cut. Fleming tried to sweep Emburey and missed, and the Kent innings was in danger of disappearing at 198 for 6. Mark Ealham hit 30 off 26 balls to give purpose to the closing overs, and the home side reached their highest score against Middlesex in the Benson and Hedges Cup. There were some strange events in the Middlesex out-cricket. Gatting strained a groin muscle, but this could not explain why Johnson did not bowl a ball while the ineffective Weekes bowled a full quota of overs. Feltham opened with Pooley and made his highest score in the competition, 37, sharing an opening stand of 70. He fell to de Silva's occasional off-spin, and, at tea,

A Gold Award for Jeremy Batty in Somerset's quarter-final victory over Gloucestershire, but little first-team cricket for the off-spinner during the season. (David Munden/Sportsline)

Middlesex were 93 for 1 from 25 overs. The accuracy of McCague and Headley made the run rate required increasingly demanding in the period after tea. McCague had been desperately unlucky earlier when Feltham was dropped twice off successive deliveries by Cowdrey at slip in his second over. At 133 for 2 in the 38th over, Middlesex's hopes were still alive, but Ramprakash then played across the line to Ealham, who had already taken the wicket of Pooley, and was bowled. Neither Gatting, batting with a runner, nor Carr could find their touch, and the Middlesex innings subsided as batsmen flailed wildly at the persistent Headley. The match lasted until the fourth ball of the 55th over when Fraser was bowled by Fleming.

In contrast, the game at Old Trafford was over after 49.4 overs of Lancashire's innings. In the absence of the injured Pollard, Nottinghamshire opened with Wileman who, playing his first Benson and Hedges Cup innings, edged the second ball of the match from Wasim Akram to Atherton at second slip. Robinson and Banton added 60 but, with Johnson also absent, the Nottinghamshire innings never gained momentum. Lewis, in one of his rare appearances of the season, hit 48 off 82 balls, but he was unable to bowl, and a target of 202 posed few problems for Lancashire. Gallian was soon out, and Atherton and Crawley were back in the pavilion with 90 scored. Lloyd and Fairbrother added 70 in 15 overs, and Lloyd, dropped when 29, went on to score 72 off 68 balls to win the match and his Gold Award.

At Headingley, Worcestershire won the toss, asked Yorkshire to bat and bowled them out in 48.5 overs on a pitch which contained more than a hint of moisture. Bevan and White were out to successive deliveries from Haynes while Lampitt took the last four wickets in 16 deliveries. One of his victims was Byas, acting-captain, who had shown admirable responsibility and craft for his

47. Yorkshire's total, their lowest in the competition, was their first under 100 in their 106 Benson and Hedges Cup matches. Worcestershire won the game before tea. They reached 89 in 22.5 overs. Moody finished the match by hitting Stemp for 2 sixes.

The match at Bristol was played in damp, cloudy conditions and went into a second day. That the match needed two days in which to be completed was due, in part at least, to the lack of flexibility of the umpires in their interpretation of the rules of the competition. Ninety minutes' play was lost in mid-afternoon, yet tea was not taken until nearly six o'clock when the Somerset innings was 25 overs old. Russell erred in deciding to bat when he won the toss, for Hodgson and Lynch were soon gone, and when the spinners took over batting became increasingly difficult. Dawson and Symonds raised hopes with a fifth-wicket stand of 33, but this was followed by further decline, and the home side were all out in 49.4 overs. Lathwell and Bowler departed early, both falling to spectacular catches by Russell, and Trescothick survived miraculously. The day ended at tea, six o'clock, with Somerset 63 for 2 from 25 overs. In 10.1 overs on the second day, they lost Trescothick and Rose and hit the 51 further runs they needed. Batty, 2 for 13 in his 11 overs, took the Gold Award. Like Ealham and Lloyd, it was his first award. It was also one of his few first-team appearances during the season.

SEMI-FINALS

13 June *at Worcester*

Worcestershire 261 for 5 (G.A. Hick 109, T.M. Moody 75 not out, T.S. Curtis 50)

Lancashire 264 for 8 (Wasim Akram 64)

Lancashire won by 2 wickets

(Gold Award – Wasim Akram)

13 and 14 June *at Canterbury*

Kent 250 for 9 (M.A. Ealham 52)

Somerset 219 for 8 (A.N. Hayhurst 69 not out, P.D. Bowler 53)

Kent won by 31 runs

(Gold Award – M.A. Ealham)

In an astonishing game at Worcester, Lancashire staged a remarkable recovery to win with four balls to spare and so reach their fifth Lord's final in six seasons. Curtis won the toss and was perfectly justified in his decision to bat first. Weston was caught at slip at 18, but Hick joined Curtis in a stand which realised 95 in 24 overs. Hick and Moody then put on 120 in 24 overs. Hick hit 2 sixes and 7 fours in his seventh Benson and Hedges Cup century, and his 109 came off 131 balls. It brought his total of runs in the competition in 1995 to 466, and it looked as though it had given Worcestershire a place in the final in spite of the fact that Wasim Akram took three wickets, one of them being the wicket of Hick, in eight balls at the close. For once, none of the Lancashire top-order batsmen produced an innings of substance and, at 135 for 6 with 17 overs to go, they looked a beaten side. Austin was out at 169, and from the last 10 overs 83 runs were needed with only three wickets standing, but the Wasim/Hegg partnership was already under way. Wasim launched an attack on Radford which brought 19 runs in an over, and when Hick, who had earlier taken two wickets, returned, he was hit for 11 in an over. When Newport finally knocked back Wasim's off stump the Pakistani all-rounder had hit 64 off 47 balls, with 6 fours and 2 sixes, and he and Hegg had added 69 in seven overs. Twenty-four runs were still needed from four overs following the departure of Wasim, and Yates, playing in place of the injured Martin, hit 19 of them off 14 balls, cutting Illingworth for the winning boundary with four balls remaining. Wasim rightly took the Gold Award, but Hegg's contribution should not be overlooked. He ran like a greyhound to give Wasim the strike, and his own 31 runs came from just 28 balls. This was exhilarating stuff.

There were not the same fireworks in Canterbury where rain took the match into a second day. Kent completed their innings on the first day and made 250 from their 55 overs. Ward and Benson made only 53 for the first wicket on this occasion, and three wickets fell for six runs to leave the home side on a perilous 59 for 3. Mushtaq Ahmed had brought about this state of affairs, having run out Benson and bowled Fleming. He also lured de Silva down the pitch in his first over after tea, but Turner missed an easy stumping. Had the chance been taken, Kent would have been 62 for 4. As it was, de Silva made an invaluable 39 before being bowled by Mushtaq's top-spinner. Cowdrey hit cleanly, but he was caught low down by Lathwell on the boundary when he swept at Batty. Llong was run out by Mushtaq when he was rightly sent back by de Silva, and Kent were 96 for 5. Ealham batted with aggression and sense, and, following the departure of de Silva, he and Marsh added 60 for the seventh wicket. These runs came in 10 overs, and Ealham's 52 included 2 sixes and 2 fours. From the last 10 overs of their innings, Kent plundered 87 runs, and their total of 250 was eminently satisfactory. It soon became apparent that this total was beyond the reach of Somerset, who found the boundary only four times in the 35 overs before lunch on the second day. They lost Trescothick to Wren's third delivery, and the left-arm seamer returned before lunch to dismiss Lathwell and Harden with successive deliveries. Bowler could never generate the necessary rate of scoring, and by the time Hayhurst hit 69 off 71 balls, the cause was lost.

Wasim Akram's violent hitting brought Lancashire a sensational victory over Worcestershire in the semi-final at New Road. (Ben Radford/Allsport)

BENSON AND HEDGES CUP FINAL
KENT *v.* LANCASHIRE, at Lord's

Fortune did not smile on Kent. Mark Benson, an integral part of their success in reaching Lord's, as both captain and opening batsman, was deemed unfit for the final, and his place was taken by David Fulton. Neil Taylor also came into the side. Like Fulton, he was playing his first Benson and Hedges Cup game of the season. Igglesden and Patel were omitted from the party of 13, and the omission of

Patel caused considerable dismay in many quarters. It left the Kent attack with little variety. As a left-arm spinner, Patel was on the brink of the England side.

In contrast, Lancashire felt that Gallian was fit to play even though he had a damaged finger, and Fairbrother also reported fit. Martin was absent through injury, but Lancashire went into the match as firm favourites.

The morning was grey and overcast, and rain delayed the start by 10 minutes. Kent had planned to bat if they won the toss, but when Marsh called correctly he reversed that decision in view of the weather. It was a piece of ill judgement, for when Kent took the field the clouds had cleared and the sun shone. Atherton leg-glanced the first ball of the match for four, an indication of Wren's general direction, and top-edged the fourth ball towards long-leg where de Silva was a fraction too slow in starting for the catch. The chance was missed, and it was the 20th over before Kent had their first success, Ealham bowling Gallian between bat and pad.

Wren had by now been withdrawn from the attack, not to return. He had bowled five wides and had given no glimpse of the form he had shown in the earlier rounds. Aravinda de Silva offered some variety with his brisk off-breaks, but one sighed for Patel. The Kent bowlers could not muster a maiden between them.

Atherton and Crawley scored 121 in 26 overs without a hint of alarm. As ever, Atherton was thoroughly workmanlike, but Crawley was the more impressive. It was the

PRIZE STRUCTURE

£137,650 of the £641,307 Benson and Hedges sponsorship of this event will go in prize money for teams or individuals.

The breakdown is as follows:

- The Champions will win £35,000 (and hold, for one year only, the Benson and Hedges Cup)
- For the Runners-up £17,500
- For the losing Semi-finalists £8,750
- For the losing Quarter-finalists £4,375

ADDITIONAL TEAM AWARDS

The winners of all matches in the Group stages of the Cup received £750.

INDIVIDUAL GOLD AWARDS

There is a Benson and Hedges Gold Award for the outstanding individual performance at all matches throughout the Cup.

These are:

In the Group matches	£200
In the Quarter-finals	£300
In the Semi-finals	£350
In the Final	£750

The playing conditions and Cup records are on the reverse.

SPECIAL ACHIEVEMENT AWARDS

First batsman to score 400 runs	£1,000
First bowler to take 20 wickets	£1,000
First wicket-keeper to equal the Benson and Hedges record of 8 dismissals in an innings	£1,000

BENSON and HEDGES CUP 1995

MARYLEBONE CRICKET CLUB

50p   50p

FINAL
KENT v. LANCASHIRE
at Lord's Ground, Saturday, July 15th 1995

Any alterations to teams will be announced over the public address system

KENT

1 D. P. Fulton	l b w b Chapple		25
2 T. R. Ward	c Hegg b Chapple		7
3 N. R. Taylor	b Yates		14
4 P. A. de Silva	c Lloyd b Austin		112
5 G. R. Cowdrey	l b w b Yates		25
6 M. V. Fleming	b Yates		11
7 M. A. Ealham	l b w b Watkinson		3
†*8 S. A. Marsh	c Crawley b Austin		4
9 M. J. McCague	not out		11
10 D. W. Headley	c Chapple b Watkinson		5
11 T. N. Wren	c Austin b Watkinson		7
	B , l-b 7, w 2, n-b 6,		15
		Total...	239

LANCASHIRE

1 M. A. Atherton	c Fulton b Headley		93
2 J. E. R. Gallian	b Ealham		36
3 J. P. Crawley	c Taylor b McCague		83
4 N. H. Fairbrother	c McCague b Headley		16
5 G. D. Lloyd	run out		12
6 Wasim Akram	run out		10
†7 M. Watkinson	c McCague b Fleming		0
8 I. D. Austin	not out		5
*9 W. K. Hegg			
10 G. Chapple			
11 G. Yates			
	B , l-b 2, w 10, n-b 7,		19
		Total...	274

FALL OF THE WICKETS

1...28 2...37 3...81 4...142 5...162 6...180 7...214 8...214 9...219 10...239

Bowling Analysis	O.	M.	R.	W.	Wd.	N-b
Wasim Akram	10	0	57	0	2	2
Chapple	10	1	55	2	...	...
Austin	11	4	36	2	...	...
Watkinson	10.1	0	42	3	...	1
Yates	11	0	42	3	...	...
	...	...	...	...	...	...
	...	...	...	...	...	...

FALL OF THE WICKETS

1...80 2...201 3...236 4...258 5...259 6...266 7...274 8... 9... 10...

Bowling Analysis	O.	M.	R.	W.	Wd.	N-b
Wren	5	0	21	0	5	...
Headley	11	0	57	2	...	3
McCague	11	0	65	1	1	...
Ealham	11	0	33	1	...	...
de Silva	8	0	36	0	2	...
Fleming	9	0	60	1	2	...
	...	...	...	...	...	...

† Captain   * Wicket-keeper

Umpires—D. R. Shepherd & N. T. Plews

Scorers—J. C. Foley, W. Davies & E. Solomon

Toss won by—Kent who elected to field

RESULT—Lancashire won by 35 runs

The playing conditions for the Benson & Hedges Cup Competition are printed on the back of this score card.

Total runs scored at end of each over :—

Kent	1	2	3	4	5	6	7	8	9	10	11	12	13	14	15	16	17	18	19	20
	21	22	23	24	25	26	27	28	29	30	31	32	33	34	35	36	37	38	39	40
	41	42	43	44	45	46	47	48	49	50	51	52	53	54	55					

Lancashire	1	2	3	4	5	6	7	8	9	10	11	12	13	14	15	16	17	18	19	20
	21	22	23	24	25	26	27	28	29	30	31	32	33	34	35	36	37	38	39	40
	41	42	43	44	45	46	47	48	49	50	51	52	53	54	55					

Reproduced by kind permission of MCC

ABOVE: *John Crawley in sumptuous form in his innings of 83. (Shaun Botterill/Allsport)*

RIGHT: *Chapple traps Fulton leg before for 25. (Shaun Botterill/Allsport)*

BELOW RIGHT: *The most glorious sight of the season – Aravinda de Silva strikes another boundary in his innings of 112. (Shaun Botterill/Allsport)*

ideal occasion for him to show that he had tightened his technique and that he now presented a slimmer, more eager physique. Pleasingly, he has discovered that runs can be scored on the off side, and there was a suggestion that the tendency to cramp all to leg had been eradicated. He revealed some exciting cover-drives and square-cuts.

Atherton heaved the first ball of the 46th over to Fulton at mid-wicket. He had faced 141 balls and hit 9 fours, and had placed Lancashire in a strong position. His dismissal heralded the customary mayhem as five more wickets fell in the last 10 overs for the addition of 73 runs. Fairbrother ran like a terrier and hit 16 off 13 balls while Crawley's innings came to an end in the 53rd over when, out of character with the technical competence of his knock, he slogged to long-on. He had faced only 89 balls for his 83 and had hit a six and 5 fours.

That Kent were not savaged beyond redemption in those closing overs was due to the tenacity and quality of their fielding. Watkinson felt that his side had fallen some 20 runs below what they had expected, but 275 was still a daunting target, and records would have to be broken if it were to be reached.

Kent's success in reaching the final had been built upon big opening partnerships, but now there was no Benson, and, in the eighth over, the prolifically scoring Ward gave a faint edge to the keeper. Fulton had hit Wasim for two leg-side boundaries, but he was leg before in the 12th over when he played back to Chapple.

Taylor has never been a batsman at ease in the limited-over game, and it was no surprise that he was becalmed. Three of Austin's first four overs were maidens, and 'Bully's' medium-pace accuracy threatened to bring the match to a limp and painfully slow death. Whatever hopes Kent had, rested in de Silva who had been in brilliant form in championship matches. He did not disappoint.

He immediately removed the threat of Austin. Twice he lifted him into the Mound Stand for six. Where Austin had

frustrated others with his length, de Silva danced down the wicket to create his own length. He flicked the ball through mid-wicket and drove to the cover boundary in regal manner. The game was electrified by the beauty of his batting.

Chapple dropped Taylor at long-on, but in the next over Taylor was yorked by Yates, who bowled his brisk off-breaks well. Cowdrey joined de Silva in a partnership which produced 61 runs in under 14 overs and which threatened to turn the game in favour of Kent. Cowdrey looked positive, the perfect ally to de Silva's brilliance. The

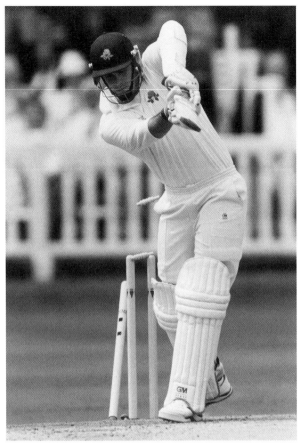

Jason Gillian, playing with an injured finger, is bowled by Mark Ealham for 36. Gallian shared an opening stand of 80 with Atherton. (Paul Sturgess/Sportsline)

Lancashire victorious. (Patrick Eagar)

stand was ripening when it was broken by rain for a time, after which Cowdrey was adjudged leg before when he swept at Yates. He had essayed the shot several times, but on this occasion umpire Shepherd decreed against him.

Now two separate games seemed to be going on at the same time. Fleming stepped away and tried to cut Yates and was bowled; Ealham hoiked across the line at Watkinson. Aravinda de Silva committed no such profanities. When we watched Atherton and Crawley we enjoyed good, honest prose; de Silva gave us the most sublime of poetry. He hit Chapple – disappointing on this showing – for six over square-leg and drove him to the cover boundary next ball to reach an exquisite century. While he was at the wicket all was possible. He had 3 sixes and 11 fours before, facing the 95th ball of his innings, he pulled Austin towards the Mound Stand only for Lloyd to take the catch on the boundary ropes. The Sri Lankan left the field, and Lord's rose to him. We had been in the presence of greatness.

It is, perhaps, necessary to define 'great', so overused has the word become. Lara's 501 against Durham in 1994 was not a *great* innings. It was a remarkable achievement against a limited attack in a match that was dead. By any standards, de Silva's 112 was a great innings. The Kent cause was all but lost when he arrived, but, with little support, he almost snatched an impossible victory. He never resorted to the slog which some see as the only means of scoring quickly in the one-day game. Not for a second in the 140 minutes that he was at the wicket did he violate the aesthetic or the technique of the game. To have seen this innings is to have been granted one of the greatest of privileges that the game has offered in the past 50 years.

Following de Silva's departure in the 49th over, there was an inevitable anti-climax. Sixty-one runs were needed from six overs and, as Marsh immediately pushed Austin into the hands of short extra-cover, the task became at once impossible. Headley chipped to fine leg, and Wren hoisted to long-on in front of the Allen Stand. Lancashire most deservedly and most positively had won. They are a team, and even one great cricketer is likely to be beaten by 11 good ones.

Aravinda de Silva became the first man to win the Gold Award in the final even though his side had lost the match. He joins Gooch and Viv Richards as the only centurions in a Benson and Hedges Cup final. The only blemishes on the day were a long-winded presentation ceremony in which trite and unnecessary interviews marred the dignity of the occasion, and reports of the match in a couple of newspapers where the emphasis was on blaming the competition for the shortcomings of the England side. They had obviously not watched de Silva's one-day magic. There is something peculiarly English in not wanting people to enjoy themselves.

BENSON AND HEDGES CUP AVERAGES

COMBINED UNIVERSITIES

BATTING	M	Inns	NO	Runs	HS	Av	100s	50s	ct/st
G.I. Macmillan	5	5	1	214	77	53.50	–	2	1
M.T.E. Peirce	5	5	–	134	44	26.80	–	–	1
I.J. Sutcliffe	3	3	–	70	39	23.33	–	–	–
J.N. Batty	4	3	2	22	11	22.00	–	–	3/1
K.R. Spiring	4	4	–	87	35	21.75	–	–	1
W.S. Kendall	3	3	–	54	23	18.00	–	–	–
U. Rashid	3	2	1	15	9	15.00	–	–	–
A.R. Whittall	4	4	–	48	21	12.00	–	–	4
C.M. Gupte	2	2	–	21	19	10.50	–	–	–
A.D. Edwards	5	4	1	21	7*	7.00	–	–	5
N. Killeen	5	4	1	14	8	4.66	–	–	1
I.G.S. Steer	2	2	–	7	4	3.50	–	–	–
A.D. MacRobert	3	2	–	6	6	3.00	–	–	2
M.S. Harvey	2	2	–	3	3	1.50	–	–	2
S.J. Renshaw	5	2	1	0	0*	0.00	–	–	1

There was one catch taken by a substitute

BOWLING	Overs	Mds	Runs	Wkts	Av	Best	4/inn
A.D. MacRobert	30	4	173	5	34.60	3-51	–
S.J. Renshaw	49	7	210	5	42.00	2-34	–
A.D. Edwards	54	6	232	5	46.40	2-51	–
N. Killeen	55	5	254	6	55.66	2-43	–
G.I. Macmillan	9.4	–	63	1	63.00	1-20	–
A.R. Whittall	40	1	209	3	69.66	2-49	–
U. Rashid	33	–	154	2	77.00	1-52	–

DERBYSHIRE

BATTING	M	Inns	NO	Runs	HS	Av	100s	50s	ct/st
D.J. Cullinan	3	3	2	106	101*	106.00	1	–	1
K.J. Barnett	3	3	1	98	58*	49.00	–	1	2
C.J. Adams	3	3	–	111	94	37.00	–	1	–
D.G. Cork	3	2	–	38	26	19.00	–	–	1
P.A.J. DeFreitas	3	2	–	37	37	18.50	–	–	3
A.S. Rollins	3	3	–	28	15	9.33	–	–	2
T.J.G. O'Gorman	3	2	–	17	16	8.50	–	–	2

Three matches: A.E. Warner 2*; D.E. Malcolm 4 (ct 1)
Two matches: C.M. Wells 3*; K.M. Krikken (ct 3)
One match: T.W. Harrison 25; A.J. Harris 5

BOWLING	Overs	Mds	Runs	Wkts	Av	Best	4/inn
D.E. Malcolm	32	1	154	11	14.00	4-34	2
P.A.J. DeFreitas	31.1	4	74	4	18.50	2-22	–
A.E. Warner	33	5	111	5	22.20	2-26	–
C.M. Wells	15	1	40	1	40.00	1-18	–
D.G. Cork	33	–	142	3	47.33	2-43	–
A.J. Harris	11	–	54	1	54.00	1-54	–
K.J. Barnett	6	2	21	–	–	–	–

DURHAM

BATTING	M	Inns	NO	Runs	HS	Av	100s	50s	ct/st
W. Larkins	5	5	–	251	123	50.20	1	1	3
J.E. Morris	4	4	1	120	62	40.00	–	2	–
M. Prabhakar	5	5	1	148	69	37.00	–	2	4
M. Saxelby	4	4	1	102	80*	34.00	–	1	–
J.I. Longley	4	4	–	62	35	15.50	–	–	1
M.A. Roseberry	5	5	–	61	27	12.20	–	–	–
J. Wood	4	4	–	36	27	9.00	–	–	–
S.J.E. Brown	3	3	–	22	12	7.33	–	–	–
J. Boiling	4	4	2	8	5*	4.00	–	–	–
A. Walker	4	4	2	5	4*	2.50	–	–	1
C.W. Scott	4	4	–	8	2	2.00	–	–	7

Two matches: J.A. Daley 17; S.D. Birbeck 1 (ct 1)
One match: D.G. Ligertwood and J.P. Searle

BOWLING	Overs	Mds	Runs	Wkts	Av	Best	4/inn
S.J.E. Brown	30.5	6	108	7	15.42	3-39	–
A. Walker	40.4	1	168	8	21.00	4-42	2
S.D. Birbeck	11	–	64	3	21.33	3-64	–
M. Prabhakar	43	3	187	5	37.40	2-36	–
J. Wood	44	4	182	4	45.50	3-50	–
J. Boiling	32	1	156	2	78.00	1-6	–
M. Saxelby	7	–	38	–	–	–	–

ESSEX

BATTING	M	Inns	NO	Runs	HS	Av	100s	50s	ct/st
G.A. Gooch	5	5	2	327	117*	109.00	2	1	1
N. Hussain	5	5	1	229	81*	57.25	–	2	1
P.J. Prichard	5	5	–	167	92	33.40	–	2	–
D.D.J. Robinson	5	4	1	99	35*	33.00	–	–	1
R.C. Irani	5	4	–	92	40	23.00	–	–	1
J.J.B. Lewis	5	5	1	52	19	13.00	–	–	2
M.A. Garnham	2	2	–	25	24	12.50	–	–	–
M.C. Ilott	5	3	–	34	21	11.33	–	–	1
P.M. Such	5	3	2	6	5*	6.00	–	–	1
N.F. Williams	3	2	–	3	3	1.50	–	–	1

Four matches: D.M. Cousins 12* (ct 1)
Three matches: R.J. Rollins 0 (ct 3)
Two matches: R.M. Pearson (ct 1)
One match: N.A. Derbyshire

BOWLING	Overs	Mds	Runs	Wkts	Av	Best	4/inn
R.C. Irani	42	5	168	8	21.00	3-40	–
P.M. Such	42	3	146	6	23.66	3-27	–
R.M. Pearson	22	2	89	3	29.66	3-46	–
M.C. Ilott	44	3	160	3	53.33	1-22	–
N.F. Williams	18.3	–	107	1	107.00	1-49	–
D.M. Cousins	25.1	1	130	1	130.00	1-46	–
G.A. Gooch	21.3	1	77	–	–	–	–

GLAMORGAN

BATTING	M	Inns	NO	Runs	HS	Av	100s	50s	ct/st
S.P. James	5	5	–	301	90	60.20	–	4	–
R.D.B. Croft	5	3	1	100	50*	50.00	–	1	1
D.L. Hemp	5	5	–	202	121	40.40	1	1	1
P.A. Cottey	5	5	2	119	38*	39.66	–	–	1
A. Dale	5	5	2	108	37*	36.00	–	–	3
M.P. Maynard	5	5	–	170	41	34.00	–	–	2
C.P. Metson	5	3	1	32	22	16.00	–	–	7
S.L. Watkin	5	2	1	11	7*	11.00	–	–	3
R.P. Lefebvre	5	3	–	30	16	10.00	–	–	2

Four matches: S.R. Barwick 10* & 0*
Three matches: G.P. Butcher 0
One match: H. Morris 9; H.A.G. Anthony 2; S.D. Thomas (ct 1)

BOWLING	Overs	Mds	Runs	Wkts	Av	Best	4/inn
S.D. Thomas	9.2	3	20	6	3.33	6-20	1
H.A.G. Anthony	11	1	40	3	13.33	3-40	–
A. Dale	33	2	131	6	21.83	3-42	–
S.L. Watkin	52	7	203	7	29.00	3-56	–
R.P. Lefebvre	50.5	5	183	6	30.50	3-42	–
R.D.B. Croft	50	4	171	5	34.20	3-33	–
S.R. Barwick	42	1	167	3	55.66	2-36	–
G.P. Butcher	2	–	12	–	–	–	–

GLOUCESTERSHIRE

BATTING	M	Inns	NO	Runs	HS	Av	100s	50s	ct/st
R.C. Russell	6	6	5	147	42*	147.00	–	–	8
A. Symonds	6	6	–	180	95	30.00	–	1	1
A.J. Wright	6	6	–	168	40	28.00	–	–	2
K.E. Cooper	6	4	3	25	16*	25.00	–	–	–
R.I. Dawson	6	6	–	147	38	24.50	–	–	1
M.W. Alleyne	6	6	–	132	42	22.00	–	–	3
T.H.C. Hancock	4	4	–	77	36	19.25	–	–	–
G.D. Hodgson	2	2	–	31	31	15.50	–	–	–
M.A. Lynch	6	6	–	76	30	12.66	–	–	6
M.C.J. Ball	6	5	–	31	12	6.20	–	–	2
J. Srinath	6	6	1	12	6	2.40	–	–	1
A.M. Smith	6	2	1	1	1*	1.00	–	–	–

BOWLING	Overs	Mds	Runs	Wkts	Av	Best	4/inn
J. Srinath	64.2	18	176	15	11.73	4-33	1
A.M. Smith	64.1	5	233	14	16.64	6-39	1
M.C.J. Ball	58	7	163	8	20.37	3-26	–
M.W. Alleyne	50	6	179	7	25.57	2-30	–
K.E. Cooper	57	7	158	4	39.50	2-41	–
R.I. Dawson	3	–	12	–	–	–	–

HAMPSHIRE

BATTING	M	Inns	NO	Runs	HS	Av	100s	50s	ct/st
J.P. Stephenson	4	4	–	246	98	61.00	–	3	–
V.P. Terry	5	4	–	141	68	35.25	–	1	3
R.A. Smith	5	4	–	129	83	32.25	–	1	1
P.R. Whitaker	2	2	–	47	42	23.50	–	–	–
G.W. White	3	2	–	37	37	18.50	–	–	–
H.H. Streak	5	4	2	32	18	16.00	–	–	2
A.N. Aymes	5	4	1	47	29	15.66	–	–	6
C.A. Connor	5	2	1	13	11	13.00	–	–	1
S.D. Udal	5	4	1	34	12	11.33	–	–	1
K.D. James	3	2	–	17	15	8.50	–	–	1
M.C.J. Nicholas	5	4	–	15	8	3.75	–	–	–

Three matches: M.J. Thursfield 0* & 4*
Two matches: J.N.B. Bovill
One match: R.J. Maru 0; R.S.M. Morris & N.G. Cowans

BOWLING	Overs	Mds	Runs	Wkts	Av	Best	4/inn
H.H. Streak	44	6	171	8	21.37	3-28	–
J.P. Stephenson	32	3	129	6	21.50	2-33	–
R.J. Maru	6	–	24	1	24.00	1-24	–
K.D. James	15	3	74	2	27.00	1-23	–
N.G. Cowans	11	1	41	1	41.00	1-41	–
C.A. Connor	44.1	10	136	3	45.33	3-36	–
M.J. Thursfield	24	2	119	2	59.50	2-40	–
J.N.B. Bovill	16.1	1	87	1	87.00	1-37	–
S.D. Udal	54	8	186	2	93.00	1-22	–
M.C.J. Nicholas	1.3	–	11	–	–	–	–
P.R. Whitaker	1	–	13	–	–	–	–

IRELAND

BATTING	M	Inns	NO	Runs	HS	Av	100s	50s	ct/st
D.A. Lewis	4	4	1	91	67*	30.33	–	1	1
S.S.J. Warke	4	4	–	59	29	14.75	–	–	1
G.D. Harrison	4	4	–	56	18	14.00	–	–	–
J.D. Curry	4	4	1	32	20	10.66	–	–	2
J.D.R. Benson	4	4	–	41	26	10.25	–	–	1
U. Graham	4	4	–	39	25	9.75	–	–	1
M. Patterson	3	3	–	12	9	4.00	–	–	–
A.R. Dunlop	2	2	–	8	7	4.00	–	–	1
O.F.X. Butler	3	3	2	3	3*	3.00	–	–	–
C.J. Hoey	3	3	1	4	4*	2.00	–	–	–
B.R. Millar	3	3	–	4	4	1.33	–	–	–
G. Cooke	2	2	–	0	0	0.00	–	–	1

One match: M.V. Narasimha Rao 14; M.P. Rea 74 (ct 1); S.G. Smyth 11; S. Ogilby 0 (ct 1)

BOWLING	Overs	Mds	Runs	Wkts	Av	Best	4/inn
O.F.X. Butler	29	2	149	5	29.80	3-53	–
M. Patterson	27	3	122	5	30.36	3-48	–
C.J. Hoey	19.1	2	97	2	48.50	1-8	–
G.D. Harrison	25	1	114	2	57.00	2-34	–
G. Cooke	11	–	62	1	62.00	1-21	–
J.D. Curry	2	–	12	–	–	–	–
M.V. Narasimha Rao	2	–	16	–	–	–	–
A.R. Dunlop	4	–	29	–	–	–	–
D.A. Lewis	11	–	65	–	–	–	–
U. Graham	29.1	2	111	–	–	–	–

KENT

BATTING	M	Inns	NO	Runs	HS	Av	100s	50s	ct/st
M.R. Benson	6	6	1	401	119	80.20	1	3	3
T.R. Ward	7	7	1	469	125	78.16	2	3	2
M.J. Walker	5	4	1	137	69*	45.66	–	1	3
P.A. de Silva	7	6	1	203	112	40.60	1	–	3
M.J. McCague	5	3	2	40	24	40.00	–	–	4
M.A. Ealham	6	5	–	105	52	21.00	–	1	1
M.V. Fleming	7	5	1	76	44*	19.00	–	–	2
G.R. Cowdrey	7	5	–	90	28	18.00	–	–	3
D.W. Headley	6	3	2	16	7*	16.00	–	–	2
S.A. Marsh	6	5	1	44	27	11.00	–	–	6
T.N. Wren	5	2	1	11	7	11.00	–	–	1
M.M. Patel	4	2	1	1	1	1.00	–	–	1

Two matches: N.J. Llong 1
One match: S.C. Willis; A.P. Igglesden; D.P. Fulton 25 (ct 1); N.R. Taylor 14 (ct 1)

KENT (cont.)

BOWLING	Overs	Mds	Runs	Wkts	Av	Best	4/inn
T.N. Wren	49	3	203	12	16.91	6-41	1
M.V. Fleming	61.4	1	268	13	20.61	3-18	–
M.A. Ealham	59.5	6	210	10	21.00	3-55	–
D.W. Headley	64	9	226	8	28.25	3-47	–
N.J. Llong	5	–	31	1	31.00	1-31	–
P.A. de Silva	38	1	128	4	32.00	2-12	–
A.P. Igglesden	11	–	45	1	45.00	1-45	–
M.M. Patel	40	5	129	2	63.50	2-29	–
M.J. McCague	53	2	249	3	83.00	1-40	–

LANCASHIRE

BATTING	M	Inns	NO	Runs	HS	Av	100s	50s	ct/st
J.P. Crawley	8	7	1	385	114	64.16	1	2	2
M.A. Atherton	8	7	1	347	93	57.83	–	2	4
J.E.R. Gallian	8	7	1	335	134	55.83	2	–	1
G.D. Lloyd	8	6	2	196	81*	49.00	–	2	2
N.H. Fairbrother	8	6	1	228	60*	45.60	–	1	6
Wasim Akram	6	3	–	76	64	25.33	–	1	1
I.D. Austin	8	4	2	42	16*	21.00	–	–	–
M. Watkinson	7	5	2	42	34*	14.00	–	–	4

Eight matches: W.K. Hegg 4* & 31* (ct 9); G. Yates 19* (ct 2)
Six matches: G. Chapple (ct 2)
Four matches: P.J. Martin
One match: A. Flintoff

BOWLING	Overs	Mds	Runs	Wkts	Av	Best	4/inn
A. Flintoff	6	2	10	1	10.00	1-10	–
N.H. Fairbrother	3	–	17	1	17.00	1-17	–
J.E.R. Gallian	21.5	3	107	6	17.83	5-15	1
I.D. Austin	78	17	274	13	21.07	4-8	1
Wasim Akram	51.1	5	239	11	21.72	3-59	–
P.J. Martin	30	6	104	4	26.00	2-35	–
G. Yates	62	1	264	10	26.40	3-42	–
M. Watkinson	68.1	3	282	7	40.28	3-42	–
G. Chapple	54	3	275	3	91.66	2-55	–
G.D. Lloyd	3	–	42	–	–	–	–

LEICESTERSHIRE

BATTING	M	Inns	NO	Runs	HS	Av	100s	50s	ct/st
W.J. Cronje	5	5	–	228	158	45.60	1	–	2
J.J. Whitaker	5	5	–	214	88	42.80	–	3	–
P.E. Robinson	4	4	–	85	54	28.33	–	1	3
G.J. Parsons	5	5	3	55	28	27.50	–	–	–
D.L. Maddy	3	3	–	81	50	27.00	–	1	1
V.J. Wells	5	5	–	120	39	24.00	–	–	3
B.F. Smith	5	5	–	77	27	15.40	–	–	2
N.E. Briers	4	4	–	46	28	11.50	–	–	–
D.J. Millns	4	2	–	7	6	3.50	–	–	–
A.D. Mullally	5	2	–	3	3	1.50	–	–	–

Four matches: A.R.K. Pierson 10* & 9* (ct 1)
Three matches: P. Whitticase 0 (ct 1)
One match: T.J. Boon 54; T. Mason 5*; J.M. Dakin 8

BOWLING	Overs	Mds	Runs	Wkts	Av	Best	4/inn
D.J. Millns	23	3	85	5	17.00	4-26	1
G.J. Parsons	43.3	4	185	8	23.12	3-46	–
T. Mason	11	2	34	1	34.00	1-34	–
V.J. Wells	27	–	154	4	36.25	2-34	–
W.J. Cronje	44	2	165	4	41.25	2-26	–
A.D. Mullally	42.4	4	160	3	53.33	3-39	–
J.M. Dakin	2	–	27	–	–	–	–
A.R.K. Pierson	22.2	1	96	–	–	–	–

MIDDLESEX

BATTING	M	Inns	NO	Runs	HS	Av	100s	50s	ct/st
M.R. Ramprakash	6	6	2	214	91*	53.50	–	2	1
P.N. Weekes	6	6	1	208	67*	41.60	–	2	–
M.W. Gatting	6	6	1	198	93*	39.60	–	1	–
D.J. Nash	6	4	1	97	54	32.33	–	1	3
K.R. Brown	6	5	1	123	75	30.75	–	1	10
J.C. Pooley	6	6	–	181	47	30.16	–	–	3
M.A. Feltham	6	3	1	52	37	26.00	–	–	1

MIDDLESEX (cont.)

BATTING (cont.)	M	Inns	NO	Runs	HS	Av	100s	50s	ct/st
J.D. Carr	6	6	–	151	47	25.16	–	–	3
J.E. Emburey	6	3	2	3	3*	3.00	–	–	–
A.R.C. Fraser	6	2	–	2	1	1.00	–	–	2

Three matches: D. Follett 4

Two matches: P.C.R. Tufnell

One match: R.L. Johnson 0

BOWLING	Overs	Mds	Runs	Wkts	Av	Best	4/inn
A.R.C. Fraser	56.2	6	198	13	15.23	4-49	1
D. Follett	24	1	100	4	25.00	2-44	–
P.N. Weekes	52	–	187	7	26.71	3-33	–
J.E. Emburey	58	7	197	5	39.40	2-23	–
M.A. Feltham	40	4	161	4	40.25	2-42	–
D.J. Nash	56	7	223	5	44.60	2-31	–
P.C.R. Tufnell	18	–	67	1	67.00	1-28	–
M.R. Ramprakash	6	–	29	–	–	–	–

MINOR COUNTIES

BATTING	M	Inns	NO	Runs	HS	Av	100s	50s	ct/st
I. Cockbain	5	1	1	122	65*	40.66	–	1	–
L. Potter	4	3	–	94	34	31.33	–	–	2
S.J. Dean	5	4	–	90	44	22.50	–	–	1
R.J. Evans	5	4	–	89	56	22.25	–	1	–
M.I. Humphries	5	4	–	62	26	15.50	–	–	3
S.C. Goldsmith	3	2	–	27	17	13.50	–	–	–
D.R. Thomas	3	3	1	21	18*	10.50	–	–	2
M.J. Roberts	2	2	–	20	20	10.00	–	–	–
P.G. Newman	3	3	–	21	13	7.00	–	–	–
S.D. Myles	3	2	–	7	7	3.50	–	–	–
M.A. Sharp	4	3	2	1	1*	1.00	–	–	–
K.A. Arnold	5	4	1	2	2*	0.66	–	–	2
R.A. Evans	4	3	–	0	0	0.00	–	–	–

Two matches: R.G. Hignett 23 (ct 1)

One match: K. Jahangir 0 (ct 1); M.G. Scothern 1 (ct 1)

BOWLING	Overs	Mds	Runs	Wkts	Av	Best	4/inn
P.G. Newman	26	3	74	4	18.50	4-29	1
L. Potter	34.2	4	112	6	18.66	4-23	1
R.G. Hignett	6	–	26	1	26.00	1-26	–
D.R. Thomas	12	–	87	3	29.00	3-34	–
M.A. Sharp	31	7	94	3	31.33	2-36	–
K.A. Arnold	38.3	9	111	3	37.00	1-18	–
S.C. Goldsmith	10	–	60	1	60.00	1-32	–
S.D. Myles	3.3	–	12	–	–	–	–
M.G. Scothern	6	–	51	–	–	–	–
R.A. Evans	24.1	3	93	–	–	–	–

NORTHAMPTONSHIRE

BATTING	M	Inns	NO	Runs	HS	Av	100s	50s	ct/st
R.J. Bailey	4	4	1	164	93*	54.66	–	2	2
A. Fordham	3	3	–	128	108	42.66	1	–	1
K.M. Curran	4	4	–	127	53	31.75	–	2	1
A.J. Lamb	3	3	–	79	41	26.33	–	–	1
J.N. Snape	2	2	1	24	23	24.00	–	–	–
A.L. Penberthy	4	4	–	76	26	19.00	–	–	2
T.C. Walton	2	2	–	35	29	17.50	–	–	1
R.J. Warren	4	4	–	53	23	13.25	–	–	5
D.J. Capel	3	3	–	29	23	9.66	–	–	–
J.G. Hughes	3	3	–	11	9	3.66	–	–	1
A.R. Kumble	4	3	–	5	3	1.66	–	–	1
M.B. Loye	2	2	–	2	2	1.00	–	–	–

Four matches: J.P. Taylor 4*, 7* & 1* (ct 1)

One match: R.R. Montgomerie 5; S.A.J. Boswell

BOWLING	Overs	Mds	Runs	Wkts	Av	Best	4/inn
S.A.J. Boswell	5	2	6	1	6.00	1-6	–
J.N. Snape	17	3	51	3	17.00	2-28	–
T.C. Walton	6	–	27	1	27.00	1-27	–
K.M. Curran	26	1	121	4	30.25	4-38	1
J.P. Taylor	28	5	107	3	35.66	1-15	–
A.L. Penberthy	32	5	111	3	37.00	3-39	–
J.G. Hughes	14.5	2	79	2	39.50	2-47	–
A.R. Kumble	37.4	1	135	3	45.00	2-40	–
R.J. Bailey	15	2	50	1	50.00	1-29	–
D.J. Capel	22	1	76	1	76.00	1-21	–

NOTTINGHAMSHIRE

BATTING	M	Inns	NO	Runs	HS	Av	100s	50s	ct/st
P. Johnson	5	4	3	142	70*	142.00	–	2	–
R.T. Robinson	6	5	1	225	84	56.25	–	2	1
P.R. Pollard	4	3	–	126	56	42.00	–	2	1
G.F. Archer	4	3	–	125	74	41.66	–	1	–
W.M. Noon	2	2	1	40	23	40.00	–	–	1
C.C. Lewis	3	2	–	56	48	28.00	–	–	1
K.P. Evans	6	4	1	69	47	23.00	–	–	1
C.L. Cairns	6	4	–	73	46	18.25	–	–	2
G.W. Mike	6	2	–	18	9	9.00	–	–	1
M.P. Dowman	4	2	1	6	6	6.00	–	–	1

Six matches: R.A. Pick 21* & 10* (ct 1); J.A. Afford (ct 1)

Four matches: B.N. French 9 (ct 3/st 1)

Two matches: J.R. Wileman 0 (ct 1)

One match: J.E. Hindson 41*; C. Banton 40

Three catches were taken by substitutes

BOWLING	Overs	Mds	Runs	Wkts	Av	Best	4/inn
C.C. Lewis	17	3	49	5	9.80	3-11	–
K.P. Evans	57.2	9	227	14	16.21	4-19	1
C.L. Cairns	46.5	1	186	10	18.60	4-47	1
G.W. Mike	60.3	10	265	5	53.00	2-73	–
J.A. Afford	63	5	236	4	59.00	2-44	–
J.E. Hindson	10	–	69	1	69.00	1-69	–
R.A. Pick	53.4	6	257	3	85.66	1-48	–
J.R. Wileman	3	–	15	–	–	–	–
G.F. Archer	6	–	44	–	–	–	–

SCOTLAND

BATTING	M	Inns	NO	Runs	HS	Av	100s	50s	ct/st
J.D. Love	3	3	1	103	54	51.50	–	1	2
G.N. Reifer	4	4	1	71	57*	23.66	–	1	–
P.D. Steindl	3	3	2	18	14*	18.00	–	–	–
M.J. Smith	4	4	–	60	35	15.00	–	–	–
J.G. Williamson	3	3	–	43	24	14.33	–	–	–
D.J. Haggo	4	3	1	28	20*	14.00	–	–	2
I.M. Stanger	4	3	–	41	27	13.66	–	–	4
S.T. Crawley	4	4	–	49	34	12.25	–	–	1
M.D. Marshall	4	4	–	40	36	10.00	–	–	–
G.B.J. McGurk	2	2	–	18	11	9.00	–	–	–
K. Thomson	2	2	–	17	17	8.50	–	–	–
J.W. Govan	3	2	–	16	14	8.00	–	–	–
A.C. Storie	3	3	–	14	12	4.66	–	–	–

One match: D. Cowan

BOWLING	Overs	Mds	Runs	Wkts	Av	Best	4/inn
D. Cowan	11	–	64	3	21.33	3-64	–
P.D. Steindl	19	–	92	3	30.66	3-43	–
M.D. Marshall	34	4	125	3	41.66	2-35	–
K. Thomson	18	–	78	1	78.00	1-32	–
J.G. Williamson	14	–	82	1	82.00	1-65	–
I.M. Stanger	34.1	3	164	1	164.00	1-55	–
G.N. Reifer	5	–	22	–	–	–	–
J.W. Govan	24.3	–	111	–	–	–	–

SOMERSET

BATTING	M	Inns	NO	Runs	HS	Av	100s	50s	ct/st
A.N. Hayhurst	6	5	2	114	69*	38.00	–	1	–
A.R. Caddick	2	2	1	38	28	38.00	–	–	–
G.D. Rose	6	6	1	185	79	37.00	–	1	–
M.E. Trescothick	6	6	–	209	122	34.83	1	–	5
R.J. Turner	6	4	2	67	27*	33.50	–	–	7
P.D. Bowler	6	6	–	169	54	28.16	–	3	2
M.N. Lathwell	6	6	–	145	74	24.16	–	1	2
S.C. Ecclestone	4	4	1	65	30	21.66	–	–	2
R.J. Harden	6	6	1	96	50	19.20	–	1	3
Mushtaq Ahmed	6	4	–	36	21	9.00	–	–	–
H.R.J. Trump	2	2	–	11	11	5.50	–	–	1

Three matches: J.D. Batty 19* & 0*

One match: J.I.D. Kerr; A.P. van Troost 5; K.A. Parsons

One catch was taken by a substitute

BOWLING	Overs	Mds	Runs	Wkts	Av	Best	4/inn
Mushtaq Ahmed	60.4	11	160	10	16.00	4-29	1
A.N. Hayhurst	25.2	4	94	5	18.80	3-2	–

SOMERSET (cont.)

BOWLING (cont.)	Overs	Mds	Runs	Wkts	Av	Best	4/inn
H.R.J. Trump	57	7	200	10	20.00	3-17	–
J.D. Batty	33	6	111	5	22.20	2-13	–
G.D. Rose	59	15	185	7	26.42	4-21	1
A.R. Caddick	19	2	69	2	34.50	1-27	–
S.C. Ecclestone	23	1	108	3	36.00	2-44	–
A.P. van Troost	9	–	70	1	70.00	1-70	–
M.N. Lathwell	0.1	–	1	–	–	–	–
P.D. Bowler	4	–	29	–	–	–	–

SURREY

BATTING	M	Inns	NO	Runs	HS	Av	100s	50s	ct/st
D.M. Ward	4	3	2	88	60*	88.00	–	2	1
N. Shahid	4	2	1	65	65*	65.00	–	1	–
A.J. Stewart	4	4	1	152	52	50.66	–	1	6/1
A.D. Brown	4	4	1	118	82	39.33	–	1	1
D.J. Bicknell	4	4	1	105	81*	35.00	–	1	2
G.P. Thorpe	2	2	–	30	25	15.00	–	–	–
A.J. Hollioake	4	2	–	26	23	13.00	–	–	3
A.C.S. Pigott	4	2	1	13	8	13.00	–	–	–

Four matches: S.G. Kenlock
Three matches: J.E. Benjamin (ct 1); M.P. Bicknell 43
Two matches: R.W. Nowell 15* (ct 1)
One match: M.A. Butcher 5; J.D. Ratcliffe 14

BOWLING	Overs	Mds	Runs	Wkts	Av	Best	4/inn
S.G. Kenlock	35	4	171	11	15.54	5-15	2
J.E. Benjamin	31	6	97	4	24.25	4-27	1
A.C.S. Pigott	36.1	2	139	5	27.80	2-52	–
M.P. Bicknell	29	5	103	3	34.33	1-14	–
R.W. Nowell	14	1	47	1	47.00	1-35	–
A.J. Hollioake	23	–	108	2	54.00	2-30	–
N. Shahid	25	–	131	1	131.00	1-59	–

SUSSEX

BATTING	M	Inns	NO	Runs	HS	Av	100s	50s	ct/st
N.J. Lenham	3	3	2	133	73*	133.00	–	1	1
C.W.J. Athey	4	4	–	295	118	73.75	1	1	–/1
J.W. Hall	4	4	–	185	67	46.25	–	2	1
F.D. Stephenson	4	3	1	68	45	34.00	–	–	–
K. Greenfield	4	3	–	43	21	14.33	–	–	1
A.P. Wells	4	4	1	42	23*	14.00	–	–	–
I.D.K. Salisbury	4	2	–	18	17	9.00	–	–	2
P. Moores	3	2	1	9	6*	9.00	–	–	1
P.W. Jarvis	2	2	–	10	8	5.00	–	–	–
C.C. Remy	2	2	–	10	7	5.00	–	–	–

Four matches: E.S.H. Giddins 0* (ct 1)
Three matches: J.D. Lewry 14*
Two matches: J.A. North 10
One match: K. Newell 35

BOWLING	Overs	Mds	Runs	Wkts	Av	Best	4/inn
F.D. Stephenson	42.1	5	176	8	22.00	3-29	–
E.S.H. Giddins	40	5	137	6	22.83	3-28	–
P.W. Jarvis	21	2	95	3	31.66	3-29	–
I.D.K. Salisbury	42	2	163	5	32.60	2-40	–
C.C. Remy	10	–	37	–	–	–	–
J.A. North	7	–	45	–	–	–	–
K. Greenfield	29	–	138	–	–	–	–
J.D. Lewry	26	–	152	–	–	–	–

WARWICKSHIRE

BATTING	M	Inns	NO	Runs	HS	Av	100s	50s	ct/st
D.P. Ostler	5	5	1	279	87	69.75	–	4	1
R.G. Twose	5	4	1	206	90	68.66	–	3	5
A.J. Moles	5	5	–	237	89	47.40	–	3	1
N.V. Knight	4	4	1	139	91	46.33	–	1	–

WARWICKSHIRE (cont.)

BATTING (cont.)	M	Inns	NO	Runs	HS	Av	100s	50s	ct/st
D.A. Reeve	4	3	1	48	28*	24.00	–	–	3
G. Welch	4	3	1	36	27*	18.00	–	–	–
T.L. Penney	4	4	1	30	12*	10.00	–	–	–
N.M.K. Smith	5	3	1	13	10	6.50	–	–	1
M. Burns	4	2	–	12	12	6.00	–	–	2/1
G.C. Small	4	2	1	3	3	3.00	–	–	1
A.A. Donald	3	2	–	2	2	1.00	–	–	–

Two matches: P.A. Smith; D.R. Brown; R.P. Davis (ct 1)
One match: M.A.V. Bell; K.J. Piper 6

BOWLING	Overs	Mds	Runs	Wkts	Av	Best	4/inn
D.R. Brown	11	2	43	3	14.33	3-43	–
P.A. Smith	11	1	49	2	24.50	2-49	–
D.A. Reeve	31.3	3	121	5	41.80	4-37	1
R.G. Twose	6	–	43	1	43.00	1-23	–
A.A. Donald	31	2	131	3	43.66	2-39	–
G.C. Small	39	5	88	2	44.00	2-24	–
N.M.K. Smith	35	1	179	4	44.75	2-77	–
G. Welch	41	1	242	2	121.00	1-24	–
R.P. Davis	7	–	30	–	–	–	–

WORCESTERSHIRE

BATTING	M	Inns	NO	Runs	HS	Av	100s	50s	ct/st
G.A. Hick	6	5	1	466	127*	116.50	3	1	3
T.M. Moody	6	5	2	209	75*	69.66	–	2	3
T.S. Curtis	6	6	1	183	54*	36.60	–	2	1
D.A. Leatherdale	4	3	1	36	29	18.00	–	–	–
G.R. Haynes	6	5	1	68	27	17.00	–	–	1
W.P.C. Weston	6	6	1	81	54*	16.20	–	1	1
S.R. Lampitt	5	2	1	14	13	14.00	–	–	2
S.J. Rhodes	6	4	1	24	12	8.00	–	–	12/2

Six matches: P.J. Newport; R.K. Illingworth 4* (ct 2); N.V. Radford 12* (ct 1)
One match: M.J. Church; Parvaz Mirza; C.M. Tolley 0

BOWLING	Overs	Mds	Runs	Wkts	Av	Best	4/inn
S.R. Lampitt	47.5	9	141	14	10.07	4-16	2
G.R. Haynes	41.5	5	144	9	16.00	3-17	–
R.K. Illingworth	59.1	7	167	9	18.55	4-27	1
T.M. Moody	10	4	19	1	19.00	1-10	–
P.J. Newport	62	13	182	9	20.22	2-9	–
G.A. Hick	12	–	46	2	23.00	2-30	–
N.V. Radford	54	7	181	6	30.16	3-23	–
Parvaz Mirza	9	–	40	–	–	–	–

YORKSHIRE

BATTING	M	Inns	NO	Runs	HS	Av	100s	50s	ct/st
M.G. Bevan	4	3	1	147	83*	73.50	–	2	1
M.D. Moxon	3	3	1	97	66*	48.50	–	1	1
M.P. Vaughan	3	3	1	87	50*	43.50	–	1	1
D. Byas	4	3	–	111	47	37.00	–	–	1
R.J. Blakey	4	3	1	38	19*	19.00	–	–	4/1
C. White	4	3	–	52	43	17.33	–	–	2
A.P. Grayson	4	2	–	32	18	16.00	–	–	2
D. Gough	4	2	–	17	14	8.50	–	–	–
P.J. Hartley	4	2	1	8	8*	8.00	–	–	1
M.A. Robinson	4	2	–	1	1	0.50	–	–	–
R.D. Stemp	4	2	1	0	0*	0.00	–	–	–

One match: S.A. Kellett 6; A. McGrath 2

BOWLING	Overs	Mds	Runs	Wkts	Av	Best	4/inn
P.J. Hartley	35.4	9	107	9	11.88	4-21	1
M.A. Robinson	37	13	68	5	13.60	2-15	–
D. Gough	39	7	120	5	24.00	2-21	–
A.P. Grayson	10	–	56	2	28.00	2-36	–
R.D. Stemp	35	4	122	4	30.50	2-28	–
C. White	27	1	135	2	67.50	1-26	–

NATWEST TROPHY

ROUND ONE

27 June *at March*

Derbyshire 289 for 3 (D.J. Cullinan 119 not out,
  W.A. Dessaur 85, C.M. Wells 51 not out)
Cambridgeshire 132 (P.A.J. DeFreitas 5 for 28)

Derbyshire won by 157 runs

(Man of the Match – D.J. Cullinan)

at Chester (Boughton Hall)

Essex 265 for 8 (P.J. Prichard 81, M.C. Ilott 54 not out,
  A.J. Murphy 4 for 48)
Cheshire 201 (R.G. Hignett 55, G.A. Gooch 5 for 8)

Essex won by 64 runs

(Man of the Match – P.J. Prichard)

at St Austell

Middlesex 304 for 8 (P.N. Weekes 143 not out)
Cornwall 200

Middlesex won by 104 runs

(Man of the Match – P.N. Weekes)

at Chester-le-Street (Riverside)

Durham 326 for 4 (S. Hutton 125, M.A. Roseberry 121)
Herefordshire 119 (J. Boiling 4 for 22)

Durham won by 207 runs

(Man of the Match – M.A. Roseberry)

at Cardiff

Dorset 191 for 4 (J.J.E. Hardy 89 not out)
Glamorgan 192 for 0 (H. Morris 105 not out, S.P. James
  74 not out)

Glamorgan won by 10 wickets

(Man of the Match – H. Morris)

at Bristol

Gloucestershire 301 for 5 (A.J. Wright 124 not out,
  R.C. Russell 59 not out)
Suffolk 177 (D.J.P. Boden 6 for 26)

Gloucestershire won by 124 runs

(Man of the Match – A.J. Wright)

at Old Trafford

Norfolk 188
Lancashire 190 for 2 (J.E.R. Gallian 101 not out)

Lancashire won by 8 wickets

(Man of the Match – J.E.R. Gallian)

Dermot Reeve holds aloft the NatWest trophy after Warwickshire's victory at Lord's. (Graham Chadwick/Allsport)

at Leicester

Hampshire 204 for 9
Leicestershire 204 for 9 (C.A. Connor 4 for 41)

Leicestershire won on faster run rate after 30 overs

(Man of the Match – A.R.K. Pierson)

at Northampton

Holland 267 for 9 (N.E. Clarke 86, A.R. Kumble 4 for 50)
Northamptonshire 269 for 3 (A. Fordham 99,
  R.R. Montgomerie 69)

Northamptonshire won by 7 wickets

(Man of the Match – N.E. Clarke)

at Trent Bridge

Scotland 171 for 9 (A.C. Storie 56, R.A. Pick 5 for 23)
Nottinghamshire 172 for 2 (P.R. Pollard 83 not out)

Nottinghamshire won by 8 wickets

(Man of the Match – R.A. Pick)

An historic occasion as Holland are photographed before their NatWest Trophy first-round match against Northamptonshire at Northampton. (Paul Sturgess/Sportsline)

at Stone

Kent 349 for 8 (N.R. Taylor 86, G.R. Cowdrey 65, T.R. Ward 53, P.F. Ridgway 4 for 62)

Staffordshire 258 for 6 (L. Potter 105 not out)

Kent won by 91 runs

(Man of the Match – L. Potter)

at The Oval

Berkshire 148 (J.E. Benjamin 4 for 20)

Surrey 151 for 1 (M.A. Butcher 79 not out, D.J. Bicknell 52 not out)

Surrey won by 9 wickets

(Man of the Match – J.E. Benjamin)

at Hove

Devon 267 for 4 (N.A. Folland 104, N.R. Gaywood 69)

Sussex 271 for 3 (N.J. Lenham 129 not out)

Sussex won by 7 wickets

(Man of the Match – N.J. Lenham)

at Edgbaston

Warwickshire 357 for 3 (N.V. Knight 151, A.J. Moles 90, D.P. Ostler 76)

Somerset 339 for 9 (R.J. Harden 104, P.C.L. Holloway 50 not out, D.A. Reeve 4 for 54)

Warwickshire won by 18 runs

(Man of the Match – N.V. Knight)

at Worcester

Worcestershire 257 for 8 (G.R. Haynes 116 not out)

Cumberland 192 for 9 (P.J. Berry 81)

Worcestershire won by 65 runs

(Man of the Match – G.R. Haynes)

at Leeds

Yorkshire 299 for 6 (C. White 113, S.A. Kellett 107)

Ireland 228 for 7 (S.J.S. Warke 82)

Yorkshire won by 71 runs

(Man of the Match – S.A. Kellett)

The first round of the 60-over knock-out competition brought no surprises. The only two first-class counties to be eliminated were Hampshire and Somerset, and they fell to Leicestershire and Warwickshire respectively. None of the 11 Minor Counties survived nor did Ireland, Scotland or the newcomers Holland, although all gave good accounts of themselves.

Some of the first-class counties had frightening moments, however, notably Essex at Boughton Hall. Tony Murphy, who last year excelled in the competition with Surrey, was mainly responsible for Essex trembling at 156 for 7, and it needed an eighth-wicket stand of 78 between Prichard and Ilott to take the first-class county to a more comfortable position. Ilott hit his first fifty in the competition, but it was Prichard who played the most vital innings. He had come in when Gooch had just become Murphy's third victim in two overs, and it was necessary for him to restore calm and order to the Essex camp before turning to attack.

Cheshire could never quite match the required run rate although, at 185 for 4, they had a good platform. Childs and Such had frustrated them, and only 52 came from 25 overs. Hignett and Gray struck some lusty blows, but the introduction of Gooch changed matters. He took 5 for 8 in 16 balls, and Cheshire's last six wickets fell for 16 runs.

Derbyshire had no problems against Cambridgeshire. Cullinan hit a century in his first NatWest Trophy match and shared a third-wicket stand of 169 with Dessaur who hit his first fifty in the tournament. Rollins had been out for 0, but this was the last moment of doubt that Derbyshire suffered. Barnett and DeFreitas proved too much for the Cambridgeshire batsmen.

Cornwall included Adam Seymour who played for Worcestershire in the 1994 Benson and Hedges Cup final, and they had early success when Lovell dismissed Pooley for one. Middlesex faltered before lunch, but Weekes reached his first century in the competition and, with support from Feltham, Emburey and Johnson, took his side to a big total. Fraser, 2 for 2 in five overs, sent back Thomas and Seymour with only 12 scored, and Cornwall never recovered.

Mike Roseberry and Stewart Hutton established a first-wicket record for the NatWest Trophy when they scored 255 against Herefordshire, the county who had joined the Minor Counties championship when Durham had attained first-class status. Both batsmen made their highest scores in the competition, and Durham's total was also their highest.

In spite of a fine 89 not out from Jon Hardy, a much-travelled cricketer, Dorset were overwhelmed by Glamorgan. Morris and James hit 192 in 40.5 overs, a first-wicket record for Glamorgan in the tournament. Morris reached his century off 112 balls.

Gloucestershire were in some trouble against Suffolk. Hodgson, Cunliffe and Lynch fell to Carter with 51 runs scored before Wright and Alleyne added 114. Symonds did not make his usual substantial contribution, but Russell joined Wright in an unbroken partnership of 107. David Boden, formerly of Essex and Middlesex, returned his best figures in any one-day competition when Suffolk were shot out for 177, but the individual award went to Wright, who added three catches to his century.

Norfolk made their highest NatWest score, but Lancashire won in 40.4 overs. Gallian came to his century with the four that won the match.

There was great tension in the match between Hampshire and Leicestershire, at Leicester. Hampshire decided to bat when they won the toss, but they could

Former Surrey bowler Tony Murphy caused Essex untold problems when he appeared for Cheshire in the first round of the NatWest Trophy. (USPA)

never quite break free of the shackles that the Leicestershire attack imposed upon them. Smith made the highest score of the day with his 45, and there was a useful 34 from Stephenson, but they never truly recovered from being reduced to 89 for 3 by Pierson, one of Leicestershire's walking wounded, playing with a broken finger.

The start of the Leicestershire innings was totally undermined by Cardigan Connor who, in an inspired spell of new-ball bowling, took 3 for 19 in nine overs. Robinson and Ben Smith took the score from 31 for 3 to 80 before Smith was caught behind off Udal, and when the pugnacious Robinson gave a return catch to Maru the score was 110.

Maddy and Dakin batted boldly before falling to good catches. When the ninth wicket went down and Pierson joined Mullally, Leicestershire were still 33 short of Hampshire's score. There were six overs remaining. The batsmen ran, played some handsome strokes and kept calm. A spanking cover-drive from Pierson meant that one run was needed from Maru's last over to level the score. Mullally scored this run, and, once it was confirmed that Leicestershire had the better run rate after the first 30 overs, Pierson blocked the last three balls to give his side victory.

The most interesting fixture of the round was that at Northampton where Holland made their debut in the competition and acquitted themselves nobly. They won the toss, batted first and were given a rousing start by Nolan Clarke – who played for Barbados from 1969 to 1977 and was making his debut in the competition at the age of 47 – and Peter Cantrell, once of Queensland. Clarke hit 10 fours, and Cantrell seven, as they put on 88. Aponso, the Sri Lankan, also batted well, and that the batting never quite maintained these early heights was due to a spell of 4 for 13 in his last six overs by Kumble.

The Dutch bowling was not of the standard of their batting but, bolstered by Lefebvre (playing for Glamorgan) and Bakker, it could be. Montgomerie and Fordham scored 125 in 33 overs for Northamptonshire's first wicket, and later Loye hit 49 off 42 balls to take them to victory with 3.1 overs to spare.

The feature of the game at Trent Bridge was a hat trick by Andy Pick. He trapped Patterson, McGurk and Salmond leg before to leave Scotland staggering on 8 for 3. Storie and Malcolm Marshall added 80, but Storie's 56 took him 152 balls and he was not out until the 59th over. Pollard and Cairns shared an unbroken third-wicket stand of 81 to take Nottinghamshire to victory in 36.3 overs.

A fourth-wicket stand of 100 between Taylor and Cowdrey provided the main substance of Kent's large total against Staffordshire. The Minor County died bravely. Laurie Potter hit 3 sixes and 8 fours as he reached his century in the last over. Potter, once of Kent, won the individual award. Earlier in the season, he had won the Gold Award against another of his former counties, Leicestershire, in a Benson and Hedges Cup match.

Surrey swamped Berkshire at The Oval. Benjamin and Rackemann proved too much for the Berkshire batsmen to cope with, and they were well supported by Alec Stewart who held six catches. Ratcliffe was out at 11, but Darren Bicknell and Butcher had the game won by the second ball of the 25th over.

Devon gave Sussex a hard fight at Hove. Gaywood and Folland scored 157 for their second wicket, and Roebuck hit 46 not out to take his side to their highest score in the competition. Lenham and Newell hit 92 in 25 overs for Sussex's first wicket, and Lenham and Greenfield made 105 for the second. Lenham went on to hit his first century in one-day competitions as Sussex won with 4.4 overs to spare.

There was a mighty meeting at Edgbaston where Warwickshire, runners-up in 1994, took on Somerset. Reeve won the toss, and Warwickshire batted. They were given a splendid start by Knight and Moles who hit 178 in 38 overs. Knight reached his first century in one-day tournaments, and his 151 came off 184 balls with 3 sixes and 14 fours. Ostler hit 4 sixes in the second-wicket stand with Knight which brought 146 in 20 overs. The last five overs of the Warwickshire innings brought 65 runs, with Knight's third fifty coming off 28 balls.

Somerset lost Lathwell, Bowler and Rose for 93. Rose had been a particular sufferer with the ball in Warwickshire's innings, conceding 91 off 11 overs. Harden and Parsons put on 134 in 22 overs, and Harden's faultless century off 103 balls gave Somerset every chance of victory. Holloway's 50 maintained the challenge and, with six overs remaining, they were still up with the required run rate, but by now they were running short of batsmen.

Man of the Match Nolan Clarke in action for Holland against Northamptonshire. (Paul Sturgess/Sportsline)

Worcestershire, the holders, were revived by Haynes' first one-day hundred. He dominated a fifth-wicket stand of 102 with Solanki. Cumberland made a dreadful start before Berry's innings gave them respectability.

Craig White and Simon Kellett made their first centuries in the competition and added 207 in 44 overs after Yorkshire had slipped to 31 for 3. Warke and Rea scored 92 for Ireland's first wicket, and the visitors had the satisfaction of making their highest score in the Natwest Trophy or the Benson and Hedges Cup. White added to his century by taking 3 for 38, catching Smyth and running out Rea.

ROUND TWO

12 July *at Chester-le-Street (Riverside)*

Gloucestershire 276 for 6 (A.J. Wright 84, M.A. Lynch 58)
Durham 117

Gloucestershire won by 159 runs

(Man of the Match – A.J. Wright)

at Chelmsford

Yorkshire 307 for 3 (S.A. Kellett 92, M.G. Bevan 91 not out,
   C. White 51 not out, D. Byas 50)
Essex 210 (D.D.J. Robinson 55)

Yorkshire won by 97 runs

(Man of the Match – M.G. Bevan)

at Old Trafford

Worcestershire 271 for 6 (T.S. Curtis 106 not out,
  G.A. Hick 87)

Lancashire 275 for 6 (S.P. Titchard 92, M.A. Atherton 70)

Lancashire won by 4 wickets

(Man of the Match – S.P. Titchard)

at Leicester

Leicestershire 197 for 7 (I.J. Sutcliffe 68)

Glamorgan 198 for 4 (D.L. Hemp 78, P.A. Cottey 61 not out)

Glamorgan won by 6 wickets

(Man of the Match – D.L. Hemp)

at Trent Bridge

Northamptonshire 352 for 8 (A. Fordham 132,
  R.R. Montgomerie 109)

Nottinghamshire 314 for 8 (P.R. Pollard 96, R.T. Robinson 73)

Northamptonshire won by 38 runs

(Man of the Match – R.J. Bailey)

at The Oval

Middlesex 304 for 7 (T.A. Radford 82, P.N. Weekes 72,
  A.J. Hollioake 4 for 53)

Surrey 225 (D.J. Bicknell 77)

Middlesex won by 79 runs

(Man of the Match – J.E. Emburey)

at Hove

Sussex 222 for 8 (J.W. Hall 70, K. Newell 52, D.G. Cork
  4 for 50)

Derbyshire 225 for 2 (C.J. Adams 109 not out, A.S. Rollins 56)

Derbyshire won by 8 wickets

(Man of the Match – C.J. Adams)

at Edgbaston

Warwickshire 262 for 7 (R.G. Twose 93 not out,
  N.M.K. Smith 65)

Kent 252 for 9 (T.R. Ward 68, S.A. Marsh 55)

Warwickshire won by 10 runs

(Man of the Match – R.G. Twose)

Durham met Gloucestershire without the aid of Manoj
Prabhakar who was unwell, weakening even further an
attack that was not of the strongest. Winning the toss
should have been an advantage to Durham for the conditions were steamy, the pitch offered variable bounce, and
Roseberry was right to ask Gloucestershire to bat first.
When Windows was leg before in Walker's first over

Durham scented a rout, but Cunliffe helped Wright to add
75, and Monte Lynch hit a brisk fifty in a third-wicket partnership of 106. Wright proved to be the rock of the visitors'
innings and when he was fourth out, in the 55th over, the
score was 230 and already looked well beyond Durham's
reach.

So it proved. Both openers were out with 16 on the
board. There were two silly run outs in the middle-order,
and Durham sank before a varied attack in 42 overs.

There are matches which can be lost before a side takes
the field, and Essex contributed massively to their own
extinction when they named their side. Incomprehensibly,
Lewis was chosen ahead of Childs or Williams. This meant
that Essex went into the match with only three front-line
bowlers – one of whom was the inexperienced Cousins –
and therefore they had put themselves in a position where
Waugh, Irani and Gooch would have to share 24 overs. In
the event, Gooch was not called upon, and Essex paid a
heavy price for their stupidity.

Yorkshire won the toss and batted on a flat, friendly
pitch, but the accuracy of Ilott and Cousins restricted them
to 25 runs in the first 15 overs. Such, who bowled
admirably, had Vaughan caught as soon as he came on, but
this brought in Byas who hit 50 off 67 balls. Byas was run
out, but Kellett remained to give the innings the substance
it needed. He was dismissed by Ilott at 187 in the 49th
over. From the last 11 overs, Bevan and White pillaged 120
runs. Bevan's 91 came off only 76 deliveries, and he hit a
six and 6 fours as well as running like a demon. White's 51
came from 28 balls with 4 fours and a six. Waugh, who
bowled a full quota of 12 overs, was murdered. He went
for 96 runs, and by the close, bowling off a shorter run, he
suggested by his body language that his interest had
waned.

Gooch and Robinson started the Essex innings at such a
rate that it seemed that they would reach their huge target
with ample time to spare. Gough was cracked to the off-
side boundary, and 28 runs were on the board in a flash.
Then there was a dreadful misunderstanding, and Gooch
departed glowering, run out for 17. The mishap had a
chastening effect on Robinson who became introspective,
yet he still managed to help Hussain to add 100 in 26
overs. The trauma had almost become a distant memory
when Hussain, batting with great authority, turned
Robinson to leg, slipped as he set off for a run and dislodged a bail. When Waugh completed a nightmare match
by slashing at Mark Robinson to be caught by Kellett for
two, Essex knew it was not their day. The last six wickets
fell for 44 runs.

Lancashire ended Worcestershire's cup hopes for the
second time in the season, winning a resounding victory
with an over to spare. There was a dreadful start for
Worcestershire when Weston was run out without facing a
ball, but Hick and Curtis added 143 for the second wicket
in 28 overs. Curtis survived throughout the 60 overs, facing 194 balls and hitting 7 fours. He made sure that
Lancashire would have to face a quite daunting target.

The Red Rose side began as though they would make
light work of the task. Titchard and Atherton scored 167 –
a Lancashire record for the competition, and by the 48th
over, with only Atherton back in the pavilion, only 62 runs

were needed. Crawley was then caught by Hick off Newport, and this brought an attack of nerves. Lloyd and Speak were run out, and Watkinson was bowled, but Wasim Akram and Ian Austin kept calm, and Wasim smashed the ball to the cover boundary for the winning hit with an over to go.

Glamorgan beat Leicestershire with six wickets and 5.4 overs to spare. Leicestershire, still weighed down by a long sick-list, meandered to 109 for 5 in 41 overs before lunch. The position would have been worse but for Iain Sutcliffe, the Oxford blue playing his first senior game for Leicestershire, who batted with responsibility. Nixon gave the innings a fillip in the afternoon, but Glamorgan were never likely to be overawed by a target of 198.

Mullally and Pierson shattered complacency when they sent back James, Morris and Maynard with 32 scored, but Hemp and Cottey added 161. Hemp, showing that his rehabilitation was complete, was caught off Macmillan with five needed, but he was rewarded with his first Man-of-the-Match honour.

At Trent Bridge, Montgomerie and Fordham scored 232 in 43 overs for Northamptonshire's first wicket. This was the county's highest partnership for any wicket in the competition. Montgomerie faced 144 balls, and Fordham 142. Bailey gave the innings a further boost, but seven wickets fell in seven overs in the inevitable mad scramble for runs.

Robinson and Pollard responded with 180 in 33 overs before Pollard was bowled by Kumble. Bailey then dismissed Robinson and Johnson in the same over, and Cairns, promoted to bolster the run rate, was bowled by Snape. Thereafter, Nottinghamshire lost their way.

Even without the injured Jason Pooley, Middlesex registered their highest score against a first-class county in the competition. Their huge total was founded on an opening partnership of 165 between Radford and Weekes, an unlikely opener who took 20 overs to reach 10. The strength of the Middlesex batting – Ramprakash, Gatting and Brown in particular – saw that 164 runs came from the last 20 overs.

Surrey, without Stewart and at a low point in form and confidence, were given some encouragement by Darren Bicknell who batted well against the seamers before chopping on to Emburey. No one else hinted at permanence. Emburey took 2 for 23 in his 11 overs, and Surrey were bowled out in 55.5 overs.

Derbyshire, too, won with contemptuous ease at Hove. They restricted Sussex to 222 on a slow track. Hall batted through 50 overs to make 70, with 7 fours, and Newell hit 52 off 76 balls, but it was the Derbyshire bowlers, Barnett and Wells in particular, who took the honours. These two were the make-shift bowlers after the Test trio of Cork, Malcolm and DeFreitas, for Griffith could not find his line, and they maintained a relentless accuracy.

Barnett was out at 45 when Derbyshire batted, but Adams and Rollins added 100 in 23 overs. Adams hit 13 fours in another sparkling hundred, and Derbyshire won with 13 balls to spare.

For the fourth time in four years, Kent's hopes of winning the NatWest Trophy ended at Edgbaston. They had every chance when, having put Warwickshire in to bat on

a two-paced pitch, they sent back Knight for 0 and Ostler for 5. Warwickshire's strength is that, in a team which really has no stars, all contribute, and Brown and Smith now added 69 in 18 overs. Then came Twose whose nudging, driving and running ensured that Warwickshire would realise 111 from their last 20 overs and that his side would reach a total which the Kent bowlers should really have been able to prevent on this pitch.

Kent were without the injured Benson and soon lost Fulton. Donald and Munton were wayward early on, and Ward punished them, but Taylor departed, and de Silva's stay was all too short. He was undone by Reeve who also accounted for Cowdrey. Munton returned to have Ward caught, and suddenly Kent declined to 200 for 8 in the 52nd over. Marsh then found a good partner in Headley. They ran and scurried until 14 were needed from the last over, but Reeve bowled Marsh with the first ball, and the rest was beyond Wren and Headley.

QUARTER-FINALS

1 August *at Derby*

Warwickshire 290 for 6 (N.V. Knight 71, D.R. Brown 58, R.G. Twose 51)

Derbyshire 174 (K.J. Barnett 53, A.A. Donald 5 for 41)

Warwickshire won by 116 runs

(Man of the Match – T.A. Munton)

at Cardiff

Glamorgan 242 for 9 (S.P. James 56)

Middlesex 176 (J.D. Carr 62, H.A.G. Anthony 4 for 25, S.L. Watkin 4 for 26)

Glamorgan won by 66 runs

(Man of the Match – C.P. Metson)

at Bristol

Northamptonshire 226 (R.J. Bailey 52, J. Srinath 4 for 38)

Gloucestershire 203 (J.P. Taylor 4 for 34)

Northamptonshire won by 23 runs

(Man of the Match – R.J. Bailey)

at Leeds

Lancashire 169 (M. Watkinson 55)

Yorkshire 170 for 8 (M.G. Bevan 60 not out)

Yorkshire won by 2 wickets

(Man of the Match – M.G. Bevan)

When Neil Smith was caught at the wicket in Devon Malcolm's first over, and the first 10 overs of the Warwickshire innings produced only 17 runs, Derbyshire could be well pleased with themselves. Spirits ran higher still when Dominic Cork joined the attack after 15 overs and had Ostler caught at mid-on off his second delivery. The Derbyshire elation was halted by Knight and Brown

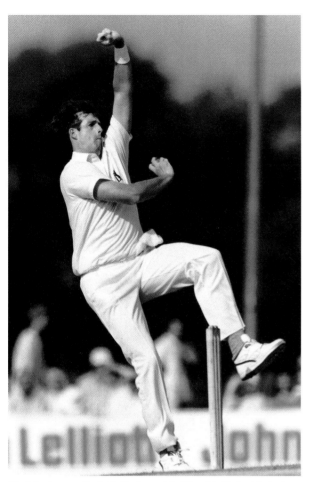

Tim Munton won the individual award in Warwickshire's victories in the quarter- and semi-finals, but injury robbed him of a place in the final. (USPA)

who added 98 in 19 overs. It was Dougie Brown who really changed the aspect of the game with his 58 off 61 balls.

Nick Knight kept up the momentum. His 71 occupied 117 balls, but he had seen Warwickshire through a difficult period, and he eventually hit a six and 5 fours. Twose, Reeve and Penney all kept the score moving, and 83 runs came from the last 10 overs. It is proof of Twose's eagerness and the general zest and commitment of the Warwickshire side that the left-hander, destined soon to play for New Zealand, hit only 1 four in an innings that spanned only 77 balls.

Derbyshire's chances of reaching the semi-final had virtually evaporated by the 13th over, by which time Rollins, Adams and Cullinan were out for 29. Colin Wells and Kim Barnett added 79, and Wells had the distinction of striking Munton for the only boundary the bowler conceded. Munton's opening spell of 12–6–13–1 deservedly won the individual award for the pitch was bland. Cork batted with a runner, and Krikken had had to give up wicket-keeping after eight overs because of a dislocated finger, so that there was every indication that this would not be

Derbyshire's day. They needed 143 runs from the last 20 overs with five wickets in hand, and when Cork was out immediately it was just left to Donald to mop up the tail. The home side surrendered in 46.5 overs.

A late-evening thunderstorm interrupted the match at Cardiff, and the game was not decided until a quarter to eight. In fact, it had been decided long before that, for Glamorgan won most convincingly. The pitch was slow and low, and it became slower and lower as the game progressed. James and Morris put on 71 for the first wicket, and James became the county record-holder for the most limited-over runs scored in a season. He was out to the penultimate delivery before lunch, and the capacity crowd showed concern when Maynard was out with only two more runs scored. Hemp, Dale, Croft and Metson made valuable contributions although Dale, like Cottey, was wastefully run out. The home side could be well content with 242 on this pitch.

Contentment increased as Steve Watkin produced an opening spell of seven overs in which he had Weekes caught at slip, trapped Ramprakash leg before third ball and conceded only nine runs. At the other end, Anthony was bowling quickly, and he had Pooley caught behind and Gatting leg before so that Middlesex were 16 for 4 in the 14th over. Carr and Brown quietened the excitement, but in eight balls either side of tea, Brown and Nash fell to reckless shots against Croft. Carr battled on valiantly, hitting 62 off 84 balls, and he and Johnson scored 67 in 15 overs. Watkin returned to dismiss them both. The storm arrived with Middlesex 153 for 8 in the 48th over. On the resumption, Anthony accounted for Emburey and Feltham, and Middlesex were out in 51.5 overs.

Metson, whose wicket-keeping was exemplary and who took a brilliant catch to dismiss Brown when he anticipated a reverse-sweep, won the Man-of-the-Match award.

When expectations are high the disappointment is the greater, and Gloucestershire suffered such disappointment at Bristol. Their season had been exciting, and they had played good cricket, but the NatWest Trophy offered their last chance of an honour. Russell decided to ask Northamptonshire to bat when he won the toss. The pitch was slow and the going was hard. Srinath accounted for both openers with 41 scored, but Bailey dropped anchor and scored 52 off 134 balls. His innings spanned 36 overs, and later events proved how important his resolution had been. He and Lamb added 62, with the captain hitting 40 of these runs off 52 balls before being run out. It seemed that Gloucestershire were on top when Curran and Capel fell to Ball in quick succession to leave the visitors trembling on 129 for 5. Warren came in to bat with a fluency out of keeping with much of the rest of the day, and hit 44 at a run a ball. In spite of this, Northamptonshire were out in 58.2 overs.

The Gloucestershire innings could never get moving. Hodgson batted for 22 overs, scoring eight off 63 balls, and after 29 overs, the home side were 66 for 3. Lynch and Alleyne lifted the tempo with 44 in 11 overs, but both fell at the same score, and it was Symonds who offered the last hope. He hit 3 sixes and 4 fours, and his 48 came off 40 balls. He and Russell put on 73 in 12 overs for the sixth wicket. When Symonds was out, bowled by Bailey,

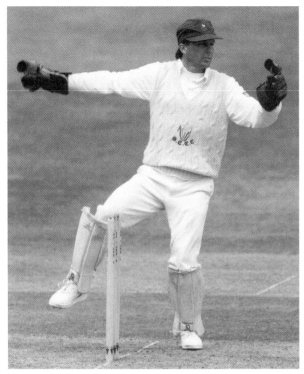

Colin Metson – a Man-of-the-Match award for his outstanding wicket-keeping for Glamorgan in the quarter-final against Middlesex. (Neal Simpson/Empics)

Gloucestershire needed 45 from seven overs, but 14 runs later Russell was out, and the last four wickets went down for six runs.

There was an argument before the start of the match at Headingley. Yorkshire announced that Gough would be in their side, and the England manager – once a Yorkshire captain and manager – criticised the decision, saying that the fast bowler should be rested and allowed to get fit for England. This did sound arrant nonsense. Yorkshire were playing their most important game of the year, and the rest of their season depended upon it. They employ Gough. They are his bread and butter, and it is they who made him a Test cricketer. Test cricket is external decoration; county cricket is the heart and lungs of the game. In the event, Gough played a vital part in Yorkshire's unexpected victory. There was a capacity crowd, and they erupted when Gough drew Atherton forward and found the outside edge for Blakey to take the catch. Gallian was soon leg before to the wonderfully accurate Robinson, who finished with 3 for 21 in 10.2 overs, and when Craig White dismissed Crawley and Lloyd in his second over, both victims of dreadful shots, Lancashire were 47 for 4 and looking doomed.

Watkinson and Fairbrother put on 70 and could have turned the game round, but shortly after lunch Fairbrother jumped out rashly at Grayson and was stumped. Wasim Akram lasted only five balls before hitting Bevan, a bowler with a strange action and a deceptive change of pace, to mid-off. Robinson returned to have Watkinson sky the ball to mid-wicket where White held a good catch, and Lancashire were out in 53.3 overs.

Yorkshire's greatest problem was their nerves, and this was reflected when Austin, cool and demanding, sent back both openers for 29. Byas and Bevan restored calm with a stand of 37 before Byas was caught behind off Yates. White fell to Watkinson for 0, and the jitters returned, but Ashley Metcalfe, recalled to the side, batted with the utmost sense and contributed an invaluable 33 runs. Blakey ran himself out, and 43 runs were needed from 10 overs with four wickets standing.

Gough brought a much-needed impetus, and he and Bevan added 23 for the eighth wicket before Gough was bowled in Austin's last over. Bevan stayed calm for 48 overs, but he was totally in charge and, in the 58th over, he hit Chapple for 10 runs off three balls. Peter Hartley won the match with three balls to spare.

SEMI-FINALS

15 August *at Cardiff*

Glamorgan 86
Warwickshire 88 for 2

Warwickshire won by 8 wickets

(Man of the Match – T.A. Munton)

at Leeds

Northamptonshire 286 for 5 (R.J. Bailey 93 not out, A.J. Lamb 63)
Yorkshire 199

Northamptonshire won by 87 runs

(Man of the Match – R.J. Bailey)

The semi-finals of the NatWest Trophy proved to be a disappointment after the excitement of the previous rounds. A packed house at Cardiff suffered bitterly. Morris was adjudged caught behind in the second over when, to all eyes but the umpire's, he was nowhere near the ball, and James was rightly caught behind when he drove loosely at Donald. Maynard and Hemp appeared to be stabilising matters until they committed suicide. Maynard was sent back by Hemp, loitered in mid-pitch and was run out. Cottey and Hemp scored 18 in 12 overs and were both out at the same total; Cottey was well caught by Piper in the last of Munton's unbroken 12 overs, which cost 18 runs and brought two wickets, and Hemp insanely tested Penney's arm and was run out by yards. Anthony went rashly, and Metson was out first ball. Croft settled for defence when he might have been better advised to hit the loose ball, and Glamorgan were out in 47 overs. It was dreadful stuff from such a keen side.

Barwick gave some pride by capturing the wickets of Knight and Smith, top scorer in the match with 32, but when Brown reverse-swept Barwick for the winning runs only 24.1 of Warwickshire's 60 overs had been used.

Robert Bailey batting for Northamptonshire in the semi-final against Yorkshire. Bailey won three Man-of-the-Match awards in succession. (Graham Chadwick/Allsport)

There was another capacity crowd at Headingley where, unfortunately, there were disturbances towards the end as Yorkshire fell apart. Northamptonshire chose to bat first, and although Montgomerie and Fordham were slow, they gave a solid foundation of 75. Montgomerie called his partner for a run that left him a yard short when Bevan's throw hit the stumps, and then Montgomerie, too, was run out when Hartley hit the stumps from deepish mid-off. This brought Lamb to the wicket at 79 for 2 in the 28th over. Suddenly the play was galvanised.

Given too much room outside the off stump, Lamb immediately found the boundary, and by the time he gave Grayson a simple return he had hit 63 off 67 balls, and he and Bailey had added 131 in 22 overs. Curran plundered well as Yorkshire put down what seemed like an endless stream of catches, and Bailey improvised intelligently, staying to the end and making 93 off 103 balls. His innings was to win him his third Man-of-the-Match award in succession.

Yorkshire never settled. Moxon was caught behind off Curran at 26. Vaughan showed promise with some delightful boundaries, but Byas was totally out of touch and becalmed. Four balls before tea, Vaughan was run out, responding unwisely and unwillingly to Byas' call for a third run to Curran.

Bevan, too, was stupidly run out, and left muttering, and the advent of Kumble caused total confusion. Metcalfe played back first ball and was comprehensively leg before. Yorkshire were 99 for 6, and whatever Blakey, Grayson, Gough and Hartley could offer, the game was decided.

NATWEST TROPHY FINAL
NORTHAMPTONSHIRE v. WARWICKSHIRE
at Lord's

Following a period of intense heat, drought and water shortages, Lord's welcomed the NatWest final with a miserable morning of constant drizzle. The ground was a quarter full, and those who had braved the weather were huddled under umbrellas. Pools of water spotted the tarpaulins which covered the playing area, and all lunched early.

At two, the rain ceased, the clouds receded and the sun shone. For Warwickshire, there was the good news that Knight had declared himself fit, but there was a late disaster. Two days before the final, Tim Munton had strained an intercostal muscle and was out of the match – a grievous blow. Munton was replaced by Bell, and Warwickshire also brought in Paul Smith for the left-arm spinner Ashley Giles who had appeared in the semi-final.

Lamb won the toss, decided to bat, and play began at three. Donald opened the bowling from the Pavilion End and soon generated a lively pace. Brown, rugged and forceful, bustled in from the Nursery End. One was reminded immediately of how many options Reeve had at his disposal – Bell, Paul Smith, Twose and himself in the quicker department and Neil Smith's off-spin. Seven bowlers is a luxury in a limited-over game, but Lamb, too, had such riches at his disposal.

Montgomerie opened Northamptonshire's account when he turned the first ball of the third over to leg for a single, but there was no air of confidence as the ball frequently passed the bat. It came as no surprise when, with the fifth ball of the fifth over, Donald drew Montgomerie forward and bowled him with a ball that moved in from outside the off stump.

Donald leaps in joy after bowling Montgomerie. (Adrian Murrell/Allsport)

Alan Fordham is bowled by Brown in a disastrous over for Northamptonshire. (Adrian Murrell/Allsport)

Taylor celebrates as Knight is caught at slip. (David Munden/Sportsline)

Two overs later, Fordham drove Brown through the covers for the first four, and then he touched Donald low past the keeper for another four. There was an edged boundary from Bailey, and the rate had climbed to above three an over.

The crucial over for Northamptonshire – and Warwickshire – was the 12th. Fordham was growing in confidence until he chopped a ball from outside off stump into his wicket. This brought in Lamb who drove extravagantly at Brown second ball and was lucky that his pad intercepted the inside edge before it hit his stumps. Unwisely, he drove loosely at Brown's next ball and was caught at slip. Lamb's three-ball innings was incomprehensible. He was desperate to do well, and one can only think that nerves got to this old campaigner on what many had hoped would be his day.

Bell came into the attack, and Neil Smith's off-spin was employed from the Pavilion End. He hustled quickly through his overs, efficient and accurate. The pitch was slow, and runs had to be worked for because the outfield tended to be as slow as the wicket. There was, too, the factor that Warwickshire were dynamic in the field, with Trevor Penney outstanding and thrilling.

Northamptonshire did not help their own cause. They ambled singles when they might have pressed for twos, but, in fairness, Bailey and Curran's main concern was reparation.

Reeve bowled from the Nursery End, and Curran hit the last ball of the 26th over back over the bowler's head for four. One had been screaming for a batsman to play this shot, but runs were hard work.

The fifty partnership arrived off the last ball of the 30th over, but two balls later, Bailey, who had enjoyed a spectacularly successful competition, essayed a cut at Neil Smith and chopped the ball into his stumps from an under edge.

The hundred came up in the 35th over, and Curran and Capel suddenly began to use their feet against Neil Smith, whose accuracy could not disguise the fact that he was not turning the ball. There was joy when Capel rocked back and pulled Reeve into the Grandstand for six, but 11 balls later, he drove inside a ball pitched on the off stump which held its line and was caught behind. After 40 overs, Northamptonshire were 112 for 5.

Neil Smith ended his spell, and Donald returned for a four-over burst at a reduced pace to a purely defensive field. Reeve and Neil and Paul Smith offered strangulation rather than movement, simply putting the ball on the spot and waiting for Northamptonshire to self-destruct which – under pressure to score more quickly – they did.

Cometh the hour, cometh the man – Dermot Reeve hits Kevin Curran for four as Warwickshire sight victory. (David Munden/ Sportsline)

Having faced 80 balls, Curran was bowled by an in-swinger which straightened to shatter his stumps. Penberthy, an elegant left-hander, promised much, and the 150 came up in the 50th over. Four balls later, Penberthy was brilliantly run out by Penney who hit the stumps with his throw and caught the batsman an inch short of the line. Even with the aid of television replay, it was a difficult decision to make.

The arrival of Snape brought a refreshing urgency as he and Warren, positive and confident, added 39 in seven overs before Snape was caught off an inside edge to the wicket-keeper. Snape's 21 had come off 28 balls while Warren had hit a six and 3 fours.

The batsmen had declined the offer of bad light when in full flow, but with Kumble in the middle, Donald bowling and nine balls remaining, the players left the field – 197 for 8.

On the Sunday, Northamptonshire wasted their last nine balls. They attempted big hits when pushes and nudges would have been more profitable. Kumble hit high to Twose, and Warren, who had batted so well on the Saturday, heaved across the line and missed next ball.

NATWEST TROPHY FINAL – NORTHAMPTONSHIRE v. WARWICKSHIRE
2 and 3 September 1995 at Lord's

NORTHAMPTONSHIRE

R.R. Montgomerie	b Donald	1
A. Fordham	b Brown	20
R.J. Bailey	b N.M.K. Smith	44
A.J. Lamb (capt)	c Ostler, b Brown	0
K.M. Curran	b Donald	30
D.J. Capel	c Piper, b Reeve	12
*R.J. Warren	b Bell	41
A.L. Penberthy	run out	5
J.N. Snape	c Piper, b Donald	21
A.R. Kumble	c Twose, b Bell	2
J.P. Taylor	not out	0
Extras	b 4, lb 9, w 11	24
		—
(59.5 overs)		200

WARWICKSHIRE

N.V. Knight	c Bailey, b Taylor	2
N.M.K. Smith	c Warren, b Taylor	2
D.P. Ostler	b Kumble	45
D.R. Brown	c Warren, b Penberthy	8
R.G. Twose	run out	68
T.L. Penney	c Montgomerie, b Penberthy	20
D.A. Reeve (capt)	not out	37
P.A. Smith	not out	4
*K.J. Piper		
A.A. Donald		
M.A.V. Bell		
Extras	b 2, lb 14, w 1	17
		—
(58.5 overs)	(for 6 wickets)	203

	O	M	R	W
Donald	12	1	33	3
Brown	10	2	35	2
Bell	8.5	1	41	2
N.M.K. Smith	12	1	23	1
Reeve	12	1	31	1
P.A. Smith	5	–	24	–

	O	M	R	W
Taylor	11.5	4	37	2
Curran	11	3	31	–
Penberthy	11	1	44	2
Kumble	12	–	29	1
Capel	12	–	40	–
Snape	1	–	6	–

FALL OF WICKETS
1–4, 2–39, 3–39, 4–89, 5–110, 6–128, 7–158, 8–197, 9–200

FALL OF WICKETS
1–5, 2–14, 3–28, 4–74, 5–122, 6–176

Umpires: H.D. Bird & M.J. Kitchen   *Man of the Match:* D.A. Reeve   *Warwickshire won by 4 wickets*

The beginning of the Warwickshire innings was awful. Against some excellent bowling from Taylor and Curran, the openers were impotent. Neil Smith was out in the fifth over when he drove wildly at Taylor and was splendidly caught in front of first slip by Warren. Knight played an innings that was indescribably bad. The technical imperfections suggested in the Test matches were magnified tenfold. His bat was ever away from his body, and he was beaten constantly outside the off stump in his vain attempts to give catches to slip or keeper. His coaches must have winced, and Essex must have wondered why they were angered by his departure. In the 11th over, having faced 34 balls and having been applauded when he made contact with the ball, he edged to second slip. It was merciful euthanasia.

Northamptonshire had gained the initiative, and when Penberthy had Brown caught behind, Warwickshire were 28 for 3 in 17 overs. At this point, Northamptonshire could have taken the game, but there were two costly misses. Ostler, on 11, was dropped at long-leg, and Twose, when six, was put down by Capel at slip – the easiest of chances. Twose might also have been caught and bowled by Kumble and, when he had scored 51, he attempted a reverse-sweep which Warren got hands to but could not hold.

Ostler and Twose put on 46 in 14.4 overs before Ostler was bowled by Kumble's top-spinner. The Indian bowled magnificently as he had done all season, but the fielding lacked the urgency and eagerness which had been characteristic of the Warwickshire out-cricket. The fielders were never attacking the ball, and the batsmen were never pressurised.

Northamptonshire hopes were kept alive when Penney drove Penberthy to deep point in the 45th over with 79 still needed, but Reeve was immediately hustling and bustling.

With 20 balls remaining and 25 runs needed, Twose was run out by Warren. The wicket-keeper fumbled the ball but recovered to hit the stumps with his throw. Reeve was mightily lucky to survive an appeal for leg before. The ball hit him on the back leg in front of middle stump, but umpire Bird must have believed that it hit the front pad. The Warwickshire captain, who was to take the individual award for his total contribution to the match, admitted later that he was rather fortunate.

Reeve moved onto the attack. He hit the ball over the top, determined his own length and decided where the ball would be driven. There is no answer to him in this mood. He hit 5 fours, and his 37 came off 47 balls. Warwickshire's joy was unconfined as they wasted good champagne in the puerile spraying ritual. Northamptonshire could rue their missed chances.

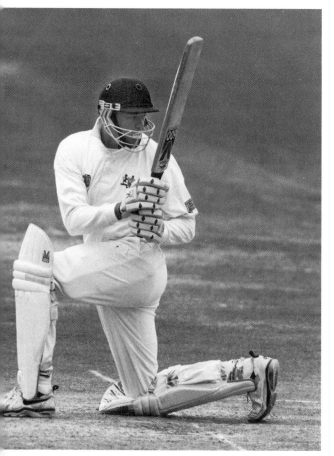

Young cricketer of the year – Andrew Symonds hit a world-record 20 sixes for Gloucestershire against Glamorgan at Abergavenny. Symonds learned his cricket in Australia and declined the invitation to tour with the England 'A' side, a decision for which he deserves commendations. (Paul Sturgess/Sportsline)

BRITANNIC ASSURANCE COUNTY CHAMPIONSHIP
and other county matches

18, 19, 20 and 21 April *at Edgbaston*

Warwickshire 240 (A.J. Moles 67, N.M.K. Smith 55 not out) and 205 (D.A. Reeve 77 not out, M.M. Patel 4 for 58, D.G. Cork 4 for 63)

England 'A' 503 (A.P. Wells 178, M.R. Ramprakash 79, M.C. Ilott 60, M.M. Patel 55, P.A. Nixon 51 retired hurt)

England 'A' won by an innings and 58 runs

The weather was unkind to the game between the reigning champions and the England 'A' side led by Alan Wells. As the umpires took the field, there was a violent hailstorm, and the start was delayed for 90 minutes. The ground was not at its welcoming best, being in a state of redevelopment, and Chapple, Cork and Stemp proved to be most unwelcoming to Warwickshire who were in a dreadful state until the last two wickets realised 77 in 14 overs. Munton was unfit, and Knight, who had been on the England 'A' tour to India – as had Piper – and who had recently been acquired by Warwickshire, was also unavailable.

Gallian was leg before in Donald's first over on the second morning. The pitch seemed a little untrustworthy, and there was a 25-minute stoppage because of snow, but Alan Wells warmed the brave spectators. He and Ramprakash added 152 for the third wicket, and Wells reached his fifty when he hit Neil Smith for 18 off four balls. Wells hit 26 fours and 5 sixes in his blistering innings and was finally out when he moved down the pitch, head in the air, and was stumped. Piper also held four catches in the innings. His rival for the England wicket-keeping spot, Nixon, batted well and was 51 not out at the end of the second day, but he did not resume on the third morning, having had his index finger broken by a ball from Donald. This was wretched luck for a man whom many thought

would win a place in the England side to play West Indies.

Ilott and Patel hit their highest first-class scores as the 'A' team passed 500. They then played a major part in reducing Warwickshire to 205 for 9 by the end of the day. Patel had a spell of 4 for 3 in five overs, and, at one time, the county side were 94 for 8. They were rallied by Reeve, Small and Donald, but Stemp caught-and-bowled Donald with the sixth ball of the final day.

27, 28, 29 and 30 April *at Derby*

Sussex 111 (D.E. Malcolm 6 for 61) and 113 (P.A.J. DeFreitas 6 for 35)

Derbyshire 603 for 6 dec. (K.J. Barnett 164, D.J. Cullinan 134, C.J. Adams 111, D.G. Cork 84 not out, A.S. Rollins 52)

Derbyshire won by an innings and 379 runs

Derbyshire 24 pts, Sussex 1 pt

at Stockton-on-Tees

Durham 177 (J.N.B. Bovill 6 for 39) and 248 (M. Prabhakar 84, J.N.B. Bovill 6 for 29)

Hampshire 194 and 205 (R.A. Smith 77, S.J.E. Brown 5 for 49)

Durham won by 26 runs

Durham 20 pts, Hampshire 4 pts

at Chelmsford

Leicestershire 253 (N.E. Briers 114, N.F. Williams 5 for 93, M.C. Ilott 4 for 78) and 432 (N.E. Briers 95, D.J. Millns 70, P. Whitticase 62 not out)

Essex 404 (G.A. Gooch 139, N. Hussain 100, P.J. Prichard 63) and 179 (G.A. Gooch 92)

Leicestershire won by 102 runs

Leicestershire 21 pts, Essex 8 pts

at Canterbury

Northamptonshire 561 for 8 dec. (R.R. Montgomerie 192, D.J. Capel 167, A.J. Lamb 54) and 7 for 1

Kent 352 (T.R. Ward 76, M.V. Fleming 61, D.J. Capel 4 for 50) and 215 (T.R. Ward 114 not out, J.P. Taylor 5 for 49)

Northamptonshire won by 9 wickets

Northamptonshire 24 pts, Kent 6 pts

at Taunton

Somerset 277 (R.J. Harden 113) and 214 (P.D. Bowler 84 not out, G.D. Rose 84, S.L. Watkin 7 for 49)

James Bovill had a magnificent start to the season with career-best bowling performances for Hampshire only to be sidelined by injury for the second half of the season. (David Munden/Sportsline)

Glamorgan 405 (R.D.B. Croft 143, M.P. Maynard 62, A. Dale 60, G.D. Rose 5 for 78) and 89 for 2

Glamorgan won by 8 wickets

Glamorgan 24 pts, Somerset 6 pts

at The Oval

Gloucestershire 392 (A. Symonds 161 not out, R.I. Dawson 51, J.E. Benjamin 4 for 77) and 207 (M.W. Alleyne 60, R.C. Russell 56, J.E. Benjamin 4 for 68)

Surrey 217 (M.A. Butcher 71) and 475 (A.D. Brown 187, A.J. Stewart 65, M.A. Butcher 51, J. Srinath 4 for 137)

Surrey won by 93 runs

Surrey 21 pts, Gloucestershire 8 pts

at Edgbaston

Warwickshire 282 (N.V. Knight 85, R.G. Twose 66, D.P. Ostler 57, J.E. Emburey 4 for 31, P.C.R. Tufnell 4 for 55) and 294 (T.L. Penney 88)

Middlesex 224 (M.R. Ramprakash 85, A.A. Donald 6 for 56) and 137

Warwickshire won by 215 runs

Warwickshire 22 pts, Middlesex 5 pts

While Australia and West Indies were still battling for supremacy in the Caribbean, the Britannic Assurance County Championship began with 14 of the 18 counties involved.

Kim Barnett's criticisms of his team's attitude and performance in 1994 seemed to have worked wonders. Barnett, in his last season as captain, won the toss and asked Sussex to bat first at Derby. The weather was cold, and the pitch was a little green. More significantly, the bowling was accurate, hostile and intelligent. Cork and Malcolm were quick and moved the ball appreciably. The Sussex response was limp and, with only three batsmen reaching double figures, they were bowled out in 39 overs, shortly after lunch. Top scorer was Neil Lenham, but he was dropped by O'Gorman off Malcolm at long-leg when on 27. He eventually fell to the same combination when he had scored 45. Malcolm bowled splendidly for his six wickets, but Cork, too, was in fine form, and Warner snapped up two wickets towards the end of the innings.

What demons the pitch had held vanished when Derbyshire batted. Having bowled 2.3 overs, Jarvis limped off with a muscle injury, all too familiar an occurrence in a career which had once promised much. Barnett and Rollins celebrated. By the end of the day, Derbyshire were 263 for 1. Rollins had fallen to Giddins on 189, but Adams was matching Barnett's aggression.

On the second day, Derbyshire reached 600 for the first time this century and claimed a first-innings lead of 492, the highest in their history. Barnett added only 12 to his overnight score, but Adams, full of flair, and Cullinan added 144 in 35 overs for the third wicket, and Cullinan and Cork 132 in 31 overs for the fifth wicket. Sussex were 68 for 4 at the end of the day, and, with Wells alone offer-

ing resistance, they subsided to DeFreitas on the third day. Cullinan had become the first Derbyshire player to score a century on his championship debut, and the Derbyshire margin of victory was the biggest in their history.

There was no such high scoring at Stockton where 17 wickets fell on the first day and where the game was also over on the Saturday. Durham went from 80 for 1 to 177 all out, and this was mainly due to the pace bowling of James Bovill, ironically of Durham University, who had never before taken six wickets in an innings. By the close, Hampshire were 126 for 7, six of their batsmen having been adjudged leg before. Udal and Streak added 72 for the eighth wicket, and Hampshire took a first-innings lead.

Prabhakar followed his three wickets with an innings of 84 which tilted the match in favour of Durham. This was compounded when, in the four overs possible before the end of the second day, Durham captured the wicket of Stephenson as one run was scored.

Hampshire, for whom Bovill had bettered his career-best figures of the first innings, needed 232 to win, and, at 147 for 3 with Robin Smith in fluent form, they looked set to reach their target. Terry was leg before offering no shot, and Smith was caught behind, both off Brown who also accounted for Nicholas. Prabhakar quickly dismissed Udal and Aymes to complete a highly satisfactory championship debut, and Durham happily won their opening championship match.

There was less satisfaction for Essex at Chelmsford in a game of dramatic turns of fortune. The first day saw some furious cricket. Put in to bat, Leicestershire were 160 for 7 from 33 overs at lunch. Neil Williams swung the ball menacingly. Rollins displayed exceptional talent behind the stumps, holding five catches – two of which were outstanding – and Ilott found accuracy after an erratic start. Briers could be excused for wondering what was happening at the other end, but eventually he found a useful partner in Pierson, and the pair added 100 for the eighth wicket. Briers reached his 29th first-class hundred, and Essex had 48 overs of the first day at their disposal.

Gooch and Prichard began merrily with a stand of 138 before the new Essex captain was caught at slip, and Lewis ran himself out. Essex closed on 150 for 2, and the game moved positively in their favour on the second day when Gooch reached his 114th first-class century. Pierson was unable to bowl for Leicestershire after ricking his neck having sent down one over, and Hussain batted quite splendidly to score the 21st hundred of his career and to remind the England selectors of his presence.

Leicestershire were 76 for 1 at the beginning of the third day, still 75 runs in arrears. Cronje was out without addition, and it seemed that the game might end in three days when the visitors slipped to 275 for 7. Whitticase, playing his first game since 1992 in place of the injured Nixon, immediately skied a catch to Gooch at mid-off, but it was dropped. Whitticase went on to reach 60 before being hit in the mouth by a ball from Williams. He was taken to hospital and lost eight teeth, but bravely returned later. He and Millns had added 114 when the accident happened.

Needing 282 in 93 overs to win the match, Essex inexplicably fell apart against a seam attack and were 117 for 8.

Such and Gooch added 62, but Leicestershire were not to be denied.

Allan Lamb won the toss at Canterbury, but he could not have been too happy when Northamptonshire lost their first five wickets for 172 on a true pitch. By the end of the day, Montgomerie and Capel had advanced the score to 343, and the former Oxford captain had reached the third century of his career.

Both batsmen went on to make the highest scores of their careers, and their sixth-wicket partnership became worth 337, only 39 short of the county record held by Subba Row and Lightfoot. Facing a daunting 561, Kent were 257 for 5 at the end of the second day, and, although there was much spirit from the late-order, they followed on 209 runs in arrears. Capel followed his highest score with four wickets. By the close of the third day, which ended early because of bad light, Kent were 192 for 7, and the match ended after 68 minutes on the fourth day. The home side had their hero in Trevor Ward, who had been in sparkling form in the Benson and Hedges Cup. He carried his bat through the innings for the first time, facing 217 balls and hitting 18 fours.

In spite of missing chances, Glamorgan soon had the upper hand at Taunton where only the patience of Harden saved the home side from humiliation. In contrast, the visitors showed great panache after capturing the last two Somerset wickets on the second morning. They plundered 405 from 93.5 overs, with Croft hitting 2 sixes and 23 fours in his first championship century. He and Maynard added 121 for the fifth wicket, and Glamorgan's zestful approach earned justified reward.

No play was possible on the third day, but Watkin quickly reduced Somerset to 59 for 5 on the fourth day. Bowler and Rose, who hit 16 fours, put on 129 for the sixth wicket, but the last four wickets went down for 26 runs. Needing 87 in 22 overs, Glamorgan romped home with 8.4 overs to spare.

There were remarkable happenings at The Oval. There was the familiar sight of Martin Bicknell being carried off in his seventh over with a calf strain, but, in spite of some brisk batting from Dawson and Lynch – playing *against* Surrey after 17 years at The Oval – Gloucestershire were reduced to 180 for 6. Then came Andrew Symonds, known to those who toured Australia with the England side. Off 140 balls, he hit 161 with 21 fours and 4 sixes. Born in Birmingham, settled in Australia, Symonds lashed the ball to all parts of the ground, and when, on the second day, Surrey were bowled out for 217, Srinath and Smith bowling impressively, the home side found themselves following on.

By the end of a third day dominated by Alistair Brown, Surrey found themselves 256 ahead. Brown's ninth century was his highest, and he hit 17 fours and 4 sixes in his usual positive manner.

Having been in a winning position, Gloucestershire found themselves facing defeat on the last morning at 44 for 5. Russell and Alleyne, captain and vice-captain, steadied the innings with a stand of 63, and there was some late hitting from Ball, but, for the first time in their history, Surrey won a championship match after being asked to follow on.

At Edgbaston, Warwickshire showed a determination to hold on to their title. Put in to bat, they were given a solid platform by Knight and Twose who added 126 for the second wicket. They were then worn down by Tufnell and Emburey, and by the brilliant slip catching of Carr who held six catches in the innings and was to hold two more in the second. Tufnell entered the match with two fingers strapped together and bowled 31.3 consecutive overs before leaving the field after damaging another finger in stopping a straight drive from Ostler.

It was pace rather than spin which deflated Middlesex, as Donald was in full cry proving his total fitness. He bowled Warwickshire to a first-innings lead of 58, which did not look sufficient until Trevor Penney made a stolid 88 in nearly five hours. Needing 353 to win, Middlesex were brushed aside by a varied attack.

FRIENDLY MATCH

27, 28, 29 April and 1 May *at Leeds*

Yorkshire 417 for 7 dec. (D. Byas 193, R.J. Blakey 77 not out, C. White 72) and 288 for 6 dec. (M.G. Bevan 108, M.D. Moxon 84, C. White 50)

Lancashire 271 (M.A. Atherton 129) and 215 (W.K. Hegg 64, D. Gough 7 for 28)

Yorkshire won by 219 runs

Yorkshire could gain great satisfaction from this 'friendly' Roses Match. Byas improved on the career-best score he had registered against Cambridge University, Australian Michael Bevan gave further evidence of his quality, Craig White showed he was fully fit, and Darren Gough returned the best bowling figures of his career.

4, 5, 6 and 8 May *at Chelmsford*

Essex 389 (G.A. Gooch 86, J.J.B. Lewis 75, R.C. Irani 63, R.K. Illingworth 4 for 80) and 332 (G.A. Gooch 165, N.V. Radford 4 for 50)

Worcestershire 276 (T.S. Curtis 76, S.J. Rhodes 54, P.M. Such 6 for 84) and 237 (T.M. Moody 79, P.M. Such 6 for 94)

Essex won by 208 runs

Essex 24 pts, Worcestershire 6 pts

at Cardiff

Northamptonshire 377 (A.J. Lamb 124, A. Fordham 57, J.N. Snape 55, N.M. Kendrick 4 for 98) and 243 (S.L. Watkin 4 for 55)

Glamorgan 334 (P.A. Cottey 116, A. Dale 61, A.R. Kumble 5 for 65) and 290 for 7 (H. Morris 109, D.L. Hemp 58, D.J. Capel 4 for 36)

Glamorgan won by 3 wickets

Glamorgan 23 pts, Northamptonshire 8 pts

at Old Trafford

Durham 249 (J.E. Morris 68, Wasim Akram 5 for 40) and 432

(J.E. Morris 169, C.W. Scott 56, J.A. Daley 55,
M. Watkinson 4 for 115)

Lancashire 370 (M. Watkinson 108, P.J. Martin 71, G. Chapple
58, J. Wood 4 for 54) and 314 for 2 (M.A. Atherton 155
not out, J.P. Crawley 81)

Lancashire won by 8 wickets

Lancashire 24 pts, Durham 5 pts

at Leicester

Yorkshire 332 (C. White 107, A.P. Grayson 73, A.D. Mullally
4 for 62) and 37 for 1

Leicestershire 147 (D.J. Millns 50 not out, P.J. Hartley 5 for 19)
and 221 (V.J. Wells 75)

Yorkshire won by 9 wickets

Yorkshire 23 pts, Leicestershire 4 pts

at Lord's

Middlesex 189 (M.R. Ramprakash 71, J.P. Stephenson
7 for 51) and 427 for 6 dec. (M.R. Ramprakash 163 not out,
J.D. Carr 129)

Hampshire 169 (D.J. Nash 4 for 61) and 242 (R.A. Smith 75,
D.J. Nash 5 for 35)

Middlesex won by 205 runs

Middlesex 20 pts, Hampshire 4 pts

at Trent Bridge

Nottinghamshire 244 (P. Johnson 65, G.F. Archer 61,
D.G. Cork 4 for 51, D.E. Malcolm 4 for 53) and 302
(P.R. Pollard 85, C.L. Cairns 64, D.G. Cork 4 for 65)

Derbyshire 312 (D.J. Cullinan 131, C.L. Cairns 4 for 83,
G.W. Mike 4 for 87) and 120 (J.E. Hindson 4 for 30,
J.A. Afford 4 for 58)

Nottinghamshire won by 114 runs

Nottinghamshire 21 pts, Derbyshire 7 pts

at Taunton

Gloucestershire 424 (M.A. Lynch 105, A.J. Wright 75,
M.W. Alleyne 71, A.R. Caddick 4 for 65) and 347 for 8
(A. Symonds 102, G.D. Hodgson 81, H.R.J. Trump 5 for 85)

Somerset 478 (P.D. Bowler 136, R.J. Harden 103,
A.N. Hayhurst 76, G.D. Rose 53, M. Davies 4 for 86)

Match drawn

Somerset 6 pts, Gloucestershire 5 pts

at Hove

Sussex 323 (A.P. Wells 107, C.W.J. Athey 62) and 343
(A.P. Wells 136, C.W.J. Athey 72, K. Greenfield 68,
D.W. Headley 7 for 58)

Kent 361 (P.A. de Silva 117, M.A. Ealham 88, F.D. Stephenson
4 for 86) and 230 (M.A. Ealham 77 not out, S.A. Marsh 59,
E.E. Hemmings 4 for 63)

Sussex won by 75 runs

Sussex 23 pts, Kent 8 pts

at Edgbaston

Warwickshire 470 (D.P. Ostler 208, D.A. Reeve 53) and 210 for
4 dec. (D.P. Ostler 66 not out)

Surrey 288 (M.A. Butcher 54, A.J. Hollioake 53, A.A. Donald
6 for 64) and 301 (A.J. Holloake 117 not out, G.C. Small
5 for 71)

Warwickshire won by 91 runs

Warwickshire 24 pts, Surrey 3 pts

All the first-class counties were engaged in the second
round of Britannic Assurance County Championship
matches, and Essex had some rejoicing after a wretched
start to the season. They scored consistently on the opening day after Prichard had won the toss and had claimed
maximum batting points by the close. With Such and
Childs bowling well in tandem, Worcestershire batted fit-
fully. Curtis was at number four, having had four stitches
in a finger damaged while fielding. He batted through 73
overs for 65 not out on the second day, but he added 11 of
the 36 scored on the third morning.

Leading by 113 on the first innings, Essex made a violent assault on the Worcestershire bowling. Gooch hit 165
off 189 balls. His innings included 21 fours and 2 sixes, and
he was severe on all bowlers. The Essex innings was over
in 71.1 overs, but they left Worcestershire a target of 446
and their bowlers plenty of time in which to bowl out the
opposition.

Such trapped Weston before the close, and the off-spinner went on to capture six wickets for the second time in the
match and to end with the best match figures of his career.

Glamorgan gained their sixth victory in six matches in
all competitions when they won a fine contest against
Northamptonshire. The first day at Cardiff belonged to the
visitors who, with Lamb hitting 21 fours and 2 sixes in his
87th first-class century, scored 359 for 9. Loye and Capel
failed to score, but all the other batsmen made useful
contributions.

As they had done in their previous match, Glamorgan
adopted a positive approach, scoring at three runs an over.
Cottey and Dale added 161 for the sixth wicket, and the
home county reached 334, having been 19 for 3 at one time.
Watkin then dismissed both openers before the close, and
to add to Northamptonshire's woes, Lamb had an injured
wrist and batted number eleven, and Ripley and
Montgomerie broke fingers. In spite of these afflictions,
they batted solidly, and Glamorgan had 14 overs and the
whole of the last day in which to score 287 to win.

At 229 for 3, all was going well, but Capel took three
wickets in four balls, and suddenly they were 242 for 6.
Morris had batted splendidly, but once again it was Cottey
who calmed nerves and took Glamorgan to victory.

Durham hit their highest-ever second-innings total, and
still found themselves trounced by Lancashire. They had
promised a big score in their first innings, but Wasim
Akram had brought it to an abrupt end by taking 4 for 6 in

33 balls. Gallian was soon out when Lancashire batted, but Chapple came in as night-watchman and stayed to add 85 with Watkinson after five wickets had gone for 105 runs. Watkinson, a leader by example, hit 108 off 122 balls with 4 sixes and 6 fours.

It was on the Saturday that John Morris led the Durham revival. His side were 51 for 3 before he added 150 with Daley, and Saxelby, Scott and Wood made valuable contributions. Brown was bowled by the first ball of the fourth day, and Lancashire went in search of 312 in 99 overs.

Atherton and Gallian put on 94 for the first wicket, and Crawley, dropped before he had scored, helped Atherton to add 179 for the second. Victory came with 16.2 overs to spare.

Yorkshire's positive start to the season continued with victory inside three days at Grace Road. Former Yorkshire batsman Phil Robinson kept wicket for Leicestershire as both Nixon and Whitticase were injured. Craig White's hundred was the feature of the first day. He was on 83 when joined by last man Mark Robinson, and he went from 86 to 100 with a straight six, an off-driven two and a six over mid-on off consecutive balls from Pierson. Earlier, Grayson had hit 73 off 93 balls.

Briers and Pierson were both dismissed before the close, 1 for 2, and on the Friday, Leicestershire descended to 47 for 7. Millns led a mini-revival, but he could not save the follow-on. Leicestershire ended the day on 102 for 5. Wells briefly delayed the inevitable on the Saturday.

The game at Lord's was also over in three days. Sixteen wickets fell on the first day, with John Stephenson returning the best bowling figures of his career. He took seven wickets for 17 runs in the space of 62 balls, and he confirmed his liking for his new county, and for Lord's.

Hampshire ended the day on 105 for 6, and the second day belonged entirely to Middlesex. The excessive swing of the opening day had disappeared, and once Pooley and Gatting had gone for 69, Carr and Ramprakash came together to add 253 at more than four runs an over. Carr reached his hundred with a six off Connor, and Hampshire's abysmal start to the season continued.

Middlesex added 105 quick runs on the third morning, and Gatting's declaration left Hampshire a target of 448. They were all out in 68 overs, with Dion Nash taking five wickets in an innings for Middlesex for the first time.

Derbyshire gave first-class debuts to Harrison and Owen, and at first all went well for the visitors to Trent Bridge. Malcolm and Cork bowled superbly on a pitch which gave them no assistance, and once a third-wicket stand of 113 between Robinson and Johnson was broken, Derbyshire took charge. Barnett and Rollins scored 43 before the close, and Nottinghamshire had had a sorry day.

The second day did not begin well for Derbyshire who lost both Rollins and Barnett for the addition of one run, but then came Cullinan. He hit 131 from 213 balls, his second century in successive county games, and Derbyshire took a lead of 68. Cullinan, who hit 17 fours and Krikken put on 74 for the eighth wicket. Krikken did not bat in the second innings as he was stricken by chicken-pox. Derbyshire had gone into the match without the injured Adams.

Due mainly to Pollard and Cairns, who had bowled

Substitute fielder Dougie Brown runs out Nadeem Shahid as Warwickshire beat Surrey by 91 runs at Edgbaston, 8 May. (Philip Wilcox)

well, Nottinghamshire reached 260 for 4, but then lost their last six wickets for 42 runs. This left Derbyshire with a target of 235 in 14 overs and the whole of the last day. Rollins was out before the close, which came with Derbyshire on 24 for 1.

Barnett and Cottam, who was playing his first game for Derbyshire, scored 37 and 32 respectively, but thereafter only DeFreitas, 11 not out, reached double figures. Derbyshire collapsed before the combined left-arm spin of Afford and Hindson.

Taunton was the scene of the first drawn match of the season in the championship. Gloucestershire scored 326 for 5 on the opening day after Wright and Hodgson put on 113 for the first wicket. This stand was followed by Monte Lynch's first century for his new county. He hit 13 fours and 2 sixes in what was his first hundred for three seasons, and he was, as ever, wonderfully entertaining. Ball led the charge on the second morning with 48 out of the 98 scored in 24 overs.

Somerset could not replicate Gloucestershire's dash. Lathwell and Trescothick went cheaply, after which Bowler and Harden batted out the day at less than 2.5 runs an over to reach 218 for 2.

The partnership was broken on the Saturday morning, by which time it was worth 193. Both Harden and Bowler reached centuries; for Bowler, who shared a fourth-wicket stand of 123 with Hayhurst, it was his first for his new county.

Gloucestershire had 18 overs at the end of the day in which they scored 47 without loss, but by then the game looked certain to be drawn. So it proved. The visitors were 129 for 4 just after lunch, and looking vulnerable, but the advent of Symonds changed the mood. Hodgson's 221-minute vigil was ended by Mushtaq, and then Symonds and Russell added 100. Symonds hit 15 fours and 2 sixes and faced 137 balls.

Adrianus van Troost had missed the match because of a back problem, and Caddick retired after bowling one over in the second innings with the recurrence of a shin injury, to leave Somerset with a depleted attack for the early weeks of the season.

Sussex showed excellent powers of recovery, bouncing back from their mauling at Derby to beat Kent. They won the toss at Hove, batted inconsistently and briskly, and were bowled out for 323. Athey provided the basis of the innings, and Alan Wells, having had a depressing season in 1994, made his second hundred in four innings to give promise of a glorious summer. Wells' good form was all-important to Sussex, for the chances of Speight's return to the side were not promising. He had contracted a virus in Spain pre-season which had defied diagnosis, and he remained weak and underweight.

The last three Sussex wickets realised 76 runs, and Kent began the second day with 18 on the board from seven overs. They raced to a first-innings lead of 38 and took maximum batting points with considerable aplomb, but their innings was a thing of fits and starts. Benson was passive for long periods, and his 45 occupied three hours. Ward's fine start to the season was punctured by Stephenson, and Walker was run out for 0. The panache was provided by Aravinda de Silva who hit a six and 19 fours in his first century for Kent. He is a brilliant batsman, and he gave notice that he would grace the English summer with his charm and dash. There was also a career-best 88 from Ealham, and, with Sussex finishing the day on 6 for 1, Kent could be well pleased with their Friday's work.

Giddins and Moores were soon back in the pavilion on the Saturday morning, to leave Sussex struggling at 42 for 3. Athey and Wells then added 103. Athey was leg before to Headley, but Greenfield helped Wells to add 161 for the fifth wicket to complete the Sussex rehabilitation. Wells completed his second century of the match and, in so doing, he became the first Sussex player to score a century in each innings at Hove since C.B. Fry in 1903.

Sussex added only two runs on the last morning before Lewry was caught off Headley. This gave Headley figures of 7 for 58, the best of his career, and well deserved. Kent were left with 99 overs in which to score 306 to win. Their chances looked good as Giddins was absent injured, and the pitch was benign. Doubts began when Stephenson had Ward caught behind for eight. The left-arm seamer Jason Lewry captured three quick wickets, and, with de Silva run out for 0, Kent were 42 for 5. The sixth wicket fell at 68, and although Marsh and Ealham put on 126, Hemmings, beginning his 30th season in county cricket, took the last four wickets to give Sussex a fine victory.

Warwickshire's determination to hold on to their title became even more apparent when they despatched Surrey as convincingly as they had disposed of Middlesex. They gave a first-class debut to Wasim Khan, but he, Moles and Twose were dismissed for 75 after the home county had been put in. Ostler then dominated a stand of 123 with Penney, and Warwickshire were 344 for 4 at the close. Ostler, 181 not out, had recorded his first century at Edgbaston.

This duly became his first double century on any ground on the Friday, and it took Warwickshire to a daunting 470. Darren Bicknell and Butcher began Surrey's innings with a stand of 76, but it lacked conviction, and the spectre of Donald was soon haunting the innings. He captured three wickets, and Surrey closed uncertainly on 168 for 5.

Donald finished with six wickets, and Surrey trailed by 182 runs on the first innings. Reeve did not enforce the follow-on, but Warwickshire pressed for quick runs. His declaration left Surrey six overs and the last day in which to score 393 runs to win. The loss of Darren Bicknell to Donald did not help their cause.

At 125 for 8, Surrey's defeat seemed imminent, but Hollioake saw that his county died fighting. Off 114 balls, in 136 minutes, he hit 117 not out. He lashed 13 fours and 3 sixes which came in the space of four balls bowled by Davis – the third ball of the four was hit for four. He and Nowell scored 76 for the ninth wicket, and with Joey Benjamin, he added 100 for the last wicket. It was a gloriously brave innings, but Warwickshire joined Glamorgan with two wins from two matches.

11, 12, 13 and 15 May *at Chesterfield*

Yorkshire 177 and 104 (P.A.J. DeFreitas 4 for 30)

Derbyshire 140 (M.A. Robinson 4 for 58) and 134
  (P.J. Hartley 9 for 41)

Yorkshire won by 7 runs

Yorkshire 20 pts, Derbyshire 4 pts

at Swansea

Glamorgan 212 (E.S.H. Giddins 6 for 87) and 270 for 7 dec.
  (M.P. Maynard 74, H. Morris 61, R.D.B. Croft 52 not out,
  F.D. Stephenson 5 for 64)

Sussex 196 (K. Newell 63, H.A.G. Anthony 4 for 47) and 256
  for 5 (C.W.J. Athey 92, J.W. Hall 85)

Match drawn

Glamorgan 5 pts, Sussex 4 pts

at Bristol

Gloucestershire 389 for 3 dec. (A.J. Wright 193, G.D.
  Hodgson 148) and 187 for 4 dec. (R.I. Dawson 53 not out)

Nottinghamshire 300 for 8 dec. (K.P. Evans 78 not out,
  M.P. Dowman 63, G.F. Archer 62, J. Srinath 4 for 34) and
  142 (A.M. Smith 4 for 51)

Gloucestershire won by 134 runs

Gloucestershire 23 pts, Nottinghamshire 4 pts

at Canterbury

Kent 575 (M.R. Benson 192, N.R. Taylor 127, P.A. de Silva 57,
  M.M. Patel 56, A.R.K. Pierson 4 for 141)

Leicestershire 303 (W.J. Cronje 124, P.E. Robinson 60 not out,
  M.J. McCague 4 for 80) and 151 (S. Herzberg 5 for 33)

Kent won by an innings and 121 runs

Kent 24 pts, Leicestershire 5 pts

at Old Trafford

Warwickshire 262 (A.J. Moles 51, P.J. Martin 4 for 68) and 297
  (Wasim Khan 78, A.J. Moles 66, D.P. Ostler 50,
  P.J. Martin 4 for 51)

Tony Wright…

…and Dean Hodgson established a record opening stand for Gloucestershire in a championship match, 361 v. Nottinghamshire, 12 May. (Clive Brunskill/Allsport)

Surrey 652 for 9 dec. (M.A. Butcher 167, A.J. Stewart 155, A.J. Hollioake 83, G.P. Thorpe 62, G.J. Kersey 55)

Surrey won by an innings and 159 runs

Surrey 24 pts, Durham 3 pts

at Worcester

Worcestershire 193 (G.A. Hick 59, A.R.C. Fraser 4 for 40, M.A. Feltham 4 for 55) and 170 (T.M. Moody 90 not out, A.R.C. Fraser 4 for 52)

Middlesex 393 (J.C. Pooley 121, K.R. Brown 99, M.W. Gatting 70, P.J. Newport 5 for 83)

Middlesex won by an innings and 30 runs

Middlesex 24 pts, Worcestershire 4 pts

Lancashire 410 (N.H. Fairbrother 129, M. Watkinson 91, R.P. Davis 5 for 118) and 150 for 4 (J.P. Crawley 56 not out)

Lancashire won by 6 wickets

Lancashire 23 pts, Warwickshire 5 pts

at Northampton

Somerset 242 (G.D. Rose 84, S.C. Ecclestone 81) and 343 (M.E. Trescothick 151, A.N. Hayhurst 58 not out, S.C. Ecclestone 50, A.R. Kumble 4 for 87)

Northamptonshire 297 (K.M. Curran 96, J.N. Snape 54 not out) and 291 for 3 (A.J. Lamb 85 not out, T.C. Walton 71, R.J. Bailey 66 not out)

Northamptonshire won by 7 wickets

Northamptonshire 22 pts, Somerset 5 pts

at The Oval

Durham 269 (M. Saxelby 68, J.A. Daley 55, M.P. Bicknell 4 for 81) and 224

Pitches in Derbyshire have long had the reputation of being pleasure beaches for seam bowlers. One influential member of the county club asserted at the end of the 1994 season that Chris Adams, Derbyshire's leading run-scorer with 969 runs, would have passed 1,500 runs had he not had to play half his matches in his own county. The problem with such pitches is that they can favour the visitors as much as they favour Malcolm, Cork, DeFreitas and Warner. So it proved in the match against Yorkshire at Chesterfield which was over inside three days.

Barnett won the toss, asked Yorkshire to bat, and his pace quartet bowled them out for 177. The visitors lost Moxon with a broken thumb, and the only stand of substance in their innings was when White and Blakey put on 71 for the fourth wicket.

Derbyshire ended the day on 122 for 7, and they had also lost Cullinan with a cracked finger. The first day had seen 15 wickets fall and two men retire hurt. Rollins, too, had retired with a hamstring problem, but he had returned with a runner to be his side's top scorer with 38.

One of the batsmen still in overnight was Andrew Bairstow – like his father David, a wicket-keeper, but, unlike his father, playing *against* Yorkshire because of Krikken's illness. Bairstow acquitted himself well enough to score 16 – riches in this match, but the Derbyshire innings was over after just 32 balls on the second day. Yorkshire then plunged to 90 for 8 before rain ended play in early afternoon.

Moxon came in at number ten to help add 14 vital runs on the third morning. He was unbeaten on six, and Derbyshire needed 142 to win. Barnett was soon caught at second slip, but Adams hit Gough for 3 fours in succession before hitting the fourth ball uppishly to cover. Cork arrived to hit the next two balls for four so that the over had produced 20 runs and one wicket.

At 76 for 2, Derbyshire looked likely winners. Only 15 overs had been bowled, and Gough had been withdrawn.

Peter Hartley, 9 for 41, including the hat trick, Yorkshire v. Derbyshire, 12–15 May. (Alan Cozzi)

Hartley then had O'Gorman caught behind, and two balls later, he trapped DeFreitas leg before. Harrison was out in identical fashion first ball, and so Hartley was on a hat trick. Cork took a single off Robinson to bring him to face Hartley. He slashed hard at a delivery just outside off stump, and Byas took a spectacular catch at slip high to his right. Hartley had taken the first hat trick of his career and when he accounted for Bairstow in his next over, Derbyshire were 77 for 7.

Rollins offered defence while Warner thrashed. Malcolm, too, hit massively, and Cullinan bravely held an end, but Peter Hartley finished with career-best figures of 16.4–4–41–9, and Yorkshire won by seven runs.

There was nothing quite so spectacular at Swansea where Keith Newell and Robert Kirtley made their first-class debuts for Sussex, and only three overs, during which James was out, were possible on the first day. There were only 58 overs bowled on the second day, and Glamorgan advanced to 173 for 8, with a draw already looking inevitable.

Giddins finished with his best bowling figures for Sussex, and the game sprang to life on the Saturday when Hamesh Anthony returned his best bowling figures for Glamorgan. With a first-innings lead of 16, Glamorgan went for quick runs. They reached 115 for 2 in 28 overs by the Saturday evening.

Maynard and Croft scored 101 in 18 overs for the sixth wicket on the Monday morning, and Morris' declaration left Sussex 64 overs in which to score 287. Athey and Hall scored 165 for the first wicket, and although Wells was out for his second 'duck' of the match and Hall and Athey

departed within 22 balls of each other, Sussex needed only 51 from seven overs with five wickets standing. Sadly, they made no attempt to get the runs.

There was no play on the first day at Bristol, and on the second, Gloucestershire scored 389 for 3. This was based on an opening stand of 361 between Wright and Hodgson, a record for the county in the championship. Young and Nicholls scored 395 against Oxford University in 1962. Wright hit 4 sixes and 17 fours in the highest score of his career while Hodgson hit 15 fours. It was Hodgson who was the first to go, caught at long-off after 365 minutes at the crease. Wright fell to Pick three overs later.

Russell declared overnight, but Gloucestershire did not dominate the third day as they had the second. Dowman and Archer scored 123 for Nottinghamshire's second wicket, but, at 221 for 7, the visitors were in some trouble. Their saviour was Kevin Evans who added 67 with Andy Pick and enabled Robinson to declare 89 runs behind.

This declaration made a result possible. The home county hit 187 for 4 off 45 overs and left Nottinghamshire 54 overs in which to make 277. When Smith dismissed both openers in his first six overs, the Nottinghamshire task became difficult. Soon they were 66 for 6, and defeat seemed imminent. French and Evans offered stout resistance before Evans was leg before to Ball, who accounted for Pick in the same manner. Pennett showed fine concentration, but French was finally beaten by Ball. Afford and Pennett held out until Afford was leg before to Smith with 28 balls remaining. So Gloucestershire claimed their first championship win of the season.

Kent also enjoyed a first championship win of the season, beating Leicestershire inside three days. Ward was out for 0, but Benson and Taylor added 192, with Taylor surprising perhaps even himself by hitting a century before lunch. He was on 74 with only 13 minutes of the morning session remaining. The introduction of Cronje and a spate of bad balls gave Taylor the chance to hit 5 fours in 10 deliveries, and he strolled to his hundred before lunch. Aravinda de Silva scored some brisk runs, and Benson ended the day unbeaten on 159 out of his side's 397 for 4.

There was no respite for Leicestershire as Patel and McCague added 95 for the ninth wicket, and Kent assembled their highest total at Canterbury. McCague quickly shot out Briers and Boon, but Cronje stayed solid in the bitterly cold weather to reach his first championship century for Leicestershire, who closed on 227 for 4.

Unfortunately, Cronje added only four to his overnight score before falling to McCague, and although Robinson batted doggedly, Leicestershire were forced to follow on. McCague, who had a good match, soon disposed of Briers and Cronje, and with these two pillars removed, the visitors disintegrated as Patel and Herzberg found help in the pitch. Herzberg, born in Surrey, but an off-break bowler of experience with Worcestershire, Western Australia and Kent, captured five wickets on his debut for Kent.

The growing power of Lancashire, and their strength in depth, was clearly evident at Old Trafford where the reigning champions were brushed aside with unexpected ease. Choosing to bat first when they won the toss, Warwickshire moved uncertainly to 246 on a cold day.

They were without Donald, Munton and Reeve because of injury, and Ostler was limping with his knee cartilage problem. Knight and Piper were also absent, but this could not detract from the fact that the Lancashire attack looked sharp and varied, and the fielding was disciplined. Their command of the day was eroded in the last 13 overs, however, when Warwickshire captured the wickets of both Atherton and Crawley as 16 runs were scored.

It was not until Fairbrother was joined by Watkinson at the fall of the fourth wicket that Lancashire reasserted themselves. The pair added 136 to take the home county into the lead and to expose, too, the Achilles heel of the reigning champions: the lack of a top-class spinner. By the end of the day, Lancashire had scored 352 for 7 and had missed a fourth batting point by just nine runs.

Hegg and Martin struck out on the Saturday, and the first-innings lead of 148 was far more than Lancashire could have anticipated. Acting captain Moles and freshman Wasim Khan fought back splendidly with an opening stand of 168, but three wickets fell for 10 runs before Ostler and Davis took the score to 194 without any more mishaps.

In fact, their stand became worth 88 on the Monday, but the last seven wickets went down to Chapple and the impressive Martin for 31 runs. Lancashire romped to victory with 15 overs to spare.

Northamptonshire displaced Glamorgan and Warwickshire at the top of the table with a fine win over Somerset. Somerset won the toss, but their decision to bat looked flawed when, against Hughes, Taylor and Curran, they plunged to 68 for 6. Rose and Ecclestone came together to add 153, with the left-handed Simon Ecclestone, the former Oxford blue, hitting the highest score of his career. Warren, pressed into service as a wicket-keeper (a position he was to occupy for the rest of the season), Fordham and Walton were all out before the close which left the game balanced – Northamptonshire 75 for 3.

Lamb was out without addition to the score on the Friday, but a sixth-wicket stand of 92 between Curran and Capel suggested a Northamptonshire recovery, and this was confirmed by Jeremy Snape who hit his second fifty in succession for the county and batted with a confidence and zest not displayed by his colleagues. Somerset ended the day on 123 for 3, and 83 of those runs had come from Trescothick.

There was considerable vitality in the England under-19 captain's 151 off 186 balls. It was his third and highest first-class century, and it contained a six and 25 fours. It augured well for the future, but then so did the performances of Lathwell, his opening partner, a couple of seasons ago.

The Somerset innings was a stop-and-go affair, the fifties of Hayhurst and Ecclestone being punctuated by the 'ducks' of Rose and Turner, and when Kumble brought the innings to a sudden end Northamptonshire had 54 overs and a day in which to score 289 to win. By the close, with Walton having raced to 71 off 83 balls, Northamptonshire were only 83 runs short of victory with seven wickets standing. Walton had hit the highest score of his career, and he and Bailey added 121 for the third wicket at more than five runs an over.

To enable Somerset to travel to Ireland for their Benson and Hedges Cup match, play began at 10.00 am on the fourth morning, and the game was all over by 10.45. The last 79 runs of the home side's score came in 8.4 overs, and Lamb finished the match by hitting Mushtaq Ahmed for 2 sixes.

The uncertainty of Durham cricket continued. They won the toss at The Oval, lost four wickets for 45 and were restored by Daley and Saxelby who added 83. Then three wickets fell for 38 before Boiling and Ligertwood stayed 29 overs for 44. Wicket-keeper Ligertwood, once briefly with Surrey, was replacing the injured Scott, and he batted into the second day to make 40.

The tedium of the Durham innings was put to shame by Surrey who rushed to 288 for 1 off 77 overs on the second day. Stewart and Darren Bicknell started with a partnership of 103. Simon Brown conceded 102 runs from 17 overs on the Friday and did not reappear on the Saturday because of tendon trouble. Depleted and dejected, Durham saw century stand follow century stand. Mark Butcher hit a career-best 167 and shared a second-wicket stand of 193 with Stewart, and Kersey hit a maiden first-class fifty. There were 25 fours and 2 sixes in Butcher's innings, while Stewart hit 25 fours and 1 six before becoming off-break bowler Jason Searle's first victim in first-class cricket.

Durham lost Roseberry and Morris for 56 runs before the close, and wickets fell regularly on the Monday. Kersey added five catches to his fifty, and the game was over just after tea. Had it been a boxing match, the referee would have stopped the contest much earlier.

Only 27.4 overs were possible on the first day at Worcester where Hick scored 50 of the home side's 78 runs. Having been put in, Worcestershire were 18 for 3 at one time. Feltham and Fraser continued successfully on the second day, and by the close of play, Middlesex had a 37-run lead for the loss of four wickets. Gatting made 70 out of an opening stand of 120 before being bowled by Richard Illingworth as he tried to cut. Jason Pooley reached his maiden first-class century before the close after Ramprakash, Carr and Weekes had gone cheaply.

When Pooley was fifth out, having added 120 with Brown, Middlesex led by 82. Nash and Feltham were dismissed by Newport, but the evergreen Emburey aided Brown in a stand worth 74. Brown deserved a century, but Newport, who bowled manfully, produced a splendid outswinger when he was on 99 and Rhodes took the catch.

Not only did Worcestershire face a deficit of 200 – much beyond expectations, but they had to bat a second time without the assistance of Hick who had damaged a finger in catching Carr on the Friday. By the close, they were 161 for 7, Moody unbeaten on 82, and the match was over 30 minutes into the fourth day.

The Worcester pitch was reported by the umpires, and Worcestershire were cautioned by the TCCB pitches committee.

18, 19, 20 and 22 May at Chester-le-Street (Riverside)

Warwickshire 424 (A.J. Moles 90, N.V. Knight 89, R.G. Twose 51, S.J.E. Brown 5 for 123) and 145 for 8 dec. (S.J.E. Brown 6 for 69)

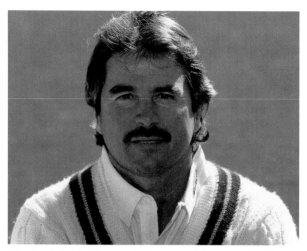

Allan Lamb, 166 for Northamptonshire against Surrey and inspiring captaincy throughout the season. (Mike Hewitt/Allsport)

Durham 313 (J.E. Morris 128, W. Larkins 58) and 145 (M. Prabhakar 66)

Warwickshire won by 111 runs

Warwickshire 22 pts, Durham 5 pts

at Southampton

Kent 207 and 288 (N.R. Taylor 87, M.J. Walker 53, S.D. Udal 5 for 81)

Hampshire 137 (M.J. McCague 5 for 47) and 319 (A.N. Aymes 60 not out)

Kent won by 39 runs

Kent 21 pts, Hampshire 4 pts

at Leicester

Derbyshire 256 (J.E. Owen 50, G.J. Parsons 4 for 55) and 173 (K.J. Barnett 71, C.M. Wells 61, A.D. Mullally 6 for 50)

Leicestershire 357 (J.J. Whitaker 120, P. Whitticase 51, D.G. Cork 5 for 74) and 73 for 1

Leicestershire won by 9 wickets

Leicestershire 24 pts, Derbyshire 6 pts

at Lord's

Lancashire 375 (G.D. Lloyd 75, J.P. Crawley 55, M.A. Atherton 54)

Middlesex 88 (Wasim Akram 6 for 35) and 112

Lancashire won by an innings and 175 runs

Lancashire 24 pts, Middlesex 4 pts

at Northampton

Northamptonshire 403 (A.J. Lamb 166, K.M. Curran 117, A.C.S. Pigott 6 for 91) and 59 (A.C.S. Pigott 5 for 20, J.E. Benjamin 5 for 37)

Surrey 263 (G.J. Kersey 64, M.A. Butcher 52, A.R. Kumble 4 for 47) and 190 (A.J. Hollioake 54 not out, D.J. Capel 4 for 62)

Northamptonshire won by 9 runs

Northamptonshire 24 pts, Surrey 5 pts

at Hove

Sussex 326 (P. Moores 86, K. Greenfield 51, M.C. Ilott 7 for 82) and 390 (K. Greenfield 121, P. Moores 94, A.P. Wells 69, M.E. Waugh 4 for 76)

Essex 185 (R.C. Irani 57 not out, E.S.H. Giddins 5 for 48) and 253 (N. Hussain 60, I.D.K. Salisbury 7 for 72)

Sussex won by 278 runs

Sussex 23 pts, Essex 4 pts

at Bradford

Glamorgan 135 and 212 (P.A. Cottey 51, P.J. Hartley 6 for 64)

Yorkshire 189 (M.P. Vaughan 74, S.L. Watkin 6 for 55) and 161 for 3 (D. Byas 57, M.G. Bevan 51 not out)

Yorkshire won by 7 wickets

Yorkshire 20 pts, Glamorgan 4 pts

A dream was realised when Durham's magnificent new cricket ground at Chester-le-Street staged its first Britannic Assurance County Championship match. More than £4 million has already been spent on the Riverside ground, and another £9 million is due to be spent to make this the most impressive of grounds. Where once was a field on the banks of the Wear, there now stands the first of the four buildings that will surround the ground. This first module is a splendid pavilion complex with luxurious changing rooms, hospitality suites and administrative offices as well as members' areas. This complex looks across the river towards Lumley Castle. There is pride and joy in an achievement which has been realised out of a genuine love of the game and out of the energy and goodwill of many people in various walks of life.

The weather did not do the occasion justice. There had been rain earlier in the week, and now there was a chilling wind. Warwickshire inevitably spoiled Durham's party by winning the toss and batting. Moles and Knight were not separated until 3.37 when Knight top-edged Wood to Roseberry at second slip. The score was 172. Moles was also dismissed before the close, but Warwickshire were secure on 240 from 87 overs.

They lost Penney, Ostler and Reeve in quick succession on the second morning, but Warwickshire have considerable resilience, and their late-order took them to 424. They were well short of maximum batting points, scoring at not much more than two an over, but their total gave every indication that they would notch up another victory. Roseberry and Larkins were gone before the close, and although Durham had reached 105, there were already shades of doubt in the batting.

It was fitting that it should be a Durham batsman who scored the first century on the Riverside ground. On a

Leicestershire's Adrian Pierson bowled well and batted doggedly to earn his county cap. (David Munden/Sportsline)

pitch which displayed irregular bounce, John Morris batted for over 4½ hours and reached his century off 200 balls. It was not one of the ex-Derbyshire batsman's more spectacular innings, but it was worthy of the occasion and infinitely valuable. Daley helped Morris to add 82 for the third wicket, and Prabhakar and Morris scored 78 for the fifth before the last five wickets went down for 31 runs.

Durham finished within 111 runs of Warwickshire's score and Brown captured four wickets in the evening session to become the first Durham bowler to reach 200 wickets. Warwickshire tottered to 76 for 4, but their lead looked significant on a pitch that was not getting any easier.

The game at the Riverside ground was, in fact, one of only two to last into a fourth day. Reeve hit briskly and declared to give Durham 10 minutes' batting before lunch. The home side were already handicapped in that Wood had been unable to bowl because of a strained back, and now Daley was out of action with a broken hand. Larkins was leg before first ball, and Roseberry was out in the next over. Saxelby went quickly, but Morris and Prabhakar added 63. It was a bright interlude in an innings of gloom.

The other beam of brightness was that Simon Brown's match figures of 11 for 192 were the best figures recorded for Durham since the county had gained first-class status.

The match at Southampton lasted just three days, and it was another tale of woe for Hampshire. Kent chose to bat first, but they were bowled out for 207, of which 35 had come from a last-wicket stand by McCague – top scorer with 38 not out – and Igglesden. Hampshire ended the day on 115 for 4 and could be content with what they had achieved.

They could be less happy with their second day's work when they lost their last six wickets for 15 runs. McCague was the principal destroyer, and wicket-keeper Simon Willis took three catches on his championship debut.

Kent were batting again with more than an hour to go before lunch on the second day, a day on which 16 wickets were to fall. Benson and Taylor offered substance and sanity after Ward's early dismissal, caught behind off Bovill. They took the score to 80 at which point Benson and de Silva fell to Stephenson. Walker joined Taylor in a stand worth 115. Neil Taylor batted with a great sense of purpose and with unusual freedom, hitting 2 sixes and 15 fours. There were useful contributions late in the day, and Kent were out for 288, which meant that Hampshire had more than two days in which to score 359 to win. Few gave them even a remote chance, but Terry and Morris made 47 of the necessary runs before the close.

Their opening stand became worth 85 on the Saturday, and both were out to Igglesden who was making one of his all-too-rare appearances. Smith and Stephenson were out soon after lunch, and Hampshire had lost their four main batsmen and were still 230 short of victory. Nicholas and White gave resistance, but the Hampshire captain was hit on the head by McCague, and when he returned White, Udal and Streak had left the scene. With Aymes, Nicholas added 31 before being taken at slip off Patel. Aymes survived and reached a half-century off 130 balls. He and Connor advanced the score from 281 to 319, but, in the last over of the day, Headley had Connor leg before and bowled Bovill. Hampshire had come closer than had been expected, but they had suffered yet another defeat.

For the third time in succession, a county match involving Leicestershire finished in three days. Leicestershire asked Derbyshire to bat first and captured the first five wickets for 99 runs. Owen and DeFreitas added 41, and John Owen hit his first fifty in first-class cricket, but the real saviours for the visitors were the last pair – Warner, 43, and Malcolm, 25 not out – who added 58.

With Briers, Maddy and Cronje falling for 73 before the close, it could be said that this last-wicket stand had tilted the game marginally in Derbyshire's favour.

Unbeaten with five on the Thursday, James Whitaker reached the 28th hundred of his career on the second day. His one Test appearance now nearly nine years in the past, Whitaker has become one of cricket's forgotten men, but he has served Leicestershire well and is destined to captain them. He did an admirable job when deputising for Briers, and responsibility seems to lift his batting. He dominated a fourth-wicket stand of 102 with Smith which put the home county back in control.

Whitticase bravely helped Whitaker to add 98 for the seventh wicket, but the effort took its toll of the wicket-keeper, returning after the facial damage he sustained at Chelmsford, and he was forced to leave the field later when feeling faint.

Derbyshire trailed by 101 on the first innings, but they were reprieved when both Barnett and Adams were dropped in the first two overs of their second innings. Parsons dismissed Adams and O'Gorman within the space of three balls, but Barnett and Wells were sound, and the visitors closed on 121 for 2.

Wells reached his first first-class fifty for Derbyshire at the age of 35, but when Barnett was out at 134 it was the first of eight wickets to fall for 39 runs, six of them to Mullally.

This burst left Leicestershire needing only 73 for victory, which was achieved for the loss of Maddy shortly before tea on the third day.

Middlesex suffered humiliation at Lord's. Gatting read that the pitch was conducive to seam rather than to spin and omitted Tufnell and brought in Johnson. Nash had Gallian caught for 0, but for the rest of the day there was consistent application from the Lancashire batsmen, and a closing score of 338 for 9 was highly satisfactory.

It became even more pleasing on the second day when Chapple and Yates, a pest of a last pair for opponents, took their partnership to 45 and won a fourth batting point. Only 52.5 overs could be bowled in the day, but they were enough to give Lancashire the chance to take an iron grip on the match. Wasim Akram bowled a full length, took four wickets, and Middlesex staggered to 78 for 7.

There was no respite on the third morning when Wasim removed Brown and Emburey, and Middlesex lost their last three wickets for 10 runs. Soon they were batting again and falling again – Wasim, Martin and Chapple each claimed three wickets in the second innings – and the match was over shortly after three o'clock.

Surrey, too, were beaten in three days in an extraordinary match at Northampton. There was nothing too unusual about the start of the match. Northamptonshire, who were giving a first-class debut to slow left-arm bowler Craig Atkins, born in Australia, won the toss, batted and lost four wickets for 101 runs. Curran then joined Lamb, and by the end of the day, the score was 363, and both batsmen had reached centuries.

The pair were separated on the second morning when their stand had become worth 282. Lamb hit 23 fours and Curran 18, and they batted with such command and purpose as to mock what was to follow. Curran was given an early life, but thereafter there were few blemishes. The last six Northamptonshire wickets, however, went down for 20 runs in the first hour of the second day.

Surrey lost Stewart and Darren Bicknell with only 14 scored. Thorpe and Mark Butcher added 72. Craig Atkins claimed his first first-class wicket when he had Butcher taken at square-leg, but it was Kumble who totally undermined the Surrey innings. In 30 overs of brisk leg-spin, he took 4 for 47. Thorpe was taken at short-leg, Holioake was frustrated into heaving at a straight ball and was leg before, and Kersey, having hit a career-best, was beaten by the snap of the flipper and was also leg before. Pigott was Kumble's fourth victim, and Surrey just managed to drag themselves past the point where they would have had to follow on.

Nine wickets were down on the second evening, and only one was scored before Kenlock fell to Taylor on the third morning. It was the first of 11 wickets to fall before lunch.

Northamptonshire were bowled out by Benjamin and Pigott in 23.3 overs. On a dry, dusty pitch, both bowlers took five wickets. They bowled well, maintaining a full length and a good line. Most of the uncertainty was in the

minds of the batsmen, as Lamb epitomised when he needlessly nudged Benjamin to second slip. Bailey alone reached double figures – he was bowled by Pigott for 13 – but the crucial stand, as it transpired, was between Atkins, 8 not out, and Taylor, 6. They added 16 for the last wicket.

The home county had anticipated an innings victory on the Friday evening, but half a day later they faced defeat as Surrey, in search of 200 for victory, were given a romping start by Darren Bicknell and Alec Stewart. In 10 overs, they overtook their hosts' second-innings score, thanks mainly to some dreadfully erratic bowling from Curran. Bicknell was the more secure of the Surrey openers, and it was no real surprise when Stewart chased a ball from Capel and was caught at second slip. Surrey were now 66 for 1, and when Kumble was introduced into the attack, perhaps somewhat belatedly, the climate of the game changed.

With his first ball, he had Bicknell caught bat-and-pad, and he quickly had Thorpe plumb leg before. Capel had found his rhythm, and Surrey moved from 80 for 1 to 83 for 5. Holioake looked confident and capable, and when Pigott stayed with him to add 37 for the seventh wicket Surrey's hopes leapt.

When the ninth wicket fell Surrey were 11 short of victory, and Holioake was faced with the problem of trying to shield Kenlock from the bowling or taking every run that was available. He chose the latter course, and Kenlock was exposed to five balls from Kumble. The young man's off bail was sent spinning by a master craftsman whose second-innings figures were 21.5–5–29–3.

Capel, too, was a hero, and his return to form and fitness was a major reason for Northamptonshire heading the county championship.

A thought should be spared for Tony Pigott: 11 for 111 in the match and brave contributions with the bat, and still he finished on the losing side.

The game at Hove, like that at Chester-le-Street, did last four days, although there were only 45 minutes needed to finish the game on the last morning.

Having arrived from Bermuda, Mark Waugh was rushed into action for Essex, a county in need of a lift in spirits. Wells won the toss, and Sussex batted on a splendid pitch, but the first honours went to Essex and to Mark Ilott. The left-arm pace bowler captured three wickets as Sussex slipped to 82 for 4. Greenfield then joined Moores in a stand worth 161. Moores has always flourished against Essex, and this time he was aided and abetted by Prichard's obsession with seam and reluctance to turn to spin. When, belatedly, he used Such, the off-spinner dismissed both Greenfield and Moores. Another burst from Ilott reduced Sussex to 262 for 8, but Ed Giddins hit the highest score of his career (34), and, aided by 54 extras, the home side climbed to 326. Giddins' previous highest score had also been made against Essex who could be well satisfied at having dismissed Sussex for under 450 on such a pitch. The fine work that the bowlers had done, however, was eroded by the batsmen. Gooch was leg before to Lewry for one, Prichard was caught off Stephenson for four, and Waugh padded up to Giddins in the last over of the day, and Essex were 50 for 3.

There was no improvement on the second day. Irani batted forcefully; others surrendered tamely to the enthusiastic Giddins. This was a wretched display by a side not at ease with itself.

Ilott and Irani again made early inroads before Wells hit 69 off 97 balls. Sussex ended the day on 169 for 4, having been 49 for 3, and they were already 310 ahead of Essex.

There was more agony for Essex on the third day. Childs was again grossly underbowled as Moores and Greenfield extended their second fifth-wicket stand of the match to 148. Childs trapped Moores leg before when the wicket-keeper was six short of his century, but Greenfield went on to his highest championship score, and his innings included 17 fours. He was caught behind off Waugh who took four of the last five wickets.

Essex could not have contemplated the target of 532, for they were soon gasping for survival. Prichard was caught by Salisbury off Stephenson, and when Salisbury himself came into the attack wickets began to tumble. He bowled Gooch, trapped Waugh leg before and had Hussain and Irani caught. Giddins dismissed Lewis for 0, and Essex ended the day on 202 for 6.

Less than 50 minutes was needed on the Monday to put them out of their misery, with leg-spinner Ian Salisbury capturing three more wickets.

Neither side could manage 200 in their first innings at Bradford where the pitch was not condemned but was deemed as being unsuitable for a four-day game. Fourteen wickets fell on the opening day. Byas, leading Yorkshire in the absence of Moxon, asked Glamorgan to bat when he won the toss, and his seam bowlers enjoyed themselves accordingly.

Yorkshire gave a first-class debut to McGrath, but he was out for 0. Vaughan and Byas added 92, and Vaughan played one of his best innings so that by the close Yorkshire led by seven runs with six wickets in hand.

In fact, Yorkshire's last eight wickets went down for 47 runs, but a lead of 54 on the first innings was a considerable achievement in the context of this match. Watkin was Yorkshire's tormentor, and Peter Hartley, very much in form, was the bowler who most disturbed Glamorgan.

The Welshmen showed considerable fight, and lost just two wickets before clearing the arrears. Three-quarters of an hour after lunch, however, they had lost six wickets and led by only 47. Cottey batted with courage and much honour through 37 difficult overs, and he was well served by Anthony and Lefebvre. The last four Glamorgan wickets realised 111 runs – riches indeed – and Yorkshire needed 159 to win.

Vaughan was leg before to a Watkin shooter, but McGrath, showing an unexpected maturity for his 19 years, played an invaluable innings of 36. Yorkshire began the Saturday needing 87 more runs, and although Byas was stumped off Croft, the match was won five minutes before lunch.

24, 25, 26 and 27 May at Tunbridge Wells

Kent 369 (P.A. de Silva 135, T.R. Ward 98, M.A. Ealham 58, H.A.G. Anthony 5 for 70) and 253 for 8 dec. (M.A. Ealham 72, N.M. Kendrick 4 for 70)

Glamorgan 352 for 8 dec. (A. Dale 133, H. Morris 114) and 269

An outstanding season for the Gloucestershire left-arm pace bowler Mike Smith, and a place in the England 'A' side to tour Pakistan. (Tom Morris)

for 8 (P.A. Cottey 85, M.P. Maynard 73, M.M. Patel 5 for 99)

Match drawn

Glamorgan 8 pts, Kent 7 pts

25, 26, 27 and 29 May at Chelmsford

Middlesex 473 (M.W. Gatting 94, J.E. Emburey 87, T.A. Radford 69, D.J. Nash 67, K.R. Brown 57) and 25 for 0

Essex 207 (R.C. Irani 69, J.E. Emburey 4 for 53) and 290 (R.C. Irani 82, P.J. Prichard 69, J.E. Emburey 4 for 71)

Middlesex won by 10 wickets

Middlesex 24 pts, Essex 3 pts

at Gloucester

Worcestershire 172 (J. Srinath 4 for 35, A.M. Smith 4 for 68) and 130 (A.M. Smith 6 for 58)

Gloucestershire 375 (R.I. Dawson 101, R.C. Russell 56, A. Symonds 52, N.V. Radford 5 for 45)

Gloucestershire won by an innings and 73 runs

Gloucestershire 24 pts, Worcestershire 4 pts

at Portsmouth

Hampshire 534 (V.P. Terry 170, R.A. Smith 120, A.N. Aymes 60)

Sussex 196 (J.P. Stephenson 4 for 45) and 232 (H.H. Streak 4 for 81)

Hampshire won by an innings and 106 runs

Hampshire 24 pts, Sussex 1 pt

at Liverpool

Lancashire 309 (S.P. Titchard 57, N.J. Speak 50, C.L. Cairns 5 for 64) and 238 for 8 dec. (S.P. Titchard 81, J.E.R. Gallian 52, J.E. Hindson 5 for 71)

Nottinghamshire 292 (R.T. Robinson 136, G.F. Archer 50) and 172 for 8 (R.T. Robinson 63)

Match drawn

Lancashire 7 pts, Nottinghamshire 6 pts

at Leicester

Leicestershire 380 (J.J. Whitaker 92, G.J. Parsons 73, V.J. Wells 58, M. Prabhakar 7 for 65)

Durham 138 (A.R.K. Pierson 5 for 48) and 151

Leicestershire won by an innings and 91 runs

Leicestershire 24 pts, Durham 3 pts

at Edgbaston

Somerset 495 (P.D. Bowler 176, P.C.L. Holloway 61) and 119 for 4 dec.

Warwickshire 314 for 4 dec. (T.L. Penney 101 not out, Wasim Khan 89, N.V. Knight 58) and 304 for 7 (A.J. Moles 131)

Warwickshire won by 3 wickets

Warwickshire 20 pts, Somerset 4 pts

at Sheffield

Yorkshire 250 (C. White 110, A.R. Kumble 4 for 63) and 252 (D. Byas 88, M.G. Bevan 50, A.R. Kumble 4 for 63)

Northamptonshire 357 (R.J. Bailey 111, D.J. Capel 72, S.D. Milburn 4 for 68) and 146 for 3

Northamptonshire won by 7 wickets

Northamptonshire 23 pts, Yorkshire 5 pts

The beautiful ground at Tunbridge Wells was the venue for Kent's game against Glamorgan which started on the Wednesday. Sadly, the weather was not as kind as the Nevill Ground deserved, and only 53 overs could be bowled on the first day when Kent scored 164 for 3. Ward scored 98 of these runs, but he had been dropped by Maynard at second slip off Watkin when he had scored nine. From that point, he played fluently, and his 50 came out of 66 for the loss of Benson. Kent also lost Taylor who was forced to retire hurt when a ball from Thomas broke a knuckle. Ward was run out when he hesitated over a single to mid-on and was beaten by Thomas' throw to the bowler.

Well as Ward had batted, his innings could not compare with that played by Aravinda de Silva on the second day. The Sri Lankan hit 23 fours in a delightful display of wristy shots and dancing feet. He and Ealham added 151 for the fourth wicket in 49 overs, but Kent lost their last six

A prolific scorer for Somerset – Richard Harden. (Paul Sturgess/ Sportsline)

wickets for 55 runs. Morris and Dale scored 155 off 43 overs before the close to seize the initiative for Glamorgan.

Both batsmen hit centuries and their opening partnership became worth 238. The rest of the side then pressed for quick runs, and maximum batting points came in 103.3 overs. Morris, who hit a six and 11 fours, declared as soon as the fourth point was won, and, by the close, Glamorgan had captured five Kent wickets for 133. As Taylor would be unable to bat, the visitors were very much in charge.

The remaining Kent wickets proved obdurate on the last day. Ealham, batting at number three, faced 170 balls for his 72, and Marsh, McCague and Headley all offered resistance. Glamorgan were set a target of 271 from what turned out to be 50 overs. A fourth-wicket stand of 89 off 14 overs between Maynard and Cottey raised their hopes, and 124 were needed from the last 20 overs. This was reduced to 22 off the last three in spite of Patel's teasing left-arm spin. Metson was run out off the last ball of the match as he ran for a bye that would have tied the scores.

Middlesex won the toss at Chelmsford and gave Essex another miserable day. Pooley was caught at slip off Waugh, and Gatting and Radford then added 146 for the second wicket. Radford, playing in his first championship match, hit 8 fours before being splendidly caught at backward point by Such. It was the off-spinner who beat Gatting through the air and bowled him when the Middlesex captain was six short of his century. There was a tranquillity about the proceedings as the visitors ended the day on 329 for 6, but the following day, Nash and Emburey extended their seventh-wicket stand to 124, with Nash hitting his highest score for Middlesex.

Essex were handicapped by the loss of Ilott with a groin strain and by their own ineptitude in the field. Tufnell and Emburey offered the ultimate gesture of contempt by adding 56 for the last wicket.

Gooch was soon bowled by Nash, and Waugh by Johnson. At 135 for 6 at the end of the second day, Essex were sinking fast. Irani hit a brave 69 and led a ninth-wicket stand of 54 with Cousins. It could not save the follow-on, and Irani was soon batting again as Essex slipped to 119 for 5. He hit his second fifty of the day, and his partnership with Ilott, who batted with a runner, went into the final day and realised 93 for the seventh wicket. Ilott was caught off Tufnell, and Emburey, bowling with the new ball, took the last three wickets – one of which was Irani's – in 11 deliveries.

The game at Gloucester ended in three days. Curtis chose to bat when he won the toss but, apart from his own 44, and 34 from Rhodes, the Worcestershire batsmen offered little against the high-quality seam attack of Srinath and Smith, ably supported by Alleyne. Srinath had proved to be an excellent investment as an overseas bowler. He had shown total commitment and had revealed that he was a new-ball expert who will test England severely in 1996. Mike Smith's bowling had advanced dramatically, with control now allied to pace and movement. There was a new-found spirit in the Gloucestershire side, and they ended the day 50 runs behind with eight wickets standing.

They tightened their grip on the match on the second morning. Robert Dawson hit his first championship century, an innings which included a six and 16 fours, and provided the backbone of the Gloucestershire innings after Lampitt had sent back Hodgson and Alleyne early in the day. Lampitt was to run into trouble later, and umpire Holder ruled that he had to be removed from the attack for persistently running on the pitch.

Symonds and Russell gave late impetus to the innings so that the home county took a lead of 203. Worcestershire's plight grew worse as they lost three for 49 before the close.

The match was over before lunch on the third day. Smith produced a career-best bowling performance and captured 10 wickets in a match for the first time.

Hampshire gained their first batting points of the season and their first win of the season in the championship, a victory that came, like that at Gloucester, in three days. John Stephenson's run of poor form with the bat continued, and Hampshire were 70 for 2. By the end of the day, they were 356 for 3, with Paul Terry and Robin Smith having shared a third-wicket partnership of 259. Both played most accomplished innings on a pitch which was not easy initially. Terry hit a six and 18 fours, and Smith hit 15 fours.

With later batsmen enjoying some slogging, Hampshire moved to 534 from 162.4 overs, and Stephenson, Streak and Bovill then reduced Sussex to 142 for 7 before the close.

The game followed a predictable pattern on the third day. An eighth-wicket stand of 68 between Salisbury, captaining Sussex for the first time, and Jarvis when the visitors followed on, was the only hindrance to Hampshire's progress.

Lancashire's strength was reduced because of England's calls for the Texaco Trophy but, following the early departure of Gallian, Titchard and Crawley added 90. Cairns, who had been unable to bowl in recent matches because of injury, dismissed them both in successive overs and started a decline which threatened to become an avalanche until Speak and Wasim put on 79 for the sixth wicket. They were both out before the close of play, and Lancashire tottered on 277 for 8.

Hegg and Chapple wrestled another batting point, but the pitch was no help to bowlers if batsmen applied themselves diligently. Such a situation was ideal for Tim Robinson who reached the 53rd century of his career off 209 balls. Lancashire rued a costly miss, for the Nottinghamshire captain was dropped at short-leg off Wasim Akram when 29. Wasim had bowled Dowman with the second ball of the innings. Archer gave Robinson good support in a second-wicket stand of 117, but thereafter the innings faded away to 244 for 5 at the close.

There was no resurgence on a third day which was reduced by rain and on which Titchard and Gallian scored 110 from 35.4 overs. This partnership lasted six runs into the last day when Lancashire plundered quick runs and set the visitors a target of 256 in 61 overs, which was generous. Dowman again went cheaply, but Wileman, in his first championship match, and Robinson put on 102. With 20 overs remaining and eight wickets in hand, Nottinghamshire needed 145, but the dismissal of Wileman, Johnson and Cairns soon sent them onto the defensive. They have not been a county noted for adventure since the departure of Clive Rice.

Leicestershire had their fourth three-day finish of the season. James Whitaker hit 92 off 122 balls on the first morning, leading his side from the uncertainty of 15 for 2. He and Briers added 106, and Whitaker's positive response to a difficult situation proved infectious. Millns and Parsons scored 98 in 36 overs for the eighth wicket, and Leicestershire closed on 349 for 8. Seven of those wickets had gone to Prabhakar who produced not only the best bowling figures of his career, but also the best figures by a Durham bowler in first-class cricket.

Durham reached 58 before losing their first wicket on the second morning. It was the first of 10 that fell for 80 runs. Five of the wickets went to off-spinner Adrian Pierson who was awarded his county cap.

Following on, Durham were 100 for 4 at the close, and the game was all over half an hour before lunch on the third day. Gordon Parsons took six catches in the match to add to his hard-hit 73.

Perhaps Warwickshire's greatest asset in winning three trophies in 1994 was their determination to go for victory in every match whatever the odds. Bowler led Somerset for the first time as Hayhurst was absent injured, and he batted for most of the first day, scoring an unbeaten 110 out of 298 for 4 after his side had been put in to bat.

Bowler and Holloway, who had made his highest score for Somerset against the county for whom he once scored a century, put on 187 in 80 overs for the fifth wicket, and Somerset crawled to 495 at less than three an over. Warwickshire hit 96 for 1 before the end of the second day, and the match seemed certain to be drawn. Bowler faced 419 balls for his 176 and hit 21 fours.

Reeve, who has his faults and his detractors, is not one to accept a draw without a fight, and, on the third day, after a first session which produced only 59 runs, 144 came in the afternoon. Penney reached his first hundred of the season, and there was more than a hint of collusion when Reeve declared 181 in arrears and, having sent Somerset spinning to 19 for 3, 'gifted' them 47 runs by bowling Moles and Wasim Khan at the end of the day.

The outcome of such negotiations meant that Warwickshire were set a target of 301 in 82 overs. Batting with a runner for most of his innings, Moles hit 20 fours and was not out until the scores were level. He gained sound support all the way through the innings, especially from Brown who hit 36 off 27 balls. Brown and Moles added 81 from 11 overs for the seventh wicket. Warwickshire won with seven balls to spare, but the win may not have pleased all of those fighting to dethrone the champions.

Reappearing for Northamptonshire after an absence of nine years in Somerset, Neil Mallender took the wicket of Byas on an opening day in Sheffield on which Yorkshire made 229 for 7 after being put in, Craig White scored a century, and rain ended play 80 minutes early. At 167 for 4, Yorkshire had looked in a good position, but three wickets for 15 runs either side of tea changed the perspective.

The pitch offered help to the seamers, but Bailey battled splendidly for Northamptonshire, taking his side to 262 for 5 at the close on the second day. He and Capel scored 112 for the fifth wicket, with Bailey offering solid defence while Capel launched an attack on the bowling which brought 72 off 97 balls, with 14 fours and a six.

Lamb did not bat until the second day because he was suffering from a ricked neck, but he made an invaluable 30, and Bailey completed his patient, most worthy century. Trailing by 107, Yorkshire kept well in touch when Byas and Bevan were sharing a third-wicket partnership of 93, but three wickets for two runs in five balls by Kumble changed the game. Yorkshire ended the day on 174 for 6.

Parker helped Bevan to add 71, and then the last four wickets fell for seven runs. The innings ended at lunch on the last day, but three hours were lost to rain, and Northamptonshire had to make 146 in 23 overs.

Capel and Fordham scored 41 in the first seven overs, but both batsmen were out within 10 balls of each other. With the boundary ringed with fielders, Lamb and Curran scored brisk runs, but 73 were needed from the last 10 overs. From the next five overs, the pair took 46. Lamb, having scorned his ricked neck, now pulled a hamstring taking the run that meant that 28 were needed from 31 balls. Batting with a runner, he was out next over, having hit 49 off 39 balls.

As the tension mounted, Bevan was reprimanded after remarks the Australian made to a colleague following an overthrow. Curran was dropped in the deep by Vaughan and responded by hitting a six which meant that six runs were needed from 11 balls. Two were needed from the last two balls, bowled by Mark Robinson. Robinson bowled a

bouncer, and the batsmen took a bye to the keeper. He bowled another bouncer with the same result, and Northamptonshire were still top of the table with victory off the last ball of an astounding match.

1, 2, 3 and 5 June *at Chester-le-Street (Riverside)*

Kent 272 for 9 dec. (P.A. de Silva 83) and 0 for 0 dec.

Durham 72 for 0 dec. and 85 (D.W. Headley 5 for 32)

Kent won by 115 runs

Kent 18 pts, Durham 4 pts

at Cardiff

Hampshire 324 (M.C.J. Nicholas 75, J.P. Stephenson 65, H.A.G. Anthony 6 for 77) and 55 for 2

Glamorgan 174 and 204 (P.A. Cottey 52)

Hampshire won by 8 wickets

Hampshire 23 pts, Glamorgan 4 pts

at Lord's

Derbyshire 267 (C.M. Wells 81, A.S. Rollins 61, A.R.C. Fraser 4 for 39) and 209 for 3 dec. (W.A. Dessaur 84 not out, A.S. Rollins 72)

Middlesex 174 (J.C. Pooley 85 not out) and 130 for 4 (M.R. Ramprakash 75 not out)

Match drawn

Derbyshire 6 pts, Middlesex 4 pts

at Trent Bridge

Nottinghamshire 314 (R.T. Robinson 101, W.M. Noon 63 not out, C.L. Cairns 50, J.H. Childs 4 for 74) and 274 for 6 dec. (M.P. Dowman 73, C.L. Cairns 68 not out, P.M. Such 4 for 87)

Essex 301 (P.J. Prichard 109, J.E. Hindson 5 for 92) and 271 (N. Hussain 106, J.E. Hindson 5 for 92)

Nottinghamshire won by 16 runs

Nottinghamshire 23 pts, Essex 7 pts

at Taunton

Yorkshire 413 (A. McGrath 84, D. Byas 66, Mushtaq Ahmed 5 for 126) and 197 for 6 dec. (M.G. Bevan 79, Mushtaq Ahmed 4 for 86)

Somerset 351 for 5 dec. (R.J. Harden 129 not out, M.N. Lathwell 61) and 261 for 3 (M.N. Lathwell 111, R.J. Harden 80 not out)

Somerset won by 7 wickets

Somerset 22 pts, Yorkshire 6 pts

at Hove

Gloucestershire 202 (A. Symonds 83, J.D. Lewry 6 for 45) and 380 for 7 dec. (A.J. Wright 139, M.W. Alleyne 91, G.D. Hodgson 52)

Sussex 482 for 7 dec. (C.W.J. Athey 163 not out,
F.D. Stephenson 106, I.D.K. Salisbury 74, N.C. Phillips
50 not out)

Match drawn

Sussex 8 pts, Gloucestershire 3 pts

at Worcester

Worcestershire 204 (J.E. Benjamin 4 for 47, C.G. Rackemann
4 for 56) and 265 for 7 dec. (G.A. Hick 120, T.S. Curtis 52)
Surrey 183 (A.D. Brown 58) and 152 (A.J. Stewart 50)

Worcestershire won by 134 runs

Worcestershire 21 pts, Surrey 4 pts

With 35 overs on the first day, 32.5 on the second and no
play possible at all on the third, the match at the Riverside
Ground was heading for oblivion. Aravinda de Silva had
scored 79 from 68 balls when rain left Kent stranded on
144 for 4 on the Thursday, and although he was dismissed
early on the second day, Kent maintained a belligerent
approach which saw them reach what turned out to be
their declaration score.

Farce took over on the last morning when, after con-
sultation, a target of 201 for Durham was agreed as being
realistic. To this end, Kent conceded 72 runs in 3.5 overs.
These were the last cheap runs of the day as Durham were
bowled out by Headley, McCague and Ealham. The Kent
seamers found much lateral movement. Prabhakar scored
35 not out, but his side subsided in 43.2 overs.

Having started the season with defeat piling upon
defeat in all competitions, Hampshire won their second
championship match in succession and accomplished it in
three days. There was a refreshing consistency in the batting with John Stephenson, who had scored only 58 runs
in the championship for Hampshire, breaking his hoodoo
with 65. As Hampshire left Glamorgan on 12 for 1, they
were well satisfied with the opening day.

Hamesh Anthony had produced his best bowling
performance for Glamorgan, but it was the combined
efforts of Connor, Bovill, Stephenson and Streak that
undermined the Welshmen. Bovill took three wickets in
four deliveries to plunge the home county to 105 for 8.
Thomas and Anthony added 61. Anthony slashed Streak
to gully, and Thomas was caught behind off Stephenson,
thus not saving the follow-on.

When Glamorgan batted again Morris hit 5 fours off
Streak, but Dale was out to Udal's first delivery, and both
Morris and Maynard were out to Connor before tea. It
seemed that the game would be over in two days, but
Cottey stood firm, and Glamorgan limped to 155 for 6 at
the close. Rain was Hampshire's only enemy, and it
delayed victory until the afternoon on the Saturday.

There were strange events at Lord's where Middlesex
again failed to win a batting point. Derbyshire laboured to
258 for 6 on the first day. There was a brief flourish from
Colin Wells, but Barnett spent 38 overs over his 30 runs,
and when Emburey bowled Rollins for 61 it was the 83rd
over, and Rollins had faced 223 balls.

The batsmen's suspicions regarding the wicket were

confirmed on the second day when 14 wickets fell before
tea. One that did not fall was that of Jason Pooley who carried his bat through the 52.5 overs of the Middlesex
innings to finish on 85 not out. Pooley had grasped his
chance of a regular opportunity in the Middlesex side, and
the left-hander was maturing with every match. He also
showed excellent qualities in the field.

Derbyshire ended the day on 83 for 1, well in command, but there was no play on the third day. Dessaur
and Rollins set up a declaration with a second-wicket
partnership of 125, but the batting, without Adams, again
lacked all flair. Set to get 303 in 71 overs, Middlesex
ground to 130 for 4 before the captains – Carr, deputising
for the injured Gatting, and Barnett – thankfully agreed to
call off hostilities.

An opening stand of 107 between Dowman, 29, and
Robinson, who hit the 54th hundred of his career, gave
Nottinghamshire an excellent platform against Essex.
Such and Childs each took a wicket to disturb the home
county's complacency, and the spinners were soon on top
of the batsmen, reducing Nottinghamshire to 218 for 8.
Without Pollard, injured, and Johnson, tending his seriously ill daughter, the Nottinghamshire batting was thin
– one does not mention Lewis who had become something
akin to a figment of all our imaginations. Noon, however,
played well, and he cajoled 96 runs from the last two
wickets.

Essex were without Ilott, but spin was to be the principal ingredient in this match. Prichard hit 100 off 156 balls
with 17 fours, but he was one of Hindson's victims as was
Childs, but not before he had added 32 for the last wicket
with Cousins and earned a third batting point.

Robinson and Dowman scored 50 in 14 overs before the
close of play, and on a third day restricted to 27 overs, they
reached their second century partnership of the match, 103,
and Nottinghamshire were brought to a halt at 114 for 1.

Cairns and Noon shared an unbroken seventh-wicket
stand of 103, with Cairns' 68 coming off 77 balls. Essex
were left 66 overs in which to score 288.

In the first 19 overs, they lost Gooch, Robinson and
Waugh for 77, but Prichard and Hussain added 108, and
Irani then gave Hussain more purposeful support.
Hussain batted with considerable skill, and he was quick
to punish anything remotely loose. He is too good a
player for England to continue to ignore. With three overs
remaining, Essex were 268 for 5, but Lewis and Rollins fell
to Hindson without addition. At the start of the penultimate over, 18 runs were needed with Hussain on strike.
He took a single but was run out when he tried to regain
the strike. Childs unnecessarily ran himself out in the last
over, and Cousins was caught at silly point off Hindson's
fifth delivery. This gave the left-arm spinner his 10th
wicket of the match, and it brought Nottinghamshire an
exceptional and unexpected victory.

Yorkshire fielded their youngest-ever opening pair for
the match against Somerset at Taunton, McGrath and
Vaughan, and they began the game with a stand of 115.
With Byas again batting well, Yorkshire hit a solid but
unspectacular 269 for 6 on the opening day.

This excessive caution gave way to some swashbuckling on the second morning as Grayson and Gough hit 79

Left-arm medium-pace bowler Jason Lewry took 6 for 45 for Sussex against Gloucestershire, 1 June, and established himself as a young bowler of immense promise. (M. Prior/Allsport)

in 22 overs, and Peter Hartley blasted all about him. The result was that Yorkshire added 144 in the pre-lunch session and were all out.

The Somerset top-order showed more urgency than their opponents had done, and the home side closed on 248 for 4 from 75 overs. Harden ran to a most able century next day after a delayed start, and his 16th four brought the fourth batting point and the declaration. The Yorkshire openers were out before the close with 32 scored, but an 'arrangement' of some kind looked inevitable if a result were to be achieved.

Yorkshire stuttered as they sought quick runs on the last day, but Bevan gave indication of better days to come. Byas' declaration left Somerset to score 260 in what transpired to be 58 overs. Trescothick immediately went to Hartley, but the Yorkshire spinners failed to pose the problems which Mushtaq and Trump had presented. Stemp was accurate, but Lathwell began to relish Vaughan and hit 21 fours in his first championship century of the season. Somerset needed 111 off the last 20 overs. Harden was again in regal form – indeed he has taken on the mantle of king of Taunton – and he hit a six and 8 fours in his unbeaten 80 which came off 109 balls. Ecclestone also thumped hard for 29 not out off 23 balls, and Somerset moved to their first championship win of the season with 13 balls to spare.

At Hove, 14 wickets fell on the first day. Left-arm fast medium bowler Jason Lewry produced the best bowling performance of his short career, and he was more than ably supported by another pace man, Ed Giddins. Gloucestershire would have suffered total humiliation but for Andrew Symonds who hit 3 sixes and 13 fours. He has quickly established himself in county cricket as one of the fiercest of hitters, competent of batsmen and toughest of competitors. The direction his career will take remains uncertain, but it is sure that he will break many bowlers' hearts and give joy to all who watch him. He and Russell

added 81 for the sixth wicket, and without this stand, Gloucestershire would have looked very sick.

Sussex did not begin well, losing four wickets for 61 runs before Athey and Moores took them to 113 by the end of the day.

Moores was out a quarter of an hour into the second day, caught behind off Srinath, but this brought in Franklyn Stephenson. Athey and Stephenson, two batsmen of violently contrasting styles, shared a sixth-wicket stand of 162. Stephenson hit 13 fours and 4 sixes in his typically roistering hundred; while Athey moved sedately to the 50th first-class century of his career and batted throughout the day. He added 127 with Salisbury, who hit the highest score of his career, and there was an unbroken stand of 75 with Phillips who flayed a maiden first-class fifty.

Gloucestershire did not join in the applause for Athey whom they believed they had caught when he was on 59. In all, the ex-Yorkshire and Gloucestershire batsman faced 478 balls and hit 20 fours.

Twelve overs beginning at five minutes to six were all that was possible on a wretched third day, and when Wright and Hodgson extended their opening stand to 132 in another 28 overs on the last morning, a draw was certain. Wright batted for 279 minutes and hit 2 sixes and 17 fours. He has refound his form and is enjoying the game since relinquishing the captaincy.

Carl Rackemann made his first appearance for Surrey and took a wicket with his 16th ball in county cricket when he bowled Weston. Worcestershire were 138 for 3 before Joey Benjamin took 3 for 5 in 12 balls. Lampitt and Rhodes added 51 in 28 overs, but the last four wickets went down for 10 runs, and Rackemann celebrated a good debut.

Surrey lost Stewart and Butcher for 34 before the end of the day, and four more wickets fell for the addition of 26 runs on the second morning. Alistair Brown and Graham Kersey then added 70 in 15 overs, with Brown hitting 5 sixes and 5 fours in his 71-ball innings and Kersey showing much sense with his 35 off 62 balls. Nowell and Joey Benjamin made useful contributions, and Surrey got to within 21 of the Worcestershire score.

The game seemed balanced until Hick hit the fastest hundred of the season to date. He reached three figures off 76 balls and, in all, hit 3 sixes and 19 fours in his 120 which came off 98 balls. Worcestershire were 178 for 3, Curtis 44 not out, when play ended on the Friday, and no play was possible on the Saturday.

Surrey were asked to make 287 in 74 overs on the last day, but Richard Illingworth strangled them with his accuracy, taking 3 for 23 in 16.1 overs and winning the match with 6.1 overs to spare. It was Worcestershire's first championship win of the season.

7, 8, 9 and 10 June *at Basingstoke*

Hampshire 319 (G.W. White 62, J.P. Stephenson 55, M.C.J. Nicholas 50, G.J. Parsons 4 for 58) and 92 for 1

Leicestershire 154 (B.F. Smith 57 not out, C.A. Connor 6 for 44, H.H. Streak 4 for 44) and 253 (B.F. Smith 67, W.J. Cronje 66, H.H. Streak 4 for 40, C.A. Connor 4 for 83)

Hampshire won by 9 wickets

Hampshire 23 pts, Leicestershire 4 pts

8, 9, 10 and 12 June *at Derby*

Derbyshire 113 (J.P. Taylor 4 for 23) and 139 (J.P. Taylor
4 for 44)

Northamptonshire 120 (D.G. Cork 9 for 43) and 135 for 6
(D.G. Cork 4 for 50)

Northamptonshire won by 4 wickets

Northamptonshire 20 pts, Derbyshire 4 pts

at Chelmsford

Essex 373 (G.A. Gooch 97, M.E. Waugh 95, N. Hussain 66,
A. Walker 8 for 118) and 243 (D.D.J. Robinson 110,
A. Walker 6 for 59)

Durham 288 (D.A. Blenkiron 94) and 149

Essex won by 179 runs

Essex 24 pts, Durham 6 pts

at Canterbury

Gloucestershire 321 (M.A. Lynch 108, A. Symonds 52,
D.W. Headley 5 for 68, M.J. McCague 5 for 68) and
266 for 8 dec. (M.A. Lynch 114, R.I. Dawson 58)

Kent 137 (A.M. Smith 6 for 66) and 346 (M.R. Benson 102,
G.R. Cowdrey 71)

Gloucestershire won by 104 runs

Gloucestershire 23 pts, Kent 4 pts

at Old Trafford

Lancashire 417 (J.P. Crawley 182, G.D. Lloyd 50) and 338 for 3
dec. (J.E.R. Gallian 158, J.P. Crawley 108)

Glamorgan 475 (M.P. Maynard 138, P.A. Cottey 124,
H. Morris 67, Wasim Akram 4 for 77) and 233 for 7
(M.P. Maynard 67, M. Watkinson 4 for 51)

Match drawn

Glamorgan 8 pts, Lancashire 6 pts

at Trent Bridge

Nottinghamshire 301 (P. Johnson 96, W.M. Noon 59,
P.J. Newport 4 for 61) and 319 (P. Johnson 73,
G.F. Archer 61, R.T. Robinson 51, S.R. Lampitt 4 for 71)

Worcestershire 360 (T.M. Moody 157, W.P.C. Weston 105) and
263 for 7 (T.M. Moody 106, G.R. Haynes 55)

Worcestershire won by 3 wickets

Worcestershire 23 pts, Nottinghamshire 5 pts

at The Oval

Surrey 221 (J.D. Ratcliffe 70, Mushtaq Ahmed 5 for 54) and
419 for 9 dec. (M.A. Butcher 102, A.W. Smith 88,
D.M. Ward 51)

*A maiden first-class century for Darren Robinson, Essex v. Durham,
9 June. Robinson won high praise for his fielding close to the wicket.
(Alan Cozzi)*

Somerset 260 (R.J. Harden 90, M.P. Bicknell 5 for 61) and
383 for 5 (P.D. Bowler 132 not out, M.N. Lathwell 75,
G.D. Rose 51)

Somerset won by 5 wickets

Somerset 22 pts, Surrey 5 pts

at Edgbaston

Warwickshire 248 (A.J. Moles 66, T.L. Penney 51,
E.S.H. Giddins 4 for 59) and 332 for 5 dec. (R.G. Twose
131 not out, N.V. Knight 74 retired hurt, D.R. Brown 50)

Sussex 361 (K. Greenfield 84, P. Moores 56, A.A. Donald
4 for 112) and 47 for 1

Match drawn

Sussex 8 pts, Warwickshire 5 pts

It was not surprising that the match between Hampshire
and Leicestershire at Basingstoke ended in three days.
Both sides were making a speciality of completing their
matches in three days, and none of Hampshire's championship matches had lasted into the fourth day. On a miserable morning, Mark Nicholas chose to bat first and,
initially, the Hampshire run rate matched the weather.
Terry, Stephenson and White laboured against the moving
ball and there was little to dispel the gloom except that

Stephenson showed signs of returning confidence with his second championship fifty for Hampshire. Nicholas pepped up the scoring, and he and White added 110 for the fifth wicket. The real jolt to the innings, however, came from Connor and Bovill with 41 for the last wicket, a stand which earned a third batting point. Connor then sent back Briers and Maddy, the Leicestershire openers, to leave the visitors reeling on 7 for 2 at the close.

There was no respite the following morning when Connor produced a spell of 4 for 5 in 13 balls to subject Leicestershire to the humiliation of 26 for 6. Streak then claimed two wickets before Ben Smith and David Millns added 73 for the ninth wicket. They could not save the follow-on, and Leicestershire were once more in trouble at 75 for 4. Smith again, this time with Cronje, stemmed the flood, the pair adding 105.

Nixon and Parsons scored 66 in 24 overs on the third morning – they had scored one the previous evening – before Streak finished the innings by taking 4 for 2 in seven balls. An opening partnership of 67 between Morris and Terry set Hampshire on the path to a comfortable victory.

Derbyshire has long been noted for producing pitches which favour seam bowlers, but the umpires refused to blame the strip at Derby for the fact that 23 wickets fell on the opening day. Four openers did not score a run between them, and Kim Barnett was caught behind twice in the day off Taylor to record the first 'pair' of his career.

The loss of Barnett and Dessaur for one in the first innings seemed a temporary hiccup as Rollins and Cullinan added 51, but Allan Lamb had a variety of seamers at his disposal, and they gnawed away at the Derbyshire innings to bring it to an end in 39.3 overs.

Generally, it was the swing rather than movement off the pitch that disconcerted batsmen, but one bowler who claimed the day as his was Dominic Cork. Justifiably disappointed at being omitted from the Test side, Cork took

the first nine of the Northamptonshire wickets to fall. Montgomerie played tentatively at an away-swinger and was bowled. Fordham went back to a ball of full length and was leg before, while Bailey steered a delivery to first slip. Lamb countered fire with fire until, having made 37, he was leg before pushing half-forward. Curran hooked to long-leg, and Capel was caught in the gully, a fate later suffered by Kumble. Penberthy was taken in the slips, and Mallender was leg before, but Warren played with good sense, mingling watchful defence with sensible aggression for his unbeaten 42. On 36, he slashed a ball towards second slip where Colin Wells was unable to hold on to the chance, surprising on a day when some outstanding catches were taken. The unlucky bowler was Dominic Cork, who was tiring. He bowled 22 consecutive overs. The last wicket was taken by Aldred who yorked Taylor, leaving Cork with figures of 22–5–43–9, his best and the best for Derbyshire for 20 years.

Derbyshire closed this eventful day on 59 for 3. This score might have suggested revival, but only nine had been added on the second morning when Harris was caught at short-leg. Dessaur was solid for his 40, but Wells was caught bat-and-pad. Hard as Cork, Krikken and the tail tried, the wickets continued to fall, and Northamptonshire needed 133 to win.

Montgomerie and Fordham were both leg before to Cork who bowled off a shorter run and kept a full length, but Bailey, Lamb and Warren proved tougher opposition. Cork had both Lamb and Warren caught behind to finish with 13 for 93, the best match figures of his career, but he finished on the losing side. The match was over before tea on the second day.

Alan Walker of Durham, formerly of Northamptonshire, found himself in the same position as Cork. He took eight wickets in an innings for the first time, and his 14 for 177 represented the first time he had taken 10 or more wickets in a match, but his side was overwhelmed by Essex.

Prichard won the toss, and, after the early loss of Robinson, Gooch and Waugh put on 191 in 49 overs. Waugh, looking as if his appetite for the game was returning, was the more aggressive, and his 95 came off 148 balls. Both batsmen were victims of Walker and left in quick succession before Hussain and Prichard added 98. The dismissal of Prichard heralded a collapse, and Essex went from 315 for 3 to 339 for 8 at the close.

Walker claimed the last two wickets on the second morning to give him the best figures recorded for a Durham bowler. Longley and Roseberry started briskly enough, but both fell victim to Irani as four wickets fell for 14 runs. The other two wickets were captured by Mark Waugh. Recovery came in the shape of Darren Blenkiron, a left-hander who had found run-scoring difficult in the first team, but whose achievements in the second eleven had earned him another chance in the championship side. He attacked from the start, was not afraid to hit in the air

Alan Walker, Durham and former Northamptonshire pace bowler, took 14 wickets in the match at Chelmsford, 7–10 June, and still finished on the losing side. (David Munden/Sportsline)

and clattered 15 fours as he reached 94 off 99 balls. His century was denied him by Irani's splendid catch at mid-on off the bowling of Cousins.

With Such and Childs beginning to find some turn, Durham ended the day on 246 for 9. Boiling and Brown added valuable runs on the Saturday morning, but the day belonged to Darren Robinson, who had played only three first-class matches before 1995. Winning the opening spot when Prichard belatedly and sensibly dropped down the order, Robinson responded with a maiden first-class century. He hit 110 out of 184 off 231 balls before being stumped as he tried to sweep the slow left-armer Cox. He hooked Prabhakar for six and hit 12 fours. Hussain was the only other Essex batsman to reach 20, but a target of 329 in 92 overs was always likely to be beyond Durham.

Larkins was absent with a broken thumb sustained in the Sunday League game, and Ligertwood opened with Longley who hit 35. Prabhakar was unbeaten on 46, but the last five Durham wickets fell for 29 runs, and they plunged to their sixth consecutive championship defeat.

There was yet another example of the kind of optimism blowing through Gloucestershire cricket with the county's performance at Canterbury. They were 42 for 4 on the opening day before Lynch and Symonds added 114. Symonds batted with customary daring to hit 52 off 63 balls, and Lynch hit 15 fours in an innings which lasted under three hours and revitalised Gloucestershire. Russell and Srinath put on 78 in 31 overs to give Kent more problems, and, in spite of the very fine bowling of McCague and Headley, the visitors reached 321 and gave further joy to their day by dismissing Ward before the close, by which time Kent had scored 13.

Only 44 overs were possible on the second day during which Kent floundered to 98 for 7. They showed more positivity on the third day, which began with Fleming hitting Smith's first ball for six. He took six off Srinath three overs later and finished on 36 not out. Smith had his revenge, claiming another six-wicket haul as the last three wickets fell for one run.

Russell did not enforce the follow-on, and Monte Lynch took the opportunity to hit his second century of the match. This is the first time that the charming 37-year-old has achieved the feat. He hit 10 fours and 3 sixes and was even quicker and more commanding than he had been in the first innings. Gloucestershire's newcomers, Lynch, Symonds and Srinath, had proved to be outstanding acquisitions. Kent were asked to make 451, and they closed on 73 for 1, having lost Ward.

With Smith striking again, they were soon 87 for 3 on the last morning, but Benson, who had spent a long time over 0 in the first innings, and Cowdrey added 126. Cowdrey's 71 came off 90 balls. Once this pair was separated – Benson being bowled by Ball, and Cowdrey falling leg before to Srinath – only Marsh offered serious resistance as Gloucestershire moved to a comfortable win.

There was a run glut at Old Trafford where Lancashire scored 378 for 8 on the opening day. Crawley made 182 in 5¼ hours, hitting 98 of the 184 runs scored between lunch and tea. Crawley faced 259 balls and hit a century in fours while Lloyd's 50 came off 47 balls.

Glamorgan lost Dale with a broken thumb on the second day, but Maynard and Cottey came together at 140 for 2 and were not separated until the score was 377. Maynard hit 14 fours, and Cottey 15, and Glamorgan took a first-innings lead of 58. This was soon wiped out as Lancashire ended the Saturday on 140 for 1.

Crawley, a slim-line version of the 1994 batsman, hit his second century of the match and added 196 with Gallian, who hit a solid 158. Watkinson's declaration left Glamorgan 61 overs in which to score 281. Metson opened in the absence of Dale, but quickly fell victim to Watkinson. Morris began well, but it was Maynard, 67 off 64 balls, and Cottey who made victory seem possible. Watkinson blunted the Glamorgan charge, however, when he had Croft, Cottey and Anthony stumped in successive overs of his off-spin.

Worcestershire recalled Damian D'Oliveira, second-team coach, for the game at Trent Bridge. Test calls and injuries had limited their options, and Nottinghamshire gave a clue to the pitch by including three spinners in their side. The home team made 277 for 9 on the first day, and D'Oliveira bowled 28 overs to take three wickets. It was Newport's medium pace that did the most damage, and it was Paul Johnson's 96 off 135 balls with a six and 12 fours that offered Nottinghamshire's strongest challenge. He was caught at slip by Moody off Lampitt with a century beckoning.

Worcestershire seized control of the game on the second day when Weston and Moody put on 227 for their third wicket. Both batsmen hit centuries, and Moody's innings included 3 sixes and 16 fours, while Weston hit 2 sixes and 12 fours. The visitors ended the second day on 279 for 3, but they lost the initiative on the Saturday when their last five wickets went down for 42 runs. Johnson was again in good form, and Nottinghamshire moved to 200 for 3 in the second innings to leave the game well balanced.

A collapse which saw the home side's last five wickets fall for 37 runs meant that Worcestershire had 60 overs in which to score 261 to win. Twice in the match, Worcestershire had been in total command only to surrender the advantage. Now they began horrendously, losing three wickets for 11 runs, but Moody had enjoyed an outstanding match. He had held five slip catches, and he followed his first-innings 157 with 106 off 101 balls. He hit 11 fours and added 151 in 31 overs with Gavin Haynes. Hindson dismissed them both, and 72 were needed from 13 overs. Rhodes scampered enthusiastically before being bowled by Evans, and D'Oliveira was run out in a dreadful mix-up with Lampitt who cut the first ball of the last over for four to win the match.

Surrey had a bad first day at The Oval when Mushtaq had a spell of 5 for 22 in 25 overs. Pigott was captaining Surrey, won the toss and batted. Surrey rushed to 130 for 1 with Ratcliffe playing his best innings for them, but then collapsed as they played across the line, ran themselves out and surrendered to good leg-spin bowling. Lathwell and Trescothick were out in the first four overs of the Somerset innings, and Bowler followed later for them to close 147 runs behind.

Richard Harden's wonderful stream of successes continued with an admirable four-hour 90. He looked set for another century until he pushed forward at Martin

Bicknell and was taken at slip. Bicknell bowled Surrey back into the game with four wickets in nine balls, and he had Trump dropped before he had scored. This was costly, for the last wicket added 46 and took Somerset into the lead. There had been a costly miss earlier when Ecclestone, who thumped an excellent 41, was dropped off Smith at slip early in his innings.

Ratcliffe and Butcher raced Surrey to 70 for 0 by the close, and their opening partnership was finally worth 111. Butcher hit his second century of the summer off 124 balls with 17 fours, and Ward and Smith, who made his highest championship score, gave further substance later in the innings. Pigott declared overnight, leaving Somerset a day in which to score 381.

Lathwell and Trescothick scored 70 for the first wicket, but the match-winner was Peter Bowler. He is not an exciting stroke-player, but he paced his innings well after rain had cost his side six overs. The fireworks were provided by Rose, 51 off 46 balls, and Ecclestone, 25 not out, and Somerset won with nine balls to spare.

Warwickshire laboured on the first day at Edgbaston. The pitch was not easy, and the Sussex pace trio of Giddins, Lewry and Stephenson bowled well. Moles batted with his usual technical competence and dedication, but the last six wickets fell for 40 runs. Warwickshire welcomed back Munton, and he, Small and Donald gave Sussex a torrid last hour during which 41 were scored and Lenham was leg before to Donald.

Most of the Sussex batting followed the Warwickshire pattern – dour and introspective, but Wells hit 10 fours as he scored 49 from 58 balls and enlivened proceedings. Moores and Greenfield put on 107 for the sixth wicket. Moores fell to the second new ball, and Greenfield's 84 occupied four hours.

Sussex added just one run on the Saturday morning before the last wicket fell, and, leading by 113, they had a joyful start to Warwickshire's second innings when Moles was caught at gully in the first over. The next 51 overs were occupied by Knight and Twose who scored 154 before rain ended play in mid-afternoon.

Knight was concussed in the Sunday League game and could not continue his innings on the Monday. Only one wicket fell before lunch, and with Twose digging in for 131 from 359 balls in seven hours, the game moved inevitably to a draw.

15, 16, 17 and 19 June *at Derby*

Derbyshire 376 (D.J. Cullinan 161, A.S. Rollins 56, Mushtaq Ahmed 5 for 107) and 168 (C.M. Wells 98, G.D. Rose 4 for 27)
Somerset 189 (D.G. Cork 4 for 40) and 434 (P.D. Bowler 138, R.J. Turner 106 not out, R.J. Harden 63)

Somerset won by 79 runs

Somerset 20 pts, Derbyshire 4 pts

Wicket-keeper Robert Turner hit a century for Somerset against Derbyshire, 17–19 June. Turner was to finish the season with 64 dismissals to his credit. (David Munden/Sportsline)

at Colwyn Bay

Glamorgan 276 (H.A.G. Anthony 58, H. Morris 53) and 332 (S.P. James 84, H. Morris 66, J.E. Emburey 4 for 97)
Middlesex 530 (K.R. Brown 147 not out, J.D. Carr 129, J.C. Pooley 125, M.R. Ramprakash 69, S.R. Barwick 4 for 116) and 79 for 2 (J.C. Pooley 50 not out)

Middlesex won by 8 wickets

Middlesex 24 pts, Glamorgan 4 pts

at Bristol

Hampshire 341 (R.A. Smith 136, K.D. James 53, A.M. Smith 4 for 76) and 175 for 6 dec.
Gloucestershire 266 for 9 dec. (R.C. Russell 82 not out, A.J. Wright 50, S.D. Udal 6 for 65) and 180 for 6

Match drawn

Hampshire 7 pts, Gloucestershire 6 pts

at Leicester

Leicestershire 381 (J.J. Whitaker 127, J.M. Dakin 101 not out) and 357 (W.J. Cronje 113, J.M. Dakin 66, R.A. Pick 5 for 82)
Nottinghamshire 364 (C.L. Cairns 99, P. Johnson 70) and 246 for 7 (G.F. Archer 122 not out)

Match drawn

Leicestershire 8 pts, Nottinghamshire 8 pts

at Luton

Essex 127 (R.J. Rollins 52 not out, D.J. Capel 5 for 29) and 107 (J.P. Taylor 7 for 50)

Mark Ilott took 9 for 19, including the hat trick, for Essex against Northamptonshire but finished on the losing side. (Alan Cozzi)

Northamptonshire 46 (M.C. Ilott 9 for 19) and 192 for 8 (A.J. Lamb 50 not out, M.C. Ilott 5 for 86)

Northamptonshire won by 2 wickets

Northamptonshire 20 pts, Essex 4 pts

at Horsham

Surrey 187 (E.S.H. Giddins 4 for 54, J.D. Lewry 4 for 77) and 501 for 8 dec. (A.J. Stewart 150, G.P. Thorpe 110, A.J. Hollioake 51, J.D. Lewry 5 for 110)

Sussex 304 (K. Newell 53, J.E. Benjamin 5 for 94) and 230 for 9 (N.J. Lenham 72, J.W. Hall 54, C.G. Rackemann 6 for 60)

Match drawn

Sussex 7 pts, Surrey 4 pts

at Worcester

Lancashire 206 (N.J. Speak 51, R.K. Illingworth 4 for 63) and 231 (J.E.R. Gallian 59)

Worcestershire 487 for 9 dec. (G.A. Hick 152, T.M. Moody 110, S.R. Lampitt 97, G. Chapple 4 for 124)

Worcestershire won by an innings and 50 runs

Worcestershire 24 pts, Lancashire 5 pts

at Leeds

Yorkshire 462 for 7 dec. (M.D. Moxon 203 not out, M.P. Vaughan 71, D. Gough 60) and 140 for 2 (M.D. Moxon 65 not out, D. Byas 58 not out)

Kent 234 (T.R. Ward 65, P.A. de Silva 52, D. Gough 4 for 34) and 365 (P.A. de Silva 115, D.P. Fulton 59, C. White 4 for 40)

Yorkshire won by 8 wickets

Yorkshire 24 pts, Kent 4 pts

Colin Wells was awarded his county cap for Derbyshire, Cullinan hit his highest score for the county, and 376 were scored from 106.1 overs on the first day. Cullinan hit 30 fours in a graceful innings, and Rollins hit 56 off 62 balls. Apart from the fact that Kim Barnett was out for his third 'duck' in succession and Adams was still absent injured, all seemed right with Derbyshire's world.

That world became even better on the second day. Cork and the rest of the pace attack were again in top form. The dangerous Bowler was out for 0 against his old county, caught by Wells running back from slip as a ball from Malcolm jumped off his glove, the resistance offered by Harden and Parsons was soon broken, and Somerset followed on 187 runs in arrears. In their second innings, they lost Lathwell and Trescothick for 20, and although Bowler and Harden, standing first and second in the national averages, took the score to 123 by the close, Derbyshire remained in command.

It was on the Saturday that the game began to change dramatically. Harden was out 37 runs into the day, and Hayhurst was forced to retire hurt third ball when he was hit on the hand by Malcolm. Bowler was subjected to some rather fierce bowling, but he hit two of Malcolm's leg-side deliveries for six and claimed 8 fours as well. When he finally fell to Malcolm, Turner stood firm, hitting a six and 10 fours in what was his highest score. He had not reached 30 in any first-class innings previously in the season. Dimond helped him in a ninth-wicket stand of 83, and Hayhurst returned only to be run out for 0. Through the two centuries, some gritty batting and wayward bowling on the part of the hosts, Somerset were able to set a target of 248. Derbyshire had 17 overs to negotiate before the end of the day, and they lost Dessaur, Cullinan and Krikken to Rose while Mushtaq trapped Rollins leg before, 28 for 4.

Wells batted for two hours and hit 98 off 117 balls with a six and 18 fours before swatting across the line and being bowled by a Mushtaq googly. Barnett finished on 16 not out, Cork made two, and DeFreitas was out second ball to a limp shot. Warner was bowled by Mushtaq, and when Bowler held a spectacular diving slip catch to dismiss Malcolm in the third over after lunch, Somerset had won. It was Derbyshire's first defeat after enforcing the follow-on since 1882, and it must have given great satisfaction to Bowler, the acting captain of Somerset, who had left Derbyshire a few months earlier after hostility between himself and Barnett.

Derbyshire called a crisis meeting of the cricket committee to discuss playing standards. Four days can be a long time in cricket.

At Colwyn Bay, Glamorgan won the toss in a championship match for the first time in 1995, but it did them little good. A partnership of 71 for the seventh wicket was the best that they could offer on the first day against

Middlesex, although they did get Weekes out before the close as the visitors scored 43.

On the second day, three Middlesex batsmen hit centuries. Jason Pooley hit the highest score of his career off 176 balls with 14 fours and 5 sixes, and he and Ramprakash added 193 for the second wicket. Gatting was run out when the bowler, Watkin, deflected Carr's drive onto the stumps, at which Brown and Carr put on 209 for the fifth wicket. Carr's 129 came off 203 balls, but Brown's hundred was reached off 162 balls, and he batted into the third day when Middlesex plundered 71 more runs.

Morris and James began Glamorgan's second innings with 147 in 59 overs, but in the remaining 41 overs of the day, 111 runs were scored as five wickets fell. Anthony was also forced to retire hurt, but he returned on the last morning.

Middlesex were set for a comfortable victory, but they were delayed by a ninth-wicket stand of 35 between Watkin and Metson. Tufnell dismissed them both, and the game was over an hour after lunch.

Gloucestershire capped Cooper, Lynch and Srinath before the match against Hampshire, and celebrated by taking the first three of the visitors' wickets for 16 runs. They then ran into Robin Smith in his most powerful mood. Solid in defence, violent in attack, he batted for four hours and hit 18 fours. He and Morris scored 117 for the fifth wicket.

Hampshire were all out on the second morning, having added 18 to their overnight score. Gloucestershire began smoothly, but, having reached 83, they lost four wickets for 38 runs. Most of the damage was done by Shaun Udal, but he was countered by 'Jack' Russell who took his side to 266 for 9 at the close.

Only seven overs were possible on the third day, and Hampshire rather lost themselves as they pressed for quick runs on the last morning. Nicholas' declaration left Gloucestershire 53 overs in which to score 251, and they slipped to 137 for 6 with 20 overs remaining before Alleyne and Srinath effectively brought the match to its end.

James Whitaker, playing better than he has done since winning his one Test cap nine years earlier, batted with sense and charm to lift Leicestershire from the depths against Nottinghamshire. Relying mainly on the drive, he hit 20 boundaries in an innings which lasted $4\frac{1}{4}$ hours. He was missed at first slip when three, and he survived to relish his dominance of a fifth-wicket stand of 113 with Nixon. The tall left-hander Dakin, playing his second championship match, took over the leading role when Whitaker departed, and he moved to a maiden first-class century on the second morning. He is 22 years old and a powerful all-rounder, a commodity in short supply at present.

Millns and Mullally had early success for Leicestershire, but Johnson and Cairns put on 150 in 29 overs for the visitors' fourth wicket. Cairns flogged the ball to all parts of the field, but favouring the leg side, before the hard-working Parsons took a leaping one-handed catch off his own bowling to dismiss the New Zealander. Leicestershire finally led by 17 runs, but it was not a good day for them. Mullally was warned for run-

ning on the pitch and was hit for 90 in 13 overs. He and the other bowlers contributed 38 runs in no-balls to the 64 extras in the Nottinghamshire total.

On the Saturday, Cronje scored his first first-class century at Grace Road, with 17 fours and a six, and shared a second-wicket stand of 144 with Briers. Five wickets then fell for 27 runs before Dakin again came to the rescue. He and Pierson added 22 more runs on the last morning, which left Nottinghamshire to make 375 in 102 overs.

This was a demanding task, but Mullally was forced to bowl 12 overs of slow left-arm rather than pace because of a side strain, and Millns, on the eve of receiving treatment for Achilles tendon trouble, bowled only eight overs. Johnson and Cairns perished to loose shots, but Archer hit his first century of the season as Nottinghamshire, all too predictably, settled for survival and a draw.

For the second time in as many matches, Northamptonshire won in two days. On the first day at Luton, 30 wickets fell, and Mark Ilott took 9 for 19, the best figures of his career and of the season. His nine wickets included the hat trick when he had Snape, Kumble and Mallender leg before to successive deliveries.

Umpires Constant and White did not report the pitch because they asserted that the rash of wickets was due to excessive swing for which the pitch, of course, could not be blamed. Lamb asked Essex to bat when he won the toss, and his bowlers were able to exploit some residual moisture in the pitch. Capel took the wickets of Prichard and Irani with his first two deliveries, but Hussain's sound technique helped him to score 27. In the event, it was Rollins who hit the day's highest score, and his first first-class fifty. His 52 came off 77 balls and included a six and 6 fours. His last-wicket stand of 39 with John Childs was the best of the innings.

Ilott, who had missed the previous two championship games through injury, reduced Northamptonshire to 45 for 5 by tea, and, with one run having been scored after the break, the last five wickets fell without addition. The last eight had fallen for seven runs. Capel, caught behind off Irani, was the only man not to fall to Ilott who had six leg befores and two batsmen bowled in his nine wickets.

Essex batted again with a lead of 81 and were bowled out in 28.1 overs for 107. Another left-arm pace bowler, Taylor, did most of the damage. The home side had two overs before the close and scored one run. Cricket has seen few days like this one.

Mallender, Loye, Bailey and Montgomerie departed with 56 runs on the board, but Warren, who shows character and tenacity in moments like this, added 38 vital runs in a stand with Lamb. Then Curran and Lamb put on 37. Capel and Snape became Ilott's 13th and 14th victims of the match, and when Kumble joined Lamb 28 were still needed. Lamb had been dropped when he offered Waugh a difficult return catch on 22, but, crucially, Kumble, who batted with a flourish, was dropped when two runs were still needed. That was Essex's last chance, and Northamptonshire took their number of championship wins to six in seven matches.

By the end of the first day at Horsham, Sussex led Surrey by 22 runs and had five wickets in hand. Surrey would have been in a worse plight had Kersey, who hit 18 off four balls from Giddins, and Rackemann not added 48 for their last wicket. Generally, the Sussex seamers dominated, with Lewry taking three wickets in four balls at one stage.

Consistent batting took Sussex to a third batting point and a lead of 117 on the second day, but this advantage was wiped out in a third-wicket stand of 243 between Stewart and Thorpe. Between lunch and tea, they scored 177 in 39 overs. This was silky-smooth batting – no violence in the aggression, just power and majesty. There was violence from Brown – three towering sixes – and Surrey ended the day on 394 for 5.

Sadly, there was no play on the third day, and Surrey hurried on the last morning to make possible a target of 385 in 79 overs. Lenham and Hall started well with a partnership of 128 even though Lenham, it was later revealed, suffered a broken bone in his left hand. Sussex lost their way after the opening partnership and seven wickets fell for 56 runs. Wells and Stephenson were beaten by Rackemann's pace, and it was the Australian who brought Surrey to the brink of victory, only for Lewry and Giddins to hold out for 21 balls.

There was drama before the start of the match at New Road. Two days earlier, Worcestershire had been beaten by Lancashire in the semi-final of the Benson and Hedges Cup when, it had seemed, the match was theirs for the taking. It was noised abroad that Tim Curtis no longer had the support of some of his players and they had lost confidence in his captaincy. Cricket grows closer to soccer every day. Failure demands a price. Past successes, however recent, count for nothing. Curtis tendered his resignation as captain of Worcestershire, and Tom Moody took over for the rest of the season.

The Australian met with immediate success, for Lancashire were bowled out for 206, and Hick and the new captain were together at the end of the day with Worcestershire 74 for 2.

Atherton had batted down the order, and Moody – rightly – refused to allow Lancashire to field a substitute because Atherton had obviously gone into the match unfit.

Moody and Hick flourished on the second day. Their partnership became worth 250, and they murdered the Lancashire attack, 206 runs coming in just over two hours. The partnership lasted 53 overs. Late in the day, Lampitt hit 97 off 150 balls to help Worcestershire to a first-innings lead of 281. Newport then bowled Speak before the close.

Only seven balls were possible in the morning session of the third day, but the clouds lifted, and Lancashire's indifferent batting performance made an early finish inevitable.

Steve Marsh captained Kent in the absence of Benson and asked Yorkshire to bat when he won the toss at Leeds. Moxon and Vaughan, finding no problems in the pitch, scored 132 for the first wicket. Byas and Moxon then scored 106 for the second, and although Bevan made only 29, Yorkshire ended the day on 346.

Moxon had been nursing a broken thumb for five weeks, and he announced his return with an innings of 203 in 8½ hours. He hit 31 fours, but Gough stole his thunder in an eighth-wicket partnership of 84. The England bowler hit 60 off 55 balls, including 10 fours and a six. His day was not yet finished, for he took four Kent wickets in

Tim Curtis relinquished the captaincy of Worcestershire in June. (Paul Sturgess/Sportsline)

five balls. This feat included the hat trick, Marsh, McCague and Wren being the victims. Following on, Kent were 12 for 0 at the close.

Kent showed every sign of being able to save the game on the third day. Aravinda de Silva raced to 115 off 150 balls with a six and 17 fours, and Kent were 266 for 3. Then he was out, and Yorkshire chewed away at the rest of the Kent batting. Ultimately, they needed 138 to win, but there was a shiver of uncertainty as Vaughan and Stemp were out with just 15 scored on the Saturday evening.

There were no more tremors on the Monday as Moxon and Byas moved briskly to victory before lunch.

22, 23, 24 and 26 June *at Chester-le-Street (Riverside)*

Derbyshire 194 (K.J. Barnett 58, S.J.E. Brown 4 for 39) and
    195 (K.J. Barnett 74, F.A. Griffith 53, S.J.E. Brown 5 for 42)

Durham 273 (J.E. Morris 99, S.D. Birbeck 75 not out,
    D.E. Malcolm 4 for 91) and 118 for 2 (J.I. Longley 50 not out)

Durham won by 8 wickets

Durham 22 pts, Derbyshire 4 pts

at Southampton

Hampshire 428 (V.P. Terry 73, M.C.J. Nicholas 73, S.D. Udal
    56) and 344 for 5 dec. (M.C.J. Nicholas 138 not out,
    P.R. Whitaker 119)

Worcestershire 289 (D.A. Leatherdale 83, J.N.B. Bovill

One of the most successful 'transfers' for many a season, Monte Lynch from Surrey to Gloucestershire. (Clive Brunskill/Allsport)

4 for 66) and 413 (G.R. Haynes 78, D.A. Leatherdale 69, W.P.C. Weston 57, S.D. Udal 5 for 144)

Hampshire won by 70 runs

Hampshire 24 pts, Worcestershire 5 pts

at Old Trafford

Lancashire 496 (M. Watkinson 161, S.P. Titchard 130, N.J. Speak 83, M.C. Ilott 5 for 86) and 106 for 0 (N.J. Speak 64 not out)

Essex 248 (G.A. Gooch 123, Wasim Akram 4 for 86) and 350 (D.D.J. Robinson 86, M. Watkinson 6 for 91)

Lancashire won by 10 wickets

Lancashire 24 pts, Essex 2 pts

at Northampton

Northamptonshire 564 (D.J. Capel 175, R.J. Warren 75, A.J. Lamb 55 retired hurt, K.M. Curran 53, M.B. Loye 51 not out)

Leicestershire 367 (B.F. Smith 112, J.M. Dakin 77, N.E. Briers 68) and 160 (N.A. Mallender 4 for 49)

Northamptonshire won by an innings and 37 runs

Northamptonshire 24 pts, Leicestershire 6 pts

at Trent Bridge

Kent 533 (P.A. de Silva 225, M.A. Ealham 121, M.J. McCague 59, S.C. Willis 53) and 287 for 3 dec. (N.R. Taylor 99 not out, T.R. Ward 59, G.R. Cowdrey 53 not out, D.P. Fulton 52)

Nottinghamshire 491 for 9 dec. (R.T. Robinson 196, P. Johnson 68, R.A. Pick 50 not out) and 331 for 7 (R.T. Robinson 88, P.R. Pollard 75)

Nottinghamshire won by 3 wickets

Nottinghamshire 23 pts, Kent 6 pts

at Bath

Somerset 178 (K.A. Parsons 59, E.S.H. Giddins 6 for 73) and 345 (P.C.L. Holloway 129 not out, E.E. Hemmings 4 for 57)

Sussex 227 (A.P. Wells 106, Mushtaq Ahmed 6 for 54, J.I.D. Kerr 4 for 68) and 172 (Mushtaq Ahmed 4 for 62)

Somerset won by 124 runs

Somerset 20 pts, Sussex 5 pts

at The Oval

Glamorgan 450 (P.A. Cottey 125, M.P. Maynard 63, H. Morris 51, S.D. Thomas 51) and 329 (M.P. Maynard 97, H.A.G. Anthony 91, N.M. Kendrick 59, C.G. Rackemann 4 for 70, M.A. Butcher 4 for 72)

Surrey 397 (N. Shahid 125, A.J. Hollioake 88, J.D. Ratcliffe 56, G.J. Kersey 54, S.D. Thomas 4 for 95) and 302 for 9 (A.D. Brown 92, J.D. Ratcliffe 72, D.J. Bicknell 53)

Match drawn

Glamorgan 8 pts, Surrey 7 pts

at Edgbaston

Yorkshire 96 (A.A. Donald 5 for 21, D.R. Brown 4 for 35) and 185 (M.P. Vaughan 65, D.R. Brown 4 for 24, T.A. Munton 4 for 63)

Warwickshire 449 (N.V. Knight 91, K.J. Piper 90, D.P. Ostler 57, T.L. Penney 50, P.J. Hartley 4 for 109)

Warwickshire won by an innings and 168 runs

Warwickshire 24 pts, Yorkshire 2 pts

Derbyshire's emergency meeting of the inner cabinet seemed to have had no immediate effect as they crashed to Durham inside three days at the Riverside Ground. Barnett won the toss and chose to bat. Derbyshire began the match without DeFreitas who, finding he was not required by England, flew north and arrived at lunch-time to find his side on 66 for 7. He hit 49 not out off 50 balls. He added 55 with Warner and 29 with Malcolm to give the Derbyshire innings some substance.

DeFreitas continued his good work when he trapped Longley leg before. Malcolm dismissed Roseberry, and three wickets for Griffith in his first 10 deliveries reduced Durham to 75 for 5 before Birbeck joined Morris to take the score to 156 by the close.

The Morris/Birbeck stand became worth 125 before Morris was leg before to Malcolm when one short of his century. Birbeck, whose previous highest score in first-class cricket had been 10, finished unbeaten on 75 off 181 balls, and Durham led by 79. This lead assumed massive proportions when Derbyshire tumbled to 87 for 7 in their second innings. Barnett, batting at number six, then found an able partner in Griffith, and the pair put on 102 before Barnett was caught behind as he attempted to cut Brown. The same bowler quickly accounted for Griffith and Malcolm, so claiming his fourth five-wicket haul of the season.

Needing 117 to win, Durham ended the day on 10 without loss, and the next day they won with no alarms to bring to a close a dreadful run of six defeats in a row in the county championship.

Hampshire, too, put the nightmares of the early season further behind them with a win over Worcestershire that, eventually, was hard-earned. A century stand for the third wicket between Terry and Nicholas was the main feature of a first day on which Worcestershire contained the home side to 314 for 6. Solanki made his championship debut for the Midland county and took the wicket of Paul Terry.

There was considerable action on the second day when Udal, Streak and Bovill were the main contributors as Hampshire realised 114 from their remaining wickets. Bovill then dismissed Curtis with the first ball of the Worcestershire innings. This was the first of four wickets for Bovill, and only Moody and Leatherdale provided significant resistance as Hampshire took a first-innings lead of 139.

On the Saturday, Hampshire took complete command of the game as Whitaker and Nicholas shared a stand of 199 after two wickets had fallen for 31 runs. The left-handed Paul Whitaker hit 17 fours in his maiden first-class hundred, and it came in $3\frac{1}{4}$ hours. In contrast, Mark Nicholas hit his 32nd hundred for his county, and he hit a six and 16 fours. The partnership between the two occupied just 52 overs, and Nicholas' declaration asked Worcestershire to make 484. They hit 41 in 20 overs before the close.

Worcestershire refused to surrender on the last day on a pitch that was still amiable. Curtis and Weston extended their opening partnership to 105, but four wickets fell for 42 runs. Haynes and Leatherdale then added 125. With five wickets standing, the visitors needed 147 from the last 20 overs, but the Hampshire spinners gnawed away at the late-order, and Hampshire won with nine balls to spare.

Worcestershire's 413 was the highest fourth-innings total recorded against Hampshire, and the aggregate of 1,474 was the highest for a Hampshire game. More importantly, it was Hampshire's fourth win in five matches.

Essex had no joy. Gallian and Speak began the Lancashire innings with a partnership of 123, but four wickets fell for 48 runs. This brought Watkinson in to join Titchard, a late replacement for the injured Fairbrother, and by the close of play the score had advanced to 322.

Both batsmen completed their centuries on the second day and extended their partnership to 225. Watkinson's 161 was the highest score of his career, and the Essex bowling and fielding was under pressure for much of the time. Ilott recovered well to take five wickets, and the veteran John Childs claimed three top batsmen.

Gooch, who batted with an assurance and serenity born of his years at the crease, and Robinson scored 129 for Essex's first wicket, but after that only Irani, 28, reached double figures. The last five wickets went down for 20 runs, and Essex followed on 248 runs in arrears. Shadford, a fast medium-pace bowler making his first-class debut, took his first wicket when he had Gooch for 0. Robinson showed more of his immense potential, and there was some vigour from the late-order. Lancashire had to make 103 to win, and they did this in a mere 25.2 overs, with the game over soon after lunch on the fourth day.

Northamptonshire gained their sixth consecutive championship victory, beating Leicestershire in a match ripe with injuries. They hit 385 for 4 on the first day, but Loye, hit on the arm, and Lamb, a broken thumb, were both forced to retire hurt. Lamb did not return although – against doctor's orders – he fielded on the last day. Loye came back at the fall of the eighth wicket and dominated a partnership of 64, reaching 50 off 47 balls. The hero, however, was David Capel who reached his second century of the summer and the highest of his career. He hit 2 sixes and 27 fours in an innings which lasted just over six hours.

Leicestershire started shakily before Briers and Smith added 137 for the fourth wicket. Briers was out just before the close, 185 for 4, but Ben Smith hit the second and higher century of his career. There were also some fireworks, but the visitors could not save the follow-on.

When Leicestershire batted a second time Cronje sustained a broken finger. He played on but was out shortly after sustaining the injury, and the game was over within an hour after lunch on the fourth day.

Nottinghamshire gave a first-class debut to spinner Afzaal, but he played no part in reducing Kent to 68 for 5 by the 20th over of the match. In the next 85 overs, de Silva and Ealham scored 315, beating the county sixth-wicket record which had stood for 68 years. Mark Ealham hit the first century of his career, an innings which was tailored to the needs of the side and which included 17 fours. Initially, he played a supportive role to Aravinda de Silva who continued to blaze his way through the shires with what was, at this juncture, the highest score of the season. He batted for 317 minutes, faced 273 balls and hit 35 fours and 2 sixes. What an inspired importation this was on the part of Kent. What delight he gave to all those privileged to see him.

Kent ended the first day on 396 for 6, and Willis and McCague hit their highest first-class scores on the second day to lift them to 533. Undaunted, the home side, too, found the pitch to their liking and were 201 for 2 by the close.

They increased their rate of scoring considerably on the third day. Robinson provided the solidity to the innings with 27 fours in his 196 which lasted $7\frac{1}{2}$ hours, and the unexpected zest came from Pick and Hindson in a 97-run ninth-wicket stand, and Robinson declared 42 runs in arrears.

Kent batted exuberantly either side of lunch on the last day, with Taylor and Cowdrey sharing an unbroken stand of 117. Taylor was left unbeaten on 99 when the declaration came after one false alarm, and Nottinghamshire were left 51 overs in which to score 330 runs.

Batting in a style different to that which he had adopted in the first innings, Robinson hit 71 in 50 minutes. He and Pollard scored 164 for the first wicket in 29 overs. The pitch remained perfect, and Cairns and Johnson kept the momentum going. Six were needed off the last over, bowled by Patel, and Wileman and Hindson won the game with three balls to spare.

At Bath, the sides were evenly balanced at the end of the first day. The pitch offered assistance to pace and spin, but it was Giddins, enjoying a good season, who led the rout of Somerset with his brisk medium pace, returning the best bowling figures of his career. Bowler was awarded his county cap before the match and was captaining Somerset in the absence of Hayhurst who had a broken hand.

Somerset were all out before tea, and Sussex had 98 for 4 by the close. With Wells giving a high-quality display, Sussex looked as if they could take a substantial lead, but the captain had no support. He was last out after completing his fourth century of the season. His 106 came out of 181 scored while he was at the wicket.

Somerset had done well to restrict Sussex to a 49-run lead, but they lost Bowler and Harden before these arrears were cleared. At 107 for 5, they were still in trouble, but Holloway was then joined by Rose. They added 93, but were separated on the third morning when only one run had been added to the score. Turner, Kerr and Trump all batted with good sense in support of Holloway, and the last four wickets realised 144 runs. Holloway reached his first century for Somerset, and Sussex were set the task of scoring 297 on a pitch that was now giving much help to the spinners. Their hopes were dead by the end of the third day when they were 156 for 8, Somerset having claimed the extra half-hour. The match was over after 14 balls on the Monday.

At The Oval, Surrey suffered on the opening day. They bowled their overs slowly so that play went beyond seven o'clock, and most of the Glamorgan batsmen – including Thomas who hit a maiden first-class fifty – plundered runs. Tony Cottey, small but eager, quick of foot and eye, hit 20 boundaries in his 4½-hour innings and took his side to a position of strength.

On the second morning, they scored only 28 more runs while losing their last three wickets, but, in spite of Ratcliffe's 56, they soon reduced Surrey to 121 for 5. Revival came through Shahid, who hit his first century for his new county, and Hollioake, the pair adding 149. Shahid and the rapidly improving Kersey then hit 114 in 20 overs, and Surrey climbed to within 53 of the Glamorgan total.

On the third day, Matthew Maynard gave one of those delightful exhibitions which have excited spectators over the years, but which have never earned him a permanent place in international cricket. In spite of his aggressive cameo, Glamorgan slipped to 189 for 7 before Anthony and Kendrick hit their highest scores in a stand of 121.

Runs had come at nearly 4.5 an over, and Surrey were batting again before the end of the day in search of a target of 383. Five to their credit overnight, Ratcliffe and Darren Bicknell hit 137 for the first wicket, and, with 24 overs remaining, Surrey had moved to 262 for 5 with Hollioake having just joined Brown, who was in rampant mood. Hollioake disappointed, steering Anthony to gully, and Brown was caught at mid-wicket off Croft as he attempted to hit a third six. Kersey dropped anchor for 15 overs to save the game, but it was Rackemann who had to survive Watkin's final over.

Warwickshire maintained their challenge on Northamptonshire when they beat Yorkshire in three days. Electing to bat first, Yorkshire were bowled out by the home side's pace-and-seam attack in 37.1 overs for a paltry 96. By the end of the day, Warwickshire had established a lead of 113 and had six wickets standing. Knight had

In his last season in county cricket before joining the media on a permanent basis, Mark Nicholas excelled for a Hampshire side which often struggled. (David Munden/Sportsline)

made his highest score since joining the Midland county from Essex.

Night-watchman Piper continued the slaughter of Yorkshire the next morning, stretching his duties into the afternoon and hitting 14 fours in his 151-ball innings. There was consistency throughout the lower-order, and Warwickshire took a lead of 353. Yorkshire reduced this by 115 without loss by the end of the day, but this was at a price.

Moxon was playing in only his second match since breaking a thumb, and it was discovered that a blow he had received when on six had caused the same injury so that he could not resume his innings on the third day. Another miserable Yorkshire batting performance saw the last seven wickets go down for six runs, the last four without a run being scored.

29, 30 June, 1 and 3 July *at Derby*

Hampshire 284 (J.P. Stephenson 93) and 167 (G.W. White 52, C.M. Wells 4 for 29, P.A.J. DeFreitas 4 for 63)

Derbyshire 295 (K.J. Barnett 76, W.A. Dessaur 67, C.J. Adams 64, K.D. James 6 for 38) and 157 for 4

Derbyshire won by 6 wickets

Derbyshire 22 pts, Hampshire 6 pts

at Ilford

Essex 328 (N. Hussain 94, M.E. Waugh 80, R.C. Irani 63) and 219 (N. Hussain 59, N.M.K. Smith 5 for 67)

Warwickshire 513 (T.L. Penney 141, D.P. Ostler 116, D.R. Brown 85) and 35 for 0

Warwickshire won by 10 wickets

Warwickshire 24 pts, Essex 6 pts

at Swansea

Glamorgan 335 (H. Morris 106, P.A. Cottey 60, M.P. Maynard 59, M. Prabhakar 4 for 47) and 336 for 9 dec. (P.A. Cottey 130, M.P. Maynard 67, D.M. Cox 4 for 141)

Durham 331 (M. Prabhakar 101, J.I. Longley 58, M.A. Roseberry 56, D.A. Blenkiron 53) and 343 for 4 (D.A. Blenkiron 145, S. Hutton 91)

Durham won by 6 wickets

Durham 23 pts, Glamorgan 7 pts

at Lord's

Middlesex 425 (M.R. Ramprakash 214, K.R. Brown 86, P.N. Weekes 62)

Surrey 209 (N. Shahid 76, J.E. Emburey 5 for 64) and 140 (J.E. Emburey 5 for 34)

Middlesex won by an innings and 76 runs

Middlesex 24 pts, Surrey 2 pts

at Trent Bridge

Somerset 366 (M.N. Lathwell 110, R.J. Harden 66, J.E. Hindson 5 for 67) and 361 (P.D. Bowler 91, S.C. Ecclestone 67, K.A. Parsons 61, J.E. Hindson 5 for 78)

Nottinghamshire 479 (R.T. Robinson 134, P.R. Pollard 120) and 8 for 0

Match drawn

Nottinghamshire 8 pts, Somerset 6 pts

at Worcester

Worcestershire 279 (G.R. Haynes 55, T.M. Moody 51, G.J. Parsons 4 for 46) and 297 (D.A. Leatherdale 51, P.J. Newport 50)

Leicestershire 359 (N.E. Briers 175 not out) and 83 (G.A. Hick 5 for 18, R.K. Illingworth 4 for 30)

Worcestershire won by 134 runs

Worcestershire 22 pts, Leicestershire 7 pts

at Middlesbrough

Yorkshire 340 (D. Byas 108, M.G. Bevan 102, J. Srinath 6 for 63) and 145 (J. Srinath 4 for 34)

Gloucestershire 276 (R.C. Russell 87, M.A. Lynch 68, M.A. Robinson 4 for 46) and 210 for 1 (A.J. Wright 107 not out, R.J. Cunliffe 51 not out)

Gloucestershire won by 9 wickets

Gloucestershire 22 pts, Yorkshire 7 pts

Derbyshire rested Dominic Cork, the Test match hero, but still managed to end their sombre run of failure by beating Hampshire inside three days. Having won the toss, Hampshire batted first and scored consistently after the early loss of Terry to reach 284 in just under 100 overs. Their innings was held together by John Stephenson who faced 212 balls and hit a six and 14 fours in what was his highest innings for his new county.

A second-wicket stand of 99 for Derbyshire was completely dominated by Chris Adams who hit 64 off 60 balls. He is an exciting batsman, and 60 of his runs came in boundaries. He may flirt with danger, but he is a joy to watch, and he would enliven international cricket. Barnett steered Derbyshire to a narrow first-innings lead in spite of the fact that Kevan James returned his best bowling figures in championship matches.

Hampshire lost their way before the end of the second day, losing Stephenson, Terry and Whitaker for 17 and closing on 69 for 3. Nicholas went without addition on the third morning, and Smith soon followed. White played purposefully, but Wells took the last four wickets to record his best bowling performance for Derbyshire, who were left with a target of 157. Dessaur and Rollins began with a partnership of 82, but there was a tremor when four wickets fell for 13 runs. Cullinan and Barnett restored order and brought victory.

Essex had an horrendous start to the game at Valentine's Park, Ilford, losing Gooch and Robinson with two runs scored. Hussain and Waugh added 152, and there were useful contributions from Prichard and Irani, who was last out on the second morning.

At lunch, Warwickshire were 88 for 2. Childs had just dismissed Knight, and the pitch was offering help to the spinners. Incomprehensibly, Prichard relied almost exclusively on his seam bowlers until late in the day, by which time Ostler and Penney had added 151 for the third wicket in 32 overs.

Leading by 18 runs at the close of play on the second day, but with only four wickets standing, Warwickshire caused havoc on the third morning. In 38 overs, they added another 167 runs. Brown and Donald – whose 44 was his highest score for Warwickshire – put on 90 for the ninth wicket, and Essex wilted as they were outplayed tactically and technically.

Batting a second time, Essex again lost both openers cheaply before Waugh and Hussain added 81. The last six Essex wickets went down to Smith and Munton for 52 runs, and Warwickshire, having claimed the extra half-hour, won with a day to spare.

Hugh Morris hit his fourth century of the season for Glamorgan and shared three-figured partnerships with Maynard and Cottey. The combined spin of Cox and Boiling restricted Glamorgan in mid-innings when five wickets fell for 45 runs. Glamorgan added 35 runs on the second morning as they lost their last two wickets.

Durham made a quick response, with Longley and Roseberry scoring 100 for the first wicket. Three wickets fell for 24 runs before Manoj Prabhakar took over. He hit his first century for Durham and was the senior partner in a fourth-wicket partnership of 84 with Hutton. He also dominated a fifth-wicket stand of 94 with Blenkiron. Durham trailed by 17 at the end of the day, but collapsed on the third morning. In all, their last six wickets fell for 29 runs.

Former wicket-keeper Piran Holloway bolstered the Somerset batting with his prolific scoring. (Clive Brunskill/Allsport)

The main feature of Glamorgan's second innings was a fourth-wicket stand of 107 between Cottey and Maynard in which both batsmen passed 1,000 first-class runs for the season. Cottey hit his fourth century of the summer – a sharp contrast to David Hemp who was dropped for this match and had scored only 352 runs in the season.

Glamorgan led by 308 at the end of the day, and when Cox had Cottey stumped on the last morning it meant that Durham had 102 overs in which to score 341 to win. Cox's dismissal of Cottey brought him a career-best 4 for 141.

There seemed no chance of a Durham victory when Watkin sent back Longley and Roseberry with 37 scored, but Hutton and Blenkiron changed the whole complexion of the match with a partnership of 177. The two left-handers played some exciting cricket, and Blenkiron, who had batted with belligerence against Essex a few weeks earlier, hit a maiden first-class hundred with 18 fours and 4 sixes. Morris helped him in a stand of 86, and with Prabhakar keeping calm, Durham won with nearly 18 overs to spare.

Surrey's stock was low, and they took drastic steps in dropping Darren Bicknell and Alistair Brown for the match at Lord's. Brown had hit 92 in the previous championship match, but it was argued that his batting lacked a sense of responsibility. A place was found for Alex Tudor who, with his fifth delivery, had Pooley leg before. Surrey then dropped four catches. Weekes was reprieved three times and, vitally, Ramprakash was missed on 11. The pair added 104, and by the end of the day Ramprakash was unbeaten for 185, and Middlesex were 356 for 4.

Ramprakash and Keith Brown made their fifth-wicket stand worth 217 on the second day, and when Ramprakash finally fell to the deserving young Tudor he had faced 337 balls and hit 37 fours. It did not save him from being dropped from the England team.

Defeat loomed for Surrey when they slipped to 180 for 9 by the end of the second day. Benjamin and Rackemann showed defiance, but they could not avert the follow-on. Stewart was hit on the hand and retired hurt, and, having reached 100 for 3, Surrey lost their remaining batsmen for 40 runs, 33 of them being scored by Kersey. Their stock had sunk even lower.

Lathwell had become a name never mentioned when people were listing their England elevens, but he jogged several memories that, at Trent Bridge two years earlier, he had played for England against Australia with a sparkling century containing 23 boundaries. Somerset really failed to profit from Lathwell's innings although Harden, as he had done all season, made a valuable contribution.

The last two Somerset wickets brought 61 runs, but Nottinghamshire could be well pleased with their second day's work. Pollard and Robinson hit 233 for their first wicket, and Robinson, in his fifth century of the season, passed 1,000 runs. Nottinghamshire had lost only three wickets when stumps were drawn, and they trailed Somerset by only 24 runs.

The home county did take a first-innings lead of 113, but they failed to score with sufficient speed on the third day. Somerset, too, did not hurry, and they lost three wickets in making 105 off 45 overs. Their task, it seemed, was simply to save the match. Bowler did his part to achieve this by batting 311 minutes for his 91, and there was dogged resistance from Parsons and Ecclestone before farce set in. Noon held five catches in Somerset's second innings.

Worcestershire's first innings against Leicestershire was a stop-start affair. Curtis and Weston scored 91 for the first wicket, and Moody and Haynes 82 for the fourth. Rhodes batted 98 minutes for nine, and, bolstered by 55 extras, Worcestershire made 279 from 102.1 overs.

Nigel Briers began his innings on the first evening, and he was still there at the end of the second day when his side were 334 for 9.

Their ninth wicket had fallen at 237, but Pierson, who made 40, joined his skipper in a partnership worth 122, the highest of the innings. Briers batted for 438 minutes and hit 22 fours. It was the fourth time in his career that he had carried his bat.

Trailing by 80 runs, Worcestershire lost both openers before clearing the deficit. Hick – for the second time in the match – and Moody both fell to leg-spinner Clarke. At 89 for 4, Worcestershire were in considerable trouble. Haynes, Leatherdale, Rhodes and Newport showed great determination, and, eventually, Leicestershire were left a target of 218, with James Whitaker unable to bat because of damaged ankle ligaments.

Briers and Boon scored 59 for the first wicket, but the rest of the batting, bereft of Whitaker and Cronje, was bemused by a pitch that was offering great encouragement to the spinners. Nine wickets fell for 24 runs. Hick returned the best bowling figures of his career with his off-spin, and the slow left-arm of Richard Illingworth proved equally effective.

At Middlesbrough, David Byas became the first batsman in the season to score 1,000 runs, beating others by a day. He and Bevan came together after Yorkshire had lost both openers for 29 and added 190. There was another batting highlight for Yorkshire when Mark Robinson passed 20 for the first time in a career which stretched back eight years.

Srinath's fine bowling halted Yorkshire's middle-order progress, and 340 was less than the home side might have expected at one time. It seemed sufficient on the second day when Robinson, Gough and Hartley bowled the

White Rose to a 64-run lead. Only Lynch and Russell gave serious resistance to the pace trio.

Srinath struck again by removing Kellett and Vaughan. Ball accounted for Byas and Bevan, and White was run out. Alleyne took two late wickets, and Yorkshire closed on 123 for 8. Gloucestershire had given another indication of the resolve and self-belief which marked their cricket in 1995. Nor did their display of resolve end there. Srinath quickly wrapped up the innings the following morning to finish with match figures of 10 for 97.

Needing 210, Gloucestershire accomplished their task with ease. Wright and Hodgson hit 96 for the first wicket, and Cunliffe joined Wright, who hit 19 fours, to score the remaining runs and to reach his first championship fifty.

5, 6, 7 and 8 July *at Maidstone*

Kent 534 (P.A. de Silva 255, G.R. Cowdrey 137, A.E. Warner 5 for 75, F.A. Griffith 4 for 89) and 339 for 9 dec. (P.A. de Silva 116, M.R. Benson 92, S.A. Marsh 57 not out)

Derbyshire 546 for 9 dec. (C.J. Adams 216, C.M. Wells 98, A.S. Rollins 82, T.N. Wren 5 for 148) and 168 for 4

Match drawn

Kent 6 pts, Derbyshire 5 pts

6, 7, 8 and 10 July *at Darlington*

Worcestershire 424 for 8 dec. (D.A. Leatherdale 93, W.P.C. Weston 80, S.J. Rhodes 70 not out, J. Boiling 5 for 119) and 25 for 0

Durham 191 (M. Prabhakar 59, P.J. Newport 5 for 45) and 255 (M. Prabhakar 59, P.J. Newport 4 for 27)

Worcestershire won by 10 wickets

Worcestershire 23 pts, Durham 2 pts

at Bristol

Gloucestershire 208 (R.C. Russell 69 not out, A.J. Wright 54, J.E. Emburey 4 for 33, R.L. Johnson 4 for 53) and 222 (M.W. Alleyne 69)

Middlesex 441 (J.C. Pooley 136, M.R. Ramprakash 133, M.W. Gatting 108, J. Srinath 6 for 78)

Middlesex won by an innings and 11 runs

Middlesex 24 pts, Gloucestershire 1 pt

at Southampton

Hampshire 429 (M.C.J. Nicholas 147, S.D. Udal 85, P.R. Whitaker 72, M.A. Robinson 4 for 72, P.J. Hartley 4 for 109) and 265 (V.P. Terry 94, P.J. Hartley 5 for 56, R.D. Stemp 4 for 68)

Yorkshire 431 for 8 dec. (M.G. Bevan 107, S.A. Kellett 86, M.P. Vaughan 66, D. Byas 62) and 265 for 7 (M.P. Vaughan 70, M.G. Bevan 56)

Yorkshire won by 3 wickets

Yorkshire 22 pts, Hampshire 5 pts

at Old Trafford

Lancashire 437 (J.P. Crawley 173, W.K. Hegg 101, Wasim Akram 50) and 280 for 9 dec. (J.P. Crawley 64, S.P. Titchard 53, R.J. Bailey 4 for 66)

Northamptonshire 290 (R.J. Warren 90, A. Fordham 62, M. Watkinson 4 for 62) and 194 (Wasim Akram 7 for 73)

Lancashire won by 233 runs

Lancashire 24 pts, Northamptonshire 4 pts

at Leicester

Leicestershire 151 (D.A. Reeve 4 for 30) and 67 (T.A. Munton 4 for 14)

Warwickshire 307 (N.M.K. Smith 67 not out, D.P. Ostler 59, G.J. Parsons 4 for 70, A.R.K. Pierson 4 for 107)

Warwickshire won by an innings and 89 runs

Warwickshire 23 pts, Leicestershire 4 pts

at The Oval

Surrey 437 (A.D. Brown 103, G.J. Kersey 64, M.A. Butcher 59, M.C. Ilott 4 for 101) and 203 (M.A. Butcher 59, D.J. Bicknell 50, P.M. Such 5 for 79, J.H. Childs 4 for 55)

Essex 493 (N. Hussain 137, M.E. Waugh 126, R.C. Irani 108, C.G. Rackemann 4 for 99) and 151 for 3 (R.C. Irani 61 not out, M.E. Waugh 59 not out)

Essex won by 7 wickets

Essex 24 pts, Surrey 6 pts

Dropped from the England side, Mark Ramprakash replied to the selectors by becoming the only batsman in the country to top 2,000 runs. He was selected for the party to tour South Africa. (Neal Simpson/Empics)

at Arundel

Sussex 134 (F.D. Stephenson 68, C.L. Cairns 8 for 47) and 149
 (C.L. Cairns 7 for 36)

Nottinghamshire 255 (R.T. Robinson 72) and 29 for 0

Nottinghamshire won by 10 wickets

Nottinghamshire 22 pts, Sussex 4 pts

While Kent still tended to struggle somewhat in the bottom half of the county championship, the achievements of
Aravinda de Silva continued to rewrite the record books.
On the first day at Maidstone, he hit his second double
century in consecutive matches, and he and Graham
Cowdrey put on 368 for the fourth wicket in 80 overs. This,
after Kent had lost Ward, Benson and Taylor for 54 runs.

Cowdrey hit his first championship century in two
seasons, and his innings contained 22 fours. He batted
with considerable authority and was more than a bit
player in a partnership which was a Kent record for any
wicket. In writing of de Silva, one has exhausted the
superlatives. He remained unbeaten on 243 at the end of
the first day out of a score of 486 for 4.

He added only 12 on the second morning when Kent's
last six wickets went down in little over an hour. He had
hit a six and 38 fours. Any idea that Derbyshire would surrender meekly quickly vanished. Rollins and Dessaur
began with a partnership of 69, and Rollins then helped
Adams to add 109. Chris Adams was unbeaten at the end
of the day with 130 to his credit.

Adams continued to thrive on the third day as he and
Colin Wells took their fourth-wicket partnership to 224.
Wells was caught behind off Igglesden two short of his
century, but Adams, who hit 3 sixes and 38 fours and faced
256 balls, went on to reach the highest score of his career.

Derbyshire took a first-innings lead of 12, and then de
Silva blazed his way to his second century of the match.
This time he was dropped early in his innings, but he and
Benson added 152 for the third wicket. The tail rallied after
a minor collapse, and Derbyshire were asked to make 328
in 48 overs. Once Adams was gone for 43, they called off
the chase.

James Boiling produced his best bowling performance
for Durham, but he suffered somewhat on the second
morning. Worcestershire batted cautiously on a slow pitch,
and their tactics proved to be correct when Leatherdale
and Rhodes took them to a position of strength. Durham
stumbled to 157 for 6 before the close.

Prabhakar added only eight to his overnight score,
and his was the first of three wickets in 25 balls to fall to
Newport at a personal cost of one run. Prabhakar was
soon in action again as Durham followed on. He raced to
fifty off 52 balls as he and Blenkiron put on 119 for the
fourth wicket. Lampitt removed them both, and
Newport took 4 for 6 in five overs to end the innings and
give him match figures of 9 for 72 on a pitch that grew
easier in pace.

Worcestershire scored the necessary runs in under two
overs, and the game was over in three days.

Three wickets in six balls without conceding a run from
Richard Johnson, and two from John Emburey, took

*David Byas – the first batsman to reach 1,000 runs in the season – a
season in which he also held 42 catches. (Paul Sturgess/Sportsline)*

Gloucestershire from 77 for 1 to 94 for 6 against Middlesex.
Russell and Ricky Williams stopped the rot with a stand of
71, but Johnson returned to have Williams caught behind.
Emburey quickly took two more wickets, and Middlesex
were batting before the end of the day with 34 to their
credit.

Weekes was out to Alleyne before lunch on the second
day, but only one more wicket fell during the day, and that
was not until Pooley and Ramprakash had added 141.
Given a regular place in the side, the left-handed Jason
Pooley had shown himself to be one of the most consistently reliable opening batsmen in the country. His confidence had soared, and his ability to move quickly into top
gear had proved a tremendous asset to his side who
always sought quick runs. He batted for $4\frac{1}{2}$ hours and hit a
six and 23 fours before being caught at mid-off off the veteran Cooper. This brought no respite to Gloucestershire for
Ramprakash and Gatting had completed centuries by the
end of the day, by which time Middlesex had scored 410.

The Ramprakash/Gatting partnership was broken on
the third morning having realised 196. Gatting's 108 came
off 177 balls with 19 fours, and Ramprakash hit 16 fours in
his 298-ball innings. In the pursuit of quick runs,
Middlesex lost their last eight wickets for 22 runs. Srinath,

who bowled well throughout, captured six of them. His final spell brought 6 for 8 in 8.4 overs.

Batting again, Gloucestershire faltered once more against a varied attack. Wickets fell regularly, and the game was over in three days.

Hampshire gave a first-class debut to Richard Dibden, an off-break bowler from Loughborough University. He was not in action on the first day when his side scored 346 for 6 and lost Stephenson with a broken finger. Following this mishap, Paul Whitaker had given life to the Hampshire innings with a six and 12 fours, and this was compounded by Udal's 85 off 124 balls with 2 sixes and 11 fours.

Throughout these fireworks Mark Nicholas remained placid, ending the day on 90. He duly completed his century on the second morning and batted for almost seven hours, hitting a six and 23 fours. Kellett and Vaughan made 135 for Yorkshire's first wicket, and Bevan and Byas added 119 for the third wicket, a partnership which stretched into the third day. Bevan hit his second century in consecutive championship matches. There were 13 fours in his innings, and Moxon declared as soon as Yorkshire passed the Hampshire total.

Hampshire were 166 for 3 at the close of play on the third day. Richard Stemp and Peter Hartley took the last seven Hampshire wickets for 65 runs on the Monday, and Yorkshire had 64 overs in which to score 264 to win. Bevan, White and Vaughan led the charge, and Hartley hit Dibden for 2 sixes when 38 were needed from the last five overs. Hartley was caught behind off Streak, but Blakey steered Yorkshire to victory with five balls remaining.

Northamptonshire suffered a dreadful hammering at Old Trafford, and Warwickshire drew level with them at the top of the table. Crawley won the toss and decided to bat while Watkinson was still on his way from Birmingham. The first blood went to Northamptonshire who took the first four Lancashire wickets for 85 runs in 27 overs. Hegg joined Crawley for the next 76 overs in a partnership that was worth 237 runs. A delighted Hegg reached the third century of his career, the first at Old Trafford. Crawley batted into the second day, and his 173 came from 367 balls in $7\frac{1}{2}$ hours. He hit 24 fours. Wasim Akram hit a ferocious 50 off 67 balls, and Northamptonshire were denied maximum bowling points for the first time.

They then lost their first five wickets for 151 before Capel joined Warren in a grim stand which, eventually, was worth 65. Capel batted 35 overs for 11 on the Friday and was out without addition the following morning. Warren was yorked by Wasim 10 runs short of what would have been a maiden first-class century, and it was left to the last pair to add six runs and avoid the follow-on. It mattered little, for Northamptonshire were batting again before the end of the day. Lancashire pressed for quick runs in spite of Speak's early dismissal, and

Watkinson's declaration left the championship leaders 10 awkward overs at the end of the day in which they lost Montgomerie.

Three hours into the fourth day, the game was over. Wasim Akram, bowling off a shorter run, still generated considerable pace and bounce and ended Northamptonshire's run of six championship wins in a row. It was also Lancashire's first victory over Northamptonshire since 1979.

Warwickshire moved level with Northamptonshire by beating Leicestershire in two days. Severely weakened by injuries, Leicestershire were in utter disarray at 56 for 7. Dermot Reeve at one time had 4 for 7 in 12 overs. The pitch presented few problems, but the Leicestershire batting looked woefully dispirited. Nixon and Parsons added 86 to restore some order, but, by the end of the day, Warwickshire, 102 for 3, were completely in command.

Unaccountably, Reeve spent 40 overs in making 14 runs. In contrast, Neil Smith hit an unbeaten 67 off 51 balls. There were 9 fours and a six in his innings, and he and Donald put on 92 for the ninth wicket to claim a third batting point. Leicestershire began their second innings 156 runs in arrears with 44 overs of the second day remaining. Ben Smith was absent with a thigh injury, and the other 10 batsmen lasted only 37.4 overs. Lacking confidence and in some cases experience, they went like lambs to the slaughter.

At The Oval, Essex played the only side lying below them in the championship table. Restored to the side,

Middlesex began the season with concern as to an opening batsman, for both Haynes and Roseberry had departed. The problem was soon solved by Jason Pooley who batted with style and aggression and won a place in the England 'A' squad to tour Pakistan. (Alan Cozzi)

Alistair Brown showed admirable restraint in hitting 103 off 209 balls, restricting himself to 10 fours. Rollins held two outstanding leg-side catches to account for Ratcliffe and Butcher who had scored 90 for the second wicket, but the Essex fielding in general gave every indication as to why the county were lying 17th in the table.

This was never more apparent than on the second morning when Surrey scored another 95 runs from the two wickets they had standing. Joey Benjamin hit his highest score, 49, and the catching and ground fielding were deplorable. The malaise seemed as if it would continue into the batting when Robinson was caught behind off Benjamin, and Gooch gave Kersey a second catch when he hung out his bat at Tudor. Vitally, Surrey failed to accept a chance offered by Mark Waugh. The Australian was on 20 when he was put down at slip by Butcher off Rackemann. The reprieve allowed Waugh to share a 208-run stand in 59 overs with Hussain. Waugh hit 23 fours and a six in his first century of the season.

Hussain reached his third, and, on the third day, Ronnie Irani lashed 17 fours and 2 sixes in his 164-ball innings. He and Hussain scored 131 for the fifth wicket in 35 overs. Hussain was the solid partner in both of the century stands, and his innings lasted 312 balls and contained 20 fours. England must be rich in batting to ignore his talent.

Surrey began their second innings placidly, and they scored at barely two an over to close on 123 for 2. By the end of the innings, Surrey averaged less than two runs an over, strokeless against the accuracy of Such and Childs. Childs conceded only 55 runs in 44 overs in spite of being hit for a six and a four by Hollioake who was captaining Surrey. Childs had him stumped, and Essex had 55 overs in which to score 148.

Richard Nowell, the young left-arm spinner, confirmed that the pitch was aiding those who could turn the ball when he accounted for Gooch, Robinson and Hussain with only 26 scored. Irani quickly put an end to Surrey's hopes. He dominated an unbroken partnership of 125 with Waugh, and Essex won with 13 overs to spare.

Like the match at Leicester, the match at Arundel was over in two days. Wells decided to bat when he won the toss, and he was top scorer among the first six batsmen – with seven – as Sussex were sent reeling to 14 for 5. This was, in effect, 14 for 6 because Lenham had retired hurt with a broken finger after being struck by a ball from Cairns. The New Zealander was to return the best figures of his career for both innings and match, and he dismissed both Salisbury and Stephenson after they had added 85 for the sixth wicket. With Robinson showing good sense and the richness of experience, Nottinghamshire had a lead of 27 with five wickets standing by the end of the day.

Cairns and the late-order extended this lead to 121 on the second morning before Sussex, without the injured Lenham, once more surrendered to the New Zealand all-rounder's pace. Five of his second-innings victims were bowled, and he finished with match figures of 15 for 83.

20, 21, 22 and 24 July *at Southend*

Somerset 421 (P.D. Bowler 196, A.N. Hayhurst 78, M.C. Ilott 4 for 84) and 139 for 3 (Mushtaq Ahmed 62 not out)

Essex 186 (P.J. Prichard 71, M.E. Waugh 56, Mushtaq Ahmed 4 for 74) and 372 (M.E. Waugh 173, Mushtaq Ahmed 4 for 142)

Somerset won by 7 wickets

Somerset 23 pts, Essex 0 pts

at Cardiff

Glamorgan 122 (T.A. Munton 5 for 42) and 122 (A.A. Donald 4 for 25)

Warwickshire 208 (D.R. Brown 52) and 37 for 1

Warwickshire won by 9 wickets

Warwickshire 21 pts, Glamorgan 4 pts

at Cheltenham

Lancashire 231 (W.K. Hegg 61) and 117 (J. Srinath 5 for 53, A.M. Smith 5 for 60)

Gloucestershire 265 (R.J. Cunliffe 92 not out, R.C. Russell 83, Wasim Akram 5 for 58, I.D. Austin 4 for 50) and 84 for 0 (M.G.N. Windows 51 not out)

Gloucestershire won by 10 wickets

Gloucestershire 22 pts, Lancashire 5 pts

at Northampton

Hampshire 560 (R.A. Smith 172, M.C.J. Nicholas 120, S.D. Udal 62 not out, P.R. Whitaker 57, A.R. Kumble 7 for 131) and 118 for 8 (A.R. Kumble 6 for 61)

Northamptonshire 321 (A.J. Lamb 88, J.P. Taylor 58, R.J. Bailey 55) and 365 (A. Fordham 120)

Match drawn

Hampshire 8 pts, Northamptonshire 4 pts

at Guildford

Surrey 239 (G.P. Thorpe 72, A.D. Brown 55) and 528 for 9 dec. (D.J. Bicknell 228 not out, G.P. Thorpe 63, N. Shahid 57, A.J. Hollioake 56, J.E. Hindson 4 for 162)

Nottinghamshire 324 (W.M. Noon 64 not out, C.L. Cairns 50, J.E. Benjamin 5 for 53) and 272 (P. Johnson 57, R.T. Robinson 52, R.W. Nowell 4 for 43)

Surrey won by 171 runs

Surrey 21 pts, Nottinghamshire 7 pts

at Hove

Leicestershire 242 (N.E. Briers 125, I.D.K. Salisbury 5 for 70) and 347 (G.I. Macmillan 103, W.J. Cronje 69, V.J. Wells 55, I.D.K. Salisbury 6 for 101)

Sussex 233 (F.D. Stephenson 80, P. Moores 58) and 293 (A.P. Wells 142, A.R.K. Pierson 4 for 96)

Leicestershire won by 63 runs

Leicestershire 21 pts, Sussex 5 pts

at Harrogate

Yorkshire 338 (M.P. Vaughan 87, D. Byas 64, M. Prabhakar
4 for 87, S.J.E. Brown 4 for 90) and 204 for 4 dec.
(M.G. Bevan 64 not out)

Durham 206 (D. Gough 4 for 57, P.J. Hartley 4 for 65) and 125
(P.J. Hartley 4 for 51)

Yorkshire won by 211 runs

Yorkshire 23 pts, Durham 5 pts

Essex suffered their greatest indignity in half a century
when they were beaten by Somerset and, for the first time,
failed to gain a single point. Somerset were fortunate to
have first use of a placid wicket and a quick outfield, and
they scored 71 in the first hour for the loss of Lathwell.
After that the batting was more somnolent. The ball rarely
passed the bat, and by the time Hayhurst was caught at
mid-on shortly before six, he and Bowler had put on 202,
and Bowler stayed until the end of the day when he was
159 from 112 overs.

Eventually, Bowler was stumped off Such for 196. He hit
23 fours and faced 384 balls, and it was his fifth and highest century of the season. His was one of 18 wickets to fall
on the second day, a sharp contrast to the two of the first
day. Bowler's innings lasted eight hours; the Essex first
innings lasted barely half that long. The pitch was now
offering help to the bowlers, and Rose broke the back of
the Essex innings by dismissing Gooch, Robinson and
Hussain (first ball) with only 28 scored. Waugh and
Prichard counter-attacked with 101 in 18 overs, but
Mushtaq and Trump began to extract some turn, and the
last six wickets went down for 36 runs.

On the third morning Essex followed on before another
large crowd who suffered early heartbreaks when Gooch,
Robinson and Hussain again went cheaply. This time there
was the compensation of a regal innings from Mark
Waugh. Prichard helped him to add 94, and Irani shared a
stand of 105, but Waugh dominated. He mingled care with
aggression and hit 19 fours in an innings which lasted 324
minutes. It was something of a surprise when he fell to the
second new ball, but Essex ended the day with a lead of
135 and two wickets standing.

Those two wickets brought only another two runs on
the Monday so that Somerset faced a target of 138. The
spinners were soon in action, and Childs immediately had
Bowler caught behind. Lathwell and Harden fell to Such,
and Somerset were 54 for 3. Their response was to pro-
mote Mushtaq Ahmed who hit 3 sixes and 5 fours as he
made 62 off 41 balls to take his side to victory with three
hours to spare.

Warwickshire moved clear at the top of the table when
they beat Glamorgan at Cardiff in what amounted to
little more than a day and a half. Glamorgan elected to
bat and soon found themselves at 26 for 7, five of the
wickets having fallen to Munton. Anthony and Kendrick
added 66. The pitch was slow, and occasional deliveries
were keeping low, but the real cause of Glamorgan's
problems was Munton's ability to swing the ball in the
humid conditions.

Warwickshire themselves experienced difficulties
against Watkin and Anthony, and when their sixth wicket
fell they led by just one run. Reeve and Piper put on 42,
but Piper was caught off Watkin, and a day on which 17
wickets fell ended with Warwickshire 47 runs in the lead.

Reeve coaxed 41 more runs out of the last three wickets
on the second morning, and Allan Donald then set about
demolishing Glamorgan with a display of high-quality
pace bowling. James edged to the keeper, and Morris was
bowled by a slower ball. Maynard got a rising ball which
went head high to Piper, Dale was caught in the gully, and
Glamorgan lunched at 29 for 4.

Cottey was absent with an injured ankle, the result of
jogging the previous evening, so Glamorgan's hopes of
survival were slim, but Croft and Hemp scored 31 in seven
overs before Hemp sliced Munton to gully. Croft was leg
before to Giles, the very promising slow left-arm bowler,
and Anthony ran himself out in suicidal fashion. In the
end, Warwickshire needed 37 to win, and they scored
these runs for the loss of Twose who was run out. Three
hours of the second day still remained when the winning
hit was made.

At Cheltenham, the game was over in three days.
Fifteen wickets fell on the first day, and that Lancashire,
having chosen to bat, were reduced to 92 for 7 had much
to do with their own ineptitude. Fairbrother, without facing a ball, and Wasim Akram were both run out risking
runs to Symonds – strong of arm and throw – and Chapple
suffered the same fate after Austin and Hegg had brought
about a revival with an eighth-wicket stand of 102. Austin
was then primarily responsible for bringing Gloucestershire staggering to 44 for 5 by the close.

Austin struck again on the second morning, bowling
Symonds before a run had been added. This brought
Russell to join Cunliffe who had gone to the wicket at 8 for
1. Together they brought Gloucestershire back to sanity
with a stand of 125. Cunliffe also received able support
from Ball and Srinath, and the home side took a first-
innings lead of 34. Cunliffe had patiently hit 9 fours and
remained unbeaten at the end on 92, his highest championship score.

Revitalised, Gloucestershire now took a firm grip on the
game. The pitch was true but, bowling unchanged for 15
overs each, Srinath and Smith destroyed the Lancashire
batting. Titchard was bowled by Smith as he tried to drive,
and Srinath had Atherton caught at cover and beat
Crawley with a quicker ball. It was intelligent bowling,
with Smith swinging the ball into the left-hander and
Srinath varying his pace and moving the ball cleverly off
the seam. They were well supported behind the stumps
and by the catching of the slip cordon where Lloyd,
Watkinson and Austin all perished. At the close,
Lancashire were 87 for 8.

Gloucestershire were not to be denied, and the game
was over just after lunch on the Saturday.

Northamptonshire's title challenge wobbled against
Hampshire, although their remarkable resilience almost
snatched an improbable victory. Hampshire scored 353 for
3 on the first day with Smith and Nicholas still at the
crease. They were aided in what became a record stand for
this fixture by some sad lapses in the field by their hosts,

and one must still tax Northamptonshire for their insistence on pressing Warren into service as a wicket-keeper.

Hampshire had given a first-class debut to opening batsman Jason Laney, and he acquitted himself well only to be overshadowed by Smith and Nicholas whose fourth-wicket stand was worth 249. Smith hit 33 fours in his 332-ball innings while Nicholas hit 2 sixes and 18 fours in facing 304 balls. Udal plundered runs towards the end of the innings, and Kumble wheeled away for 57.5 overs to take 7 for 131, his best figures for Northamptonshire.

Montgomerie and Fordham were soon out, but Bailey and Lamb scored briskly in adding 133, only for Lamb to be out just before the close. Night-watchman Paul Taylor batted valiantly for 276 minutes before being eighth out, but he could not save the follow-on, and Northamptonshire batted again 239 runs in arrears.

They entered the last day still 99 runs behind with eight wickets standing. Lamb was out in the seventh over of the day, but Fordham extended his innings to nearly six hours, and there was much help from the rest of the order. The innings was not ended until 15 minutes before the last 20 overs were due to be called, so that Hampshire's task was to score 127 in 22 overs if they wanted to win. At 86 for 2, they had a chance, but four wickets fell for 15 runs, and when Kumble began the last over 15 were still needed. Hampshire lost two wickets in that over, and Kumble took the final honours of a grand match.

Surrey's miserable run came to an end at Guildford. They had marginally the better of the first day, but their batting was uneven, and they relied heavily on Thorpe, Brown and Hollioake for their 239 in 62.1 overs. They captured four Nottinghamshire wickets very quickly to send the visitors down to 55 for 4. Archer and Cairns halted the slide with a stand of 89, but Cairns was bowled by Benjamin in the last over of the day, and Surrey had the advantage.

They held this advantage as Nottinghamshire plummeted deeper on the second morning, descending to 181 for 7. Wayne Noon then took command, scoring 62 for the eighth wicket with Hindson and 73 for the ninth with Pick. Boosted by 51 extras, which included eight wides and 26 no-balls, Nottinghamshire had snatched a lead of 85.

Thorpe made a brisk 63, but the hero of Surrey's second innings was Darren Bicknell. He had not enjoyed the best of seasons, but now he proceeded to make the highest score in a first-class match at Guildford. His 228 not out came off 497 balls and included a six and 34 fours. It also took Surrey to the highest total ever recorded in a county game on the ground. By the end of the third day, Nottinghamshire were 37 for 2 and, in spite of the fact that Benjamin was absent injured, they succumbed on the Monday, with spinner Nowell returning the best figures of his embryo career.

There had been much optimism at Hove at the start of the season, but Sussex slid to the bottom of the table by mid-July, and it was apparent that all was not well. Omitted from the side in recent matches, Eddie Hemmings decided to retire and although, technically, he was available to play for Sussex until the end of the season, none thought that he would be seen on the first-class cricket field again. An off-spinner who played for three different counties and who captured more than 1,500 wickets,

Former Surrey wicket-keeper David Ligertwood had a long and successful run in the Durham side. (David Munden/Sportsline)

Hemmings is one of the very best of men. He played cricket for 30 years, and he wants to put something back into the game in a coaching role. The game itself would be foolish to turn its back on such a man.

Sussex's troubles did not end with the loss of Hemmings, for, a few days later, Norman Gifford gave up his post as manager of the county because of the lack of success on the field. Cricket grows closer to football every day.

Nor did things on the field get any better. Nigel Briers was last out for Leicestershire, having batted through 90.1 overs for his 125 out of 242. The second-highest scorer was Mullally with 22, and he and Briers added 64 for the ninth wicket. Salisbury took the first five wickets to fall in the space of six overs at a personal cost of nine runs.

It was seam that undid Sussex as they lost their first five wickets for 40 and were 101 for 6 before Moores and Stephenson put on 72. Holding a slender lead, Leicestershire lost Briers just before the close of the second day, but on the Saturday Macmillan – the Oxford captain making his championship debut for Leicestershire – hit a roaring hundred off 110 balls. He took 24 off one over from Phillips, added 137 for the fourth wicket with Cronje and generally treated the Sussex attack with disdain. Salisbury took six wickets to bring his match figures to 11 for 171, but Sussex were left needing 357 to win, and they lost both openers before the end of the day.

Wells played a splendid innings on the last day, facing 222 balls and hitting 2 sixes and 22 fours, but the next highest scorer was Newell with 28. Parsons and Pierson, in particular, nagged away, and Sussex crumbled, one point adrift at the bottom of the table.

Nine points above them stood Durham who were beaten for the eighth time in the season when they lost convincingly at Harrogate. Losing the toss did not help, and although they did not score briskly, Yorkshire scored steadily with all but Robinson reaching double figures.

Durham fielded a young side, many of them local products, and the game was evenly balanced when they ended the second day on 113 for 3 with Prabhakar and Blenkiron together. Unfortunately, Roseberry had been forced to retire with an injured hand and, although he returned later, the Durham innings followed a familiar pattern, with the last five wickets going down for 52 runs.

Yorkshire batted with purpose in their second innings, and there was a maturity about their approach which Durham lacked. Byas' declaration left the visitors seven uncomfortable overs before the close. With Roseberry unable to bat because of the injury – now diagnosed as a broken knuckle, Ligertwood opened and was leg before to Hartley for 0.

To end a match short of a player had become part of Durham's pattern for the season, and they duly fell before Yorkshire's rampant seam attack on the last day. The win took Yorkshire to the unexpected heights of fourth place.

27, 28, 29 and 31 July at Derby

Derbyshire 392 (C.M. Wells 106, C.J. Adams 83, K.M. Krikken 61, R.D.B. Croft 6 for 120) and 372 for 8 dec. (A.S. Rollins 118, C.M. Wells 51, H.A.G. Anthony 4 for 97)

Glamorgan 248 (S.D. Thomas 51 not out) and 321 (S.P. James 96, A.J. Harris 4 for 84)

Derbyshire won by 195 runs

Derbyshire 24 pts, Glamorgan 5 pts

at Cheltenham

Essex 244 (N. Hussain 85, R.C. Irani 54, A.M. Smith 7 for 70) and 437 (D.D.J. Robinson 123, M.E. Waugh 80, R.C. Irani 68, N. Hussain 65)

Gloucestershire 400 (A. Symonds 123 not out, M.A. Lynch 111, M.W. Alleyne 77) and 285 for 7 (M.W. Alleyne 141, A. Symonds 57, M.C. Ilott 4 for 81)

Gloucestershire won by 3 wickets

Gloucestershire 24 pts, Essex 5 pts

at Leicester

Leicestershire 503 (W.J. Cronje 163, G.I. Macmillan 122, B.F. Smith 51, M.P. Bicknell 5 for 117)

Surrey 218 (M.A. Butcher 65, N. Shahid 51, A.R.K. Pierson 5 for 80) and 248 (A.J. Tudor 56, G.J. Kersey 54, A.D. Mullally 5 for 47, A.R.K. Pierson 4 for 133)

Leicestershire won by an innings and 37 runs

Leicestershire 24 pts, Surrey 4 pts

at Lord's

Middlesex 602 for 7 dec. (M.R. Ramprakash 205,

M.W. Gatting 101, P.N. Weekes 80, J.D. Carr 78, D.J. Nash 50 not out)

Sussex 201 (A.P. Wells 61, F.D. Stephenson 55) and 115

Middlesex won by an innings and 286 runs

Middlesex 24 pts, Sussex 2 pts

at Trent Bridge

Yorkshire 256 (M.P. Vaughan 61, D. Byas 60) and 163 (C.L. Cairns 4 for 32, J.E. Hindson 4 for 65)

Nottinghamshire 403 (R.T. Robinson 124, P. Johnson 65, R.D. Stemp 4 for 108) and 18 for 2

Nottinghamshire won by 8 wickets

Nottinghamshire 23 pts, Yorkshire 5 pts

at Taunton

Lancashire 429 (N.H. Fairbrother 132, N.J. Speak 76, Wasim Akram 61, Mushtaq Ahmed 4 for 127) and 6 for 0

Somerset 161 (P.D. Bowler 57, G. Keedy 4 for 35) and 273 (A.N. Hayhurst 70 not out, G. Yates 4 for 67)

Lancashire won by 10 wickets

Lancashire 24 pts, Somerset 4 pts

at Edgbaston

Northamptonshire 152 (D.J. Capel 50, A.A. Donald 4 for 41, T.A. Munton 4 for 67) and 346 (A. Fordham 101, R.J. Warren 70, A.A. Donald 6 for 95)

Warwickshire 224 (R.G. Twose 140, D.J. Capel 7 for 44) and 267 (N.M.K. Smith 75, D.A. Reeve 74, A.R. Kumble 7 for 82)

Northamptonshire won by 7 runs

Northamptonshire 20 pts, Warwickshire 5 pts

at Worcester

Worcestershire 332 (T.M. Moody 87) and 335 for 7 dec. (G.A. Hick 74, S.J. Rhodes 54 not out)

Kent 320 (G.R. Cowdrey 94, D.P. Fulton 59, D.W. Headley 54, G.R. Haynes 4 for 33) and 286 (G.R. Cowdrey 77, S.A. Marsh 67 not out, R.K. Illingworth 4 for 89)

Worcestershire won by 61 runs

Worcestershire 23 pts, Kent 7 pts

Colin Wells hit his first championship century for Derbyshire on the opening day of the match against Glamorgan. Chris Adams dominated the early part of the Derbyshire innings with a mighty square-drive for six off Thomas and 17 fours in his 83. In spite of his rousing knock, Derbyshire were 177 for 6, and it needed a stand of 140 between Krikken and Wells to lift the innings. Wells hit 16 fours in his confident century, and some hard hitting from Griffith took Derbyshire to maximum batting points at nearly four runs an over. Croft's six wickets were reward for accuracy and perseverance.

A varied array of swing bowling and an even more

varied array of ill-chosen shots helped Glamorgan to slip to 90 for 6 on the second day, but Cottey, Anthony and Thomas – who made a career-best score – were the main reasons as to why 158 came from the last four wickets and the follow-on was avoided. Derbyshire roared to 166 for 2 before the close, and Adrian Rollins reached a maiden first-class century on the third day. His first fifty came off 177 balls, but his next took only 60 deliveries.

Barnett's declaration left Glamorgan the mammoth task of scoring 517 to win. They did well on the Saturday, losing only Morris as 156 were scored, but determination was not enough on the Monday when DeFreitas cut short James' innings and Harris, the young seamer, finished with the best bowling figures of his developing career.

Essex gave another disappointing performance at Cheltenham where Gloucestershire were led by Alleyne. He won the toss, asked Essex to bat and saw four wickets go down for 88. Hussain and Irani added 122, but the last five wickets fell for 34 runs, emphasising the length of the Essex tail. The match was a triumph for Michael Smith, the left-arm medium-pace bowler, who had been sweeping all before him throughout the season and now bettered the career-best performances established earlier in the season by taking 7 for 70.

Gloucestershire were 115 for 3 at the close and were handicapped by the loss of Cunliffe who had broken a thumb while fielding. His absence was not noticed as Gloucestershire routed the Essex attack in conditions which should have favoured the bowlers. Lynch blasted his way to 111 off 147 balls with a six and 18 fours, and his dismissal only served to prompt Symonds to unleash his powers. He hit 18 fours and 4 sixes, and his century came at a run a ball. Gloucestershire led by 156, which Essex had reduced to eight for the loss of Gooch by the close.

On the Saturday, Darren Robinson hit the second and higher century of his career. He shared a stand of 126 with Hussain, and Waugh and Irani played well to take Essex to 437, thereby setting Gloucestershire a target of 282. The home side had been handicapped by Srinath's inability to bowl.

By the end of the day, Essex seemed in control. Wright, Windows, Ricardo Williams and Lynch were out, Cunliffe would again be unable to bat, and Gloucestershire had scored only 62. Alleyne and Symonds quickly righted the position on the Monday with a stand of 141. Alleyne played a most responsible innings, batting for 251 minutes and hitting 21 fours in his 141. He was seventh out when he cut uppishly at Ilott who had done the damage on the Saturday evening, but by then Gloucestershire were only 19 short of victory, and Essex suffered their ninth defeat in 12 matches.

Surrey's revival proved to be short-lived as they crashed to defeat at Leicester in three days. Gregor Macmillan hit his second championship century in three innings, and he and Hansie Cronje devastated the Surrey attack in a third-wicket stand of 195 in 37 overs. Macmillan forced the pace from the start, hitting 2 sixes and 9 fours as he reached his hundred off 121 balls. The tall 25-year-old hit another boundary before being caught at long-off off a long-hop bowled by Nowell. Leicestershire had 431 by the end of the day, added another 72 for the last three wickets

the next morning, and then reduced Surrey to 202 for 9. The only substance to their innings was a fourth-wicket stand of 105 between Butcher and Shahid.

Surrey fared no better on the third day. They limped to 126 for 8 when they followed on before Tudor, a maiden first-class fifty, and Kersey belted their way to a stand of 65. Pierson suffered, but he could look back with contentment on a match that brought him nine wickets to take him past 50 for the season. The match was over before tea, and every aspect of the Surrey cricket was woeful.

Middlesex scored 415 for 2 in 102 overs on the first day against Sussex at Lord's after they had been put in to bat. On the second day, Ramprakash went to his second double century of the season as he and Gatting extended their third-wicket partnership to 242. Stephenson had retired from the attack with a twisted ankle. The slaughter continued until Gatting declared half an hour after lunch. With Nash and Johnson showing considerable fire and energy, Sussex slumped to 53 for 5. Stephenson, batting with a runner, and Wells scored 77 before Tufnell mopped up the tail.

Sussex were worse in their second innings than in the first, and the match was over just after lunch on the third day. The South Coast side remained bottom of the table, and the Middlesex challenge for the title was firmly on course.

Nottinghamshire, too, won in three days. Vaughan and Byas scored 95 for Yorkshire's second wicket, but the rest of the batting offered little against a varied Nottinghamshire attack. Tim Robinson hit his sixth hundred of the summer, shared a third-wicket stand of 128 with Johnson, and the home side took total command. Batting a second time, Yorkshire collapsed to the spin of Hindson and the pace of Cairns. Nottinghamshire won with more than a day to spare although the decision to send in Chapman and Afzaal to hit off the 17 runs required did give Vaughan the chance to capture two wickets.

There was yet another three-day finish at Taunton. In the absence of Watkinson, Atherton and Crawley, Wasim Akram led Lancashire for the first time, won the toss and batted. Fairbrother and Speak hit 177 for the third wicket. Fairbrother's innings included 6 sixes and 17 fours, and he bludgeoned a hundred between lunch and tea, destroying the Somerset spinners. There was a whirlwind contribution from Wasim Akram, but it was Austin and Keedy who deflated the Somerset first innings. By the end of the second day, the home side were 152 for 4 in their second innings, still 116 runs adrift.

They showed more resilience on the third morning, but the Lancashire spinners accepted punishment with a smile and captured the wickets. The game was over by lunch, and it ended with a statistical oddity. Lancashire needed six to win. Bowler bowled a no-ball which Gallian hit to the boundary, leaving the occasional off-spinner with no overs, no maidens, six runs and no wickets!

Edgbaston saw one of the very greatest of county matches, and the outcome left Warwickshire just two points ahead of Northamptonshire at the top of the table. Electing to bat, Northamptonshire lost six wickets for 69. Capel and Warren added 51, but Donald took two wickets in three balls. Capel attacked and extracted

27 from the last wicket with Taylor before becoming Munton's fourth victim.

To an opening stand of 67 with Twose, Wasim Khan contributed only 17, and this set the pattern of the Warwickshire innings. By the close, they had a lead of seven for the loss of six wickets, and Twose was unbeaten on 98. His partnership with Neil Smith for the seventh wicket was worth 36, and Smith's 18 was the second-highest score of the innings. Roger Twose carried the Warwickshire batting through 78.5 overs before hooking Capel to long-leg to be last out. It was a mighty effort, characteristic of Twose and of Warwickshire.

That Northamptonshire remained in touch was due to David Capel who returned the best bowling figures of his career in a season which had seen him revitalised. Warwickshire still had the upper hand, and Montgomerie, Bailey and Loye were out before the arrears of 72 had been wiped off. Fordham stayed, reached one of the most important centuries of his career before the close, by which time Northamptonshire had snatched a lead of 182 and had four wickets standing.

He was out early next morning, his 101 having come from 243 balls with 16 fours. Warren gave excellent support and, with tension growing and nerves fraying, the last three Northamptonshire wickets realised 68 invaluable runs. Warwickshire needed 275 to win.

Hughes soon removed Wasim Khan, and Capel bowled Twose with the score on 32. Kumble had already joined the attack, and he mesmerised the batsmen as he had done so often in the season, taking four wickets and sending Warwickshire reeling to 53 for 6. There was every prospect of Northamptonshire winning a resounding victory in three days, but Neil Smith and Dermot Reeve gave formidable resistance, and by the end of the day they had advanced the score to 161.

So play started on the Monday with the home side needing 114 more runs to win the game and the tension apparent. Reeve and Smith were not separated until the last day was 80 minutes old and their stand was worth 148. Smith cut Kumble for four to bring up the 200, but two balls later, the Indian maestro bowled him. Piper was out two overs after lunch, with the score at 225, when he lunged forward at Kumble and gave a return catch. Vitally, three runs later, after nearly five hours at the wicket, Reeve was caught neither forward nor back to Kumble and popped up the ball for Bailey to dive and hold the catch. Northamptonshire were elated. Nine wickets were down, and Warwickshire were still 47 runs short of their target.

Kumble missed a return chance offered by Donald, and the last pair nudged and clouted their way nearer to victory. Kumble was tiring after bowling 20 overs on the trot, and anxiety was showing. Capel, one of the game's many heroes, was brought back and, with a ball of full length, he trapped Munton leg before. Donald remained unbeaten on 27. Like Munton, he had played a worthy innings after producing fast bowling of the highest quality.

A great match ended in victory to Northamptonshire by seven runs – and there are those in the administration of cricket and in the media who would emasculate the game and deny us this.

The game at Worcester could not provide such excitement although it did give us a debutant in Stanford – a slow left-arm bowler deputising for the injured Patel in the Kent side – to match Anurag Singh, the batsman who made his debut for Warwickshire. Moody won the toss, Worcestershire batted and made 332 on the first day before taking two Kent wickets for 30.

At 193 for 7 on the second day, Kent looked in danger of facing a big first-innings deficit. Headley joined Cowdrey in a stand of 84 before Cowdrey was stumped off Illingworth. Cowdrey had played another excellent innings including 16 fours and a six in a season in which other Kent batsmen had struggled and injuries had been plentiful. Headley hit his first fifty for Kent, and he led Kent to within 12 of the Worcestershire score. As Curtis was out before the end of the day, the visitors could claim to have taken the initiative. That initiative was surrendered on the third day when Hick, Moody, Haynes, Leatherdale and Rhodes presented a blend of solidity and aggression. Moody's declaration left Kent a target of 348.

They negotiated seven overs on the Saturday evening, but the openers were soon separated on the Monday. Ward was totally subdued. Cowdrey played another good innings, and Marsh tried to muster the tail, but Kent had long since lost the battle.

Adrian Rollins hit a maiden century for Derbyshire against Glamorgan, 29 July, and followed this with a double century a few weeks later. (Paul Sturgess/Sportsline)

3, 4, 5 and 7 August *at Colchester*

Essex 662 for 7 dec. (N. Hussain 145, G.A. Gooch 142,
M.E. Waugh 136, R.J. Rollins 85, R.C. Irani 78)
Hampshire 255 (J.E. Stephenson 94, P.M. Such 8 for 93)
and 153 (J.P. Stephenson 63, J.H. Childs 6 for 36)

Essex won by an innings and 254 runs

Essex 24 pts, Hampshire 3 pts

at Canterbury

Surrey 559 (G.P. Thorpe 152, D.J. Bicknell 146,
A.J. Hollioake 90, M.P. Bicknell 61, M.M. Patel 6 for 206)
and 252 for 7 dec. (A.D. Brown 124 not out,
M.A. Butcher 52)
Kent 410 (T.R. Ward 101, N.J. Llong 59, S.A. Marsh 57,
R.W. Nowell 4 for 105) and 380 for 8 (N.J. Llong 118,
G.R. Cowdrey 98, P.A. de Silva 89, R.W. Nowell 4 for 144)

Match drawn

Surrey 8 pts, Kent 5 pts

at Lytham

Lancashire 355 (S.P. Titchard 60, M. Watkinson 58,
J.E.R. Gallian 53, Wasim Akram 52, I.D.K. Salisbury
6 for 107) and 215 (J.P. Crawley 70, P.W. Jarvis 5 for 55)
Sussex 317 (A.P. Wells 105, C.W.J. Athey 57, N.C. Phillips 52,
M. Watkinson 7 for 140) and 193

Lancashire won by 60 runs

Lancashire 24 pts, Sussex 7 pts

at Lord's

Middlesex 587 (M.W. Gatting 148, J.C. Pooley 133,
K.R. Brown 83, P.N. Weekes 80, M.R. Ramprakash 62,
R.A. Pick 5 for 119)
Nottinghamshire 285 (C.L. Cairns 115, P.C.R. Tufnell 5 for 74)
and 116 (A.R.C. Fraser 4 for 41)

Middlesex won by an innings and 186 runs

Middlesex 24 pts, Nottinghamshire 5 pts

at Northampton

Durham 148 (A.R. Kumble 5 for 26) and 268 (W. Larkins 112,
S. Hutton 57, J.N. Snape 5 for 65, A.R. Kumble 4 for 75)
Northamptonshire 492 for 5 dec. (R.J. Bailey 132,
A.J. Lamb 97, J.P. Taylor 86, A. Fordham 79)

Northamptonshire won by an innings and 76 runs

Northamptonshire 24 pts, Durham 1 pt

at Scarborough

Yorkshire 600 for 4 dec. (D. Byas 213, C. White 107 not out,
M.G. Bevan 89, M.P. Vaughan 88, M.D. Moxon 51) and 231
for 3 dec. (D. Byas 69, M.P. Vaughan 61)
Worcestershire 453 for 5 dec. (T.S. Curtis 169 not out,
S.J. Rhodes 72 not out, T.M. Moody 64, W.P.C. Weston 52)

and 189 for 5 (W.P.C. Weston 68, D.A. Leatherdale
67 not out)

Match drawn

Yorkshire 6 pts, Worcestershire 5 pts

There were three centuries on the opening day at Castle
Park where Essex amassed 452 in 110 overs. Gooch, who
passed 1,000 runs for the season, and Hussain scored 176
in 44 overs for the second wicket, and Hussain, impressing
with every innings and showing admirable selectivity, was
then joined by Waugh in a stand which realised 185 in 43
overs. Waugh rushed to his hundred off 127 balls while
Gooch took 150 deliveries and Hussain 225.

There was no respite for Hampshire on the second day
as Essex batted until 3.00 pm and reached the highest score
ever made in a first-class game at Castle Park. Rollins hit a
career-best 85, and Irani belted his way to 1,000 runs in the
season.

Facing a daunting total, Hampshire showed great determination and ended the day on 148 for 3. This was mainly
due to John Stephenson who, batting against his former
county, hit the first two balls he received for four. He was
unbeaten on 71 at the close of play and looked certain to
reach a century, but he was bowled trying to sweep Such.
The off-spinner finished with career-best figures of 8 for
93, and claimed two more wickets when Hampshire followed on. In all, he sent down 54 overs on the Saturday.

Childs also exploited the conditions admirably, and
Essex claimed the extra half-hour when Hampshire lost
eight second-innings wickets. Childs dismissed Connor,
but Udal and Dibden held out until the Monday.

The match was over in 17 balls on the fourth day when
three extras were scored. Such had Dibden caught, which
left the newcomer with no runs in his four first-class
innings.

A second-wicket stand of 260 between Darren Bicknell
and Graham Thorpe took Surrey to 345 for 2 on the first
day at Canterbury. Thorpe did not add to his overnight
score on the second day, and when Patel took three wickets in nine balls Kent were very much back in the game.
Hollioake and championship debutant Kennis put on 98,
and Martin Bicknell flayed the bowling for 61. Min Patel
became only the second Kent bowler to concede 200 runs
in an innings, but he bowled just under 60 overs and took
six wickets. Kent were 154 for 4 at the close, and salvation
seemed a long way off.

Trevor Ward completed his century on the third day,
and the middle-order worked hard to draw closer to
Surrey's total, but when the ninth wicket fell the score was
336, still 74 short of avoiding the follow-on. A remarkable
last-wicket partnership between Headley and Patel
brought those 74 runs, and the game threatened to stand
on its head when Headley bowled Darren Bicknell and
Thorpe with the first two balls of Surrey's second innings.
Butcher and Brown restored order, and Brown became the
fourth centurion of the match on the Monday morning.
Kent were left 78 overs in which to score 402.

Fulton and Ward went quickly, but Llong and de Silva
engaged in a thrilling stand which brought 173 in 31 overs.

The Sri Lankan again delighted with his magic, and his runs came off 91 balls, while Llong hit the highest score of his career. Both fell to the very occasional left-arm slows of Darren Bicknell who finished with 3 for 80 off 15 overs. Graham Cowdrey maintained the Kent challenge with 98 off 87 balls, but when he was stumped off Darren Bicknell with 26 needed from 13 balls the home side settled for a draw.

At Lytham, the last five Lancashire wickets added 208 runs, and the Red Rose county took a firm grip on the game when Keedy bowled Peirce before the close. The left-hander from Durham University had appeared for Combined Universities in the Benson and Hedges Cup, but was making his first-class debut.

On the second day, Athey and night-watchman Phillips made their second-wicket stand worth 99, and with Wells hitting a six and 10 fours in his fifth championship century of the summer, Sussex came to within 38 of the Lancashire score. They might well have done even better had Watkinson not taken 3 for 5 in 11 balls in mid-innings.

Sussex were very much in control when Salisbury dismissed both Atherton and Austin before the close, and when Jarvis produced a spell of 5 for 17 before lunch on the third day there was every prospect of a Sussex win. In search of 254, they moved with some comfort to 135 for 3, only to lose three quick wickets – one of which was that of Wells – and close on 145 for 6.

The match was all over in half an hour on the Monday, with Wasim Akram taking three of the last four wickets.

At Lord's, Middlesex beat Nottinghamshire inside three days. It was their fifth consecutive victory, their fourth by an innings. The only blemish was that Tufnell was reported and fined for gestures he made to the crowd.

The match began with Jason Pooley making a hundred before lunch off 94 balls. He and Weekes put on 157 for the first wicket in 36 overs. Ramprakash's outstanding form continued, and Gatting punched a third consecutive century as he added 213 for the fifth wicket with Brown. Middlesex had 500 on the board at the end of the day.

They made brisk runs the next morning, but the honours on the second day went to Chris Cairns who restored some pride to Nottinghamshire with a century off 150 balls. He was unbeaten on 106 at the end of the day, by which time Nottinghamshire had lost eight wickets for 263 runs.

Tufnell took the last two wickets on the Saturday morning, and Nottinghamshire were disposed of in under 50 overs when they batted again. Nottinghamshire were going through a difficult period, but it was no surprise when they announced that they were releasing their England all-rounder Chris Lewis. It was said that he wanted to come to London, and Surrey were said to be interested. The doubt was as to how much cricket he would play. There were no tears at Trent Bridge.

Like Middlesex, Northamptonshire won in three days and with Warwickshire idle, they went top of the table, 16 points clear of Middlesex. Sussex remained bottom although Durham, Northamptonshire's victims, were only one point above them. The seamers began the demolition of Durham and, inevitably, Kumble completed it. Montgomerie and Fordham then scored 107 for the home county's first wicket. Both fell to Cox, and Northampton-

shire ended the day one run behind with eight wickets standing.

They did not lose their third wicket until nearly half an hour after lunch on the second day when night-watchman Paul Taylor was caught off Cox for 86, the highest score of his career. His partnership with Bailey was worth 146, and his departure only let in Lamb who hit 97 in 112 minutes and helped Bailey to add 155. Bailey, as often in the season, was the backbone of the Northamptonshire innings, and his 132 occupied 277 balls and contained a six and 13 fours.

Lamb declared when his side had a lead of 344, and Larkins and Hutton reduced this by 68 runs before the end of the day. They were not separated until they had scored 181, Durham's first century opening stand of the season. Larkins hit a fine century against his old county, but five Durham wickets fell in 38 balls for the addition of only 11 runs. Thereafter, the Northamptonshire spinners took control, and Jeremy Snape returned the best bowling figures of his career.

There was never a chance of a three-day finish on the placid turf of Scarborough. Martyn Moxon returned from his second thumb-break of the season, and Michael Vaughan was awarded his county cap. The pair combined to score 118 for the first wicket. On the second day, David Byas reached the first double century of his career to give the final statistical confirmation to his wonderful summer. He shared a third-wicket stand of 180 with Bevan and a fourth-wicket partnership of 207 with White. Byas faced 376 balls and hit 27 fours. Worcestershire were 188 for 2 from 60 overs at the end of the second day, and Moody declared once the follow-on was saved on the third day. Curtis batted more than eight hours for his unbeaten 169 and shared an unbroken sixth-wicket stand of 155 with Rhodes. Stemp bowled 57.5 overs and took 2 for 128.

Set a target of 379 in 71 overs, Worcestershire were 31 for 4 before Weston and Leatherdale put on 116. The pitch had long since decided that this game would be all about statistics.

10, 11, 12 and 14 August *at Chester-le-Street (Riverside)*

Middlesex 307 (J.D. Carr 89) and 397 for 5 dec.
   (M.R. Ramprakash 155, J.D. Carr 81 not out,
   J.C. Pooley 64)
Durham 204 (M. Prabhakar 86, D.J. Nash 5 for 47,
   R.L. Johnson 5 for 50) and 114 (R.L. Johnson 5 for 48)

Middlesex won by 386 runs

Middlesex 23 pts, Durham 5 pts

at Swansea

Essex 422 (R.J. Rollins 133 not out, N. Hussain 103,
   G.A. Gooch 102, R.D.B. Croft 6 for 104) and 244
   (N. Hussain 80, N.M. Kendrick 4 for 79, R.D.B. Croft
   4 for 87)
Glamorgan 339 (P.A. Cottey 76, D.L. Hemp 66,
   M.P. Maynard 61, M.C. Ilott 5 for 53) and 180
   (P.A. Cottey 53, J.H. Childs 5 for 60)

Somerset won by 8 wickets

Somerset 23 pts, Kent 6 pts

at The Oval

Surrey 409 (N. Shahid 139, G.J. Kersey 83, M.A. Butcher 57, M.A. Robinson 4 for 64) and 175 (M.A. Butcher 62, C.E.W. Silverwood 5 for 62)

Yorkshire 366 (M.G. Bevan 153 not out, M.D. Moxon 63, C.G. Rackemann 4 for 64) and 217 (M.D. Moxon 90, A.J. Hollioake 4 for 22)

Surrey won by 1 run

Surrey 24 pts, Yorkshire 8 pts

at Kidderminster

Derbyshire 471 (K.J. Barnett 169, T.W. Tweats 78 not out, D.J. Cullinan 65, Parvaz Mirza 5 for 110) and 279 for 4 dec. (D.J. Cullinan 101 not out, C.M. Wells 55 not out, C.J. Adams 54)

Worcestershire 234 (T.S. Curtis 70, D.E. Malcolm 5 for 65) and 467 for 9 (T.M. Moody 168, S.J. Rhodes 71, D.A. Leatherdale 66, D.E. Malcolm 5 for 114)

Match drawn

Derbyshire 8 pts, Worcestershire 3 pts

Essex won by 147 runs

Essex 23 pts, Glamorgan 6 pts

at Southampton

Hampshire 225 and 221 (J.S. Laney 61, N.M.K. Smith 6 for 72)

Warwickshire 535 for 8 dec. (Wasim Khan 181, K.J. Piper 99, T.L. Penney 85, D.A. Reeve 77 not out, C.A. Connor 5 for 121)

Warwickshire won by an innings and 89 runs

Warwickshire 24 pts, Hampshire 3 pts

at Leicester

Leicestershire 235 (J.J. Whitaker 63, W.J. Cronje 55, V.J. Wells 51, Wasim Akram 6 for 72) and 282 (V.J. Wells 78, B.F. Smith 53, Wasim Akram 6 for 93)

Lancashire 303 (J.E.R. Gallian 76, A.D. Mullally 4 for 64) and 218 for 6 (N.J. Speak 64, Wasim Akram 50 not out)

Lancashire won by 4 wickets

Lancashire 23 pts, Leicestershire 5 pts

at Northampton

Northamptonshire 321 (A. Fordham 82, D.J. Capel 58) and 312 (K.M. Curran 84)

Gloucestershire 293 (M.A. Lynch 104, A. Symonds 56, A.R. Kumble 6 for 76) and 131 (J.P. Taylor 4 for 17)

Northamptonshire won by 209 runs

Northamptonshire 23 pts, Gloucestershire 6 pts

at Taunton

Kent 271 (N.J. Llong 100, G.R. Cowdrey 52, Mushtaq Ahmed 5 for 106) and 119 (Mushtaq Ahmed 6 for 38)

Somerset 338 (P.D. Bowler 85, A.P. Igglesden 5 for 92) and 53 for 2

Middlesex's win at Chester-le-Street was their sixth in a row and left them second in the table, just 16 points adrift of Northamptonshire with a game in hand. The win was harder to achieve than the scores would suggest, for Middlesex struggled at first on a pitch which was lively and aided the seamers. Carr's 89 rallied the side and took Middlesex to a third batting point. He faced 129 balls and hit 18 fours before being caught at mid-wicket off Walker. The first six Middlesex wickets had all gone to catches at slip or behind the stumps, and the visitors were delighted to reach that third batting point.

There was more delight when Roseberry and Morris fell to Johnson in the first four deliveries of the Durham innings. Hutton and Boiling were out early on the second morning to leave the home side in despair at 29 for 4. Larkins and Prabhakar added 124. Both fell to Johnson, and Durham then succumbed to Nash who took four for two in 15 balls. Trailing by 103 on the first innings, Durham then took a fearful hammering from Pooley and Ramprakash after Weekes had gone for 12. Pooley reached 1,000 runs in his first full season, and when he was caught off Boiling in the 21st over the score was 125.

Ramprakash reached his century before the end of the day, and Gatting's declaration on the Saturday left Durham a target of 501. They were 82 for 2 when rain ended play early, and, troubled by the pitch, the bowling of Johnson and Nash and the absence of Walker, they disintegrated inside an hour on the Monday morning for the addition of only another 32 runs.

The Essex revival continued with victory at Swansea. They lost Robinson early on the first morning, but Hussain and Gooch added 189 for the second wicket. It was the off-spin of Croft that was mainly responsible for bringing about a collapse as five wickets fell for 56 runs. Rollins and Ilott stopped the rot, and on the second day Robert Rollins hit the first century of his career. His innings included 3 sixes and 14 fours, and he was the principal reason for the last four wickets realising 167 runs.

Ilott bowled James with his third delivery before Morris and Hemp put on 129. The pair fell to the spinners in successive overs shortly before tea, but Cottey and Maynard scored briskly before Cottey was caught at backward point off Gooch, the seventh bowler tried. Glamorgan were still nine runs short of saving the follow-on when play ended for the day.

That target was safely passed, but Essex took a first-innings lead of 83 on a pitch that was now beginning to show signs of aiding the spinners. With Gooch bowled first ball by Watkin and Robinson caught at slip off Anthony, Essex lost some of the initiative, but Hussain again batted admirably. He played with more aggression than in the first innings, hitting 2 sixes and 10 fours before becoming one of Kendrick's four victims.

Essex scored only 17 runs on the Monday as their last three wickets fell, but Childs and Such were soon in action after Williams and Ilott had dismissed the Glamorgan openers. Glamorgan lunched at 78 for 2, but only three runs had been added after the break before Hemp and Maynard went to successive deliveries. This began a slide which was never halted, with the veteran left-arm spinner John Childs bowling particularly well.

Warwickshire's determination to retain their title was never more in evidence than in the three-day victory over Hampshire. Electing to bat when they won the toss, Hampshire fell in 88 overs to a varied attack which looked even more potent for the arrival of left-arm spinner Ashley Giles. The champions soon lost Twose and Ostler, but the second day was a triumph for the left-handed Wasim Khan who compensated for the absence of Moles and Knight with an eight-hour innings of 181. Night-watchman Piper scored briskly before being bowled by Udal one short of his century, and Wasim Khan and Penney added 208 for the fourth wicket at four runs an over.

Reeve produced his customary spice on the third morning and declared with a lead of 310. Terry and Laney responded with an opening partnership of 111, but thereafter, as Neil Smith's off-breaks began to bite, Hampshire slid to another innings defeat.

Lancashire, too, won in three days although not without some difficulty. With Wasim Akram in fiery form, they took control on the first day after Whitaker and Cronje had put on 104 for Leicestershire's first wicket. Wells also presented Lancashire with problems and he gave more problems on the second day after Lancashire had taken a first-innings lead of 68 and Wasim had sent back Macmillan, Briers and Cronje for 45. Wells and Smith added 103, but Wells added only 13 to his overnight score on the Saturday morning. Wasim Akram again bowled magnificently –

inspired, it seemed, in the role of captain – and he finished with match figures of 12 for 165. Lancashire's successful season owed much to his total commitment and consistently fine form.

Needing 215 to win, Lancashire were moving along steadily at 101 for 1 with Gallian and Speak looking untroubled when five wickets fell for 61 runs. With Wasim and Austin together and only the tail to come, a Lancashire victory looked improbable. Austin countered the off-spin of Pierson, who had taken three wickets in six overs, while Wasim attacked Parsons and Wells. He finally hit Pierson for two boundaries which brought up his fifty and won the match, an appropriate climax for an outstanding all-round performance.

Northamptonshire kept ahead of the pack with what was eventually a comfortable win over Gloucestershire. The first day ended very much in favour of the home side. In spite of the absence of Smith, Gloucestershire bowled well and it was consistent application by the Northamptonshire batting rather than any huge partnership which brought the three batting points. Fordham negotiated the early dangers of an uneven bounce and a moving ball, and Capel and Snape offered belligerence in the late middle-order. Vital, too, was a last-wicket stand of 40 between Kumble, 29 not out, and Hughes, 16. Kumble was then soon in action as a bowler, taking two of the three wickets that fell in 15 balls as Gloucestershire slumped to 22 for 3.

There was a time when such a score would have heralded an early Gloucestershire demise, but that was not the way of the 1995 vintage. They descended to 98 for 6 before Lynch and Symonds rallied them with a stand of 99 in 21 overs. Lynch batted brilliantly as he had done for most of the season, and he hit his fifth century of the summer. His runs came from 121 balls, and his aggression and demeanour gave confidence to his side. He may be in the twilight of his career, but he is vastly entertaining, an exciting fielder and a tremendous asset to the side.

It was mainly through his efforts that the Northamptonshire lead was restricted to 28, and when Gloucestershire claimed five wickets for 120 runs by the close, the game was in the balance.

Night-watchman Taylor stayed long enough to help add an invaluable 75 with Curran, and Kumble, who once more had bowled immaculately, now produced another resolute batting display. His 40 not out off 42 balls was vital in bringing 66 for the last two wickets and virtually putting the game out of Gloucestershire's reach.

With Lamb ringing the changes in his attack, Gloucestershire floundered as they went in search of a target of 341. They were 127 for 8 on the Saturday evening, and the game ended after three overs on the Monday with Taylor taking the last two wickets.

The power of the overseas player was clearly demonstrated at Taunton where Mushtaq Ahmed took 11 for 144 and Somerset beat Kent in three days. There were two significant events on the first day – Nigel Llong reached his second century in successive innings, and Adrianus van Troost was removed from the Somerset attack on the instructions of umpire Barry Dudleston for persistent intimidatory bowling. It was not van Troost's first brush with the law, yet one wonders whether he is guilty of vicious intent or simply lacks control. Having reached 220 for 5, Kent disappointed in being all out for 271, and Somerset, after losing Lathwell for two, reduced this by 77 runs by the end of the day.

Their batting displayed a consistency which had avoided Kent, although they seemed obsessed by defence and failed to score at three runs an over on a sweltering day when bowlers toiled. Kent fielded well, and Igglesden produced his best bowling of the season. Somerset led by 67, and, at the close, Kent were 41 for 1.

This gave no indication as to what was to come. On the Saturday, after an uneventful start to the day, Kent lost their last eight wickets for 35 runs in 48 minutes, the result of some excellent leg-spin bowling from Mushtaq and some inexplicably inept batting from Kent. Somerset lost Lathwell and Bowler, but scored the 53 they needed for victory in 10 overs.

There was high drama at The Oval. Darren Bicknell was caught behind with one run on the board, and Butcher and Shahid then added 136. Catches were dropped and a stumping missed, and Shahid hit a six and 25 fours in the highest score of his career. Brown and Hollioake made useful contributions, and Kersey showed his batting had benefited from a regular place in the side with a career-best 83. Yorkshire's reply was founded on Bevan's third century in six innings, and they came to within 43 of the Surrey total.

For two days, the pitch had been a batsman's dream, but it became slower and slower, and with Yorkshire using the conditions intelligently, Surrey were bowled out for 175. Mark Butcher batted maturely, and Hollioake and Kersey again proved their worth as batsmen with responsible innings. Medium-pacer Chris Silverwood returned the best figures of his career, and he bowled intelligently to be well worthy of his five wickets. Needing 219 to win, Yorkshire were 74 for the loss of Vaughan on the Saturday evening and seemingly set for victory.

That victory looked certain when, shortly after lunch on the last day, with Bevan and Moxon together, they were 185 for 3. Bevan then hit Nowell low to mid-on where Shahid took the catch. This was hardly disaster, but at 194, Moxon, a century beckoning, sliced Nowell to point. Kellett was leg before at the same score, and three runs later, Blakey prodded at a ball from the reliable Rackemann and was caught behind. This created considerable tension, and Hamilton and Silverwood tried to restore calm with nudges and deflections which brought Yorkshire to within four of their target with three wickets still standing. Hollioake brought himself on in place of Nowell, and Silverwood turned his first ball into the hands of square-leg. The next ball Stemp slogged wildly and insanely to extra-cover. This brought in one of the game's most noted rabbits, Mark Robinson. He survived the hat trick, and two were scored before, on the last ball of Hollioake's next over, Robinson was struck on the pad. The bowler appealed for leg before but umpire Willey gave not out, and Robinson claimed that he had got bat on ball. It was an unfortunate claim, for the ball had rebounded to slip where Butcher held the catch. Surrey had won an extraordinary match by one run, and not for the first time

in the season Yorkshire had snatched defeat from the jaws of victory.

The bat dominated all four days at Kidderminster. Derbyshire won the toss and hit 355 for 4 on the first day. The wickets that fell were due to batting errors or complacency, and Barnett seized the day to make 169, his 46th first-class century. They accumulated more runs on the Friday, with Tim Tweats making a career-best 78 not out, and Parvaz Mirza gaining honours for Worcestershire with the best bowling performance of his career.

Worcestershire closed on 180 for 5 and were all out in 75 minutes on the Saturday for the addition of only 54 runs. Barnett chose not to enforce the follow-on – which might well have brought victory – but batted again. Cullinan hit a superb century, his fourth of the season, with 2 sixes and 11 fours, and there were sparkling efforts from Adams and Wells. Eventually, Barnett set Worcestershire a target of 517. They were 27 for 1 when the rain came.

The home side gave a splendid account of themselves on the Monday. Moody and Leatherdale made 159 in 33 overs after three wickets had gone for 82, and Moody and Rhodes added 102 for the sixth wicket. Moody hit a six and 22 fours and faced 183 balls for his 168. In spite of this, when Thomas joined Parvaz Mirza for the last wicket, nine overs remained. They emulated their colleague Richard Illingworth at Trent Bridge, although neither was handicapped by a broken finger, and saved the game without undue fuss.

17, 18, 19 and 21 August *at Chester-le-Street (Riverside)*

Somerset 333 (R.J. Turner 65, A.R. Caddick 61) and
    390 for 5 dec. (A.N. Hayhurst 107, R.J. Harden 100 not out,
    R.J. Turner 71 not out, K.A. Parsons 69)
Durham 221 (C.W. Scott 55, A.R. Caddick 8 for 69) and 216
    (J.E. Morris 50, Mushtaq Ahmed 5 for 60)

Somerset won by 286 runs

Somerset 23 pts, Durham 5 pts

at Bristol

Derbyshire 463 (A.S. Rollins 200 not out, J.C. Adams 68,
    K.J. Barnett 68) and 104 (J. Srinath 5 for 25)
Gloucestershire 351 (A. Symonds 71, A.J. Wright 56 not out,
    M.G.N. Windows 56) and 217 for 7 (T.H.C. Hancock
    79 not out, A.E. Warner 5 for 62)

Gloucestershire won by 3 wickets

Gloucestershire 21 pts, Derbyshire 8 pts

at Old Trafford

Yorkshire 505 (M.G. Bevan 95, A.A. Metcalfe 79, D. Byas 76,
    C.E.W. Silverwood 50) and 96 for 1 (M.D. Moxon 50 not out)
Lancashire 238 (J.P. Crawley 83, M.A. Atherton 61) and 361
    (M.A. Atherton 100, J.P. Crawley 58)

Yorkshire won by 9 wickets

Yorkshire 24 pts, Lancashire 4 pts

Middlesex 410 (M.W. Gatting 136, J.C. Pooley 95,
K.R. Brown 53, M.J. McCague 4 for 81) and 201
(D.W. Headley 4 for 32, M.M. Patel 4 for 78)

Kent 265 (P.A. de Silva 88, T.R. Ward 59, P.C.R. Tufnell
4 for 73) and 206 (P.A. de Silva 60, P.C.R. Tufnell 5 for 76)

Middlesex won by 140 runs

Middlesex 24 pts, Kent 4 pts

Nottinghamshire 166 (C.L. Cairns 52, T.A. Munton 5 for 37)
and 272 (P. Johnson 120 not out, C.L. Cairns 83,
T.A. Munton 5 for 79)

Warwickshire 414 (T.L. Penney 144, Wasim Khan 68,
C.L. Cairns 4 for 81) and 28 for 0

Warwickshire won by 10 wickets

Warwickshire 24 pts, Nottinghamshire 4 pts

Sussex 326 (A.P. Wells 108, K. Greenfield 99, M.T.E. Peirce 60,
P.J. Newport 5 for 66) and 267 (N.J. Lenham 84,
A.P. Wells 55, P.A. Thomas 4 for 78)

Worcestershire 170 (J.D. Lewry 6 for 43) and 348
(W.P.C. Weston 111, S.J. Rhodes 51 not out,
I.D.K. Salisbury 5 for 139)

Sussex won by 75 runs

Sussex 23 pts, Worcestershire 4 pts

Durham slipped to another three-day defeat and to the bottom of the championship table. It had all begun so brightly when James Lawrence, a left-arm pace bowler from Darlington and 18 years old, bowled in lively fashion and had Bowler and Rose caught at slip as Somerset moved uneasily to 114 for 5. Somerset's sting was in the tail, and 121 runs came from the last three wickets with Caddick, Turner and van Troost to the fore. Caddick, in only his fourth championship match of the season, gave Durham more agony when he had Roseberry caught behind for 0 and bowled Hutton for 4.

Durham closed on 34 for 2, and disaster struck the next morning when three wickets fell at 64. The score advanced to 98 for 7 before Scott and Killeen, who made his best score of 48, put on 102 in 20 overs. Both became victims of Caddick whose figures of 8 for 69 in 19.4 overs suggested that fitness was complete and the force was with him again.

With a lead of 112, Somerset inflicted more pain on Durham as they punished an attack weakened by injury and never strong at the best of times. Andy Hayhurst hit his first century of the summer, and he declared once Richard Harden completed his hundred. Harden had retired hurt at 26 on the Friday, but showed no discomfort the following day. Turner also enjoyed himself again, and he and Harden shared an unbroken stand of 123.

Requiring 503 to win, Durham soon lost Roseberry to Caddick who again bowled well. Roseberry had had a most unhappy first season as captain of Durham. He had been injured for much of the time and had lost form and confidence. Morris hit a brisk fifty, and there was late resistance from Prabhakar, but Mushtaq Ahmed was too potent for the rest, and Durham suffered their 11th defeat of the season.

Adrian Rollins began the match at Bristol by sharing century stands with Barnett and Adams. Unbeaten on 129 at the end of the first day, Rollins carried his bat for 200, an innings which lasted more than nine hours and included 29 fours. Rollins' maiden century had come only a few weeks earlier.

Gloucestershire temporarily lost Wright when he was struck on the arm by a ball from Malcolm, but their batsmen were not afraid to hit the ball and displayed a positive approach. Symonds blasted 71 in 63 minutes, and he and Alleyne put on 93 in 18 overs, but, with five wickets standing, the home side trailed by 215 runs at the end of the second day. Wright returned. Ball showed resolution. And the follow-on was avoided.

Srinath now bowled Gloucestershire back into the game. He immediately bowled Rollins and had Tweats caught at slip. Ball – who opened the attack with Srinath, bowling his off-breaks – accounted for Wells, and Srinath had Adams caught, trapped Cork leg before and bowled DeFreitas. Derbyshire were 65 for 6.

Barnett was batting at number eight due to a stomach upset, and his ninth-wicket stand of 26 with Warner offered some comfort. Warner then took four wickets as Gloucestershire, in search of 217, scored 78. On the Monday, Hancock stood firm and shared a vital partnership with Russell which added 85 for the seventh wicket and took Gloucestershire to within two runs of victory. Derbyshire could only muse on another defeat from a position which had been favourable and look to their batsmen for more discipline.

The inconsistency of Yorkshire continued. Having lost to Surrey by one run in a game they should have won and having made a miserable exit from the NatWest Trophy at the semi-final stage, they recovered within two days to score 393 for 5 in 110 overs on the first day at Old Trafford and to give their closest rivals a sound drubbing. With Metcalfe displaying further rehabilitation and Silverwood following his career-best bowling against Surrey with his maiden first-class fifty, Yorkshire passed 500. An attack lacking Hartley and Gough then destroyed Lancashire for 238 on a pitch that held no demons. Stemp, who had not enjoyed the best of seasons, bowled well and took 3 for 50.

Following on, Lancashire showed greater determination and batted throughout the third day to reach 346 for 7. Atherton, batting at number five, completed his century on the Monday, but defeat for Lancashire was inevitable, especially when Wasim Akram did not bowl because of a strain.

With Northamptonshire idle, Middlesex moved to the top of the championship when they beat Kent. Kent began brightly with Headley trapping Weekes leg before for 0, and McCague having Ramprakash taken at short-leg for 8, but they soon wilted as Pooley and Gatting added 189.

Both batsmen were dropped, and the Kent fielding became very ragged, with Marsh far below his best behind the stumps. To add to Kent's woes, Headley was later banned from the attack by umpire Jesty for running on the pitch.

Gatting was his usual pugnacious self – squat, compact and bristling with determination – while Pooley was mightily impressive. The left-hander once hit Herzberg for 4 fours in one over, and he should have had a century, but he sacrificed himself for his captain. Gatting called him for a third run when the skipper was on 99, and Pooley paid the price.

Middlesex batted into the second morning, and McCague finished with four wickets which were well deserved. Kent were 205 for 5 at the close, but only Ward and de Silva had shown confidence. They avoided the follow-on, and Headley and Patel then whittled away at the Middlesex second innings to leave Kent with a target of 347.

The Lord's wicket was not known for its durability in 1995, and when Fulton and Ward were out on the Saturday evening defeat for Kent looked certain. Aravinda de Silva demonstrated an adaptability to the conditions which was beyond the technique of his colleagues, and Kent duly tumbled to Tufnell and Emburey on the Monday.

Warwickshire moved relentlessly into second place with yet another three-day victory. Nottinghamshire won the toss and batted first at Trent Bridge, but Munton and Donald wrought havoc, and four men were out for 44 before Johnson and Cairns added 84. This was the only partnership of any substance, and by the end of the day, Warwickshire were within 27 runs of Nottinghamshire's score for the loss of Knight and Ostler.

On the second day, Trevor Penney, enjoying some

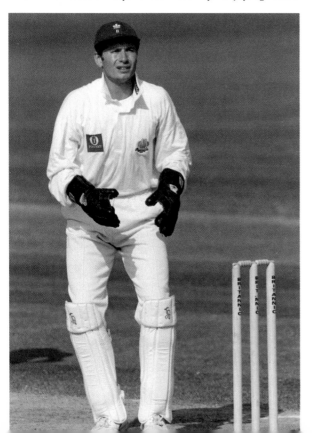

fortune from missed chances, hit his third century of the season. At 279 for 7, Warwickshire were still short of a third batting point, but Giles and Munton, in particular, supported Penney in seeing that the last three wickets realised 135 runs. The last 14 overs of the innings brought 73 for the last wicket between Munton and Penney, who hit 3 sixes and 23 fours in his 200-ball innings.

Nottinghamshire were soon in trouble again, closing at 66 for 4, and, with Banton sustaining a broken arm before he had scored, it was left once more to Johnson and Cairns to give some respectability in a stand of 151. Cairns hit 5 sixes and 8 fours in his 83, and Johnson's first first-class hundred of the season, like Penney's innings, included 3 sixes and 23 fours. It was of little avail for the game was over in mid-afternoon, the sixth time in seven matches that Warwickshire had won in three days.

There was luxury of a different kind for Sussex who gained their first championship win for three months. Victory seemed far away when they lost Athey and Lenham for 22 on the first morning at Eastbourne, but Alan Wells and the left-handed Toby Peirce put on 111 in 30 overs. Peirce made a maiden championship fifty, and when he was caught off Newport, who bowled well throughout the day, Greenfield came in to bat with an ease of timing and fluency of stroke that was totally engaging. He hit a six and 18 fours and faced 143 balls, the last of which saw him caught at slip off Lampitt. It was one of four splendid catches that Hick took during the day. The fall of Wells, who hit 18 fours and brimmed with confidence, heralded decline, and the last six wickets went down for 46 runs.

An outstanding display of left-arm swing bowling from Jason Lewry, who took a career-best 6 for 43, took Sussex to a first-innings lead of 156, which was increased by 199 by the close of play on Friday. Three wickets fell as only 12 runs were added on the Saturday. Moores and Salisbury brought relief in a stand of 42 before the last three wickets went down for 14 runs, and Worcestershire were left with a target of 424.

With the pitch offering help to the spinners, Salisbury posed a threat, but Weston played with care and confidence to reach a century before the close of play when Worcestershire, having lost four wickets, were 197 short of their target. Weston was leg before on the Monday without addition to his score while Solanki added only one before falling to Salisbury. Lewry was injured and unable to bowl, and Rhodes defied Sussex for 156 balls for his unbeaten 51, but Salisbury's long stint, 51.5 overs, was rewarded with five wickets, and Sussex came off the bottom of the table.

23, 24, 25 and 26 August *at Abergavenny*

Glamorgan 334 (S.D. Thomas 78 not out, D.L. Hemp 71, H. Morris 67, M.C.J. Ball 4 for 54, J. Srinath 4 for 74) and 471 (M.P. Maynard 164, D.L. Hemp 157, H. Morris 62, J. Srinath 9 for 76)

Graham Kersey held a regular place in the Surrey side and claimed more dismissals than any other wicket-keeper in the country. (David Munden/Sportsline)

Gloucestershire 461 (A. Symonds 254 not out,
R.C.J. Williams 52) and 293 for 9 (A. Symonds 76,
M.W. Alleyne 64, M.A. Lynch 56 not out, S.D. Thomas
5 for 99)

Match drawn

Gloucestershire 8 pts, Glamorgan 7 pts

24, 25, 26 and 28 August *at Derby*

Surrey 349 (N. Shahid 74, J.D. Ratcliffe 68, P.A.J. DeFreitas
4 for 104) and 167 for 3 (J.D. Ratcliffe 65, D.J. Bicknell 50)

Derbyshire 181 (K.J. Barnett 72, A.J. Tudor 5 for 32,
M.P. Bicknell 4 for 48) and 333 (C.J. Adams 101,
T.W. Harrison 61 not out)

Surrey won by 7 wickets

Surrey 23 pts, Derbyshire 4 pts

at Hartlepool

Durham 177 (P.W. Jarvis 4 for 46, E.S.H. Giddins 4 for 57)
and 271 (S. Hutton 98, E.S.H. Giddins 6 for 87,
P.W. Jarvis 4 for 104)

Sussex 498 for 8 dec. (C.W.J. Athey 108, N.J. Lenham 104,
J.W. Hall 100, N. Killeen 5 for 118)

Sussex won by an innings and 50 runs

Sussex 24 pts, Durham 2 pts

at Portsmouth

Hampshire 154 (Wasim Akram 7 for 52) and 352
(J.P. Stephenson 127, A.N. Aymes 60)

Lancashire 293 (S.P. Titchard 77) and 214 for 5
(G.D. Lloyd 97 not out)

Lancashire won by 5 wickets

Lancashire 22 pts, Hampshire 4 pts

at Canterbury

Essex 472 (N. Hussain 186, G.A. Gooch 105, M.E. Waugh 58)

Kent 178 (M.V. Fleming 61, M.C. Ilott 6 for 58, N.F. Williams
4 for 38) and 282 (P.A. de Silva 95, T.R. Ward 64, R.C. Irani 5
for 62)

Essex won by an innings and 12 runs

Essex 24 pts, Kent 1 pt

at Northampton

Nottinghamshire 527 (R.T. Robinson 209, G.F. Archer 158,
A.R. Kumble 4 for 118) and 157 (A.R. Kumble 5 for 43)

Northamptonshire 781 for 7 dec. (R.J. Warren 154,
A. Fordham 130, A.J. Lamb 115, D.J. Capel 114 not out,
K.M. Curran 70, R.R. Montgomerie 69)

Northamptonshire won by an innings and 97 runs

Northamptonshire 21 pts, Nottinghamshire 5 pts

*A young batsman rich in promise – Northamptonshire's Russell Warren,
who hit 154 in his county's astonishing victory over Nottinghamshire,
24–8 August. (Mike Hewitt/Allsport)*

at Weston-super-Mare

Somerset 293 (P.C.L. Holloway 117) and 368 for 6 dec.
(R.J. Harden 124, K.A. Parsons 78, P.C.L. Holloway
51 not out)

Leicestershire 350 (W.J. Cronje 213, A.R. Caddick 4 for 90)
and 313 for 8 (P.A. Nixon 79, A.R.K. Pierson 50,
Mushtaq Ahmed 4 for 150)

Leicestershire won by 2 wickets

Leicestershire 24 pts, Somerset 6 pts

at Edgbaston

Warwickshire 462 (R.G. Twose 191, P.J. Newport 4 for 98) and
69 for 0

Worcestershire 177 (T.S. Curtis 75 not out, T.M. Moody 62,
A.F. Giles 5 for 23) and 350 (S.J. Rhodes 81 not out,
T.M. Moody 78, N.M.K. Smith 5 for 162)

Warwickshire won by 10 wickets

Warwickshire 24 pts, Worcestershire 4 pts

at Leeds

Middlesex 516 for 9 dec. (M.R. Ramprakash 235,
K.R. Brown 67, P.N. Weekes 53)

Yorkshire 250 (M.D. Moxon 104, J.E. Emburey 4 for 75) and
241 (M.D. Moxon 78, J.E. Emburey 7 for 82)

Middlesex won by an innings and 25 runs

Middlesex 24 pts, Yorkshire 3 pts

There were four days of glorious cricket at Abergavenny,
and a heap of records tumbled. Rain delayed the start and
more rain brought an early lunch. Dalton fell to the fourth
ball of the day after which Hemp and Morris put on 145 in
160 minutes. The combined attack of Srinath and Ball
caused problems for the batsmen, and seven wickets fell
for 58 runs before Thomas and Kendrick stopped the rot.
They added 73 for the ninth wicket, and Watkin joined

Thomas in a last-wicket stand worth 58. Darren Thomas finished with a career-best 78 not out.

Glamorgan continued to have the better of exchanges when they reduced Gloucestershire to 79 for 5 – and then came Andrew Symonds. He and reserve wicket-keeper Richard Williams put on 213 in 41 overs. Symonds reached his century off 86 balls and passed 1,000 runs for the season. He was unbeaten on 197 at the end of the second day, and Gloucestershire led by 39 runs with three wickets standing.

That lead was extended by another 88 runs on the third day as Symonds moved to the first double century of his career, the most amazing innings of his amazing summer. His 254 came off 206 balls, and it contained 22 fours and 16 sixes. His 16 sixes took him past John Reid's 32-year-old world record, and debate as to whether he should represent England or Australia reached fever pitch.

Undaunted by what their bowlers had suffered the Glamorgan batsmen themselves began to enjoy the charms of the Abergavenny wicket, and Hemp and Maynard reached centuries before the end of the day, by which time Glamorgan had a 293-run lead.

The stand between Maynard and Hemp for the third wicket was ended when it was worth 306. Both contributed to the boundary tally, Maynard hitting 3 sixes and 21 fours, and Hemp – whose 157 was a career-best score – hit 2 sixes and 24 fours. The last eight Glamorgan wickets fell for 47 runs, seven of them to Srinath who finished with a remarkable career-best achievement of 9 for 76. His contribution to Gloucestershire's successful season was the equal to that of Symonds.

Gloucestershire needed 345 to win in 79 overs, but rain deprived them of 13 of those overs. This was unfortunate as Alleyne and Symonds added 121 in 19 overs for the fourth wicket and looked as if they might bring off a spectacular victory. Symonds was leg before to Watkin for 76 which included 4 sixes so that he established another world record with 20 sixes in a match. In the end, Lynch and Pike batted out time, and a draw was probably the best result in a match of records and incident.

A forceful innings of 68 by Jason Ratcliffe and another good performance by Nadeem Shahid were the highlights as Surrey moved to 268 for 6 against Derbyshire on a first day deprived of 28 overs through showers and bad light. Positive batting by the tail-enders took Surrey to within sight of a fourth batting point, but they were denied by DeFreitas. The Surrey bowlers were not to be denied. Kim Barnett apart, Derbyshire had no answer to Alex Tudor and Martin Bicknell, but, as so often, the Derbyshire batsmen contributed much to their own destruction. Following on, they lost Barnett and Rollins before the close and still needed another 77 to make Surrey bat again.

On the third day, Chris Adams delighted with his stroke-play in his third century of the season, and Tom Harrison, a left-hander who looks full of promise, saw that the last three wickets raised 103. Harrison's highest score proved in vain, for Surrey were victors in the last over of the extra half-hour. Ratcliffe and Darren Bicknell scored 132 for the first wicket.

Durham presented another sorry performance, and defeat by Sussex left them firmly rooted at the bottom of the championship table. They won the toss, batted and were bowled out by Jarvis, Giddins and Kirtley in 64.1 overs. Athey and Peirce scored 114 for the first Sussex wicket; Athey and Hall 120 for the second; and Hall and Lenham 137 for the third. It was all too easy, and Durham did not claim a bowling point until the 108th over.

There was some consolation on the third day for Durham when the 19-year-old Neil Killeen completed his first five-wicket haul, but by then Sussex had a lead of 321. Durham made 170 for 2 before rain ended play early.

It could not save them on the final day when Jarvis and Giddins again combined to capture the last eight wickets for 83 runs. Hutton gave some hope in an innings of 98 and was settling as an opener, but confidence was very low, and the support of the faithful was being severely tested.

Hampshire succumbed to another inspired bowling performance by Wasim Akram, and by the end of the first day, Lancashire had established a lead of 18 with six wickets standing. Wasim quickly removed Terry, bowled in the opening over, and trapped Stephenson leg before offering no shot. Returning for a second spell shortly before lunch, he was mainly instrumental in the removal of the last six Hampshire wickets for 55 runs. He bowled a full length at a very brisk pace.

Lancashire's batting – without Atherton, Gallian and Crawley, their first three – was a rather patchwork affair, and it was left to the familiar faces of Austin and Hegg to stretch the lead to 139. Steve Titchard again proved his reliability with an innings of 77 in just under six hours which gave substance when there was a threat of subsidence.

Hampshire gained considerable cheer from John Stephenson's first first-class century for the county in a season which had not been easy for him. He and Aymes put on 124 in 2½ hours for the seventh wicket. Lancashire were left to make 214 to win and were 77 for the loss of Titchard and Fairbrother on Saturday evening. Speak and Flintoff were out early on the Monday, and Hegg was forced to retire hurt after being hit on the hand by a ball from Streak. Lancashire had problems, but Austin was again defiant, and Graham Lloyd made his best championship score of the season, 97 off 89 balls, to steer the Red Rose to victory.

Essex had refound confidence, form and teamwork and were finishing the season strongly. Their sixth win of the season came at Canterbury. They romped to maximum batting points on the opening day. Gooch hit his fourth century in consecutive matches, and he and Robinson put on 101 for the first wicket, 92 of them before lunch. Gooch hit a six and 16 fours before being stumped, but this only subjected Kent to Hussain and Waugh who added 117 for the third wicket.

Hussain's most impressive and mature innings ended the next morning when he was leg before to McCague, and Kent were soon batting and losing wickets. Williams took four wickets before – inevitably, it seemed – limping off with hamstring problems, and at one point Kent were 35 for 5. Ilott had, in fact, taken three of those wickets, and he was to finish with 6 for 58, making Essex thankful that he had been released from the England squad at The Oval.

Nasser Hussain topped the Essex batting averages, fielded brilliantly and forced his way back into reckoning for the England side. He was chosen to lead the 'A' party to Pakistan. (Alan Cozzi)

Montgomerie and Fordham hit 149 in 44 overs before the close, but a predictable pattern looked to be developing: Northamptonshire would declare if and when they saved the follow-on and look for a run chase on the last afternoon.

Allan Lamb's thinking was more positive. He looked for no favours nor declarations from opponents. On the third day, Northamptonshire feasted on runs, and on some quite dreadful bowling and fielding by Nottinghamshire. The opening partnership reached 188 before Cairns, who bowled very fast and should be immune from the criticism levelled at the rest of the attack, had Montgomerie taken at slip, who was lying rather deep. Fordham had completed his ground work before he fell to Pick, but by then Lamb was peppering the off-side boundary on his way to the 89th first-class century of his career. Warren, a lovely batsman in the making, hit his first first-class hundred, and with Capel and Curran plundering at will, 219 runs came in the final session on the Saturday evening.

On the last morning, Northamptonshire added 72 runs in 8.3 overs without loss. David Capel completed his century off only 87 balls.

Lamb had decided that his only means of success was to allow his bowlers the best part of a day in which to bowl out Nottinghamshire on a pitch which had produced 1,308 runs for the loss of 17 wickets in 35 minutes over three days' play. There seemed no difficulty in the visitors batting out the day even when Pollard was bowled by Curran with the score on 24.

Archer and Robinson were unruffled, playing Kumble off the front foot and looking efficient to the extent almost of boredom. At 72, Robinson went back fatally to Kumble and was bowled. Five balls later, Johnson lobbed back a simple return catch to Kumble off a leading edge. In the next over, Archer was leg before to Capel, and Nottinghamshire were now 72 for 4. Worse was to follow. Cairns was taken at short-leg off Kumble. Dowman was splendidly caught in the gully by Snape off Curran, and Hindson was caught behind down the leg side off the same bowler. The score was now 90 for 7, and an unthinkable win seemed imminent.

Noon proved obdurate against his old county, and he thwarted the bowling for 47 overs. Pick stayed with him for 17 overs until Kumble had him taken in the leg-trap; Chapman dropped anchor for 21 overs before he was taken at leg slip off Taylor. This brought in Afford, a noted 'rabbit', with five overs remaining. Runs had no meaning as fielders crowded round the bat, as they had done for most of the day. With 17 balls to go, Kumble trapped Afford leg before, and Northamptonshire had won a remarkable victory. Bowling virtually unchanged since mid-day, Kumble finished with figures of 39.1 overs, 21 maidens, five wickets for 43 runs. Wonderful bowling, and inspiring leadership by Lamb.

There was drama, too, at Weston-super-Mare, although not of such import as that at Northampton. A truncated

Another to enjoy the day was Robert Rollins who held five catches behind the stumps.

Kent's only resistance came from de Silva and Fleming, who added a brisk 93 for the sixth wicket, and Marsh who tried to cajole something from the tail, but the follow-on could not be saved, and Benson was victim to Irani before the close.

Ronnie Irani took four more wickets on the Saturday to complete the first five-wicket haul of his career. He is a very useful cricketer. As Kent died, the last rites were illuminated by de Silva. He hit a six and 16 fours and made 95 off 96 balls. He could not save his side from a three-day defeat, but he made sure that they died gloriously.

It was destined that Northamptonshire should end the 1995 season without a trophy, yet no side gave more entertainment, nor – under Lamb's inventive and intelligent captaincy – pulled off more sensational victories. The win at Edgbaston was still fresh in people's minds, and Kumble was the leading wicket-taker in England, yet, at the end of the first day against Nottinghamshire, Northamptonshire were pointless. Robinson had a double century to his name, and his side were 353 for 1 from 100 overs.

Twenty runs into the second day, Robinson, Johnson and Cairns had gone, but Archer batted for more than seven hours, and the Nottinghamshire innings lasted until tea. Catches were missed, and there were lapses in the field. Luck and form, it appeared, had deserted the title challengers. There was comfort in the fact that

John Childs reached 1,000 wickets in first-class cricket. (Allsport)

first day saw Piran Holloway and Simon Ecclestone score 104 for Somerset's fifth wicket. Holloway enjoyed some luck in making 117, but he displayed enough class and a variety of strokes to confirm what a splendid addition he had become to the Somerset batting.

Leicestershire batted with considerably more enterprise than the home county due to the mastery of Hansie Cronje. His 213 was not a chanceless innings, but it was full of majesty and power, evidenced by his 6 sixes, and the next highest scorer was Briers with 49.

Harden and Parsons shared a third-wicket stand of 198 when Somerset batted again, but the loss of 60 overs to rain over the first three days was certain to have an influence on the outcome of the match. It convinced Hayhurst that a declaration was necessary, and he gave Leicestershire 83 overs in which to score 312 to win. Wells and Briers could not bat before five wickets had fallen, for they had been off the field nursing injuries on the Saturday evening, and Pierson opened with Macmillan. It was a productive move, for the pair put on 52, and Pierson stayed 245 minutes for his 50. He was fifth out when 51 were needed from 19.5 overs. Nixon, 79 off 89 balls, had dominated a partnership of 96 for the fifth wicket, and his was one of three wickets to fall for eight runs before Wells and Mullally steadied matters.

Warwickshire had the unusual experience of being taken to the fourth day. Dougie Brown was capped before the game with Worcestershire, but the first day belonged to Roger Twose who – as against Northamptonshire – dominated the innings. He batted into the second morning, and the second-highest score to his excellent 191 was the 71 extras, 45 of them being no-balls.

Only two batsmen reached double figures in Worcestershire's first innings, Curtis who carried his bat through the 69.2 overs and Moody with whom he added 106 for the third wicket. The last eight wickets fell for 31 runs, and Ashley Giles, a most valuable addition to the Warwickshire attack, returned his best figures in a championship match. Worcestershire followed on and lost Weston for 0 before the close.

They survived doggedly on the Saturday with Moody and Leatherdale sharing a fifth-wicket partnership of 96. Eight wickets were lost before an innings defeat was avoided, but the last pair, Rhodes and Thomas, survived until the Monday.

The eighth and ninth wickets had realised 105 runs, and Rhodes and Thomas extended their last-wicket stand to 40 before Thomas fell to Munton. It was the first time Thomas had reached double figures in his brief career. Twose and Wasim Khan briskly hit off the required runs, and the game was over in two hours on the Monday. Warwickshire remained five points behind Middlesex and six ahead of Northamptonshire. Each side had three games to play.

Middlesex moved on relentlessly. Ramprakash dominated, and they made 346 for 4 on the first day at Headingley. Ramprakash's partnership with Brown became worth 170 on the second morning, and the batsman whom England had temporarily discarded made the highest score of his career. He batted with care and purpose hitting 31 fours and a six in an innings which lasted eight hours. Content when his side passed 500, Gatting declared 45 minutes after lunch.

Vaughan was out first ball, but, with Bevan and Byas playing minor roles, Moxon took his side to 202 for 3 at the close. They did not fare so well on the Saturday. Emburey and Tufnell used the conditions to good effect, and the Yorkshire late-order sank without trace – a familiar pattern in 1995. The last seven wickets fell for the addition of 40 runs after Moxon had shown that sound technique, patience and application were able to counter the wiles of the Middlesex spinners and bring runs.

He demonstrated his ability and fine form once more when Yorkshire were forced to follow on. He and Vaughan put on 95 for the first wicket, and he had added 65 for the second with Byas when Tufnell got a ball to turn sharply and find the edge of Moxon's bat for Carr to take the catch.

The second Yorkshire innings followed the same path as the first. Bevan fell to Emburey without addition to the Saturday evening score of 179, and Byas and White were out at the same score, 210. This started the avalanche, the last seven wickets falling for 31 runs.

Emburey bowled splendidly for his seven wickets while Tufnell confirmed that he remains the best left-arm spinner in England, bowling White with a quicker ball to add to the scalps of Moxon and Vaughan he had claimed on the Saturday evening. The Yorkshire batting against the two Middlesex spinners was poor to the point of embarrassing.

This was Middlesex's eighth consecutive win, and during this run they had dropped only one point. Their problem now was that their two remaining home matches were at Uxbridge, a batsman's paradise, and the first of their opponents was Northamptonshire.

29, 30, 31 August and 1 September *at Chelmsford*

Essex 326 (M.E. Waugh 121 not out, G.A. Gooch 68,
P.A.J. DeFreitas 5 for 66) and 386 for 8 dec.
(M.E. Waugh 121, G.A. Gooch 94, P.J. Prichard 93,
T.W. Harrison 4 for 153)

Derbyshire 290 (P.A.J. DeFreitas 91, P.M. Such 5 for 86,
J.H. Childs 4 for 81) and 166 (C.J. Adams 61, J.H. Childs
4 for 39, P.M. Such 4 for 93)

Essex won by 256 runs

Essex 23 pts, Derbyshire 6 pts

at Leicester

Glamorgan 439 for 5 dec. (S.P. James 230 not out,
M.P. Maynard 103) and 194 for 5 dec. (H. Morris 61,
M.P. Maynard 53, A.R.K. Pierson 4 for 80)

Leicestershire 351 for 6 dec. (B.F. Smith 94,
G.I. Macmillan 85, N.E. Briers 73) and 285 for 4
(W.J. Cronje 99, J.J. Whitaker 65, B.F. Smith 62 not out)

Leicestershire won by 6 wickets

Leicestershire 22 pts, Glamorgan 6 pts

at Uxbridge

Northamptonshire 479 (R.J. Bailey 157, R.J. Warren 79,
R.R. Montgomerie 50) and 238 for 6 dec. (R.J. Bailey 119,
J.E. Emburey 5 for 101)

Middlesex 351 for 4 dec. (M.R. Ramprakash 111,
M.W. Gatting 83) and 277 for 6 (P.N. Weekes 127 not out,
J.C. Pooley 74)

Match drawn

Middlesex 5 pts, Northamptonshire 5 pts

at Trent Bridge

Hampshire 333 (P.R. Whitaker 68)

Nottinghamshire 154 (S.D. Udal 5 for 85) and 172
(S.D. Udal 6 for 85)

Hampshire won by an innings and 7 runs

Hampshire 22 pts, Nottinghamshire 3 pts

at The Oval

Surrey 221 (G.P. Thorpe 61, A.J. Hollioake 51,
G. Chapple 4 for 44) and 239 (A.W. Smith 51)

Lancashire 391 (J.E.R. Gallian 110, N.J. Speak 72,
M.A. Atherton 61, M.P. Bicknell 5 for 107) and 71 for 1

Lancashire won by 9 wickets

Lancashire 24 pts, Surrey 3 pts

at Edgbaston

Warwickshire 278 (Wasim Khan 68, J. Lewis 4 for 64) and
11 for 0

Gloucestershire 124 (A.A. Donald 5 for 37) and 162

Warwickshire won by 10 wickets

Warwickshire 22 pts, Gloucestershire 4 pts

at Worcester

Somerset 425 (A.R. Caddick 92, P.C.L. Holloway 74,

A valuable addition to the Warwickshire attack – Ashley Giles. (Paul Sturgess/Sportsline)

G.D. Rose 53, P.J. Newport 5 for 105) and 275 for 3
(P.D. Bowler 130 not out, P.C.L. Holloway 80)

Worcestershire 670 for 7 dec. (T.M. Moody 155,
T.S. Curtis 129, G.A. Hick 128, D.A. Leatherdale 81,
W.P.C. Weston 60)

Match drawn

Worcestershire 7 pts, Somerset 4 pts

Essex confirmed their late-season surge with a victory
over Derbyshire that took them to fifth place in the table –
unthinkable heights two months earlier. On a rain-
interrupted first day, Essex scored 315 for 9 from 86 overs.
Gooch looked set for a century and had made 68 with 3
sixes and 7 fours when he edged DeFreitas to Harrison.
Hussain, too, looked set for a big score before being caught
behind off Cork. The wicket-keeper, Derbyshire's fourth of
the season, was Steven Griffiths, formerly of Somerset second XI, who was neat and impressive in all that he did.
The Essex innings was in danger of falling apart, but it was
rescued by Mark Waugh, who, with little assistance, took
his side to a third batting point.

The Derbyshire innings was a strange affair with batsmen vying with each other to see who could hit the ball in
the air most times. Adrian Rollins was two short of his fifty
when he swung at Such and was caught by brother Robert,
one-handed above his head. Cullinan twice hit Childs for

Tony Cottey – a Glamorgan stalwart. (David Munden/Sportsline)

six and was then caught at long-off trying to hit a third. Childs had another victim when Cork skied the ball in the air and wicket-keeper Rollins took the catch to give the left-arm spinner his 1,000th wicket in first-class cricket, a notable achievement for one of the game's most popular and nicest of men.

Derbyshire had lost three wickets for eight runs and had plunged to 137 for 6 when DeFreitas, captain in the absence of Barnett who was unwell, came to the wicket. He launched a violent attack on the bowling and reached 86 off 74 balls. Childs decided to bowl over the wicket and to pitch the ball outside DeFreitas' leg stump. The batsman became subdued and constantly played the ball with his pad. The result was that one delivery hit pad and bat and was taken at silly point.

DeFreitas' innings took Derbyshire to within 36 of the Essex total, and they captured the wicket of Robinson before the close. Hussain, too, was out quickly on the third morning, but DeFreitas had now withdrawn from the match because his young daughter had been hurt in a domestic accident. Gooch, Waugh – who hit his second century of the match – and Prichard punished the bowling mercilessly. Runs came at more than four an over, and Malcolm limped out of the attack with an injury. The one bright spot for Derbyshire was the bowling of left-arm spinner Tom Harrison who took some heavy punishment but captured four wickets. He looked capable of plugging the yawning gap on the Derbyshire staff that needed to be filled by a spinner, but the administration thought otherwise and released him.

A target of 423 was always going to be beyond the capabilities of Derbyshire, and it became mission impossible when they closed on 38 for 3. In spite of Chris Adams' brave and bold 61, Childs and Such quickly finished the rout on the last morning.

Essex had given a first-class debut to fast bowler Ashley Cowan who had been on the staff since 1994. He bowled little in the match and did not take a wicket but looked lively.

There was no play on the first day at Leicester, and on the second day, Stephen James hit the first double century of his career and shared a third-wicket stand of 242 in 54 overs with Matthew Maynard. James had enjoyed a magnificent season in limited-over cricket, but he has always carried the reputation of being simply a hitter, which is rather unfair. The Leicestershire bowling was inept, but he played some glorious strokes and hit 35 fours in an innings which was often played in poor light. Maynard's 103 came off 157 balls, and he and James provided some highly entertaining cricket.

Morris, who was to relinquish the Glamorgan captaincy at the end of the season, declared at the overnight score, and Leicestershire's response was positive. Macmillan and Briers began with a stand of 153, and there were useful contributions from Whitaker and Cronje before Bev Smith hit 94 off 112 balls. Briers, who was also retiring from captaincy, declared as soon as Smith was out and four batting points had been won.

Leicestershire's task on the last day was to score 283 in 69 overs on a slow pitch. Using a heavy bat for the first time, Cronje hit 99 off 96 balls to make light of the work. Smith reached 50 off 37 balls, and he and Cronje added 145 in 24 overs. Victory came with 7.3 overs to spare.

The game which decided the championship was played at Uxbridge. This was unfortunate in that whereas Lord's pitches consistently provided a result, the wicket at Uxbridge was notorious for its placidity and unfriendliness to bowlers. Middlesex entered the match on the back of eight wins in succession while Northamptonshire had captured the public imagination and neutral support with deeds of heroism and victories against the odds. Lamb won the toss and Northamptonshire batted on a slow pitch. They made 237 for 3 in a first day on which 24 overs were lost to drizzle and bad light. Bailey and Fordham had added 97 for the second wicket, and Bailey was unbeaten on 98, but it was a day of tension and preliminary jousting rather than high drama.

There was progression on the second day when eight wickets fell, but the pace of the match was already suggesting a draw, particularly as more time was lost to bad light. Northamptonshire's run rate increased, and Bailey and the so-promising Warren scored 158 for the fourth wicket. Warren had suffered in trying to keep wicket to Kumble, and Ripley was restored to the side for this match so that Warren could be relieved of duties he never sought.

Bailey provided the backbone to the innings. He hit 2 sixes and 11 fours in a knock which lasted six hours. He was responsible and tenacious, and he made sure that his side got four batting points. Kumble hit merrily at the close, and Northamptonshire could be well content with their score. They had the bonus of capturing the wicket of Pooley before the end of the day, but Kumble, who had been given the new ball for one over, could find no joy. Emburey's three wickets had cost him 124 runs in 46.2 overs, and Tufnell had gone wicketless.

A third-wicket stand of 137 between Gatting and Ramprakash gave substance to the Middlesex innings, with Ramprakash continuing the amazing form that he had shown since losing his place in the England side after the Lord's Test. His 111 in the first innings at Uxbridge brought his total of runs in the past 10 championship innings to 1,163.

Gatting's declaration conceded a lead of 128 to Northamptonshire, and even the capture of the wicket of Fordham before the close did not change the belief that the match was destined to be drawn.

On the last morning, Bailey hit his second hundred of the match – the first time he has achieved the feat of a century in each innings – and Lamb declared at 2.15, leaving Middlesex 55 overs in which to score 367. Northamptonshire could not have been surprised by Pooley's 74 off 66 balls, but they could not have expected Weekes' first hundred of the season off 135 balls. The pair scored 126 for the first wicket, and there was a scent of victory. Pooley was caught off Kumble, and both Ramprakash and Gatting were run out in trying to take runs to short third man. Snape and Kumble now bowled in tandem, and fielders clustered round the bat. Carr was caught at mid-wicket, Brown was caught behind, and Emburey perished in the leg-trap, but it was never going to be difficult to survive on this pitch, and the match was drawn. This was a result that suited neither side, and it virtually handed the championship to Warwickshire who were operating on a very different kind of pitch at Edgbaston.

For Nottinghamshire, the season had turned to misery. Hampshire laboured to 198 for 4 from 90 overs on a shortened first day at Trent Bridge. Afford and Cairns were missing from the Nottinghamshire attack, but medium-pacer Wileman had a pre-lunch spell which brought him 2 for 2 from 13 overs, 11 of which were maidens. Stephenson was leading Hampshire in this game, and he must have been well pleased when the later order, Udal in particular, scored with more abandon even though a third batting point eluded them. Udal then combined with Maru to reduce the home side to 142 for 9 at less than two an over by the end of the second day.

The follow-on was not avoided, and Nottinghamshire fared no better against the spinners in their second innings than they had done in the first. Udal finished with match figures of 11 for 170, his best of the season, and Maru, whose appearances in the first team have become a rarity, took 6 for 84 from 56 overs. The pitch aided the spinners, but this was a woeful performance by Nottinghamshire, and the match was over in less than three days.

Woeful is a word that many are applying to Surrey cricket. With further unrest growing among members, the county side suffered another big defeat – this time at the hands of Lancashire. Crawley kept wicket for Lancashire in the absence of the injured Hegg, and he caught Butcher off Martin. This was one of four wickets to fall for 44 runs before Thorpe and Holloake added 113. Runs came at

nearly four an over, but wickets tumbled almost as quickly, and even though more than 20 overs were lost on the first day, Lancashire, 39 for 0 at the close, could be well satisfied with their work.

Gallian crawled to a century in five hours on the second day, and to add to Surrey's troubles, they were without Alex Tudor who had strained a side muscle. Lancashire lost only two wickets in passing the Surrey score, and Surrey were then faced with the prospect of Atherton coming in at number five.

Even without Wasim Akram, there is strength in the Lancashire late middle-order, and Surrey found themselves trailing by 171 runs on the first innings in spite of capturing the last four Red Rose wickets for four runs.

Martin and Chapple swung the ball appreciably. Watkinson bowled both seam and spin, and Green, the young medium-pacer making his first-class debut, had the satisfaction of bowling Thorpe. Lancashire were left needing 69 runs to win and had scored 19 of them for the loss of Titchard when they came off for bad light. The victory was completed the following morning.

For Surrey, facing another extraordinary general meeting and a winter of discontent, there was the comfort of Martin Bicknell's five-wicket haul, and that Neil Sargeant, in his first game of the season, held six catches.

There was no play on the first day at Edgbaston so that Warwickshire, in effect, won in two days. They batted first and scored consistently until losing their last three wickets without scoring a run. In all, the last five wickets fell for 20 runs, and Warwickshire took only two batting points. Gloucestershire were giving a debut to Jonathan Lewis, a medium-pacer who was once on Northamptonshire's staff. He was hit for 4 fours in one over by Ashley Giles, but he had Giles caught on the boundary in his next over and finished with two wickets in successive deliveries.

Gloucestershire's joy at Lewis' 4 for 64 was short-lived, for they slipped to 54 for 4 by the close, with Piper catching the first three batsmen. The position became worse on the next morning when Donald was in fiery form and only Symonds offered serious resistance. Astonishingly, Gloucestershire failed to avoid the follow-on. There was then a serious blow for Warwickshire as Munton retired with a strain after bowling one ball. The injury was to keep him out of the NatWest Trophy final and out of the two remaining championship matches. Such is the strength and variety of the Warwickshire attack that they managed without him. Wright was steadfast for 59 overs for his 47, and Symonds again impressed, but the Warwickshire target was nine. The holders went 12 points clear at the top of the table, and only Derbyshire, lying 15th, and Kent, lying 16th, stood between them and another championship.

Somerset scored 267 for 6 from 84 overs on the first day at Worcester with Holloway playing a stolid innings of 74 in 242 minutes. Rose offered more flamboyance, but the batting honours went to Caddick who on the second day, hit 92 – the highest score of his career – off 137 balls as 142 runs were added for the last three wickets. There was to be little joy for Caddick apart from this. He had Weston caught behind to break an opening stand of 111, but thereafter, in common with the rest of the Somerset attack, he toiled on a lifeless pitch which brought a feast of runs.

Hick (a century off 139 balls), Moody (155 from 156 deliveries) and Curtis (129 off 388 balls), all improved their batting averages. Hayhurst was out for 0 on the last day, but Bowler scored his sixth century of the season. It was four days 'full of sound and fury, Signifying nothing.'

6, 7 and 8 September *at The Oval*

New South Wales 398 for 7 dec. (M.J. Slater 69,
   M.A. Taylor 61, K.J. Roberts 53)

Surrey 57 for 1

Match drawn

Surrey's 150th anniversary celebrations, like much of their season, fell rather flat. The worthy attempt to entertain New South Wales as part of the festival was ruined by rain which prevented any play on the second and third days. There was some exciting batting from Australia's openers, Slater and Taylor, who scored 133 for the first wicket, and New South Wales made their runs in less than 80 overs. The match was interesting in that Surrey gave a first-class debut to wicket-keeper Jason Knott, son of the former England keeper Alan. Jason caught Roberts off Rackemann.

7, 8, 9 and 11 September *at Cardiff*

Glamorgan 417 for 6 dec. (H. Morris 166 not out,
   P.A. Cottey 57, R.T. Bates 4 for 138) and 213 for 0 dec.
   (H. Morris 104 not out, S.P. James 101 not out)

Nottinghamshire 319 for 6 dec. (G.F. Archer 110) and 122
   (R.D.B. Croft 5 for 47)

Glamorgan won by 189 runs

Glamorgan 22 pts, Nottinghamshire 5 pts

at Bristol

Gloucestershire 350 for 6 dec. (A.J. Wright 117,
   M.W. Alleyne 84, R.C. Russell 66 not out) and 77 for 0 dec.
   (A. Symonds 54 not out)

Durham 172 for 7 dec. (S. Hutton 60, J. Lewis 4 for 34) and
   236 (J.E. Morris 70, M.C.J. Ball 5 for 65, J. Lewis 4 for 87)

Gloucestershire won by 19 runs

Gloucestershire 23 pts, Durham 2 pts

at Southampton

Somerset 333 (R.J. Turner 66 not out, P.C.L. Holloway 65,
   C.A. Connor 5 for 79) and 0 for 0 dec.

Hampshire 36 for 0 dec. and 190 for 5 (J.S. Laney 73,
   Mushtaq Ahmed 4 for 57)

Match drawn

Hampshire 4 pts, Somerset 3 pts

at Old Trafford

Lancashire 269 for 8 (M.A. Atherton 82, N.H. Fairbrother 52,
   M.M. Patel 4 for 109)

v. Kent

Match drawn

Kent 3 pts, Lancashire 2 pts

at Uxbridge

Middlesex 338 (M.R. Ramprakash 158) and 212 for 2 dec.
   (M.R. Ramprakash 111 not out)

Leicestershire 300 for 5 dec. (V.J. Wells 124, W.J. Cronje 84,
   P.C.R. Tufnell 5 for 102) and 249 (W.J. Cronje 53, J.J.
   Whitaker 51, P.C.R. Tufnell 5 for 100, J.E. Emburey 4 for 81)

Middlesex won by 1 run

Middlesex 21 pts, Leicestershire 7 pts

at Northampton

Worcestershire 196 (A.R. Kumble 6 for 63) and 237 for 6 dec.
   (W.P.C. Weston 89, K.M. Curran 4 for 78)

Northamptonshire 174 for 9 dec. (R.J. Warren 64,
   S.R. Lampitt 4 for 34) and 265 for 5 (A. Fordham 126)

Northamptonshire won by 5 wickets

Northamptonshire 20 pts, Worcestershire 4 pts

at Edgbaston

Derbyshire 268 (D.J. Cullinan 121) and 122 (A.A. Donald
   5 for 65)

Warwickshire 387 for 8 dec. (T.L. Penney 137 not out,
   D.A. Reeve 67, D.P. Ostler 62) and 5 for 0

Warwickshire won by 10 wickets

Warwickshire 24 pts, Derbyshire 5 pts

at Scarborough

Sussex 357 for 8 (N.J. Lenham 86, K. Greenfield 85,
   A.P. Wells 76)

v. Yorkshire

Match drawn

Sussex 4 pts, Yorkshire 3 pts

Three balls at Uxbridge was the only play possible anywhere in the country on the Thursday, and rain was to interfere with several matches in the days that followed.

Glamorgan were galvanised by retiring skipper Hugh Morris who reached the highest score of his career on the Saturday before declaring. Nottinghamshire suffered an early disaster when Paul Pollard was taken to hospital with a serious groin injury. It was the end of what had not been a lucky season for him. Following the departure of Pollard, much rested on Archer who hit 2 sixes and 13 fours in his 110. He shared a third-wicket stand of 86 with Johnson who was leading Nottinghamshire. Johnson was due to succeed Robinson as captain in 1996. He declared 98 runs in arrears, but his bowlers failed to capture a wicket on the Saturday evening.

Indeed, Morris and James extended their opening partnership to 213 in 51.3 overs on the Monday. Morris completed a century in each innings for the third time in his career, and he set Nottinghamshire a target of 312 in 65 overs. With Pollard absent, the visitors were relying heavily on Robinson, Archer and Cairns, but the first two fell to Croft, and Cairns was stumped off Kendrick immediately after tea. Noon gave resistance, but Thomas returned to capture three of the last four wickets which went down for 12 runs.

Co-operation between the captains brought a result at Bristol where only 53 overs were possible on the second day after a blank first. Wright, as so often, provided the rock for the Gloucestershire innings while Alleyne and Russell brought the fourth batting point with their aggression. Hutton, doing well as an opener, and Longley added 100 for Durham's first wicket, but seven wickets then fell for 38 runs.

Durham declared at their Saturday score, and wicket-keeper Scott and batsman Longley then bowled 7.2 overs to Symonds and Wright from which 77 runs were scored. This resulted in Russell setting Durham a target of 256 in 65 overs, which, with Srinath now on his way back to India, was generous. Durham cruised to 127 for 1 with Morris in control, but, inevitably, they fell apart, and seven wickets fell for 52 runs before Brown gave late resistance. He was last out, caught at mid-off to become Ball's fifth victim with 10 balls remaining. Jon Lewis brought his total of wickets to 12 in three innings in his first two first-class matches.

Play did not start at Southampton until the Saturday, and forfeiture and declaration were unable to conjure a result. At Old Trafford, 100 overs on the Saturday was the extent of the match so that Lancashire's lingering hopes of taking the title were washed away.

Middlesex kept theirs alive in dramatic fashion at Uxbridge. Only 68 overs were possible on the Friday, but that was enough time for Ramprakash to register his eighth century of the season, his second in eight days at Uxbridge. His innings was all the more meritorious in that Weekes and Pooley were out for 12, and no other batsman could find his touch on a drab day. The Leicestershire spinners, Pierson and Brimson, posed problems, and Tufnell emulated them, taking all five wickets that fell when Leicestershire batted. In spite of Tufnell's efforts, the honour went to Wells and Cronje whose third-wicket stand of 185 denied the star-studded Middlesex attack, and they seized the initiative for Leicestershire.

Whitaker declared when his side had gained their third batting point, and Middlesex had to score quickly to keep the game alive. Ramprakash hit his second hundred of the match off 69 balls – it was his third in 10 days at Uxbridge – and he excelled once more, although he was aided by some friendly bowling in the later stages of his innings. Gatting's declaration left Leicestershire two sessions in which to score 251 runs.

The visitors seemed well set for victory when Whitaker and Cronje shared a third-wicket stand of 95 at five runs an over, and at one point, with some 45 overs remaining, Leicestershire needed 120 to win with eight wickets standing. Tufnell hit Cronje's off stump and had Smith caught bat-and-pad to alter the complexion of the match. At tea, Leicestershire were 145 for 4 with 34 overs left.

When Whitaker was brilliantly caught at short-leg by Pooley off Emburey Middlesex nosed ahead, and when the eighth wicket fell Leicestershire were 37 short of their target. The advance in Pierson's batting had been one of the features of Leicestershire's season, and he now displayed admirable calm and sound technique. From 10 overs, 28 were needed, but Brimson was bowled by Tufnell at 237. The target was now 14 from five overs, and two no-balls and an overthrow helped reduce the gap to two runs with 10 balls to go. Had sense prevailed… But it did not. Mullally went for glory, hitting Tufnell high to the square-leg boundary where Emburey judged the catch, and the brave Pierson could only fling down his bat in despair, frustration and anger at human folly.

Middlesex's hopes of the title remained alive – just, but Northamptonshire's disappeared even though they beat Worcestershire. They were not helped by the fact that only 43 overs could be bowled on the second day after the blank first. The Saturday was an historic day for Northamptonshire and for the great Anil Kumble. He began it by taking a catch at fine leg to get rid of Lampitt, and he later trapped Haynes leg before and bowled Radford with his top-spinner. This brought his total number of wickets for the season to 99, and when Solanki drove to extra-cover and Snape plucked a catch out of the air the Indian leg-spinner had become the first spinner for 12 years to take 100 wickets in a season and the first bowler of any type for four years to accomplish a feat that was once common. With only 17 championship matches now played, it is no easy task to take 100 wickets on pitches which are often in favour of the batsmen.

Sadly, Northamptonshire's batsmen were unable to follow Kumble's inspiration, and Warren and Ripley were the only men to reach 20. Lamb declared 22 runs in arrears, and although Kumble made Curtis his 101st victim before the end of the day, Worcestershire were on top.

Moody played his part in keeping the game alive by offering Northamptonshire a target of 260. Fordham hit 17 fours and a six in his fourth century of the summer, and he and Lamb put on 127 for the third wicket. Capel finished the match with successive sixes off Lampitt, but, to the chagrin of Northamptonshire, Warwickshire were already out of reach.

The reigning champions had a fuller day than most on the Friday and collected four bowling points as Derbyshire charged to 268 in 85.4 overs. While most of those around him floundered, Daryll Cullinan batted imperiously, mocking a pitch with variable bounce and help for spin, and hitting 20 fours, a six and – by courtesy of overthrows – a seven as he made 121 out of 171 while he was at the wicket.

Warwickshire lost Knight to the first ball of their innings, but on the Saturday, a sixth-wicket stand of 168 between Reeve and Penney brought the pace and the substance to the innings that Warwickshire always seek. Penney hit his fourth hundred of the season and became the first Warwickshire batsman to reach 1,000 runs, a testimony to the teamwork and commitment, the support for each other which is the very essence of the Warwickshire success. Neil Smith and Piper also blazed away to advantage, and, after what had been an indifferent start, Warwickshire were able to declare at 387 for 8 from 101 overs. This gave them 11 overs at Derbyshire before the close, and, in fading light, that was enough time for Donald to york Barnett, to have night-watchman Griffiths caught first ball at slip by the tumbling Ostler and to have Rollins caught by Twose at gully. Base, the second night-watchman, stayed, and Derbyshire had 31 on the board by the end of what – for Warwickshire – had been a perfect day.

The only surprise on the last day was that Warwickshire had to bat again to score four runs. Once the partnership between Adams and Cullinan had been broken, there was little to delay them. In eight overs, Adams and Cullinan played some lovely strokes, as is their custom, and added 48, but, having hit Smith for six, Adams was caught at mid-off. Cullinan fell to the wily Reeve, and it was all over 15 minutes before lunch.

At Scarborough, Sussex gave Robin Martin-Jenkins his first-class debut, but only on Saturday was play possible, and he was unbeaten on 0. Sussex were 21 for 2 before Neil Lenham and Alan Wells added 163. Greenfield and Salisbury also batted with conviction, and the clouds seemed to be passing from Sussex's overcast season.

Craig White was injured while bowling his first over and did not play in Yorkshire's final match.

14, 15, 16 and 18 September *at Derby*

Derbyshire 267 (P.A.J. DeFreitas 94 not out) and 325
(K.J. Barnett 88)
Lancashire 155 (I.D. Austin 80 not out, D.G. Cork 7 for 61) and 155 (J.P. Crawley 52, A.E. Warner 6 for 21)

Derbyshire won by 282 runs

Derbyshire 22 pts, Lancashire 4 pts

---

at Chester-le-Street (Riverside)

Durham 424 (W. Larkins 121, J.E. Morris 109,
M.A. Roseberry 53, J.A. Daley 50, R.T. Bates 5 for 88)
Nottinghamshire 190 (D.B. Pennett 50, A. Walker 4 for 29)
and 220 (W.M. Noon 52 not out, J. Boiling 5 for 73,
S.J.E. Brown 4 for 61)

Durham won by an innings and 14 runs

Durham 24 pts, Nottinghamshire 3 pts

---

at Chelmsford

Essex 313 (R.J. Rollins 63, N. Hussain 58, P.J. Prichard 54) and
270 (P.J. Prichard 104, R.J. Rollins 77, D. Gough
4 for 94, P.J. Hartley 4 for 105)
Yorkshire 309 (D. Byas 98, R.A. Kettleborough 55, M.C. Ilott
4 for 97) and 185 (P.M. Such 5 for 89)

Essex won by 89 runs

Essex 23 pts, Yorkshire 7 pts

---

at Canterbury

Warwickshire 468 for 6 dec. (N.V. Knight 174, R.G. Twose
109 not out, N.M.K. Smith 54, Wasim Khan 51)

Kent 239 (G.R. Cowdrey 103, D.A. Reeve 5 for 30) and 124
(A.A. Donald 4 for 43)

Warwickshire won by an innings and 105 runs

Warwickshire 24 pts, Kent 3 pts

---

at Leicester

Gloucestershire 196
Leicestershire 57 for 1

Match drawn

Leicestershire 4 pts, Gloucestershire 0 pts

---

at Taunton

Somerset 376 (A.N. Hayhurst 71, R.J. Harden 63,
K.A. Parsons 62, A.R.C. Fraser 5 for 56) and 323 for 7 dec.
(J.C. Hallett 111 not out, M.E. Trescothick 59)
Middlesex 350 for 3 dec. (M.W. Gatting 122 not out,
M.R. Ramprakash 115, J.C. Pooley 90) and 262 for 6
(P.N. Weekes 79, M.R. Ramprakash 73, J.D. Batty 4 for 70)

Match drawn

Middlesex 7 pts, Somerset 4 pts

---

at The Oval

Hampshire 185 (M.P. Bicknell 4 for 65) and 152
(M.C.J. Nicholas 53, M.P. Bicknell 4 for 60)
Surrey 71 for 2 dec. and 175 for 2 (N. Shahid 77 not out,
D.J. Bicknell 75)

Match drawn

Surrey 4 pts, Hampshire 0 pts

---

at Hove

Sussex 331 (P. Moores 89 not out, C.W.J. Athey 56,
R.S.C. Martin-Jenkins 50, D.J. Capel 4 for 102) and
132 for 2 dec. (I.D.K. Salisbury 67 not out)
Northamptonshire 41 for 1 dec. and 36 for 0

Match drawn

Northamptonshire 4 pts, Sussex 3 pts

---

at Worcester

Worcestershire 79 for 1
v. **Glamorgan**

Match drawn

No points

With their 14th victory of the season, Warwickshire retained the Britannic Assurance County Championship. As had become their habit, they beat Kent inside three days. Reeve won the toss, and Knight and Wasim Khan, who had been an admirable deputy for the injured Moles for more than half the season, scored 148 for the first wicket. More than 20 overs were lost to rain on the opening day, but Warwickshire passed 300 and set the basis of victory. Knight obliterated the memories of his dreadful innings in the NatWest final with his first first-class century for his adopted county. He is, perhaps, a less fluid and open batsman than in his early days with Essex, but he has taken on a more solid look, and he times the ball sweetly as his 2 sixes and 21 fours indicated in the highest of his eight centuries.

On the Friday, the solidity was provided by Roger Twose in his last first-class innings for Warwickshire before joining the New Zealand national side. He duly reached his 15th first-class hundred, his fourth of the 1995 season. He is a most valuable cricketer, one of those who is always contributing to the game. England's loss is New Zealand's gain. He should prosper. Penney and Neil Smith added the fireworks to the Warwickshire innings, and Reeve declared five minutes before lunch. He himself shared the new ball with Donald in the absence of Munton and Brown, and he had Benson caught behind and Walker taken at mid-off. Llong was also caught behind, off Donald, and Ward swung at a straight ball from Bell and was bowled. Kent were 20 for 4.

Cowdrey, who had begun the season without a first-team place, demonstrated why he had been Kent's most successful home-grown batsman of the summer with a century which shamed his colleagues. He added 72 with Ealham and 85 with Fleming, but he became Reeve's fourth victim, and Kent followed on as had seemed likely since lunch on the first day.

Play could not restart until the Saturday afternoon. Kent were 18 for 0 from 10 overs, but 39 overs later, they were all out. They batted two short, both Cowdrey and Igglesden being injured, but one felt that a hundred men would not have halted the Warwickshire tide. Donald took the final wicket when he had Patel caught at slip. He sank to his knees and was engulfed by the other Bears.

Donald is a great bowler, but Warwickshire success is founded on total team effort. Every man contributes. They played much of the season without two vital players, Moles and Munton, but the gaps were filled. They are led with intelligence and drive, and they thrive on self-belief and total commitment. They do not complain about too much cricket or about anything else that it has become customary to complain about. Moaning saps performance. Mr Illingworth should note that, perhaps.

Warwickshire will be without Donald and Twose next year. It is probable that Lara will return, although he is unlikely to score the number of runs that he did in 1994, and unless another county can match Warwickshire's joy, commitment and what Dermot Reeve calls 'self-esteem', the championship will remain at Edgbaston.

The winning of the championship in 1995 had more merit for Warwickshire than it had had the previous year in that the opposition was stronger, and Middlesex and Northamptonshire were splendid challengers who shared an approach to the game that was similar to that of the champions. At Taunton, Middlesex had to watch the rain fall on the first day, and Somerset batted into the third day, depriving Middlesex of a fourth bowling point. The response to this was some devastating batting. Pooley hit 90 off 80 balls, Gatting 122 off 104, and Ramprakash 115 off 134. They moved to maximum batting points in 55.4 overs,

Keith Piper takes a catch as Warwickshire move closer to victory over Kent – and to the championship. (Allsport)

Gatting and Ramprakash having added 176 in 23 overs. The Somerset bowling was brutalised. Hallett went for 52 runs in four overs; Batty for 135 in 18.4.

It all proved to be of no avail. Jeremy Hallett, generally a tail-ender, opened the Somerset second innings because Bowler was unwell and, fed by bowlers like Brown and Pooley, he hit a maiden century. Middlesex were set a target of 350 in 63 overs and were 178 for 1 at one time, but this was followed by a collapse and by rain.

The match marked the end of the career of John Emburey, although he is likely to take up a coaching appointment and may be seen occasionally in first-class cricket in the future. Umpire Peter Wright also stood in a match for the last time.

Northamptonshire were even less fortunate than Middlesex as rain plagued their game at Hove and no play was possible on the last day so that declarations in an effort to secure a result proved futile. There was joy for Robin Martin-Jenkins who hit 50 in his second first-class innings, his first having been 0 not out at Scarborough.

All that was possible at Worcester was 18 overs on the Saturday, and there was no play after the first day at Leicester. Martin Bicknell bowled well at The Oval where Mark Nicholas said farewell with a fifty, but rain ended any hope of a result, for there had been no play on the Saturday. Neither Hampshire nor Surrey could draw any comfort from the season, and Surrey's gloom deepened with the resignation of chairman Brian Downing. One cannot always agree with his priorities, but he is a good man and he helped raise much money for the game and for Surrey.

For Durham, the season ended on a high note. They beat Nottinghamshire by an innings inside three days. Larkins, who was not being offered a new contract, and Morris shared a second-wicket stand of 180, and, back in the side after a disappointing season of injury, Daley hit 50. Pick and Pennett hit 85 for Nottinghamshire's last

Allan Donald falls to his knees as Patel is caught at slip. Warwickshire have beaten Kent and retained the Britannic Assurance County Championship. (Allsport)

Only 22 balls were possible on the Saturday, but on the Monday, again scoring at a furious pace, Prichard and Rollins extended their sixth-wicket partnership to 147. Rollins, who had enjoyed a very good first full season, hit 77 off 83 balls. Prichard sped to a worthy century, and 182 runs came in 29.1 overs in the morning session. Needing 275 from 73 overs, Yorkshire reached 91 for 2 before losing their last eight wickets to spinners Such and Childs in 70 minutes either side of tea.

With their fifth victory in succession, Essex clinched fifth place in the table, and the prize money of £4,000. This had not seemed remotely possible earlier in the year, and credit must go to Prichard who had led his side through a very difficult period and had salvaged some pride and honour.

So the sun set on an eventful season which contained some good and exciting cricket in all competitions, and at international level. One hopes and prays that those who administer and constantly reshape the structure and the rules will just allow the rest of us to get on with the game unaltered for a few years. Let us try to build on and enjoy what we have and end the constant moaning. As Scarlett O'Hara would have said, 'Tomorrow is another day.'

wicket, but they could not save the follow-on, and Boiling took Durham to victory with his first five-wicket haul for the county.

At Derby, 18 wickets fell on the first day. Colin Wells and Phillip DeFreitas put on 73 for Derbyshire's seventh wicket, with DeFreitas hitting 94 off 99 balls. Dominic Cork then swung into action, and Lancashire were reduced to 51 for 7, and 80 for 8, before a swashbuckling 80 from Ian Austin took them to 155.

Derbyshire showed unusual consistency when they batted a second time, and Kim Barnett, in his last match as captain, scored 88. Lancashire batted dreadfully, but this should not detract from the performance of the 38-year-old Allan Warner who took a career-best 6 for 21 on the last day of the season and bowled his side to victory as if in celebration of his benefit and of the new contract he had been offered.

The first day at Chelmsford saw some whirlwind batting from Essex and some wayward bowling from Yorkshire. Essex scored at more than 4.5 runs an over, and Yorkshire finished on 53 for 1. Byas and McGrath added 74 for their fourth wicket, and Kettleborough hit 55 in his first game of the season. The tail brought them to within four of the Essex score, and Yorkshire seized the initiative when they captured five wickets before the close on Friday for only 41.

BRITANNIC ASSURANCE COUNTY CHAMPIONSHIP FINAL TABLE

| | P | W | L | D | Bonus Pts | | |
					Bt	Bo	Pts
Warwickshire (1)	17	14	2	1	49	64	337
Middlesex (4)	17	12	2	3	51	62	305
Northamptonshire (5)	17	12	2	3	41	57	290
Lancashire (10)	17	10	4	3	48	61	269
Essex (6)	17	8	9	0	42	58	228
Gloucestershire (12)	17	8	4	5	45	50	223
Leicestershire (2)	17	7	8	2	41	61	214
Yorkshire (14)	17	7	8	2	39	55	206
Somerset (11)	17	7	5	5	40	49	201
Worcestershire (15)	17	6	7	4	29	57	182
Nottinghamshire (3)	17	5	9	3	41	54	175
Surrey (7)	17	5	8	4	34	55	169
Hampshire (13)	17	5	8	4	32	56	168
Derbyshire (17)	17	4	10	3	39	64	167
Sussex (8)	17	4	7	6	37	51	152
Glamorgan (18)	17	3	8	6	40	57	145
Durham (16)	17	4	13	0	20	53	137
Kent (9)	17	3	10	4	40	44	132

(1994 positions in brackets)

AXA EQUITY AND LAW LEAGUE
and minor one-day competitions

FRIENDLY MATCH

30 April *at Leeds*

Yorkshire 221 for 4 (A.P. Grayson 82 not out,
M.P. Vaughan 71)
Lancashire 130

Yorkshire won by 91 runs

This 40-over Roses Match saw Yorkshire win with ease.
Vaughan and Grayson added 110 for their third wicket.
Lancashire welcomed the return of Wasim Akram who
played his first game of the season after arriving in
England on the Sunday morning.

7 May *at Chelmsford*

Worcestershire 253 for 6 (T.M. Moody 106, G.A. Hick 80)
Essex 75 (P.J. Newport 5 for 32)

Worcestershire (4 pts) won by 178 runs

at Cardiff

Northamptonshire 194 for 8 (T.C. Walton 56, K.M. Curran 50)
Glamorgan 195 for 6 (S.P. James 93 not out)

Glamorgan (4 pts) won by 4 wickets

at Old Trafford

Lancashire 249 for 7 (M.A. Atherton 103, G.D. Lloyd 63)
Durham 165 (M.A. Roseberry 54)

Lancashire (4 pts) won by 84 runs

at Leicester

Leicestershire 200 for 7 (V.J. Wells 79)
Yorkshire 170 (R.J. Blakey 61)

Leicestershire (4 pts) won by 30 runs

at Lord's

Middlesex 244 for 4 (M.R. Ramprakash 64, K.R. Brown 54 not
out, P.N. Weekes 50 not out)
Hampshire 207 for 9 (M.A. Feltham 5 for 51)

Middlesex (4 pts) won by 37 runs

at Trent Bridge

Derbyshire 219 for 6 (D.J. Cullinan 64, K.J. Barnett 51)
Nottinghamshire 198 (P.R. Pollard 57)

Derbyshire (4 pts) won by 21 runs

at Taunton

Somerset 217 for 9
Gloucestershire 219 for 4 (A.J. Wright 63, M.A. Lynch 50)

Gloucestershire (4 pts) won by 6 wickets

*The Sunday League begins. Marcus Trescothick in action for Somerset
against Gloucestershire, 7 May. (Ben Radford/Allsport)*

at Hove

Kent 225 for 9 (T.R. Ward 70, M.R. Benson 53)
Sussex 218 for 5 (K. Newell 76 not out)

Kent (4 pts) won by 7 runs

at Edgbaston

Surrey 192 for 5 (G.P. Thorpe 60, A.J. Hollioake 54 not out)
Warwickshire 145 (A.J. Hollioake 4 for 22)

Surrey (4 pts) won by 47 runs

The Sunday League began in fine weather, and only at
Trent Bridge and Edgbaston could the fielding side manage just 39 overs before time was called.

Essex had not begun the season well. They were out of
the Benson and Hedges Cup, had lost their first
championship match, and there were rumbles of discontent among their supporters. Those rumbles grew thunderous when, in their opening match against
Worcestershire, they suffered the heaviest Sunday
League defeat in their history. The match had started
promisingly for them. Darren Cousins bowled well and,
having discomforted both Weston and Moody, he bowled

Weston in the 11th over with the score on 40. What followed was massacre as Moody and Hick put on 160 in 21 overs. Hick, having reached 50 with three successive fours off Such, hit 8 fours and a six in his 73-ball innings. Essex steadied somewhat after his departure, but Moody's 106 came off as many deliveries, and he hit 4 sixes and 7 fours. He and Leatherdale were out to successive balls from Such.

Any hopes that Essex had rested on Gooch, but he was run out for two, and, having reached 32 for 1, the home county lost five wickets as three runs were scored. Their 75 all out was their second-lowest score in the history of the Sunday League. The return of Mark Waugh was awaited eagerly.

In contrast, the success of Glamorgan continued. Hamesh Anthony had arrived from the Caribbean to bolster their strength, and he took 3 for 40 as Northamptonshire were restricted to 194 on a good pitch. The Glamorgan innings was anchored by Steve James, whose place in the side had been in doubt before the season began. He batted throughout 39 overs, and when the last over arrived, bowled by Penberthy, Glamorgan needed five, and James and Anthony scored these runs with three balls to spare.

Mike Atherton's rich vein of form in the earlier part of the season was confirmed with a century off 94 balls. Put in to bat, Lancashire were 63 for 3 before Atherton and Lloyd added 140 in 21 overs. Durham lost Larkins run out for two and never looked like reaching their target. Richard Green, an all-rounder from Warrington, took 3 for 38 on his debut.

Having suffered a three-day championship defeat and humiliation at the hands of Minor Counties in the Benson and Hedges Cup, Leicestershire regained some pride with a solid win over Yorkshire. They were put in to bat and were given a good start by Wells and Briers who scored 90 in 19 overs. Thereafter they faltered as Briers became the first of five batsmen to be run out. He was a victim of brilliant fielding by Bevan.

Yorkshire's hopes diminished rapidly when they slipped to 80 for 6. Blakey and Gough offered positive resistance, but the visitors were all out in 38.3 overs.

The misery of Hampshire was compounded when they suffered their sixth defeat in as many matches in all competitions. At Lord's, Connor dismissed Gatting and Pooley with only 33 scored, but Ramprakash and Carr hit 97 in 17 overs for the third wicket. Weekes, 50 off 48 balls, and Brown, 54 off 46, shared an unbroken stand of 113 in 15 overs for the fifth wicket to take Middlesex to a formidable 244.

The Hampshire innings never had the necessary momentum, and the visitors lost placidly as Mark Feltham returned his best figures in the Sunday League.

Cullinan hit 3 sixes and 6 fours and, with Barnett and Adams, gave the Derbyshire innings substance against Nottinghamshire. This seemed to matter little, however, as Pollard raced to 50 off 49 balls, and Nottinghamshire reached 170 for 4, Johnson and Cairns having added 58 in 10 overs. Cairns was then caught on the mid-wicket boundary, and Johnson became the first of four Nottinghamshire batsmen to be run out. From 170 for 4,

the home county subsided to 178 for 8. There was brief resistance from Mike and Hindson, but Nottinghamshire were bowled out in 36.1 overs.

Lynch and Symonds were again to the fore for Gloucestershire. Facing a target of 218, Gloucestershire lost Hancock at 5, but Lynch and Wright added 104. Three wickets fell as 38 runs were scored before Alleyne and Symonds combined to hit 72 runs in seven overs to take Gloucestershire to victory over Somerset with four overs to spare.

The closest encounter came at Hove where Kent won by seven runs. Once again, the foundation for the Kent success was built upon an opening stand between Ward and Benson. This time they scored 136, while the Kent score was boosted by 43 extras, 27 of which were wides. One over from Giddins contained six wides and a no-ball.

Keith Newell hit his highest Sunday League score, but the Sussex innings never found the necessary impetus.

Warwickshire's defence of their Sunday League title began badly. Reeve retired from the attack with a back injury after bowling 17 balls and was unable to bat, while Ostler was hampered by a leg strain. Thorpe and Holloake put on 105 for Surrey's fifth wicket, and a brief shower reduced the visitors' allotted number of overs to 39.

Neil Smith was out for 0 when Warwickshire went in search of a modest target, but Ostler and Moles crashed the ball about to suggest an easy win. This proved to be deceptive, for, of the remaining batsmen, only Twose reached double figures, and the home side were out with four of their overs unused.

14 May at Chesterfield

Yorkshire 167 for 7 (A.E. Warner 4 for 14)
Derbyshire 108

Yorkshire (4 pts) won by 59 runs

at Swansea

Sussex 132
Glamorgan 133 for 1 (M.P. Maynard 69 not out)

Glamorgan (4 pts) won by 9 wickets

at Bristol

Gloucestershire 115 (J.R. Wileman 4 for 21)
Nottinghamshire 117 for 6

Nottinghamshire (4 pts) won by 4 wickets

at Canterbury

Leicestershire 235 for 5 (N.E. Briers 108 not out)
Kent 239 for 6 (G.R. Cowdrey 92 not out)

Kent (4 pts) won by 4 wickets

at Old Trafford

Warwickshire 193 for 8
Lancashire 196 for 5 (G.D. Lloyd 50 not out)

Lancashire (4 pts) won by 5 wickets

at Northampton

Northamptonshire 195 for 7
Somerset 198 for 8 (P.D. Bowler 57)

Somerset (4 pts) won by 2 wickets

at The Oval

Durham 189 for 8
Surrey 190 for 3 (A.D. Brown 79)

Surrey (4 pts) won by 7 wickets

at Worcester

Worcestershire 199 for 6 (T.M. Moody 57)
Middlesex 122

Worcestershire (4 pts) won by 77 runs

Put in to bat at Chesterfield, Yorkshire suffered a spell of 3 for 5 in four overs by Allan Warner and dithered towards 104 for 6. Some lusty blows from Gough and Blakey took the score to 167 before Gough was run out off the last ball of the innings. The Yorkshire total was also helped along by the fact that Derbyshire bowled 21 wides. Yorkshire conceded 12 wides, but this was probably just as well, for 'extras' claimed the third highest score in a Derbyshire innings which ended in 32.4 overs and included three run outs. Peter Hartley had starred in Yorkshire's championship win the previous day, and he caused the home side more embarrassment with 2 for 7 in six overs.

Glamorgan showed more good form in the limited-over game when they crushed Sussex. Croft opened the home county's bowling and perplexed Sussex to the extent that he took 2 for 13 in eight overs, and they plummeted to 46 for 6. Salisbury rallied them with 48 not out, and they lasted until the second ball of the final over of their quota. Glamorgan took only 23.4 overs to score the runs needed, with James and Maynard sharing an unbroken second-wicket stand of 124.

The match at Bristol was reduced to 33 overs after rain, but Wileman produced his best Sunday League bowling figures, and Gloucestershire lasted only 30.2 overs. Cairns hit fiercely for Nottinghamshire to win with four balls to spare.

Nigel Briers carried his bat through the 40 overs of the Leicestershire innings, but the inevitable air of martyrdom surrounded the Leicestershire captain as his side lost. Kent slipped to 70 for 3 before de Silva and Cowdrey hit 110 in 16 overs. Cowdrey hit 92 off 63 balls, and his final boundary off the last ball of the match won Kent the four points.

Warwickshire were beaten for the second Sunday in succession, and Lancashire, their conquerors, appeared to be gaining strength in all competitions. The Warwickshire batting promised more than it achieved, but the pitch was slow and the bowling accurate. Lancashire lost Atherton and Crawley in bizarre circumstances. Atherton played a ball from Brown hard into the ground from whence it bounced high into the air and dropped onto the stumps. Crawley was caught on the boundary by Neil Smith who held the ball above his head. After discussion the catch was allowed as Smith had lifted his heel and not touched the boundary rope. Such diversions failed to disturb

Lancashire who were without Fairbrother and Watkinson but still won with 15 balls to spare.

Somerset cut things finer at Northampton. They needed seven from the final over, and it was Mushtaq Ahmed who hit the final ball of that last over, bowled by Kumble, for four.

Surrey beat Durham with 29 balls to spare. Brown reached his fifty off 39 balls and dominated an opening stand of 56 with Darren Bicknell. Stewart and David Ward scored the last 53 runs required, and Ward made 32 of them. This likeable and enthusiastic cricketer was not used to the best advantage by Surrey.

A second win in as many matches raised Worcestershire's spirits. Moody batted delightfully to score 57 off 74 balls, and Haynes and Leatherdale made useful contributions on a pitch that was never easy. Middlesex lasted 33.3 overs, but the game was virtually over when they subsided to 92 for 6 in the 23rd.

21 May *at Chester-le-Street (Riverside)*

Durham 132 for 9
Warwickshire 130 for 9

Durham (4 pts) won by 2 runs

at Southampton

Kent 276 for 5 (G.R. Cowdrey 105 not out, M.R. Benson 92)
Hampshire 210 for 6

Kent (4 pts) won by 66 runs

at Leicester

Leicestershire 217 (V.J. Wells 50)
Derbyshire 194 for 8 (T.J.G. O'Gorman 57, A.R.K. Pierson 5 for 36)

Leicestershire (4 pts) won by 23 runs

at Lord's

Middlesex 155 for 9
Lancashire 158 for 2 (J.P. Crawley 75, J.E.R. Gallian 51 not out)

Lancashire (4 pts) won by 8 wickets

at Northampton

Surrey 256 for 5 (D.J. Bicknell 76)
Northamptonshire 242 for 7

Surrey (4 pts) won by 14 runs

at Hove

Essex 217 for 8 (M.C. Ilott 56 not out)
Sussex 204 for 9

Essex (4 pts) won by 13 runs

at Leeds

Yorkshire 157 (D. Byas 54)
Glamorgan 155 for 8

Yorkshire (4 pts) won by 2 runs

The first Sunday League match to be played at Durham's new Riverside Ground was watched by a crowd of more than 6,000. They had an early disappointment when Larkins fell to Reeve for 0, and Durham's final score of 132 hardly gave confidence for victory. It was, however, made from only 38 overs – all that Warwickshire could manage in 2½ hours. This was mainly due to the fact that they sent down 15 wides, one of which went for four. A total of 26 extras was most welcome to Durham, for only Prabhakar's 32 bettered this. Knight gave Warwickshire a sound start with 44, but there were three 'ducks' in the middle-order, and nine wickets went down for 117. Bell and Small edged close to the required target, but never quite close enough, and the large crowd went home happy.

A magnificent 105 off 62 balls from Graham Cowdrey was the principal reason for Kent's success over Hampshire. The score was 80 for 3 when Cowdrey joined Benson, and the pair added 145 in 16 overs for the fourth wicket. Benson was run out for 92, but Cowdrey finished unbeaten on his highest Sunday League score, having hit 3 sixes and 12 fours.

Cowdrey's part in Kent's victory was not over as, in the 13th over of the Hampshire innings, with the score on 67, he took a spectacular tumbling catch to dismiss Stephenson who was captaining Hampshire for the first time. Robin Smith was bowled by Headley, and Cowdrey ran out Morris as the Hampshire innings went into decline. With three wins out of the three matches, Kent led the table with Lancashire and Surrey.

Leicestershire off-spinner Adrian Pierson produced the best Sunday League bowling figures of his career to propel his side to victory over Derbyshire. Having been put in to bat, Leicestershire were bowled out in 39 overs for 217, a total that owed much towards the end to a seventh-wicket stand of 42 between Maddy and Nixon, who was returning to the side after his injury sustained while playing for England 'A'. The stand was particularly important as three wickets had just fallen for 13 runs.

Adams was caught behind off Parsons in the opening over when Derbyshire batted, but Cork and O'Gorman then added 118. Pierson dismissed the pair with successive deliveries, and from that point, Derbyshire lost touch with the required run rate.

Middlesex completed a thoroughly miserable weekend at Lord's when they were trounced by Lancashire who won with 9.2 overs to spare. Gatting chose to bat first, but his side's innings never really got started. Pooley was caught at slip in Wasim's first over. Carr was caught behind by Crawley, who took over the keeper's role because Hegg was injured, and Weekes alone – with 45 – offered serious resistance. He hit three of the four boundaries scored in the Middlesex innings, but it was an unbroken stand of 31 between Johnson and Fraser for the last wicket which saved total embarrassment. It was the highest stand of the innings.

Atherton hit 18 of the first 20 before being leg before to Fraser, and Gallian and Crawley added 122 in 22 overs. Crawley hit 75 off 80 balls. His innings included a six and 8 fours, and he overshadowed the more stately Gallian.

An opening stand of 81 in 13 overs between Darren Bicknell and Alistair Brown laid the foundation for a good

Graham Cowdrey, 105 not out against Hampshire, 21 May, and Kent's leading batsman in their AXA Equity and Law League triumph. (Neal Simpson/Empics)

Surrey score at Northampton. Late in the innings, David Ward and Adam Hollioake hit hard and often, and 63 runs came in the last five overs. Hollioake's 49 not out came off 20 balls.

This burst really took the game out of Northamptonshire's reach. They batted solidly to climb to 202 for 7, and Warren and Snape shared an unbroken stand of 40 which never looked as if it would deny Surrey victory.

Essex gained their first Sunday League win of the season and had to stage a recovery to do so. After 29 overs, they were 134 for 6, but Mark Ilott hit his first fifty in the competition, Robinson gave good support, and they assembled 217 for 8 in their 40 overs. Three of the Essex wickets fell to Paul Jarvis who was returning after being injured in the opening county match of the season.

Sussex looked as if they had a substantial enough basis to win at 123 for 4, but Such and Waugh clawed away at their middle-order, and they fell 13 runs short of the Essex score.

Glamorgan were beaten in a tactical battle at Headingley. They were content when they bowled out Yorkshire in 39.2 overs. Watkin was particularly successful with 3 for 16 in his eight overs, but the field-settings for Croft could have been more intelligent and saved valuable runs in a low-scoring match.

Morris and Cottey gave substance to the Glamorgan innings, but Maynard, Croft and Hemp went cheaply as concern grew about the run rate. Dale was resolute, and six runs were needed when Gough bowled the last over. Lefebvre was run out, and Dale needed to hit the last ball for three to win the game. A delivery of very full length was too fast for Dale's attempted pull, and the batsman's stumps were shattered.

28 May *at Chelmsford*

Essex 178 for 6 (P.J. Prichard 54, G.A. Gooch 50,
    M.W. Gatting 4 for 44)
Middlesex 176 for 9

Essex (4 pts) won by 2 runs

at Gloucester

Worcestershire 225 for 3 (T.S. Curtis 82 not out,
    T.M. Moody 65)
Gloucestershire 178 for 8 (R.C. Russell 56 not out,
    N.V. Radford 5 for 57)

Worcestershire (4 pts) won on faster scoring rate

at Portsmouth

Sussex 206 for 7 (K.D. James 4 for 35)
Hampshire 198 for 9 (M.C.J. Nicholas 66, F.D. Stephenson
    4 for 47)

Sussex (4 pts) won by 8 runs

at Tunbridge Wells

Glamorgan 180 for 6 (P.A. Cottey 52, D.W. Headley 4 for 59)
Kent 169 (S.R. Barwick 6 for 49)

Glamorgan (4 pts) won by 11 runs

at Old Trafford

Nottinghamshire 172 for 5 (R.T. Robinson 63)
Lancashire 173 for 6 (G.D. Lloyd 59 not out)

Lancashire (4 pts) won by 4 wickets

at Leicester

Durham 160 for 9
Leicestershire 126 for 1 (V.J. Wells 66 not out)

Leicestershire (4 pts) won on faster scoring rate

at Edgbaston

Warwickshire 260 for 7 (N.M.K. Smith 71, R.G. Twose 58)
Somerset 177 for 5

Warwickshire (4 pts) won on faster scoring rate

at Sheffield

Northamptonshire 145 for 4
v. Yorkshire

Match abandoned

Yorkshire 2 pts, Northamptonshire 2 pts

Rain was unkind to the fourth round of matches in the Sunday League, causing the abandonment of the match at Sheffield after 31.4 overs had been bowled. At Chelmsford, Essex were 147 for 4 after 34.4 overs when rain caused an interruption, and the match was reduced to 37 overs. From the 14 balls that were left to them after the rain, Essex conjured 31 runs, with Gooch hitting 15 runs in an over from Johnson, nearing 8,000 Sunday League runs. Andrew bowled seven wides in his first two overs, and Feltham hit 4 fours to give Middlesex 43 in nine overs for their first wicket. Gatting and Farbrace showed good form, and Gatting threatened to win the match until, on 46, he skied Andrew to Prichard in the penultimate over. Radford was left to hit three off the last ball to win the game for Middlesex, but he could not manage it.

Worcestershire batted their full 40 overs at Gloucester, and Curtis and Moody put on 110 in 18 overs for the second wicket. Rain reduced the home side's target to 181 in 32 overs, and they seemed well beaten when they slumbered to 91 for 5 in 22. Russell led the revival with a six and 6 fours in his 56 off 36 balls. He was ever inventive and made victory seem possible. Radford bowled the last over with Gloucestershire needing 14. Russell hit 2 fours, but Ball, needing to hit three off the last ball, was spectacularly caught by Tom Moody.

Hampshire's barren run in the Sunday League continued when they were beaten by Sussex. The margin was really greater than eight runs suggests, for Hampshire did not hit a boundary between the 15th and 26th overs, and only Mark Nicholas' spirited 66 saw them approach their target.

Glamorgan ended Kent's 100% record in one-day matches for the season, winning by 11 runs in a match which was reduced to 23 overs. Glamorgan were asked to bat first and were well served by Morris and James who scored 52 for the first wicket in eight overs before the rain. The resumption meant a dash for 15 overs, and Cottey, 52 off 34 balls, and Dale, who hit Headley for successive sixes, led the way. A total of 180 was highly commendable. Kent lost five wickets for 54 runs before Ealham hit 4 sixes and Fleming three, but the target proved beyond them as Steve Barwick kept his head amid the carnage to take 6 for 49 from seven overs.

Lancashire went clear at the top of the table by beating Nottinghamshire with an over to spare. The visitors made 172 for 5 from 39 overs and must have thought that they were close to victory when they reduced Lancashire to 94 for 6. Lloyd, 59 off 57 balls, and Austin, 36 off 39 balls, then hit 79 in 12 overs to win the match and to leave Lancashire unbeaten in all competitions.

Leicestershire restricted Durham to 160 for 9 in 40 overs and had reached 126 for 1 in 25 overs when rain stopped play. This meant that they had already reached the revised target by the time a restart was possible. Maddy, 3 for 31, took his first Sunday League wickets.

Neil Smith made his highest Sunday League score when he opened for Warwickshire against Somerset, and he made possible a formidable total of 260 for 7. Two rain interruptions reduced Somerset's target to 189 in 29 overs, and they made a brave attempt to win, but they were thwarted mostly by Tim Munton who took 3 for 45 in his first competitive match of the season.

4 June *at Chester-le-Street (Riverside)*

Durham v. Kent

Match abandoned

Durham 2 pts, Kent 2 pts

at Cardiff

Glamorgan 238 for 2 (S.P. James 87, M.P. Maynard 58 not out)

Hampshire 125

Glamorgan (4 pts) won by 113 runs

at Lord's

Derbyshire 152 for 9 (A.R.C. Fraser 5 for 32)

Middlesex 128

Derbyshire (4 pts) won by 24 runs

at Trent Bridge

Essex 267 for 4 (M.E. Waugh 89, P.J. Prichard 57, G.A. Gooch 55 not out)

Nottinghamshire 155 for 8 (R.A. Pick 58 not out)

Essex (4 pts) won by 112 runs

at Taunton

Yorkshire 213 for 6 (M.G. Bevan 80)

Somerset 215 for 7 (G.D. Rose 60 not out)

Somerset (4 pts) won by 3 wickets

at Hove

Gloucestershire 166 for 4 (M.A. Lynch 58)

Sussex 168 for 4 (A.P. Wells 70 not out, F.D. Stephenson 54)

Sussex (4 pts) won by 6 wickets

at Worcester

Surrey 126 (G.R. Haynes 4 for 21)

Worcestershire 129 for 1 (T.M. Moody 73 not out, G.A. Hick 51 not out)

Worcestershire (4 pts) won by 9 wickets

The weather was again unkind and wiped out the match at Chester-le-Street. At Cardiff, a full quota of 40 overs was possible although Hampshire lasted only 32.1 of theirs. James and Morris began with a partnership of 106 in 21 overs which set the platform for Maynard to hit 58 off 57 balls. Hampshire quickly subsided to 20 for 4, and there was no effective recovery. Colin Metson, the Glamorgan wicket-keeper, held four catches and made two stumpings.

The game at Lord's was reduced to 31 overs. Put in to bat, Derbyshire offered consistency with seven players and 'extras' reaching double figures. Angus Fraser had a best bowling performance in the Sunday League, but he was let down by his batsmen. Middlesex were 83 for 8 before Feltham and Emburey put on 42. In spite of their efforts, Middlesex were bowled out in 28.4 overs.

Essex stirred remembrance of things past when Waugh and Prichard scored 126 for the first wicket. Waugh's 89 came off 91 balls, and Gooch made an unbeaten 55 off 37 balls. Nottinghamshire slipped to 71 for 8, and the contest was over, but Pick and Wileman shared an unbroken partnership of 84 against some friendly bowling.

Bevan reached another landmark with his highest Sunday League score, but it was overshadowed by the fact that Somerset passed Yorkshire's score with 10 balls to spare. A fifth-wicket stand of 56 between Harden and Rose helped Somerset to recover from an uncertain start, and Rose and the hard-hitting Ecclestone then added 58.

At Hove, rain delayed the start and the match was reduced to 21 overs. Gloucestershire, asked to bat first, set a daunting target, but Stephenson and Alan Wells came together for Sussex after Greenfield and North had gone for 23. They added 84 in eight overs, and Sussex won with nine balls to spare.

Worcestershire won their fourth game in a row as they crushed Surrey by nine wickets. Surrey won the toss and chose to bat first, but they surrendered to Haynes who returned his best one-day bowling figures. Surrey were out for 126, and this included a sixth-wicket stand of 44 between Hollioake and Butcher. Worcestershire lost Curtis in the first over, but Moody – 73 off 85 balls with 2 sixes and 8 fours – and Hick – 51 off 63 balls with a six and 5 fours – rushed them to victory in 24.4 overs.

4 June *at Edgbaston*

Rest of the World XI 235 for 8 (S.R. Waugh 52, W.J. Cronje 51)

Warwickshire 232 for 6 (N.M.K. Smith 51)

Rest of the World XI won by 3 runs

As part of their triple-triumph and centenary celebrations, Warwickshire staged a 50-over match against an international eleven led by Ian Healy. Cronje and Steve Waugh scored 102 in 19 overs for the World XI's third wicket. Warne, Slater, Rhodes, Boon, Malcolm Marshall, Simmons, Andy Flower and Tim May were in the international side.

11 June *at Derby*

Northamptonshire 200 for 6 (K.M. Curran 60, R.J. Bailey 58)

Derbyshire 200 for 9 (C.M. Wells 73)

Match tied

Derbyshire 2 pts, Northamptonshire 2 pts

at Chelmsford

Durham 116 for 6

Essex 116

Match tied

Essex 2 pts, Durham 2 pts

at Canterbury

Gloucestershire 136 for 8

Kent 140 for 5 (M.V. Fleming 55)

Kent (4 pts) won by 5 wickets

at Basingstoke

Leicestershire 204 for 9

Hampshire 123 for 3

Hampshire (4 pts) won on faster scoring rate

at Old Trafford

Glamorgan 162 (G. Yates 4 for 40)

Lancashire 153

Glamorgan (4 pts) won by 9 runs

at Trent Bridge

Nottinghamshire 216 for 5 (R.T. Robinson 82)

Worcestershire 155 (T.S. Curtis 54)

Nottinghamshire (4 pts) won by 61 runs

at The Oval

Surrey v. Somerset

Match abandoned

Surrey 2 pts, Somerset 2 pts

at Edgbaston

Warwickshire 180 for 8 (P.A. Smith 85, N.V. Knight 59,
F.D. Stephenson 5 for 38)

Sussex 166 (N.M.K. Smith 6 for 33, P.A. Smith 4 for 39)

Warwickshire (4 pts) won by 14 runs

The rain continued to cause havoc with the Sunday League, and the match at The Oval was abandoned without a ball being bowled. Forty overs were possible at Derby where the two sides contrived to score 400 runs. In the championship match, which was over in two days, they managed just 407 for the loss of 36 wickets. A fourth-wicket stand of 96 in 16 overs between Curran and Bailey formed the backbone of the Northamptonshire innings while Derbyshire owed much to Colin Wells who, although batting with a runner, hit his first Sunday League fifty for his adopted county. The last over arrived with Derbyshire needing 14 to win, and Taylor bowling. Paul Aldred, a Sunday League novice, hit a six, a four and a two, but he could manage only a bye off the last ball, and the match was tied.

There was the same result at Chelmsford where rain reduced the match to 26 overs. Durham lost Larkins with a broken thumb, and Essex conceded 10 wides – criminal in a shortened match, unprofessional at any time. The home side batted poorly, and the last over arrived with the last pair together and nine runs needed. Seven runs came from Prabhakar's first five deliveries, but Jonathan Lewis was run out by Walker's throw from the third-man boundary when he went for a second run that would have won the match.

At Canterbury, 37 overs were possible, but Kent needed only 27.1 in which to pass Gloucestershire's total. In the gloom, Fleming hit 2 sixes and 5 fours. Monte Lynch, who hit a century in each innings in the championship game

which straddled the Sunday League one, was out to the first ball of the match.

Leicestershire batted a full 40 overs at Basingstoke, but two interruptions for rain reduced Hampshire's target to 123 in 24 overs. They won with seven balls to spare thanks to an undefeated 42 from Mark Nicholas.

Lancashire suffered their first defeat in any competition in a tense match at Old Trafford. Morris chose to bat when he won the toss, and he and James took Glamorgan to 47 in the 10th over before James was bowled by Yates. This wicket had the effect of inhibiting the visiting batsmen, and Maynard gave Austin a return catch when he tried to break free from the shackles that were being imposed. Morris was caught behind as he attempted to cut Yates, and Hemp was run out in a mix-up with Cottey. When Croft fell to Wasim Akram it seemed unlikely that Glamorgan would top 150, but Watkin and Barwick added an improbable and invaluable 21 for the last wicket. The innings ended on the second ball of the 40th over.

Lancashire were soon in dire straits. Crawley played on, Fairbrother was run out by Watkin, and Gallian, Speak and Lloyd all perished as five wickets fell for 58 runs in 21 overs. Wasim and Watkinson added 39, but with Hegg and Chapple – the last pair – together, 34 were still needed from 24 balls. Hegg played admirably, and Chapple supported splendidly until being caught off the first ball of the last over. The Glamorgan fielding and catching were outstanding, and the Welshmen well deserved to go top of the table.

Worcestershire lost their unbeaten Sunday record when they were brushed aside in a 38-over match at Trent Bridge, but Warwickshire won their second match in succession. The game at Edgbaston was reduced to 34 overs, and Warwickshire soon found themselves 10 for 2. Knight, capped before the match, and Paul Smith added 129 for the third wicket, and Paul Smith's 85 came off only 86 balls. Sussex began with a stand of 83, but collapsed to 166 all out as Neil Smith returned his best Sunday League figures. Knight was injured when he collided in the field with Penney. Penney suffered a suspected broken nose but held on to the ball to catch Salisbury off Neil Smith while Knight was detained in hospital overnight with concussion.

18 June *at Derby*

Somerset 212 for 7 (M.N. Lathwell 55, K.A. Parsons 52 not out)

Derbyshire 193 for 6 (D.J. Cullinan 76 not out)

Somerset (4 pts) won by 19 runs

at Colwyn Bay

Glamorgan 249 for 6 (H. Morris 100)

Middlesex 220 (M.W. Gatting 50, S.R. Barwick 5 for 30)

Glamorgan (4 pts) won by 29 runs

at Bristol

Gloucestershire 223 for 7 (M.W. Alleyne 70)

Hampshire 219 for 5 (R.S.M. Morris 87, R. Smith 55)

Gloucestershire (4 pts) won by 4 runs

Leicestershire 285 for 8 (N.E. Briers 54, J.R. Wileman 4 for 71)
Nottinghamshire 275 for 7 (P.R. Pollard 74)

Leicestershire (4 pts) won by 10 runs

at Luton

Essex 216 for 6 (P.J. Prichard 81, R.C. Irani 50)
Northamptonshire 111

Essex (4 pts) won by 105 runs

at Horsham

Sussex 222 for 7
Surrey 212 (G.P. Thorpe 53, I.D.K. Salisbury 4 for 39)

Sussex (4 pts) won by 10 runs

at Worcester

Worcestershire 189 for 8 (G.A. Hick 80 not out)
Lancashire 190 for 3 (N.H. Fairbrother 99 not out,
   J.P. Crawley 54)

Lancashire (4 pts) won by 7 wickets

at Leeds

Kent 161 (T.R. Ward 63)
Yorkshire 75

Kent (4 pts) won by 86 runs

Cullinan hit his highest Sunday League score for Derbyshire, and Dominic Cork celebrated being named in the England party for the second Test by scoring 36 in an opening partnership of 63 with Kim Barnett, but Derbyshire fell 19 runs short of Somerset. Keith Parsons hit his first Sunday League fifty, and he and Holloway added 80 after five wickets had gone for 129. Parsons also bowled an economic spell.

Glamorgan maintained their place at the top of the table by beating Middlesex. James and Morris started the match with 92 in 17 overs, and the Glamorgan captain went on to reach an impressively crafted 100 off 118 balls. He was out in the 38th over, having hit 2 sixes and 11 fours.

Watkin and Lefebvre proved to be a restrictive pair of opening bowlers, and Weekes and Pooley found it difficult to give the Middlesex innings the required momentum. Pooley was bowled by Barwick, and Ramprakash fell to a spectacular catch on the boundary by Lefebvre. James also held a fine catch to account for Weekes. Brown and Gatting added a spirited 88 for the fifth wicket. Gatting batted with a runner because of a pulled calf muscle, and when he was out, with five overs remaining and 58 runs still needed, the Middlesex cause was lost.

Mark Alleyne's 70 off 62 balls gave the Gloucestershire innings a necessary lift at Bristol. Hampshire were given a good basis when Morris and Whitaker scored 60 for the first wicket, and Morris, who hit a competition best, and Smith then added 119 for the second wicket at almost six an over. The former Essex and Middlesex bowler David Boden tilted the game in Gloucestershire's favour when he

dismissed Smith, Nicholas and Morris inside three overs, and when Keech was run out Hampshire fell five short of their target.

Leicestershire batted with consistency against Nottinghamshire, and Maddy gave the innings final impetus with 4 fours and 3 sixes in his 48 off only 21 balls. Nottinghamshire were beaten by 10 runs, but they had much to cheer them. Pollard played his first game for six weeks after injury and hit 74 off 70 balls with 12 fours, and Chris Cairns took three wickets in his first spell of bowling for more than a fortnight because of a side strain.

The infamous Luton pitch posed no problem for the Sunday match. Prichard gave Essex a good foundation and Irani hit 50 off 26 balls. He scored 24 off the penultimate over of the innings, bowled by David Capel, and he then dismissed both openers.

The match at Horsham marked the debut for Sussex of Robin Martin-Jenkins, son of the writer and broadcaster. A fast medium-pace bowler, Martin-Jenkins had a good debut, bowling his seven overs for 35 runs and the prize wicket of Alec Stewart. Surrey bowled only 37 overs in the time allowed, and the Sussex top scorer was 'extras' with 48, of which 12 were wides and 10 no-balls. Surrey never really looked like approaching their target as Salisbury took three wickets in four balls.

Worcestershire contributed much to their own defeat by Lancashire. Hick reached his eighth half-century in limited-over cricket during the season, but received scant support. Speak and Gallian were out with 24 scored, but Crawley and Fairbrother put on 115. Illingworth was hit for 52 in six overs, but he twice had Fairbrother dropped. The left-hander went on to hit 12 fours and a six in his 99 off 90 balls, and Lancashire won with eight balls to spare.

Kent, led for the first time by Aravinda de Silva, were bowled out in 38.1 overs for 161, a bitter disappointment when one considers that they had 88 on the board after 14 overs and that Ward scored 63 off 71 balls. The disappointment was soon over as Yorkshire were reduced to 38 for 7. Eventually, the home county were bowled out for 75, their second-lowest score in the competition. Igglesden, Wren and Ealham each had three wickets.

25 June *at Chester-le-Street (Riverside)*

Durham 113
Derbyshire 114 for 5 (D.J. Cullinan 52 not out)

Derbyshire (4 pts) won by 5 wickets

at Southampton

Hampshire 275 for 9 (M. Keech 98, P.R. Whitaker 97,
   S.R. Lampitt 4 for 43)
Worcestershire 275 for 9 (T.M. Moody 108, H.H. Streak 4 for 56)
Match tied

Hampshire 2 pts, Worcestershire 2 pts

at Old Trafford

Essex 200 (M.E. Waugh 83, N. Hussain 73)
Lancashire 201 for 7 (S.P. Titchard 53)

Lancashire (4 pts) won by 3 wickets

at Northampton

Leicestershire 246 for 5 (N.E. Briers 82, W.J. Cronje 67 not out, P.A. Nixon 53)

Northamptonshire 205 for 7 (R.J. Bailey 61 not out, A. Fordham 53)

Leicestershire (4 pts) won by 41 runs

at Trent Bridge

Kent 194 (G.R. Cowdrey 80)

Nottinghamshire 195 for 1 (P. Johnson 104 not out, P.R. Pollard 81 not out)

Nottinghamshire (4 pts) won by 9 wickets

at Bath

Sussex 197 for 8

Somerset 181 (R.J. Harden 69, J.D. Lewry 4 for 29)

Sussex (4 pts) won by 16 runs

at The Oval

Surrey 152 (S.L. Watkin 4 for 40)

Glamorgan 154 for 1 (S.P. James 80 not out, M.P. Maynard 52 not out)

Glamorgan (4 pts) won by 9 wickets

at Edgbaston

Warwickshire 175 for 6 (R.G. Twose 69 not out, G.M. Hamilton 4 for 27)

Yorkshire 56 (A.A. Donald 6 for 15)

Warwickshire (4 pts) won by 119 runs

Paul Smith bowls Richard Stemp as Yorkshire collapse to 56 all out in their Sunday League game against Warwickshire, 25 June. (Philip Wilcox)

Durham gave a dismal display against Derbyshire, occupying 39 overs in scoring 113. Warner took 3 for 14 in his eight overs. Derbyshire lost both openers for five and Wells at 21, but Barnett and Cullinan added 64, and Cullinan took them to victory with three overs to spare.

At Southampton, Whitaker and Keech hit their highest Sunday League scores and put on 158 in 16 overs for Hampshire against Worcestershire. Lampitt claimed them both as he took four wickets in nine balls. Moody hit 5 sixes and 7 fours in his 108 which came off only 76 balls. It was an innings of exceptional quality, but when he was caught off Maru 113 were still needed off 16 overs. Nine were needed from the last over, and when Radford was bowled by Streak two were needed from the last ball. Newport could manage only one, and the match was tied.

Lancashire's biggest Sunday crowd since August 1991 saw the home side beat Essex with an over to spare. Titchard was awarded his county cap before the start of the match, but it was Essex who produced the early celebrations. Waugh and Hussain scored 119 for the second wicket, and Waugh's 83 came off 89 balls. He reached his fifty by hitting Keedy for six. At 141 for 2 in the 28th over, Essex were in a strong position. Gooch helped Hussain to take the score to 176 before being run out, and this heralded a collapse, the last eight wickets falling for 24 runs.

Titchard and Gallian began Lancashire's challenge with a stand of 87. Four wickets then fell for 18 runs. Watkinson and Lloyd restored order with a partnership of 58. They left in quick succession, and it was left to Wasim Akram's 22 off 17 balls to settle the issue.

Briers and Nixon scored 144 for Leicestershire's first wicket at Northampton, and this was followed by Cronje's 67 off 48 balls. The home side were never in touch with the required run rate.

Kent's AXA Equity and Law League title hopes suffered a severe setback when they were destroyed by Nottinghamshire. Bowled out for 194 in 40 overs, having been 91 for 6, Kent dismissed Robinson at eight, but then suffered Pollard and Johnson taking Notts to victory with 33 balls to spare. Johnson's hundred came off 84 balls and included 15 fours.

In spite of Harden and Parsons scoring 89 for Somerset's fourth wicket, Somerset were beaten in front of a large festival crowd enjoying the sun at Bath. Lewry produced his best Sunday League bowling figures for Sussex.

Surrey were brushed aside by league-leaders Glamorgan at The Oval. Bowled out in 38.5 overs for a miserable 152, with only David Ward giving the innings any substance, Surrey saw their own bowling demolished. Maynard hit 42 off 29 balls, and James raced to fifty off 37 balls. The pair shared an unbroken partnership of 80 as Glamorgan won with 19.5 overs to spare.

Yorkshire completed a dreadful weekend at Edgbaston. All seemed well at first when they reduced Warwickshire to 46 for 4. Reeve and Twose added 84 in 20 overs of what was a 38-over innings. Byas and Vaughan scored 36 for Yorkshire's first wicket, but then they lost all 10 wickets for 20 runs. Their last eight wickets went down for 12 runs in 11 overs. It was Yorkshire's lowest total in the Sunday

League, and Allan Donald, in his 48th match in this competition, returned his best bowling figures. Yorkshire were not enjoying Sundays.

2 July *at Derby*

Hampshire 154 for 8
Derbyshire 159 for 5 (D.G. Cork 57)

Derbyshire (4 pts) won by 5 wickets

at Ilford

Essex 201 for 7 (N. Hussain 55)
Warwickshire 160 for 7 (M.C. Ilott 4 for 27)

Warwickshire (4 pts) won on faster scoring rate

at Swansea

Glamorgan 212 for 6 (S.P. James 87)
Durham 213 for 5 (M.A. Roseberry 94, M. Prabhakar 64)

Durham (4 pts) won by 5 wickets

at Lord's

Middlesex 180 for 3 (M.R. Ramprakash 85 not out)
Surrey 40 for 4

Match abandoned

Middlesex 2 pts, Surrey 2 pts

at Trent Bridge

Somerset 253 for 6 (R.J. Harden 61, M.N. Lathwell 53)
Nottinghamshire 257 for 4 (P.R. Pollard 132 not out)

Nottinghamshire (4 pts) won by 6 wickets

at Worcester

Worcestershire 142 for 8 (T.M. Moody 52)
Leicestershire 114

Worcestershire (4 pts) won by 28 runs

at Middlesbrough

Yorkshire 235 for 4 (M.G. Bevan 103 not out)
Gloucestershire 142

Yorkshire (4 pts) won by 93 runs

'Extras' was top scorer in the Hampshire innings at Derby with 32, of which 20 were wides, although it must be stated that the Derbyshire bowlers also produced some straight balls. Andrew Harris discovered two good deliveries to account for Smith and Nicholas, and his eight impressive overs cost only 19 runs. Cork and Adams began Derbyshire's innings with a partnership of 53, and Cullinan was again a mid-innings rock with an unbeaten 46 which took his side to victory with 15 balls remaining.

Warwickshire gained their fourth Sunday League win in succession when they overcame Essex in a rain-affected match at Ilford. Essex made 201 from 39 overs, but the start

The fastest century in the history of the Sunday League – Mark Ealham, 100 off 44 balls for Kent against Derbyshire at Maidstone. (Neal Simpson/Empics)

of the Warwickshire innings was delayed by rain and their target was reduced to 160 from 31 overs. Twose hit 47 off 61 balls, and the reigning champions won with eight balls to spare.

Glamorgan received a nasty shock when they were surprisingly beaten by Durham at Swansea. Morris and James gave Glamorgan another rapid start with 68 in 14 overs, but three wickets fell for 16 runs. Dale helped James bring back order with a partnership of 50, and Croft and James added 57 in eight overs before James was yorked by Prabhakar in the 37th over.

John Morris and Roseberry scored 42 in 12 overs before Roseberry and Prabhakar lifted the tempo in a stand of 152 in 24 overs. Lefebvre dismissed them both and trapped Hutton leg before, and then was carried off on a stretcher with a groin strain. Six runs were needed from Barwick's last over, and Barwick had Longley stumped by Metson. Blenkiron needed to hit two from the last ball. He was struck on the pad, and the batsmen took a leg-bye. Maynard's throw at the stumps missed, and the batsmen ran an overthrow to win the match.

No such excitement at Lord's where Middlesex hit 180 off 35 overs. Rain reduced Surrey's target to 165 off 32 overs, but they were 40 for 4 from 15 when more rain ended the match.

Paul Pollard hit his highest Sunday League score – 132 not out with 14 fours in 38.5 overs – to take Nottinghamshire to victory over Somerset at Trent Bridge. He shared stands of 69 with Johnson, and 77 with Cairns. Somerset had reached a commendable 253 in 40 overs, with the momentum of the innings coming from a third-wicket stand of 90 in 13 overs between Harden and Rose. Nottinghamshire gave a debut to Jamie Hart, a 19-year-old pace bowler. He took the wicket of Ecclestone.

Worcestershire revived their sagging challenge with victory over Leicestershire in a low-scoring game at New Road. Moody hit 52 off 76 balls, but there was little else to enthuse about in the batting. Leicestershire wanted only 49 from their last 10 overs, but they lost their last six wickets for 17 runs. Hick took three wickets in five balls.

Michael Bevan hit a six and 10 fours in his 103 off 108 balls, and he followed this with 3 for 21 in 5.1 overs to help bring to an end Yorkshire's poor run and to gain some revenge over Gloucestershire who had beaten Yorkshire inside three days in the championship match.

9 July *at Darlington*

Worcestershire 272 for 5 (G.A. Hick 130)

Durham 193 (J.E. Morris 74)

Worcestershire (4 pts) won by 79 runs

at Bristol

Middlesex 200 (M.W. Gatting 63, R.C. Williams 4 for 51)

Gloucestershire 203 for 4 (M.W. Alleyne 60 not out)

Gloucestershire (4 pts) won by 6 wickets

at Southampton

Yorkshire 264 for 2 (M.G. Bevan 97 not out, D. Byas 78, C. White 50 not out)

Hampshire 245 for 7 (R.A. Smith 115, G.M. Hamilton 4 for 38)

Yorkshire (4 pts) won by 19 runs

at Maidstone

Kent 253 for 7 (M.A. Ealham 112)

Derbyshire 249 for 7 (C.J. Adams 79)

Kent (4 pts) won by 4 runs

at Old Trafford

Northamptonshire 201 (D.J. Capel 57 not out, Wasim Akram 4 for 29)

Lancashire 200 for 8 (J.P. Crawley 53)

Northamptonshire (4 pts) won by 1 run

at Leicester

Warwickshire 277 for 4 (R.G. Twose 64 not out, D.P. Ostler 58, N.M.K. Smith 57)

Leicestershire 165

Warwickshire (4 pts) won by 112 runs

at The Oval

Essex 271 for 6 (P.J. Prichard 78, N. Hussain 68 not out)

Surrey 210 for 9 (M.C. Ilott 4 for 30)

Essex (4 pts) won by 61 runs

at Arundel

Sussex 241 for 6 (K. Greenfield 102, C.W.J. Athey 52)

Nottinghamshire 229 for 6 (J.R. Wileman 51 not out)

Sussex (4 pts) won by 12 runs

Graeme Hick hit his highest Sunday League score. His 130 against Durham came off 81 balls and included 2 sixes and 12 fours. Durham succumbed in 36 overs.

Ricardo Williams produced his best bowling figures in one-day cricket, and Gloucestershire beat Middlesex with seven balls to spare.

Byas and Bevan shared a second-wicket stand of 118 for Yorkshire against Hampshire, and after Byas was stumped off Udal, White – who hit 50 off 24 balls – joined Bevan in an unbroken partnership of 91. Robin Smith hit 2 sixes and 9 fours in a fine 115, but when he was caught at the wicket off Hamilton Hampshire lost their way.

Maidstone again proved a paradise for batsmen. Kent were 105 for 5 when Mark Ealham came to the wicket, and his arrival brought an explosion in the scoring rate. He hit 9 fours and 9 sixes to reach his century off 44 balls, so establishing a new record for the Sunday League. He was missed three times, but it was an astonishing performance. Derbyshire did not surrender meekly. Chris Adams, guilty of missing Ealham, hit 79 off 79 balls, and by the time the last ball arrived Derbyshire needed six to win, but Krikken could manage only one.

It was a sad day for Lancashire at Old Trafford. Able to play because the Test match had finished early, Martin was carried from the field with torn ankle ligaments after bowling two overs. Capel hit 57 off 52 balls, and consistent batting took Northamptonshire to 201 before Bowen was leg before to Wasim Akram on the fifth ball of the 40th over. Atherton and Speak scored 60 from 12 overs, and Crawley and Fairbrother hit 67 in 14. Four wickets then went down in five overs for 13 runs as spinners Kumble and Bailey exerted pressure on the batsmen. Four runs were needed from Bailey's last over of the match, and three off the last four balls, a task which Yates found beyond him.

Leicestershire were demolished by Warwickshire. Twose and Reeve scored 85 in the last eight overs of the visitors' innings, and Reeve then took three wickets as Leicestershire were bowled out in 38.2 overs.

Prichard and Waugh began Essex's innings against Surrey with a partnership of 123. Hussain played another fine knock, sharing a fifth-wicket stand of 64 with Robinson, and Essex reached 271 for 6 in 38 overs. Benjamin conceded 71 in his eight overs, and Butcher 25 from three. Surrey never approached the required rate and were well beaten.

In contrast to the championship match, there were runs galore at Arundel where Keith Greenfield hit his first century in one-day cricket, a fine knock which brought him 102 off 103 balls. He and Athey put on 113 for the third wicket. Sussex's score of 241 was not beyond the reach of Nottinghamshire whose score at the end of the 37th over was 197 for 5, identical to the Sussex score at the same stage. Noon hit 18 of the 19 runs scored in the 38th over, but Stephenson and Lewry tightened up, and the visitors finished 13 runs short of their target.

16 July *at Derby*

Sussex 198 (A.P. Wells 85)
Derbyshire 1 for 2
Match abandoned
Sussex 2 pts, Derbyshire 2 pts

at Chester-le-Street (Riverside)

Durham 170 for 5 (J.A. Daley 53 not out)
Hampshire 174 for 6 (K.D. James 62 not out)
Hampshire (4 pts) won by 4 wickets

at Chelmsford

Essex 211 for 6 (N. Hussain 58, R.C. Irani 50)
Leicestershire 186 for 5
Essex (4 pts) won on faster scoring rate

at Taunton

Somerset 196 for 9 (P.D. Bowler 65, S.L. Watkin 4 for 42)
Glamorgan 16 for 0
Match abandoned
Somerset 2 pts, Glamorgan 2 pts

at The Oval

Surrey 265 for 2 (G.P. Thorpe 112, D.J. Bicknell 102 not out)
Gloucestershire 246 for 8 (R.C. Russell 76 not out)
Surrey (4 pts) won by 19 runs

at Edgbaston

Middlesex 100 for 4
Warwickshire 82 for 2
Warwickshire (4 pts) won on faster scoring rate

18 July *at Canterbury*

Kent 235 for 7 (M.A. Ealham 89 not out)
Northamptonshire 238 for 2 (K.M. Curran 119 not out, R.R. Montgomerie 60)
Northamptonshire (4 pts) won by 8 wickets

One had to feel sympathy for Sussex's Ed Giddins at Derby. Sussex scored 198 and were bowled out in 39.4 overs. Giddins opened the Sussex bowling, conceded a wide and then bowled Cork with an in-swinging yorker. Next ball, he trapped Rollins leg before. Eager for his hat trick, Giddins was denied by a downpour before the next batsman could get to the wicket, and the match was abandoned.

Hampshire made hard work of chasing Durham's meagre 170 at the Riverside Ground. They reached 51 for 1 in the 11th over and found themselves 61 for 5 in the 14th. Kevan James and Adrian Aymes stopped the rot by adding 109 before Aymes was bowled by

Prabhakar with the scores level. Hampshire won with four balls to spare.

Essex were somewhat fortunate at Chelmsford. Hussain continued his good form, and Irani hit 50 from 56 balls. The pair put on 90 in 19 overs. Leicestershire moved to 186 for 5 in 35.4 overs, at which point rain fell as soon as Prichard had brilliantly caught Dakin. The game did not resume, and Essex were declared the winners. Had Leicestershire scored three more runs, the match would have been theirs. The win took Essex to second place in the table.

Glamorgan, too, could feel aggrieved. They restricted Somerset to 196 in 40 overs and had scored 16 in three overs when rain ended their match. The two points kept them ahead of the pack at the top of the table.

There was some relief for the suffering Surrey fans at The Oval. Darren Bicknell and Graham Thorpe established a Surrey second-wicket record for the competition when they made 203 in 32 overs. Bicknell's hundred came in 119 balls, and Thorpe hit 6 sixes and 4 fours in reaching his century off 90 balls. Gloucestershire slipped to 90 for 6 before Russell and Dawson helped them to respectability.

Rain delayed the start of the match at Edgbaston, and there was more rain after the Middlesex innings had lasted for 24.3 of their allotted 33 overs. This meant that Warwickshire's target was reduced to 80 in 20 overs. They won in 16.1 overs, but Middlesex protested strongly that the weather had not been good enough for the game to resume.

As Kent were engaged in the Benson and Hedges Cup final, their fixture was delayed until the Tuesday; for Kent, it was another day of disappointment. They seemed to have set Northamptonshire a challenging target. Ealham hit 9 fours and 3 sixes in his unbeaten 89 which came off 74 balls, and there were good contributions from Cowdrey and de Silva, who was given a hero's welcome. The hero of the day, however, was Kevin Curran who made his first one-day hundred and shared a second-wicket stand of 138 in 23 overs with Montgomerie. Curran and Loye hit the last 80 runs in eight overs, and Northamptonshire won with 19 balls to spare. Curran's 119 off 101 balls included 2 sixes and 15 fours.

COSTCUTTER CUP
at Harrogate

SEMI-FINALS

17 July

Nottinghamshire 215 for 6 (P.R. Pollard 101)
Yorkshire 187 for 8
Nottinghamshire won by 28 runs

Nottinghamshire spoiled the Harrogate Festival by knocking out the home side in a match reduced to 37 overs. Pollard took the individual award for his 101 off 107 balls.

18 July

Essex 185 for 7

Gloucestershire 187 for 5 (M.A. Lynch 62)

Gloucestershire won by 5 wickets

Overnight rain reduced the second match to 31 overs. Gloucestershire won with three balls to spare. Monte Lynch took the Man-of-the-Match award for steadying the winners after Alleyne had gone at three.

FINAL

19 July

Nottinghamshire 181 (M. Davies 5 for 22)

Gloucestershire 182 for 6

Gloucestershire won by 4 wickets

With the full 55 overs possible for the first time in three days, Nottinghamshire contrived to get bowled out in 47.4 overs. Their destroyer was slow left-arm bowler Davies who took 5 for 22 in 10 overs. This made Gloucestershire's task comparatively easy, but they lost Alleyne and Windows for 13, and then slipped to 103 for 6. Ricardo Williams and Russell steered them to victory, and Davies took the individual award.

23 July *at Southend*

Somerset 211 for 4 (A.N. Hayhurst 64 not out, R.J. Harden 60)

Essex 212 for 6 (N. Hussain 57)

Essex (4 pts) won by 4 wickets

at Cardiff

Warwickshire 190 for 8 (N.V. Knight 80)

Glamorgan 182 (S.P. James 50)

Warwickshire (4 pts) won by 8 runs

at Cheltenham

Lancashire 182 for 9

Gloucestershire 183 for 5

Gloucestershire (4 pts) won by 5 wickets

at Northampton

Hampshire 155 for 9

Northamptonshire 161 for 3 (R.R. Montgomerie 58)

Northamptonshire (4 pts) won by 7 wickets

at Guildford

Surrey 268 for 8 (G.P. Thorpe 66, D.J. Bicknell 58)

Nottinghamshire 267 for 6 (R.T. Robinson 70, C.L. Cairns 69)

Surrey (4 pts) won by 1 run

at Hove

Leicestershire 262 for 8 (P.A. Nixon 84, D.L. Maddy 69)

Sussex 263 for 3 (P. Moores 89 not out, C.W.J. Athey 61 not out, K. Greenfield 56, F.D. Stephenson 50)

Sussex (4 pts) won by 7 wickets

at Leeds

Yorkshire 133 (S.J.E. Brown 4 for 20)

Durham 137 for 3 (M. Prabhakar 55)

Durham (4 pts) won by 7 wickets

Essex moved to the top of the AXA Equity and Law League by beating Somerset at Southchurch Park. Somerset were 73 for 3 before Harden and Hayhurst added 101. Prichard was out for 0 when Essex batted, and, although Waugh, Hussain and Gooch saw them to 139 for 2, four wickets then fell for 22 runs. Harvey Trump's off-spin was their undoing, but Irani and Ilott countered with a blistering attack which saw Essex win with three balls to spare.

Warwickshire drew level with Glamorgan in second place by beating the Welshmen in Cardiff. Knight celebrated his selection for the England party with his highest Sunday League score, but the innings sagged in the middle, and it was left to Paul Smith and Piper to revive fortunes. Glamorgan seemed to be cruising to victory at 146 for 3, but their last seven wickets went down for 36 runs.

Lancashire suffered a thoroughly miserable weekend in Cheltenham. Gloucestershire had won the championship match in three days and now they won the Sunday League match with 13 balls to spare. Mike Smith was rightly rewarded for his outstanding season with the award of his county cap, and he dismissed Atherton and Titchard with only 20 scored. None of the Lancashire batsmen could establish himself. At 154 for 7 in the 36th over, they were struggling, and matters got worse when Hegg was run out at 159. Austin marshalled the remaining resources and hit the last two balls of the innings, bowled by Smith, for six.

Gloucestershire began soundly enough, but they stuttered in mid-innings. Symonds restored their confidence with 47 off 34 balls which included 18 off one over from Chapple.

Northamptonshire won their third Sunday League game in a row, beating Hampshire with 9.3 overs to spare, but Surrey's win over Nottinghamshire was far more exciting. Darren Bicknell and Graham Thorpe scored 112 in 20 overs for Surrey's second wicket, a partnership which was the backbone of Surrey's substantial score. Pollard and Robinson began Nottinghamshire's challenge with a partnership of 111, and Cairns brought impetus to the innings with 69 off 39 balls. When Hollioake began the last over 11 runs were needed, but Wileman and Pick could manage only three from the first five balls before Wileman pulled the last for six to leave Surrey winners by one run.

After 20 overs, Leicestershire were 80 for 5. Nixon and Maddy then added 136 in 16 overs to set Sussex a formidable target. Wells went cheaply, but Greenfield and Stephenson added 104 in 13 overs. This was followed by a violent partnership of 152 in 19 overs between Athey and Moores which won the match. Moores hit 89 off 58 balls, his highest score in any of the one-day competitions.

Durham bowled out Yorkshire in 39.1 overs and passed Yorkshire's score with 6.5 overs remaining. Simon Brown produced his best Sunday League bowling figures, and Prabhakar hit 5 fours and 2 sixes in his 55.

30 July *at Derby*

Glamorgan 247 (R.D.B. Croft 66 not out, S.P. James 60,
P.A. Cottey 56)
Derbyshire 251 for 9 (C.J. Adams 67, C.M. Wells 67,
S.L. Watkin 4 for 38)
Derbyshire (4 pts) won by 1 wicket

at Cheltenham

Essex 303 for 7 (R.C. Irani 101 not out, M.E. Waugh 78,
G.A. Gooch 51, R.C. Williams 4 for 57)
Gloucestershire 235 (M.W. Alleyne 58, M.J. Cawdron 50,
S.J.W. Andrew 4 for 40)
Essex (4 pts) won by 68 runs

at Leicester

Surrey 180
Leicestershire 181 for 3 (J.J. Whitaker 65 not out)
Leicestershire (4 pts) won by 7 wickets

at Lord's

Middlesex 163 for 9
Sussex 164 for 3 (K. Greenfield 77)
Sussex (4 pts) won by 7 wickets

at Cleethorpes

Yorkshire 194 (M.G. Bevan 56)
Nottinghamshire 197 for 5 (P.R. Pollard 95)
Nottinghamshire (4 pts) won by 5 wickets

at Taunton

Lancashire 268 for 2 (G.D. Lloyd 88 not out, N.H. Fairbrother
86 not out)
Somerset 181 (A.N. Hayhurst 70 not out)
Lancashire (4 pts) won by 87 runs

at Edgbaston

Warwickshire 222 for 6 (R.G. Twose 62, N.M.K. Smith 60)
Northamptonshire 198 for 9
Warwickshire (4 pts) won by 24 runs

at Worcester

Worcestershire 164 for 8 (T.S. Curtis 68)
Kent 168 for 2 (M.V. Fleming 70)
Kent (4 pts) won by 8 wickets

Ronnie Irani, the Essex all-rounder, hit his first Sunday League century, a ferocious 101 against Gloucestershire at Cheltenham. Irani won a place in the England 'A' party to tour Pakistan. (Paul Sturgess/Sportsline)

Glamorgan's challenge floundered at Derby, and Essex went two points clear at the head of the table. Electing to bat first, Glamorgan lost Morris and Maynard for 12, both victims of DeFreitas. James and Cottey then added 109, and when Dale and Croft put on 86 for the sixth wicket it seemed that Glamorgan had reached a winning score. Malcolm took the wicket of Dale, but it cost him 73 runs from his eight overs. He was to have his revenge. In spite of rip-roaring innings by Adams and Wells, Derbyshire needed seven from the last three balls of the match, bowled by Barwick – never one to give runs easily. Malcolm hit him for six over mid-wicket, missed the next ball and clouted four off the last.

Ronnie Irani hit 101 off 47 balls to set up Essex's big victory over Gloucestershire. He hit 6 sixes and 5 fours, and his century was the third fastest in the history of the Sunday League. The home side were 63 for 5, but Michael Cawdron, a tall left-hander educated at Cheltenham College, hit 50 on his debut to help give respectability.

Surrey were bowled out in 38.2 overs at Leicester, and the home side won with 17 balls to spare. Sussex maintained their challenge as they beat Middlesex with two overs to spare. Middlesex gave debuts to Fay, a medium-pace bowler, and to Rashid, a slow left-arm bowler with tremendous powers of hitting, as he displayed for the England Under-19 side against South Africa.

After an uneven batting display Yorkshire were

brushed aside by Nottinghamshire. Pollard and Cairns scored 113 for Nottinghamshire's third wicket, and victory came with seven balls to spare.

Lancashire kept in pursuit of the pack by routing Somerset. Gallian and Titchard began with a partnership of 60, but the fireworks came in an unbroken stand of 179 in 19 overs for the third wicket between Fairbrother and Lloyd. Simon Ecclestone conceded 56 runs in four overs. Somerset were never in the hunt.

In spite of the fact that the fourth Test match was being televised from Old Trafford with England in a winning position, a large crowd saw Warwickshire win their eighth Sunday League game in a row to go second in the table. Ostler went for 0, but Twose and Neil Smith provided substance for the Warwickshire innings in a third-wicket stand of 97. Penney's 42 not out off 32 balls gave the spice in the closing overs. Northamptonshire stumbled to 114 for 6, and the game was kept alive by Warren and Penberthy who hit 69 in eight overs. Three wickets then fell for six runs, and the cause was lost.

Kent ousted Worcestershire from the leading pack by winning comfortably at New Road. The home side's batting was sluggish, with Curtis surviving 38 overs for his 68. In contrast, Fleming hit a six and 9 fours in his 70 which came off 44 balls, and Kent won with 16 balls to spare.

6 August *at Colchester*

Essex 235 for 5 (N. Hussain 66, M.E. Waugh 55)
Hampshire 199 for 9

Essex (4 pts) won by 36 runs

at Canterbury

Kent 301 for 7 (P.A. de Silva 124, T.R. Ward 123)
Surrey 246 (A.J. Hollioake 93, D.W. Headley 6 for 42)

Kent (4 pts) won by 55 runs

at Old Trafford

Lancashire 166 for 8
Sussex 144 (Wasim Akram 4 for 16)

Lancashire (4 pts) won by 22 runs

at Lord's

Middlesex 149 for 9
Nottinghamshire 148 for 9

Middlesex (4 pts) won by 1 run

at Northampton

Durham 191 for 7
Northamptonshire 163 (N. Killeen 5 for 26)

Durham (4 pts) won by 28 runs

at Scarborough

Worcestershire 251 for 4 (G.A. Hick 113 not out)
Yorkshire 218 for 9 (M.G. Bevan 101)

Worcestershire (4 pts) won by 33 runs

A capacity crowd at Colchester saw Essex maintain their lead at the top of the table with a comfortable win over Hampshire. Hussain hit 66 off 68 balls with 4 fours and a six, and the home side went to 235 in 39 overs. In spite of Nicholas hitting Peter Such for consecutive sixes, Hampshire were never in a position to challenge Essex.

Trevor Ward and Aravinda de Silva established a Kent record for any wicket in the Sunday League by scoring 241 for the second wicket against Surrey. Pressed into service as a bowler, Ratcliffe conceded 77 runs in seven overs. Dean Headley produced his best Sunday League bowling figures, and, in spite of Adam Hollioake making his highest Sunday League score, Surrey were well beaten.

Sussex's tale of woe continued when they lost ground in the Sunday League, going down to Lancashire in a match they should have won. Lancashire batted badly after a good start which took them to 90 for 1 in the 21st over. The loss of seven wickets for 31 runs undid the fine work of Atherton and Crawley, but Hegg and Yates hit lustily in the closing overs to add 45. A total of 166 hardly looked defensible, however, and when Franklyn Stephenson was batting a Sussex victory looked certain. He was splendidly caught by Crawley off Yates to reduce Sussex to 56 for 3, and with Wasim Akram taking 4 for 16 in seven overs, Sussex tumbled headlong to defeat.

Middlesex edged off the bottom with a thrilling win over Nottinghamshire. They were defending an even smaller total than Lancashire, and when Nottinghamshire, seeking 150, were 88 for 2, defeat for the home side looked imminent. Tufnell bowled a fine containing spell in which he conceded only 13 runs from his eight overs, and Cairns and Pollard were out in quick succession. There were two run outs in five balls, but with five overs to go, Nottinghamshire still had four wickets in hand and needed just 34. Weekes contained, and the last over arrived with 15 required. Nash bowled straight, and although Pick hit a huge six over long-off, Middlesex snatched victory by one run.

Northamptonshire included Michael Foster in their Sunday League side against Durham. It was his first game since joining the county from Yorkshire. Loye hit 7 fours in his 28, but Killeen's best one-day bowling performance and four catches by Jason Boiling took Durham to victory.

There were two centuries at Scarborough where Worcestershire always seemed in control over Yorkshire. Hick's unbeaten 113 came off 83 balls and included 2 sixes and 12 fours. He and Leatherdale added 114 in 14 overs for the fourth wicket, and Worcestershire scored 91 from their last 10 overs. Bevan began slowly but increased in momentum to reach his hundred off 90 balls. Yorkshire were always below the required run rate and finished well adrift of the visitors.

13 August *at Chester-le-Street (Riverside)*

Durham 180 for 9 (J.E. Morris 51)
Middlesex 181 for 3 (M.R. Ramprakash 54 not out)

Middlesex (4 pts) won by 7 wickets

at Pontypridd

Essex 236 for 9 (G.A. Gooch 65)

Glamorgan 237 for 6 (H. Morris 80, M.P. Maynard 54)

Glamorgan (4 pts) won by 4 wickets

at Southampton

Warwickshire 226 for 7 (N.M.K. Smith 55, D.A. Reeve 50)
Hampshire 159 for 9

Warwickshire (4 pts) won by 67 runs

at Leicester

Lancashire 198 for 7 (J.E.R. Gallian 51)
Leicestershire 202 for 4 (W.J. Cronje 93 not out)

Leicestershire (4 pts) won by 6 wickets

at Northampton

Northamptonshire 227 for 8 (A. Fordham 57)
Gloucestershire 175 for 9 (A.L. Penberthy 4 for 29)

Northamptonshire (4 pts) won by 52 runs

at Taunton

Somerset 166 for 7 (G.D. Rose 59, M.A. Ealham 4 for 21)
Kent 170 for 1 (P.A. de Silva 105 not out, T.R. Ward 52 not out)

Kent (4 pts) won by 9 wickets

at The Oval

Surrey 308 for 6 (A.D. Brown 100, D.J. Bicknell 68)
Yorkshire 296 for 8 (M.G. Bevan 60, D. Byas 59,
    A.A. Metcalfe 50)

Surrey (4 pts) won by 12 runs

at Worcester

Derbyshire 163 (Parvaz Mirza 4 for 27)
Worcestershire 164 for 0 (T.M. Moody 98 not out, T.S. Curtis
    58 not out)

Worcestershire (4 pts) won by 10 wickets

Highly successful quick bowler in all forms of cricket, Ed Giddins of Sussex, 16 wickets in the Sunday League and a place in the England 'A' party to tour Pakistan. (Paul Sturgess/Sportsline)

Middlesex climbed four points clear of the bottom of the Sunday League by beating Durham with 25 balls to spare. Middlesex included Fay and Yeabsley in their attack and batted Owais Shah at number five in the absence of Gatting.

Essex's title hopes suffered a severe setback at Pontypridd when they were beaten by Glamorgan. Having scored 236 in 40 overs, Essex seemed secure, but an opening stand of 133 between James and Morris lifted the home side's chances. Five wickets then went down for 35 runs, and Glamorgan needed 69 from the last 10 overs. Dale and Maynard took them to within 11 runs of victory before Maynard fell to Ilott, and 10 were needed from the last over. This came down to two from two balls. Croft pushed Waugh to mid-wicket where Gooch fielded and threw at the stumps. The ball missed the wicket and went for overthrows to give Glamorgan the game.

Meanwhile Warwickshire moved into third place – two points behind Essex with two games in hand – when they trounced Hampshire. A second-wicket stand of 98 between Neil Smith and Dominic Ostler gave the Warwickshire innings substance, but five men were out for 133. Reeve, inevitably, changed the game with 50 off 59 balls, and he then took three of the first four wickets to leave Hampshire in a forlorn situation.

Lancashire's challenge was surprisingly halted at Leicester where the home county won with 27 balls to spare. Wells bowled tightly and took three wickets, and Cronje hit an unbeaten 93 off 89 balls to win the game. The match was originally started on a pitch that was declared too dangerous by umpires and captains and was transferred to another track. The full 40 overs were bowled in the Lancashire innings.

A weakened Gloucestershire attack was unable to contain Northamptonshire while Kent joined Essex at the top of the table with a resounding victory at Taunton. Igglesden and Ealham reduced Somerset to 18 for 5 before Rose and Ecclestone added 106. Facing a target of 167, Kent lost Fleming in the opening over, but then came de Silva. With another breathtaking display of audacious stroke-play, the Sri Lankan hit 105 off 81 balls with 5 sixes and 16 fours, and Kent won with 10.5 overs to spare.

Alistair Brown hit 100 off 79 balls and shared an opening stand of 184 with Darren Bicknell to set up Surrey's victory over Yorkshire. The visitors battled well but were always short of the required run rate.

Worcestershire kept their title hopes alive when they beat Derbyshire with five overs to spare. Parvaz Mirza again showed lively and promising form with the wickets of Adams, Rollins, Griffith and Warner. Derbyshire were bowled out for 163 on the fifth ball of the final over, and Moody and Curtis hit off the runs without being separated.

20 August *at Chester-le-Street (Riverside)*

Durham 202 for 6 (J.I. Longley 92, D.A. Blenkiron 56)

Somerset 205 for 5 (R.J. Harden 100 not out)

Somerset (4 pts) won by 5 wickets

at Bristol

Gloucestershire 138

Derbyshire 142 for 2 (K.J. Barnett 57 not out)

Derbyshire (4 pts) won by 8 wickets

at Old Trafford

Lancashire 210 for 7 (N.H. Fairbrother 60 not out)

Yorkshire 174 for 9 (R.J. Blakey 53 not out)

Lancashire (4 pts) won by 36 runs

at Lord's

Kent 219 for 8 (G.R. Cowdrey 101 not out,
    A.R.C. Fraser 4 for 18)

Middlesex 173 (J.C. Pooley 51, P.A. de Silva 4 for 28)

Kent (4 pts) won by 46 runs

at Trent Bridge

Nottinghamshire 219 for 5 (P. Johnson 82, R.T. Robinson 67)

Warwickshire 222 for 6 (D.R. Brown 78 not out)

Warwickshire (4 pts) won by 4 wickets

at Eastbourne

Worcestershire 197 for 9 (W.P.C. Weston 80)

Sussex 117

Worcestershire (4 pts) won by 80 runs

Longley and Blenkiron made their best Sunday League scores and shared a second-wicket stand of 104 for Durham against Somerset, but they still finished on the losing side. John Morris had broken his thumb the previous day and, with Roseberry absent, Bainbridge returned to lead the side. Durham had hopes of victory when Somerset were 110 for 4, but Rose joined Harden in a stand of 85, and Harden, who had hit a century on the Saturday, steered Somerset to their target with four balls to spare.

Derbyshire bowled out Gloucestershire in 38 overs at Bristol and, with Adams and Barnett scoring 85 for the first wicket, Derbyshire won with 16 balls to spare.

Lancashire revived title hopes which had flagged the week before when they won the Roses battle at Old Trafford. Warnings against drunkenness preceded the game which, initially, was highlighted by Neil Fairbrother's unbeaten 60 off 58 balls. The second vital contribution to Lancashire's victory was Glen Chapple's three wickets in the opening five overs of the Yorkshire innings. As the wickets were those of Moxon, Byas and Vaughan, the value of Chapple's contribution can be easily measured. When Austin had Bevan caught, Yorkshire were doomed.

Kent maintained their lead at the head of the table with a comfortable win at Lord's. At the start of the match, Kent had many problems. They lost Ward for one and, having reached 124 for 3, they lost three wickets without a run being scored, all three falling in the first over of Fraser's second spell. In the last nine overs of the innings, however, Cowdrey stormed to a chanceless century off 81 balls, and 79 vital runs were added.

Weekes and Pooley began Middlesex's reply with 81 in 15 overs. Aravinda de Silva dismissed them both and had Ramprakash brilliantly caught at long-off by Walker. Middlesex went from 132 for 3 to 137 for 7, and their cause was lost.

Warwickshire stayed just two points behind Kent with a game in hand when they won their 10th game in succession, beating Nottinghamshire at Trent Bridge with three balls to spare. They were fined for bowling only 38 overs in their allotted time. Nottinghamshire were much indebted to Paul Johnson for their 219. He hit 5 sixes and 7 fours. Warwickshire lost Knight early, but they always kept up with the required run rate. Dougie Brown's 78 off 67 balls was his highest score in one-day cricket, and he guided Warwickshire to the last over when six were needed. Piper hit the third ball of Cairns' over to the cover boundary to bring victory.

Worcestershire held on to third place with a win at Eastbourne. They began dreadfully, losing the top four in the batting order for 26 in the first nine overs. Weston lifted spirits by coming in at number six and staying until the last over for his 80. He and Rhodes were the main reasons why Worcestershire scored 47 in the last five overs. Newport soon undermined the Sussex innings by sending back Lenham and Stephenson, and the home side never recovered.

27 August *at Derby*

Surrey 269 for 7 (N. Shahid 101, D.J. Bicknell 91,
    F.A. Griffith 4 for 56)

Derbyshire 251 for 7 (A.S. Rollins 126 not out)

Derbyshire (4 pts) won on faster scoring rate

at Hartlepool

Sussex 89 for 3

v. Durham

Match abandoned

Durham 2 pts, Sussex 2 pts

at Ebbw Vale

Glamorgan 153 (S.P. James 78, M.W. Alleyne 5 for 28)
Gloucestershire 154 for 4 (A. Symonds 69)

Gloucestershire (4 pts) won by 6 wickets

at Portsmouth

Lancashire 196 for 8
Hampshire 181 for 7 (P.J. Martin 4 for 29)

Lancashire (4 pts) won by 15 runs

at Canterbury

Kent 221 for 6
Essex 200 (N. Hussain 83, M.E. Waugh 51, M.J. McCague 5 for 41)

Kent (4 pts) won by 21 runs

at Northampton

Northamptonshire 249 for 6 (R.R. Montgomerie 60, M.B. Loye 57 not out, R.J. Bailey 52)
Nottinghamshire 250 for 3 (P. Johnson 136 not out, C.L. Cairns 70)

Nottinghamshire (4 pts) won by 7 wickets

at Weston-super-Mare

Leicestershire 232 for 7 (B.F. Smith 115)
Somerset 236 for 6 (P.D. Bowler 76, P.C.L. Holloway 66)

Somerset (4 pts) won by 4 wickets

at Worcester

Worcestershire 157 for 7 (T.S. Curtis 62)
Warwickshire 155 for 8

Worcestershire (4 pts) won by 2 runs

at Leeds

Yorkshire 161 for 8 (M.G. Bevan 81)
Middlesex 143 (O.A. Shah 64, D. Gough 4 for 35)

Yorkshire (4 pts) won by 18 runs

Nadeem Shahid and Darren Bicknell scored 190 in 25 overs for Surrey's second wicket against Derbyshire. Shahid's first Sunday League century came off 84 balls. A brief shower reduced Derbyshire's target to 249 from 37 overs, and they won with 13 balls to spare. This was thanks to Adrian Rollins who reached his first Sunday League hundred off 68 balls and finished on 126 not out.

Rain caused the abandonment of the game at Hartlepool when the Sussex innings was 14.2 overs old. At Ebbw Vale, Steve James continued his form as the most prolific scorer in one-day cricket, but he had little support as Mark Alleyne strangled the Glamorgan innings with his 5 for 28 in eight overs. Gloucestershire were having some problems when Andrew Symonds came in and hit 7 sixes and 4 fours in his innings of 69 which came off 35 balls.

Gloucestershire's victory came with 10.5 overs to spare.

Bottom-of-the-table Hampshire appeared to be in a winning position against Lancashire. Chasing a target of 197, they needed 90 from the last 18 overs with eight wickets standing. Peter Martin showed that he had returned to full fitness by taking three wickets in four overs and changing the course of the match.

Any lingering hopes that Essex still had of winning the Sunday League disappeared with defeat at Canterbury. Kent did not seem to have made a winning score when they ended at 221 for 6 in 39 overs. Their batsmen had promised more, and only a sixth-wicket stand of 61 between Ealham and Llong gave the innings any substance. Prichard was well caught and bowled by Igglesden in the third over, but Waugh and Hussain added 90 for the second wicket, and although Gooch was caught behind for one, another large partnership – 73 between Hussain and Irani – seemed to have made sure of an Essex victory. Both batsmen were out at 175, and Robinson and Rollins were out to consecutive deliveries from McCague nine runs later. The tail disintegrated, and Kent remained four points clear at the top of the table.

Northamptonshire scored well against Nottinghamshire but the visitors raced to victory with 6.4 overs to spare. Johnson and Cairns put on 158 in 16 overs for the third wicket. Johnson's undefeated 136 came off 98 balls, and he hit 5 sixes and 14 fours. Cairns also hit 5 sixes, and he took 22 off one over by Robert Bailey. His 70 included 5 fours and came off 44 balls.

Caddick limped off the field at Weston-super-Mare with a recurrence of his shin injury, but Somerset still beat Leicestershire for whom Ben Smith hit 115 off 95 balls. Somerset needed 84 from the last 10 overs and won with two balls to spare.

Warwickshire's run of 10 consecutive wins was brought to an end by neighbouring Worcestershire who moved into second place behind Kent. The pitch was slow and the scoring low so that Curtis' 62 off 99 balls was an invaluable innings, and Worcestershire's 157 from 39 overs was a little more respectable than it may appear. Warwickshire began comfortably, but Moody took three wickets and his side fielded splendidly to frustrate and harry their opponents. Reeve enjoyed stands with Twose and Paul Smith which brought 65 runs in 14 overs, and 25 were needed from the last six overs. Newport and Lampitt bowled admirably, and the last over arrived with eight needed by Warwickshire. Three came from the first three balls before Newport bowled Piper with the fourth. Donald and Small could manage only singles from the last two, and Worcestershire were the victors.

The match at Headingley was reduced to 37 overs. Michael Bevan hit 81 and took 3 for 35, and Gough took 4 for 35 as Middlesex were bowled out in 36.4 overs. The 16-year-old Owais Shah made an impressive 64 for the losers.

3 September *at Chelmsford*

Essex 196 for 7 (G.A. Gooch 63 not out)
Derbyshire 172 (C.J. Adams 54)

Essex (4 pts) won by 24 runs

at Leicester

Glamorgan 212 for 6 (S.P. James 80, D.L. Hemp 74)
Leicestershire 215 for 6 (B.F. Smith 78 not out, V.J. Wells 50)

Leicestershire (4 pts) won by 4 wickets

at Trent Bridge

Nottinghamshire 240 for 5 (C.L. Cairns 101, G.F. Archer 53)
Hampshire 244 for 5 (R.S.M. Morris 64, J.S. Laney 53)

Hampshire (4 pts) won by 5 wickets

at The Oval

Surrey 189 for 9
Lancashire 190 for 4 (J.E.R. Gallian 62)

Lancashire (4 pts) won by 6 wickets

at Worcester

Worcestershire 174 for 7 (G.A. Hick 72)
Somerset 106 (G.A. Hick 4 for 21)

Worcestershire (4 pts) won by 68 runs

5 September *at Uxbridge*

Middlesex 233 for 6 (M.R. Ramprakash 103, M.W. Gatting 68)
Northamptonshire 158 for 4

Northamptonshire (4 pts) won on faster scoring rate

at Edgbaston

Gloucestershire 111 for 6
Warwickshire 112 for 6

Warwickshire (4 pts) won by 4 wickets

Graham Gooch hit 63 off 52 balls for Essex against Derbyshire and played a major part in the visitors' astonishing collapse. Barnett and Adams scored 101 for their first wicket in 24 overs, only for the side to be all out in the next 14.2 overs for 172.

Glamorgan had led the AXA Equity and Law League earlier in the season, but their season fell further apart when they went down to Leicestershire who won with nine balls to spare. Ben Smith had another fine day for the home side, hitting 2 sixes and 5 fours in his 78 off 59 balls.

A century off 75 balls by Chris Cairns was not enough to bring Nottinghamshire victory over Hampshire for whom Morris and Laney scored 119 for the first wicket in 20 overs.

There was another lack-lustre performance by Surrey at The Oval. They were without Hollioake but still failed to call on David Ward – incomprehensible in view of the batting they offered. All the Lancashire bowlers bowled well, with Wasim Akram to the fore on his last appearance of the season. He took 3 for 30. Gallian and Crawley scored 76 in 17 overs for Lancashire's second wicket, and Wasim and Lloyd took the Red Rose to victory with 15 balls to spare.

There was some excellent all-round cricket from Hick in Worcestershire's victory over Somerset. He hit 72 off 87 balls on a pitch which did not allow for stroke-play. Harden batted manfully for Somerset, but they were

never in the hunt against the off-spin of Hick and Worcestershire's accurate seam attack.

The matches involving the NatWest finalists were played on the Tuesday and both were affected by rain. Ramprakash hit 103 off 118 balls for Middlesex, but Northamptonshire's target was reduced to 158 in 27 overs, and they won amid gloom and dampness with four balls to spare.

Gloucestershire were 111 for 6 in 32.2 overs when rain ended their innings. As Symonds was unbeaten on 38 off 26 balls, they could feel ill-used. Warwickshire had the relatively simple task of scoring 112 off 32 overs to win. They were 13 for 3 and 36 for 4, but Knight, who carried his bat for 36, Penney and Piper saw them home with 23 balls to spare.

With two matches remaining, Kent and Worcestershire had 46 points, and Lancashire and Warwickshire 44. The title would not be decided until the last Sunday of the season.

 TETLEY BITTER FESTIVAL
at Scarborough

4 September

Nottinghamshire 298 for 6 (R.T. Robinson 76 not out, C.L. Cairns 62)
Yorkshire 177 (S.A. Kellett 64, R.J. Chapman 4 for 41)

Nottinghamshire won by 121 runs

5 September

Kent 328 for 7 (G.R. Cowdrey 145, M.R. Benson 94)
Durham 276 (P.D. Collingwood 74, S. Hutton 53)

Kent won by 52 runs

6 September

Nottinghamshire 197 for 9 (C.L. Cairns 62 not out)
Kent 137

Nottinghamshire won by 60 runs

Nottinghamshire were worthy winners of the Tetley Bitter Festival Trophy for they played some very entertaining cricket. In the semi-final of this 50-over competition, Chris Cairns hit 5 sixes in his 62 which lasted only 35 minutes and came off just 28 balls. He gave a similar blast in the final which rain reduced to 40 overs. He hit 62 off 46 balls with 3 sixes and 3 fours. Kent were bowled out in 33.2 overs. Graham Cowdrey, outstanding against Durham, was top scorer with 39.

10 September *at Cardiff*

Glamorgan v. Nottinghamshire

Match abandoned

Glamorgan 2 pts, Nottinghamshire 2 pts

at Bristol

Gloucestershire v. Durham

David Bowden, Gloucestershire's fast-bowling recruit from Essex. (Neal Simpson/Empics)

Match abandoned
Gloucestershire 2 pts, Durham 2 pts

at Southampton

Hampshire *v.* **Somerset**

Match abandoned

Hampshire 2 pts, Somerset 2 pts

at Old Trafford

Lancashire 126
Kent 128 for 3

Kent (4 pts) won by 7 wickets

at Uxbridge

Middlesex *v.* **Leicestershire**

Match abandoned

Middlesex 2 pts, Leicestershire 2 pts

at Northampton

Worcestershire 118 for 1 (T.M. Moody 56)
v. **Northamptonshire**

Match abandoned

Northamptonshire 2 pts, Worcestershire 2 pts

at Edgbaston

Derbyshire 81 for 5
v. **Warwickshire**

Match abandoned

Warwickshire 2 pts, Derbyshire 2 pts

at Scarborough

Sussex 164 for 8 (N.J. Lenham 56 not out)
Yorkshire 165 for 3 (A. McGrath 72)

Yorkshire (4 pts) won by 7 wickets

The penultimate Sunday of the season was most unkind to two of the counties with title aspirations. Worcestershire had scored 118 for 1 from 22.1 overs when rain ended their encounter at Northampton, while Warwickshire had Derbyshire reeling at 81 for 5 after 25 overs at Edgbaston when play was halted. Four other matches never got started, but the game at Old Trafford went its full course, and Kent went two points clear at the top of the table with a fine win over Lancashire.

Watkinson chose to bat when he won the toss, and Atherton and Gallian gave the home side a sound start with 45 runs in 13 overs. Igglesden dismissed them both as three wickets went down for one run. The score crept to 60 for 4 at which point Watkinson and Fairbrother added 40 in seven overs. They became Marsh's fourth and fifth catches of the innings, and the last six Lancashire wickets went down for 26 runs due to some accurate, aggressive bowling and some tigerish fielding.

Kent lost Ward and Benson for 22, but Cowdrey and de Silva – playing his last game for Kent – added 76. Cowdrey was caught by Lloyd for 44, but de Silva was unbeaten for 40 as Kent won with 8.4 overs unused.

Yorkshire's victory over Sussex had little impact on the league table, but it was significant in that McGrath and Vaughan, the Yorkshire openers – both under 21 – scored 114 in 27 overs for the first wicket. Yorkshire won with a ball to spare.

The finale to the season would see Kent entertain Warwickshire at Canterbury while Worcestershire would host Glamorgan. Kent, Warwickshire and Worcestershire could all still win the title.

FRIENDLY MATCH

10 September *at The Oval*

Surrey *v.* **New South Wales**

Match abandoned

Surrey's plans to celebrate their 150th anniversary with matches against New South Wales were ruined by the weather. The first-class match had to be abandoned after the first day, and the one-day game scheduled for the Sunday was abandoned without a ball being bowled.

17 September *at Derby*

Derbyshire 119 for 4 (C.M. Wells 66)
v. **Lancashire**

Match abandoned

Derbyshire 2 pts, Lancashire 2 pts

at Chester-le-Street (Riverside)

Durham 203 for 7 (J.E. Morris 52)

Nottinghamshire 206 for 8 (C.L. Cairns 75 not out)

Nottinghamshire (4 pts) won by 2 wickets

at Chelmsford

Essex 82 for 6

Yorkshire 86 for 1

Yorkshire (4 pts) won by 9 wickets

at Canterbury

Kent 166 (N.J. Llong 51, D.A. Reeve 4 for 22)

Warwickshire 167 for 5 (N.M.K. Smith 55)

Warwickshire (4 pts) won by 5 wickets

at Leicester

Leicestershire *v.* Gloucestershire

Match abandoned

Leicestershire 2 pts, Gloucestershire 2 pts

at Taunton

Somerset 132

Middlesex 114 for 3

Middlesex (4 pts) won on faster scoring rate

at The Oval

Hampshire 166 for 6 (M. Keech 70)

Surrey 109 for 4

Surrey (4 pts) won on faster scoring rate

at Hove

Northamptonshire 193 (P.W. Jarvis 6 for 29)

Sussex 180 (P. Moores 63, A.P. Wells 56)

Northamptonshire (4 pts) won by 13 runs

at Worcester

Worcestershire 145 for 6 (W.P.C. Weston 63)

Glamorgan 3 for 0

Match abandoned

Worcestershire 2 pts, Glamorgan 2 pts

The Sunday League had a damp and soggy climax, and Kent won their first trophy for 17 years by virtue of Worcestershire's game against Glamorgan being washed out in mid-afternoon. The Worcestershire innings was brought to an end after 37.1 overs, and it had been rescued by Weston who celebrated the award of his county cap with an innings of 63. Ten balls of Glamorgan's innings were all that was possible before the rain returned.

The 10-over thrash at Derby had to be abandoned after the home side had batted, and Yorkshire won a similarly limited encounter at Chelmsford with two balls to spare.

Both Middlesex and Surrey won by reaching reduced targets while there was no play at all at Leicester. Middlesex included the England Under-19 wicket-keeper David Nash, who made two catches and a stumping. His Under-19 international colleague Umer Rashid took two wickets.

Chris Cairns hit 75 off 59 balls and enabled Nottinghamshire to beat Durham off the last ball of a match that went the full distance, and Northamptonshire won a strange encounter at Hove. Chasing a target of 194, Sussex were going strongly until four wickets fell for two runs in mid-innings, and they lost by 13 runs. This was hard on Paul Jarvis who took 6 for 29 and hit 12 not out.

All attention was focused on Canterbury where, the previous day, Warwickshire had clinched the Britannic Assurance County Championship and where now Kent could clinch the Sunday League. The match did not go according to script. Graham Cowdrey, batting with an injured finger, played some fine shots as he had done all season, and Llong hit 51 off 48 balls, but there was little else to commend in a disappointing display. Reeve had asked Kent to bat first on a slow pitch, and he did most of the damage with his best Sunday bowling performance of the season.

Warwickshire romped to 81 for 0 in 12 overs, but slipped to 104 for 4 in the 21st over. Roger Twose, in his last innings for the county before emigrating to New Zealand, steered Warwickshire to victory with 6.4 overs to spare. In spite of this, Kent were champions because of their faster run rate, and while one felt sympathy for Worcestershire in the abandonment of their game against Glamorgan, a league is won by performances over a period of 17 matches. Kent needed some comfort from a season which had seen them finish bottom of the county championship for the first time in 100 years.

AXA EQUITY AND LAW LEAGUE FINAL TABLE

	P	W	L	T	NR	Pts
Kent (3)	17	12	4	0	1	50
Warwickshire (1)	17	12	4	0	1	50
Worcestershire (2)	17	11	3	1	2	50
Lancashire (4)	17	11	5	0	1	46
Essex (17)	17	10	6	1	0	42
Glamorgan (7)	17	8	6	0	3	38
Leicestershire (10)	17	8	7	0	2	36
Derbyshire (8)	17	7	6	1	3	36
Surrey (6)	17	7	8	0	2	32
Sussex (15)	17	7	8	0	2	32
Nottinghamshire (11)	17	7	9	0	1	30
Yorkshire (5)	17	7	9	0	1	30
Northamptonshire (13)	17	6	8	1	2	30
Somerset (16)	17	5	9	0	3	26
Gloucestershire (18)	17	5	10	0	2	24
Durham (9)	17	4	9	1	3	24
Middlesex (14)	17	4	11	0	2	20
Hampshire (12)	17	3	12	1	1	16

(1994 positions in brackets)

YOUNG AUSTRALIA TOUR

The Young Australia side selected for the short tour of England was a strong one, containing as it did eight players who had appeared at international level. The party was captained by Stuart Law who had led Queensland to triumph in the Sheffield Shield. The rest of the party was: A.C. Gilchrist, J.L. Langer and J. Angel (Western Australia); M.L. Love, M.L. Hayden and M.S. Kasprowicz (Queensland); R.T. Ponting and S. Young (Tasmania); M.T.G. Elliott and B. Williams (Victoria); P.E. McIntyre, S.P. George and M.A. Harrity (South Australia).

3 July *at Trowbridge*

Young Australia 328 for 5 (M.L. Hayden 159, S.G. Law 61)
NCA England XI 265 for 8 (S.J. Dean 146 not out)

Young Australia won by 63 runs

The tour began with a 55-over game against some very capable amateur cricketers. Matthew Hayden hit 12 fours and a six in his 173-ball innings, and he and Law added 168 in 24 overs for the third wicket. Steve Dean carried his bat through the NCA innings, faced 157 balls, hit 2 sixes and 23 fours and took the individual award.

5, 6 and 7 July *at Taunton*

Young Australia 380 (A.C. Gilchrist 122, S. Young 110, R.T. Ponting 54, M.E. Trescothick 4 for 36, G.D. Rose 4 for 50) and 386 for 3 dec. (M.L. Love 181, M.L. Hayden 67, R.T. Ponting 52 not out)
Somerset 306 for 9 dec. (M.N. Lathwell 89, P.C.L. Holloway 59 not out, B.D. Williams 4 for 79) and 430 (K.A. Parsons 105, M.N. Lathwell 84, G.D. Rose 71)

Young Australia won by 30 runs

The opening first-class match of the tour was rich in entertainment. Hayden was caught off Rose on the first ball of the match. Ponting hit 54, but five wickets were down for 156. This brought together Adam Gilchrist, the wicket-keeper, and Shaun Young, an up-and-coming all-rounder. In 28 overs, they savaged 195 runs. Young hit 3 sixes and 16 fours, and Gilchrist – a surprise choice ahead of Tasmania's Atkinson – hit 8 sixes and 13 fours. Their running between the wickets was electric, and their stroke-play thrilling. Young was caught at long-on to give Trescothick his first wicket in first-class cricket, and he celebrated this by dismissing Gilchrist, Angel and McIntyre with successive balls to complete a hat trick. The Australians were all out by four o'clock, having hit 380 off 68 overs.

Lathwell hit 89 off 81 balls, and by the close, Somerset were 176 for 4. They continued to score at a ferocious rate on the second day, and declared 74 runs in arrears, having made 306 in 52.3 overs.

Martin Love followed this by hitting 181 off 190 balls with 24 fours and 3 sixes. He and Hayden scored 169 for the first wicket. Law declared at the overnight score, and

the last day was given to Somerset to score 461 if they wanted to win.

They made a valiant effort. Parsons hit a maiden first-class hundred, and Rose batted with his customary aggression, but Somerset fell 30 runs short of the visitors.

8, 9 and 10 July *at Neath*

Glamorgan 362 for 6 dec. (P.A. Cottey 123 not out, D.L. Hemp 88, M.P. Maynard 56) and 286 (S.P. James 116, P.E. McIntyre 4 for 75)
Young Australia 261 (J.L. Langer 111 not out, R.D.B. Croft 4 for 45) and 179 for 5 (M.T.G. Elliott 89 not out)

Match drawn

Tony Cottey hit his fifth century of the season, and he and Maynard added 133 in 32 overs for Glamorgan's fifth wicket. Perhaps more importantly for the county side, David Hemp hit 14 fours and a six in an innings which showed a return of form and confidence after a miserable start to the season. Justin Langer hit a century and carried his bat on the second day. He held the Young Australians together after Love was out at 22 and others rushed headlong to their doom. Barwick broke a finger while fielding.

Batting a second time, Glamorgan lost their last eight wickets for 63 after James' 116 off 157 balls. Needing 388 in 76 overs, the tourists were 179 for 5 in 44.4 overs when rain ended play.

12 July *at Reading*

Young Australia 316 for 5 (R.T. Ponting 120, M.T.G. Elliott 62, S.G. Law 54, J.L. Langer 52)
Minor Counties 245 for 8 (S.D. Myles 50 not out)

Young Australia won by 71 runs

Ponting hit 120 off 119 balls in this 55-over match which again showed the Australians' batting strength.

18 July *at Leeds*

Yorkshire 224 for 6 (M.P. Vaughan 76, D. Byas 73)
Young Australia 156 (A.C. Gilchrist 51, A.C. Morris 5 for 32)

Yorkshire won by 68 runs

The tourists suffered their first defeat of the tour. They were bowled out in 45.5 overs.

19, 20 and 21 July *at Chesterfield*

Derbyshire 191 (J.E. Owen 65, M.A. Harrity 4 for 37) and 316 for 8 dec. (T.A. Tweats 58, D.G. Cork 50 not out)
Young Australia 234 (A.C. Gilchrist 105 not out) and 276 for 6 (M.L. Love 108, R.T. Ponting 64)

Young Australia won by 4 wickets

A steamy day at Queen's Park saw Derbyshire in trouble at 40 for 4, the havoc having been wrought by Angel and Harrity. Owen helped to bring more comfort to the county side with the highest score of his career, racing to fifty off 44 balls.

Young Australia were not without problems against Harris, Aldred and Malcolm, and they were 107 for 7 before Gilchrist and Williams took the score to 171 by the end of an eventful day.

The eighth-wicket pair were separated on the second morning by which time their partnership was worth 76. Adam Gilchrist played an impressive innings and reached his century off 105 balls. It was mainly due to him that the tourists took a lead of 43 on the first innings. Derbyshire lost Rollins and Adams before these arrears were wiped out. The rest of the order settled down to bat consistently, and Tweats reached a maiden first-class fifty.

Derbyshire added 26 runs to their overnight score on the last day, and Cork's declaration left Young Australia 51 overs in which to score 274. Love hit a hundred off 99 deliveries, and victory came with five balls to spare.

22, 23 and 24 July at Worcester

Worcestershire 397 (S.J. Rhodes 122 not out, W.P.C. Weston 62, N.V. Radford 50) and 198 for 6 dec.

Young Australia 332 for 3 dec. (R.T. Ponting 103 not out, J.L. Langer 88, M.L. Love 53 not out) and 220 for 9 (J.L. Langer 72 not out)

Match drawn

Worcestershire occupied the first day at New Road and confirmed the general view that the Australian bowling was not as good as their batting. That said, the county side were reduced to 160 for 6 and owed a great debt to Rhodes who hit the eighth and highest century of his career. He and Radford added 118 for the eighth wicket. Rhodes hit 2 sixes and 17 fours, and Radford 2 sixes and 5 fours in his first fifty for three years.

There was some highly entertaining batting from the Australians on the Sunday. Ponting reached 103 off 136 balls and shared century partnerships with Langer and Love.

Moody eventually asked the tourists to make 264 in 45 overs. They lost their first three wickets for 38. Ponting and Langer added 67, but four wickets fell for 23 runs, and, in the end, Langer and McIntyre resisted for 50 balls to save the game.

26 July at Cheltenham

Young Australia 262 for 4 (S.G. Law 76 not out, M.T.G. Elliott 51)

Gloucestershire 265 for 8 (M.W. Alleyne 102 not out, A. Symonds 50)

Gloucestershire won by 2 wickets

Rain reduced the match from 55 to 48 overs. Alleyne's century off 109 balls set up Gloucestershire's victory which Cooper completed on the third ball of the last over.

28, 29, 30 and 31 July at Southampton

Young Australia 527 for 7 dec. (M.L. Hayden 146, S.G. Law 134, R.T. Ponting 87, A.C. Gilchrist 62) and 21 for 0

Hampshire 100 (M.S. Kasprowicz 5 for 19) and 446 (V.P. Terry 104, J.P. Stephenson 89, H.H. Streak 69, A.N. Aymes 61)

Young Australia won by 10 wickets

Having lost Elliott for 0, the Australians plundered runs on the opening day. Hayden, who hit 19 fours and 4 sixes, and Law, 24 fours, scored 239 for the third wicket, and Ponting and Gilchrist shared a century stand on the Saturday. Hampshire, 71 for 2, lost four wickets for three runs as they collapsed before former Essex pace bowler Kasprowicz. Following on, the county side were indebted to Stephenson and Terry – top scorers in the first innings – who put on 199 for the second wicket. Streak hit the highest score of his career, 69 off 76 balls with 14 fours, but the Australians could not be halted. The game was completed on the Sunday, leaving a day unused.

3, 4, 5 and 6 August at Leicester

Young Australia 220 (S. Young 62, A. Sheriyar 4 for 55) and 146 (M.T.G. Elliott 50, A. Sheriyar 6 for 30, A.D. Mullally 4 for 51)

Leicestershire 323 (J.J. Whitaker 103, W.J. Cronje 53, J. Angel 4 for 93) and 45 for 6 (M.S. Kasprowicz 4 for 17)

Leicestershire won by 4 wickets

The tourists were beaten in two days, but Leicestershire paid a high price for their victory. Sutcliffe, the talented Oxford blue, broke a wrist while fielding, and the injury threatened to bring an end to his season.

5 August at Leicester

Young Australia 236 for 6 (M.L. Hayden 103, R.T. Ponting 63)

Leicestershire 179 for 9 (P.E. Robinson 75)

Young Australia won by 57 runs

Following the humiliation of being beaten in two days, Young Australia agreed to play a 40-over match on the Saturday which had been scheduled as the third day of the four-day game. In fact, Leicestershire bowled only 38 overs, and the substance of the Young Australia innings came from a second-wicket stand of 154 between Hayden and Ponting. Hayden's 103 came off 111 balls with 3 sixes and 7 fours.

8 August at The Oval

Young Australia 322 for 6 (S.G. Law 163, R.T. Ponting 71)

Surrey 143 (N. Shahid 63, S. Young 5 for 39)

Young Australia won by 179 runs

YOUNG AUSTRALIA FIRST-CLASS AVERAGES

BATTING

	M	Inns	NO	Runs	HS	Av	100s	50s
A.C. Gilchrist	8	11	3	495	122	61.87	2	2
J.L. Langer	7	12	3	516	149	57.33	2	2
M.L. Love	7	13	2	510	181	46.36	2	1
R.T. Ponting	7	12	2	460	103*	46.00	1	4
M.L. Hayden	7	14	2	551	178	45.91	2	1
S.G. Law	7	11	2	397	134	44.11	1	1
M.T.G. Elliott	6	12	3	357	89*	39.66	–	3
J. Angel	6	7	4	103	29*	34.33	–	–
S. Young	7	10	–	228	110	22.80	1	1
M.S. Kasprowicz	5	6	2	65	43*	16.25	–	–
S.P. George	3	3	–	46	29	15.33	–	–
B.D. Williams	5	6	1	72	28	14.40	–	–
M.A. Harrity	5	3	–	18	18	6.00	–	–
P.E. McIntyre	8	8	1	26	13	3.71	–	–

BOWLING

	Overs	Mds	Runs	Wkts	Av	Best	10/m	5/inn
M.S. Kasprowicz	175.1	42	599	27	22.18	5-19	–	1
S. Young	128	36	359	16	22.43	3-23	–	–
M.T.G. Elliott	7	2	23	1	23.00	1-23	–	–
J. Angel	179.5	39	709	27	26.25	4-31	–	–
P.E. McIntyre	296.5	70	1018	34	29.94	5-38	–	1
B.D. Williams	134.3	26	446	14	31.85	4-79	–	–
M.A. Harrity	135.2	33	497	13	38.23	4-37	–	–
S.P. George	72	6	419	7	59.85	3-91	–	–
R.T. Ponting	10	1	36	–	–	–	–	–

FIELDING FIGURES

39 – A.C. Gilchrist (ct 34/st 5); 13 – S.G. Law; 10 – M.L. Love; 7 – R.T. Ponting; 6 – J.L. Langer and J. Angel; 4 – M.T.G. Elliott, S. Young and P.E. McIntyre; 3 – subs; 2 – M.L. Hayden and M.A. Harrity; 1 – S.P. George.

This 55-over match was an embarrassment and a farce. Surrey claimed that due to injuries they could field only four first-team players, and they included six cricketers who had never appeared for Surrey before. Law hit 163 off 126 balls and added 176 in 29 overs for the third wicket with Ponting. Most of the Surrey regulars reported fit for the four-day game two days later.

11, 12, 13 and 14 August *at Hove*

Young Australia 580 for 8 dec. (M.L. Hayden 178, J.L. Langer 149, M.T.G. Elliott 79, A.C. Gilchrist 64 not out) and 9 for 1
Sussex 109 and 479 (D.R.C. Law 115, N.J. Lenham 94, N.C. Phillips 53, J. Angel 4 for 68)

Young Australia won by 9 wickets

Another match scheduled for four days was over in three. Hayden and Elliott, the two left-handers, began the match with 116 in 22 overs. Hayden batted throughout the first day, a blend of patience and aggression, and hit 3 sixes and 24 fours. He was out on the second morning without adding to his score. His fourth-wicket partnership with Justin Langer was worth 261.

Young Australia declared after four scintillating sessions and bowled out Sussex in a session and 35 minutes. Following on, the county did not lose a wicket on the Saturday evening, but the tourists whittled away on the Sunday and they looked certain to claim an innings victory. That they did not was due to Danny Law who hit a maiden first-class century with 3 sixes and 18 fours. His 115 came off 121 balls, and he followed this belligerent innings by dismissing Matthew Hayden before Young Australia could score the nine they required.

17, 18, 19 and 20 August *at Edgbaston*

TCCB XI 191 (P.E. McIntyre 5 for 38) and 101 (J. Angel 4 for 31)
Young Australia 258 (S.G. Law 70, R.D.B. Croft 5 for 58) and 35 for 1

Young Australia won by 9 wickets

What was meant to be the show-piece finale of the Young Australian tour was all over in two days. A sub-standard pitch – not unusual at Edgbaston in 1995 – and a TCCB XI that was hardly representative of England's second eleven made the Australians feel somewhat slighted and disgruntled. They dealt with the occasion in the best way possible. The spinners thrived on the first day, and Stuart Law hit an elegant 70 on the second day. Young Australia's tail, with Kasprowicz hitting cleanly, wagged furiously, and the last five wickets doubled the score. Angel then dismissed Butcher and Maynard in his opening over, and the game was virtually settled.

Adam Gilchrist, who had a highly successful tour, claimed 10 victims in the match – seven catches and three stumpings. Six of his victims came in the second innings.

Five wins and one defeat in eight first-class outings meant a satisfactory tour for the Australians whose batting was stronger than their bowling. On the evidence of the itinerary and the opposition, however, one doubts whether England is capable of staging an 'A' tour.

The TCCB XI was: H. Morris (capt), M.P. Maynard, P.A. Cottey and R.D.B. Croft (Glamorgan); M.A. Butcher and A.J. Hollioake (Surrey); D.J. Capel (Northamptonshire); P.A. Nixon (wicket-keeper), A. Sheriyar, A.R.K. Pierson and A.D. Mullally (Leicestershire). All of the players were chosen from counties who were not engaged in a championship match.

OXFORD AND CAMBRIDGE UNIVERSITIES

13, 14 and **15** April *at Cambridge*

Yorkshire 479 for 3 dec. (D. Byas 181, M.D. Moxon 130, M.G. Bevan 113 not out, C. White 50 not out) and 165 for 3 dec. (A.P. Grayson 59, M.P. Vaughan 52 retired hurt)

Cambridge University 174 (J. Ratledge 56) and 52 for 4

Match drawn

at Oxford

Durham 322 for 9 dec. (J.E. Morris 99, M.A. Roseberry 90, D.P. Mather 4 for 65, A.D. MacRobert 4 for 93) and 137 for 3 dec. (J.A. Daley 53 not out)

Oxford University 183 (S.J.E. Brown 4 for 54) and 93 for 3

Match drawn

As has become customary, the first-class season in England began with matches involving the two oldest universities. As has also become customary, those matches were drawn, yet the early indications from the two sides were much more in favour of Oxford than of Cambridge. Gregor Macmillan, the Oxford captain, had seven old blues at his disposal, and he and Sutcliffe were both con-

The season's first centurion – Martyn Moxon, 130 for Yorkshire against Cambridge University. (Paul Sturgess/Sportsline)

tracted to Leicestershire while Kendall was with Hampshire. Cambridge did not possess a player contracted to a first-class county, and the captain, Andrew Whittall, cousin of the Zimbabwe Test all-rounder, faced considerable problems. These were evident on the opening day at Fenner's when Martyn Moxon hit the first century of the season and was quickly followed by David Byas who reached the highest score of his career. The pair added 235 after Vaughan had had his off stump knocked back by Haste in the third over of the day. There was also a century from Yorkshire's new overseas signing, Michael Bevan. Bevan had hit a century against a Western Province XI on a pre-season tour of South Africa, so that he could be said to have made a most impressive start. Having seen his side score 479 in 96.3 overs and White reach fifty, Moxon declared.

The Cambridge scoring provided a sharp contrast. The undergraduates were bowled out for 174 in 93.2 overs. Ratledge battled bravely after being struck on the thumb, and Clarke and Churton both sustained finger injuries. Moxon did not enforce the follow-on, and the game dribbled to a draw on the Saturday, with Cake displaying a class not shown by his team-mates.

Things were rather different in The Parks where Michael Roseberry led Durham in a first-class match for the first time. He celebrated with 90 as he and Morris added 163 runs for the second wicket. Durham ended a serenely beautiful first day on 272 for 4, which had come at less than three runs an over. They encountered some good bowling by left-arm medium-pace freshman David Mather from Cheshire, and by Angus MacRobert from Western Province.

Durham batted into the second day, and Oxford began their innings well enough before collapsing from 124 for 2 to 183 all out. Durham then settled for batting practice and the game died.

18, 19 and **20** April *at Cambridge*

Lancashire 245 for 4 dec. (N.J. Speak 116, J.P. Crawley 74) and 243 for 4 dec. (G.D. Lloyd 117)

Cambridge University 168 for 8 dec. (R.A. Battye 65) and 144 for 2 (R.T. Ragnauth 65 not out)

Match drawn

at Oxford

Glamorgan 360 for 5 dec. (H. Morris 125, M.P. Maynard 86) and 229 for 4 dec. (A. Dale 121)

Oxford University 157 (W.S. Kendall 52, R.P. Lefebvre 6 for 45) and 105 for 1 (G.I. Macmillan 53 not out)

Match drawn

The weather turned unpleasantly cold and damp as the universities engaged in two rather aimless encounters. Speak and Lloyd succeeded where others failed at

Michael Roseberry took over the captaincy of Durham and led the county for the first time in the match against Oxford University. (David Munden/Sportsline)

Fenner's, but Cambridge ended the match on an encouraging note as Ragnauth and Cake shared an unbroken stand of 101. Lancashire were without Chapple, playing for the England 'A' side at Edgbaston, and Wasim Akram who had not yet arrived in England, but they gave a debut to Gary Keedy, the left-arm spinner whom they had acquired from Yorkshire.

Glamorgan were in joyful mood in The Parks. Hugh Morris shrugged off the poor form of 1994 with a century. The Glamorgan captain, a stone lighter than of yore, shared a second-wicket stand of 162 with Maynard. The Welshmen had returned from Zimbabwe only 48 hours earlier, but they showed no sign of fatigue as Roland Lefebvre returned the best bowling figures of his career on the second day. There was another century, this time by Dale, but Oxford ended happily enough. Glamorgan's one problem proved to be that Morris was troubled by back pains and returned to Cardiff for examination and treatment.

27, 28 and **29** April *at Cambridge*

Nottinghamshire 413 for 8 dec. (C.L. Cairns 110, R.T. Robinson 101, P. Johnson 73, K.P. Evans 53,

A.R. Whittall 4 for 131) and 245 for 0 dec. (M.P. Dowman 102 retired hurt, C. Banton 80 not out, G.W. Mike 54 not out)
Cambridge University 91 and 218 for 6 (A.R. Whittall 81 not out, J. Ratledge 65)

Match drawn

at Oxford

Worcestershire 320 for 7 dec. (W.P.C. Weston 100, T.S. Curtis 81) and 186 for 2 dec. (D.A. Leatherdale 92, G.R. Haynes 55)
Oxford University 225 (C.M. Gupte 60, A.C. Ridley 50, P.J. Newport 4 for 51) and 123 for 6 (I.J. Sutcliffe 57)

Match drawn

On the first day at Fenner's, Nottinghamshire made 413 for 8 off 87.3 overs and captured two Cambridge wickets for 11 runs before the close. Robinson hit a century off 164 balls, but the most cheering aspect for the county side was that New Zealander Chris Cairns made his highest score for Nottinghamshire and equalled the best score of his career. His hundred came off 65 balls, and he hit 7 fours and 7 sixes. Two of those sixes were hit out of the ground. He followed this by taking 2 for 7 in eight overs as the University were tumbled out for 91. Robinson did not enforce the follow-on, and Colin Banton and the left-handed Matthew Dowman scored 159 for the first wicket before Dowman, having completed a maiden first-class century, retired with a conveniently injured back. Banton, born in South Africa, was making his first-class debut. Whittall and Birks shared an unbroken stand of 110 after six wickets had fallen for 108 and saved the game for Cambridge.

Weston and Curtis scored 163 for Worcestershire's first wicket in The Parks where, interestingly, Oxford included Michael Jarrett who had won his blue at Cambridge in 1992 and 1993. Weston hit 8 fours and 2 sixes in his century. Gupte and Ridley batted well for Oxford whose last seven wickets went down for 55 runs. Eventually, they were set a target of 282 to win, but lost Macmillan and Gupte without a run scored. Sutcliffe and Ridley added 73, stopped the rot, and the match was drawn.

11, 12 and **13 May** *at Cambridge*

Essex 260 (N. Hussain 68, A.R. Whittall 5 for 67) and 168 for 8 dec. (J.J.B. Lewis 60, A.R. Whittall 6 for 46)
Cambridge University 175 for 8 dec. (R.Q. Cake 61) and 164 for 8 (R.A. Battye 64)

Match drawn

at Oxford

Hampshire 331 for 6 dec. (M.C.J. Nicholas 120, A.N. Aymes 62 not out, G.W. White 57)
Oxford University 317 for 1 dec. (I.J. Sutcliffe 163 not out, C.M. Gupte 119)

Match drawn

Essex gave a first-class debut to Andrew Hibbert and included Nicholas Derbyshire, their new recruit from Lancashire, in their side. Hussain, captaining Essex for the first time, lost the toss, and shared a second-wicket stand of 98 with Lewis after his side was put in. With Whittall in excellent form, Cambridge University bowled out a county side for the first time in two seasons, and they then had the spirit to declare 85 runs in arrears after a rather dreary batting display. It was enlightened only by Russell Cake who had been absent from the side because of his final examinations. There was more joy for Cambridge in the performance of Andrew Whittall, who took 5 for 8 in 22 balls in Essex's second innings. He finished with career-best figures of 6 for 46 and with match-best figures for his off-breaks, 11 for 113. Needing 254 to win in 192 minutes, Cambridge were fortunate to draw after the later order had been perplexed by John Childs.

Hampshire had had a miserable start to the season, but Nicholas did win the toss for the first time in eight games when his side visited The Parks. Only 16 overs were possible on the first day, when Hampshire lost Morris and scored 35. That score was increased to 331 for 6 by the end of the second day, with Nicholas having hit 17 fours in his 120. It was a chilly day, and the batting did little to warm spectators. On the final day, Sutcliffe and Gupte established an Oxford first-wicket record against a county when they scored 283. Gupte hit the third century of his career, but Sutcliffe's 163 not out was his first.

14 May *at Cambridge*

Oxford University 329 for 6 (I.J. Sutcliffe 101, C.M. Gupte 90, G.I. Macmillan 63)
Cambridge University 217 (J. Ratledge 65)

Oxford University won by 112 runs

The first one-day Varsity match for the Johnson Fry Trophy was won convincingly by Oxford. In 55 overs, they scored at nearly six runs an over and overwhelmed the light blues. The tone was set by Iain Sutcliffe and Chinmay Gupte who followed their marvellous partnership against Hampshire the previous day with 204 for the first wicket at five runs an over. Gregor Macmillan then hit 63 off 27 balls, and from that point on, helped by four dropped catches and some erratic bowling, Oxford were in total control.

18, 19 and 20 May *at Oxford*

Nottinghamshire 303 for 6 dec. (G.W. Mike 66 not out, C. Banton 63, J.E. Hindson 53 not out) and 243 for 3 dec. (M.P. Dowman 107, W.M. Noon 66)
Oxford University 280 for 5 dec. (W.S. Kendall 74, A.C. Ridley 71) and 108 for 3

Match drawn

Noon led Nottinghamshire for the first time, and his side scored consistently on the opening day, with Mike and Hindson hitting career-best scores. Gupte and Sutcliffe continued their exotic partnership with 70 off 15 overs in the first hour on the second morning. They were separated at 90, but Ridley, who reached his highest first-class score, and Kendall added 126 for the third wicket. Dowman followed his hundred against Cambridge with a career-best 107 on the last day, dominating an opening stand of 168 with Noon.

25, 26 and 27 May *at Oxford*

Derbyshire 261 for 2 dec. (W.A. Dessaur 119 not out, C.M. Wells 115) and 95 for 5
Oxford University 97 and 258 (M.E. Cassar 4 for 54)

Derbyshire won by 5 wickets

Oxford suffered their first defeat of the season when they lost to Derbyshire in The Parks. Derbyshire gave a trial debut to Wayne Dessaur, who had been with Nottinghamshire and who had scored two centuries for his former county. He hit the third century of his career on his debut for Derbyshire and shared a second-wicket stand of 203 with Colin Wells. Medium-pacer Alan Richardson, making his first-class debut, dismissed Gupte and Sutcliffe

Wayne Dessaur hit a century on the occasion of his debut for Derbyshire, against Oxford University in The Parks. He was the fourth Derbyshire player to score a century on his debut. The former Nottinghamshire batsman was given a contract for the season. (Laurence Griffiths/Empics)

before the close, and the students collapsed miserably on the second day. Following on, they were 152 for 6, but the tail wagged appreciably. Karl Krikken, the Derbyshire wicket-keeper, held six catches in Oxford's second innings, and his side won in spite of reversing the batting order when they went in search of 95.

2, 3 and 5 June *at Oxford*

Oxford University 320 for 9 dec. (C.M. Gupte 97, W.S. Kendall 94, A. Sheriyar 5 for 61) and 83 for 1 dec.

Leicestershire 0 for 0 dec. and 404 for 5 (A. Habib 174 not out, D.L. Maddy 131)

Leicestershire won by 5 wickets

No play was possible on the second day in The Parks after the University had scored 320 for 9 on the opening day. Gupte and Macmillan had scored 102 for the third wicket, and Gupte and Kendall 139 in 35 overs for the fourth. Leicestershire forfeited their first innings, and Oxford declared after a second innings which lasted 16 overs. Stephen Bartle, making his first-class debut, conceded 42 runs in two overs. He bowled 10 no-balls and a wide. Set to make 404 in 83 overs, Leicestershire achieved a remarkable victory with four balls to spare. The win was made possible mainly through Darren Maddy and Aftab Habib who shared a second-wicket partnership of 192 in 39 overs. Habib, formerly of Middlesex, was playing his second game for Leicestershire and, like Maddy, reached a maiden first-class hundred.

9, 10 and 11 June *at Cambridge*

Middlesex 327 for 5 dec. (J.D. Carr 116 not out, P.N. Weekes 58) and 104 for 0 dec. (T.A. Radford 51 not out)

Cambridge University 230 for 8 dec. (R.A. Battye 70 not out, R.T. Ragnauth 52, A.A. Khan 4 for 51) and 49 for 4 (K.J. Shine 4 for 23)

Match drawn

The most interesting feature of the drawn game at Fenner's was the debut for Middlesex of leg-break bowler Amer Ali Khan who was born in Pakistan. Rain determined that the match would be reduced to batting practice, but Kevin Shine took four wickets in his first seven overs on the last afternoon to suggest that a result might be possible.

16, 17 and 18 June *at Cambridge*

Warwickshire 300 for 3 dec. (A.J. Moles 98, R.G. Twose 96) and 208 for 5 dec. (Wasim Khan 91, P.A. Smith 57, D.R. Brown 53)

Cambridge University 220 for 7 dec. (R.Q. Cake 75, R.A. Battye 50) and 119 for 3

Match drawn

An opening stand of 192 in 66 overs between Moles and

Darren Maddy scored a maiden first-class century in Leicestershire's remarkable victory over Oxford University, 5 June. (David Munden/Sportsline)

Twose took Warwickshire to a strong position after Whittall had put them in. Munton declared at 300, and he himself dismissed Ragnauth for 0, but, on the second day, Churton and Cake added 119 for the University's third wicket, and, thereafter, the game turned into batting practice as seems the custom when counties play the universities. Wasim Khan, in his first season in first-class cricket, made his highest score.

20, 21 and 22 June *at Oxford*

Middlesex 303 for 7 dec. (P.N. Weekes 143, K.R. Brown 70) and 167 for 1 dec. (J.C. Pooley 100 not out, D.J. Nash 50 not out)

Oxford University 202 (J.D. Ricketts 63, C.W. Taylor 4 for 15) and 97 for 4

Match drawn

Once Mike Gatting had decided that it was too late in life to become an opening batsman, Middlesex decided that the left-handed Paul Weekes should be tried in the position. He responded by hitting the highest score of his career, against Oxford in The Parks, and his 143 included 20 fours. He and Brown added 154 for the third wicket. Brown was one of three batsmen to fall to Richard Yeabsley, on the Middlesex staff, who was only now play-

An inspiring captain of Oxford University – Gregor Macmillan. (David Munden/Sportsline)

ing his first game of the summer for Oxford because of examinations. Oxford slipped to 70 for 7 on the second day, but Justin Ricketts made the highest score of his career and added 58 for the ninth wicket with Townsend. Pooley reached his third first-class hundred of the season on the last day, which was mostly a tranquil and meaningless day's cricket.

23, 24 and 25 June *at Bristol*

Gloucestershire 378 for 7 dec. (R.J. Cunliffe 190 not out, R.C.J. Williams 90)
Oxford University 125 (K.E. Cooper 4 for 34) and 191 (I.J. Sutcliffe 53)

Gloucestershire won by an innings and 62 runs

Asked to bat first, Gloucestershire were reduced to 144 for 6, but Bob Cunliffe then found an able partner in Richard Williams. The left-handed Williams has proved himself a most efficient deputy behind the stumps for 'Jack' Russell, and now he batted with vigour to help Cunliffe add 184 for the seventh wicket. Both batsmen reached the highest scores of their careers, and their partnership extended into the second day. Alleyne differed from other captains in that he sought victory rather than batting practice, and he

enforced the follow-on when the University were dismissed for 125. Cooper, the Gloucestershire veteran, had match figures of 7 for 40.

1, 2 and 3 July *at Folkestone*

Kent 409 for 7 dec. (D.P. Fulton 116, M.V. Fleming 100, S.C. Willis 82) and 108 for 3 dec.
Cambridge University 142 (R.A. Battye 63, M.M. Patel 4 for 43) and 207 (R.T. Ragnauth 82, M.M. Patel 6 for 74)

Kent won by 168 runs

When Matthew Fleming joined Kent in 1989 it was common knowledge in cricketing circles that he had been brought in to captain the side. That knowledge has proved to be inaccurate, but he led Kent for the first time in the match at Folkestone, the county's first game on the ground for four years. Fleming opened his scoring with a six and completed his first hundred of the summer with his 16th four. He was caught in the deep next ball. Fulton was more circumspect in reaching his first century of the season, but he also hit 16 fours in his 116 which came off 172 balls. He and Fleming added 173 for the third wicket. Wicketkeeper Willis hit a career-best 82 off as many deliveries, and Kent became totally dominant. Needing 376 to win, Cambridge fell to Patel, but not before Ragnauth had made the highest score of his career and shared a third-wicket stand of 100 with Cake.

 THE VARSITY MATCH

This proved to be one of the very best of Varsity matches in recent years, appropriate in that this was the 150th anniversary game. Whittall won the toss, and Cambridge batted. There was a short boundary on the Tavern side so that accurate bowling was essential. Unfortunately, the Oxford bowlers erred in direction and were punished accordingly. Ragnauth and Churton gave the light blues their best start of the season, and Ratledge, dismissed first ball in both innings in 1994, batted just under three hours for his 67. He and Cake added 102 for the third wicket.

Cake, the best batsman in the Cambridge side, took 2½ hours to reach his first fifty, but his second came off 44 balls, and he went from 68 to 90 in the 91st over of the day when he hit consecutive balls from Mather – left-arm medium pace – into the Mound Stand for 6, 4, 6, 6. He was caught finally off Sutcliffe who, thereby, took his first wicket in first-class cricket.

Cambridge then disappointed, closing on 284 for 8, having been 267 for 4. They were all out for 295 on the second morning, with How, who had entered the match without a first-class run or wicket to his name, again being dismissed for 0.

Whittall took an inspired gamble when he chose to open the Cambridge attack with his off-breaks. He quickly dismissed the dangerous Gupte, and with Haste in fine form, finishing with a career best, Oxford were reeling at 15 for 3. The left-handed Sutcliffe batted magnificently for

OXFORD UNIVERSITY v. CAMBRIDGE UNIVERSITY
5, 6 and 7 July 1995 at Lord's

CAMBRIDGE UNIVERSITY

	FIRST INNINGS		SECOND INNINGS	
R.T. Ragnauth	c Ricketts, b MacRobert	35	c Ridley, b Kendall	14
*D.R.H. Churton	c Sutcliffe, b Ricketts	31	c Townsend, b Kendall	1
J. Ratledge	c Ridley, b Mather	67	c MacRobert, b Yeabsley	8
R.Q. Cake	c Ricketts, b Sutcliffe	101	b MacRobert	43
J.P. Carroll	c Townsend, b Ricketts	17	(6) lbw, b Yeabsley	13
R.A. Battye	c Townsend, b Ricketts	6	(7) c Macmillan, b MacRobert	1
A.R. Whittall (capt)	lbw, b MacRobert	2	(8) c and b Yeabsley	17
N.J. Haste	c Townsend, b Yeabsley	6	(5) c Malik, b Yeabsley	0
A.N. Janisch	not out	4	not out	18
J.W.O. Freeth	c Malik, b MacRobert	13	c Mather, b Ricketts	1
E.J. How	lbw, b MacRobert	0	b Mather	0
Extras	b 5, lb 7, w 1	13	b 4, lb 6	10
		—		—
		295		126

OXFORD UNIVERSITY

	FIRST INNINGS		SECOND INNINGS	
C.M. Gupte	c Ragnauth, b Whittall	5	(3) not out	13
I.J. Sutcliffe	c Ragnauth, b Janisch	71	(1) c Churton, b How	52
A.C. Ridley	c Churton, b Haste	2		
G.I. Macmillan (capt)	lbw, b Haste	2	(2) not out	113
W.S. Kendall	c Whittall, b Haste	41		
H.S. Malik	c Whittall, b Haste	64		
R.S. Yeabsley	c Ragnauth, b Haste	3		
J.D. Ricketts	c Cake, b Janisch	10		
A.D. MacRobert	c Ratledge, b Janisch	7		
*C.J. Townsend	not out	9		
D.P. Mather				
Extras	b 4, lb 11, w 2, nb 2	19	b 6, lb 2, w 2, nb 2	12
		—		—
	(for 9 wickets, dec.)	233	(for 1 wicket)	190

	O	M	R	W	O	M	R	W
MacRobert	23	8	41	4	23	5	55	2
Mather	17	3	70	1	0.1	–	0	1
Yeabsley	18	6	45	1	19	7	34	4
Ricketts	29	8	59	3	12	5	14	1
Kendall	5	2	7	–	8	2	13	2
Malik	5	1	24	–				
Macmillan	13	3	26	–				
Sutcliffe	4	1	11	1				

	O	M	R	W	O	M	R	W
Whittall	19	7	47	1	13	3	19	–
Haste	19	4	73	5	9	–	51	–
How	8	2	32	–	4	–	24	1
Janisch	12	2	38	3	6	–	22	–
Freeth	12	1	28	–	14	1	52	–
Battye					0.4	–	14	–

FALL OF WICKETS

1–57, 2–83, 3–185, 4–215, 5–267, 6–267, 7–276, 8–276, 9–295
1–14, 2–19, 3–30, 4–33, 5–55, 6–60, 7–81, 8–103, 9–106

FALL OF WICKETS

1–10, 2–13, 3–15, 4–89, 5–174, 6–183, 7–196, 8–215, 9–233
1–143

Umpires: K.E. Palmer & B. Dudleston

Oxford University won by 9 wickets

$3\frac{1}{2}$ hours, and he shared stands of 74 with Kendall and 85 with Malik. Oxford sought quick runs, and Macmillan declared 62 runs in arrears. His ploy worked as Kendall and Yeabsley sent Cambridge tottering to 40 for 4 by the close, and, for the first time, the game was tilted in favour of the dark blues.

Another fine batting effort from Cake, who stayed for $2\frac{1}{2}$ hours for his 43, took Cambridge to 126 and meant that Oxford had 54 overs in which to score 189 to win the match.

Macmillan and Sutcliffe opened and scored 143 for the first wicket to make victory a formality. Sutcliffe was caught behind off How, who had again been out for 0, so that the bowler from Dr Clalliner's Grammar School at last claimed a first-class wicket. Macmillan finished unbeaten on 113 which came off 115 balls. He hit 11 fours and finished the match with 2 sixes into the Mound Stand off Battye.

It was a fitting way to end a splendid match.

FIELDING FIGURES

10 – D.R.H. Churton (ct 7/st 3) and R.T. Ragnauth
6 – A.R. Whittall
4 – J.P. Carroll, J. Ratledge and R.Q. Cake
3 – R.A. Battye
2 – J.W.O. Freeth, A.N. Janisch, M.J. Birks and Sub (st 2)
1 – L.P. Clarke, N.J. Haste and E.J. How

CAMBRIDGE UNIVERSITY

BATTING

	M	Inns	NO	Runs	HS	Av
R.T. Ragnauth	8	16	1	335	82	22.33
R.Q. Cake	7	14	3	511	101	46.45
J. Ratledge	8	16	0	358	67	22.37
J.P. Carroll	8	15	2	292	42	22.46
R.A. Battye	6	14	2	391	70*	32.58
D.R.H. Churton	6	10	1	118	39	11.80
L.P. Clarke	8	13	2	17	14	5.66
A.R. Whittall	8	13	2	185	81*	16.81
N.J. Haste	7	10	4	83	16	13.83
A.N. Janisch	7	8	1	38	18*	9.50
J.W.O. Freeth	7	6	1	35	18	7.00
D.E. Stanley	2	6	4	10	6	2.50
M.J. Birks	2	3	2	43	23*	43.00
M.I. Yeabsley	2	3	1	10	6	0.50
E.R. Hughes	2	1	1	0	0	0.00
E.J. How	4	4	2	0	0*	0.00

Match totals (Total / Wickets / Result) by fixture:

Fixture	Total	Wickets	Result
v. Yorkshire (Cambridge) 13–15 April	174 / 52	10 / 4	D
v. Lancashire (Cambridge) 18–20 April	168 / 144	8 / 6	D
v. Nottinghamshire (Cambridge) 27–9 April	91 / 218	6 / 10	D
v. Essex (Cambridge) 11–13 May	175 / 164	8 / 8	D
v. Middlesex (Cambridge) 9–11 June	230	8	D
v. Warwickshire (Cambridge) 16–18 June	220 / 119	7 / 7	D
v. Kent (Folkestone) 1–3 July	142 / 207	10 / 10	L
Varsity Match (Lord's) 5–7 July	295 / 126	10 / 10	L

BOWLING

Fixture	N.J. Haste	L.P. Clarke	A.N. Janisch	A.R. Whittall	J.W.O. Freeth	J. Ratledge	J.P. Carroll	E.R. Hughes	M.I. Yeabsley	E.J. How	R.A. Battye
v. Yorkshire (Cambridge) 13–15 April	12-2-58-1	7-0-55-1	23-2-112-0	25.3-7-111-1	26-3-111-1	3-0-26-0					
v. Lancashire (Cambridge) 18–20 April	15-3-47-0		12-1-48-0	21-7-46-3	6-1-21-0						
v. Nottinghamshire (Cambridge) 27–9 April	21-9-30-2 / 15-2-58-1		17-1-69-1 / 18-5-44-1	26-6-83-1 / 16-2-76-0	15-5-61-0 / 10-0-62-2		12-1-43-0				
v. Essex (Cambridge) 11–13 May	18-4-56-3		19-2-91-2 / 17-0-64-0	32.3-8-131-4 / 27-9-67-5	7-0-47-0 / 10-1-23-0		5-1-29-0	13-1-62-1 / 13-2-48-0	4-0-32-1	13-3-28-0	
v. Middlesex (Cambridge) 9–11 June	10-1-22-1 / 24-6-67-2		14-3-42-0 / 11-1-48-0	17.4-8-46-6 / 25-6-92-1	28.3-6-64-2 / 16-5-41-1		6-1-22-0		5-0-24-0	7-1-29-0 / 14-0-39-0	
v. Warwickshire (Cambridge) 16–18 June	11-3-28-0 / 11-2-41-0		10-1-23-0	30-4-108-2 / 16-1-48-3	29.4-7-83-1 / 17.2-2-43-1		3-0-4-0	24-2-98-1	9-3-28-1	8-0-28-0 / 15-3-75-0	
v. Kent (Folkestone) 1–3 July	9-2-31-0 / 18-2-74-3		7-0-55-0 / 11-2-43-1	20-3-104-2 / 8-3-17-1	1-0-1-0	1.4-0-16-1		4-0-26-0		6-0-44-0 / 8-2-32-0	0.4-0-14-0
Varsity Match (Lord's) 5–7 July	5-1-19-0 / 19-4-73-5		8-1-24-2 / 12-2-38-3 / 6-0-22-0	19-7-47-1 / 13-3-19-0	12-1-28-0 / 14-1-52-0					4-0-24-1	
Bowler's average	197-41-655-18 / 36.38	7-0-55-1 / 55.00	185-21-723-10 / 72.30	328.4-85-1064-29 / 36.68	210.3-33-721-8 / 90.12	4.4-0-42-1 / 42.00	26-3-98-0 / —	54-5-234-2 / 117.00	18-3-84-2 / 42.00	75-9-299-1 / 299.00	0.4-0-14-0 / —

OXFORD UNIVERSITY BATTING

Batting	M	Inns	NO	Runs	HS	Av
G.I. Macmillan	10	15	2	357	113*	27.46
I.J. Sutcliffe	10	18	3	673	163*	44.86
C.M. Gupte	9	16	3	472	119	33.71
A.C. Ridley	10	16	1	375	71	25.00
W.S. Kendall	10	15	2	442	94	34.00
H.S. Malik	8	10	1	160	64	17.77
N.F.C. Martin	2	3	1	10	7	5.00
A.D. MacRobert	9	9	2	80	29	11.42
J.D. Ricketts	10	11	1	148	63	14.80
C.J. Townsend	6	6	1	72	27	24.00
D.P. Mather	8	6	3	19	8*	6.33
J.M. Attfield	6	8	2	76	23*	12.66
M.E.D. Jarrett	7	11	4	137	40	19.57
J. Windsor	2	3	1	28	14	14.00
R.S. Yeabsley	3	3	–	13	4	3.25

OXFORD UNIVERSITY BOWLING

Match	Byes	Leg-byes	Wides	No-balls	Total	Wks
v. Durham (Oxford) 13–15 April		5	1	4	322	9
v. Glamorgan (Oxford) 18–20 April		6			137	3
v. Worcestershire (Oxford) 27–9 April	4	8	2	16	360	5
		8	1	4	229	4
v. Hampshire (Oxford) 11–13 May		5	3		320	7
	2	3	1		186	4
	1				331	6
v. Nottinghamshire (Oxford) 18–20 May		8		10	303	6
v. Derbyshire (Oxford) 25–7 May	2	4		2	243	3
		6	1	2	261	4
v. Leicestershire (Oxford) 2–5 June		4			95	5
		6	2		404	5
v. Middlesex (Oxford) 20–2 June	2	4	1	4	303	7
	3	1			167	1
v. Gloucestershire (Bristol) 23–5 June		3	1	2	378	7
VARSITY MATCH (Lord's) 5–7 July	5	7	1		295	10
	4	6			126	10

Bowler's average

Bowler	O–M–R–W	Av
A.D. MacRobert	264–37–843–18	46.83
N.F.C. Martin	23–2–123–1	123.00
D.P. Mather	227.1–49–710–18	39.44
J.D. Ricketts	224.5–34–732–17	43.05
G.I. Macmillan	129.3–12–460–5	92.00
H.S. Malik	152–22–539–6	89.83
W.S. Kendall	76–13–233–8	29.12
J.M. Attfield	87.3–12–310–3	103.33
I.J. Sutcliffe	9–1–31–1	31.00
J. Windsor	41.4–12–93–3	31.00
R.S. Yeabsley	85–16–277–8	34.62

FIRST-CLASS AVERAGES

BATTING

	M	Inns	NO	Runs	HS	Av	100s	50s
R.J. Cunliffe	7	8	3	412	190*	82.40	1	2
M.R. Ramprakash	20	32	3	2258	235	77.86	10	7
A. Habib	3	5	2	230	174*	76.66	1	–
J.C. Hallett	2	4	1	229	111*	76.33	1	–
M.D. Moxon	13	23	8	1145	203*	76.33	3	8
A.A. Metcalfe	4	4	1	200	100	66.66	1	1
P.A. de Silva	16	30	–	1781	255	59.36	7	7
D. Byas	20	37	3	1913	213	56.26	4	10
A.J. Lamb	16	26	4	1237	166	56.22	3	6
A. Symonds	18	31	5	1438	254*	55.30	4	9
T.M. Moody	18	31	2	1600	168	55.17	5	7
M.G. Bevan	20	34	5	1598	153*	55.10	6	7
N. Hussain	19	35	1	1854	186	54.52	6	10
A.P. Wells	18	30	2	1524	178	54.42	7	4
M.W. Gatting	16	22	1	1139	148	54.23	5	3
R.T. Robinson	18	32	–	1728	209	54.00	7	5
P.D. Bowler	19	33	3	1619	196	53.96	6	5
P.C.L. Holloway	12	22	6	863	129*	53.93	2	6
R.A. Smith	12	23	2	1117	172	53.19	3	4
H. Morris	18	33	3	1574	166*	52.46	6	8
M.E. Waugh	16	29	2	1392	173	51.55	5	6
J.C. Pooley	18	30	4	1335	136	51.34	5	6
G.A. Gooch	18	34	1	1669	165	50.37	7	6
W.J. Cronje	16	28	1	1362	213	50.44	4	7
T.L. Penney	19	27	3	1198	144	49.91	4	4
Wasim Khan	13	23	6	847	181	49.82	1	6
G.A. Hick	16	27	3	1193	152	49.70	4	5
N.V. Knight	13	23	5	887	174	49.27	1	7
R.J. Harden	19	35	6	1429	129*	49.27	5	6
P.A. Cottey	19	33	3	1465	130	48.83	5	7
J.D. Carr	20	29	6	1098	129	47.73	4	3
J.P. Crawley	18	31	2	1377	182	47.48	3	10
S.C. Ecclestone	7	12	2	472	81	47.20	–	3
A.J. Wright	18	34	4	1401	193	46.70	4	5
R.Q. Cake	7	14	3	511	101	46.45	1	2
R.G. Twose	19	30	4	1186	191	45.61	4	3
D.J. Cullinan	14	26	4	1003	161	45.59	5	1
M.P. Maynard	20	36	1	1590	164	45.42	3	12
K.J. Barnett	17	31	3	1251	169	44.67	2	7
R.C. Russell	17	26	4	977	91	44.40	–	8
A.J. Moles	9	16	–	710	131	44.37	1	6
G.R. Cowdrey	13	22	1	930	137	44.28	2	6
M.A. Atherton	18	31	1	1323	155*	44.10	4	6
J.A. Daley	7	12	2	435	55	43.50	–	4
I.J. Sutcliffe	14	24	4	847	163*	42.35	1	5
J.J. Whitaker	15	25	–	1055	127	42.20	3	5
K.R. Brown	19	27	4	970	147*	42.17	1	7
A.D. Brown	16	29	4	1054	187	42.16	3	3
N.R. Taylor	7	12	2	421	127	42.10	1	2
N.E. Briers	15	27	2	1046	175*	41.84	3	3
R.J. Warren	16	27	5	914	154	41.54	1	5
D.P. Ostler	18	26	2	983	208	40.95	2	6
G.P. Thorpe	16	30	–	1223	152	40.76	2	9
S.J. Rhodes	20	33	8	1018	122*	40.72	1	7
T.S. Curtis	20	35	5	1221	169*	40.70	2	7
C.J. Adams	15	27	–	1096	216	40.59	3	5
S.P. James	15	28	3	1011	230*	40.44	3	2
C.L. Cairns	17	30	1	1171	115	40.37	2	7
G.F. Archer	17	32	3	1171	158	40.37	3	4
M.C.J. Nicholas	19	33	3	1210	147	40.33	4	4
D.J. Bicknell	15	28	3	997	228*	39.88	2	4
N.J. Lenham	15	25	3	867	128	39.40	2	4
N. Shahid	14	25	2	900	139	39.13	2	5
R.J. Bailey	18	30	3	1038	157	38.44	4	2
S.C. Willis	3	4	–	153	82	38.25	–	2
J.E. Morris	19	35	1	1297	169	38.14	3	6
A.J. Stewart	10	18	1	647	151	38.05	2	2
M.A. Lynch	17	29	2	1026	114	38.00	5	2
P. Whitticase	3	5	1	150	62*	37.50	–	2
J.E.R. Gallian	18	33	3	1122	158	37.40	2	4
D.A. Leatherdale	18	30	3	993	93	36.77	–	8
M.A. Butcher	18	34	1	1210	167	36.66	2	10
A.J. Hollioake	18	32	2	1099	117*	36.63	1	8
A. Fordham	16	29	1	1025	130	36.60	4	4
R.C. Irani	18	34	2	1165	108	36.40	1	9
D.A. Reeve	16	22	4	652	77*	36.22	–	5
C.M. Wells	16	30	3	976	115	36.14	2	6
K.M. Curran	17	27	3	863	117	35.95	1	4
C.W.J. Athey	15	27	1	929	163*	35.73	2	5
D.J. Capel	19	29	3	926	175	35.61	3	3
G.I. Macmillan	17	26	3	817	122	35.52	3	3
W.P.C. Weston	20	35	1	1207	111	35.50	3	7
T.A. Radford	6	11	4	244	69	34.85	–	2
C.M. Gupte	10	18	2	554	119	34.62	1	3
A.N. Hayhurst	17	29	5	825	107	34.37	1	5
P. Johnson	17	30	1	996	120*	34.34	1	8
P.N. Weekes	20	31	2	995	143	34.31	2	6
J.P. Stephenson	17	30	4	892	127	34.30	1	6
M.P. Dowman	9	18	2	548	107	34.25	2	2
A.S. Rollins	17	33	1	1095	200*	34.21	2	5
W.A. Dessaur	8	16	2	478	119*	34.14	1	2
M. Watkinson	18	29	3	887	161	34.11	2	3
A.R. Caddick	6	7	–	237	92	33.85	–	2
P.J. Prichard	18	33	1	1080	109	33.75	2	5
N.J. Llong	9	16	–	538	118	33.62	2	1
M.W. Alleyne	19	32	2	1007	141	33.56	1	7
D.P. Fulton	8	16	1	502	116	33.46	1	4
M.R. Benson	13	21	–	702	192	33.42	2	1
N.J. Speak	17	30	2	919	116	32.82	1	7
M.P. Vaughan	21	39	1	1244	88	32.73	–	10
W.S. Kendall	11	16	2	457	94	32.64	–	3
R.A. Battye	8	14	2	391	70*	32.58	–	5
J.D. Ratcliffe	9	17	–	550	75	32.35	–	5
W. Larkins	13	23	–	737	121	32.04	2	1
M. Prabhakar	17	31	3	896	101	32.00	1	5
S.P. Titchard	13	24	2	697	130	31.68	1	5
K.A. Parsons	16	28	2	821	105	31.57	1	6
M.N. Lathwell	17	33	–	1033	111	31.30	2	5
C. White	19	33	5	874	110	31.21	3	3
R.J. Turner	19	30	7	717	106*	31.17	1	4
B.F. Smith	18	31	5	802	112	30.84	1	6
G.D. Rose	16	25	–	771	84	30.84	–	6
G.D. Hodgson	9	17	–	524	148	30.82	1	2
V.P. Terry	20	35	2	1012	170	30.66	2	3
N.H. Fairbrother	14	23	3	602	132	30.10	2	1
S.D. Thomas	11	15	4	331	78*	30.09	–	2
T.R. Ward	18	32	1	932	114*	30.06	2	6
F.D. Stephenson	13	23	–	690	106	30.00	1	2
A.N. Aymes	20	33	9	720	62*	30.00	–	5
M.V. Fleming	10	16	1	447	100	29.80	1	2
W.M. Noon	17	31	6	745	66	29.80	–	5
P.R. Pollard	11	19	2	506	120	29.76	1	2
P.R. Whitaker	13	21	–	624	119	29.71	1	3
M.A. Ealham	18	31	1	891	121	29.70	1	4
J.M. Dakin	8	13	2	326	101*	29.63	1	2
A. Dale	12	23	2	622	133	29.61	2	1
G.J. Kersey	15	28	4	708	83	29.50	–	6
K. Newell	10	19	2	500	135	29.41	1	2
J.S. Laney	9	17	1	470	73	29.37	–	4
C. Banton	7	14	4	292	80*	29.20	–	2
S. Hutton	12	23	1	634	98	28.81	–	4
V.J. Wells	14	24	1	654	124	28.43	1	3
D.R. Brown	15	20	2	506	85	28.11	–	4
A. McGrath	5	10	–	280	84	28.00	–	1
W.K. Hegg	18	28	4	669	101	27.87	1	2
D.A. Blenkiron	9	17	1	446	145	27.87	1	2
G.D. Lloyd	14	23	2	584	117	27.80	1	3
J.N. Snape	13	16	3	361	55	27.76	–	2
S.A. Marsh	16	28	2	688	67*	27.52	–	4
K. Greenfield	19	32	1	853	121	27.51	1	5

FIRST-CLASS AVERAGES – continued

BATTING

	M	Inns	NO	Runs	HS	Av	100s	50s
R.R. Montgomerie	14	24	1	632	192	27.47	1	2
D.L. Hemp	18	32	–	872	157	27.25	1	4
P.J. Newport	18	23	8	404	50	26.93	–	1
F.A. Griffith	8	13	4	240	53	26.66	–	1
S.D. Birbeck	4	6	2	106	75*	26.50	–	1
K.M. Krikken	11	16	5	288	61	26.18	–	1
C.W. Scott	7	13	1	311	56	25.91	–	2
S.R. Lampitt	17	25	6	488	97	25.68	–	1
D.J. Millns	8	14	2	307	70	25.58	–	2
R.J. Rollins	19	35	3	809	133*	25.28	1	4
G.W. White	15	24	2	554	62	25.18	–	3
J.D. Batty	4	6	1	125	45*	25.00	–	–
A.C. Ridley	10	16	1	375	71	25.00	–	2
J.E. Owen	4	8	–	200	65	25.00	–	2
M. Keech	2	4	–	100	41	25.00	–	–
P.A. Smith	3	5	–	124	57	24.80	–	1
R.C.J. Williams	5	9	–	223	90	24.77	–	2
M.A. Roseberry	16	29	2	669	90	24.77	–	4
J.I. Longley	9	18	1	420	58	24.70	–	2
G.R. Haynes	18	30	–	737	78	24.56	–	4
J.W. Hall	12	22	–	537	100	24.40	1	2
G.W. Mike	5	9	3	143	66*	23.83	–	2
R.I. Dawson	9	16	1	355	101	23.66	1	3
M.P. Bicknell	9	12	3	213	61	23.66	–	1
K.P. Evans	7	13	2	260	78*	23.63	–	2
K.J. Piper	16	19	2	398	99	23.41	–	2
N.M.K. Smith	18	23	2	486	75	23.14	–	4
G. Yates	7	9	2	162	42*	23.14	–	–
A.L. Penberthy	4	6	1	115	73	23.00	–	1
B. Parker	4	8	1	161	40	23.00	–	–
T.H.C. Hancock	8	13	1	275	79*	22.91	–	1
I.D. Austin	13	22	4	412	80*	22.88	–	1
S.A. Kellett	6	11	1	228	86	22.80	–	1
J.P. Carroll	8	15	2	292	42	22.46	–	–
J. Ratledge	8	16	–	358	67	22.37	–	3
R.D.B. Croft	20	36	4	716	143	22.37	1	1
R.T. Ragnauth	8	16	1	335	82	22.33	–	3
A.J. Dalton	5	10	1	201	46	22.33	–	–
Wasim Akram	14	22	3	423	61	22.26	–	4
D.D.J. Robinson	17	32	–	712	123	22.25	2	1
I.D.K. Salisbury	18	30	3	599	74	22.18	–	2
P. Moores	19	32	2	660	94	22.00	–	5
M.C.J. Ball	18	28	9	417	48	21.94	–	–
M.T.E. Peirce	6	10	–	219	60	21.90	–	1
J.P. Taylor	18	21	8	284	86	21.84	–	2
D.G. Cork	18	31	4	589	84*	21.81	–	3
J.J.B. Lewis	7	14	–	299	75	21.35	–	2
A.W. Smith	9	13	–	272	88	20.92	–	2
M.G.N. Windows	9	17	2	313	56	20.86	–	2
D.J. Nash	19	25	4	433	67	20.61	–	3
P.A.J. DeFreitas	16	26	3	474	94*	20.60	–	2
T.A. Tweats	8	16	1	308	78*	20.53	–	2
J.I.D. Kerr	13	19	2	349	80	20.52	–	1
S.D. Udal	18	29	4	512	85	20.48	–	3
R.S.M. Morris	10	18	–	368	47	20.44	–	–
J.E. Emburey	17	20	1	387	87	20.36	–	1
N.C. Phillips	6	10	1	183	53	20.33	–	3
A.R. Kumble	17	21	5	321	40*	20.06	–	–
P.J. Martin	13	17	2	300	71	20.00	–	1
M.E.D. Jarrett	7	11	4	137	40	19.57	–	–
G. Chapple	15	21	6	292	58	19.46	–	1
G.J. Parsons	18	28	2	501	73	19.26	–	1
J.R. Wileman	8	16	4	230	43	19.16	–	–
D.R.C. Law	8	13	–	248	115	19.07	1	1
M.E. Trescothick	12	22	–	417	151	18.95	1	1
K.D. James	12	21	3	341	53	18.94	–	1
A.E. Warner	14	22	8	265	43	18.92	–	–
V.S. Solanki	6	9	1	150	36	18.75	–	–
P.A. Nixon	18	30	5	461	79	18.44	–	2
D. Gough	14	19	1	332	60	18.44	–	1

BATTING

	M	Inns	NO	Runs	HS	Av	100s	50s
M.J. McCague	14	25	6	344	59	18.10	–	1
A.P. Grayson	9	14	1	235	73	18.07	–	2
C.P. Metson	17	23	9	253	26*	18.07	–	–
H.A.G. Anthony	14	25	1	433	91	18.04	–	2
R.A. Pick	17	26	4	395	50*	17.95	–	1
M. Saxelby	7	14	–	251	68	17.92	–	1
A.R.K. Pierson	20	32	10	392	50	17.81	–	1
H.S. Malik	8	10	1	160	64	17.77	–	1
A.A. Donald	15	16	5	194	44	17.63	–	–
T.C. Walton	4	7	1	104	71	17.33	–	1
R.J. Blakey	20	29	6	398	77*	17.30	–	1
N.A. Mallender	7	10	3	121	49*	17.28	–	–
H.R.J. Trump	16	22	10	207	47	17.25	–	–
N.M. Kendrick	15	21	4	291	59	17.11	–	1
A.R. Whittall	8	13	2	185	81*	16.81	–	1
D.L. Maddy	9	17	1	264	131	16.50	1	–
M.M. Patel	18	29	6	376	56	16.34	–	2
P.W. Jarvis	9	13	2	177	38	16.09	–	–
R.K. Illingworth	14	19	9	160	23*	16.00	–	–
C.A. Connor	17	27	6	336	33	16.00	–	–
D.G.C. Ligertwood	12	21	2	303	40	15.94	–	–
M.J. Church	5	9	1	126	35	15.75	–	–
J. Srinath	15	24	4	314	44	15.70	–	–
T.J.G. O'Gorman	5	8	–	125	39	15.62	–	–
C.E.W. Silverwood	7	9	2	106	50	15.14	–	1
H.H. Streak	19	28	3	378	69	15.12	–	1
C.G. Rackemann	13	20	12	120	20*	15.00	–	–
R.L. Johnson	12	13	2	164	29*	14.90	–	–
M.B. Loye	7	10	1	134	51*	14.88	–	1
J.D. Ricketts	10	11	1	148	63	14.80	–	1
Mushtaq Ahmed	17	23	2	311	62*	14.80	–	1
T.J. Boon	6	12	–	177	38	14.75	–	–
N.V. Radford	10	11	2	130	50	14.44	–	1
D.W. Headley	14	23	5	253	54	14.05	–	1
M.C. Ilott	17	29	4	350	60	14.00	–	1
N. Killeen	7	13	3	137	48	13.70	–	–
A.J. Tudor	5	9	–	123	56	13.66	–	1
P.J. Hartley	18	23	4	256	38	13.47	–	–
J.E. Hindson	17	28	5	309	53*	13.43	–	1
U. Afzaal	7	12	2	134	37	13.40	–	–
J. Boiling	18	32	7	312	69	12.48	–	1
M.J. Walker	9	14	1	162	53	12.46	–	1
J.E. Benjamin	12	18	4	174	49	12.42	–	–
S.L. Watkin	16	23	9	174	30	12.42	–	–
D.R.H. Churton	6	10	–	118	39	11.80	–	–
S.J.E. Brown	18	30	6	278	36	11.58	–	–
T.W. Harrison	5	10	1	102	61*	11.33	–	1
M.A. Feltham	14	15	4	115	25	10.45	–	–
D.M. Cousins	9	16	4	121	18*	10.08	–	–
J.D. Lewry	12	19	4	150	34	10.00	–	–

(Qualification – 100 runs, average 10.00)

BOWLING

	Overs	Mds	Runs	Wkts	Av	Best	10/m	5/inn
A.A. Donald	535.3	136	1431	89	16.07	6-56	1	6
D.A. Reeve	312	118	661	38	17.39	5-30	–	1
J. Lewis	67.4	12	209	12	17.41	4-34	–	–
K.E. Cooper	103	32	228	13	17.53	4-34	–	–
J. Srinath	568.4	146	1661	87	19.09	9-76	2	5
Wasim Akram	518.1	108	1598	81	19.72	7-52	3	7
T.A. Munton	373.5	119	952	48	19.83	5-37	1	3
C.L. Cairns	375.5	89	1035	52	19.90	8-47	1	3
D.G. Cork	586.5	111	1800	90	20.00	9-43	1	4
R.L. Johnson	301.4	79	812	40	20.30	5-48	1	2
A.R. Kumble	899.4	261	2143	105	20.40	7-82	2	8
S.M. Milburn	69	15	204	10	20.40	4-68	–	–
A.M. Smith	415.3	104	1275	59	21.61	7-70	1	4
J. Wood	97.4	25	303	14	21.64	4-54	–	–
P.C.R. Tufnell	678.1	207	1634	74	22.08	6-111	1	5

FIRST-CLASS AVERAGES – continued

BOWLING

	Overs	Mds	Runs	Wkts	Av	Best	10/m	5/inn
A.F. Giles	146.5	46	354	16	22.12	5-23	–	1
P.J. Newport	548	147	1551	69	22.47	5-45	–	4
A.J. Tudor	83.3	7	320	14	22.85	5-32	–	1
P.J. Hartley	549	120	1861	81	22.97	9-41	1	4
J.E. Emburey	708.4	198	1701	74	22.98	7-82	2	5
V.J. Wells	139.3	33	438	19	23.05	3-28	–	–
D.J. Capel	358.2	70	1206	51	23.64	7-44	–	2
M.P. Bicknell	286	65	986	41	24.04	5-61	–	3
M.C. Ilott	582.4	126	1897	78	24.32	9-19	2	6
P. Aldred	108.2	23	375	15	25.00	3-47	–	–
J.E. Benjamin	420.4	85	1326	53	25.01	5-37	–	3
N.A. Mallender	142.2	32	427	17	25.11	4-49	–	–
A.J. Harris	85.5	16	354	14	25.28	4-48	–	–
I.D. Austin	363.4	113	889	35	25.40	4-50	–	–
A.R. Caddick	183.1	34	613	24	25.54	8-69	1	1
M.T. Brimson	110	24	310	12	25.83	2-11	–	–
J.H. Childs	678.2	184	1757	68	25.83	6-36	–	2
D.E. Malcolm	461.4	82	1692	65	26.03	6-61	1	3
P.J. Martin	349.5	96	922	35	26.34	4-51	–	–
J.D. Lewry	350.1	62	1247	47	26.53	6-43	–	3
D. Gough	414.5	89	1365	51	26.76	7-28	1	1
A.P. Igglesden	171.2	37	563	21	26.80	5-92	–	1
P.M. Such	784.4	173	2064	77	26.80	8-93	2	6
A.E. Warner	375.1	90	1050	39	26.92	6-21	–	1
R.K. Illingworth	524	172	1212	45	26.93	4-30	–	–
S.L. Watkin	590.4	144	1755	65	27.00	7-49	1	2
M.A. Feltham	273	72	783	29	27.00	6-41	–	1
J.N.B. Bovill	251.3	62	814	30	27.13	6-29	1	2
D.R. Brown	311.4	71	1011	37	27.32	4-24	–	–
R.G. Twose	108	29	301	11	27.36	3-30	–	–
A. Sheriyar	189	27	799	29	27.55	6-30	1	2
P.W. Jarvis	228.4	45	719	26	27.65	5-55	–	1
S.R. Lampitt	494.1	124	1524	55	27.70	4-34	–	–
M. Prabhakar	579.1	165	1439	51	28.21	7-65	–	1
A.D. Mullally	583.4	172	1700	59	28.81	6-50	–	2
D.W. Headley	430.5	101	1276	44	29.00	7-58	–	3
J.P. Taylor	573.4	122	1713	59	29.03	7-50	–	2
D.J. Nash	460.1	90	1512	52	29.07	5-35	–	2
M.J. McCague	424.2	79	1457	50	29.14	5-47	–	2
A.R.C. Fraser	592.1	156	1632	56	29.14	5-56	–	2
P.A.J. DeFreitas	591.1	128	1751	60	29.18	6-35	–	1
M. Watkinson	622.4	158	1910	65	29.38	7-140	1	2
E.E. Hemmings	177.5	51	442	15	29.46	4-33	–	–
E.S.H. Giddins	596.4	110	2004	68	29.47	6-73	1	4
G.J. Parsons	579.2	178	1570	53	29.62	4-46	–	–
Mushtaq Ahmed	952	286	2821	95	29.69	6-38	2	7
C.G. Rackemann	457	114	1430	48	29.79	6-60	–	1
G.C. Small	182.5	48	507	17	29.82	5-71	–	1
M.A. Robinson	483.1	133	1375	46	29.89	4-46	–	–
A.C.S. Pigott	209.3	50	667	22	30.31	6-91	1	2
A.R.K. Pierson	637.1	135	2115	69	30.65	5-48	–	2
H.H. Streak	516.4	118	1629	53	30.73	4-40	–	–
A. Walker	285.3	53	958	31	30.90	8-118	1	2
I.D.K. Salisbury	558.2	130	1674	54	31.00	7-72	1	5
R.A. Pick	490.2	105	1602	51	31.41	5-82	–	2
F.D. Stephenson	361.2	73	1113	35	31.80	5-64	–	1
H.A.G. Anthony	397.5	70	1402	44	31.86	6-77	–	2
K.M. Curran	357.1	84	1202	37	32.48	4-78	–	–
C.M. Wells	110	25	326	10	32.60	4-29	–	–
J.E.R. Gallian	129.5	17	533	16	33.31	3-14	–	–
S.D. Udal	628.2	136	1864	55	33.89	6-65	1	5
G. Chapple	380.1	81	1229	36	34.13	4-44	–	–
J.E. Hindson	692	165	2219	65	34.13	5-67	2	5
T.N. Wren	205.4	31	785	23	34.13	5-148	–	1
S.J.E. Brown	589.3	117	1951	57	34.22	6-59	1	4
C.A. Connor	556.2	116	1954	57	34.28	6-44	1	3
A.J. Hollioake	230.3	46	721	21	34.33	4-22	–	–
R.D.B. Croft	847	209	2353	68	34.60	6-104	1	4
S.C. Ecclestone	105	20	383	11	34.81	2-31	–	–
C.E.W. Silverwood	147.1	23	630	18	35.00	5-62	–	1

BOWLING

	Overs	Mds	Runs	Wkts	Av	Best	10/m	5/inn
N.M.K. Smith	460	105	1375	39	35.25	6-72	–	3
M.C.J. Ball	577.2	140	1481	42	35.26	5-49	–	2
N.F. Williams	188.4	31	743	21	35.38	5-93	–	1
M.M. Patel	788	194	2336	66	35.39	6-74	1	3
N.V. Radford	220.1	46	780	22	35.45	5-45	–	1
G.D. Rose	436	93	1402	39	35.94	5-78	–	1
F.A. Griffith	190.4	42	614	17	36.11	4-89	–	–
N.J. Haste	197	41	655	18	36.38	5-73	–	1
J.P. Stephenson	358	62	1316	36	36.55	7-51	–	1
A.R. Whittall	328.4	85	1064	29	36.68	6-45	1	2
R.T. Bates	115.1	32	369	10	36.90	5-88	–	1
K.P. Sheeraz	225.1	36	888	24	37.00	6-67	1	2
C. White	273.4	49	934	25	37.36	4-40	–	–
M.A. Ealham	384.2	95	1151	30	38.36	3-37	–	–
D.M. Cox	129.5	28	422	11	38.36	4-141	–	–
R.P. Davis	216.4	54	576	15	38.40	5-118	–	1
A.P. van Troost	145.3	23	624	16	39.00	5-120	–	1
J.N. Snape	231	53	747	19	39.31	5-65	–	1
D.P. Mather	227.1	49	710	18	39.44	4-65	–	–
R.W. Nowell	424.5	120	1264	32	39.50	4-43	–	–
K.J. Barnett	218.2	42	635	16	39.68	3-51	–	–
M.P. Vaughan	272.4	64	876	22	39.81	3-32	–	–
G.R. Haynes	272	76	840	21	40.00	4-33	–	–
G. Keedy	505	128	1498	37	40.48	4-35	–	–
J.I.D. Kerr	280.1	43	1134	28	40.50	5-82	–	1
D.J. Millns	205.2	27	792	19	41.68	3-47	–	–
K.P. Evans	238.1	60	590	14	42.14	3-66	–	–
M.W. Alleyne	421.5	125	1228	29	42.34	3-59	–	–
M.A. Butcher	234.5	37	935	22	42.50	4-72	–	–
J.D. Ricketts	224.5	34	732	17	43.05	3-30	–	–
H.R.J. Trump	596.2	173	1745	40	43.62	5-85	–	1
G. Yates	136	33	494	11	44.90	4-67	–	–
K.D. James	233.2	51	857	19	45.10	6-38	–	1
N. Killeen	195.3	30	767	17	45.11	5-118	–	1
R.C. Irani	361.5	72	1222	27	45.25	5-62	–	1
W.J. Cronje	256.2	79	688	15	45.85	3-42	–	–
R.D. Stemp	721.1	220	1929	42	45.92	4-68	–	–
M.E. Waugh	255.5	66	789	17	46.41	4-76	–	–
N.M. Kendrick	389.5	102	1255	27	46.48	4-70	–	–
A.D. MacRobert	264	37	843	18	46.83	4-41	–	–
P.A. Thomas	386.4	67	1554	33	47.09	5-70	–	1
J.A. Afford	314.5	67	990	21	47.14	4-58	–	–
Parvaz Mirza	175.1	40	661	14	47.21	5-110	–	1
S.D. Thomas	303.3	51	1356	28	48.42	5-99	–	1
S.R. Barwick	233.5	58	681	14	48.64	4-116	–	–
M.M. Betts	194.5	31	853	17	50.17	3-35	–	–
A.N. Hayhurst	139.2	21	519	10	51.90	2-39	–	–
P.N. Weekes	258.4	55	679	13	52.23	3-26	–	–
D.M. Cousins	176	23	640	12	53.33	3-73	–	–
V.J. Pike	195.3	39	592	11	53.81	3-72	–	–
J. Boiling	599	149	1702	27	63.03	5-73	–	2
A.W. Smith	165.3	27	647	10	64.07	3-112	–	–
R.J. Chapman	179.2	23	777	11	70.63	3-119	–	–
A.N. Janisch	185	21	723	10	72.30	3-38	–	–
D.B. Pennett	208.1	34	812	10	81.20	3-136	–	–

(Qualification – 10 wickets)

LEADING FIELDERS

65 – G.J. Kersey (ct 60/st 5); 64 – R.J. Turner (ct 54/st 10); 63 – R.J. Blakey (ct 59/st 4); 62 – R.J. Rollins (ct 53/st 9); 61 – K.J. Piper (ct 59/st 2); 58 – S.J. Rhodes (ct 51/st 7); 56 – A.N. Aymes (ct 53/st 3); 54 – C.P. Metson (ct 47/st 7); 52 – R.C. Russell (ct 50/st 2); 51 – K.R. Brown (ct 45/st 6); 48 – P.A. Nixon (ct 46/st 2); 45 – P. Moores (ct 43/st 2); 43 – K.M. Krikken (ct 42/st 1); 42 – J.D. Byas; 39 – J.D. Carr; 37 – W.M. Noon (ct 32/st 5); 36 – D.G.C. Ligertwood (ct 33/st 3); 34 – N. Hussain and S.A. Marsh (ct 32/st 2); 31 – T.M. Moody; 30 – V.P. Terry; 28 – R.J. Warren (ct 27/st 1); 27 – R.R. Montgomerie; 26 – N.V. Knight; 25 – D.D.J. Robinson, M.A. Lynch, J.C. Pooley and D.P. Ostler; 24 – R.C.J. Williams; 23 – M.P. Maynard, T.R. Ward, G.I. Macmillan and A.J. Stewart; 22 – K.M. Curran and G.A. Hick; 21 – J.P. Crawley and R.J. Bailey; 20 – P.N. Weekes and A.D. Brown

DERBYSHIRE CCC

BATTING

	v. Sussex (Derby) 27-30 April	v. Nottinghamshire (Trent Bridge) 4-8 May	v. Yorkshire (Chesterfield) 11-15 May	v. Leicestershire (Leicester) 18-22 May	v. Oxford University (Oxford) 25-7 May	v. Middlesex (Lord's) 1-5 June	v. Northamptonshire (Derby) 8-12 June	v. Somerset (Derby) 15-19 June	v. Durham (Chester-le-Street) 22-6 June	v. Hampshire (Derby) 29 June – 3 July	v. Kent (Maidstone) 5-8 July	v. Young Australia (Chesterfield) 19-21 July	M	Inns	NO	Runs	HS	Av
K.J. Barnett	164 –	28 37	6 3	11 71	– –	30 14	0 –	0 16*	58 74	76 22*	23 16*	– –	17	31	3	1251	169	44.67
A.S. Rollins	52 –	15 5	38 3	– –	– –	61 72	42 8	56 11	76 6	6 43	82 29	8 12	17	33	1	1095	200*	34.21
C.J. Adams	111 –	0 24	44 17	– –	– –	– –	– –	– –	9 1	64 13	216 43	7 5	15	27	–	1096	216	40.59
D.J. Cullinan	134 –	131 0	1* 1*	– –	– –	10 –	23 25	161 1	10 0	0 34*	35 20	– –	14	26	4	1003	161	45.59
T.J.G. O'Gorman	17 –	39 4	13 24	11 0	17 –	– –	– –	– –	– –	– –	– –	– –	5	8	–	125	39	15.62
D.G. Cork	84* –	8 2	9 24	5 1	– –	28 –	10 16*	3 2	– –	– –	– –	22 50*	12	22	3	383	84*	20.15
P.A.J. DeFreitas	4 –	0 11*	25 0	28 3	– –	2 –	– –	– –	49* 24	8 –	20 –	– –	15	24	3	450	94*	21.42
C.M. Wells	2* –	– –	– –	8 61	115 –	81 22	7 2	47 98	15 4	10 0	98 45*	– –	16	30	5	976	115	36.14
A.E. Warner	– –	– –	9* 33	43 0	– –	0* –	11 8	28* 5	22 2*	– –	5 –	– –	14	22	8	265	43	18.92
K.M. Krikken	– –	36* –	– –	– –	2* 15*	24 –	0 17	27 0	3 0	23* –	11 –	– –	11	16	5	288	61	26.18
D.E. Malcolm	– –	13 5	8 18	25* 0*	– –	0 –	– –	– –	14 0	2 –	– –	4* –	12	18	4	110	25*	7.85
J.E. Owen	– –	4 6	– –	50 11	– –	– –	– –	– –	– –	– –	– –	65 45	4	8	–	200	65	25.00
T.W. Harrison	– –	1 • 6	9 0	2 0	– –	– –	– –	– –	– –	– –	– –	– –	5	10	1	102	61*	11.33
A.C. Cottam	– –	13 32	– –	– –	– 36	– –	7 2	– –	– –	5 –	– –	26 22	5	6	–	95	36	15.83
A.D. Bairstow	– –	16 0	– –	5 4	– –	– –	– –	– –	– –	– –	– –	– 46	8	16	2	478	119*	34.14
W.A. Dessaur	– –	– –	– –	– –	119* 2	4 84*	0 40	28 –	1 21	67 37	29 0	0 7	7	12	–	97	33	8.08
P. Aldred	– –	– –	– –	– –	– 13	5 –	0 0	– –	– –	– –	– –	32 29	4	6	3	47	14*	15.66
M.E. Casser	– –	– –	– –	– –	– 7	– –	– –	– –	– –	– –	– –	– –	2	3	–	68	32	22.66
A.J. Harris	– –	– –	– –	– –	– 13*	5* 5	– –	– –	– –	– –	– –	8 14*	4	6	3	47	14*	15.66
A. Richardson	– –	– –	– –	– –	– 4	– –	– –	– –	– –	– –	– –	– –	1	1	–	4	4	4.00
T.W. Tweats	– –	– –	– –	– –	– –	– –	– –	7 17	– –	– –	– –	– –	8	16	1	308	78*	20.53
F.A. Griffith	– –	– –	– –	– –	– –	– –	0 53	14 –	10* –	– –	– –	3 58	8	13	4	240	53	26.66
S.P. Griffiths	– –	– –	– –	– –	– –	– –	– –	– –	– –	– –	– –	– –	5	9	–	75	20	8.33
S.J. Base	– –	– –	– –	– –	– –	– –	– –	– –	– –	– –	– –	– –	1	2	1	17	10	17.00
Byes	4	5 4	4	4		1	4		4		2 6	4 9						
Leg-byes	22	1 5	2 4	2 4		8 8	7 12	6 8	4 7	4	14 4	10 10						
Wides	1	1	1	16 2		4	1 4		3	1	1 1	5						
No-balls	8	18 2	4		2	14 4	2	8 4	2 2		3	12 4						
Total	603	312 120	140 134	256 173	261 95	267 209	113 139	376 168	194 195	295 157	546 168	191 316						
Wickets	6	10 10	9† 10	10 10	2 5	10 3	10 10	10 4	10 10	10 4	9 4	10 8						
Result	W	L	L	L	W	D	L	L	L	W	D	L						
Points	24	7	4	6		6	4	8	4	22	5	–						

BATTING

	v. Glamorgan (Derby) 27-31 July	v. Worcestershire (Kidderminster) 10-14 August	v. Gloucestershire (Bristol) 17-21 August	v. Surrey (Derby) 24-8 August	v. Essex (Chelmsford) 29 August – 1 September	v. Warwickshire (Edgbaston) 7-11 September	v. Lancashire (Derby) 14-18 September	M	Inns	NO	Runs	HS	Av
K.J. Barnett	25 46	169 43	68 16	72 14	– –	– –	42 88	17	31	3	1251	169	44.67
A.S. Rollins	10 118	43 6	200* 0	4 32	48 13	14 11	17 24	17	33	1	1095	200*	34.21
C.J. Adams	83 27	26 54	68 12	10 101	12 61	1 28	21 38	15	27	–	1096	216	40.59
D.J. Cullinan	0 41	65 101*	– –	– –	30 0	121 37	7 15	14	26	4	1003	161	45.59
T.J.G. O'Gorman	– –	– –	– –	– –	– –	– –	– –	5	8	–	125	39	15.62
D.G. Cork	– –	– –	29 0	– –	31 5	21 0	4 29	12	22	3	383	84*	20.15
P.A.J. DeFreitas	4 0	10 55*	5 25	2 11	91 –	– –	94* 39	15	24	3	450	94*	21.42
C.M. Wells	106 51	10 –	5 0	2 23	19 8	14 9	45 14	16	30	5	976	115	36.14
A.E. Warner	7 –	23 –	6* 16*	4* 11	– –	7 4*	1 20	14	22	8	265	43	18.92
K.M. Krikken	61 25	– –	– –	– –	– –	– –	20 24*	11	16	5	288	61	26.18
D.E. Malcolm	– –	0 –	0 0	– –	2* 18	– –	– –	12	18	4	110	25*	7.85
J.E. Owen	– –	– –	– –	– –	– –	– –	5 14	4	8	–	200	65	25.00
T.W. Harrison	– –	– –	– –	19 61*	0 4	– –	– –	5	10	1	102	61*	11.33
A.C. Cottam	– –	– –	– –	– –	– –	– –	– –	5	6	–	95	36	15.83
A.D. Bairstow	– –	– –	– –	– –	– –	– –	– –	3	6	–	73	26	12.16
W.A. Dessaur	– –	– –	– –	– –	– –	– –	– –	8	16	2	478	119*	34.14
P. Aldred	– –	– –	– –	17 22	– –	33 0	0 0	7	12	–	97	33	8.08
M.E. Casser	2 –	– –	– –	– –	– –	– –	– –	2	3	–	68	32	22.66
A.J. Harris	– –	– –	– –	– –	– –	– –	– –	4	6	3	47	14*	15.66
A. Richardson	– –	– –	– –	– –	– –	– –	– –	1	1	–	4	4	4.00
T.W. Tweats	17 40	78* 2	24 4	0 0	20 33	3 2	– –	8	16	1	308	78*	20.53
F.A. Griffith	40* 0*	26 –	11 23	33 12	12 6*	– –	– –	8	13	4	240	53	26.66
S.P. Griffiths	– –	8 –	9 2	3 20	16 0	17 0	– –	5	9	–	75	20	8.33
S.J. Base	– –	– –	– –	– –	– –	7* 10	– –	1	2	1	17	10	17.00
Byes	5	4	14	1 4	4	6 4	5						
Leg-byes	11 11	4 8	5 6	5 5	5 11	8 7	6 13						
Wides	4 6	2	3	1 1	1	1 1	1						
No-balls	22 2	16 16	16	8 16	4 2	4	6 4 2						
Total	392 372	471 279	463 104	181 333	290 166	268 122	267 325						
Wickets	10 8	10 4	9† 10	10 10	10 9	10 10	10 10						
Result	W	D	L	L	L	L	W						
Points	24	8	4	4	6	5	22						

AXA EQUITY AND LAW LEAGUE – AVERAGES

BATTING

	M	Inns	NO	Runs	HS	Av	100s	50s	ct/st
M.M. Krikken	10	8	6	124	29	62.00	–	–	9/1
D.J. Cullinan	12	11	3	365	76*	45.62	–	3	4
J.E. Owen	4	4	1	91	45	30.33	–	–	–
C.J. Adams	15	15	1	387	79	27.64	–	3	8
K.J. Barnett	16	15	3	313	53*	26.08	–	2	2
C.M. Wells	13	12	–	295	73	24.58	–	3	5
T.J.G. O'Gorman	6	5	1	89	57	22.25	–	1	–
D.G. Cork	13	13	2	232	57	21.09	–	1	4
A.S. Rollins	15	14	1	271	126*	20.84	1	–	6
P. Aldred	8	3	2	18	11*	18.00	–	–	1
P.A.J. DeFreitas	12	10	–	167	28	16.70	–	–	5
T.A. Tweats	9	5	1	60	19	15.00	–	–	7
W.A. Dessaur	2	2	–	23	18	11.50	–	–	–
T.W. Harrison	6	5	1	40	15	10.00	–	–	3
F.A. Griffith	10	5	1	23	12	5.75	–	–	3
D.E. Malcolm	9	5	3	11	10*	5.50	–	–	1
A.E. Warner	13	7	1	26	11	4.33	–	–	2
A.J. Harris	10	2	1	3	3	3.00	–	–	3

Two matches: S.J. Base 5*

One match: A.D. Bairstow 0 (ct 3); A. Richardson did not bat

BOWLING

	Overs	Mds	Runs	Wkts	Av	Best	5/inn
A.E. Warner	82	8	300	20	15.00	4-14	–
A.J. Harris	60.4	2	321	13	24.69	3-15	–
D.G. Cork	84	2	392	15	26.13	3-38	–
F.A. Griffith	60	3	316	12	26.33	4-56	–
D.E. Malcolm	66	–	317	12	26.41	2-23	–
S.J. Base	8	–	55	2	27.50	2-55	–
C.M. Wells	48	2	236	8	29.50	3-31	–
P. Aldred	39.4	1	237	8	29.62	3-28	–
P.A.J. DeFreitas	91.1	7	349	11	31.72	2-15	–
K.J. Barnett	22	–	92	2	46.00	2-32	–
T.A. Tweats	4	–	27	–	–	–	–
A. Richardson	6	–	41	–	–	–	–
T.W. Harrison	4	–	41	–	–	–	–

BOWLING

Opponent (Venue) Date	D.E. Malcolm	D.G. Cork	P.A.J. De Freitas	A.E. Warner	A.C. Cottam	K.J. Barnett	T.W. Harrison	C.M. Wells	A.J. Harris	T.W. Tweats	P. Aldred	F.A. Griffith	Byes	Leg-byes	Wides	No-balls	Total	Wkts
v. Sussex (Derby) 27–30 April	16-2-61-6 / 15-0-56-3	9-4-12-2 / 7-2-19-1	5-2-13-0 / 18-6-35-6	8.4-1-17-2										8 / 2	1	4 / 2	111 / 113	10 / 10
v. Nottinghamshire (Trent Bridge) 4–8 May	21.1-2-57-3	21.2-4-51-4	19-4-49-1		6-1-30-0 / 6-1-20-0	20-6-52-1 / 11-0-38-1	17-3-49-0						20	7 / 7	3	1 / 6	244 / 302	10 / 10
v. Yorkshire (Chesterfield) 11–15 May	18-3-69-3	14-3-40-2	11-3-32-1 / 14.5-2-30-4	11-3-32-1 / 3-0-8-1										12	5	2	177 / 104	9A / 10
v. Leicestershire (Leicester) 18–22 May	11-3-41-3 / 24-4-100-2	26-3-74-5	25.1-9-64-2 / 13-3-27-0	21-3-57-1 / 5-0-15-0				7-1-13-0			10-4-24-2 / 14.3-4-36-1			17 / 2	4	10 / 2	357 / 73	1 / 10
v. Oxford University (Oxford) 25–7 May		11-6-18-0			6.3-2-5-2 / 17-6-29-1	2.1-1-6-1 / 4-1-3-0 / 21-9-60-1	7-2-23-0	16-3-36-3 / 12-5-33-2					9	7		8	97	10B
v. Middlesex (Lord's) 1–5 June	11.5-3-37-3 / 15-4-30-0	15-4-49-2 / 15-3-39-1	13-4-37-2 / 11-3-20-1	13-3-37-3 / 9-4-15-1		1-0-4-0								14 / 6	1	14 / 16	258 / 174	4 / 10
v. Northamptonshire (Derby) 8–12 June		22-5-43-9		16-2-57-0 / 5-2-15-0				7-0-18-0			6-1-16-0 / 5.3-0-12-1 / 8-0-37-2		6	15		8	130 / 120	6 / 10
v. Somerset (Derby) 15–19 June	18-3-76-3	20.3-5-50-4	12-5-16-2 / 31-5-84-1	12-3-44-1 / 24-5-61-1		24-4-51-3							1	12	1 / 2	12 / 12	135	6
v. Durham (Chester-le-Street) 22–6 June	25.1-127-3 / 27.1-4-91-4	22-2-73-2	8-1-46-0	29-6-74-0 / 10.2-1-33-1	8-3-31-0						8-2-26-3 / 6-0-22-1	8-2-26-3 / 6-0-22-1	6 / 13	19 / 5	4	26 / 8	189 / 434	10 / 10C
v. Hampshire (Derby) 29 June – 3 July	4-1-15-0		26.4-7-60-3 / 26.4-10-63-4	38-10-75-5 / 28-7-65-3	21.1-1-103-1 / 15-2-73-0	1-1-0-0 / 10-0-56-0 / 28-3-75-3		13-2-43-2 / 11-5-29-4 / 17-4-50-0			24-5-66-2 / 10-2-26-1	24-5-66-2 / 10-2-26-1	7 / 8	2 / 11	1 / 2	8 / 4	273 / 118	10 / 2
v. Kent (Maidstone) 5–8 July	22-5-58-2 / 20-6-40-1		20-0-88-0 / 26-1-95-3								25.4-3-89-4 / 11-1-28-0	25.4-3-89-4 / 11-1-28-0	15	3	3 / 6	10 / 4	284 / 167	10C / 10D
v. Young Australia (Chesterfield) 19–21 July	19-1-77-3 / 10-1-62-1	5.4-1-19-0 / 10-4-36-1	26-1-95-3	15-5-44-3 / 12-6-27-0				2-1-4-2 / 10-5-22-1	19-4-83-3 / 7.1-1-50-0 / 14.4-1-84-4	9-0-45-1	11.5-2-47-3 / 5-2-27-0	14-1-60-0	6 / 9	1	1	2 / 2	534 / 234	10D / 10E
v. Glamorgan (Derby) 27–31 July			21-2-84-3 / 26-8-74-2	19.2-8-42-1 / 21-6-62-5		19.4-8-48-2 / 20.2-4-40-1 / 16-2-69-1 / 21.1-3-66-1						19-10-30-1 / 10-2-20-1 / 20-5-84-1 / 17-3-79-2	8	6 / 8	3 / 3	20 / 26	276 / 248	10E / 6
v. Worcestershire (Kidderminster) 10–14 August	24-8-65-5 / 30-6-114-5		10-1-47-0 / 23-1-102-1										7	13	6	6	321 / 234	10 / 10
v. Gloucestershire (Bristol) 17–21 August	22-6-86-2 / 8-1-31-0	11-1-36-1 / 12-2-40-1	28.2-8-72-3 / 31.5-11-68-1	21-6-62-5 / 15-5-32-0								1-0-8-0	8 / 10	10	3	18	467	9
v. Surrey (Derby) 24–8 August			13-2-38-0 / 22-3-66-5		17-6-30-1	17-6-30-1	12-4-35-1 / 10-3-22-0 / 30-7-153-4	7-2-36-0 / 5-0-20-0 / 7-0-39-0 / 17-2-40-0 / 13-3-29-1		6.4-1-23-1 / 6-0-19-0 / 13-1-57-1 / 9-1-50-1	21-4-89-3 / 8-3-11-0	19-6-53-1	1	7	1	14 / 8	351 / 217	10 / 7
v. Essex (Chelmsford) 29 August – 1 September	23-4-107-3 / 6-0-19-1	21-3-68-2 / 19-2-71-1	4-0-16-0									6-2-23-0	5 / 1	12 / 6	1 / 8	12 / 10	350 / 167	10 / 3
v. Warwickshire (Edgbaston) 7–11 September		21-4-49-2 / 1-0-1-0		22-3-81-1		3-0-17-0					16-3-45-2 / 0.3-0-4-0		8 / 7	8 / 3	2 / 5	8 / 22	326 / 386	8F / 8G
v. Lancashire (Derby) 14–18 September		18.1-3-61-7 / 9-1-43-0	10-3-35-1 / 14-2-59-2	9-2-56-2 / 7.5-3-21-6				1-0-1-0			2-0-27-1		2 / 5	10	1	10	387 / 5	0 / 9H
Lancashire cont.																	155 / 155	
Bowler's average	411.1-75-1472-60 / 24.53	364.4-74-1020-57 / 17.89	564.1-125-1636-58 / 28.20	375.1-90-1050-39 / 26.92	79.3-16-291-4 / 72.75	218.2-42-635-16 / 39.68	76-19-282-5 / 56.40	110-25-326-10 / 32.60	85.5-16-354-14 / 25.28	43.4-3-194-4 / 48.50	108.2-23-375-15 / 25.00	190.4-42-614-17 / 36.11						

A M.D. Moxon retired hurt
B A. Richardson 10-2-27-3, 9-1-13-0. M.E. Casser (2) 24-9-54-4
C C.J. Adams 6-3-8-0
D C.J. Adams 9-0-39-0. W.A. Dessaur 4-1-16-0
E M.A. Casser 0.2-0-1-0, 6-0-36-1. W.A. Dessaur (2) 3-0-8-1
F A.S. Rollins 3-1-19-1
G S.J. Base 17-2-99-1
H S.P. Titchard retired hurt

DURHAM CCC

BATTING	v. Oxford University (Oxford) 13–15 April		v. Hampshire (Stockton) 27–30 April		v. Lancashire (Old Trafford) 4–8 May		v. Surrey (The Oval) 11–15 May		v. Warwickshire (Chester-le-Street) 18–22 May		v. Leicestershire (Leicester) 25–9 May		v. Kent (Chester-le-Street) 1–5 June		v. Essex (Chelmsford) 8–12 June		v. West Indians (Chester-le-Street) 17–19 June		v. Derbyshire (Chester-le-Street) 22–6 June		v. Glamorgan (Swansea) 1–3 July		v. Worcestershire (Darlington) 6–10 July		M	Inns	NO	Runs	HS	Av
M.A. Roseberry	90	–	19	0	44	13	5	7	25	2	25	4	41*	6	23	18	79	20	10	36*	56	18	22	5	16	29	2	669	90	24.77
M. Saxelby	16	5	4	18	19	31	68	5	16	9	2	22					29	7							7	14	–	251	68	17.92
J.E. Morris	99	–	4	28	68	169	5	9	128	25	38	41	–	4	4	7	75	0	99	3	7	45*	13	37	19	35	1	1297	169	38.14
J.A. Daley	20	53*	25	33	27	55	55	49	31	–															7	12	2	435	51	43.50
J.I. Longley	37	11											31*	0	21	35	0	7	7	50	58	4	9	32	9	18	1	420	58	24.70
S. Hutton	15	21															39	8	18	19*	26	91	7	0	12	23	1	634	98	28.81
C.W. Scott	0	41*	20	1	22	56																			7	13	1	311	56	25.91
J. Boiling	0	–	14*	0	6*	1	18	1	14*	11	0	4	–	10	24	1	8*	69			0	–	17*	0	18	32	7	312	69	12.48
J. Wood	19*	–	2	8	4	40*			5	8															4	7	2	86	40*	17.20
A. Walker	0	–											–	4	5	8	1*	29	6	–			4	19	11	16	3	102	29	7.84
S.J.E. Brown	16*	–	0	8*	2	0	33	26	1	15	6	13	–	1	32*	7			6	–	0	–	0	5	18	30	6	278	36	11.58
W. Larkins			47	31	23	19	2	28	58	0	27	26	–	4	22	–									13	23	–	737	121	32.04
M. Prabhakar			7	84	21	1	23	41	27	66	18	7	–	35*	4	46*			2	–	101	24*	59	59	17	31	3	896	101	32.00
M.M. Betts			8	6	0	5			2	0*	0*	0	–	0			–	11*	1	–			0	1*	9	15	5	55	14	5.50
S.D. Birbeck							0	10			4	1							75*	–	16*	–			4	6	2	106	75*	26.50
D.G.C. Ligertwood							40	28*	2	2	3	26*	–	3	25	17	40	38	1	–	2	–	19	7	12	21	2	303	40	15.94
J.P. Searle							2*	0																	1	2	1	2	2*	2.00
D.A. Blenkiron											3	0	–	4	94	0	24	9			53	145	19	34	9	17	1	446	145	27.87
D.M. Cox															5	0					1	–			3	5	–	23	17	4.60
N. Killeen																	2	35							7	13	3	137	48	13.70
P. Bainbridge																			0	–					2	3	–	4	4	1.33
R.M.S. Weston																									3	6	–	15	9	2.50
J.R. Lawrence																									1	2	1	7	7*	7.00
Byes			1			7					1			4	7		2		13		4	4		8						
Leg-byes	5	6	7	8	7	18	3	3	2	3	10	3		4	3	4	13	2	5	2	1	8	5	13						
Wides	1		5	4		1	3	3		4	1	4		2	3		1		4				1	1						
No-balls	4		14	19	6	16	12	14	2					4	16	6	51	24	26	8	6	4	16	34						
Total	322	137	177	248	249	432	269	224	313	145	138	151	72	85	288	149	364	259	273	118	331	343	191	255						
Wickets	9	3	10	10	10	10	10	10	10	9†	10	10	0	10	10	9‡	9	10	10	2	10	4	10	10						
Result	D		W		L		L		L		L		L		L		D		W		W		L							
Points	–		20		5		3		5		3		4		6		–		22		23		2							

BATTING	v. Yorkshire (Harrogate) 20–4 July		v. Northamptonshire (Northampton) 3–7 August		v. Middlesex (Chester-le-Street) 10–14 August		v. Somerset (Chester-le-Street) 17–21 August		v. Sussex (Hartlepool) 24–8 August		v. Gloucestershire (Bristol) 17–11 September		v. Nottinghamshire (Chester-le-Street) 14–18 September		M	Inns	NO	Runs	HS	Av
M.A. Roseberry	16	–			0	28	0	4					53	–	16	29	2	669	90	24.77
M. Saxelby															7	14	–	251	68	17.92
J.E. Morris	46	4	21	0	2	0	38	50	25	21	3	70	109	–	19	35	1	1297	169	38.14
J.A. Daley	0	37*											50	–	7	12	2	435	51	43.50
J.I. Longley									34	35	48	1			9	18	1	420	58	24.70
S. Hutton	21	26	13	57	9	14	4	34	0	98	60	44	10	–	12	23	1	634	98	28.81
C.W. Scott							55	1	31	24	0	28	32	–	7	13	1	311	56	25.91
J. Boiling	18	4	2	14	10	2	12	13	18	18	3*	0*	0	–	18	32	7	312	69	12.48
J. Wood															4	7	2	86	40*	17.20
A. Walker	12	2			0	–			1	4*	–	5	2*	–	11	16	3	102	29	7.84
S.J.E. Brown	5	5	21*	0*	0	5	14*	2	1	1	–	36	17	–	18	30	6	278	36	11.58
W. Larkins			18	112	41	33	14	20	19	43	1	28	121	–	13	23	–	737	121	32.04
M. Prabhakar	35	4	1	46	86	8	9	45	11	0	15	9	2	–	17	31	3	896	101	32.00
M.M. Betts	7*	14													9	15	5	55	14	5.50
S.D. Birbeck															4	6	2	106	75*	26.50
D.G.C. Ligertwood	13	0	23	2	9	3									12	21	2	303	40	15.94
J.P. Searle															1	2	1	2	2*	2.00
D.A. Blenkiron	7	8	15	5	26*	0									9	17	1	446	145	27.87
D.M. Cox			17	0											3	5	–	23	17	4.60
N. Killeen			0	3	2	0*	48	19	19*	4	5*	0	0	–	7	13	3	137	48	13.70
P. Bainbridge			4	0											2	3	–	4	4	1.33
R.M.S. Weston							0	4	0	0	2	9			3	6	–	15	9	2.50
J.R. Lawrence							0	7*							1	2	1	7	7*	7.00
Byes	12			10	1	4	16	4					5							
Leg-byes	7	13	3	17	8		5	7	9	10	1		11							
Wides	1					9		6	3	5	8	2								
No-balls	6	8	10	2	10	8	6		6	8	26	4	12							
Total	206	125	148	268	204	114	221	216	177	271	172	236	424							
Wickets	10	9¶	10	10	10	9•	10	10	10	10	7	10	10							
Result	L		L		L		L		L		L		W							
Points	5		1		5		5		2		2		24							

FIELDING FIGURES

36 – D.G.C. Ligertwood (ct 33/st 3)
18 – C.W. Scott
17 – M.A. Roseberry
11 – J. Boiling and W. Larkins
9 – J.E. Morris and M. Prabhakar
6 – S.J.E. Brown and S. Hutton
5 – M. Saxelby, J.A. Daley and R.M.S. Weston
4 – N. Killeen and A. Walker
3 – J.I. Longley and D.A. Blenkiron
2 – M.M. Betts
1 – P. Bainbridge, S.D. Birbeck and sub

† J.A. Daley absent hurt
‡ W. Larkins absent hurt
¶ M.A. Roseberry absent hurt
• A. Walker absent hurt

AXA EQUITY AND LAW LEAGUE – AVERAGES

BATTING	M	Inns	NO	Runs	HS	Av	100s	50s	ct/st
P.D. Collingwood	2	2	1	37	33*	37.00	–	–	–
J.A. Daley	6	6	2	129	53*	33.25	–	1	1
J.E. Morris	14	13	1	342	74	28.50	–	3	3
M. Prabhakar	12	12	–	324	69	27.00	–	2	2
M.A. Roseberry	9	9	–	237	94	26.33	–	2	3
J.I. Longley	9	8	–	203	92	25.37	–	1	1
P. Bainbridge	6	5	2	62	31*	20.66	–	–	1
J. Boiling	14	7	4	62	21*	20.66	–	–	12
D.A. Blenkiron	9	8	1	131	56	18.71	–	1	3
A. Walker	10	5	2	48	15*	16.00	–	–	1
S. Hutton	11	10	–	156	34	15.60	–	–	2
W. Larkins	10	9	1	121	42	15.12	–	–	5
D.C.G. Ligertwood	11	9	3	84	31	14.00	–	–	15/2
C.W. Scott	4	3	1	24	14	12.00	–	–	3
S.D. Birbeck	5	4	–	48	23	12.00	–	–	–
M. Saxelby	4	4	–	44	23	11.00	–	–	–
N. Killeen	8	4	1	27	20	9.50	–	–	1
S.J.E. Brown	11	8	3	27	7	5.40	–	–	5
M.M. Betts	9	4	4	33	14*	–	–	–	1

One match: J.P. Searle did not bat

BOWLING	Overs	Mds	Runs	Wkts	Av	Best	5/inn
S.J.E. Brown	76.5	4	321	17	18.88	4-20	–
M. Saxelby	13	–	61	3	20.33	3-18	–
N. Killeen	56.4	3	248	12	20.66	5-26	1
M. Prabhakar	87	6	377	17	22.17	3-30	–
M.M. Betts	64.1	2	302	11	27.45	3-39	–
S.B. Birbeck	25	2	109	3	36.33	1-14	–
A. Walker	74.3	1	386	9	42.88	3-23	–
P. Bainbridge	26	–	158	3	52.66	3-56	–
J. Boiling	72	3	333	6	55.50	2-22	–
D.A. Blenkiron	17	–	111	1	111.00	1-25	–
J.P. Searle	2	–	19	–	–	–	–
P.D. Collingwood	11	–	53	–	–	–	–

BOWLING

Bowling analyses shown as overs–maidens–runs–wickets. Where two innings were bowled, figures are separated by " / ".

Match	S.J.E. Brown	J. Wood	J. Boiling	A. Walker	M. Saxelby	M. Prabhakar	M.M. Betts	M.A. Roseberry
v. Oxford University (Oxford) 13–15 April	23.4-8-54-4 / 8.2-2-7-1	15.5-5-37-1 / 8.4-1-11-1	25-13-29-2 / 12-7-7-0	8-2-43-0 / 8-1-38-1	5-2-15-1 / 6-0-25-0			
v. Hampshire (Stockton) 27–30 April	21-6-50-1 / 21.3-8-49-5	9.2-3-31-2	6-3-13-0					
v. Lancashire (Old Trafford) 4–8 May	25-6-72-3	18.4-4-54-4	18-4-61-1		1-0-3-0 / 3-0-16-0	22-9-36-3 / 22-8-50-2	8.2-3-35-3 / 11-2-51-1	
v. Surrey (The Oval) 11–15 May	17-0-102-0	21-3-88-2	36-7-150-2			23-8-49-1 / 32-8-116-0	12-1-75-0	1.4-0-7-0
v. Warwickshire (Chester-le-Street) 18–22 May	41-11-123-5	14-6-25-1	37-6-86-0		5.4-0-29-1	38.4-13-62-2 / 30-7-65-7	27-6-103-2 / 27-8-73-0	
v. Leicestershire (Leicester) 25–9 May	25-3-69-6 / 21.5-2-85-2		2-0-15-0 / 26-6-78-1		4-0-12-0			
v. Kent (Chester-le-Street) 1–5 June	17-4-69-3			17-4-52-2		23.5-2-83-3	10-0-61-1	
v. Essex (Chelmsford) 8–12 June	33-6-87-1 / 14-4-27-0		18-4-66-0 / 7-1-26-0	39.2-8-118-8 / 23.1-5-59-6		21-4-40-0 / 18-3-56-2		
v. West Indians (Chester-le-Street) 17–19 June			21-6-91-0	24-7-100-1	13-3-38-0		16-1-112-3 / 3-1-8-1	1-0-5-0
v. Derbyshire (Chester-le-Street) 22–6 June	16-5-39-4 / 16.4-4-42-5			3-1-8-0 / 14.5-2-42-2		14-0-45-1 / 22.1-12-47-4	10-2-44-1 / 8-2-37-1	
v. Glamorgan (Swansea) 1–3 July	13-2-49-0		24-10-51-2 / 34-7-102-1	10-3-22-1		15-6-23-2		
v. Worcestershire (Darlington) 6–10 July	27-5-88-0 / 1-0-13-0		32-14-119-5	27-4-79-0				
v. Yorkshire (Harrogate) 20–4 July	27-7-90-4 / 11-1-35-2		38-13-80-1	18.1-3-42-1 / 14-4-68-0		27.5-11-87-4 / 13-7-15-1	23-1-74-2 / 0.3-0-12-0	
v. Northamptonshire (Harrogate) 3–7 August	22-4-96-0		19-2-74-0 / 29-6-84-0			26-8-73-1	9-0-35-0 / 2-0-9-0	
v. Middlesex (Chester-le-Street) 10–14 August	27-4-103-2 / 13-2-66-1		12-4-29-2 / 26-1-114-2	17-4-65-3 / 14-3-36-0		23-8-61-2 / 20-6-71-2		
v. Somerset (Chester-le-Street) 17–21 August	28.2-2-107-1		11-5-17-1 / 28-7-80-0			23-6-59-3 / 17-3-40-2		1-0-7-0
v. Sussex (Hartlepool) 24–8 August	9.1-1-31-0 / 29.5-1-111-0		31-9-56-0	17-2-85-1		29-5-85-2		
v. Gloucestershire (Bristol) 7–11 September	24.3-6-79-0		16-0-70-2	19-2-72-1		15-4-33-0		
v. Nottinghamshire (Chester-le-Street) 14–18 September	10-1-50-1 / 22-5-61-4		8-2-32-0 / 29-6-73-5	12-2-29-4		17-4-38-3 / 9.4-2-24-1		
Bowler's average	589.3-117-1951-57 34.22	97.4-25-303-14 21.64	599-149-1702-27 63.03	285.3-53-958-31 30.90	37.4-5-138-2 69.00	579.1-165-1439-51 28.21	194.5-31-853-17 50.17	3.4-0-19-0 –

Match	S.D. Birbeck	J.P. Searle	D.A. Blenkiron	D.M. Cox	N. Killeen	P. Bainbridge	J.R. Lawrence	R.M.S. Weston	Byes	Leg-byes	Wides	No-balls	Total	Wkts
v. Oxford University (Oxford)										5 / 5		12 / 10	183 / 93	10 / 3
v. Hampshire (Stockton)										16 / 8	1	25 / 10	194 / 205	10 / 10
v. Lancashire (Old Trafford)									12	3	3	16	370	10
v. Surrey (The Oval)	22-3-119-3	36-3-126-2							3 / 4	4	2	12	314	9
v. Warwickshire (Chester-le-Street)										6	3	8	652	10
v. Leicestershire (Leicester)	16-1-55-0		4-0-16-0							13 / 2	1	4 / 12	424 / 145	10 / 8
v. Kent (Chester-le-Street)			4-1-10-1	12-3-46-0 / 27-7-72-2						8	4	2	380	10
v. Essex (Chelmsford)									2	7	1	6	272 / 0	9 / 0
v. West Indians (Chester-le-Street)					20-2-109-1					3		4	373	10
v. Derbyshire (Chester-le-Street)	6-1-20-1 / 6-0-28-0		6-0-27-0	26-8-54-2 / 38.5-6-141-4		5-2-5-1				4 / 7	2	4 / 2	243 / 462	10 / 5
v. Glamorgan (Swansea)	14-1-49-0									7			16	1
v. Worcestershire (Darlington)									1	10 / 12	6	6	194 / 195	10 / 10
v. Yorkshire (Harrogate)				26-4-109-3					9 / 2	10	2	2	335 / 336	10 / 9
v. Northamptonshire (Harrogate)					21-3-72-1	10-0-50-0			1	3 / 6	1	2	424 / 25	8 / 0
v. Middlesex (Chester-le-Street)					17.2-6-47-1 / 20-2-83-0				8	2 / 1	2 / 3	2	338 / 204	10 / 5
v. Somerset (Chester-le-Street)			2-0-11-0		19-3-83-3		16-5-44-2 / 24-3-79-1	15.1-2-41-1 / 7-0-29-0	4	21	3	2	492	10
v. Sussex (Hartlepool)					21-2-96-1 / 29.4-118-5				4	14	2	18	307 / 397	10 / 5
v. Gloucestershire (Bristol)					28-8-85-3				2	9	9	6	350 / 77	6 / 0B
v. Nottinghamshire (Chester-le-Street)					6.1-0-20-2 / 14-0-54-0				8	13 / 8	1		190 / 220	10 / 10
Bowler's average	64-6-271-4 67.75	36-3-126-2 63.00	16-1-64-1 64.00	129.5-28-422-11 38.36	195.3-30-767-17 45.11	15-2-55-1 55.00	40-8-123-3 41.00	22.1-2-70-1 70.00						

A S. Hutton 2-0-13-0.
B C.W. Scott 3.2-0-30-0. J.J. Longley 4-0-47-0.

FIELDING FIGURES

62 – R.J. Rollins (ct 53/st 9)
34 – N. Hussain
25 – D.D.J. Robinson
19 – M.E. Waugh
12 – G.A. Gooch
11 – P.M. Such
10 – P.J. Prichard
9 – J.J.B. Lewis
6 – J.H. Childs
4 – M.C. Ilott
3 – D.M. Cousins
2 – subs
1 – A.P. Cowan

AXA EQUITY AND LAW LEAGUE – AVERAGES

BATTING	M	Inns	NO	Runs	HS	Av	100s	50s	ct/st
N. Hussain	17	17	1	634	83	39.62	–	7	6
M.E. Waugh	16	16	0	608	89	38.00	1	5	8
G.A. Gooch	17	17	2	453	65	30.20	–	5	5
P.J. Prichard	17	17	0	513	81	30.17	–	4	5
R.C. Irani	17	17	2	419	101*	27.93	1	2	4
M.C. Ilott	14	12	6	138	56*	23.00	–	1	4
D.D.J. Robinson	17	17	0	239	38	17.07	–	–	6
R.J. Rollins	9	11	3	88	28*	11.62	–	–	22
R.M. Pearson	5	2	1	7	4*	7.00	–	–	1
D.M. Cousins	16	4	2	12	7	6.00	–	–	–
S.J.W. Andrew	9	2	0	9	7	4.50	–	–	2
J.J.B. Lewis	16	5	1	11	18	2.75	–	–	8

One match: M.A. Garnham 0; N.F. Williams 0; A.P. Cowan 0*

BOWLING	Overs	Mds	Runs	Wkts	Av	Best	5/inn
M.C. Ilott	96.2	–	442	22	22.09	4-27	–
G.A. Gooch	17	1	101	4	22.25	2-27	–
S.J.W. Andrew	45	2	203	9	22.55	4-40	–
R.C. Irani	112	6	543	22	24.68	3-32	–
P.M. Such	100	4	491	19	25.84	3-41	–
D.M. Cousins	112	7	506	18	28.11	3-20	–
M.E. Waugh	80.3	1	462	15	30.80	3-20	–
R.M. Pearson	25	–	162	3	54.00	2-67	–
D.D.J. Robinson	2	–	19	–	–	–	–
A.P. Cowan	4	–	20	–	–	–	–
N.F. Williams	4	–	25	–	–	–	–

ESSEX CCC — BATTING (season averages)

	M	Inns	NO	Runs	HS	Av
G.A. Gooch	18	34	1	1669	165	50.57
P.J. Prichard	18	33	1	1080	109	33.75
J.J.B. Lewis	7	14	–	299	75	21.35
N. Hussain	17	35	1	1854	186	54.52
D.D.J. Robinson	17	32	–	712	123	22.25
R.C. Irani	18	34	3	809	133*	25.28
R.J. Rollins	19	35	3	1165	108	36.40
M.C. Ilott	16	28	4	290	37	12.08
N.F. Williams	9	12	2	90	17	9.00
P.M. Such	18	16	8	121	18*	10.08
D.M. Cousins	18	30	8	214	32	9.72
J.H. Childs	17	28	11	113	24	6.64
A.J. Hibbert	1	2	–	31	18	15.50
M.A. Garnham	1	2	–	48	41	24.00
R.M. Pearson	2	2	–	27	17	13.50
N.A. Derbyshire	2	4	–	47	17	15.66
S.J.W. Andrew	4	1	–	4	4	1.75
M.E. Waugh	15	28	2	1347	173	51.80
A.P. Cowan	2	4	1	47	22	15.66

BOWLING

	M.C. Ilott	N.F. Williams	R.C. Irani	D.M. Cousins	P.M. Such	J.H. Childs	S.J.W. Andrew	R.M. Pearson	N.A. Derbyshire	M.E. Waugh	G.A. Gooch	A.P. Cowan	Byes	Leg-byes	Wides	No-balls	Total	Wkts
v. Leicestershire (Chelmsford) 27-30 April	23-2-78-4	18.3-3-93-5	6-0-38-0	8-0-26-1	6-1-14-0								1	4		18	253	10
	28-5-104-2	25.2-3-93-3	15-4-60-0	29-3-73-3	44-13-90-2	36-10-77-3							8	11	3	10	432	10
v. Worcestershire (Chelmsford) 4-8 May	8-1-32-1		11-0-35-0	7-2-34-0	38.4-9-84-6	22.3-9-60-3							1	6			276	10
	11-2-32-1		4-0-18-0	3-0-27-0	33-3-94-6								2	5		6	237	10
v. Cambridge University (Cambridge) 11-15 May				15-2-38-0		14-6-28-3	15-6-24-1	19.3-5-58-3	11-4-18-1				4	7	4	4	175	8
				6-2-18-2		15.5-6-39-3	4-1-13-0	20-5-77-3	5-0-10-0					3	3	44	164	8
v. Sussex (Hove) 18-22 May	26-7-82-7	23-0-71-1	13-2-73-0	13-1-47-0	12-2-43-2	7-2-18-0				9-2-33-0				6	4	6	326	10
	27-6-75-3	13-1-60-1			21-4-72-0	25-6-53-2				17-3-76-4			4	4	3	24	390	10
v. Middlesex (Chelmsford) 25-9 May	34.1-7-95-2	17-3-53-1	33-6-90-2		37-9-72-2	24-1-99-2				14.1-8-52-1			2	10	1		473	10
					5.1-2-8-0	5-1-17-0											25	0
v. Nottinghamshire (Trent Bridge) 1-5 June		23-5-64-1	6-1-31-1		26-5-94-3	36-10-74-4				22-7-40-1	4-1-17-0		1	11		2	314	6
			2-0-11-0		35-10-87-4	39-6-115-2			5-1-20-1	14-2-58-0			7	2		2	274	6
v. Durham (Chelmsford) 8-12 June	10.1-2-19-9	25-6-86-2	14-2-41-1		10-4-17-1	22-8-32-2				22.5-5-65-3				5	3	16	288	
	22-0-86-5	12-4-35-1	6-1-29-0		12.2-2-44-2	6-0-19-3				13-6-19-3	4-1-17-0			4		6	149	9A
v. Northamptonshire (Luton) 15-19 June	31.2-4-86-5	6-2-18-1	4-0-9-0		24-5-83-0	36-10-88-3	18-2-67-0			17-4-47-2			4	2	1	8	46	10
	5-0-16-0	28-4-85-2			8-0-31-0	9.2-1-48-0	1-0-3-0			20-1-63-0			10	14	6	2	192	10
v. Lancashire (Old Trafford) 22-6 June	23-7-78-1	15-1-66-2	15-4-48-1		45-5-122-2	28-3-104-2				2-0-6-0	3-0-17-1		15	18	1	18	496	8
	2.4-0-18-0	2-0-12-0								15.4-3-45-1				5			106	10
v. Warwickshire (Ilford) 29 June – 3 July	29-7-101-4	28-6-96-2	13-2-52-0		22.4-3-51-3	27-6-80-1				10-1-40-0			9	8		10	513	10
	19-7-44-1	5-2-12-0			36.4-12-79-5	44-19-55-4				3-2-1-0			8	5			35	0
v. Surrey (The Oval) 6-10 July	31-9-84-4	26-6-94-0	15-5-31-1		34.1-9-75-2	37-10-84-3				18-6-38-0			4	11		8	437	10
	3-0-8-0	2-0-10-0			16-2-60-2	17.4-3-54-1				2-0-5-0						2	203	10
v. Somerset (Southend) 20-4 July			17-0-75-2		2-1-5-0	5-1-31-0				20-5-85-1			2	2		14	421	10
			17-5-46-2		10-1-54-0	6.5-0-29-0							12	7		16	139	9B
v. Gloucestershire (Cheltenham) 27-31 July	26-8-81-4	18.4-1-105-1			49.1-18-93-8	39-9-101-2											400	
	15-8-31-0	18-2-73-1			37-9-100-3	28-15-36-6							2	4	1		285	7
v. Hampshire (Colchester) 3-7 August	4-0-23-0	4-1-14-0	3-0-14-1		28.5-9-67-3	26-8-103-1				4-1-13-0	3-2-4-1			13	1		255	10
	25.5-7-53-5		9-2-32-0		24-2-79-2	22.1-2-60-5							4	7		18	153	10
v. Glamorgan (Swansea) 10-14 August	10-2-18-2	9-1-23-0			24-6-48-2	28-15-36-6					4.4-0-22-2		8	1	2	4	339	10
	9-1-56-1	4-1-14-1			16-2-76-0			21-2-78-1			5-0-22-0		5	6			255	10
v. West Indians (Chelmsford) 19-21 August	21.3-5-58-6	13.1-4-38-4	18-1-88-2	13-1-63-0				20.3-1-89-0		4-0-24-0		6-0-29-0	6	9	3		180	
			11.5-2-53-0	4-0-30-0								2-1-5-0	4	1	1		366	0C
v. Kent (Canterbury) 24-8 August			20-0-62-5		26.5-6-86-5	18-2-66-1				20.1-8-55-1	6-1-15-2		4	2		4	260	10
			2-1-3-0		28.3-7-93-4	25-6-81-4					4-0-15-0			5			178	10
v. Derbyshire (Chelmsford) 29 August – 1 September	21-3-81-1					30-18-39-4											282	10
	12-2-71-1														1	2	290	10
v. Yorkshire (Chelmsford) 14-18 September	8-0-14-1		16-6-36-1		17.5-3-54-3	14-3-36-1				8-2-25-0		11-1-53-1	4	11	1	4	166	9D
	26-7-97-4		5-2-6-1		17.5-4-89-5	13-3-31-3						5-0-26-0		8		2	309	10
11-2-27-1																		
Bowler's average	551.4-117-1761-77 / 22.87	188.4-31-743-21 / 35.38	361.5-72-1222-27 / 45.25	176-23-640-12 / 53.33	748.4-174-2064-77 / 26.80	678.2-184-1757-68 / 25.83	38-9-107-1 / 107.00	81-13-302-7 / 43.14	21-5-48-2 / 24.00	255.5-66-789-17 / 46.41	29.4-4-112-6 / 18.66	24-2-113-1 / 113.00						

A W. Larkins absent hurt
B R.J. Cunliffe absent hurt
C D.D.J. Robinson 1-0-7-0
D P.A.J. DeFreitas absent

FIELDING FIGURES

- 54 — C.P. Metson (ct 47/st 7)
- 22 — M.P. Maynard
- 14 — P.A. Cottey and D.L. Hemp
- 12 — S.P. James
- 8 — R.D.B. Croft and S.L. Watkin
- 7 — A. Dale
- 6 — N.M. Kendrick, H.A.G. Anthony and subs
- 5 — A.D. Shaw (ct 3/st 2) and H. Morris
- 4 — S.D. Thomas and A.J. Dalton
- 3 — S.R. Barwick

† A. Dale retired hurt
‡ P.A. Cottey absent hurt

AXA EQUITY AND LAW LEAGUE – AVERAGES

BATTING	M	Inns	NO	Runs	HS	Av	100s	50s	ct/st
S.P. James	16	16	5	815	93*	74.09	—	8	6
R.D.B. Croft	16	11	2	196	66*	39.20	—	1	6
H. Morris	16	15	2	434	100	33.38	1	1	7
P.A. Cottey	15	14	4	287	56	28.70	—	2	7
M.P. Maynard	16	14	3	315	69*	28.63	—	3	7
A. Dale	12	9	1	212	48	26.50	—	1	3
S.D. Thomas	3	1	—	19	19	19.00	—	—	—
D.L. Hemp	15	11	—	164	74	14.90	—	—	10
R.P. Lefebvre	14	3	1	23	10*	11.50	—	—	1
S.R. Barwick	14	3	2	11	9	11.00	—	—	1
S.L. Watkin	14	3	1	17	13*	8.50	—	—	3
H.A.G. Anthony	16	4	1	22	7	3.66	—	—	2
C.P. Metson	16	4	1	7	3	2.33	—	—	20/7

BOWLING	Overs	Mds	Runs	Wkts	Av	Best	5/inn
S.R. Barwick	99.4	4	451	30	15.03	6-49	2
S.L. Watkin	125.1	4	508	32	15.87	4-38	—
R.P. Lefebvre	76.3	3	313	16	19.56	3-29	—
S.D. Thomas	19	—	94	4	23.50	3-44	—
R.D.B. Croft	115	5	516	20	25.80	3-28	—
H.A.G. Anthony	75	1	404	11	36.72	3-40	—
P.A. Cottey	15	—	91	2	45.50	1-8	—
A. Dale	69.1	4	421	9	46.77	2-30	—

BOWLING

	S.L. Watkin	R.P. Lefebvre	A. Dale	R.D.B. Croft	N.M. Kendrick	G.P. Butcher	P.A. Cottey	S.D. Thomas	D.L. Hemp	H.A.G. Anthony	S.R. Barwick	A.P. Davies	Byes	Leg-byes	Wides	No-balls	Total	Wkts
v. Oxford University (Oxford) 18–20 April	21-6-59-3	18.3-6-45-6	7-2-8-0	7-5-3-1	11-8-10-0	7-2-23-0							4	5			157	10
	8-3-11-0		4-0-12-0	5-4-5-0	15-5-23-0	9-3-22-0								3		2	105	1
v. Somerset (Taunton) 27–30 April	28.1-6-55-3	22-7-36-0	4-2-12-0	21-13-26-1	7-3-17-1								4	4	9		277	10
	24.2-9-49-7	16-5-34-0	4-2-12-0	14-3-36-0	10-4-21-0				3-0-9-1				1	7	1	4	214	10
v. Northamptonshire (Cardiff) 4–8 May	23.1-5-74-3		15-2-54-1	34-11-78-2	33-11-98-4			26-5-98-3						1	1	2	377	10
	23.2-5-55-4			32-9-60-2	33-13-62-3			13-0-51-0 / 13-2-66-0					4			2	243	10
v. Sussex (Swansea) 11–15 May	19-3-45-1		15-4-60-1	8.3-0-37-3	20-8-56-1			17-4-56-1	2-0-10-1	19-4-47-4			1	5			196	5
	17-2-49-2		13-3-38-2	9.2-2-37-0	10-1-48-0					12-0-57-1				5		2	256	5
v. Yorkshire (Bradford) 18–22 May	23-6-55-6	12-4-34-0	6-2-21-0	4-2-8-1						16-1-49-1				5			189	10
	12-3-88-1	17-6-30-0	10-4-31-1	15.1-4-28-2			1-0-5-0			11-1-40-0				4	2	4	161	3
v. Kent (Tunbridge Wells) 24–7 May	30-5-98-2			25-8-63-0	13-2-37-0			13-0-61-0	2-1-8-0	24.1-6-70-5				1	1	2	369	9A
	15-2-40-0			23-7-47-2	37-17-70-4			12.4-0-53-1		16-6-36-1				4		6	253	10
v. Hampshire (Cardiff) 1–5 June	19-5-44-2			24-3-60-0	14-3-45-0			16-3-61-1		23.3-3-77-6			3	2			324	10
	5-0-14-2							3-1-8-0		3-0-17-0			7			2	55	1
v. Lancashire (Old Trafford) 8–12 June	23.4-4-67-2		6-0-28-0	29-4-93-3	9-0-58-0		10-0-50-0		3-0-19-1	15-2-62-0	30-8-78-2		5	4		8	417	10
	11-5-24-0		1.5-0-16-0	40-3-132-2			3-0-13-0		7-0-26-0	21-6-57-0						6	338	10
v. Middlesex (Colwyn Bay) 15–19 June	33-11-87-1		16-2-50-1	38-5-135-2	15-1-82-0				3-0-10-0	13-2-56-1	40.5-6-116-4			8		6	530	10
	6-1-22-1			6-1-18-0	4-0-21-1									6			79	1
v. Surrey (The Oval) 22–6 June	20-6-82-3			22-4-72-1	13-1-59-0			19-3-95-4		15.5-2-75-2	27-7-74-2		2			2	397	10
	23-9-43-3		7-1-33-0	41-18-94-3	4-3-2-0			14-2-79-1		24-7-55-2	23-8-74-0		20	12		6	302	9
v. Durham (Swansea) 29 June – 3 July	17-2-78-2			30-6-108-2			1-0-2-0	13-1-74-2		21.2-5-65-3	20-6-62-2		4		1	4	331	10
				26-5-94-1			2.1-0-10-0	5-0-25-0		14-2-75-1			4	9	1		343	4
v. Young Australia (Neath) 8–10 July			7-0-14-1	23.4-11-45-4	11-1-61-0								4	1	1	2	179	5
			2-0-19-0	19-2-56-2	18.4-3-73-3								4	8	1	14	261	10
v. Warwickshire (Cardiff) 20–4 July	18-6-59-3		8-1-19-0	21-4-44-0	12.1-1-18-2					21-2-62-3			4	1	1	4	208	10
				6.1-0-26-0	6-1-11-0				1-0-3-0				4	2		22	37	1
v. Derbyshire (Derby) 27–31 July	25-4-100-1			43.3-9-120-6	24-2-100-0			16-4-77-0	2-0-21-0	16-3-63-3				11	4	2	392	10
	26-9-70-1			47-20-77-0				18.5-2-98-2	2-1-14-0	17-0-97-4	11-6-19-0		5	11	6		372	8
v. Essex (Swansea) 10–14 August	30-4-111-1			41.3-7-104-6	24-2-100-0			29-6-79-3		29-6-79-3			4	5	1	4	422	10
				26.5-8-87-4	24-4-79-4					11-2-49-1			2	1		10	244	10
v. Gloucestershire (Abergavenny) 23–6 August	24-3-122-3		7-0-20-1	26.5-6-90-3	10-0-66-1			18-3-100-1		18-3-81-2						8	461	10
				19-5-70-1	4-0-20-0			17-0-99-5		10-1-45-0	26.5-7-78-3		3	5		8	293	10
v. Leicestershire (Leicester) 29 August – 1 September	7-1-34-0			37-5-131-1				21-5-83-1			25-7-87-0			10		2	351	6
				18.3-1-96-2				8-1-39-1					4				285	4
v. Nottinghamshire (Cardiff) 7–11 September	10-2-49-1			18-3-62-1	21-4-92-2			19-7-62-1		15-3-45-1	16-2-46-1			9			319	6
				23.1-6-47-5	11-3-26-1			13-7-28-3		4-0-14-0			4	9			122	9B
v. Worcestershire (Worcester) 14–18 September				2-2-0-0				8-1-43-1		5-0-19-0		3-0-17-0	4	3		4	79	1
Bowler's average	590.4-144-1755-65 · 27.00	85.3-28-179-6 · 29.83	144.5-28-472-6 · 52.44	829.1-206-2289-63 · 36.33	389.5-102-1255-27 · 46.48	16-5-45-0 · –	32.1-2-109-1 · 109.00	303.3-51-1356-28 · 48.42	22-2-110-3 · 36.66	397.5-70-1402-44 · 31.86	233.5-58-681-14 · 48.64	3-0-17-0						

A N.R. Taylor retired hurt
B P.R. Pollard absent hurt

AXA EQUITY AND LAW LEAGUE – AVERAGES

BATTING

	M	Inns	NO	Runs	HS	Av	100s	50s	ct/st
R.C. Russell	12	10	4	280	76*	46.66	–	2	10/1
R.C. Williams	8	6	2	148	40	37.00	–	–	3
R.C.J. Williams	3	–	–	33	19	33.00	–	–	3/1
A. Symonds	15	15	3	391	69	30.07	–	1	6
M.W. Alleyne	15	15	3	352	70	29.33	–	1	5
M.A. Lynch	14	14	–	320	58	22.85	–	2	5
A.J. Wright	15	15	–	310	63	22.14	–	2	2
G.D. Hodgson	3	3	1	44	29	22.00	–	–	1
M.J. Cawdron	3	3	–	58	50	19.33	–	1	1
T.H.C. Hancock	5	4	–	58	32	14.50	–	–	2
R.I. Dawson	13	12	2	136	45	13.60	–	–	2
K.P. Sheeraz	3	3	1	26	14*	13.00	–	–	1
M.C.J. Ball	14	9	7	84	20	12.00	–	–	4
M.G.N. Windows	7	7	1	67	29	9.57	–	–	–
J. Lewis	3	1	1	5	5	5.00	–	–	–
J. Srinath	6	4	1	13	11	4.33	–	–	3
D.J.P. Boden	3	3	–	6	5	2.00	–	–	–
A.M. Smith	10	3	3	12	3	2.00	–	–	–

Two matches: K.E. Cooper did not bat
One match: R.J. Cunliffe 10; M. Davies did not bat

BOWLING

	Overs	Mds	Runs	Wkts	Av	Best	5/inn
A. Symonds	14	4	61	4	15.25	3-38	–
J. Srinath	43.5	4	213	11	19.36	3-27	–
M.A. Lynch	3	–	23	1	23.00	1-23	–
J. Lewis	22.3	4	94	4	23.50	3-27	–
R.C. Williams	53	5	361	11	32.81	4-51	–
M.W. Alleyne	92.1	5	475	14	33.92	5-28	1
D.J.P. Boden	18.1	1	103	3	34.33	3-34	–
A.M. Smith	74.4	7	347	9	38.55	2-23	–
K.P. Sheeraz	76	1	369	9	41.00	2-20	–
M.C.J. Ball	78	3	424	10	42.40	2-37	–
R.I. Dawson	5.2	–	51	1	51.00	1-19	–
K.E. Cooper	12	1	66	1	66.00	1-35	–
M.J. Cawdron	35	3	134	1	134.00	1-23	–
M. Davies	8	–	35	–	–	–	–
M.G.N. Windows	8	–	49	–	–	–	–

GLOUCESTERSHIRE CCC

BATTING (season averages summary)

	M	Inns	NO	Runs	HS	Av
A.J. Wright	18	34	4	1401	193	46.70
G.D. Hodgson		17	1	524	148	30.82
M.A. Lynch		29	2	1026	114	38.00
R.I. Dawson		16	0	355	101	23.66
M.W. Alleyne		31	3	1007	254*	33.56
A. Symonds		32	5	1438	141	55.30
R.C. Russell		24	5	778	87	43.22
J. Srinath		28	4	314	44	15.70
M.C.J. Ball		24	9	417	48	21.94
K.E. Cooper		5	4	36	32	9.00
A.M. Smith		11	7	37	22	4.11
M. Davies		7	4	77	22	25.66
K.P. Sheeraz		8	1	8	2	1.14
D.J.P. Boden		8	1	2	2	2.00
V. Pike		15	8	42	22	8.40
R.J. Cunliffe		13	3	412	190*	82.40
M.G.N. Windows		9	1	256	79*	22.91
T.H.C. Hancock		3	1	275	56	18.28
R.C. Williams		60	1	60	22	8.57
R.C.J. Williams		5	3	223	90	24.77
J. Lewis		9	3	3	3	1.00

BOWLING

	J. Srinath	A.M. Smith	M.C.J. Ball	K.E. Cooper	M.W. Alleyne	R.C. Williams	K.P. Sheeraz	J. Lewis	M. Davies	A. Symonds	D.J.P. Boden	V. Pike	Byes	Leg-byes	Wides	No-balls	Total	Wks
v. Surrey (The Oval)	26–5–83–3	26.4–11–60–3	5–1–9–0	20–7–22–2	13–4–35–1								1	7		20	217	10
27–30 April	33.3–4–137–4	31–6–90–3	46–2–128–2	24–4–65–0	13–2–42–0									9	2	18	475	10A
v. Somerset (Taunton)	26.3–3–81–3		38–6–87–0		33–9–89–1								3	12		12	478	10B
v. Nottinghamshire (Bristol)	22–8–34–4	25–7–72–2	38.1–11–97–2		12–2–40–0				30–10–86–4	4–0–8–0			4	5		4	300	8
11–15 May	14–3–37–0	16.2–6–51–4	19.7–49–5										6	1		8	142	10
v. Worcestershire (Gloucester)	21–9–35–4	21.1–6–68–4	1–0–1–0		25–16–36–2		33–3–107–1		1–1–0–0				6	1		4	172	10C
25–9 May	13–4–35–2	18.2–5–57–6	16–10–23–2		4–1–11–0				30–2–79–1				1	3			130	10
v. Sussex (Hove)	34–9–113–1	35–6–142–1	24–5–74–1		33–17–59–3		13–2–52–0							10	5	26	482	7D
v. Kent (Canterbury)	19–9–35–3	26–11–66–6	1–1–0–0		10–2–25–1				1–0–4–0				1	6		12	137	10
8–12 June	28.1–4–109–3		33–9–72–2		7–0–36–2				14–1–51–0				4	3	1	29	346	10
v. Hampshire (Bristol)	18–4–50–1	27–6–76–4			19–7–41–0							28–2–94–2	4	4		10	341	10
15–19 June	15–8–22–2	14–4–45–1										12–1–52–2		6		13	125	10
v. Oxford University (Oxford)			4.5–1–14–1	15–5–34–4	2–1–4–0, 12–3–27–2	12–3–26–1			19.2–8–36–0		22–2–73–2, 12–2–50–1		8	9		4	175	10
23–5 June			20.4–33–1, 32.7–112–1	11–7–6–3	13–2–46–0	20.3–7–44–3			8–3–28–0, 4–3–4–1		12–1–38–3, 13.4–5–26–1		4	7	2	10	191	10
v. Yorkshire (Middlesbrough)	24–5–63–6	24.2–4–80–3	13–3–33–2		11–6–21–2	22–2–83–0							11		1	20	340	10
29 June –3 July	9.3–3–34–4	12–1–52–0											4	7	1	10	145	10
v. Middlesex (Bristol)	34.4–14–78–6		27–5–95–0	28–7–92–3	23–5–88–1								1	4		10	441	10
v. Lancashire (Cheltenham)	20–4–62–1	22.1–6–66–2	7–1–15–1		17–8–31–2							19–7–49–1	4	4	1	6	231	10
20–4 July	22–4–53–5	22.3–6–60–5										1–1–0–0		3	1	6	117	10
v. Essex (Cheltenham)	13–4–60–1	23.4–7–70–7	12–2–31–1		10–2–30–1	16–4–46–0				10–5–13–0			4	7	3	30	244	10
27–31 July	17.5–2–53–4	21.2–1–55–1	39–8–129–3		22–2–82–1	23–9–94–1							1	10		36	437	10
v. West Indians (Bristol)		11.2–1–57–3	30.4–10–61–2		11–2–40–0, 16–3–64–2	10–1–68–1	16.1–4–67–6, 20–5–44–5			3–0–13–1			7	13	1	2	193	10
5–7 August					13.5–3–42–1, 15–3–41–2		22–3–63–2, 17.2–59–2						8	13	2	2	321	10
v. Northamptonshire (Northampton) 10–14 August	25–5–81–3	25.5–83–3	16–5–49–3							1–0–2–0		20–1–69–1	14	6	5	16	312	9
v. Derbyshire (Bristol)	26.3–6–61–3	21–10–56–0	23–10–35–1		23–5–81–2		22–6–89–3			5–3–12–0		18–3–72–3, 49–16–107–0		6	3		463	10
17–21 August	31–5–120–3		22.2–5–52–3				23–3–103–1, 14–3–72–1					8–1–21–1	13	13	5	30	334	10
v. Glamorgan (Abergavenny)	15–9–25–5	33.9–54–4	33–9–54–4		17–5–59–0		18–3–77–1	9.3–1–31–1		15–1–52–0		9.3–1–31–1	13	13	3	6	104	10E
23–6 August	20–6–74–4, 21–3–76–9	26–8–74–0	26–8–74–0		12–3–59–0		2–0–4–0					31–6–97–0	6	8	2	10	471	10
v. Warwickshire (Edgbaston) 29 August – 1 September	19–6–50–3	11–4–24–1	5–0–24–0		18–7–51–2		12–1–76–1	18.2–6–64–4, 12–0–7–0						1	1	26	278	10
v. Durham (Bristol) 7–11 September		2–0–12–0	4–0–9–0		12–5–28–1		9–1–47–1	15–4–34–4, 24–1–87–4							8	4	11	0
v. Leicestershire (Leicester) 14–18 September			20.2–0–65–5	5–2–9–1	5–0–20–0		4–0–28–0	9–1–17–0						3	2	4	172	7
Bowler's average	568.4–146–1661–87 19.09	415.3–104–1275–59 21.61	577.2–140–1481–42 35.26	103–32–228–13 17.53	421.5–125–1228–29 42.34	103.3–26–361–6 60.16	225.1–36–888–24 37.00	67.4–12–209–12 17.41	107.2–28–288–6 48.00	38–9–100–1 100.00	59.4–10–187–7 26.71	195.3–39–592–11 53.81					236 57	10F 1

A M.A. Lynch 2–0–3–0
B R.I. Dawson 7–4–5–0
C R.I. Dawson 6–2–18–0
D R.I. Dawson 2–0–5–0
E T.H. Hancock 2–0–15–0
F T.H. Hancock 3–1–5–0

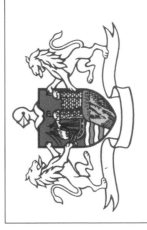

AXA EQUITY AND LAW LEAGUE – AVERAGES

BATTING	M	Inns	NO	Runs	HS	Av	100s	50s	ct/st
J.S. Laney	4	4	–	161	53	40.25	–	1	–
K.D. James	12	9	4	173	62*	34.60	–	1	3
R.S.M. Morris	13	13	–	422	87	32.46	–	2	3
A.N. Aymes	16	13	6	221	41	31.57	–	–	23
M. Keech	12	12	–	348	98	29.00	–	1	4
M.C.J. Nicholas	11	11	1	264	66	26.40	–	1	2
R.A. Smith	8	8	–	211	115	26.37	1	–	2
H.H. Streak	8	8	5	154	32*	25.66	–	–	1
G.W. White	11	11	2	222	59	24.66	–	1	5
P.R. Whitaker	11	11	1	224	97	22.40	–	2	4
R.J. Maru	8	3	2	16	9*	16.00	–	–	1
J.P. Stephenson	11	10	–	140	37	14.00	–	–	3
V.P. Terry	8	8	–	95	33	11.87	–	–	2
S.D. Udal	14	11	4	59	15*	8.42	–	–	1
M.J. Thursfield	6	3	1	12	7	6.00	–	–	–
C.A. Connor	12	5	1	18	8	4.50	–	–	–

Two matches: J.N.B. Bovill 0 (ct 1); N.G. Cowans 2*

BOWLING	Overs	Mds	Runs	Wkts	Av	Best	5/inn
C.A. Connor	90	–	463	16	28.93	2-23	–
P.R. Whitaker	10	–	59	2	29.50	2-32	–
H.H. Streak	112	2	656	22	29.81	4-56	–
K.D. James	86	6	393	13	30.23	4-35	–
R.J. Maru	63.3	7	332	7	47.42	2-56	–
J.P. Stephenson	65.3	2	398	8	49.75	2-31	–
S.D. Udal	95	9	537	9	59.66	2-31	–
J.N.B. Bovill	11	–	66	1	66.00	1-36	–
M.J. Thursfield	44	3	224	3	74.66	2-26	–
M. Keech	4	–	33	–	–	–	–
M.C.J. Nicholas	10	–	64	–	–	–	–
N.G. Cowans	14	–	76	–	–	–	–

HAMPSHIRE CCC — BATTING (season averages)

	M	Inns	NO	Runs	HS	Av
J.P. Stephenson	17	30	4	892	127	34.30
V.P. Terry		35	2	1012	170	30.66
R.S.M. Morris	10	18	1	368	47	20.44
R.A. Smith	12	15	1	812	172	58.00
M.C.J. Nicholas	15	33	3	1210	147	40.33
G.W. White	15	24	2	554	62	25.18
A.N. Aymes		33	9	720	62*	30.00
S.D. Udal	20	29	4	512	85	20.48
H.H. Streak	18	28	3	378	69	15.12
C.A. Connor	19	27	6	336	33	16.00
J.N.B. Bovill		10	5	90	31	18.00
P.R. Whitaker	17	21	1	624	119	29.71
D.P.J. Flint	13	3	2	17	17*	15.33
M.J. Thursfield		3	1	46	30	
K.D. James	12	21	3	341	53	18.94
R.R. Dibden	5	7	5	0	0*	0.00
J.S. Laney	9	17	1	470	73	29.37
R.J. Maru	2	3	1	8	7	4.00
T.C. Middleton	2	5	1	48	31	12.00
M. Keech	2	4	–	100	41	25.00

(The full match-by-match batting scores for each fixture — v Durham, Middlesex, Oxford University, Kent, Sussex, Glamorgan, Leicestershire, Gloucestershire, Worcestershire, Derbyshire, Yorkshire, Northamptonshire, Young Australia, Essex, Warwickshire, West Indians, Lancashire, Nottinghamshire, Somerset, Surrey — together with byes, leg-byes, wides, no-balls, totals, wickets, results and points — are recorded in the detailed grids alongside these averages.)

BOWLING

	C.A. Connor	H.H. Streak	J.N.B. Bovill	S.D. Udal	J.P. Stephenson	M. Keech	R.J. Maru	M.J. Thursfield	D.P.J. Flint	P.R. Whitaker	K.D. James	R.R. Dibden	Byes	Leg-byes	Wides	No-balls	Total	Wkts
v. Durham (Stockton)	15-3-39-1	15-4-45-1	15.2-8-39-6	7-3-19-0	9-2-27-1								1	7	5	14	177	10
27–30 April	17-2-66-3	16-2-46-1	16.5-8-29-6	22-3-68-0	9-2-31-0									8	4	19	248	10
v. Middlesex (Lord's)	22-8-44-3	7-0-37-0	10-1-40-0	4-1-8-0	18-4-51-7									9	3	6	189	10
4–8 May	30-3-113-2	26-6-80-1	20.2-3-64-2	6-1-25-0	19-1-90-1								7	10	1	6	427	6A
v. Oxford University (Oxford)		16.4-1-58-0	20-1-73-1	29-5-51-0				21-6-48-0	18-5-59-0	6-2-15-0				13		6	317	1
11–13 May																		
v. Kent (Southampton)	13.3-3-52-2	10-3-31-2	12-2-62-1	14-7-21-2	13-4-37-2									4		18	207	10
18–22 May	13.2-2-42-1	14-3-46-0	15-2-59-2	19-2-81-5	15-1-55-2									5		14	288	10
v. Sussex (Portsmouth)	25-6-64-1	10.3-3-22-2	21-5-60-3		14-3-45-4								1	4		14	196	10
25–9 May	15.5-4-43-3	17-4-81-4	13-3-43-0		19-3-64-3									1		9	232	10
v. Glamorgan (Cardiff)	12-2-60-2	13-5-29-3	18-6-51-3	3-1-5-0	8.4-1-27-2								1	5		16	174	10
1–5 June	13-2-44-6	14.1-4-41-3	10-4-24-1	21-8-41-2	12-5-27-2									5	1	14	204	10
v. Leicestershire (Basingstoke)	17-4-65-2	9.3-1-44-4		6-3-5-0	4-1-19-0								1	6		14	253	10
7–10 June			14-3-48-0	15-1-46-2	6-2-7-0									7	1	16	144	9
v. Gloucestershire (Bristol)	25-9-83-4	24-6-58-1	26-8-57-0	34-10-65-6	4-1-19-0								2	4		15	266	10
15–19 June	15-3-42-1			18.3-1-66-2	18-5-44-1								4	2		2	180	6B
v. Worcestershire (Southampton)	13-2-26-1	18-2-74-2	15-2-66-4	19-3-70-2	3-0-10-0			19-5-59-1	9-4-12-0	2-0-6-0	12-1-51-0		7	7		10	289	10
22–6 June		14-2-61-1	25-6-99-1	46.3-13-144-5				6-0-23-0	23-7-52-2		4-0-28-1		4	3	1	8	413	10
v. Derbyshire (Derby)	19-4-89-2	24.2-7-57-3		18-4-36-0	13-0-66-1						17-2-60-2	32-9-87-0		1		12	157	4
29 June – 3 July	13-1-54-0	9-2-43-1		0.3-0-5-0	12-2-51-3						15-4-35-1			9	7	4	295	8
v. Yorkshire (Southampton)	36-9-107-2	13-3-55-2		36-8-96-1	17-0-66-1						15.1-2-38-6	8-1-36-2	9	4	14	14	431	7
6–10 July	15.1-1-52-1	21-7-47-2		21-1-79-3	10-2-44-0						14-6-20-1		1	10	1	16	265	8
v. Northamptonshire (Northampton) 20–4 July	13-3-47-2	22-1-70-1		31-6-107-3	12-1-45-0		18-6-41-1				20-7-68-2			4		4	321	10
	26-8-74-2			44-13-127-3			31.5-14-74-2				9-3-25-1		9	8		6	365	7
v. Young Australia (Southampton) 28–31 July	23-3-121-2			26-3-116-2							20-7-98-0	25.3-10-62-2	7			12	527	7
				3-2-5-0								2.4-0-16-0		10	3		21	
v. Essex (Colchester)	28-5-124-1	27-5-88-0		55-8-183-2	16-2-68-1					1-0-5-0	15-4-49-0	23-0-132-2	4			10	662	7
3–7 August						10.3-0-43-1				1-0-4-1			1	8	2		535	8C
v. Warwickshire (Southampton)	40-10-121-5	35-12-98-1		26-4-83-1	23-4-99-0	10-0-55-1					16-1-72-0			14	4	10	696	6
10–14 August													11			16		
v. West Indians (Southampton)	18-0-116-1	18-4-53-0			20-0-107-0			26-2-108-3			26-1-137-1	12-0-95-0		9		12	293	10
16–18 August														9		2	214	5
v. Lancashire (Portsmouth)	27-10-68-1	25.2-4-77-3		22-9-46-3	19-5-48-1		33-19-38-3				15-4-45-2		1	5			154	10
24–8 August	11-3-32-0	13-5-36-2		7-0-51-0	14-5-57-1		23-8-46-3				6.1-1-28-2			9	2		172	10
v. Nottinghamshire (Trent Bridge)	23.3-4-79-5	6-3-9-1		34-10-85-5	1-0-1-0						4-1-9-0		4			14	333	0
29 August – 1 September		12-4-25-1		28.5-5-85-6	24-6-74-3						15-1-61-0		4	5	1		0	0
v. Somerset (Southampton)	8-1-35-0	22.4-7-76-2		7-1-30-0									3	5			71	2
7–11 September		8.1-0-28-2											3	2	1		175	2
v. Surrey (The Oval)	9-1-52-1	9-1-30-1		5-0-15-0	9.2-1-56-0						3-1-17-0							
14–18 September																		
Bowler's average	556.2-116-1954-57 34.28	516.4-118-1629-53 30.73	251.1-62-814-30 27.13	628.2-136-1864-55 33.89	358-62-1316-36 36.55	20.3-0-98-2 49.00	105.5-47-199-9 22.11	72-13-238-4 59.50	50-16-123-2 61.50	10-2-30-1 30.00	233.2-51-857-19 45.10	103.1-20-428-6 71.33						

A G.W. White 3-0-22-0. M.C.J. Nicholas 5-0-16-0.
B G.W. White 1-1-0-0.
C M.C.J. Nicholas 2-0-10-0.

KENT CCC

BATTING

	v. Northamptonshire (Canterbury) 27-30 April		v. Sussex (Hove) 4-8 May		v. Leicestershire (Canterbury) 11-15 May		v. Hampshire (Southampton) 18-22 May		v. Glamorgan (Tunbridge Wells) 24-7 May		v. Durham (Chester-le-Street) 1-5 June		v. Gloucestershire (Canterbury) 8-12 June		v. Yorkshire (Leeds) 15-19 June		v. Nottinghamshire (Trent Bridge) 22-6 June		v. Cambridge University (Folkestone) 1-3 July		v. Derbyshire (Maidstone) 5-8 July		v. West Indians (Canterbury) 19-21 July		M	Inns	NO	Runs	HS	Av
T.R. Ward	76	114*	13	8	0		0	8	98	31	4		6	17	65	29	23	59			21	19	3	0	18	32	1	932	114*	30.06
M.R. Benson	42	13	45	17	192		13	47	14	31	10		0	102			16	–			19	92			13	21	–	702	192	33.42
M.J. Walker	34	13	0	1	5		9	53	6	24	6	–							2	0*					9	14	1	162	53	12.46
P.A. de Silva	2	13	117	0	57		28	0	135	5	83		3	4	52	115	225	16			255	116	18	102	16	30	–	1781	255	59.36
N.R. Taylor	30	6	13	5	127		24	87	13*						10	15		99*			5	8			7	12	2	421	127	42.10
M.V. Fleming	61	5	9	27							22		36*	14	10	15			100				8	4	10	16	1	447	100	29.80
M.A. Ealham	28	3	88	77*	38		23	8	58	72	21		33	27	1	36	121	–			35	1	5	26	18	31	1	891	121	29.70
S.A. Marsh	37	23	24	59	41				13	24	47		8	40	22	29					3	57*	3	12	16	28	3	688	67*	27.52
M.M. Patel	3	2	10	1	56		17	28	21*	0	32		26	0	14*	19	13	–	4	6	8	13	5	12*	17	28	6	321	56	14.59
D.W. Headley	1	0	19	0	1*		0	5	2	29*			0	0*	13	5					7	15	0*	17	14	23	5	253	54	14.05
M.J. McCague	0*	7			35		36*	17	1	23	15*		4	18	0	11*	59	–					0*	4	14	25	5	344	59	18.10
T.N. Wren			8*	23											0	0	4*	–			0*	3*	0	4	7	11	4	60	23	8.57
S. Herzberg					0	–							0	17											3	4	1	61	18	8.71
S.C. Willis					17	1											53	–	82	–					3	4	–	153	82	38.25
A.P. Igglesden					18	15*	2	5*											–	–	10	6			7	9	4	62	18	12.40
G.R. Cowdrey									19				2	71			0	53*	41	48	137	0	20	43	13	22	1	930	137	44.28
D.P. Fulton															21	59	2	52	116	8*			5	89	8	16	1	502	116	33.46
N.J. Llong															19	30			3	19					9	16	–	538	118	33.62
J.B.D. Thompson																			40*	13*			4	5	3	6	2	83	40*	20.75
E.J. Stanford																									2	2	1	4	4	4.00
Byes	8	4	1							3			1	4			4				6	3	4	1						
Leg-byes	16	11	8	1	11		4	5	1	4	7		4	7	7	1	4	7			7	7	3	4						
Wides		1	2	5	4				1	4	4			1				1			2	6	2							
No-balls	14	4	6	8			18	14	4	2	12	29	12	4	12	6		6			10	4	16	10						
Total	352	215	361	230	575		207	288	369	253	272	0	137	346	234	365	533	287	409	108	534	339	95	331						
Wickets	10	10	10	10	10		10	10	9†	8	10	0	10	10	10	10	10	3	7	3	10	9	10	10						
Result		L		L	W		W		D		W		L		L		L		W		D		L							
Points		6		8	24		21		7		18		4		7		7		20		6		2							

BATTING

	v. Worcestershire (Worcester) 27-31 July		v. Surrey (Canterbury) 3-7 August		v. Somerset (Taunton) 10-14 August		v. Middlesex (Lord's) 17-21 August		v. Essex (Canterbury) 24-8 August		v. Lancashire (Old Trafford) 7-11 September		v. Warwickshire (Canterbury) 14-18 September		M	Inns	NO	Runs	HS	Av
T.R. Ward	12	19	101	16	5	33	59	0	8	64	–	–	8	13	18	32	1	932	114*	30.06
M.R. Benson			2	18					0	12	–	–	2	15	13	21	–	702	192	33.42
M.J. Walker													7	2	9	14	1	162	53	12.46
P.A. de Silva	11	5	0	89	42	0	88	60	45	95					16	30	–	1781	255	59.36
N.R. Taylor															7	12	2	421	127	42.10
M.V. Fleming	0	10	47	0	5	7	4	13	61	3			37	35	10	16	1	447	100	29.80
M.A. Ealham	0	10	47	0	5	7	4	30	4	30	–	–	36	33	18	31	1	891	121	29.70
S.A. Marsh	1	67*	57	6	10	3	24	0	36*	12	–	–	15	15	16	28	3	688	67*	27.52
M.M. Patel			26	–			0*	3	2	0*			0*	0	17	28	6	321	56	14.59
D.W. Headley	54	8	47*	1*	3	0	10	37	6	12	–	–			14	23	5	253	54	14.05
M.J. McCague	8	23					11	19	6	0			12	0*	14	25	6	344	59	18.10
T.N. Wren	13	5													7	11	4	60	23	8.57
S. Herzberg			5	4*	3	18	3	11*							5	9	2	61	18	8.71
S.C. Willis															3	4	–	153	82	38.25
A.P. Igglesden					6*	0*					–	–			7	9	4	62	18	12.40
G.R. Cowdrey	94	77	28	98	52	9	14	13	0	8	–	–	103	–	13	22	1	930	137	44.28
D.P. Fulton	59	21	0	19	16	14	16	5							8	16	1	502	116	33.46
N.J. Llong	44	20	59	118	100	24	14	38	4	43	–	–	2	1	9	16	–	538	118	33.62
J.B.D. Thompson					17	4									3	6	2	83	40*	20.75
E.J. Stanford	0*	4													2	2	1	4	4	4.00
Byes	2	5	5	3			4	6	4	1			8	1						
Leg-byes	3	2	5	4	2	3	13	5	1	2			2	6						
Wides			4		2				1				1							
No-balls	18	20	24	4	8		2	2					6	2						
Total	320	286	410	380	271	119	265	206	178	282			239	124						
Wickets	10	10	10	8	10	10	10	10	10	8‡			10	7						
Result		L		D		L		L		L		D		L						
Points		7		5		3		4		3		3		3						

AXA EQUITY AND LAW LEAGUE – AVERAGES

BATTING

	M	Inns	NO	Runs	HS	Av	100s	50s	ct/st
G.R. Cowdrey	15	14	3	593	105*	53.90	2	2	7
M.A. Ealham	15	13	–	369	112	36.90	1	1	4
P.A. de Silva	15	15	2	473	124	36.38	2	–	3
T.R. Ward	16	16	1	483	123	32.20	1	3	5
M.R. Benson	9	9	–	255	92	28.33	–	2	2
N.R. Taylor	2	2	–	47	34	23.50	–	–	–
M.V. Fleming	16	16	1	305	70	20.33	–	2	4
N.J. Llong	12	10	2	132	51	16.50	–	1	2
S.A. Marsh	14	10	4	92	22*	15.33	–	–	23/1
M.J. Walker	9	8	2	77	24*	12.83	–	–	2
S.C. Willis	2	2	–	25	13	12.50	–	–	2
M.J. McCague	14	8	3	51	14	10.20	–	–	2
A.P. Igglesden	11	5	1	16	13	8.00	–	–	3
D.P. Fulton	4	4	–	24	11	6.00	–	–	1
D.W. Headley	14	3	1	10	6*	5.00	–	–	3
T.N. Wren	6	3	3	10	4*	–	–	–	–

Two matches: J.B.D. Thompson 0* (ct 1)

BOWLING

	Overs	Mds	Runs	Wkts	Av	Best	5/inn
D.W. Headley	107	3	533	24	22.20	6-42	1
M.J. McCague	95.3	2	483	21	23.94	5-40	1
M.A. Ealham	100.3	7	433	17	25.47	4-21	–
A.P. Igglesden	76	9	270	10	27.00	3-11	–
M.V. Fleming	88	3	496	15	33.06	2-14	–
T.N. Wren	38	1	178	5	35.60	3-20	–
N.J. Llong	11	–	74	2	37.00	2-7	–
P.A. de Silva	57	1	297	8	37.12	4-28	–
J.B.D. Thompson	13	–	79	2	39.50	2-27	–
G.R. Cowdrey	1	–	7	–	–	–	–

BOWLING

Kent first-class bowling, 1995. Analyses are given as overs–maidens–runs–wickets; where a bowler sent down two innings in a match the figures are shown on successive lines (here separated by " / ").

Match	M.J. McCague	D.W. Headley	M.V. Fleming	M.A. Ealham	M.M. Patel	P.A. de Silva	T.N. Wren	S. Herzberg	A.P. Igglesden	N.J. Llong	J.B.D. Thompson	E.J. Stanford	Byes	Leg-byes	Wides	No-balls	Total	Wkts
v. Northamptonshire (Canterbury) 27–30 April	22–2–105–2		23–5–87–0	33–10–114–3	43–6–122–2								11	10	18	14	561	8
v. Sussex (Hove) 4–8 May		25–4–69–2	7–1–23–1 / 10–2–23–0	21–4–58–2 / 4–0–16–0	2.3–1–3–1 / 29.2–7–79–3	3–0–4–0 / 2–0–12–0	15–1–62–2 / 22–3–68–2						5 / 6	15 / 8	1 / 1	2 / 10	7 / 323	1 / 10
v. Leicestershire (Canterbury) 11–15 May	20–3–80–4 / 7–0–22–2	26.4–9–58–7 / 20–5–65–2		6–1–21–0	34–10–102–1 / 22.5–3–79–1	16–1–62–0							3 / 1	6 / 6		4 / 4	343 / 303	10 / 10
v. Hampshire (Southampton) 18–22 May	16–4–47–5	9–2–28–0 / 10–2–34–1		5–3–3–0 / 10–4–15–1	19–3–59–3 / 30–9–62–2	16.5–4–42–1 / 4–1–5–1		13–2–45–1 / 15.4–4–33–5	11.2–2–40–2 / 14–3–47–2				5	9	1		151 / 137	10 / 10
v. Glamorgan (Tunbridge Wells) 24–7 May	31–8–70–2	22.4–3–64–3 / 21.3–4–85–0		14–5–20–0 / 5–1–15–0	37–9–94–3 / 21–2–99–5	1–0–6–0			16–2–67–2 / 3–0–22–0				5 / 4	17 / 11	1		319 / 352	10 / 8
v. Durham (Chester-le-Street) 1–5 June	20–2–64–2 / 16–1–83–0	9–0–44–1			27–3–100–0 / 26–7–71–2								4			4	269 / 72	8 / 8
v. Gloucestershire (Canterbury) 8–12 June	16–4–29–3 / 25–5–68–5	19.2–4–32–5 / 25.1–8–68–5	4–1–10–0	8–1–16–1 / 10–3–30–0	18.5–6–63–1 / 8.2–2–31–0	8–2–24–0 / 5–1–15–0	28–5–93–4 / 9–2–37–1	8–0–31–0 / 7–1–56–0					4 / 6	4 / 8	2	4 / 2	85 / 321	0A / 10
v. Yorkshire (Leeds) 15–19 June	8–3–26–1 / 32–7–77–2	8–3–36–1	9–0–39–1 / 16–3–45–0	12–2–45–3 / 26–7–109–0		27–7–59–0 / 4–0–30–0	27–4–75–1						6	9	2	8	266 / 462	10 / 8
v. Nottinghamshire (Trent Bridge) 22–6 June	9–2–27–1 / 30–3–122–2	8–1–36–0		4–1–22–0 / 22–6–78–3	48.3–14–137–3 / 16.3–0–107–1		12–1–67–0 / 10–4–23–2						6	9	2		140 / 491	7 / 2
v. Cambridge University (Folkestone) 1–3 July	10–0–53–2			8–0–51–2	25–14–43–4 / 36.2–14–74–6		4–3–3–1 / 29.4–4–148–5		18–9–27–3 / 11–2–35–1	1–0–4–0 / 8–0–37–0	8–3–10–2	10.5–2–33–1 / 16–5–42–0	4 / 14	16 / 11	4		331 / 142	9 / 7
v. Derbyshire (Maidstone) 5–8 July	17–2–80–1 / 8–0–50–1			21–5–70–1 / 3–0–4–0	27–6–84–0 / 12–4–22–1	20–3–68–1 / 6–2–9–0	7–0–24–2		22–6–80–1 / 6–0–24–0		11–1–72–2 / 7–3–23–2		1 / 3	11 / 14			207 / 546	10 / 10
v. West Indians (Canterbury) 19–21 July	16.4–7–64–2 / 6–1–29–1		15–0–41–1	17–4–37–3	20–5–43–0 / 2.3–0–13–0	1–0–4–0 / 1–0–3–0	16–1–67–1 / 3–0–17–1						2 / 6	8 / 5	1 / 2	4 / 12	168 / 337	3B / 4
v. Worcestershire (Worcester) 27–31 July	19–4–74–3 / 7–2–24–2	20–5–53–3 / 18–7–51–1		18.2–5–48–3 / 12–0–43–0	59.5–10–206–6 / 31–8–93–3	16–5–39–1 / 27–1–71–0	13–2–57–0 / 10–1–44–1	30–6–92–2 / 8–0–32–1		4–1–12–0 / 11–3–29–0		14–2–49–0 / 37–10–96–2	19	7 / 7	3		92 / 332	4 / 10
v. Surrey (Canterbury) 3–7 August		26–6–76–0 / 26–7–67–2		32–9–71–2 / 5–0–28–0		11–1–31–0 / 16–4–40–0		18–5–51–0	26–2–92–5 / 4–0–21–2		12–1–52–0		4 / 1	14 / 3		4 / 11	559 / 252	7 / 7
v. Somerset (Taunton) 10–14 August		3–0–12–0	4–0–12–0	15–6–32–2		1–0–8–0			1.4–0–12–0	1.4–0–12–0			1	3	4	8	338 / 53	10 / 0
v. Middlesex (Lord's) 17–21 August	32–8–81–4 / 7–1–17–0	20–5–74–2		23–5–63–1 / 5–2–13–1	29.5–9–87–2 / 21–2–78–4	13–2–35–0		16–3–61–0	26–2–92–5 / 4–0–21–2	12–0–57–1	12–1–52–0	37–10–96–2	3 / 2	6 / 3	3	10 / 2	410 / 201	10 / 10
v. Essex (Canterbury) 24–8 August	31.4–8–91–2	11.4–3–32–4 / 35–10–95–2	26–5–93–3	14–2–43–0	37–11–113–2	5–0–30–0							4	3	1	14	472	10
v. Lancashire (Old Trafford) 7–11 September	18–2–74–1	13–3–32–0	4–0–12–0	11–5–23–1	39–10–109–4			13–2–30–1	13–2–30–1	20–5–47–0		77.5–19–220–3	10	6	3	8	269	8
v. Warwickshire (Canterbury) 14–18 September	18–2–74–1	13–2–63–0	13–2–63–0	20–4–63–1	29–7–95–1				27–5–78–2	14–2–75–0			11	9	1	4	468	6
Bowler's average	424.2–79–1457–50 — 29.14	430.5–101–1276–44 — 29.00	127–19–436–6 — 72.66	384.2–95–1151–30 — 38.36	753.2–182–2268–61 — 37.18	215–36–641–5 — 128.20	205.4–31–785–23 — 34.13	115.4–21–401–9 — 44.55	171.2–37–563–21 — 26.80	71.4–11–273–3 — 91.00	38–8–157–6 — 26.16	77.5–19–220–3 — 73.33						

A T.R. Ward 1.5–0–36–0. G.R. Cowdrey 2–0–36–0.

B G.R. Cowdrey 1–0–10–0. T.R. Ward 2–0–7–0. S.A. Marsh 2–1–8–0.

AXA EQUITY AND LAW LEAGUE – AVERAGES

BATTING

BATTING	M	Inns	NO	Runs	HS	Av	100s	50s	ct/st
N.H. Fairbrother	14	13	4	412	99*	45.77	–	3	3
I.D. Austin	15	11	8	137	36*	45.66	–	–	5
G.D. Lloyd	17	15	5	432	88*	43.20	–	4	3
J.E.R. Gallian	14	13	1	385	62	32.08	–	3	5
M.A. Atherton	14	13	1	245	53	30.62	–	1	3
S.P. Titchard	6	6	–	168	53	28.00	–	1	–
J.P. Crawley	14	13	–	362	75	27.84	–	3	1
W.K. Hegg	16	10	4	123	29*	20.50	–	–	21/1
N.J. Speak	9	8	–	159	36	19.87	–	1	1
A. Flintoff	2	2	–	34	22	17.00	–	–	1
M. Watkinson	15	12	3	145	26	16.11	–	–	7
Wasim Akram	15	12	2	159	32	15.90	–	1	4
G. Yates	13	6	3	40	24*	13.33	–	–	1
G. Chapple	13	6	6	14	8	7.00	–	–	–
P.J. Martin	11	3	1	3	2	1.50	–	–	–

Four matches: G. Keedy did not bat
Two matches: R.C. Green did not bat

BOWLING

BOWLING	Overs	Mds	Runs	Wkts	Av	Best	5/inn
Wasim Akram	112.5	7	415	29	14.31	4-16	–
J.E.R. Gallian	25.5	1	150	8	18.75	2-11	–
R.C. Green	13	–	62	3	20.66	3-38	–
I.D. Austin	108.3	9	462	18	25.66	3-30	–
P.J. Martin	74	6	314	12	26.16	4-29	–
G. Chapple	87.2	2	400	15	26.66	3-36	–
G. Yates	79.2	3	415	15	27.66	4-40	–
M. Watkinson	94.5	4	449	16	28.00	2-29	–
N.H. Fairbrother	6	–	33	1	33.00	1-33	–
G. Keedy	24	–	128	1	128.00	1-40	–

LANCASHIRE CCC — BATTING (season summary)

BATTING	M	Inns	NO	Runs	HS	Av
M.A. Atherton	12	19	1	835	155*	46.38
N.J. Speak	17	30	2	919	116	32.82
J.P. Crawley	15	25	1	1277	182	53.20
N.H. Fairbrother	14	23	3	602	132	30.10
G.D. Lloyd	14	23	2	584	117	27.80
M. Watkinson	15	25	2	731	161	31.78
I.D. Austin	13	22	4	412	80*	22.88
W.K. Hegg	18	28	4	669	101	27.87
G. Yates	9	13	2	248	71	23.14
P.J. Martin	10	11	2	162	42*	27.55
G. Keedy	14	17	12	73	15*	14.60
J.E.R. Gallian	15	28	3	1088	158	43.52
S.P. Titchard	13	24	2	697	130	31.68
G. Chapple	14	22	6	275	58	19.64
Wasim Akram	14	20	1	423	61	22.26
D.J. Shadford	2	2	–	7	7	3.50
A. Flintoff	2	1	–	7	7	—
R.J. Green	1	1	–	1	1	1.00

BOWLING

Match	P.J. Martin	I.D. Austin	M. Watkinson	G. Keedy	G. Yates	N.J. Speak	J.E.R. Gallian	Wasim Akram	C. Chapple	M.A. Atherton	D.J. Shadford	N.H. Fairbrother	A. Flintoff	R.J. Green	Total	Wkts
v. Cambridge University (Cambridge) 18–20 April	14-5-36-1 / 7-0-23-1	17-8-36-1 / 5-3-2-0	16-6-27-3 / 10-4-19-0	16-7-21-1 / 16-3-57-1	20-9-37-2 / 10-3-19-0										168 / 144	8 / 2
v. Yorkshire (Leeds) 27 April – 1 May	22-5-75-1	27-7-70-1	20-5-86-2	13-2-56-0	20-2-81-2 / 18-4-88-1	3-0-20-0	10-3-47-1 / 9-2-56-2								417 / 288	7 / 6
v. Durham (Old Trafford) 4–8 May	18-6-47-2		17-3-50-1 / 17-2-70-1	15-3-41-1 / 25-2-85-1			1-0-1-0 / 7-1-27-1	20.3-8-40-5 / 32-6-112-2	19-6-43-1 / 24.4-8-68-2						249 / 432	10 / 10
v. Warwickshire (Old Trafford) 11–15 May	17.5-3-68-4 / 19.3-4-51-4		36-6-115-4 / 21-9-45-1	28-11-65-3 / 24-7-53-2	15-1-85-0			16-3-47-2 / 20-7-65-0	11-0-31-0 / 18-3-46-3	1-0-1-0					262 / 297	10 / 10
v. Middlesex (Lord's) 18–22 May	16-9-10-1 / 9.3-3-31-3		32-10-55-1	27-9-52-2			10.5-3-24-2 / 7-1-20-1	19-4-35-6	8-4-14-1						88 / 112	10 / 10
v. Nottinghamshire (Liverpool) 25–9 May		29-9-63-3	15-3-55-1	19.5-5-61-3			3-0-11-0	12-6-74-3	12-1-35-0						292	10
v. Glamorgan (Old Trafford) 8–12 June		26-3-81-1	13-5-27-1 / 31.1-7-103-3	28-6-106-1			5-1-16-0	9-1-24-0 / 25-6-77-4	8-3-25-1 / 18-3-85-0						172 / 475	10 / 8
v. Worcestershire (Worcester) 15–19 June		5-3-7-1	18-4-51-4 / 23.4-2-102-1	12-0-74-2	15-1-85-0		17-1-77-1	13.4-2-42-0 / 30-7-79-3	12-4-35-0 / 32-2-124-4						233 / 487	9[A] / 7
v. Essex (Old Trafford) 22–6 June		18.4-5-50-2	19-6-39-3	13-5-24-2 / 26-3-82-0	8-2-36-0 / 6-0-24-1		8-1-24-1 / 4-0-12-0	25-5-86-4 / 22-4-79-2	9-2-26-0		7-1-19-0 / 11-1-36-1				248 / 350	9 / 10
v. Northamptonshire (Old Trafford) 6–10 July		26-10-50-4 / 5-0-19-0	28.5-13-91-6 / 34-13-62-4	18-6-35-1 / 10-4-20-2				26-4-99-3 / 22.5-7-73-7	10-4-18-0 / 14-5-31-0						290 / 194	10 / 10
v. Gloucestershire (Cheltenham) 20–4 July		7-3-14-3	18-3-60-1 / 19-3-64-1	18-4-61-0				23.5-6-58-5	7-3-12-0			0.5-0-14-0			265 / 84	10 / –
v. Somerset (Taunton) 27–31 July		16-6-32-2	5-1-20-0	6-2-16-0 / 17.1-6-35-4	8-0-24-0 / 14-3-67-4		3-0-13-0	14-1-58-2 / 9.1-0-37-1	7-1-25-1 / 12-2-46-1						161 / 273	10 / 10
v. Sussex (Lytham) 3–7 August		15-7-16-1 / 13-9-13-2	40.2-10-140-7	22-6-81-2		1-0-6-0	2-2-0-0	14-4-26-1 / 16-3-34-3							317 / 193	10 / 10
v. Leicestershire (Leicester) 10–14 August	11-3-34-0 / 15-4-47-2	17-7-39-2	24-5-82-3	35.5-5-102-1 / 16-4-45-2			4-0-12-0	20-4-72-6							235 / 282	10 / 10
v. Yorkshire (Old Trafford) 17–21 August		21-1-79-2 / 17-3-60-0	30-7-117-3	19-8-36-1	17-9-33-1		4-0-11-1	27-5-93-6 / 32-3-104-3	27-5-87-1 / 7-1-32-0						505 / 96	10 / 1
v. Hampshire (Portsmouth) 24–8 August	5-2-10-0 / 28-12-43-2	4-0-9-0	4-0-17-0	18-8-43-0			4-4-28-0	16-4-52-7 / 27.1-4-104-3	22-4-73-3 / 16-4-44-4				4-0-15-0 / 7-0-24-0		154 / 352	10 / 10
v. Surrey (The Oval) 29 August – 1 September	20-3-59-2 / 14-6-24-3	29-8-51-2	18-6-61-3	24-7-90-3			3-0-14-0		19.1-4-66-3		7.5-1-40-2 / 4-1-12-0			10-1-40-2 / 10-1-47-1	221 / 239	10 / 10
v. Kent (Old Trafford) 7–11 September				3.5-1-22-0			5-1-14-3	15-0-93-2				1-1-0-0			267	Ab.
v. Derbyshire (Derby) 14–18 September	19-5-76-2 / 19-5-47-2	14-4-48-2 / 25-5-82-2	9-1-30-1 / 10.4-3-33-2	14-3-46-0			11-0-65-3	14-2-80-1							267 / 325	10 / 10
Bowler's average	254.5-75-681-30 / 22.70	363.4-113-889-35 / 25.40	529.4-137-1621-57 / 28.43	505-128-1498-37 / 40.48	136-33-494-11 / 44.90	4-0-26-0 / –	117.5-16-477-16 / 29.81	518.1-108-1598-81 / 19.72	361.1-75-1188-33 / 36.00	1-0 / –	29.5-4-107-3 / 35.66	1.5-1-14-0 / –	11-0-39-0 / –	20-2-87-3 / 29.00		

A A. Dale retired hurt

AXA EQUITY AND LAW LEAGUE – AVERAGES

BATTING	M	Inns	NO	Runs	HS	Av	100s	50s	ct/st
B.F. Smith	14	13	2	479	115	43.54	2	3	3
V.J. Wells	12	12	1	418	79	38.00	–	4	3
N.E. Briers	13	13	1	446	108*	37.16	1	3	3
W.J. Cronje	13	13	3	357	93*	35.70	–	2	2
J.J. Whitaker	9	8	1	221	65*	31.57	–	2	4
P.A. Nixon	13	10	1	260	84	28.88	–	1	10/4
D.L. Maddy	15	10	2	197	69	24.62	–	1	7
G.J. Parsons	11	8	5	65	26*	21.66	–	–	3
J.M. Dakin	11	8	6	157	45	18.62	–	2	7
A.R.K. Pierson	8	4	1	36	21*	18.00	–	–	1
A. Habib	7	7	1	15	15	15.00	–	–	7
P.E. Robinson	7	7	1	86	28	14.33	–	–	1
I.J. Sutcliffe	4	4	–	14	14	14.00	–	–	1
G.I. Macmillan	4	4	–	46	38	11.50	–	–	3
T.J. Mason	11	3	1	17	10*	11.00	–	–	–
A.D. Mullally	14	4	1	19	10*	6.33	–	–	3
V.P. Clarke	10	3	1	6	6	3.00	–	–	1

BOWLING	Overs	Mds	Runs	Wkts	Av	Best	5/inn
G.J. Parsons	101	10	419	20	20.95	3-22	–
A.R.K. Pierson	37	1	235	11	21.36	5-36	1
J.M. Dakin	43.2	1	255	10	25.50	3-23	–
D.L. Maddy	78	5	435	15	29.00	3-29	–
V.J. Wells	37	7	234	7	33.42	3-32	–
W.J. Cronje	98	3	466	11	42.36	3-37	–
A.D. Mullally	101.2	6	486	10	48.60	2-23	–
T.J. Mason	69	3	359	6	59.83	2-41	–
D.J. Millns	4	–	27	–	–	–	–
J. Ormond	6	–	41	–	–	–	–

One-match: D.J. Millns, P. Whitticase and J. Ormond did not bat

LEICESTERSHIRE CCC — BATTING (season aggregates)

Player	M	Inns	NO	Runs	HS	Av
T.J. Boon	6	12	–	177	38	14.75
N.E. Briers	15	28	2	1046	175*	41.84
W.J. Cronje	16	27	1	1362	213	50.44
J.J. Whitaker	15	25	1	1055	127	42.20
P.E. Robinson	6	6	1	99	60*	19.80
V.J. Wells	14	24	–	654	124	28.43
G.J. Parsons	18	28	8	501	73	19.26
P. Whitticase	3	3	–	150	62*	37.50
A.R.K. Pierson	19	30	9	382	70	18.19
A.D. Mullally	18	14	6	150	22	25.58
D.J. Millns	8	18	5	307	50	6.81
B.F. Smith	18	31	5	802	112	30.84
P.A. Nixon	16	27	4	150	50	16.50
D.L. Maddy	8	17	6	264	131	16.34
A. Habib	8	5	2	376	174*	76.66
J.M. Dakin	13	13	4	230	101*	29.63
V.P. Clarke	7	7	2	326	29	9.16
A. Sheriyar	10	10	1	55	29	6.55
S. Bartle	7	5	1	59	32	32.00
M.T. Brimson	7	5	3	32	25	20.00
T. Mason	1	–	–	40	–	–
J. Ormond	1	1	–	–	–	–
C.D. Crowe	3	2	1	10	9	5.00
I.J. Sutcliffe	3	4	–	63	34	15.75
G.I. Macmillan	6	10	1	389	122	43.22

BOWLING

Opponent / Date	D.J. Millns	A.D. Mullally	G.J. Parsons	V.J. Wells	W.J. Cronje	A.R.K. Pierson	A. Sheriyar	J.M. Dakin	V.P. Clarke	J. Ormond	T. Mason	M.T. Brimson	Byes	Leg-byes	Wides	No-balls	Total	Wkts
v. Essex (Chelmsford) 27–30 April	31-6-120-2	32-7-93-1	31-9-84-1	20.2-5-60-3	13-4-29-1	1-0-9-0							13	9	1	2	404	10
v. Yorkshire (Leicester) 4–8 May	15-3-47-3 / 27-3-90-2	13.4-2-33-3 / 24.1-9-62-4 / 4.1-0-21-1	19-6-34-1 / 15-5-31-0	9-0-26-2 / 7-1-25-0	12-3-20-1 / 12-3-33-0	16-1-77-3 / 4-1-13-0							8	6	1 / 6	4	332 / 37	10 / 1
v. Kent (Canterbury) 11–15 May	25-3-123-2	36-7-113-2	28-6-96-1	15-4-44-0	9-2-47-0	47.5-11-141-4							4	11	4	8	575	10
v. Derbyshire (Leicester) 18–22 May	13-0-66-2 / 1.1-0-15-0	20-3-81-1 / 23-10-50-6	19.2-5-55-4 / 22-6-64-2	11-3-31-2 / 6.3-3-12-2	9-6-15-1 / 4-1-14-0	5-1-15-0 / 21.3-8-48-5							4	3 / 10	4	16 / 2	256 / 173	10 / 10
v. Durham (Leicester) 25–9 May	12-3-29-2 / 8.2-0-29-2	17-6-32-3 / 18-9-24-2	7-4-18-0 / 21-9-23-2	0.4-0-2-1	6.2-1-10-1	26-8-63-3 / 18-2-80-0							1	10	4	32	138 / 151	10 / 10
v. West Indians (Leicester) 30 May – 1 June	18-2-67-1		21-9-23-2 / 9-3-20-1			4-2-15-1	24-1-146-2 / 7-4-41-1	20-2-94-2 / 6-1-27-0	7-0-49-0 / 8.1-0-35-1				5	4	1	2	468 / 143	7 / 4
v. Oxford University (Oxford) 2–5 June							21.5-6-61-5	17-2-54-1 / 2-1-1-1	8-2-28-0 / 6-2-17-0	17-6-65-2		14-3-41-1	4	14	6 / 1	12	320 / 83	9 / 1A
v. Hampshire (Basingstoke) 7–10 June	21-0-95-1 / 5-0-14-0	22-8-43-3 / 8-5-5-0	24.4-9-58-4 / 7-2-32-0	17-6-48-0 / 4-1-10-0		15-1-50-2 / 5-0-26-1		3-1-14-0					12	13 / 5	1	10 / 2	319 / 92	10 / 1
v. Nottinghamshire (Leicester) 15–19 June	20.5-4-75-2	13-0-90-2	26-8-75-2 / 20.4-6-49-2	5-1-25-0 / 9-6-8-0	5-1-25-0 / 9-6-8-0	29-8-61-3		9-2-20-2 / 13-2-51-0					10	14	2 / 6	38 / 4	364 / 246	10 / 7B
v. Northamptonshire (Northampton) 22–6 June	8-3-22-0	23-6-63-0	38-12-106-2	11-3-26-1	11-3-26-1	40-12-104-3 / 44.2-7-141-3	32-3-152-3						8	17		12	564	9C
v. Worcestershire (Worcester) 29 June – 3 July		28-14-47-1 / 25-7-46-1	24.1-5-46-4 / 23-6-57-2			15-6-34-2 / 23-5-47-3	13-1-62-2 / 15-2-39-1	7-0-19-0	15-3-48-1 / 22.3-3-72-3		19-4-57-0		9 / 15	14 / 21	4	28	279 / 297	10 / 10
v. Warwickshire (Leicester) 6–10 July		27-11-76-2	23-7-70-4			34.4-10-107-4			7-0-35-0		6-0-22-0		8	7		6	307	10D
v. Sussex (Hove) 20–4 July		17-3-53-2	20-8-29-3	13.4-5-24-2	16-7-40-2	6-0-24-0						19-4-52-1	2	14		6	233	10
v. Surrey (Leicester) 27–31 July		17-5-50-1 / 14-5-35-0	23-11-58-3 / 20-10-46-3	4-1-12-0 / 7-2-23-2	13-3-44-1 / 4-1-17-0	29.1-5-96-4 / 38.1-10-80-5						3-2-6-1 / 6-2-7-0	17 / 3	10 / 7	1 / 2	2 / 4	293 / 218	10 / 10
v. Young Australia (Leicester) 3–6 August		18-9-47-5 / 13-2-51-4	8-2-27-0	5-1-25-0 / 3-0-20-0	4-0-10-1 / 4-2-2-0	25-4-133-4	11-2-55-4					5.2-2-31-1	7	3		8	248	10
v. Lancashire (Leicester) 10–14 August		14-2-61-2 / 24-6-64-4	3-0-5-0 / 14-4-41-1	7.1-2-28-3 / 5-1-19-1	15.6-37-0 / 5-1-16-0	13-2-47-1 / 4-0-26-0	11.3-3-30-6 / 17-3-50-1					5-1-14-2 / 2-0-12-0	1 / 15	5 / 8	5	4 / 12	303 / 218	6 / 6
v. Somerset (Weston-super-Mare) 24–8 August		8-5-12-0 / 17-8-50-1	18-4-82-1 / 20-7-47-1	14-4-50-1 / 7.1-1-29-0	16-8-33-2 / 19-6-42-3	22-2-110-2 / 21.4-3-99-3	7-1-15-1 / 12.4-4-46-3						3 / 14	1 / 9			293 / 368	5 / 5
v. Glamorgan (Leicester) 29 August – 1 September		24-7-100-2 / 30-7-132-2	23-5-59-1 / 22-5-97-1	25-5-56-1	25-5-56-1	6-1-27-1 / 27.5-10-67-0	10-1-60-0	3-0-23-0 / 2-0-8-0				18-2-56-1	12 / 5	8 / 2	4 / 7	2 / 8	439 / 194	2E / —
v. Middlesex (Uxbridge) 7–11 September		2-1-2-0 / 0-0-32-1	19-5-40-3	11-2-42-0	11-2-42-0	11-1-53-0 / 19-2-80-4		8-2-35-0 / 4-1-11-0				25.4-3-60-2 / 3-0-20-1	8 / 1	5 / 3	1 / 1	2	338 / 212	10
v. Gloucestershire (Leicester) 14–18 September		15-2-53-2	4-1-17-0 / 20.3-7-44-3	8-0-54-0 / 5-1-10-0	8-0-54-0 / 5-1-10-0	28-4-116-3 / 2-1-1-0 / 20-6-50-3		5-1-13-0				9-5-11-2	4	3	3	4	176	10
Bowler's average	205.2-27-792-19 / 41.68	577-169-1646-58 / 28.37	579.2-178-1570-53 / 29.62	139.3-33-438-19 / 23.05	256.2-79-688-15 / 45.86	622.1-134-2040-67 / 30.44	182-27-757-29 / 26.10	99-15-370-6 / 61.66	73.3-10-284-5 / 56.80	17-6-65-2 / 32.50	25-4-79-0 / —	110-24-310-12 / 25.83						

A   S. Bartle 2-0-42-0

B   B.F. Smith 1-1-0-0.   D.L. Maddy 2-0-5-0

C   A.J. Lamb retired hurt

D   C.D. Crowe 3-2-4-0

E   B.F. Smith 10.3-1-69-1.   D.L. Maddy 4-0-36-0

AXA EQUITY AND LAW LEAGUE – AVERAGES

BATTING

	M	Inns	NO	Runs	HS	Av	100s	50s	ct/st
M.R. Ramprakash	13	13	3	485	103	48.50	1	3	4
M.W. Gatting	10	9	—	298	68	33.11	—	3	4
K.P. Dutch	3	2	1	33	21*	33.00	—	—	1
P.N. Weekes	16	15	—	405	50*	27.00	—	1	6
K.R. Brown	15	14	3	279	54*	25.36	—	1	16/4
O.A. Shah	3	3	1	86	64	21.50	—	—	1
D.J. Nash	5	3	—	35	30	17.50	—	—	1
T.A. Radford	3	3	1	34	12*	17.00	—	—	—
A.R.C. Fraser	12	7	5	34	12*	17.00	—	—	—
R.A. Fay	6	4	2	34	12*	17.00	—	—	1
J.C. Pooley	14	14	1	215	51	16.53	—	1	6
P. Farbrace	4	4	1	46	26	15.33	—	—	—
J.C. Harrison	3	2	1	15	13*	15.00	—	—	1
M.A. Feltham	12	8	1	102	35	14.57	—	—	4
D.J. Nash	13	8	5	109	35	13.62	—	—	—
J.E. Emburey	13	6	3	40	14*	13.33	—	—	6
J.D. Carr	16	16	—	149	27	9.31	—	—	1
R.L. Johnson	4	3	—	31	18*	6.20	—	—	1
U.B.A. Rashid	4	3	1	14	8	4.66	—	—	—
P.C.R. Tufnell	6	4	2	7	5	3.50	—	—	1
J.P. Hewitt	1	1	—	3	3	3.00	—	—	—

One match: R.S. Yeabsley (ct 1); D.C. Nash (ct 2/st 1); D. Follett (ct 1)
did not bat

BOWLING

	Overs	Mds	Runs	Wkts	Av	Best	5/inn
J.C. Harrison	1	—	3	1	3.00	1-3	—
R.S. Yeabsley	3	—	13	1	13.00	1-13	—
M.W. Gatting	9.4	—	53	4	13.25	4-44	—
D. Follett	7	—	27	2	13.50	2-27	—
A.R.C. Fraser	80.4	10	267	19	14.05	5-32	1
M.R. Ramprakash	2.2	—	20	1	20.00	1-18	—
M.A. Feltham	57.5	—	278	13	21.38	5-51	1
D.J. Nash	85	4	365	16	22.81	3-34	—
J.P. Hewitt	9	—	53	2	26.50	2-31	—
P.C.R. Tufnell	43	3	192	7	27.42	3-43	—
U.B.A. Rashid	26	2	118	4	29.50	2-34	—
P.N. Weekes	78.1	3	321	10	32.10	4-41	—
J.E. Emburey	43	—	223	5	44.60	2-15	—
R.A. Fay	37	3	155	3	51.66	2-32	—
R.L. Johnson	52	5	312	5	62.40	2-54	—
K.P. Dutch	12	—	57	—	—	—	—

MIDDLESEX CCC — BATTING (Averages)

	M	Inns	NO	Runs	HS	Av
M.W. Gatting	16	22	1	1139	148	54.23
J.C. Pooley	18	30	1	1335	136	51.34
M.R. Ramprakash	17	27	4	2157	235	89.87
J.D. Carr	20	29	6	1098	129	47.73
P.N. Weekes	20	31	2	995	143	34.31
K.R. Brown	19	27	4	970	147*	42.17
D.J. Nash	19	25	4	433	67	20.61
J.E. Emburey	16	19	1	379	87	21.05
A.R.C. Fraser	13	13	4	73	20	8.11
D. Follett	1	2	1	5	4*	5.00
P.C.R. Tufnell	17	15	9	65	23*	8.12
M.A. Feltham	14	15	4	115	25	10.45
R.L. Johnson	12	13	1	164	29*	14.90
T.A. Radford	6	11	4	244	69	34.85
J.C. Harrison	6	6	4	95	46*	47.50
P. Farbrace	2	3	—	17	16	8.50
K.J. Shine	2	2	1	6	6	6.00
A.A. Khan	2	—	—	—	—	—
K.P. Dutch	1	—	—	—	—	—
C.W. Taylor	1	1	1	1	1*	—
R.A. Fay	1	1	—	1	1	—

BOWLING

This is a rotated full-page bowling-analysis table. Bowler columns (left to right): A.R.C. Fraser, D.J. Nash, H.R. Ramprakash, J.E. Emburey, P.C.R. Tufnell, P.N. Weekes, M.A. Feltham, R.L. Johnson, K.J. Shine, C.W. Taylor, A.A. Khan, K.P. Dutch, followed by Byes, Leg-byes, Wides, No-balls, Total, Wks. Innings figures are stacked per match.

Match (date)	Fraser	Nash	Ramprakash	Emburey	Tufnell	Weekes	Feltham	Johnson	Shine	Taylor	Khan	Dutch	Byes	Leg-byes	Wides	No-balls	Total	Wks
v. Warwickshire (Edgbaston) 27–30 April	17-6-49-0	12-0-60-1		20.1-9-31-4	31.3-13-55-4	5.3-2-19-0							11	7		2	282	10A
	22-5-50-3	17-5-51-2		22.1-7-49-2	28-9-91-3									8	1	6	294	10
v. Hampshire (Lord's) 4–8 May	20-6-46-0	20-6-61-4		11-4-17-1	5.2-1-16-3		14-4-25-2							4		2	169	10
	19-3-60-3	13-4-35-5		13-2-44-1	17-4-55-1		5-1-36-0						5	4		10	242	10
v. Worcestershire (Worcester) 11–15 May	19.4-4-52-4	17-1-64-1		1-0-3-0	3-1-15-1	1-0-4-0	13-5-27-3							7			193	9B
	24-7-85-0	23-4-85-3		2-0-11-0		8-2-16-0	22-5-55-4	22.3-3-67-3					4	1	1	2	170	10
v. Lancashire (Lord's) 18–22 May	24-7-85-0			17-5-51-3	3-1-15-1		13-5-27-3							5		8	375	10
v. Essex (Chelmsford) 25–9 May	24-10-39-4	12-4-35-1		26-6-53-4	20.1-9-33-2	10-4-12-1	9-2-30-0	13-4-41-2						3			207	10
	20.1-1-64-2	17-5-49-0		30-8-72-4	22-5-66-3	20-4-43-1		12-1-38-1					1	11		12	290	10
v. Derbyshire (Lord's) 1–5 June		21.2-5-50-2		28-10-52-2	23-10-54-0	6-0-20-0	16-4-44-2						1	8	4	14	267	10
		15-1-46-1		13-4-30-0	11-5-13-0	10-3-21-0	10-2-26-0							8	4	4	209	3
v. Cambridge University (Cambridge) 9–11 June						19-3-42-1		16.5-9-24-3	13-1-43-0		23-5-51-4		4	9		2	230	8C
						2-0-5-0		6-2-10-0	10-4-23-4		4-0-7-0					4	49	4
v. Glamorgan (Colwyn Bay) 15–19 June	16-5-33-1	13-4-46-0		32-11-79-3	25.5-10-61-3	14-4-29-0	14.3-5-39-2	14-3-47-2		8-4-15-4			12	10	16		232	10
	14-6-19-0	14-2-41-3		48-17-97-4	36.3-10-105-3	9-2-12-0	5-3-6-0	8-3-17-0		3-0-11-0			1	12	3		202	10
v. Oxford University (Oxford) 20–22 June		11-1-31-0			3-1-15-1			17-2-51-1			29-9-56-3						97	4D
								7-3-14-0			18-8-28-1		2	7	1		209	10
v. Surrey (Lord's) 29 June – 3 July	17-3-50-2	7-2-24-1		27.3-9-64-5	22-10-32-2	4-0-21-0	20-8-46-2	5-1-18-0						7			140	9E
	10-3-22-0	5-0-35-0		16.4-5-34-5	19-8-30-3	9-1-20-2	11-2-32-2	4-2-12-1						4		4	208	10
v. Gloucestershire (Bristol) 6–10 July		17-5-35-0		27.1-12-33-4	11-2-26-2	4-0-21-0	24-3-84-0	21-6-53-4					6	10		2	222	10
		14-0-49-1		22-9-46-0	40-8-111-6	9-1-20-2		16-4-34-3						9			456	10
v. West Indians (Lord's) 22–4 July		24.5-4-93-1	2.2-0-17-1			19-2-74-1	19.5-4-81-6	24-3-84-0	14-1-65-2					6			213	9
					17-2-47-3	3-0-21-1	4-0-16-0	8-2-33-0	6-0-42-1			1-1-0-0		6		6	201	10
v. Sussex (Lord's) 27–31 July		11-0-47-3		24-8-59-1	18.2-8-30-2	6-0-26-3	3-1-6-0	14-1-64-3				1-1-0-0		1		10	115	10
		7-0-37-3		7-2-15-1	26.2-5-74-5	4-1-7-0		13-7-15-2					9	14		22	285	10
v. Nottinghamshire (Lord's) 3–7 August		11-3-20-2		5-0-25-0	13-6-29-2			15-5-48-2					6	2		8	116	10
		7-2-20-2			15-7-32-0			7-2-4-3-1					1	8		10	204	10
v. Durham (Chester-le-Street) 10–14 August	20-7-24-2	20.5-6-47-5			34.2-6-73-4	2-1-2-0	9-1-41-0	18-4-50-5					4		9	4	114	9F
	14-4-37-2	10.1-4-29-3		19-2-71-1	28.4-5-76-5	14-2-36-1	12-3-33-1	17-3-48-5					6	13	1	2	265	10
v. Kent (Lord's) 17–21 August	37-7-106-3	19.5-5-50-2		21-3-63-2	38-10-68-3	1-0-3-1	19-8-28-1	4-0-13-1						5		5	205	10
	9-1-36-0	4-0-10-0		36.5-10-75-5	41-17-69-3	14-2-36-1	4-2-6-0						14	10		12	250	10G
v. Yorkshire (Leeds) 24–8 August	14-1-35-0	6-0-22-1		44.4-13-82-7	8.4-2-34-0		31-7-72-2						10	7		8	241	8
	10-1-40-1	8-2-36-0		46.2-9-124-3	26.3-5-100-5		5.3-0-31-1							25		24	479	10
v. Northamptonshire (Uxbridge) 29 August – 1 September		27-6-90-2		25-7-101-5	37-7-102-5	2-1-1-0	2-0-8-0						4	3		3	238	6H
		4-0-16-0		19-2-54-0	37.7-81-4	2-1-0-0	19-6-69-1						12	8		10	300	5I
v. Leicestershire (Uxbridge) 7–11 September	23-5-56-5	2-1-4-0		32-7-81-4	24-7-57-1								1	11		18	249	10
		23-4-78-1		30.1-6-76-1	7-5-8-0	5-2-4-0							4	4	4	8	376	10
v. Somerset (Taunton) 14–18 September	5-1-31-0	4-1-28-0	20-2-91-3	12-4-27-2									4	1		2	323	7J
Bowler's average	404.2-104-1069-40 / 26.72	460.1-90-1512-52 / 29.07	22.2-2-108-4 / 27.00	678.4-191-1619-74 / 21.87	668.1-207-1634-74 / 22.08	258.4-55-679-13 / 52.23	273-72-783-29 / 27.00	301.4-79-812-40 / 20.30	43-6-173-7 / 24.71	11-4-26-4 / 6.50	76-24-142-8 / 17.75	14-7-24-0 / —						

A D. Follett 17-4-61-1, 13-2-34-0
B G.A. Hick absent hurt
C K. Mare 9-0-37-0
D P. Farbrace 1-1-0-0.   T.A. Radford 1-1-0-1
E A.J. Stewart retired hurt
F A. Walker absent hurt
G R.A. Fay 3-0-25-0
H M.W. Gatting 4.2-0-23-0
I M.W. Gatting 0.4-0-8-0
J K.R. Brown 15-0-114-1.   J.C. Pooley 4-0-15-0

AXA EQUITY AND LAW LEAGUE – AVERAGES

BATTING

	M	Inns	NO	Runs	HS	Av	100s	50s	ct/st
M.B. Loye	13	12	4	332	57*	41.50	—	1	2
A.J. Lamb	2	2	—	82	48	41.00	—	—	1
K.M. Curran	14	13	1	424	119*	35.33	1	2	1
R.J. Bailey	16	13	3	340	61*	34.00	—	3	6
R.R. Montgomerie	12	11	—	339	60	30.81	—	3	3
D.J. Capel	14	12	3	264	57*	29.33	—	1	7
A. Fordham	14	13	—	336	56	25.84	—	2	4
T.C. Walton	9	9	—	224	56	24.88	—	1	4
D.J. Sales	4	3	—	40	27*	20.00	—	—	1
J.N. Snape	16	10	6	76	17*	19.00	—	—	6
R.J. Warren	15	12	2	186	44*	18.60	—	—	16/2
A.L. Penberthy	14	10	1	106	44	11.77	—	—	2
M.N. Bowen	4	3	1	14	7*	7.00	—	—	1
M.J. Foster	4	3	1	14	9	7.00	—	—	—
A.R. Kumble	10	3	1	11	8	5.50	—	—	3
D. Ripley	3	2	—	10	5	5.00	—	—	3/—
S.A.J. Boswell	4	1	—	2	0*	2.00	—	—	—
J.G. Hughes	2	1	—	0	0*	0.00	—	—	1
J.P. Taylor	7	2	—	15	9*	—	—	—	4

Four matches: N.A. Mallender did not bat.
One match: K.J. Innes did not bat; C.S. Atkins did not bat; A.R. Roberts 4

BOWLING

	Overs	Mds	Runs	Wkts	Av	Best	5/inn
N.A. Mallender	23	—	75	4	18.75	2-21	—
A.R. Kumble	69	2	347	16	21.68	3-25	—
J.G. Hughes	14	—	71	3	23.66	2-39	—
M.N. Bowen	32	1	148	6	24.66	2-11	—
A.L. Penberthy	93.3	4	455	18	25.27	4-29	—
R.J. Bailey	47	3	290	11	26.36	3-28	—
A.R. Roberts	3.5	—	33	1	33.00	1-33	—
S.A.J. Boswell	23	—	104	3	34.66	3-49	—
K.M. Curran	75	2	400	10	38.10	1-20	—
J.N. Snape	76	2	381	10	38.10	2-25	—
M.J. Foster	21	—	124	3	41.33	2-30	—
D.J. Capel	59.1	1	275	6	45.83	3-23	—
J.P. Taylor	62	6	367	4	91.75	2-55	—
T.C. Walton	3	—	26	—	—	—	—
K.J. Innes	6	—	29	—	—	—	—
C.S. Atkins	4.2	—	38	—	—	—	—

NORTHAMPTONSHIRE CCC

BATTING — part 1 (season summary with fixtures Apr–Jul)

Fixtures covered: v. Kent (Canterbury) 27–30 April; v. Glamorgan (Cardiff) 4–8 May; v. Somerset (Northampton) 11–15 May; v. Surrey (Northampton) 18–22 May; v. Yorkshire (Sheffield) 25–9 May; v. West Indians (Northampton) 3–5 June; v. Derbyshire (Derby) 8–12 June; v. Essex (Luton) 15–19 June; v. Leicestershire (Northampton) 22–6 June; v. Lancashire (Old Trafford) 6–10 July; v. Hampshire (Northampton) 20–4 July; v. Warwickshire (Edgbaston) 27–31 July.

Player	M	Inns	NO	Runs	HS	Av
R.R. Montgomerie	14	24	1	632	192	27.47
A. Fordham	16	29	1	1025	130	36.60
R.J. Bailey	18	30	3	1038	157	38.44
M.B. Loye	7	10	—	134	51*	14.88
A.J. Lamb	16	26	4	1237	166	56.22
K.M. Curran	17	27	3	863	117	35.95
D.J. Capel	18	27	3	897	175	37.37
D. Ripley	6	6	—	90	40	22.50
A.R. Kumble	17	21	5	321	40*	20.06
J.G. Hughes	5	6	1	32	16	6.40
J.P. Taylor	18	21	8	284	86	21.84
J.N. Snape	13	16	5	360	55	27.76
R.J. Warren	16	27	5	914	154	41.54
T.C. Walton	4	6	1	104	71	23.00
A.L. Penberthy	4	7	1	115	73	17.28
C.S. Atkins	7	10	3	13	8*	13.00
N.A. Mallender	7	2	—	121	49*	17.28
A.R. Roberts	1	2	—	21	11	10.50

Match results: v. Kent — W (24 pts, Total 561/7 dec); v. Glamorgan — L (4 pts, Totals 377 & 243); v. Somerset — W (22 pts, Totals 297 & 291); v. Surrey — W (24 pts, Total 403); v. Yorkshire — W (23 pts, Totals 357 & 146); v. West Indians — D (Total 281); v. Derbyshire — W (20 pts, Totals 120 & 135); v. Essex — W (20 pts, Totals 46 & 192); v. Leicestershire — W (24 pts, Total 564); v. Lancashire — L (4 pts, Totals 290 & 194); v. Hampshire — D (4 pts, Totals 321 & 365); v. Warwickshire — W (20 pts, Totals 152 & 346).

BATTING — part 2 (season summary with fixtures Aug–Sep)

Fixtures covered: v. Durham (Northampton) 3–7 August; v. Gloucestershire (Northampton) 10–14 August; v. Nottinghamshire (Northampton) 24–8 August; v. Middlesex (Uxbridge) 29 August – 1 September; v. Worcestershire (Northampton) 7–11 September; v. Sussex (Hove) 14–18 September.

Player	M	Inns	NO	Runs	HS	Av
R.R. Montgomerie	14	24	1	632	192	27.47
A. Fordham	16	29	1	1025	130	36.60
R.J. Bailey	18	30	3	1038	157	38.44
M.B. Loye	7	10	—	134	51*	14.88
A.J. Lamb	16	26	4	1237	166	56.22
K.M. Curran	17	27	3	863	117	35.95
D.J. Capel	18	27	3	897	175	37.37
D. Ripley	6	6	—	90	40	22.50
A.R. Kumble	17	21	5	321	40*	20.06
J.G. Hughes	5	6	1	32	16	6.40
J.P. Taylor	18	21	8	284	86	21.84
J.N. Snape	13	16	5	360	55	27.76
R.J. Warren	16	27	5	914	154	41.54
T.C. Walton	4	6	1	104	71	23.00
A.L. Penberthy	4	7	1	115	73	17.33
C.S. Atkins	7	10	3	13	8*	13.00
N.A. Mallender	7	2	—	121	49*	17.28
A.R. Roberts	1	2	—	21	11	10.50

Match results: v. Durham — W (24 pts, Total 492/5 dec); v. Gloucestershire — W (23 pts, Totals 321 & 312); v. Nottinghamshire — W (21 pts, Total 781/7); v. Middlesex — D (5 pts, Totals 479 & 238); v. Worcestershire — W (20 pts, Totals 174 & 265); v. Sussex — D (4 pts, Total 41).

BOWLING

Match	J.P. Taylor	J.G. Hughes	D.J. Capel	A.R. Kumble	K.M. Curran	J.N. Snape	R.J. Bailey	A.L. Penberthy	C.S. Atkins	N.A. Mallender	T.C. Walton	A.R. Roberts	Byes	Leg-byes	Wides	No-balls	Total	Wkts
v. Kent (Canterbury) 27-30 April	20-2-82-1	17-1-72-1	12.2-1-50-4	33-11-74-2	9-2-50-2								8	16		14	352	10
v. Glamorgan (Cardiff) 4-8 May	21.2-7-49-5	9-1-31-1	5-0-30-2	27-4-60-2	11-3-30-0								4	11	1		215	10
	13.3-4-51-3		11-3-36-4	32-9-65-5	13-4-40-0								12	13	1	8	334	10
v. Somerset (Northampton) 11-15 May	22.3-5-63-0	18-4-69-3	11-4-27-0	41-9-94-2	5-0-21-0	8-0-45-0	19-6-45-1						9	10		2	290	7
	17-7-37-2		14-2-49-2	14-2-45-1	13-1-48-2	14-2-32-0	7-0-25-0							4		4	242	10
v. Surrey (Northampton) 18-22 May	24-7-71-2		5-2-22-1	30-9-87-4	15-0-61-2	8.2-3-12-2		15-1-56-2					13	16		4	343	10
	17.4-4-53-2		18-3-62-4	30-12-47-4	12-4-28-0	9-1-46-0		5-1-15-0					8	11			263	10
v. Yorkshire (Sheffield) 25-9 May	13-1-42-3		15-8-25-2	21.5-5-29-3	3-0-29-0		2-2-0-0						4	5		2	190	10
	27.2-6-92-2		7-1-32-0	28-6-63-4	12-4-21-1					17-4-38-1			3	7		4	250	10
v. West Indians (Northampton) 3-5 June	20.3-4-74-3		11-1-37-1	31-12-63-4	10-5-23-2	5-0-14-1	1-0-4-0	11-1-36-0		15-4-29-0			2	1	2		252	10
	15-4-28-2					19-6-66-0	8-1-27-1			12-3-45-0	8-2-26-0					10	268	5A
v. Derbyshire (Derby) 8-12 June	13-6-23-4		5-0-19-0	12-4-26-2	10.3-1-36-3			6-3-6-2		5-0-22-1			1	7	1		113	10
	13.5-1-44-4		10-4-18-2	10-2-39-2	6-1-15-0			1-0-5-0		10-2-33-2				12	1	2	139	10
v. Essex (Luton) 15-19 June	10-1-18-2		14.1-3-29-5	2-0-7-0	4-0-22-0					8-0-22-1				4		2	127	10
	14.1-2-50-7		6-0-24-0	9.2-2-3-3	6-1-24-1					8-3-22-2				6			107	10
v. Leicestershire (Northampton) 22-6 June	11-1-51-1		15-1-65-1	38-10-70-1	10-3-32-2	16-8-34-1	8-2-16-1			16-3-59-2			14	27			367	10
	28-4-97-3		7-2-26-0	23-3-95-1	19.3-7-49-2					14.2-3-49-4			14	1		6	160	10
v. Lancashire (Old Trafford) 6-10 July	11-1-42-2		12-3-59-1	57.5-21-131-7	5-0-26-0		4-1-22-0			23-5-63-3		11-2-45-0	7	12		6	437	10
	25-7-79-0			10.5-1-61-6	24-7-91-1		16.3-4-66-4		11-4-46-1	3-1-8-0			16	10			280	9
v. Hampshire (Northampton) 20-4 July	7-0-25-0	7-2-32-0	18.5-3-44-7	29-7-69-3	3-0-14-2		21-4-88-0			11-4-37-1			4	6	1	10	560	8
	17-3-41-0	12-3-29-1	19-9-26-2		7-0-26-0	18-4-53-0	1-0-10-0							4		4	118	8
v. Warwickshire (Edgbaston) 27-31 July	31-6-78-0	11-2-29-0	13-4-23-1	42-16-82-7	5-1-17-0								8	12		8	224	10
	11-0-27-1	4-0-19-0	3-0-22-0	16.5-6-26-5	12-4-40-2		4-1-16-0							11		8	267	10
v. Durham (Northampton) 3-7 August	15-6-33-1	8-2-25-0	7-2-18-1	41-14-75-4	11-4-20-0	27.4-5-65-5							10	3		10	148	10
	13-7-17-4	4-0-14-1		24.2-7-76-6	12-1-82-2	11-0-48-1							1	17		2	293	10
v. Gloucestershire (Northampton) 10-14 August	27-8-59-1		23-1-84-2	21-6-53-1	6-3-7-1	12-5-14-2	8-0-27-0							6	1	6	131	10
			8-3-16-1	50-15-118-4	29.1-5-97-3	14-2-59-0							9	4		18	527	10
v. Nottinghamshire (Northampton) 24-8 August	15-3-40-1		11-2-38-0	39.1-21-43-5	19-7-39-3	4-3-1-0	3-2-4-0	14-1-59-0					6	15	1	8	157	4
	20.3-3-78-1		5-0-30-0	39-5-127-1	19-5-47-0	18-3-48-2							6	8		8	351	10
v. Middlesex (Uxbridge) 29 August – 1 September	3-1-17-0		7-0-21-0	23.3-2-111-2	4-1-24-0	18-4-82-2	1-0-7-0						7	6		6	277	6
			9-0-39-0		14-3-45-2	5-3-5-1							1	11		2	196	6
v. Worcestershire (Northampton) 7-11 September	8-0-32-0			31.2-12-63-6	18-3-78-4	5-2-4-0	1-0-4-0						7	7		2	237	6
				21-3-70-2	10-4-20-0	15-2-83-1							7	3	1		331	10
v. Sussex (Hove) 14-18 September	17.2-6-52-0		25-4-102-4	35-13-68-3		4-0-36-1	10-1-42-1							6			132	2B
Bowler's average	573.4-122-1713-59 29.03	90-15-320-7 45.71	349.2-69-1166-48 24.29	899.4-261-2143-105 20.40	357.1-84-1202-37 32.48	231-53-747-19 39.31	114.3-21-403-8 50.37	52-7-177-4 44.25	11-4-46-1 46.00	142.2-32-427-17 25.11	8-2-26-0 –	11-2-45-0 –						

A A. Fordham 1-1-0-1
B A. Fordham 6-0-51-0

AXA EQUITY AND LAW LEAGUE – AVERAGES

BATTING	M	Inns	NO	Runs	HS	Av	100s	50s	ct/st
P.R. Pollard	10	10	2	577	132*	71.12	2	1	5
P. Johnson	15	15	2	617	136*	47.46	2	4	5
C.L. Cairns	15	14	2	615	101	47.30	1	4	—
J.R. Wileman	16	13	8	226	51*	45.20	—	1	8
R.T. Robinson	16	16	1	488	82	30.50	—	4	8
W.M. Noon	15	10	4	154	34	25.66	—	—	12/2
R.A. Pick	5	5	2	76	58*	25.33	—	—	2
K.P. Evans	5	5	2	62	26*	20.66	—	—	1
G.F. Archer	16	15	2	213	53	16.38	—	1	9
C.C. Lewis		14		14	14	14.00	—	—	4
J.E. Hindson	16	5	2	37	14	11.33	—	—	4
M.P. Dowman	16	4	2	22	9	9.25	—	—	3
G.W. Mike	6	3	1	10	9	5.00	—	—	—
U. Afzaal	6	2		2	2	2.00	—	—	3
D.B. Pennett	11	4	2	2	2	2.00	—	—	1

Two matches: J. Hart did not bat.
One match: C. Banton 1; B.N. French and I. Riches did not bat

BOWLING	Overs	Mds	Runs	Wkts	Av	Best	5/inn
U. Afzaal	34	1	165	8	20.62	2-25	—
G.F. Archer	23	4	127	6	21.16	2-16	—
C.L. Cairns	82.2	4	451	20	22.55	3-34	—
J.R. Wileman	81.2	7	476	17	28.00	4-21	—
D.B. Pennett	74	2	420	15	28.00	3-27	—
G.W. Mike	45	2	234	8	29.25	2-21	—
K.P. Evans	31.2	2	163	4	40.75	2-26	—
J.E. Hindson	102	6	527	11	47.90	3-47	—
R.A. Pick	96	4	434	9	48.22	2-13	—
R.J. Chapman	32	1	212	4	53.00	2-36	—
J. Hart	12	1	87	1	87.00	1-48	—
I. Riches	3	—	21	—	—	—	—

NOTTINGHAMSHIRE CCC — BATTING (season summary)

BATTING	M	Inns	NO	Runs	SH	Av
M.P. Dowman	9	18	2	548	107	34.25
R.T. Robinson	18	32	1	1728	209	54.00
P. Johnson	17	30	1	996	120*	34.34
C.L. Cairns	17	30	1	1171	115	40.37
C. Banton	7	14	4	292	80*	29.20
K.P. Evans	7	13	2	260	78*	23.63
G.W. Mike	5	7	3	143	66*	23.83
J.E. Hindson	17	28	5	309	53*	13.43
B.N. French	2	3	1	19	16	9.50
R.A. Pick	17	26	9	395	57	17.95
J.A. Afford	7	11	8	57	15*	9.50
P.R. Pollard	19	32	3	506	120	29.76
G.F. Archer	17	32	2	1171	158	40.37
W.M. Noon	17	31	6	745	66	29.80
D.B. Pennett	8	12	8	89	50	22.25
J.R. Wileman	8	16	4	230	43	19.16
L.N. Walker	4	7	5	42	24	21.00
R.T. Bates	4	2	2	50	11	7.14
M.G. Field-Buss	8	4	—	4	2	2.00
R.J. Chapman	8	11	2	78	22	9.75
U. Afzaal	7	12	2	134	37	13.40
N.A. Gie	3	6	—	98	34	16.33

BOWLING

BOWLING	C.L. Cairns	R.A. Pick	G.W. Mike	J.A. Afford	J.E. Hindson	K.P. Evans	C. Banton	D.B. Pennett	G.F. Archer	R.J. Chapman	M.G. Field-Buss	J.R. Wileman	R.T. Bates	U. Afzaal	M.P. Dowman	Byes	Leg-byes	Wides	No-balls	Total	Wkts
v. Cambridge University (Cambridge) 27-9 April	8-4-7-2 / 4-1-6-1	16.4-6-22-3 / 11-4-26-3	3-2-1-0	19-12-23-3 / 19-7-47-0	9-4-15-2 / 19.5-4-44-2	7-2-17-0 / 18-3-59-0										1	5			91	10
																1	10		18	218	6
v. Derbyshire (Trent Bridge) 4-8 May	26-6-83-4 / 4-0-17-0	19.1-7-76-2 / 11-2-41-0	18.5-4-87-4	27-5-57-1 / 27.5-8-58-4	10-0-36-1 / 25-11-30-4	24-7-43-0 / 7-4-6-1	5-0-25-0									5	1	1	2	312	9A
																4	5			120	3
v. Gloucestershire (Bristol) 11-15 May			19-2-72-0 / 7-3-21-0	31-5-83-0 / 11-1-55-1	25-6-70-2 / 11-3-31-0	20-5-39-1 / 8-1-22-2		17-0-93-0 / 8-1-36-1 / 13-1-69-1 / 4-1-12-0	4-0-9-0							8	9		12	389	
																	12		2	187	
v. Oxford University (Oxford) 18-20 May			12-1-32-2 / 6-0-19-1										3-2-2-0			1	9		14	280	
																5				108	
v. Lancashire (Liverpool) 25-9 May	24.4-2-64-5 / 12-2-30-0	21-9-50-2 / 8-2-20-0		34-9-83-1 / 25-3-99-2	9-0-49-0 / 16-5-71-5	24-5-55-2 / 6-0-15-0 / 20-7-46-0		12-1-47-0 / 3-0-11-1		12-1-47-0 / 3-0-11-1	12-2-49-0 / 13-5-28-1	6-3-3-0					8	1	16	309	10
																	3		6	238	8
v. Essex (Trent Bridge) 1-5 June	11-1-40-2	20-4-64-2 / 8-0-33-0		17-5-52-1	31.1-4-92-5	12-1-37-0										1	6		4	301	10
																	6			271	
v. Worcestershire (Trent Bridge) 8-12 June		18-4-60-2 / 8-2-35-2 / 21.5-3-81-3		18-0-86-2 / 35-8-71-3 / 10-0-53-0	27.5-1-105-5 / 35.1-9-85-3 / 23-4-86-2 / 33-9-80-2	19-7-61-2 / 14.1-2-46-2 / 27-9-66-3				14-2-78-2 / 13.2-3-63-2	28-7-66-0 / 4-0-29-0					4	13	1	4	360	10
																7	7	2	18	263	7
v. Leicestershire (Leicester) 15-19 June		30-4-82-5	23-6-62-0		36-11-111-2	32-7-78-1			3-0-9-0					26-4-91-0		5	9	1	12	381	10
					18-3-85-1											6	17		6	357	10
v. Kent (Trent Bridge) 22-6 June	26-9-71-3	27.1-6-75-3 / 15-1-53-1			23-5-72-0			35-5-136-3 / 13-3-56-1				20-4-59-0 / 6-1-26-0		19-4-73-0 / 29-8-73-2			7			533	3
																	7		6	287	10
v. Somerset (Trent Bridge) 29 June – 3 July	27-6-73-2 / 27-10-55-0	9-1-46-0 / 12-1-54-1			25.3-6-67-5 / 44-20-78-5			18-4-64-1 / 15-2-63-1 / 6-1-30-0	2-0-10-2			10-5-25-0 / 8-4-21-1		28-11-63-0			18		12	366	10
																	11	1		361	10
v. Sussex (Arundel) 6-10 July	16.5-4-47-8	13-6-37-1 / 13.2-3-41-2			9-3-17-0 / 3-1-15-0				6-1-16-0					4-0-18-0		6			4	134	9B
														7-0-40-0			3	1	3	149	9
v. Surrey (Guildford) 20-4 July	17.1-3-53-3 / 30-11-97-1	15-2-40-3 / 21-7-76-0			10-0-53-1 / 54-12-162-4			7-0-27-1	13-3-36-0 / 30-6-119-3 / 8-0-36-0 / 4-0-19-0					21-7-53-0 / 19-5-41-2		3	10	3	2	239	10
																	12	5	9	528	10
v. Yorkshire (Trent Bridge) 27-31 July	17.4-36-2 / 13-5-32-4	18-2-66-3 / 6-1-12-1			21.2-7-67-3 / 22.3-10-65-4									8-1-14-0		9	10	2	4	256	10
																10	10	2	10	163	10
v. Middlesex (Lord's) 3-7 August	31-4-103-3	28-3-119-5			18-0-121-0		3-1-12-0	27.4-5-119-2 / 20-5-61-0	11-1-41-0 / 9-2-29-1 / 4-2-8-0					10-0-64-0			8		12	587	10
v. Warwickshire (Trent Bridge) 17-21 August	24.1-7-81-4	27-10-65-3 / 4.4-0-20-0			26-5-105-1				12-3-45-0					11-2-52-1		13	8	4	15	414	10
																				28	0
v. Northamptonshire (Northampton) 24-8 August	26-4-65-1	24-3-119-1		41-4-223-3	33-4-160-2					21-1-109-0					5-0-30-0	9	21	10	24	781	7
v. Hampshire (Trent Bridge) 29 August – 1 September		24-6-72-3			38.3-13-90-3			22-4-57-1	4-0-11-0			27-16-33-2	21-8-52-1			13	5	1	4	333	10
v. Glamorgan (Cardiff) 7-11 September	13-3-39-0	13.4-4-47-0			17-3-73-1 / 19-1-84-0			18-4-70-1 / 7.3-1-28-0	6-0-29-0 / 1-0-4-0	15-0-75-0			34-9-138-4 / 24-2-89-0			18	3	1	6	417	6
																5	3			213	0
v. Durham (Chester-le-Street) 14-18 September		27-8-70-0						23-4-75-0	17-2-50-3			18-3-50-1	33.1-11-88-5			5	11		12	424	10
Bowler's average	375.5-89- 1035-52 19.90	490.2-105- 1602-51 31.41	88.5-18- 294-7 42.00	314.5-67- 990-21 47.14	692-165- 2219-65 34.13	238.1-60- 590-14 42.14	8-1- 37-0 –	208.1-34- 812-10 81.20	79-11- 261-6 43.50	179.2-23- 777-11 70.63	57-14- 172-1 172.00	95-36- 217-4 54.25	115.1-32- 369-10 36.90	182-42- 582-5 116.00	5-0- 30-0 –						

A K.M. Krikken absent hurt
B N.J. Lenham retired hurt, absent hurt

AXA EQUITY AND LAW LEAGUE – AVERAGES

BATTING

	M	Inns	NO	Runs	HS	Av	100s	50s	ct/st
R.J. Harden	14	14	4	491	100*	37.76	1	3	3
G.D. Rose	13	13	1	365	60*	30.41	–	2	3
A.N. Hayhurst	10	10	3	210	70*	30.00	–	1	2
S.C. Ecclestone	9	9	2	196	45*	28.00	–	2	5
P.D. Bowler	14	14	0	349	76	24.92	–	3	1
K.A. Parsons	11	11	1	242	52*	24.20	–	1	5
H.R.J. Trump	15	6	5	21	6*	21.00	–	–	4
P.C.L. Holloway	10	9	2	145	66	20.71	–	1	1/1
R.J. Turner	12	9	–	96	19	19.20	–	–	9/4
M.N. Lathwell	15	15	–	284	55	18.93	–	2	3
Mushtaq Ahmed	14	12	5	118	23*	16.85	–	–	1
M.E. Trescothick	8	8	–	82	27	10.25	–	–	2
J.I.D. Kerr	9	4	–	21	8	5.25	–	–	1

Five matches: A.R. Caddick 1 and 22*
Two matches: A.P. van Troost 9 (ct 1); J.D. Batty 3; J.C. Hallett 2

BOWLING

	Overs	Mds	Runs	Wkts	Av	Best	5/inn
J.C. Hallett	12	2	80	4	20.00	3-33	–
A.R. Caddick	28	2	127	5	25.40	3-41	–
K.A. Parsons	47	2	213	8	26.62	2-16	–
H.R.J. Trump	102	5	511	17	30.05	3-37	–
J.I.D. Kerr	57	1	335	11	30.45	3-52	–
A.N. Hayhurst	21.3	1	112	3	37.33	2-17	–
Mushtaq Ahmed	99.1	3	492	10	49.20	3-40	–
S.C. Ecclestone	45	0	306	6	51.00	2-21	–
A.P. van Troost	11	1	80	1	80.00	1-41	–
G.D. Rose	91.5	4	487	6	81.16	1-34	–
J.D. Batty	13	4	70	–	–	–	–

SOMERSET CCC

BATTING

	M	Inns	NO	Runs	HS	Av
M.N. Lathwell	17	33	1	1033	111	31.30
M.E. Trescothick	12	22	–	417	151	18.95
P.D. Bowler	19	33	3	1619	196	53.96
R.J. Harden	19	35	6	1429	129*	49.27
A.N. Hayhurst	17	29	5	825	107	34.37
R.J. Turner	19	30	7	717	106*	31.17
G.D. Rose	16	25	0	771	84	30.84
Mushtaq Ahmed	16	23	7	311	62*	14.80
A.R. Caddick	6	7	2	237	92	33.85
H.R.J. Trump	16	22	10	207	47	17.25
A.P. van Troost	6	11	3	82	34	10.25
K.A. Parsons	16	28	2	821	105	31.57
S.D. Ecclestone	7	12	2	472	81	47.20
P.C.L. Holloway	12	22	6	863	129*	53.93
J.C. Hallett	2	4	1	229	111*	76.33
J.I.D. Kerr	13	19	2	349	80	20.52
J.D. Batty	4	6	1	125	45*	25.00
M. Dimond	1	2	–	33	26	16.50

BOWLING

	A.R. Caddick	A.P. van Troost	Mushtaq Ahmed	H.R.J. Trump	G.D. Rose	A.N. Hayhurst	M.E. Trescothick	M.N. Lathwell	P.D. Bowler	S.D. Ecclestone	K.A. Parsons	J.I.D. Kerr	Byes	Leg-byes	Wides	No-balls	Total	Wks
v. Glamorgan (Taunton) 27–30 April	14–3–60–0	15.5–3–72–3	35–4–135–1	10–1–57–0	19–2–78–5									3	3	10	405	10
	4–0–17–1	3–0–24–1	6.2–1–47–0											1		7	89	2
v. Gloucestershire (Taunton) 4–8 May	28.3–4–65–4	4–0–21–0	46–12–141–3	21–3–56–0	26–4–93–2	10–1–31–1	1–0–3–0	8–2–8–0	5–2–9–0				1	13	6	8	424	10
			37–16–115–2	40–16–85–5	12–2–49–0	13–6–26–1	10–1–37–0						7	7	1	2	347	7
v. Northamptonshire (Northampton) 11–5 May	1–0–4–0		29–6–77–3	19.3–8–38–1	23–7–67–3	12–2–39–2					4–0–25–1		4	15	1	2	297	10
			22.4–3–110–1	14–4–46–1	16–5–65–0	4–0–16–0					9–1–38–1		10	8			291	8
v. West Indians (Taunton) 19–21 May			16–3–77–3	19–4–70–1	15–5–37–0	14–0–83–2	5–2–10–0				15–2–51–1			8	2		449	3
			8–2–28–0	12.4–3–32–2	10–2–53–1	3–0–19–0	5–1–23–0							1			176	3
v. Warwickshire (Edgbaston) 25–9 May			38–14–89–1	27–4–87–0	22–12–29–0	4–2–11–0			2.2–1–10–0		3–0–13–0	21–7–44–1	10	10		2	314	4A
			35–7–116–3	15.5–3–52–2	15–0–56–1							11–2–50–1	12	6	2	2	304	7
v. Yorkshire (Taunton) 1–5 June			51–16–126–5	35–8–77–2						16.3–3–53–2		23–6–71–1	5	13			413	10B
			29.3–7–86–4	21–6–68–1						3–0–10–0		2–0–4–0	7	5			197	6
v. Surrey (The Oval) 8–12 June			32.1–16–54–5	8–2–26–0	14–1–44–1	8–3–15–1				5–1–29–1		16–5–47–2	1	1		4	221	10
			42.1–13–107–5	39–21–67–2	24–4–101–1	4–0–19–1				3–1–12–1		16–4–64–2	5	11		8	419	10C
v. Derbyshire (Derby) 15–19 June			23–10–64–3	1–0–10–0	21–5–76–2		3–0–18–0				10–4–28–1	5–0–38–0		8		8	376	10
			31–13–54–6		16–5–27–4						4–1–11–2	20.1–6–68–4	4	8	2	4	168	10
v. Sussex (Bath) 22–6 June			27.2–10–62–4	19–6–38–2	25–4–74–0						5–1–14–0	10–6–16–1	4	5		8	227	10
			43–18–81–3	41–16–75–2	13–1–47–3							20–3–98–2	2	14	9		172	
v. Nottinghamshire (Trent Bridge) 29 June – 3 July			56–16–142–4	22–7–85–0	15–4–50–4	11–0–44–0	4–1–36–4	1–0–6–0	6–0–30–0		9–1–35–0	15–2–83–1		6		18	479	10D
			1–0–8–0	27–5–109–2	10–0–45–0		4–1–11–1					4–0–26–0						8	0
v. Young Australia (Taunton) 5–7 July			26.4–9–74–4	16–7–30–3	9–2–37–3	4–0–15–0		12–2–52–1		20.3–6–48–2		6–1–51–0	8	6		2	380	10D
					4–0–14–1							9–0–58–0	11			2	386	10
v. Essex (Southend) 20–4 July	6–0–35–0		45.2–16–127–4	32.2–8–88–2	17–4–43–2						1–0–5–0	9–1–44–0	12	18	1	2	186	10
v. Lancashire (Taunton) 27–31 July	27–7–94–3	28–6–87–3		33–10–113–2	9–1–34–1	2–1–12–0					3–0–23–1			8	4	10	429	0E
																	6	
v. West Indians (Taunton) 2–4 August		19–5–53–2	30.3–9–106–5	11.4–3–38–1	5–2–11–0	4.2–0–16–0		1–0–1–0	0–0–6–0		3–2–8–0	14–1–82–5	4	2	5	6	230	10
		19.1–1–120–5		34–10–95–2	2–0–9–0	3–2–2–0		3–1–15–1				6–0–45–0		5	3	6	386	9F
v. Kent (Taunton) 10–14 August		10.4–4–35–1		22–4–69–2	13–2–59–0					14–4–31–2	17–2–77–0			2	2	8	271	10
				8.2–3–15–3	16–1–39–2					3–0–17–1							119	10
v. Durham (Chester-le-Street) 17–21 August	19.4–1–69–8	10–2–23–0	19–8–38–6									9–0–51–2	4	5		6	221	10
												9–1–29–1	16	7	3		216	10
v. Leicestershire (Weston-super-Mare) 24–8 August	21–4–62–2	5–0–33–0	10–1–36–0		19–7–47–1	27–2–121–2					4–0–13–0		4	6	3	6	350	10
	23–3–90–4	12–0–45–1	17.4–8–60–5										4	3	1		313	8
v. Worcestershire (Worcester) 29 August – 1 September	19–5–65–1		30.5–5–122–3	12–7–13–0	4–3–3–0				3–0–13–1			7–0–33–0	4	7			670	7G
												4–4–35–0		6		14		
v. Hampshire (Southampton) 7–11 September		19–2–111–0	32.5–5–150–4	12–1–79–1	12–2–43–0	6–2–11–0	1–0–5–0				1–0–5–0	5–0–10–0	1	1		10	36	0H
					13–5–42–1	7–0–27–1						8–0–51–0	1	14		10	190	31
v. Middlesex (Taunton) 14–18 September			60–17–192–2	23–3–127–1	17–1–30–1	3–0–12–0					5–1–21–0		2	8		12	350	J
			31–14–57–4															
Bowler's average	183.1–34– 613–24 25.54	145.1–23– 624–16 39.00	935–286– 2821–95 29.69	596.2–173– 1745–40 43.62	436–93– 1402–39 35.94	139.2–21– 519–10 51.90	33–6– 143–5 28.60	25–5– 82–2 41.00	16.2–3– 68–1 68.00	105–20– 383–11 34.81	105–16– 458–6 76.33	280.1–53– 1134–28 40.50						

A J.C. Hallett 8–1–22–2, 2–0–12–0
B J.D. Batty 21–5–57–0, 9–2–20–1
C M. Dimond 10–1–54–0, 4–1–16–1
D J.D. Batty 6–0–69–1, 25–1–128–0
E P.C.L. Holloway 1–1–0–0
F J.D. Batty 17–2–104–1. J.C. Adams retired hurt
G P.C.L. Holloway 1–0–12–0
H R.J. Harden 1–0–17–0
I   J.C. Hallett 4–0–52–0. J.D. Batty 18.4–0–135–0
J   J.D. Batty 15–3–70–4

AXA EQUITY AND LAW LEAGUE – AVERAGES

BATTING	M	Inns	NO	Runs	HS	Av	100s	50s	ct/st
N. Shahid	13	12	5	322	101	46.00	1	–	5
D.J. Bicknell	13	13	–	545	102*	45.41	1	4	4
A.J. Hollioake	15	14	4	412	93	41.20	–	4	5
A.J. Tudor	2	2	1	40	29*	40.00	–	–	2
A.C.S. Pigott	7	3	2	35	19*	35.00	–	–	2
G.P. Thorpe	10	10	–	342	112	34.20	1	3	1
A.D. Brown	16	16	–	462	100	28.87	1	1	7
A.J. Stewart	5	5	1	114	44*	28.50	–	–	7
A.W. Smith	9	5	1	129	42	21.50	–	–	2
D.M. Ward	9	9	1	162	49	20.25	–	1	–
M.P. Bicknell	11	5	–	86	25	17.20	–	–	–
C.G. Rackemann	11	5	3	31	15*	15.50	–	–	1
J.D. Ratcliffe	3	3	1	31	31	15.00	–	–	–
M.A. Butcher	14	14	2	108	29	14.40	–	–	4/1
G.J. Kersey	8	6	–	54	24	9.00	–	–	4
J.E. Benjamin	8	4	1	19	13	6.33	–	–	–
N.F. Sargeant	3	2	–	13	9	4.00	–	–	3
S.G. Kenlock	12	5	1	13	9	3.25	–	–	–

Two matches: R.W. Nowell 0 (ct 1)
One match: G.J. Kennis 5; J.M. De La Penna 2*

BOWLING	Overs	Mds	Runs	Wkts	Av	Best	5/inn
D.J. Bicknell	6	2	39	2	19.50	1-11	–
A.C.S. Pigott	46.4	1	243	10	24.30	3-31	–
A.J. Hollioake	77.1	4	483	17	28.41	4-22	–
A.W. Smith	64	–	328	9	36.44	3-51	–
J.E. Benjamin	48	1	282	7	40.28	3-36	–
M.P. Bicknell	74	4	349	8	43.62	3-43	–
A.J. Tudor	7	–	48	1	48.00	1-19	–
C.G. Rackemann	79	2	404	8	50.50	3-36	–
S.G. Kenlock	78	6	455	9	50.55	2-36	–
M.A. Butcher	62.3	1	455	8	56.87	2-35	–
J.D. Ratcliffe	13	–	110	1	110.00	1-15	–
N. Shahid	13	–	72	–	–	–	–
G.P. Thorpe	1	–	14	–	–	–	–
J.M. De La Penna	4	–	27	–	–	–	–
R.W. Nowell	8	–	31	–	–	–	–

SURREY CCC — BATTING (season summary)

BATTING	M	Inns	NO	Runs	HS	Av
D.J. Bicknell	15	28	3	997	228*	39.88
A.J. Stewart		13	1	534	151	44.50
M.A. Butcher	17	32	2	1185	167	38.22
A.D. Brown	16	29	4	1054	187	42.16
A.J. Hollioake	14	30	2	1094	117*	39.07
N.Shahid	14	25	4	900	139	39.13
G.J. Kersey	15	28	4	708	83	29.50
M.P. Bicknell	11	20	11	213	61	23.66
R.W. Nowell	9	12	2	134	27	7.44
S.G. Kenlock	4	8	2	50	12	8.33
J.E. Benjamin	12	18	4	174	49	12.42
G.P. Thorpe	10	18	–	717	152	39.83
A.C.S. Pigott	6	11	3	76	19	7.60
C.G. Rackemann	13	20	12	120	20*	15.00
J.D. Ratcliffe		17	–	550	75	32.35
D.M. Ward	3	4	–	66	51	16.50
A.W. Smith	5	13	3	272	88	20.92
A.J. Tudor				123	56	13.66
G.J. Kennis		3	–	47	29	23.50
J.M. De La Pena	2	2	1	8	2*	4.00
N.F. Sargeant	2	2		6	6	–
J.A. Knott	1					

BOWLING

	M.P. Bicknell	J.E. Benjamin	S.G. Kenlock	A.J. Hollioake	R.W. Nowell	N. Shahid	A.C.S. Pigott	M.A. Butcher	J.M. De La Penna	C.G. Rackemann	A.W. Smith	A.J. Tudor	Byes	Leg-byes	Wides	No-balls	Total	Wks
v. Gloucestershire (The Oval) 27–30 April	6.3–3–17–0	24.5–5–77–4	26–3–105–2	19.3–2–84–2	19–5–73–1	5–0–29–0							–	7	–	6	392	10
		24–8–68–4	19–2–71–2	9–2–11–0	20–11–34–2	7–0–30–2							2	1	1	8	207	10
v. Warwickshire (Edgbaston) 4–8 May		31–5–82–2		16–3–55–2	46–13–119–1	6–0–49–0	34–12–92–3	16–2–62–0					8	3	2	46	470	10
		12–2–33–0		13–2–42–1	12–1–51–1		4–0–19–0	9–1–35–2					6	3	1	18	210	4[A]
v. Durham (The Oval) 11–15 May	26–12–81–4	22.1–3–57–3	16–0–67–1	5–1–12–0	16–7–38–1		20–6–46–1	13–3–32–1					–	6	3	12	269	10
	18–8–32–3	20–3–64–2		4–1–7–2	32–9–71–3		11–2–26–0	3–0–21–0					4	3	3	14	224	10
v. Northamptonshire (Northampton) 18–22 May		24.3–2–79–3		13–1–36–0	21–3–62–0		31–7–91–6	16–4–53–0					–	11	2	14	403	10
							11.3–4–20–5	9–0–32–1					1	4	–	4	59	10
v. Worcestershire (Worcester) 1–5 June	19–8–61–5	19.3–7–47–4		4–0–11–1	7–4–17–0		17–5–36–0	7.5–1–43–3		18.5–5–56–4			4	1	–	8	204	10
	7.2–1–31–0	22–6–65–2		7–2–20–0	5–0–28–0			4–0–26–0		17–6–34–1			1	2	2	6	265	7
v. Somerset (The Oval) 8–12 June		26–6–94–5		1–0–5–0			13–2–68–1	4–1–18–0		21–5–58–2	15–3–51–1		3	2	1	10	260	10
		17–3–60–2		6–0–23–0			15.5–4–36–2			18–6–63–2	36–7–123–2		2	11	–	12	383	10
v. Sussex (Horsham) 15–19 June		36–1–108–1		12–3–28–1	14–8–24–0	5–1–18–0	16.1–3–79–1	15–3–54–1		10.5–3–40–1	5–2–7–0		9	11	3	28	304	10
v. Glamorgan (The Oval) 22–6 June		8.5–1–27–0		10–4–21–0	16–4–56–1	10–1–54–1	22–3–84–1	16–1–72–4		27–8–60–6			–	8	–	20	230	10
		30–8–66–2		16.2–6–40–3		9–1–45–0	14–2–70–2	16–1–56–1		29–6–102–3	9–2–47–0		–	8	–	16	450	9
v. Middlesex (Lord's) 29 June – 3 July				7.1–1–34–0	40–10–103–2	3–0–15–0				21.4–6–70–4		19–1–63–3	6	5	3	6	329	10
				26.3–7–77–2	20–1–71–3					28–9–73–2			–	11	5	6	425	10[B]
v. Essex (The Oval) 6–10 July		25–3–120–1		5–0–23–0	22–10–43–4	3–0–13–0		11–1–38–0		34–10–99–4		18–2–77–3	12	8	2	20	493	10
		4–1–13–0			12.1–7–35–2	4–0–15–0				10–3–36–0		4–0–9–0	3	4	–	4	151	3
v. Nottinghamshire (Guildford) 20–4 July		20.1–4–53–5	24–5–88–2	7–4–12–1		19–4–87–2		5–1–10–0		25–2–98–1			3	15	8	25	324	10
v. Leicestershire (Leicester) 27–31 July			12–3–45–0	13–2–55–0	19.3–2–93–1					20–6–73–3			5	7	1	12	272	10
	34–3–117–5			3–0–15–0		10–3–29–2				22–3–55–0	24–1–112–3	15–1–57–1	–	4	2	18	503	10
v. Kent (Canterbury) 3–7 August	26–4–98–2				28.1–6–105–4	7–0–36–0			19–2–112–3	26.3–9–64–4			5	5	4	24	410	10[C]
	16–2–82–1				35–6–144–4	8–1–47–0			4–1–20–0	26–8–63–2	7–0–43–0		3	4	–	4	380	8
v. Yorkshire (The Oval) 10–14 August	17–6–48–4		20–7–50–1	12–1–49–1	23–6–66–0			9–3–32–1	19–5–53–3	12–1–58–0	19–6–47–2		3	6	1	16	366	10
	26.5–4–99–3		2–0–14–0	10–2–22–4		2–1–1–0		9–4–32–1	2–0–23–0	20–6–74–1			4	1	–	12	217	10
v. Derbyshire (Derby) 24–8 August				6–2–17–1	17–7–41–2	10–3–29–2		4–0–20–0		24.1–4–77–2	3–1–5–0		1	5	1	8	181	10
	36.2–7–107–5					9–1–34–0		12–5–47–2		7–1–25–0	16–3–53–0	9.4–2–32–5	4	5	1	16	333	10
v. Lancashire (The Oval) 29 August –1 September	13–1–79–0	19–1–82–2				3–0–12–0				12–3–36–1	5–0–19–0	12–0–70–2	–	7	4	34	392	10[D]
v. New South Wales (The Oval) 6–8 September	6–1–9–1					6–2–23–1						5.5–1–12–0	–	–	–	8	71	1[E]
	19–3–65–4	10.1–1–62–3						8–0–70–1		16–4–58–3	21.3–2–104–2		4	–	2	38	398	7
v. Hampshire (The Oval) 14–18 September	15–2–60–4	13.2–3–32–3								11–0–58–2			–	4	–	34	185	10
Bowler's average	286–65–986–41 / 24.04	420.4–84–1326–53 / 25.01	119–20–440–8 / 55.00	230.3–46–721–21 / 34.33	424.5–120–1264–32 / 39.50	120–16–547–8 / 68.37	209.3–50–667–22 / 30.31	234.5–37–935–22 / 42.50	44–8–208–6 / 34.66	457–114–1430–48 / 29.79	165.3–27–647–10 / 64.70	83.3–7–320–14 / 22.85						

A A.J. Stewart 3–0–18–0
B G.P. Thorpe 6–2–17–0
C G.J. Kennis 3–3–0–0.   D.J. Bicknell 6–4–2–0, 15–0–80–3
D G.P. Thorpe 17–2–42–2
E D.J. Bicknell 2.3–1–6–0

FIELDING FIGURES

45 – P. Moores (ct 43/st 2)
17 – I.D.K. Salisbury
11 – K. Greenfield
10 – N.J. Lenham
9 – A.P. Wells
8 – P.W. Jarvis
6 – C.W.J. Athey and D.C.R. Law
5 – J.W. Hall and M.T.E. Peirce
4 – F.D. Stephenson
3 – K. Newell, E.S.H. Giddins and N.C. Phillips
2 – R.J. Kirtley, J.D. Lewry and subs
1 – E.E. Hemmings

† N.J. Lenham retired hurt, absent hurt

AXA EQUITY AND LAW LEAGUE – AVERAGES

BATTING	M	Inns	NO	Runs	HS	Av	100s	50s	ct/st
P. Moores	17	16	8	383	89*	47.87		2	17/4
C.W.J. Athey	11	10	2	279	61*	34.87		2	2
K. Newell	10	8	1	207	76*	29.57		1	2
A.P. Wells	15	15	1	403	85	28.78		3	4
K. Greenfield	17	17	0	488	102	28.70	1	3	9
N.J. Lenham	9	9	1	193	56*	24.12		1	3
J.W. Hall	6	6	0	128	47	21.33			2
F.D. Stephenson	15	15	1	292	54	20.85		2	4
D.C.R. Law	15	12	7	112	41*	18.66			2
I.D.K. Salisbury	17	11	1	151	48*	15.10			5
P.W. Jarvis	12	8	4	57	13*	14.25			1
J.A. North	6	6	1	60	32	12.00			1
J.D. Lewry	7	5	2	17	7*	5.66			2
R.S.C. Martin-Jenkins	9	5	1	12	10	3.00			1
N.C. Phillips	7	3	1	2	2	1.00			1
E.S.H. Giddins	16	7	2	2	1*	0.40			—

Three matches: R.J. Kirtley 2
One match: M.T.E. Peirce 7

BOWLING	Overs	Mds	Runs	Wkts	Av	Best	5/inn
P.W. Jarvis	68.4	3	336	18	18.66	6-29	1
J.D. Lewry	61.1	5	290	14	20.71	4-29	—
K. Greenfield	28.4	2	146	7	20.85	3-34	—
F.D. Stephenson	97	7	434	20	21.70	5-38	1
I.D.K. Salisbury	98	7	478	20	23.90	4-39	—
R.S.C. Martin-Jenkins	100.1	4	548	16	34.25	2-1	—
E.S.H. Giddins	53	5	286	5	57.20	2-41	—
J.A. North	11	1	61	1	61.00	1-39	—
R.J. Kirtley	11	1	69	1	69.00	1-49	—
N.C. Phillips	16	1	69	1	69.00	1-35	—
K. Newell	9	—	58	—	—	—	—

SUSSEX CCC

BATTING

	v. Derbyshire (Derby) 27–30 April	v. Kent (Hove) 4–8 May	v. Glamorgan (Swansea) 11–15 May	v. Essex (Hove) 18–22 May	v. Hampshire (Portsmouth) 25–9 May	v. Gloucestershire (Hove) 1–5 June	v. Warwickshire (Edgbaston) 8–12 June	v. Surrey (Horsham) 15–19 June	v. Somerset (Bath) 22–6 June	v. West Indians (Hove) 1–3 July	v. Nottinghamshire (Arundel) 6–10 July	v. Leicestershire (Hove) 20–4 July	M	Inns	NO	Runs	HS	Av
N.J. Lenham	45	11 0	17 92	8 21	7 7	0 163*	13 20*	21 72	32 8	128	0* 4	21 21	15	25	3	867	128	39.40
C.W.J. Athey	0 0	62 72	85		17 32		42	41 54			4 4	18 0	15	27	1	929	163*	35.73
J.W. Hall	0 0	19 0	0		30	15	49 1	47 21	106	21	7 0	0 35	16	22	0	537	100	24.40
A.P. Wells	10 46*	107 136	2 85	10 15	30 32	8	84 56	29 26	43 20	21 45	7 0	15 142	16	27	2	1343	142	51.65
K. Greenfield	7 5	68	8 0	5 69	8	4	12	0 1	6 0		0 46	8 8	19	32	5	853	121	27.51
P. Moores	1 0	0 5	12 16*	51 121	23 17	26		25 0	9 21	32	68 40	58 13	19	23	1	660	94	22.00
F.D. Stephenson	19 10	48 29	30 16	86 18	19 17	106						80	13	23	0	690	106	30.00
C.C. Remy	4								4 23		38		1	2	0	5	4	2.50
I.D.K. Salisbury	4 8	9	33	25 18		74	10 20	11 0		0 0	1 0*	9 5	18	30	12	599	74	22.18
P.W. Jarvis	4*				38 28			0 6*	8* 1*			5 6	13	19	2	177	38	16.09
E.S.H. Giddins	5	9 5	20	34 4	1		1*	31* 11*	11 13	0*	4* 13	0*	18	27	12	137	34	9.13
J.D. Lewry		3		7* 7				4 2	18 12				12	19	9	150	34	10.00
E.E. Hemmings	1	0*	63 34*	33 10	0* 3*		89	53	10 0	135	13 11	7 28	7	15	7	70	18	14.00
K. Newell			2*		24 35								10	19	0	500	135	29.41
R.J. Kirtley	34	34				50*				43		4 5	8	10	2	183	53	20.33
N.C. Phillips	4*												6	8	0	248	115	19.07
D.C.R. Law	5						0*						6	13	1	219	60	21.90
M.T.E. Peirce													6	10	1	23	22	11.50
A.D. Edwards													1	2	2	50	50	50.00
R.S.C. Martin-Jenkins													2	2	1			
Byes	8	5	1	4	1		4	9	2	3		2						
Leg-byes	1	15		3	4	10	15	3	4	5	3	9						
Wides	4	8		6	4			2	5	1	3	1						
No-balls	2	2	2	44	14	26	18	28	8		4	6						
Total	111	323 343	196 256	326 390	196 232	482	361	304 230	227 172	446	134 149	233 293						
Wickets	10	10 10	10 D	10 10	10 10	7	10 8	10 10	10 10	W	9† 10	10 10						
Result	L	W	D	W	L		D	D	L		L	L						
Points	10	23	4	23	1	8	8	7	5		4	5						

BATTING

	v. Middlesex (Lord's) 27–31 July	v. Lancashire (Lytham) 3–7 August	v. Young Australia (Hove) 11–13 August	v. Worcestershire (Eastbourne) 17–21 August	v. Durham (Hartlepool) 24–8 August	v. Yorkshire (Scarborough) 7–11 September	v. Northamptonshire (Hove) 14–18 September	M	Inns	NO	Runs	HS	Av
N.J. Lenham	0 16	8 57	21 40	0 3		86 9	28 56	15	25	3	867	128	39.40
C.W.J. Athey	17		94 40	33	104 108		6* 41	15	27	1	929	163*	35.73
J.W. Hall	61 4	105 0	26		100	76	40	16	22	0	537	100	24.40
A.P. Wells	4 0	0 7		108 0		85 7	10 89*	16	27	2	1343	142	51.65
K. Greenfield	55 13	24* 10	6 41	99 5	45 6		10 20	19	32	5	853	121	27.51
P. Moores			53	12 18	29*	43 23*	67*	19	23	1	660	94	22.00
F.D. Stephenson	22* 16	26 11	115	0* 5*	18			13	23	0	690	106	30.00
C.C. Remy		1* 0*	44	0 0				1	2	0	5	4	2.50
I.D.K. Salisbury	0 10		22	12		23*	10	18	30	12	599	74	22.18
P.W. Jarvis					1*			13	19	2	177	38	16.09
E.S.H. Giddins								18	27	12	137	34	9.13
J.D. Lewry				9 7		0 0		12	19	9	150	34	10.00
E.E. Hemmings				16 60	2 44	6	2	7	15	7	70	18	14.00
K. Newell		52 17	8 44				20 14	10	19	0	500	135	29.41
R.J. Kirtley	16 19	3	1 22			0*	50	8	10	2	183	53	20.33
N.C. Phillips								6	8	0	248	115	19.07
D.C.R. Law								6	13	1	219	60	21.90
M.T.E. Peirce								6	10	1	23	22	11.50
A.D. Edwards								1	2	2	50	50	50.00
R.S.C. Martin-Jenkins								2	2	1			
Byes	6	12		4	14		6						
Leg-byes	1	15 11		4	9	6	3 1						
Wides	6	4	14 6		8	16							
No-balls	10			10 8	18								
Total	201 115	317 193	109 479	326 267	498	357	331 132						
Wickets	10 10	10 10	10 10	10 10	8	8	10 D						
Result	L	L	W	W	W	D	D						
Points	10	—	—	24	24	4	3						

BOWLING

Opponent (venue), date	F.D. Stephenson	P.W. Jarvis	E.S.H. Giddins	I.D.K. Salisbury	D.R.C. Law	C.W.J. Athey	K. Greenfield	J.D. Lewry	E.E. Hemmings	R.J. Kirtley	K. Newell	N.C. Phillips	Byes	Leg-byes	Wides	No-balls	Total	Wks
v. Derbyshire (Derby) 27–30 April	29-3-117-2	2.3-0-11-0	41-2-157-3	41-13-118-0		2-0-15-0	13.1-1-45-0						4	22	1	8	603	6A
v. Kent (Hove) 4–8 May	31-9-86-4		27-3-94-1	21.3-2-76-2				21-3-73-2	11-3-23-0				1	8	2	4	361	10
	13-4-49-1			20-5-63-1				13-1-54-3	19.1-4-63-4				5	1	5	6	230	10
v. Glamorgan (Swansea) 11–15 May	12.5-2-42-1		28-7-87-6	2-0-3-0				17-6-31-2		11-3-28-1			4	16	6	10	212	10
	17-4-64-5		23-1-74-1	11-1-58-1				11-1-46-0		1-0-4-0			2	20	1	6	270	7
v. Essex (Hove) 18–22 May	23-6-66-2		13.1-2-48-5	13-5-23-2									4	3	3	14	185	10
	6-1-24-1			27-7-72-7				7-0-33-0			10-3-22-0		12	10	3	2	253	10
v. Hampshire (Portsmouth) 25–9 May	27-7-62-1	28-3-111-2	33-7-91-3	31-2-123-1		3-1-9-0					15-3-35-0		1	5	4	8	534	10
v. Gloucestershire (Hove) 1–5 June	16-4-39-0		17.2-2-79-3	8-1-33-1				17.2-3-45-6	20-4-77-1				5	11	1	14	202	10
	11-2-34-1		29-2-96-2	34-7-85-3				19-2-72-0	25.4-4-81-2			18-2-67-0	4	10	2	16	380	7B
v. Warwickshire (Edgbaston) 8–12 June	15-6-35-3		26.4-7-59-4	13-4-30-0			4-0-26-0	20-5-63-2					5	3	3	10	248	10
	24-4-68-1		25-10-53-2	12-2-28-0				23-5-81-0			2-0-24-0		1	21	1	4	332	6
v. Surrey (Horsham) 15–19 June	11.3-1-46-2		11-0-54-4	24-4-106-1				16-3-77-4	4-1-6-0				12	16	3	10	187	10
	9-0-60-0		23-4-129-2	8-2-16-2				19.2-0-110-5	23-5-90-0				4	4	1	2	501	8
v. Somerset (Bath) 22–6 June	15-2-48-0		21.5-2-73-6	28-6-76-2				12-2-27-2					4	2	2	2	178	10
	24-6-72-1		20-3-67-2	8-2-25-2				13-0-53-1					2	7	1	4	345	10
v. West Indians (Hove) 1–3 July	9-1-23-2	16-4-51-3		24-9-69-3	10-5-11-1			21-6-62-2	43-18-57-4				2	4	3	6	186	10
	6-1-23-2	10-2-39-0							3-1-7-0				8	3	5	22	139	10
v. Nottinghamshire (Arundel) 6–10 July	19-3-33-3	18-6-59-2	27-7-76-3	28-9-70-5				10.3-2-38-4	15-4-33-4				4	6		8	255	10
			4-0-16-0						9-4-23-0				7	5		2	29	0
v. Leicestershire (Hove) 20–4 July	15.1-4-32-2		26-7-60-1	33-5-101-6		2-0-11-0	4-0-11-0	15-3-45-1			4-1-11-0	3-0-7-0	5	18		8	242	10
	15-2-44-0	21.1-1-63-2	15-5-101-6	37-7-129-2	21-4-115-2			3.2-0-9-0			9-1-35-0	15-8-38-0	13	6		22	347	7
v. Middlesex (Lord's) 27–31 July	12.5-1-48-0		28.1-2-121-0					33-8-116-3					4	5		6	602	10C
v. Lancashire (Lytham) 3–7 August		19-4-56-1	16-4-49-1	33-5-107-6								20.3-2-106-2	4	2		8	355	10
		14-2-55-5	5-1-10-0	23-7-53-2								21.2-3-78-3	8	3		6	215	10
v. Young Australia (Hove) 11–13 August			22-6-75-1		13-0-73-0 / 13-0-4-1							40-11-157-1	4	9			580	8D, E
v. Worcestershire (Eastbourne) 17–21 August			20-1-55-3		10-1-46-1 / 12-1-41-1								8	3			170	10
v. Durham (Hartlepool) 24–8 August		21-6-46-4	34-9-84-2	10-3-20-0	2-0-13-0			31-4-139-3		18-6-42-1		36-8-64-2	1	10			348	10
		29-5-104-4	19.1-5-57-4	51.5-19-139-5				19.4-7-43-6		8-2-29-0							177	10
v. Yorkshire (Scarborough) 7–11 September			26.4-6-87-6					2-0-9-0									271	Ab.
v. Northamptonshire (Hove) 14–18 September		2-1-4-0	5-2-22-1									1-0-4-0	1	3		6	41	1
		2-0-6-0	4-0-26-0	11-3-28-0													36	0F
Bowler's average	361.2-73-1113-35 31.80	228.4-45-719-26 27.66	596.4-110-2004-68 29.47	558.5-130-1674-54 31.00	69.3-11-303-6 50.50	7-1-35-0 –	21.1-1-82-0 –	350.1-62-1247-47 26.53	177.5-51-442-15 29.46	38-11-103-2 51.50	40-8-127-0 –	154.5-34-521-8 65.12						

A C.C. Remy 22.3-4-114-0
B N.J. Lenham 2-0-10-1
C M.T.E. Peirce 6-1-14-0
D N.J. Lenham 4-0-17-0. M.T.E. Peirce 3-0-16-0. A.D. Edwards 22-4-83-3
E A.D. Edwards 1-0-4-0
F R.S.C. Martin-Jenkins 3-1-11-0

WARWICKSHIRE CCC

BATTING

	v. England 'A' (Edgbaston) 18–21 April		v. Middlesex (Edgbaston) 27–30 April		v. Surrey (Edgbaston) 4–8 May		v. Lancashire (Old Trafford) 11–15 May		v. Durham (Chester-le-Street) 18–22 May		v. Somerset (Edgbaston) 25–9 May		v. Sussex (Edgbaston) 8–12 June		v. Cambridge University (Cambridge) 16–18 June		v. Yorkshire (Edgbaston) 22–6 June		v. Essex (Ilford) 29 June – 3 July		v. Leicestershire (Leicester) 6–10 July		v. Glamorgan (Cardiff) 20–4 July		M	Inns	NO	Runs	HS	Av
A.J. Moles	67	13	31	0	2	35	51	66	90	22	16	131	66	0	98	–	22	–			24	–	33	–	4	–	9	16	–	710	131	44.37
R.G. Twose	29	25	66	26	26	7	0	4	51	2	5	39	27	131*	96	–	7	–	24	–	33	–	14	–	19	30	4	1186	191	45.61
T.L. Penney	14	14	0	88	38	26	25	0	48	8	101*	12	51	16	37*	–	50	–	141	–	14	–	14	–	19	27	3	1198	144	49.91
D.P. Ostler	26	2	57	12	208	66*	11	50	18	7			31	7	46	–	57	–	116	–	59	–	20	20*	18	26	2	983	208	40.95
G. Welch	0	2																							1	2	–	2	2	1.00
D.A. Reeve	0	77*	7	10	53	20*					4	47	23*	19			21	–	9	–	14	–	36	–	16	22	4	652	77*	36.22
K.J. Piper	8	0							24	30*		0*	3	4	–	2	90	–	10	–	5	–	28	–	16	19	2	398	99	23.41
D.R. Brown	9	3					47	7	33	8		36*	13	50	–	53	27	–	85	–	44	–	52	–	15	20	2	506	85	28.11
N.M.K. Smith	55*	18	4	11	40	–	21	0				5	3	11	–	0	32	–	0	–	67*	–	0	–	18	23	2	486	75	23.14
G.C. Small	10	12	6*	4	3	–			6*	6*			15	10*											6	9	4	72	15	14.40
A.A. Donald	16	33	3	1*	4*	–							6	–			0*	–	44	–	24	–	2	–	15	16	5	194	44	17.63
N.V. Knight			85	72					89	4			4	74*			91	–	40	21*	21	–	5	13*	11	19	5	798	174	57.00
Wasim Khan					19	25	38	78			58	18	89	23	16*	91			3	6*	1	–			13	23	6	847	181	49.82
M. Burns			1	35	8	–	28	6																	3	5	–	78	35	15.60
R.P. Davis			13	9	10	–			0	30	6	11*	–	–											6	8	2	79	30	13.16
P.A. Smith							13	7	44	3			–	57											3	5	–	124	57	24.80
M.A.V. Bell									0*	–															3	1	1	0	0*	–
T.A. Munton													1*	–			13	–	0*	–	4	–	2*	–	11	10	6	66	19*	16.50
A. Giles																							24	–	6	5	–	84	32	16.80
A. Singh																									1	2	–	12	7	6.00
Byes			11		8	6			15				10	12	4	5	2	1	15		8		4							
Leg-byes	6	6	7	8	3	6	6	11	13	2	10	6	10	6	4	1	5		18	5	7		2							
Wides			1		2	1	1	1			2	1		2	1				1				1							
No-balls			2	6	46	18	16	16	4			2	14	16		2	34		18	2	6		14							
Total	240	205	282	294	470	210	262	297	424	145	314	304	248	332	300	208	449		513	35	307		208							
Wickets	10	10	10	10	10	10	10	10	10	10	4	7	10	5			10		10	0	10		10							
Result	L		W		W		L		W		W		D		D		W		W		W		W							
Points	–		22		24		5		22		20		5		–		24		24		23		21							

FIELDING FIGURES

61 – K.J. Piper (ct 59/st 2)
25 – D.P. Ostler
19 – N.V. Knight
17 – D.A. Reeve and Wasim Khan
10 – M. Burns (ct 9/st 1)
9 – T.L. Penney
7 – R.G. Twose, A.A. Donald and D.R. Brown
6 – N.M.K. Smith
5 – R.P. Davis and A.J. Moles
3 – T.A. Munton
2 – M.A.V. Bell and subs
1 – P.A. Smith and A. Singh

AXA EQUITY AND LAW LEAGUE – AVERAGES

BATTING	M	Inns	NO	Runs	HS	Av	100s	50s	ct/st
R.G. Twose	17	15	4	436	69*	38.72	–	4	3
N.V. Knight	12	10	–	345	80	38.33	–	2	4
N.M.K. Smith	17	16	–	504	71	31.50	–	5	8
D.A. Reeve	15	13	4	230	50	25.55	–	1	4
K.J. Piper	15	9	6	73	27*	24.33	–	–	24/2
D.P. Ostler	14	13	1	290	58	24.16	–	1	4
A.J. Moles	5	5	–	103	46	20.60	–	–	–
P.A. Smith	15	12	1	211	85	19.18	–	1	2
G.C. Small	4	3	2	17	17	17.00	–	–	1
D.R. Brown	17	16	3	212	78*	16.30	–	1	2
T.L. Penney	16	13	2	176	42*	16.00	–	–	7
M. Burns	2	2	–	8	7	4.00	–	–	1
A.A. Donald	11	3	3	14	5*	–	–	–	–
R.P. Davis	2	2	2	3*	–	–	–	–	2

Eleven matches: T.A. Munton (ct 2) did not bat
Seven matches: M.A.V. Bell 8* (ct 1)
Three matches: A.F. Giles (ct 2) did not bat
Two matches: M. Asif Din 4 (ct 1)
One match: G. Welch 24; Wasim Khan 1 (ct 1)

BOWLING	Overs	Mds	Runs	Wkts	Av	Best	5/inn
P.A. Smith	60	3	295	20	14.75	4-39	–
A.A. Donald	84.4	5	311	19	16.36	6-15	1
D.A. Reeve	82.1	3	355	19	18.68	4-22	–
M.A.V. Bell	47	1	206	10	20.60	3-25	–
N.M.K. Smith	78	3	386	18	21.44	6-33	1
T.A. Munton	82	7	324	14	23.14	3-45	–
G.C. Small	32	4	126	4	31.50	3-23	–
R.P. Davis	16	–	64	2	32.00	2-30	–
D.R. Brown	77	2	355	10	35.50	2-41	–
R.G. Twose	22.5	–	112	2	56.00	1-14	–
G. Welch	3	–	19				

BATTING

	v. Northamptonshire (Edgbaston) 27–31 July		v. Hampshire (Southampton) 10–14 August		v. Nottinghamshire (Trent Bridge) 17–21 August		v. Worcestershire (Edgbaston) 24–8 August		v. Gloucestershire (Edgbaston) 29 August – 1 September		v. Derbyshire (Edgbaston) 7–11 September		v. Kent (Canterbury) 14–18 September		M	Inns	NO	Runs	HS	Av
A.J. Moles	140	16	12	–	44	–	191	37*	10	1*	24	–	109*	–	9	16	–	710	131	44.37
R.G. Twose															19	30	4	1186	191	45.61
T.L. Penney	1	0	85	–	144	–	44	–	43	–	137*	–	47	–	19	27	3	1198	144	49.91
D.P. Ostler	0	14	0	–	47	–	9	–	30	–	62	–	8	–	18	26	2	983	208	40.95
G. Welch															1	2	–	2	2	1.00
D.A. Reeve	14	74	77*	–	1	–	44	–	35	–	67	–	0	–	16	22	4	652	77*	36.22
K.J. Piper	0	10	99	–	18	–	40	–	17	–	20	–			16	19	2	398	99	23.41
D.R. Brown	0	4	1	–			5	–	29*	–	0	–			15	20	2	506	85	28.11
N.M.K. Smith	18	75	21	–	14	–	0	–	8	–	29	–	54	–	18	23	2	486	75	23.14
G.C. Small															6	9	4	72	15	14.40
A.A. Donald	9	27*	4*	–	3	–	18	–							15	16	5	194	44	17.63
N.V. Knight					6	18*					0	5*	174	–	11	19	5	798	174	57.00
Wasim Khan	17	3	181	–	68	10*	21	26*	68	9*	4	0*	51	–	13	23	6	847	181	49.82
M. Burns															3	5	–	78	35	15.60
R.P. Davis															6	8	2	79	30	13.16
P.A. Smith															3	5	–	124	57	24.80
M.A.V. Bell															3	1	1	0	0*	–
T.A. Munton	0*	10	–	–	19*	–	17*	–	0	–					11	10	6	66	19*	16.50
A. Giles			32	–	10	–	2	–	16	–					6	5	–	84	32	16.80
A. Singh	5	7													1	2	–	12	7	6.00
Byes		8	1		13		8		6		7		11							
Leg-byes	12	11	8		8		18		6		10		9							
Wides			4		4					1	5		1							
No-balls	8	8	10		15		45	6	10		22		4							
Total	224	267	535		414	28	462	69	278	11	387	5	468							
Wickets	10	10	8		10	10	10	0	10	0	8	0	6							
Result	L		W		W		W		W		W		W							
Points	5		24		24		24		24		24									

BOWLING

Bowlers' season analyses (O–M–R–W)

Bowler	Match-by-match analyses (O–M–R–W)	Season total (O–M–R–W)	Avge
A.A. Donald	24-6-68-1; 22-3-56-6; 17-3-48-2; 25.5-3-64-6; 2.4-0-13-1; 29-3-112-4; 5-0-23-0; 12.1-3-21-5; 20-4-55-1; 25.4-5-70-3; 17-3-49-3; 21-9-38-3; 6-3-15-0; 15-4-49-2; 10-3-25-4; 16-8-41-4; 39.1-10-95-6; 21-8-48-3; 19-7-50-2; 25-6-78-3; 25-5-57-3; 24.2-13-47-2; 12.4-1-37-5; 16.2-8-22-3; 18-5-42-3; 16.4-4-65-5; 17-3-48-2; 15-0-43-4	535.3-136-1431-89	16.07
G.C. Small	23-7-63-0; 20-2-52-2; 12-4-25-3; 20-9-38-1; 19.3-7-71-5; 27-7-76-3; 11.4-2-32-1; 29-9-74-2; 18-0-74-0; 2.4-1-2-0	182.5-48-507-17	29.82
G. Welch	17-1-80-2	17-1-80-2	40.00
D.R. Brown	26-4-121-2; 22-4-63-2; 11.2-0-47-1; 24.2-7-65-3; 12.3-1-62-3; 40-7-140-2; 11-4-27-2; 21.5-6-55-3; 10-4-25-0; 7-1-23-1; 12-2-35-4; 8.4-4-24-4; 13-0-52-0; 4-0-23-0; 14-8-22-2; 8-2-16-1; 7-0-31-1; 23-9-51-2; 4-0-16-0; 8-2-25-0; 9-3-27-2; 12-2-52-2; 3-1-9-0	311.4-71-1011-37	27.32
N.M.K. Smith	24-4-111-2; 5-1-18-1; 15-3-44-3; 27-6-76-1; 12-0-63-0; 42-11-112-0; 2-0-14-0; 27-6-52-1; 3.1-0-12-0; 7-4-15-0; 20-7-33-1; 16-6-41-0; 6-1-20-0; 31-10-87-2; 23.1-4-67-5; 8-1-22-0; 3-1-3-0; 0.4-0-1-1; 10-2-23-1; 21-4-72-0; 3-0-15-1; 33.2-10-72-6; 14-5-49-0; 8-2-27-0; 40.5-16-2-5; 3-0-7-1; 10-4-18-3; 26.4-4-83-2; 11-1-33-2; 4-1-19-0; 2-1-3-0	460-105-1375-39	35.25
D.A. Reeve	18.2-5-41-2; 7.2-1-25-1; 2-1-4-0; 15-5-37-2; 0.2-0-1-0; 28-11-59-2; 15-7-24-3; 31-9-69-0; 4-2-8-0; 2-1-7-0; 16-4-37-3; 7-1-21-0; 23-13-30-4; 10.4-4-17-2; 6-5-1-1; 3-1-6-0; 12-4-26-1; 6-1-25-0; 6-4-6-0; 8.3-5-9-1; 15-2-48-1; 4-2-6-1; 14-5-27-3; 7.5-3-51-1; 8-3-16-1; 2-1-4-3; 18-7-30-5; 4-2-3-0	312-118-661-38	17.39
R.P. Davis	15-4-60-0; 7-3-10-1; 25-7-58-0; 31-8-93-0; 53.2-13-118-5; 15.1-2-40-1; 2-1-14-0; 28.5-8-77-3; 10-2-25-2; 21.2-6-62-2; 8-4-19-1	216.4-58-576-15	38.40
R.G. Twose	11-0-50-3; 1-1-0-0; 20-6-51-3; 22-5-67-2; 4-3-2-0; 14-5-29-0; 5-1-14-2; 7-0-26-1; 2-0-5-0; 2-0-14-0; 4-2-12-0; 4-2-9-0; 1-1-0-0; 8-1-20-0; 3-2-2-0	108-29-301-11	27.36
P.A. Smith	8-2-28-0; 3-0-12-1; 18-5-45-1; 6-1-22-2; 8-2-29-0	43-10-136-4	34.00
M.A.V. Bell	29-10-77-1; 9-1-34-1; 18-7-59-2; 16-5-68-2; 8-2-27-1	80-25-265-7	37.85
A.J. Moles	7-0-22-0	7-0-22-0	–
Wasim Khan	7-1-22-0	7-1-22-0	–
T.A. Munton	28-7-59-3; 5-1-15-0; 15-4-46-2; 5-3-6-0; 9-2-26-1; 22-6-63-4; 27-7-66-1; 16-7-47-2; 11.5-5-25-1; 10-4-14-4; 13-3-42-5; 12-2-46-1; 20.3-6-47-4; 29-8-83-2; 27-8-61-2; 16-5-43-1; 23-10-37-5; 27.5-9-79-5; 13-4-32-2; 27.3-15-47-2; 16-3-48-1; 0.1-0-0-0	373.5-119-952-48	19.83
A. Giles	8-4-13-1; 9.3-3-14-1; 11-2-32-2; 15-5-30-1; 16-3-52-1; 1-0-10-0; 15.2-7-23-5; 27-6-52-0; 4-2-3-0; 9-3-20-1; 11-1-64-1; 20-10-41-3	146.5-46-354-16	22.12

Innings extras and totals

Match (venue, dates)	Byes	Leg-byes	Wides	No-balls	Total	Wks
v. England 'A' (Edgbaston) 18–21 April	5	14	3	14	503	9A
v. Middlesex (Edgbaston) 27–30 April	5	8		9	224	10
	2	8	1	6	137	10
v. Surrey (Edgbaston) 4–8 May	10	5	3	10	288	10
	4	8		14	301	10
v. Lancashire (Old Trafford) 11–15 May	5				410	4
	1	2	1	2	150	10
v. Durham (Chester-le-Street) 18–22 May		3		2	313	9B
	7	9	4	14	145	4
v. Somerset (Edgbaston) 25–9 May	4	15	2		495	1
	4	4		18	119	7
v. Sussex (Edgbaston) 8–12 June	7				47	3
	1	4		6	220	10
v. Cambridge University (Cambridge) 16–8 June	5	5		2	119	9C
		6		16	96	10
v. Yorkshire (Edgbaston) 22–6 June	4	2	1	18	185	10
	2	8			328	10
v. Essex (Ilford) 29 June – 3 July	1	12		12	219	9D
		16	2	2	151	10
v. Leicestershire (Leicester) 6–10 July	4	7		12	67	9E
		3		6	122	10
v. Glamorgan (Cardiff) 20–4 July	9	1	1	6	122	6
	12	11	2	20	152	10
v. Northamptonshire (Edgbaston) 27–31 July	9	6		4	346	10
	9	11		10	225	10
v. Hampshire (Southampton) 10–14 August	4	5		4	221	10
	7	7		4	166	9F
v. Nottinghamshire (Trent Bridge) 17–21 August		6	1	2	272	10
		16			177	10
v. Worcestershire (Edgbaston) 24–8 August	3	1		10	350	10
	6	3		18	124	10
v. Gloucestershire (Edgbaston) 29 August – 1 September	4	8			162	10
	8	7	1	6	268	10
v. Derbyshire (Edgbaston) 7–11 September		2	1	6	122	
		6		2	239	
v. Kent (Canterbury) 14–18 September	1	6		2	124	8G

A P.A. Nixon retired hurt
B I.A. Daley absent hurt
C M.D. Moxon retired hurt
D B.F. Smith absent ill
E P.A. Cottey absent hurt
F C. Benton retired hurt
G C.R. Cowdrey, A.P. Igglesden absent hurt

FIELDING FIGURES

58 – S.J. Rhodes (ct 51/st 7)
31 – T.M. Moody
16 – G.A. Hick
15 – D.A. Leatherdale
14 – W.P.C. Weston
11 – S.R. Lampitt
10 – G.R. Haynes
8 – T.S. Curtis and V.S. Solanki
5 – Parvaz Mirza
4 – subs
3 – M.J. Church and R.K. Illingworth
2 – P.J. Newport and D.B. D'Oliveira
1 – K.R. Spring, C.M. Tolley and P.A. Thomas
† G.A. Hick absent hurt

AXA EQUITY AND LAW LEAGUE – AVERAGES

BATTING	M	Inns	NO	Runs	HS	Av	100s	50s	ct/st
G.A. Hick	11	11	4	551	130	78.71	2	4	6
T.M. Moody	17	17	1	797	108	53.13	3	4	6
T.S. Curtis	16	16	3	480	82*	36.92	–	5	5
W.P.C. Weston	13	10	1	279	80	31.00	–	2	5
S.R. Lampitt	16	13	6	168	29*	24.85	–	–	3
D.A. Leatherdale	13	10	1	199	47	22.11	–	–	3
C.M. Tolley	7	4	2	44	30	22.00	–	–	1
G.R. Haynes	17	14	1	229	41	17.61	–	1	7
N.V. Radford	12	7	3	60	21	15.00	–	–	8
S.J. Rhodes	17	10	3	75	31*	10.71	–	–	17/7
V.S. Solanki	9	6	2	33	12	8.25	–	–	4
P.J. Newport	16	5	5	18	15*	6.00	–	–	2
M.J. Church	6	5	1	25	14	5.00	–	–	–
Parvaz Mirza	13	3	3	9	2*	–	–	–	–
R.K. Illingworth	7	2	2	0	0*	–	–	–	2

One match: D.B. D'Oliveira and J.E. Brinkley did not bat

BOWLING	Overs	Mds	Runs	Wkts	Av	Best	5/inn
G.A. Hick	28.3	1	125	13	9.61	4-21	–
D.B. D'Oliveira	8	–	45	3	15.00	3-45	–
S.R. Lampitt	90.5	3	382	21	18.19	4-43	–
Parvaz Mirza	65	–	337	17	19.82	4-27	–
G.R. Haynes	100.4	8	403	19	21.21	4-21	–
T.M. Moody	19	–	69	3	23.00	3-25	–
N.V. Radford	57.5	4	301	13	23.15	5-57	1
P.J. Newport	106	10	409	17	24.05	5-32	1
R.K. Illingworth	49.5	6	196	8	24.50	2-3	–
J.E. Brinkley	8	–	24	–	–	–	–
V.S. Solanki	3	–	32	–	–	–	–

WORCESTERSHIRE CCC — BATTING (season summary)

Batting	M	Inns	NO	Runs	HS	Av
W.P.C. Weston	20	35	1	1207	111	35.50
T.S. Curtis	20	35	5	1221	169*	40.70
G.A. Hick	11	17	1	790	152	49.37
G.R. Haynes	18	30	3	737	93	24.56
D.A. Leatherdale	18	30	3	993	93	36.77
M.J. Church	5	9	–	126	35	15.75
S.J. Rhodes	20	33	8	1018	122*	40.72
S.R. Lampitt	17	23	8	488	97	25.68
P.J. Newport	18	23	8	404	50	26.93
R.K. Illingworth	10	11	4	91	23*	13.00
J.E. Brinkley	2	1	1	14	14*	–
A. Wylie		4	1	14	5*	4.66
T.M. Moody	18	31	2	1600	168	55.17
N.V. Radford	10	11	2	130	50	14.44
P.A. Thomas	14	15	4	57	25	5.18
C.M. Tolley	3	5	–	62	24	12.40
D.B. D'Oliveira	3	4	–	59	25	14.75
V.S. Solanki	6	10	2	150	36	18.75
Parvaz Mirza	6	10	2	39	18*	4.87
K.R. Spring	1	2	–	4	3	2.00

BOWLING

Match	P.J. Newport	J.E. Brinkley	S.R. Lampitt	R.K. Illingworth	W.P.C. Weston	G.R. Haynes	Parvaz Mirza	A. Wylie	N.V. Radford	D.A. Leatherdale	G.A. Hick	T.M. Moody	P.A. Thomas	D.B. D'Oliveira	V.S. Solanki	T.S. Curtis	Byes	Leg-byes	Wides	No-balls	Total	Wks
v. Oxford University (Oxford) 27–9 April	21-7-51-4 / 7-5-7-2	14-3-49-0 / 12-2-50-1	17-6-49-3 / 8-0-24-2	21.4-7-47-2 / 16-6-21-1	1-0-4-0 / 2-2-0-0	10-3-19-1 / 8-4-15-0										2-1-3-0		6	1	24	225	10
v. Essex (Chelmsford) 4–8 May	27.5-5-83-1			47-20-80-4		10-6-26-1		12-1-51-0 / 5-0-27-0	20-3-82-2 / 11.1-1-50-4	10-2-43-2 / 8-1-36-2 / 8-0-32-0							7	3	1	14	123	6
v. Middlesex (Worcester) 11–15 May	8-0-48-0		28.3-4-87-1	24-3-93-2 / 19-5-46-2		7-2-31-2 / 11-2-36-0		18-6-65-1			8-0-40-0	5-3-12-1					4	17	6	4	389	10
v. West Indians (Worcester) 16–8 May	29-4-83-5		16-1-49-1						7-1-28-0	1-0-2-0			16-4-70-5				5	7 / 28	1	6 / 13	332 / 393	10 / 10
v. Gloucestershire (Gloucester) 25–9 May	12-2-48-0 / 17-2-72-0		24.3-5-80-3	14.3-4-30-3		10-2-33-0			16.1-4-45-5				15-0-78-0				1	11	1	8	241	9
v. Surrey (Worcester) 1–5 June	16-7-37-3 / 14-6-29-2		20-5-58-3 / 14-4-43-3	22.3-5-63-2		14-7-31-2 / 8-5-13-0											3	1		30	375	10
v. Nottinghamshire (Trent Bridge) 8–12 June	26.4-5-61-4 / 20-8-61-3		22-6-59-2	15.3-4-51-2 / 16.1-7-23-3		12-3-31-1 / 6-1-15-1			11-2-33-1 / 10-2-38-0 / 9-1-40-0		4-2-3-1	3-0-7-0		28-4-88-3 / 37-3-122-2				8 / 7	1	2	183	10
v. Lancashire (Worcester) 15–19 June	18-8-35-2		23.1-7-71-4 / 16.4-6-44-2		1-0-7-0	4-0-10-1				1-0-10-0								3 / 8		16	152	10
v. Hampshire (Southampton) 22–6 June	21-7-48-2 / 31-8-95-2		11.4-1-42-3 / 29.4-10-73-3	26-11-63-4 / 18-6-36-1	1-0-1-0 / 4-0-24-0	25-8-68-2 / 17-2-56-1						8-0-45-1	30-5-98-2 / 11-3-37-1 / 17.1-3-62-2		19-4-76-1 / 18-3-70-1			6 / 2	1	10 / 18	301	10
v. Leicestershire (Worcester) 29 June – 3 July	10-4-23-0 / 23-4-72-2		17.4-4-66-1	43-13-89-3 / 16.5-8-30-4		3-1-6-0	18-5-68-2 / 5-2-7-0				21-4-47-0 / 13-6-18-5		4-0-7-0 / 10-2-32-0		4-1-18-0 / 12-4-20-0		6 / 8	9 / 5	2	16 / 16	319	9A
v. Durham (Darlington) 6–10 July	6-2-12-0 / 22.4-8-45-5		9-1-19-1 / 21-8-56-3			8-2-21-2 / 11-0-39-0	17-3-51-1 / 14-2-79-3		19.5-3-81-1 / 12-2-45-3			10-2-32-0 / 5-2-9-0	5-2-9-0		4-1-18-0 / 12-4-20-0		8	13 / 9	1	10 / 18	206	10
v. Young Australia (Worcester) 22–4 July	11-3-27-4		12-1-48-0 / 11-3-52-3		5-0-29-0	10-1-45-0	16-3-63-1 / 10-2-41-0					1-0-4-0 / 1-1-0-0	11-0-75-2				8	7	3	16 / 8	231	10
v. Kent (Worcester) 27–31 July	17.3-5-46-3 / 20-4-64-3		17-4-52-0 / 18-4-53-2	39-12-92-2 / 34.5-7-89-4		14-6-33-4 / 2-1-2-0					3-0-26-0 / 7-1-26-0 / 30-6-93-0 / 12-5-25-1		22-7-66-0 / 13-2-45-0				2 / 5	3 / 2 / 5	1	16	428	5B
v. Yorkshire (Scarborough) 3–7 August	21-2-70-1 / 6-2-10-1		26-4-92-1 / 7-0-35-0	38-9-112-0 / 12-5-32-0	7.4-0-26-0	22-6-91-1 / 8-1-45-1						4-0-13-1	18-2-86-0 / 13-2-79-0				8	9 / 4	1	24 / 12	344	9C
v. Derbyshire (Kidderminster) 10–14 August	22-6-66-5 / 18-8-32-3					23-11-50-0 / 9-0-40-1	32.5-10-110-5 / 14-2-56-0		32-8-92-2 / 14-5-32-1			6-2-10-0	29-1-116-2 / 18-4-69-2	34-7-89-0 / 14.5-1-70-0			4	8 / 4	1	18 / 20	359	10
v. Sussex (Eastbourne) 17–21 August	29-8-98-4 / 6-1-17-0		20-5-78-3 / 12-5-23-1				16-6-47-0 / 12-4-44-1				15-1-50-0 / 18-5-45-0	14-2-67-2	14-2-67-2				8	4	1	28 / 10	83	10
v. Warwickshire (Edgbaston) 24–8 August	33.2-7-105-5		36-15-74-2 / 7-3-17-0			13-2-49-0 / 3-0-15-0	18.2-3-95-1					14-6-23-2 / 3.1-1-6-0	17-2-64-1 / 5-1-20-0		3-1-14-0 / 8-1-33-0 / 16-1-80-0 / 4-0-26-0		8	18	2	16 / 6	191	9
v. Somerset (Worcester) 29 August – 1 September	9-4-11-0		12-4-34-4						20-5-70-1 / 14-2-64-1		9-3-23-0 / 16-2-66-1	5-2-14-0 / 17-5-48-0	17-3-84-2 / 9-4-29-1			1-0-5-0	6	6 / 14	2	10 / 16	255	3
v. Northamptonshire (Northampton) 7–11 September	10-3-32-2					4-0-20-0			14-3-39-0			9-4-29-1	14-2-50-2		2-0-10-1 / 2-0-12-0		2	7	1	6	332	10
v. Glamorgan (Worcester) 14–18 September	15-2-63-1		11.2-2-70-3						10-4-41-1			5-0-27-0	6-1-26-0				4	2	1 / 2	14 / 18	220 / 286	10 / 10
Bowler's average	548-147-1551-69 / 22.47	26-5-99-1 / 99.00	494.1-124-1524-55 / 27.70	424-132-997-39 / 25.56	21.4-2-91-0 / —	272-76-840-21 / 40.00	175.1-40-661-14 / 47.21	35-7-143-1 / 143.00	220.1-46-780-22 / 35.45	28-3-123-4 / 30.75	156-35-462-8 / 57.75	72.1-20-209-5 / 41.80	386.4-67-1554-33 / 47.09	113.5-15-369-5 / 73.80	88-15-359-5 / 119.66	3-1-8-0 / —						

A M.A. Atherton absent hurt
B C.M. Tolley 4-0-23-0
C J.J. Whitaker absent hurt

AXA EQUITY AND LAW LEAGUE – AVERAGES

BATTING	M	Inns	NO	Runs	HS	Av	100s	50s	ct/st
M.G. Bevan	17	16	3	706	103*	54.30	2	5	5
R.J. Blakey	17	11	3	276	61	34.50	–	2	15/2
D. Byas	17	16	1	399	70	26.60	–	3	6
A.A. Metcalfe	12	9	7	131	50	26.20	–	1	4
C. White	20	20	1	235	50*	23.50	–	1	3
M.P. Vaughan	14	13	1	243	46	20.25	–	1	4
B. Parker	11	9	–	118	28	16.85	–	–	3/1
G.M. Hamilton	3	4	2	30	17	15.00	–	–	1
S.A. Kellett	2	2	–	14	13*	14.00	–	–	1
C.E.W. Silverwood	6	3	–	14	7	14.00	–	–	1
A.P. Grayson	14	10	2	87	33*	10.87	–	–	3
D. Gough	7	7	–	76	30	10.85	–	–	2
P.J. Hartley	12	7	–	43	15*	8.60	–	–	1
M.D. Moxon	7	4	–	23	11	5.75	–	–	1
R.D. Stemp	15	7	–	21	11	5.25	–	–	–
M.A. Robinson	15	7	3	15	7	3.75	–	–	1
A.C. Morris	8	6	–	5	3	0.83	–	–	2
G.M. Hamilton									

Two matches: A. McGrath 72 (ct 2); R.A. Kettleborough 7

BOWLING	Overs	Mds	Runs	Wkts	Av	Best	5/inn
C.E.W. Silverwood	38	7	182	10	18.20	3-31	–
M.G. Bevan	43.1	2	234	12	19.50	3-21	–
R.A. Kettleborough	6	–	43	2	21.50	2-43	–
G.M. Hamilton	48	–	249	11	22.63	4-27	–
P.J. Hartley	77.4	2	327	14	23.35	2-7	–
D. Gough	65.4	9	292	11	26.54	4-35	–
A.P. Grayson	68	2	329	11	29.90	2-9	–
M.A. Robinson	100.1	5	478	14	34.14	2-27	–
A.C. Morris	19	3	72	2	36.00	1-8	–
R.D. Stemp	47	5	234	6	39.00	2-41	–
C. White	72	5	361	9	40.11	2-15	–
S.M. Milburn	24	1	118	2	59.00	2-29	–
M.P. Vaughan	6	–	31	–	–	–	–

YORKSHIRE CCC — BATTING (season averages)

	M	Inns	NO	Runs	HS	Av
M.D. Moxon	13	23	8	1145	203*	76.33
M.P. Vaughan	20	38	1	1235	88	33.37
D. Byas	20	37	1	1913	213	56.26
M.G. Bevan	20	34	5	1598	153*	55.10
C. White	17	29	5	848	110	35.33
R.J. Blakey	20	29	6	398	77*	17.30
A.P. Grayson	9	14	1	235	73	18.07
P.J. Hartley	18	23	4	256	59	13.47
G.M. Hamilton	3	4	–	59	29	29.50
R.D. Stemp	18	24	8	179	22*	8.52
M.A. Robinson	20	20	8	75	23	6.25
D. Gough	11	13	1	259	60	21.58
A. McGrath	5	10	–	280	84	28.00
B. Parker	4	8	–	161	40	23.00
S.M. Milburn	3	6	1	15	7	3.00
A.C. Morris	6	11	–	228	86	22.80
S.A. Kellett	7	9	2	106	50	15.14
C.E.W. Silverwood	7	9	2	—	—	—
A.A. Metcalfe	4	4	1	200	100	66.66
R.A. Kettleborough	1	2	–	59	55	29.50

BOWLING

BOWLING	P.J. Hartley	G.M. Hamilton	M.A. Robinson	C. White	R.D. Stemp	M.P. Vaughan	A.P. Grayson	M.G. Bevan	D. Gough	S.M. Milburn	A.C. Morris	C.E.W. Silverwood	D. Byas	A.A. Metcalfe	Byes	Leg-byes	Wides	No-balls	Total	Wks
v. Cambridge University (Cambridge) 13–5 April	20-6-36-2	22.2-9-41-3	14-2-32-1	16-7-31-2	18-8-23-1	3-1-5-0										6			174	10
v. Lancashire (Leeds) 27 April – 1 May	16-2-56-2	6-4-14-0	5-2-4-1	8-0-38-1	9-2-11-0	9-2-14-1	8-6-5-2	6-4-4-0									2	4	52	4
	16.4-2-74-3		19-9-47-3	7-0-32-0	7-1-23-0	7-2-31-0		2-0-16-0	17-4-52-3						1	8	8	14	271	9A
v. Leicestershire (Leicester) 4–8 May	20-12-19-5		10-2-33-0	7-0-32-0	12-3-44-0	7-1-0-0			17-7-28-7							3		6	147	10
	10-2-38-1		11.4-3-42-1	1-0-2-1	13-5-34-0	16.1-5-32-3			18-7-46-3						1	3			221	10
v. Derbyshire (Chesterfield) 11–15 May	9-0-27-2		8-3-15-1	6-1-16-0	28-12-49-3				23-5-67-2							4	2	4	140	9B
	16.4-4-41-9		17-6-58-4	3-0-15-0					17-3-38-3							4	8		134	10
v. Glamorgan (Bradford) 18–22 May	11.1-2-45-2		17-6-37-2	7-3-12-2	3-0-7-1	3-1-8-0		5-2-18-0	14-2-72-1							3			135	10
			11.5-2-40-2	7-0-35-0	8-6-13-0	5-1-20-0		3-1-5-0	16-6-32-2	26-8-68-4					5	3		8	212	10
v. Northamptonshire (Sheffield) 25–9 May	32-7-87-3		29-6-86-2	15-5-41-1	18-7-34-0				11-1-44-1	5-0-26-1						3			357	10
	10-0-61-1			4-0-34-0												5	1	20	146	10
v. Somerset (Taunton) 1–5 June	12-3-49-1		18-5-57-1	5-0-25-0	27-7-77-2	17-4-52-1	6-4-5-0	3-1-5-0	16.3-5-72-0						2	4	2	6	351	5
	5.5-0-33-1		2-0-16-0		19-2-69-2	11-1-57-0	8-1-33-0		10-1-40-0						11	5		12	261	5
v. Kent (Leeds) 15–19 June	10-2-35-2		17.3-3-68-2	8-1-24-0	17-4-69-2	1-1-0-0	6-1-22-0		19-8-34-4						4	4	1	6	234	10
	20-5-68-2		21-3-57-2	14.4-2-40-4	23-10-93-1	4-0-18-0	1-0-9-0		17-1-56-0	22-5-50-3					4	7		34	365	6
v. Warwickshire (Edgbaston) 22–6 June	26.3-6-109-4		26-7-74-1	23-4-53-0	33-7-120-1	11-3-29-1									4	5	1		449	10
v. Gloucestershire (Middlesbrough) 29 June – 3 July	17-4-71-2		17-4-46-4	7.5-0-33-1	4-2-9-0	5-2-21-0	3-1-6-0	7-2-15-1	20-5-76-3						4	16		22	276	10
	10-0-39-0		12.1-4-32-0	5-2-14-0	26-13-65-0	12-4-31-1		4-2-8-0	9-4-17-0						2	4		12	210	9C
v. Hampshire (Southampton) 6–10 July	35.1-7-109-4		36-15-72-4	20-3-78-1	16-1-83-0	4-1-12-0		7-1-31-0	10-1-40-0		13-4-51-0				24	7	2	24	429	10
	19-5-56-5		16-2-60-0	13-3-34-1	25.1-6-68-4	5-0-19-0		2-1-5-0	19-8-34-4	6-0-21-0	4-1-11-0				10	7		6	265	10
v. Durham (Harrogate) 20–4 July	26-6-65-4		11-3-22-1	16-3-30-1	7-3-13-0				26-7-57-4						12	13		8	206	10
	20-6-51-4		9-4-17-1	4-2-16-2					15.3-7-28-2						9	16		8	135	9D
v. Nottinghamshire (Trent Bridge) 27–31 July	30-8-75-0		22-8-54-1		57-20-108-4	21.5-4-44-2						17-2-72-2				4			403	0
					57.5-24-128-2	37-10-114-2													18	0
v. Worcestershire (Scarborough) 3–7 August	11-2-49-1		22-9-50-0	6-0-24-0	17-7-39-0	4.4-1-10-2						9-2-49-0			2	6	1	24	453	5
	14-1-53-2		5-1-15-0	4-3-5-0	41-12-103-1	11-3-27-0						11-3-33-1			4	2		12	189	5
v. Surrey (The Oval) 10–14 August		14-2-72-1	24.8-8-64-4		18-6-37-3	8-3-22-2		10-0-37-0		10-2-39-1		22-3-94-3			10	10	3	12	409	10
		8-1-29-1	12-4-22-0	5-1-22-0	24-8-50-3	16-3-58-2		12-1-52-1		6-0-21-0		16.1-2-62-5			12	4		2	175	10
v. Lancashire (Old Trafford) 17–21 August		13-5-25-2	9.2-2-23-3	15.1-2-52-3	36-11-58-2	12-1-52-1		6-0-31-0				8-1-40-0			4	7	1	10	238	10
		12-3-43-0	13-4-40-0	25.4-4-80-3	39-3-140-3							12-3-42-2			2	3		16	362	10
v. Middlesex (Leeds) 24–8 August	28-7-57-0		17-4-54-1									24-4-85-1				15		8	516	9
v. West Indians (Scarborough) 30 August – 1 September	19-2-101-2		15-1-80-3	10.3-3-70-2	17-4-55-1	2-0-23-0		6-0-39-0	16-1-95-2			6-1-44-0	6-1-37-0	6-0-46-0		2		28	426	10
	7-1-38-1		7-1-21-0	0.5-0-2-0	17-3-76-0			15-5-55-3	11-3-40-1								1	12	356	4
v. Sussex (Scarborough) 7–11 September	23-9-70-3				21.1-1-73-0	13-2-59-2		17-4-42-1	17-4-42-1			22.3-9-94-3				6		16	357	8
v. Essex (Chelmsford) 14–18 September	16-1-80-3			24-9-56-2	24-9-56-2	2-0-23-0		4-0-14-1	16-1-80-2			12-0-73-2		6-0-46-0	4	6		20	313	10
	20-5-105-4				8-1-33-0	22-5-65-1			18.5-1-94-1			10-2-36-2				2		8	270	10
Bowler's average	549-120-1861-81 · 22.97	75.2-24-224-7 · 32.00	483.1-133-1375-46 · 29.89	257.4-49-858-25 · 34.32	690.1-208-1860-38 · 48.94	272.4-64-876-22 · 39.81	32-13-80-2 · 40.00	99-24-351-6 · 58.50	344.5-83-1110-45 · 24.66	69-15-204-10 · 20.40	17-5-62-0 · –	147.1-23-630-18 · 35.00	6-1-37-0 · –	6-0-46-0 · –						

A P.J. Martin absent ill
B D.J. Cullinan retired hurt
C J.P. Stephenson retired hurt
D M.A. Roseberry absent hurt